ADAPTIVE CRUISE CONTROL

PT-132

Edited by

Ronald K. Jurgen

Published by
SAE International
400 Commonwealth Drive
Warrendale, PA 15096-0001
U.S.A.
Phone (724)776-4841
Fax (724)776-0790

For permission and licensing requests contact:

SAE Permissions
400 Commonwealth Drive
Warrendale, PA 15096-0001-USA
Email: permissions@sae.org
Fax: 724-776-3036
Tel: 724-772-4028

SAE International is committed to preserving ancient forests and natural resources. We elected to print *Adaptive Cruise Control PT 132* on 30% post consumer recycled paper, processed chlorine free. As a result, for this printing, we have saved:

7 Trees (40' tall and 6-8" diameter)
2,886 Gallons of Wastewater
1,161 Kilowatt Hours of Electricity
318 Pounds of Solid Waste
625 Pounds of Greenhouse Gases

SAE International made this paper choice because our printer, Thomson-Shore, Inc., is a member of Green Press Initiative, a nonprofit program dedicated to supporting authors, publishers, and suppliers in their efforts to reduce their use of fiber obtained from endangered forests.

For more information, visit www.greenpressinitiative.org

All SAE papers, standards, and selected books are abstracted and indexed in the Global Mobility Database.

For multiple print copies contact:

SAE Customer Service
Tel: 877-606-7323 (inside USA and Canada)
Tel: 724-776-4970 (outside USA)
Fax: 724-776-0790
Email: CustomerService@sae.org

ISBN-10 0-7680-1792-0
ISBN-13 978-0-7680-1792-2

Library of Congress Catalog Card Number: 2006932572
SAE/PT-132

SAE Order No. PT-132

Printed in USA

ADAPTIVE CRUISE CONTROL

Other SAE books in this series:

Electronic Braking, Traction, and Stability Controls, Volume 2
by Ronald K. Jurgen
(Product Code: PT-129)

Multiplexing and Networking, Volume 2
by Ronald K. Jurgen
(Product Code: PT-128)

Automotive Software
by Ronald K. Jurgen
(Product Code: PT-127)

Electronic Engine Control Technologies, Second Edition
by Ronald K. Jurgen
(Product Code: PT-110)

Sensors and Transducers, Second Edition
by Ronald K. Jurgen
(Product Code: PT-105)

Electric and Hybrid Electric-Vehicles
by Ronald K. Jurgen
(Product Code: PT-85)

On- and Off-Board Diagnostics
by Ronald K. Jurgen
(Product Code: PT-81)

Electronic Transmission Controls
by Ronald K. Jurgen
(Product Code: PT-79)

Multiplexing and Networking
by Ronald K. Jurgen
(Product Code: PT-78)

Electronic Steering and Suspension Systems
by Ronald K. Jurgen
(Product Code: PT-77)

Electronic Braking, Traction, and Stability Controls
by Ronald K. Jurgen
(Product Code: PT-76)

Navigation and Intelligent Transportation Systems
by Ronald K. Jurgen
(Product Code: PT-72)

INTRODUCTION

Adaptive Cruise Control: Still Evolving

A conventional cruise control system maintains a user-set vehicle speed. Adaptive cruise control (ACC), by contrast, adjusts vehicle speed to provide a specified spacing between the vehicle with ACC and a preceding vehicle. There is no need for driver intervention. ACC takes advantage of the functions of several existing electronic control units (e.g., engine control) and adds a sensor "for measuring the distance, relative speed, and lateral position of potential target vehicles using laser optics or millimeter waves. This component often contains the logic for controlling vehicle movement. The latter is effected by commands to ECUs for engine and brake control electronics. Existing components are also used or adapted for operator use and display."[1]

ACC was introduced in the automotive market by Mitsubishi in 1995 and has been evolving steadily since then. One of the most recent applications is in the 2007 Mercedes-Benz S550. Its ACC system maintains an appropriate following distance to the traffic ahead, but in doing so, it controls up to 40 percent of the car's maximum braking power, as well as the speed. The system can bring the car to a complete stop, if necessary.[2]

The authors of the 63 ACC papers presented herein address progress and problems in their designs of ACC systems and components. Their papers are presented in two main sections. The first section contains papers dealing with an overview of ACC systems. The second section deals with ACC sensors and is subdivided into ACC Sensors Overview, ACC Radar Sensors, and Miscellaneous ACC Sensors. A final paper by Peter M. Knoll of Robert Bosch GmbH in Germany discusses the current state of ACC and what can be expected in the future, including the role of the next-generation ACC, ACCplus.

As is usually the case when attempting to categorize papers, arbitrary decisions must be made. Many of the ACC papers herein cover both systems and sensors. The category in which each paper was placed was predicated on the main thrust of that paper. It is hoped that this approach will be helpful to the reader.

Some of the many ACC developments described in the papers herein are as follows:

- An ACC system that uses "vehicle-to-vehicle communication to improve string stability substantially and to obtain natural vehicle behavior with a smaller degree of longitudinal acceleration/deceleration." (2006-01-0348)

- "A new control device located e.g. at the steering wheel enables the driver to create additional inputs in terms of acceleration or deceleration to the assistance system. Acceleration is the third cinematic dimension in addition to velocity and distance which are already influenced by the driver while using ACC." (2006-01-0346)

- "Although many different types of Adaptive Cruise Control (ACC) have been developed to maintain a constant headway between lead and following vehicles, little is known about the dynamic performance of such controllers during cornering and in adverse environmental conditions." (2005-01-0403)

- "The current improvement in data precision means that direct use of geometry information from the databases in the form of a series of polygons or related curvature information is not far off. The fusion of data with the currently accepted dynamic course prediction of ACC systems results in considerable improvements in tract prediction suitable for long, straight stretches of road as well as very curved sections." (2004-01-1744)

- "The automatic braking function can be achieved by various means; some methods include an intelligent brake booster, electric calipers, stored hydraulic fluid pressure, etc." (2004-01-0255)

- "We have developed an automobile millimeter-wave radar that uses switched digital beam forming and a high-resolution null-scanning algorithm for application to the radar. Due to the characteristics of these technologies, the developed radar provides a superior azimuth resolution of 3 degrees or less, which promises improvement of obstacle detection performance. Moreover, since the developed radar is implemented in compact body and requires low computing power feasible with an automobile microprocessor, it has high prospects for installation in popular and small cars." (2006-01-1463)

- "A new method to track a target vehicle in non-uniform conditions has been developed. It is based on the locus on the phase chart between the azimuth angle and relative velocity, which are obtained from the radar and host vehicle information. It can express the path of the target vehicle in non-uniform conditions exactly since the locus can be expressed theoretically." (2003-01-0013)

- "This paper describes a multi-beam infrared sensor technology (*IDIS*®) with unprecedented robustness to environmental influences, which was originally designed for the comfort application Adaptive Cruise Control (ACC). The paper shows that beside ACC, an optimal functionality for safety applications such as Precrash and Collision Mitigation can be provided by the *IDIS*® sensor, which has a good lateral resolution by principle and can clearly identify width and outlines of vehicles and road obstacles." (2006-01-0347)

1. Winner, Hermann, "Adaptive Cruise Control," in *Automotive Electronics Handbook, Second Edition,* Ronald K. Jurgen, editor, McGraw-Hill Inc., New York, NY, 1999, pp. 30.1–30.30.

2. Sabatini, Jeff, *The New York Times*, May 28, 2006.

* * * * * * * * * *

This book and the entire Automotive Electronics Series are dedicated to my friend Larry Givens, a former editor of SAE's monthly publication, *Automotive Engineering International.*

Ronald K. Jurgen, Editor

TABLE OF CONTENTS

INTRODUCTION

ADAPTIVE CRUISE CONTROL (ACC) SYSTEMS

ACC SENSORS

Overview

ACC Radar Sensors

Miscellaneous ACC Sensors

ACC NOW AND IN THE FUTURE

ADAPTIVE CRUISE CONTROL (ACC) SYSTEMS

2006-01-0800

Effect of Computational Delay on the Performance of a Hybrid Adaptive Cruise Control System

Junmin Wang
Southwest Research Institute and The University of Texas at Austin

Raul G. Longoria
The University of Texas at Austin

ABSTRACT

This paper investigates the effect of real-time control system computational delay on the performance of a hybrid adaptive cruise control (ACC) system during braking/coasting scenarios. A hierarchical hybrid ACC system with a finite state machine (FSM) at the high-rank and a nonlinear sliding mode controller (SMC) at the low-rank is designed based on a vehicle dynamics model with a brake-by-wire platform. From simulations, parametric studies are used to evaluate the effect of the bounded random computational delay on the system performance in terms of tracking errors and control effort. The effect of the computational delay location within the control system hierarchy is also evaluated. The system performance generally becomes worse as the upper boundary of the computational delay increases while the effect of the computational delay located at the high-rank controller is more pronounced. In this paper, these results are also contrasted against those found by applying a computational delay compensation technique in the high-rank controller.

INTRODUCTION

Control systems are usually implemented using real-time digital computers, which conduct control tasks by executing a sequence of instructions. Execution of these instructions does not occur instantaneously, as may be assumed during the control system design phase. Computational delay (CD) refers to the computational time required for a computer to complete a control algorithm. The CD for a control system is defined as the period from when the control algorithm is triggered to the generation of a corresponding control command. In general, the computational delay of the control system arises from the fact that the real-time digital computer needs to handle the data-dependent conditional branches, resource sharing delays, processing exceptions, interrupt handling, as well as regular computation simultaneously [1]. For example, it is reported in [2] that the execution of an adaptive robot computed torque control algorithm requires 17 milliseconds on a MC68000 microprocessor. The concept of computational delay for a discrete-time control system is illustrated in Figure 1.

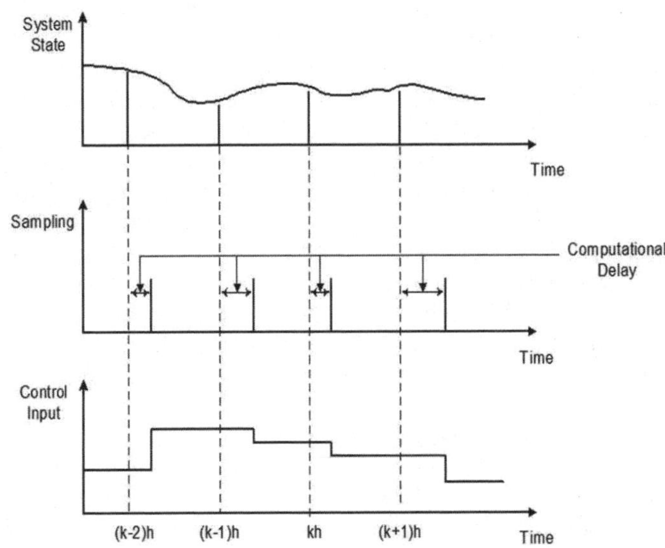

Figure 1. The computational delay of the real-time control system

The computational delay decreases considerably with the increasing speed of the hardware. On the other hand, to meet growing demands, complexities in control system algorithms (e.g. artificial intelligence, knowledge-based control, hybrid control) and sampling frequency continue to increase dramatically, requiring significant amounts of computational time compared to the sampling period. Therefore, it is important to quantify the effect of computational delay on the performance of a control system.

Of late, vehicle control systems have become more and more sophisticated and many different advanced vehicle control systems continue to appear in the market, such as ACC, traction control system (TCS), electronic stability program (ESP), direct yaw-moment control

(DYC), and so on. As all these systems are implemented on computers, the effect of computational delay on the system performance requires attention. Analysis of the effect of computational delay can be helpful in allocation of hardware resources for system design and evaluation of system performance.

Recently, the effects of computational delay on control systems have attracted research efforts reported in the literature. Yang [3] compared the effect of computational delay on the performance of a linear robotic control system. The results show that the closed-loop system performance with an adaptive controller designed without considering the computational delay is even worse than that with a simple fixed parameter controller due to the large computational time. The computational delay in this work was treated as a fixed time delay, which did not reflect its random nature. Shin and Cui [1] studied the effect of computational delay on conventional real-time control systems. A quantitative analysis was made based on an example of the computed torque control of a robot. An upper bound for the computational delay that the system performance can tolerate was derived. Nilsson, et al. [5] studied the effect of a randomly varying computational delay on a linear control system and proposed a LQG optimal control based on a stochastic description of the computational delay. Anderson and Reed [6] presented the results of a simulation study of the effect of computational delay modeled as certain percentage of sampling period, on a robot manipulator controller. It was shown that computational delay stability boundaries directly depend on the sampling frequency for both the step response and trajectory tracking cases. In addition, given the fact that the computational delay is inherent to real-time control systems, several approaches have been suggested to compensate for it as well [7-9].

Most of the research results reported are for linear systems. Hybrid control systems (involving the interactions between continuous dynamic system and discrete event-driven automation) have recently been studied to improve system performance and fulfill the increasing demands in many engineering areas [10]. However, the complex nature of these control systems has made it difficult to predict and/or evaluate the system performance as well. A study of the effect of computational delay on the performance of a hybrid control system has not been found in the literature. As pointed out in [1, 3, 4, 6], it is difficult to generally analyze the effects of computational delay for different control systems, and insight requires case-by-case evaluation.

The rest of this paper is organized as follows. In the next section, a vehicle longitudinal braking dynamic model is established. Based on this model, a hybrid ACC system is designed, which includes a low-rank nonlinear sliding mode controller and a high-rank supervisory controller. The performances of these controllers without computational delay are verified in simulation. The subsequent section examines the effects of computational delay and its location (within the control system hierarchy) on the performance of this hybrid control system using simulation studies. A computational delay compensation technique is then designed for the high-rank controller, and the performance is compared with the uncompensated system. Finally, conclusive remarks are given in the last section of the paper.

DESIGN OF HYBRID ACC SYSTEM

This section describes the design of a hybrid adaptive cruise control system, which will be used as a platform to evaluate the effect of the computational delay on system performance.

HYBRID ADAPTIVE CRUISE CONTROL

As opposed to a conventional cruise control system, which maintains a user-set vehicle speed as a regulation problem, the ACC is a tracking control system that adjusts vehicle speed to a desired value according to specified spacing policies [11-13]. One ACC speed policy is to track the speed of the preceding vehicle in the same lane; this is a so-called constant-gap policy. This paper uses this policy in the scenario where only the brake is applied for both the current vehicle and the preceding one for simplicity. Recently, some intelligence has been built into the regular ACC system to improve performance [15-17], which essentially makes the ACC a hybrid control system. From a practical point of view, it is not very wise/necessary for the ACC vehicle to actively track the speed of the preceding vehicle at all times, especially during a braking/coasting situation. The following subsections describe a hybrid ACC design that conducts the brake only when it is necessary. The system could potentially save energy compared to a conventional ACC system. This system consists of a supervisory controller and a speed-tracking controller in hierarchy.

Brake-by-Wire

The advanced automotive brake-by-wire technology usually employs the electromechanical braking system, which dispenses with the brake fluid and hydraulic line completely. The braking force at each wheel is generated directly by a high-performance electric motor controlled by an ECU individually. The system can perform all the vehicle brake and stability functions, as required by anti-lock braking system (ABS), traction control system (TCS), vehicle stability control (VSC), and adaptive cruise control (ACC) etc.

Supervisory Control Design

The supervisory controller dictates the ACC vehicle to perform either braking or coasting. The goal is to avoid unnecessary brake actions, and therefore save energy. Define the speed error, $v_{err} = v\_p - v\_c$, with v_p being the speed of the preceding vehicle and v_c the current vehicle speed. When the ACC vehicle is in a "coasting" state, if the speed error is less than the threshold value, $v\_errThrC2B$ (a negative value), or the spacing s is less than $s\_\min C2B$, then the state will be switched to a brake state to reduce the ACC vehicle speed to more effectively track the v_p. In the "brake" state, if the speed error is small enough, $v_{err} > v\_errThrB2C$, then the state is switched back to "coasting", which disables the brake action and allows the ACC vehicle to potentially run at a higher speed than the preceding one.

There is a potential for chattering whenever a switching interface exists in a control system. Such chattering is usually caused by noise in the signal used to determine the switching condition, discrepancies between the modeled and actual values of the interface, as well as other reasons. To avoid chattering in this controller, two threshold values, $v\_errThrC2B$ and $v\_errThrB2C$, are used to construct a hysteresis band between the brake and coasting states. This supervisory controller can be implemented by a finite state machine (FSM) as shown in Figure 2.

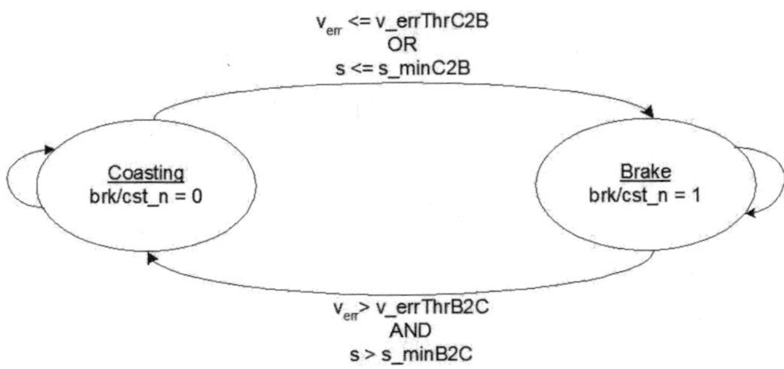

Figure 2. Finite state machine for the supervisory controller of the hybrid ACC system

This discrete control system can be described by the equation, $q^+ = G(q, v)$, where, $q, q^+ \in \{Coasting, Brake\}$ is the discrete state of the system and $v \in \{C2B = [(v_{err} \le v\_errThrC2B) OR (s \le s\_\min C2B)],$ $B2C = [(v_{err} > v\_errThrB2C) AND (s > s\_\min B2C)]\}$ is the discrete input space. A transition function, G, is defined as,

$q^+ = Brake$, when $q = Coasting$ AND $v = C2B$

$q^+ = Coasting$, when $q = Brake$ AND $v = B2C$

Notice that, for a complete ACC system, there should be an "acceleration" state that has not been considered in this paper for simplicity sake.

<u>Modeling the Vehicle Braking Longitudinal Dynamics</u>

This subsection describes the modeling of the vehicle longitudinal braking dynamics. The longitudinal slip is defined as the relative difference between a driving wheel's circumferential velocity and the vehicle's absolute velocity, v, as [18],

$$s = \frac{\omega R - v}{\max(v, \omega R)}, \tag{1}$$

where ω is the wheel angular velocity, and R is the tire effective radius.

The brake-by-wire actuators usually have an associated built-in closed-loop controller to accept the brake torque command as an input and regulate the actual brake torque [19]. The dynamics of this kind of actuator can be approximately modeled as a first-order system with sufficient accuracy [14, 20],

$$\tau_b \dot{T}_b + T_b = T_b^d, \tag{2}$$

where τ_b is the time constant for the actuator control system, T_b is the braking torque applied to the wheel, and the T_b^d is the desired braking torque dictated by the higher level controller.

The motion of the wheel during braking is determined by the force from the ground and braking torque. It can be represented as,

$$J_w \dot{\omega}_w = -T_b + RF_g, \tag{3}$$

where, J_w is the moment of inertia of the wheel, ω_w is the wheel angular velocity, and F_g is the force from ground, which is equal to the sum of friction force and rolling resistance. Ignoring the lateral dynamics, the vehicle longitudinal motion can be described by,

$$M\dot{v} = -nF_g - D_a v^2, \tag{4}$$

where, v is the vehicle longitudinal absolute speed, $D_a = 0.5 C_d \rho A$ is the vehicle air drag coefficient with C_d being the aerodynamic friction coefficient, ρ being the air density, and A being the vehicle frontal area. The wind speed is assumed to be zero. The number n is the number of braking wheels of the vehicle. Since the rolling resistance is generally small compared with both the braking force and air drag force at high speed, it is ignored here. The force from the ground can then be described as,

$$F_g = N\mu(s), \tag{5}$$

where, N is the normal force acting on the tire due to the vehicle weight, and $\mu(s_x)$ is the tire-road friction coefficient. The friction coefficient is a nonlinear function of the amount of slip at that tire-road interface. One famous model that describes this relationship is the so-called "Magic Formula" tire model developed by Pacejka

[21]. However, as an experimental model, there are many parameters that need to be defined in the Magic Formula tire-road friction model, and the format of the model is complicated as well. A simplified model is given in [19] as,

$$\mu(s) = ks \text{, for } s \le s_t \tag{6}$$
$$\mu(s) = ks_t \text{, for } s > s_t,$$

where, k is a constant related to the road surface friction condition [22]. In this paper, we focus on the normal braking condition (small slip ratio range) rather than ABS mode in which slip ratio is greater. In this case, the specified model should describe the tire-road friction coefficient with sufficient accuracy.

Combining the equations (1)-(6) with, $x_1 = v$, $x_2 = \omega_w$, and $x_3 = T_b$ as the states, the nonlinear vehicle longitudinal state-space model is,

$$\begin{aligned}
\dot{x}_1 &= -\frac{gk\ (x_1 - x_2 R)}{x_1} - \frac{D_a}{M} x_1^2 \\
\dot{x}_2 &= -\frac{x_3}{J_w} + \frac{RMgk\ \ (x_1 - x_2 R)}{4 J_w x_1} \\
\dot{x}_3 &= -\frac{x_3}{\tau_b} + \frac{T_b^d}{\tau_b}
\end{aligned} \tag{7}$$

where T_b^d is the control input to the system, and $x_1 = v$ is the output. It is assumed that there are four braking wheels, and the vehicle weight is equally distributed on the front and rear axes. In addition, the effect of pitching on the distribution of front and rear normal forces is ignored.

Design of the Low-Rank Sliding Mode Controller (SMC)

Sliding mode control (SMC) offers a robust control approach to deal with system uncertainties and modeling error. A low-rank sliding mode tracking controller is designed based on the nonlinear model developed above with the desired brake torque, T_b^d, as the input and the vehicle longitudinal speed, $x_1 = v$, as the output. The following coordinated transformation is used for the model described in equation (7) as,

$$\begin{aligned}
z_1 &= x_1 \\
\dot{z}_1 &= z_2 = \dot{x}_1 = -\frac{gk\,(x_1 - x_2 * R)}{x_1} - \frac{D_a}{M} x_1^2 \\
\dot{z}_2 &= z_3 = \frac{d}{dt}\left[\frac{-gk\,(x_1 - x_2 R)}{x_1} - \frac{D_a}{M} x_1^2\right] \\
&= \frac{Rg^2 k^2 x_2}{x_1^2} - \frac{g^2 k^2 R^2 x_2^2}{x_1^3} - \frac{gkRD_a x_2}{M} - \frac{gkRx_3}{J_w x_1} + \frac{g^2 k^2 R^2 M}{4 J_w x_1} \\
&\quad - \frac{g^2 k^2 R^3 M x_2}{4 J_w x_1^2} + \frac{2 D_a gk x_1}{M} + \frac{2 D_a^2 x_1^3}{M^2}
\end{aligned}$$

$$\begin{aligned}
\dot{z}_3 &= \frac{d}{dt}(z_3) = \frac{1}{4J_w M^2 x_1^4}(-8J_w M^2 x_1 R g^2 k^2 x_2 + 12 J_w M^2 g^2 k^2 R^2 x_2^2 \\
&+ 4M^2 gkR x_1^2 x_3 - M^3 g^2 k^2 R^2 x_1^2 + 2M^3 g^2 k^2 R^3 x_1 x_2 + 8J_w M D_a gk x_1^4 \\
&+ 24 J_w D_a^2 x_1^6)\left(-\frac{gk(x_1 - x_2 R)}{x_1} - \frac{D_a}{M} x_1^2\right) + \frac{1}{4J_w M x_1^3}(4J_w MRg^2 k^2 x_1 - \\
&8J_w M g^2 k^2 R^2 x_2 - 4J_w gkRD_a x_1^3 - g^2 k^2 R^3 M^2 x_1)\left(-\frac{x_3}{J_w} + \frac{RMgk(x_1 - x_2 R)}{4J_w x_1}\right) \\
&+ \frac{gkRx_3}{J_w x_1 \tau_b} - \frac{gkR}{J_w x_1 \tau_b} T_b^d \\
&= f(x) - g(x) T_b^d
\end{aligned} \tag{8}$$

Thus the relative order of the system is, $r = 3$. To ensure the speed tracking ability of the system, we can define the sliding surface as,

$$\begin{aligned}
S &= \left(\frac{d}{dt} + P\right)^{r-1} \tilde{z}_1 = \ddot{\tilde{z}}_1 + 2P\dot{\tilde{z}}_1 + P^2 \tilde{z}_1 \\
&= z_3 - \ddot{x}_{1d} + 2P(z_2 - \dot{x}_{1d}) + P^2 (z_1 - x_{1d})
\end{aligned} \tag{9}$$

where, $\tilde{z}_1 = z_1 - x_{1d}$, and P is a positive number determining the control gain. The derivative of the sliding surface becomes,

$$\begin{aligned}
\dot{S} &= \dot{z}_3 - \dddot{x}_{1d} + 2P(z_3 - \ddot{x}_{1d}) + P^2 (z_2 - \dot{x}_{1d}) \\
&= f(x) - g(x) T_b^d - \dddot{x}_{1d} + 2P(z_3 - \ddot{x}_{1d}) + P^2 (z_2 - \dot{x}_{1d})
\end{aligned} \tag{10}$$

The control law then can be set as,

$$T_b^d = g(x)^{-1}[f(x) - \dddot{x}_{1d} + 2P(z_3 - \ddot{x}_{1d}) + P^2 (z_2 - \dot{x}_{1d}) + K\,\mathrm{sgn}(S)] \tag{11}$$

Consider the candidate Lyapunov function, $V = \frac{1}{2} S^2$, and its derivative,

$$\dot{V} = S\dot{S} = S[f(x) - g(x) T_b^d - \dddot{x}_{1d} + 2P(z_3 - \ddot{x}_{1d}) + P^2 (z_2 - \dot{x}_{1d})] \tag{12}$$

By choosing the K large enough, we can guarantee that $\dot{V} = S\dot{S} \le -\eta |S|$ ($\eta > 0$), and the sliding surface is attractive.

In practice, to reduce the chattering effect caused by the switching of the SMC around $S = 0$, a continuous approximation with a thickness of Φ around the switching surface is used to smooth out the control input discontinuity. The approximation function is defined as,

$$sat(S/\Phi) = \begin{cases} S/\Phi, & \text{if } |S| < \Phi \\ \mathrm{sgn}(S/\Phi), & \text{if } |S| \ge \Phi, \end{cases} \tag{13}$$

with Φ being a positive number. The control law is then modified as,

$$T_b^d = g(x)^{-1}[f(x) - \ddot{x}_{1d} + 2P(z_3 - \ddot{x}_{1d}) + P^2(z_2 - \dot{x}_{1d}) + Ksat(S/\Phi)] \quad (14)$$

In the above SMC, it is assumed that the controller has full-state feedback, which means all the system states, v, ω_w, and T_b, are assumed to be available for the controller. In practice, the wheel rotational speed, ω_w, is very easy to measure. The vehicle longitudinal speed can be estimated accurately by using a sensor fusion technique that incorporates signals from both an accelerometer and a GPS [23]. By using an accelerometer to measure the vehicle deceleration in real-time, the brake torque, T_b, can be estimated reasonably well. However, these efforts are not the focus of this paper, and the states will be assumed to be available for direct feedback to the controller.

It needs to be pointed out that the SMC controller designed above is based on the assumption that the system is in continuous time domain and the control action can switch at infinite frequency. However, when implementing this controller in a computer, a fixed sampling rate is used and switching frequency is therefore limited, which means that the control T_b^d is constant during the sampling interval and changes only at the moment of sampling time. This type of action may not be able to guarantee that the system states are maintained inside the defined neighborhood Φ around the sliding surface. There have been several approaches proposed for the design of discrete-time sliding mode control (DSMC) [24-26]. However, for the system with high sampling rate and large time constant (relative to the sampling period), the effect of the sampling will be diminished [27, 28] and the above control law is used in the simulation.

The performance of this controller is verified in simulation. Figure 3 shows a comparison between the desired speed and actual speed along with the applied brake torque, wheel slip, and friction coefficient. As one can see, the controller can perform the task well. The wheel slip is relatively small and is in the linear region of the slip-friction function, which makes the equation (6) valid. Notice that no computational delay is considered in this simulation.

Hybrid ACC System

In this hybrid ACC system, to ensure fast response of the low-rank controller to a request from the supervisory controller, the low-rank controller takes the output of the supervisory controller, brk/cst_n, as an interrupt with high priority, while it samples other signals with fixed sampling rate. Figure 4 shows the simulation results and Table 1 compares the peak error, root mean square error (RMSE), and control effort between the conventional and hybrid ACC.

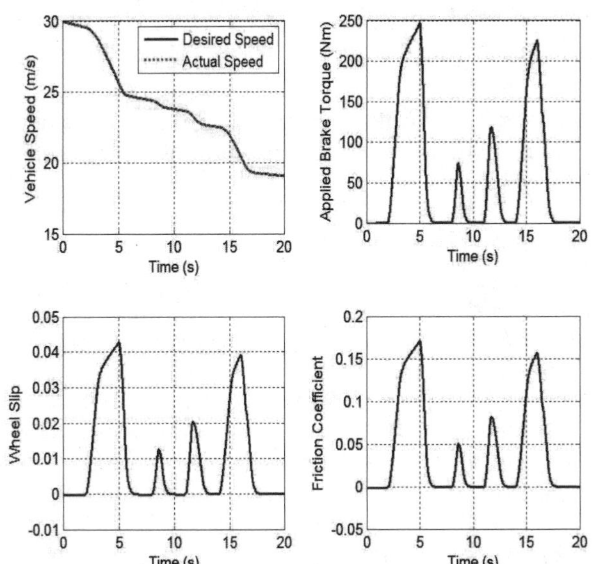

Figure 3. Simulation results of the conventional nonlinear ACC controller (sampling at 200 Hz)

Notice that the error of the hybrid ACC is mainly generated during the coasting mode, in which the speed tracking is disabled. However, in the 20 seconds simulation, the hybrid ACC reduces more than 12% control effort compared with that of the conventional ACC.

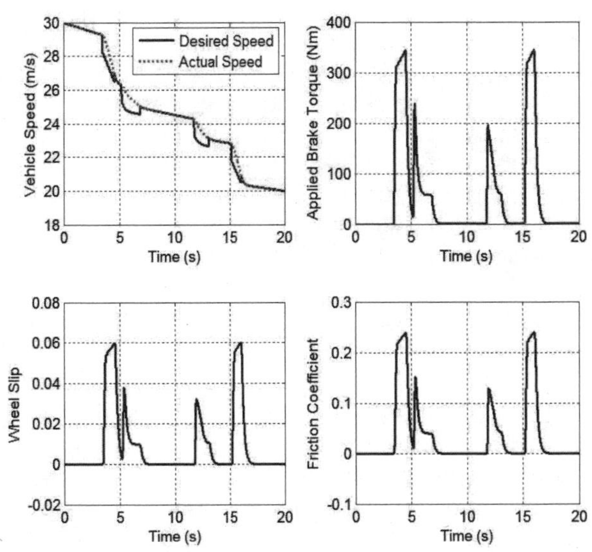

Figure 4. Simulation results of the hybrid ACC (sampled at 200 Hz)

Table 1. Comparison of conventional and hybrid ACC (no computational delay)

	Peak Error (m/s)	RMSE (m/s)	Control Effort (kJ)
Conventional (No CD)	0.037	0.003	94.53
Hybrid (No CD)	1.13	0.205	82.92

EFFECT OF THE COMPUTATIONAL DELAY ON THE PERFORMANCE OF THE HYBRID ACC

This section investigates the effect of the computational delay on the performance of the hybrid adaptive cruise control system.

COMPUTATIONAL DELAY

For the hybrid ACC system, computational delay can arise from several sources. For example, the low-rank brake controller must perform the regular braking task in addition to other control modes, such as ABS, traction control, and stability control. This requires the brake controller to monitor additional sensor signals, detect critical conditions, and respond, communicate, and cooperate with other controllers (e.g. powertrain controller, steering controller etc.) at similar or different ranks all in real-time. These time-consuming processes, along with the calculation of the ACC control algorithm, cause computational delay in the regular brake control task. Besides, for the high-rank controller, the information coming from low-rank controller and/or sensors are usually through a network (such as CAN bus). The communication delay of the network may vary significantly in magnitude depending on the load of the network. We consider this communication delay as part of the computational delay in this paper.

The computational delay can be described as a random number [1, 5, 29]. In [5], it is modeled as a random number uniformly distributed on the interval $[0, \lambda h]$ where, h is the sampling period and $0 \le \lambda \le 1.0$ is a bounded value. The same approach is adopted in this paper, but the interval of the random number is changed to $[0.05h, \lambda h]$, with $0.1 \le \lambda \le 1.0$, because all the computation will realistically take at least a minimum amount of time assumed here to be $0.05h$.

ANALYSIS OF THE EFFECT OF COMPUTATIONAL DELAY

For linear discrete-time systems analyzed with Z-transforms, computational delays can only be assumed to be zero or a whole sampling period. This does not reflect the random nature of computational delay. For nonlinear systems, the standard frequency-domain analysis methods cannot be applied. As suggested in [6], simulation is an effective approach to evaluate the effect of computational delay. In this subsection, the effect of CD will be roughly analyzed, while simulation results will be presented in the following subsection.

When computational delay is purely located in the high-rank supervisory controller, it affects the hybrid ACC system performance by delaying the decision making output brk/cst_n an amount of time ε. Since the number of the states is finite in the high-rank controller, its effect will only occur during the state transition, namely from brake to coasting state or from coasting to brake state in this case. For transition from brake to coasting state, computational delay of the brk/cst_n will cause the low-rank SMC to perform "unnecessary" braking for a time period ε, which causes "unnecessary" use of brake energy and reduces the benefit of the hybrid ACC. For transition from coasting to brake state, computational delay of the brk/cst_n will postpone brake action, and this increases initial speed error for the low-rank SMC and sacrifices safety.

When the computational delay is purely located in the low-rank SMC controller, which is implemented in discrete-time with a sampling period, h, the sliding surface between samples for the case of no computational delay can be approximately evaluated as,

$$S(t_k+h)=S(t_k)+\int_{t_k}^{t_k+h}\dot{S}(t)dt \approx S(t_k)+\int_{t_k}^{t_k+h}\left[\dot{S}(t_k)+\ddot{S}(t_k)(t-t_k)\right]dt$$

$$=S(t_k)+\dot{S}(t_k)h+\frac{1}{2}\ddot{S}(t_k)h^2 \tag{15}$$

Substituting the control law equation (14) into equation (10) leads to,

$$S(t_k+h)\approx S(t_k)+Ksat[S(t_k)/\Phi]h+\frac{1}{2}\ddot{S}(t_k)h^2 \tag{16}$$

Given the fact that h is usually small, the high order term can be ignored and the distance between $S(t_k)$ and $S(t_k+h)$ is mainly determined by $\dot{S}(t_k)=Ksat\,[S(t_k)/\Phi]$ and the sampling interval, h. If computational delay is considered, the sliding surface between samples can be evaluated as (the subscript c denotes the CD case.),

$$S_c(t_k+h)=S_c(t_k)+\int_{t_k}^{t_k+\varepsilon}\dot{S}_c(t)dt+\int_{t_k+\varepsilon}^{t_k+h}\dot{S}_c(t)dt$$
$$\approx S_c(t_k)+\int_{t_k}^{t_k+\varepsilon}\left[\dot{S}_c(t_k)+\ddot{S}_c(t_k)(t-t_k)\right]dt$$
$$+\int_{t_k+\varepsilon}^{t_k+h}\left[\dot{S}_c(t_k+\varepsilon)+\ddot{S}_c(t_k+\varepsilon)(t-t_k-\varepsilon)\right]dt \tag{17}$$
$$=S_c(t_k)+\dot{S}_c(t_k)\varepsilon+\frac{1}{2}\ddot{S}_c(t_k)\varepsilon^2+\dot{S}_c(t_k+\varepsilon)(h-\varepsilon)$$
$$+\frac{1}{2}\ddot{S}_c(t_k+\varepsilon)(h-\varepsilon)^2$$
$$=S_c(t_k)+\dot{S}_c(t_k)\varepsilon+\dot{S}_c(t_k+\varepsilon)(h-\varepsilon)$$
$$+\frac{1}{2}\left[\ddot{S}_c(t_k)\varepsilon^2+\ddot{S}_c(t_k+\varepsilon)(h-\varepsilon)^2\right]$$

As opposed to the case of no computational delay, $\dot{S}_c(t_k)$ is evaluated at time t_k with state $x(t_k)$ and control input of last sample, $T_{bc}^d(k-1)$. The $\dot{S}_c(t_k+\varepsilon)$ is evaluated at time $t_k+\varepsilon$ with state $x(t_k+\varepsilon)$ and control input of the current sample, $T_{bc}^d(k)$. Notice that due to the state and control input mismatch, the nonlinear terms in equation (10) cannot be cancelled out at either t_k or $t_k + \varepsilon$. Comparing equation (15) and (17) it can be found that the computational delay acts on the SMC like a disturbance, which could lead the $S_c(t_k + h)$ further from the desired manifold than $S(t_k + h)$. However, according to equation (14), the more diverged $S_c(t_k + h)$ at $t_k + h$ will generate a more effective $T_{bc}^d(k+1)$ to try to bring the surface back to zero faster. If the control gain is big enough and the sampling rate is much faster than the system time constant, then the computational delay will just expand the thickness of the sliding surface and the divergence of the surface caused by the CD is limited.

When there are computational delays located at both the high-rank and low-rank controllers, their effects on the system performance will be greater than if CD is located only at high-rank or low-rank controller. As mentioned above, the effect of the CD on the high-rank controller will arise only during the state transition, but it affects both the tracking and control energy. With the delay at the low-rank controller, the sliding surface will diverge from the desired surface for a longer time during the state transition, which could increase the tracking error and cause more control energy to bring the surface back later.

Since the computational delay is bounded within the sampling period, if the sampling rate is much faster than the system time constant (which is the time constant of the brake actuator here), then the system state will not diverge as much from the desired by the delayed control actions within the delay time.

SIMULATION STUDIES

The hybrid ACC system developed in the previous section is simulated in Matlab/Simulink for evaluating the effect of the computational delay and its location on the performance of this hybrid control system in terms of peak error, RMSE, and control energy. Four different hybrid ACC systems: without computational delay (No CD), computational delay at the low-rank controller only (LR CD), computational delay at the high-rank controller only (HR CD), and computational delay at both low-rank and high-rank controllers (HLR CD) are compared.

Figure 5, Figure 6, and Figure 7 show the simulation results of the peak error, RMSE, and control energy, respectively, for different λ values at a sampling rate of 200 Hz. As expected, the peak error, RMSE, and the control energy generally increase with the upper bound of the computational delay. The performance has deteriorated most at the HLR CD case and the least at the LR CD case. Comparing the HR CD and LR CD cases, one can find that the effect of the computational delay located at the high-rank controller is more pronounced than that located at the low-rank controller.

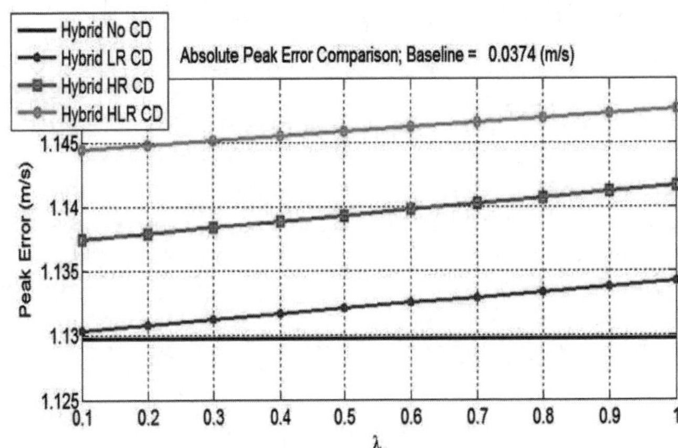

Figure 5. Peak error for different λ values (200 Hz)

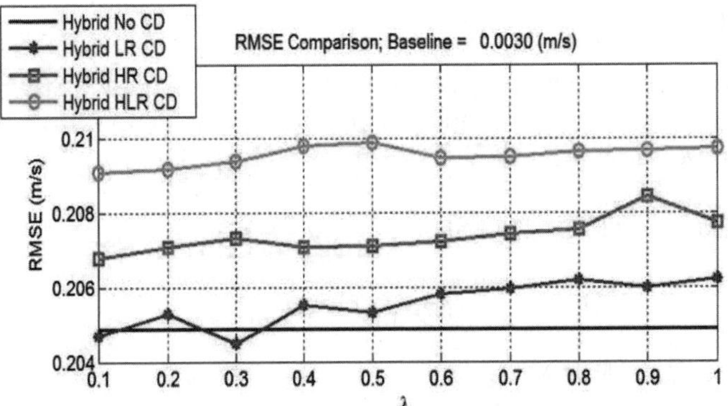

Figure 6. RMSE for different λ values (200 Hz)

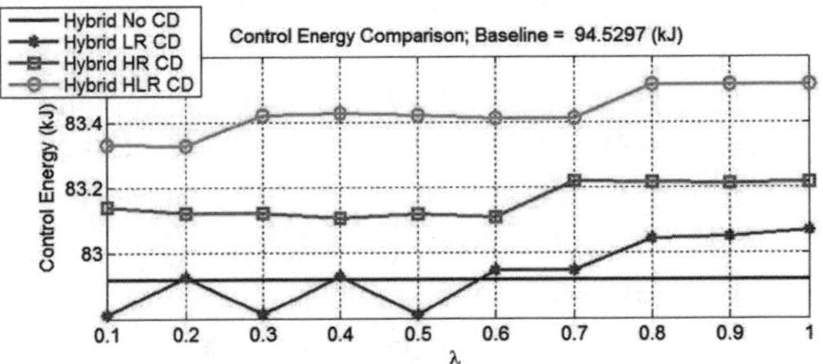

Figure 7. Control energy for different λ values (200 Hz)

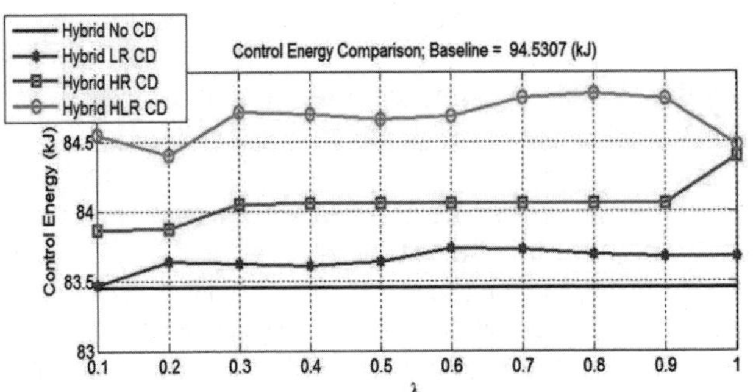

Figure 8. Control energy for different λ values (100 Hz)

Similar simulations were conducted for slower sampling rates as well. The same general trend was found. As the sampling rate is reduced, the baseline performance is degenerated and the computational delay upper bound is increased, which causes more deterioration of the performance when computational delay exists in the system. Figure 8 shows simulation results for the control energy at sampling rate of 100 Hz.

COMPENSATION OF THE COMPUTATIONAL DELAY

Knowing that the computational delay at the high-rank supervisory controller deteriorates the system performance greater than that at the low-rank controller, a simple computational delay compensation technique is designed for the high-rank controller to improve the system performance.

As described before, the supervisory controller switches between the coast and braking states based on two variables, speed error, $v_{err}(t)$, and spacing, $s(t)$. However, the switching decision will be postponed by the computational delay, ε. To compensate for the computational delay associated with the decision making process, we can employ lead compensation to form two new variables,

$$\hat{v}_{err}(t+\varepsilon) = v_{err}(t) + \dot{v}_{err}(t) \times \varepsilon ,$$

$$\hat{s}(t+\varepsilon) = s(t) + \dot{s}(t) \times \varepsilon , \quad (18)$$

for the state transition in the FSM, where, $\dot{v}_{err}(t)$ and $\dot{s}(t)$ are the derivatives of the v_{err} and spacing s at time t, respectively. $\hat{v}_{err}(t+\varepsilon)$ and $\hat{s}(t+\varepsilon)$ can approximately predict the $v_{err}(t+\varepsilon)$ and $s(t+\varepsilon)$ at time t, respectively. The switching decision made based on these new variables at time t and received by the low-rank controller at time $t+\varepsilon$ is approximately the same as the one made based on $v_{err}(t+\varepsilon)$ and $s(t+\varepsilon)$. Therefore, the effect of the computational delay at the high-rank controller can be compensated.

The performance of the compensated system is compared with that of the one without compensation in simulation. The HLR CD case is used for the comparison. The compensation is applied only at the high-rank controller while there is still the same computational delay at the low-rank controller for both systems. Figure 9 shows the simulation results, which generally indicate that the compensated system exhibits better performance in terms of smaller RMSE, smaller peak error, and less control effort, especially for the high computational delay region where the effect of the CD is significant.

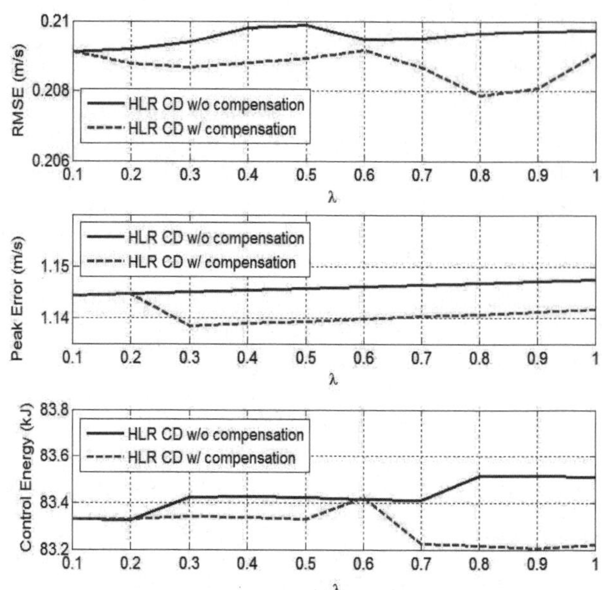

Figure 9. Comparison of the system without and with computational delay compensation at high-rank controller

CONCLUSIONS

The effect of the computational delay on the performance of a hybrid ACC control system is evaluated. The bounded computational delay affects the performance of this hybrid control system in terms of peak error, RMSE, and control energy. The performance generally deteriorates as the upper bound of the computational delay increases. It is also noticed that the effect of the computational delay at the high-rank controller is more pronounced than that at low-rank controller.

The hybrid ACC system with a computational delay compensator applied at the high-rank controller shows improved performance compared with that of the one without compensation. The effect of the computational delay on the system performance also depends on the sampling rate compared to the system time constant.

REFERENCES

1. Shin, K.G., and Cui, X., 1995, "Computational Time Delay and Its Effects on Real-Time Control Systems," *IEEE Transactions on Control System Technology*, Vol. 3, No. 2, pp. 218 - 224.
2. Lee, C.S.G., and Lee, B.H., 1984, "Resolved Motion Adaptive Control for Mechanical Manipulators," *Journal of Dynamic Systems, Measurement, and Control*, Vol. 106, No. 2, pp. 134 – 142.
3. Yang, T.C., 1994, "On Computational Delay in Digital and Adaptive Controllers," *Proceedings of the International Conference on Control*, Vol. 2, pp. 906 – 910.

4. Long, M.L., Carroll, J.J., and Mukundan, R., 1997, "Comments on 'Computing Time Delay and Its Effects on Real-Time Control Systems'," *IEEE Transactions on Control System Technology*, Vol. 5, No. 3, pp. 379.
5. Nilsson, J. Bernhardsson, B., and Wittenmark, B., 1998, "Stochastic Analysis and Control of Real-time Systems with Random Time Delays," *Automatica*, Vol. 34, No. 1, pp. 57 – 64.
6. Anderson, J.N., and Reed, B. L., 1990, "The Effects of Computational Delay on the Model-Based Control of Manipulators," *Proceedings of IEEE Southeastcon*, pp. 103 – 107.
7. Ovaska, S. J. and Vainio, O., 1997, "Predictive Compensation of Time-Varying Computing Delay on Real-Time Control Systems," *IEEE Transactions on Control System Technology*, Vol. 5, No. 5, pp. 523 – 526.
8. Rattan, K.S., 1989, "Compensating for Computational Delay in Digital Equivalent of Continuous Control Systems," *IEEE Transactions on Automatic Control*, Vol. 34, No. 8, pp. 895 – 899.
9. Mita, T., 1985, "Optimal Digital Feedback Control Systems Counting Computation Time of Control Laws," *IEEE Transactions on Automatic Control*, Vol. 30, No. 6, pp. 542 – 548.
10. Savkin, A., Evans, R., 2002, "Hybrid Dynamical Systems: Controller and Sensor Switching Problems," Birkhauser.
11. Wang, J. and Rajamani, R., 2004, "Should Adaptive Cruise Control Systems be Designed to Maintain a Constant Time-Gap between Vehicles?" *IEEE Transactions on Vehicular Technology*, Vol. 53, No. 5, pp. 1480 – 1490.
12. Wang, J. and Rajamani, R., 2004, "The Impact of Adaptive Cruise Control (ACC) Systems on Highway Safety and Traffic Flow," *Journal of Automobile Engineering, Proceedings of the Institution of Mechanical Engineers, Part D*, Vol. 218, Issue 2, pp. 111 – 130.
13. Wang, J. and Rajamani, R., 2002, "Adaptive Cruise Control System Design and Its Impact on Traffic Flow," *Proceedings of American Control Conference*, pp. 3690 – 3695.
14. Johansen, T.A., Petersen, I., Kalkkuhl, J., and Ludemann, J., 2003, "Gain-Scheduled Wheel Slip Control in Automotive Brake Systems," *IEEE Transactions on Control System Technology*, Vol. 11, No. 6, pp. 799 – 811.
15. Godbole, D.N., Lygeros, J., Sastry, S., 1994, "Hierarchical Hybrid Control: an IVHS Case Study," Proceedings of the 33rd *IEEE Conference on Decision and Control*, Vol. 2, pp. 1592 – 1597.
16. Choi, H.C., Hong, S.K., 2002, "Hybrid Control for Longitudinal Speed and Traction of Vehicles," *Proceedings of the 28th IEEE Conference*, Vol. 2, pp. 1675 – 1680.
17. Godbole, D., Kourjanskaia, N., Sengupta, R., and Zandonadi, M., 1998, "Methodology for an Adaptive Cruise Control Study Using the SHIFT/Smart-AHS Framework," *Proceedings of IEEE International Conference on Systems, Man and Cybernetics*, Vol. 4, pp. 3217 – 3222.
18. "Vehicle Dynamics Terminology," SAE J670e, Society of Automotive Engineers.
19. Anwar, S., 2003, "Brake-Based Vehicle Traction Control via Generalized Predictive Algorithm," *SAE Paper 2003-01-0323*.
20. Oh, B., Hwang, W., Song, B., 2000," Simulator for Forward Collision Warning and Avoidance System," *Proceedings of FISITA World Automotive Congress*, pp. 1-6.
21. Pasterkamp, W.R., and Pacejka, H.B., 1997, "The Tyre as a Sensor to Estimate Friction," *Vehicle System Dynamics*, Vol. 27, pp. 409 – 422.
22. Gustaffson, F., 1997, "Slip-Based Tire-Road Friction Estimation," *Automatica*, Vol. 33, No. 6, pp. 1087 – 1099.
23. Wang, J., Alexander, L., and Rajamani, R., 2004, "Friction Estimation on Highway Vehicles Using Longitudinal Measurements," *Journal of Dynamic Systems, Measurement, and Control*, Vol. 126, pp. 265 – 275.
24. Furuta, K., 1990, "Sliding Mode Control of Discrete System," *System & Control Letters*, Vol. 14, pp. 145 – 152.
25. Spurgeon, S. K., 1991, "Sliding Mode Control Design for Uncertain Discrete-Time Systems," *Proceedings of 30th IEEE Conference on Decision and Control*, pp. 2136 – 2141.
26. Sira-Ramirez, S., 1991, "Non-linear Discrete Variable Structure Systems in Quasi-Sliding Mode," *International Journal of Control*, Vol. 54, pp. 1171 – 1187.
27. Sarpturk, S.Z., Istefanopulos, Y., Kaynak, O., 1987, "On the Stability of Discrete-Time Sliding Mode Control Systems," *IEEE Transactions on Automatic Control*, Vol. 32, No. 10, pp. 930 – 932.
28. Young, K. D., Ozguner, U., 1999, "Sliding Mode: Control Engineering in Practice," *Proceedings of the American Control Conference*, pp. 150 – 162.
29. Luck, R. and Ray, A., 1990, "An Observer-based Compensator for Distributed Delays," *Automatica*, Vol. 26, No. 5, pp. 903 – 908.

LIST OF VARIABLES

v_{err}:	Vehicle speed error
v_p:	Speed of the preceding vehicle
v_c:	Speed of the current vehicle
$v\_errThrC2B$:	Speed error threshold value for transition from cruise to brake
s:	Spacing between vehicles
$s\_\min C2B$:	Minimum spacing value for transition from cruise to brake
$v\_errThrB2C$:	Speed error threshold value for transition from brake to cruise
S:	Tire longitudinal slip ration

v: Vehicle speed

ω_w: Wheel rotational speed

R: Tire effective radius

τ_b: Time constant for brake-by-wire actuator

T_b: Braking torque

T_b^d: Desired braking torque

J_w: Wheel rotational moment of inertia

F_g: Force from the ground

M: Vehicle mass

D_a: Vehicle air drag coefficient

μ: Tire road friction coefficient

ε: Computational delay

h: Sampling period

CONTACT

Junmin Wang is a Research Engineer at Southwest Research Institute and a Ph.D. Candidate at The University of Texas at Austin. He can be reached by email: junmin.wang@swri.org. Raul G. Longoria is an Associate Professor in the Department of Mechanical Engineering at The University of Texas at Austin and can be reached by email: r.longoria@mail.utexas.edu.

2006-01-0348

A Study of String-Stable ACC Using Vehicle-to-Vehicle Communication

Yoshinori Yamamura and Yoji Seto
Nissan Motor Co., Ltd.

ABSTRACT

A study was made on a control method for an adaptive cruise control (ACC) system that uses vehicle-to-vehicle communication to achieve a substantial improvement in string stability and natural headway distance response characteristics at lower levels of longitudinal G. A control system using model predictive control was constructed to achieve this desired ACC vehicle behavior. Control simulations were performed using experimental data obtained in vehicle-following driving tests conducted on a proving ground course using a platoon of three manually driven vehicles. The results showed that the proposed ACC system satisfactorily achieved higher levels of required ACC performance.

INTRODUCTION

The major objective of the adaptive cruise control (ACC) systems [1], [2] commercialized at present is to reduce the driver's workload. However, in addition to that function, it is envisioned that as the use of ACC systems becomes more widespread in the future, they will have to support vehicle behavior which works to improve traffic flow. An important property of headway distance control with respect to improving road transportation efficiency by suppressing traffic flow disruptions and density variations is string stability. This refers to the property whereby changes in a preceding vehicle's speed are not amplified and propagated to following vehicles. This study examined an ACC control method capable of substantially improving string stability through the use of vehicle-to-vehicle communication, which has been the focus of research and development efforts toward practical implementation in various countries in recent years.

The vehicles envisioned as the target of the ACC system described here are ones driven by human drivers in front of the host vehicle. The system uses vehicle-to-vehicle communication to detect the operating status of each vehicle, including its speed, position and other conditions, and controls the host vehicle's speed accordingly so as to obtain natural vehicle behavior. Control is performed in such a way that the response characteristic of the host vehicle's speed does not overshoot the lead vehicle's speed. As a result, string stability is maintained between the lead vehicle and the host vehicle, and decline in the driving speed of the platoon is suppressed. Such performance is achieved even in situations where the string stability of multiple intermediate vehicles between the lead vehicle and the host vehicle is relatively poor.

As one control method for obtaining the above-mentioned vehicle behavior, an ACC system was constructed in this study using a model predictive control method. This paper describes the effectiveness of the system and presents experimental and simulation results to illustrate its performance.

STRING STABILITY

The nomenclature used here is defined as indicated in Figure 1. The integer i=0, 1, •••, n-1 represents the i-th vehicle in a platoon consisting of n number of vehicles. The notation v_i is the velocity of the i-th vehicle, and d_i is the headway distance between the i-th vehicle and the i+1-th vehicle. The n-1-th vehicle is regarded as the lead vehicle, and the 0-th vehicle is the tail-end vehicle in the platoon.

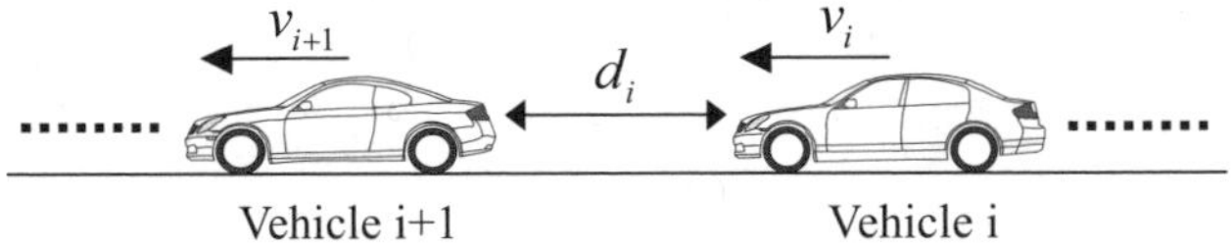

Figure 1 Vehicle string

Assuming that the i-th vehicle controls the headway distance by using only information received from the i+1-th vehicle, then the transfer function from the lead vehicle's velocity v_{n-1} to the tail-end vehicle's velocity v_0 can be expressed by the following equation:

$$\frac{v_0(s)}{v_{n-1}(s)} = G_0(s) \cdot G_1(s) \cdot \cdots \cdot G_{n-2}(s) \qquad (1)$$

where $G_i(s)$ is the velocity transfer function when the i-th vehicle uses information from the i+1-th vehicle to control the headway distance. The relationship between v_i and v_{i+1} is given as

$$v_i(s) = G_i(s) \cdot v_{i+1}(s) \tag{2}$$

In maintaining a constant headway distance, the steady-state gain of $G_i(s)$ should be 1 because the velocity of the i-th vehicle and that the i+1-th vehicle are equal under a steady-state condition. However, if many vehicles in the platoon are traveling in a manner such that the gain characteristic of $G_i(s)$ becomes larger than 1 at a certain frequency, a slight change in the lead vehicle's velocity can be amplified and propagated from one vehicle to the next, with the result that the tail-end vehicle may experience a situation where it has to stop. In order to prevent such amplification and propagation of velocity changes, the following expression is defined:

$$\|G_0(s)\|_\infty \le 1, \ \|G_1(s)\|_\infty \le 1, \ \cdots, \ \|G_{n-2}(s)\|_\infty \le 1 \tag{3}$$

One possible approach here is to make the H_∞ norm of the velocity transfer function of each vehicle less than 1, or another approach is to define the following equation:

$$\|G_0(s) \cdot G_1(s) \cdot \cdots \cdot G_{n-2}(s)\|_\infty \le 1 \tag{4}$$

It is clear that the H_∞ norm of the product of the transfer functions should be made less than 1 [3]. However, a platoon is generally formed of vehicles, including those operated manually by their drivers, that have various headway distance control characteristics. Accordingly, on ordinary roads it would be extremely difficult to form a platoon that would satisfy Eq. (3).

Here, we consider a case where the host vehicle, fitted with the ACC system that performs headway distance control using only information on the vehicle directly in front of it and is traveling at the tail-end of a vehicle string as shown in Fig. 2.

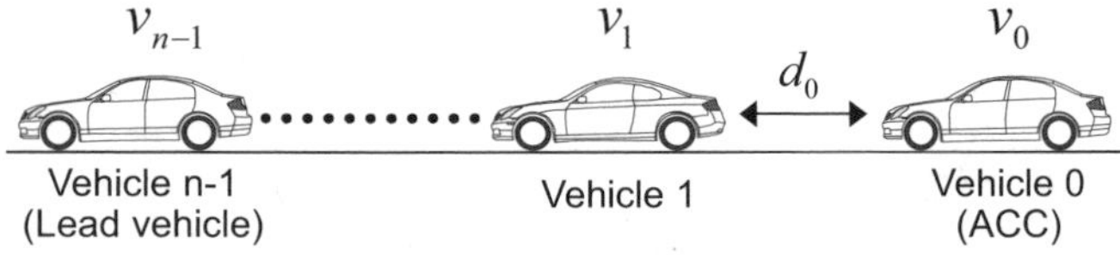

Figure 2 Vehicle string including ACC

In this case, if the ACC control characteristics can be designed such that they absorb the velocity overshoot characteristics of the multiple preceding vehicles, then the H_∞ norm of the total velocity transfer function from the lead vehicle to the tail-end vehicle can be kept below 1 and Eq. (4) will hold true. However, there is concern that ride comfort may deteriorate because the characteristics of $G_0(s)$ are very sensitive to changes in the velocity of the preceding vehicle and to noise in the headway distance sensor.

STRING-STABLE ACC USING VEHICLE-TO-VEHICLE COMMUNICATION

Consider a platoon consisting of n number of vehicles like that shown in Fig. 2 where it is assumed that all of them are fitted with a vehicle-to-vehicle communication system. The ACC vehicle is again the tail-end vehicle. In this case, the ACC vehicle can obtain information on the operating status of the multiple preceding vehicles via vehicle-to-vehicle communication. That capability makes it possible to keep the H_∞ norm of the velocity transfer function from the lead vehicle to the controlled vehicle below 1 without causing ride comfort to deteriorate, even in situations where the string stability of the vehicles between them is relatively poor.

In the case of the platoon in Fig. 2, we assume that the tail-end ACC vehicle is controlled such that the transfer function from the lead vehicle's velocity v_{n-1} to its own velocity v_0 becomes $G_{0L}(s)$. If the H_∞ norm of $G_{0L}(s)$ is determined so that it is less than 1, this platoon will have string stability from the lead vehicle to the ACC vehicle. In this case, the response of d_0 relative to v_{n-1} is given by

$$\frac{d_0(s)}{v_{n-1}(s)} = \frac{1}{s}\{G_1(s) \cdots G_{n-2}(s) - G_{0L}(s)\} \tag{5}$$

It is clear from Eq. (5) that the transient response of the headway distance d_0 when v_{n-1} changes is dependent on the difference in response characteristics between the velocity transfer characteristics of the in-between vehicles $G_1(s)$ ••• $G_{n-2}(s)$ and the response characteristics of $G_{0L}(s)$. If a platoon contains many vehicles whose velocity transfer characteristics include dead time, d_0 will tend to increase initially and then decrease in a situation where the lead vehicle decelerates from a steady speed. In case d_0 increases extremely, the driver of the ACC vehicle may feel that the vehicle behavior is unnatural.

CONTROL SYSTEM DESIGN

REQUIREMENT OF HEADWAY DISTANCE CONTROLLER

When vehicle-to-vehicle communication is used to accomplish ACC control as outlined above, the behavior of the controlled vehicle changes according to the behavior of preceding vehicles that are not directly visible to the controlled vehicle's driver. From the driver's viewpoint, such behavior may seem unnatural because his/her vehicle starts to decelerate at an early timing, even though the vehicle directly ahead is not decelerating. It is desirable to design the control system such that, in relation to greater deceleration by an unseen preceding vehicle, the controlled vehicle begins to decelerate at an earlier timing and slows down at a smaller rate of deceleration so as to maintain the desired headway distance to the vehicle directly in front of it. Accordingly, the key point for the design of the control system is to suppress any unnatural feeling in the headway distance response and furthermore to accomplish it at the smallest rate of deceleration possible, while ensuring string stability with the lead vehicle. The above-mentioned requirements can be summed up as follows:

(1) The H_∞ norm of the transfer function from the lead vehicle's velocity v_{n-1} to the host vehicle's velocity v_0 should be less than 1.

(2) The response characteristic of the headway distance d_0 between the host vehicle and the vehicle directly ahead of it should not give the driver any unnatural feeling.

(3) The conditions in (1) and (2) above should be accomplished at a small rate of deceleration.

DESIGN OF HEADWAY DISTANCE CONTROLLER

In order to satisfy the three requirements noted above, it is necessary to be able to predict platoon behavior. For example, consider that one of the vehicles ahead of the ACC vehicle decelerates for some reason. In this case, it is important to predict how that deceleration will be propagated through the platoon to the vehicle just ahead of the ACC vehicle and to determine the optimum control input accordingly. A headway distance controller using model predictive control was constructed in this study as one example of a control technique for meeting the above-mentioned requirements. A block diagram of the ACC system is shown in Fig. 3.

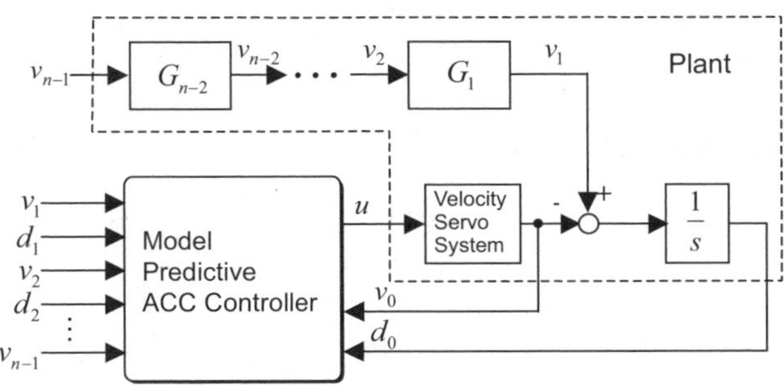

Figure 3 Block diagram of ACC system

With model predictive control, the operational state qualities of the platoon at the present time t are regarded as the initial values and a mathematical model is used to predict the future behavior of the plant in the interval from time t to t+T. An input trajectory is calculated at every sampling time for obtaining the optimal cost function during this interval. Among the optimum input trajectories calculated from time t to t+T, the value at time t is used as the actual input to the plant.

Plant

The plant is the portion enclosed in the dashed line in Fig. 3. In the velocity servo system it is assumed that the host vehicle's velocity v_0 relative to the velocity command value u matches the first-order system shown in the following equation.

$$\dot{v}_0 = -\omega_v \cdot v_0 + \omega_v \cdot u \tag{6}$$

The relative velocity between the host vehicle and vehicle 1 (the vehicle directly ahead of it) is given by

$$\dot{d}_0 = v_1 - v_0 \tag{7}$$

The vehicle-following behavior of i-th vehicle's driver is denoted as G_i, which is modeled as follows:

$$\dot{v}_i = k_{v\_i} \cdot v_i + k_{d\_i} \cdot d_i + k_{r\_i} \cdot v_{i+1} \tag{8}$$

$$\dot{d}_i = v_{i+1} - v_i \tag{9}$$

where

$$k_{d\_i} = 2 \cdot \zeta_{d\_i} \cdot \omega_{d\_i},$$
$$k_{r\_i} = \omega_{d\_i}^2,$$
$$k_{v\_i} = -k_{d\_i} \cdot T_{h\_i} - k_{r\_i}$$

The values of ω_{d_i} and ζ_{d_i} are varied according to the headway distance d_i and the relative velocity v_{i+1}-v_i so that they match the characteristics of a typical driver. The notation T_{h_i} is the time headway for the driver of the i-th vehicle.

Summarizing the expressions from Eq. (6) to Eq. (9), we can express the vehicle behavior of the platoon in the form of the following equation.

$$\dot{x} = f(x,\ u,\ t) \tag{10}$$

where x is a vector having the composition as shown in equation below.

$$x^T = [v_0 \quad d_0 \quad v_1 \quad d_1 \quad \cdots \quad v_{n-1}] \tag{11}$$

Cost Function

The cost function is given by

$$J = \int_t^{t+T} L(x(\tau),\ u(\tau))d\tau \tag{12}$$

$$L(x,\ u) = q_0\left(-d_0 + T_{h0}\cdot v_0\right)^2 + \sum_{k=1}^{n-1} q_k\left(v_k - v_0\right)^2 + r\left(u - v_{ref}\right)^2 \quad (13)$$

where t is the present time, T is the length of the prediction horizon and q_0, •••, q_{n-1} and r are parameters showing the weighting. The first term on the right-hand side of Eq. 13 is for evaluating the extent to which the time headway to the vehicle directly ahead of the host vehicle coincides with the target value T_{h0}. It serves to prevent the spacing to the vehicle directly ahead from becoming too close or too distant. The second term on the right-hand side is for evaluating the extent to which the relative velocity between the host vehicle and the multiple vehicles ahead is suppressed to zero. The third term on the right-hand side is for evaluating the extent to which the velocity command value u agrees with the velocity reference model v_{ref}, which is given by

$$v_{ref} = G_{mv}(s)\cdot v_{n-1} \quad (14)$$

where

$$G_{mv}(s) = \frac{\left(2\cdot\zeta_{mv}\cdot\omega_{mv} - \omega_{mv}^2\cdot T_{h0L}\right)\cdot s + \omega_{mv}^2}{s^2 + 2\cdot\zeta_{mv}\cdot\omega_{mv}\cdot s + \omega_{mv}^2} \quad (15)$$

In Eq. (15), T_{h0L} is the headway time between the lead vehicle and the host vehicle, and ω_{mv} and ζ_{mv} are design parameters used for setting the response characteristics. In order to satisfy the requirements mentioned earlier, ω_{mv} and ζ_{mv} were set in this study so that the acceleration or deceleration of the host vehicle was minimized.

Optimization of Headway Distance Control

Here we will consider the problem of finding the control input u of the system in Eq. (10) so as to minimize the cost function in Eq. (12) in the interval from time t to t+T. Using adjoint variables λ, we define a Hamiltonian as shown in the equation below.

$$H(x,u,\lambda,t) = L(x,u,t) + \lambda^T\cdot f(x,u,t) \quad (16)$$

Based on the minimum principle, the necessary condition for the control input u* and its corresponding trajectory x* to be optimal is that there must exist a λ * that satisfies the conditions below in relation to u* and x*.

$$\dot{x}^* = f\left(x^*,u^*,t\right),\ x^*(t) = x_0 \quad (17)$$

$$\dot{\lambda} = -H_x\left(x^*,u^*,\lambda^*\right),\ \lambda^*(t+T) = 0 \quad (18)$$

$$H\left(x^*,u^*,\lambda^*,t\right) = \min_{u\in U} H\left(x^*,u,\lambda^*,t\right) \quad (19)$$

In this study, we used the following algorithm to find the optimal solution satisfying these conditions.

Step 0: Set the values of e_J and e_u. Letting j=0, assign a nominal control input $u^{(0)}$. Then, calculate the trajectory $x^{(0)}$ and cost function $J(u^{(0)})$ relative to $u^{(0)}$, and let j=1.

Step 1: Using $x^{(j-1)}$ and $u^{(j-1)}$ found above, integrate the following differential equation in the inverse time direction.

$$\dot{\lambda}^{(j-1)} = -H_x\left(x^{(j-1)},u^{(j-1)},\lambda^{(j-1)}\right),\quad \lambda^{(j-1)}(t+T) = 0 \quad (20)$$

Step 2: Find $u^{(j)}$ and $x^{(j)}$ that satisfy the following equations.

$$u^{(j)} = Arg\ \min_{u\in U}\left[H\left(x^{(j)},u,\lambda^{(j-1)},t\right) + \left(u-u^{(j-1)}\right)^T \mu^{(j)}\left(u-u^{(j-1)}\right)\right] \quad (21)$$

$$\dot{x}^{(j)} = f\left(x^{(j)},u^{(j)},t\right),\ x^{(j)}(t) = x_0 \quad (22)$$

where $\mu^{(j)}\geq 0$.

Step 3: Calculate the following equation.

$$J\left(u^{(j)}\right) = \int_t^{t+T} L\left(x^{(j)},u^{(j)},t\right)dt \quad (23)$$

If $J(u^{(j)})>J(u^{(j-1)})-e_J$, make a correction so that $\mu^{(j)}$ becomes larger and return to Step 2. If that is not true, execute Step 4.

Step 4: If $||u^{(j)}-u^{(j-1)}||< e_u$ holds true, it is judged to be the solution that satisfies the optimality condition, and the calculation is completed. If it does not hold true, let j=j+1 and return to Step 1.

CONTROL SIMULATIONS AND DRIVING TESTS

COMPARATIVE SIMULATIONS WITH RADAR-BASED STRING STABILITY CONTROL

Simulations were conducted to compare the proposed string-stable ACC system using vehicle-to-vehicle communication and a string-stable ACC system that uses a headway distance radar sensor to detect the information needed for headway distance control only from the preceding vehicle directly ahead of the host vehicle. The simulations assumed a situation where the lead vehicle of a four-vehicle platoon traveling at a steady speed decelerates, followed by deceleration of the other vehicles in turn. The ACC vehicle is the tail-end vehicle of the platoon.

The results obtained are shown in Figure 4. Comparing the results for the two systems, it is seen that with the proposed ACC there was no vehicle velocity overshoot and also that the deceleration rate was substantially reduced even in situations where the string stability of the intermediate vehicles was relatively poor. It is also seen that the headway distance did not increase to an extreme degree.

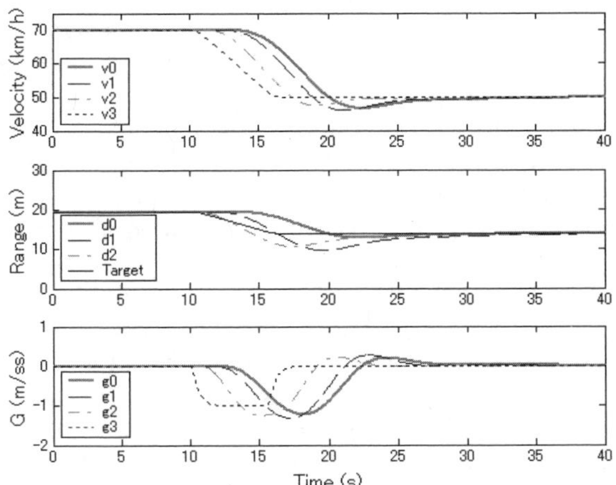

(a) Headway distance sensor type

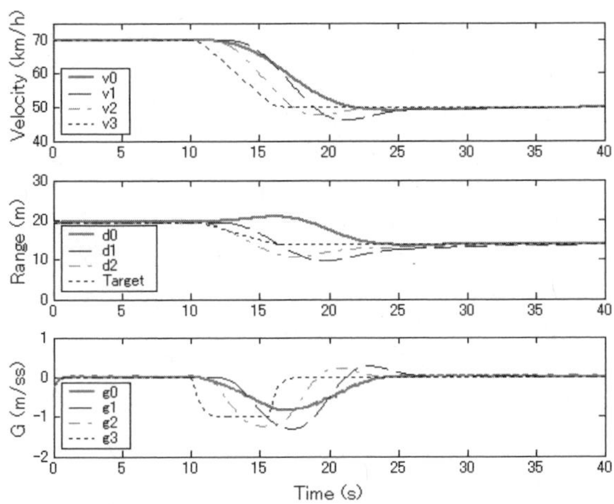

(b) Vehicle-to-vehicle communication type

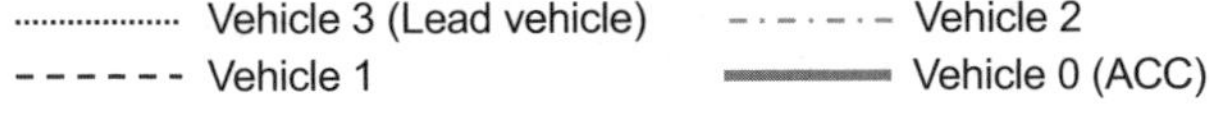

Figure 4 Simulation results for response characteristics comparison

DRIVING TESTS AND CONTROL SIMULATIONS USING TEST DATA

The control system used here requires a model of the following behavior of the intermediate vehicles between the lead vehicle and the host vehicle. Therefore, driving tests involving a platoon of three vehicles were conducted on a proving ground course, and data were measured concerning driver following behavior in manual driving. The parameters were identified and a model was created of driver following behavior. That model was then used to configure the control system.

The configuration of the experimental vehicle system is shown in Figure 5. The position of the host vehicle as detected by real-time kinematic (RTK)-GPS, operating data and other information were exchanged with other vehicles by means of a vehicle-to-vehicle communication system.

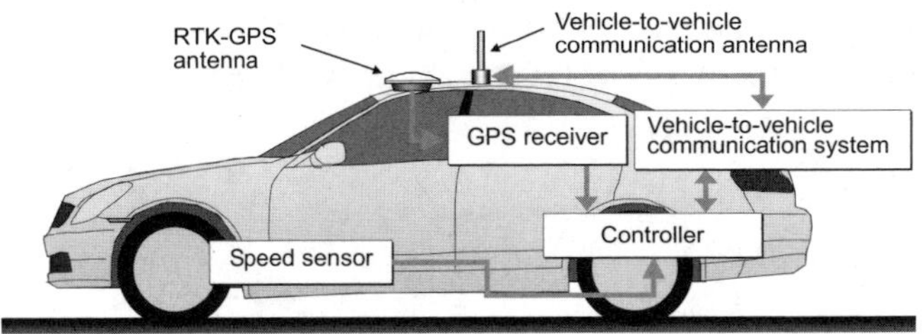

Figure 5 Configuration of experimental vehicle system

As illustrated in Figure 6, the test data used were for manual driving in which three test vehicles followed one another in a platoon; simulations were conducted for a scenario where the tail-end ACC vehicle followed the other three vehicles.

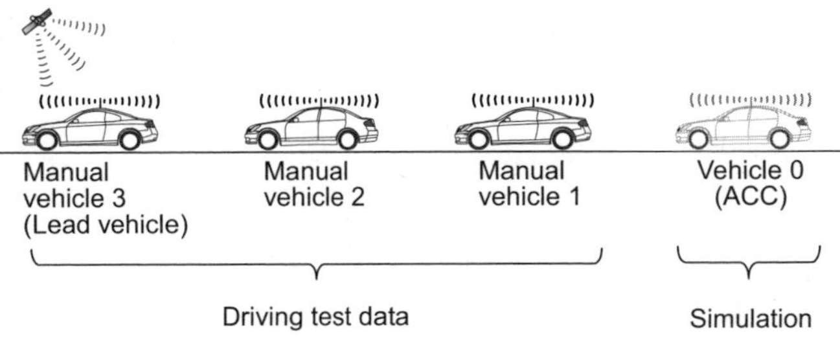

Figure 6 Image of ACC simulation using driving test data

The results obtained in the simulations using the test data are shown in Figure 7. The velocity of the lead vehicle was reduced from 70 km/h to 50 km/h at two different rates of deceleration: (a) 1 m/s^2 and (b) 2 m/s^2. The results indicate that, following deceleration by the lead vehicle, the velocity of the two intermediate vehicles fell below that of the leader, whereas that of the ACC vehicle did not, and its rate of deceleration was better controlled than that of the two intermediate vehicles. One especially notable result is that the rate of deceleration of the ACC vehicle was kept to approximately one-half of that of the vehicle directly ahead of it. An acceptable value for the increase in the headway distance to the vehicle ahead with the proposed system is an aspect that will be examined in future driving tests. However, judging from these simulation results, the increase in the headway distance can be controlled relatively well, so it is presumed that the driver of the ACC vehicle would not perceive any appreciable degree of unnatural vehicle behavior. There still remains a slight steady-state deviation from the target headway distance, which indicates that the method of weighting the cost function in Eq. (12) needs some further improvement. In these simulations, the cost function was weighted using a constant value. However, it is thought that the weight should be varied according to the operational status of the multiple vehicles ahead in order to satisfy the requirements imposed on the headway distance controller with respect to the different dynamic conditions of the preceding vehicles.

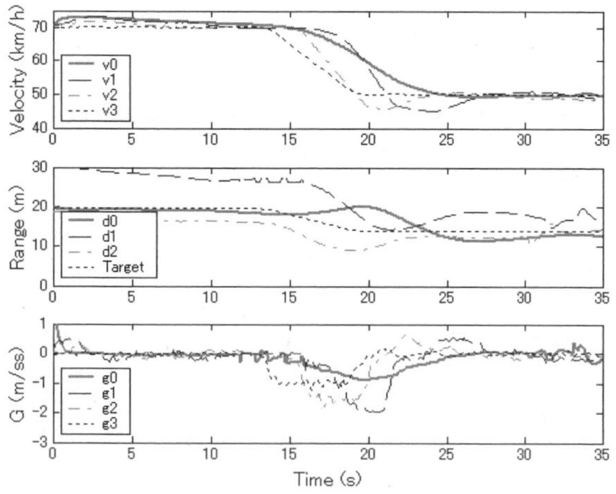

(a) Lead vehicle deceleration 1 m/s^2

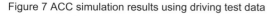

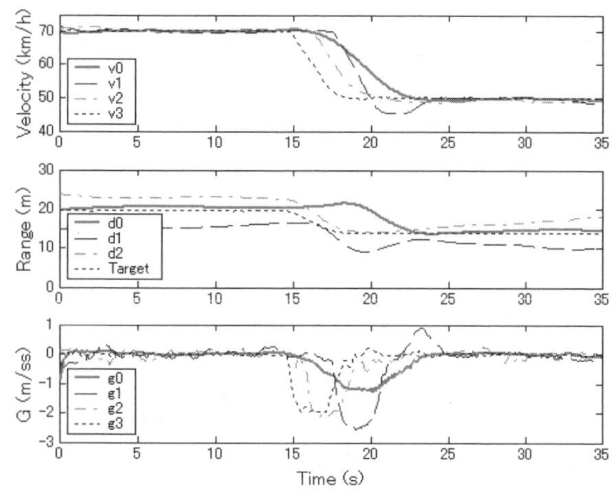

(b) Lead vehicle deceleration 2 m/s^2

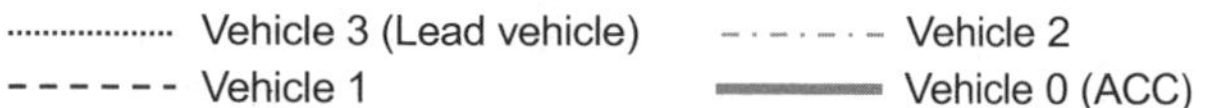

Figure 7 ACC simulation results using driving test data

CONCLUSION

This paper has described the control system for an ACC system that uses vehicle-to-vehicle communication to improve string stability substantially and to obtain natural vehicle behavior with a smaller degree of longitudinal acceleration/deceleration. As one control strategy for obtaining such improvements, a control system was constructed in this study using a model predictive control method. ACC simulations were conducted using test data recorded for driver following behavior in manual driving in a three-vehicle platoon on a proving ground coarse. The results showed that, in simulations involving deceleration by the lead vehicle of a four-vehicle platoon, the proposed system achieved higher levels of required ACC performance with respect to string stability, little unnatural headway distance response behavior and reduction of the rate of deceleration. With the aim of satisfying higher levels of required performance under a wide variety of driving situations, future research will examine a control system capable of accommodating the diverse response characteristics of intermediate vehicle drivers. It is planned to address this issue by improving the weighting method and adding constraints, among other measures.

REFERENCES

1. T. Iijima, et al., "Development of Adaptive Cruise Control with Brake Actuation", SAE Technical Paper No. 2000-01-1353 (2000).
2. Y. Yamamura, et al., "Development of an Adaptive Cruise Control System with Stop-and-Go Capability", SAE Technical Paper No. 2001-01-0798 (2001).
3. C. Liang and H. Peng, "String Stability Analysis of Adaptive Cruise Controlled Vehicles", JSME International Journal Series C, Volume 43, No.3, September 2000, pp. 671-677.

2006-01-0346

InterActive Cruise Control - A New Driver Interaction Concept for Adaptive Cruise Control Systems

Christoph Mayser[1], Karl Naab[2] and Walter Kagerer[1]
[1] BMW Group, Driver Assistance and Active Safety Systems / System Development
[2] BMW Group, System Architecture and Design / Driver Assistance Systems

ABSTRACT

Already established driver assistance systems like Cruise Control or Adaptive Cruise Control are based on the delegation of a part of the driving task to the system. Instead of keeping a suitable speed the driver is just monitoring the correct function of the assistance system. In situations when the system is fulfilling the task in a way the driver doesn't accept she / he has to deactivate it. Adding a new input element the driver gains the possibility to create additional inputs in terms of acceleration or deceleration to the assistance system. This allows the driver to modify the system behavior in different driving situations without deactivating the system. The relationship between driver and system shifts from "delegation" to "co-operation". This paper explains principal aspects of the technical realization and presents the results of a study regarding the first contact of subjects with an enhanced Adaptive Cruise Control.

INTRODUCTION

Traffic density is rising due to a constantly increasing number of vehicles combined with an infrastructure that is not growing equivalently. Therefore the driving task today has become more and more difficult. Further, the additional distraction of the driver through the use of cell phones and other communication devices while driving has intensified the problem. Within the last two decades, the automotive industry has started developing technical systems with the goal to assist the driver, accordingly to increase driving comfort and driving safety [1].

DRIVER ASSISTANCE

The basic idea of driver assistance is to support the driver according to her / his expectations. This characteristic can be compared to an electronic co-pilot that assists the driver performing the driving task. The first technical systems introduced into the market were chassis management systems (figure 1) like Anti Blocking Systems (ABS) or Dynamic Stability Control (DSC). They support the driver by taking over control for a very short time to regain stability of the vehicle. Nowadays driver information systems like Navigation Systems have been introduced into the market as well. These systems inform the driver and are capable of recommending certain actions; however, the driver remains in charge, deciding for her- / himself whether to use the supplied information.

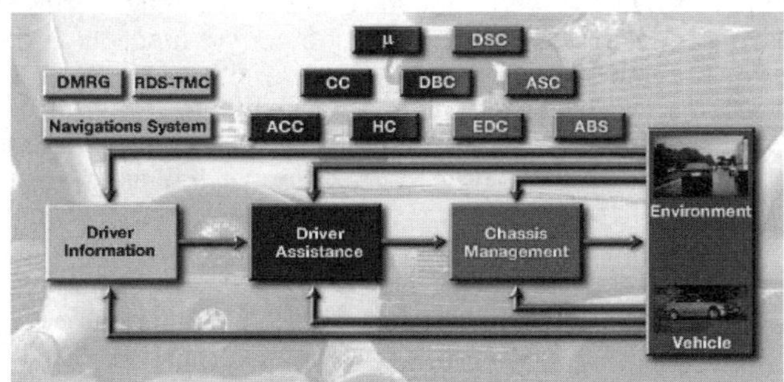

Figure 1: Classification of technical systems that are supporting the driver (Abbreviations: ABS: Anti Blocking System, EDC: Electronic Damping Control, ASC: Anti Skid Control, DSC: Dynamic Stability Control, DBC: Dynamic Brake Control, HC: Heading Control, μ: Friction Detection, CC: Cruise Control, ACC: Active Cruise Control, RDS-TMC: Radio Data System – Traffic Message Channel, DMRG: Dual Mode Route Guidance)

With the introduction of systems like Cruise Control (CC) the notion "Driver Assistance" was established. These types of driver assistance systems do not aim at automating the driving task. At the driver's request, the Cruise Control performs actions according to the rules of the driver. Instead of the task of maintaining a suitable speed the driver has the task of monitoring the correct functioning of the assistance system. This monitoring effort should be less than the effort to perform the driving task itself. The driver can intervene at any given time and still has full responsibility for the driving task. To reduce the driver's workload, the characteristic of an assistance system has to follow the mental model of the driver [2]. Thus, the possibilities of turning the system on and off as well as a high transparency of the different system states and limitations are important features.

Furthermore, the driver's interface to the assistance system should be easy to understand [3].

The more recently introduced driver assistance systems often enhance features of already established ones. Active Cruise Control (ACC), for example adds the feature of controlling the following distance between vehicles to Cruise Control [4]. Since both systems are assisting the driver in longitudinal vehicle guidance the driver expects a well-done integration between these two systems [5].

FROM ADAPTIVE TO INTERACTIVE CRUISE CONTROL

The driver has different controls to activate a Cruise Control system. Basically she / he sets or changes the **desired driving speed** and the system is maintaining the velocity of the vehicle. Using Adaptive Cruise Control there is an additional control to set the **desired following distance**. Now the system is maintaining the velocity and furthermore the distance to the leading vehicle. Driving with Cruise Control or Adaptive Cruise Control the driver is monitoring the correct functioning of the assistance system and therefore she / he is in the passive role of a supervisor. The driver can intervene at any given time, but every intervention overrules the system. After pressing the brake pedal the assistance system is deactivated and the driver has to reactivate it to pass back the control to the assistance system. After pressing and releasing the gas pedal the system is reactivated automatically, but during this intervention it has no impact on the driving task. Changes the traffic situation in front of the vehicle in the same moment, e.g. the leading vehicle is decelerating, Adaptive Cruise Control is not maintaining the following distance, since the driver took over control by pressing the gas pedal. Therefore, either the assistance system or the driver is performing the task.

Adaptive Cruise Control is based on a radar sensor which detects objects in forward traffic. The sensor itself has a range of 2 – 150 m and an angular coverage of +/- 4° [4]. The quality of sensors, used in the industry improved since the first generation of ACC, e.g. nowadays the angular coverage is +/- 8°. ACC is reacting on slower objects, which are moving in the same lane the own vehicle is driving. Therefore the system has to predict the own path using vehicle dynamics and has to select objects according to their relevance. Is a preceding vehicle out of the range of the sensor or not within the predicted path of the own vehicle ACC is maintaining the desired driving speed instead of a safe following distance.

Approaching a slower vehicle with Adaptive Cruise Control can lead to situations in which the driver has to regain the control on the driving task by deactivating the assistance system. Figure 2 illustrates the situation "approaching a significantly slower vehicle". ACC is maintaining the desired driving speed since the vehicle is out of the range of the radar sensor (figure 2, top). The leading vehicle is selected as the relevant object when it is within the range of the radar sensor. Because of the significant difference in velocity the deceleration initiated by ACC is not comfortable for the driver or – even worse – ACC is not able to reduce the velocity within a safe distance to the preceding vehicle (figure 2, bottom). In this case ACC presents a visual and acoustical warning to the driver and she / he has to intervene by pressing the brake pedal. After the critical situation is solved the driver has to reactivate the assistance system.

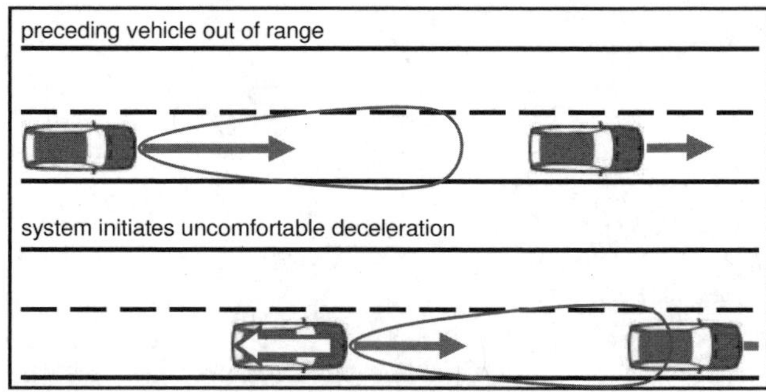

Figure 2: approaching a significantly slower vehicle with Adaptive Cruise Control (Velocity indicated by filled arrows, deceleration indicated by a hollow arrow)

Because of the fact that Cruise Control is not maintaining a safe following distance to other vehicles at all each situation "approaching a slower preceding vehicle" can be compared to the situation described above. The driver has to deactivate the assistance system to avoid a critical situation. After the preceding vehicle changed to a different lane Cruise Control can be reactivated by the driver.

Another limitation of Adaptive Cruise Control is explained in figure 3, which illustrates the situation "lane change of a preceding vehicle". Passing slower cars on the right lane should not cause a system reaction in form of deceleration since these cars are not in the lane of the ACC vehicle and therefore they should not be selected as relevant objects / preceding vehicles (figure 3, top). Is one of the drivers on the right lane performing a lane change, his vehicle will be selected after entering the predicted path of the ACC vehicle. The short distance and the lower velocity may cause a deceleration initiated by the system that is not comfortable for the driver (figure 3, bottom). Is the velocity of the vehicles similar, ACC will adjust the following distance with a comfortable deceleration, but the following distance may be very short during this adjustment process. The driver will probably deactivate the system for a moment to fall back and reactivate it after the situation is clarified.

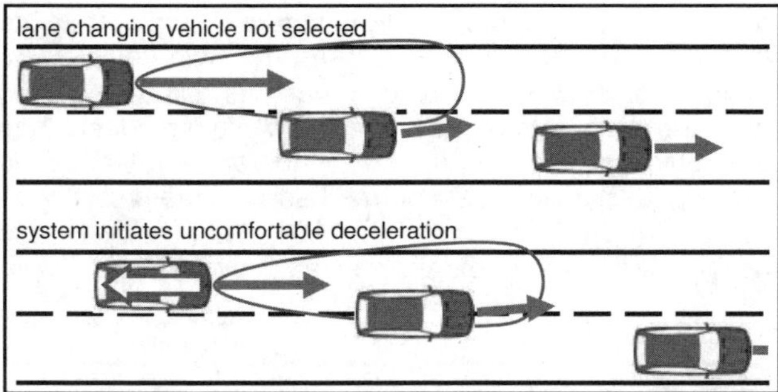

Figure 3: lane change of a preceding vehicle with Adaptive Cruise Control (Velocity indicated by filled arrows, deceleration indicated by a hollow arrow)

Both examples have in common that normally the driver is realizing the traffic situation earlier than ACC is able to interpret it correctly. Therefore she / he would take action like a moderate deceleration to solve the situation very comfortable while ACC is still maintaining the previously desired driving speed. Since ACC shows a later reaction the system would have to initiate a higher deceleration. To avoid critical or uncomfortable situations the driver needs to deactivate the system.

An approach to handle the situations "approaching a significantly slower vehicle" and "lane change of a preceding vehicle" more comfortable is to integrate sensors with a better performance to the ACC system. Using a radar sensor with a wider range and / or a wider angular coverage or adding an optical sensor with an image processing unit to the system could be sufficient technical solutions for the discussed problem. Since the prediction of the own path will be less reliable with the increasing preview area an ACC system will still show unexpected behavior in certain situations even with more sophisticated sensor concepts.

But in other situations even technical improvement might not avoid uncomfortable moments for the driver. Figure 4 illustrates the situation "passing a preceding vehicle". The ACC system follows the preceding vehicle maintaining a safe distance (figure 4, top). During the lane change maneuver, ACC is still maintaining the following distance, even if the ACC vehicle already entered the passing lane. After the driver completed the lane change, ACC detects the previously preceding vehicle is not relevant anymore and accelerates to the originally selected driving speed (figure 4, bottom). With the increasing velocity the ACC system passes the slower vehicle on the right lane.

But in the same situation the driver would intend to accelerate during the lane change to enter the passing lane with a higher speed, even if she / he is not obeying a safe following distance during this maneuver. The driver is able to take this risk, because she / he has a better overview on the complex traffic situation than the assistance system. Since the intention of the driver can not be detected by a system so far, driver expectation and system behavior will be different in these situations.

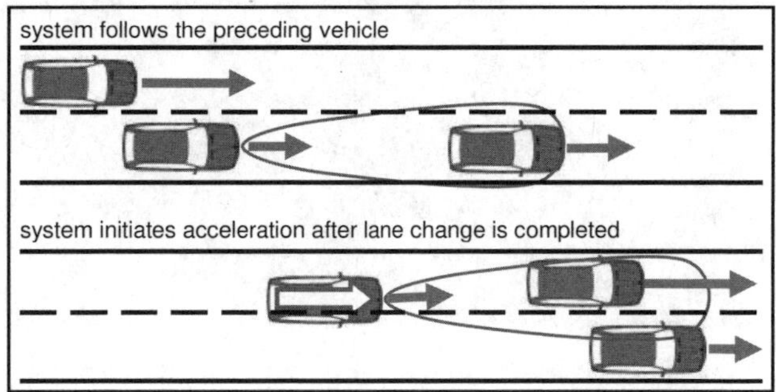

Figure 4: passing a preceding vehicle with Adaptive Cruise Control (Velocity indicated by filled arrows, deceleration indicated by a hollow arrow)

A new control device located e.g. at the steering wheel enables the driver to create additional inputs in terms of **acceleration or deceleration** to the assistance system. Acceleration is the third cinematic dimension in addition to velocity and distance which are already influenced by the driver while using ACC. The user input is added to the acceleration or deceleration required by the ACC system during normal operation. Therefore it allows the driver to modify the system behavior temporarily in certain situations without deactivating the system. Integrating this additional control it is not necessary anymore to switch off the assistance system for a wide range of driving situations. In critical situations the driver can still deactivate the system by pressing the brake pedal or pushing the OFF button.

A bi-directional lever is a practical solution for this input element. The driver produces inputs by shifting the lever in forward or in backward direction, which is interpreted as acceleration or deceleration. In a test vehicle this lever was integrated into the control area at the right hand side of the steering wheel (figure 5). Furthermore controls to set the desired speed as well as the desired following distance were placed in the same area. Finally a button to deactivate the enhanced assistance system manually was added to the steering wheel. With this concept the driver can reach all controls while keeping her / his hands at the steering wheel.

Figure 5: controls for interActive Cruise Control at the steering wheel (Top left: OFF button; top right: bi-directional lever for acceleration and deceleration; bottom left: control to select desired following distance; bottom right: control to select desired driving speed)

Using the lever the driver actively influences the previously discussed situations "approaching a significantly slower vehicle" and "lane change of a preceding vehicle". Figure 6 shows the same scenario as already presented in figure 2. Before the preceding vehicle is within the range of the radar sensor, the driver has analyzed the situation. Now she / he reduces the driving speed by adding a moderate deceleration using the lever. When the preceding vehicle is within the range of the radar sensor, the difference in velocity between the two vehicles is already reduced. The driver releases the lever and passes back the complete control to the assistance system. ACC reduces the velocity down to the speed of the preceding vehicle and starts to maintain a safe following distance. The complete situation was solved in co-operation between the driver and the assistance system.

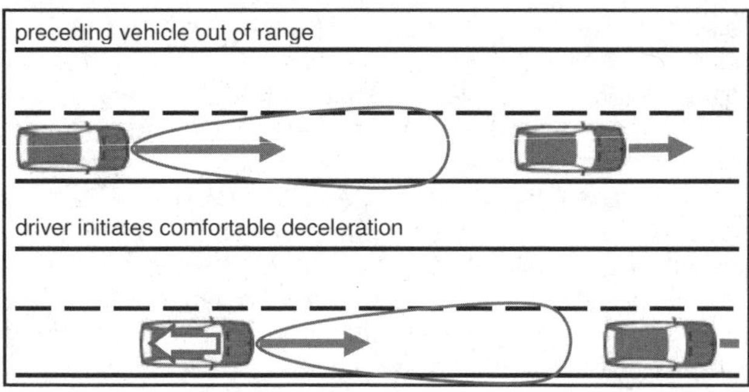

Figure 6: approaching a significantly slower vehicle with interActive Cruise Control (Velocity indicated by filled arrows, deceleration indicated by a hollow arrow)

Even the situation "passing a preceding vehicle" explained in figure 4 can be solved in co-operation using the added input element. The driver can reduce the distance by pushing the lever while she / he is still following the preceding vehicle (figure 7, top). After the faster car on the left lane passed the own vehicle, the driver begins the lane change maneuver. On the passing lane the own vehicle has already a higher speed than the vehicle on the right lane. Now the driver releases the lever and passes the control back to the assistance system (figure 7, bottom). ACC takes over and accelerates to the originally desired driving speed.

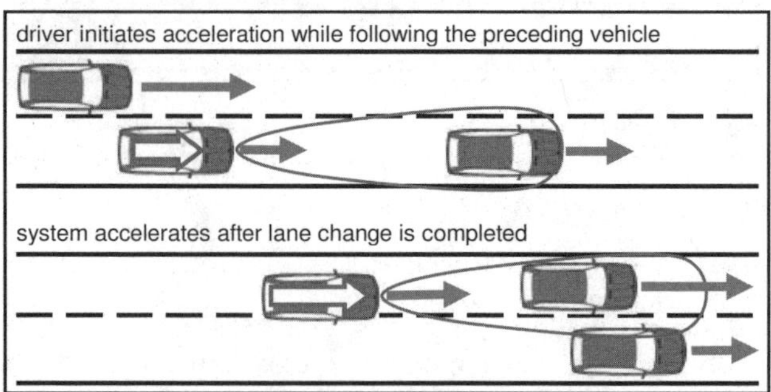

Figure 7: passing a preceding vehicle with interActive Cruise Control (Velocity indicated by filled arrows, deceleration indicated by hollow arrows)

In the moment the assistance system is not performing according to the mental model of the driver, she / he has the possibility to modify its behavior. Now the driver interacts with the system and begins to actively form the driving situation. Using a standard ACC system the driver has to deactivate the system and has to regain complete control on the driving task. The driver always has to decide whether the system is performing the driving task or she / he is doing it by her- / himself. Adding the lever as an additional input device for acceleration and deceleration the system characteristic changed from Adaptive Cruise Control (ACC) to interActive Cruise Control (iACC).

SYSTEM DESCRIPTION

To implement interActive Cruise Control the desired acceleration indicated by the lever has to be integrated into the existing Adaptive Cruise Control structure [6]. A normal ACC generates an acceleration command (a_{system}) to achieve the nominal distance (d) in case of a preceding vehicle or the nominal speed (v) in case of free flow. In this process the driver is not directly involved in the control loop, she / he only pre-selects the nominal values (d_{driver}) and (v_{driver}) by appropriate controls.

The main aspect of interActive Cruise Control is the more intensive co-operation between the driver and the assistance system. Figure 8 shows the principle of such a co-operative approach. In this case the resulting acceleration command ($a_{vehicle}$) consists of a combination of the ACC system output and the driver intention.

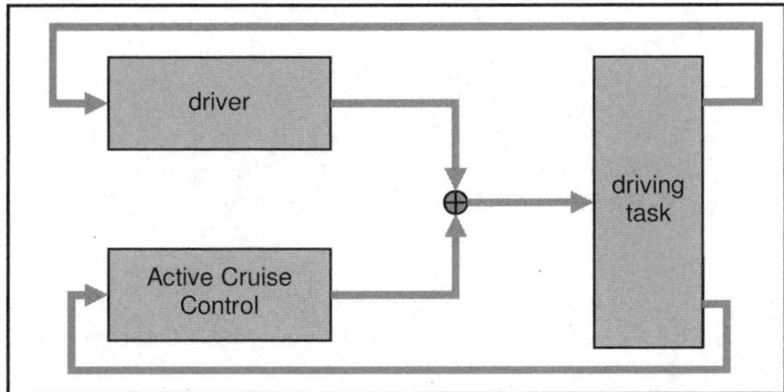

Figure 8: driver – vehicle co-operation for interActive Cruise Control

The lever shown in Figure 5 enables the driver to give additional acceleration or deceleration commands (a_{driver}), which modify the ACC system commands (a_{system}) accordingly. A possible design of a correlation between the lever angle (α_{lever}) and the resulting acceleration / deceleration ($a_{vehicle}$) is shown in Figure 9. The linear correlation is only one example; it can also be progressive, declining, symmetric or asymmetric. A weighting function is generated by the lever angle (Figure 10), which scales the ACC output (a_{system}). Additionally, a term (a_{driver}) is added depending on the lever position. If the lever is in idle position the ACC has the full control and ($a_{vehicle}$) is equivalent to (a_{system}). By pressing the lever to its positive or negative maximum the driver gets full control over the acceleration command ($a_{vehicle}$). In the range between the two extremes the driver can modify the acceleration command ($a_{vehicle}$) continuously.

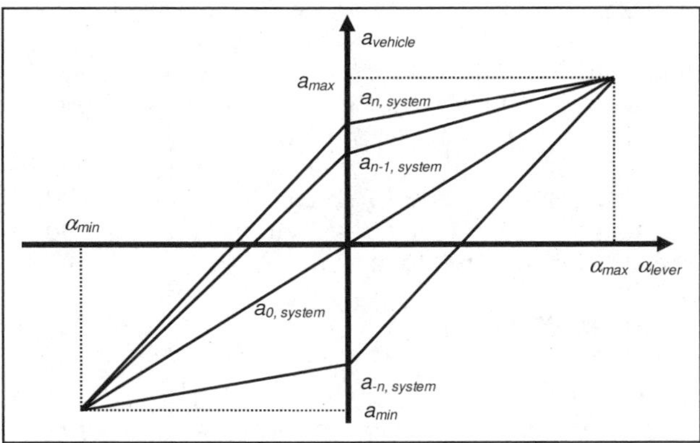

Figure 9: correlation lever-angle to acceleration and deceleration

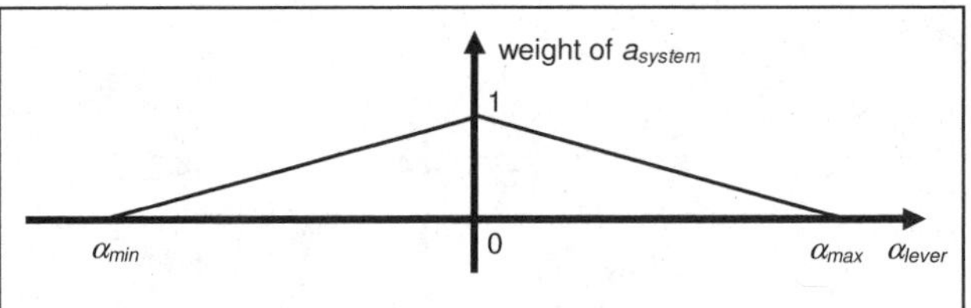

Figure 10: resulting weight of a_{system}

Figure 11 illustrates the integration principal of such a driver input to an existing Adaptive Cruise Control structure. The overlay of a_{driver} looks like an external disturbance to a_{system} within the control loop. The controller design has to ensure that this input is not compensated by the usual disturbance compensation mechanisms that are necessary to achieve accurate stationary control behavior for distance and speed. PI controller structures are not suitable. Therefore state estimation technique is proposed, which is able to distinguish between different types of disturbances within the control loop to compensate them selectively if needed.

Using this controller design to integrate manual acceleration it is possible for the driver to handle driving situations as "approaching a significantly slower vehicle", "lane change of a preceding vehicle" and also situations like "passing a preceding vehicle" without pressing the brake pedal and deactivating the assistance system. Therefore iACC is an adequate system in longitudinal control to support the driver according to her / his needs.

EVALUATION

A user study was performed to receive a feedback on interActive Cruise Control and to evaluate the impact of the system on the driving behavior of the subjects. 41 male participants were invited to the research with the previously introduced system integrated in a BMW sedan. The participants were between 35 and 55 years old and had experience in driving with Adaptive Cruise Control. After a short explanation of the input controls and the basic idea of the system the participants had the opportunity to familiarize themselves with the system. During the test drive on a predefined route the participants were requested to instantly give feedback. Furthermore all subjects were asked for feedback at the end of the test drive. Because the evaluation took place on public roads with equal parts on major highways and rural roads there was no possibility to create special driving scenarios. All comments during and after the test drive were classified in five categories (very positive, positive, neutral, negative, very negative) of overall feedback to interActive Cruise Control.

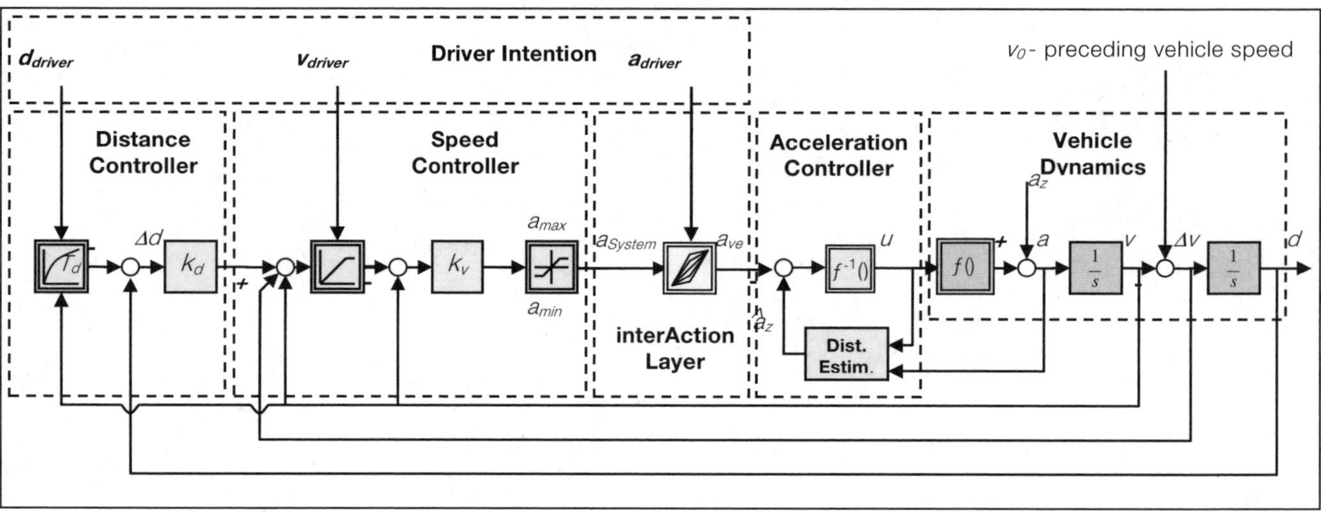

Figure 11: integration principal of the driver input to an existing ACC structure

Almost every other of the participants (48.8%) described iACC as useful enhancement of ACC. The possibility to actively form driving situations without deactivating the system was the main argument for the positive feedback. 19.5% reported a very positive feedback, because the time of usage of the assistance system is significantly increased. A negative feedback on the system was given by 7.3% of the subjects. This group saw a disadvantage in the additional input controls and the eventually higher response times to activate the brake pedal in emergency situations. 24.4% of the participants gave a neutral feedback.

In a second experiment 19 participants without experience with Cruise Control or Adaptive Cruise Control were invited to prove if the results of the first experiment are correlated to the driving experience with ACC. Within this group there a large number (68%) of participants did not give any feedback on iACC at all. These subjects were probably concentrated on the ACC system itself. Furthermore they didn't know the limitations of ACC and therefore they couldn't see the potential of an enhanced system with an additional input device.

Participants with a rich experience on ACC know the limitations of the system very well. Probably they are estimating the potential of usage for interActive Cruise Control based on their experience with the conventional ACC system.

CONCLUSION

A driving experiment was performed to investigate the acceptance of the test persons to the introduced operating device and its impact on driving with Adaptive Cruise Control. More than two thirds (68.3%) of the participants which rated interActive Cruise Control at all gave a positive feedback on the system. Using the new input element the driver can actively form the driving situation in co-operation with the system, her / his role shifts from a supervisor to a partner of the assistance system. This might result in a longer time the assistance system is in use and therefore in a better support for the driver.

On the other hand the experiment created some important remarks. For example what is the impact of an additional manual control device on the drivers reaction time in critical situations? After using the lever for more and more driving situations it might be difficult for the driver to recognize that she / he has to use the brake pedal for emergency breaking. Furthermore it is not clear if the driver is able and is interested to handle another additional input device to control the acceleration and deceleration of his vehicle. This question has to be investigated in a long term study.

REFERENCES

1. G. Reichart, R. Haller, K. Naab. (1995). "Towards future driver assistance systems". *Automotive Technology International.* pp. 25 – 29
2. D. A. Norman. (1983). "Some Observations on Mental Models". D. Gentner & A. L. Stevens (Eds.): *Mental Models.* pp. 7 – 14. Lawrence Erlbaum Associates Hillsdale, New Jersey. pp. 7 – 14.
3. R. Haller. (2000). „Wie erreicht man bei Fahrerassistenz, dass der Fahrer Herr der Situation bleibt?". H. Bubb (Ed.): *Ergonomie und Verkehrssicherheit.* Herbert Utz Verlag, München. pp. 64a – 64h
4. W. Prestl, T. Sauer, J. Steinle, O. Tschernoster. (2000). The BMW Active Cruise Control ACC. SAE

2000-01-0344, SAE Congress 2000, Detroit, Michigan.
5. M. Schraut, K. Naab, T. Bachmann. (2000). “BMW’s driver assistance concept for integrated longitudinal support”. Proceedings of 7th ITS World Congress on Intelligent Transport Systems. Turin, Italy.
6. K. Naab. (1999). „Geschwindigkeits- und Abstandsregler“. Seminar Abstandsregelung. Haus der Technik. Essen. Germany.

CONTACT

BMW Group
Christoph Mayser
80788 Munich
Germany
email: christoph.mayser@bmw.de

BMW Group
Karl Naab
80788 Munich
Germany
email: karl.naab@bmw.de

BMW Group
Walter Kagerer
80788 Munich
Germany
email: walter.kagerer@bmw.de

2006-01-0141

Adaptive Cruise Control for Heavy-Duty Vehicles: A Torque-Based Approach

Sorin C. Bengea, Peter B. Eyabi and Michael P. Nowak
Eaton Corporation, Innovation Center

Richard M. Avery and Robert O. Anderson
Eaton Corporation, Vehicle Solutions

ABSTRACT

Adaptive cruise control (ACC) has been demonstrated to improve driver comfort, safety and highway traffic flow. It also has the potential to reduce fuel consumption and vehicle emissions. In addition to maintaining constant time headway under various driving scenarios, a commercial ACC system should be robust against varying vehicle and road parameters and radar measurement inaccuracies to ensure consistent performance and wide-scale application. The robustness property is particularly critical for heavy-duty vehicle applications where the vehicle mass can vary significantly. The paper presents a torque-based ACC system for heavy-duty vehicles that achieves a significant level of parameter robustness. The torque control is realized through the application of SAE J1939 engine torque limiting commands and through the activation of the engine retarder (engine/compression brake). Both simulation and road test results are provided to demonstrate the performance of the ACC system.

INTRODUCTION

For heavy-duty vehicle application, a practical ACC system must be insensitive to the time-varying system parameters. This is important for two reasons.

First, parameters such as road grade, rolling resistance, and vehicle mass vary each trip. For example, depending on the payload, the mass of a heavy-duty vehicle can vary by over 400% [4]. Therefore to provide consistent performance the effect of these parameters on the behavior of the ACC system should be minimal. In addition to driver acceptance and satisfaction, this also has important safety implications. Consistency in the ACC performance is necessary for improving the driver's understanding of the system's capabilities and limitations, which is especially important for emergency situations when driver intervention may be required.

Second, for commercial adoption of the technology, the controller should not be overly sensitive to specific vehicle configurations, such as specific engine or transmission characteristics. This allows application on diverse vehicle platforms and configurations while minimizing integration and maintenance costs.

Advances in ACC systems are demonstrated not only by the diversity of technologies on which such systems are based [2] (radar, laser, stereo camera), but also by the vast literature published on various ACC control techniques. The paper [4] provides an excellent overview of the latest developments in ACC systems and their impacts on traffic safety and flow. Actually, ACC control techniques are widely used in the literature as an intermediate step towards platoon control. Although the requirements for platoon control are more stringent, similar techniques can be employed for general ACC applications.

For improving controller robustness and overcoming the limitations of PID controllers, various control techniques have been proposed. Several control approaches such as backstepping, adaptive and model predictive control are compared in [4]. In [1], fuzzy control techniques are applied for specification of comfort demands. In [3], controller gains are generated as solutions of an optimization problem. In the majority of the published literature, the control signals are the throttle and brake signals.

This paper develops a torque-based ACC algorithm where the control signal is the torque at the engine. The desired engine indicated torque is realized either through the application of engine torque limiting commands (positive desired torque) or by activating the engine retarder (negative desired torque), via the J1939 bus. The use of torque limiting, as opposed to torque control, implies that the ACC system operates in conjunction with the conventional cruise control system (CCC). The ACC system limits the torque requests commanded by the CCC system and therefore only has the capacity to reduce the vehicle velocity from the driver selected CCC set speed. Naturally, this provides an additional safety feature. The main feature of the system is that it mitigates the amount of controller parameter tuning required for each installation and enhances the overall performance under the range of potential vehicle configurations and driving conditions.

This paper provides an overview of the development and validation of the ACC system in MATLAB/Simulink [1] and is organized as follows: The first section describes the Simulink environment created for simulation analysis. The second section provides an overview of the ACC system. The third section provides simulation results for two of the most common traffic scenarios. In the fourth section, vehicle following performance results from actual road tests are presented. The paper concludes with a summary.

SIMULATION ENVIRONMENT

Fig. 1 displays a high-level view of the Simulink modeling environment. It is composed of three main sub-models: radar model, heavy-duty truck model and the ACC system.

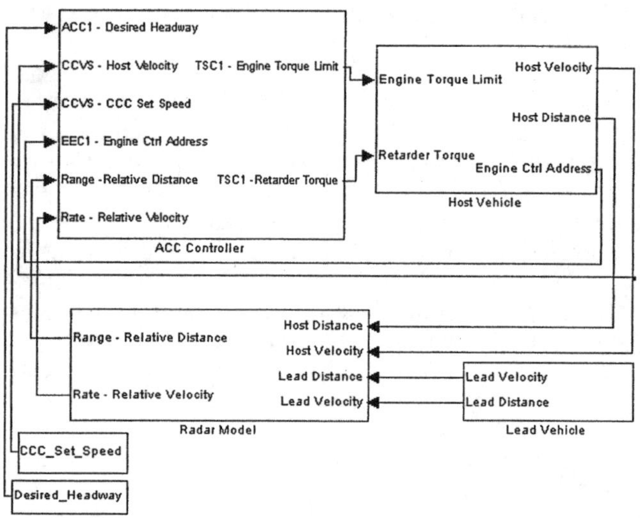

Figure 1: Simulink simulation environment.

RADAR MODEL: The radar model calculates the relative distance (range) and relative velocity (range rate) with respect to the host vehicle given the lead vehicle velocity profile. The characteristics of the radar signals: latency, resolution, sampling frequency and noise were based on commercial ACC radar systems.

HEAVY-DUTY TRUCK DYNAMIC MODEL: The longitudinal dynamic truck model is designed to predict torque and speed characteristics of the drivetrain for different engine torque commands. In general, for ACC algorithm development, the truck model can be simplified significantly. However to appropriately evaluate the robustness of the controller with respect to vehicle parameters, one of the main objectives of the study, the model fidelity was chosen to be sufficiently detailed. The model subsystems include the engine, transmission, vehicle longitudinal model and the conventional cruise control system. The model subsystems are briefly summarized below.

Engine Dynamics. A mean value engine model was used to predict engine behavior. This model neglected most of the fast dynamics due to combustion and the reciprocating motion of engine. The combustion dynamics was represented by a static map, with engine torque command (or throttle command) and starter torque as inputs and net indicated torque as output. The engine retarder (compression brake) was modeled by three levels of retarding torque at the engine: retarder low, medium and high. The levels correspond to the number of cylinders used for retardation: two, four and six, respectively, assuming a six cylinder engine.

Transmission Dynamics. The transmission was modeled as a lumped parameter system. The effects of gear ratio change on the effective inertia of the transmission were taken into consideration. However, the fast dynamics due to transient events within the transmission was neglected. The effective transmission and final drive efficiencies were taken into consideration to account for frictional losses along the driveline.

Vehicle Longitudinal Dynamics. The following assumptions were made to simplify the longitudinal vehicle model: the crankshaft and transmission are infinitely stiff, the propeller shaft and drive shaft are infinitely stiff, the vehicle lateral motion was neglected and the vehicle mass was lumped at the center of gravity. The wheel torque losses were accounted for as tractor body damping, aerodynamic drag, rolling resistance, and resistance due to road grade.

Conventional Cruise Control (CCC) System. As previously mentioned, the primary method for controlling the vehicle speed is through engine torque limiting or by activating the engine retarder. The ACC system operates in conjunction with the conventional cruise control system (CCC) limiting the torque requests commanded by the CCC system. Therefore to effectively simulate the ACC performance the CCC has to be realistically modeled. The CCC was modeled as PI controller with the ability to deal with actuator constraints.

[1]Matlab and Simulink are registered trademarks of The MathWorks, Natick, MA.

ADAPTIVE CRUISE CONTROL SYSTEM

The objective of the ACC system is to generate a desired engine torque command such that when implemented by the engine controller, performance requirements are met for a variety of traffic scenarios. The closed loop system was designed to achieve both transient and steady state performance requirements, e.g. overshoot, settling time, steady state error, etc. A thorough specification of the performance requirements is beyond the scope of this paper, however the primary steady-state requirement is simply to maintain a specific desired following distance given by

$$d_{rel}^{des} = h\ v_{host} \tag{1}$$

Where v_{host} is the velocity of the host vehicle and the parameter h is referred to as the desired *time headway*. Fig. 2 depicts the lead and host vehicles, their velocities, and the inter-vehicle distance.

The uniqueness of the approach followed in this work is that control commands are entirely based on the desired engine indicated torque and therefore allows for seamless switching between positive and negative torque commands. More specifically, negative desired torque commands are actuated by appropriately activating the three levels of engine retardation and positive torque is realized through engine torque limit commands. Both commands are realized via the J1939 Torque/Speed Control 1 (TSC1) message. As indicated in Fig. 1, the ACC system inputs

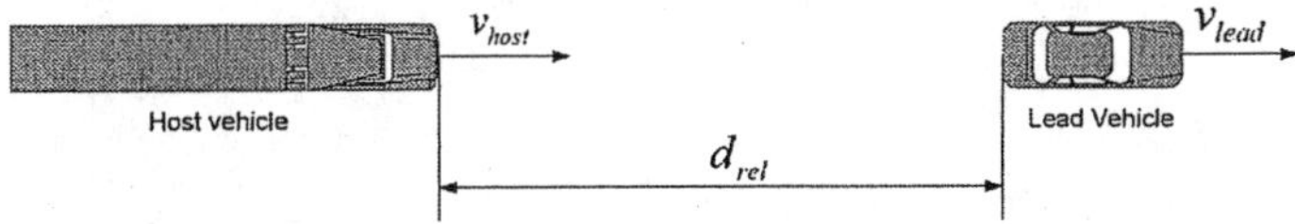

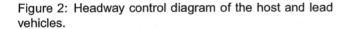

Figure 2: Headway control diagram of the host and lead vehicles.

and outputs were specified to match the available J1939 CAN bus signals as to directly facilitate the real-time implementation of the controller using the rapid-prototyping hardware. The ACC system consists of two primary components: a supervisory controller and a main controller. These modules are discussed in more detail in the following subsections.

Supervisory Controller The supervisory controller provides high-level system control primarily for handling the acquisition and loss of lead vehicle targets. At the core of the supervisory controller is a three-state operational state machine determining the proper state of the system: *No Control*, *Distance Control*, or *Resume to CCC Set Speed* state. During the *Distance Control* state, the supervisory controller provides low pass filtered versions of the relative distance and velocity radar measurements to the main controller. For the *Resume to CCC Set Speed* state, the distance error (difference between actual relative distance and desired distance) is set to zero and relative velocity is set to the difference between the current vehicle speed and a desired "resume speed". The resume speed is a calculated speed that slowly ramps up from the initial vehicle speed (when entering this state) to the CCC set speed. The supervisory controller also provides appropriate logic to handle speed-matching conditions (zero-Doppler) where the lead vehicle target is temporarily lost during vehicle following situations.

Main Controller The main controller generates the desired engine torque signal based on radar measurements, vehicle and road parameters. This torque command consists of two components: a steady-state component and a transient-error-dependent component:

$$T_{engine} = T_{engine\_steady} + \Delta T_{engine} \tag{2}$$

The steady-state torque, T_{engine_steady}, is the torque required to maintain constant speed immediately after lead-vehicle target acquisition. This torque component is a function of the lead vehicle speed, and estimated host vehicle and road parameters. In designing the second component, ΔT_{engine}, of (2) two factors are considered: (i) compensation for inaccuracies in the estimated vehicle and road parameters; and (ii) generation of the appropriate dynamic torque required for headway control.

The component ΔT_{engine} operates during the transient response, when the host vehicle speed and distance do not have the desired steady-state values; this torque compensates for the errors related to both relative velocity and distance defined as follows:

$$v_{rel} = v_{lead} - v_{host} \tag{3}$$

$$d_{rel} = d_{lead} - d_{host} \tag{4}$$

Similarly to [5], the overall error is defined as $\epsilon = v_{rel} + C_d\ \Delta d_{rel}$, where $\Delta d_{rel} = (d_{rel} - d_{rel}^{des})$, d_{rel}^{des} is given by (1), and C_d is a weighting coefficient between the velocity and distance control objectives, respectively. The torque ΔT_{engine} acts to minimize the overall system error and it implicitly compensates for model inaccuracies.

The dynamic performance of the closed loop system is dependent on the controller parameters. Some constraints on these parameters can be determined as a result of the expected performance in certain driving scenarios. For example, in some scenarios (such as lead vehicle cut-in scenarios where the lead vehicle speed is significantly greater than the host) it is desirable that the ACC system would not affect the host speed. Assuming that the host speed was constant previous to these scenarios, the requirement is that the ACC system maintains the constant vehicle speed. Assuming knowledge of the vehicle parameters, this implies that ΔT_{engine} must be equal to zero. Therefore, upon utilization of the values of v_{rel} and d_{rel}, a constraint on the controller parameters can be derived.

The proposed control law formulation enables the controller to quickly adapt to aggressive traffic scenarios, such as close vehicle cut-in situations, while not being overly aggressive during steady-state vehicle following situations resulting in smooth control performance. The simulation results presented in the next section also demonstrate that the controller's performance is robust against imprecise knowledge of the vehicle and road parameters.

SIMULATION PERFORMANCE

The ACC system was simulated for a variety of common traffic scenarios of which two are presented here. For the tests, only the parameters specific to the particular scenario (host and lead velocities, CCC set speed, initial separation distance and desired headway) were modified. The controller parameters and settings were identical for all tests. As discussed previously, the desired engine torque computed by the controller consists of a steady-state component and a transient-error-dependent component. The steady-state component is a function of the vehicle and road parameters which are unknown and vary across vehicle platforms and road conditions. One of the primary goals of this work is to develop a control approach that is robust to variations in these parameters. Therefore, the parameters used to calculate the steady-state torque were set corresponding to the greatest potential mismatch between them and the actual values of the model. More specifically, the parameters used for the steady-state torque were set equal to their actual values plus (or minus) the maximum amount of uncertainty typically encountered for that particular parameter. The sign of the uncertainly (i.e. whether added or subtracted from the actual value) was randomly determined. For example, the uncertainty for the rolling resistance coefficient, effective tire radius and aerodynamic drag coefficient were estimated at 50%, 10% and 20%, respectively. A nominal vehicle mass of 13,608 kg (30,000 lb) was also used for the steady-state torque calculation.

The following scenarios are investigated in this paper:

1. Normal Approach: The host vehicle approaches the lead vehicle from behind. The initial host velocity is greater than the lead vehicle velocity.
2. Vehicle Cut-In: The lead vehicle cuts in front of the host vehicle. The initial host velocity is greater than the lead vehicle velocity.

For each scenario, the performance is evaluated at two mass extremes: a tractor-only configuration of 9,071 kg (20,000 lb) and a tractor-trailer configuration of 38,555 kg (85,000 lb). All of the simulations start with the host vehicle under steady-state CCC conditions at the CCC set speed.

NORMAL APPROACH: For the normal approach scenario the desired time headway is set at a normalized value of 0.6, the road grade is zero degrees and the initial separation distance is beyond the radar range. Figs.

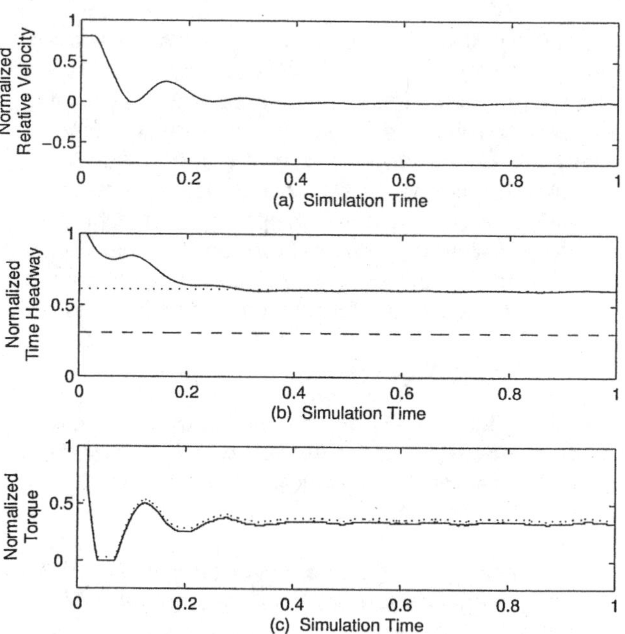

Figure 3: Simulation performance for the normal approach scenario for the tractor configuration (9,071 kg): (a) relative velocity $(v_{host} - v_{lead})$, (b) actual headway (solid), desired headway (dotted), lower headway threshold (dashed), (c) ACC torque command (solid), CCC torque command (dotted).

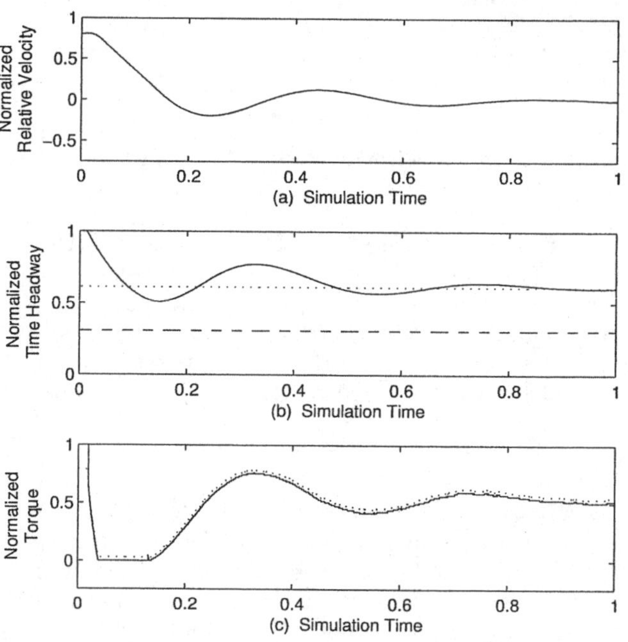

Figure 4: Simulation performance for the normal approach scenario for tractor-trailer configuration (38,555 kg): (a) relative velocity $(v_{host} - v_{lead})$, (b) actual headway (solid), desired headway (dotted), lower headway threshold (dashed), (c) ACC torque command (solid), CCC torque command (dotted).

3 and 4 display the performance for the tractor and the tractor-trailer configurations, respectively. Each figure displays three different graphs. The uppermost graph displays the normalized relative velocity (host velocity - lead velocity) with respect to elapsed simulation time. In the middle plot of Figs. 3 and 4, the solid trace displays the normalized actual time headway with respect to simulation time. The actual headway is defined as $h_{act} = d_{rel}/v_{host}$. Also indicated in the graph is the desired headway (dotted) and a lower headway threshold (dashed). The lower headway threshold is set at half the desired headway and is a useful indicator of when significant deceleration is necessary. In the bottom graph, the solid trace is the normalized desired engine torque command output of the ACC system. Positive torque values reflect engine torque limit commands and negative values are the desired retarder torque commands. The dotted trace is the conventional cruise controller's requested engine torque command. Unless otherwise noted, all the simulation results will be presented in the same format.

It is observed that initially when the lead vehicle is beyond the radar range, the CCC is in control of the vehicle maintaining constant velocity. Immediately upon acquiring the lead vehicle target, the controller quickly reacts by limiting the torque to zero, effectively defueling the engine until the velocities are approximately equal, after which the controller applies torque limiting to provide a gradual reduction of the headway to the desired value while maintaining a safe headway distance. In fact, it is noted that only the tractor-trailer configuration results in a headway less than the desired at any point during the approach. In this case the headway error is minimal and persists only for a brief period. From the figures it is also observed that the CCC logic designed to deal with engine torque constraints realizes a CCC torque command slightly greater than the ACC torque limit command when the ACC is in control of the engine. This provides the appropriate switching from ACC back to the CCC system for certain traffic scenarios tested.

VEHICLE CUT-IN: For the vehicle cut-in scenario the desired headway is also set at 0.6 and the road grade is again zero degrees. The normalized cut-in separation headway for the tractor-only configuration is 0.27 and 0.47 for the tractor-trailer configuration. The cut-in headway values were selected such that the vehicle could avoid a collision by applying the full retarding torque of the engine retarder. In fact, this happens to be one of the most demanding scenarios for the controller. Figs. 5 and 6 display the performance of the tractor and tractor-trailer configurations, respectively. In each figure, the retarder (engine brake) is active when the torque is negative. On the relative velocity plot (uppermost), the portion of the trace that corresponds to the time periods when the retarder is active are highlighted.

The results demonstrate the initial application the engine retarder immediately after the cut-in event. The applica-

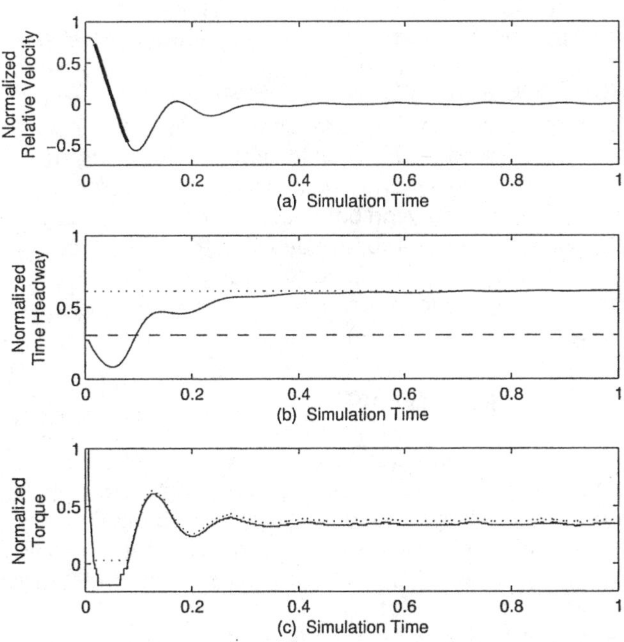

Figure 5: Simulation performance for the vehicle cut-in scenario for the tractor configuration (9,071 kg): (a) relative velocity $(v_{host} - v_{lead})$, (b) actual headway (solid), desired headway (dotted), lower headway threshold (dashed), (c) ACC torque command (solid), CCC torque command (dotted).

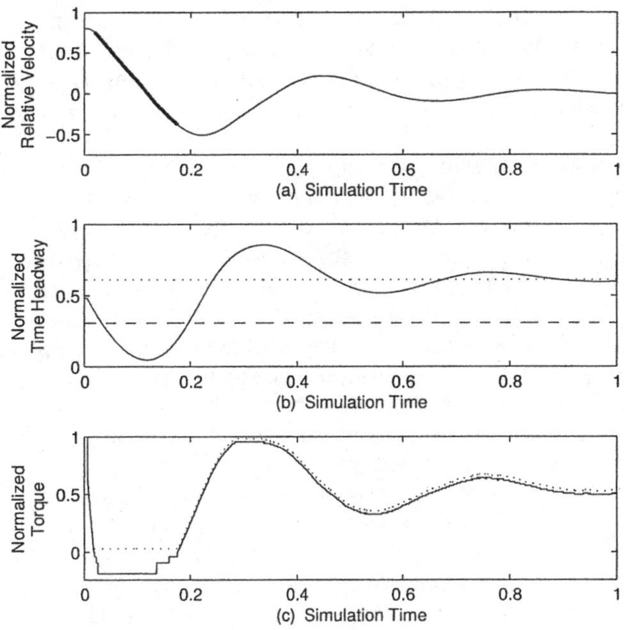

Figure 6: Simulation performance for the vehicle cut-in scenario for the tractor-trailer configuration (38,555 kg): (a) relative velocity $(v_{host} - v_{lead})$, (b) actual headway (solid), desired headway (dotted), lower headway threshold (dashed), (c) ACC torque command (solid), CCC torque command (dotted).

tion of the various levels of the retarder is evident as well as the smooth transition to positive torque limiting values. In both figures it is observed that the retarder is active primarily when the actual headway is less than the lower headway threshold. It is also observed that the tractor-trailer configuration exhibits some oscillations before convergence. It is important to note that in addition to the magnitude of the velocity oscillations, the convergence time was also a key design parameter and the results presented represent a compromise between the two that best meets the desired performance requirements. The oscillations could be reduced at the expense of increasing the convergence time.

ROAD TEST PERFORMANCE

The Mathwork's Real-Time Workshop tools were utilized in implementing the control strategy on a rapid prototyping hardware platform, an xPC Target, for evaluation on a heavy-duty test truck. Two different road tests were conducted in order to evaluate the performance of the ACC system with respect to vehicle mass. The tests were: tractor-only configuration (approximately 8,600 kg or 19,000 lb) and tractor with a heavy unloaded trailer (approximately 25,000 kg or 55,000 lb). The same controller parameters were used for both tests and were essentially identical to those used in the simulations. For both tests the ACC system exhibited very good performance. The controller performed very well under steady-state headway control conditions, attaining almost constant relative distance, even under varying road grade conditions. The dynamic performance was also good, providing an appropriate level of aggressiveness for vehicle cut-in and approach scenarios while effectively transitioning between engine torque limit commands and the various levels of retardation.

For comparison with the simulation results, Figs. 7 and 8 display the steady-state headway control performance of the ACC system for the two configurations. For both cases, the data was collected over a 4 minute interval when the evaluation truck was following a lead vehicle that likely had its cruise control set at 97 km/h (60 mph) on a stretch of road that had a varying road grade profile. The uppermost plot displays the normalized relative velocity (rate) from the radar unit. The middle plot displays the normalized actual headway as calculated using the relative distance (range) measurement from the radar. The desired headway for the tests is 0.65 as indicated by the dotted line. The bottom plot shows a normalized trace of the J1939 actual torque value (byte 3 of the J1939 Electronic Engine Controller #1: EEC1 message). It is observed that for both cases the headway is consistently controlled to coincide with its desired value.

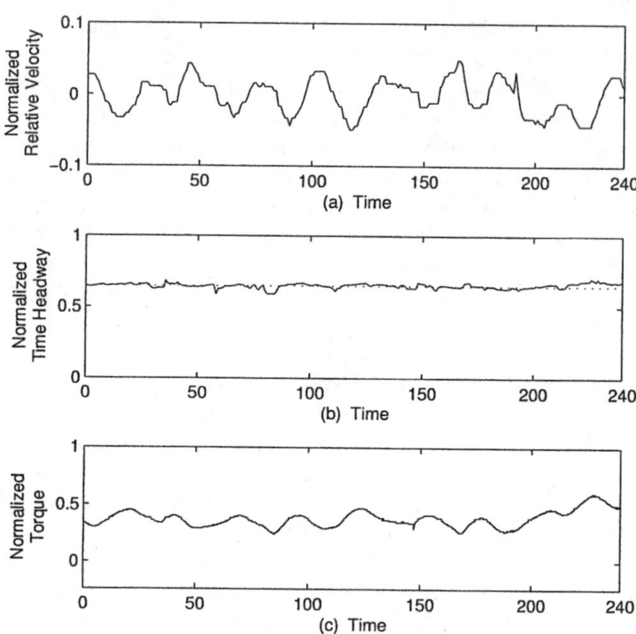

Figure 7: Road test performance under steady-state headway control for the tractor configuration (8,600 kg): (a) relative velocity ($v_{host} - v_{lead}$), (b) actual headway (solid), desired headway (dotted), (c) J1939 actual torque.

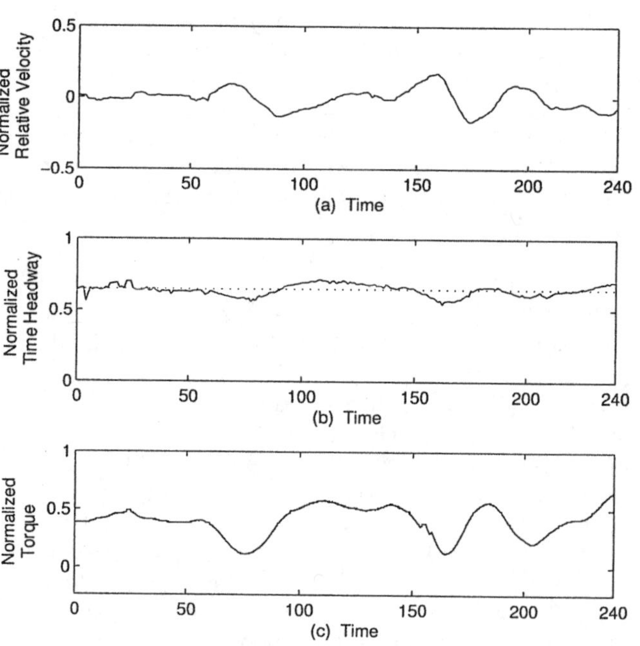

Figure 8: Road test performance under steady-state headway control for the tractor-trailer configuration (25,000 kg): (a) relative velocity ($v_{host} - v_{lead}$), (b) actual headway (solid), desired headway (dotted), (c) J1939 actual torque.

SUMMARY

The paper presents a robust ACC system. The uniqueness of the controller is that it consists of two engine torque components. This control law formulation enables the controller to quickly adapt to aggressive traffic scenarios while being less aggressive during steady-state vehicle following conditions, resulting in stable control performance. The controller required essentially no parameter adjustment when moving from simulation to road testing and between the different weighting conditions of the road tests. This result, along with the robustness of the controller (with respect to the the primary vehicle parameters) demonstrated in the simulations, suggests that this control strategy could easily be exported and realized in different vehicle platforms with minimal adjustments.

ACKNOWLEDGMENTS

The authors wish to thank the Eaton Vehicle Solutions team for their support and cooperation throughout this project.

REFERENCES

[1] St. Germann and R. Isermann. "Nonlinear distance and cruise control for passenger cars". *Proceedings of American Control Conference, Seattle, Washington*, 5:3081–3085, 1995.

[2] W.D. Jones. "Keeping Cars from Crashing". *IEEE Spectrum*, pages 40–45, September, 2001.

[3] C-Y. Liang and H. Peng. "Optimal Adaptive Cruise Control with Guaranteed String Stability". *Vehicle System Dynamics*, 31:313–330, 1999.

[4] A. Vahidi and A. Eskandarian. "Research Advances in Intelligent Collision Avoidance and Adaptive Cruise Control". *IEEE Transanctions on Intelligent Transportation Systems*, 4(3):143–153, September, 2003.

[5] D. Yanakiev and I. Kanellakopoulos. "Longitudinal Control of Automated CHVs With Significant Actuator Delays". *IEEE Transanctions on Vehicular Technology*, 50(5):1289–1297, September, 2001.

2005-01-1483

Development of Adaptive Cruise Control With Low Speed Following Capability

Kenichi Egawa, Kou Satou, Masahiro Tozawa, Takayuki Ida and Tetsuya Ojika
Nissan Motor Co., Ltd.

ABSTRACT

This paper presents a newly developed adaptive cruise control system with low-speed following capability that is designed to reduce the driver's workload in low-speed driving such as in congested traffic. This system incorporates a forward-looking sensor with a wider range of view for improved detection of a preceding vehicle in the same lane. It also has a control algorithm that achieves natural vehicle behavior without any disconcerting feeling, as a result of being constructed on the basis of analyses of driving behavior characteristics at low speed like that of congested traffic. Evaluations conducted on a driving simulator have confirmed that the system is effective in reducing the driver's workload.

INTRODUCTION

Advances made in the development of driver assistance systems in recent years have led to the implementation of adaptive cruise control (ACC) and lane-keeping support (LKS) systems on production vehicles. ACC systems are intended to reduce the driver's workload by automatically adjusting the headway distance to the vehicle ahead to match the flow of traffic in driving environments where vehicle speeds change. [1] However, their scope of use has so far been limited to the medium to high speed range. We have developed an ACC system with low-speed following capability that can follow a preceding vehicle even at low speeds such as when driving in congested traffic. This system is designed to extend the operating range of ACC and reduce the driver's workload further so as to provide greater practicality and driving comfort.

In order to ensure the market acceptance of this system, it is essential that the system be able to achieve natural vehicle behavior consistent with drivers' expectations in the same way as conventional ACC systems. Another requirement for attaining widespread acceptance among users is that the system must incorporate functions corresponding to actual traffic conditions.

This paper describes the concept and utility of the system along with presenting experimental results that show its effectiveness.

SYSTEM FEATURES

Low-speed following capability serves to maintain a pre-set headway distance to a preceding vehicle in the host vehicle's lane according to the driving speed. It operates up to a driving speed of approximately 40 km/h when following the vehicle ahead at a slow speed such as when traveling in congested traffic. Because this operating mode does not incorporate a set cruising speed function like that of conventional ACC systems, it is deactivated when a preceding vehicle is not detected. In situations where the vehicle ahead decelerates and continues to slow down until coming to a stop, the system is deactivated once the driving speed falls below approximately 5 km/h. The driver of the host vehicle must always act to stop the vehicle. In view of the driving speed changes that occur between the low-speed range and the medium- to high-speed range in actual traffic environments, the system incorporates a function for automatically switching between the conventional ACC mode and the low-speed following mode, so as to provide enhanced practicality and convenience. A transition from the low-speed following mode to the conventional ACC mode is made only if the driver has pre-set a vehicle speed for ACC, thus ensuring that the driver's intentions are reflected in the operation of the system.

A diagram of the system configuration is shown in Fig.1. The brake actuator is shared with an ACC system already in use on production vehicles. A laser radar is used as the sensor for measuring the distance to the vehicle ahead. A new laser radar was developed to improve the driving environment recognition performance, including expanding the area of detection, compared with the sensor used in the conventional ACC system.

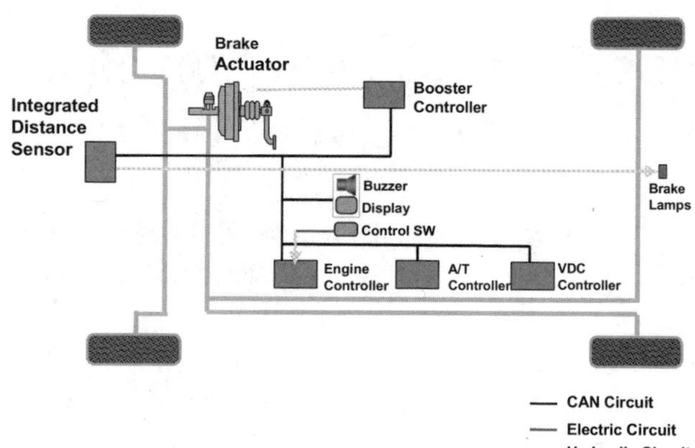

Fig. 1 Configuration of system

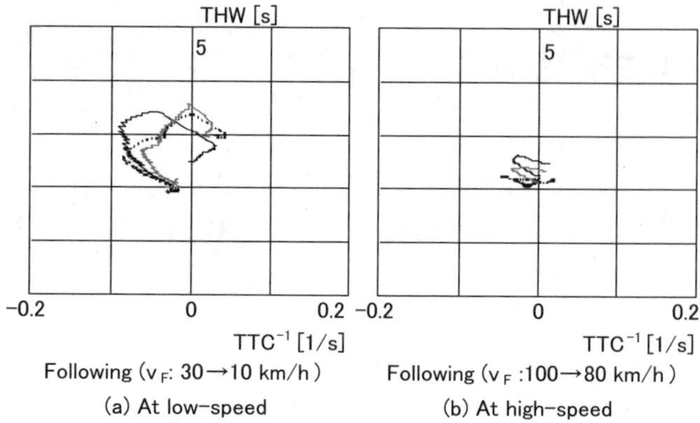

Fig. 2 Trajectories during following

DESIGN OF HEADWAY DISTANCE CONTROLLER

ANALYSIS OF DRIVERS' LOW-SPEED DRIVING CHARACTERISTCS

The low-speed driving characteristics of well-mannered drivers were analyzed in order to construct a headway distance controller that would provide vehicle behavior consistent with drivers' expectations. Marked differences in driving behavior characteristics were observed in a comparison between low-speed following and following in the speed range in which conventional ACC is used [2]. Figure 2 shows trajectories for the time headway (THW) and the inverse of the time to collision (TTC^{-1}) in low-speed and high-speed following situations when the preceding vehicle decelerated at approximately 2 m/s^2. Using the headway distance dR, the preceding vehicle's velocity vF, the host vehicle's velocity vP and the relative velocity vR, TTC and THW are defined as

$$TTC = \frac{d_R}{v_R} \quad (1)$$

$$THW = \frac{d_R}{v_F} \quad (2)$$

The host vehicle's velocity and the relative velocity in that situation are shown in Fig. 3. Both Figs. 2 and 3 superimpose the experimental results for three driving scenarios.

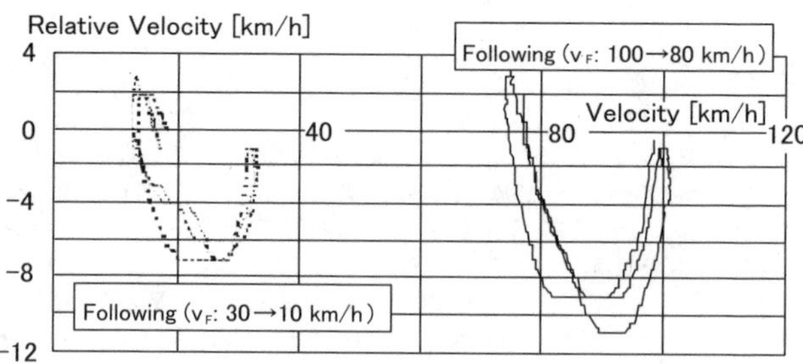

Fig. 3 Relative velocity during following

The results shown in Fig. 2 indicate that the trajectories are larger at lower speeds than higher speeds. On the other hand, the results shown in Fig. 3 indicate that while following the vehicle ahead at a low speed, the host vehicle decelerates faster relative to the deceleration of the preceding vehicle to avoid increasing the relative velocity. At a glance, it would seem to suggest that in the low-speed range drivers tolerate a larger negative TTC^{-1} value and drive in a relaxed manner. In actuality, though, TTC^{-1} invariably shows a large negative value because of the shorter headway distance in the low-speed range, even though drivers decelerate faster at low speeds than they do at high speeds

CONFIGURATION OF HEADWAY DISTANCE CONTROLLER

One distinct feature revealed by this examination of driving behavior characteristics is that drivers respond faster when following a preceding vehicle at low speed compared with their response in the high-speed range. This indicates that the host vehicle's velocity must respond more quickly to changes in the preceding vehicle's velocity. Accordingly, the control system was constructed to simulate this faster response when following the vehicle ahead at low speed, while the control algorithm for approaching and cut-in situations was designed in the same way as that of the conventional ACC system. In this study, a two-degree-of-freedom control system incorporating a phase compensator was adopted for headway distance control. This section describes the control system designed for following control. [3]

PLANT

In designing the headway distance controller, a robust model-matching method was used to construct a vehicle velocity control system that would be little affected by changes in the road gradient, vehicle weight and other factors. The target response of the headway distance in relation to the preceding vehicle's velocity is specified by the natural frequency ω_{MD}, damping factor ζ_{MD} and time headway T_{HW}. The vehicle velocity control system is designed such that the transfer characteristic of the host vehicle's velocity V_{SP} in relation to the vehicle velocity command V_{SPC} is given as shown in Eq. (3) below.

$$G_{MV}(s) = \frac{\omega_{MV}}{s + \omega_{MV}} \tag{3}$$

Letting V_{PR} denote the preceding vehicle's velocity, the response of the headway distance L_D relative to the vehicle velocity command V_{SPC} is obtained with the following equation:

$$L_D = \frac{1}{s} \cdot \{V_{PR} - G_{MV}(s) \cdot V_{SPC}\} \tag{4}$$

PHASE COMPENSATOR

Figure 4 shows a block diagram of the controller configuration in relation to the plant in Eq. (4). The phase compensator $G_{FF}(s)$ is determined so that the transfer function $G_{VD}(s)$ from the preceding vehicle's velocity V_{PR} to the headway distance L_D coincides with the desired transfer function $G_{MD}(s)$ from the preceding vehicle's velocity V_{PR} to the headway distance L_D. The transfer function $G_{VD}(s)$ is given by

$$G_{VD}(s) = \frac{1}{s}\left\{1 - G_{FF}(s) \cdot \frac{G'_{MV}(s)}{1 - G'_{MV}(s)}\right\} \tag{5}$$

Letting the right-hand term of Eq. (5) be equal to $G_{MD}(s)$ and solving for $G_{FF}(s)$, we obtain the following equation:

$$G_{FF}(s) = \frac{\{1 - G'_{MV}(s)\} \cdot \{1 - sG_{MD}(s)\}}{G'_{MV}(s)} \tag{6}$$

When $G_{MD}(s)$ is given as a quadratic system, $G_{MD}(s)$ must be expressed in the form of the following equation in order for $G_{FF}(s)$ to be proper:

$$G_{MD}(s) = \frac{s + \omega_{MD}^2 \cdot T_{HW}}{s^2 + 2 \cdot \zeta_{MD} \cdot \omega_{MD} \cdot s + \omega_{MD}^2} \tag{7}$$

where T_{HW} is the target headway time.

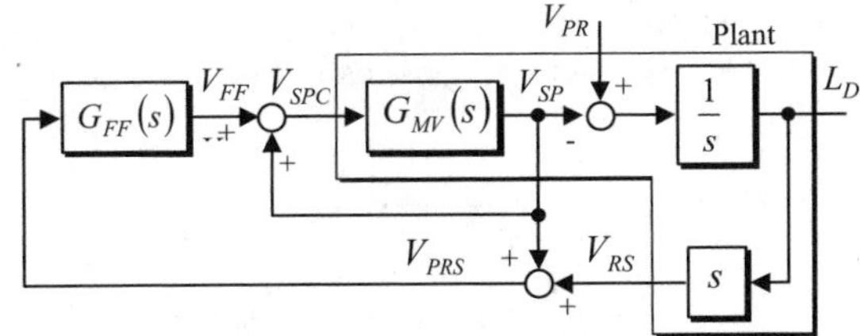

Fig. 4 Phase compensator

FEEDBACK COMPENSATOR

Feedback compensation serves to converge error between the actual headway distance or relative velocity and the reference model to zero. Such error originates in variation of the characteristics of the vehicle velocity control system accompanying a delay by the headway distance sensor in detecting the relative velocity or as a result of vehicle parameter variation. The feedback compensator output V_{FB} is calculated with the following equation:

$$V_{FB} = -k_L \cdot \{G_{MD}(s) \cdot V_{PRS} + -L_D\} - k_{VR} \cdot \{s \cdot G_{MD}(s) \cdot V_{PRS} - V_{RS}\} \tag{8}$$

where k_L and k_{VR} denote the feedback gain of the headway distance and relative velocity, respectively. The target vehicle velocity, representing the control input, is calculated with Eq. (9). A block diagram of the overall headway distance control system is given in Fig. 5.

$$V_{SPC} = V_{FF} + V_{FB} + V_{SP} \tag{9}$$

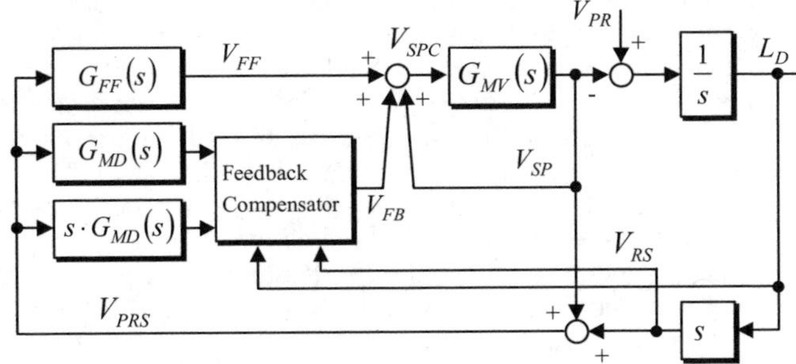

Fig. 5 Block diagram of headway distance controller

The control characteristics were tuned on the basis of simulations, and the constants were approximately determined so as to be consistent with the experimental data on driving behavior characteristics. Then, the controller described above was installed in an experimental vehicle and tests were conducted to fine-tune the constants further. Driving tests were conducted to confirm the performance of the controller. The trajectories obtained with the controller and for manual driving in a following situation are compared in Fig. 6. As is clear from the results, the trajectory obtained with the controller agrees well with the characteristics of manual driving. These results confirmed that the controller is capable of simulating the driving characteristics of human drivers.

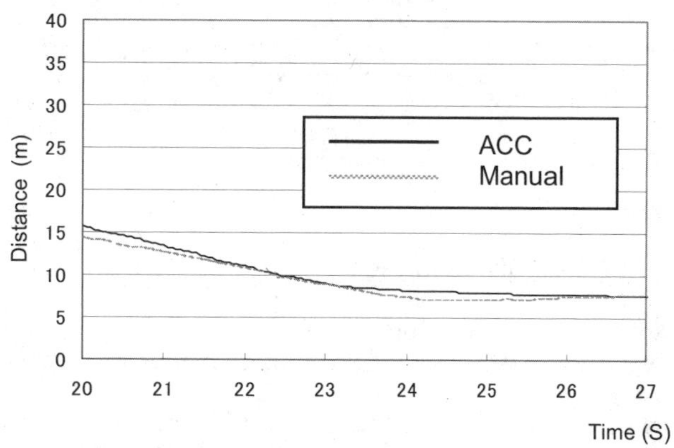

Fig. 6 Comparison of ACC driving and manual driving

TRANSITION BETWEEN LOW- AND HIGH-SPEED FOLLOWING MODES

In view of real-world traffic environments, it is necessary to have control procedures that match the conditions of both low- and high-speed driving, inasmuch as the driving circumstances of these speed ranges differ substantially. Accordingly, the control procedures differ between the two modes in cases where the laser radar does not detect a preceding vehicle. In the conventional ACC mode designed for the high-speed range, the host vehicle accelerates to the speed pre-set by the driver and travels at that steady speed. In contrast, following control is deactivated in the low-speed following mode designed for slow travel such as in congested traffic. Depending on how the vehicle speed range allowed for the operation of each mode is set, it can be expected that there will be trade-offs between convenience and ease of mode recognition by the driver. If the vehicle speed range allowed for the operation of each mode is set at different speed ranges, it can be assumed that mode recognition confusion will probably not occur, but the system might not be so convenient to use.

However, in order to construct a system that is well suited to real-world traffic environments and will be more convenient and practical to use, it is necessary to switch smoothly between the high- and low-speed operating ranges defined for the system. With respect to this issue, simulation results obtained in our research has shown the potential for improving convenience without hindering the driver's recognition of the operating mode. [4] [5]

Mode recognition by the driver was evaluated using an experimental vehicle. In this evaluation, tests were conducted to assess the subjects' level of understanding of the system [6]. Specifically, after each driving session in which the subjects executed a specified driving pattern, they were asked 19 questions about the system's control procedure, display indications and audible warnings. The rate of correct answers to the questions was calculated to determine their level of understanding. The test subjects were not told the correct answers to the questions, as they were expected to gain an understanding of the system based solely on their experience of using it. The driving patterns noted here constituted one evaluation cycle: a pattern of repeated transitions between the two control modes, a pattern involving following a preceding vehicle in the ACC speed range and acceleration to the driver's pre-set speed when the preceding vehicle was not detected, and a pattern involving following in the low-speed mode and deactivation of control when the preceding vehicle was not detected. The subjects were alerted to a transition between control modes by a buzzer and a dashboard indicator lamp. The levels of understanding shown by three typical test subjects are plotted in Fig. 7. All the test subjects acquired a better understanding of the system as their cumulative driving distance increased. Everyone showed an understanding of the system after driving approximately 50 km. The results confirmed that the presence of multiple modes did not interfere with mode recognition so long as the test subjects were able to recall the differences between the control modes.

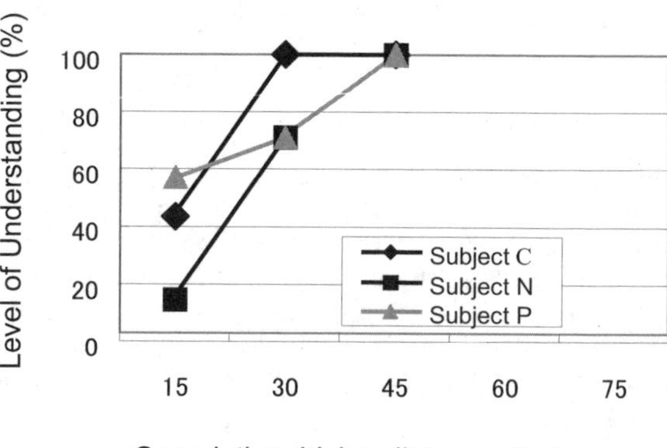

Fig .7 Level of understanding shown by three typical test subjects

EVALUATION OF LOW-SPEED FOLLOWING CAPABILITY

A driving simulator was used in evaluating the system because of the need to measure data in traffic environments allowing good reproducibility. In the evaluations, attention was focused on both the drivers' physical and mental loads. The driver's operational workload was used an index of the physical load. For the mental load index, Low frequency Component (LF: near 0.1 Hz), which corresponds to Mayer-wave-related sinus arrhythmia (MWSA) that indicates the level of activity of the cardiac sympathetic and parasympathetic nerves and originates in the Mayer wave of the blood pressure, was used in the evaluations. It has been reported that there is a correlation between LF and driver behavior. [7] [8]

DRIVER'S OPERATIOAL WORKLOAD

Measurements were made of accelerator usage time and brake pedal usage time on the driving simulator with and without use of the system under conditions that simulated congested traffic. Both experienced and beginning drivers were used as test subjects in order to consider differences stemming from the length of their driving experience. The results are shown in Fig. 8. The results for each driver indicated that accelerator and brake pedal usage times decreased when the system was used. These results confirmed that the system has the effect of reducing the physical effort involved in operating these pedals.

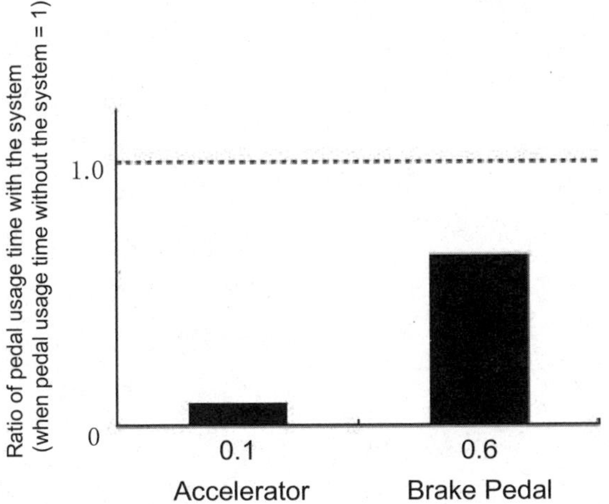

Fig. 8 Comparison of Accelerator usage time and Brake pedal usage time (Average of all subjects)

DRIVERS' MENTAL WORKLOAD

The foregoing results indicated that the use of the system reduced the drivers' physical workload. That reduction, however, must not result in a marked increase in the mental load. In order to examine the mental load involved, LF measurements were made under the same simulated driving conditions. The mental load index was expressed as (LF mean value with or without the use of the system)/(LF under a calm condition with the eyes open). The results are shown in Figs. 9-10. Typical results are shown in Figs. 9 and 10. The LF values for both the experienced and beginning drivers showed no significant difference between driving with the system and driving without it. In other words, No heightened mental workload, such as excessive stress, was observed when the system was used.

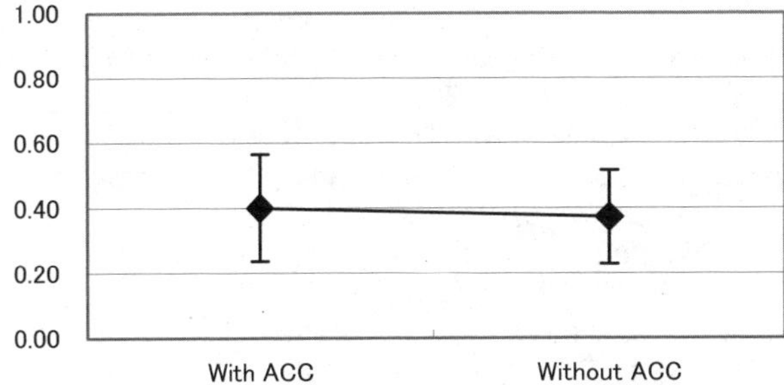

Fig. 9 Relative comparison of LF (Experienced driver)

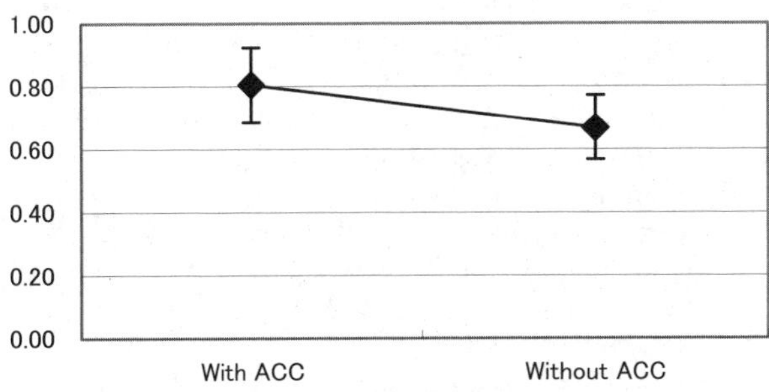

Fig . 10 Relative comparison of LF (Beginning driver)

CONCLUSION

A headway distance sensor with a wider range of view and a headway distance control algorithm that accurately simulates the driving behavior characteristics of human drivers have been developed to provide the capability for following a preceding vehicle at low speed such as when driving in congested traffic. By designing the control system to match real-world traffic environments, a more practical and convenient low-speed following capability has been achieved. The results of evaluations conducted on a driving simulator confirmed that the driver's physical load (operational effort) was reduced without any attendant increase in mental load, thereby reducing the driver's workload. If driver support systems, such as this low-speed following capability, are to gain acceptance in the field, it is essential that they do not give drivers any unnatural feeling. Although they might appear to be the same, driving behavior characteristics differ considerably between the high-speed range (region of conventional ACC operation) and the low-speed range (region of low-speed following mode). While it can be taken for granted that driver support systems will continue to advance in the coming years, it will also be necessary to undertake further research to gain a better understanding of driving behavior characteristics

REFERENCE

1. T. Iijima, et al., "Development of Adaptive Cruise Control with Brake Actuation", SAE Technical Paper No. 2000-01-1353 (2000).
2. Y.Yamamura, et al., "Development of Adaptive Cruise ControlSystem with stop-and-go capability", SAE Technical Paper No. 2000-01-0798 (2001).
3. Y. Yamamura , et al., "A Design Method For String Stable ACC" ITSWC 2002/1
4. T. Inagaki, et al., "Mode Awareness of a Dual-Mode Adaptive Cruise Control system", Proceedings of JSAE Annual Congress 20035621(2003)
5. M. Ito, et al., " Contributing Factors for Mode Awareness of a Vehicle with a Low-Speed Range and a High-speed Range ACC System", Proceedings of JSAE Annual Congress 20045700 (2004)
6. Y.Takae, et al., "A Study for Driver's Trust in Low Speed ACC System" , Proceedings of JSAE Annual Congress 20035531(2003)
7. F. Atsumi, "Evaluation of mental condition on drivers by analysis of heart rate variability - measurement of mental stress and drowsiness by indexes of autonomic nervous system - " , Proceedings of SAE, 9437601(1994,No946)
8. I.Kageyama, et al., "A Modeling of the heart Rate Variability to Estimate Mental Work Load " Proceedings of the 7th Transportation and Logistics, JSME (1998)

2005-01-0430

A Study of Drivers' Trust in a Low-Speed Following System

Yasuhiko Takae, Makoto Iwai, Masanori Kubota and Takayuki Watanabe
Nissan Motor Co., Ltd.

ABSTRACT

Driving tests were conducted using an experimental vehicle equipped with an adaptive cruise control system incorporating low-speed following capability in order to evaluate drivers' trust in a driver support system. The results revealed that the drivers' trust in the system declined in cases where the control algorithm produced vehicle behavior that was inconsistent with their expectations. However, that decline in trust ceased to be observed as the drivers' understanding of the system improved. This result suggests a correlation between their understanding of the system and trust in it.

INTRODUCTION

A great deal of research and development work has been done in recent years on driver support systems, such as Adaptive Cruise Control (ACC) system, with the aim of reducing the driver's workload by assisting with the execution of a portion of the driving task. Even though these systems are designed to assist drivers with the execution of certain driving operations, suitable intervention by the driver is still required depending on the driving conditions. Accordingly, it is essential for drivers to have an appropriate level of trust in such systems. In other words, if drivers overly rely on these systems, there is a possibility that they might be remiss in intervening suitably to control the vehicle even though the systems are not able to function properly. Conversely, if drivers do not have sufficient trust in such systems, they are apt not to use them. This means that it is important to evaluate drivers' trust in driver support systems to ensure their proper use. In previous research studies, subjective evaluations have been carried out to assess the degree of trust that operators and pilots have in automated control systems for industrial plants and aircraft [1-11]. However, there are no examples in the literature of studies that have examined drivers' trust in driver support systems.

Therefore, an effort was made in this research to evaluate drivers' trust in a driver support system, using as an example a system that is designed to control the host vehicle so that it follows a preceding vehicle when traveling at low speeds.

EXPERIMENTAL PROCEDURE

DRIVER SUPPORT SYSTEM

The driver support system used in this study is a device that functions to control the host vehicle so that it follows a vehicle ahead in the same lane when traveling at a low speed in congested traffic. The principal components making up the system are shown in Fig. 1. When a vehicle ahead is detected in the host vehicle's lane by the radar sensor indicated in the figure, the system operates the throttle and brake actuators so that it follows the preceding vehicle at the headway distance preset by the driver. If the driver depresses the brake pedal, the operation of the system is cancelled.

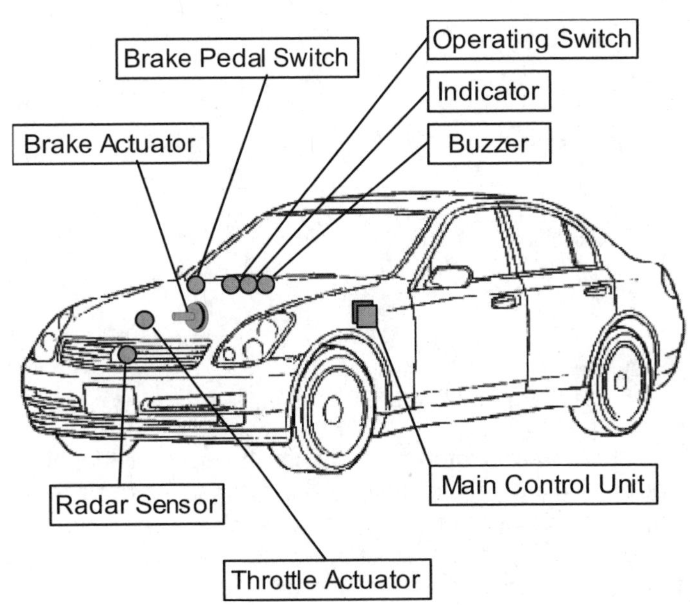

Fig. 1 System Overview

TEST SUBJECTS

The test subjects who participated in the evaluations were 32 individuals, 25 men and 7 women, who possessed a driver's license and ranged in age from 19-69. The total evaluation period for each subject was one month. The subjects drove for one hour a day in congested traffic on roads in the Tokyo area. During the first week of the month-long evaluation period, the subjects drove without using the system. That was followed by three weeks of driving with the system. The details of the study were explained to all of the subjects prior to beginning the evaluation, and they all signed a consent form before taking part in the driving sessions.

EVALUATION INDICES

Trust in the System

As shown in Fig. 2, an 11-step subjective evaluation scale, divided into increments of 10 from 0 (no trust) to 100 (complete trust), was created in reference to previous studies [3] as an index for evaluating the subjects' trust in the system. The subjects were asked to rate their trust in the system at the end of the driving session each day. When the subjective ratings showed a decline in trust, the subjects were asked about the reasons.

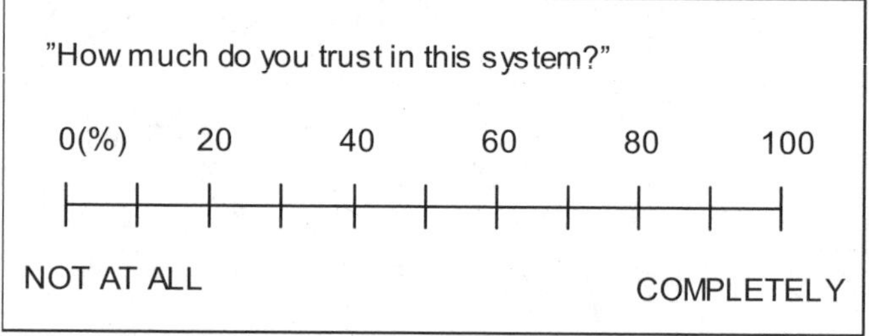

Fig. 2 Subjective Scale for Evaluating Trust in the System

Understanding of the System

A test was conducted to measure the subjects' level of understanding of the system, in order to observe how their understanding improved as they accumulated experience with the system in the course of driving. This test consisted of a total of 27 questions. The following 3 questions of this test were asked regarding the basic operation of the system:

- Whether or not following control is deactivated when the driver depresses the brake pedal
- Whether or not following control is deactivated in situations where the system cannot detect a preceding vehicle, such as when the host vehicle is cornering on a winding road or changing lanes
- Whether or not the operation of the system is understood when another vehicle cuts in front of the host vehicle

Other 24 questions were about the system's control procedure, display indications and audible warnings. The percentage of correct answer rate to these questions was calculated in assessing the subjects' level of understanding of the system. The test was administered to the subjects after the conclusion of each daily driving session. The subjects were not told whether their answers were right or wrong, nor were they told the correct answers. The intention was for the subjects to gain an understanding of the system only through their experience of using it.

Recorded Images

Video cameras were used to record the following images in order to observe the subjects' driving behavior.

- Face images in order to observe the subjects' facial expression and whether they were inattentive to driving or not
- Images of the indicator showing the operational status of the system
- Images of the traffic situation in front of the host vehicle
- Images of the foot position in order to observe the position of the foot during driving

The images taken at these four locations were used in analyzing the subjects' driving behavior. Typical examples of the images recorded during a driving session are shown in Fig. 3.

Camera 1 (Face Angle) Camera 2 (System Indicator)

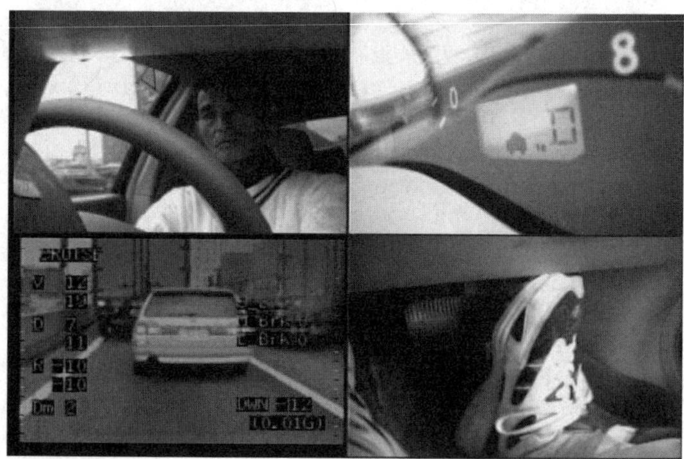

Camera 3 (Front View) Camera 4 (Foot Position)

Fig. 3 Examples of the Images Recorded by Video Cameras

RESULTS

STATISTICAL ANALYSISES

Figure 4 shows the graphs of the all subjects' average trust and the level of understanding on each experiment trial days. The trust and the level of understanding show tendencies to increase and stable with increasing in experiment trial days from the appearance of the figure. In addition, the stable trust value was individually different, i.e., the average was 68, the minimum at 20, and the maximum at 92. So, the trust was statistically analyzed based on 2 age groups (age range 19-40 and 43-69 group), and gender groups (male and female groups), for explaining what affects the trust. As a result, there are no significant differences between each age groups, and gender groups. From this result, the trust seemed to be affected each subject's criterion for evaluating trust than age and gender factors.

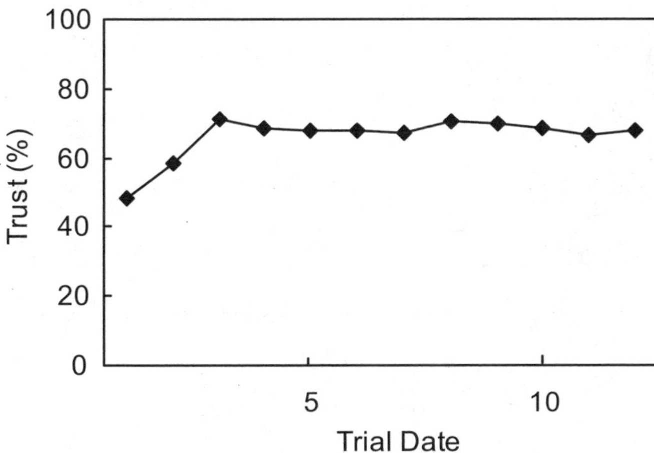

(a) Dynamics of Trust

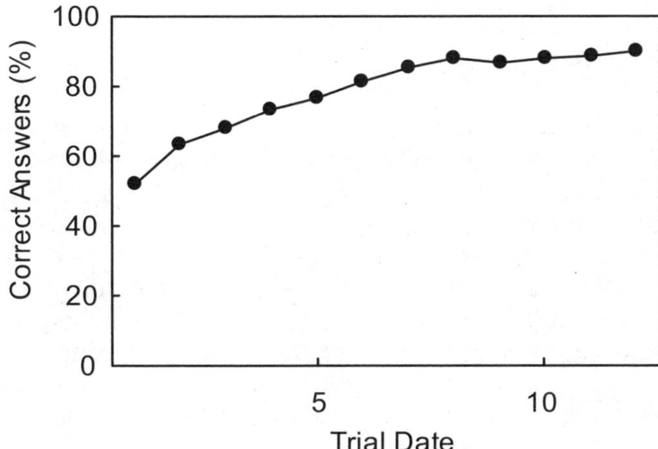

(b) Dynamics of the Average Correct Answer Rate in the Test of Understanding

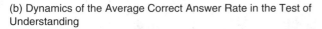

Fig. 4 Average Trust and Correct Answers Rate in the Test of Understanding

CHANGE IN TRUST

As one example of the change in the subjects' trust in the system, the results recorded for one subject (subject 1) are shown in Fig. 5. This subject was a 66-year-old man who had been driving for 36 years.

The subject's trust in the system was at a low level initially, but it rose as the person accumulated more mileage in the driving sessions. However, the subject's trust declined at point (1) in the figure. The subject explained that he reduced his trust rating in that driving session because the system's timing for accelerating/decelerating the host vehicle while following the vehicle ahead seemed unnatural compared with his own operation of the accelerator pedal. It was assumed from this result that trust in the system might decline if the subjects' expectations did not coincide with the actual operating behavior of the system. Subsequently, however, subject 1's trust in the system rose again and remained stable, which presumably indicates that the subject's expectations came to coincide with the actual behavior of the system as the person gained more experience with the operation of the system.

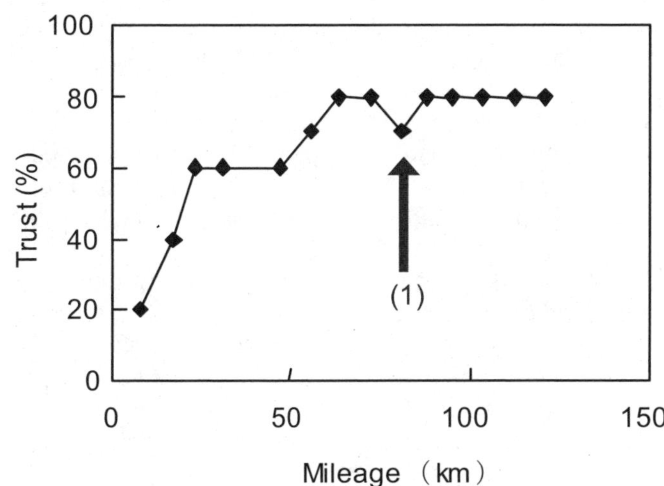

Fig. 5 Dynamics of the Trust of Subject 1

TRUST AND LEVEL OF UNDERSTANDING

The trust evaluation results for another subject (subject 2) were examined from the standpoint of trust and learning about the system through experience. This subject was a 22-year-old woman who had been driving for three years. So as to make more detailed analysis, the percentage of correct answer rate was calculated from the basic 3 questions and other 24 questions individually.

Figure 6 presents graphs of this subject's trust and level of understanding. Both trust and the level of understanding show general tendencies to increase and remain stable with increasing mileage. These same tendencies were also observed for the other subjects as well. A close examination of the change in trust shows a decline at point (2). When asked about this decline, subject 2 gave the following explanation. She mentioned that she did not know at what point the target of following control would change in cases where another vehicle cut in front of the host vehicle. While it was following a preceding vehicle, she felt that the headway distance was closer than what she had expected. That was the reason why she lowered her level of trust in the system. After that learning experience, though, subject 2 did not lower her trust rating again even in cases where the same sort of cutting-in occurred as at point (2).

Looking at this subject's level of understanding at point (2), it is seen that her understanding of the basic items, which included a question about the operation of the system when cutting-in occurred, reached 100%, and it subsequently remained at that level. It is therefore inferred that the cutting-in event at point (2) improved this subject's understanding of how the system operated in cutting-in situations. After that, the timing for changing the target of following control in cutting-in situations never caused subject 2 to reduce her trust in the system. This implies that there was a close relationship between the subject's trust in the system and her level of understanding of it.

An examination of the subsequent change in trust for subject 2 shows a decline at point (3). Upon confirming with the subject why she lowered her trust rating, she explained that she did so out of dissatisfaction with the system because she wanted following control to be performed over a wider speed range. At that point, her understanding of the system was already at a rather high level. It is therefore presumed that a heightened expectation of the system specifications caused subject 2 to reduce her trust rating, rather than a sense of betrayal stemming from a lack of understanding of the system's operating behavior.

These results suggest that people's understanding and expectations of a system affect the improvement and stability of their trust in the system.

Also, when multiple regression analysis of trust was done about this subject, the following of prediction equation was obtained.

$$\text{Trust} = 23.67 + 0.35 \times \text{Correct Answers of Basic Items (\%)} + 0.62 \times \text{Correct Answers of Other Items (\%)}$$

Contribution ratio R and Correlation coefficient R^2 was 0.794 and 0.630 respectively. This R and R^2 suggested trust strongly related understanding of a system.

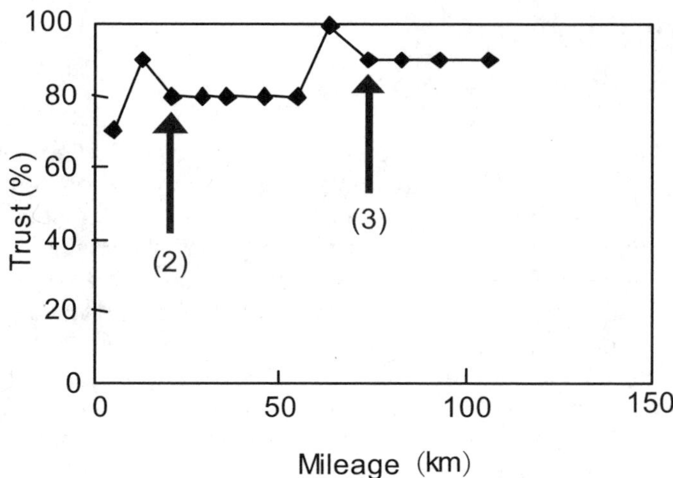

(a) Dynamics of Trust

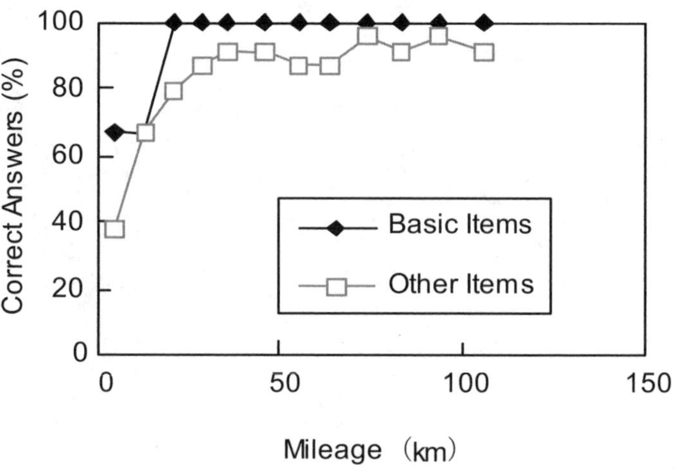

(b) Dynamics of the Correct Answer Rate in the Test of Understanding

Fig. 6 Results for Subject 2

DRIVING BEHAVIOR

Subject 1's trust in the system showed a greater degree of change compared with subject 2, and also the level at which his trust finally stabilized was different. Similarly, the other subjects also tended to show differing levels of trust in the system. An investigation was then made of the relationship between this variation in the subjective ratings of trust and the subjects' behavior thought to relate to the trust in the system. Inattentive driving and braking timing were examined for each subject, as examples of driving behavior thought to relate to the trust.

The duration of Inattentive driving was identified from the recorded face images. Inattentive driving was defined as a change in the orientation of a subject's face, such as when turning the head sideways to look at the outside scenery. Looking in the rearview mirror, checking the outside mirrors and other actions to confirm safety were excluded from the definition. An investigation was made of the data for durations of inattention lasting one second or longer. The recorded face images showed that the subjects were inattentive to driving under relatively stable traffic flow conditions regardless of whether the system was On or Off. No significant statistical difference was found for any of the subjects between the On and Off states of the system.

Braking timing was investigated as a distance and a relative speed in cases where cutting-in occurred while the host vehicle was following a preceding vehicle. The braking timing when cutting-in occurred was examined statistically with and without the system. No significant difference was found for any subject. These results suggest that the subjects exercised the same level of caution in driving with the system as they did when the system was turned Off. These imply that differences in the absolute evaluation ratings do not mean that the subjects' level of trust on the system differed. In other words, the assignment of a rating as an absolute value on a subjective scale of trust differs from one individual to another. Accordingly, it is important to ascertain the phenomena that are present when the level of trust changes or remains stable.

CONCLUSION

This paper has described an evaluation of drivers' trust in a driver support system, based on the results of driving tests conducted with a vehicle fitted with a system that controls the host vehicle so that it follows a preceding vehicle at low speeds. The results made clear the following points.

- When the control algorithm produced vehicle behavior that was inconsistent with the subjects' expectations, they felt suspicious and their trust in the system declined. However, their reduced trust in the system gradually recovered.
- It was found that the subjects' level of understanding of the system contributed to improving their trust in the system and the stability of their trust.
- Variation in the absolute rating of trust does not necessarily indicate that the degree of trust differs.

ACKNOWLEDGMENTS

The authors would like to thank Professor T. Inagaki and Associate Professor H. Furukawa of University of Tsukuba for their many valuable suggestions concerning the evaluation method, data analysis and other aspects of this research.

REFERENCES

1. B. M. Muir: Trust between Humans and Machines, and the Design of Decision Aids. The International Journal of Man-Machine Studies, Vol. 27, pp. 527-539, 1987.
2. B. M. Muir: Trust in Automation. Part 1. Theoretical Issues in the Study of Trust and Human Intervention in Automated Systems. Ergonomics, Vol. 37, No. 11, pp. 1905-1922, 1994.
3. B. M. Muir and N. Moray: Trust in Automation. Part 2. Experimental Studies of Trust and Human Intervention in a Process Control Simulation. Ergonomics, Vol. 39, No. 3, pp. 429-460, 1996.
4. J. Lee and N. Moray: Trust, Control Strategies and Allocation of Function in Human-Machine Systems. Ergonomics, Vol. 35, No. 10, pp. 1243-1270, 1992.
5. J. Lee and N. Moray: Trust, Self-confidence, and Operators' Adaptation to Automation. The International Journal of Human-Computer Studies, Vol. 40, pp. 153-184 1994.
6. R. Parasuraman, R. Molloy, and I. Singh: Performance Consequences of Automation-induced "Complacency". The International Journal of Aviation Psychology, Vol. 3, No. 1, pp. 1-23, 1993.
7. T. Inagaki, N. Moray, and M. Itoh: Trust and Time-Criticality: Their Effects on the Situation-Adaptive Autonomy. Proceedings of International Symposium on Artificial Intelligence, Robotics, and Intellectual Human Activity Support for Nuclear Applications, pp. 93-104, 1997.
8. T. Inagaki, N. Moray, and M. Itoh: Trust, Self-confidence and Authority in Human-Machine Systems. Proceedings of 7th IFAC/IFIP/IFORS/IEA Conference on Analysis, Design and Evaluation of Man-Machine Systems, pp. 491-496, 1998.
9. M. Itoh, Y. Takae, T. Inagaki, and N. Moray: Experimental Study of Situation-Adaptive Human-Automation. Preprints of the 7th IFAC MMS, pp. 371-376, 1998.
10. T. Inagaki, Y. Takae, and N. Moray: Automation and Human-Interface for Takeoff Safety: Proceedings of the 10th International Symposium on Aviation Psychology, pp. 402-407, 1999.
11. T. Inagaki, Y. Takae, and N. Moray: Decision Support Information for Takeoff Safety in the Human-Centered Automation: An Experimental Investigation of Time-Fragile Characteristic. Proceedings of IEEE International Conference on Systems, Man, and Cybernetics, No. 1, pp. 1101-1106, 1999.

CONTACT

Contact the author by email;

y-takae@mail.nissan.co.jp

or write to

Yasuhiko Takae, Ph. D

1-1, Morinosatoaoyama, Atsugi-shi, Kanagawa

243-0123, Japan

2005-01-0403

Dynamic Performance of Adaptive Cruise Control Vehicles

Robin A. Auckland, Oliver M. J. Carsten, Martin C. Levesley and David A. Crolla
The University of Leeds, UK

Warren J. Manning
Manchester Metropolitan University, UK

ABSTRACT

Although many different types of Adaptive Cruise Controller (ACC) have been developed to maintain a constant headway between lead and following vehicles, little is known about the dynamic performance of such controllers during cornering and in adverse environmental conditions. There are currently no standard guidelines for the use of ACC systems in such scenarios. Use of the controller in adverse weather or cornering conditions may lead to braking and handling instabilities, or unwanted accelerations being transmitted to the driver in the forms of pitch and roll. These dynamic characteristics are especially important when one considers that ACC systems are being marketed not as safety devices but to aid driver comfort. This paper presents an ACC algorithm that can be tuned to provide desirable dynamic characteristics as well as high-quality kinematic results. The performance of the controller is evaluated using a high-fidelity 9 degree of freedom vehicle model. Firstly the longitudinal performance of the ACC vehicle is examined through a range of straight line simulations with different environmental conditions and levels of acceleration, to investigate the safety of such systems and the pitch accelerations experienced by the driver. The controller is then tested using curved road simulations to examine the effects of ACC on cornering performance as well as the roll accelerations generated.

INTRODUCTION

Advanced Driver Assistance Systems (ADAS) have been developed over the past few years to remove workload from the driver, making driving an easier mental and physical activity; whilst also increasing the safety of the vehicle by removing the driver from some control decisions. Much of the recent ADAS research concerns Adaptive Cruise Control (ACC) systems, which are now available on a wide range of passenger vehicles. ACC systems consist of a simple cruise control system (basic speed control), combined with a forward-looking radar to monitor the time gap (headway) from the vehicle in front. The system can then either assume speed control mode, if no vehicle is found by the radar, or following mode, where a constant time gap is maintained between the following and lead vehicles. ACC systems are the most common form of ADAS as they require no inter-vehicle communication or modernised highway infrastructure. The aim of ACC is to remove the vehicle following driving task at highway speeds; although recent developments such as 'Stop and Go' should allow the longitudinal motion of the vehicle to be controlled from standstill to max speed. This research is mainly concerned with high speed manoeuvres as it is in this area that the largest forces are generated and largest accelerations are experienced.

Much of the engineering research concerned with these ACC systems looks primarily at the control strategies and hardware needed to implement a successful system. While this is valid, ACC's are now available on a wide range of production vehicles and some of the issues overlapping the engineering/psychological boundary remain un-resolved. It is the aim of this paper to tackle some of these issues including:

- Safe handling implications of a vehicle that adjusts longitudinal velocity independent of lateral velocity.
- The performance of ACC in low friction conditions.
- Rolling and pitching accelerations and the implications on driver comfort levels.

ISSUES WITH ACC

ENGINEERING FACTORS

Manufacturers from all over the world are currently introducing ACC systems. They are currently marketed as a comfort device and offered as an optional extra on high specification models, but trends show that as the cost of systems is reduced over the next few years ACC will become more commonplace [1]. With this increased use of the system and the introduction of other types of vehicle automation (lane tracking, lane changing) it is necessary to fully explore the performance of the system and the effects it will have on the driver. Some of the large manufacturers have published literature on the implementation of ACC on their vehicles ([2], [3] and [4]), while others have discussed the control algorithm used ([5]). Large scale field operational tests have also been undertaken with positive feedback from the test drivers ([6]). With all of this research and ACC systems in use on public roads it may seem unproductive to research the subject further, but current research neglects some issues which are key to the long term success of Adaptive Cruise Control.

Central to these problems are the literature and training provided by the vendor to the customer. Currently no training is given to drivers who purchase a new ACC system, and while the dealer may inform the customer of the usefulness of the system to maximise selling potential, information on its functions and guidelines for its use may only be delivered in the owner's manual. These guidelines differ from one manufacturer to the next with regards to suitable weather conditions and road geometry in which to use the system. Audi suggest their system 'should not be used on winding roads or in adverse weather conditions such as fog, ice or heavy rain.'[7], whereas Visteon marketing information insists their system, 'Maintains consistent performance in poor visibility conditions and maintains continuous performance during road turns and elevation changes.'[8]. Although the specification of these systems may differ, it is unlikely that the functionality of the two will be so diverse. These misleading guidelines may cause the driver to disable the system or worse use the system in unsuitable conditions.

Considering the range of environmental conditions to which the system may be subject to, research has shown that the millimetre wave radar used in all ACC's will work in all conditions from ice and snowfall to dry roads in bright sunshine [9]. The problems arise at the vehicle dynamics level, where the vehicle may not be able to convert the braking force applied by the controller into a tractive force on the road due to a low coefficient of friction. This may result in a rear end collision if the driver does not fully understand the capabilities of the system, especially when small headway gaps are being used.

Next we shall consider the claims of some manufacturers regarding the system's performance on curved roads. Again while the radar may work in such situations problems may arise with the vehicle dynamics. The International Standard for ACC [10] prescribes a minimum bend radius around which the system should be able to perform depending on its classification (Table 1).

Performance Class	Curve Radius Capability (m)
II	≥ 500
III	≥ 250
IV	≥ 125

Table 1 – ACC Curve Performance Classifications [10]

Systems are tested around curved tracks to asses the controller's acceleration and braking performance, although there is no provision for the weather conditions during testing and no assessment of the vehicle's handling performance during these tests. Experienced test drivers may be able to control the vehicle through the steering wheel alone whereas the unsuspecting common driver may be surprised by sudden acceleration or braking whilst cornering, this could lead to instability of the vehicle and lane departure.

The two previous points concern safety issues of the vehicle when an ACC system is implemented. The third point concerns the comfort of the driver, which is especially important as ACC systems are currently marketed as a comfort device rather than a safety aid. Some research has briefly touched on acceptable comfort levels. Ioannou [11] makes some estimation as to acceptable levels of longitudinal acceleration and jerk or 'driving comfort constraints'. The controller's response is filtered to ensure that the vehicle remains within these acceleration limits. But the full dynamic response of the vehicle is neglected throughout the literature. The pitching behaviour of the vehicle may be severely affected by a repetitive accelerating and decelerating behaviour on straight roads. When this is combined with lateral movement the rolling behaviour of the vehicle may also be affected. These rolling and pitching accelerations are directly linked to the levels of comfort experienced by the driver.

VEHICLE DYNAMICS MODELLING

Previous research into ACC vehicle simulation has almost exclusively been conducted using 3 degree of freedom bicycle models with linear tyre models, where the lateral and yaw motions of the vehicle are considered along with the longitudinal. These models can provide excellent results for straight line following and basic cornering, but accuracy is lost in the nonlinear handling regime. For the purpose of this research it is this area which is of interest as this is where the stability of the vehicle will come into question. To accurately simulate the vehicle performance in this region a non-linear Pacejka's 'Magic Formula' tyre model [12, 13] was used.

To accurately model vehicle handling and all accelerations experienced by the driver a sophisticated 9 degree of freedom vehicle model is used throughout the simulations. Longitudinal ($x,u,\dot{u}$), lateral ($y,v,\dot{v}$) and yaw ($\psi,r,\dot{r}$) motions of the vehicle body are calculated as well as its roll ($\phi,\dot{\phi},\ddot{\phi}$) and pitch ($\theta,\dot{\theta},\ddot{\theta}$) motions. A longitudinal wheel slip ratio (ω) is calculated for each tyre to ensure accurate acceleration and deceleration behaviour. These degrees of freedom are described in figures 1-3.

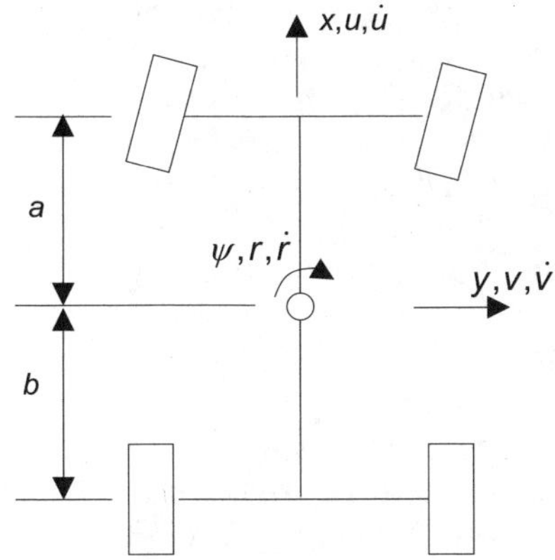

Figure 1 – Longitudinal, Lateral and Yaw Degrees of Freedom

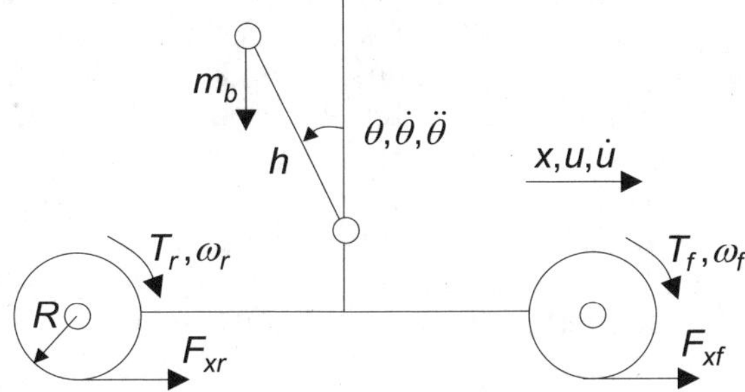

Figure 2 – Pitch and Wheel Slip Degrees of Freedom

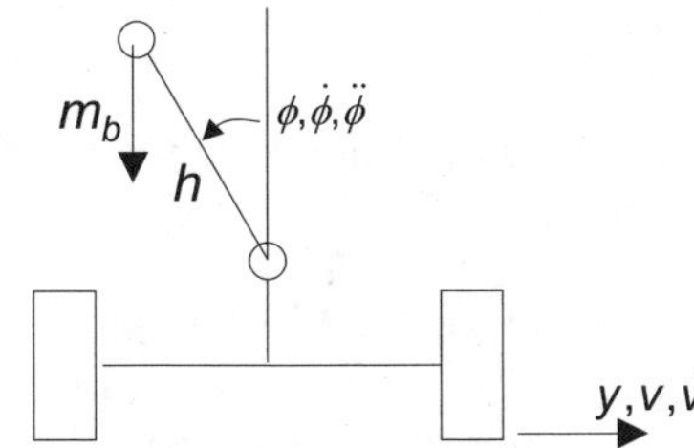

Figure 3 – Roll Degree of Freedom

A Lagrangian approach was used to derive the following equations of motion for the system:

$$m_t(\dot{u}-vr)-(am_f-bm_r)r^2-m_b\left(h_r r\dot{\phi}+h_p\ddot{\theta}\right)=\sum F_x$$

$$m_t(\dot{v}+ur)+(am_f-bm_r)\dot{r}+m_b\left(h_p r\dot{\theta}+h_r\ddot{\phi}\right)=\sum F_y$$

$$(am_f-bm_r)(\dot{v}+ur)+\left(m_f a^2+m_r b^2+I_{zz}\right)\dot{r}+m_b\left(h_r u\dot{\phi}-h_p v\dot{\theta}\right)=\sum M_z$$

$$\left(I_{yy}+m_b h_p^2\right)\ddot{\theta}+C_\theta\dot{\theta}+\left(K_\theta-m_b g h_p\right)\theta+h_p^2\dot{\phi}r+m_b h_r(\dot{v}+ur)=d_f F_{xf}-d_r F_{xr}$$

$$\left(I_{xx}+m_b h_r^2\right)\ddot{\phi}+C_\phi\dot{\phi}+\left(K_\phi-m_b g h_r\right)\phi-h_r^2\dot{\theta}r+m_b h_r(\dot{v}+ur)=d_f F_{yf}-d_r F_{yr}$$

$$\kappa=\frac{u_w-R\dot{\omega}}{u_w}$$

This vehicle model was tested without any control to validate is correlation with the real vehicle and previous simulations. A simple PID Adaptive Cruise Control system was then applied to the vehicle model. This controller was based on the research of Ioannou [11] which has been used regularly in other ACC research. The controller has the following primary objectives:

1) To keep the desired vehicle spacing (headway) S_d, if we let the subscripts l and f denote lead and following vehicles S_d can be given as:

$$S_d = Hu_f$$

Where H is the time headway.

2) To ensure similar lead and following velocities

$$u_f \approx u_l$$

Also given in [11] are two secondary control objectives relating to the ride comfort requirements:

1) $a_{min} \le \dot{u}_f \le a_{max}$ Where a_{min} and a_{max} are -0.2g and 0.1g respectively.

2) The absolute value of jerk $\ddot{u}_f$, should be as small as possible.

As with every model some assumptions are made to simplify the simulation and ensure model stability for a range of tests. It was decided that the throttle angle to wheel torque model should be removed from the simulations. Instead the controller directly controls the amount of torque applied to each of the rear wheels. This is the same case for the brake model. These two non-linear relationships are beyond the scope of this research as the dynamic performance of the vehicle is more important than the intricacies of the controller.

Given equations of motion for the vehicle models, the vehicle parameters from a luxury saloon and the control parameters, Matlab/Simulink was employed to simulate the system's performance in a range of manoeuvres discussed in the next section.

EVALUATION OF ACC

To fully investigate the performance of the ACC system is was necessary to conduct a combination of both longitudinal and lateral manoeuvres. The straight line (longitudinal) simulations will examine the systems performance in adverse weather conditions; where as the lateral simulations will look more at the handling performance of the vehicle equipped with and without ACC.

STRAIGHT LINE SIMULATIONS

The main objectives of the longitudinal tests were to investigate:

- The effect of different weather conditions on the headway response of the vehicle.
- The pitching behaviour of the vehicle under ACC operation and its impact on driver comfort.

For the purpose of all simulations it is assumed that the lead vehicle is not equipped with an ACC system. It is therefore able to generate accelerations larger than the following vehicle (assuming no following driver intervention). In all simulations both vehicles are Initially travelling at 31m/s (70mph) with a constant time headway gap of 1.5s (46.5m at 31m/s).

A) As discussed earlier there is some inconsistency in the acceptable range of conditions in which ACC systems can be used. For this reason it was chosen to investigate ACC system performance through a range of environmental conditions, characterised through coefficients of friction (μ) given in Table 2 for the pure rolling case.

Surface	Co-eff Of Friction (μ)
Dry Asphalt	0.8
Wet Asphalt	0.4
Icy or Snowy Road	0.2

Table 2 – Surface Coefficients of Friction [14]

The lead vehicle was given a range of decelerations from -0.5m/s^2 to -2.0m/s^2 and the following vehicles headway and velocity performance were monitored.

B) Currently ACC systems are marketed as a comfort aid rather than a safety device. When using ACC Driver workload is reduced, but the comfort levels of the driver matter not only on his/her workload but also the accelerations he/she will experience. For this reason the pitching behaviour of the vehicle is investigated to measure any differences between the uncontrolled response of the vehicle and that of the vehicle with an ACC system.

In the test the lead vehicle decelerates at 2.5m/s^2 for 6s after which time the resultant speed (21m/s) is maintained. For the standard case (no ACC) it is assumed that the following driver can track this deceleration and perform the same manoeuvre.

For the simulation with control the deceleration level of the lead vehicle is outside that which can be achieved by the following vehicle with ACC. It is therefore possible to monitor the systems performance outside its applicable range as would happen without intervention from the driver.

COMBINED LATERAL AND LONGITUDINAL SIMULATIONS

While the longitudinal performance of the system was considered in the previous tests it is also necessary to look at the effects of ACC on the cornering performance of a vehicle, given the ACC system is a purely longitudinal control device any lateral control of the vehicle must be performed by the driver. Any change in longitudinal speed of vehicle caused by an ACC system will have a direct effect on its lateral response. These effects are investigated in the following tests.

C) From the international standard for ACC [10] the minimum bend radius around which the system should function is a curve of radius 125m. The sophisticated vehicle model is given a constant speed of 31m/s (70mph) to simulate a curve during motorway driving and the steer angle is found with which the vehicle will follow a path of radius 150m. Simulations are then undertaken to demonstrate the following vehicles lateral and longitudinal performance when the lead vehicle accelerates through the curve and brakes through the curve. The path tracking performance is observed as well as the effect on vehicle roll accelerations which have an adverse effect on the level of driver comfort.

RESULTS

STRAIGHT LINE SIMULATIONS

The results from the straight line simulations are shown in figures 4, 5 and 6 on the following page. Each set of graphs corresponds to a different level of acceleration. The top plot on each set of axes corresponds to the distance in metres between the lead and following vehicles. The lower plot corresponds to the time gap in seconds between the lead and following vehicle. In all of the simulations the deceleration of the lead vehicle begins at 2 seconds and stays constant for 6 seconds at which point the deceleration level returns to zero.

A) In this first set of simulations the aim was to asses what impact differing levels of friction would have on the ACC vehicle's performance. Figure 4 shows the response of the vehicle to a deceleration of 0.5m/s^2 for dry roads (μ=0.8), wet roads (μ=0.4), and icy roads (μ=0.2). At this low level of deceleration the response of the vehicle is excellent for all surface characteristics. To all intents and purposes the outputs are identical for all values of μ, the time headway remains near constant and the distance headway is reduced quickly and smoothly.

Figure 5 shows the response of the vehicle to a deceleration of 1.0m/s^2 for dry roads (μ=0.8), wet roads (μ=0.4), and icy roads (μ=0.2). Again for dry, wet and icy roads the response of the system is near identical. Distance headway is reduced smoothly with only a minor fluctuation in the headway time throughout the manoeuvre.

Figure 6 shows the response of the vehicle to a deceleration of 2.0m/s^2 for dry roads (μ=0.8), wet roads (μ=0.4) and icy roads (μ=0.2). -2.0m/s^2 is the maximum acceleration level that the ACC system can achieve due to the limits employed on the controller suggested by Ioannou [11]. Under dry and wet road conditions the system performs well with minor variations in time headway; but when tested on icy roads the headway response can be seen to diverge and oscillate. Although in this case the two vehicles do not collide the system becomes unstable. This is due to the vehicle not being able to generate the required braking forces at these lower levels of friction.

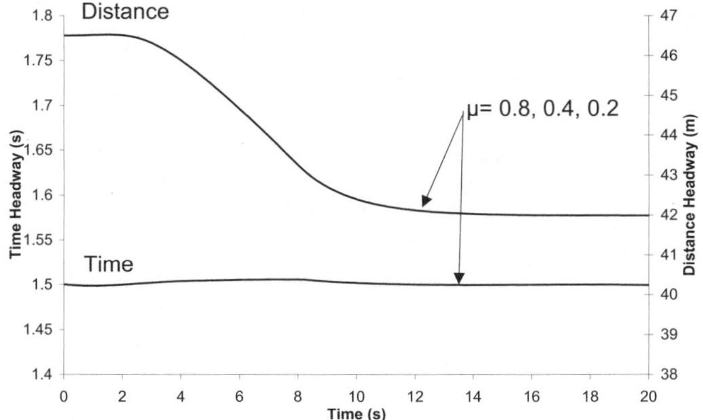

Figure 4 -Headway for Dry, Wet and Icy at $\dot{u}_L$ = -0.5m/s^2

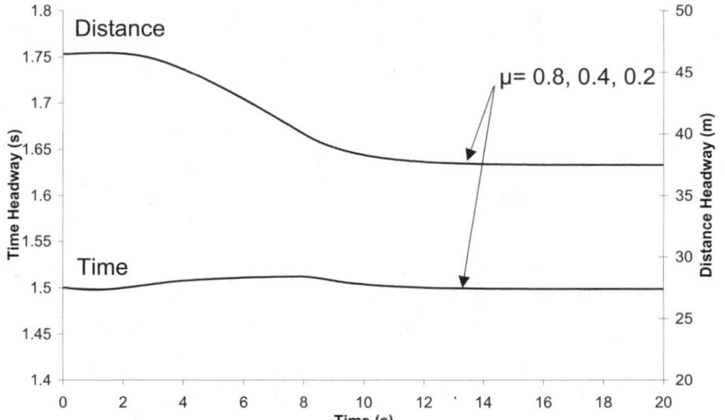

Figure 5 -Headway for Dry, Wet and Icy at $\dot{u}_L$ = -1.0m/s^2

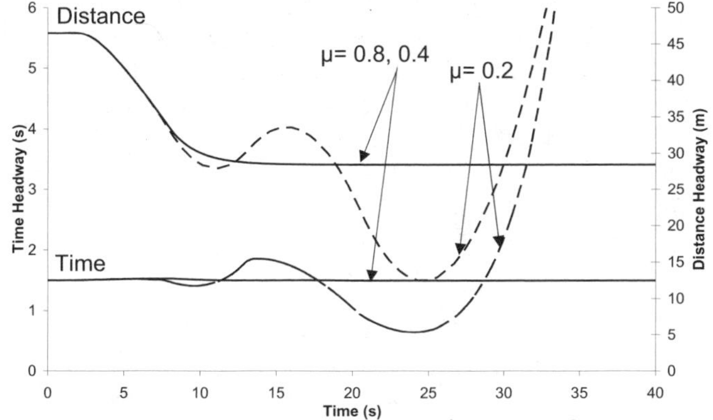

Figure 6 -Headway for Dry, Wet and Icy at $\dot{u}_L$ = -2.0m/s^2

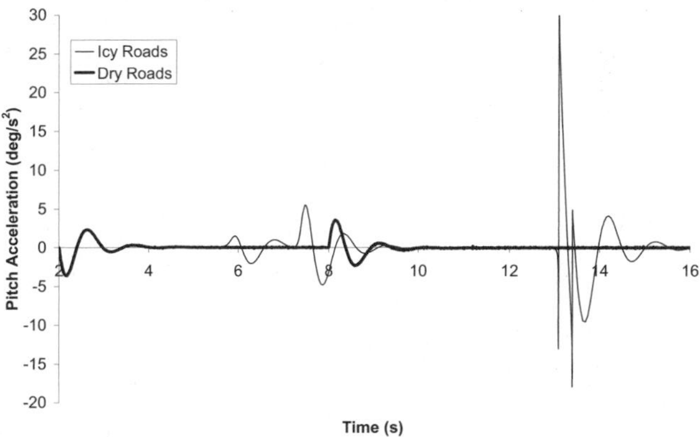

Figure 7 – Pitch Accelerations on Dry and Icy Roads

Figure 7 shows the pitching accelerations that would be experienced by the vehicle body (i.e. the driver and passengers) during a 2.0m/s^2 deceleration (the same manoeuvre as figure 6) here it can be seen that the instabilities of the controller in icy conditions cause a large increase in the levels of pitch acceleration. These accelerations may be uncomfortable for the driver.

B) In test B the pitching performance of the vehicle was investigated by subjecting the following vehicle to a deceleration of 2.5m/s^2 (just beyond the controller's limits). This caused a slight overshoot in the control of the time headway as the levels high levels of acceleration could not be maintained by the controller. Figure 8 shows that in recovering from this overshoot the following vehicle experiences instantaneous levels of pitch acceleration above 40deg/s^2 compared to 5deg/s in the driver controlled case (constant deceleration of 2.5m/s^2).

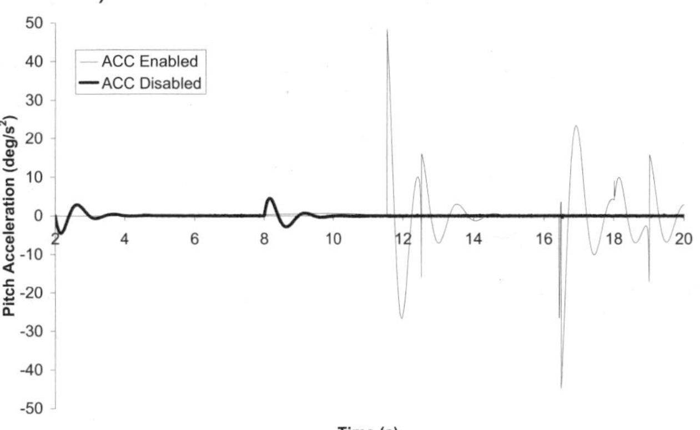

Figure 8 – Pitch Accelerations with ACC enabled and Disabled

C) The aim of this range of simulations was to investigate the performance of the vehicle around a curve. The effects of the ACC system on the path taken and the levels of roll acceleration experienced by the driver. Looking at Figure 9 it can be seen that the desired trajectory of the following vehicle is significantly affected by the introduction of longitudinal acceleration during the manoeuvre. Whilst the stability of the vehicle is never in question the lateral position of the vehicle on the road may vary by up to 5m at the exit of a medium

(100m long) 150m radius bend. This error will result in lane departure unless the driver counteracts the ACC input using either a change in steer angle or longitudinal input (throttle/brake).

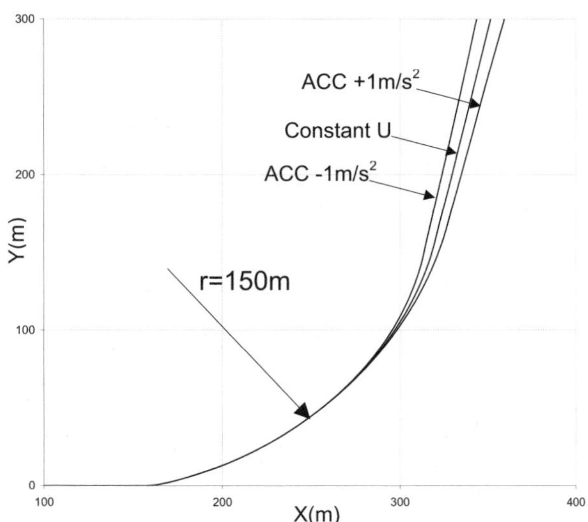

Figure 9 – Trajectory around 150m radius corner for ACC system.

The body roll accelerations were monitored throughout these combined lateral and longitudinal simulations; figure 10 shows that there is little variation in these values due to ACC interaction, the only minor difference in value of roll acceleration occurs at 3 seconds. This fluctuation is small when compared to the initial peak in all cases. It can therefore be assumed that ACC systems have do not cause a decrease in driver comfort levels due to roll accelerations.

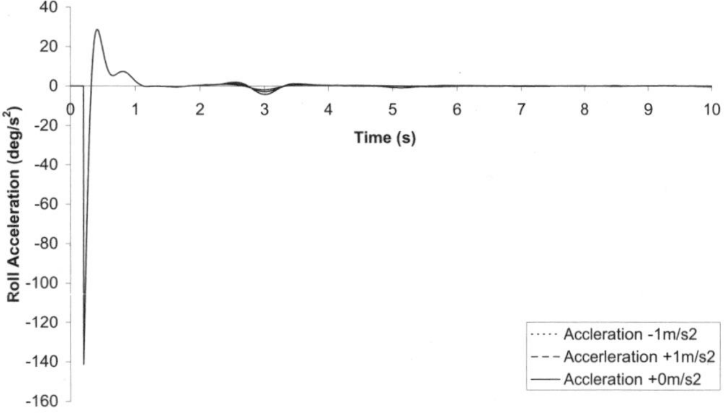

Figure 10 – Body Roll Accelerations during combined Lateral and Longitudinal Simulations

CONCLUSION

The full dynamic response of Adaptive Cruise Controllers has been investigated. Longitudinal simulations have demonstrated that poor environmental conditions (low coefficients of road friction) have a detrimental effect on the deceleration performance of the controller, it is therefore suggested that future control schemes are designed to overcome this fundamental flaw. The levels of pitch accelerations experienced by the driver are also increased with the use of ACC systems. This is especially noticeable when the systems maximum accelerations levels are exceeded. This increased sophistication of the vehicle model has shown some problems with ACC systems which have been overlooked in previous simulations.

Lateral simulations have shown that ACC systems cause an error in path tracking which without driver intervention could lead to lane departure. The roll accelerations experienced by the driver are negligible and have little effect on the driver comfort levels.

It is suggested that drivers new to Adaptive Cruise Control vehicles are fully informed of its performance characteristics. Driver training may also be of use in highlighting possible scenarios in which driver intervention is required.

REFERENCES

1. Zwaneweld P J, Van Arem B, Bastianensen E G H J, Soeteman J J, et al., *Development Scenarios For Advanced Driver Assistance Systems.* 1999, TNO - Department of Traffic: 97 Schoemakerstraat 2628 VK Delft.

2. Prestl W, Sauer T, Steinle J, and Tschernoster O, *The BMW Active Cruise Control ACC.* SAE 2000 World Congress - Journal of Passenger Car - Electronic and Electrical Systems 2000.

3. Richardson M, Corrigan D, King P, Smith I, et al., *Application of Control System Simulation in the Automotive Industry.* IEE Seminar on Tools for Simulation and Modelling. 2000. pp. 8/1 - 8/13.

4. Masuda H, Hirosima Y, and Ito T, *Development of Daihatsu ASV2.* IEEE Intelligent Vehicles Symposium, 2000. 2000. pp. 708 - 713.

5. Iijima T, Higashimata A, Tange S, Mizoguchi K, et al., *Development of an Adaptive Cruise Control System with Brake Actuation.* SAE 2000 World Congress - Journal of Passenger Car - Electronic and Electrical Systems 2000.

6. Fancher P, Ervin R, Sayer J, Hagan M, et al., *Intelligent Cruise Control Field Operational Test.* 1998, The University of Michigan Transportation Research Institute: Ann Arbor, Michigan 48109-2150 USA.

7. Audi, *Glossary -Adaptive Cruise Control.* 2004: Ingolstadt, Germany.

8. Visteon, *DRIVER AWARENESS - Adaptive Cruise Control.* 2004: Dearborn MI USA.

9. Abou-Jaoude R, *ACC radar sensor technology, test requirements, and test solutions.* IEEE Transactions on Intelligent Transportation Systems. 2003. Vol:4. 3:3, pp. 115 - 122.

10. ISO/FDIS, *Transport Information and Control Systems — Adaptive Cruise Control Systems — Performance Requirements and Test Procedures.* 2002: Geneva.

11. Ioannou P, Xu Z, Eckert S, Clemons D, et al., *Intelligent Cruise Control: Theory and Experiment.* IEEE Conference on Decision and Control. 1993. Vol:2. pp. 1885 - 1890.

12. Pacejka H B, *Tyres and Vehicle Dynamics.* 2002: Oxford, Butterworth-Heinemann.

13. Pacejka H B and Besselink I J M, *Magic Formula Tyre Model with Transient Properties.* Vehicle System Dynamics 1997. 27(Suppl):27(Suppl), pp. 234 - 249.

14. Sakai S-I and Hori Y, *Advanced Vehicle Motion Control Of Electric Vehicle Based On The Fast Motor Torque Response.* 5th International Symposium on Advanced Vehicle Control. 2000.

2004-01-1744

Functional Optimization of Adaptive Cruise Control Using Navigation Data

Martin Brandstaeter, Willibald Prestl and Guenter Bauer
BMW Group, Munich

ABSTRACT

The paper explains how driver assistance systems, using ACC as an example, can take advantage of navigation data. The operational concept of the assistance function has to be designed according to the particular properties of this additional data source. Even with the quality of navigation data available today, BMW's ACC system can be enhanced by dynamics, which adapt to the situation, providing even more benefit for the customer.

INTRODUCTION

BMW offers assistance functions such as Active Cruise Control [1], for current vehicle models. ACC supports the driver by eliminating the need to make monotonous fine adjustments to the driving distance from preceding vehicles. BMW achieves this by automating sub-functions within the speed and distance control. Further assistance functions concerning lateral guidance will follow at a later stage.

In spite of occasionally heated debate, customers accept the assistance functions because they recognize the need for them. Most of the criticism arises where their function deviates subjectively from expectations. As long as drivers are not tired, distracted or inattentive, it is desirable for them to experience the outcome of their own driving abilities at the steering wheel. By this yardstick, they subjectively measure the capability of the assistance functions.

In order to drive a vehicle well, the driver needs concrete information about the driving environment in addition to well-founded training, experience and the ability to perform routine functions. Ideally, he or she is able to estimate a situation fully and completely and then make the correct decisions about how to act. The driving environment is based on the one hand on the position, movement and type of the other vehicles on the road, and on the other hand on the route and the nature of the road, on traffic regulations, weather, visibility etc.

However, because of the limitations of their sensors, driver assistance functions at best possess only part of the information needed to describe the whole situation, Fig. 1. Consequently, the driver will always experience a deficit in his or her expectations if the subjectively perceived information does not correspond to the full picture of the driving environment.

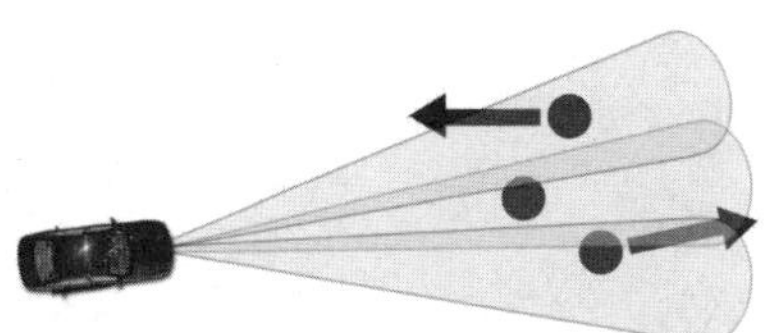

Fig. 1: Drivers View / ACC View (beneath)

In this context we can think of navigation systems and their associated databases as additional forward-looking environment sensors, which make part of the missing information available. The geometry of the road surface and other information about the road, such as its type and the number of lanes or restrictions, results in an estimation of the driving environment. This gives rise to opportunities for optimizing the driver assistance functions, which we present here using Active Cruise Control as an example.

ACC SYSTEM LIMITATIONS

ACC systems receive information from long-range sensors about the position and movement of objects on the road in a relatively narrow field of view of approx. ± 4° to ± 8° over a distance of about 150 meters, Fig. 2. If a vehicle equipped with ACC follows a vehicle in front in the same lane, then *this* is the main feature of the driving situation. The distance control is targeted at this vehicle. The data available on the position and movement of the vehicle in front allow it to be followed conveniently in a way that satisfies the driver's expectations.

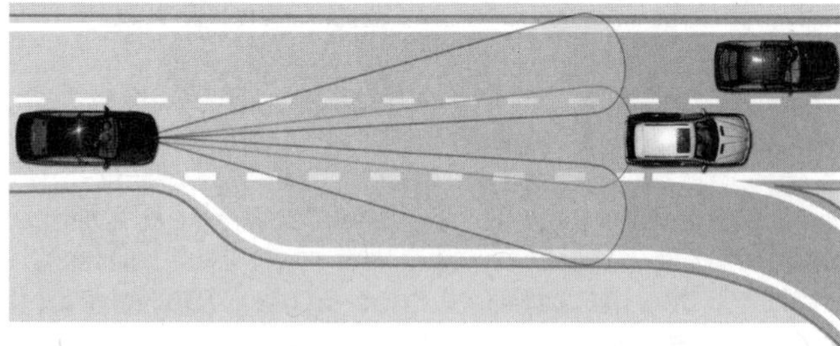

Fig. 2: ACC Function

However, greater demands are imposed by what initially appears to be trivial: the clear road, i.e. when there is no vehicle driving in front in the same lane, and the transition from being behind one to having no vehicle in front. Can the system really be sure that there is not a vehicle in the same lane, perhaps one that cannot be seen because of visual obstructions, for example, in tight bends? Does the system suppose that the road ahead is clear although there is a vehicle moving in the same lane, which is not identified correctly as occupying that lane, because the topography of the road is not known?

Geometrical limitations in the field of view and the absence of forward-looking data on the course of the road can therefore result in uncertainties when assessing the situation. This is where we currently encounter system limitations.

However, even correctly identifying a simple situation such as changing to a clear lane poses the question of the correct system reaction. The system has to adjust the driver's desired speed, which was typically pre-selected to be higher than the speed maintained when following the vehicle in front. In this case, what is the correct rate of acceleration?

Current ACC systems always have to work with a compromise layout, which is acceptable in different situations, because information on the current driving environment, such as the type of road or its course is missing. The driver, on the other hand, obviously includes this information in his own decision-making. For example, acceleration controlled by the ACC when changing to a clear lane on a straight highway may sometimes be judged to be too sluggish, whereas the same acceleration on a winding country road or the exit lane from a highway can in some circumstances be felt to be dynamic to the point of uncertainty, Fig. 3. If the dynamic of one situation is applied, then loss of comfort automatically occurs in other situations. The driver, however, expects system dynamics to adapt continuously and automatically to the current situation.

Here too, missing information about the environment manifests itself as significant system limitations, which make it difficult to refine and optimize the system's behavior further until it matches the customer's expectations.

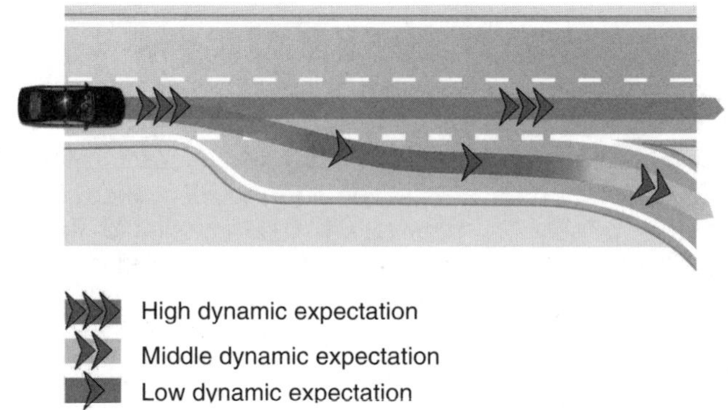

Fig. 3: Anticipated dynamics

Attempts to satisfy the driver's situation-related expectations indirectly by altering the dynamic behavior of the active cruise control according to the chosen distance from the preceding vehicle do not solve the central issue. The desire for dynamic progress when driving on a clear road and the selected distance when driving behind other vehicles are not actually related to each other either causally or inherently. Conversely it is not meaningful to have to accept, for example, a lower vehicle-following distance in order to obtain a higher dynamic on fast roads.

POTENTIAL FOR OPTIMIZING THE ACC FUNCTION USING NAVIGATION SYSTEM DATABASES

With the rapid further development of data quality and the degree of coverage achieved by navigation system databases, precise prediction of the track of the road will be possible in the medium-term. In the future further functions can be built up on this basis.

However, even without precise descriptions of bends in the road, we can already achieve considerable improvements by making use of currently available data sources. The basis for this is structural information, classification of bends and attributive road data such as the type of road or number of lanes. From these data we have developed functions which influence both the layout of the control dynamic and the recognition of traffic objects.

In this way we can comply with the increased dynamic demand on highways and also the demand for a broad sensor recording area on single-lane roads, Fig. 4.

We can already set a narrow recognition field on the current lane of highways, and reduce the dynamic on twisting sections of road. However, this is not about reacting to an individual bend. Consequently, the result is not some kind of automatic speed reduction to a supposedly safer or more comfortable speed in the bend; instead, the dynamic form of the ACC is adjusted while leaving its basic function otherwise unchanged.

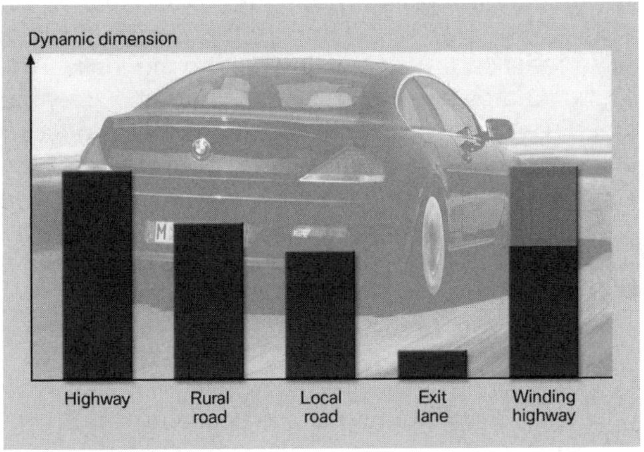

Fig. 4: Dynamic steps

COMMUNICATION CONCEPT AND SYSTEM INTEGRATION

For the original navigation functions such as route planning, reports and turning indications, the vehicle's current position needs to be related to a stored map. This comparison is called 'mapmatching'. It supplies most of the navigation data required by the ACC functions, and also keeps additional navigation system costs within limits. Nevertheless, there are a few conditions which need to be taken into account with regard to the navigation interface.

Navigation systems in today's vehicle concepts are typically located near the vehicle's communication, audio and multimedia functions. For this reason there can be a long way, in terms of onboard network topology, to the navigation data users such as the active cruise control. If the communication path leads from the navigation system to the ACC via several gateways, then on the one hand the communication load must be matched to the weakest bus, and on the other hand the system must be in a position to recognize delays or to compensate for them more effectively, Fig. 5.

To protect the buses, redundant data is not sent. The solution presented here makes a distinction between synchronous and asynchronous data. Synchronous, i.e. cyclical data are only used to produce a relative link to an already asynchronous prediction transmitted on demand.

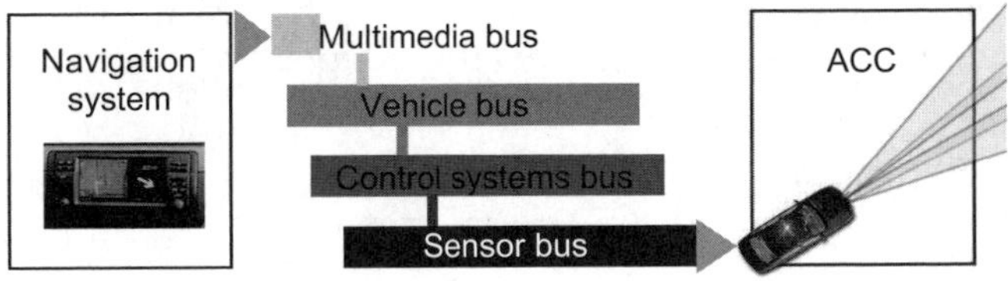

Fig. 5: System configuration

It is obvious that other control devices, such as active lighting or transmission control, may also represent meaningful functions using the navigation data. A peer-to-peer solution between the navigation system and each individual navigation data user cannot be considered, as this places too much of a burden on the bandwidth of the CAN buses. We therefore use broadcast technology, which permits resynchronization in the event of data loss.

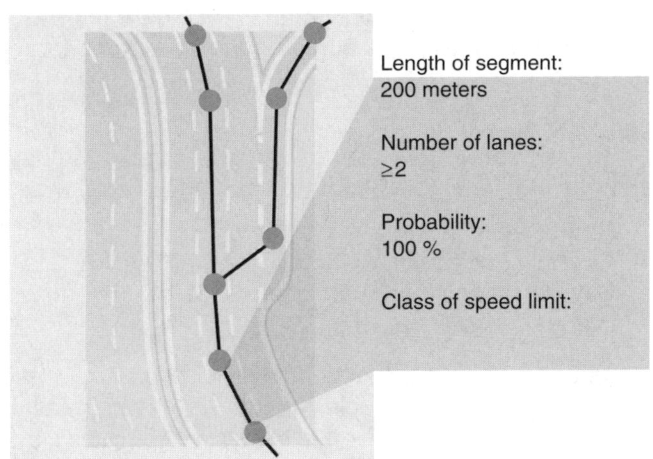

Fig. 6: Tree structure

The transmitted road prediction contains reachable sections of road together with geometric data and attributes which either have a minimum distance from the current position or which can be reached within a specific period of time. This also means that all data are available at junctions. The data representation is a living tree, which the navigation system dynamically expands or contracts, Fig. 6. As the match position progresses within this tree, the matching sections of road and turn-offs are removed from the root of the tree and new sections added to the branches step by step. This solution has several advantages. One of these is that the data are available independently of a planned route. Moreover, the journey can immediately be continued from the new position on the tree, even if the most likely route is departed from. This ensures the claim to the highest possible availability. Construction and deconstruction of the tree are not time-critical, as they take place at points that have already been passed or which will only become of current significance at some future time. At junctions, the navigation system calculates and transfers the probability of which road is being driven on. This information can be used for the tree segment transfer sequence, as well as for the probability-related parameter adaptation discussed below.

APPROACHES TO SOLUTIONS FOR DYNAMIC SITUATION-RELATED ADAPTATION

Traffic movements consist of an incalculable number of different conditions. A person can react to each situation appropriately. In the ideal situation, he or she takes the right action. However, a technical system cannot, at least from today's viewpoint, depict these possibilities completely and fully. As far as problems specific to ACC are concerned, we therefore classify roads into three categories:

- Well-built highways
- Less important rural and main roads
- Roads through villages and stretches with many bends

A combination of attributes in an "AND"-gate increases recognition quality and ensures a function appropriate to the situation.

Highways

Features of highways are, Fig. 7:

- Road classification in a high category
- Physical separation of the directions of travel
- Several lanes in each direction of travel
- Higher speed limits

A method of construction ideally suited to traffic requirements and mostly clear traffic conditions result in the driver expecting a high dynamic, i.e. a quick and decisive reaction to the change from following a vehicle to driving in a clear lane, as well as rapid control of the selected speed.

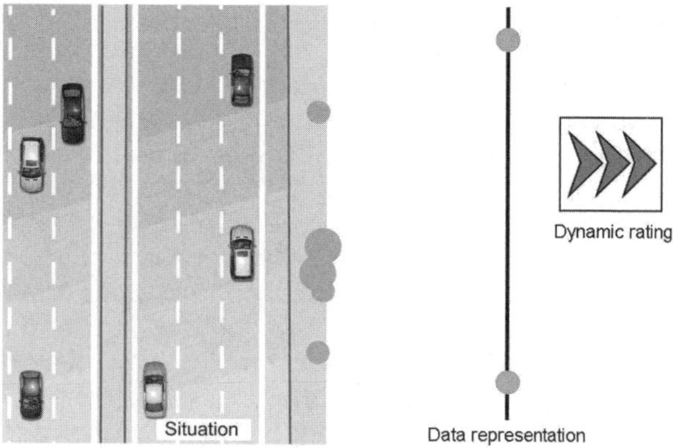

Fig. 7: Highways

If the road has several lanes and runs more or less straight, adjustment to a narrow lane prediction width is possible. The space in which the targeted vehicle can be recognized as relevant can also be narrower. This results in quicker "de-targeting" from the vehicle in front when changing lanes, and also fewer false reactions to vehicles in neighboring lanes.

Rural roads

A rural road has the following characteristics, Fig. 8:

- One lane in each direction of travel
- Not classified in the lower road category
- Road speed classification not in the lower band

The dynamic expectation corresponds here to what is currently called "Standard ACC": a moderate dynamic in a changing situation, and acceleration to the desired speed with the emphasis on comfort. There is no limit to the width of the lane prediction, as there is no question of a false reaction to vehicles in neighboring lanes. This makes the journey behind the vehicle in front quieter and smoother. The system also recognizes vehicles quickly on bends.

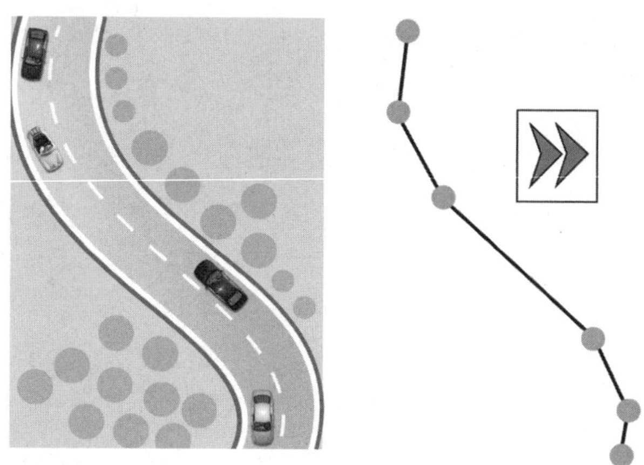

Fig. 8: Rural roads

Local roads

The local roads category has the following characteristics, Fig. 9:

- Road classification in the lowest category
- Single lane
- Low speed limits

A compromise in the application, which should cover all conditions imaginable, has, in some situations and as already mentioned, an uncomfortable dynamic effect on the driver. Frequently unclear traffic situations on this type of road call for restrained tuning of the dynamic parameters.

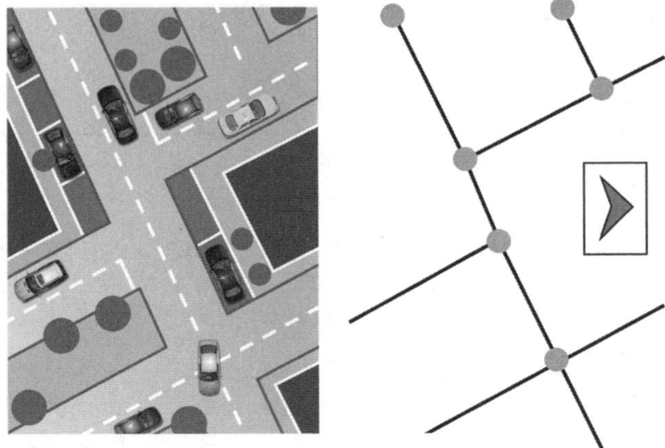

Fig. 9: Local roads

Examination of the character of bends

The dynamic steps presented here relate to straight or at least mostly straight stretches of road. Investigations [2] show that speed selection depends primarily on how many bends the stretch of road possesses. The unit for this winding characteristic is defined as the sum of all changes in angle per length of road.

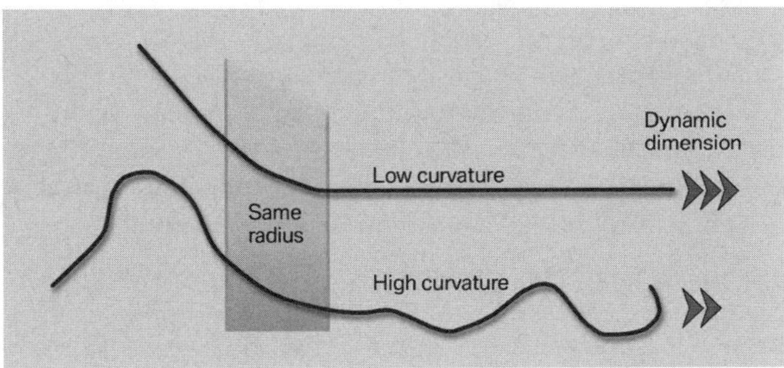

Fig. 10: Winding roads

Bends with the same radius are driven through more quickly compared with very twisting stretches of road if the curvature intensity of the entire section of road is low, Fig. 10. The bend configuration of the road can therefore also be a measure of the driver's dynamic awareness. If the ACC and navigation system are linked, the resulting geometric behaviors can be used to control the dynamic. On a stretch of road which is less twisting, the ACC vehicle can make use of the full dynamic. The dynamic is reduced at the same rate as the intensity of the bends in the road increases. On very winding roads the dynamic is set at the lowest level, even for a highway.

The winding nature of the road is determined by examining a specific stretch of road ahead of and behind the vehicle. This means that only the decisive stretch of road for the current situation, and consequently for the driver, is taken into account. The result is harmonious overall behavior of the ACC control system with good adaptation to the current situation.

Exit handling

When the driver exits a highway, he or she often observes a deviation between the technically correct control of an ACC system without navigation links and what the driver expects.

If the driver intends to exit the highway, he will move into the lane from which the exit lane branches off, generally several hundred meters in advance. This can also be on the left hand side, as there are exits which leave to the left even when driving on the right. Let us assume that the driver is driving behind a truck until he reaches the exit, and also that he or she has previously set a higher speed than that at which the truck in front is driving. If the truck continues along the highway, the ACC will no longer have a target as soon as the driver changes to the exit lane. Consequently, the ACC will now accelerate the vehicle comfortably to the pre-set speed. Although technically correct, this reaction seems implausible to the driver, because most exits are curved and he is expected to disengage the ACC in such situations. The dynamic tuning on highways strengthens this effect even more. As a rule, having driven at speed on the highway, a driver will no longer accelerate on the exit lane. However, if the navigation data presumes that the driver is going to leave the highway, the inappropriate acceleration on the exit lane can be suppressed, Fig. 11.

Unfortunately, a satisfactorily precise determination of the vehicle's position on the exit lane is currently seldom possible. In order to decide whether the driver intends to turn off or carry on, further characteristics are necessary. Appropriate here are the vehicle's speed, use of the turn indicator or a route planned in the navigation system. If such characteristics suggest that the driver is going to exit from the highway, then acceleration is prevented. If the vehicle continues on the highway, acceleration remains active.

Fig. 11: Exit

Probability-supported parameter adaptation

If the ACC is connected to a navigation system, there are many opportunities for influencing the system. Besides influencing recognition, the solution presented here focuses mainly on a situation-dependent dynamic interpretation.

Having analyzed the navigation data, a probability is determined for the current situation. This controls the level of intervention, Fig. 12.

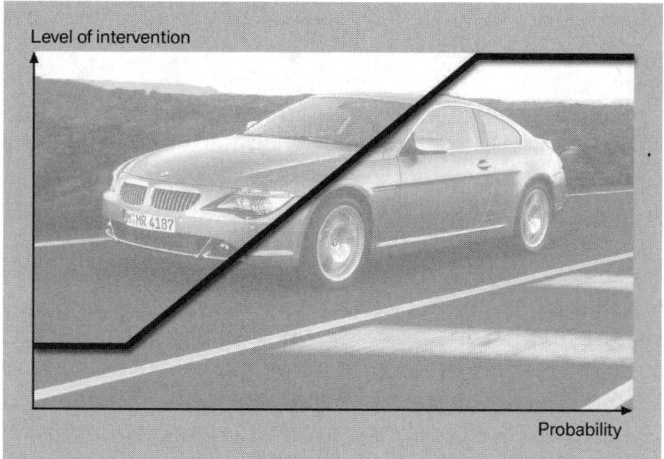

Fig. 12: Level of intervention

For example, the probability that the driver will leave the highway via an exit increases after a certain distance, and reaches its maximum value in the area of the exit at the correct speed with a flashing turn indicator and a planned route. Given these assumptions, the dynamic is set to the lowest level.

Using a sliding scale of probabilities from values acquired from the navigation system, from plausibilities and from driver inputs, parameter interventions can also be derived on a sliding scale. This prevents jerky movements and levels which could restrict comfort.

Each effect on a parameter requires an interface in the software of the ACC control unit. Function development and the tuning of the appropriate parameters show how the ACC dynamic can be influenced. The software module, which analyzes the navigation data, adjusts to these influences. The connection with the navigation system does not therefore fundamentally change the functionality of the ACC; it only tunes the available functions to match the current situation.

It behaves in a similar way with changes in the recognition of traffic objects. The parameters for influencing lane width and curvature can be matched to the current situation, for example to the maximum lane width on single-lane roads.

LAYOUT CRITERIA

The use of digitalized road data for vehicle management leads immediately to the following basic problems:

- Due to changes in the road network, such as construction sites or traffic calming, actual conditions may disagree with the data. Data are often out of date as soon as they have been published.
- Data may be incomplete, incorrectly captured or contain errors.

Neither the manufacturer of the vehicle, nor the manufacturer of the navigation system or the original data supplier can comprehensively check, assess and guarantee the quality of the data.

Clear matching of the vehicle's position to certain data cannot always be guaranteed. Therefore, ambiguities must be tolerated, at least in the short term.

In view of this it must be fundamentally assumed that the representation of data can deviate from reality and result in function errors. In terms of the function concept, this results in the following interpretation characteristics:

- The use of data is only meaningful if, from the driver's point of view, the assistance system does not generate incorrect reactions that are uncomfortable or critical compared with the initial situation, and if the positive effect of avoided shortcomings is a clear improvement over any further possible incorrect reactions.
- Data errors must not result in vehicle control interventions that are critical to safety. In the ACC application this clearly means limiting acceleration or deceleration to tried and tested values that can always be controlled by the driver.
- The use of database-supported functions is to be linked to an adequate assessment of quality during operation. Poor or missing information demands a meaningful basic function as a fallback level.

APPROACHES TO QUALITY ASSESSMENT

Whereas conventional map data on average only achieve an absolute geometrical accuracy of 30 meters or more, the next data generation will be considerably more accurate. For the purposes of investigation there are already maps available which guarantee an absolute geometric point accuracy of better than five meters and a relative point-to-point accuracy of better than one meter.

For the functions derived from these, the accuracy of the data and, of course, how up to date the maps are play an important role.

The navigation system determines the quality of the mapmatching. All the necessary quality information is available for the matching process. Initially, a general map match quality is available. Here, data on the course of the road and dynamic journey data such as yaw rate or speed are compared with the pattern of historic match positions. If, for example, both of these agree with each other to a large extent over the last two minutes, if the GPS position is available and if the permissible distance to the current match position is not exceeded, the value of the general match position should approach 100%. Implausible repositioning, i.e. a jumping to and from match positions, should also be taken into account as a reducing factor, Fig. 13.

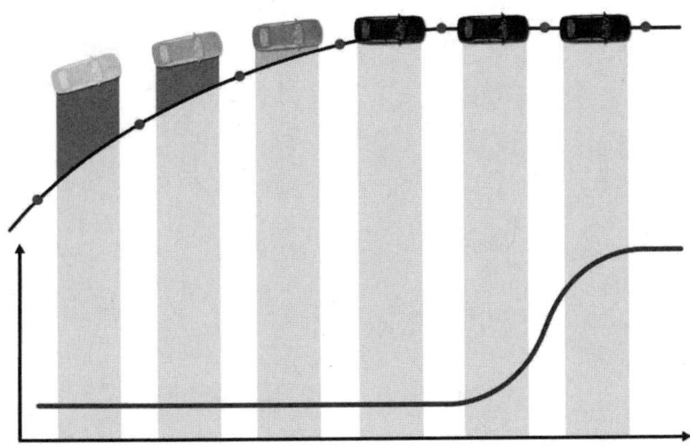

Fig. 13: Match quality

A further characteristic is uniqueness, Fig. 14. If a low value is present, this quality information shows that there are alternatives in the immediate vicinity, for example, parallel alternative routes, which make a certain probability for an alternative match position possible.

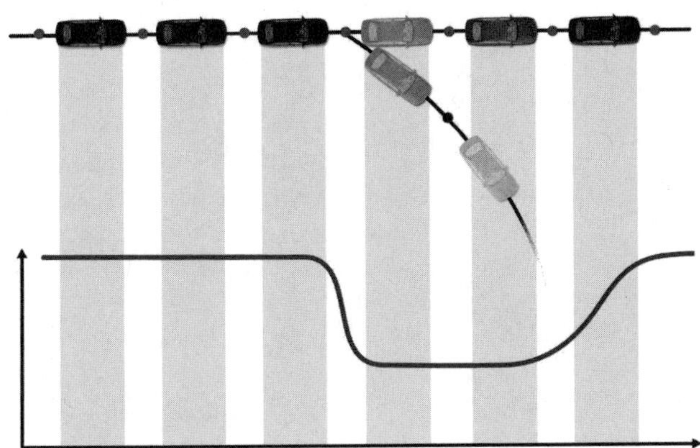

Fig 14: Uniqueness

An important measure for all functions relevant to position is distance accuracy. An error in distance measured in meters indicates a possible obstruction on the road. Interventions will start sooner or end later by this distance, to ensure that the function is available reliably and at the right place.

The level of parameter adaptation is carried out in accordance with the quality criteria. If these are poor, parameter adaptation reverts to the basic parameterization of the ACC system.

FUTURE POTENTIAL

In addition to the attribute and structure data, the current improvement in data precision means that direct use of geometry information from the databases in the form of a series of polygons or related curvature information is not far off. The fusion of data with the currently accepted dynamic course prediction of ACC systems results in considerable improvements in track prediction suitable for long, straight stretches of road as well as very curved sections. Further possibilities arise in connection with camera-based lane recognition systems. These can supply the relative position of the car on the lane and the course taken by the lane, but only up to mid-range distances of about 70 meters. Curvature prediction from the navigation data can supply a forward projection of up to 200 meters. This brings significant advantages in comfort, and in particular means that many functions for the predictive reduction and avoidance of the consequences of accidents are possible for the very first time.

LITERATURE

[1] Willibald Prestl, Thomas Sauer, Joachim Steinle, Oliver Tschernoster: The BMW Active Cruise Control. SAE Technical Paper Series 2000-01-0344. SAE 2000 World Congress, Detroit, Michigan, March 6-9, 2000.

[2] Köppel Gerhard, Bock Hans: Fahrgeschwindigkeit in Abhängigkeit von der Kurvigkeit (Driving speed depending on Curvature). Forschungsbericht in „Forschung Straßenbau und Straßenverkehrstechnik“ Heft 269, 1979. Hrsg. Bundesminister für Verkehr, Abteilung Straßenbau, Bonn-Bad Godesberg.

2004-01-1243

Hardware-In-the-Loop Simulator with Auto Building Vehicle Model for Adaptive Cruise Control System

Masanori Ichinose, Atsushi Yokoyama and Takaomi Nishigaito
Mechanical Engineering Research Laboratory, Hitachi, Ltd.

Hiroyuki Saito and Daisuke Iwanuma
Automotive Systems, Hitachi, Ltd.

ABSTRACT

A Hardware-In-the-Loop simulator with a vehicle-ready Electronic Control Unit (ECU) coupled with a vehicle model, simulating a real vehicle movement in real time, was developed. The simulator was used to validate the ECU software and hardware components of the Adaptive Cruise Control (ACC) system.

The authors have modularized each vehicle component so that the entire vehicle model can be rebuilt automatically by selecting each component. This feature enables flexible and rapid building of the virtual vehicle. As a result, the simulator with auto building vehicle model allowed the development and validation of the ACC control system for various vehicle configurations.

INTRODUCTION

An Intelligent Transport System (ITS) improves safety, transportation efficiency, and comfort through advanced electronic and communication technologies. Adaptive Cruise Control (ACC) is now in practical use as a preliminary system proceeding complete implementation of ITS. An ACC system not only maintains the vehicle speed to the driver's selected target speed, but also maintains the following distance by using radar to measure relative speed and distance between the two vehicles. When the vehicle approaches the preceding vehicle, it is slowed down by engine braking or by electronically activated wheel braking. Then, if the preceding vehicle pulls away, the vehicle is accelerated to once again regain the chosen cruise speed by actuating the throttle valve. The ACC system is currently available as an opinion on high-end models; however, the ACC system availability is expected to be extended to many types of vehicles. The main issue facing for adaptation of ACC systems is to further reduce cost and reduce time-to-market without sacrificing safety and performance. It is necessary to cut the time spent on testing the actual vehicle. Especially, the fail-safe function of an ACC system must be verified by simulating a failure state, without having to use an actual vehicle. Accordingly, we have developed a Hardware-In-the-Loop simulator that can be applied to many types of vehicles by using the auto-building vehicle model for rapid development of the ACC systems.

The developed simulator performs vehicle-dynamics analysis in real time. The dynamics is calculated according to the throttle and brake controlled by a real Electronic Control Unit (ECU). The simulator then feeds the analysis results back to the ECU as simulated sensor information. It includes a high-speed and highly precise vehicle model, which can simulate a real vehicle dynamics in real time. It also includes a function for simulating a failure state for testing fail-safe functions. In this paper, the outline of the simulator, the auto-building vehicle model, and the simulation result of the developed simulator are described.

OUTLINE OF THE ACC SIMULATOR

SYSTEM CONFIGURATION

The ACC simulator connects the brake booster, which controls braking pressure, and the actual ECU. This simulation set-up is known as an HIL (Hardware-In-the-Loop) simulation. An outline of the ACC simulator is shown in Figure 1. It consists of a host-vehicle model, a preceding-vehicle model, which is set at a required speed, and a radar model, which outputs the distance between the vehicles. Within the environment imitated in the simulation, the ECU works as if it were loaded on an actual vehicle. The ECU outputs an engine-torque-demand signal and a brake-control-demand signal. The simulator then inputs the engine-torque-demand and brake-pressure signal into the vehicle model. The vehicle model runs virtually and outputs the distance between the two vehicles and the vehicle operating conditions to the ECU.

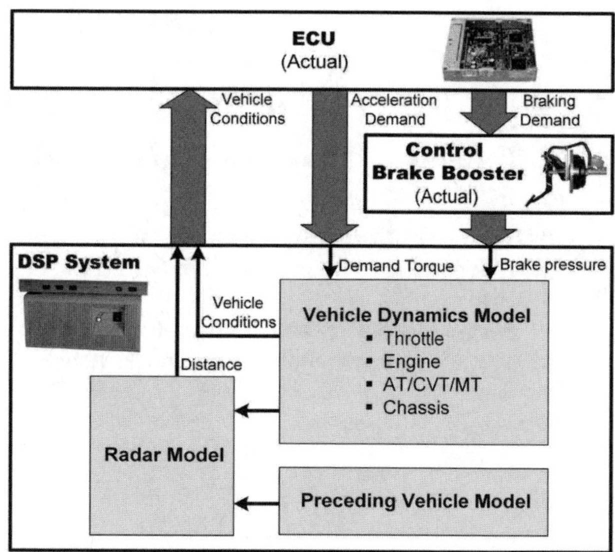

Figure 1. ACC Simulator

VEHICLE MODEL

The vehicle model used in this simulator is shown in Figure 2. Calculation of vehicle dynamics in real time is necessary for the HIL simulation. An original vehicle model was therefore developed to lighten the calculation load. It was created on MATLAB by Mathworks Inc. and consists of an electronically controlled throttle model, a drivetrain model of the engine and transmission, a brake model, and a chassis model. The electronically controlled throttle model determines the throttle angle according to the inputted engine-torque-demand. The drivetrain model calculates drive torque according to the throttle angle. The brake model calculates brake torque using the pressure generated by the brake booster. The chassis model calculates vehicle position, vehicle speed, and wheel speed using the calculated drive torque and brake torque. Each model is explained in the following paragraphs.

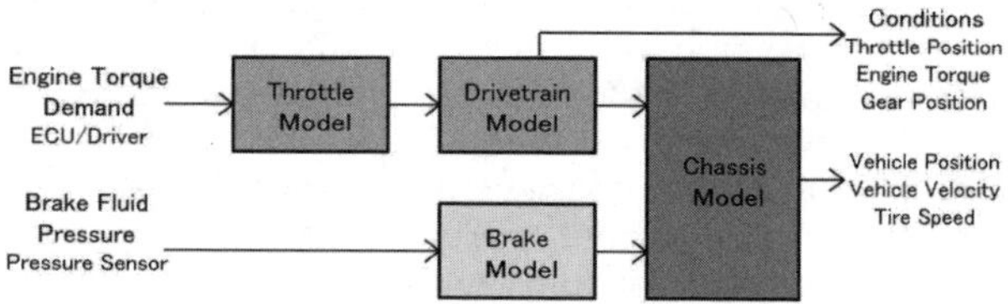

Figure 2. Vehicle Model

Electronically Controlled Throttle Model

The electronically controlled throttle model determines the throttle angle from the engine-torque-demand, which is transmitted from the ECU via a Controller Area Network (CAN). The model consists of a reverse map of an engine characteristic and a first-order delay system. The simulator refers the throttle angle to the reverse map by the engine-torque-demand and calculated engine revolution speed. The first-order delay system simulates the delay time of the throttle mechanism.

Drivetrain Model

The drivetrain model calculates the required drive-torque from the throttle angle. It consists of the engine model and transmission model, as shown in Figure 3. The engine model calculates the rotation speed of the crankshaft from the engine torque using an engine-characteristic map. The simulator refers the engine torque to the map by the throttle angle and the engine revolution speed. After the engine revolution speed is calculated, the input-shaft revolution speed of the torque-converter is calculated from the engine revolution speed, and the output-shaft revolution speed of the torque-converter is calculated from the vehicle speed. Output-shaft torque is then calculated from the torque-ratio of the torque-converter, which is referred to the map by the ratio of the input and output shaft-revolution speeds. Furthermore, the gear-select logic determines the gear ratio of the gearbox.

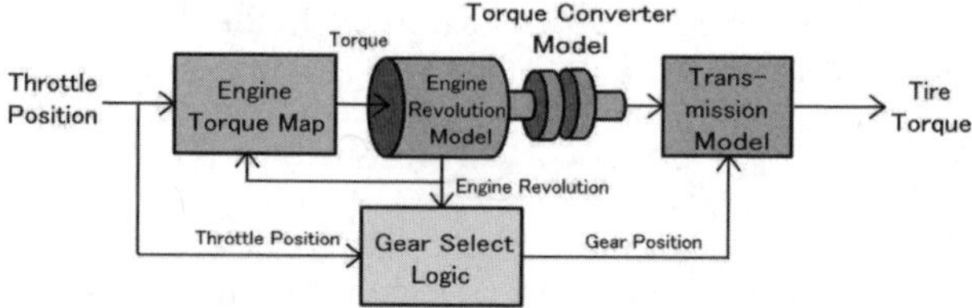

Figure 3. Drivetrain Model

Brake Model

The brake model determines braking torque from the pressure generated by the brake booster. Braking torque is calculated from piston thrust, pad area, the diameter of the rotor, and the friction coefficient of the brake pad.

Chassis Model

The chassis model determines the vehicle position, vehicle speed, and wheel speed from the braking torque and drive torque. The chassis model is approximated as a one-dimension model in which mass acceleration is calculated from drive torque and braking torque as shown in Figure 4. Moreover, the running resistance is modeled as the sum of air resistance and rolling resistance.

Air resistance is proportional to the square of vehicle speed. The proportionality constant of air resistance is derived from the airflow resistance coefficient (Cd) of the vehicle under test. The rolling resistance was determined by experiment on an actual vehicle.

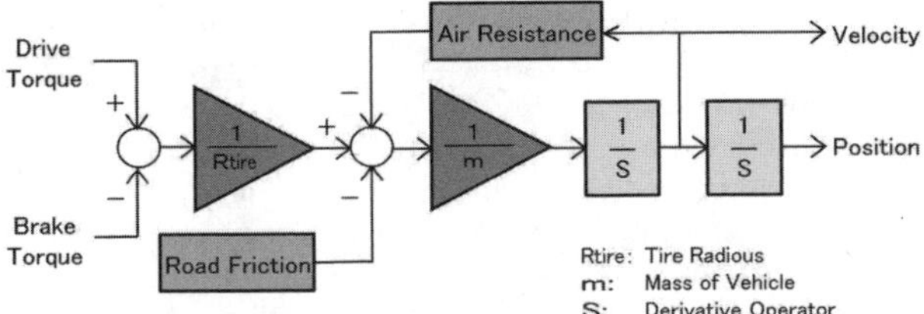

Figure 4. Chassis Model

CONTROL BRAKE BOOSTER

The ACC system controls braking pressure electrically by means of a brake booster [1]. The brake booster has a solenoid that enables it to control braking pressure, and the brake pressure is controlled by an electric signal (i.e., not by stepping on the brake pedal).

ECU INTERFACE

The ECU interface connects the ECU and the simulation system. It converts the ECU-signal voltage level to a computer one, and it includes the power-supply circuit of the ECU.

CONTROL PC

The Control PC operates the vehicle, displays the experimental state, and saves data. It can also setup of distance and speed of the host and preceding vehicles. The created operation screen of the simulator control panel is shown in Figure 5.

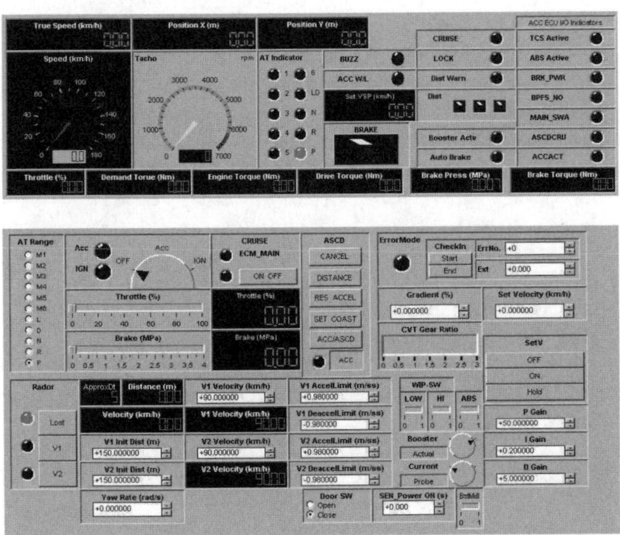

Figure 5. Simulator Control Panel

AUTOMATIC VEHICLE-MODEL ASSEMBLY

The vehicle model within the simulator was modularized to facilitate the evaluation and development process of both control logic software and hardware for a large number of different vehicle types and configurations. Figure 6 shows the concept of the auto-building vehicle model. In a conventional way of building models, separate vehicle models were made for each type of vehicle. Instead, the auto-building vehicle model includes many component types so that the appropriate component type for the targeted vehicle structure can be selected. In detail, each of the vehicle component configurations (i.e. engine type, transmission type, chassis type, and drive-configuration) is stored in a separate individual subsystem, and the appropriate

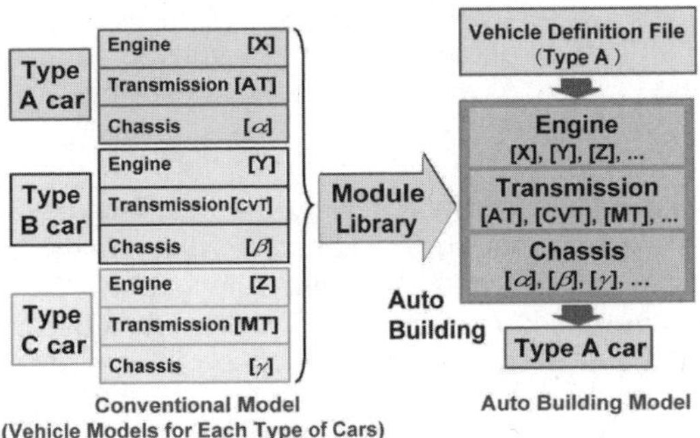

Figure 6. Auto-building Vehicle Model

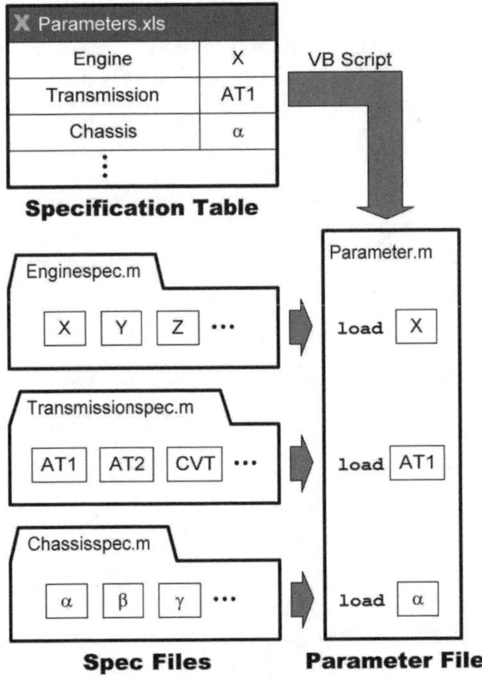

Figure 7. Procedure of Making Parameter File

component for the modeled vehicle is called from the 'parameter file' before the simulation run. For ease of creating the 'parameter file', the parameters for each target-vehicle component specification are selected from the 'specification table'. Figure 7 shows the procedure for creating the 'parameter file'. The user only needs to edit the 'specification table' file and the parameter file is created automatically. The simulator then automatically 'rebuilds' the vehicle from each selected component and parameter. This feature enables flexible and rapid building of a virtual vehicle. This software structure allowed the authors to evaluate many different vehicle platforms efficiently and accurately.

SIMULATION RESULTS

VERIFICATION OF VEHICLE MODEL

To verify the accuracy of the vehicle model, its calculated results were compared with actual vehicle measurements.

The parameters compared were the running resistance of the chassis model, the transfer characteristic of the drivetrain model, and the gear-select logic. Coasting experiment in the N range and D range were performed, and the results are shown respectively in Figures 8 and 9.

In the case of N range coasting, deceleration is dominated by the running resistance of the vehicle. The declination of simulated vehicle speed shown in Figure 8 is almost the same as that of the experimental results, so it can be considered that the running resistance of the model, which is the sum of air resistance and rolling resistance, is correct.

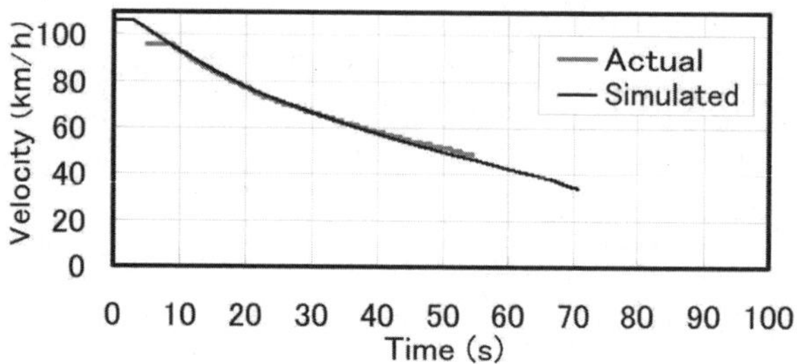

Figure 8. Coasting Data (N Range)

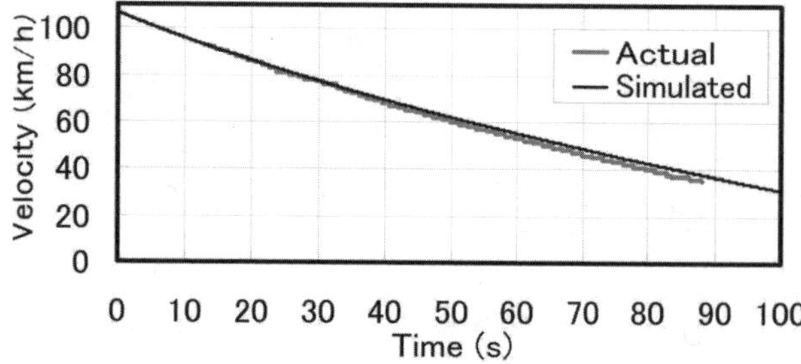

Figure 9. Coasting Data (D Range)

Figure 9 shows the results for D-range coasting. In this case, deceleration is dominated by running resistance and engine braking. As for engine braking, the engine characteristic and the transmission characteristic, e.g., characteristics of the torque converter, timing of shifting gears, and timing of lock-up, also influence deceleration. The declination of simulated vehicle speed shown in Figure 9 is almost the same as that of the experimental results, so it is clear that the drivetrain model is correct.

VERIFICATION OF HIL SIMULATOR

To check that the closed loop characteristic of a simulator is the same as an actual vehicle, the following experiment was performed. The distance data measured by a radar mounted on an actual vehicle was given to the HIL simulator, and the simulation result were compared with the actual vehicle measurements. An actual vehicle following a preceding vehicle under various conditions was tested, and the distance between the two vehicles was measured by the radar. The measured data was then input into the HIL simulator, and a closed-loop examination was performed. Accordingly, the validity of the closed-loop-controlled result was confirmed by comparing with the simulated result with that measured from of an actually controlled vehicle.

The simulation results for the case that the speed of the preceding vehicle is repeatedly increased and decreased between 80 to 100 km/h are shown in Figure 10. Figure 10(a) shows the velocity of the preceding vehicle and the host vehicles. Figure 10(b) shows the distance between the two vehicles. The speed of the host vehicle changes according to the fluctuations in the speed of the preceding vehicle. And the simulated host vehicle speed is nearly the same as the speed of an actual vehicle. This means that the simulator can reproduce the dynamics of an actual vehicle well. In addition, the trajectory of the controlled system is shown in Figure 10(c), the horizontal axis represents the relative speed between two vehicles, and the vertical axis represents the distance between two vehicles. From this figure, the relation between the inputted distance and the controlled speed of the simulated vehicle is about the same as that for the actual vehicle. This means that the simulator has allowed the validation of the ACC control system without the need for testing real vehicles.

Furthermore, the simulated engine revolution (Figure 10 (d)), the turbine revolution of the torque converter (Figure 10(e)), the engine-torque-demand from the ACC ECU (Figure 10(f)), and the brake-pressure-demand from the ACC ECU (Figure 10(g)) all agree well with the corresponding values from the actual vehicle. These results show that the simulation is precise enough to substitute for an actual vehicle.

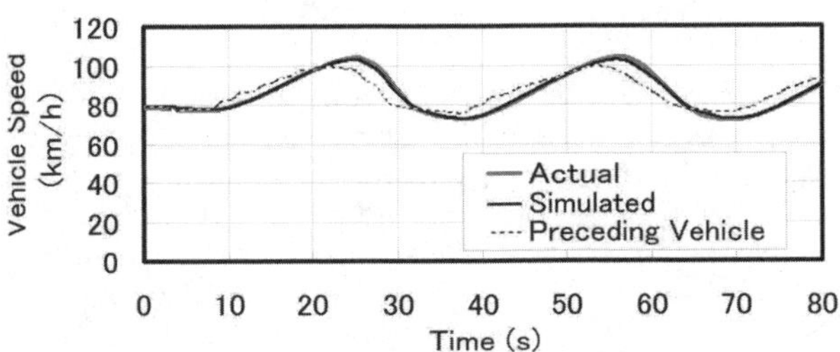

(a) Velocity of the Vehicles

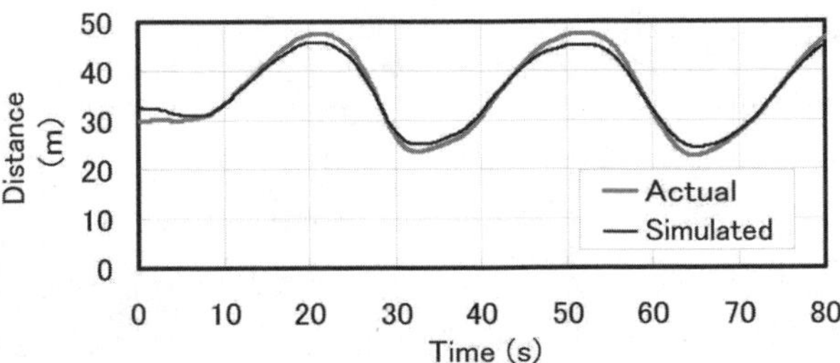

(b) Distance Between Preceding Vehicle and Following Vehicle

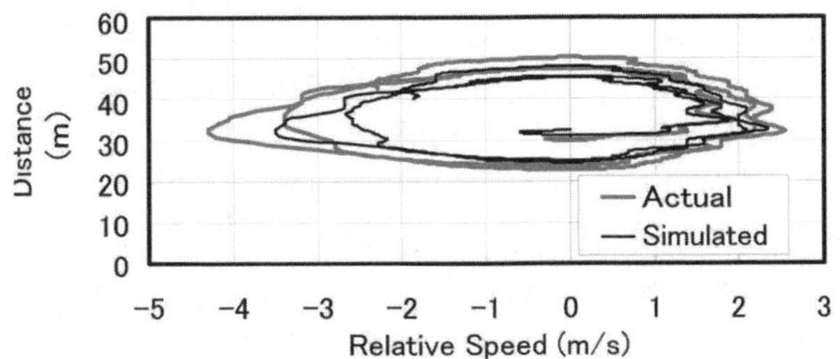

(c) Trajectory of The Controlled System

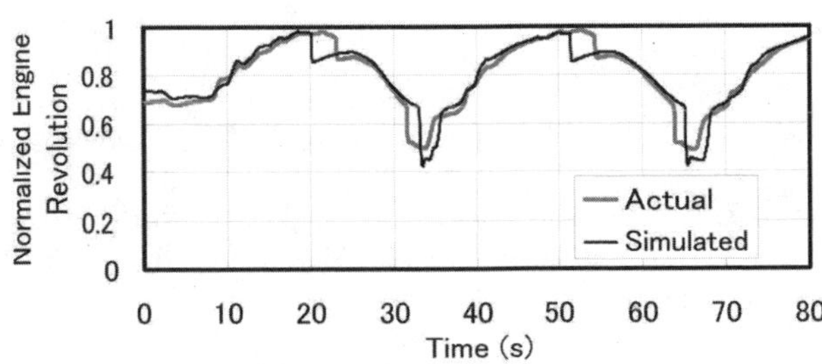

(d) Engine Revolution

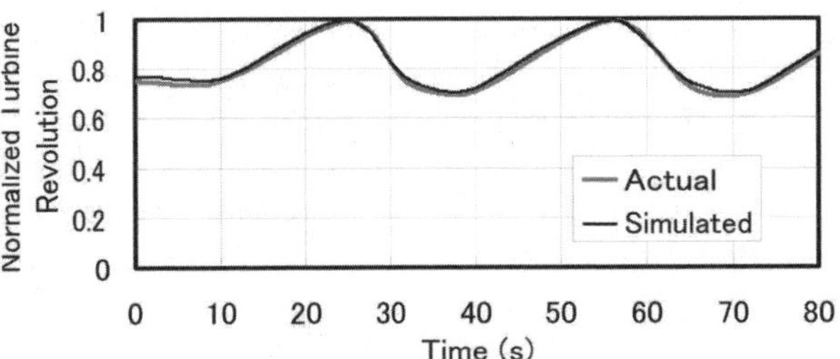

(e) Torque Converter Turbine Revolution

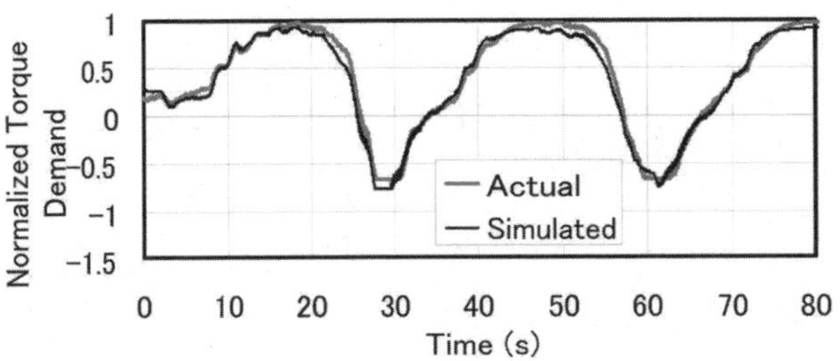

(f) Engine Torque Demand

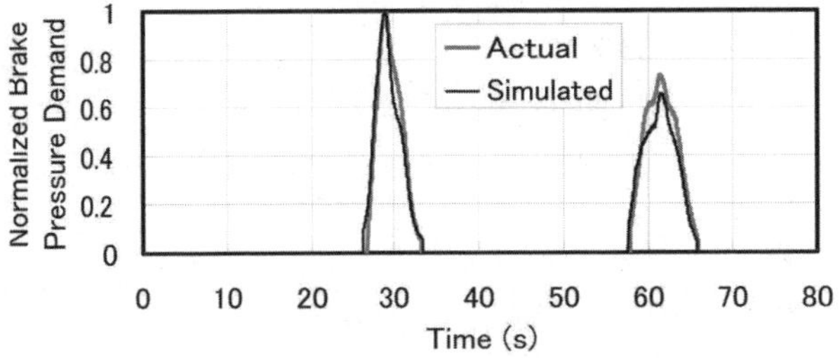

(g) Brake Pressure Demand

Figure 10. Simulation Results

PRACTICAL USE OF ACC SIMULATOR

CONTROLLER TUNING BY HIL SIMULATOR

By running virtual experiments with the ACC simulator, the controller can be tuned by connecting it to an actual ACC ECU. The controller parameters can be changed in accordance with the simulation results, and the simulation is run over again. For example, the response of a vehicle model that is controlled by the tuned ECU is shown in Figure 11. It shows the result when the preceding vehicle running at 90 km/h slows down to 50 km/h. As shown in Figures 11(a) and (b), if the preceding vehicle slows down, the distance between two vehicles decreases. The ECU detects this decrease, and slows down to keep the distance between the two vehicles constant. Figure 11(c) shows the slowdown by engine braking in terms of engine torque demand. On the other hand, brake demand is output when the engine braking cannot attain the required deceleration. As shown in Figure 11(d), brake-control-demand for automatic braking was output and the deceleration reached its target. These results show that the HIL simulation including the actual ECU can validate the workings of the ECU, and can tune up the control parameter to the targeted vehicle.

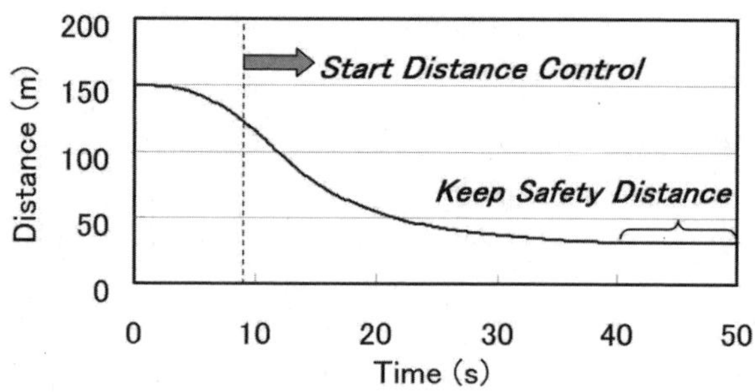

(a) Distance between Preceding Vehicle and Following Vehicle

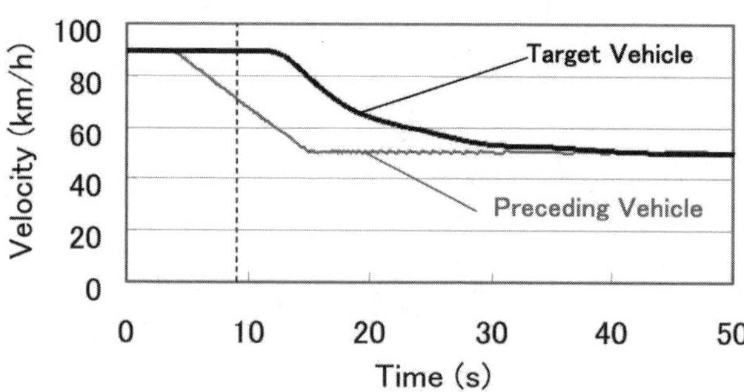

(b) Vehicle Speed

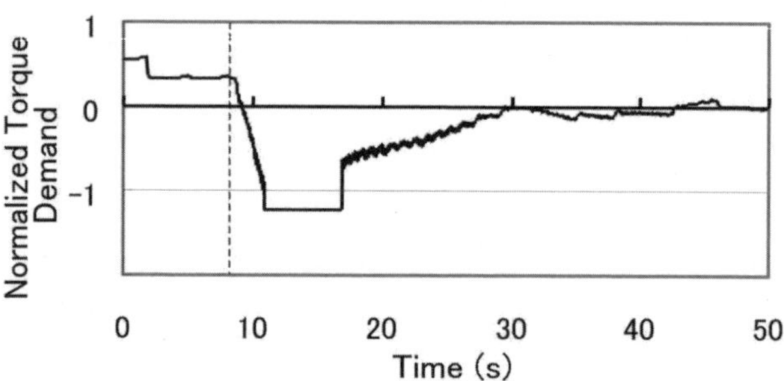

(c) Engine Torque Demand

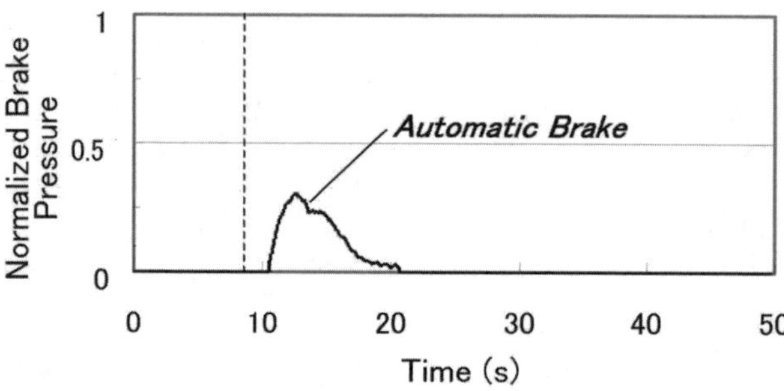

(d) Brake Fluid Pressure

Figure 11. Examination Result

DEBUGGING OF FAIL-SAFE LOGIC

Debugging the software program in the ACC ECU requires that abnormal fail-safe operation as well as regular operation are checked. The simulator can easily simulate failure of the radar, the engine or the transmission. To let a failure occur in an actual vehicle is difficult because it is dangerous. Accordingly, for checking the fail-safe operation, a function for starting failure mode via the operation panel was added to the simulator. To select failure from a large number of failure patterns, a "failure mode number" is input into the control panel. Figure 12 shows the procedure of failure-mode operation. Various failures can be simulated intentionally and the fail-safe function can be safely checked by the simulator.

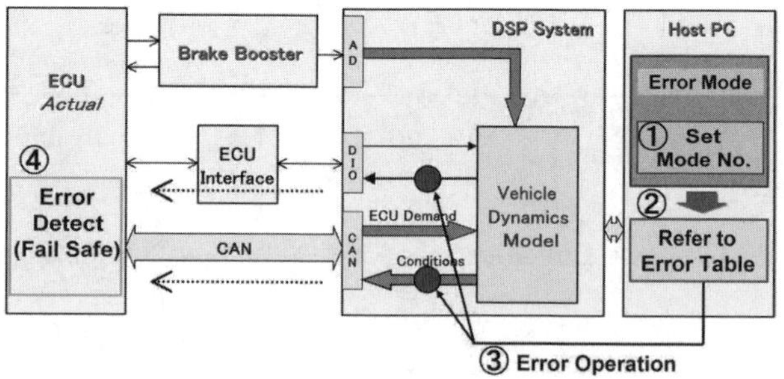

Figure 12. Process of Fail-Safe Validation

CONCLUSION

A Hardware-In-the-Loop (HIL) simulator for rapidly evaluating real-world ACC logic software and hardware was developed. The simulator incorporates a virtual vehicle model and can calculate vehicular movement in real time. The virtual vehicle model is connected via virtual sensor and actuator signals to the real world ECU. Furthermore, auto-building the vehicle model allowed us to construct a large number of different vehicles efficiently. For validation of the simulator, both real world and virtual vehicles were run under similar conditions, and it was found that the virtual vehicle movement sufficiently matched that of the real vehicle. The HIL simulator was then used to evaluate the fail-safe algorithms of the ACC control system. The HIL simulator allowed the development and validation of the ACC control system without the need for a real vehicle.

REFERENCES

1. T.Iijima, et al.: Development of An Adaptive Cruise Control System With Brake Actuation, SAE 2000 World Congress
2. H.Hanselmann: Hardware-In-The-Loop Simulation as a Standard Approach for Development, Customization, and Production Test, SAE Technical Paper 930207
3. K.Bill, et al.: Smart Booster – New Key Element for Brake Systems with Enhanced Function Potential, SAE Technical Paper 950760

2004-01-1111

Predictive Safety Systems – Steps Towards Collision Mitigation

Peter M. Knoll and Bernd-Josef Schaefer
Robert Bosch GmbH, Driver Assistance Systems Business Unit

Hans Guettler and Michael Bunse
Robert Bosch GmbH, Restraint Systems Business Unit

Rainer Kallenbach
Robert Bosch GmbH, Automotive Electronics Division

ABSTRACT

Sensors to detect the vehicle environment are being used already today. Ultrasonic parking aids meanwhile have a high customer acceptance, and ACC (Adaptive Cruise Control) systems have been introduced in the market recently. New sensors are being developed at rapid pace. On their basis new functions are quickly implemented because of their importance for safety and convenience.
Upon availability of high dynamic CMOS imager chips Video cameras will be introduced in vehicles. A stereo capable Computer platform with picture processing capability will explore the high potential of functions. Finally, sensor data fusion will improve significantly the performance of the systems.
At the end of the 1980s this insight led to the vision of highly efficient street traffic, demonstrated in the "Prometheus" funded project. But at that time the electronic components necessary for these systems – highly sensitive sensors and extremely efficient micro-processors – were not yet ready for high-volume series production and automotive applications.

INTRODUCTION

Almost every minute, on average, a person dies in or caused by a crash. In 1998 more then 93,000 persons have been killed in the Triad (Europe, USA and Japan) in road traffic accidents leading to a socioeconomic damage of more then 600 bil. EUR.
The EU Commission has defined a demanding goal by cutting the number of killed persons to half until the year 2010. Bosch wants to contribute significantly to this goal by developing Driver Assistance Systems in close cooperation with the OEMs and thus, reduce the frequency and the severity of road accidents.
An important aspect of developing active and passive safety systems is the capability of the vehicle to perceive and interpret its environment, recognize dangerous situations and support the driver and his driving maneuvers in the best possible way.

TRAFFIC ACCIDENTS – CAUSES AND MEANS TO MITIGATE OR AVOID THEM

In critical driving situations only a fraction of a second may determine whether an accident occurs or not. Studies [1] indicate that about 60 percent of front-end crashes and almost one third of head-on collisions would not occur if the driver could react one half second earlier. Every second accident at intersections could be prevented by faster reactions.

DRIVER ASSISTANCE SYSTEMS FOR VEHICLE STABILIZATION

Only recently, statistic material has been published [2] showing that the accident probability for vehicles equipped with the ESP system (ESP=Electronic Stability Program) is significantly lower than for vehicles without ESP. Fig. 1 shows the high collision mitigation potential of this system.
Additional improvement is expected from systems like PRE-SAFE from DaimlerChrysler. PRE-SAFE combines active and passive safety by recognizing critical driving situations with increased accident possibility. It triggers preventive measures to prepare the occupants and the vehicle for possible crash by evaluating the sensors of the ESP and the Brake Assist.

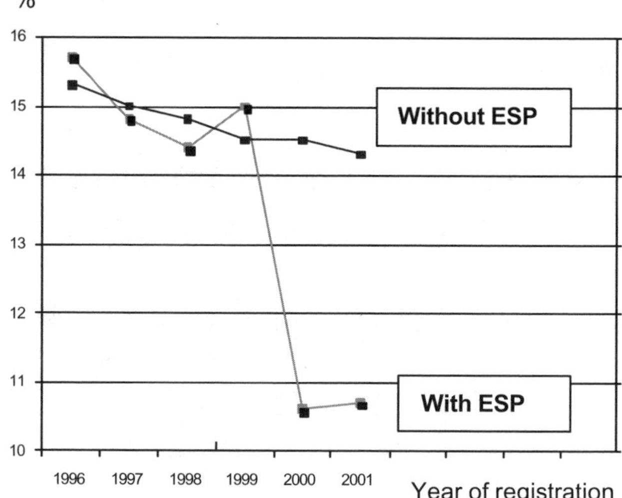

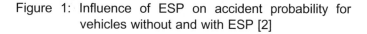

Figure 1: Influence of ESP on accident probability for vehicles without and with ESP [2]

To protect best passengers from a potential accident, reversible belt-pretensioners for occupant fixation, passenger seat positioning and sunroof closure are activated.

Like the vehicle interaction with the vehicles dynamic with ESP, the release of collision mitigation means can be activated only in the case when a vehicle parameter went out of control or when an accident happens. Today, airbags are activated in the moment when sensors detect the impact. Typical reaction times last 5 ms. In spite of the extremely short time available for the release of accident mitigation means, there is no doubt that airbags have contributed significantly to the mitigation of road accidents and, in particular, fatalities. But due to the extremely short time between the start of the event and the possible reaction of a system the potential of today's systems is limited.

Bosch as supplier of the ESP is proud of the achieved improvements but we want to achieve even more with a new generation of safety systems, being currently under development. These are the so called "predictive" driver assistance systems. They expand the detection range of the vehicle by the use of surround sensors. With the signals of these sensors objects and situations in the vicinity of the vehicle can be enclosed into the calculation of collision mitigating and collision avoiding means.

COMPONENTS OF PREDICTIVE DRIVER ASSIS-TANCE SYSTEMS

Today, the components for the realization of these systems – highly sensitive sensors and powerful microprocessors - are available or under development with a realistic time schedule, and the chance for the realization of the "sensitive" automobile is fast approaching. Soon sensors will scan the environment around the vehicle, derive warnings from the detected objects, and perform driving maneuvers all in a split second faster than the most skilled driver.

Electronic surround sensing is the basis for numerous driver assistance systems – systems that warn or actively intervene. Fig. 2 shows the detection areas of different sensor types.

Until now, due to the limited availability of sensors, only a few driver assistance systems could be established on the market up to now. One example is the Park Pilot from Bosch, which monitors objects at near range with the help of ultrasound technology. Sensors integrated in the bumper forward an acoustic or optical warning to the driver as soon as he approaches an obstacle. In the meantime, this system is widely used and has high acceptance with the customer. It is already in series-production in many vehicles [5].

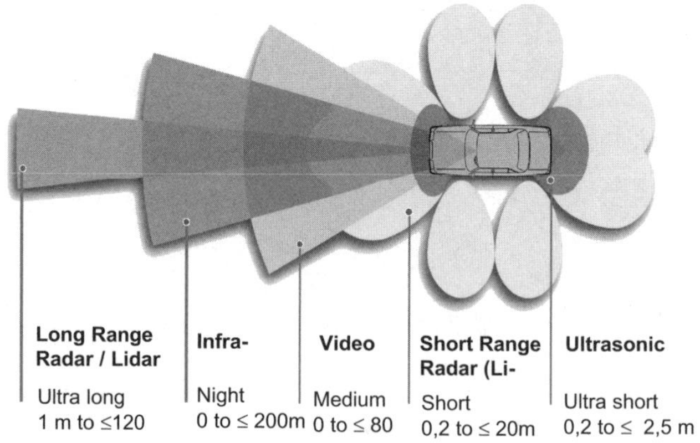

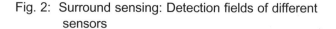

Fig. 2: Surround sensing: Detection fields of different sensors

Upon availability of appropriate sensors, new systems will be introduced in future vehicles. Their spectrum will range from warning systems to systems with vehicle interaction [4].

ULTRASONIC SENSORS

Reversing and Parking Aids today are using Ultra Short Range Sensors in ultrasonic technology. They have a detection range of approx. 1,5m. They have gained high acceptance with the customer and are found in many vehicles. The sensors are mounted in the bumper fascia. When approaching an obstacle the driver receives an acoustical and/or optical warning. The next generation of ultrasonic sensors will have a detection range of approx. 2.5m, and will thus, explore new applications like Parking Space Measurement and Semiautonomous Parking.

LONG RANGE RADAR 77 GHz

The 2nd generation Long Range Sensor with a range of approx. 120m is based on FMCW Radar technology. The narrow lobe with an opening angle of ± 8° detects obstacles in front of the own vehicle and measures the distance to vehicles in front. The CPU is integrated in the sensor housing. The sensor is multi target capable and can measure distance and relative speed simultaneously. The angular resolution is derived from the signals from 4 Radar

lobes. Series introduction was made in 2001 with the first generation. Figure 3 shows the 2nd generation sensor. It will be introduced into the market in March, 2004. At that time this Sensor&Control Unit will be the smallest and lightest of its kind on the market.
The antenna window for the mm-waves is a lens of plastic material which can be heated to increase the availability during winter season. The unit is mounted in air cooling slots of the vehicle front end or behind plastic bumper material by means of a model specific bracket. Three screws enable the alignment in production and in service [4].

Fig 3: 77 GHz Radar sensor with integrated CPU for Adaptive Cruise Control

The information of this sensor is used to realize the ACC function (Adaptive Cruise Control). The system warns the driver from following too close or keeps automatically a safe distance to the vehicle ahead. The set cruise speed and the safety distance is controlled by activating brake or accelerator. At speeds below 30 km/h the systems switches off with an appropriate warning signal to the driver.
In future, additional sensors (Video, Short Range Sensors) will be introduced in vehicles. They allow a plurality of new functions.

SHORT RANGE SENSORS

Besides ultrasonic sensors, 24 GHz radar sensors (Short-Range-Radar (SRR)-Sensors) or Lidar sensors can be used in future to build a „virtual safety belt" around the car with a detection range between 2 and 20m, depending on the specific demand for the function performance. Objects are detected within this belt, their relative speeds to the own vehicle are calculated, and warnings to the driver or vehicle interactions can be derived.
Today, there is still a limitation for the introduction of the 24 GHz UWB (Ultra Wide Band) Radar imposed by the pending release of the frequency band for the mentioned applications. This release has been given in 2002 for the USA. In Europe this process is still going on and under intensive discussion, mainly opposed by the established services such as Earth Exploration Satellite Services, Radio Astronomy and Fixed Services. A worldwide harmonization is necessary.

VIDEO SENSOR

Figure 4 shows the current setup of the Robert Bosch camera module.
The camera is fixed on a small PC board with camera relevant electronics. On the rear side of the PC board the plug for the video cable is mounted. The whole unit is shifted into a windshield mounted adapter.
CMOS technology with non linear luminance conversion will cover a wide luminance dynamic range and will significantly outperform current CCD cameras. Since brightness of the scene cannot be controlled in automotive environment, the dynamic range of common CCD technology is insufficient and high dynamic range imagers are needed.

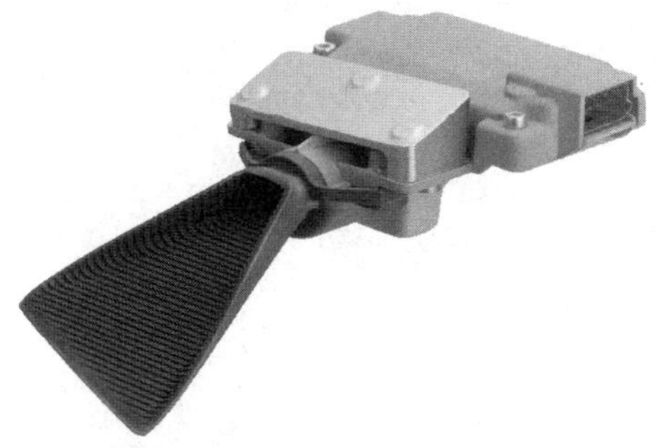

Fig. 4: Video camera module

SURROUND SENSING SYSTEMS AND DRIVER ASSISTANCE SYSTEMS

Based on the various sensor technologies, a plurality of application areas are possible for driver assistance systems.

LONG RANGE RADAR SYSTEM

Inattention is the cause of 68% of all rear end collisions! In 11% besides inattention following too closely is the cause, 9% of the rear end collisions are caused by following too closely alone. These statistics [6] show that 88% of rear end collisions can be influenced by longitudinal control systems. We assume a stepwise approach from convenience systems to safety systems where the first step has been made with the Adaptive Cruise Control.

- Step 1:
  Longitudinal Control (Adaptive Cruise Control)

  ACC and next ACC generations control the speed of a vehicle and control automatically the safety distance to a vehicle in front.

- Step 2:
  Predictive Safety Systems (PSS)

  Systems based on ACC interact with the vehicle in critical situations to avoid (in the best case) a potential accident or to mitigate the consequences of an unavoidable accident.

- Step 3:
  Systems for active collision avoidance

  Accidents are avoided by active interaction with the vehicle (longitudinal, lateral interaction and interaction with the engine management. This is still a vision.

THE FIRST STEP: ADAPTIVE CRUISE CONTROL (ACC)

Figure 5 shows the basic function of the ACC system.
With no vehicle in front or vehicle in safe distance ahead, the own vehicle cruises at the speed which has been set by the driver (Fig. 5, up). If a vehicle is detected, ACC adapts automatically the speed in such a way that the safety distance is maintained (Fig. 5, middle) by interaction with brake and accelerator. In case of a rapid approaching speed to the vehicle in front, the system additionally warns the driver. If the car in front leaves the lane the own vehicle accelerates to the previously set speed (Fig. 5, below).

Fig. 5: Basis function of ACC

In order to avoid excessive curve speeds the signals of the ESP system are considered simultaneously. ACC will reduce automatically the speed. The driver can override the ACC system at any time by activating the accelerator or with a short activation of the brake.
The current system of the first generation is active at speeds beyond 30 km/h. To avoid too many false alarms, stationary objects are suppressed.
Bosch develops the system further: With the improved ACC this convenience function can be used also on smaller highways. The 2nd generation of the ACC will come on the market in early 2004. The next step in functionality will come with the Low Speed Following (LSF) function, with a fusion of the data of the long range radar with a short range sensor. This function will allow to brake the vehicle down to speed zero and to reaccelerate after a drivers confirmation. In a further step the fusion of ACC LSF with a Video camera will allow a complete longitudinal control at all vehicle speeds, and also in urban areas with a high complexity of road traffic scenery.

The today's ACC system is a convenience function supporting the driver to drive more relaxed. Starting from 2005 on, Bosch will extend the functionality of ACC to „Predictive Safety Systems“, and enter, thus, into the field of safety systems.

THE SECOND STEP: PREDICTIVE SAFETY SYSTEMS

Predictive safety systems will pave the way to collision avoidance with full interference in the dynamics of the vehicle. They are partly based on signals derived from additional sensors, allowing to integrate the vehicle's surrounding. From the measurement of the relative speed between detected obstacles and the own vehicle, dangerous situations can be recognized in an early state. Warnings and stepwise vehicle interactions can be derived.
Figure 6 shows the shocking analysis of the braking behavior during collisions. In almost 50% of the collisions the drivers do not brake at all. An emergency braking happens only in 39% of all vehicle – vehicle accidents, and in 31% of the accidents with no influence of another vehicle, respectively.

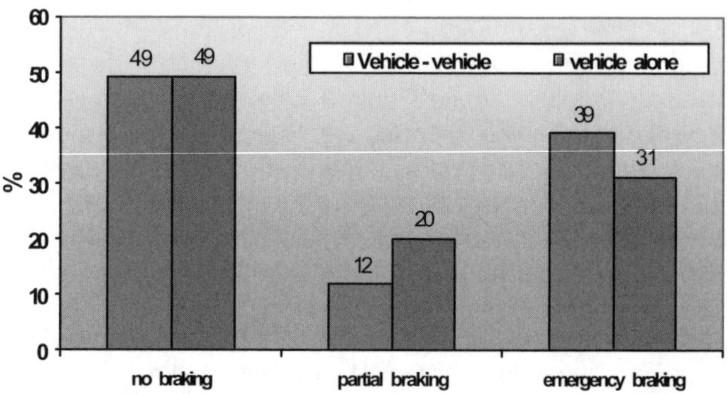

Fig. 6: Braking behavior during collision accidents [3]

This analysis confirms that inattention is the most frequent cause for collision type accidents and shows the high collision avoidance and collision mitigation potential of predictive driver assistance systems if the braking process of the driver can be anticipated or a vehicle interaction can be made by the vehicle's computer.
The introduction of predictive safety systems comes most likely with convenience systems where safety systems will use the same sensors. From 2005 on Bosch will extend ACC as the most important component of predictive safety systems to safety systems. If ACC recognizes a dangerous traffic situation the brake can be prefilled and the brake assist system can be prepared for a potential emergency braking. Future developments will incorporate functions to warn the driver very effectively and to perform automatic emergency braking.

In case of an emergency braking important fractions of a second can be used for a maximum reduction of kinetical energy.

VIDEO SYSTEM

The above mentioned Video technology will first be introduced for convenience functions that provide transparent behavior to and intervention by the driver. Fig. 7 shows the basic principle of operation for a video system.

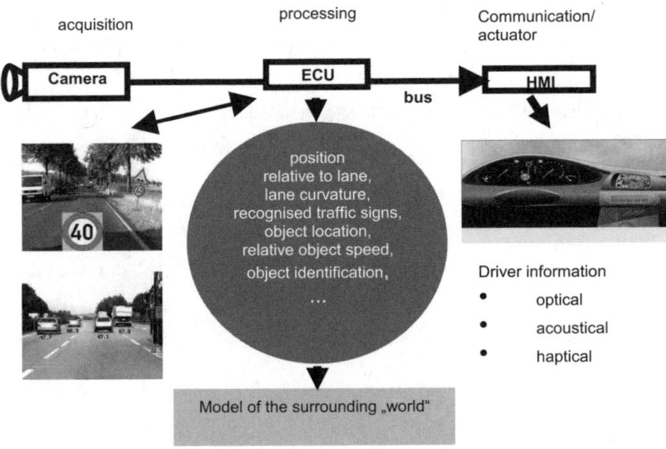

Fig. 7: Basic principle of a video sensor and functions being considered

The enormous potential of video sensing is intuitively obvious from the performance of human visual sensing. Although computerized vision has by far not achieved similar performance until today, a respectable plurality of information and related functions can readily be achieved by video sensing:

- lane recognition and lane departure warning, position of own car within the lane,
- traffic sign recognition (speed, no passing, ...) with an appropriate warning to the driver,
- obstacles in front of the car, collision warning
- vehicle inclination for headlight adjustments.

New methods of picture processing in conjunction with high dynamic imagers in future will further improve the performance of these systems [4]. Besides the measurement of the distance to the obstacle the camera can assist the ACC system by performing an object detection or object classification. Special emphasis is put on the night vision improvement function in the introduction phase of Video technology.
A high benefit can be achieved with a tail camera if objects approaching quickly from behind are detected, and the driver gets a warning signal when he intends to pass.

OUTLOOK

Figure 8 shows the enormous range of driver assistance systems on the way to the „Safety Vehicle". They can be sub-divided into two categories:

- Safety systems with the goal of collision mitigation and collision avoidance,
- Convenience systems with the goal of semiautonomous driving.

Driver support systems without active vehicle interaction can be viewed as a pre-stage to vehicle guidance. They only warn the driver or suggest a driving maneuver. One example is the parking assistant of Bosch. This system will give the driver steering recommendations when parking in order to park optimally in an automatically determined, prior measured parking space. Another example is the Night Vision Improvement system. As more then 40% of all fatalities occur at night this function has high potential for saving lives. Lane departure warning systems and systems detecting obstacles in the blind spot can also contribute significantly to the reduction of accidents as almost 40% of all accident are due to unintended lane departure.
ACC, which has already been introduced to the market, belongs to the group of active convenience systems and will further be developed to a functionality which allows driving in all speed ranges and in urban areas as well. If longitudinal guidance is augmented by lane-keeping assistance (also a video-based system for lateral guidance), and making use of complex sensor data fusion algorithms, automatic driving is possible in principle.

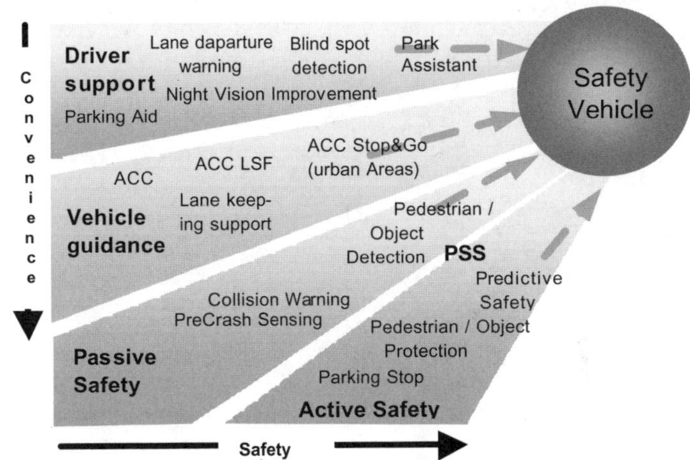

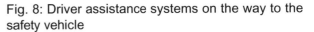

Fig. 8: Driver assistance systems on the way to the safety vehicle

Passive safety systems contain the predictive recognition of potential accidents and the functions of pedestrian protection.
The highest demand regarding performance and reliability is put on active safety systems. They range from a simple parking stop, which automatically brakes a vehicle before reaching an obstacle, to computer-supported control of complex driving maneuvers to avoid collisions. For example, the automatic emergency braking feature intervenes if a crash is unavoidable. In its highest levels of refinement, active systems intervene in steering, braking and engine management to avoid colliding with an obstacle. Here, the vision goes to the collision avoiding vehicle, making computer assisted driving maneuvers for crash avoidance.

CONCLUSION

The European Union has put the right emphasis on the e-Safety program with the vision to reduce fatalities to 50% until the year 2010. Car makers and suppliers have responded to the Commissions program and try to make their contributions to reach the goal [5].

The accident-free traffic, in our opinion, will remain a vision but we at Bosch see a plurality of means for a step wise introduction of convenience and safety systems for collision mitigation and future accident avoidance.

REFERENCES

[1] Enke, K.: „Possibilities for Improving Safety Within the Driver Vehicle Environment Loop, 7th Intl. Technical Conference on Experimental Safety Vehicle, Paris (1979)

[2] Anonymous statistics of accident data of the 'Statistisches Bundesamt (German Federal Statistics Institution), Wiesbaden, Germany (1998 – 2001)

[3] Statistics from the 'Gesamtverband der Deutschen Versicherunswirtschaft e.V." (Association of the German Insurance Industry) (2001)

[4] Seger, U.; Knoll, P.M.; Stiller, C.: "Sensor Vision and Collision Warning Systems", Convergence, Detroit (2000)

[5] Knoll, P.M.: Fahrerassistenzsysteme – Realer Kundennutzen oder Ersatz für den Menschen? VDI, Deutscher Ingenieurtag, Münster, Germany (2003)

[6] NHTSA Report (2001)

CONTACT

peter.knoll@de.bosch.com

2004-01-0757

Constraint-Driven Simulation-Based Automatic Task Allocation on ECU Networks

Paolo Giusto
Automotive Team - Cadence Design Systems, Inc.

Gary Rushton
E/E Vehicle Systems – Visteon Corporation

ABSTRACT

With the increasing number of ECUs in modern automotive applications (70 in high end cars), designers are facing the challenge of managing complex design tasks, such as the allocation of software tasks over a network of ECUs. The allocation may be dictated by different attributes (performance, cost, size, etc.). The task of validating a given allocation can be achieved either via static analysis (e.g., for cost, size) and/or dynamic analysis (e.g. via performance simulation – for timing constraints). This paper brings together two key concepts: algorithmic and optimization techniques to be used during static analysis and virtual integration platforms for simulation-based exploration. The two concepts together provide the pillars for a constraint-driven / simulation-based approach, tailored to optimize the entire ECU network according to a cost function defined by the user.

INTRODUCTION

In order to satisfy different drivers' needs such as performance, comfort, safety, and to meet stringent time to market and cost requirements, the automotive industry is increasingly using *configurable platforms* (mechanical, electrical/electronic) to implement safety-critical sophisticated applications such as adaptive cruise controls (Figure 1). These applications are implemented on complex distributed architectures where data messages are exchanged between Electronic Control Units (ECUs) via high-speed, fault-tolerant, serial buses (e.g., Flexray, TTP). The increasing functional complexity and chassis requirements (sensors/actuators allocation) have led to an increase in the number of ECUs (between 6 for a low-end and 35 for a high-end model, see Figure 2) and to the usage of multiple buses in terms of different

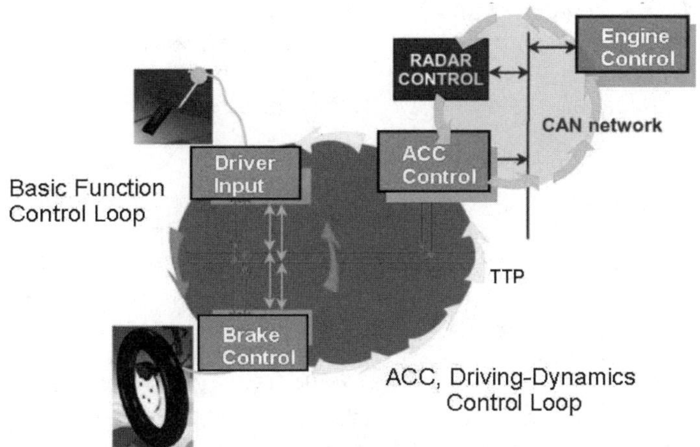

Figure 1: Adaptive Cruise Control

bandwidth requirements (10Mbs for a dependable fault tolerant communication protocol).

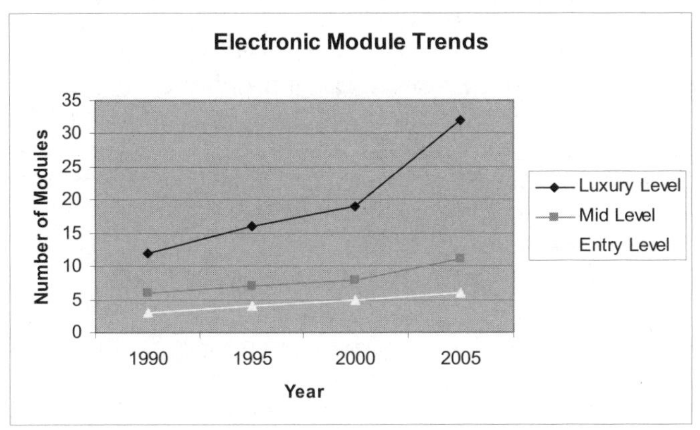

Figure 2: Electronic Module Trends

In this paper, we have identified two design issues. First, the OEM system architect often decides the distributed target electronic architecture (ECUs, buses, sensors, actuators, etc) *very early* in the design cycle, when not much information is available (HW is often not available), while the *validation of it is performed quite late,* only after sub-systems' HW/SW implementations become available. Thus, integration issues are discovered when changes are very expensive. Moreover, resilience to faults can only be checked via expensive and not easily repeatable tests on physical prototypes. Secondly, the communication between the car manufacturers (OEM) - playing the role of system integrator once the sub-systems have been delivered - and the providers of the sub-systems (e.g. engine control), is often a source of misunderstandings regarding the intended functional and non-functional requirements the sub-system has to provide in terms of timing, cost, and safety.

Besides, OEM and Tier1 system architects are facing the challenge of managing complex design tasks, such as the allocation of software tasks over a network of ECUs (SW binding). The trend toward the standardization of SW platform APIs consistent with OSEK specifications for communication among ECUs (e.g. COM and FTCom) and with application software processing and scheduling (e.g. OSEK Time) makes it possible to distribute the functionality (application SW) across different ECUs.

When looking at the vehicle as a system, the distributed nature of these applications also provides potential for optimizations that can be achieved via an efficient use of HW resources (e.g. a smaller number of ECUs). This optimization, carried out by system architects, is applicable to both OEM and Tier1 suppliers. While the Tier1 goal is to provide an optimized platform that can be re-used for different products by different OEMs, the OEM is more concerned with creating a platform that can be shared across vehicles.

In this paper we illustrate how two key concepts, algorithmic and optimization techniques for static analysis [1][2][3], and simulation-based virtual integration platforms [4][5][6] coupled together, provide the pillars for a constraint-driven and simulation-based approach, tailored to optimize the entire ECU network according to a cost function defined by the user. In the rest of the paper, we describe the concepts and the technologies aimed at realizing such an approach into an innovative tool flow in more detail.

THE VIRTUAL INTEGRATION PLATFORM

In [6], the concept of a virtual integration platform was introduced. In a nutshell, the Cadence Automotive System Design Platform (Figure 3) supports a distributed model-based system design process based upon several orthogonal concepts:

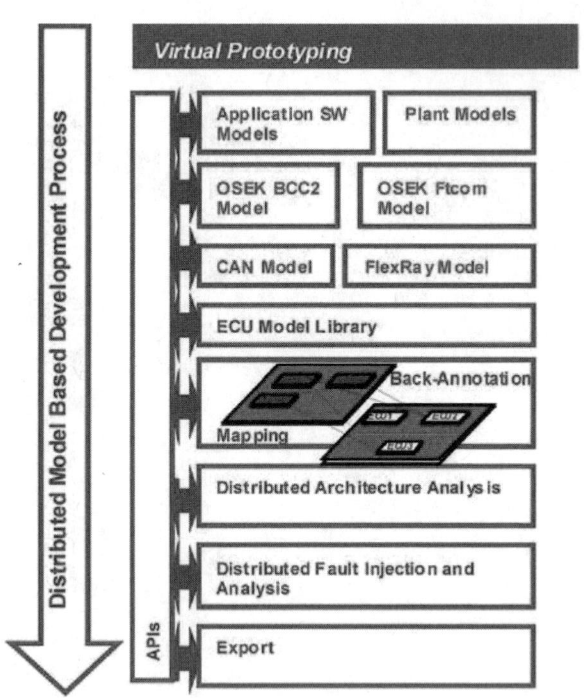

Figure 3: Cadence Automotive Platform

- A design shift from physical integration to virtual integration of models (Figure 4)

The extension of a single ECU model-based system design paradigm, in which the transformation from a design representation to its implementation is automatic.

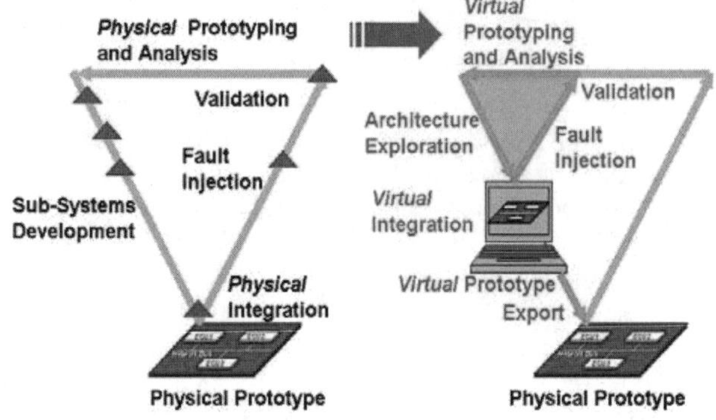

Figure 4: Design Shift

- The separation between executable models of control algorithms and the high level/abstract performance/functional models of the architectural resources including the network communication stack
- Binding control algorithm tasks to HW resources
- Binding functional abstract communications (signals and shared variables) to network protocol stack models

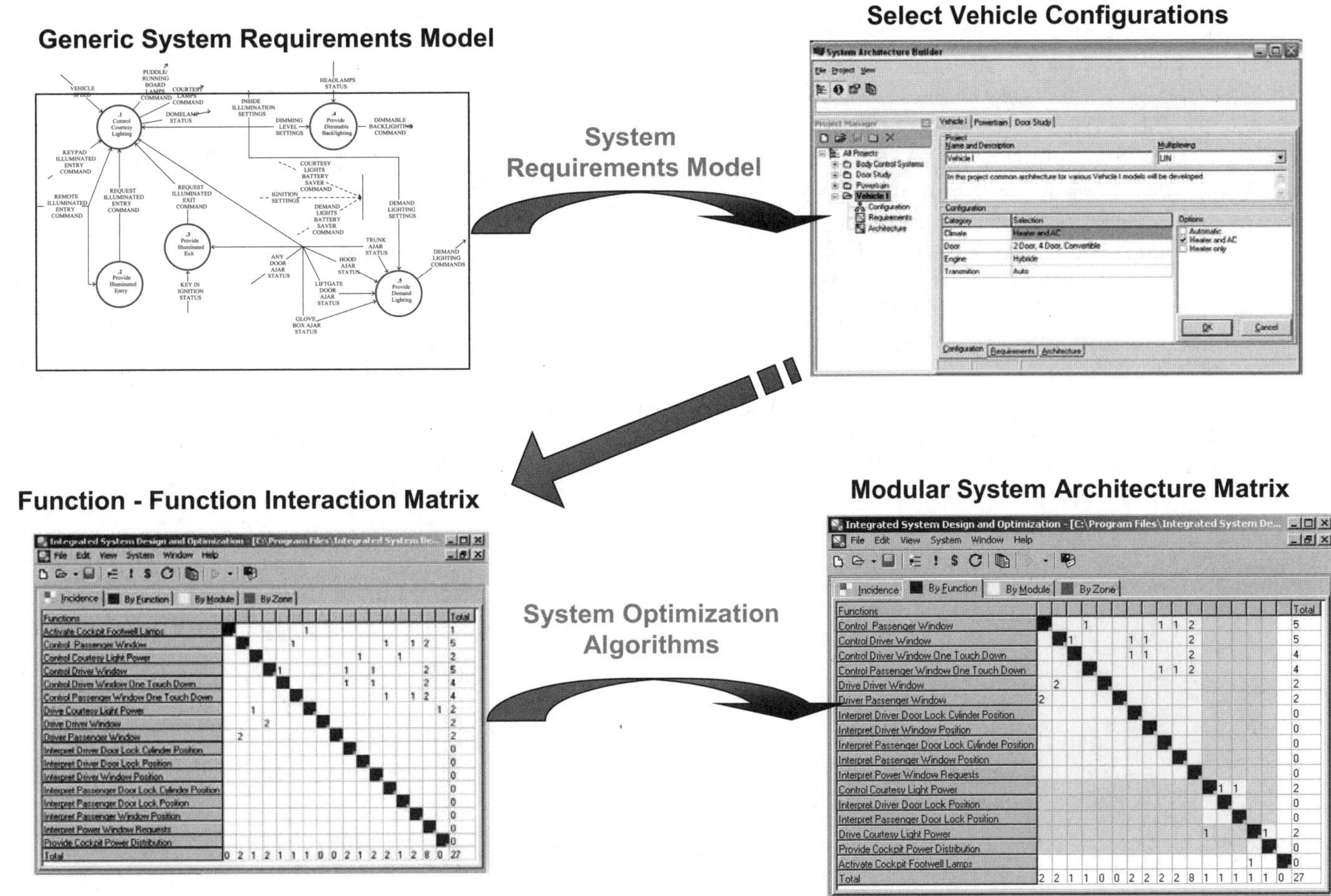

Figure 5: ISDO Tool

- Automatically annotating the control algorithm tasks and communications with timing performance formulae for dynamic computation (at simulation time) of the message transmission latencies over the network bus as well as the SW scheduling execution times due to shared resources (buses, CPUs)

- Simulating the bound virtual platform (e.g. representing a possible candidate distribution of functionality over the network) for verification purposes under regular conditions and/or with fault injection (e.g. data corruption, abnormal task delay, etc)

Notice that the virtual integration platform relies on providing library elements for both functionalities and architectural resources. The platform provides links with the most popular tools for algorithmic development and simulation, thus enabling the seamless import of such models and their composition in the overall distributed complex control function. The platform also provides models of popular communication protocols such as CAN. One important aspect, the XML-based programming capabilities provided by the platform, constitutes the core of the linkage between the Cadence Automotive Platform itself and the Visteon Integrated System design and Optimization (ISDO) static analysis tool (described in the next section). This aspect is detailed later in the paper.

ISDO TOOL FLOW

In [3], new approaches and software algorithms were presented that allow vehicle Electrical, Electronic and Software (EES) system design engineers to develop modular architectures / modules that can be shared across vehicle platforms (for OEMs) and across OEMs (for suppliers). The methodology uses matrix clustering and graph-based techniques. The ISDO software tool (Figure 5) allows system design experts to build a low cost EES architecture that can be shared across multiple vehicle platforms. The ISDO software builds an optimal system architecture for a given set of system features and feature take rates by grouping (integrating) system functions into physical modules and determining the best possible tradeoffs between system overhead costs, give away costs, and wiring costs. Also in [3], a new approach is presented that allows system developers to identify common modules in EES architectures that can be shared across multiple vehicle platforms. In a nutshell, the ISDO tool flow can be described as follows:

- Import the system requirements model into a specified database using predefined templates to create various vehicle configurations

- Automatic creation of the *function-function interaction matrix* once the requirements for each vehicle configuration are identified

- User pre-defined, or carryover, modules: the user can select functions from the incidence matrix and group them into predefined modules. This step makes sure that in the final vehicle architecture the functions of carryover, or predefined modules, will appear in a single cluster/module.

- Applying optimization algorithms to the function-function interaction matrix to identify optimal functional grouping in the vehicle architecture.

decomposition and function interface definition (signals and shared variables)

- Next, the ISDO tool is used to allocate functions to modules

- Next, the allocation is exported by the ISDO tool and imported by the Cadence Automotive Platform environment and simulated

- If the simulation results are satisfactory, the designer can (optionally) refine the design, provided that he/she does not modify the function interfaces, by replacing the coarse grain functional models used during the simulation in the Cadence Automotive Platform with more detailed models imported from other tools (e.g. Simulink) and re-importing them with the Cadence Platform

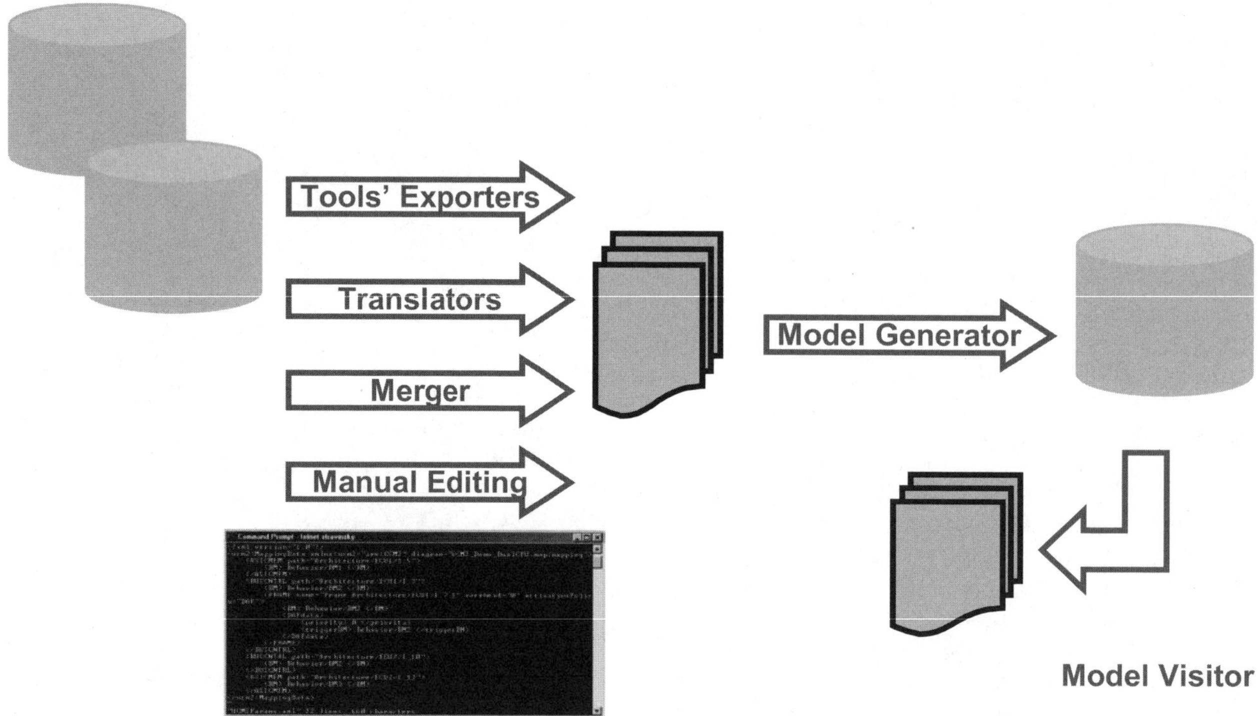

Figure 6: XML-Based Design Representation

INTEGRATED TOOL FLOW

The Cadence Automotive Platform and the Visteon ISDO tool are complementary in that, while the former provides a powerful dynamic analysis environment, the latter provides powerful static allocation mechanisms. Therefore, good results are produced when the tools are coupled together in the following sequence:

- The system design expert starts from a description of the overall complex control algorithm by performing the functional

XML-BASED DESIGN REPRESENTATION

In the Cadence Automotive Platform, a design is represented in an isomorphic fashion. First, an XML-based representation is used to describe the functionality (excluding the primitive block models), the architecture, the software execution architecture (SEA), meaning the set of tasks with their activation policies and priorities, the software and communication binding information, the fault scenarios' descriptions, and the simulation set-up. The XML representation is manipulated via a Cadence-defined scripting language, to, for instance, define/update/change a binding of tasks to a set of ECUs. Once all the needed manipulations have been performed, the XML representation is then

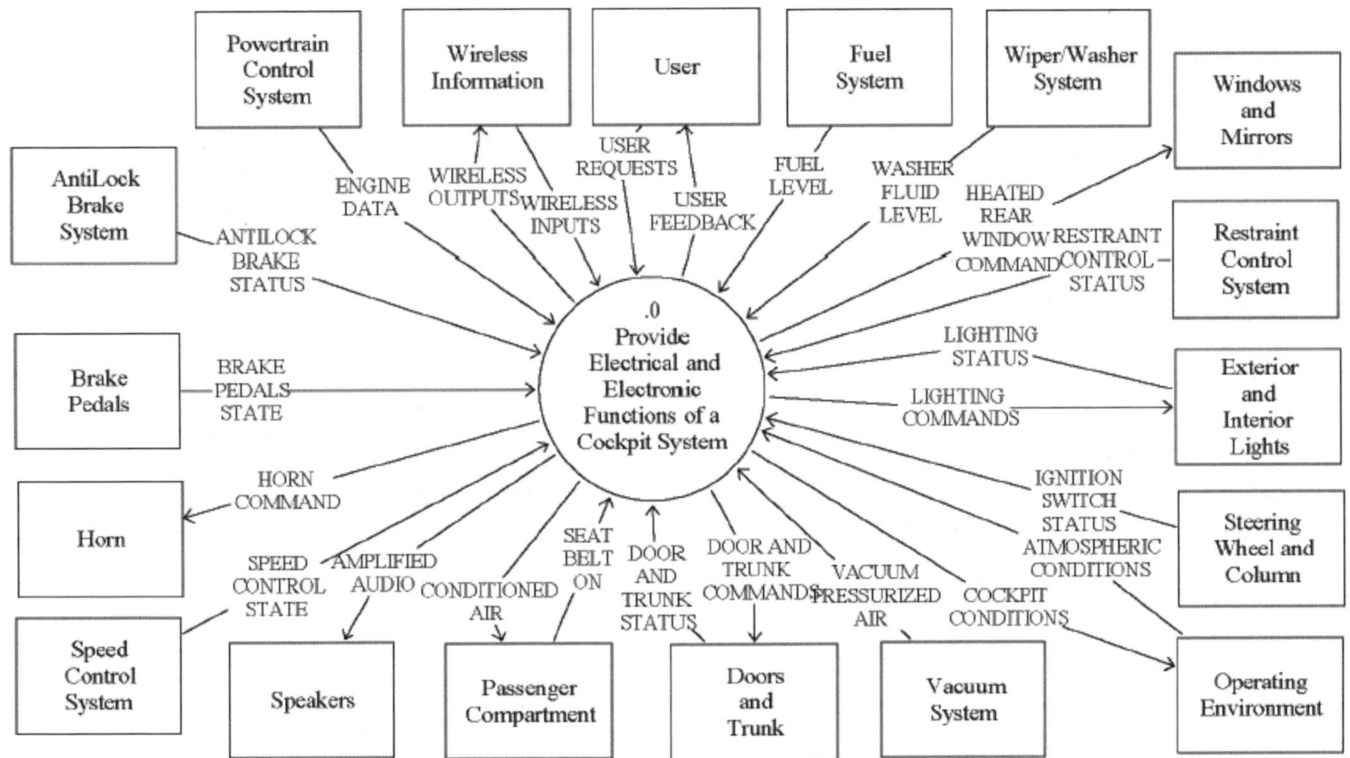

Figure 6: Top Level Hierarchical Context Diagram

compiled into a simulatable representation (Figure 6) [6]. Notice that the XML-based representation includes information about the functions' interfaces with their activation mechanisms (via signals or periodic timers) and shared variables. A very important piece of information is represented by the Software Execution Architecture (SEA). In fact, in order to be scheduled and simulated, the functions have to be assigned to tasks, which in turn, are assigned to ECU scheduler models during the binding step (OsekTime for the Cadence Automotive Platform). Once the user has programmed with scripting language the type of communication protocol model that has to be used to simulate the network traffic, the Cadence Automotive Platform engine automatically determines the network bus communication matrix. In fact, at this point of the design flow, it is known which messages are sent by an ECU to which other ECUs, because the software tasks that send messages to the bus controllers and receive them from them have been assigned to the ECUs themselves within the Visteon ISDO tool. The engine provides the user with an automatic configuration of the network. For each bus cluster, a communication cycle with arbitration is provided, while each frame is activated via a triggering mechanism. Notice that the user can modify the configuration, as part of the XML manipulations, via the scripting language.

YOURDON DE MARCO REPRESENTATION

In the ISDO tool, a design is translated from hierarchical context diagrams (Yourdon-DeMarco methodology) (Figures 7-8) to an XML-based format. The hierarchy is used to manage complexity. Notice that the context diagrams are not executable, since the wired connections between functions do not have any execution semantics (e.g. hardware interrupts). They are meant to represent the logical flow of data (information, material, or energy) between functions. Moreover, there is no definition of SEA and no executable models for the functions themselves. Since the purpose of the Visteon ISDO tool is to perform static analysis and allocation of functions to modules (hereafter either the term *modules* or ECUs are used with the same meaning) the tool does not need executable semantics for its design representation, since no simulation is performed. It is therefore important to implement a linkage between the ISDO design representation and the Cadence Platform representation to simulate a given allocation. This is explained in the next section.

COMMUNICATION MATRIX IMPORT

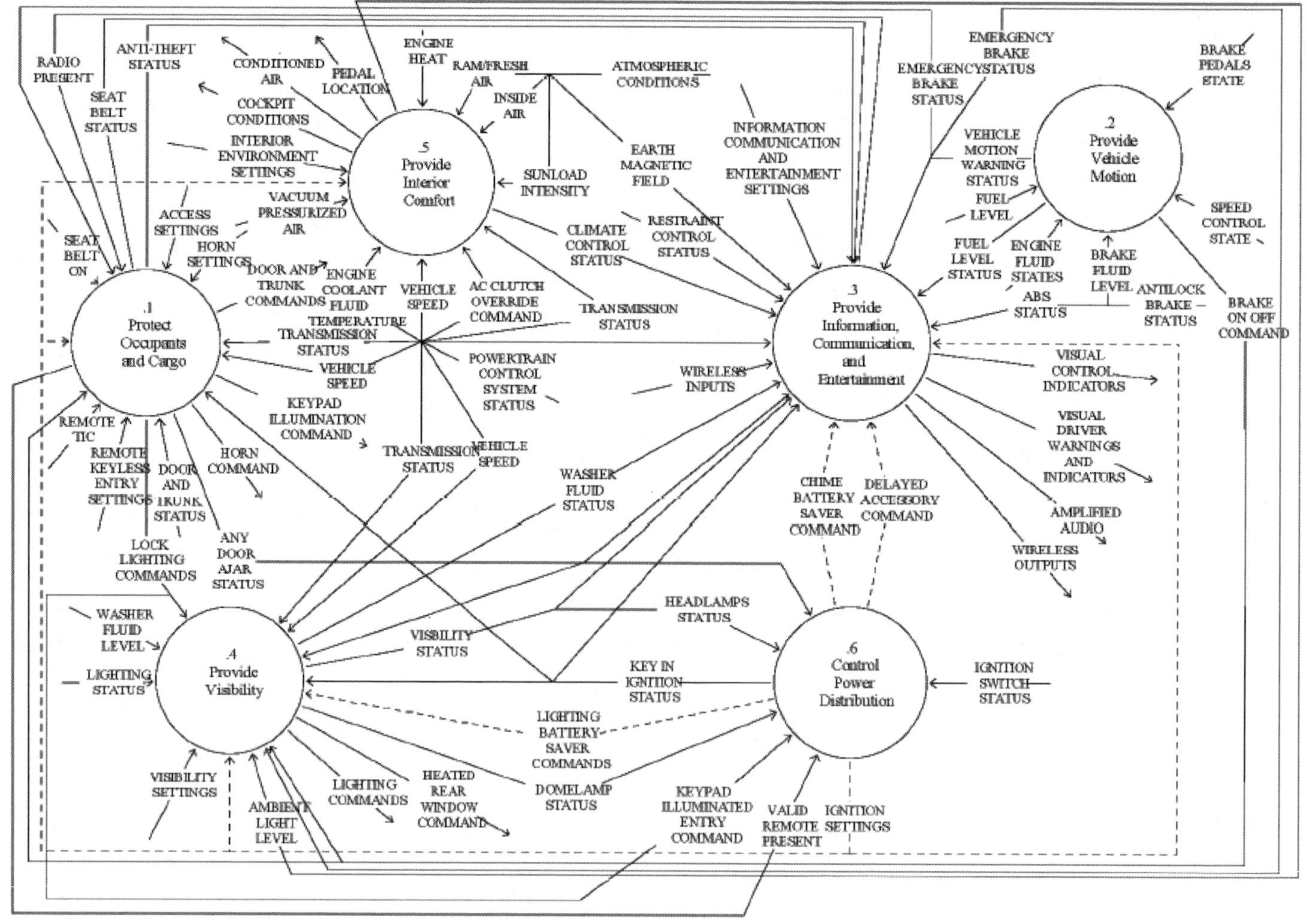

Figure 8: Next Level Hierarchical Context Diagram

An efficient way of importing the Visteon ISDO design representation to simulate a given functional allocation is via the communication matrix import. The communication matrix is a representation that does not take into account the original design hierarchy – the communications are represented with respect to the ECUs instantiated in the network cluster. Therefore, if one is able to annotate the communication matrix by itself with information about the activation policy of the messages being broadcast, then this representation can be used to automatically create a simulatable design in the Cadence Automotive Platform. Notice that the usage of the communication matrix is equivalent to flattening the original design hierarchy – which was irrelevant for simulation purposes anyway, since it was only used for managing design complexity. Therefore, we envision the following flow (Figure 9 at the end of the paper) between the two environments:

- First, the ISDO tool determines the allocation of functions to modules
- Second, the allocation is transformed by the ISDO tool into an equivalent XML-based communication matrix
- Third, the designer annotates (for instance with an XML editor of choice or via Java API based command) the messages in the communication matrix with activation policy information (e.g. periodic vs. triggered): this is needed in order to simulate the network traffic.
- Fourth, the Cadence Automotive Platform reads in the communication matrix and compiles into a set of XML based representations (again see Figure 9)
    - An architecture XML that represents a single-cluster network of ECUs connected via a network bus (ECU=Module)
    - A functional XML that represents a trivial functional network, in which a set of *transactor* behaviors are used to generate network traffic, one transactor per ECU

- A SEA XML that represents the trivial assignment of one transactor to a task
- A binding XML that represents the mapping of each single transactor task to one ECU
- A simulation set-up XML initially empty, later on updated to include any probing of given metrics (e.g. bus load)

- Fifth, the five XML representations are compiled into a simulatable representation and the simulation with data collection and analysis can take place.

Notice that in this flow design exploration is provided with respect to analyzing a given allocation of functionality vs. specific attributes of interest, such as the network traffic. It is important to notice that since the original hierarchy is not preserved, should the user want to explore a different task organization, this step must be performed in the Visteon ISDO tool. The steps described above should then be repeated. However, it is also important to note that, since there is no function executable specification in ISDO, once a specific allocation has been validated via simulation, it makes sense to refine the coarse grain transactor models by importing finer models from a tool such as Mathworks/Simulink via dSPACE Target Link code generation. At this point, the designer would be able to explore different software execution architectures and further refine the target implementation model. Note also that the flow is independent of the communication protocol model being used for the simulation – the user can replace a general yet highly programmable model such as the Universal Communication Model (UCM) [4] with a more refined model for CAN (included in the Cadence Automotive Platform) and utilize error injection capabilities provided by the Cadence Automotive Platform.

CONCLUSION

In this paper, we have presented a novel flow that couples together a static analysis tool for functional allocation and a simulation environment to verify a given allocation. The flow is aimed at reducing the design cycle time by using highly integrated and programmable simulation models and algorithms for static allocation. The final result is a validated functional allocation that can be handed over to sub-system software developers. We are envisioning extending the automatic generation of the simulatable design to multi-cluster networks (e.g. LIN plus CAN) by incrementally importing communication matrixes and composition via gateways to realize a complete virtual car analysis environment.

ACKNOWLEDGMENTS

The authors would like to thank Pascal Bornat and Jean-Yves Brunel from Cadence Design Systems, Velizy, France, Alberto Ferrari from Parades, Rome, and Luciano Lavagno from Politecnico di Torino, Turin, Italy for their contributions to the paper.

REFERENCES

1. Zakarian, A. and Rushton G. J. (2001), “Development of Modular Electrical Systems”, IEEE/ASME Transaction on Mechatronic,
2. Rushton, G., Zakarian, A., and Grigoryan, T. (2002), “Algorithms and Software for Development of Modular Vehicle Architectures”, SAE World Congress 2002-01-0140.
3. Rushton, G., Zakarian, A., and Grigoryan, T. (2003), “Development of Modular Electrical, Electronic, and Software System Architectures for Multiple Vehicle Platforms “, SAE 2003-01-0139
4. Thilo Demmeler, Paolo Giusto (2001), “A Universal Communication Model for an Automotive System Integration Platform”, Design Automation and Test Europe Congress 2001
5. Thilo Demmeler, Barry O'Rourke, Paolo Giusto (2002) “Enabling Rapid Design Exploration through Virtual Integration and Simulation of Fault Tolerant Automotive Application”, SAE World Congress 2002, SAE 02AE-76.
6. Paolo Giusto, Jean-Yves Brunel, Alberto Ferrari, Eliane Fourgeau, Luciano Lavagno, Alberto Sangiovanni Vincentelli (2003), “Virtual Integration Platforms for Automotive Safety Critical Distributed Applications”, Conference International Su les Systemes Temps Reel (RTS) 2003

CONTACTS

Paolo Giusto has a Bachelor Degree in Computer Science from the University Of Turin, Italy and a Masters Degree in Information Technology from CEFRIEL, Milan, Italy. He has over 12 years of industrial experience and is currently working as the Automotive Team marketing director with Cadence Design Systems. Previously, with Magneti Marelli, he visited the EECS Department at University of California at Berkeley as an Industrial Fellow, working on hw-sw co-design methodologies for embedded systems. Previously, with Cadence, he worked as technical leader on system level design methodologies and tool sets with particular focus on safety-critical automotive distributed applications. (giusto@cadence.com).

Gary Rushton has over 18 years of commercial and military electrical/electronic systems engineering experience. He has an MS in Automotive Systems Engineering from the University of Michigan. He is currently working as an electrical/electronic systems engineering technical fellow with Visteon Corporation. As an engineer with Visteon Corporation, he has worked on audio software, subsystem product development/design, diagnostics, vehicle system architectures, and cockpit system design. Previously, with General Dynamics, he worked on avionics systems for the F-16 and vetronics systems for the Abrams M1A2 tank. (grushton@visteon.com).

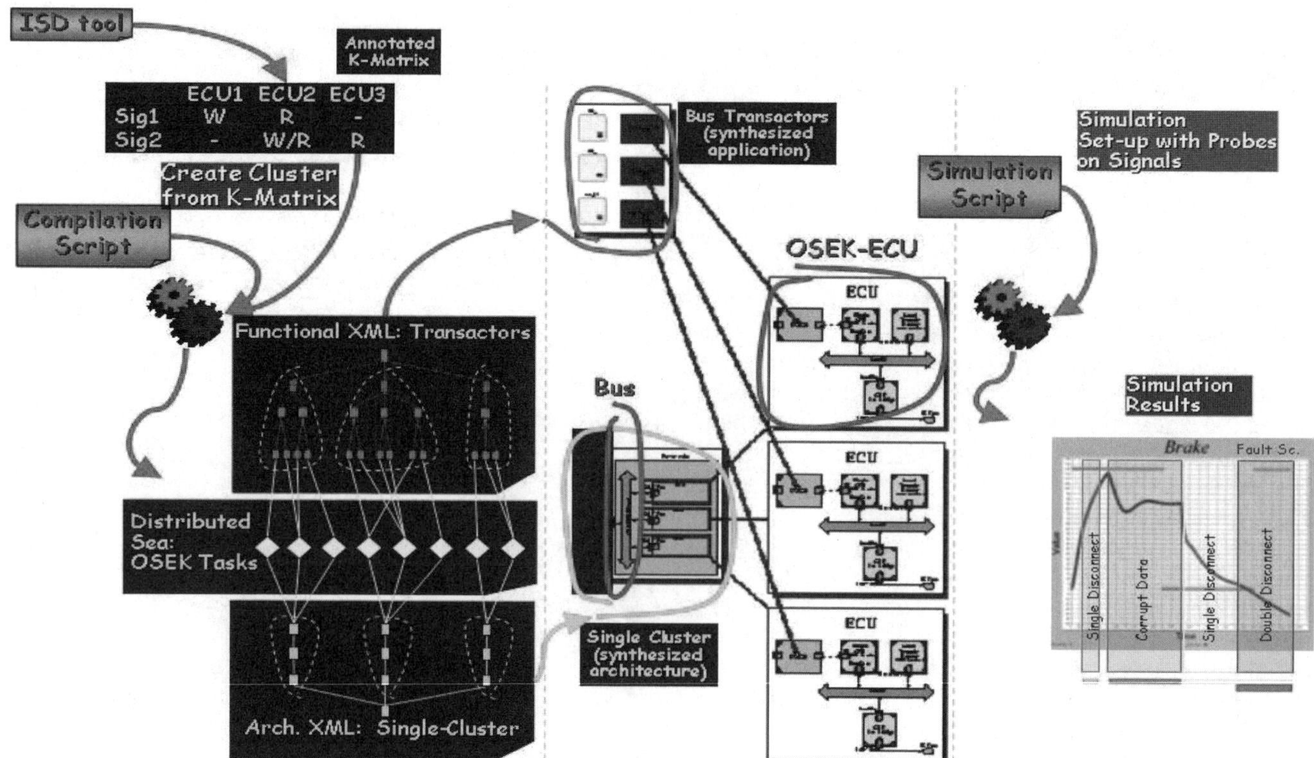

Figure 9: The Novel Flow

2004-01-0255

Performance, Robustness, and Durability of an Automatic Brake System for Vehicle Adaptive Cruise Control

Deron Littlejohn, Tom Fornari, George Kuo, Bryan Fulmer, Andrew Mooradian, Kevin Shipp, Joseph Elliott and Kwangjin Lee
Delphi Corporation

Margaret Richards
Michigan State University

ABSTRACT

Adaptive Cruise Control (ACC) technology is presently emerging in the automotive market as a convenience function intended to reduce driver workload. It allows the host vehicle to maintain a set speed and distance from preceding vehicles by a forward object detection sensor. The forward object detection sensor is the focal point of the ACC control system, which determines and regulates vehicle acceleration and deceleration through a powertrain torque control system and an automatic brake control system. This paper presents a design of an automatic braking system that utilizes a microprocessor-controlled brake hydraulic modulator. The alternatively qualified automatic braking means is reviewed first. The product level requirements of the performance, robustness, and durability for an automatic brake system are addressed. A brief overview of the presented system architecture is described. The control methodology of generating brake pressure via a hydraulic modulator to achieve the vehicle deceleration requested by ACC controller is then introduced. The paper includes a description of two Pulse Width Modulated (PWM) solenoid control designs and applications as an important technology to ensure the automatic braking performance. The implementation of moding the automatic brake system with ABS, Traction Control, and Vehicle Stability Control is revealed at the vehicle system level. Vehicle test data will be presented as insight to the braking performance and robustness. The control-related system durability will also be examined and discussed under vehicle testing profiles. Vehicle integration system test data summarizes and concludes the practice and value of the presented automatic brake system for vehicle adaptive cruise control.

INTRODUCTION

ACC is a system that uses a forward radar sensor to determine the distance between the host vehicle and a target vehicle. The system is intended to match the speed of the target vehicle by reducing the throttle and/or applying the brakes without requiring the driver to adjust the cruise control settings. Figure 1 shows the components and subsystems required to implement ACC.

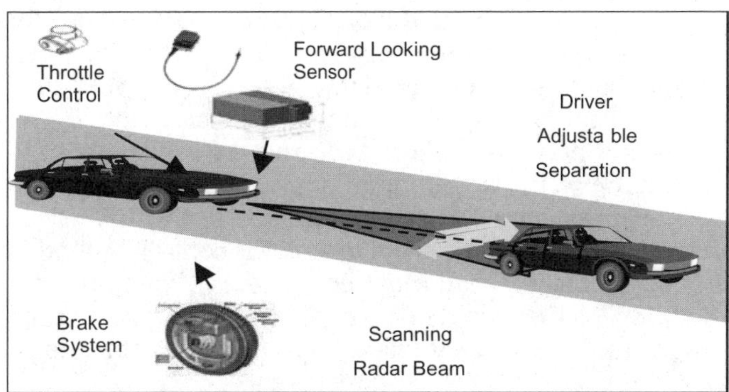

Figure 1 The Components of the ACC System

There are several ways to implement ACC on a vehicle and this paper will discuss some typical implementation schemes. The automatic braking function can be achieved by various means; some methods include an intelligent brake booster, electric calipers, stored hydraulic fluid pressure, etc. This paper details implementation based upon stored hydraulic fluid pressure; however, brief descriptions of other methods are given first. One method to regulate wheel brake pressure utilizes an intelligent/smart booster. Wheel pressure is regulated by a solenoid valve that controls air flow into the booster air chamber, which generates differential pressure across the booster's diaphram. This method generates little audible noise and is also very smooth; however, there is additional risk of mechanical failure plus the brake pedal drops during an autobraking event. One prior method of generating brake pressure with the hydraulic modulator is the traditional operation of traction control. When the pump, Prime Valve and Isolation Valve are energized together, brake fluid is delivered under pressure to the wheel brakes. The fluid flow from the master cylinder into the pump is regulated by the Prime Valves. The Isolation Valve is located on the high pressure side of the pump to prevent the fluid from returning to the master cylinder. The wheel brake pressure is regulated by the Apply Valves and Release Valves. The Apply valves are energized to block the in-flow of fluid to the brake to control the rate of the pressure increase, while the Release Valves are energized to control the rate of the pressure decrease. This method of controlling the wheel brake pressure is suitable for traction control and vehicle stability where noise and harshness are less of a concern. In the automatic braking mode of ACC, the noise and harshness would typically be unacceptable.

An alternate method to regulate the wheel brake pressure is through ON/OFF control of the Prime and Isolation Valves. Wheel pressure is increased by regulating the fluid supply to the pump through Prime Valve modulation and pressure is decreased by releasing fluid through the Isolation Valves. This method generates much less noise, but it is not as smooth as required for auto braking.

The chosen method to control the wheel brake pressure is through the use of a hydraulic pump (modulator), prime valve, and Variable Isolation Valve (VIV). The VIV operates as a pressure regulating valve where the blow-off pressure is proportional to the applied PWM duty cycle. To increase wheel brake pressure, the Prime Valve and pump are energized, and the PWM signal to control the VIV is set appropriately to hold/build the desired pressure. To release pressure, the VIV PWM duty cycle is reduced. This modulator control method is smoother, quieter, and more cost effective than the prior methods. The remainder of this paper gives some insight to the implementation, performance, robustness, and durability of this chosen method.

THE PRESENTED SYSTEM OVERVIEW

Hydraulic Mechanization

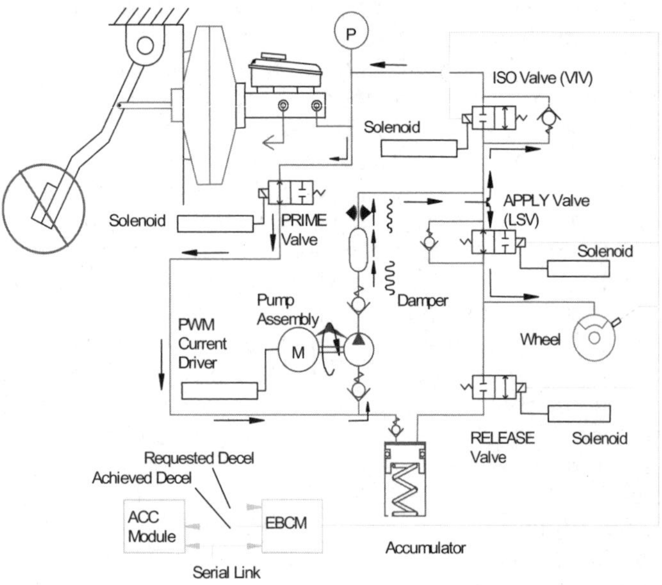

Figure 2 The Mechanization of Hydraulic Modulator

Figure 2 depicts the mechanization of the ABS/TCS/VSE controlled brake system capable of performing ACC Automatic Braking without driver input on the braking pedal. The ABS Controller commands the motor in the modulator to pump brake fluid from the master cylinder into the wheel brake lines through the energized and opened PRIME solenoid valves. ACC Automatic Brake utilizes PWM-driven variable isolation valves (VIV) to regulate the pressure level on the wheel brake hydraulic lines. Delphi VIV technology provides the characteristic of throttling the braking flow through the orifice of the solenoid valve with extremely low-pressure jumps. The result achieves smooth, uniform, and low-vibration vehicle deceleration. The VIV provides an attractive linear flow control of the solenoid valves where the blow-off pressure is proportional to the applied current. That overcomes the technologic limitations of conventional ON/OFF style solenoid valves, which are used in most of today's industrial market. Additional key features of the VIV hardware are the capabilities to match the deceleration control stability requirements of ACC automatic brake through synchronizing pressure control with ABS/TCS/VSE subsystems which basically utilize APPLY and RELEASE valves for wheel brake pressure regulation. To meet the low noise requirement, a PWM-driven motor control circuit is equipped to effectively minimize the noise level from pump piston impact.

Vehicle System Integration

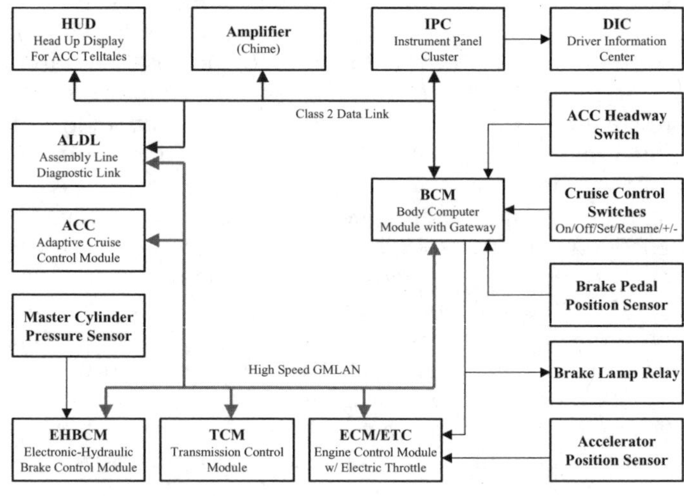

Figure 3 The Architecture of Vehicle System Integration

Figure 3 indicates the block diagram of implementing the ACC vehicle integration system. To maintain the vehicle headway and cruise speed, the ACC controller issues the requested deceleration or acceleration commands through a high-speed serial link to the EHBCM and ECM. The ACC Automatic Brake System is assigned to fulfill the task of achieving the desired deceleration level beyond the maximum decelerating capability available from the powertrain system. In ACC autobraking mode, when the driver applies the brake pedal, the automatic braking action is phased out. This transition is done and secured by monitoring the signals from brake pedal position sensor and master cylinder pressure sensor. Input to the electric throttle from the driver and the ACC module for speed maintenance is differentiated within the ECM. The ECM reports the driver's throttle input during ACC autobraking activation to the EHBCM via the high-speed serial link. When the ECM reports the driver's throttle input, ACC autobraking phases out. If the decel request from the ACC module persists once the driver's throttle input goes away, then ACC autobraking resumes. A brake lamp relay is included in the system for the purpose of signaling the tail brake warning light in the ACC automatic braking events.

AUTOBRAKING SYSTEM PERFORMANCE

Control Design

The key control design of the Automatic Brake system is to achieve the required performance through vehicle deceleration tracking control. The vehicle deceleration, which is derived from the fusion of wheel speed signals subject to possible wheel slips/spins or active brake control, is used as the feedback to guide the tracking schemes. To match the product requirements, a sequence of control sessions is adopted to take advantage of the dedicated hardware technologies, VIV and PWM Motor, to regulate the braking pressures at all 4 wheels. Figure 4 cascades the high-level flow of the wheel brake pressure control.

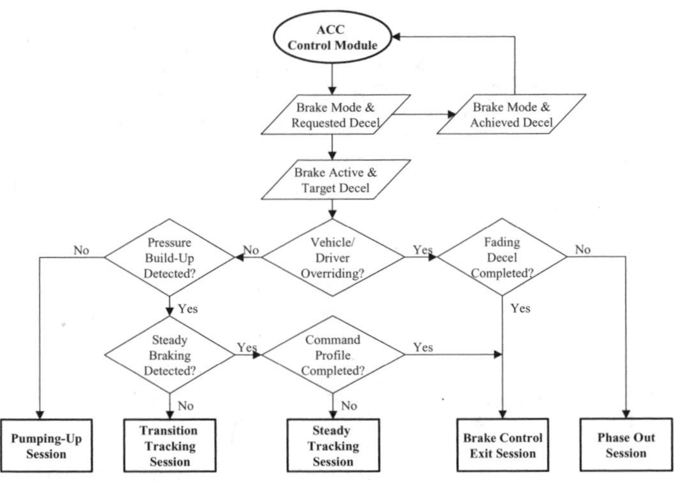

Figure 4 The Cascade of the Wheel Pressure Control

The pressure control scheme starts with a pumping up session that applies a temperature compensation based open-loop command to the VIVs and PWM Motor to maximize response time. After the detection of the pressure buildup, a closed-loop transient tracking session takes over to pilot the VIV blow-off pressure to achieve the vehicle deceleration target with minimum overshoot. Next, a steady tracking session with learning process follows to generate smooth, quiet, and low-vibration deceleration, which also helps to avoid misleading feedback due to rough road disturbances or emergency braking cycles. In the event of a driver's override or system failure, an open-loop phase out session is used to fade out the wheel brake pressures to satisfy the requirement for a smooth transition. In addition, a brake control exit session is executed to remove any residual upstream vacuum or downstream pressure relative to the modulator to ensure repeatable performance.

Vehicle Testing and Responses

The Automatic Brake control design is validated in the target production vehicle, which is equipped with Delphi's Adaptive Cruise Control Module with Forward Detection Sensor and Delphi's DBC7.2 brake system. The DBC7.2 brake system for the target production vehicle has capabilities for Antilock Braking (ABS), Traction Control (TCS), Electronic Stability Control (ESC) and Adaptive Cruise Control Automatic Braking. A variety of tests and evaluations were performed to achieve the production requirements on automatic braking deceleration – responsive, precise, smooth, low-noise, low-vibration, decent transition, uniform/stable, and robust. Fundamental tests, such as Rubber-Band Cruising, Lane Changes, Lane Cut-in, Tailing Stopping, Ride and Handling Cruise, Brake Overriding, Throttle Overriding, etc., were executed on proving ground tracks. Public Road Tests were done to verify the integrated system performance and to monitor the brake thermal reaction. The vehicles were exposed to low temperature and winter surfaces to confirm the response time and subsystem moding (ABS/ESC) with the Automatic Braking. Figure 5 shows data collected through a CAN Analyzer. The graph demonstrates the decel tracking response and precision during lane-cut-in tailing. It also displays the Automatic Braking capability to track the deceleration commands after transition from speed control mode (acceleration in this case) to braking mode.

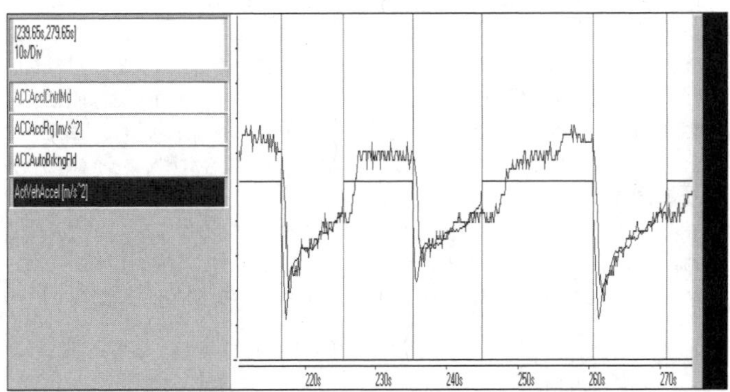

Figure 5 The Deceleration Tracking in Event of Lane-Cut-In Tailing.

AUTOBRAKING SYSTEM ROBUSTNESS

Modeling and Simulation Technology

The simulation of this system was run using a co-simulation between Matlab, Simulink, AMESim and CarSim. The brake control algorithm was generated using an s-function, in Simulink, which was created using Visual C++. This s-function derives the modulator commands based on the requested deceleration and the vehicle's behavior.

AMESim offers an environment for simulating mechanical, fluid and thermo-fluid systems. In this simulation, the pressure on each brake caliper was derived based on modulator commands, which are developed within the Simulink model. The AMESim model contains two pumps, one to run each side of the diagonally split braking system. The volumetric efficiency of each of these pumps was varied to understand the vehicle yaw and stability effects.

CarSim can be used for simulating and animating the behavior of four-wheel vehicles. The user may define a three-dimensional environment for the vehicle to travel in and various parameters of the vehicle. It can provide graphical outputs of specified parameters, a data file, or an animation of the vehicle in its environment. AMESim and CarSim generate s-functions when they are compiled; these s-functions are put into Simulink to interface with the brake control algorithm.

Simulation Results

When the model is run, CarSim allows the user to define the friction of the surface upon which the vehicle is traveling. Using this feature the simulated vehicle was driven on a straight path with a high coefficient of friction surface, to simulate a dry surface. It was run again with a split coefficient of friction surface, to simulate a vehicle that had its left wheels on a dry surface while its right wheels were on an icy surface.

CarSim also allows the user to vary the amount of steering. The tests were first run with a fixed steering wheel angle input. Then they were each run a second time with a simulated driver corrected steering. This simulated the driver having a one second preview. In each of the tests, the volumetric efficiency on the two pumps was varied to the most extreme case that is typically seen. After each condition had been tested, the yaw of the vehicle for each run was plotted. This shows the severity of changes in the pump efficiency based on yaw in a diagonally split braking application.

The yaw for a high coefficient of friction surface is shown in Figure 6.

The simulation was run for five seconds and the deceleration rate was requested when the time was equal to one second until the end of the simulation. The lower volumetric efficiency was on the pump that drives fluid to the left front and right rear brake corners, this explains the vehicle's movement to the right without the driver correcting the steering. The dark line depicts the case in which the simulated driver tried to correct steering. The driver over steers slightly, but is able to maintain the straight path with little effort. The lighter line is the case when the steering angle is fixed. This level of yaw is very minimal and could easily be corrected by a driver with very little effort.

This same test was run on a surface with a split coefficient of friction. The yaw in each case was again measured and plotted with respect to time. This plot is shown in Figure 7.

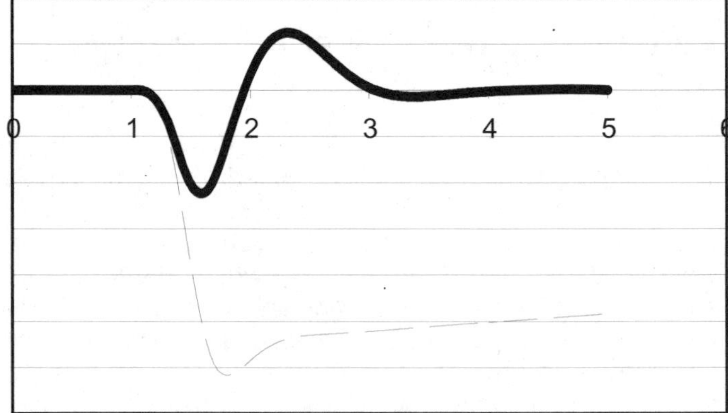

Figure 6 Yaw vs. Time on a Surface with High Coefficient of Friction.

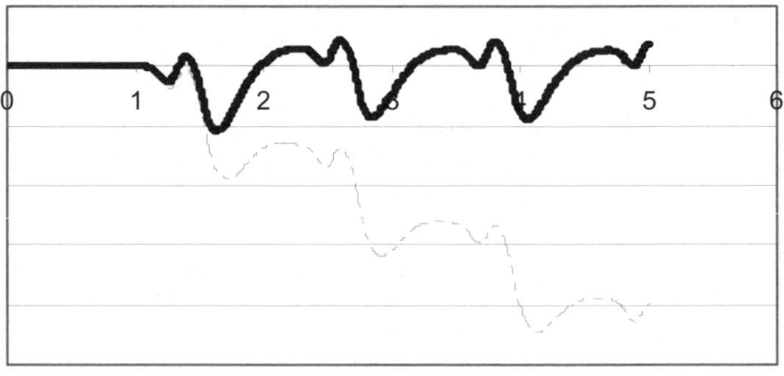

Figure 7 Yaw vs. Time on a Surface with Split Coefficient of Friction.

It is important to note that the right wheels of the vehicle are on a surface that is very slippery; this causes the vehicle to enter an antilock braking event when braking is requested. It is continually entering and exiting an antilock braking event for the remainder of the simulation. This causes the waves that are shown in Figure 7. Once again the right front and left rear brake corners are run by the greater pump efficiency. The dark line is the case in which the driver corrects the steering, while the lighter line is the instance in which the steering wheel is fixed. With the driver corrected steering the yaw is still very minimal, without the driver's correction the yaw is still within a safe range. Based on this simulation Delphi feels very confident in their brake control algorithm in this application.

AUTOBRAKING SYSTEM DURABILITY

Usage Profile Study

A question arose regarding what should be a reasonable hardware usage profile to be defined in the production specification for the presented ACC Automatic Brake System. This issue affects the system durability testing to meet the product platform requirements. Though a thought was to induct the profile by interpolating the conventional cruise control brake usage envelope based on SAE or an OEM data inventory, the deviations of driver's overriding projection and system turned-on acceptance ruled out using this method. There is also the complication of trying to estimate how many of the base brake applications that are required to disengage the conventional cruise control system will be inherited by the ACC system. Another plot was to refer the automatic braking profile to the existing market vehicles equipped with ACC systems, which use intelligent boosters as the automatic braking mechanisms. However, the discrepancies of the deceleration command limitation, speed range availability, powertrain braking capability, headway setting sensibility (sensitivity?), forwarding defense algorithm, and of course commercial secret obstacles this direct importing door.

Therefore a customer-supplier joint effort was initiated to study the usage profile in a development car equipped with the targeted product ACC system. The test vehicle was driven in a variety of situations and road conditions. There were 86 separate test drives completed, which resulted in 3,246 test miles of ACC activation being logged. A total of 847 Automatic Braking events were recorded during the 3,246 miles. The data was taken at different daily timing, at different speeds by different drivers in an attempt to simulate as many different driving situations as possible. The drive routes ranged from heavy urban street traffic in and around Detroit

Metro, Michigan and Dayton Metro, Ohio to high-speed rural interstate travels. Figure 8 shows the automatic event percentage and the deceleration request bands, which was from extrapolating the data across the standard 100,000 miles vehicle life cycle.

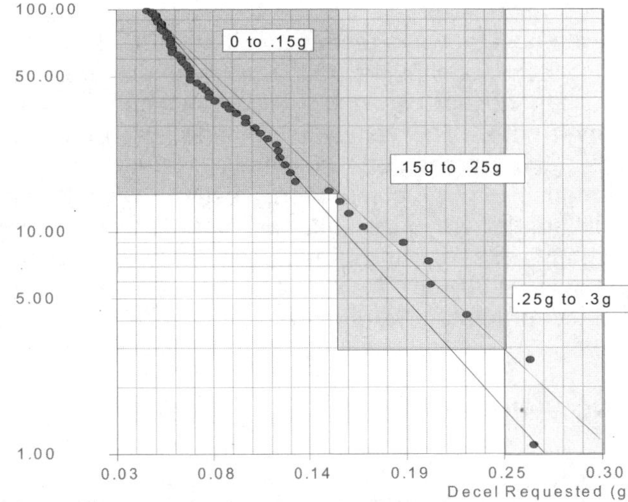

Figure 8 Autobraking Events vs Requested Decel

Component Durability Verification (DV)

In process of the presented Automatic Braking component Development Verification, the real-time vehicle control data corresponding to requested commands in the above study were broken down into 3 event-cycle-equivalent time domain profiles to fit practically for feasible chamber testing. Figure 9 displays the VIV valve input profiles which have linearly ramp-up and ramp-down signals to respectively represent the average energizing durations of pressure control. These 3 profiles were run in a chamber at four season temperatures evenly with the individually equivalent event cycle numbers and pre-set trigger waiting times. To minimize the hydraulic modulator noise, similar profiles with PWM commands proportional to these VIV signal levels were utilized to drive the hydraulic motor for the DV testing. The specification-met cycle numbers were accomplished in the chamber.

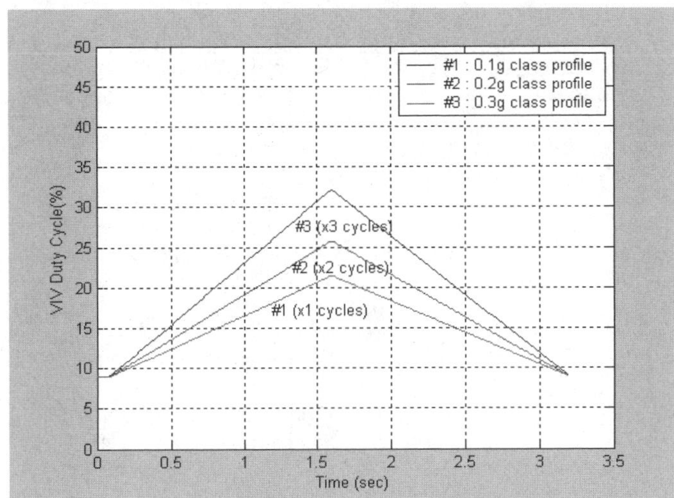

Figure 9 The VIV PWM Signals for the HCU DV Testing

CONCLUSION

There are several ways to implement an ACC automatic brake system for vehicle adaptive cruise control. The hydraulic-modulator-based implementation was examined here. The vehicle integration system testing verifies the presented automatic brake system performance. The component testing reveals its durability under brake life usage profiles. The simulation technology proves the automatic braking control robustness subject to driver, environment and manufacturer related disturbances.

ACKNOWLEGEMENTS

We wish to acknowledge the technician team in the Vehicle Test and Instrumentation departments who supported vehicle builds and testing.

CONTACT INFORMATION

Deron C. Littlejohn
Delphi Energy and Chassis Systems
M/S 483-3DB-210
12501 E. Grand River
Brighton, MI 48116-9326
Phone: 810-494-4428
Fax: 810-494-4458
Email: deron.littlejohn@delphi.com

REFERENCES

1. McLaughlin, S.: Measurement of Driver Preferences and Intervention Responses as Influenced by Adaptive Cruise Control Deceleration Characteristics, Thesis, Virginia Polytechnic Institute and State University, Blacksburg, Virginia; June 29, 1998
2. "Surface Transportation Act Boosts Intelligent Systems, Says I.T.S. America President," Top Tech Stories Washington, June 10, 1999 http://techmall.com.techdocs/TS980610-9.html
3. Hatipoglu, C.; Ozguner, U.; Sommerville, M.: "Longitudinal Headway Control of Autonomous Vehicles," Proceedings of the 1996 IEEE International Conference on Control Applications, New York, NY; 1996; p.721-6
4. Shein, E.; Mausner, E.: "Deployment and Commercialization of Cost and Safety-effective Autonomous Intelligent Cruise Control System," Microwaves and RF Conference Proceedings, Nexus Media, Swanley, UK; 1995; p. 124-31
5. Bryan Riley, George Kuo, Brian Schwartz, Jon Zumberge, Kevin Shipp; Development of a Controlled Braking Strategy for Vehicle Adaptive Cruise Control, SAE 2000 World Congress; March 2000
6.. Brakes for the Future, *Automotive Engineer*, September, 1998

DEFINITIONS, ACRONYMS, ABBREVIATIONS

ACC	Adaptive Cruise Control
ABS	Anti-lock Brake System
TCS	Traction Control System
ESC	Electronic Stability Control
EBCM	Electronic Brake Control Module
PWM	Pulse Width Module
VIV	Variable Isolation Valve
LSV	Linear Solenoid Valve

2004-01-0175

Tracking a Preceding Vehicle for Adaptive Cruise Control Using a Block Matching Method

Eui Yoon Chung, Jee Yeong Kim, Eugene Chang, Jin Min Chun and In Sik Lee
R&D Division for Hyundai Motor Company & Kia Motors Corporation

ABSTRACT

Adaptive cruise control (ACC) systems, which detect distance of a preceding vehicle and a radar-mounted vehicle using the radar, are available from automobile manufacturers. The distance and a relative velocity of the preceding vehicle and the radar-mounted vehicle can be estimated by analyzing a millimeter-wave signal obtained through the radar. Due to a characteristic of the radar and the relative velocity between the preceding vehicle and the radar-mounted vehicle, it is difficult to detect and track the preceding vehicle in the same lane where the radar-mounted vehicle is moving. In this paper, an algorithm is proposed to solve the above difficulties. The proposed algorithm separates a radar-search range into several blocks. And it detects and tracks a preceding object as a detected block of the several blocks. Applying this algorithm and assigning priority among the blocks, the searching range for the targeting vehicle and response time of the system are reduced.

INTRODUCTION

Intelligent vehicle technologies are rapidly growing worldwide. They have been recognized as technologies that are enabling enhancement in road transport operational efficiency, and increasing driving pleasure. Intelligent vehicle technologies are being developed to the driver assistance concept to assist human beings while driving the vehicle, or the autonomous driving/intelligent vehicle concept to enable a vehicle to drive autonomously along the road, with no or limited assistance from humans [1].

Driver assistant systems are emerging as a solution to the driver to release stress, to improve the control of vehicles and so to reduce the number of accidents and fatalities. Moreover, some of these systems can help to improve the traffic flow as well.

Adaptive cruise control (ACC) techniques are one of the vehicle technologies which are being developed to the driver assistance concept as a safety and comfort feature.

ACC stand for 'adaptive cruise control' and refers to extension of conventional cruise control to higher level of sensors and control, including detection of vehicles in front of the equipped car, and distance regulation with the relevant targets. It first was called ICC(intelligent cruise control) or AICC(autonomous intelligent cruise control). The final acronym of ACC is more representative of the great number of highway situations the system can cope with.

Nowadays, first generation of ACC system has been introduced to the market as a first step towards collision avoidance. Some luxuries vehicles makers in Europe and Japan have already implemented it.

ACC is a comfort system which can also contribute to reduce the number of accidents since a significant part of rear-end collisions are caused by driver inattention and following too closely.

In any case, concerning the new driver assistance systems a lot of improvements and advance are needed in terms of sensor and power capacity to be able to understand perfectly the environment around the car and then to take the best decisions. Sensors, on the one hand, need to measure accurately the distance and relative speed to preceding vehicles, be easily and cheaply producible, and must meet the strict requirement of the automotive market. On the other hand, the signal processing must guarantee the desired resolution of the processed data while keeping rigorous timing constraints [2].

Sensor specifications also have an impact on control and driver acceptance. Main defaults are selection and deselection time of the targets. When the ACC vehicle changes lane, the driver expects the system to accelerate as soon as no vehicle is present in the expected trajectory. But tracking algorithm use filtering and deselection of target some times occurs when the ACC vehicle is in the second lane, with no more obstacles ahead, which is unacceptable for the driver.

To correct errors is needed signal processing technology.

In this paper we present a method that is determination and tracking preceding targets. The proposed algorithm separates a radar-search range into several blocks. And it detects and tracks a preceding object as a detected block of the several blocks. A target number is assigned at the region block where the radar-search range is divided by means of a radar signal based on the distance information from input radar signals. Based on the radar signal to be input, it is searched the neighbor region block, to find and to compare the former target.

MAIN SECTION

ADAPTIVE CRUISE CONTROL OVERVIEW

An ACC is a comfort system that enhances the functionality of standard cruise control system and is suited to be used in highways. It automatically adjusts the vehicle speed in order to maintain a driver-specified adjustable distance behind a preceding vehicle

A forward-looking detection sensor (radar or laser) is used to monitor the traffic in front of the ACC-vehicle assessing the distance, angular position and relative speed to possible targets. Fig. 1 is described the ACC function mode. If no obstacle is detected, the car accelerates to the desired speed as in conventional cruise control function. In case that a vehicle is detected, a safety distance is kept actuating over the throttle or applying the brakes if necessary. The system operates under a limited speed range.

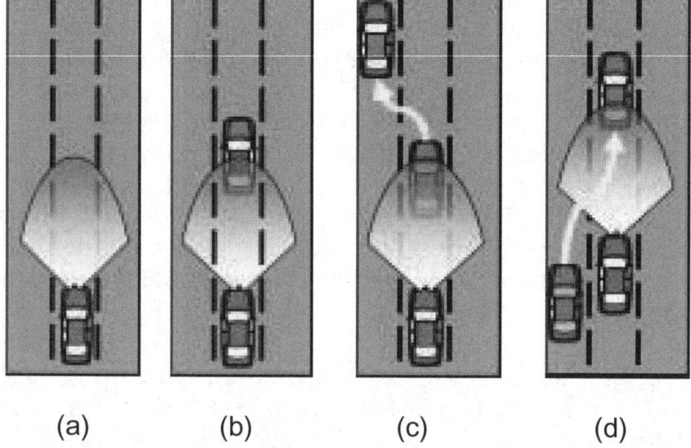

(a) (b) (c) (d)

Fig. 1 ACC function mode.(a) Normal cruise mode. (b) A vehicle is detected, a safety distance is kept. (c) A vehicle is changed a lane, the car accelerates to the desired speed. (d) If a vehicle changes into a lane, the car activates a brake, and is kept a safety distance.

Selection of the relevant preceding vehicle is the first and essential step in ACC. The distance sensor supplies the distance, relative speed and angle of multiple objects representing different preceding vehicles. Combination of expected trajectory and preceding vehicles' positions produces the most relevant target to be considered by ACC longitudinal control law.

PROPOSED ALGORITHM OVERVIEW

In this paper, we present a method which is determined multiple targets in search range, and tracking the targets. To tracking the target need radar signal which is continuous and exact. Unfortunately, radar is lost target at times. Also radar detects a wrong number of radar wave. The proposed algorithm separates a radar-search range into several blocks. And it detects and tracks a preceding object as a detected block of the several blocks as shown Fig. 2. Fig. 2 shows a concept of proposed algorithm. Searching range of millimeter wave radar is separates some blocks.

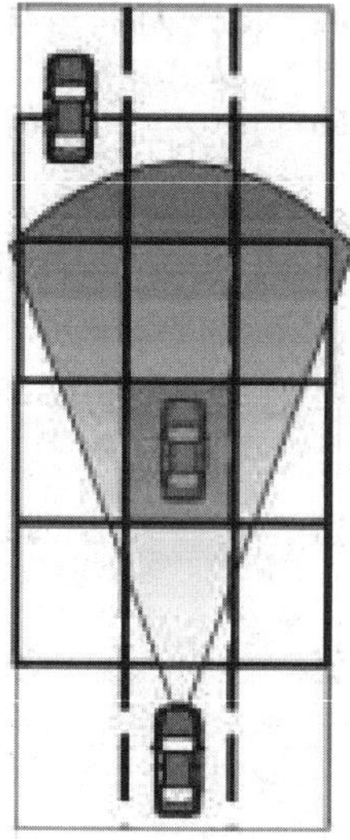

Fig. 2 Target tracking using block matching method.

A vehicle detected by radar is calculated and assigned a block, and then searched neighbor blocks which are stored previous target data, to tracking.

It is reduced searching time to tracking that target detected is assigned block and is tracked.

The proposed algorithm is consist of determination of target block and tracking of target in Fig. 3. A vehicle is assigned a block from input signal with a distance and angle of preceding vehicle. After a vehicle is assigned a block, Assigned block is comparing neighbor block to find a direction of target. Data of each target is updating Target Database. ACC main control unit is get a target data to control a vehicle.

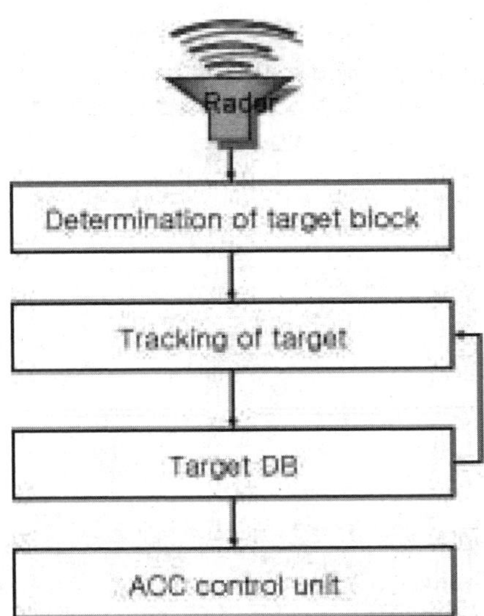

Fig.3 Blockdiagram of proposed algorithm.

DETERMIN A TARGET TO BLOCK

The millimeter wave radar detects a distance and angle of preceding vehicle in Fig. 4. We calculate a block of coordinate from that data using trigonometric function.

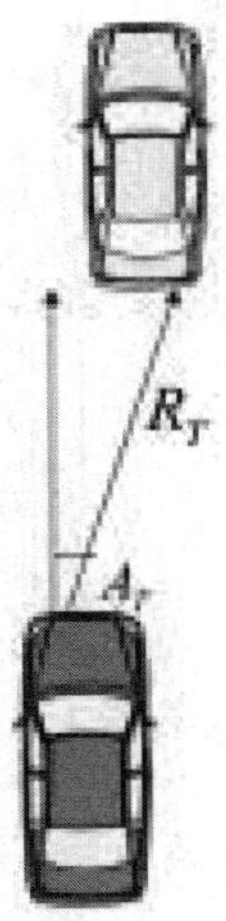

Fig. 4 Output signal of millimeter wave radar.

Tb_x, Tb_y *of* block is given by

$$Tb_x = \frac{R_T A_T C \pm L/2}{L}, \qquad (1)$$

$$Tb_y = \frac{R_T - C_i}{B} \qquad (2).$$

Where R_T is a distance which is from ACC vehicle to target vehicle. A_T is an angle in Fig. 4. C is a coefficient is $Sin1^\circ$ (=0.0175). Change rate of A_T is very small and it change lineally in proportion to $Sin1^\circ$. L is a width of lane of road. B is longitude of block as shown Fig. 5. It is bigger than a vehicle. The number of assigned block is proportion to search range. Target which is detected with radar is assigned block is reduced searching area to tracking a target

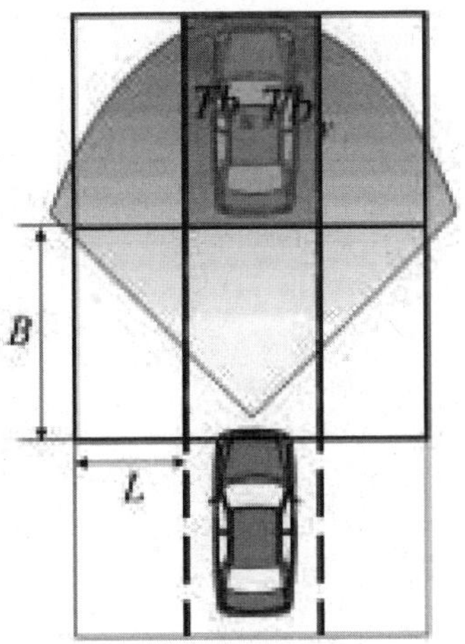

Fig. 5. Coordinate of assigned block.

TRACKING ALGORITHM USING BLOCK MACHING METHOD

To control a ACC vehicle, we know a direction of a target vehicle assigned block and is tracking a target vehicle. Proposed tracking method is block matching method. It is compare neighbor block. Assigned block compare neighbor blocks to find which is a previous block assigned.

Fig. 6 is showed the flowchart of proposed tracking algorithm. After input a target assigned block, Compare assigned block is existence of previous target. If target existed, target is updated in target DB. Elsewhere target isn't existing a block. Assigned block is compared neighbor block to find previous target which is moved.

Sampling time of radar is faster than move a vehicle. So vehicle cannot jumped a neighbor block. To find previous target is only compared neighbor blocks. In target DB, each target has a velocity, a distance, an angle, a coordinate of assigned block, a direction of progress and frequency of assigned block.

Because we separate a block and use a block matching method, we reduced searching time a target in searching range of radar.

Also, a frequency of assigned block is needed for compensation of lost time which is missing a target by radar.

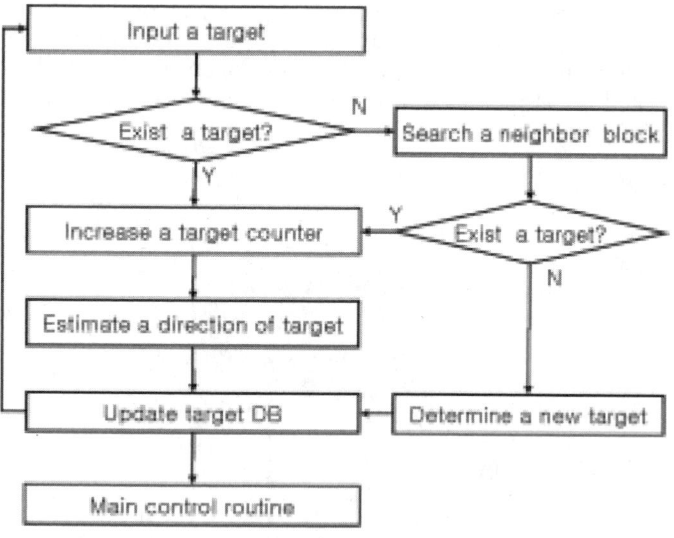

Fig. 6. Flowchart of tracking algorithm.

EXPERIMENTS AND RESULTS

The proposed algorithm installed in a production vehicle equipped with radar based ACC. We make a data logger program to experiment in Fig. 7. It shows a distance of target which is detected. Also a graph of distance of each target is proportion to time. Fig. 8 shows a example image frame of experiments.

Fig 7. Image of data logger.

Because of specification of millimeter wave radar, wrong target is detected in Fig. 9 (a). Proposed algorithm is this problem is reduced using a counter of target block. If counter is zero. Target is eliminated. That result is shown in Fig.9 (b).

Fig. 10 shows a distance graph. Fig. 10 (a) shows that target is changed confusing of radar signal but (b) shows that proposed algorithm is not confused target because of target tracking using block matching method.

Fig 8. Image frame of CCD camera.

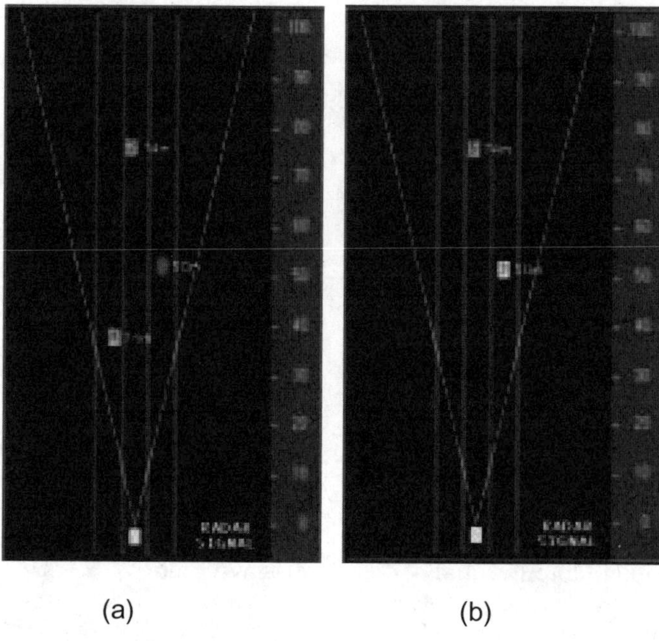

(a) (b)

Fig. 9. Target image of radar detected. (a) diagram of radar signal. Number 4 is a target wrong detected. (b) diagram of proposed algorithm.

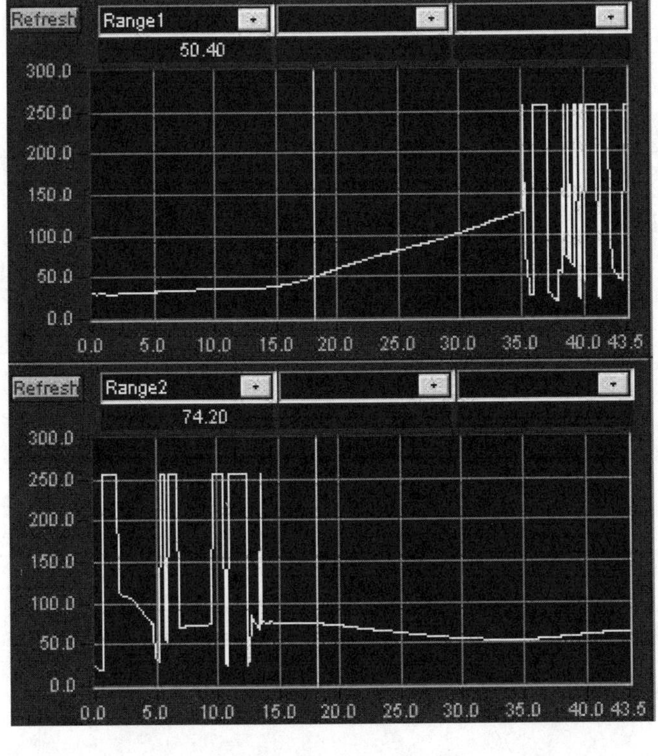

(a)

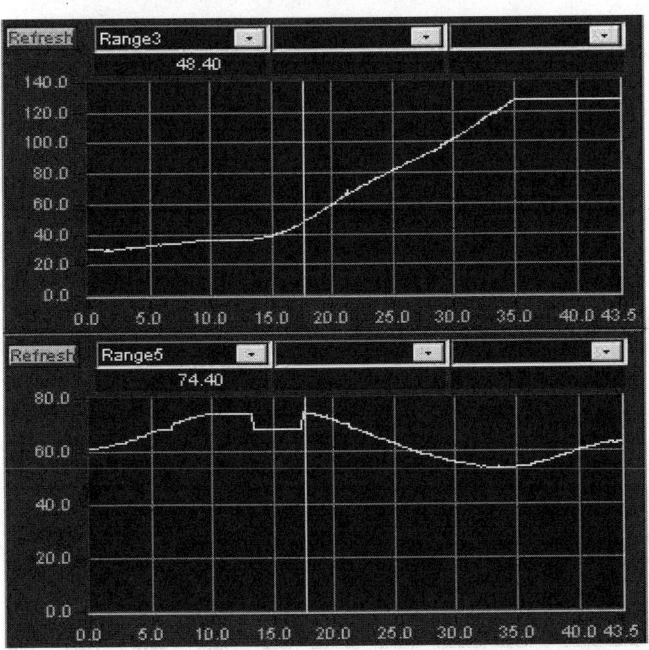

(b)

Fig. 10 Distance graph of target distance. (a) distance of radar signal (b) distance of proposed algorithm.

CONCLUSION

Adaptive cruise control (ACC) systems, which detect distance of a preceding vehicle and a radar-mounted vehicle using the radar, are available from automobile manufacturers. Due to a characteristic of the radar, t is difficult to detect and track the preceding vehicle in the same lane where the radar-mounted vehicle is moving. In this paper, an algorithm is proposed to solve the above difficulties. The proposed algorithm separates a radar-search range into several blocks. And it detects and tracks a preceding object as a detected block of the several blocks. Applying this algorithm and assigning priority among the blocks, the searching range for the targeting vehicle and response time of the system are reduced.

In the future work, we will study combine with STOP & GO system. Also To more accurate control ACC system, we needed study of sensor fusion with long range radar , short range radar and vision system.

REFERENCES

1. D. Maurel, S. Donikian, “ACC systems overview and examples,” *Intelligent vehicle technologies*, Warrendale, PA: SAE, 2001, pp.423-424
2. F. Sanchez, M. Seguer, A. Freixa, P. Andress, K. Sochaski, and R. Holze, “From Adaptive Cruise Control to Active Safety Systems,” *SAE Technical Paper* 2001-01-3245, 2001.
3. H. Winner, S. Witte, W. Uhler, B. Lichtenberg, “Adaptive Cruise Control System Aspects and Development Trends,” *SAE Technical Paper* 961010, 1996.

2003-01-2262

Characterizing the Capability of a Rear-End Crash Avoidance System

Jonathan Koopmann and Wassim G. Najm
Volpe National Transportation Systems Center

ABSTRACT

This paper presents a framework to characterize the capability of an automotive rear-end crash avoidance system that integrates forward crash warning and adaptive cruise control functionalities. This system characterization describes the operational performance of the system and its main components in the driving environment, based on data to be collected from instrumented vehicles driven by volunteer subjects as their own vehicles under real-world conditions. This characterization is pursuing a number of objectives dealing with the capability of system components including the forward-looking sensor suite, alert logic, automatic vehicle controls, and driver-vehicle interface. A number of subobjectives and concomitant measures are delineated. Examples are provided to illustrate the analysis process of this framework based on data recently collected from system verification tests.

INTRODUCTION

This paper describes a framework to characterize the capability of an automotive Rear-End Crash Avoidance System (RECAS) that integrates Forward Crash Warning (FCW) and Adaptive Cruise Control (ACC) functionalities. The FCW function alerts the driver of impending rear-end crashes with a lead vehicle ahead. The ACC function performs the automatic speed control of conventional cruise control and enables the maintenance of set time gap in the presence of a slower lead vehicle. This integrated system will be installed on ten Buick LeSabre vehicles to be driven by 78 volunteer drivers from the general public over a ten-month period as part of the Automotive Collision Avoidance System Field Operational Test (ACAS FOT) project [1]. Each subject will drive an instrumented RECAS-equipped vehicle for a period of four weeks, as his or her own vehicle. During the first week of driving, the RECAS is disabled to collect baseline-driving data. The RECAS is enabled during the remaining three weeks for 66 subjects to gather driver-vehicle-system performance data. For the other 12 subjects, the RECAS is enabled for the second and third weeks, and later disabled in the fourth week. Numeric, video, and audio data will be recorded from many sensors onboard the instrumented vehicle, including forward looking radar, forward view and driver face cameras, Global Positioning System (GPS), and a variety of in-vehicle sensors. In addition, subjective data will be obtained from surveys and focus groups.

This paper focuses on characterizing the system performance and capability, one of the four major goals adopted for the RECAS evaluation using data from the field test described above [2,3]. These four goals are:

1. Achieve a detailed understanding of RECAS safety benefits
2. Determine driver acceptance of RECAS
3. Characterize RECAS performance and capability
4. Assess RECAS deployment potential and price.

The first goal seeks to estimate potential reductions in rear-end crashes and harm caused by crash related injuries if all light passenger vehicles in the United States (U.S.) were equipped with RECAS. The second goal examines driver acceptance in terms of the compatibility between the driver's expectations and RECAS performance as well as the degree to which drivers express interest in acquiring a RECAS system for their personal vehicle. The third goal, the main focus of this paper, deals with the operational performance and capability of the RECAS, and describes how the RECAS and its individual components perform safety-related functions in the driving environment. Price, introduction date, and deployment rate of RECAS in the U.S. vehicle fleet comprise the fourth goal of the evaluation.

Next, this paper describes the RECAS and its components, as well as an alternative rear-end crash warning algorithm to be evaluated along with the system. After, this paper delineates the framework for addressing the system capability goal of the evaluation. Subsequently, data sources are identified and examples of preliminary system performance data are presented. This paper concludes with a summary of remarks about the system characterization results presented herein.

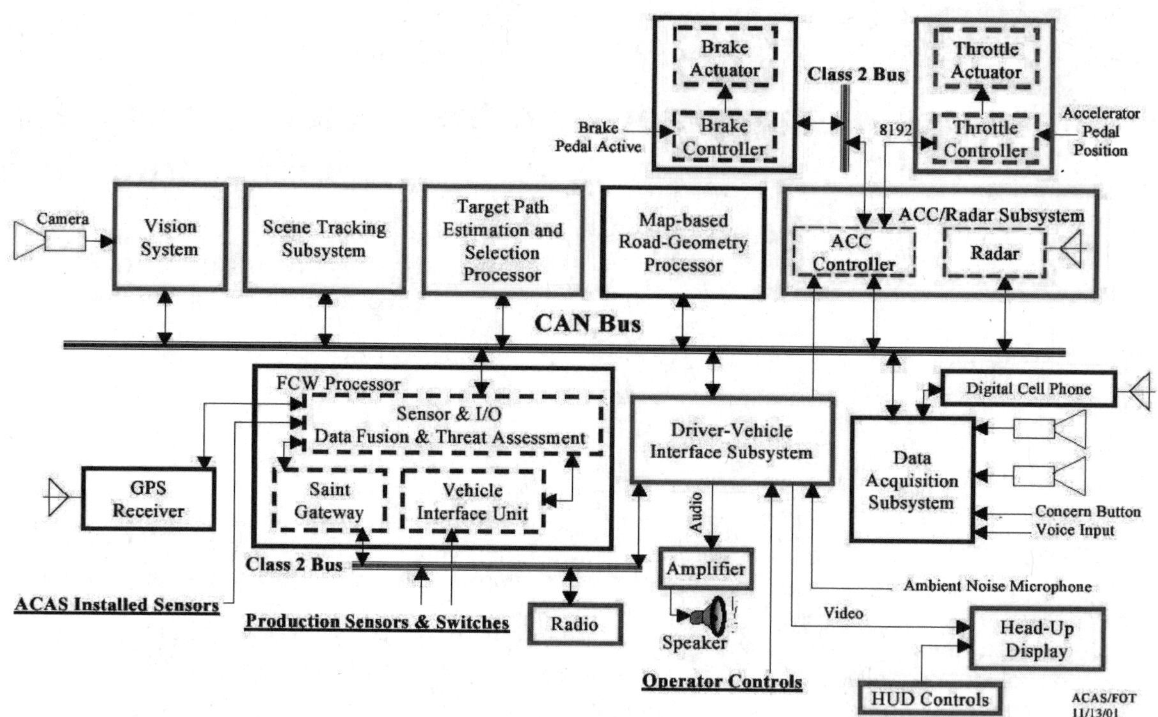

Figure 1.
Physical Layout of the ACAS Vehicle

SYSTEM DESCRIPTION

The RECAS provides two functionalities to the driver, FCW and ACC, which assist the driver via alerts and automatic control of the vehicle. Figure 1 presents the physical architecture, components, and connections of the system [4]. The system combines signal inputs from the forward-looking radar, forward vision, GPS receiver coupled with a map database, and in-vehicle sensors to detect and track targets, track lane boundaries, and predict upcoming road geometry. Data fusion is carried out to determine if vehicles or objects ahead are in the path of the host vehicle. A threat assessment algorithm evaluates the threat of in-path obstacles and decides whether or not to issue a crash imminent alert if necessary.

The radar tracks up to 15 targets simultaneously and generates target information such as range, range rate, acceleration, azimuth angle, and target status. The forward vision system utilizes a Charged-Coupled Device (CCD) camera to extract upcoming road geometry ahead of the host vehicle and estimate the vehicle's lateral lane position and heading. Forward roadway information from the vision system is combined with radar data to reduce the incidence of false alerts from roadside objects during curve entry/exit and lane change maneuvers. This process is assisted by a Differential GPS (DGPS) receiver and digital map database, which provides an additional source of road geometry information.

Data from radar, vision, DGPS/map, and in-vehicle sensors such as speed and yaw rate, are combined in a data fusion process to determine the host vehicle state and eliminate conflicts from multiple data input sources. A path prediction and target selection algorithm then forecasts where the host vehicle is going and what objects or vehicles are encountered in its path of travel. Targets deemed in-path are classified as either Closest In-Path Stationary object/vehicle (CIPS) or Closest In-Path (moving) Vehicle (CIPV). Subsequently, the threat assessment algorithm makes a decision about warning the driver on these in-path targets by issuing graded cautionary alerts based on a driver selected sensitivity setting or a crash imminent alarm based on a fixed threshold. Cautionary visual alerts are sent to the driver via Head-Up Display (HUD) on the lower portion of the windshield below the driver view of the roadway. Crash imminent alerts are conveyed to the driver via visual icon and an alert tone from a separate speaker in the vehicle as shown in Figure 1.

The ACC allows the driver to select a desired speed in a similar fashion to conventional cruise control, and to set a time gap between the host vehicle and the lead vehicle in six settings between 1 and 2 seconds. The ACC maintains the set speed when no vehicle ahead is impeding the forward movement of the host vehicle. However, the ACC switches from automatic speed control to distance control when a slower lead vehicle is present, by maintaining the selected time gap via throttle and brake applications. The ACC only responds to moving vehicles and its maximum braking capacity is limited to 0.3 g.

A proprietary rear-end crash warning algorithm provides alert signals to the driver-vehicle interface of the RECAS during the field test. At the same time, another warning algorithm is running "silent" in the background using similar sensor data; its alerts are recorded but not transmitted to the driver. The evaluation will analyze and compare the performance of both algorithms during the baseline driving portion of the field test as explained later in this paper. The input parameters of the alternative silent algorithm consist mainly of the host vehicle velocity, host vehicle acceleration, and relative acceleration, range, and range rate [5]. In a standard mode operation, the algorithm calculates a projected miss distance to the lead vehicle every 100 ms based upon these inputs. If the projected miss distance falls below a particular miss-distance threshold, then the alert corresponding to the new condition is issued. The algorithm issues early, intermediate, and imminent alerts based upon sensitivity levels selected by the driver. Reaction time of 1.5 s, which includes driver and system delays, and a maximum braking level of -0.55g define the boundary for imminent alerts. Table 1 presents the assumed host vehicle braking capability corresponding to driver selected sensitivity and algorithm alert level. The imminent alert is the same regardless of driver-selected sensitivity. Assumed brake level values allow an aggressive driver to receive later alerts requiring more severe deceleration, closer allowable following distances, and fewer overall alerts. Brake levels for "Far" sensitivity enable a conservative driver to be warned earlier and perform moderate braking maneuvers. The standard mode of the alternative algorithm covers scenarios when the lead vehicle is stopped, moving slowly, or braking and sufficient distance is available to accurately estimate lead vehicle deceleration. Close following situations initiate a separate tailgating algorithm that issues an imminent alert when lead vehicle deceleration is -0.2 g or greater.

Table 1.
Assumed Host Vehicle Maximum Braking Capability

	Assumed Host Vehicle Maximum Braking Capacity (g)		
Warning Sensitivity	Alert Level		
	Early	Intermediate	Imminent
Near	0.38	0.45	0.55
Mid	0.32	0.40	0.55
Far	0.27	0.35	0.55

SYSTEM CAPABILITY

The main focus of this paper is to present a framework for characterizing the capability of the RECAS and its major components including the sensor suite, decision making subsystem (alert logic), automatic control, and driver-vehicle interface. This framework addresses the adequacy, reliability, and consistency of RECAS safety-related functions. Figure 2 illustrates the four objectives and associated subobjectives dealing with specific portions of RECAS functionality. These objectives and subobjectives describe the quality of the system to either alert the driver in a timely manner and/or apply automatic controls when required. Qualitative data will be collected to address the dark-shaded subobjectives shown in Figure 2 because their measures depend on individual driver subjective response to RECAS signals.

The first objective characterizes the performance of the forward-looking sensor in detecting and tracking in-path obstacles. To meet this objective, we will examine how well the system detects Closest In-Path Targets (CIPT's), tracks CIPT's, and rejects Out-Of-Path Targets (OPT's). Measures for CIPT detection and tracking include the number of CIPT's detected, missed, lost, or intermittently detected divided by the total number of CIPT detected. The OPT rejection is measured by the

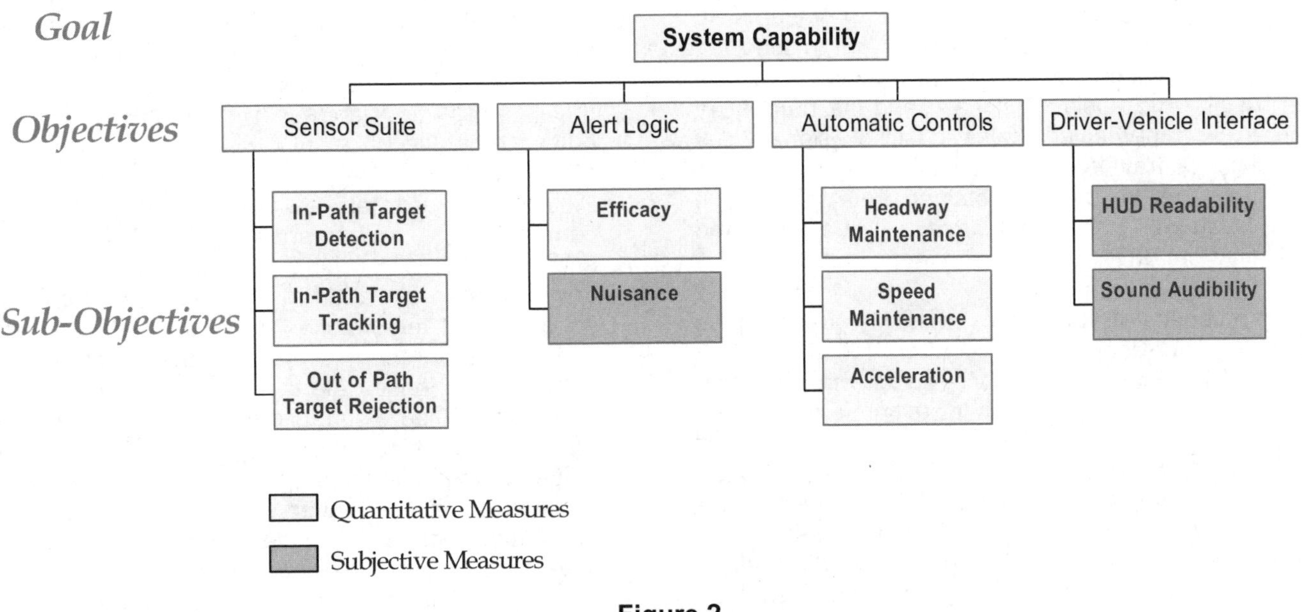

Figure 2.
Analysis of RECAS Capability

number of OPT's rejected divided by the total number of OPT's encountered. Sensor suite measures will be derived from the field test, on-road independent test using an instrumented FOT vehicle, and "system-level verification" tests.

The second objective examines the performance of the warning logic in alerting the driver to driving conflicts that might lead to imminent rear-end crashes. The two subobjectives of the warning logic performance are the ability of the system to issue a correct signal and the driver perception of the alert usefulness. The RECAS issues a "true" signal (warning/deceleration) when the host vehicle is on a rear-end crash course with a CIPT (i.e., situations requiring a signal). On the other hand, a "false" signal is issued when the host vehicle is not on a rear-end crash course with a CIPT or due to OPT's (i.e., situations not requiring a signal). System efficacy is measured by:

1. Number of "true positive" signals over the number of all situations requiring a signal
2. Relative frequency of "false negative" signals
3. Number of "false positive" signals over the number of all situations not requiring a signal
4. "False alarm" rate
5. "True alarm" rate.

These measures will be captured from FOT data triggered either manually by the driver or automatically by an alert. Other measures will also be considered such as the time interval between crash imminent alerts and the number of alerts per vehicle distance traveled. The second subobjective of the alert logic performance is a qualitative measurement of driver perceived nuisance alerts. A driver may distinguish a "true positive" alert as a "nuisance" if it were judged either "too early" or not necessary. In contrast, a different driver may perceive the same "true positive" alert as late. Measures to capture driver opinion of system signals will include the number of "nuisance" or "too late" signals per the number of all "true positive" signals, and the number of "nuisance" and perceived "false positive" signals per vehicle distance traveled. As indicated in Figure 2, these measures cannot be directly obtained from the vehicle sensors; instead, these measures will be collected subjectively from driver surveys and focus groups.

The third objective of the system capability goal portrays ACC automatic longitudinal control functions that encompass time gap maintenance, speed maintenance, and acceleration/deceleration under dynamic conditions. Headway and speed maintenance measures are based on the error between the set value and actual value under steady state conditions. ACC performance under transient state conditions is captured by the host vehicle longitudinal acceleration and jerk per automatic braking or acceleration event. The average, standard deviation, minimum, and maximum values of these measures will also be determined. To supplement this vehicle-measured data, subjective data will also be gathered from the FOT surveys concerning driver comfort during automatic acceleration or deceleration.

Assessment of the Driver-Vehicle Interface (DVI) is the final objective of the system capability goal. To properly convey information to the driver, the HUD must be visible and alert tones must be audible in all conditions. Respective measures include the contrast ratio of light intensity between HUD brightness and ambient light, and the contrast ratio of decibels (dB's) between the alert tone and ambient noise. This objective will be supported by data from system verification tests conducted in all lighting and noise conditions, independent tests, and post-test FOT surveys. Surveys will give a qualitative measure of the drivers' ability to see and read the HUD in widely varying lighting conditions, with different sight treatments (i.e. eye glasses, sun glasses, etc.), and with assorted sight ailments such as cataracts. Qualitative data from surveys will also be used to capture the drivers' ability to perceive and hear auditory alerts during different levels of outside noise such as conversation or with the use of hearing aides.

EVALUATION OF AN ALTERNATIVE WARNING ALGORITHM

In conjunction with the analysis of the RECAS-embedded alert algorithm, the evaluation will examine and compare the performance of a non-proprietary warning algorithm described earlier in this paper. As previously discussed, the RECAS functionality is not active during the first week of driving in the field test; however, the warning algorithms are running in the background and their warnings are recorded. Although this period is intended to provide baseline driving information and allow the driver to acclimate to the basic vehicle functions, it offers the additional benefit of algorithm data collection without driver response to the RECAS-issued warnings affecting the alternative algorithm. Unfortunately, the limited scope of the field test does not allow data collection while the alternative algorithm is providing alerts directly to the driver so as to gauge driver response to true and nuisance alerts.

Figure 3 illustrates the logic for examining and comparing the performance of the RECAS-embedded and alternative warning algorithms during baseline driving. When a warning is issued, driver response will be examined for braking, steering, or a combination of both. Alerts will then be classified based on the intensity of driver response. Alerts followed by a high intensity response will be distinguished if the driver commences an intense braking or steering maneuver after the alert as determined by high longitudinal or lateral acceleration. In contrast, if the driver performs relaxed or normal brake/steer actions after the alert, then the alerts will be categorized by the low intensity response. If an alert is issued and the driver does not respond, the sensor data is examined for CIPT detection. The alert is marked "no response alert" when a CIPT was detected and video

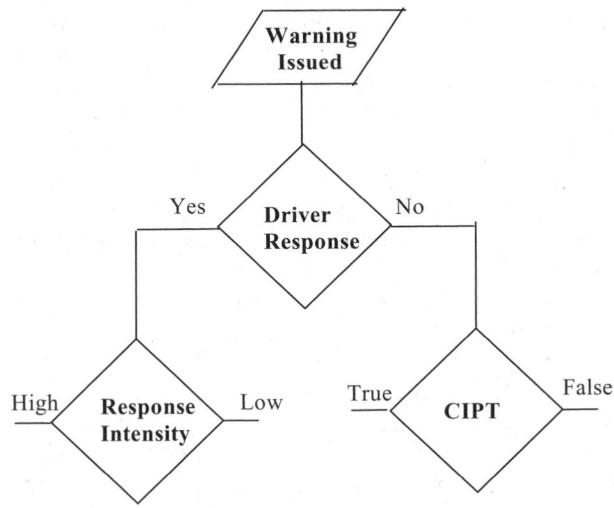

Figure 3.
Analysis Flowchart of "Warning Events"

review reveals the target was an OPT or a non-threatening CIPT. If there was no driver response, no CIPT detection, and a target does not appear in the video, the alert is classified as "sensor problem". When no warning is issued but the driver makes a high intensity response, sensor data is examined for CIPT identification. CIPT detection events will be labeled as "miss alert". On the other hand, if there is no CIPT detection the occurrence will be marked as "sensor problem". In both cases, the video will be examined to determine the cause of the high intensity response and confirm sensor operation.

DATA SOURCES

The characterization of system capability will rely on data to be collected from three separate test sets: system-level verification tests prior to the FOT, the FOT, and separate independent tests conducted to evaluate areas not fully covered by the first two test sets. Table 2 correlates the subobjectives to test data sources.

SYSTEM VERIFICATION TESTS

System-level verification tests were conducted in a controlled environment to validate system functionalities before the system was allowed to proceed to the FOT. These tests consisted of a series of controlled tests on a test track or vehicle proving ground and a pre-specified eight-hour driver on selected public roads. The sensor suite and the warning logic were examined through a number of scenarios involving the host vehicle and other vehicles in typical driving scenarios such as braking, accelerating, and passing on straight and curved roadways. Scenarios included alert tests and nuisance tests with the vehicle operating under FCW and ACC modes. Detailed results of selected tests will be discussed in the exemplary performance data section of this paper. Analysis of the DVI is partially served by the verification tests, where visual and audio devices are confirmed to function as designed. The main portion of the DVI analysis will be based on data gathered from FOT surveys.

FIELD OPERATIONAL TEST

The FOT is the primary source of data for the evaluation. Data from the FOT contain numerous quantitative measures such as vehicle sensor information, but also include survey information completed by the subjects after finishing their four-week drive. Vehicle sensor data are captured at a constant 10 Hz rate from an onboard Data Acquisition System (DAS). In addition, the host vehicle is equipped with two cameras to monitor the forward view from the vehicle and the face of test subjects. The forward view update rate is once every second or 10 Hz for about 8 seconds if triggered by a crash-imminent alert. Vehicle sensor data will provide valuable insight into automatic controls, while video data will be utilized for alert efficacy measures. FOT driver surveys will be a key source of information for alert logic

Table 2.
Test Versus "System Capability" Subobjectives

<table>
<tr><th>Subobjective</th><th>FOT</th><th>System Verification</th><th>Independent Test</th></tr>
<tr><td>Closest in Path Target Detection</td><td rowspan="3"></td><td rowspan="3">•</td><td rowspan="3">•</td></tr>
<tr><td>Closest in Path Target Tracking</td></tr>
<tr><td>Out of Path Target Rejection</td></tr>
<tr><td>Alert Efficacy</td><td>Video Clips</td><td rowspan="2">•</td><td rowspan="2"></td></tr>
<tr><td>Alert Nuisance</td><td>Surveys</td></tr>
<tr><td>ACC Headway Maintenance</td><td rowspan="2">DAS</td><td rowspan="3"></td><td rowspan="3"></td></tr>
<tr><td>ACC Speed Maintenance</td></tr>
<tr><td>ACC Acceleration</td><td>DAS + Surveys</td></tr>
<tr><td>HUD Readability</td><td>Surveys</td><td>•</td><td>•</td></tr>
<tr><td>Sound Audibility</td><td>Surveys</td><td>•</td><td>•</td></tr>
</table>

nuisance measures, DVI performance, and ACC acceleration/deceleration comfort. Surveys were designed for both pre- and post-FOT by a collaboration of the project partners. Questions pertaining to the alert logic performance ask subjects to rate the timing of true positive alerts and to rate how often the FCW issued a false warning, unnecessary warning, or useful warning. Moreover, subjects are requested to describe events that elicited, in their opinion, false or useful alerts. Automatic control issues were addressed by soliciting drivers' perception of the deceleration provided by the ACC when following other vehicles or the acceleration provided by the ACC when passing other vehicles. To address the DVI, subjects are asked to rate how easy it was to see the HUD and hear the alerts.

INDEPENDENT TESTS

Additional tests, independent of the FOT, will be conducted to examine sensor detection, tracking, and rejection in alternative target rich environment, as well as DVI performance in various road and lighting conditions. These tests will utilize one of the spare FOT vehicles to conduct tests at a test track and on public road drives on a variety of roadway types with continuous video data recording. Sensor function data will be examined for CIPT performance as well as OPT rejection. This information will be used to supplement public road data gathered from system verification tests. DVI performance will also be observed and any information or alert that is either not visible or audible will be noted.

EXEMPLARY PERFORMANCE DATA

To demonstrate the analysis process, examples are provided below based on a limited set of data collected from a recent RECAS verification test. The out-of-path target rejection performance of the forward-looking sensor is examined using data from the public road drive of the verification test. In addition, the efficacy of crash imminent alerts issued by the alternative non-proprietary crash warning algorithm is discussed based on data gathered from test track trials.

OUT-OF-PATH TARGET REJECTION

The RECAS vehicle verification test included a 188-mile route encompassing rural and urban interstate, arterial, and local roadways. This public road test was conducted to measure false alerts under real-world conditions. Alerts observed during the test were judged based upon numeric vehicle data and forward video scenes. Examples of potential scenarios that could cause "true alerts" include:

1. Lead vehicle braking and turning left on a rural, straight, two-lane roadway.
2. Lead vehicle braking to exit to the right of a straight, urban, multi-lane freeway.
3. Lead vehicle braking on a straight, arterial, multi-lane roadway.

Table 3 provides an example of how the data will be classified to demonstrate the overall rejection of the system sensors and the ability of the alert logic to effectively filter out nuisance alerts. Alerts caused by overhead object such as tunnel entrances, bridges, and overhead signs were the first category examined during the 188-mile road drive. Next, alerts caused by vehicle movement such as host vehicle passing and lane change, and lead vehicle turning were analyzed for possible nuisance alerts. Categorizing these alerts as either nuisance or true alerts is difficult due to varying driver perception of usefulness. The third scenario of interest was alerts triggered by roadside objects at curve entrance. Potential sources of alerts on curve entry include drainage grates, roadside furniture, support columns within a tunnel or bridge, and most commonly mailboxes. Correctly identifying objects on curves, particularly at the entrance and exit points, is the most difficult task for a forward collision warning system. In total, these situations typically cause a large percentage of the nuisance alerts.

ALERT LOGIC PERFORMANCE

The efficacy of the alert logic performance exhibited by the non-proprietary algorithm (alternative to RECAS-embedded algorithm) is analyzed in three different driving conflicts that precede most rear-end crashes:

1. Lead vehicle stopped: Four scenarios, seven trials each – Following (host) vehicle traveling at 26 m/s, 21 m/s, 17 m/s, and 19 m/s.
2. Lead vehicle moving at slower speed: Three scenarios, seven trials each – Following/lead vehicle speed combinations at 21/4 m/s, 21/11 m/s, and 26/18 m/s.
3. Lead vehicle decelerating: One scenario, seven trials each – Host vehicle following lead vehicle at 21 m/s and lead vehicle suddenly braking at –0.3 g.

Table 3:
Example of Data Classification for Examining Out-Of-Path Target Rejection

	Overhead Objects	Objects at Curve Entry		Host Veh. Passing	Lane Change	Lead Veh. Turning
		Mailboxes	Other			
Total # Encountered	A	C	E	G	I	K
Nuisance Alerts	B	D	F	H	J	L
Rejection Ratio	(A-B) / A	(C-D) / C	(E-F) / E	(G-H) / G	(I-J) / I	(K-L) / K

The warning algorithm issued a crash imminent alert in a consistent manner as designed across all trials in all scenarios. Figures 4.1, 4.2, and 4.3 summarize the results of these tests by highlighting the outline of the warning logic in each of the three driving conflicts respectively. Each point on these curves represents the average warning range observed from all trials in one particular scenario.

To get a preliminary picture of how drivers might appreciate the timing of this alert logic, the outline of crash imminent alerts in each of the three driving conflicts was compared to "last-second" hard braking boundaries derived from human factors studies of driver braking performance [6]. Figures 4.1, 4.2, and 4.3 display these boundaries based on modified 50 percentile statistics of the data representing the hard braking onset range chosen by the subjects in the human factors experiments. These experiments gathered performance data from test-track controlled studies in which subjects were instructed to wait to conduct a maneuver (brake or steer) at the last possible moment in order to avoid colliding with a vehicle ahead using soft or hard intensity [7,8]. As seen in Figure 4.1 and 4.2, the warning logic accommodates about 50% of the drivers. In other words, the subjects who normally brake hard above the dotted line would not judge the alerts as "too early" if they were inattentive to the driving task. Few of them though might consider them as "too late". In contrast, these alerts are deemed "too early" for the drivers who normally brake hard below the dotted line. In the lead vehicle-decelerating scenario shown in Figure 4.3, the warning point (from one scenario) occurred much later than the 50-percentile point. Thus, the alert might be considered "too late" for many drivers. It should be noted that this discussion reflects a rough look at the performance of the alert logic, keeping in mind that the real evaluation of the alert logic will be based on objective and subjective data to be collected from the subjects as they drive the RECAS-equipped vehicles during the field test.

CONCLUSION

A framework was presented to characterize the capability of an automotive rear-end crash avoidance system. The system capability represents one of four major goals to be pursued by an evaluation effort to assess the overall effectiveness and readiness of this system. The evaluation will be based on objective and subjective data to be collected from a field test in which volunteer subjects will drive RECAS-equipped vehicles gained from system operation and driver performance with the system. Finally, this paper presented system performance data that are preliminary in nature so as to illustrate the analysis process of the framework. Based on system verification test results, minor upgrades are implemented to enhance the performance and reliability of the system before the launch of the field operational test.

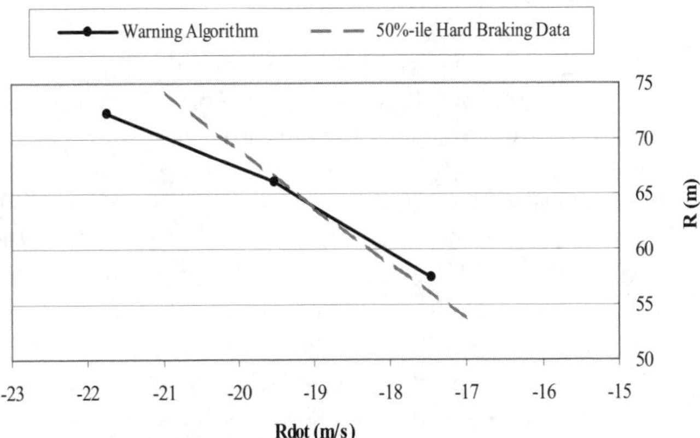

Figure 4.1. Performance of Alert Logic in Lead Vehicle Stopped Scenario

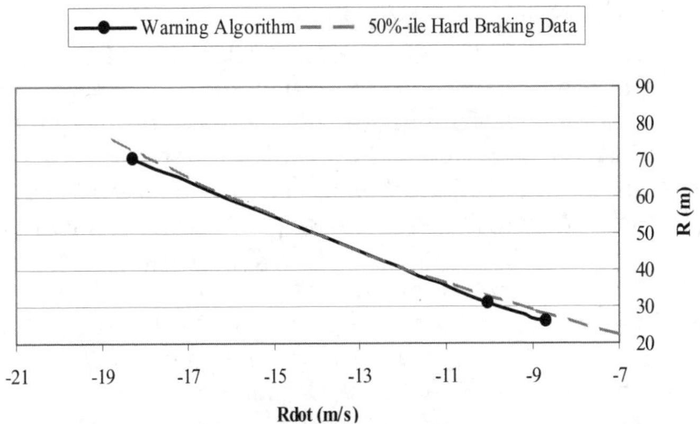

Figure 4.2. Performance of Alert Logic in Lead Vehicle Slower Scenario

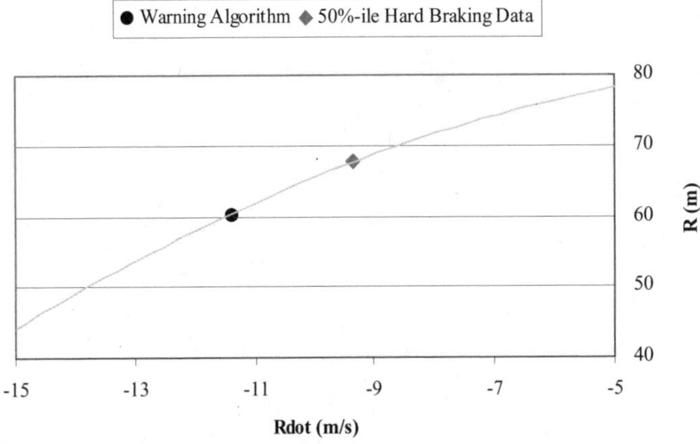

Figure 4.3. Performance of Alert Logic in Lead Vehicle Decelerating Scenario

REFERENCES

1. Ference, J.J., "Rear-End Collision Warning System Field Operational Test – Status Report". Paper No. 321, 17th International Technical Conference on the Enhanced Safety of Vehicles, Amsterdam, The Netherlands, June 2001.
2. Najm, W.G., Stearns, M.D., and Boyle, L. Ng, "Detailed Plan for an Independent Evaluation of the Automotive Collision Avoidance System Field Operational Test". Project Memorandum, DOT-VNTSC-HS116-PM-01-09, U.S. Department of Transportation, Volpe Center, March 2001.
3. Najm, W.G., Stearns, M.D., and Boyle, L. Ng, "Evaluation Framework for an Automotive Rear-End Crash Avoidance System Field Operational Test". 12th ITS America, Long Beach, CA, May 2002.
4. General Motors and Delphi-Delco Electronic Systems, *PHASE I INTERIM REPORT: Automotive Collision Avoidance System Field Operational Test*. DOT HS 809 453, May 2002.
5. Brunson, S.J., Kyle, E.M., Phamdo, N.C., and Preziotti, G.R., *Alert Algorithm Development Program, NHTSA Rear-End Collision Alert Algorithm, Final Report*. DOT HS 809 526, September 2002.
6. Smith, D.L., Najm, W.G., and Lam, A.H., "Analysis of Braking and Steering Performance in Car-Following Scenarios". SAE 2003 World Congress, Paper No. 2003-01-0283, Detroit, MI, March 2003.
7. Kiefer, R., LeBlanc, D., Palmer, M., Salinger, J., Deering, R., and M. Shulman. *Development and Validation of Functional Definitions and Evaluation Procedures for Collision Warning/Avoidance Systems*. Report DOT HS 808 964, August 1999.
8. Kiefer, R.J., Cassar, M.T., Flannagan, C.A., LeBlanc, D.J., Palmer, M.D., Deering, R.K., and Shulman, M.A., *Forward Collision Warning Requirements Project Task 1 Final Report: Refining the CAMP Crash Alert Timing Approach by Examining 'Last-Second' Braking and Lane-Change Maneuvers Under Various Kinematic Conditions*. Interim Report, NHTSA, USDOT, Washington, D.C., in press.

DEFINITIONS, ACRONYMS, ABBREVIATIONS

ACAS: Automotive Collision Avoidance System

ACC: Adaptive Cruise Control

CCD: Charged-Coupled Device

CIPS: Closest In-Path Stationary object/vehicle

CIPT: Closest In-Path Target

CIPV: Closest In-Path (moving) Vehicle

DAS: Data Acquisition System

DGPS: Differential Global Positioning System

DVI: Driver-Vehicle Interface

FCW: Forward Collision Warning

FOT: Field Operational Test

GPS: Global Positioning System

HUD: Head-Up Display

OPT: Out-of-Path Target

RECAS: Rear-End Crash Avoidance System

2002-01-1882

A Smart Rotary Actuator for Forward-Looking, Radar Based, Adaptive Cruise Control

A. M. Madni, J. B. Vuong, M. Lopez and R. F. Wells
BEI Technologies, Inc.

ABSTRACT

Common methods for achieving rotary motion and control in mechanical systems are by using stepper motors or linear actuators with conversion linkages to produce the required rotational movement. This paper describes a voice coil rotary actuator with an integrated sensor feedback system. A specific, system designed to provide oscillatory, small angle motion at 5 Hz is described, but the concepts and principles are readily adaptable to many different and varied applications.

INTRODUCTION

Mechanical systems for providing controlled rotary position and motion are often complicated and prone to backlash and wear. Stepper motors will precisely provide accurate position and motion control but generally operate in open-loop mode requiring external controllers which must have non-volatile memory to retain actual position information. To overcome these deficits, a smart rotary actuator has been developed which uses a voice coil and an integrated feedback sensor. In this integrated package, the sensor and actuator share a common shaft/bearing assembly to provide a limited-angle direct drive with hysteresis-free motion and very high acceleration rates. Linear torque vs. current control characteristics are achieved by using a built-in sensor for servo motion control operation. This paper describes the application of the smart actuator technology to a forward-looking, radar based, adaptive cruise control (ACC) for automotive applications.

The ACC system utilizes the smart rotary actuator to control the angular velocity and position trajectory of a radar platform that senses objects in a vehicle's path and helps maintain a driver-selected spacing between the vehicle and the objects ahead.

VOICE COIL ACTUATORS

Voice coil actuators are direct drive, limited motion devices that utilize a permanent magnet field and a coil winding (conductor) to produce a force or torque proportional to the current applied to the coil. These non-commutated electromagnetic devices are used in linear and rotary motion applications requiring high acceleration rates and linear torque and force response characteristics, or high frequency back-and-forth actuation [1].

The electromechanical conversion mechanism of the voice coil actuator is governed by the Lorentz force principle. This states that if a current-carrying conductor is placed in a magnetic field, a force will act upon it. The magnetic flux density, B, the current, I, and the orientation of the field and current vectors determine the magnitude of this force. Furthermore, if a total of N conductors (in series) of length L are placed in the magnetic field, the force acting upon the conductors is given by Equation (1):

$$F=kBLIN, \quad (1)$$

where k equals a constant.

Figure 1 is a simplified illustration of this principle.

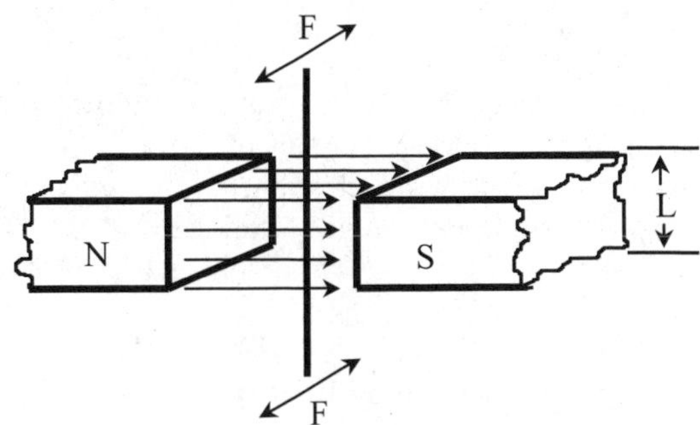

Figure 1. Lorentz Force Principle

In Figure 1, the direction of the force generated is a function of the direction of current and magnetic field vectors. Specifically, it is the cross product of the two vectors. If current flow is reversed, the direction of the force on the conductor will also reverse. If the magnetic field and the conductor length are constant, as they are in a voice coil actuator, then the generated force is directly proportional to the input current.

Equation (1) can be restated as follows: a device that contains a permanent magnet field and a coil winding moving in the field will produce a **force proportional to current** [carried in the coil].

Rotary Voice Coils

A rotary voice coil actuator consists of a tubular coil of wire that has been "flattened" or shaped into a flat tube coil of wire, an arc-shaped core with a rectangular cross section, and two arc-shaped magnet/field plate assemblies. Figure 2 depicts a typical rotary voice coil actuator.

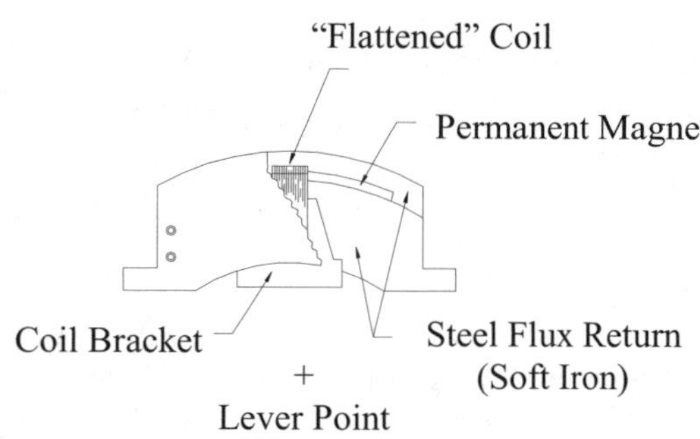

Figure 2. Typical Rotary Voice Coil Actuator

The typical motion trajectory of this device is about a specified lever point, as shown in Figure 2, and within a specified displacement angle. An application of force about a lever point is the cross product of force and radius, or torque. As such, this device can also be referred to as a limited angle torquer or a sector torquer.

Two-Wire Control

The voice coil actuator is a single-phase, "two-wire" device. Application of a voltage across the leads attached to the two ends of the coil will generate a current in the coil, causing the coil to move axially along the air gap. The direction of movement is determined by the direction of current flow in the wire.

The single-phase rotary voice coil actuator allows direct drive, smooth motion, along the path of an arc. No rotor sensing feedback devices or electronic commutators are required to maintain uninterrupted motion over the rated stroke, as with a fully rotational three-phase brushless DC motor.

Closed-Loop, or Servo Control Operation

Voice coil actuators have linear force or torque vs. current characteristics, low electrical and mechanical time constants, and a high electrical to mechanical energy conversion rate. These hysteresis-free, non-preferred coil position devices produce a level of smoothness and controllability that make voice coils ideal devices for use in many servo modes, including positioning, velocity regulation, and force/torque blocks.

In its simplest form, the voice coil is used as a ***force generator***, where velocity and position are not critical considerations. In this servo mode, an operational amplifier is used to adjust the current level applied to an actuator, based on the signal generated from some feedback element That senses force either directly or indirectly. Figure 3 illustrates the force mode block diagram.

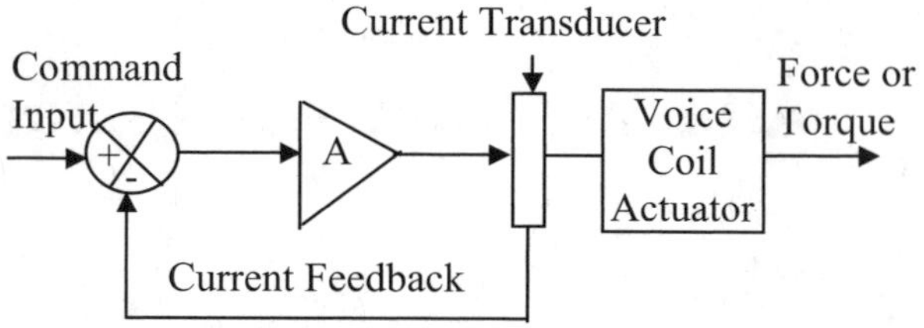

Figure 3. Basic Control Loop

In the ***position control*** mode, feedback elements are added to the system to sense velocity and position.

Consider, for example, a point-to-point move that is accomplished with a trapezoidal velocity profile. This means that the coil will be accelerated during the first one-third of the move profile, run at constant speed during the second third, and decelerated during the last one-third of the move profile, coming to rest at a specific location. In this case, the system must measure and control velocity and position throughout the move profile. This may be accomplished with a feedback sensor system that provides velocity and shaft position information. Two different sensor technologies, potentiometric and capacitive, have been chosen for this application. They both provide position **plus** velocity feedback information and are described in detail in following paragraphs. Figure 4 illustrates the velocity/position servo mode block diagram.

THE POTENTIOMETRIC SENSOR

A potentiometric sensor consists of a resistor which is used as a potential divider. The resistor has a DC voltage applied across the end terminals and a ratiometric measurement is obtained with a sliding contact that "taps" the voltage at any intermediate point across the length of the resistor. With this technique, the ohmic value of the resistor is not important. Provided that the resistance varies linearly from one end to the other, the output voltage is simply proportional to the ratio of the distances of the contact position from one end and the overall resistor length. For the application described herein, a conductive plastic (CP) resistive paste was silk-screen printed onto a polyamide substrate and temperature cured to provide the resistive element for the sensor. The performance and durability specifications for the sensor generated several conflicting requirements. For example, the sensor must have long life, produce an output with accuracy/linearity to within ± 1% of true position, have frictional torque below 0.6 ozf.ins. (4.2 mN.m), survive 100 million operating cycles and have very low electrical noise. Some specific design conflicts are:

- Low electrical noise requires high contact force.
- Long life requires low contact force.
- Low torque requires low contact force.

Additionally, the cyclical profile of the motion required for the scanning radar application has a triangular wave-

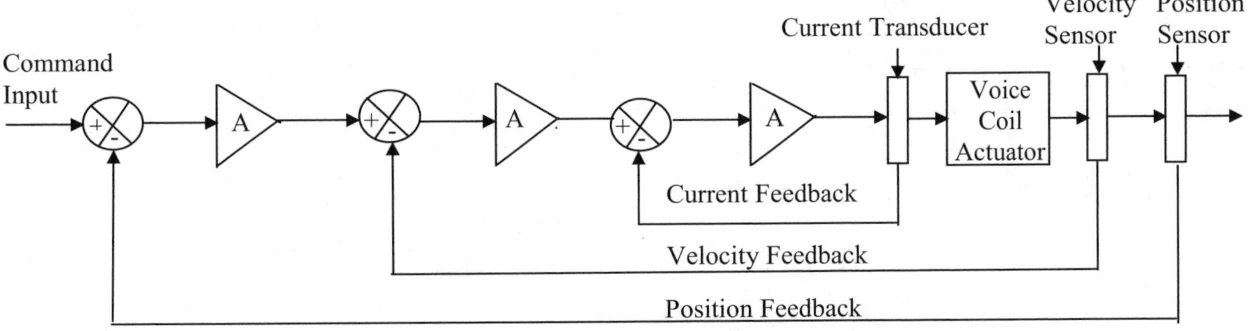

Figure 4. Velocity and Position Control Loop

form which generates very high acceleration and deceleration forces at the travel endpoints. These high forces tend to "dig" the contacts into the conductive plastic resistor at the 2 extreme limits of travel which can cause localized wear regions and progressively increasing noise spikes. The final configuration for the sensor is shown in Figure 5. The use of gold alloy contacts, tightly controlled contact height (to set contact force) and a specially formulated resistive ink which provides low-noise and long life, were used to develop a sensor which meets the performance requirements.

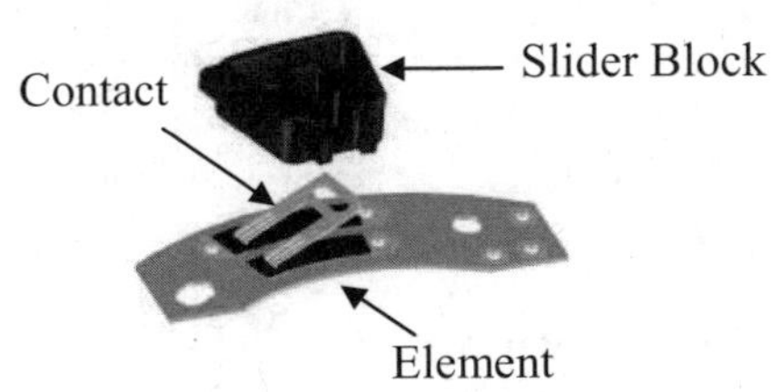

Figure 5. Potentiometric Sensor Components

A second generation sensor which has much longer life and close to zero actuation torque, has been developed using capacitive sensing technique. This new sensor will be used as an alternative where longevity and/or actuation torque limitations cannot be readily met by the potentiometric technology.

THE CAPACITIVE SENSOR

Two identical metal plates of area (a) that are arranged in a parallel configuration with respect to each other, separated by a distance (d) and filled with a dielectric media (with a dielectric constant (e)) between them, forms a capacitor as shown in Figure 6. The value of the capacitance C in such an arrangement is given by the equation:

$$C = K \cdot e \cdot \frac{a}{d} \text{ (farad)} \qquad (2)$$

where K is a constant, e is the dielectric constant which depends on dielectric properties of the medium between the two plates, a is the common (overlapping) area of the two plates, and d is the gap width between the two plates.

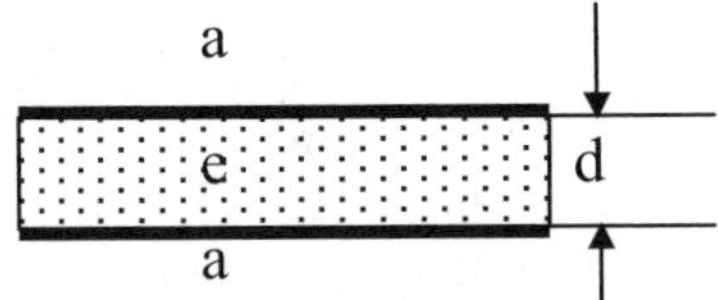

Figure 6. Basic Capacitor

When the two parallel plates (of area a) are separated by a fixed distance, with a fixed dielectric media, a fixed value capacitor is formed. A change in any one of these three parameters may be used in the sensing process [2]. As an example, when either the distance d or dielectric constant e between the plates is varied, a variable capacitor is formed. However, it is easier to move a piece of dielectric material in-and-out between the plates than to change the separation of the plates.

A displacement sensor can be constructed by sliding a piece of dielectric material such as Teflon with a dielectric constant of 4, in-and-out of the parallel plates as shown in Figure 7. However, this design approach is not suitable for real life applications due to environmental effects such as humidity. The dielectric constant of air is equal to 1 in dry conditions, however, when the humidity increases, the media will no longer be pure air but a mixture of air and water molecules which will have a dielectric constant greater than 1. This will result in significant displacement errors.

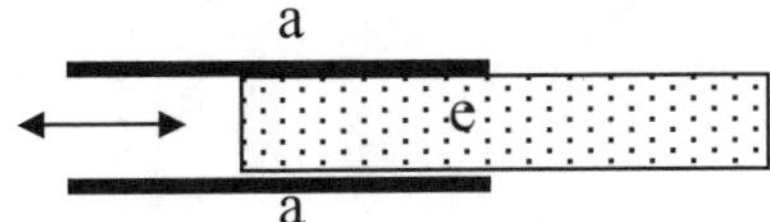

Figure 7. Variable Capacitor

In order to overcome this problem, a ratiometric capacitive sensor has been developed as shown in Figure 8. Two identical plates A and B are arranged side-by-side and in parallel to plate C which has the same width as that of A and B and twice the length of A or B, to form the capacitors C1 and C2. The length of the dielectric material D is a little larger than the length of A or B.

When D is completely between A and C, the value of C1 is maximum, and C2 is minimum. As soon as D starts sliding out of A and into B, the capacitance of C1

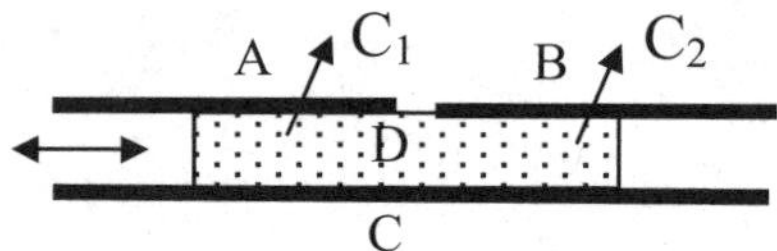

Figure 8. Ratiometric Capacitive Sensor

decreases and C2 increases. When D is completely between B and C, the value of C1 is minimum and C2 is maximum. The characteristic of this construction can be defined by the ratiometric formula of C2/C1. A simple bridge circuit for the capacitive-type sensor is shown on Figure 9.

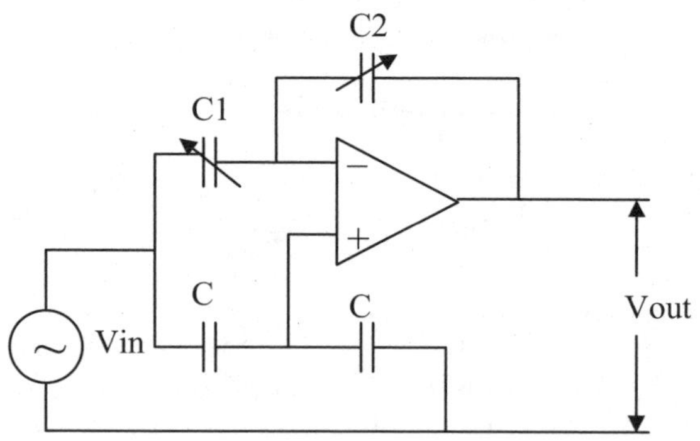

Figure 9. Signal Conditioning Circuit for Capacitive Sensor

The output is defined by the equation,

$$Vout = \tfrac{1}{2}(1 - C2/C1)Vin \qquad (3)$$

when C1 = C2, Vout = 0

Although the circuit above is adequate and provides an output that would be proportional to the changes of C1 and C2, with the current advances in Application Specific Integrated Cirucuit (ASIC) technology, a typical off-the-shelf capacitive sensor driver as shown in Figure 10 is readily available and provides an ideal signal conditioning circuit.

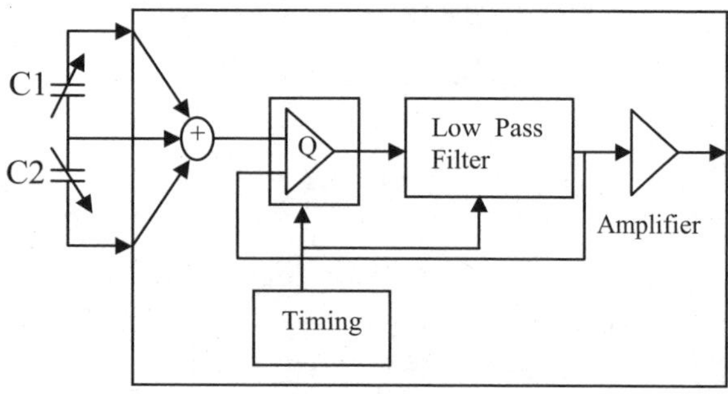

Figure 10. Typical ASIC Capacitive Sensor Signal Conditioning Circuit

The output characteristic of this signal conditioning circuit is:

$$Vout = Gain \cdot [(C1-C2)/(C1+C2)] \cdot Vin \qquad (4)$$

Since the sensor is based on a ratiometric arrangement, environmental effects such as humidity, temperature, etc. will not have a significant effect on the accuracy due to the fact that the value of C1 and C2 will track (increase and decrease proportionally) each other.

Linear Capacitive Sensor

A linear displacement sensor can be constructed in accordance with Figure 8. Two identical copper plates (A and B) and a common copper plate (C) are fabricated on a G-10 material with the typical printed circuit board (PCB) processing. A Delrin slider (D) is machined out from a Delrin block. The mechanical layout of the device is shown in Figure 11.

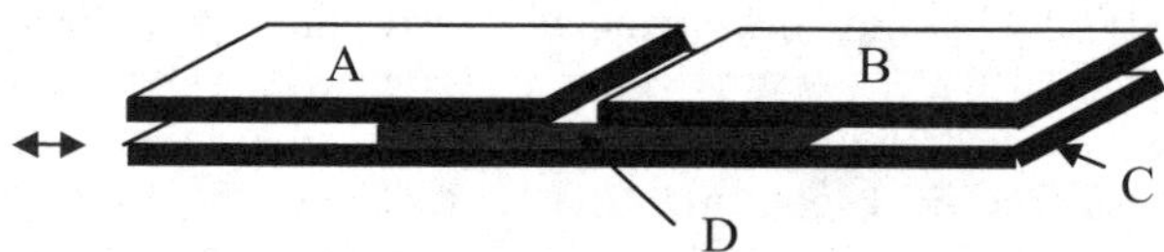

Figure 11. Linear Capacitive Sensor

In order to generate a decent value (easily processable) of the capacitance for the signal conditioning circuit, a high dielectric material such as Delrin or Polyvinylidene Flouride is used for the slider and a minimum spacing (d) between the plates is selected according to equation 2. A typical of 0.050″ to 0.060″ spacing is an optimum number for the manufacture.

Rotary Capacitive Sensor

A rotary capacitive sensor has the same basic structure of the linear sensor. Instead of rectangular plates, a circular design is applied to the rotary unit as shown in Figure 12.

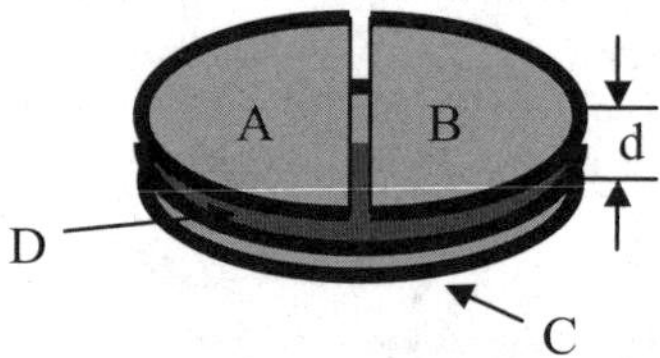

Figure 12. 180º Rotary Capacitive Sensor

Since the rotor (slider) can only cover a maximum angle of 180 degrees (half of a full circle), the output of this kind of sensor will repeat itself every 180 degrees. However, for smaller angular displacements, a narrow angle sensor can be achieved easily by reducing the angle of the plates as shown in Figure 13.

Figure 13. Narrow Angle Capacitive Sensor

THE SMART ROTARY ACTUATOR

There is yet a level of integration higher than a dual velocity/position sensing system: a velocity/position sensing system with the feedback sensor (potentiometric or capacitive) imbedded in the voice coil actuator assembly. The system consists of a rotary voice coil actuator with a standard bottom magnet/field plate assembly, a special top magnet/field plate assembly, and a cover, containing the resistive elements of the potentiometer (or capacitive plates for the non-contacting sensor) that snaps onto the assembled top and bottom parts. The sliding contact assembly for the potentiometric sensor (or the moving plate for the variable capacitor) are attached to the rotary arm of the actuator. There are two leads for power, and two leads for the sensor feedback signal, in one integrated package. Figure 14 shows the smart rotary actuator with an integral sensor, while table 1 provides the major performance specifications.

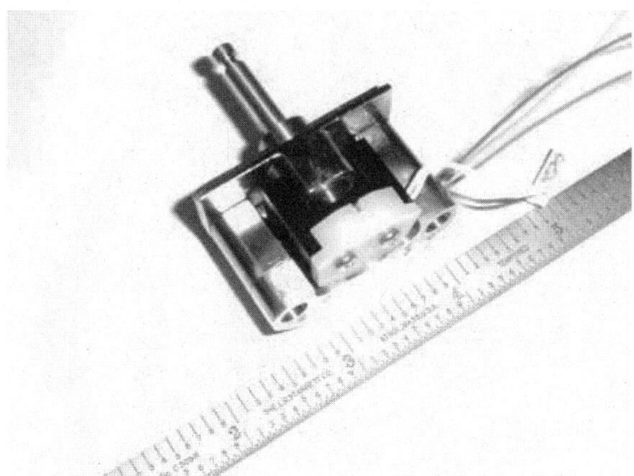

Figure 14. Smart Rotary Actuator with an Integral Position Sensor

Table 1. Sensor Performance Specifications

Parameter	Requirement
Peak Torque, T_p	8 oz. in.
Continuous Torque, T_c	± 3 oz. in.
Frequency	5 Hz
Stroke	± 7.5° Arc
Frictional Torque (Sensor)	4.2 mN.m (max)
Durability	100 Million cycles
Operating Temp. Range	-40 to +85°C
Maximum Coil Temp.	155°C
Electrical Noise	20 mV RMS (Max)
Linearity Tolerance	± 2%

Figure 15 shows the test equipment used to check the sensor's linearity. The sensor is placed in the motorized test fixture and connected to a regulated voltage supply. During the test, the computer controls the rotation of the sensor assembly over the full 15 degree range. The computer also monitors the output signal and compares the sensor output with rotational angle. From these data, the deviation from true linearity is computed and displayed on the computer screen together with the upper and lower allowable tolerance limits.

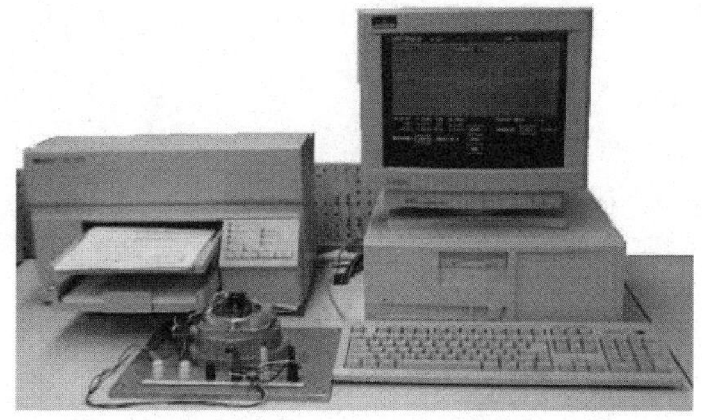

Figure 15. Linearity Tester

Figures 16 (a) – (d) show the results of the linearity characteristics for four different actuators with built-in capacitive sensors, at 25° C. While the ACC application required a ± 2% linearity error, the actuators tested, demonstrated ±0.5% linearity error at room temperature. Figure 17 shows the linearity characteristics of the acutator over temperature.

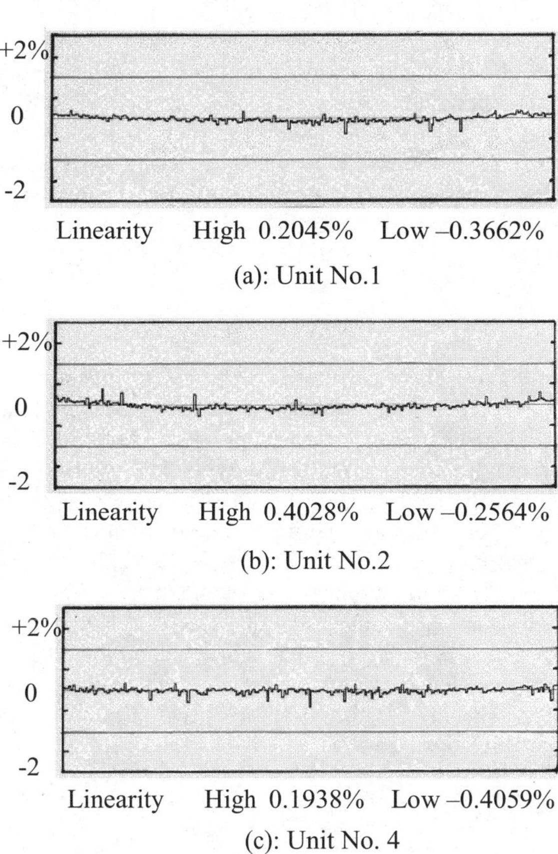

Linearity High 0.2045% Low –0.3662%

(a): Unit No.1

Linearity High 0.4028% Low –0.2564%

(b): Unit No.2

Linearity High 0.1938% Low –0.4059%

(c): Unit No. 4

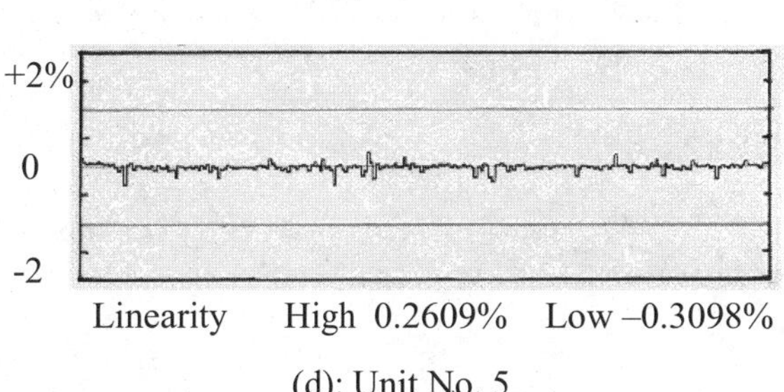

Linearity High 0.2609% Low –0.3098%

(d): Unit No. 5

Figure 16. Linearity Characteristics at 25°C

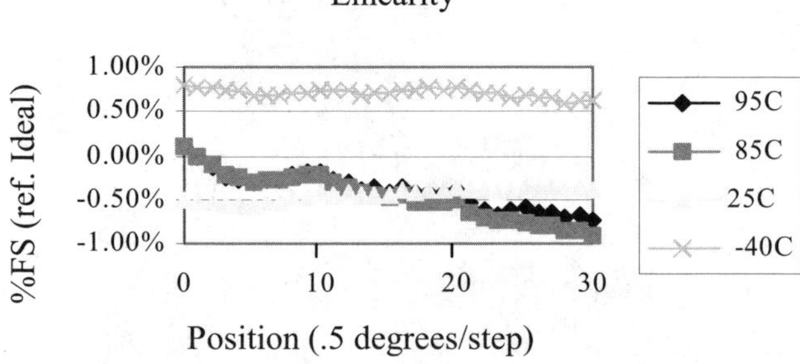

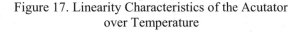

Figure 17. Linearity Characteristics of the Acutator over Temperature

FUTURE WORK

Further work is continuing in the development of the non contacting sensor which will provide significant improvements in total actuator life and which is necessary for high frequencies and longer stroke applications than those systems described in this paper.

A third non-contacting sensor option is also being studied. The Non-contacting Angular Position Sensor (NCAPS) as fully described in references [3, 4, 5] has several advantageous features. It is highly immune to EMI/RFI interference, has very wide manufacturing tolerances and is will provide a good low cost alternative to the capacitive sensor

CONCLUSION

The Adaptive Cruise Control (ACC) system that uses the smart rotary actuator required an actuator that could operate over a +/- 7.5 degree sector angle, at a scan mode of 5 Hz. A bulkier, heavier, noisy brush-type DC motor-based system was replaced with a new, smart actuator system that offers various desirable features. These include multiple target tracking (up to 15 objects); a mechanically scanned sensor for detection of small vehicles in congested traffic; a path algorithm that maintains target vehicles through curves and distinguishes between target vehicles and other objects; and a system that performs in fog and rain, automatically maintains spacing at high speeds, and resumes to set speeds when lanes clear.

ACKNOWLEDGEMENT

The authors wish to thank Linet Aghassi for her help in the preparation of this manuscript.

REFERENCES

[1] Kimco Magnetics Division, a BEI Technologies, Company, "Voice Coil Actuators, An Applications Guide", 1995.

[2] Silva, C. de, "Sensor/Transducer Technology, Part 9, Capacitive and Piezoelectric Sensors, Measurement and Control", Issue 202, pp.49-63., October 2000.

[3] Madni, A. M., Vuong, J. B., Hansen, R. K. & Wan, L. A., "A Non Contact Angular Position Sensor (NCAPS) for Motion Control Applications", Proceedings, UKACC International Conference on Control 2000, paper 34, September 2000.

[4] Madni, A. M., Vuong, J. B., Wells, R. F., "The Next Generation Position Sensing Technology, Part 1: Theory and Design", Sensors, The Journal of Applied Sensing Technology, Vol. 18, No. 3. pp. 42-55, March 2001.

[5] Madni, A. M., Vuong, J.B., Wells, R. F., "The Next Generation Position Sensing Technology, Part 2: Differential Displacement and Linear Capabilities", Sensors, The Journal of Applied Sensing Technology, Vol. 18, No. 4. pp. 61-65, April 2001.

2002-01-1601

Development of a Haptic Braking System as an ACC Vehicle FCW Measure

Bryan Riley, George Kuo, Todd Nethercutt, Kevin Shipp and Matthew Smith
Delphi Automotive Systems

ABSTRACT

This work examines the development and implementation of a pulsing brake control system as part of a Forward Collision Warning (FCW) System for an Adaptive Cruise Control (ACC) prototype vehicle. The brake pulse is a likely candidate to be employed with visual and auditory cues in the event of an imminent collision alert level when the driver is not in ACC mode.

INTRODUCTION

ACC has been developed over the past several years and has recently been introduced in both the USA and European markets. The ACC function automatically maintains a safe distance and level of speed between the host vehicle and preceding vehicles. Several studies, including the work of the Crash Avoidance Metrics Partnership (CAMP) and the ongoing Automotive Collision Avoidance System / Field Operational Test (ACAS/FOT) program have investigated the appropriateness of the vehicle-alerting-driver interface for FCW systems. Additionally, the integration of ACC and sophisticated Forward Collision Warning (FCW) Systems include defining the minimum requirements and implementation of feedback components to drivers to ensure consistency in the operating characteristics of ACC Systems. These feedback components may consist of any combination of visual, audio, and haptic stimuli as a means of immediately notifying the driver of a potential collision into the rear end of any preceding car. The haptic sensory system can be defined as the system through which an individual can sense the world adjacent to his body.

To maximize the probability that a warning will be correctly understood, display designers use redundant coding across multiple sensory modalities. Redundancy provides an important advantage to the display because it insures that there is a greater chance that factors degrading one modality will not degrade another. The stimulus-response compatibility design axiom proposes that a display is more effective when the stimulus and intended response are compatible, and suggests that a series of brake pulses may offer a promising solution for alerting drivers of a potential collision with the lead vehicle.

Several studies have investigated the potential of using a brake pulse as a haptic stimulus in the context of ACC and FCW programs (e.g., Intelligent Cruise Control/ Field Operational Test ICC/FOT, ACAS FOT, and the CAMP program) and the results show some promise. In the ICC FOT and ACAS FOT programs, participants described the deceleration stimulus as an effective and appropriate cue. The CAMP study revealed that the brake pulse provided an advantage to the FCW system by slowing the vehicle during the period before the driver could react. Although there has been little research yet that is directly focused on the effectiveness of haptic braking, it appears to be a promising candidate for the future.

It is likely that a significant percentage of rear-end crashes are preventable by the use of FCW systems. Results from this prototyped haptic brake control study is based on triangular pulses driving brake pressure control at the corner. Specifically, we investigate a brake pulse oscillating between predefined levels, the relationship providing an early alert to the driver and introducing limited deceleration of the vehicle prior to the drivers input.

TECHNOLOGY FOR EFFECTIVE AUTOMOTIVE COLLISION WARNING

As part of the CAMP project, a brake modulation system was modified and installed in a collision warning prototype vehicle. This brake subsystem was capable of applying up to 0.30g vehicle deceleration for speeds up to 90kph on hi-mu roads. The application was on a front wheel drive vehicle, and brake pressure was applied to the front axle only. The conventional base brake system and ABS available on the vehicle remained unaffected during driver initiated braking. The haptic braking function and the add-on brake modulation are both overridden by intervention of the brake or throttle. The ABS and traction control systems will override the alerting operation when the brake pulse is activated. This work provided insight relative to defining a pulse brake profile as well as what drivers may perceive as acceptable. The brake pulse intensity and duration varied from driver to driver. A pulse of approximately 0.2 g decel for 600ms was shown to be clearly noticeable while not shifting the driver out of their driving positions.

PROTOTYPE HAPTIC BRAKE VEHICLE

Description of Haptic Test Vehicle

The vehicle used for Haptic Braking development and testing was a 2000 Buick LeSabre. This vehicle was equipped with Delphi Brake Controls version 7.2, four-wheel disc brakes, and a 3.8L V6 engine.

The DBC 7.2 brake system for this vehicle has capabilities for antilock braking, traction control, vehicle stability enhancement (VSE), tire inflation monitoring (TIM), adaptive cruise control autobraking and haptic brake application. Figure 1.0 indicates the Electronic Control Unit (ECU) that incorporates the algorithm and the Brake Pressure Modulator Valve (BPMV).

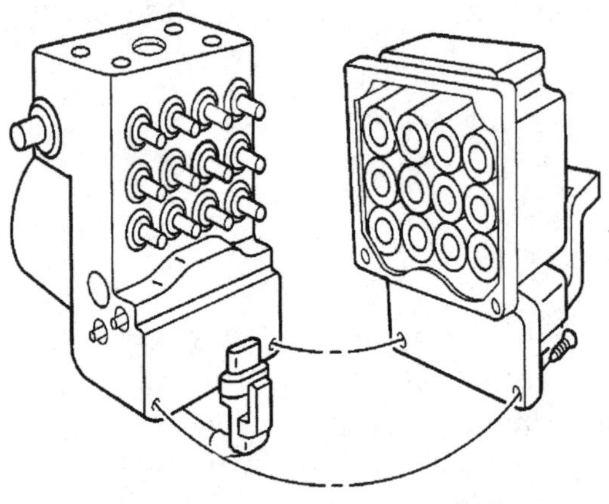

Figure 1.0 Electronic Control Unit / 12 Valve Brake Pressure Modulator Valve

This unit has the capability to modulate hydraulic line pressure independently to all four wheels in order to maintain vehicle control during ABS.

It also has the ability to build pressure without driver brake input in the event of a Traction Control situation or for VSE. This ability to build pressure is what enables haptic braking to function. The modulator creates pressure via the pump and the motor and then applies that pressure in a set schedule of pulses to the wheels. These pulses can be customized with respect to frequency, amplitude, as well as duration.

Software Interface and Operation

The prototype development vehicle was equipped with a development electronic controller which allows ease of software changing, calibration and vehicle data logging. The haptic braking control software was then able to be loaded into the brake controller memory and be re-flashed with algorithm refining or calibration change. To activate the haptic braking events, a vehicle serial interface (VSI) box was used to allow communication with the brake controller from a laptop computer through the assembly line data link (ALDL) connector under the driver's sidekick panel. Table 1.0 indicates a range of the predefined profiles for study. The haptic brake control parameters are frequency, amplitude, and duration. The experimenter may select and download to the ECU any combination of profiles for evaluation.

Table 1.0 Haptic Brake Input Profiles

Message ID	Frequency (Hz)	P-P Amplitude (g)	Duration (sec.)
H03A01D3, E3, F3, G3	3	0.1, 0.2, 0.3, 0.35	2, 4, 6, 8
H03A01D5, E5, F5, G5	5	0.1, 0.2, 0.3, 0.35	2, 4, 6, 8
H03A01D8, E8, F8, G8	8	0.1, 0.2, 0.3, 0.35	2, 4, 6, 8
H03A01D12, E12, F12, G12	12	0.1, 0.2, 0.3, 0.35	2, 4, 6, 8

Tests and Road Setup

A variety of tests and evaluations were performed to check the haptic braking functions. Due to the sensitive nature of being able to feel the brake pulses, a flat and straight road surface was selected to minimize road/driver inputs. This allowed the operators to focus on brake pulse/driver inputs. The wide variety of brake pulse schedules creates many different sensations, from a large heavy pulse to many small frequent pulses. The resulting feel ranged from small chatterbumps (or slightly rough pavement) to large rumblestrips. The next step in the development testing was to check the driver's response relative to the combined effect of road surface and braking pulse, which represent the real-world traffic input. These tests were conducted without the forward radar-based sensor that is capable of detecting and tracking vehicular traffic, and the forward vision –based sensor which detects and tracks lanes.

HAPTIC BRAKING CONTROL AND IMPLEMENTATION

The goal of the haptic braking alert feature is to provide a jerk rate and decel level of autobraking that will be sufficient to cause a 95th percentile driver to respond in such time that corrective action can be taken. A handshake architecture is established where the brake controller receives the discrete command from the ACC controller regarding haptic brake enable/disable and the desired braking profile. The Electronic Control Unit (ECU) of the ABS provides a constant 2000 Hz PWM signal to drive the DBC7.2 VIVs (Variable Isolation Valves) with variable duty cycles to regulate wheel pressures for closed-loop vehicle decel tracking control. The determination of the variable duty cycles is by the total decel tracking error of PID controller based on filtered vehicle decel feedback. Figure 2.0 shows the typical patterns of the testing control input to VIV and the vehicle response.

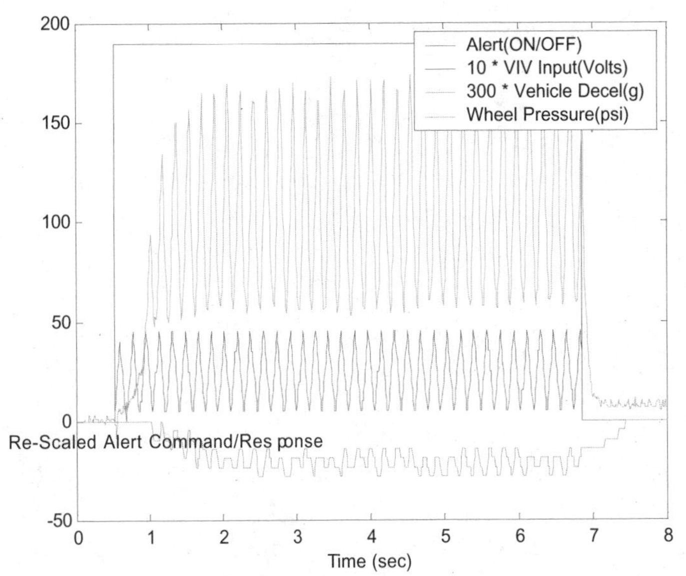

Figure 2.0 Alert Testing Command and Vehicle Response

Figure 3.0 depicts a block diagram of the control scheme and Figure 4.0 displays the Control Algorithm Simulation Model.

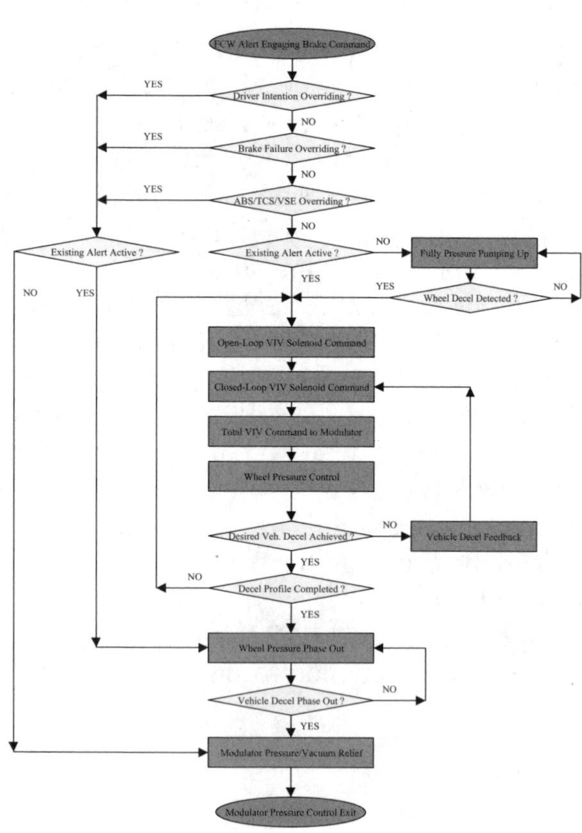

Figure 3.0 Block Diagram of Haptic Braking Control

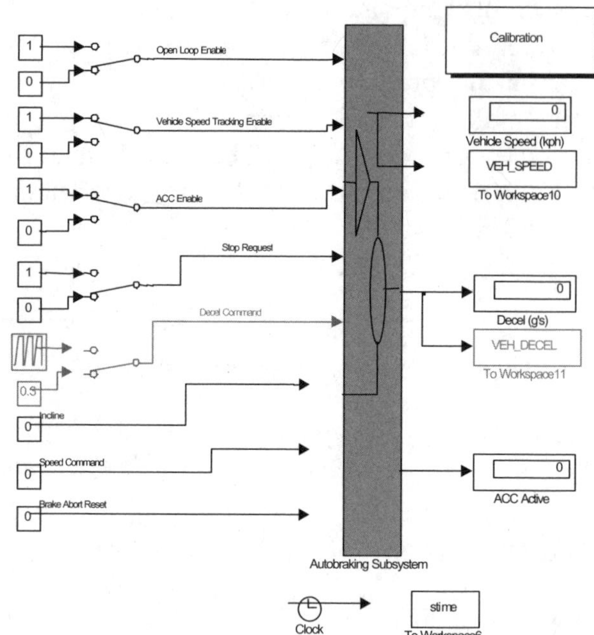

Figure 4.0 Control Algorithm Simulation Model

The control design criteria is targeted for 0.32g/sec decel jerk rate damped up and down by a linear, stepped, or sinusoidal input. A smooth transition and low resistance to the driver taking over the brake pedal is pivotal to this implementation. As part of the haptic braking process, the driver should not perceive any noise from the actuator.

A constant-interval Haptic Braking Pulse command will interrupt the closed-loop control, which tracks the requested decel commands from the ACC Controller. This periodical VIV input command will create the discrete decel for the Alert function. Due to the characteristic of hydraulic compliance, alternatively increasing/decreasing decel jerks are not recommended and the haptic braking scheme does not apply in the initial pressure pump-up session.

Driver input has priority over the decel control during the ACC Autobraking, i.e., the accelerator or brake pedal input will override the ACC Autobraking. A double-lock assurance of the driver intention is adopted based on powertrain brake switch, master cylinder pressure, PCM throttle position, and predicted engine torque.

The Haptic Braking Pulse Decel Alert exits when driver intervention is detected. However, when the driver intervenes with the brake pedal, auto braking will not cease instantly. A delay is used to prevent loss of decel and allows for smooth transition from autobraking to manual braking. Moding with individual driving patterns, smooth road surfaces and rough road surfaces was considered. Active Stability Enhancement or detection of a Split-Coefficient road surface will override the Haptic Brake Alert while the ACC Autobraking is still active. ACC Moding with ABS, DRP, and VSE systems will be included in this Pulse-Decel based ACC/FCW. The emergency braking systems (ABS/VSE) have higher priorities than Pulse Decel

Alert at any time during the ACC Autobraking. The haptic braking alert feature can be enabled/disabled by a button located on the instrument panel. Subjective measures such as overall impression, effectiveness and potential for annoyance, were recorded while participants drove the vehicle and experienced the differing levels of brake pulses.

EVALUATION AND SUMMARY

The Haptic Brake Control test vehicle was driven and evaluated by seven engineers. The primary objective was to subjectively evaluate the pulse-braking feel on the vehicle as an important component of the Driver Vehicle Interface (DVI). Different sets of frequency, amplitude, and duration of the pulse were selected as inputs to the ECU. Five out of seven participants indicated an overall favorable impression, whereas the two remaining participants did not specify whether their overall impression was favorable or unfavorable. All seven indicated that the alert was effective and that the noise and vibration were not overly annoying. Four participants concluded that 5Hz selection provided the best feel and feedback. Three participants indicated that the higher frequencies felt similar to rumble strips. Most participants appeared to favor the 0.2 g pulse, however, two participants indicated that a 0.1 g pulse would be sufficient to capture the driver's attention. The haptic brake prototype vehicle was also observed during a test-braking scenario by participants in a trailing vehicle. The observable performance of the haptic test vehicle was considered normal. There were no perceptible jerks or dives observed during test rides with any of the selected test profiles in Table 1.0.

The vehicle testing did not lead to a determination of the optimal frequency, amplitude, and duration for the brake pulse. All individuals evaluating the system agreed that the brake pulse was an effective way of providing an alert however; the vehicle testing matrix and the evaluation criteria of alert effect must be improved. Haptic braking is still a premature candidate and much research is still required to investigate the safety implications, however, the data that has been collected thus far indicates that haptic braking may be an effective and appropriate stimulus to accompany the visual and auditory stimuli for an FCW warning.

CONTACT INFORMATION

H. Bryan Riley, Ph.D.
Delphi Automotive Systems
M/S 484-400-208
5725 Delphi Dr.
Troy, Michigan 48098
Phone: 248 813-2568 Email: bryan.riley@delphiauto.com

C. George Kuo
Delphi Energy and Chassis System
M/S 483-3DB-210
Technical Center Brighton
12501 E. Grand River
Brighton, Michigan 48116

Todd Nethercutt
Delphi Energy and Chassis Systems
M/S 483-3DB-210
Technical Center Brighton
12501 E. Grand River
Brighton, Michigan 48116

Kevin Shipp
Delphi Energy and Chassis Systems
M/S 483-3DB-210
Technical Center Brighton
12501 E. Grand River
Brighton, Michigan 48116

Matthew R. Smith
Delphi Delco Electronics Systems
World Headquarters
M/S E110
P.O Box 9005
Kokomo, Indiana 46904

ACKNOWLEDGEMENTS

We wish to thank Jim DeBrincat for supporting the vehicle build and checkout.

REFERENCES

1. Fancher, Z. Bareket, and R. Ervin, "Human-Centered Design of an ACC –With-Braking and Forward –Crash Warning Systems", P. Proceedings of AVEC 2000 5th Int'l Symposium on Advanced Vehicle Control August 2000.

2. McLaughlin, S.: Measurement of Driver Preferences and Intervention Responses as Influenced by Adaptive Cruise Control Deceleration Characteristics, Thesis, Virginia Polytechnic Institute and State University, Blacksburg, Virginia; June 29, 1998

3. NHTSA Benefits Working Group, " Preliminary Assessment of Crash Avoidance System Benefits" NHTSA Report . Washington, DC October 1996

4. Intelligent Cruise Control Field Operational Test, Final Report. Vol. I & II DOT HS 88 849 NHTSA , May 1998

5. Barber, P.; Clarke, N.: "Advanced Collision Warning Systems," IEE Colloquium on Industrial Automation and Control: Applications in the Automotive Industry (Digest No. 1998/234). IEE, London, UK; 1998; p. 21-29.

6. B. Wang, M. Abe, and Y. Kano,"A Research and Design of Vehicle Dynamics Control Algorithm Adapted to the Aged Driver", Proceedings of AVEC 2000 5th Int'l Symposium on Advanced Vehicle Control August 2000.

7. B. Siruru, "Do Collision Warning Systems Reduce Accidents", UTC, Sept./Oct. 1998.

8. Smith, M. "Automotive Collision Avoidance System Field Operational Test: Warning Cue Implementation Summary Report." DTN22-99-H-07019 NHTSA, June, 2001.

9. Kiefer, R., Leblanc, D., Palmer, M., Salinger, J., Deering, R., and Shulman, M. (1999, May). "Forward collision warning systems final report: Definition and validation of functional definitions and evaluation procedures for collision warning/avoidance systems" (Cooperative Agreement No. DTNH22-95-R-07301). Farmington Hills, MI: Collision Avoidance Metrics Program.

10. Wickens, C.D., Gordon, S.E., & Liu, Y. "An Introduction to Human Factors Engineering", Longman: New York, 1998.

11. Fancher, P., et. al., "Intelligent Cruise Control Field Operational Test (Final Report), NHTSA, Report Number DOT HS 808 849, May 1998.

DEFINITIONS, ACRONYMS, ABBREVIATIONS

ABS	Anti-lock Brake System
ACC	Adaptive Cruise Control
ACAS/FOT	Adaptive Cruise Control System / Field Operational Test
ALDL	Assembly Line Data Link
DBC	Delphi Brake Control
BPMV	Brake Pressure Modulator Valve
DRP	Dynamic Rear Proportioning
DVI	Driver Vehicle Interface
CAMP	Crash Avoidance Metrics Partnership
ECU	Electronic Control Unit
FCW	Forward Collision Warning
ICC	Intelligent Cruise Control
PCM	Powertrain Control Module
PWM	Pulse Width Modulation
TCS	Traction Control System
VIV	Variable Isolation Valve
VSE	Vehicle Stability Enhancement
VSI	Vehicle Serial Interface

2001-01-3245

From Adaptive Cruise Control to Active Safety Systems

Francisco Sánchez, Marc Seguer and Antoni Freixa
SEAT, S.A.

Peter Andreas, Klaus Sochaski and Raimond Holze
Volkswagen AG

ABSTRACT

Once the adaptive cruise control systems are already in the market in Japan and Europe, the evolution of these comfort systems is logically going towards implementing new additional functions and safety strategies in order to detect and actuate in case of emergency. This transition has to be done in clear and precise steps to assure an easy adaptation to each improvement.

Driver assistance systems will play a major role in the future to minimise the risk and consequences of accidents and to increase the driving comfort level. The impact of such systems on traffic and society is briefly commented.

This paper discusses the need of new driver assistance systems and a possible roadmap for them. After a short introduction of present Adaptive Cruise Control (ACC), and based on them, next possible functions are described.

Afterwards the possible technical implementation of this new advanced functions is presented, discussing the different dangerous or ambiguous scenarios against the vehicle could be faced. The necessary inputs to recognise the situations unequivocally are identified in order to implement a satisfactory actuation of the vehicle. According to this requirements, the characteristics demanded to the system are extracted and a possible architecture is proposed.

First tests carried out with a research prototype prepared by SEAT and the VW-Group Electronic Research Department are also reported.

Finally, in the summary section, the main conclusions are highlighted.

INTRODUCTION

As far as automotive traffic is concerned, accidents, fluency and environmental damage are the main problems that have to be solved. Concerning this, it is important to remark that more than 50.000 people die every year in the EC due to traffic accidents[1]. In the case of USA, figures are quite similar: 40,000 deaths, more than 3 million injuries, and over $150 billion in economic losses [2] .

Figure 1 shows the evolution of fatalities in Spain due to traffic accidents[3]. Although there has been a big improvement regarding the number of fatalities per million vehicles, there is still a big effort to do in order to improve safety.

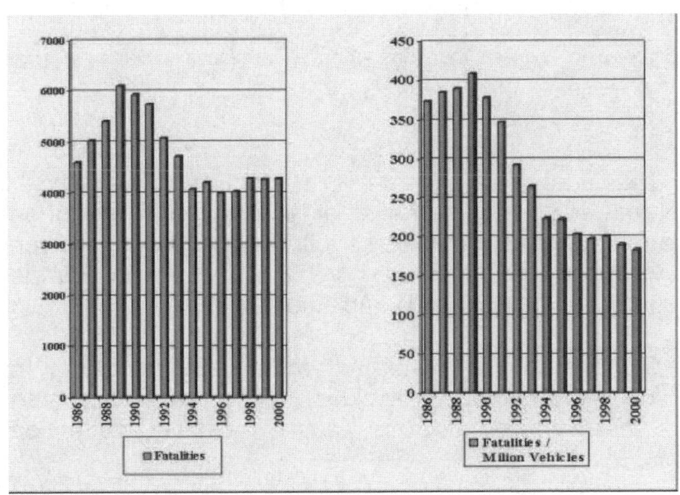

Fig.1 – Number of fatalities in Spain due to traffic accidents

The important advances in electronics, software processing and telecommunications permit the deployment of new systems in the automotive field that could help to overcome the above mentioned problems.

Driver assistant systems are emerging as a solution to the driver to release stress, to improve the vehicle's control and so to reduce the number of accidents and fatalities. Moreover, some of these systems can help to improve the traffic flow as well.

The new main driver assistance systems which are in a development or research step are summarised in the figure 2.

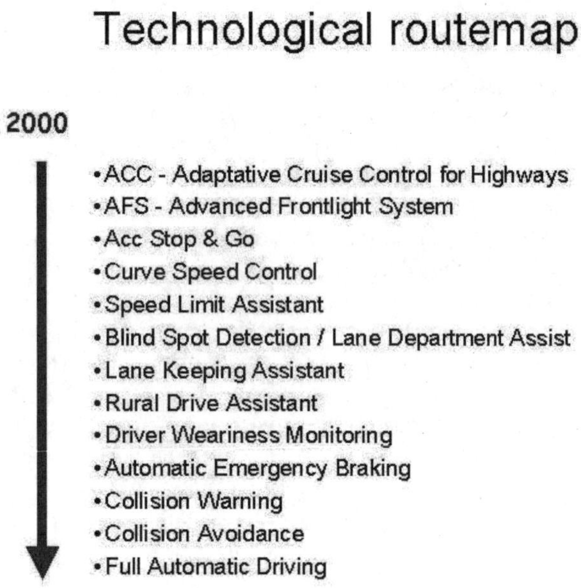

Technological routemap

2000

- ACC - Adaptative Cruise Control for Highways
- AFS - Advanced Frontlight System
- Acc Stop & Go
- Curve Speed Control
- Speed Limit Assistant
- Blind Spot Detection / Lane Department Assist
- Lane Keeping Assistant
- Rural Drive Assistant
- Driver Weariness Monitoring
- Automatic Emergency Braking
- Collision Warning
- Collision Avoidance
- Full Automatic Driving

Fig.2 – Technological routemap for driver assistance systems

Nowadays, first generation of ACC systems has been introduced to the market as a first step towards collision avoidance. Some luxuries vehicles makers in Europe and Japan have already implemented it.

ACC is a comfort system which can also contribute to reduce the number of accidents since a significant part of rear-end collisions are caused by driver inattention and following too closely.

The ability of ACC-Systems to increase comfort, safety and traffic fluency has been extensively tested and demonstrated with different prototypes in the framework of several research projects like PROMETHEUS or DRIVE in Europe, SSVS or ASV in Japan or IVHS in USA [4] .

According to the conclusions of an acceptability study carried out by VW-Research [5], ACC reduces fatigue and therefore allows the driver to travel longer distances and to concentrate better on the whole traffic situation, reducing driving stress in heavy traffic.

In any case, concerning the new driver assistance systems a lot of improvements and advances are needed in terms of sensor and power capacity to be able to understand perfectly the environment around the car and then to take the best decisions. Also a big effort has to be done to improve the electric/electronic architecture in the car. Only in this way, it will be possible to give important steps towards new safety and collision avoidance systems.

In this paper we present a description of the improvements on driver assistant systems that could be achieved.

MAIN SECTION

1 - PRESENT ADAPTIVE CRUISE CONTROL

An ACC is a comfort system that enhances the functionality of a standard cruise control function and is suited to be used in highways. It automatically adjusts the vehicle speed in order to maintain a driver-specified adjustable distance behind a lead vehicle.

A forward-looking detection sensor (radar or laser) is used to monitor the traffic in front of the ACC-vehicle assessing the distance, angular position and relative speed to possible targets. If no obstacle is detected, the car accelerates to the desired speed as in a conventional cruise control function. In case that a vehicle is detected, a safety distance is kept actuating over the throttle or applying the brakes if necessary. The system operates under a limited speed range. Actual ACC systems on the market works between 40 and 160 km/h. A maximum braking deceleration of around $2.5m/s^2$ is usually implemented. Additionally, most of the car manufacturers provide this ACC system with an acoustic advise in case system deceleration is not able to avoid a collision.

The driver remains fully responsible of operating the car if an urgent braking is needed. The driver can also override the system at any time by applying the accelerator. Though taking the foot off the accelerator, the system will continue to control the vehicle speed. For safety reasons, the driver can turn off the system at any time by either pushing the ACC-switch off or by applying the brake.

Figure 3 shows the overall ACC system architecture.

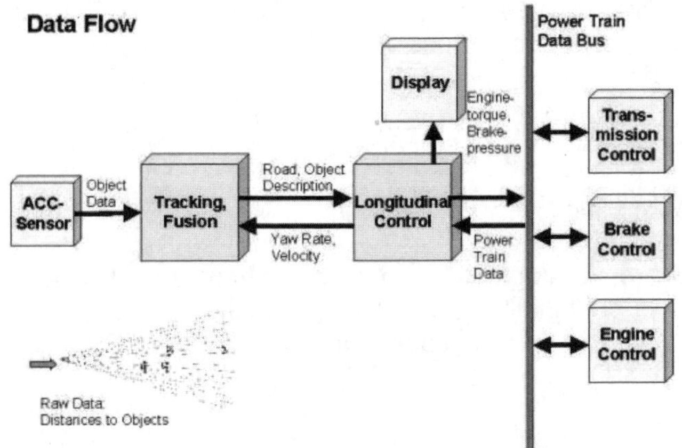

Fig.3 – Present ACC system architecture

2 - NEXT REQUIREMENTS FOR DRIVER ASSISTANCE SYSTEMS

2.1 – Additional new functions

As explained in the introduction section, a big effort has to be carried out in order to achieve the final objective of collision avoidance. In any case, taking as a basis the present ACC systems and as a first approach, several new functions and improvements could be developed.

- Stop&Go

  This function allows the driver to comfortably achieve null speed following a lead vehicle but it does not recognise any static object that suddenly could appear on its way.

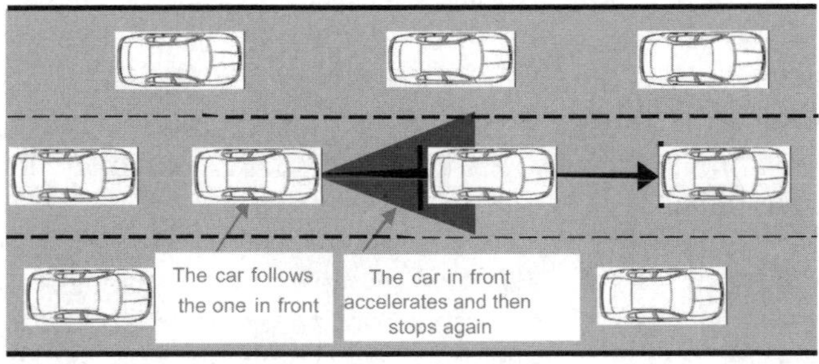

Fig.4 – Stop&Go functionality

Recognition of stationary objects and vehicles As an extension of the ACC stop&go functionality, it will be desirable to identify static objects in the vehicle trajectory at the end of a traffic jam, reacting properly to this situation.

- Curve assistant

  With the help of the digital map from the navigation system, it is possible to identify the curve before the vehicle is actually entered it. The speed can be automatically adjusted. A vision system can also improve the detection of the road course.

- Speed limit assistant

  Speed limit advises seem to be a clear way to reduce traffic accidents. Road condition sensors and image recognition sensors can give outstanding driver information. For example, a CCD or a CMOS camera, combined with an image processing system, can detect traffic signs, informing the driver and reducing the speed of the vehicle.
  In any case, final decision depends always on the driver.

- Blind spot detection /Lane change assistant

  Errors when overtaking are some of the important causes of traffic accidents. The use of short range sensors combined with some sort of long range sensor (radar, lidar or an image processing system) to monitor the rear and blind spot of the vehicle could provide a warning in the event that the driver overlooks a potential danger while changing lines.

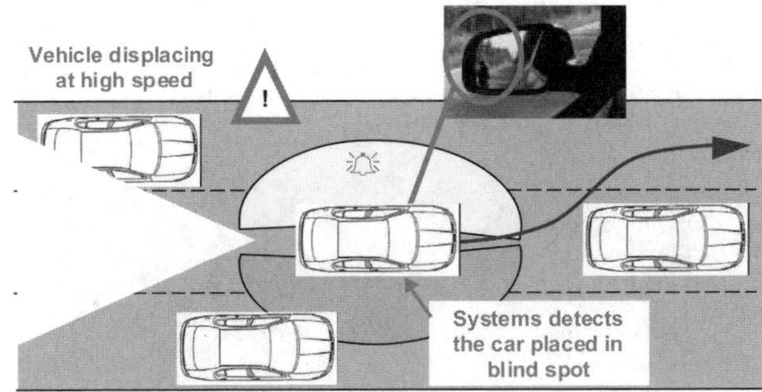

Fig.5 – Blind spot detection / lane change assistant

- Lane keeping assistant

Reliable detection of lane borders can assist and support the driver with lane keeping. Sensing and controlling of the lateral vehicle position reduces the workload of the driver. The driver is allowed to concentrate more on traffic management and changing conditions. Giving a haptik feedback about the lateral vehicle position to the driver or applying a slight direction dependant force to the steering wheel makes lane keeping an easier task for the driver.

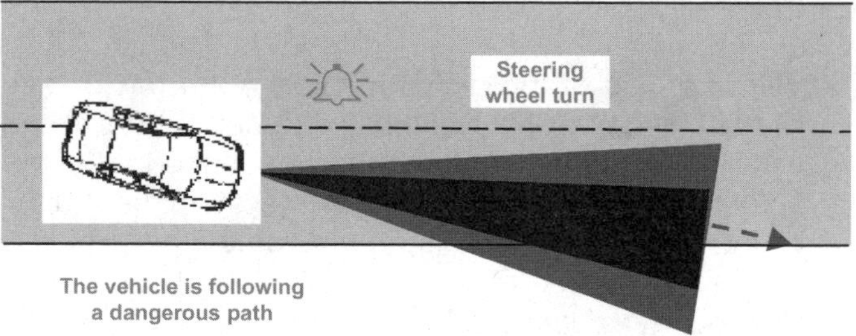
Steering
wheel turn
The vehicle is following
a dangerous path

Fig.6 – Lane keeping assistant

- Automatic emergency braking

  Research studies [6] show that in extreme situations, drivers react in many cases either too late or in a wrong way. In those cases, when a collision is not possible to avoid, the best procedure is to apply the breaks with the maximal force in order to minimize the consequences of the accident.

  To carry out properly this functionality the following aspects has to be considered:

- Sensors to detect position, contour and relative speed of possible obstacles.
- To know own vehicle dynamics
- To be sure that there is no vehicle maneuver to avoid the collision.

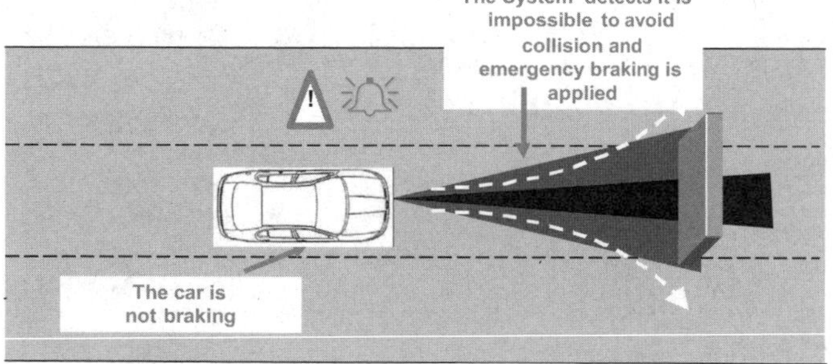
The System detects it is
impossible to avoid
collision and
emergency braking is
applied
The car is
not braking

Fig-7 – Emergency braking

2.2 – Technical implementation

Due to some system limitations, the use of present ACC systems is restricted to highways. Also ACC operates in a limited range speed (usually over 30 Km/h).

In this section, we explain how to implement some of the above explained new driver assistance functions like ACC Stop&Go, stationary object detection, curve assistant and speed limit assistant. The combination of all this functions lead us to an advanced ACC system capable to operate not only in highways but also in rural roads.

2.2.1. ACC sensor capabilities

Recognition of curve contour

As stated in figure 8, usually a curve is characterised by static objects like guard railings, pillars, trees, buildings, etc., that marks the curve contour.

The signal processing of the ACC sensor produces a simple but nevertheless representative picture of the situation, detecting the different objects with its main characteristics like position, width, relative speed, etc.

Fig.8 – Normal curve in a rural road

Then it is possible to implement a curve contour algorithm to identify the distance to the curve an the curve radius.

Figure 9 shows the situation as viewed by the sensor, in this case, a multibeam laser sensor, which beam geometry is characterised by the grey lines. The red line shows the predicted vehicle trajectory coming from the car sensors. The blue vertical lanes show the present detected objects. The blue extended line represent the curve contour. With this information, it is possible to identify the curve start point and therefore the distance between the vehicle an the curve. Taking into account also the curve radius, suitable speed can be applied to the vehicle.

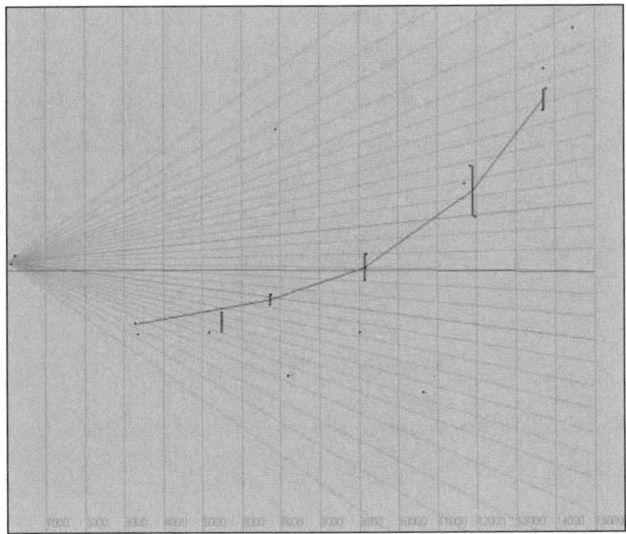

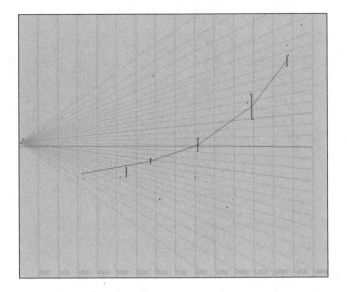

Fig.9 – Sensor view of the curve

Valuation of stationary objects concerning its relevance

An important requirement for an advanced ACC system is the ability to detect unequivocally stationary objects in the own driving path (for instance, at the end of a traffic jam).

The ability of the sensor to detect the curve contour allows the system to recognise irrelevant standing objects on the roadside.

Nevertheless, the use of external information related to the route ahead, like the navigation system information, could significantly improve the detection reliability of relevant stationary objects.

2.2.2 Improvements with the navigation system

Use of navigation system in driver assistance systems

Navigation systems are based on digital road maps and they can be used to plan a route and for guiding purposes. The data included describes the geometry of the route as well as other characteristics. A description of the probable route ahead of the vehicle can actually be calculated based on the position of the vehicle, which is determined by a satellite navigation system that uses a digital map. This "Predictive Navigation Data" can be used by the driving assistance systems as sensory data to perform functions and assist other sensory systems. Such systems are presently fully developed in Europe. The primary condition for the use of such systems is high precision digital maps.

The preparation of the data for such maps is in the process of being obtained, and will be available in the near future.

Use of predictive road data for speed assistant

Present cruise control systems have the disadvantage that they are not suitable for roads with frequent curves. Before reaching a curve that should be driven with a low velocity, the driver must reduce the pre-established cruise control speed or brake in order to ensure that the vehicle does not surpass the maximum transversal acceleration on the curve. After the curve, the speed set previously should be reactivated.

The use of the navigation system makes it possible to estimate the possible route of the driver. This is referred to as the Electronic Horizon. The geometry of the route and the curves are indicated on the digital map (see figure 10) with a set of polygons. This data can be prepared, directly or with intermediate steps that include calculations for interpolation, in a format suitable for the longitudinal regulation of the vehicle. The essential contents are the distance to the curve and the curve radius.

Other possible contents of digital maps are data related to speed limits. This kind of information could be used to warn the driver or in order to act directly to reduce the speed of the car.

Figure 11 shows a measurement register recorder when driving on the route shown in figure 10. VdriverDem is the speed set by the driver (100 Km/h). The route path includes two curves and an entrance into a city. The distance to the curve is shown by DistCurveCont and this valued decreases progressively. The curve radius is indicated by RadiusCurvePredFlash, and the resulting maximal curve speeds are shown as VmaxCurvePred. After the two curves, there is a city indicator. The distance is represented by DisToPlaceCont. The result speed is VfilKmh.

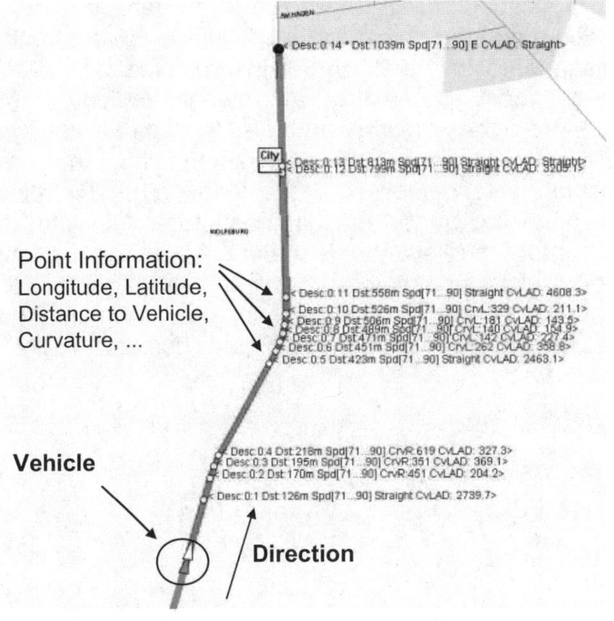

Fig.10 – Electronic Horizon

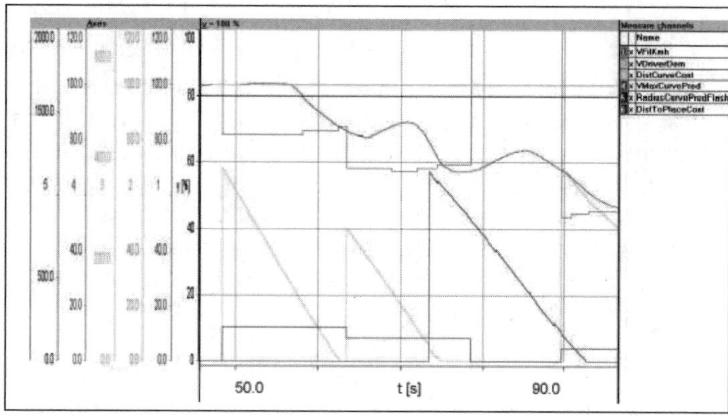

Fig.11 – Register of measurements of speed regulation when driving around curves

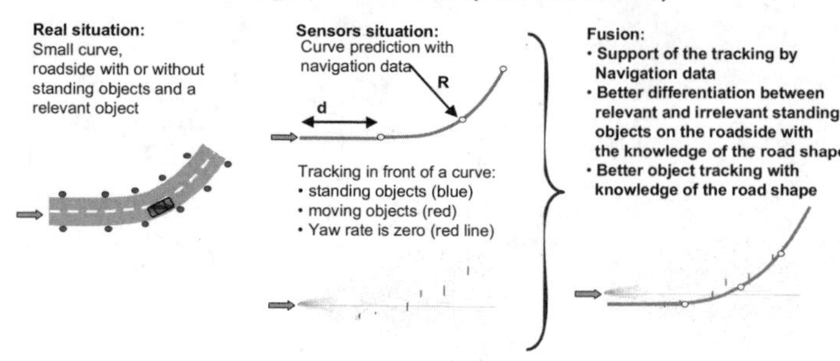

Fig-12 – Use of road prediction data to support object tracking

Use of predictive road data to support the object tracking of the ACC sensor

With the data provided by the ACC-sensor, it is possible to determine among the different recognised objects in front of the vehicle, the relevant one and to track it. In the case of several lanes, the vehicle driving in the same lane should be chosen. If the recognition of relevant stationary objects is required, the task becomes more complicated. The basis to select the relevant object is a very good knowledge of the driving path in front of the vehicle. In first generation ACC systems, this is determined by extrapolation of the mean curvature measured by a yaw rate sensor. This method leads to erroneous assignment in transition points, like for instance before a curve.

To prevent this kind of problems, it is possible to use the navigation system to predict the driving path and therefore to support the tracking process. Figure 12 shows a situation in a rural road. If our vehicle is before the curve and the object is already inside the curve, then it disappears in the driving path predicted by the yaw rate sensor, because the yaw rate still indicates zero. Therefore, the driving path is straight and some irrelevant standing objects outside the road are considered as objects in the driving path. The driving path predicted by the navigation systems facilitates the tracking of the relevant object and the right interpretation of the irrelevant standing objects on the roadside. For a proper behaviour of this method, the navigation data must be accurate enough and a unit for data fusion is required.

Figure 13 shows the data flow for the data fusion. The distance sensor provides the raw data on the objects detected in front of the vehicle, including the stationary objects. The data from the yaw rate and the route provided by the navigation system are used to predict the driving path. This information is processed in a control unit that calculates the tracking. The use of the raw data provided by the distance sensor has also the advantage that the irrelevant standing objects on the roadside can also be used to improve the prediction of the driving path.

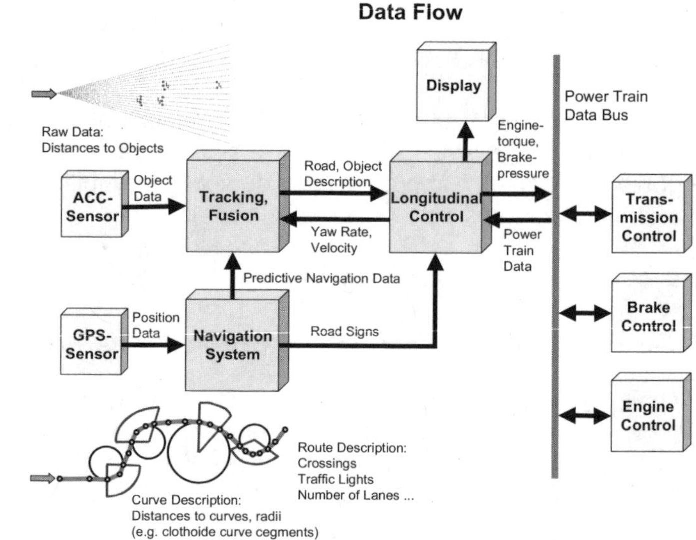

Fig-13 – Data flow for data fusion

Use of sensor data to verify curves

The use of digital maps to control the speed in the curve and to support the object tracking, has the problem of the information updating. Although in future systems the map can be updated in real time by telemetry, in the case of a change in the road geometry due to public works, it could happen that a vehicle takes the curve with a speed may be too high, and this could cause a dangerous situation. As described in the previous section, the ACC-sensor detects the obstacles on the margin (figure 14). After the recognition of a curve contour based on the sensor data, the curve radius can be estimated. If there is no correlation between this data and the information coming from the navigation system, it is assumed that such data is not correct and a break correction can be applied to limit the lateral acceleration in the curve.

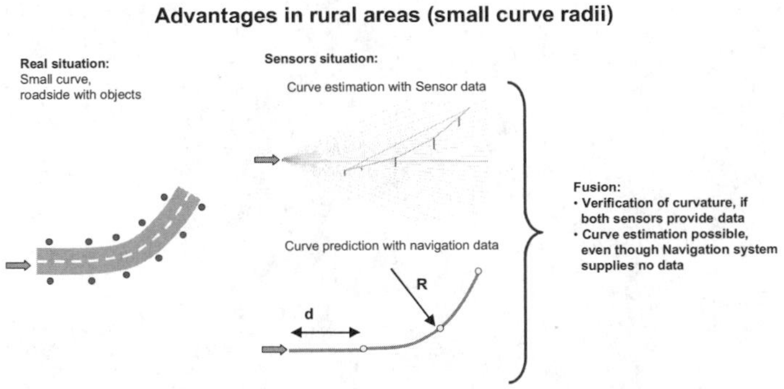

Advantages in rural areas (small curve radii)

Real situation:
Small curve,
roadside with objects

Sensors situation:
Curve estimation with Sensor data
Curve prediction with navigation data
d
R

Fusion:
- **Verification of curvature, if both sensors provide data**
- **Curve estimation possible, even though Navigation system supplies no data**

Fig-14 – Fusion of sensor and road prediction data to verify the curve contour

2.2.3 Improvements through Image processing

The ACC functionality can be improved by using a camera and an image processing system to recognise traffic signs and road lines.

The traffic sign recognition (TSR) function shown in figure 15 can be used instead of the navigation system data. The major advantage of the TSR in comparison to the predictive navigation data (PND) is the updating of the data, if the PND systems works with a static data base.

Fig-15 – Traffic sign recognition through image processing

The optical detection of the road lines, serves as support to track objects. The road shape is calculated and sent through the vehicle bus system. These data offers an improvement for the driving path prediction. Although they cover a more limited area, they are similar to the predictive data from the navigation system. The data coming from both sources, combined with the information provided by the yaw rate sensor and the recognition of the road boundaries calculated by the ACC sensor, can be merged in the tracking control unit.

Object tracking can also be performed with the image processing system. With a stereo camera is also possible to calculate the position of the objects in front of the vehicle. This object information can also be merged with the raw data detected by the ACC sensor to provided additional information, specially for the nearby area.

Fig-16 – Lane recognition and object detection through image processing

2.3 – Proposed architecture

Figure 17 shows the proposed architecture for an advanced ACC system. The information coming from the different sensors (camera, ACC sensor, navigation data) is processed in a fusion and tracking unit. The longitudinal control unit takes into account this data together with the driver inputs, in order to send through the power train data bus the required actions for the break, transmission and engine systems.

System Components

Camera
Video Data
Image Processing
TSR
Display
Power Train Data Bus
Lane Description
ACC-Sensor
Object Data
Tracking, Fusion
Road, Object Description
Longitudinal Control
Yaw Rate, Velocity
Engine-torque, Brake-pressure
Power Train Data
Trans-mission Control
Brake Control
Road Description
GPS-Sensor
Position Data
Navigation System
Road Signs
Engine Control

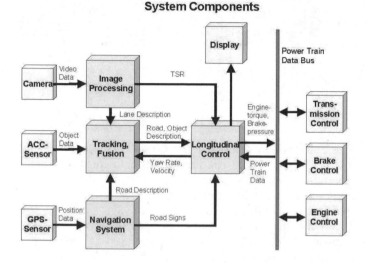

Fig-17 – Proposed architecture for an advanced ACC system

3 – PROTOTYPE DESCRIPTION AND FIRST TRIALS

3.1 – Prototype description

SEAT has introduced some of the above described driver assistant systems in a research Toledo Advanced ACC prototype (see figure 18). The implemented functions are the following:

- ACC Stop and Go
- ACC full speed range operation (from null to 160 Km/h)
- Stationary object detection
- Speed curve assistant
- Speed limit assistant
- Lane keeping assistant

In order to achieve the different functionality, several sensors have been introduced:

- A multibeam laser long-range distance sensor in the headlamp with a view angle of 30 degrees and a distance of 150 m depending on the weather conditions.
- A short-range distance scanning laser. It controls an angle of 180º around with an the vehicle and it reaches a maximum distance of 50 m.
- GPS receiver and a navigation system based in NavTech map database with enhanced geometry and additional attributes.
- Traffic Sign Recognition sensor based on a CCD-Camera.
- Lane Department Recognition sensor also based on CCD technology
- Vehicle dynamic sensors – ABS, ESP, etc.

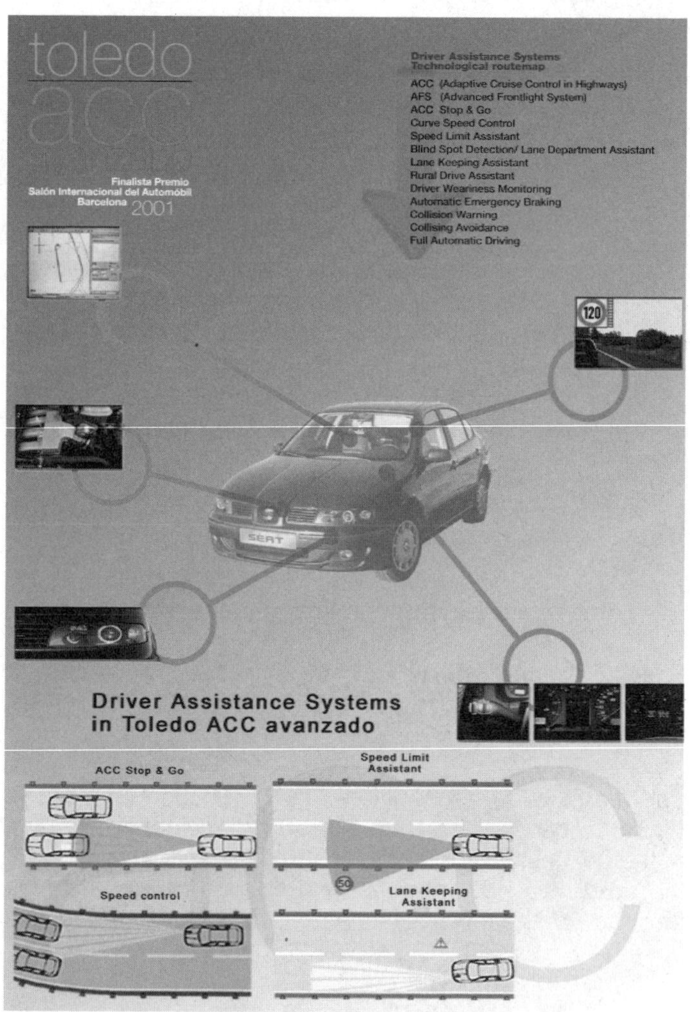

Fig-18 –Advanced ACC SEAT Toledo

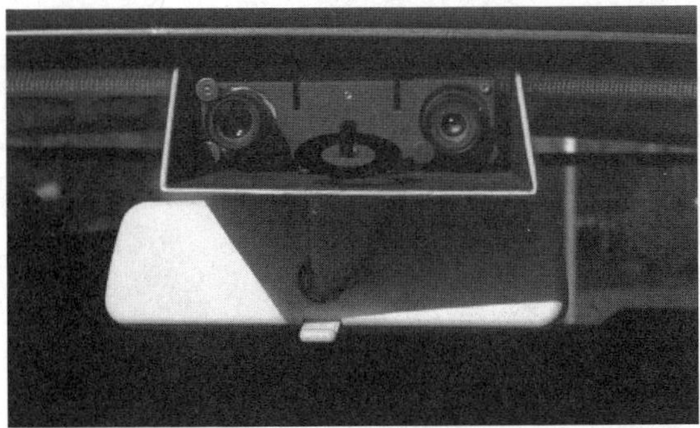

Fig-19 – Traffic sign and lane detection cameras

The information coming from the different sensors is processed by an electronic control unit that taken into account also the dynamic vehicle situation and the driver desires, issues the outputs for the brake system and the engine control unit.

Figure 20 shows the switches to select the ACC modus, and the display, integrated in the instrument cluster, to inform the driver on the ACC status.

All relevant data related to the advanced ACC system flows along the CAN network.

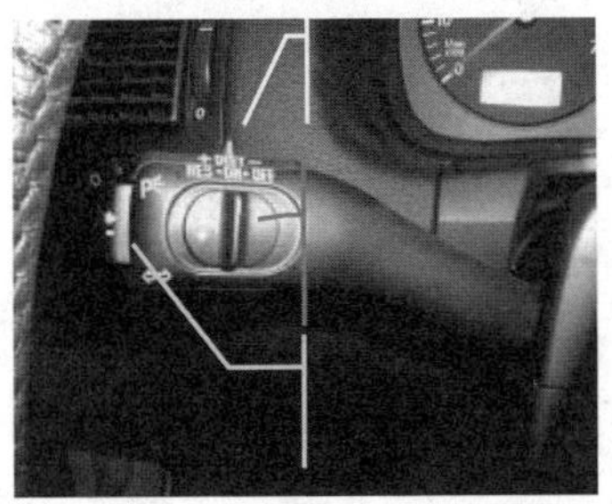

Fig. 20 – Handle control and display integrated in the instrument cluster

3.2 – First results

In order to analyse the behaviour of the whole system several tests have been carried out in the area of Barcelona, obtaining very good results in the different trials done so far, not only in highways but also in rural roads. Nevertheless, extensive tests are needed in the future to identify and to study the different situations against the vehicle could be faced.

Figure 21, 22 and 23 show the implementation of the new functions: ACC Stop&Go, extended speed operation, curve assistant, speed limit assistant and lane keeping support.

Fig. 21. Lane keeping assistant

Fig. 22. Speed limit assistant

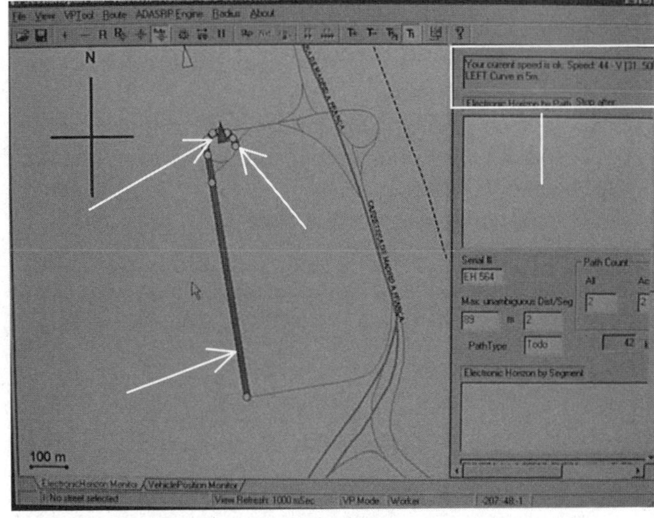

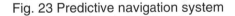

Fig. 23 Predictive navigation system

CONCLUSION

Driver assistance systems are emerging as a solution to improve safety and comfort levels in automotive traffic.

In this paper, the need and advantages of driver assistance systems and a possible road map have been presented.

Taking as a basis present ACC systems already in the market, the next steps and functions have been introduced, discussing in detail a possible technical implementation and a possible system architecture.

First trials and results carried out by SEAT with an advanced ACC research prototype have been also presented.

Concerning next steps, it is foreseen to improve the behaviour of the system in terms of software and to implement additional driver assistance functions. Also an acceptance study will be carried out to analyse customer requirements and recommendations.

Nevertheless for a proper introduction of advanced driver assistance systems, it is necessary to follow an integrated approach considering technical, ergonomic and legal aspects as proposed in [7]. Simulation tools will help also to accelerate the development process.

REFERENCES

1. J.P.Pauwelussen, H.B. Pacejka. "Smart Vehicles". Swets&Zeitlinger. 1995.
2. G.R.Widmann, W.A.Bauson,S.W.Alland. "Development of Collision Avoidance Systems at Delphi Automotive Systems". IEEE International Conference on Intelligent Vehicles. 1998
3. www.dgt.es
4. F.Sánchez. "Hacia El Automóvil Inteligente". STA Nº124. 1996
5. A.Bastian, P.Andreas, R.Holze, C.Sochaski, F.Sánchez, M. Sala, A.Freixa. "Challenges and Requirements for the Second Generation Adaptive Cruise Control Systems".
6. S.Kopischke. "Entwicklung einer Notbremsfunktion mit Rapid Prototyping Methoden". TU Braunschweig. ISBN 3-89653-782-2.
7. 2nd Response User Forum Workshop. 11Th & 12Th December 2000. Munich.

2001-01-3244

Adaptive Cruise Control System Using CVT Gear Ratio Control

Junsuke Ino, Takeshi Ishizu and Hideki Sudou
Nissan Motor Co., Ltd.

Akira Hino
JATCO TransTechnology Co., Ltd.

ABSTRACT

This paper describes a newly developed adaptive cruise control (ACC) system using continuously variable transmission (CVT) gear ratio control. This system provides excellent headway distance control performance at a reasonable cost. With this system, headway distance is measured with a laser radar, and the throttle position and CVT gear ratio are controlled under both acceleration and deceleration situations.

The new ACC system consists of a target headway distance calculator, a headway distance controller, a vehicle velocity controller and a drive torque controller. Using a drive torque control method that was newly developed based on integrated control of engine torque and the CVT gear ratio, the following benefits are obtained.

(1) It provides smoother acceleration and deceleration.

(2) It maintains the target vehicle velocity on steep uphill and downhill grades.

As a result, sufficient ACC performance can be attained even in 2.0-liter class vehicles. This paper describes the system features, design concept and benefits of the system, which are illustrated with simulation and experimental results.

INTRODUCTION

In recent years, the development of autonomous vehicle control systems has been vigorously advanced with the aim of reducing drivers' workload in expressway driving. As leading examples of this trend, ACC systems that control the headway distance to a preceding vehicle have been produced in the past few years. An ACC system adjusts the headway distance to a preceding vehicle by controlling the host vehicle's velocity within the velocity range selected by the driver. It can contribute to a reduction of driver fatigue by reducing the frequency of brake and accelerator pedal operations.

As an initial example of intelligent transportation systems (ITS), we have now developed an ACC system for use on vehicles fitted with a CVT. Because a CVT controls the gear ratio continuously, it facilitates smooth and continuous deceleration control based on engine braking. Furthermore, it can provide the required drive torque for acceleration while maintaining an engine operating point that is suitable for fuel consumption. This is possible because the engine operating point can be freely set within the CVT gear ratio range. Therefore, satisfactory ACC performance can be attained in expressway driving even in 2.0-liter class vehicles without using an automatic brake actuator. The new ACC system has already been implemented on production vehicles.

SYSTEM FEATURES

The system configuration is shown in Fig. 1. This system is composed of a distance sensor that measures the headway distance to a preceding vehicle, a cruise control unit that controls the headway distance and vehicle velocity, a throttle actuator that controls the throttle angle, and a CVT controller that controls the CVT gear ratio.

The newly developed ACC controls the host vehicle's velocity within the velocity range selected by the driver so as to maintain a certain set distance to a preceding vehicle. It can accelerate and decelerate the host vehicle by controlling not only the throttle but also the CVT gear ratio.

The headway distance sensor is a scanning-type laser radar operating at a wavelength of 870 nm. By receiving a vehicle velocity and a steering angle information from a cruise control unit, the laser radar calculates a headway distance and a relative velocity to a preceding vehicle. It can detect preceding vehicles at a distance of one hundred meters and a velocity of one hundred kilometers an hour by picking up the light reflected from a reflector at the rear of a vehicle. Even on curves, the sensor can accurately detect a preceding vehicle by estimating the road curvature based on multiple delineators installed along the road. If a road does not have such delineators, the ACC vehicle estimates the radius of curvature from the steering angle.

In general, the optical type sensor used for this ACC system, such as laser radar, has disadvantage of detection performance as compared with the radio wave type sensor, such as millimeter-wave radar, for example, even when the rear reflector of a preceding vehicle is duty or during rainy day or splashing following a rain. However, a laser radar is cheaper than a millimeter-wave radar, having performance sufficient as ACC except for bad weather case.

The system is operated by steering wheel-mounted control switches. A driver can choose from three headway distance settings, long, medium and short, corresponding to the traffic conditions.

The operational status of the system is shown by a dashboard indicator. If the headway distance to a preceding vehicle becomes too short, the system alerts the driver by sounding a buzzer and flashing the indicator.

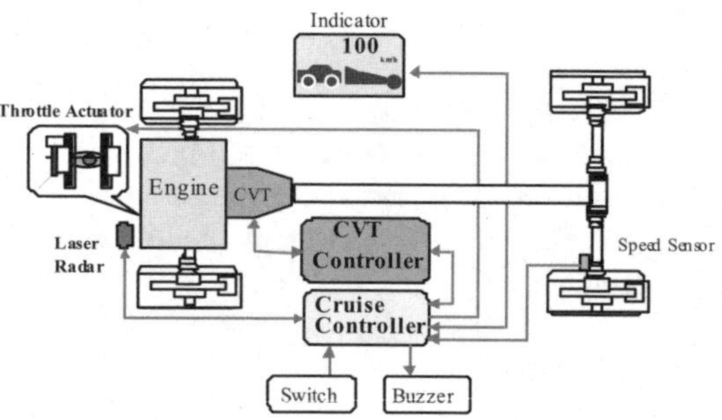

Fig. 1 ACC System Configuration

DESIGN OF CRUISE CONTROL UNIT

The newly developed ACC system described here is configured hierarchically as shown in Fig. 2. It mainly consists of ;

· a target headway distance calculator that determines the target distance from the operating state of the ACC vehicle and a preceding vehicle

· a headway distance controller that calculates the vehicle velocity command for achieving the target headway distance

· a vehicle velocity controller that determines the drive and braking torque so that the actual velocity of the ACC vehicle matches the velocity command

· a drive torque controller that distributes the drive torque command to the target engine torque and the target CVT gear ratio.

Here, the headway distance controller has already been designed.[1)] Therefore, we designed a vehicle velocity controller and a drive torque controller.

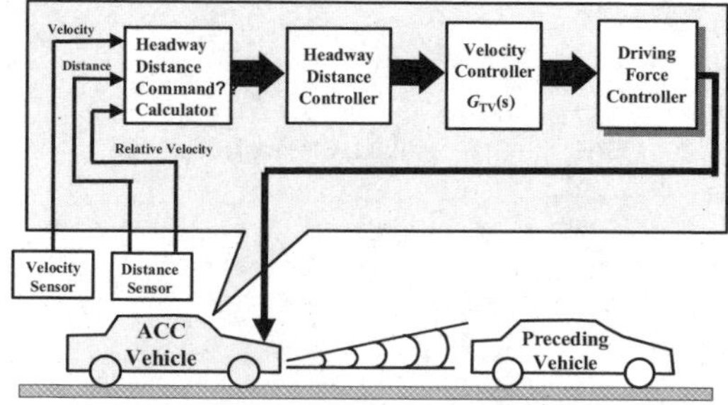

Fig. 2 Construction of Adaptive Cruise Control System

DESIGN OF VEHICLE VELOCITY CONTROL

As shown in Fig. 3, the velocity controller is composed of a robust compensator that gets rid of the influence of external disturbances like the road grade and a model-matching compensator that controls the driving force so that the actual vehicle velocity becomes the designer's desired response.[2)] Here, since the plant is the vehicle after driving force control is performed, the transfer characteristic can be expressed as

$$v_A(t) = G_{P0}(s)e^{-L_V s} f_C(t) = \frac{1}{m_V} \cdot \frac{1}{s} e^{-L_V s} f_C(t) \quad (1)$$

where m_V is the vehicle mass, s is an integration term, L_V is the dead time when the target drive torque , f_C is input and the actual vehicle velocity v_A is output.

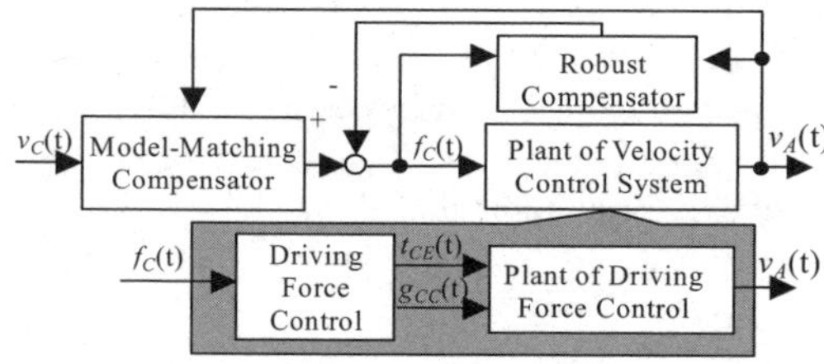

Fig. 3 Diagram of Vehicle Velocity Control

DESIGN OF DRIVING FORCE CONTROL

If vehicle velocity control is performed by using a CVT, the transmission interferes with the engine, and hunting may occur. A drive torque unit that is controlled based on integrated control of engine torque and the CVT gear ratio was newly designed to resolve this problem. A block diagram of the control algorithm is shown in Fig. 4.

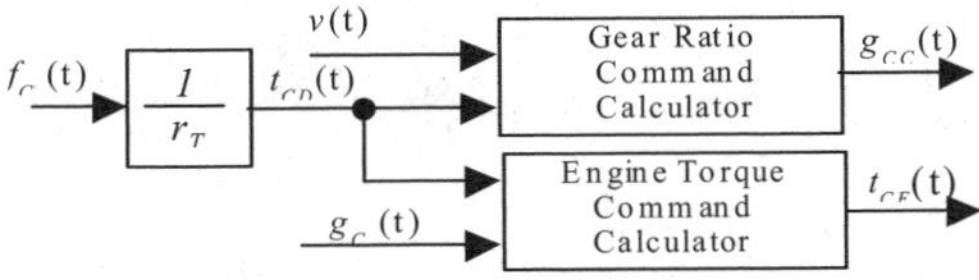

Fig.4 Diagram of Driving Force Control

The drive torque control unit consists of a target engine torque calculator that computes the target engine torque from the target drive torque and actual CVT gear ratio and a target CVT gear ratio calculator that computes the target CVT gear ratio from the target drive torque and vehicle velocity.[3)]

Target engine torque calculator

Engine output torque is transmitted to the drive shaft through the CVT and final drive. Therefore, the engine torque command t_{CE} is calculated from the driving force command f_{CD} as shown below by using the CVT gear ratio g_C, tire radius r_T and final gear ratio g_f.

$$t_{CE}(t) = \frac{f_{CD}(t)}{g_f \cdot r_T \cdot g_C(t)} = \frac{t_{CD}(t)}{g_f \cdot g_C(t)} \quad (2)$$

where, t_{CD} is drive torque.

Target CVT gear ratio calculator

This calculator computes the engine speed command n_C from the drive torque command t_{CD} and vehicle velocity v. Therefore, the target CVT gear ratio g_{CC} is determined from the calculated result and vehicle velocity v. As explained below, the engine speed command is calculated differently depending on whether the drive torque is positive or negative .

1) With positive drive torque

If the drive torque command is positive, the engine speed command is determined on the basis of the CVT gear ratio characteristic, taking into account both drivability and fuel consumption. This is because there are innumerable combinations of engine speed and engine torque for attaining the target output, which is the product of the drive torque command and vehicle velocity.

2) With negative drive torque

Under a condition of zero throttle angle, engine speed is determined uniformly relative to arbitrary engine torque levels (as shown in Fig. 5). Accordingly, the engine speed for attaining the target output is found from the point of intersection of the target engine torque line and the engine characteristic line.

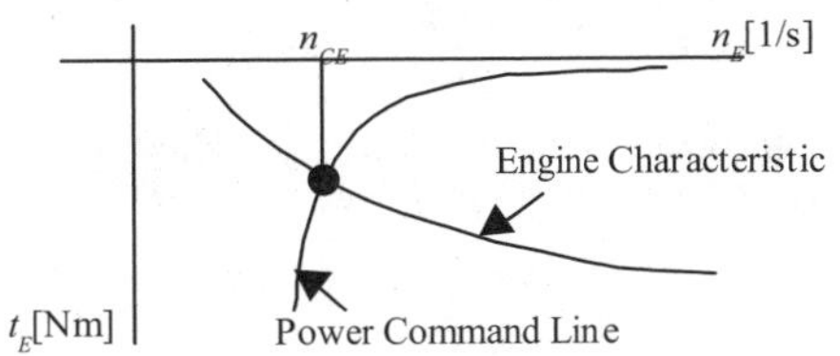

Fig. 5 Method of Calculating Engine Speed Command

DESIGN OF HEADWAY DISTANCE CONTROL

Based on an analysis of driving behavior characteristics and drivers' actions in adjusting the headway distance in various driving situations, the following two characteristics were identified as being important factors in vehicle control performance.

(1) To be able to arbitrarily set the response until the target headway distance reaches the actual headway distance after the ACC vehicle begins to follow a preceding vehicle.
(2) To be able to arbitrarily set the response when the ACC vehicle maintains the selected headway distance to a preceding vehicle.

In the ACC system with automatic brake actuation, a two-degree-of-freedom control system based on the reference model shown in Fig. 6 was adopted to satisfy the performance requirements above. As a result, these characteristics can be determined independently.[1)] That is, the headway distance response is compensated by a phase compensator, and stability against external disturbances is controlled by a feedback compensator.

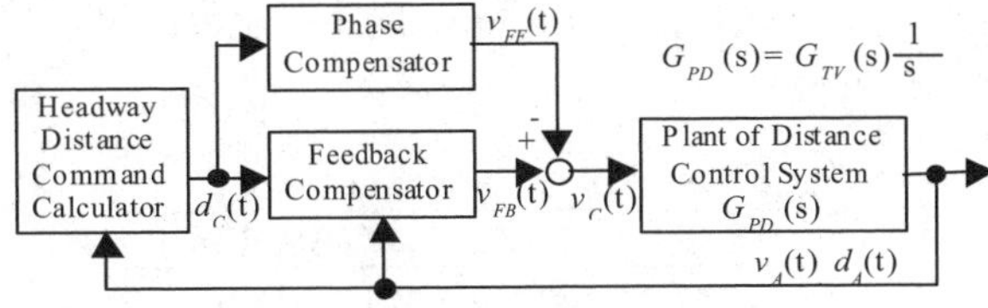

Fig. 6 Diagram of Distance Control System

SIMULATION RESULTS

The control performance of the velocity controller designed with the foregoing method was confirmed by simulation. The conditions simulated were typical driving patterns incorporated in the velocity control system.

Experimental conditions

· acceleration control: 16 m/s→27 m/s (acceleration: 0.6m/s^2)

· deceleration control: 27 m/s→16 m/s (deceleration: 1.0 m/s^2)

The simulation results are shown in Fig. 7. In both the acceleration and deceleration situations, the actual vehicle velocity nearly corresponded with the standard response. This indicates that the vehicle velocity response satisfies the required performance and that the system can provide the specified acceleration and deceleration without any hunting of engine torque and the CVT gear ratio.

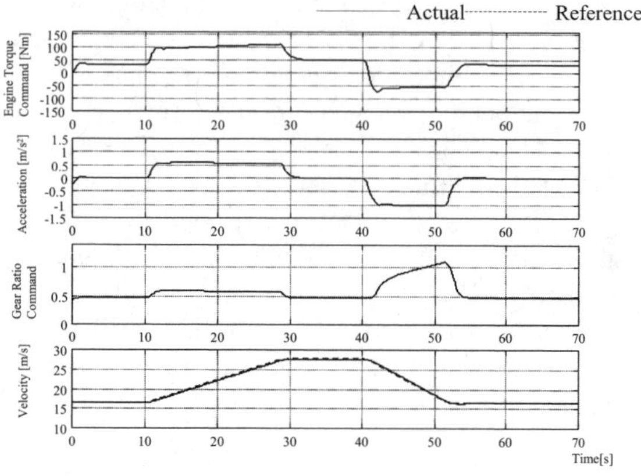

Fig. 7 Simulation Results

VEHICLE EXPERIMENT

Using a test vehicle having the specifications shown in Table 1, tests were conducted to confirm the control performance.

Table 1 Test Vehicle Specifications

Vehicle	Nissan U14 (BlueBird)
Throttle Actuator	Pump Vacuum Type
Transmission	CVT
Distance Sensor	Laser Radar

Velocity control performance confirmation

1) Acceleration and deceleration response test

Experimental conditions

· Acceleration control: 16 m/s→27 m/s (acceleration: 0.6 m/s^2)

· Deceleration control: 27 m/s→16 m/s (deceleration: 1.0 m/s^2)

The results obtained with the CVT speed ratio set in the top ratio range without any driving force control are shown in Fig. 8-(a). The results obtained with driving force control are shown in Fig. 8-(b). When the CVT gear ratio was fixed, the target engine torque saturated under both acceleration and deceleration. As a result, the target vehicle response was not obtained.

On the other hand, when the CVT gear ratio and engine torque were controlled by driving force control, sufficient driving force was obtained and the target vehicle response was attained as a result.

These results corresponded well with the simulation.

They suggest that CVT control would provide large benefits in under-2.0-liter class ACC vehicles.

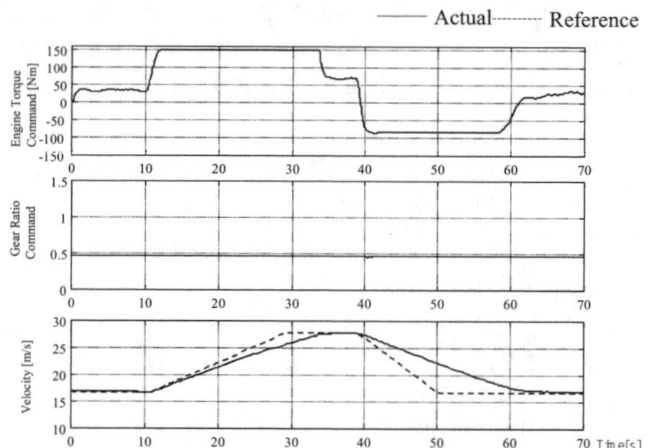

(a) Fixed Gear Ratio (without Driving Force Control)

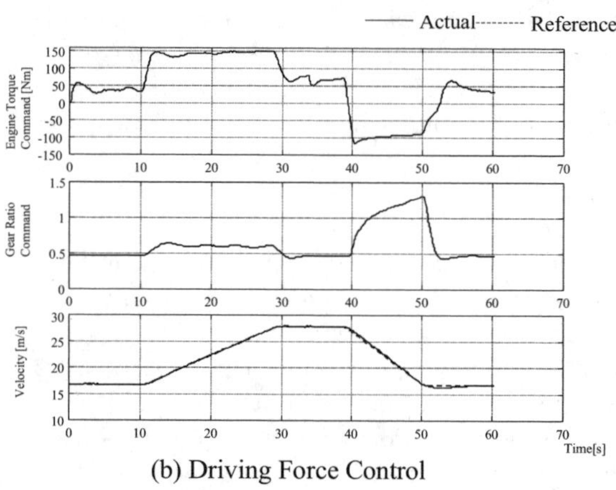

(b) Driving Force Control

Fig. 8 Experimental Results for Acceleration Response

2) Stability against external disturbances
Experimental conditions
• Downhill grade (0-5%) and a constant speed of 16 m/s

The results obtained with the CVT gear ratio set in the top range are shown in Fig. 9-(a). The results obtained with driving force control are shown in Fig. 9-(b). When the CVT gear ratio was fixed, the necessary drive torque for eliminating the influence of external disturbances due to the change in the road grade was not obtained. As a result, the vehicle velocity deviated from the target velocity.

On the other hand, when the CVT gear ratio and engine torque were appropriately controlled by driving force control, sufficient driving force was obtained to maintain a constant velocity even on a steep downhill grade.

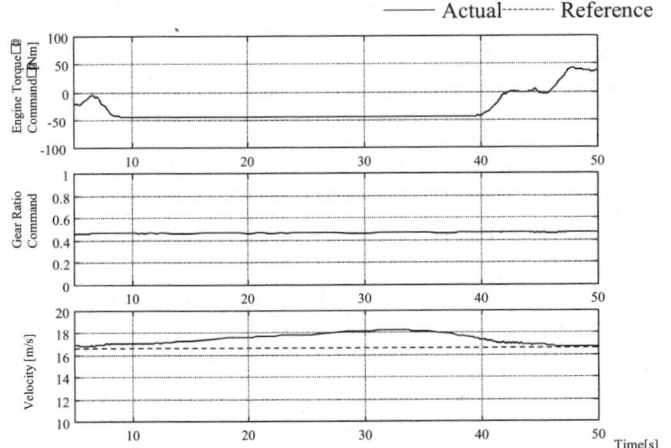

(a) Fixed Gear Ratio (without Driving Force Control)

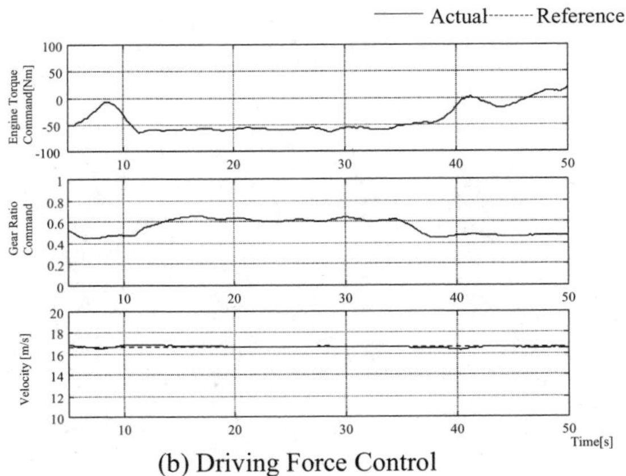

(b) Driving Force Control

Fig. 9 Experimental Results for Stability

Confirmation of headway distance controller performance

The test results obtained with the newly designed driving force controller confirmed that the velocity controller attained the specified transfer function by controlling the CVT gear ratio and engine torque. Therefore, vehicle tests involving typical driving situations were conducted to confirm the performance of the ACC system.

1) Approach situation
Experimental conditions
The response until the ACC vehicle (traveling at 27 m/s) reaches a target headway distance after recognizing a preceding vehicle (traveling at 19 m/s) 100 meters ahead.

2) Situation of following a passing vehicle
Experimental conditions
The response until the ACC vehicle (traveling at 22 m/s) reaches a target headway distance after being passed by a vehicle (traveling at 27 m/s) and then following it at a distance of 20 m.

The experimental results are shown in Figs. 10 and 11. The headway distance and the relative vehicle velocity corresponded well with the standard model in both the acceleration and deceleration situations, confirming that this ACC system provides satisfactory performance.

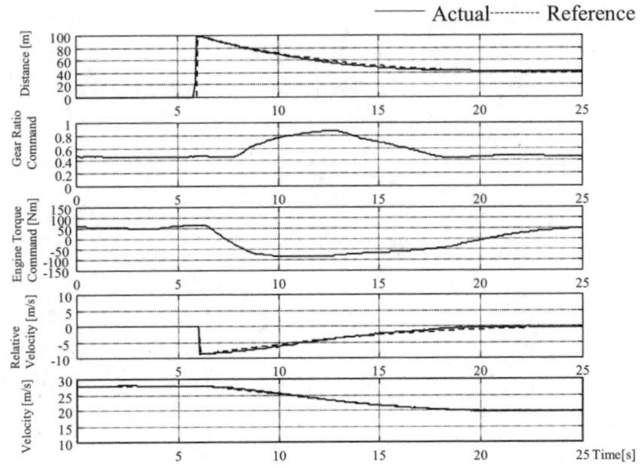

Fig. 10 Approach Test

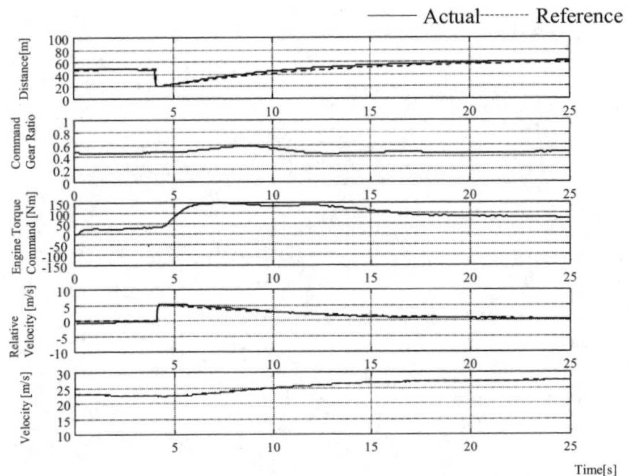

Fig. 11 Following a Passing Vehicle Test

CONCLUSION

A new ACC system was examined using a CVT with the aim of expanding the application of ACC systems. Using a drive torque control method that was newly developed based on integrated control of engine torque and the CVT gear ratio according to engine characteristics known in advance, a ACC system has been developed that provides the following benefits.

(1) It provides smoother acceleration and deceleration.
(2) It maintains the target vehicle velocity on steep uphill and downhill grades.

As a result, sufficient ACC performance can be attained even in 2.0-liter class vehicles.

REFERENCES

1) A. Higashimata, et al., Design of Headway Distance Control System for ACC JSAE Review, No. 22 (2001).
2) H. Nakamura, et al., Effectiveness of Robust Control Method for Automotive Powertrain Control IPC-10 paper No. 99066 (1999).
3) S. Katakura, et al., Study of Integrated Engine-CVT Control (in Japanese with English summary) JSAE Review, No. 61 (1998).

2001-01-0798

Development of an Adaptive Cruise Control System with Stop-and-Go Capability

Yoshinori Yamamura, Masahiko Tabe, Minoru Kanehira and Takuya Murakami
Nissan Motor Co., Ltd.

ABSTRACT

An Adaptive Cruise Control system with stop-and-go capability has been developed to reduce the driver's workload in traffic jams on expressways. Based on an analysis of driving behavior characteristics in expressway traffic jams, a control system capable of modeling those characteristics accurately has been constructed to provide natural vehicle behavior in low-speed driving. The effectiveness of the system was evaluated with an experimental vehicle, and the results confirmed that it reduces the driver's workload. This paper presents an outline of the system and its effectiveness along with the experimental results.

INTRODUCTION

In recent years, research and development work has moved forward on vehicle control systems, which control vehicle dynamics based on driving environment information, including the headway distance and the host vehicle's lateral position. These systems are aimed at reducing the driver's workload by assisting with the execution of driving tasks. As a leading example of such systems, Nissan has been offering an Adaptive Cruise Control (ACC) system in production vehicles since 1999 [1]. This system uses a millimeter-wave radar and an electronically controlled brake booster. The ACC system can adjust the headway distance or the host vehicle's speed according to the traffic flow such as under driving conditions where vehicle speeds frequently change. This makes it possible to reduce frequent acceleration or deceleration actions by the driver in such circumstances for more comfortable driving that is less tiring.

Based on the original system, a more advanced ACC System with stop-and-go capability has been developed. This system reduces the driver's workload by controlling the headway distance and provides more comfortable driving in congested expressway traffic as well as during high-speed cruising. Generally, the headway distance is shorter and a preceding vehicle's speed changes more frequently in low-speed driving than in high-speed cruising. In addition, drivers must act to adjust the distance to a vehicle ahead that is stopping or has already stopped. These factors make it difficult to design a headway distance controller that would satisfy the target following characteristics at low speeds using the same control procedure as that of the high-speed range. Based on an analysis of driving behavior characteristics in low-speed driving, a control system was constructed to model those characteristics, making it possible to achieve natural vehicle behavior.

This paper describes the ACC system design concept, results of an analysis of driving behavior characteristics at low speeds, including stop-and-start driving, and the headway distance control system. Experimental results are also presented to illustrate the performance of the system and its effectiveness.

The advanced ACC system operates in the high-speed range in the same manner as the original system. The following sections describe how the new system operates in the low-speed range.

FEATURES OF THE SYSTEM

The ACC system with stop-and-go capability is activated by a steering wheel switch and controls the headway distance when the headway distance sensor detects a preceding vehicle. The system stops the host vehicle and keeps it stationary so long as the preceding vehicle is stopped. The driver starts off again from a stationary state in the same way as with a conventional vehicle. Stop control is deactivated by stepping on the accelerator pedal. The system resumes headway distance control when the driver releases the accelerator above a predetermined speed. Since the ACC system with stop-and-go capability does not have a conventional cruise control mode at low speed, it is deactivated when the headway distance sensor does not detect a vehicle ahead.

The maximum speed, maximum longitudinal acceleration and deceleration, and steady-state headway distance were determined as explained below in reference to the results of an investigation of driving behavior in congested metropolitan expressway traffic.

Maximum speed: The maximum speed is 30km/h, which was set on the basis of the average speed measured in congested expressway traffic.

Maximum longitudinal acceleration: The maximum longitudinal acceleration is $1.0 m/s^2$, which was determined on the basis of the acceleration distribution found in congested expressway traffic.

Maximum longitudinal deceleration: The maximum longitudinal deceleration is $2.5 m/s^2$, the same as the original ACC system.

Steady-state headway distance: The steady-state headway distance is set a little longer on the basis of the average headway distance measured in congested expressway traffic. The driver can set the distance at three levels, 20 m, 23 m or 25 m, at a speed of 30 km/h, and at 4 m, 4.5 m or 5.0 m at a speed of 0 km/h.

Figure 1 shows the system configuration. The system calculates the engine torque command and brake hydraulic pressure command in order to make the actual headway distance coincide with the target value. It uses the same type of brake actuator and millimeter-wave radar as the original ACC system. A laser radar unit and a camera are used as short headway distance sensors in addition to millimeter-wave radar. Selective use of these sensor signals according to different measurement conditions achieves more accurate measurement of short distances. These commands and the vehicle signals used in calculating them are transmitted to and received from each ECU through a Controller Area Network (CAN).

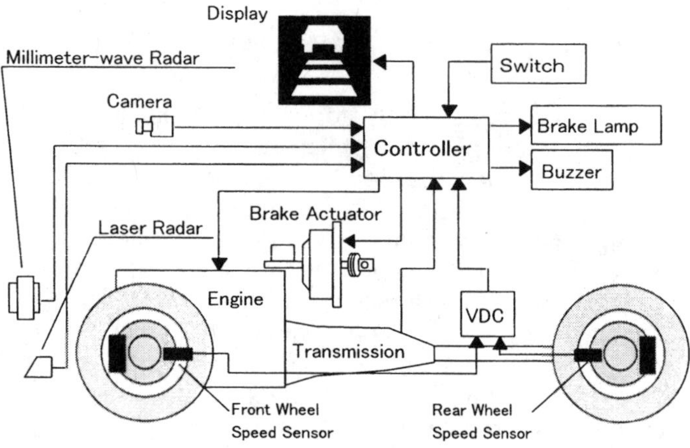

Fig. 1 Configuration of the ACC system

DESIGN OF HEADWAY CONTROL UNIT

ANALYSIS OF DRIVING BEHAVIOR CARACTERISTICS AT LOW SPEED

The first step in designing the headway distance control algorithm for low-speed driving, including stopping the host vehicle, was to analyze driving behavior characteristics of well-mannered drivers. The aim of the analysis was to achieve natural vehicle behavior that would not feel strange to the driver.

Let us consider the process of following a preceding vehicle. Following begins when a driver becomes aware of and closes on a preceding vehicle or when another vehicle cuts in front. Subsequently, the driver follows the vehicle ahead at nearly a constant headway distance. Generally, the headway distance is lengthened by decelerating. However, the headway distance can not be extended by deceleration if the preceding vehicle stops. Keeping this point in mind, an analysis was made of driving behavior characteristics in various scenarios.

<u>Driving behavior characteristics with a moving preceding vehicle</u>

At the start of following

Cambridge Basic Research has reported that the use of perceptual variables such as the time headway (THW) and the time to collision (TTC), rather than the headway distance or relative velocity, is more effective in analyzing driving behavior characteristics when following a preceding vehicle [2],[3]. Letting d_R denote the headway distance, v_F the velocity of the preceding vehicle and v_R the relative velocity, THW and TTC are defined as

$$THW = \frac{d_R}{v_F} \tag{1}$$

$$TTC = \frac{d_R}{v_R} \tag{2}$$

In the following discussion, driving behavior characteristics are explained in terms of THW and TTC, which are variables that are readily perceivable by the driver. In order to circumvent the singularity of TTC around infinity, the inverse of TTC (TTC^{-1}) is used.

Figure 2(a) shows the trajectories of TTC^{-1} and THW when approaching a slower preceding vehicle from a distance, and Fig. 2(b) shows their trajectories when another vehicle cuts in front of the host vehicle. In all cases, the trajectories ultimately converge to THW=THW* and TTC^{-1} =0 and the host vehicle follows the vehicle ahead at nearly a constant time headway (THW*). It is observed that the state space shows nearly the same trajectories regardless of the vehicle speed so long as the preceding vehicle is detected under the same TTC^{-1} and THW conditions. Under the cut-in condition shown in Fig. 2(b), it is also observed that the host vehicle driver decelerates faster in low-speed driving than in high-speed driving so that the value of TTC^{-1} is not reduced. This suggest that the driver makes a more determined effort to maintain a suitable headway distance because the distance to the vehicle ahead is shorter in low-speed driving.

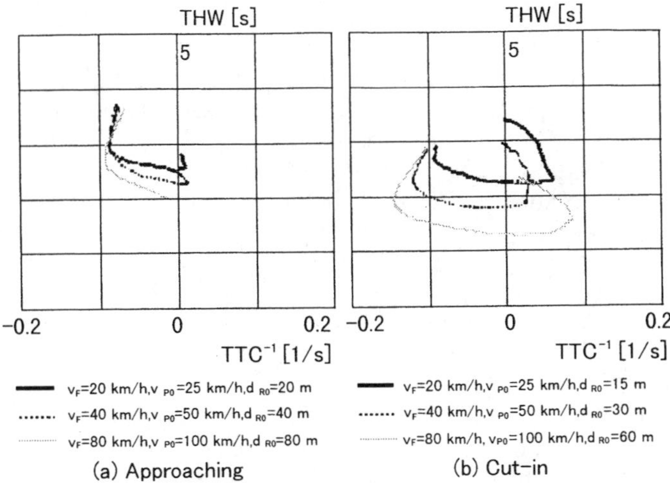

Fig. 2 Trajectories for approaching and cut-in situations

During following

Figure 3 shows the trajectories in the state space when the preceding vehicle decelerates at about 2 m/s^2 during following. The vehicle velocity and relative velocity at this time are shown in Fig. 4. These figures show the results obtained in three experiments. The results show that both trajectories are smaller than those of the cut-in situation and that the trajectories are larger at lower speeds than higher speeds. These results would seem to suggest that the driver behaves calmly in low-speed driving, permitting a large negative value of TTC^{-1}. However, the results shown in Fig. 4 indicate that the host vehicle decelerates faster relative to the deceleration of the preceding vehicle to avoid increasing the relative velocity when following at a low speed. This also indicates that the shorter headway distance in low-speed driving causes the inverse of the time to collision to become a large negative value in spite of the faster deceleration than in the high-speed range.

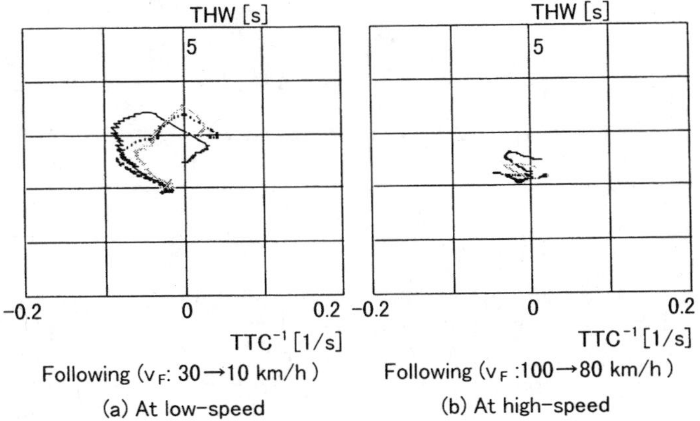

Fig. 3 Trajectories during following

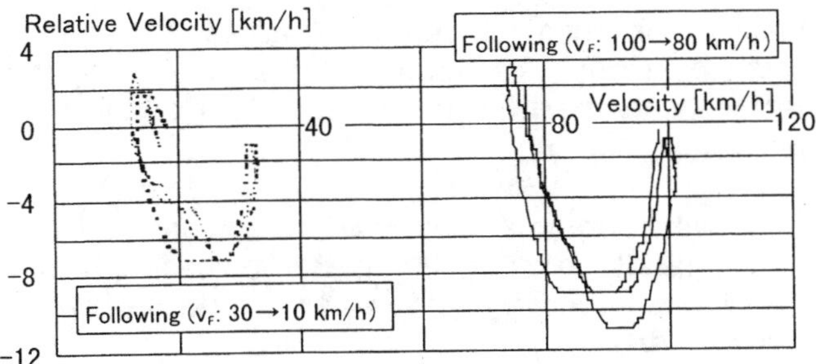

Fig. 4 Relative velocity during following

Driving behavior characteristics with a stationary preceding vehicle

Driving behavior characteristics were analyzed focusing on the time changes of TTC^{-1} with the aim of keeping THW from becoming infinite at a vehicle speed of zero. Figure 5(a) compares the trajectories of TTC^{-1} when approaching a stationary vehicle from a distance and when approaching a slow-moving vehicle. The results show that TTC^{-1} has a larger negative value when approaching a stationary vehicle than a moving vehicle. This suggests that the driver maintains a longer headway distance as a precautionary measure for avoiding the possibility of a shorter distance if the preceding vehicle decelerates. In contrast, the driver tends to approach a stationary vehicle at a shorter headway distance because it is not necessary to predict any further change in its motion. As seen in Fig. 5(b), the same tendency can be confirmed during following when the preceding vehicle continues decelerating until it stops.

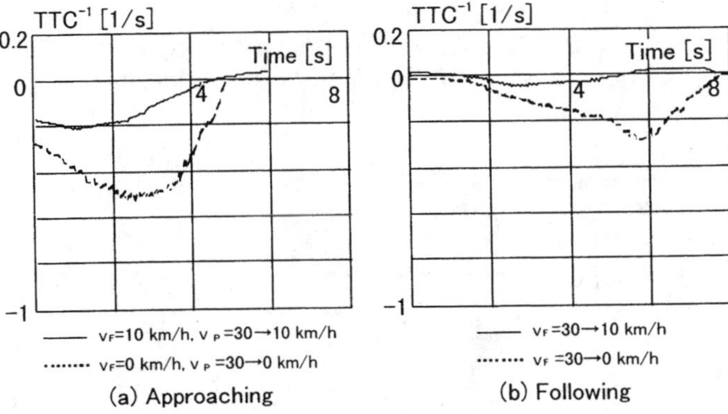

Fig. 5 TTC^{-1} trajectories for manual driving

CONTROLLER DESIGN

From these results, driving behavior characteristics can be summarized as follows:

(1) For approach and cut-in situations at the start of following, drivers show slower response until the actual

headway distance reaches the final adjusted headway distance. Under these conditions, the state space shows nearly the same trajectories regardless of the vehicle speed.

(2) While following a preceding vehicle, drivers respond more quickly to changes in the preceding vehicle's velocity. However, a relatively calm response is allowed at high speeds.

(3) When approaching a stationary vehicle, drivers tend to maintain a higher relative velocity than when approaching a moving vehicle.

In order to model the controller on these characteristics, the headway distance control system has been constructed using the concept of a two-degree-of-freedom control method. This approach achieves both the desired response in relation to the command signal and stability against external disturbances (in this case, changes in the preceding vehicle's velocity).

Figure 6 shows a block diagram of the control system. The feed-forward compensator calculates the target headway distance d_T and the target relative velocity v_{RC} at the start of following. It also calculates the velocity command v_{FF} that makes the actual headway distance and the actual relative velocity coincide with the target values. The sum of the target headway distances, including d_T at the start of following, d_{C0} during following and d_S at stopping, results in the target headway distance d_C. The feedback compensator calculates the velocity command v_{FB} that makes the actual headway distance d_R coincide with the target value d_C. As a result, the feed-forward compensator compensates for a slow response at the start of following, and the feedback compensator compensates for a quick response in relation to changes in the speed of the preceding vehicle during following. Each block is explained in more detail below.

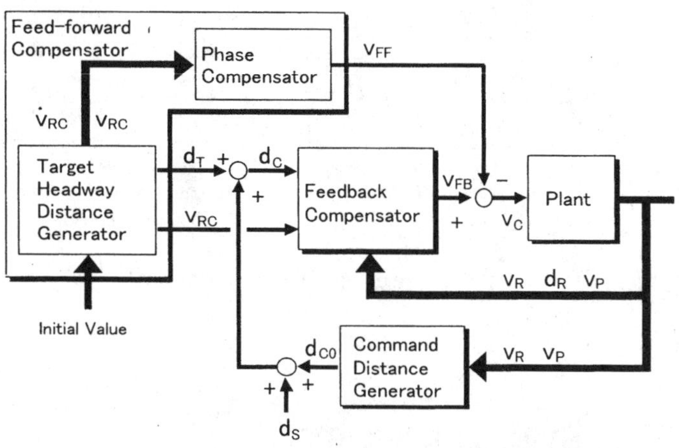

Fig. 6 Block diagram of control system

PLANT

As the first step in designing the headway distance control system, the velocity servo system was constructed using a robust model-matching method [4] that is unaffected by changes in the vehicle weight or the road gradient. The transfer function of the velocity servo system is given by equation (3).

$$G_V(s) = \frac{\omega_V}{s + \omega_V} \tag{3}$$

where s is the Laplace operator. As a result, the response of the actual headway distance d_R in relation to the velocity command v_C is obtained as

$$d_R(s) = \frac{1}{s}\{v_F(s) - G_V(s)v_C(s)\} \tag{4}$$

where v_F is the velocity of the preceding vehicle.

FEEDBACK COMPENSATOR

Figure 7 shows the feedback compensator of the headway distance controller. The target headway distance input to the feedback compensator is given by

$$d_C = d_{C0} + d_T + d_S \tag{5}$$

In order to keep the time headway t_{HW} in relation to the preceding vehicle velocity v_F, d_{C0} is given by

$$d_{C0} = t_{HW} \cdot v_F \tag{6}$$

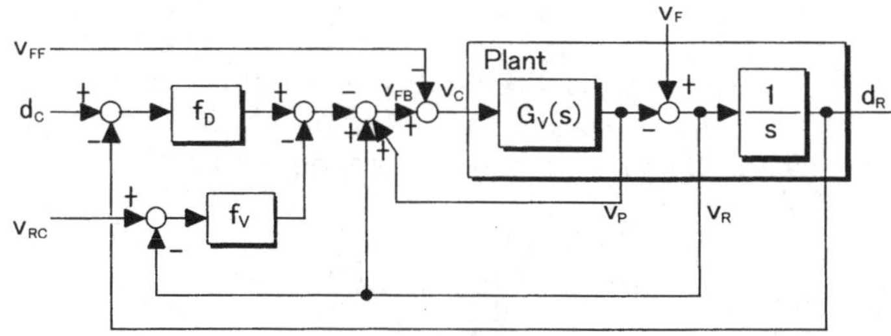

Fig. 7 Feedback compensator of headway distance controller

As will be described later, d_T is set for the initial value at the beginning of headway distance control, and then converges to zero. Since d_T and v_{RC}, the latter being the derivative of the former, become zero during following, by applying the feedback control given by equation (7), the response of d_R in relation to v_F is obtained as equation (8).

$$v_{FB} = f_V(v_{RC} - v_R) - f_D(d_C - d_R) + v_R + v_P \tag{7}$$

$$d_R = \frac{p + \omega_V f_D t_{HW}}{p^2 + \omega_V (1 - f_V) p + \omega_V f_D} v_F + d_S \quad (8)$$

where p is the differential operator. Here, the relation between the feedback gains f_V and f_D and the natural frequency ω_{FB} and the damping factor ζ_{FB} is given by

$$f_D = \frac{\omega_{FB}^2}{\omega_V} \quad (9)$$

$$f_V = 1 - \frac{2\zeta_{FB}\omega_{FB}}{\omega_V} \quad (10)$$

Equation (8) indicates that ω_{FB} should be set high to minimize the effects of the changes in the speed of the preceding vehicle. In addition, to obtain an accurate stopping distance, ζ_{FB} should be set greater than a predetermined value to avoid overshooting. However, increasing these values degrades ride comfort when following a preceding vehicle at a constant velocity. ω_{FB} and ζ_{FB} are provided as gain schedules corresponding to the relative speed and the error between d_C and d_R, making it possible to obtain both good following response in relation to the target headway distance and comfortable driving.

FEED-FORWARD COMPENSATOR

Figure 8 shows a block diagram of the feed-forward compensator. The reference model $G_M(s)$, which provides driving behavior characteristics at the start of following, is given as the following second-order system.

$$G_M(s) = \frac{\omega_M^2}{s^2 + 2\varsigma_M \omega_M s + \omega_M^2} \quad (11)$$

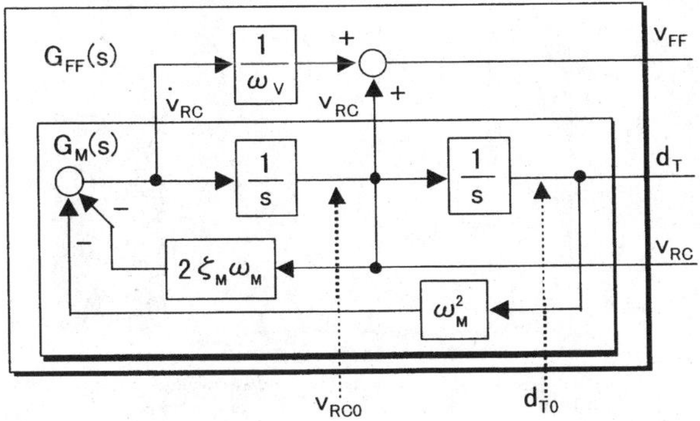

Fig. 8 Feed-forward compensator of headway distance controller

The input signal to $G_M(s)$ is always set to zero. The state variables v_{RC} and d_T are set to initial values of v_{RC0} and d_{T0} at the beginning of headway distance control. Therefore, each state variable converges to zero in relation to the natural frequency ω_M, and damping factor ζ_M, respectively. Driving behavior characteristics at the start of following are obtained to tune ω_M, and ζ_M in relation to the error between the final adjusted headway distance ($d_{C0}+d_S$) and the actual headway distance d_R, and the relative velocity v_R. In order to calculate the velocity command which provides the headway distance response at the start of following without a feedback compensator, the feed-forward compensator has been constructed using the inverse system of the plant $G_P(s)$ and $G_M(s)$. The feed-forward compensator is given by

$$G_{FF}(s) = \frac{G_M(s)}{G_P(s)} \quad (12)$$

EXPERIMENTAL RESULTS

DRIVING TESTS

The control gains were tuned on the basis of computer simulations so that the control characteristics would match the experimental data on driving behavior characteristics. Then, the controller was implemented in an experimental vehicle, which was used to fine-tune the gains further.

Figures 9 to 11 show the results of driving tests conducted to confirm the performance of the control system. Figure 9 compares the vehicle behavior when controlled by the ACC system and by a test driver. These results indicate that the trajectories obtained with headway distance control agree with those of the driver.

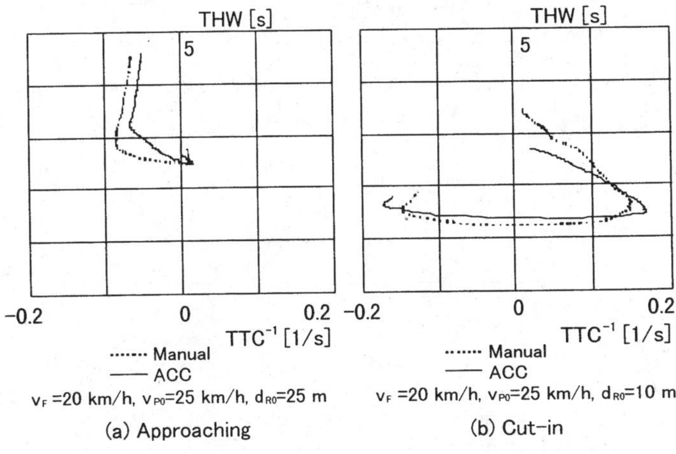

Fig. 9 Comparison of trajectories for ACC driving and manual driving

Figure 10(a) shows the response characteristics of TTC^{-1} when approaching a preceding vehicle. A larger negative value is seen for TTC^{-1} in relation to a stationary vehicle than a moving vehicle. Figure 10(b) shows the response characteristics of TTC^{-1} in relation to deceleration by the preceding vehicle during following. A larger negative value is also seen here for TTC^{-1} when the preceding vehicle comes to a stop. These results, compared with Fig. 5, indicate that headway distance control achieves almost the same vehicle behavior characteristics as those seen for the test driver.

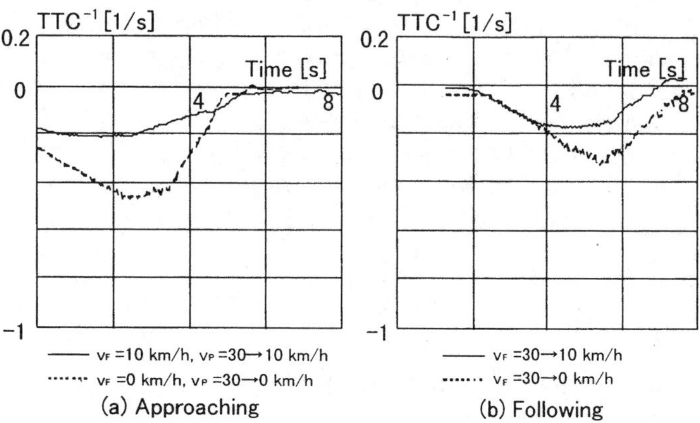

Fig. 10 TTC^{-1} trajectories for ACC driving

Figure 11 shows the response characteristics for headway distance and velocity when the preceding vehicle comes to a stop. A comparison is made between ACC driving and manual driving. Both sets of response characteristics show good agreement, thus confirming that the headway distance control system models driving behavior characteristics well.

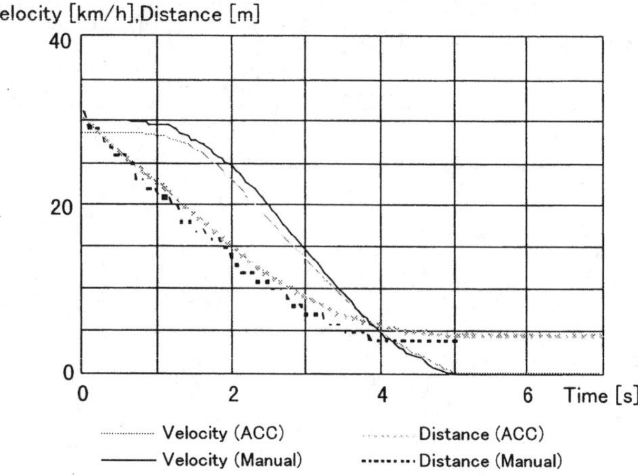

Fig. 11 Comparison of response characteristics for ACC driving and manual driving

DRIVER'S WORKLOAD

To evaluate the effect of the system on reducing the driver's workload, measurements were made of driver fatigue and stress. For measuring fatigue, a test was conducted to measure the electromyogram of the right leg. An RRV test was conducted to measure stress.

The pulse wave of an electrocardiogram is referred to as the R-wave and the interval between heartbeats is called the R-R interval. RRV is the variance of the R-R interval. The value of RRV becomes smaller with increasing psychological stress [5].

In this test, drivers were given the task of following a preceding vehicle on a proving ground course under conditions that simulated traffic congestion. Figure 12 shows the measured electromyograms. The muscular load was reduced compared with manual driving, indicating that the ACC system can reduce fatigue when driving in congested traffic.

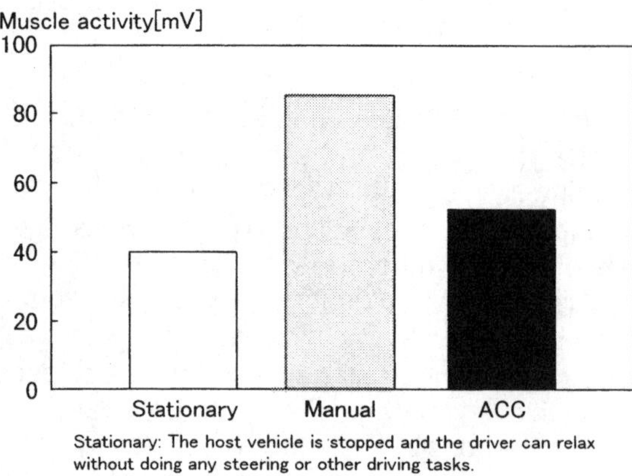

Fig. 12 Comparison of electromyograms for ACC driving and manual driving

Figure 13 shows the measured RRV. The larger RRV value obtained with the ACC system indicates that this system can relieve the excessive stress felt by drivers when adjusting the headway distance in congested traffic.

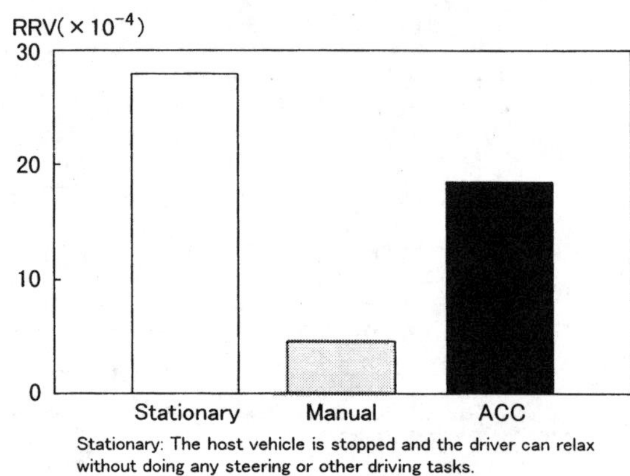

Fig. 13 Comparison of RRV data for ACC driving and manual driving

CONCLUSION

An ACC system with stop-and-go capability has been developed to reduce the driver's workload in controlling the headway distance at low speeds such as in congested traffic. The characteristics of low-speed driving were made clear by analyzing driver behavior in typical driving conditions, focusing on the time headway and time to collision. The control system was constructed to model driving behavior characteristics accurately. Tests were conducted with an experimental vehicle equipped with the control system. The results showed that the desired characteristics were obtained. In addition, measured electromyograms and RRV results indicated that the driver's workload was reduced in low-speed driving.

As seen in the relation between conventional cruise control and ACC, the technology for sensing the driving environment has the potential to expand the capabilities of conventional vehicle control systems dramatically. The integration of existing vehicle control systems with further technological innovations, including techniques for sensing the driving environment, onboard information and communications systems, and advances in human-machine interfaces, should make it possible to expand the functions and intelligence of vehicles, resulting in more comfortable driving and more efficient use of the road network.

REFERENCES

1. T. Iijima, et al., "Development of Adaptive Cruise Control with Brake Actuation", SAE Technical Paper No. 2000-01-1353 (2000).
2. R. Boer, "An Iterative LQ-Tracker for State Dependent Cost Functions: A Case Study in the Design of Human Centered Automation", International Conference on Robotics and Automation, ICRA2000.
3. M. A. Goodrich, E. R. Boer, and H. Inoue, "A Characterization of Dynamic Braking Behavior with Implications for ACC Design", Proceedings of the Intelligent Transportation Systems Conference (1999).
4. Y. Yamamura, et al., "Robust control system for electric rear wheel steering actuator", Proceedings of the Institution of Mechanical Engineers (1994), pp. 15-21.
5. H. Mouri, et al., "An investigation of driver stress induced by vehicle handling characteristics", Technical Notes/JSAE Review 15 (1994), pp. 248-250.

2000-01-1353

Development of an Adaptive Cruise Control System with Brake Actuation

Tetsuya Iijima, Akira Higashimata, Satoshi Tange, Kazutaka Mizoguchi, Hiroshi Kamiyama, Kiyohisa Iwasaki and Kenichi Egawa
Nissan Motor Co., Ltd

ABSTRACT

An adaptive cruise control (ACC) system has been developed by using an electronically controlled vacuum booster for smooth brake control and millimeter-wave radar that operates effectively even in rainy weather. The headway control unit was designed based on an analysis of driving behavior characteristics and achieves natural vehicle behavior that does not seem strange to drivers. This paper presents an outline of the system along with the results of simulations and driving tests. The effectiveness of the system was evaluated with a driving simulator and in vehicle tests, and the results verified that it reduces the driver's workload.

INTRODUCTION

Vigorous efforts have been made in recent years to research and develop autonomous vehicle control systems that are designed to reduce the driver's workload by assisting with the execution of driving tasks. Adaptive cruise control (ACC) represents a leading example of such systems, and work on the implementation of ACC technology is expected to be accelerated in the next few years. An ACC system can be regarded as one that autonomously adjusts the host vehicle's speed according to the flow of traffic such as under driving conditions where vehicle speeds are frequently changing. The adoption of ACC would free drivers from the need to accelerate or decelerate constantly in such circumstances, allowing them to enjoy more comfortable driving with less fatigue.

If ACC systems are to find marketplace recognition as a new concept and be widely accepted by drivers, they must be able to operate under the widest possible range of driving environments. Another essential requirement will be to provide natural vehicle behavior that does not deviate from drivers' expectations.

We have examined the performance required of ACC from these viewpoints, taking into account compatibility with Japanese market needs, and have developed an ACC system that uses millimeter-wave radar technology to achieve brake control capability.

This paper describes the design concept and effectiveness of the system and presents experimental and simulation results to illustrate its performance.

FEATURES OF ACC SYSTEM

An ACC system uses the speed selected by the driver as an upper limit for automatically controlling the host vehicle's speed so as to maintain a certain set distance to a preceding vehicle. The newly developed system presented here adopts a millimeter-wave radar unit as the headway distance sensor and can decelerate the host vehicle by controlling not only the throttle but also the brakes. The configuration of the system is shown schematically in Fig.1.

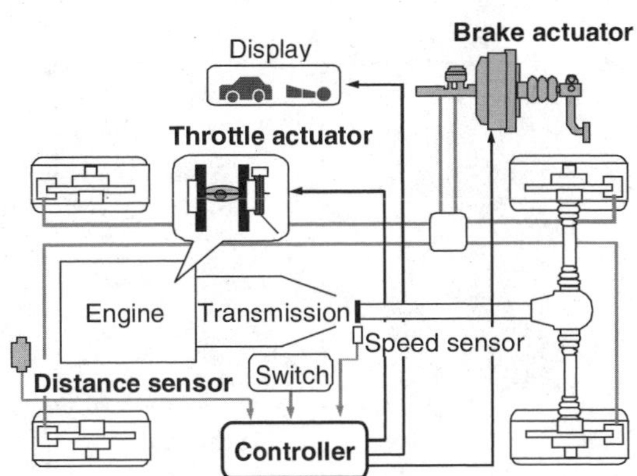

Figure 1. Configuration of ACC system

The magnitude of braking deceleration G was investigated in expressway driving, which is expected to be the principal driving environment for the use of ACC. It was found that braking to 2.5 m/s^2 accounted for approximately 90% of the frequency of maximum deceleration (Fig.2). Theaintains a certain set distance brake control capability in addition to throttle control would substantially expand the potential range of ACC use.

An electronically controlled vacuum booster is used as the brake control unit, and the operation of an atmospheric air valve is continuously controlled by a solenoid to control the brake pressure. The brake actuator achieves smooth braking force control similar to a driver's operation of the brake pedal, making it well suited to the attainment of natural deceleration behavior that does not seem strange to the driver.(1)

The headway distance sensors used for ACC are usually optical devices such as laser radar or radio-wave devices like millimeter-wave radar. Millimeter-wave radar has the advantage of providing highly reliable detection of forward objects even in adverse conditions, such as during rainy weather, splashing caused by a preceding vehicle or when the rear reflector of a forward vehicle is dirty.(2) It is thought that such performance can secure a high level of practicality under Japan's weather conditions, which are characterized by rainfall of over 1 mm during one day on more than 100 days a year.

DESIGN OF HEADWAY CONTROL UNIT

ANALYSIS OF DRIVING BEHAVIOR CHARACTERISTICS – An ACC system is expected to provide headway distance control consistent with drivers' expectations of vehicle behavior. A practical approach to achieving such control performance would be to model the driving behavior of experienced, well-mannered drivers and then conduct tests with a large number of subjects to verify that the control algorithm does not cause unnatural vehicle behavior. In line with this approach, an analysis was first made of driving behavior characteristics when drivers act to adjust the distance to a preceding vehicle.

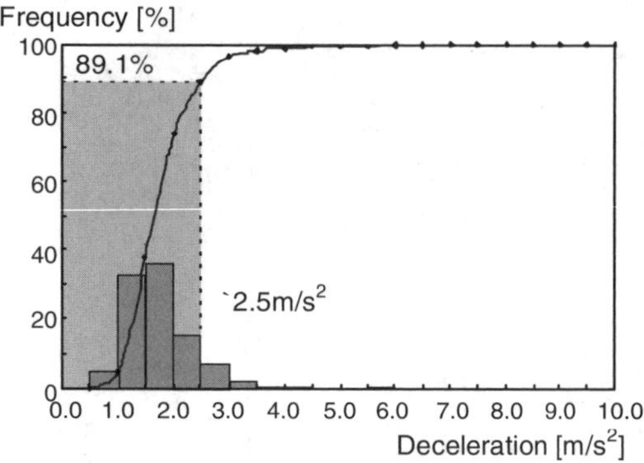

Figure 2. Magnitude of braking deceleration in expressway driving

Two objectives can be considered for a driver's action of adjusting the headway distance. One objective is to make the relative velocity with the preceding vehicle approach zero and the other is to make the distance to the preceding vehicle approach a distance predetermined by the driver. Analyses of driver behavior were conducted at Cambridge Basic Research using a test vehicle and a driving simulator. A time-series observation of the participating drivers' actions revealed a close correlation between the headway time and the collision time margin.(3) Here, the collision time margin refers to the value obtained by dividing the headway distance to the preceding vehicle by the relative velocity between the vehicles. Driver behavior in adjusting the headway distance was then analyzed by focusing on the deviation between the final adjusted headway distance and the actual headway distance during the adjustment process (referred to here as the target headway distance deviation) and changes in relative velocity.

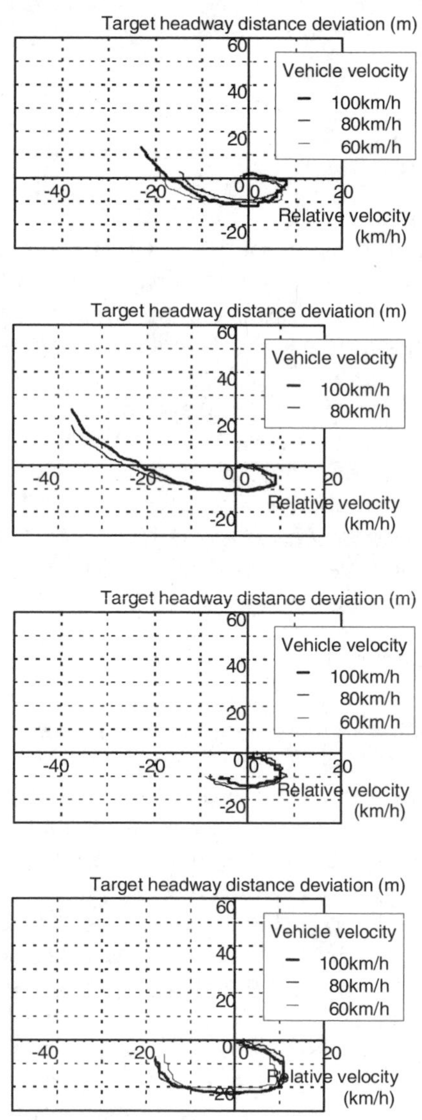

Figure 3. Phase plane trajectories of driving behavior

Driver behavior in adjusting the headway distance to a target distance after becoming aware of a preceding vehicle was examined first in tests in which a slower moving vehicle cut in front of the host vehicle. The characteristics of the test subjects' behavior were analyzed in phase planes expressed in terms of the target headway distance deviation and relative velocity. It was observed that the trajectories of their driving behavior in these phase planes generally tended to converge to the target headway distance in smooth leftward-oriented curves. This means that the subjects avoided decelerating abruptly and converged the vehicle to the target headway distance in smooth driving actions. It was also observed that the phase planes showed the same tendencies regardless of the vehicle speed, so long as the preceding vehicle was discovered under the same phase plane condition (Fig.3).

Driving behavior characteristics were then investigated focusing on a situation where the preceding vehicle changed speed within a range of a low relative velocity while the two vehicles were traveling at nearly a constant headway distance. The results indicated that the subjects acted more quickly to adjust the headway distance when following the preceding vehicle at slower speeds or at shorter distances. It was observed that their driving behavior was characterized by an effort to achieve a smooth flow of driving actions according to the vehicle speed and the headway distance involved.

CONFIGURATION OF HEADWAY CONTROL UNIT – The results of the foregoing analyses of driving behavior characteristics revealed that the headway distance control performed by the ACC system must be tuned with respect to two characteristics. One is the control characteristic of the trajectory at the start of following, and the other is the control characteristic while following a preceding vehicle. The first characteristic determines a trajectory for converging the headway distance to the target value after the driver of the host vehicle becomes aware of a preceding vehicle. The second characteristic is the response of the host vehicle to changes in the speed of the preceding vehicle while following the latter at the target headway distance.

Accordingly, a two-degree-of-freedom model was used to design the headway control unit so that these two characteristics could be determined independently. The headway control unit was positioned at a higher level above the vehicle speed control unit.[4]

DESIGN AND TUNING OF HEADWAY CONTROL UNIT – This section explains the design of the headway control unit. A block diagram of the control algorithm of this ACC system is shown in Fig.4.

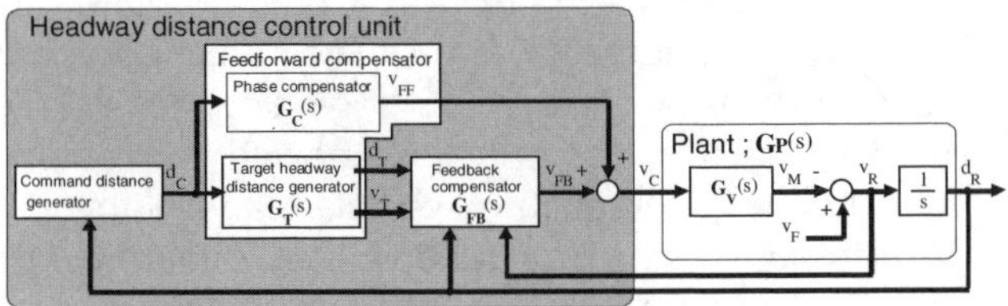

Figure 4. Block diagram of control system

As the first step in designing the headway control unit, the transfer function $G_V(s)$ of the vehicle speed control unit was set as shown in Eq.(1) below.

$$v_M(s) = G_V(s) \cdot v_C(s)$$
$$G_V(s) = \frac{\omega_V}{s + \omega_V} \tag{1}$$

The transfer function $G_P(s)$ of the object of control (plant) used in the control system design is expressed by Eq.(2) using the transfer function and its integral of the vehicle speed control unit.

$$G_P(s) = \frac{1}{s} G_V(s) \tag{2}$$

Accordingly, the transfer function $G_M(s)$ of the entire control system, i.e., the characteristic from the input of the set headway distance to the output of the actual headway distance, can be expressed as

$$\begin{aligned} d_R(s) &= G_M(s) \cdot d_C(s) \\ &= \frac{G_P(s)G_T(s)G_{FB}(s) + G_C(s)G_P(s)}{1 + G_P(s)G_{FB}(s)} d_C(s) \end{aligned} \tag{3}$$

The feed-forward compensator is designed so that the transfer function of the entire system $G_M(s)$ is made to coincide with the transfer function $G_T(s)$ that determines the response of the target headway distance. To accomplish that, it is composed of $G_T(s)$ and a phase compensator, which consists of the inverse system of the transfer function $G_P(s)$ of the plant and $G_T(s)$. The phase compensator $G_C(s)$ is given by

$$G_C(s) = \frac{G_T(s)}{G_P(s)} \tag{4}$$

The transfer function $G_T(s)$ of the target headway distance response serves to determine the control characteristic of the trajectory at the time the host vehicle begins following a preceding vehicle. As the following equation indicates, it is defined as the response characteristic of a second-order system.

$$G_T(s) = \frac{{\omega_{nT}}^2}{s^2 + 2\varsigma_T \omega_{nT} s + {\omega_{nT}}^2} \tag{5}$$

The feedback compensator acts to reduce any deviation that occurs between the actual headway distance and the target distance due to changes in the speed of the preceding vehicle or for other reasons during following. Its transfer function is given by the following expression.

$$v_{FB}(s) = G_{FB}(s) \cdot (d_T(s) - d_R(s))$$
$$G_{FB}(s) = sf_V - f_D \tag{6}$$

Based on the analysis of driving behavior characteristics, the target response of the control characteristic of the trajectory at the onset of following was expressed in terms of the target headway distance deviation and relative velocity. A simulation was then run to examine a control system for achieving the target response, and the control characteristics were finalized in validation tests conducted with an actual vehicle.

The control characteristic of the trajectory during following was determined by tuning the feedback control characteristic so that the timing for the onset of headway distance adjustment when the preceding vehicle changes speed would match the timing of the driver's action to adjust the distance.

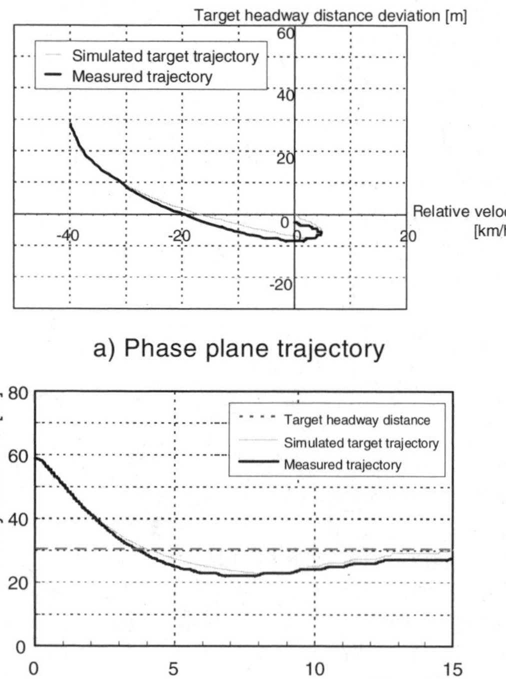

a) Phase plane trajectory

b) Time series history

Figure 5. Result of driving test

Fig.5 shows the result of driving test conducted with an actual vehicle. It is seen that the target trajectory set on the basis of the simulation results agreed well with the trajectory obtained with the test vehicle.

EVALUATION OF ACC SYSTEM

The evaluation of an ACC system requires the acquisition of data under traffic environment conditions allowing a high degree of reproducibility. To meet that requirement, tests were conducted on a proving ground and with a driving simulator so that the traffic environment could be set as desired.(5) Measurements were made of the driver's workload and of the vehicle behavior to verify the effectiveness of ACC.

DRIVER'S CONTROL INPUTS – The driver's control inputs were measured for a vehicle equipped with the ACC system and for a vehicle fitted with a conventional cruise control system under identical traffic flows set with the driving simulator. As seen in Fig.6, the results indicated that ACC reduced the frequency of the driver's accelerator and brake pedal operations compared with the vehicle equipped with conventional cruise control. The frequency of operating the control switches was also markedly reduced in the ACC-equipped vehicle. These results confirmed that the ACC system effectively reduces annoying control inputs by the driver.

DRIVER'S WORKLOAD – The steering entropy method, which is a technique for measuring variation in the steering angle during driving, was used to evaluate the driver's workload.(6) Ordinarily, drivers try to execute smooth steering maneuvers by estimating the situation ahead as they drive along. However, when some additional task other than steering is imposed on the driver, the smoothness of steering maneuvers is lost in proportion to the magnitude of the extra task, resulting in larger discontinuities in steering behavior. The steering entropy method focuses on this characteristic as an index of the driver's workload.

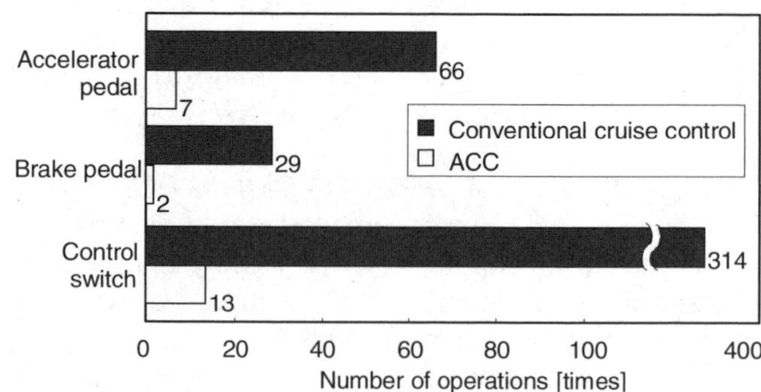

Figure 6. Driver's control inputs (driving speed : 80-100km/h; driving time : 70min)

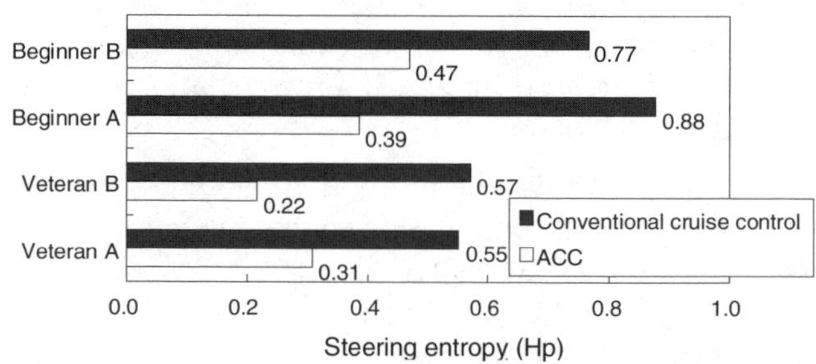

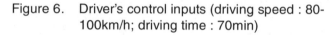

Figure 7. Variation in steering angle among drivers

Steering entropy measurements were made with the ACC-equipped vehicle and the conventional cruise control-equipped vehicle while following a preceding vehicle that changed speeds according to a predetermined pattern during test course driving. The tests were conducted with veteran drivers and beginning drivers. As indicated in Fig.7, all the subjects showed less steering entropy with the ACC-equipped vehicle than with the conventional cruise control-equipped vehicle, confirming that the driver's workload was reduced with the former system.

VEHICLE LONGITUDINAL G – Measurements were made of vehicle longitudinal G as an index of acceleration/deceleration behavior when the veteran drivers and beginning drivers followed a preceding vehicle that changed speeds according to a predetermined pattern during test course driving. The results were compared with the acceleration/deceleration behavior of the ACC-equipped vehicle.

The frequency response results in Fig.8 show that the ACC-equipped vehicle kept longitudinal oscillations in the frequency region below 2 Hz to the same level as the veteran drivers. This confirms that the operation of the ACC system eliminates unnecessary acceleration/ deceleration, enabling vehicle occupants to enjoy a smooth, comfortable ride.

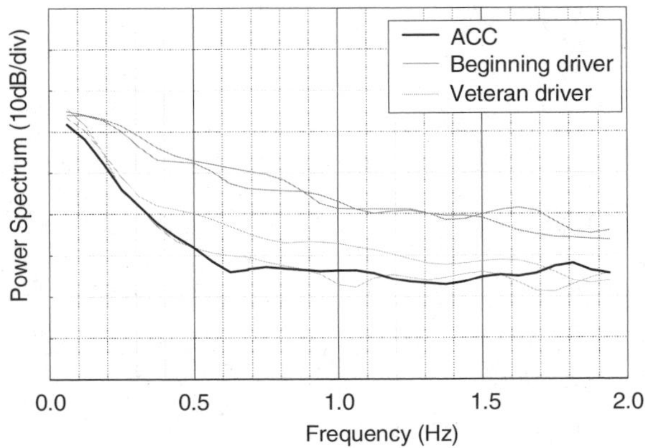

Figure 8. Frequency characteristics of vehicle longitudinal G

CONCLUSION

If ACC is to find acceptance in the marketplace as a system with a high level of practicality, it will have to be capable of operating under a wide range of driving environments and be able to adjust the vehicle speed without causing drivers to feel unnatural vehicle behavior. By using millimeter-wave radar and an electronically controlled vacuum booster, a control algorithm has been developed that is capable of modeling driving behavior characteristics. This has led to the development of an ACC system that can adapt well to typical driving behavior under Japan's traffic environment conditions. The results of tests conducted with an actual vehicle and a driving simulator confirmed that this system reduces the driver's workload for more comfortable driving.

Autonomous vehicle control systems that assist with the execution of driving tasks and reduce the driver's workload show one direction for the future evolution of vehicles. It is projected that R&D work on technologies in this field will proceed at an increasingly faster pace in the next few years, and the resulting synergies with ongoing innovations in onboard information and communications devices will dramatically expand the functions and capabilities of vehicles.

REFERENCES

1. K. Bill, et al., “Smart Booster—New Key Element for Brake Systems with Enhanced Function Potential”, SAE Technical Paper No. 950760 (1995), pp. 27-34.
2. Rolf Adomat, et al., “Radar Based Automotive Obstacle Detection System”, SAE Technical Paper No. 940904 (1994).
3. M. A. Goodrich, et al., “Semiotics and Mental Models (Modeling Automobile Driver Behavior)”, IEEE Joint Conference (1998), pp. 771-776.
4. T. Ieko, et al., “Design of a 2-Degree-of-Freedom Slip Speed Control System for an Automotive Automatic Transmission”, Transactions of the Society of Instrument and Control Engineers, Vol. 34, No. 11 (1998) (in Japanese).
5. T. Yamamura, et al., “Development of a Driving Simulator with a Bounded Oscillation Mechanism”, Proceedings of the 75th Annual Meeting of the Japan Society of Mechanical Engineers (IV), (1998), pp. 406-407 (in Japanese).
6. O. Nakayama, et al., “Development of a Steering Entropy Method for Evaluating Driver Workload”, SAE Technical Paper No. 1999-01-0892 (1999).

2000-01-1300

The N.A.I.C.C. Project: A Navigation Aided Intelligent Cruise Control System

Jean-Philippe Lauffenburger, Jérome Baujon, Michel Basset and Gérard Léon Gissinger
University of Haute Alsace

ABSTRACT

Developing a knowledge-based predictive driver-aid system requires a strategy that meets the needs and goals, as well as rigorous methods. This paper presents the strategy adopted and the first results obtained in the development of the Navigation Aided Intelligent Cruise Control (N.A.I.C.C.) system. Once the vehicle is located on the route, this new copilot can:

1. define the travel direction and the vehicle speed,
2. determine the distance to the next bend and its characteristics,
3. predict the optimal speed to negotiate the next bend considering the road profile, the constraints given by the driver and the information provided by the sensors mounted on the vehicle.

Then, used in the warning mode ("Driver Alarm Mode"), N.A.I.C.C. informs the driver of the danger of the situation (excessive speed) or, in the intervention mode ("Velocity Control Mode"), N.A.I.C.C. adapts the speed to the predicted reference. In this latter operating mode, N.A.I.C.C. can be considered as an advanced intelligent cruise control system. Real experiments were carried out with the laboratory test car to validate each module described.

INTRODUCTION

Ever increasing traffic forces the driver to treat a growing amount of information and, at the same time, to take more, and quicker, decisions. Thus, in critical situations, the amount of information may exceed the driver's effective treatment capability. Recent analyses have shown that the driver is responsible for 85% of car accidents. M. Kopf showed that the reasons could be divided into 2 different parts: the perception of the information and the appraisal of the situation's gravity [1]. Thanks to the improvements in computer technologies, the driver can now be assisted in the detection and/or correction of a critical situation with the help of on-board systems [2]. These systems essentially act in the appraisal of the situation's gravity [3, 4], but they can also replace the driver in some tasks to limit the driver's workload and so, enhance driving safety and comfort. Most of the systems developed in this way act in the field of lateral and longitudinal control [5, 6]. The current strategy adopted by car manufacturers as well as psychologists in the development of a copilot consists in replacing the driver for simple tasks (speed regulation...) and in assisting him as much as possible for more complicated ones (situation's gravity estimation...). The problems that remain now are mainly caused by the driver's unpredictability and by varying driving conditions like grip or even weather conditions.

Driving a vehicle on a road is similar to the regulation of a technical process. The system, composed of the vehicle, the driver and the road, has to be considered as a closed-loop system in which the driver performs the entire regulation function [7, 8]. During this task, the driver has to perform stabilization, guidance and navigation tasks (see Figure 1). The stabilization and guidance levels can be represented with an AND/OR-Graph which separates the longitudinal and the lateral part of the control level and shows the actuators needed [1].

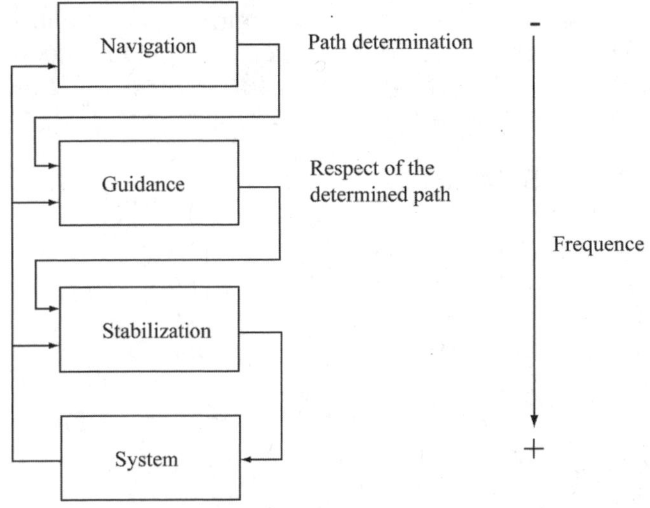

Figure 1. Hierarchical description of the driving task

Driver-aid systems[1] are designed to act almost like a human driver and are integrated into the "driver+vehicle+road" control loop. Therefore, the responsibility or task allocation of the copilot and of the driver have to be clearly defined. The development of an assistance system must specify the level of interaction between the driver and this system among 5 different levels:

- Information,
- Advice,
- Warning,
- Support,
- Intervention.

The main reason for car accidents in which the driver's responsibility is involved is inappropriate driving speed [3] due to a bad estimation of the system's limits (combination of the road shape, the vehicle's potential and the driver's capabilities). In the field of intelligent assistance systems, the I.D.A.S. (Intelligent Driver Aid System) project has been developed to improve the driver's safety and driving comfort on any type of roads. I.D.A.S. is including the DRI.MO. (DRIver MOdeling) project and the N.A.I.C.C. (Navigation Aided Intelligent Cruise Control) project. N.A.I.C.C. acts at the stabilization level described in Figure 1. This paper only presents the longitudinal part of the N.A.I.C.C. project whose aim is to warn the driver in the case of inappropriate driving speed and to adapt the vehicle's speed to the driving situation (bend,...). This new approach to supervision includes the early detection of inappropriate driving speed which could lead to critical driving situations. N.A.I.C.C. is based on:

1. an accurate vehicle location, via data fusion between a GPS system and a Dead-Reckoning (DR) algorithm combined to a new Bézier based digital map database,
2. the accuracy of the neuro-fuzzy real-time velocity estimator providing the longitudinal and the lateral velocities needed in the DR algorithm,
3. a cruise control system.

After the presentation of the laboratory test car and its measurement units (GPS, gyroscopes...), each module of the N.A.I.C.C. will be described more precisely and simulation results will be shown and discussed.

LIST OF SYMBOLS

V_L	Longitudinal velocity	m/s
V_T	Lateral velocity	m/s
$\dot{\psi}$	Yaw rate	rad/s
ψ	Yaw angle	rad
γ_L	Longitudinal acceleration	m/s²
γ_T	Lateral acceleration	m/s²
θ_{Pap}	Throttle valve angle	%
α_V	Steering-wheel angle	°

[1] The expression "Driver-aid systems" has to be taken in the sense of Copilot.

MEASUREMENTS

All the experiments were carried out with the instrumented laboratory test car (a Renault Megane 2.0l 16 valves) on a test track to ensure maximum safety.

THE TEST CAR

Currently available sensors – The different sensors and measurement parameters needed are shown in Figure 2. The longitudinal and lateral velocities (V_L, V_T) are measured during the validation period by an optical cross-correlation sensor located at the rear center of the vehicle. Afterwards, this sensor will be replaced by a real-time speed estimator developed by the laboratory [9]. The piezoelectric vibrating gyroscope, the microprocessor-controlled fluxgate compass and the accelerometers are located near the center of gravity of the test car. They measure respectively the yaw rate ($\dot{\psi}$), the yaw angle (ψ), and the longitudinal and transversal accelerations (γ_L, γ_T).

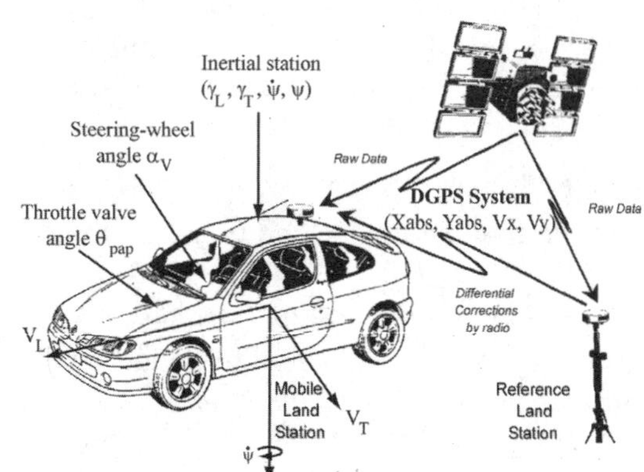

Figure 2. Sensors and measurement parameters in the instrumented laboratory car

The DGPS system – The Global Positioning System (GPS) is a satellite-based radio-navigation system which determines the absolute position with an accuracy of some hundred meters [10]. The use of 2 GPS receivers allows more accurate position determination. This technique is known as Differential GPS (DGPS). One receiver is used as a reference station with known coordinates while the other rotates around it. The calculated position of the reference is compared with the known coordinates to generate a differential correction signal which is transmitted to the remote receiver. This reduces the position error to 10^{-2} meters. In a first step, the N.A.I.C.C. positioning module is based on a DGPS in order to validate the concepts developed (data fusion, map-matching...) but the final N.A.I.C.C. prototype uses a less accurate conventional GPS system.

Acquisition hardware – The real-time data acquisition hardware is based on a DSP board and I/O boards linked, via Ethernet, to a PC in which the data are stored. A sampling frequency of 50Hz for all the sensors except the DGPS (10Hz), has been chosen for the tests.

THE TEST TRACK – The bird's-eye view plotted in Figure 3 describes the track used to develop and validate the N.A.I.C.C. system. This track located near the University is composed of bends whose radii of curvature cover a large field of possibilities (from 30m to 150m). The particularity of this track is that it is only represented by straight lines and bends with constant curvatures (no clothoïdes were used to connect the straight lines to the bends). During the tests, only the so called "slow part" of the track (represented in black in Figure 3) has been used.

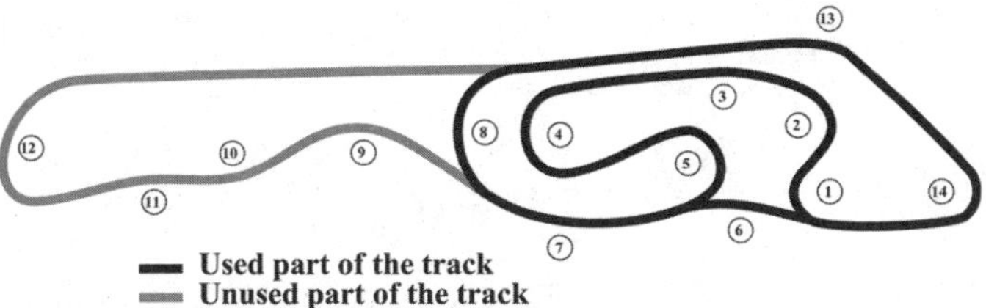

Figure 3. The test track

THE N.A.I.C.C. SYSTEM

GENERAL DESCRIPTION – The N.A.IC.C. project includes 2 research activities: the longitudinal and lateral control of a car. The longitudinal part of the N.A.I.C.C. is shown in Figure 4. The general idea is to combine a navigation system like the ones available on the market [11] and a real-time velocity estimator to finally develop a warning and intervention system. In order to predict the velocity needed to perform a given driving situation (bend negotiation,...) or to detect inappropriate speed in time, a precise position of the vehicle is required. Therefore, the positioning module, the map-matching algorithm and the digital database are most important. The optimal speed is predicted by taking account of the road characteristics, the constraints given by the driver (driving style, speed reference...) some information provided by the sensors mounted on the vehicle and the real-time velocity estimator. Afterwards, N.A.I.C.C. informs the driver of the situation's gravity or finally adapts the speed to the reference determined thanks to the cruise control system.

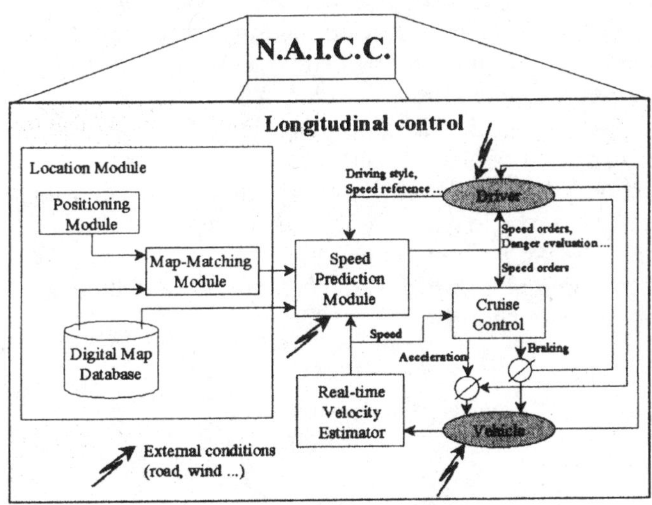

Figure 4. Structure of the N.A.I.C.C. longitudinal controller

The lateral control, based on the generation of a reference trajectory with fuzzy-logic optimized polar polynomial curves, will be presented in a future paper.

THE POSITIONING MODULE – A single sensor cannot provide an accurate vehicle position. Therefore, complementary and redundant information for all driving situations are necessary. These are obtained by multisensor integration and fusion [12, 13, 14, 15]. Each sensor has its own capabilities and independent failures; the aim of the fusion is to compensate for the failures. In the case of the vehicle's heading determination, a relative sensor (a gyroscope whose signal is integrated, for example) is generally combined with an absolute sensor (GPS). The positioning module developed in the currently available navigation systems are based on GPS and Dead-Reckoning (DR) data [12, 16, 17] fused via some filtering methods (centralized or decentralized Kalman filters, federated filters...) [18, 19]. These 2 positioning techniques operate complementarily because of their nature (absolute and relative positioning techniques).

The Dead-Reckoning method – It is a technique that determines the vehicle coordinates relative to a starting/reference point (x_0, y_0). At a time t_n, the position of the vehicle (x_n, y_n) is given by:

$$\begin{cases} x_n = x_0 + \sum_{i=0}^{n-1} d_i . \cos\theta_i \\ y_n = y_0 + \sum_{i=0}^{n-1} d_i . \sin\theta_i \end{cases} \tag{1}$$

where d_i and θ_i are respectively the distance and the absolute heading of the displacement between the time t_{n-1} and t_n. The DR method is a recursive and thus an accumulative process. The calculated point is altered by the errors and the drift of the sensors. If not compensated for, the calculated position will be less and less accurate.

The previous relation can be expressed relatively to the equipment of the test car which estimates the longitudinal and lateral velocities instead of the distance traveled:

$$\begin{cases} x_n = x_0 + T.\sum_{i=0}^{n-1} (V_{L_i}.\cos\psi_i - V_{T_i}.\sin\psi_i) \\ y_n = y_0 + T.\sum_{i=0}^{n-1} (V_{L_i}.\sin\psi_i + V_{T_i}.\cos\psi_i) \end{cases} \tag{2}$$

where T is the sampling time of the acquisition hardware.

Figure 5 describes the position determination with DR of 5 laps on the test track. The observable drift is mainly due to the use of the gyroscope in the calculation of the heading angle. A study by J. Borenstein showed a drift rate of approximately 10°/min for the model used in the tests [20].

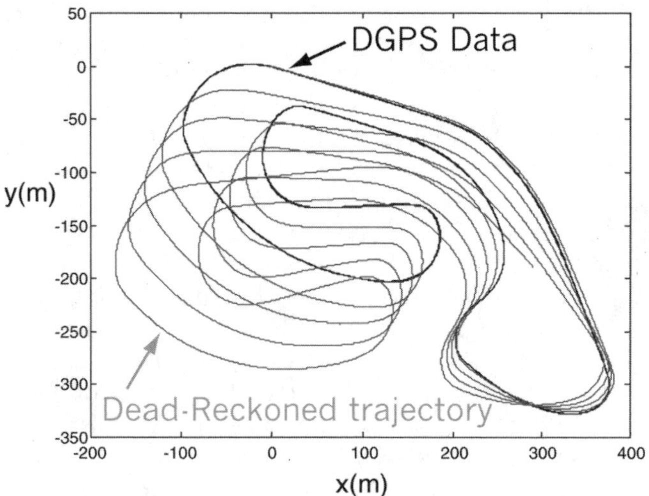

Figure 5. Trajectory reconstruction with DR

The fusion technique – Accurate vehicle positioning is necessary for best performance of the N.A.I.C.C. system. Therefore, the fusion algorithm presented in Figure 6 has been implemented.

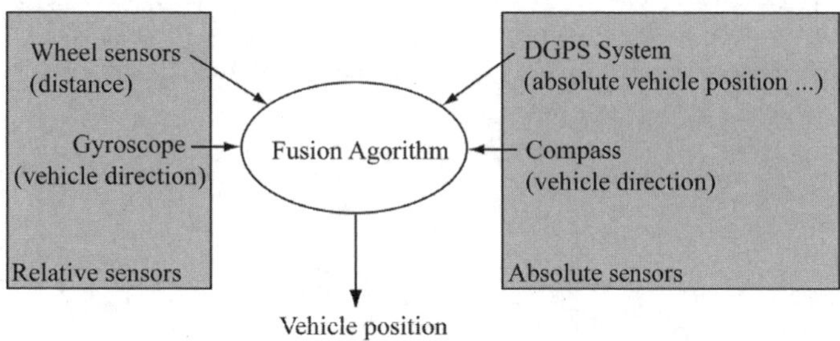

Figure 6. Fusion of absolute and relative sensors

The approach is very simple and consists in using the DGPS data when the signals are available, and switching to DR when the number of visible satellites is not sufficient to ensure an accurate position. Moreover, the DGPS data are used in the initialization of the DR routine; the last available DGPS point is taken as the initial point of the DR recursive equation shown above. As shown in Figure 7, the initialization of the recursive routine with the latest available GPS point improves considerably the dead-reckoned trajectory.

If the DGPS signal quality is poor for a longer time, the DR estimated position and thus the vehicle location are subjected to the sensor drifts previously mentioned. A technique then consists in initializing the DR routine - once every 20 acquisition points - with the accurate map-matched point. This increases the position module results considerably. Thanks to both the DGPS accuracy and the use of the map-matched location in the DR, this real-time positioning module gives satisfactory results.

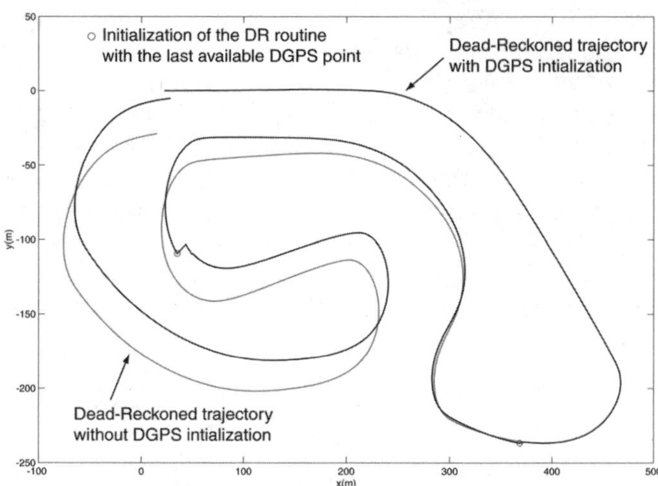

Figure 7. DR using DGPS data

Results – The DGPS/DR positioning module has been tested and validated with the trajectory described in Figure 5. Losses of DGPS data were simulated several times for each round. Figure 8 shows the results and illustrates the position jumps obtained with this approach every time the module switch from DR to DGPS.

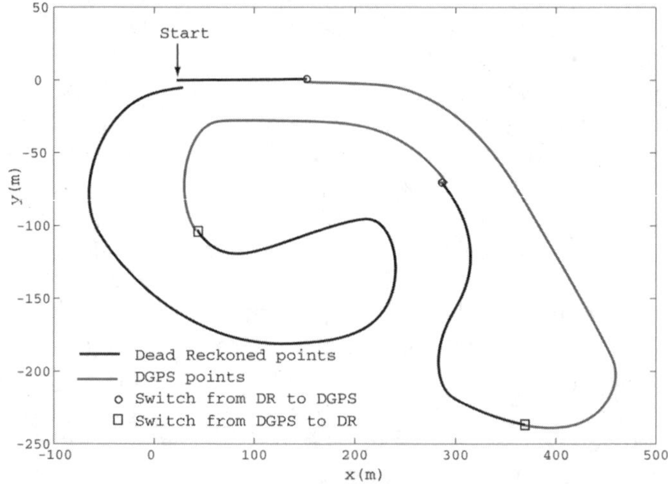

Figure 8. Real time DGPS/DR positioning

Here, on the one hand, the absolute position accuracy of the DGPS is used to provide feedback to correct the DR errors, and on the other hand, the DR system provides the position information when the DGPS signal's accuracy is degraded. This auto-correction enhances the performance in vehicle positioning. In the literature, some authors developed [16] sensor auto-calibration algorithms in order to increase the precision of the whole system. Thanks to the high accuracy of the DGPS and also of the original Bézier based digital map, these techniques are not necessary.

THE BEZIER BASED DIGITAL MAP DATABASE – The digital map database is of the utmost importance for a system that involves map-related functions like matching the trajectory and the known road or determining the optimal speed to perform a given driving task. Traditionally, the road data are represented by line segments whose endpoints (nodes) and shapes are defined in terms of longitude, latitude and sometimes relative altitude. Any road is represented by a sequence of straight lines chosen to approximate the real curvature of the road. An accuracy of about 15 meters can be reached with this technique. A precise description of this method can be found in [10]. To increase accuracy, especially when representing the curvature of the road (bend), an important number of shape points are required. This requires a serious increase in the necessary storage memory.

In the N.A.I.C.C. project, the road curvature is the most important information provided by the database. On the one hand, it is used to determine whether or not the vehicle is on a straight line, on the other hand, to predict the optimal driving speed. Thus, a better approximation tool is needed. The Bézier curves are chosen because they allow a parametric description of the curve [21]. It is then possible to approximate double definitions and almost any type of curves. Moreover, thanks to this parametric description, the necessary storage memory need not be as important as with a traditional database structure. Here, the basic idea is to consider every road as a bend, a straight line being a particular bend with an infinite radius of curvature. So, this type of representation can be used to define the road axis.

This original database structure has been tested and validated in ideal conditions (i.e. on the test track) and is now applied to the digitalization of classic road networks. Further studies will point out the effectiveness of this approach in terms of accuracy in the road representation and also of necessary storage memory.

THE MAP-MATCHING MODULE – This module is primordial to obtain an accurate location of the vehicle. It is based on the original database structure evoked above and allows a precise location of the dead-reckoned position of the vehicle.

Principle – When the DGPS signal is not available, the DR method is active. As shown earlier, this method is considerably affected by the inaccuracies and drifts of the on-board sensors. Thus, the errors in the positioning module grow with the traveled distance due to the recursive form of the calculation technique. That is why the DR position matches the nearest point on the digital map. Several Map-Matching (MM) methods have been developed so far; they can be divided into 2 categories: MM using geometric information only or using both geometric and topological information. A detailed description can be found in [22].

The Map-Matching algorithm – The N.A.I.C.C. MM Module is based on an algorithm using only geometric information called "Geometric Point-to-Point Matching" [22]. The idea is to match the point given by the positioning module and the "closest" point of a Bézier curve in the road network. In a point-to-point matching procedure, it is only necessary to calculate the distance (i.e. the polar radial) between the dead-reckoned point and each point in the database, and finally store the closest point found along the road. Compared with a traditional point-to-point algorithm, the present one is more efficient because of the high definition of the database. Moreover, the point can be approximated to any point of the Bézier curve and not only to a node or an intermediate point as is the case for conventional algorithms.

Results – The trajectory resulting from the DGPS/DR positioning module (see Figure 8) and the Bézier description of the test track road axis have been map-matched. The ensuing vehicle location is described in Figure 9. Due to the drift introduced by the use of the DR method for a long time, it appears that the trajectory and the inappropriate roads are matched, twice. The initialization of the DR routine with a previous map-matched point resolves this problem.

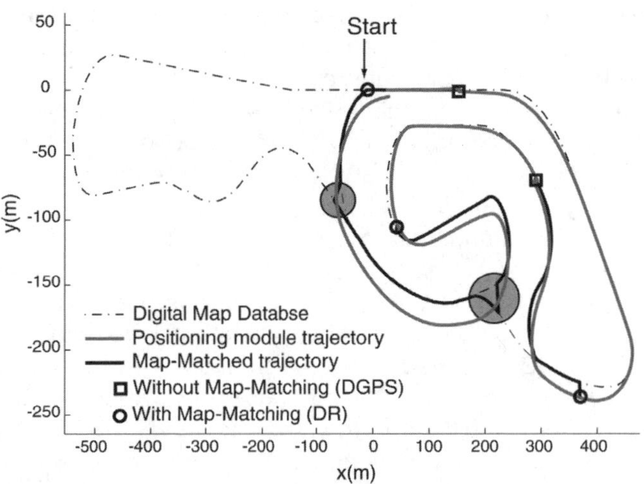

Figure 9. Vehicle location by Map-Matching

Once a precise location of the vehicle is obtained and with the help of the database comments, it is easy to determine whether or not the vehicle will have to negotiate a bend soon. Taking account of the road characteristics, the time (distance) to the next bend, the estimated velocity and different constraints given by the driver, the Speed Prediction Module predicts an optimal driving speed.

THE SPEED PREDICTION MODULE – The aim of the N.A.I.C.C. longitudinal controller is multiple: it can be used as a warning system or as a controller system. The optimal speed predicted by the Speed Prediction Module is compared with the estimated vehicle speed and, in the first utilization procedure, the system warns the driver of the inappropriate speed. In the second configuration, the system automatically adjusts the vehicle speed via a cruise control system.

Structure of the Speed Prediction Module – From the location module (positioning + MM modules), the Speed Prediction Module receives 2 main pieces of information:

- the distance to the next bend/intersection,
- the radius of curvature of this bend.

To compute the appropriate speed, some more data are required:

- driver characteristics,
- the speed limit of the current road,
- vehicle parameters (braking and acceleration potential),
- the current speed of the vehicle.

The Finite State Machine – The determination of the velocity is modeled by a finite state machine first described by [23] and adapted to the N.A.I.C.C. system. Figure 10 shows the state graph of the speed predictor.

The state machine begins in state 1. At this time, the vehicle accelerates until it reaches the desired velocity depending on the road type, say 90km/h. Once the desired speed $v_{desired}$ is reached, the state machine switches to state 2, "Approaching the curve". The basic idea in the N.A.I.C.C. system is to compute the distance which separates the vehicle from the next curve it will have to negotiate, no matter if it is still in a bend or not. In state 2, the optimal velocity for the bend is determined according to the vehicle's and driver's characteristics (braking capabilities, supported transversal acceleration...). Simultaneously, the module calculates the braking distance $d_{braking}$ required to obtain the desired velocity before the bend. The purpose is based on the "Time to Line Crossing" (TLC) concept introduced by Godthelp [24] applied to the calculation of the distance remaining before the braking sequence. If the distance between the vehicle and the next curve d_{curve} is shorter than or equal to the braking distance, the state machine changes to state 3 and the brake maneuver is performed until the speed variation[2] is less than 10% of the predicted speed. If the desired curve velocity is achieved, the state machine switches into state 4. In this state, the velocity is hold constant until the vehicle has reached the end of the current bend. At this time, two solutions are possible:

1. the curve is followed by a straight-line and the vehicle can reaccelerate. The state machine changes to state 1 in order to achieve the desired speed,
2. the curve is immediately followed by a second one and the state machine switches to state 2.

The main improvement of the state machine presented here is the capability to treat successive curves.

[2] The speed variation represents the difference between the desired speed and the actual vehicle speed.

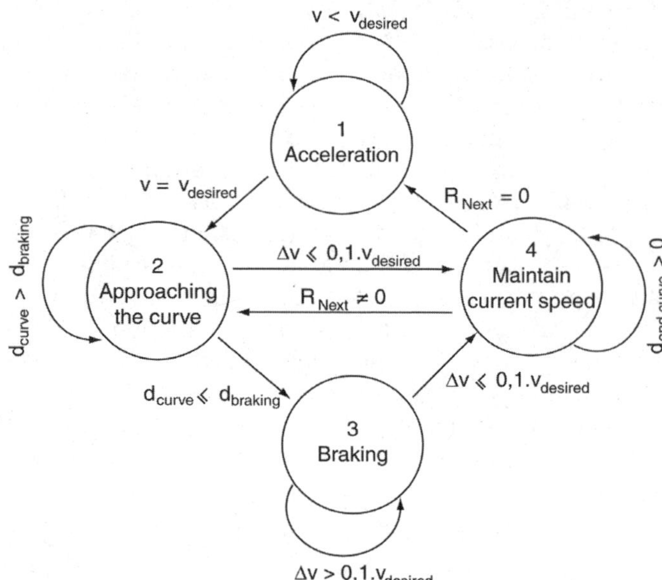

Figure 10. State graph of the Speed Prediction Module

Results – The results presented in this section have been obtained with the laboratory test car on the test track in Figure 3. The driving style implemented in the Speed Prediction Module (via the driver dependent parameters) is of the "rally" type. In the validation phase, two types of drivers are available: the "normal" one and the "rally" driver; but in the current utilization of N.A.I.C.C., only the "normal" configuration is implemented. The maximum speed has been fixed to 80km/h in order to respect the safety conditions. During these tests, N.A.I.C.C. has been used as a warning system and no special driving conditions were imposed. Figure 11 describes the vehicle speed recorded during one round and the speed shape given by the N.A.I.C.C. system. The difference observable at the beginning of the acquisition is due to the sensor calibration period that the test-driver had to perform.

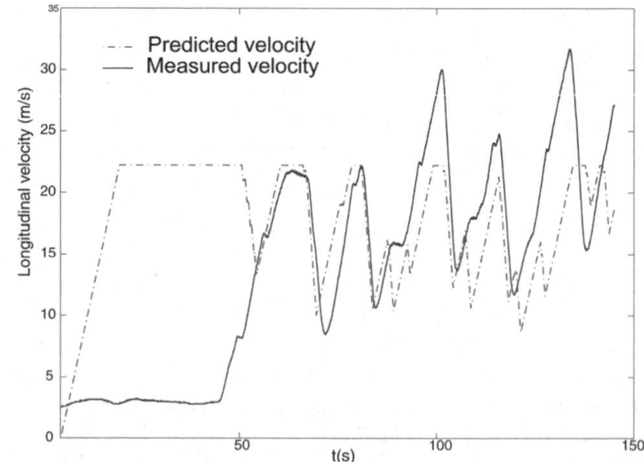

Figure 11. N.A.I.C.C. vs test-driver

During these tests, it was assumed that the N.A.I.C.C. system acts on the gear box and on the braking system (ABS). In this first approach, the aim was to study the feasibility of the speed prediction with given constraints (low-cost sensors, real-time conditions...).

CONCLUSION

The design of an assistance system is a complex task which needs a well-structured approach. First, the system requirements have to be properly identified in order to highlight the system architecture. Then, the necessary tasks have to be determined (vehicle positioning, map-matching...) in order to specify the corresponding modules and finally select the suitable hardware and software tools to develop the system.

A new intelligent driver-aid system has been described. The Navigation Aided Intelligent Cruise Control system is based on a positioning module, a map-matching algorithm and a digital map database, a real-time velocity estimator and a speed prediction module. The aim of this system is the early detection of inappropriate driving speed conditions. Thus, a precise location of the vehicle is primordial. In the positioning module, an absolute sensor (DGPS in the validation phase) is associated with a relative position determination algorithm (Dead-Reckoning). A simple fusion technique increases position accuracy. The development of an original database structure based on the Bézier curves allows a highly accurate vehicle location. Thanks to the additional information stored in this database, an easy to compute finite state machine has been implemented to determine the optimal driving speed, taking account of the road characteristics, weather conditions and driver dependent parameters.

Various feasibility and validation tests were carried out first on the test track, then on traditional roads. All the modules described in this paper have been validated successively in real-time conditions.

The N.A.I.C.C. system proposes two operating modes: the "Driver Alarm Mode" or the "Velocity Control Mode". The present paper has described N.A.I.C.C. in its warning mode and given the results. The next step will consist in validating N.A.I.C.C. as an intervention system, in its "Velocity Control Mode". Furthermore, to improve this driver-aid system, external real-time varying parameters, like grip, the driver's intrinsic parameters and his workload must be taken into account.

REFERENCES

1. M. Kopf, "Ein Beitrag zur Modellbasierten, Adaptativen Fahrerunterstützung für das Fahren auf deutschen Autobahnen", Fortschrittberichte VDI, Reihe 12: Verkehrstechnik / Fahrzeugtechnik, N°203, 1994, Düsseldorf, Germany.
2. R. Onken, "The Compelling Evolution of operator assisting systems", Gärtner Stein Widdel Mensch-Maschine-Systeme und neue Informationstechnologien, FGAN-FAT, 1993, Wachtberg-Werthoven, Germany.
3. P.E. An, C.E. Harris, "An Intelligent Driver Warning System for Vehicle Collision Avoidance", IEEE Transactions on System, Man and Cybernetics, 1996, vol. 26, N°2, pp. 254 – 261, ISBN 0018-9472.
4. I. Giraud, P. Laurence, M. Fervel, G.L. Gissinger, "Real Time Fault Detection and Diagnosis: Application to the Critical Behavior of a Road Vehicle", Proceedings of the International Symposium on Advanced Vehicle Control, June 24 – 28, 1996, vol. 2, pp. 1267 – 1276, Aachen, Germany.
5. K. Naab, G. Reichart, "Driver Assistance Systems for Lateral and Longitudinal Vehicle Guidance – Heading Control and Active Cruise Support -", Proceedings of the International Symposium on Advanced Vehicle Control, October 24 – 28, 1994, pp. 449 – 454.
6. P. Protzel, R. Holve, J. Bernasch, K. Naab, "Fuzzy Distance Control for Intelligent Vehicle Guidance", Proceedings of the 12th Annual Meeting of the North American Fuzzy Information Processing Society, August 22 – 25, 1993, pp. 87 – 91, Allentown PA.
7. P. Laurence, M. Basset, G.L. Gissinger, "Lateral Vehicle Behavior: Comparison of Subjective/Objective Assessment Using the Choquet Integral", submitted to Vehicle System Dynamics, 1999.
8. H.-M. Gass, H. Glasser, B. Heissing, B. Mäusbacher, "Electronic Driving Aids", Proceedings of the International Symposium on Advanced Vehicle Control, June 24 – 28, 1996, Aachen, Germany.
9. A. Porcel, C. Runde, M. Basset, G.L. Gissinger, "Neuro-Fuzzy Approach to Real-Time Total Velocity Vector Estimation of a Passenger Car Covering Critical Situations", Proceedings of the IFAC Workshop on Advances in Automotive Control, 1998, Colombus, pp. 29 – 36.
10. Y. Zhao, "Vehicle Location and Navigation Systems", 1997, Artech House Publisher, Boston-London, ISBN 0-89006-861-5.
11. M.L.G. Toone, "CARIN, A Car Information and Navigation System", Philips Technical Review, 1987, vol. 43, N°11/12, pp. 317 – 329.
12. H. Degawa, "A New Navigation System with Multiple Information Sources", Proceedings of the Vehicle Navigation and Information Systems Conference, 1992, VNIS'92, pp. 143 – 149.
13. K. Watanabe, K. Kobayashi, F. Munekata, "Multiple Sensor Fusion for Navigation Systems", Proceedings of the Vehicle Navigation and Information Systems Conference, 1994, VNIS'94, pp. 575 – 578.
14. C.A. Scott, C.R. Drane, "Increased Accuracy of Motor Vehicle Position Estimation by Utilizing Map Data, Vehicle Dynamics and Other Information Sources", Proceedings of the Vehicle Navigation and Information Systems Conference, 1994, VNIS'94, pp.585 – 590.
15. R.C. Luo, M.G. Kray, "Multisensor Integration and Fusion for Intelligent Machines and Systems", Norwood, NJ: Ablex Publishing Corp., 1995.
16. W.W. Kao, "Integration of GPS and Dead-Reckoning Navigation Systems", Proceedings of the IEEE-IEE Vehicle Navigation and Information Systems, 1991, VNIS'91, SAE, pp. 635 – 643.
17. P.G. Mattos, "Integrated GPS and Dead-Reckoning for Low-Cost Vehicle Navigation and Tracking", Proceedings of the Vehicle Navigation and Information Systems Conference, 1994, VNIS'94, pp. 569 – 574.

18. M.A. Abousalem, E.J. Krakiwsky, “A Quality Control Approach for GPS-Based Automatic Vehicle Location and Navigation Systems”, Proceedings of the Vehicle Navigation and Information Systems Conference, 1993, VNIS’93, pp. 466 – 470.

19. E.J. Krakiwsky, C.B. Harris, R.V.C. Wong, “A Kalman Filter for Integrating Dead-Reckoning, Map-Matching and GPS Positioning”, Proceedings of the IEEE Position Location and Navigation Symposium, 1988, pp. 39 – 46.

20. J. Borenstein, L. Feng,”Gyrodometry: A New Method for Combining Data from Gyros and Odometry in Mobile Robots”, IEEE International Conference on Robotics and Automation, 1996, Mineapolis, pp. 423 – 428.

21. P. Bézier, “Courbes et Surfaces”, Mathématiques et CAO, vol. 4, 2nd Edition, Hermes, 1987, Paris, France, ISBN 2-86601-080-9.

22. D. Bernstein, A. Kornhauser, “Map Matching for Personal Navigation Assistants”, The Transportation Research Board, 77th Annual Meeting, January 11 – 15, 1998, Washington.

23. R. Majjad, “Hybride Modellierung und Identifikation eines Fahrer-Fahrzeug Systems”, Dissertation, Universität Fridericiana Karlsruhe, 1997.

24. H. Godthelp, P. Milgram, G.J. Blaauw, “The Development of a Time-Related Measure to Describe Driving Strategy”, Human Factors, vol. 26, N°3, 1984, pp. 257 – 268.

CONTACT

Gérard Léon Gissinger
ESSAIM / MIAM Laboratory, 12 rue des frères Lumière, F – 68093 MULHOUSE Cedex, Tel. (33) 3 89 33 69 40, Fax. (33) 3 89 33 69 49,
e-mail: g.gissinger@essaim.univ-mulhouse.fr

DEFINITIONS, ACRONYMS, ABBREVIATIONS

CC: Cruise Control
DGPS: Differential Global Positioning System
DR: Dead-Reckoning
DSP: Digital Signal Processing
DRI.MO.: Driver Modeling
GPS: Global Positioning System
I.D.A.S.: Intelligent Driver Aid System
MM: Map-Matching
N.A.I.C.C.: Navigation Aided Intelligent Cruise Control
TLC: Time to Line Crossing

2000-01-0345

Comparison of Lidar-Based and Radar-Based Adaptive Cruise Control Systems

Glenn R. Widmann, Michele K. Daniels, Lisa Hamilton, Lawrence Humm, Bryan Riley, Jan K. Schiffmann, David E. Schnelker and William H. Wishon
Delphi Automotive Systems

ABSTRACT

Since the late 1980s, Delphi Automotive Systems has been very involved with the practical development of a variety of Collision Avoidance products for the near- and long-term automotive market. Many of these complex collision avoidance products will require the integration of various vehicular components/systems in order to provide a cohesive functioning product that is seamlessly integrated into the vehicle infrastructure. One such example of this system integration process was the development of an Adaptive Cruise Control system on an Opel Vectra. The design approach heavily incorporated system engineering processes/procedures. The critical issues and other technical challenges in developing these systems will be explored. Details on the hardware and algorithms developed for this vehicle, as well as the greater systems integration issues that arose during its development will also be presented. Actual on-road test results of the Adaptive Cruise Control system are discussed and compared for the two types of sensors.

INTRODUCTION

Adaptive Cruise Control (ACC) is the first milestone on the road to Automotive Collision Warning System products. Worldwide interest and a rapidly developing market for ACC shall result in the near-term introduction of this product on a wide range of vehicular platforms. These products will require the integration of various systems, such as brake, throttle, steering, engine management, harness, and detection sensor systems. The complexity and system-level nature of ACC makes it an excellent product to demonstrate the system engineering principles.

The critical path to a successful ACC system is the introduction of a new automotive component that has the capability to detect/sense the various target vehicle ahead of the host-vehicle, and assess/measure the kinematic attributes of each target (e.g.: distance, relative velocity, etc.). This "smart" device is a sophisticated forward-looking detection sensor using either infrared laser or millimeter wave signals. Delphi Delco Electronics Systems plans to offer two types of **Forewarn®** ACC products. The significant difference between these products is the type of detection sensor being utilized, namely radar and lidar. Delphi Automotive Systems is one of the few companies that has the capability to offer both types of object detection technology.

Recently, Delphi Automotive Systems developed a fully functioning ACC vehicle, on an Opel Vectra. This vehicle was configured to provide ACC functionality using either type of object detection technology. This mechanization provided a unique opportunity to compare the capabilities of either detection sensor technology, as utilized in an ACC system, while operating with the exact same environmental conditions (e.g.: traffic patterns, roadway geometry/surfaces, weather conditions, etc.).

This vehicle was developed for both demonstrations (e.g.: trade shows, etc.) and provide a practical on-road laboratory/engineering development platform as a means to explore future ACC design enhancements (e.g.: different implementation schemes, next generation systems, etc.). As such, this ACC-vehicle needed to satisfy dual conflicting utilization. In order to demonstrate the exciting properties of ACC to the general public, this vehicle must possess a "show-car" quality environment, along with providing a rugged, reliable, stable operation. This required the ACC system to be seamlessly integrated into the vehicle infrastructure, while presenting a Human-Machine Interface that appeared production intent. Also, the ACC system architecture must be robust, flexible and extensible in order to provide future engineering development investigations. These goals were met in this ACC system design for an Opel Vectra.

Four Delphi Divisions formed a team to accomplish this developmental vehicle. Each division contributed advanced technologies/components/systems that complemented the ACC system. In a fast paced development effort of 5-months, the team relied heavily on incorporating system engineering processes/procedures to formulate the design and enacting creative rapid prototyping design techniques and strategies.

COLLISON AVOIDANCE VISION

Tremendous progress has been made since the 1960's with regard to vehicle safety. Early safety approaches emphasized precaution (e.g.: surviving a crash) and focused on such passive devices as seat belts, air bags, crash zones, and lighting. These improvements have dramatically reduced the rate of crash-related injury severity and fatalities. For example, the fatality rate per hundred million vehicle miles traveled has fallen from 5.5 to 1.7 in the period from the mid-1960s to 1994. However, in spite of these impressive improvements, each year in the United States, motor vehicle crashes still account for a staggering 40,000 deaths, more than 3-million injuries, and over $150 billion in economic losses [1]. Greater demand for improvements in vehicular transportation safety, fueled by government and consumers alike, are compelling the automotive manufacturing community to constantly seek to develop innovative technologies and products which can assist in achieving further crash statistics reductions. The emphasis of these future systems will migrate from a passive safety system (e.g.: crash precaution) to active safety system (e.g.: crash prevention).

Consequently, the introduction of collision warning/avoidance systems have the potential to represent the next significant leap in vehicle safety technology by attempting to actively warn drivers of a potential impending collision event, thereby; allowing the driver adequate time to take appropriate corrective actions in order to mitigate, or completely avoid, the event. Crash statistics and numerical analysis strongly suggest that collision warning systems will be effective. Crash-related data collected by the U.S. National Highway Traffic Safety Administration (NHTSA) show approximately 88% of rear-end collisions are caused by driver inattention and following too closely. These types of crash events could derive a positive beneficial influence from such systems. In fact, NHTSA countermeasure effectiveness modeling has determined that these types of headway detection systems can theoretically prevent 37% to 74% of all police reported rear-end crashes [2][3].

Delphi Delco Electronics Systems involvement in Collision Avoidance systems is through its **Forewarn®** product line, which includes forward, side & rear object detection systems. The collision avoidance product roadmap begins with ACC (Fig 1). Each succeeding product will provide increased functionality over the preceding product. The various combinations of sub-systems will eventually yield a complete family of collision avoidance products, such as: ACC, Lane Change, Lane Keeping, Parking Aid. These systems will be introduced based on variety of factors (e.g.: technology maturity, packaging, costs, etc.) [4].

The development processes for each of these products are not unique, but fit within a common framework which builds upon the achievements of the preceding subsystem. A hierarchical structure has been developed that guides all of the integration and development processes toward Collision Avoidance (Fig 2). Information from the primary active sensing sub-systems (e.g.: GPS/Map, forward/side/rear sensors) and vehicle sensors (e.g.: speed, yaw, etc.) are processed by the "System Processing Module" in order to reconstruct the traffic environment about the host-vehicle. Within this module, sensor fusion techniques are employed to assess, evaluate, and combine the parametric information yielded from all the active sensing sub-systems, in conjunction with the host-vehicle states, into reliable parametric features which are used to improve the performance of object detection, tracking, in-path target identification & selection. Sophisticated model-based scene tracking techniques will be employed to improve the in-path target identification process [5]. Once the in-path target has been identified, situational awareness procedures evaluate if this target presents a potential threat to the host-vehicle. If a potential threat does occur, appropriate smooth corrective vehicle control actions and Human-Machine Interfaces are implemented in order to minimize the risk. Selective instrument panel switches (e.g.: windshield wiper, radio adjustments, etc.) are continually monitored and are used to further enhance the threat assessment processes.

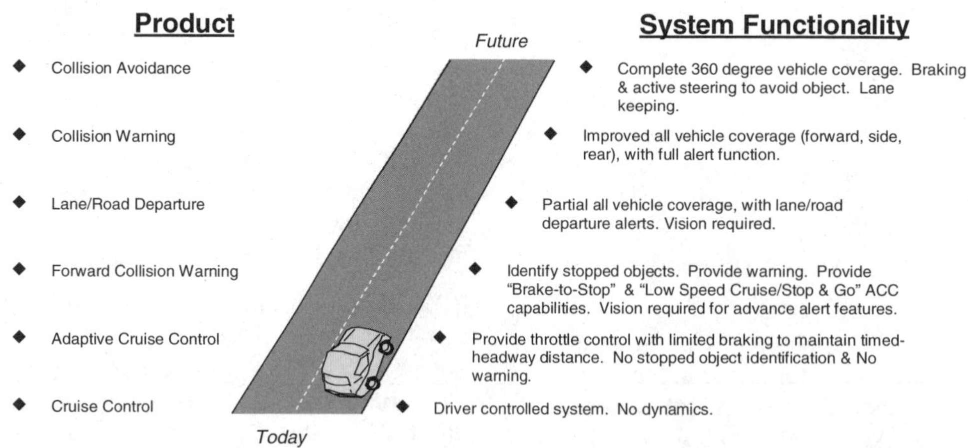

Figure 1. Collision avoidance system evolution.

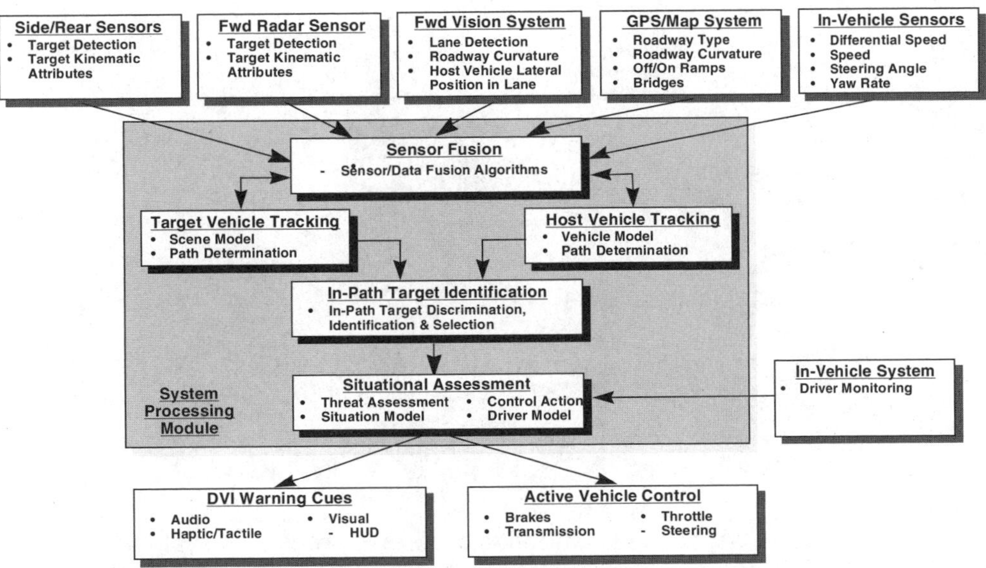

Figure 2. Conceptual architecture of collision avoidance system.

This architecture will be seamlessly integrated into the vehicle infrastructure to provide a cohesive collision avoidance product that is envisioned to provide 360° coverage about the host-vehicle (Fig 3). The "Collision Avoidance Processor" provides the functionality of the "System Processing Module".

ACC SYSTEM OVERVIEW

SYSTEM DESCRIPTION – The ACC system is designed to be a customer convenience product that will enhance the functionality of a conventional cruise control function. The ACC system will relieve the driver of the distracting (but certainly necessary) tasks of observing speed and maintaining a proper headway in irregular traffic patterns (e.g.: speed up/down, etc.). As such, the ACC system will allow the driver to direct his/her attention to observing/reacting to the dynamically changing forward traffic behavior (e.g.: cut-in, lane changes, etc.) in the presence of various weather conditions (e.g.: rain, fog, etc.). The system's intended operation is on highway-like roadway (i.e.: high speed) environments. It is designed to make freeway driving a more comfortable and pleasant experience.

In the U.S., the conventional cruise control function has widely been accepted and nearly 90% of all vehicles have it as an option. This is largely because the U.S. has vast rural areas where there is sparse traffic and urban regions where the traffic situations commonly permit near constant speed. However, in regions that have irregular traffic patterns, with frequent speed variations, the cruise control function is seldom used. These patterns represent the typical traffic environment throughout both Europe and Japan (and ever increasingly heavily congested U.S. cities). As such, a greater majority of European- and Japanese-based vehicles do not even feature conventional cruise control systems. The ACC system is intended to positively impact this situation.

The ACC system has the capability to identify the in-lane vehicle ahead of the host-vehicle, and automatically adjust its speed (by automatic limited application of brakes or throttle) in order to maintain a driver-specified adjustable "gap" distance behind this in-lane vehicle. The size of the "gap" distance is based upon a driver-specified "timed-headway" (e.g.: 1-s, 2-s, etc.) distance. In all driving scenarios, the driver controls the full operation of the ACC system and has ultimate control of the vehicle when required.

The critical key to a successful ACC system is the introduction of a new automotive component that has the capability to detect/sense the various target vehicles ahead of the host-vehicle, and assess/measure the kinematic attributes of each target (e.g.: distance, relative velocity, etc.). This "smart" device is a sophisticated forward-looking detection sensor using either infrared laser or millimeter wave signals.

FUNCTIONAL MECHANIZATION – An ACC system can be represented by an architecture (Fig 4), that is comprised of 5 major functional elements:

a. *Object Detection*: Provide the functionality for (i) object detection processing, (ii) attribute parameter estimation, from the transmitting/ receiving waveforms of a sophisticated sensor (e.g.: lidar, radar).
b. *Multi-Target Tracking*: Provide the capability to group the collective detected objects into distinct targets, according to similar attributes (i.e.: distance and relative velocity). Each new object detection will either be merged into existing targets or form a new target, characterized by its own kinematic attributes.

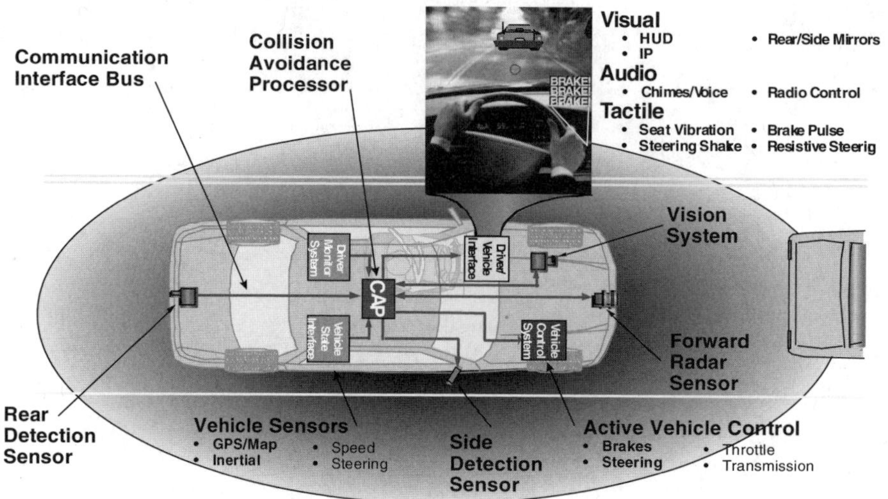

Figure 3. Vehicle mechanization of collision avoidance system.

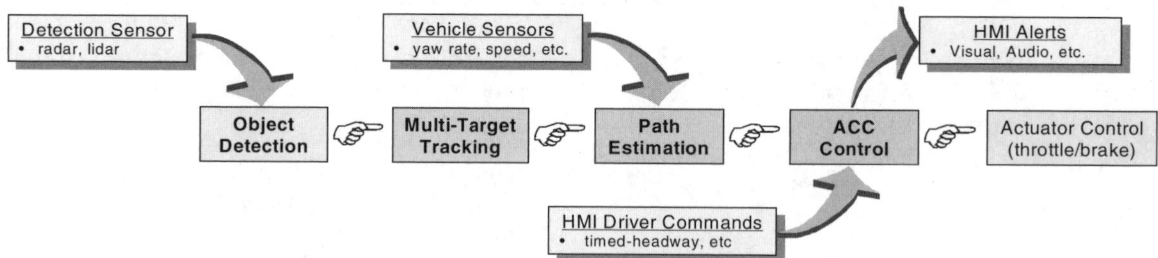

Figure 4. ACC signal processing architecture.

c. *Path Estimation*: Provide the functionality for: (i) yaw rate processing, (ii) roadway curvature estimation, (iii) object/host path estimation, and (iv) lane assignment identification/classification (e.g.: identify in-path target).

d. *ACC Control*: Responsible for determining the correct control action (i.e.: acceleration/deceleration command) based upon the traffic pattern, and supplying the HMI response (e.g.: visual or audio alerts).

e. *Actuator Control*: The brakes or throttle execute the required control action in response to the desired ACC control signal.

VEHICLE MECHANIZATION – The Vectra was mechanized to demonstrate ACC functionality using either type of detection technology (e.g.: radar or lidar). As such, the ACC/vehicle system was integrated according to the mechanization shown in Fig 5. The main communication interface between each subsystem was an optical 500-kbps CAN. However, not all of the components used this protocol. Consequently, translator boxes were developed to resolve this issue.

This decentralized design approach was pursued in order to provide a more efficient implementation. Each major functional signal processing feature (e.g.: multi-target tracking, path estimation, ACC-control, etc) was isolated in its own processor. This allowed the system engineers the freedom to develop (e.g.: algorithm development, test & debug) each complex signal processing functional block without the various time-consuming concerns associated with merging all of the other software blocks into a single fixed-based processor. Also, when software upgrades were required, it would only affect a specific processor. This significantly reduced debugging complexity and greatly assisted in reducing the development time.

Although this "pipeline chaining" methodology increased the delay time between "detection sensor" to "ACC-control", it was proven not to adversely effect the ACC system performance. In a production intent ACC-system, all of these features would be implemented in a single module configuration.

DETECTION SENSORS

SENSOR REQUIREMENTS – The minimum sensor requirements for the ACC system are based on the ability to provide smooth adequate vehicle control that can be accommodated without the need for driver intervention. The minimum subset requirements are a function of:

- Maximum timed-headway
- Maximum allowable longitudinal deceleration
- Maximum difference in velocity
- Minimum closest approach
- Maximum allowable lateral acceleration
- Maximum operating velocity

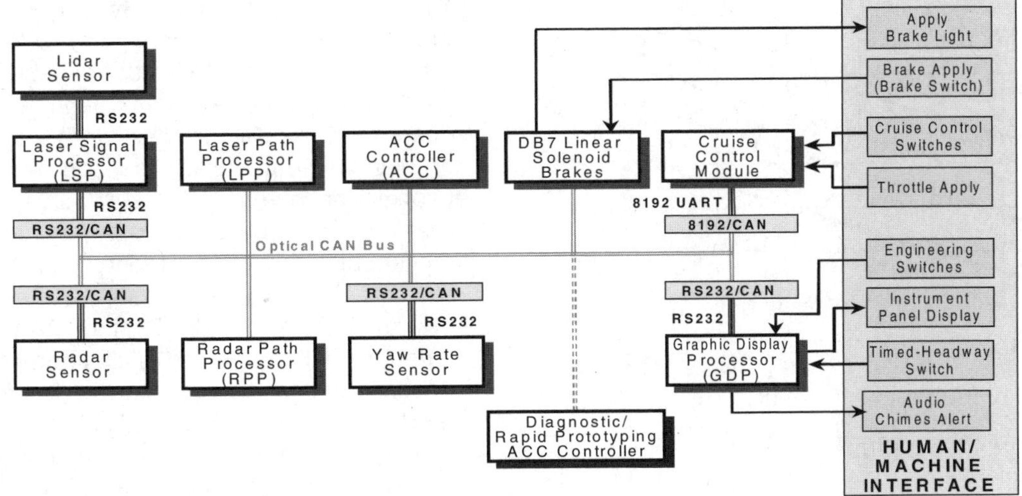

Figure 5. Vehicle mechanization of collision avoidance system.

A reasonable ACC design guideline which assists in defining the maximum sensor range is based on the selectable timed-headway. Fig 6 illustrates the following distance as a function of host-vehicle speed and timed-headway. Thus, if the maximum allowable ACC set-speed is 100-mph, with a 2-s timed-headway, then the required following distance is ≈90-m. However, in order to maintain continuous steady-state ACC-control, the sensor range will need to exceed the following range by an appropriate amount (e.g.: 10%). Thus, for this analysis, the maximum sensor detection range would be ≈100-m.

In addition for the system being capable to maintain a steady state timed-headway control, the system is also required to be able to reasonably react as the host-vehicle approaches a lead-vehicle traveling at a much slower speed. That is, without driver intervention, the ACC system should have the capability to slow the host-vehicle to a reasonable distance that is no closer than a given minimum distance (e.g.: this might violate the desired timed-headway) to the lead-vehicle and then be able to successfully re-establish the appropriate timed-headway. Fig 7 provides the required sensor range as a function of the point of closest approach to the lead-vehicle as a function of the difference in vehicle velocities, given a maximum ACC-brake deceleration of 0.2g. As shown, a maximum sensor range of 80-to-100 m is again required for a velocity difference of 30-to-40 mph, while assuming a closest point of approach of 20-to-30 m.

The minimum azimuth sensor field-of-view (FOV) required is based on providing ACC operation through curves. The FOV requirement is driven by the minimum roadway curvature (e.g.: radius-of-curvature) and maximum range. Highway design standards establish the minimum roadway curvature as a function of vehicle speed (Fig 8) [6]. These standards are conservatively based on maximum lateral acceleration of 0.13g. The minimum sensor FOV as a function of range and radius-of-curvature (Fig 9).

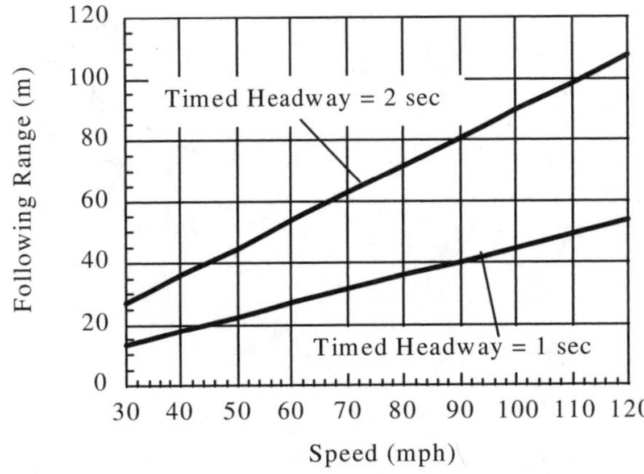

Figure 6. Steady-state ACC following range.

Figures 6-9 are used to determine the sensor FOV. For example, at a speed of 55-mph the ACC following distance is 50 m (Fig 6) and the minimum radius-of-curvature is 300 m (Fig 8) which leads to a minimum sensor FOV of ±5° (Fig 9). The situation of approaching a lead-vehicle with a large difference in velocity leads to a similar requirement. Given a host-vehicle speed of 70-mph, lead-vehicle speed of 35-mph (e.g., 35 mph differential speed), and closest point of approach of 30-m, the required sensor range is 90-m (from Fig 6) and the minimum radius-of-curvature is 500-m (see Fig 8) which also leads to a minimum sensor FOV of ±5°.

Additional FOV (e.g.: overscan) is generally needed to accommodate mechanical or electrical misalignment of the antenna relative to the sensor enclosure (e.g.: ±0.5^{o}) and mechanical misalignment of the sensor enclosure caused by installation tolerances during automotive assembly (e.g.: ±2°). Otherwise, precise alignment either by mechanical or RF means is required during installation which would be time consuming and costly. Accounting for these tolerances leads to a desirable sensor FOV of ≈15°.

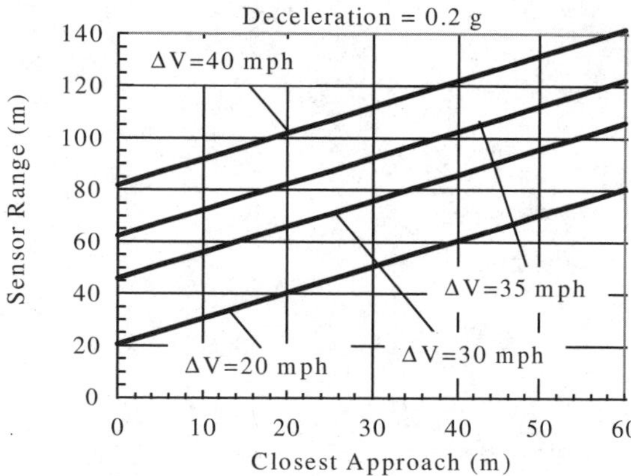

Figure 7. Required sensor range for slower lead-vehicle.

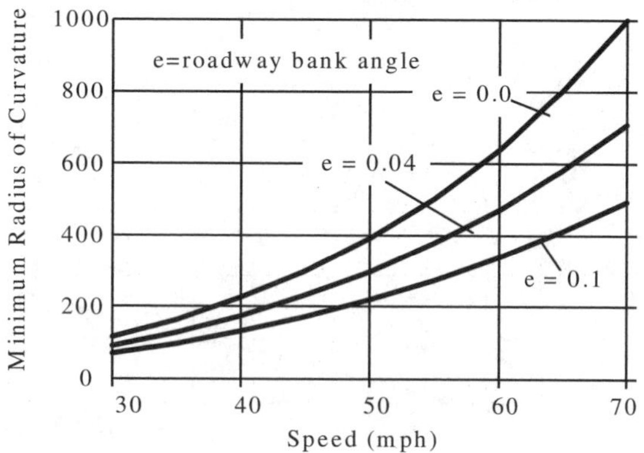

Figure 8. Minimum speed on a curve.

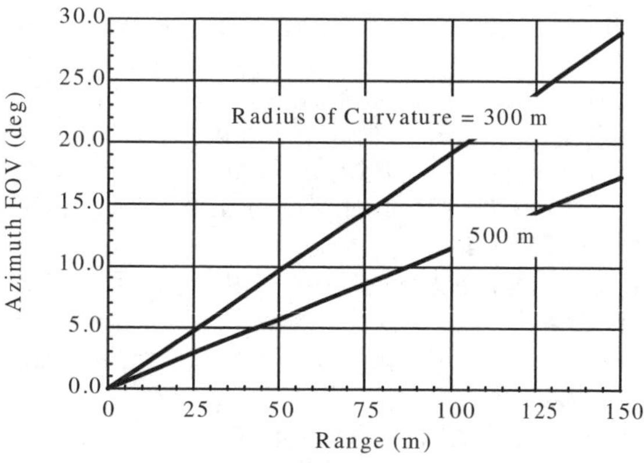

Figure 9. Azimuth FOV requirement.

SENSOR DESCRIPTION – Two types of **Forewarn®** detection sensors were used to provide ACC functionality on the Vectra. The ACC-radar sensor (e.g.: ACC-1) was a matured production component, while the ACC-lidar sensor (e.g.: ACC-L) was still in the early stages of sensor development. Each sensor performs a scanning action to provide angular accuracy and a large object detection zone. Other types of mechanization for detection sensors have been used for ACC applications [8].

Forewarn® ACC-1 Radar System – The ACC-1 sensor is a mechanically scanning millimeter-wave radar device. The sensor has a single narrow beamwidth (e.g.: ≈2°) antenna, which is mechanically swept to provide a "Detection Region" (Fig 10). The sensor azimuth-FOV is 15° and the elevation-FOV is 4°. Typically, an ACC application requires only 10° of coverage for proper functionality. Consequently, the sensor provides more coverage than is required for effective ACC operation. This extra FOV coverage comprises 5°and is provided as a means to allow for the automatic electronic compensation of any possible mechanical misalignments of the ACC-1 module.

The ACC-1 sensor has extensive capability to detect multiple objects within the single narrow beam. Within this beam, the detected objects could be a combination of "real" targets (i.e.: various range occurrence of vehicles, motorcycles, etc.) and "clutter" (i.e.: guard rails, poles, signs, etc.). As the antenna is scanned across the Detection Region, over 40 individual transmit/receive beams are executed to detect and characterize the forward environment. Consequently, at the scan conclusion, the existence of over 80 detected "beam objects" are possible.

A FMCW waveform, operating at a 76.5 GHz carrier frequency, is used to directly measure both the distance and relative velocity parameters of each detected "beam object". The sensor completes one full scan action, processes the raw detections, and updates "beam object" kinematic data, within 100-ms.

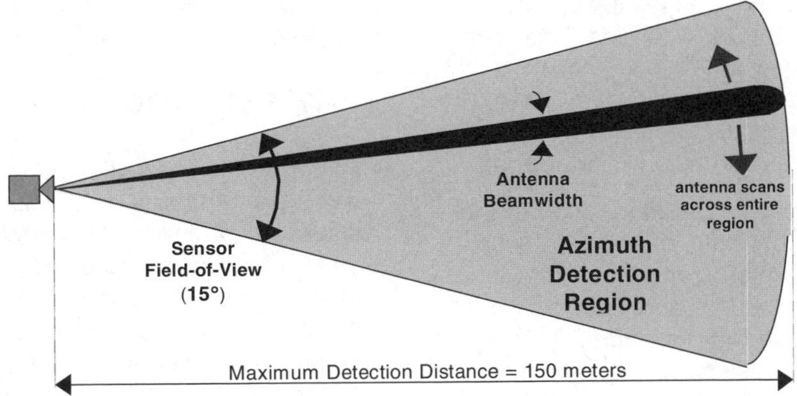

Figure 10. ACC-1 Scan Characteristic & Azimuth Detection Region.

Forewarn® ACC-L Lidar System – The ACC-L sensor is an electronic switched-beam scanning multi-channel lidar device, comprised of 12 stationary transmitters. This device is an engineering unit version of the eventual production-intent sensor that will be comprised of 16 transmitters in order to provide a larger azimuth-FOV.

The sensor has no moving parts/elements. Two lenses are used to optically disperse/project/transmit each of the 12 narrow-beamwidth (e.g.: ≈1°) laser beams to different closely-spaced, non-overlapping regions to form the Detection Region (Fig 11). The detection envelope is covered by sequentially switching between the beams. The angular coverage by a single beam does not overlap the coverage of its adjacent beams. Additionally, no detectable angular separation exists between the edges of adjacent beams. Consequently, the azimuth-FOV is ≈12° and elevation-FOV is ≈3°.

The ACC-L sensor has extensive capability to detect multiple objects within each narrow laser beam. Within a beam, these objects could be a combination of "real" targets (i.e.: various range occurrence of vehicles, motorcycles, etc.) and "clutter" (i.e.: guard rails, poles, signs, etc.). As the system scans across the Detection Region, the sensor provides the capability to detect up to six objects within each beam channel for a total of 72 "beam objects".

The lidar uses a pulse signal to directly measure only the distance parameter of each "beam object". The sensor completes one full scan action, processes raw detections, and updates "beam object" data, within 50-ms.

MULTI-TARGET TRACKING

A sophisticated multi-target tracking procedure is used to group all of the detected "beam objects" into distinct targets (i.e.: multiple grouped beam objects), according to similar attributes (e.g.: distance & relative velocity). Each new "beam object" will either be merged into existing targets or form a new target.

Each target will be characterized by its kinematic attributes (i.e.: distance, relative velocity, centroid angle, and angular extent). Kalman filter estimation techniques are used to smooth the measured data and improve accuracy. The combination of the scanning action and narrow beamwidth RF/Laser signals result in the ability to discriminate closely spaced objects, with highly accurate angle and angular extent information to be collected about target.

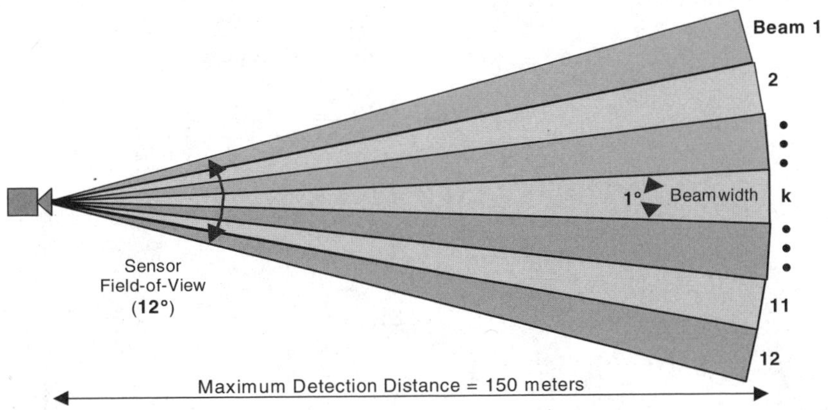

Figure 11. ACC-L Scan Characteristic & Azimuth Detection Region.

There are some interesting differences in the approach to trackfile management with radar and lidar sensors. These arise primarily because of (1) differences in the types of objects which are visible to the two sensors (e.g.: rain/snow, embedded roadway retro-reflectors); and (2) the lack of Doppler range-rate information with the lidar.

With the laser, the lack of range-rate information in the raw detections increases the difficulty of accurate detection-to-track correlation. Correlation must be done in a range-only domain with the laser, as opposed to a combined range/range-rate domain with the radar. With the radar, a detection from a stopped object can immediately be recognized as such, and can be discarded if stopped objects are not of interest. With the lidar, all raw detections must be tracked and observed for a number of scans before an accurate range-rate can be calculated and that object's motion status (e.g.: stopped, moving) assessed. This added process occupies nontrivial amounts of memory and computational throughput.

Such is the case of retro-reflective lane markings found in many roads. These retro-reflectors are invisible to the radar, but are highly visible to the laser. Many of these may be in the field-of-view, and all must be tracked in order to recognize them as inconsequential stopped objects and to prevent their raw detections from being incorrectly correlated to important "real" target objects, thereby corrupting range and range-rate estimates for those objects.

Another interesting phenomenon requiring special lidar trackfile handling occurs with many roadside guard rails. The radar can immediately recognize the guard rail as being an inconsequential stopped object by the Doppler shift in the raw detections. On the other hand, these crash barriers can appear to the laser to be a nearly continuous reflective strip which appears to be moving at the same speed as the host-vehicle, due to the primary reflection traveling down the guardrail as the host-vehicle moves. Additionally, in situations where the nearby road itself is visible to the laser, this event can also happen. Rain and snow can also appear to the laser to be nearby objects moving at the same speed as the host-vehicle. Proper interpretation of these returns requires extra processing in the trackfile manager.

PATH ESTIMATION/TARGET SELECTION

In conjunction with the curve sensor, this module provides the capability to identify the in-lane target for consideration by the ACC-control module. This procedure attempts to resolve the proper selection/identification of the lane assignment (i.e.: correctly identifies the in-path target as in-path and rejects the adjacent-lane targets as in-path). This is a highly complex problem. The ability to effectively accomplish this task is highly dependent on the sensor performance (i.e.: beamwidth, angle resolution, angle accuracy, target detection, target attributes, etc.), in conjunction with variety of non-deterministic real-world driving issues: (a) complex roadway geometry (e.g.: straight roadway, constant/non-constant curvature roadway, curved-entry/exit, etc.), (b) driver behavior (e.g.: lane change, rapid cut-in, relative position in lane, etc.), and (c) other complex driver/system-induced noise issues (e.g.: in-lane weaving/hunting by driver, over compensation in curves by driver, roadway crown, yaw rate noise, sensor misalignment, chassis misalignment, etc.).

ACC CONTROL STRUCTURE

The ACC-control is functionally responsible for determining the proper control action based upon the traffic scenario. The ACC-control (Fig 12) consists of two modes of operation: "Cruise Mode"/"Velocity Control" and "Follow Mode"/"Distance Control" [7][8]. In the absence of any in-lane lead-vehicle, the ACC-control will provide "speed control" with respect to the selected set-speed, just like the conventional cruise control function. In the presence of an in-lane lead-vehicle, depending on the traffic condition, the ACC-control will provide "Distance Control" to automatically adjust the ACC-vehicle speed (by commanding braking and throttle controls) in order to maintain the specified timed-headway "gap" distance behind the lead-vehicle. The ACC-control will automatically smoothly switch between the two modes based upon the traffic situation.

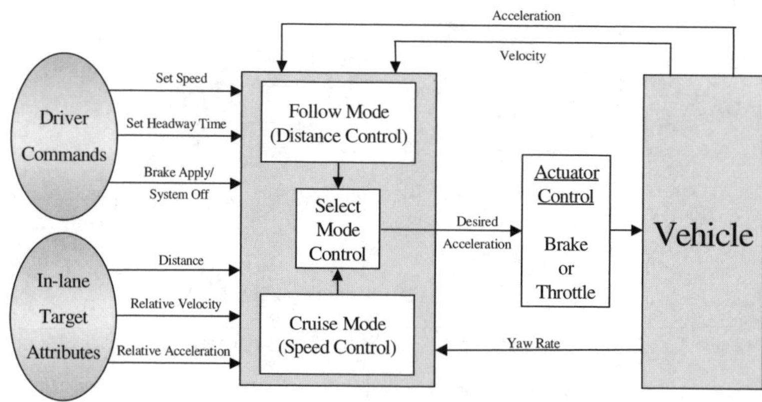

Figure 12. ACC Control Structure.

The ACC controller output variable is an indication of desired vehicle acceleration/ deceleration, which is provided to the appropriate brake or throttle controller units. The driver controls the full operation of the ACC system. The system can be engaged between 30 and 160-km/h. The driver selects the "set-speed" and "timed-headway" (e.g.: 1, 1.5, or 2 s).

Fig 13 presents one of the possible implementation schemes for a "Follow Mode" control architecture [7] [9-13]. The baseline system response is prescribed by a "gain scheduling" approach in which "*m*" multiple n^{th} order linear controllers, $G_k(s)$, of the form:

$$G_k(s) = (a_n s^n + \bullet\bullet\bullet + a_2 s^2 + a_1 s + a_0)$$

$$\div (b_n s^n + \bullet\bullet\bullet + b_2 s^2 + b_1 s + b_0);$$

$$\text{for } k = 1, \ldots, m \qquad (1)$$

are used. The output of the gain-schedule-controller is an acceleration-like command (e.g.: change of the velocity per 20-ms update rate). The switching between the "*m*" linear control structures is dependent on the traffic behavior/characteristics of the in-lane lead-vehicle. Furthermore, several non-linear boundary control layers are used to mold the system response to provide behavior which more closely mimic actual humans driving behaviors/ characteristics. Consequently, the linear controllers are used to establish stable, robust, predictable performance and the nonlinear control elements are used to marginally alter the system response from entering into undesirable regions of performance.

The basic strategy of the ACC-control is to bring the ACC-vehicle to a steady-state following condition (e.g.: both the timed-headway is maintained and matches the same speed as the lead-vehicle). This condition is represented by $\Delta V_{desired} \equiv 0$, which also corresponds to when the system is operating at the null set-point (e.g.: $X_{offset} = V_{relative} = A_{relative} \equiv 0$). Accordingly, the brakes will not be activated until the condition $\Delta V_{desired} < 0$ is satisfied.

This linear control approach is acceptable for steady-state follow traffic patterns, but does not provide adequate performance in the presence of other types of traffic patterns without further enhancements. For example, this type of linear control structure does not allow brake activation until the set-point variables are less than zero (e.g.: which typically occurs when the timed-headway distance is violated). Consequently, when the ACC-vehicle encounters a significantly slower lead-vehicle, the driver perceives the resultant brake action is "too late", since the braking action does not occur until the headway is violated. As such, a nonlinear gain, K_T (e.g.: $K_T \in [1,C]$, where C>1), was added to the design in order to scale the desired "timed-headway" for the purpose to artificially "push-out" the "timed-headway" distance which forces a quicker brake application. As the ACC-vehicle slows down and approaches the lead-vehicle speed (e.g.: approaching steady-state following conditions), this gain would also be reduced until it has no additional system effect. The value of this nonlinear gain is dependent on relative acceleration, relative velocity, and distance.

Several other nonlinear functions are incorporated into the ACC-controller design for the purpose of human factors. A nonlinear feed-forward compensation is used to supply more brake action in the presence of a very near encounter events with the lead-vehicle (e.g.: cut-in). A non-linear limit function is used to control the "jerk" characteristics. Most drivers feel uncomfortable with large jerks. Another non-linear limit function is used to control the "speed-up/slow-down" behavior of the ACC-vehicle, in the presence of (a) large lateral accelerations, or (b) when the lead-vehicle performs a lane-exit maneuver and you want to limit the speed in approaching the next in-lane lead-vehicle.

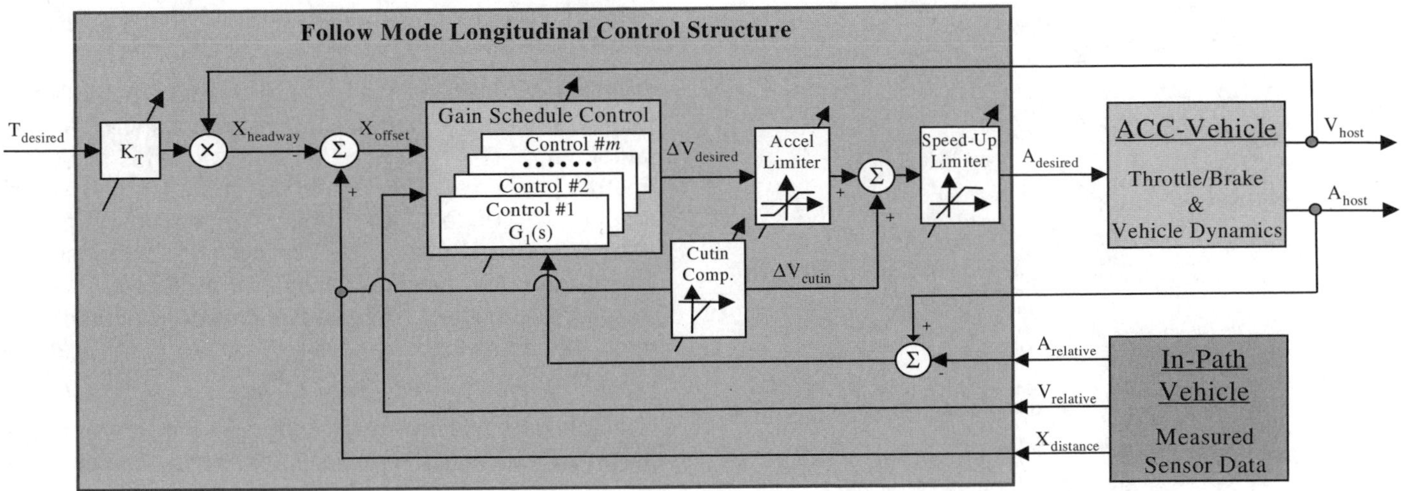

Figure 13. ACC follow-mode control structure with vehicle/target dynamics.

Each linear controller is designed to meet a specific overall vehicle system performance that correlates to a specific traffic pattern scenario. For instance, while in a steady-state following traffic scenario, the selected linear controller is designed to exhibit a "critically-damped" performance characteristic. This type of controlled response tends to inhibit/suppress any type of oscillatory type behavior due to nominal slight speed-up/slow-down oscillatory behavior of the lead-vehicle. While operating in transient following behaviors (e.g.: approaching/departing lead-vehicles), the selected linear controllers are designed to exhibit varying levels of "underdamped" performance characteristics, which then allow the ACC-vehicle to respond quickly to these dynamically changing traffic patterns. Consequently, the resultant controlled-vehicle response will behave very similar to a second-order system. The control gain set (a_k , b_k), for a specific linear controller, $G_k(s)$, are chosen using standard linear-control pole-assignment techniques.

The switching between the various Follow Mode control surfaces (e.g.: linear controllers with different response characteristics) and Cruise Mode was determined according to the relationships shown in Fig 14. The gain schedule switching surfaces between adjacent linear controllers are selected to provide smooth control response and avoid controller "kicks" at the switch transition. Hysteresis was also introduced to avoid "flickering" between the Cruise and Follow Mode states.

BRAKE SYSTEM

The controlled braking technology is accomplished using production components within a rapid prototyping environment. This brake system (DBC 7) provides smooth and quiet braking through a 4-channel hydraulic actuator with the associated electronics.

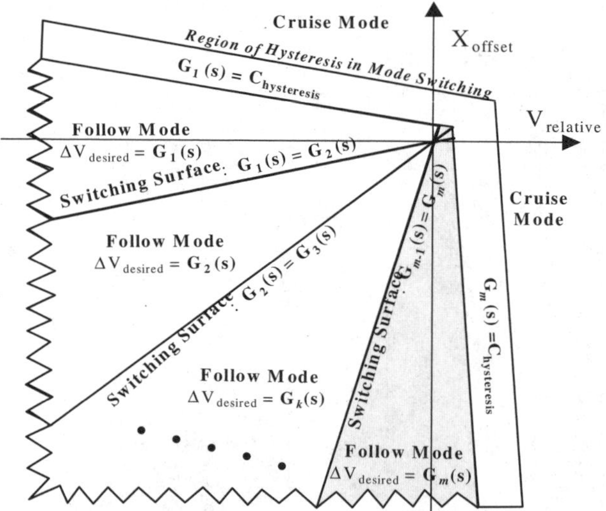

Figure 14. ACC mode switching characteristics.

The goal of automatic braking development, installation and testing required characterization of the base braking performance of the production vehicle prior to making any modifications. The mechanization of the brake system utilized both existing signals and sensors on the vehicle. The major components of the DBC 7 brake intervention system consist of a pump, motor, brake fluid storage accumulator, and several special purpose, sophisticated solenoid valve configurations. The hydraulic modulator and electronic controller unit is capable of ABS, TCS and vehicle stability enhancement. The controller is designed with a fail-safe CPU and is available with flash codes and serial communications (CAN).

The braking system was to be controlled in response to a deceleration command (up to a maximum ACC braking action). The desired headway is accomplished/maintained by an arbitration of between deceleration (braking control) and acceleration (throttle control) maintains the desired headway. This implies the brake dynamics must be at least as fast as the engine/throttle dynamics.

The primary function of the brake system is to close the loop on vehicle deceleration based on a command from the ACC-control by autonomously actuating the brake mechanisms at the wheels. For this development effort, a Modular Development System (MDS) is utilized as a brake controller, which interfaces the modulator to the system. The MDS contains the CPU and memory. The advantage of the MDS is that it "see" the program memory which allows: (a) SW to be viewed, (b) log software variables, and (c) allows modified SW to be quickly/easily downloaded (which are all invaluable for system debug and tuning).

Much of the OEM vehicle wiring is utilized through the wiring interface box that provides a connection to various signals, such as wheel speeds and vehicle speed out to the speedometer. An additional wire harness was installed to provide the connections to the rest of the system. The brake system also controls the illumination of the vehicle brake lamps.

In this implementation, a dSpace™ rapid prototyping system was utilized to perform the brake deceleration control algorithm. The dSpace™ system provides a development environment dedicated to control systems engineering. Models and code written in Simulink™, Matlab™ and C can all be combined and compiled into the target DSP processor within the dSpace™, so that advanced functions and models can be executed in real time, variables can be viewed and logged, and code changes can be made "on-the-fly".

This braking system was tested at a proving ground facility on controlled high coefficient surfaces. The calibration and moding of ACC and ABS was refined for robustness. Measured vehicle data in response to a commanded deceleration profile are provided in Fig 15. This data corresponds to smoothing and quiet braking upon commands from the ACC processor. It was observed that small commanded changes in deceleration were not detectable by the driver.

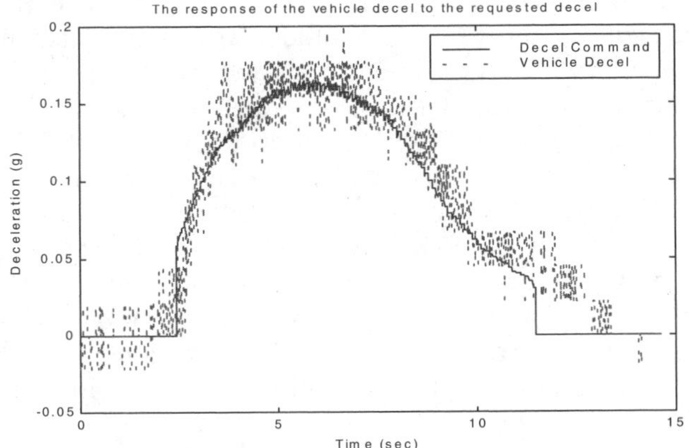

Figure 15(a).Brake Performance.

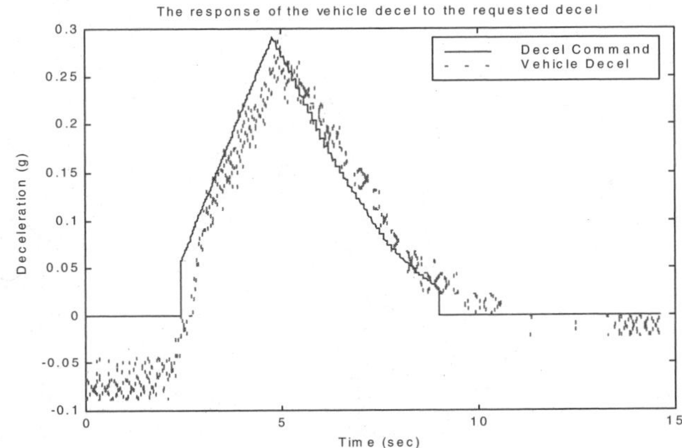

Figure 15(b).Brake Performance.

HUMAN-MACHINE INTERFACE (HMI)

The HMI consists of both the standard interfaces used with a conventional cruise control system (e.g.: set-speed/tap-up & resume/tap-down cruise control switches, brake apply) and several other enhancements in order to account for ACC operation. A rocker-style switch was installed in the cockpit which is used to allow selection of three timed-headway settings (e.g.: 1-, 1.5- & 2-s). Furthermore, the instrument cluster was modified to provide some convenient visual displays which indicate ACC operation, set-speed, and Follow Mode. These enhancements were chosen to be simple, easily understood, and intuitive to the driver, while presenting an ACC-HMI that is seamlessly integrated into the vehicle infrastructure and appears production intent.

The instrument cluster was modified to include a display and a series of diodes surrounding the speedometer (Fig 16). The illumination of a specific diode indicates the selected set-speed. It can be changed in 5-km/h increments by the driver using the cruise control stock switches. The absence of an illuminated diode indicates the ACC system is not engaged/activated. The display provides an indication the ACC-system is operating in the Follow Mode, by the presence of a vehicle-icon. The absence of this icon, along with an illuminated set-speed diode, indicates the ACC is operating in the Cruise Mode. The indication of the selected timed-headway is provided by the number of bars/chevrons presented below the vehicle-icon (e.g.: 1 bar ≡ 1-s, 2 bars ≡ 1.5-s, 3 bars ≡ 2-s). If the lead-vehicle performs a maneuver (e.g.: slows down, etc), which results in the ACC-vehicle to begin operating below the minimum ACC operating speed (e.g.: 30-km/h), the driver will be alerted by a flashing vehicle icon (on the display), along with an audible chime. This alert signifies the ACC system will be automatically disengage within 5-s.

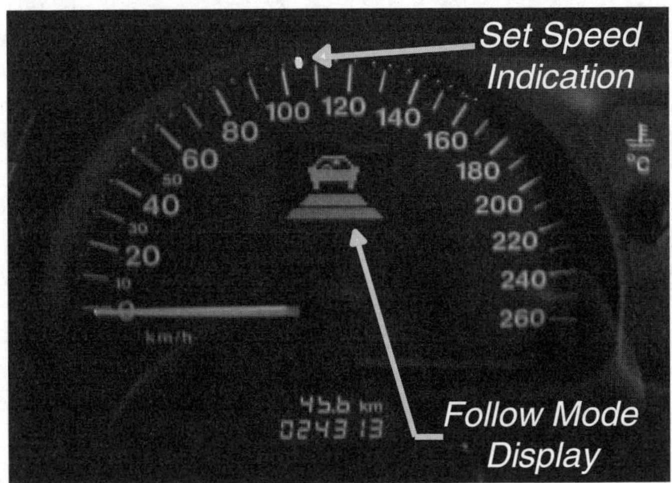

Figure 16. HMI visual display.

ON-ROAD ACC PERFORMANCE

The ACC-vehicle was mechanized to demonstrate ACC functionality using either type of detection technology (e.g.: lidar & radar). The system mechanization was also designed to allow both sensors to simultaneous operate while one sensor was used as the primary ACC sensor. This provided us with an unique opportunity to: (a) dynamically switch between both sensors to demonstrate the ACC performance for each ACC controlling sensor, and (b) collect and compare data from both detection sensors in the target detection and assessment (e.g.: range, etc.) for the exact same environmental scenario (e.g.: traffic patterns, roadway geometry, weather conditions, etc.).

SCENARIO 1 (HIGH DIFFERENTIAL SPEED ENCOUNTER; NEAR CONSTANT SPEED LEAD-VEHICLE): – The ACC-vehicle was operating in a 1-s timed-headway gap with a set-speed of 44-m/s. The ACC-vehicle is operating in the Cruise Mode, traveling with a constant speed of 44-m/s, when it encounters an in-lane lead-vehicle traveling at a slightly increasing speed of 30-m/s. This equates to an initial speed differential of 14-m/s. Fig 17 illustrates the response of the radar-based ACC system. The lead-vehicle is identified as an in-path vehicle at approximately 110-m. The ACC-control switches into the "Follow Mode" and the ACC-vehicle immediately starts to slow down as it approaches the lead-vehicle, until it reaches the steady-state condition (i.e.: matches lead-vehicle speed and maintains the proper timed-headway gap distance). The timed-headway gap distance (i.e.: $X_{headway} = V_{host}\ T_{headway}$) is presented as a reference point. This observed ACC behavior exhibits the typical response of a second order system, thereby validating the theoretical control system analysis.

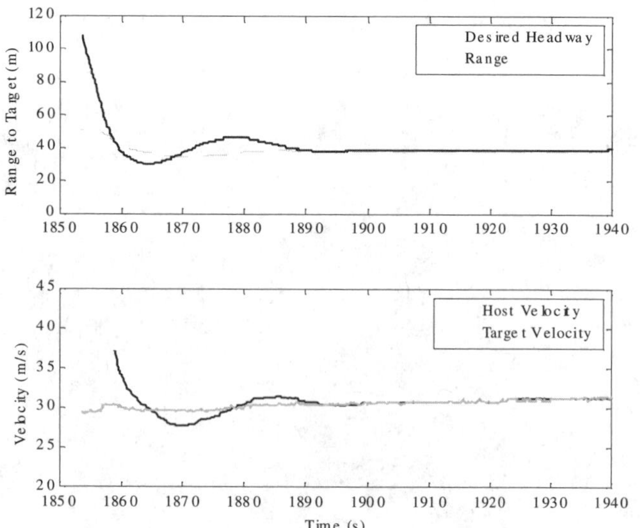

Figure 17. ACC system response (Scenario 1).

Fig 18 presents a comparison between the radar and lidar sensor assessed detection. It illustrates that both sensors provide similar performance and have reported the same distance and relative velocity paramters. The velocity measurement was slightly noisier for the lidar sensor since it does not directly measure the velocity parameter (unlike the radar sensor) and must estimate the velocity from successive observation of the measured distance parameter. In general, the noise floor is not significant and it naturally filtered out by the low filter characteristics of the ACC-vehicle behavior and is not felt by the driver. Also, the lead-vehicle is identified as an in-path vehicle at approximately 105-m for the radar and approximately 95-m by the lidar. This distance difference is directly related to the longer timing issues associated with the velocity estimation process undertaken by the lidar multi-target tracking procedure. Target information is not passed onto the path and ACC-control procedures until the target-track has matured (e.g.: velocity estimate is stable and achieves a certain limit of accuracy). This is to ensure the ACC-control will not provide a "kick" output response as a result of reacting to an erroneous transient velocity estimate. Since the lidar does not automatically measure velocity, then this estimation process takes some time. However, in-depth analysis of the raw detection data shows the radar and lidar both started to detect the target at the same range. Improvements to the estimation procedure are actively being pursued to reduce this time period (and consequently report targets quicker to the ACC-control procedure).

As a performance comparison between the two sensors, Fig 19 presents the difference in the measured "distance" and measured-radar / estimated-lidar "relative velocity" parameters. As reported by the two sensors, a slight constant distance difference (approximately 2-m) is observed in the perceived target distance. This distance differential is created by a slight measurement bias in one of the sensors. However, this bias effect does not affect the overall ACC system performance and is not perceptible by the driver. As observed, the differential velocity data shows very minor differences between the two sensors (e.g.: typically < 0.5-m/s). The "difference" performance results shown for this scenario is typical and is the same for the other scenarios.

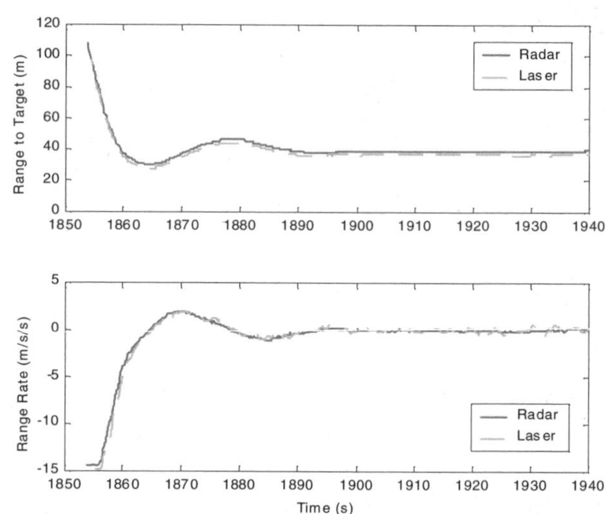

Figure 18. Sensor Performance Comparison (Scenario 1).

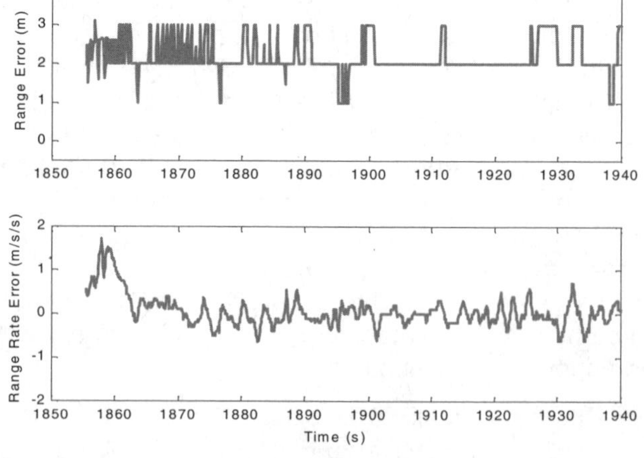

Figure 19. Sensor Performance Comparison (Scenario 1).

SCENARIO 2 (HIGH DIFFERENTIAL SPEED ENCOUNTER; ACCELERATING LEAD-VEHICLE): – The ACC-vehicle was operating in a 1-s timed-headway gap with a set-speed of 44-m/s. The ACC-vehicle operating in the Cruise Mode, traveling with a constant speed of 44-m/s, when it encounters an accelerating in-lane lead-vehicle traveling at an initial speed of 35-m/s. This equates to an initial speed differential of 9-m/s. Fig 20 illustrates the response of the radar-based ACC system. The lead-vehicle is identified as an in-path vehicle at approximately 120-m (although the radar detected the target at a more distant range). The ACC-control switches into the "Follow Mode" when it is assessed the ACC-vehicle is required to slow down as it approaches the lead-vehicle. Since the speed differential was not very severe, the "Follow Mode" criterion is not satisfied until the distance is ≈75-m. This correctly mimics human driving behavior, since most drivers do not necessarily start slowing down for near-speed lead-vehicles at very long distances. The ACC-vehicle eventually slows down to match/track the accelerating in-lane target velocity and remains at an appropriate timed-headway gap distance.

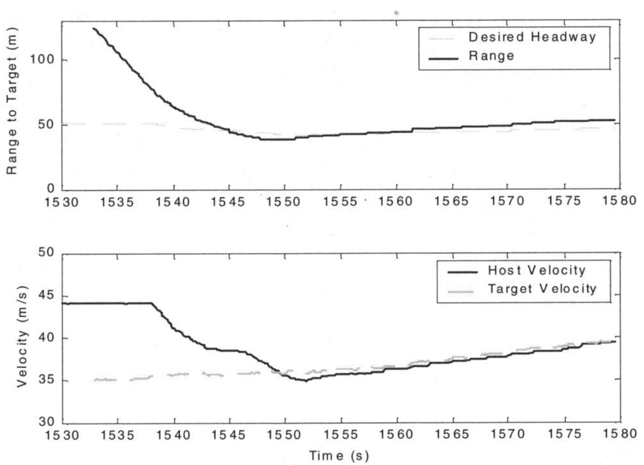

Figure 20. ACC system response (Scenario 2).

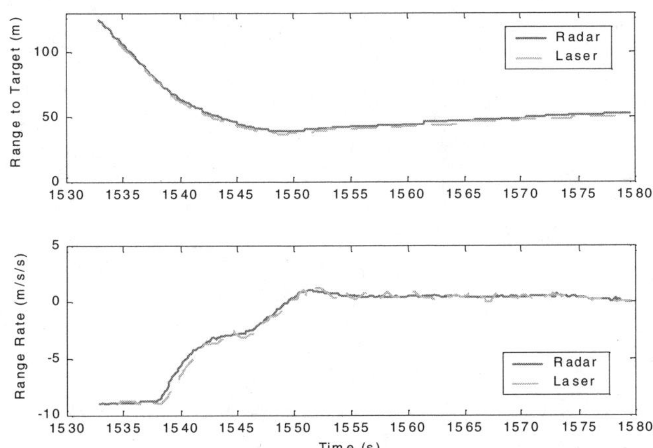

Figure 21. Figure 21: Sensor Performance Comparison (Scenario 2).

Fig 21 presents a comparison between the radar and lidar sensor assessed detection. It illustrates again that both sensors correctly measure the same distance and relative velocity performance.

SCENARIO 3 (NEAR-RANGE LANE-ENTRANCE AND LANE-EXIT MANEUVERS): – The ACC-vehicle was operating in a 1-s timed-headway gap with a set-speed of 44-m/s. The ACC-vehicle operating in the Cruise Mode, traveling with a constant speed of 44-m/s, when the adjacent-lane lead-vehicle traveling at an increasing speed of 31-m/s, performs a lane change maneuver into the ACC-vehicle lane. This equates to an initial speed differential of 13 m/s. Fig 22 illustrates the response of the radar-based ACC system. The lead-vehicle changed into the ACC-vehicle lane at approximately 80-m. The ACC-control switched into the "Follow Mode" and the ACC-vehicle immediately starts to slow down as it approaches the ead vehicle. Approximately, 6-s after the initial lane change maneuver, the lead-vehicle executes another lane change maneuver and exits the ACC-vehicle lane. At this point (i.e.: T ≡ 256-s), the ACC-control reverts back into the Cruise Mode and the ACC-vehicle begins to appropriately speed-up to achieve its previously specified set-speed.

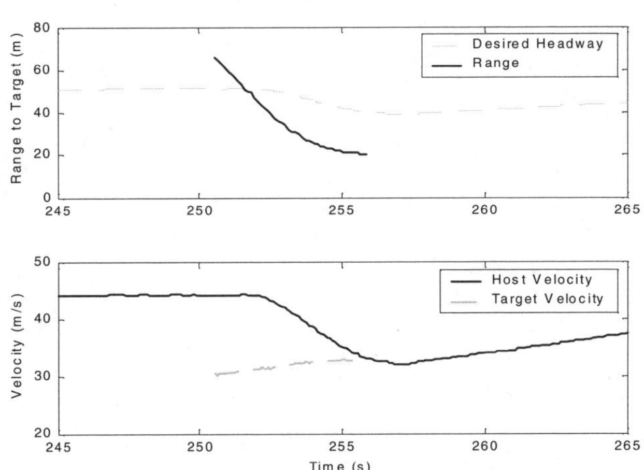

Figure 22. ACC system response (Scenario 3).

CONCLUSIONS

This paper discussed the technical and practical issues in the development/integration of a fully operational ACC system on a vehicular platform. This vehicle was uniquely configured to provide ACC functionality using either lidar- or radar-based object detection technology. This vehicle mechanization provided a unique opportunity to compare the capabilities of either detection sensor technology, as utilized in an ACC system, while operating with the exact same environmental conditions (e.g.: traffic patterns, roadway geometry/surface, weather conditions, etc.). The object detection sensors and ACC-system performance was examined for several real-world driving scenarios. In general, there are no significant differences that can be perceived by the driver while using an ACC system, which uses either object detection technology.

REFERENCES

1. J.L. Blincoe; *The Economic Cost of Motor Vehicle Crashes 1994*, U.S. Department of Transportation (Report DOT HS 808-425), 1996.
2. R. Knipling, et al.; *Rear End Crashes: Problem Size Assessment and Statistical Description*, U.S. Dept of Transportation (NHTSA Technical Report HS807-994), Springfield, VA, 1993.
3. R. Knipling, et al.; *Assessment of IVHS Countermeasures for Collision Avoidance: Rear End Crashes*, U.S. Dept of Transportation (NHTSA Technical Report HS807995), Springfield, VA, 1993.
4. G.R. Widmann, W.A. Bauson & S.W. Alland; Collision Avoidance Activities at Delphi Automotive Systems; *IEEE Conf. on Intelligent Vehicles '98*, Stuttgart Germany, 1998.
5. J. Schiffmann & G.R. Widmann; Model-Based Scene Tracking using Radar Sensors for Intelligent Automotive Vehicle Systems, *IEEE Intelligent Transportation Systems Conf.*, Boston, MA, 1997.
6. American Association of State Highway and Transportation Officials (AASHTO); *A Policy on Geometric Design of Highways and Streets*, AASHTO, Washington DC, page 174, 1984.
7. G. Widmann, M. Daniels, L. Hamilton , L. Humm, B. Riley, J. Schiffmann, D. Schnelker & W. Wishon; Adaptive Cruise Control: Forging Components into Systems, and Systems into a Company, *Techcon '99*, Kokomo, Indiana, 1999.
8. R.K. Jurgen; Automotive Electronics Handbook (2nd edition), McGraw-Hills, 1999.
9. P. Ioannou & Z. Xu; Throttle and Brake Control System for Automatic Vehicle Following, *IVHS Journal*, Vol. 1(4), 1994.
10. A. Bjornberg; "Design of Control Algorithms for Intelligent Cruise Control", Ph.D. Thesis, Chalmers Univ. of Tech., Goteborg, Sweden, Oct. 1994.
11. R. Mayr; Nonlinear vehicle distance control in longitudinal direction, *Int. J. of Systems Science*, Vol. 27, No. 8, 1996.
12. Y. Seto, T. Murakami, H. Inoue & S. Tange; Developments in Headway Distance Control Systems, *Automotive Engineering International*, Aug 1998.
13. P. Fancher, R. Ervin & S. Bogard; Operational testing of Adaptive Cruise Control, *Automotive Engineering International*, Sept 1998.

2000-01-0344

The BMW Active Cruise Control ACC

Willibald Prestl
BMW Group, Chassis Development/Vehicle Guidance Systems

Thomas Sauer
BMW Group, Electronics/By Wire Systems

Joachim Steinle and Oliver Tschernoster
BMW Group, Chassis Development/Vehicle Guidance Systems

ABSTRACT

With series introduction of Adaptive Cruise Control (ACC) systems, automotive industry at present makes a step towards a new category of vehicle control systems. For the first time in automotive history these systems make use of information about the surrounding traffic situation. This information is provided by new kinds of sensors and is being processed using intelligent algorithms. Thus new driver assistance functions are integrated in the car, ACC being the first representative of such kind of functions.

This contribution describes possibilities and also limits of today´s available technology on the example of the BMW ACC system, called „Active Cruise Control".

INTRODUCTION

BMW is soon launching in Europe its new Active Cruise Control ACC in the 7-series, an innovative driver assistance system, which provides a new distance control function as a convenience feature in addition to the velocity control of the well known standard Cruise Control. It is especially useful in dense highway traffic situations where the driver gets a new kind of support, making the task of fine tuning of both velocity and distance easier. It thus reduces the driver's workload and allows greater concentration on other driving tasks.

With the introduction of ACC systems on the market [6, 7], at the same time an important step is made towards a new category of vehicle control systems, which use not only data from within the car for control functions, but also data from new sensors, which provide information about the traffic situation surrounding the vehicle for new kinds of driver assistance functions in vehicle guidance.

The BMW ACC system, which is currently the smallest and lightest fully integrated radar based ACC system on the market, will be described in system philosophy and design as well as in its underlying technology. The system has been developed in close cooperation with Robert Bosch GmbH.

THE ACC FUNCTION

BASIC FUNCTIONS – The main functional enhancement of ACC, compared to standard Cruise Control CC, results from the ability of sensing forward traffic. Dependent on the situation, ACC changes automatically between two basic function modes: set speed control and follow control.

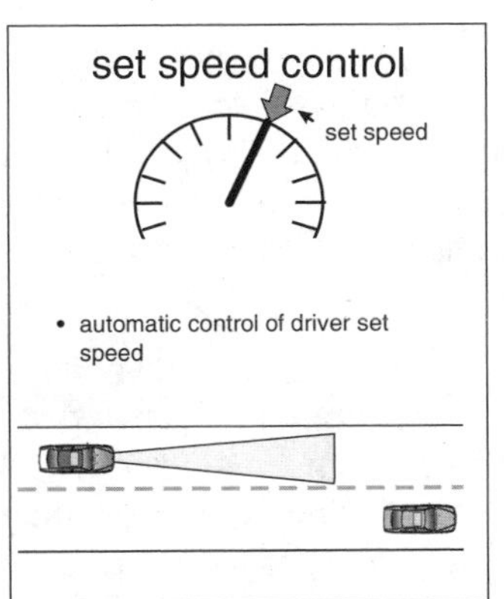

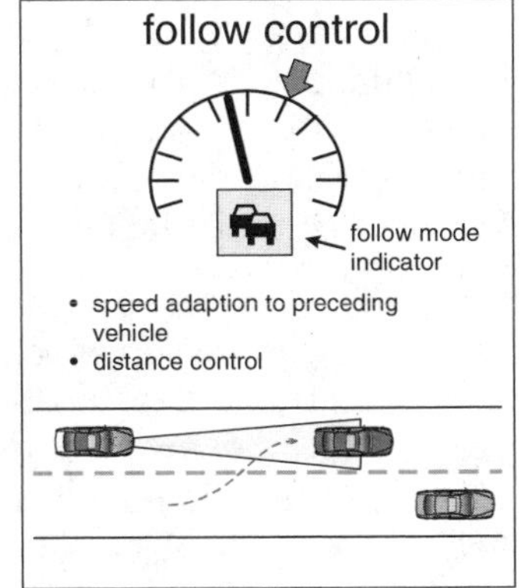

Figure 1. ACC basic function modes

In set speed control, with no preceding vehicle detected, speed is controlled according to the set speed exactly like CC does. In the follow control mode, with a slower preceding vehicle in the same lane, speed is reduced to that of the preceding vehicle and an appropriate distance is controlled automatically. If necessary, moderate braking by automatic brake actuation is used for deceleration.

These basic functions could be realized in many different shapes, but actually, system character and realization in detail is defined by capabilities and limits of ACC systems of the first generation.

SYSTEM CAPABILITIES AND LIMITS – Compared to the driver, who cannot estimate headway and relative velocity of preceding vehicles very accurately, ACC systems have much more precise data about surrounding traffic objects available as long as they are within the field of view [2]. They can be used for a very precise and sensitive distance control function.

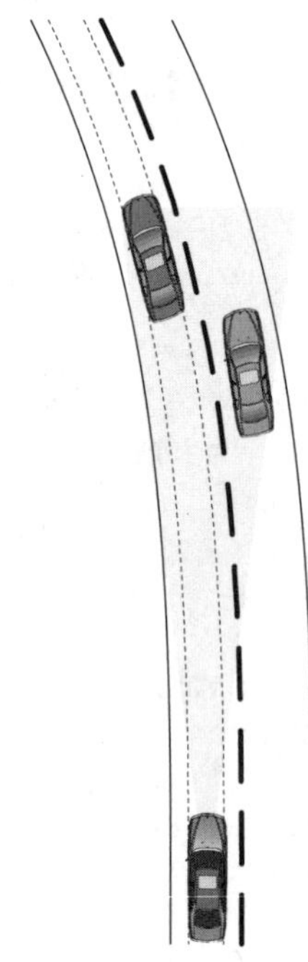

Figure 2. Lane prediction and object selection

But the mere object detection capability is not sufficient for situation interpretation, as needed for the ACC function. Object data must be correlated with the driver's future driving intentions to decide about their relevance for ACC control [4]. For example in a situation like in Figure 2.

that means to decide which one of the detected vehicles is the right target for distance control. Not knowing its own future trajectory or that of the other vehicles, ACC object selection is based on the hypothesis that objects become relevant objects, if they are in the same lane as the ACC vehicle. Lane prediction and object selection are thus central functions of all ACC systems.

State of the art technique for series application however does not allow a precise look ahead lane detection. Instead, a lane prediction, based on the current vehicle dynamic state is used, assuming for instance, that current trajectory curvature is representative for lane prediction in typical distance control range. This works very well on highways and major country roads, but especially under transient conditions, e.g. the road changing from straight to curve, uncertainty in object/lane assignment can occur, leading to misinterpretation of the traffic situation. Therefore the great variety of stationary objects besides the lane (traffic signs, beacons, trees, parking vehicles) might be assigned false to the lane. To avoid erroneous reactions in longitudinal control, which would be necessarily hard on stationary objects, these objects must be ignored for control functions, which would lead to brake actuation. In addition to the limitations in field of view, the limited certainty of situation interpretation is the most restrictive system limit of ACC systems.

FUNCTION DESIGN AND SYSTEM PHILOSOPHY – Due to the above described system limits, ACC systems clearly must be classified as convenience systems, which can provide assistance to the driver in a lot of situations, but never can relieve the driver of his/her responsibility for vehicle guidance. The driver always has full responsibility for the driving task [1, 3, 8].

To make this comprehensible for the driver based on his/her ACC driving experience an intentional limitation in functionality, especially in deceleration capability, is part of system philosophy and function layout. This ensures that system limits are reached frequently, where take over of longitudinal control by the driver is necessary, and thus they are easy to learn for the driver.

Furthermore, it is necessary to limit the systems deceleration and acceleration capability in order to avoid irritation of the driver and the surrounding traffic in case of inappropriate control reactions. In practical use a range of $-2.0 m/s^2$ to $+1 m/s^2$ was found to be a suitable compromise between customer benefit, convenience and safety requirements. In general, it is necessary that the driver is allowed to override the system at any time by throttle or brake without any conflicts with system functions. This ensures that the driver can easily and safely take over longitudinal control in every situation.

Primary safety functions like collision warning, which need an absolutely reliable situation interpretation, are not feasible with ACC systems of 1st generation and are thus not included in the BMW ACC function.

SYSTEM DESCRIPTION

ACC SYSTEM NETWORK – For safe, comfortable, reliable and economical realization of the ACC function in a vehicle, a complex system network is needed, which makes high demands on the vehicle's infrastructure. Figure 3 shows the ACC functional network solution in the BMW 7-series vehicles:

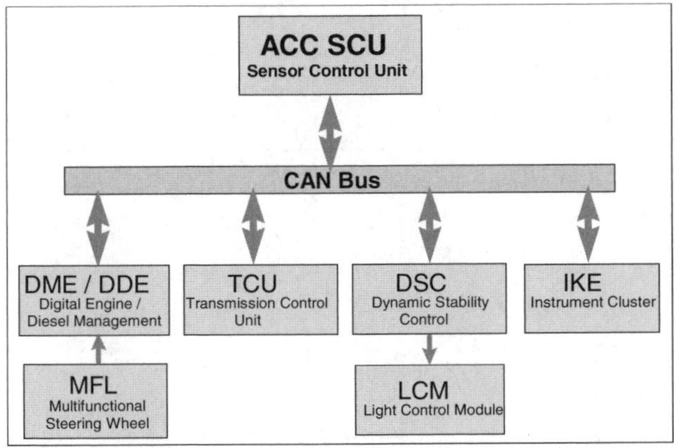

Figure 3. ACC System Network

From the realization point of view, ACC is an integrated system with distributed functionality in different partner electronic control units (ECUs). This is a special challenge for the whole development process, but also implies major technical consequences, e.g. concerning the safety relevant data exchange via 500 kBaud CAN-Bus, the diagnostics and fail safe concept for the whole system.

ACC SENSOR CONTROL UNIT – The BMW ACC system is based on the Bosch ACC Sensor Control Unit, SCU, currently the smallest and lightest ACC set in series production worldwide.

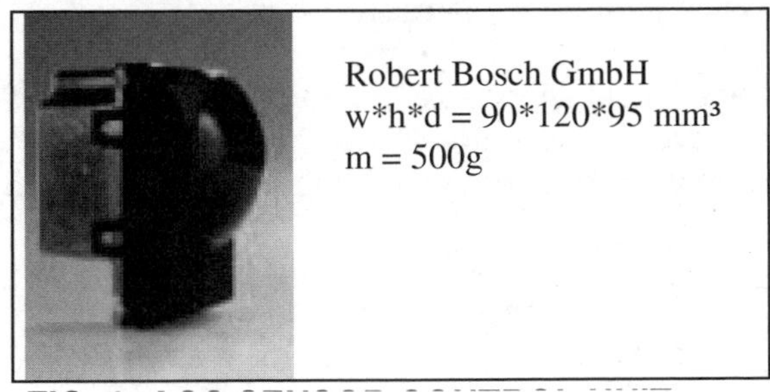

Figure 4. ACC Sensor Control Unit

The fully integrated solution has advantages in vehicle package, costs and reliability compared with systems being split into sensor front end and electronic control unit.

The ACC SCU comprises full ACC longitudinal control function (distance, velocity and acceleration control) as well as communication via CAN Bus in the system network, all diagnostics and self-test functions and the 76 GHz radar components with according signal processing functions as described below.

The sensor consists of 2 parts: the radar front end with transmitter and receiver and the digital processing unit.

Radar front end – The main component of the transmitter is a Gunn oscillator which produces a frequency modulated signal with a center frequency of 76 GHz (wavelength ≈ 4 mm). This signal is radiated by an antenna consisting of 3 patches and a dielectrical lens (see Fig. 4) for beam focusing. This results in a 3 beam antenna characteristic: the center beam is parallel to the direction of the vehicular motion, the left and right beam are displaced by an azimuthal angle of +/- 2.5° to that axis.

The reflected signal is received by the same antenna. For each of the 3 beams there is an own receiver channel. A special radio frequency component separates the transmitter from the receiver signal. Consecutively, the receiver signal is mixed with the Gunn oscillator signal resulting in the difference frequency of the 2 inputs. This is the intermediate frequency (IF) signal which is amplified and digitally converted.

Table 1. Technical data of radar sensor

transmitter frequency	76 GHz - 77 GHz
average output power	1 mW
transmitted bandwidth	200 MHz
range coverage	2 m - 150 m
range rate coverage	+/- 60 m/s
azimuthal coverage	+/- 4°
vertical beam width	+/- 2°

Digital processing unit – The 2 digital signal processors (DSPs) control the radar transmitter, i.e. they activate the transmitter every 100 msec (= 1 update cycle) for a period of 10 msec and they determine the frequency modulation. However, their main task is the processing of the IF-signals of the 3 receiver channels.

Radars determine the range to a target via the traveling time of the reflected wave:

range = total range/2 = traveling time*speed of light/2.

The FMCW (Frequency Modulation Continuous Wave)-Radar measures the traveling time indirectly via the difference frequency between the transmitter output, whose frequency linearly increases (Fig. 5: ramp 1) or decreases (Fig. 5: ramp 2), and the receiver signal. One of the DSPs performs a spectral analysis of the IF-signals. A peak in the spectrum corresponds to a target. If there is no relative motion (range rate) between the radar and the target, the difference frequency (= position of the peak) is proportional to the target range. Generally, there is a relative motion resulting in a Doppler shift of the receiver signal. By considering the difference frequency from ramp 2 the components of the range and the range rate can be separated. However, this strategy applies only for a 1-target-situation. Multi target capability is achieved by further ramps with different slopes of frequencies.This processing step is performed for each receiver channel.

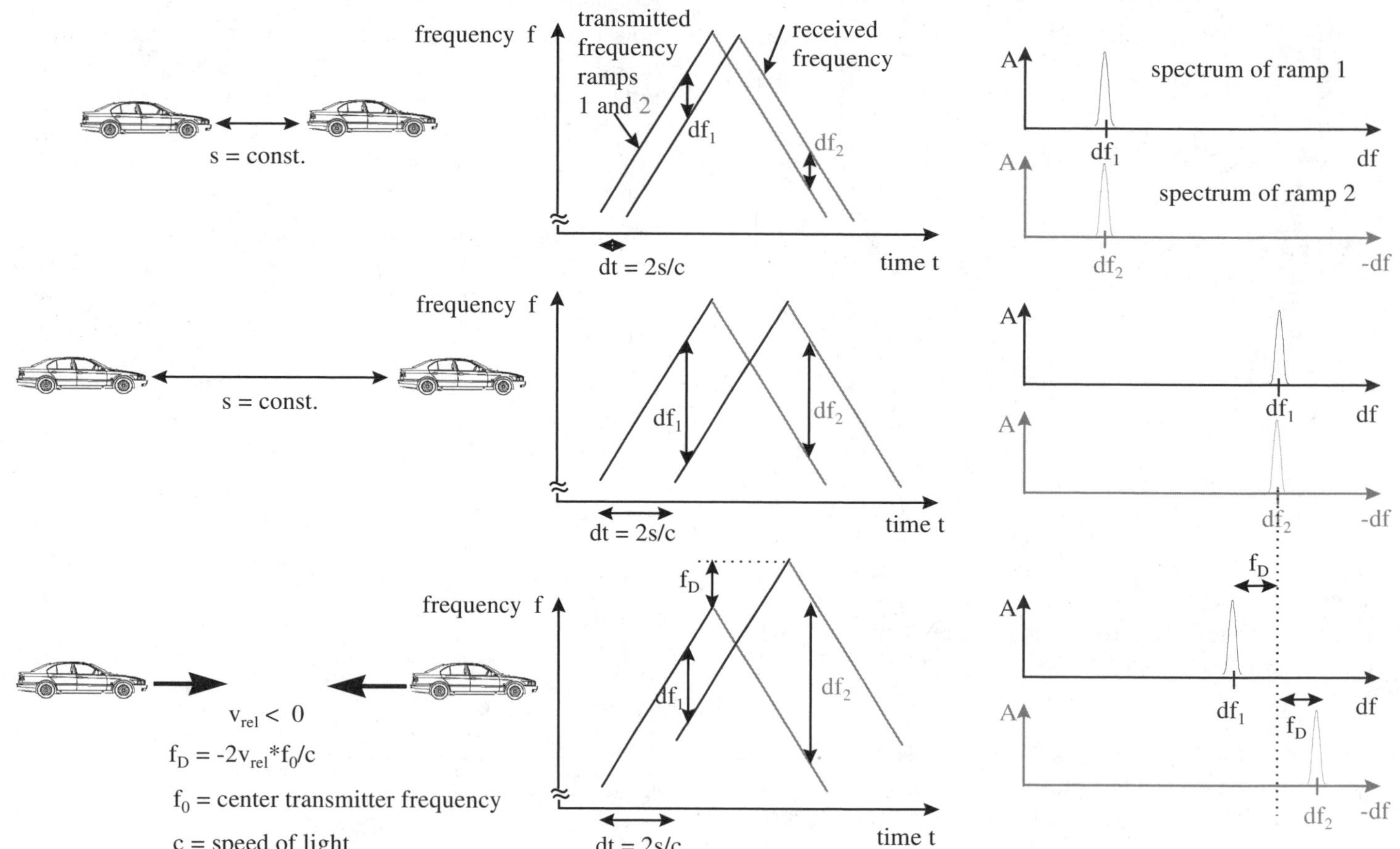

Figure 5. FMCW-Radar with increasing and decreasing frequency ramps

The azimuthal angle with respect to the radar axis is determined by comparing the amplitudes of the target peaks in the 3 receiver channels with the antenna characteristic. Therefore, in each radar sensor its specific antenna characteristic is stored which indicates the 3 receiver amplitudes for an ideal isotropic scatterer for the whole angular coverage.

The angle with the best fit between measured and stored amplitudes is assigned to the detected target.

Vehicles, especially trucks, consist of several radar scatterers which result in several target detections. These detections must be clustered into a single object. In order to avoid scatterers from different objects being clustered, only such scatterers are combined whose range and angle are located in the same cluster cell and which have the same range rate.

From update cycle to update cycle the locations of each clustered object are collected and smoothed in form of a trajectory. This tracking also allows the prediction of the object position in case of a detection loss.

Finally, a list with range, range rate and azimuthal angle of each detected object is provided to the subsequent control unit.

Beside these localization tasks the radar processing unit executes several self-surveillance routines so that malfunctions can be detected and the appropriate action taken.

DME/DDE – For ACC acceleration control, the engine is seen as a torque actuator. Torque requests are sent from ACC to a specific ACC torque interface function, which has been developed for Digital Engine Control DME and DDE of 7-series cars. Engine and ECU together act as an intelligent actuator, performing the ACC request by throttle/injection control and providing additional information about engine state, like current clutch torque. Also driver inputs from the Multifunctional Steering Wheel MFL are provided by DME/DDE on CAN-Bus.

TCU – ACC is preferably combined with an automatic transmission, because ACC works in a wide range of velocity making it necessary to change gears during ACC use. BMW´s Transmission Control Unit, TCU, has been extended by specific ACC shift maps and ACC specific functions to assure gear shifts, perfectly fitting to all ACC situations. TCU also provides data about the current gear and torque converter state for the ACC longitudinal control.

DSC – The BMW Dynamic Stability Control, DSC, provides all relevant vehicle dynamics data: velocity, acceleration and yaw-rate, which are used in lane prediction and longitudinal control of ACC.

DSC is also used as brake actuator in cases when coasting is not sufficient for ACC control and braking is necessary. DSC provides a deceleration interface on CAN Bus with a function called Electronically Controlled Deceleration, ECD. Using the DSC hydraulic unit, brake pressure is applied to the brakes by ECD to follow exactly the ACC deceleration command value. Using the DSC hydraulic unit is a particularly cost effective way for active braking [5].

If active braking occurs, brake lights are activated by DSC via the Light Control Module, LCM.

HUMAN MACHINE INTERFACE (HMI)

System Operating – Operation of the BMW ACC will be very familiar to BMW drivers with experience in Cruise Control use. The BMW Multifunctional Steering Wheel, MFL, has buttons for activation/deactivation, setting speed with increments and decrements of 10 kph as well as for resume function.

In active control mode, a selection from 3 distance programs (time gaps 2,0s - 1,4s - 1,0s) is always available for the driver by scrolling the programs with the resume key. Longest distance is the default setting at every first activation.

Instrument-Cluster – The instrument cluster with its ACC specific functions is an important part of the ACC human machine interface.

Figure 6. ACC specific instrument cluster

ACC activation state (standby and active control) is indicated to the driver by an ISO symbol (2) during the whole time of activation. In active control mode, the set speed is indicated by means of LEDs (1) around the speedometer scale in a quasi analog manner, which has proved to be an optimal ergonomic solution.

A follow mode indicator (object detected indicator) (4) informs the driver about the current ACC mode (set speed or follow mode) and especially alerts him/her to expect certain system reactions after a mode change.

Pictographs in the BMW Check Control display (3) show the currently chosen distance program while the driver is scrolling through the programs.

In situations requiring deceleration values that exceed the system capabilities of ACC it can be helpful to indicate when take over by the driver is necessary. This is especially helpful during the driver's ACC learning phase. Indication is done by flashing of the object detected indicator (4). But practical experience shows that drivers are very sensitive to the kinesthetic feedback of a beginning deceleration, which leads the drivers attention directly to the traffic scene, where ACC experienced users know very well when to take over. So normally experienced drivers don´t need a take over indication. This is also one reason for not having an audible take over alarm, which comprises high risk to be misunderstood as a collision warning function, which it cannot be due to the reasons explained above.

In case of a system failure, the Check Control display (3) is also used for failure indication combined with an audible alarm. In addition, the transition of normal ACC function to failure mode gives a strong kinesthetic feedback to the driver leading to an intuitive take over action.

CONTROL FUNCTIONS

DRIVING COURSE PREDICTION AND TARGET OBJECT SELECTION – In order to select the correct target object, ACC needs to predict the car´s future trajectory. As there is no vision system to detect lane boundaries, ACC relies on the current vehicle state: With the measurement of the vehicle´s yaw rate and speed, the actual turning radius is calculated [4].

This works well under stationary conditions, i.e. on a straight or when the car is already in a curve. However, when the curvature is changing, the prediction is not very accurate. To improve the prediction, the movement of all detected objects is taken into account. With suitable filters and within sensible boundaries, the additional curvature resulting from the detected objects is superimposed onto the curvature from the vehicle´s own movement. This improves the target selection at the entrance and exit of a curve significantly.

After calculating the actual curvature of the driving course prediction the lateral offset of each detected object can be determined as a function of distance.

With the lateral offset the plausibility for lying in the ACC car´s driving course prediction is calculated for each object. This driving course plausibility reaches a maximum when the object is definitely in the ACC car´s lane, or a minimum when it´s definitely in the adjacent lane with fuzzy transitions. These transitions are very sharp in the near range and become smoother with distance increasing. Such a plausibility distribution takes into account that the driving course prediction is loosing its accuracy proportional to the distance of an object.

The objects with the highest plausibility and the ones that are closest to the ACC vehicle are chosen for feeding the Follow Controller with their data. The controller calculates the necessary acceleration for an appropriate reaction. The object with the lowest acceleration value (i.e. the one that requires the highest deceleration) becomes the target object.

LONGITUDINAL CONTROL FUNCTIONS – The ACC controller can be separated into four basic parts (Fig. 7):

- Situation specific control functions: Set Speed Controller SSC, Follow Controller FOC and Curve Speed Controller CSC. Each of these modules gives desired values for acceleration and jerk.
- Combination and selection respectively as well as limitation of the situation specific control values in the Mixer MIX. The result is the overall desired acceleration value.
- Conversion of the acceleration value into desired values for the actuator systems (engine, brakes) in the Longitudinal Controller LOC
- actuator systems that realise controller output (electronic throttle, electronic brake control)

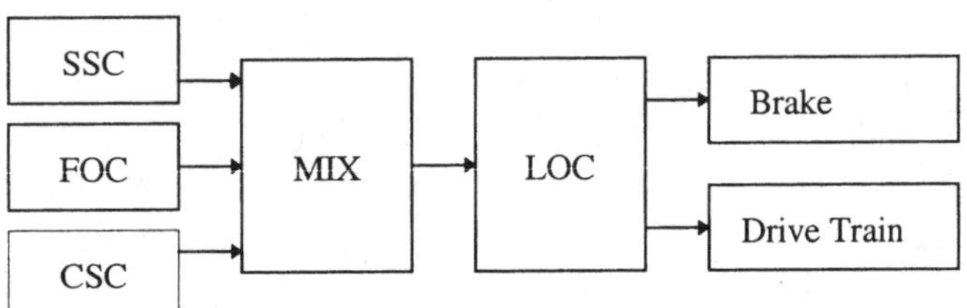

Figure 7. ACC controller structure

Set Speed Controller SSC: – This part works very similar to a conventional cruise control and is basically a proportional controller evaluating the difference between actual and set speed with certain limitations. The difference is that the brakes can also be activated in order to keep a certain speed when driving downhill.

Follow Controller FOC: – The main module of the Follow Controller is based on characteristic lookup tables that ensure human-like behavior depending on the object´s distance and relative velocity that controls the stationary follow mode. It tries to bring the ACC vehicle into a stationary state where the distance equals the desired time gap and the relative velocity equals zero. Deviations from this point result in desired relative velocities based on characteristic curves. Multiplication with the controller gain gives the necessary acceleration values.

The second module is a Slow-Down Controller that controls fast approaching manoeuvres. Its output depends on the relative velocity and the distance that can be used to slow down. It also depends on the time gap setting allowing softer deceleration with a wide time gap and harder braking for a short setting.

Curve Speed Controller CSC: – Curves need a special treatment. This is due to the fact that the ACC sensor has a very limited angular field of view and loses the objects with increasing curvature. A simple acceleration back to the set speed is not appropriate as the target object is usually still there. Also the lateral acceleration could reach too high values. Therefore the speed in curves is controlled according to a comfortable level of lateral acceleration (which decreases with increasing speed) based on the yaw rate signal.

Mixer MIX and Longitudinal Controller LOC: – The Mixer basically selects the minimum of all inputs and takes care of smooth transitions by jerk limiting acceleration changes. It also limits the maximum acceleration and deceleration values according to vehicle speed.
With the acceleration value coming from the Mixer the Longitudinal Controller LOC first has to decide whether to control the drive train or the brakes. By calculating the vehicle dynamics and with information about the minimum available engine torque and the transmission factor of the drive train the minimum acceleration with engine coasting only can be calculated. If further deceleration is required, the brakes come into effect. A hysteresis ensures that frequent changes between engine and brake control are avoided. In the nominal vehicle dynamics an incline adaptation accounts for downhill forces and/or changes in wind drag or vehicle mass (like driving with a trailer).

TECHNICAL SAFETY CONCEPT

From a technical point of view, the requirements concerning the safety concept have to be very strong, as the command values from ACC to its subsystems (engine and brake control) are regarded as safety relevant. This means on the one hand that every system being a part of the network has to be inherently safe, and on the other hand that failures in each part of the distributed system must be detected and have to result in a safe shut down state.

SAFETY CONCEPT IN DISTRIBUTED SYSTEMS – ACC and its subsystems communicate with each other via the CAN Bus, which is excellently suitable for transmitting safety relevant information because of its hardware and protocol properties.

Furthermore the interface has been designed in a way, that enables the actuator ECU´s to monitor the ACC SCU´s requests continuously in two aspects: command values being up to date, consistent and plausible.

MONITORING MEASURES – We have to distinguish ACC SCU internal monitoring measures as well as measures for the whole system´s function, both on hardware level and functional level.

Before ACC can be activated by the driver some self tests during an initial phase have to be performed. Further tests regularly take place while ACC is active.

Some important monitoring measures on the hardware level refer e.g. to the components generating the high frequency signals as well as the evaluation circuits for the incoming radar signals and both microprocessors inside the ACC Sensor and Control Unit. The latter ones perform some mutual monitoring, in order to ensure that the other processor is still working and creating consistent and plausible outputs.

Checks regarding the system function are performed by the radar-sensor unit (e.g. to find out whether the detection capability is reduced or the sensor is misaligned) as well as by the regulation unit (e.g. plausibility of ACC command values compared with the vehicle's reaction).

In addition to that, the regulating functions of ACC and its subsystems are designed in a cooperative way. If e.g. an anti skid control or a vehicle stability control function intervenes, the ACC function will be terminated in a proper way in order to make the driver take over the longitudinal control of the vehicle, if the road is slippery.

SHUT-DOWN MECHANISM FOR A SYSTEM WITH DISTRIBUTED FUNCTIONS – Failure detection inside the ACC unit or in the whole system network leads to a shut-down reaction informing the driver in a visual, audible and kinesthetic way, that the ACC function is not available anymore.

Dependent on the kind of failure and the driving situation, system performance shall temporarily be maintained on the highest possible functional level until the driver has taken over the vehicle control again. That means e.g. not to shut down ACC completely, if a currently performed deceleration can be brought reliably to an end. In other cases the system is shut down immediately by setting all ACC command values to zero. Both states are fail safe, preventing active acceleration.

In case of any failure the communication between the control units within the ACC system network is being maintained if possible. Thus, each device can inform the others if a failure is detected. As a consequence, every participant changes into the failure mode and a synchronous shut down process of the whole network is guaranteed. As long as the failure exists, the driver cannot turn on ACC again.

CONCLUSION

The BMW Active Cruise Control system described above has been designed as a comfort system, supporting the driver in follow situations by a headway control function added to the speed control function of a conventional Cruise Control.

The system has been presented with its human machine interface, with basic technical data and functions, as well as with specific functions for special driving situations. Especially, functional limits of the system and the necessity of driver intervention in critical situations have been pointed out.

Technology and properties of the 76 GHz Radar as the key component of the system have been presented. Furthermore the functional cooperation in a CAN bus network of altogether five different control systems has been shown.

The implementation of the braking function for ACC using the hydraulic aggregate of BMW´s Dynamic Stability Control DSC has been described as a particularly economical solution.

Finally an approach to the safety concept of the combined sensor control unit and of the whole system network has been presented.

REFERENCES

1. Naab, K.; Reichart, G.: Driver Assistance Systems for Lateral and Longitudinal Vehicle Guidance - Heading Control and Active Cruise Support. Proc. of AVEC ´94, 1994, pp.449-454
2. Naab, K.; Hoppstock, R.: Sensor Systems and Signal Processing for Advanced Driver Assistance. Seminar on Smart Vehicles, Delft, The Netherlands, February 13-16, 1995, Sweets&Zeitlinger, 1995.
3. Winner, H.; Witte, S.; Uhler, W.; Lichtenberg, B.: Adaptive Cruise Control System, Aspects and Development Trends. SAE Technical Paper 961010.
4. Winner, H.: Adaptive Cruise Control. Beitrag in: Jurgen, R. (Editor): Automotive Electronics Handbook, 2nd Edition, Mc Graw Hill Inc., 1999.
5. Konik, D.; Müller, R.; Prestl, W.; Toelge, T.; Leffler, H.: Elektronisches Bremsenmanagement als erster Schritt zu einem integrierten Chassis Management. ATZ 101 (1999) 4 und 102 (1999) 5.
6. Selzle, H. (Editor): Mit Abstand vorne. Automobil Produktion, Sonderausgabe Mercedes Benz S-Klasse, November 1998.
7. ATZ / MTZ Sonderheft Die neue S-Klasse (DaimlerChrysler S-Klasse), Oktober 1998
8. Winner, H.; Witte, S.; Uhler, W.; Lichtenberg, B.: System Aspects of Adaptive Cruise Control Systems, Proceedings of ATA-EL 95, Belgirate, Italy, May 9-10,1995

CONTACT

BMW Group
Dr. Willibald Prestl
Dept. EF-14
80788 Munich
Germany
e-mail: willibald.prestl@bmw.de

2000-01-0109

Development of a Controlled Braking Strategy For Vehicle Adaptive Cruise Control

Bryan Riley, George Kuo, Brian Schwartz and Jon Zumberge
Delphi Automotive Systems

Kevin Shipp
N. C. State Univ.

ABSTRACT

Adaptive Cruise Control (ACC) technology is presently on the horizon as a convenience function intended to reduce driver workload. This paper presents an implementation of a brake algorithm, which extends the production cruise control feature. A brief overview of the system architecture and subsystem interfaces to the forward-obstacle detection system, throttle and engine management controls are described. Considerations of moding ACC with ABS and Traction Control are presented at the vehicle level. This development activity is presented in two major phases. Both phases of this development project utilize CAN controllers and transceivers to implement requirements for limited access highway driving. The initial phase of development requires the brake control to follow a deceleration command and operate "open-loop" to the vehicle controller. Vehicle test data capturing smooth stops on high coefficient surfaces is presented as insight to the braking performance of the vehicle. A follow-on project extends the controlled braking requirements to "brake to a stop" as well as perform low speed cruise scenarios. The paper includes a description of rapid prototyping as an important tool to ensure the quality of the development software and reduce integration cost with core algorithms. Vehicle data summarizing autonomously controlled braking from current development vehicles will be presented.

INTRODUCTION

The number of automobiles travelling U.S. roads and highways increase on a daily basis. Unfortunately, traffic congestion and the number of automobile accidents also increase. There is an ever-pressing need to regulate traffic flow and make driving much safer. The automobile industry develops more intelligent vehicles every year. These advancements allow many people to foresee a completely autonomous vehicle in the not-so-distant future. There are several organizations that promote the development of safer, more intelligent vehicles. The U.S. government's support of the development of more intelligent vehicles is evident by the Surface Transportation Act (STA) passed just recently. The STA "will provide direction, stability, and growth for Intelligent Transportation Systems (ITS) that save lives, time, and money as we enter the new millennium," says a leading authority in ITS. Intelligent Transportation Systems include advanced technologies that help drivers avoid accidents, reduce traffic jams, and improve traffic flow. One particular topic of ITS is intelligent cruise control also called adaptive cruise control (ACC). ACC is an extension of the existing cruise control feature, which links together a forward obstacle detection system for monitoring traffic directly in front of the vehicle, the cruise control system (throttle), the brake system, and the driver's input as to a desired cruise control set speed. Identical criteria are used to determine following distance to the preceding vehicle. The main objectives of ACC are improved traffic flow and increased driver comfort while reducing the driver's workload.

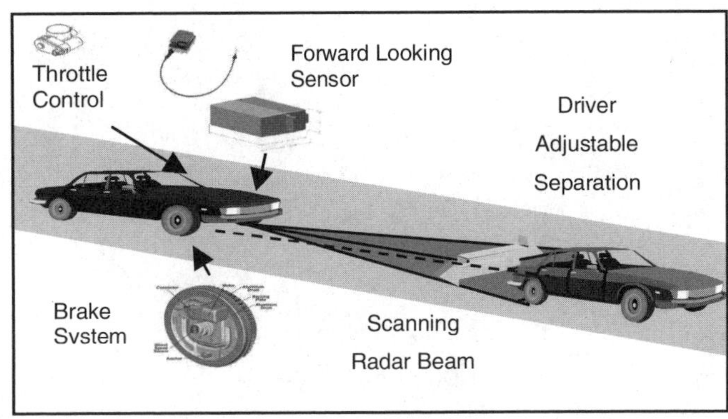

Figure 1. The subsystems of the ACC vehicle

There are many different ways to implement ACC on a vehicle, and this paper will discuss some typical implementation schemes. Figure 1 shows the components and subsystems used to achieve ACC on a host vehicle. In particular, the implementation method chosen by Delphi Automotive Systems will be discussed. The discussion of our implementation is broken up into two phases. Phase I goes into some detail of the basic ACC control algorithm and implementation, and Phase II discusses a control algorithm used to extend the basic ACC functionality to stop-and-go highway traffic.

HYDRAULIC MECHANIZATION

Figure 2 depicts the mechanization of the controlled braking system capable of ABS (Anti-lock brake System), TCS (Traction Control System), and VSE (Vehicle Stability Enhancement). The system performs ACC Autobraking without driver input on the braking pedal. The ABS Controller signals the motor in the modulator to pump brake fluid from the master cylinder into the wheel braking lines through the PRIME solenoid valves, which are opened by energizing their coils. The result achieves smooth and quiet vehicle deceleration. ACC Autobraking utilizes PWM-driven variable isolation valves (VIV) to regulate the pressure level on the hydraulic lines between wheel brake corners and isolation valves. VIV technology provides the characteristic of throttling the braking flow through the orifice of solenoid valve with extremely low-pressure jumps. The VIV provides an attractive alternative to the control of the solenoid valves where the applied voltage is proportional to fluid flow. Secondly, VIV technology overcomes the limitations of conventional ON/OFF style solenoid valves available in today's industrial market. Additional key features of the VIV hardware are to match the deceleration control requirements on quiet, smooth, and uniform autobraking for ACC, traditional traction control, and Collision Avoidance.

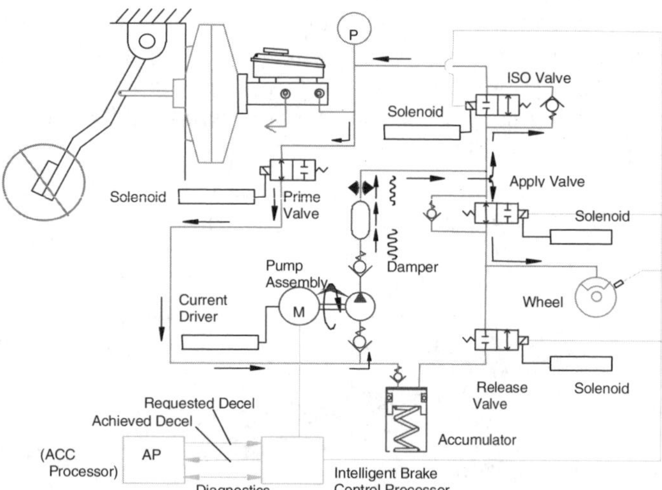

Figure 2. Hydraulic Mechanization

PHASE I: BASIC ACC FUNCTIONALITY AND IMPLEMENTATION

ACC requires driver inputs such as desired cruising speed and desired following distance in terms of timed headway. Once the cruising speed is selected and the trailing time (i.e. low, medium, and high) is entered, the driver input is complete. The ACC system performs throttle control, which allows the vehicle to travel at a constant set speed, assuming there is no traffic within the desired following distance. The vehicle will continue to cruise at the set speed until one of three things occurs. The three inputs, which disrupt the system, are:

1. Driver applies the brake – ACC is deactivated;
2. Driver increases speed – ACC remains active, but the system will return to previous (slower) set speed if a new cruising speed is not set once the driver ceases to accelerate; or
3. Forward obstacle detection system senses a slower vehicle in the path of the host vehicle.

Input number three poses a challenge to the ACC system to maintain the desired following distance. When a slower vehicle is detected, the ACC system evaluates the speed of the lead vehicle and transitions to a following mode in which it attempts to maintain the specified headway behind the lead vehicle via issuing throttle and/or brake commands. Throttle control for deceleration is typically performed when decel commands from the ACC processor are less than 0.1g, but this is heavily dependent upon the size of the host vehicle and type of engine. Therefore, this paper focuses on ACC decel commands in reference to the brake system, which is imperative in Phase II of ACC development. Once the slower moving vehicle is detected and a decel command is sent from the ACC Processor to the brake system via CAN bus, the brake system attempts to achieve the commanded decel. The brake system's reaction to the decel command is dependent upon the control algorithm used and the vehicle hardware used for implementation. Decel control for ACC braking is typically performed using a "Smart" booster, brake-by-wire, or an ABS modulator. Decel control using a "Smart" booster is done by controlling the air flow valve of the booster, thereby regulating the vacuum inside the booster. Decel control using a brake-by-wire implementation is performed by sending a brake command to the actuator at each wheel, which applies braking to the wheels. Decel control using the modulator is done by regulation of wheel pressure through solenoid valves within the modulator. The team chose to use the modulator approach to perform decel control. Modulator based decel control was selected because of the variable isolation valve (VIV) technology. Smooth and quiet vehicle decel is achieved as a result of successful VIV control. The metrics of success are the cost to implement the system, the vibration that the steering wheel and body of the vehicle is subject to when performing decel, and the noise level of the system when performing decel. Utilization of VIV results in a very quiet system, because the pressure is built-up and released in a gradual manner. Large, abrupt pressure changes may cause vibration of the brake lines, which may ultimately cause vibration in the steering column and body. Such vibrations cause the system to be noisy. And most importantly, if the vehicle to be equipped with ACC already has an ABS modulator, then the modulator based decel control comes at no additional hardware when the ABS modulator is equipped with VIVs. Replacement or the addition of hardware in order to implement the other methods is very costly. Figure 3 and Figure 4 show vehicle test data capturing braking pressures and smooth decel in response to commanded decel levels. After the initial application of the brakes, the downstream pressure at the wheels depicted as "PRESLF," "PRESRF," "PRESLR," and "PRESRR" in Figure 3 endorse smooth deceleration. Smooth deceleration is defined as non-jerky braking. Wheel pressure gradients greater than 30psi are typically felt as clunky or jerky by the driver. The pressure profiles displayed in Figure 3 have pressure gradients £20psi; therefore, exhibiting smooth deceleration. This shows the ability of the brake system to handle both, tracking of decel and, at the same time, maintain braking that is pleasing to most drivers.

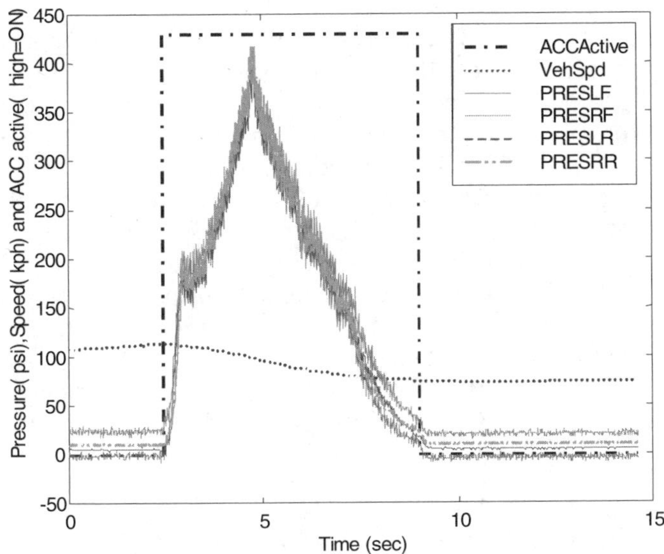

Figure 3. Response of vehicle wheel pressures in ACC autobraking.

Signals recorded in Figure 4 are ACC active flag (ACC Active), decel command from ACC controller and the effective vehicle decel. The decel command is captured as the signal "ACC Command," while the signal "VehDecel" captures the decel achieved as shown in Figure 3. The vehicle decel curve exhibits the VIV response capability in the transition from acceleration to deceleration. It also indicates the excellent performance of the decel feedback close-loop tracking control during the entire decelerating period.

The forward obstacle detection system uses a scanning millimeter wave forward looking radar (FLR). Information is transmitted between the ACC Processor the other subsystems over a CAN bus. Decel commands sent from the Adaptive Cruise Control Processor (ACCP) are inputs to the control algorithm that is loaded into the Autobox microprocessor. The outputs from the control algorithm are sent to the brake controller over the CAN.

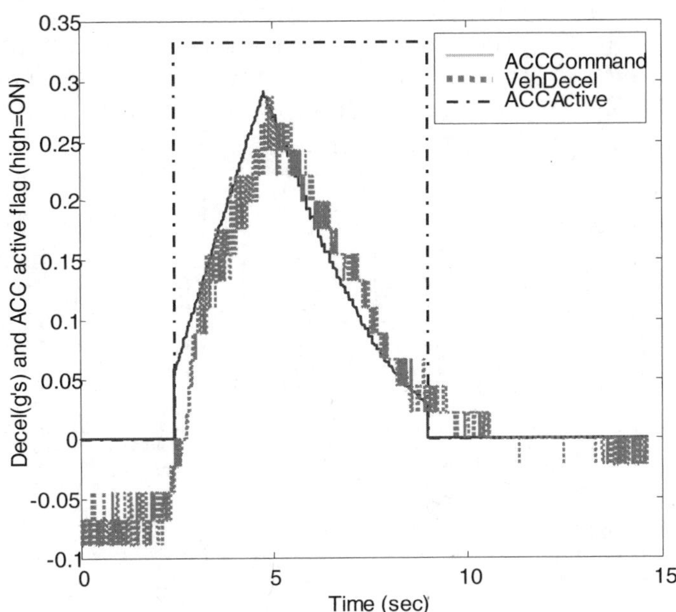

Figure 4. Decel tracking control performance in ACC Autobraking

The brake controller then sends PWM commands to the modulator in order to achieve the commanded decel. An ACC system is typically active for speeds above 20kph, and it is deactivated when the decel command forces speeds below 20kph. Phase II of ACC algorithm was developed in order to deal with decel commands requiring vehicle speeds less than 20kph including "brake to a stop."

PHASE II: STOP AND GO

The key Stop-and-Go features added to the basic ACC control algorithm address traffic jam situations, which requires low-speed cruise, braking to a stop and gradual release of the brakes once traffic flow resumes. The original ACC control area encompassed vehicle control over the traditional cruise control speeds. The figure below shows the additional speed ranges required for Stop-and-Go functionality.

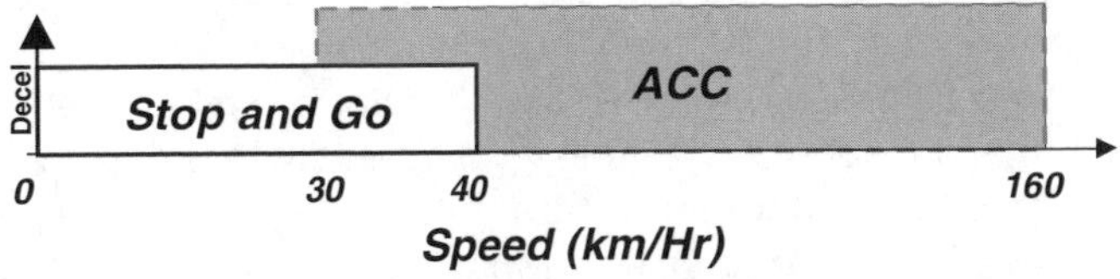

Some overlap in functionality is expected to provide a seamless Stop-and-Go ACC system.

The features associated with the use of ACC in traffic jams requires closed-loop control of vehicle speeds down to zero kph, zero speed brake apply (brake hold) and smooth pressure release for transitions from stop to go.

Rapid development and verification of the additional phase II control algorithm required the utilization of a rapid prototyping system (RPS). The RPS allows for hardware-in-the-loop simulation as well as actual interaction with real systems and hardware on the vehicle. Extensive bench simulations were run where the "Vehicle Interface" and "Brake Modulator" blocks shown in Figure 5 were replaced by a bench simulator shown in Figure 6.

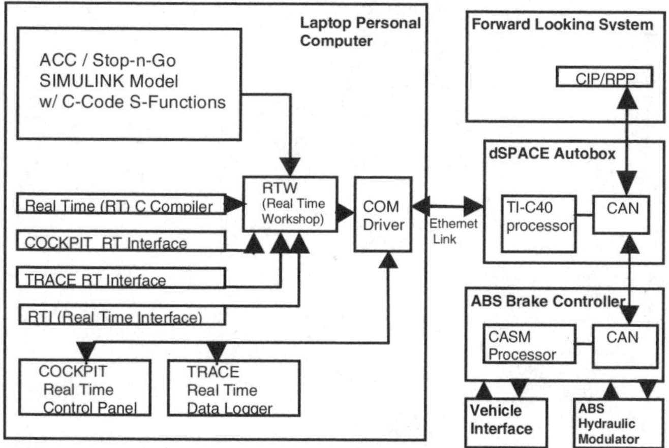

Figure 5. SIMULINK Model and RPS Block Diagram

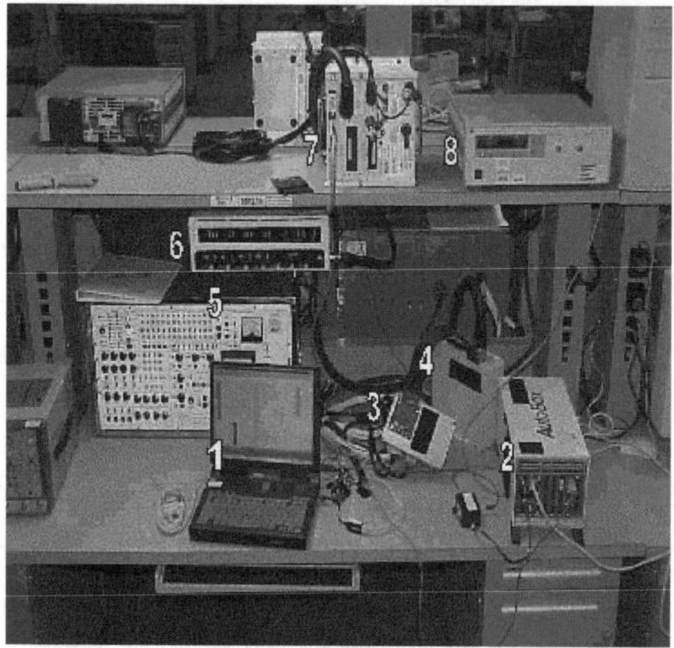

Figure 6. ACC Algorithm Bench and Test Setup

Using the RPS for bench (Figure 5) simulations allows for any major concerns within the control algorithm design to be resolved before tests are run in a vehicle. This approach saves much time and money throughout the verification process. The main focus of the bench simulations are to detect and resolve any design conflicts relative to the hardware prior to vehicle algorithm testing. For example, if for some reason, a routine in the control algorithm produces an output that could be potentially damage the actual hardware (i.e. the brake modulator), then detection of such problems on the bench save money and time required for replacing hardware. The bench also serves to verify the protocol developed for the CAN permits information to be transferred, absent of errors or timing concerns, throughout the network. Equipment shown are:

1. PC used for to development control algorithm
2. DSpace Autobox Hardware
3. DBC 7.x Development Controller
4. CASM G C-POD
5. Bench Simulator
6. Display Unit
7. MDS
8. POWER SUPPLY

CLOSED-LOOP VEHICLE SPEED CONTROL: LOW SPEED CRUISE

There are countless reasons for highway traffic to flow at speeds well below designated speed limits. The basic ACC algorithm deactivates at vehicle speeds around 25kph, requiring the driver to resume control of the vehicle. The low-speed cruise capability of the Stop-and-Go extension to ACC provides closed-loop vehicle speed control for speeds below 25kph. This addition enables the vehicle to maintain the desired headway at very low speeds. Figure 7 shows the results of commanding a cruising (tracking) speed of 3kph. As shown in the figure, the system does a good job of tracking such a low speed, even with passive wheel speed sensors. Predictions suggest that using active wheel speed sensors will produce even better results.

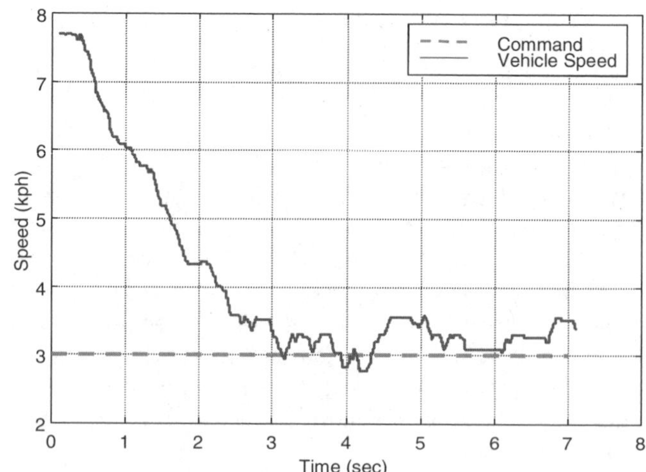

Figure 7. Vehicle Speed Tracking

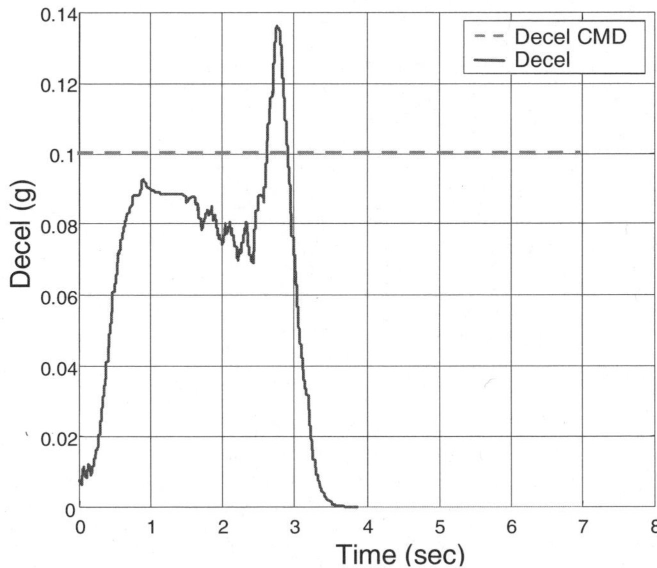

Figure 8. Stop Request at 0.1g

STOP REQUESTS

Unwanted as it may be, standstill traffic is encountered frequently on our highways. The Stop-and-Go algorithm also provides a stop request function. The stop request function commands a braking torque level based on the brake severity level dictated by the ACCP. Figure 8 shows the results of a stop request, at a brake severity level of 0.1g, from an idle speed just below 10kph. Figure 8 isolates the stop request command and the achieved decel of the vehicle. Data plotted in Figure 8, indicates the tracking performance degrades near the end of a stop. The accuracy of the wheel speed sensors at low speeds (the estimate of vehicle accelerations is based on the wheel speeds) is a primary cause of the degradation. Once a stop is obtained and traffic begins to flow, a gradual pressure release is desired so that the driver experiences a smooth transition. Recorded vehicle data shows the gradual pressure release as it applies to “go”. This smooth transition is shown in Figure 9. This data indicates that as the vehicle speed slowly increases a smooth transition from "stop" to "go" occurs.

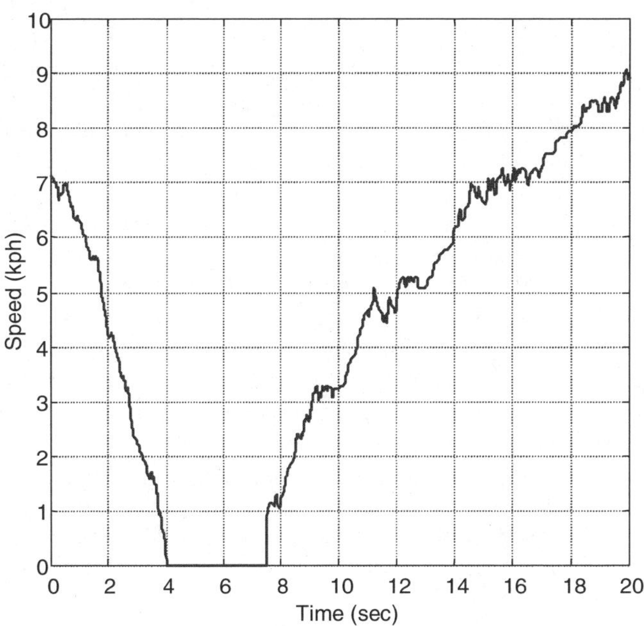

Figure 9. Vehicle response to the “STOP” and “GO”

CONCLUSION

There are several ways to implement an ACC brake control algorithm. The modulator-based implementation was examined here. The RPS proves to be very efficient in the development and verification of control algorithms because of the cost and time savings. The addition of Stop-and-Go to the ACC control algorithm is a step closer to the vision of an autonomous vehicle. While the features of Stop-and-Go increase driver convenience and reduce driver workload, they are not a substitute for an attentive driver.

ACKNOWLEDGEMENTS

We wish to acknowledge the technician team in the Vehicle Test and Instrumentation departments who supported vehicle builds and testing.

REFERENCES

1. McLaughlin, S.: Measurement of Driver Preferences and Intervention Responses as Influenced by Adaptive Cruise Control Deceleration Characteristics, Thesis, Virginia Polytechnic Institute and State University, Blacksburg, Virginia; June 29, 1998
2. "Surface Transportation Act Boosts Intelligent Systems, Says I.T.S. America President," Top Tech Stories Washington, June 10, 1999 http://techmall.com.techdocs/TS980610-9.html
3. Hatipoglu, C.; Ozguner, U.; Sommerville, M.: "Longitudinal Headway Control of Autonomous Vehicles," Proceedings of the 1996 IEEE International Conference on Control Applications, New York, NY; 1996; p.721-6
4. Shein, E.; Mausner, E.: "Deployment and Commercialization of Cost and Safety-effective Autonomous Intelligent Cruise Control System," Microwaves and RF Conference Proceedings, Nexus Media, Swanley, UK; 1995; p. 124-31
5. Barber, P.; Clarke, N.: "Advanced Collision Warning Systems," IEE Colloquium on Industrial Automation and Control: Applications in the Automotive Industry (Digest No. 1998/234). IEE, London, UK; 1998; p. 21-9
6. Widmann, Glenn et al.; Comparison of Lidar-based and Radar-based Adaptive Control Systems, SAE 2000.
7. Brakes for the Future, *Automotive Engineer*, September, 1998

CONTACT INFORMATION

H. Bryan Riley, Ph.D.
Delphi Chassis Systems
M/S 483-400-511
5725 Delphi Drive
Troy, MI 48098-2815
Phone: 248-813-2406
Fax: 248-813-2410
Email: bryan.riley@delphiauto.com

George Kuo, Ph.D.
Delphi Chassis Systems
M/S 483-3DB-210
Technical Center Brighton
12501 E. Grand River
Brighton, Michigan 48116
Phone: 810 494-4776

Brian Schwartz
Delphi Delco Electronics Systems
M/S 483-3DB-210
Technical Center Brighton
12501 E. Grand River
Brighton, Michigan 48116
Phone: 810 494-5896
Fax: 810 494-4456

Jon Zumberge
Delphi Chassis Systems
1435 Cincinnati St
Dayton, Ohio 45305
Phone: 937 455-6309

Kevin Shipp
ECE Dept.
N.C. State Univ.
Raleigh, NC 27695
Keshipp@unity.ncsu.edu

DEFINITIONS, ACRONYMS, ABBREVIATIONS

ABS: Anti-lock Brake System
ACC: Adaptive Cruise Control
ACCP: Adaptive Cruise Control Processor
CAN: Controller Area Network
CA DBC: Delphi Brake Control
CASM G C-Pod: Configurable Application Specific Module
DspaceTM: Company that produces software and hardware used for RPS
FLR: Forward Looking Sensor
ITS: Intelligent Transportation System
MDS: Modular Development System
PWM: Pulse Width Module
PRESLF: Left Front Wheel Pressure
PRESRF: Right Front Wheel Pressure
PRESLR: Left Rear Wheel Pressure
PRESRR: Right Rear Wheel Pressure
RPS: Rapid Prototyping System
STA: Surface Transportation Act
TCS: Traction Control System
VIV: Variable Isolation Valve
VSE: Vehicle Stability Enhancement

1999-01-2950

Safety Benefits Estimation of an Intelligent Cruise Control System Using Field Operational Test Data

Wassim G. Najm, Marco P. daSilva and Christopher J. Wiacek
Volpe National Transportation Systems Center

ABSTRACT

The potential safety benefits of an Intelligent Cruise Control (ICC) system are assessed in terms of the number of rear-end crashes that might be avoided on U.S. freeways if all vehicles were equipped with such a system. This analysis utilizes naturalistic driving data collected from a field operational test that involved 108 volunteers who drove ten passenger cars for about 68 and 35 thousand miles in manual and ICC control modes, respectively. The effectiveness of the ICC system is estimated at about 17 percent based on computer simulations of two rear-end precrash scenarios that are distinguished by whether the following vehicle encounters a suddenly-decelerating or slow-moving lead vehicle. The ICC system has the potential to eliminate approximately 13 thousand police-reported rear-end crashes on U.S. freeways, using 1996 national crash statistics.

INTRODUCTION

The widespread effect of fully-deployed Intelligent Cruise Control (ICC)-like systems on the rate of rear-end crashes on the nation's highways is estimated based on real-world driving data collected from a field operational test (FOT). A total of 108 randomly-invited citizens drove a fleet of 10 ICC-equipped passenger vehicles as their personal car for a two-week period (84 participants) and for a five-week period (24 participants) [1]. The vehicles were put into naturalistic use without constraining where, when, or how each participant drives. Each driver was also free to choose between operating the vehicle manually or with conventional cruise control during the first week and between manual or ICC driving during the second or subsequent weeks. The ICC system was engaged in approximately 35 thousand miles out of a total of 114 thousand miles driven in this FOT.

The ICC system utilized in the FOT can be described in terms of the sensor, the processor/controller, and the driver's interface. The sensor was a near-infrared device that measured distance and closure rate to vehicles in the lane ahead, steering its beam right or left as needed to follow the lane curvature. The processor/controller acted on the sensory data to modulate the throttle and also to downshift the transmission as required to satisfy the driver-selected minimum for headway or spacing to a vehicle ahead. The vehicle had a modest deceleration available for controlling headway (0.07g maximum) since brakes were not incorporated into this ICC system. The driver's interface included three minimum headway buttons installed on the dashboard, ranging from "closer" to "farther", and conventional cruise control buttons located on the steering wheel.

This paper provides an estimate of the potential safety benefits of the ICC system on U.S. freeways, based on a general methodology to assess the national safety benefits of new prototype, advanced-technology collision avoidance systems. This methodology is founded on estimating the effectiveness of a system to eliminate or ameliorate crash severity in driving situations that are characterized in national crash databases [2]. The estimated system effectiveness is then applied to data from national crash databases to estimate the number and severity of crashes that would have been eliminated were the system been in place when crash data were collected. This general methodology was applied in a previous study to appraise the potential safety benefits of rear-end, lane change, and single vehicle roadway departure crash countermeasure systems, using experimental data obtained from limited driving tests on public roads and in driving simulators *with* and *without* the assistance of a crash avoidance system [3][4].

Next, this paper describes the methodology used to assess the widespread impact of the ICC system on rear-end crashes. Relevant rear-end crash statistics follow, which were derived from the 1996 General Estimates System (GES) national crash database. After, this paper delineates driver/vehicle/system data used as input to the safety benefits assessment models. Later, this paper discusses the results of computer simulations that estimated the effectiveness of the ICC system under different travel speed conditions. Finally, a summary and concluding remarks are presented about the findings of the widespread safety benefits of the ICC system.

WIDESPREAD SAFETY BENEFITS ASSESSMENT METHODOLOGY

The widespread safety benefits of the ICC system are projected in terms of the number of rear-end crashes that might be avoided, because the ICC system automatically controls the gap between the host and lead vehicles. Moreover, the instrumentation package on-board the ICC-equipped vehicle in the field operational test (FOT) collected detailed data on the dynamics of car-following. In addition, the widespread safety impact analysis examined only the driving situations where the lead vehicle was moving. To avoid the problem of distinguishing roadway features, such as overpasses, as vehicle, the ICC system was designed to not respond to stopped or very slow-moving vehicles (lead vehicle speed < 1/3 host vehicle speed). Thus, the analysis in this paper does not apply to rear-end crashes with stopped vehicles.

The number of rear-end crashes that might be avoided with the use of the ICC system, B, was estimated by:

$$B = SE \times N_{wo}$$

where:

SE = Total ICC system effectiveness in all relevant rear-end pre-crash scenarios.

N_{wo} = Number of relevant rear-end crashes without ICC system intervention.

The total ICC system effectiveness was calculated as:

$$SE = \sum_{i=1}^{2} \left(\sum_{j=1}^{8} E(i,j) \times P(i,j) \times u_{ICC}(j) \right) \times F(i)$$

where:

i = Index to two rear-end pre-crash scenarios addressed by ICC system.

j = Index to eight following-vehicle speed-bins.

E(i,j) = Absolute effectiveness of a driver using the ICC system in preventing a rear-end crash in pre-crash scenario i within speed bin j.

P(i,j) = Probability that a relevant rear-end crash will be of pre-crash scenario i within speed bin j.

$u_{ICC}(j)$ = Proportion of time the ICC system was engaged within speed bin j.

F(i) = Fraction of relevant rear-end crashes in pre-crash scenario i relative to the relevant rear-end crash size.

The safety benefits of the ICC system are assessed in two rear-end pre-crash scenarios that were distinguished by whether the following vehicle encountered a suddenly-decelerating or slow-moving lead vehicle. In both pre-crash scenarios, the following vehicle was assumed to be initially traveling at a constant speed. Moreover, the driver of the following vehicle was assumed to apply emergency braking in response to the sudden deceleration, or the constant lower speed of the lead vehicle. To better equate traffic conditions across manual and ICC control modes, the ICC system effectiveness was estimated in eight travel speed bins: 25 - 35⁻, 35 - 45⁻, 45 - 55⁻, 55 - 60⁻, 60 - 65⁻, 65 - 70⁻, 70 - 75⁻, and ≥ 75 MPH. It is noteworthy that the ICC system was automatically disengaged in the FOT when the speed of the host vehicle fell below 25 MPH.

Figure 1 shows a high-level block diagram for estimating the total effectiveness of the ICC system, SE. The 1996 GES crash database was queried to obtain rear-end crash statistics for P(i,j) and F(i). The ICC FOT database provided values for ICC system usage rates, $u_{ICC}(j)$. Values for E(i,j) were estimated using computer simulations of kinematic models representing the two rear-end pre-crash scenarios. The parameter E(i,j) is mathematically expressed as:

$$E(i,j) = 1 - \frac{p_w(i,j)}{p_{wo}(i,j)}$$

where $p_w(i,j)$ and $p_{wo}(i,j)$ denote the probabilities of a rear-end crash in pre-crash scenario i within speed bin j *with* and *without* the assistance of the ICC system, respectively. These crash probabilities were estimated by Monte Carlo computer simulations using data primarily from the FOT. Monte Carlo simulation is appropriate for obtaining estimates of the crash probability where (a) a model of the driving environment under study is available, and (b) sufficient data are available to estimate parameters in the model. Models of the two rear-end pre-crash scenarios were simulated using kinematic representations of vehicle movements, and simple time delays of driver reaction and vehicle braking. These models determined if a crash occurred in each of the two scenarios for some given initial conditions. A crash was counted only if the relative speed at impact between the following and lead vehicles was over 5 MPH. Finally, the market penetration of the ICC system in the vehicle fleet was assumed at 100 percent in this analysis. That is, for any given simulation, the following vehicle was always equipped with ICC — whether the system was turned on was based on the observed usage of the test participants during the FOT.

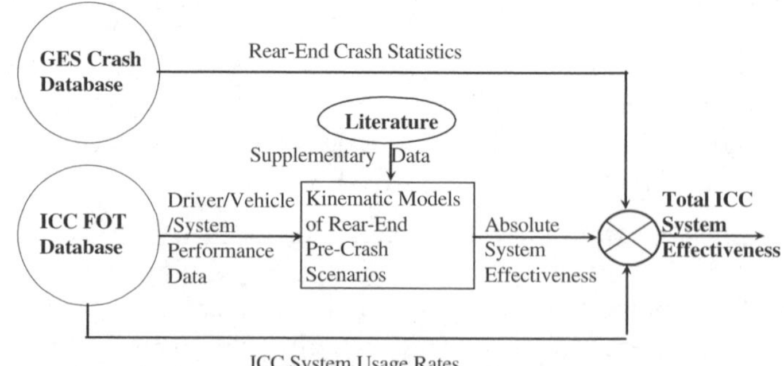

Figure 1. Block Diagram for Estimating ICC System Effectiveness

REAR-END CRASH STATISTICS

The rear-end crash type encompasses multi-vehicle crashes that occur when the front of a following vehicle strikes the rear of a lead vehicle, both traveling in the same lane. According to 1996 GES statistics, rear-end crashes accounted for about 26.5 percent of all police-reported (PR) collisions in the U.S. or approximately 1.816 million crashes [5]. Of these rear-end crashes, about 8.5 percent or 154 thousand PR crashes occurred on freeways. Table 1 lists the relative frequency of three pre-crash scenarios that happened immediately prior to these rear-end crashes. These scenarios are solely based on the dynamic state of the lead vehicle that preceded the crash and disregard the following vehicle dynamic state. The analysis in this paper excludes the pre-crash scenario where the lead vehicle was stopped because the ICC system did not respond to stationary objects. This pre-crash scenario involving a stopped lead vehicle accounts for over one third of all rear-end crashes on U.S. freeways, and thus will be important to consider in evaluation of crash avoidance systems. The ICC system in the FOT was evaluated only for its car following properties where the lead vehicle was moving.

Figure 2 shows the distribution of PR rear-end crashes for rear-end pre-crash scenarios 1 and 3, on freeways, arranged by the travel speed of the following vehicle. Crash statistics on travel speed of the following vehicle were obtained from the *Travel Speed* variable in the GES database. *Travel Speed* indicates the travel speed of the following vehicle before the driver's realization of the impending danger. It should be noted that about 60 percent of the actual speed data in the 1995 and 1996 GES databases were coded as "unknown". Moreover, a significant majority of PR rear-end crashes occurred below the posted speed limit, which may indicate that traffic was congested at the time of the crash [6].

Table 1. Definition and Relative Frequency of Rear-End Pre-Crash Scenarios on Freeways (Based on 1996 GES)

No.	Scenario Definition	Relative Frequency
1	Lead vehicle suddenly decelerates in front of following vehicle.	42.9%
2	Lead vehicle was stopped in traffic lane when encountered by following vehicle.	36.3%
3	Lead vehicle was moving at constant, lower speed than following vehicle.	20.8%

Rear-end crashes involving travel speeds below 25 MPH were not considered in this analysis because the ICC system did not operate below this speed. About 27 percent and 17 percent of PR rear-end crashes on freeways fall below this speed for pre-crash scenarios 1 and 3, respectively. Thus, the number of relevant rear-end crashes targeted by the ICC system, N_{wo}, was estimated at about 75 thousand PR crashes as indicated in Table 2. Consequently, the fractions of relevant PR rear-end crashes, F(i), were 0.6421 and 0.3579 respectively for pre-crash scenarios 1 and 3. Table 3 shows the probabilities that a relevant PR rear-end crash was of either pre-crash scenario within any of the eight speed bins, P(i,j).

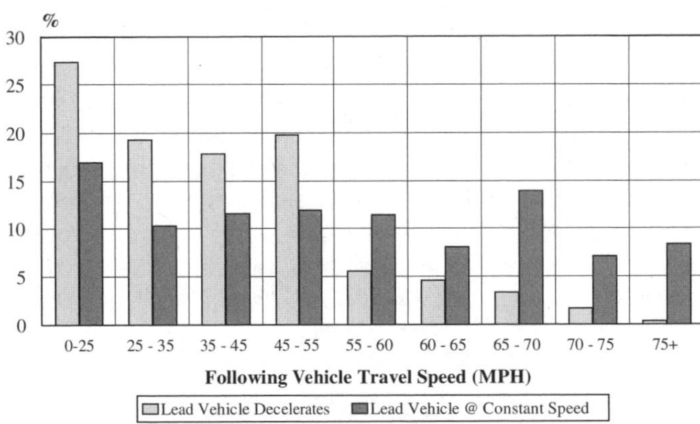

Figure 2. Distribution of Police-Reported Rear-End Crashes by Following Vehicle Travel Speed for Two Pre-Crash Scenarios on Freeways (Based on 1995-1996 GES)

Table 2. Size Derivation of PR Rear-End Crashes on Freeways Targeted by the ICC System (Based on 1996 GES)

PR Rear-End Crashes	Frequency (thousands)	% of Total
Total	1816	100
Freeways	154	8.5
Freeways, excluding lead vehicle stopped	98	5.4
Freeways, excluding lead vehicle stopped and travel speeds below 25 MPH	75	4.1

Table 3. Probabilities of Pre-Crash Scenarios Per Travel Speed Bin (Based on 1995-1996 GES)

Speed (MPH)	Scenario 1	Scenario 3
$25 - 35^-$	0.2651	0.1236
$35 - 45^-$	0.2463	0.1386
$45 - 55^-$	0.2735	0.1461
$55 - 60^-$	0.0772	0.1386
$60 - 65^-$	0.0626	0.0974
$65 - 70^-$	0.0459	0.1685
$70 - 75^-$	0.0230	0.0861
≥ 75	0.0063	0.1011

FIELD OPERATIONAL TEST DATA

The field operational test (FOT) provided data on the usage rates of the ICC system and on the performance of the driver/ICC-equipped vehicle in both manual and ICC control modes on freeways. The data were collected from 106 FOT participants (freeway data were not available for 2 drivers) in naturalistic driving conditions. Manual control data were obtained during the first week of driving. ICC control data were gathered during the second and later weeks of driving, including all ICC settings: 1.0, 1.4, and 2.0 second time-headway settings. Table 4 shows the proportions of time the ICC system was engaged by the FOT drivers on freeways in the presence of a valid lead vehicle target in eight different travel speed bins. Driver/vehicle/system performance data consisted of the following variables: ICC-equipped (following) vehicle speed, range, range-rate to a valid lead vehicle, driver braking reaction time, and lead vehicle deceleration. These variables were supplemented by the "emergency deceleration" variable, which was characterized by data from the literature. All these variables were used as input to Monte Carlo computer simulations to estimate the probability of a crash in two rear-end precrash scenarios for manual and ICC driving modes.

Data triads of following vehicle speed, range, and range-rate to a valid lead vehicle were sampled directly from the ICC FOT database, without regard to driver, trip, or headway setting, to preserve the inter-dependency among these variables. Data on driver braking reaction time were derived from a sample of video clips captured during freeway travel in the FOT. Figure 3 shows the mean braking reaction time as a function of time headway (range/vehicle speed) for both manual and ICC control modes on freeways. A lognormal distribution was utilized to generate random numbers for the braking reaction time in Monte Carlo simulations [7]. As seen in Figure 3, the correlation between driver braking reaction time and time headway is consistent with the results of another study that reported a decrease in braking reaction time as coupled vehicles drew closer together [8]. The lead vehicle deceleration variable was described in the simulations using the braking deceleration levels exhibited by the ICC-equipped vehicle in the FOT during manual control mode on freeways. Brake-only deceleration data of the ICC-equipped vehicle were used because they were easily identified in the ICC FOT database. Thus, the simulated deceleration levels in the "lead vehicle suddenly decelerating" pre-crash scenario were limited to observed decelerations resulting from brake pedal activation by the ICC-equipped vehicle, in manual control on freeways at travel speeds over 25 MPH. Figure 4 shows a histogram of these brake-only deceleration levels. Finally, the emergency deceleration variable was modeled as a normal distribution with a mean of 0.6g and a standard deviation of 0.1g, bounded by a minimum value of 0.3 g and a maximum value of 0.8 g. These values were obtained from the literature to simulate hard braking by the following vehicle in order to avoid hitting the lead vehicle [9].

Table 4. Proportion of Time ICC System Was Engaged as a Function of Travel Speed

Speed (MPH)	$u_{ICC}(j)$
25 – 35^-	0.0114
35 – 45^-	0.0620
45 – 55^-	0.2477
55 – 60^-	0.4945
60 – 65^-	0.6481
65 – 70^-	0.6961
70 – 75^-	0.6823
≥ 75	0.5891

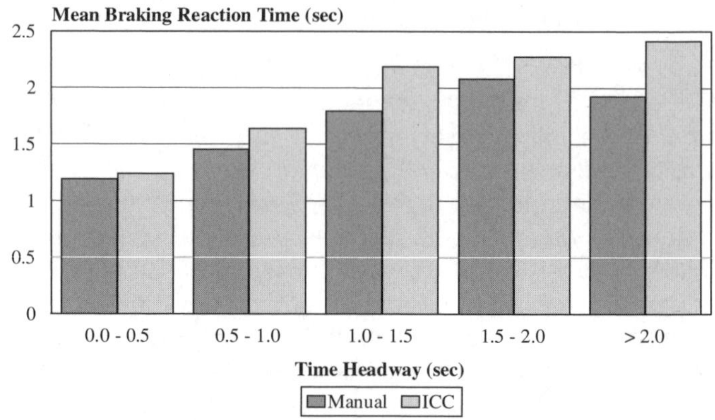

Figure 3. Relationship between Driver Braking Reaction Time and Time Headway

RESULTS OF MONTE CARLO SIMULATIONS

Computer simulations were executed to estimate the probabilities of a crash in the "lead vehicle suddenly decelerating" and the "lead vehicle moving at lower speed" rear-end pre-crash scenarios for both manual and ICC driving. Approximately one hundred thousand Monte Carlo computer simulations were run for each of the two rear-end pre-crash scenarios in each of the eight speed bins, and for each control mode, for a total of 3,200,000 runs. Figure 5 illustrates the effectiveness of the ICC system in preventing PR rear-end crashes on freeways, preceded by the two pre-crash scenarios, in each of the eight travel speed bins. These effectiveness values take into account rear-end crash rates and proportions of time the ICC system was used in each travel speed bin.

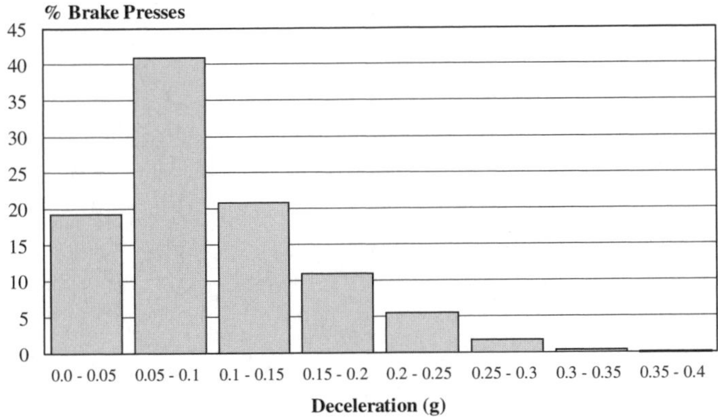

Figure 4. Histogram of Brake-Only Deceleration Levels in Manual Driving on Freeways at Speeds over 25 MPH

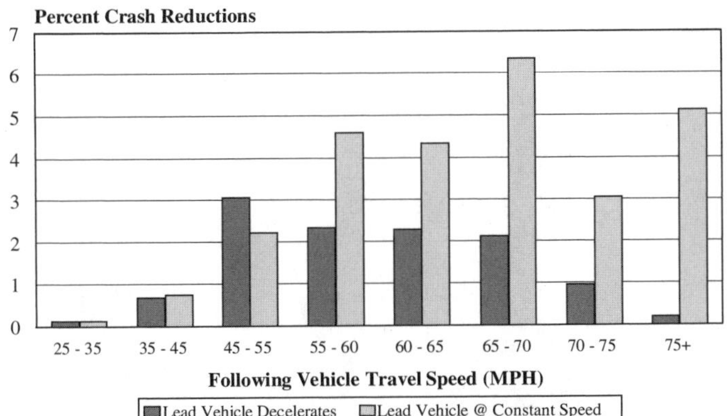

Figure 5. ICC System Percent Effectiveness in Preventing Crashes in Two Rear-End Pre-Crash Scenarios

Assuming the ICC system was "on" when the scenarios began, police-reported rear-end crashes on freeways would have been reduced by about 11.8 percent and 26.6 percent respectively for the pre-crash scenario where the lead vehicle suddenly decelerates in front of the following vehicle and for the scenario where the lead vehicle is traveling at a speed lower than the following vehicle. Taking the two scenarios together, the effectiveness of the ICC system was estimated at about 17 percent for rear-end crashes on freeways at travel speeds above 25 MPH, assuming (a) all vehicles were equipped with the system, and (b) the system was used with the same frequency as was observed in the FOT. Assuming these results generalize to the case of full system deployment, the ICC system could have reduced the number of police-reported rear-end crashes on freeways by about 13 thousands in 1996. This projected benefit is based on 1996 GES crash statistics.

SUMMARY AND CONCLUDING REMARKS

A methodology was presented and applied to project the potential safety benefits of an ICC system, using primarily driver/vehicle/system performance data collected from instrumented vehicles in a field operational test. The ICC system effectiveness in reducing rear-end crashes on freeways was estimated at about 17 percent, taking into consideration pre-crash scenarios that involve a lead vehicle either suddenly decelerating or slow moving when encountered by the following vehicle. Monte Carlo computer simulations were utilized to estimate the probability of a crash in these two pre-crash scenarios for both manual and ICC control modes. However, the simulations only considered lead and following vehicle behavior, not the effects of the ICC system on traffic flow, or the appropriateness of using the ICC system under various traffic conditions. This paper did not consider, for instance, the effects of the ICC system on the stability of strings of equipped vehicles, as has been discussed in [10]. Thus, the results reported here are limited to crash risk between a lead and following vehicle, when range, range-rate, and speed are considered.

The ICC system has the potential to reduce more rear-end crashes if road classes other than freeways were considered in this paper. It should be noted that test drivers were observed in the FOT to engage the ICC system for small proportions of time on arterials, state highways, and unclassified roads. Finally, additional safety benefits could be accrued through the use of ICC systems if such systems detected and responded to stationary objects in the forward path of the equipped vehicle.

REFERENCES

1. Fancher, P., Ervin, R., Sayer, J., Hagan, M., Bogard, S., Bareket, Z., Mefford, M., and Haugen, J., Intelligent Cruise Control Field Operational Test, Final Report, Volume I: Technical Report, UMTRI-98-17, May 1998.
2. Burgett, A.L., DOT's Approach to ITS Safety Evaluations, Workshop Proceedings on Safety Evaluation of Intelligent Transportation Systems, ITS America and the National Highway Traffic Safety Administration, Reston, VA, May 1995.
3. NHTSA Benefits Working Group, Preliminary Assessment of Crash Avoidance Systems Benefits, Version II, National Highway Traffic Safety Administration, U.S. Department of Transportation, December 1996.
4. Najm, W.G. and Burgett, A.L., Benefits Estimation for Selected Collision Avoidance Systems, Fourth World Congress on Intelligent Transport Systems, Berlin, Germany, October 1997.
5. Najm, W.G., Wiacek, C.J., and Burgett, A.L., Identification of Precrash Scenarios for Estimating the Safety Benefits of Rear-End Collision Avoidance Systems, Fifth World Congress on Intelligent Transport Systems, Seoul, Korea, October 1998.
6. Wiacek, C.J. and Najm, W.G., Driver/Vehicle Characteristics in Rear-End Precrash Scenarios Based on the General Estimates System (GES), 1999 SAE International Congress & Exposition, paper no. 1999-01-0817, Detroit, MI, March 1999.
7. Taoka, G.T., Brake Reaction Times of Unalerted Drivers, ITE Journal, March 1989.
8. Davis, D., Schweizer, N., Parosh, A., Lieberman, D., and Apter, Y., Measurement of the Minimum Reaction Time for Braking Vehicles, Wingate Institute for Physical Education and Sport, Israel, 1990.
9. Henderson, R.L., Driver Performance Data Book, DOT HS 807 126, 1987.
10. Bogard, S., Fancher, P., Ervin, R., Hagan, M., and Bareket, Z., Performance of a String or Cluster of ACC-Equipped Cars, UMTRI-98-28, July 1998.

1999-01-2887

Influence of ACC in Stop&Go Mode on Traffic Flow

David Maurel and Michel Parent
INRIA

Stéphane Donikian
IRISA-CNRS

ABSTRACT

Adaptive Cruise Control (ACC) techniques are now being put on the market as a safety and comfort feature. These ACC actually do not work at low speed, mostly because of limitations of the radar sensors being used. Using simple optical sensors, INRIA has demonstrated that it is possible to implement ACC in Stop&Go mode. Renault and other partners involved in the Urban Drive Control European project also implemented Stop&Go using radar and lidar sensors. This mode which could also include lateral control would be more useful to the driver faced with recurrent congestion. Detailed simulations which include the control algorithm of this ACC mode try to assess the impact of such systems on traffic flow.

INTRODUCTION

Research on ACC systems started more than 15 years ago. These systems extend the conventional cruise control by also enabling the driver to automatically follow a slower preceding vehicle. Thus the vehicle can automatically flow with other cars in dense traffic while keeping a safe distance. During the PROMETHEUS program, simple following behavior as well as platoon stability or impact on traffic flows have been considered.

Until mid-90s, ACC systems were developed for highway driving assistance, but could not handle urban traffic situations, because of sensors difficulties in analyzing the front-car scene. Latest developments in radar sensors and sensor fusion made prototyping of ACC in Stop&Go mode possible, for example at INRIA or in the Urban Drive Control European project.

INRIA developed a simulation tool for fine traffic assessment in real traffic situations. This includes detailed vehicle models as well as software tools to describe complete and realistic urban environments including cyclists and pedestrian.

INRIA SIMULATOR (SSE)

INRIA is not a specialist on transportation technology. Instead it specializes in software tools and control technology. The SSE simulator has been built with two goals. The first goal is to develop new software tools to program simulators which model the environment and the objects which move in this environment. The second objective is to use this simulator to test vehicle control technologies which are under development for the automotive industry. In particular, we wanted to test if the ACC control techniques developed in the automotive industry lead to safe and comfortable behavior. We also wanted to estimate the effects of this technology on traffic flow.

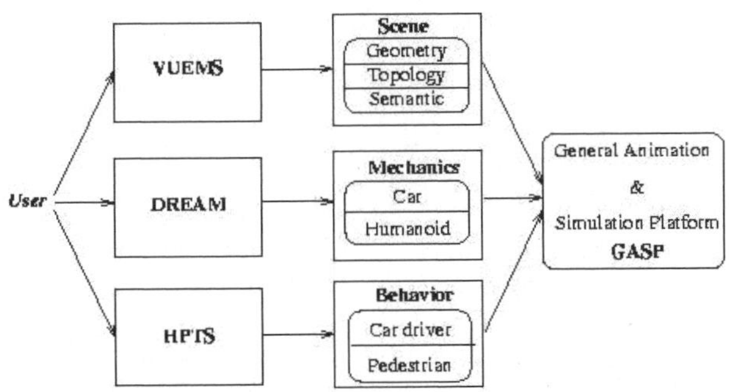

Figure 1. SSE architecture

SSE is composed of a set of modeling tools (Figure 1):

- VUEMS (Virtual Urban Environment Modeling System) to model the road network as realistically as possible, by using cartographic databases and scanned maps. VUEMS produces two complementary outputs: the 3D geometric representation of the scene and its symbolic representation used by sensors and behavioral entities;
- DREAM to specify the mechanics of entities like vehicles or humanoids but also trams, trucks or bicycles;

- HPTS to specify the behavior of entities such as a car driver or a pedestrian. HPTS is based on Hierarchical Parallel Transition Systems and is able to manage both reactive and cognitive aspects, including temporal characteristics like the reaction time.
- GASP is our simulation platform which integrates all these models and take into account real time synchronization and data-flow communication between cooperative processes distributed on an heterogeneous network of workstations and parallel machines. ACC algorithms have been integrated in the low level motion control model and have replaced (when active) the longitudinal control of the vehicle performed by the driver.

STOP&GO ALGORITHM

The controller used for this assessment was developed by Renault for the Urban Drive Control European project. It is based on an ACC algorithm, with specific Stop&Go evolutions. The algorithm structure is shown on Fig.2.

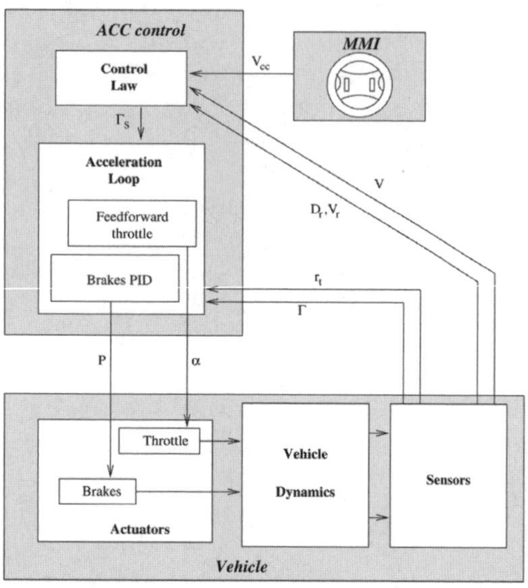

Figure 2. ACC algorithm structure

Preceding vehicles' distance and relative speed are measured by a distance sensor, based on radar or lidar, or a fusion of both technologies. The most relevant vehicle ahead is selected, considering lane positions and yaw rate.

Four main scenarios were considered for Stop&Go behavior tuning:

1. Following of a vehicle driving at low speed in congested traffic,
2. Following of a vehicle decelerating to stop,
3. Following of a vehicle starting from stop,
4. Complete stop in front of a fixed obstacle.

Each of these scenarios implied evolutions of the control law and the acceleration loop. Attention focused on driving comfort in urban traffic, which highly depends on distance setup and acceleration levels.

DISTANCE SETUP – Computation of the distance setup must be adapted to urban conditions. In ACC mode on highway, distance setup is proportional with vehicle speed :

$$D_{setup} = h*V + D_0$$

D_{setup} : distance setup,

h : headway time,

V : vehicle speed,

D_0 : distance offset.

But in congested traffic, the driver behavior is appreciably different. During a starting phase, for example, the driver will intend to keep the distance with the preceding car almost constant.

The distance setup for Stop&Go mode takes this behavior into account, as shown on Fig. 3.

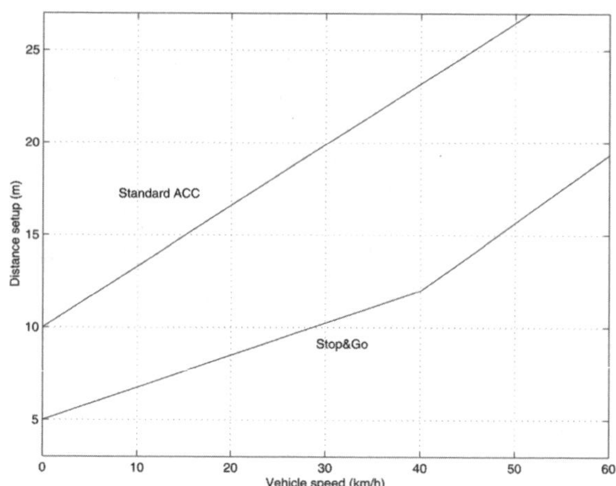

Figure 3. Distance setup in ACC and Stop&Go mode

As figure 3 shows, distance following policy in Stop&Go mode can be compared with the driver keeping the highest distance from the preceding vehicle. This is mainly due to sensor delays and limited deceleration in automatic control, which implies higher reaction time for the automated vehicle.

REGULATION PARAMETERS – The gains of the control law were tuned to ensure comfort and safety in urban traffic. Transitions between throttle and brakes control were also adapted for new operating points of the engine.

ASSESSMENT OF THE STOP&GO CONTROL

Stop&Go behavior was evaluated in simulation using two scenarios: single-lane platoon-following and urban multi-lane traffic with traffic light control. We also evaluated the influence of multiple percentages of ACC-equipped vehicles.

STOP&GO BEHAVIOR IN PLATOON – Simulations of a five vehicles platoon in close following situation with Stop&Go control and with manual driving show the impact of automatic driving : speed profile is not altered by electronic control, but Stop&Go trends to reduce dispersion of the following distance policy. As shown on Fig. 4, real drivers following distance extend from 15 to 40m, at 100 km/h.

REAL-TRAFFIC SIMULATIONS – Impact of ACC in Stop &Go mode on traffic flow was also investigated with simulations on a highly-travelled avenue inside Paris.

Simulation test site is Boulevard Sebastopol, a one-way, three-lanes and traffic-light controlled avenue with several crossing lanes. We focused on a 500 meters section, with one crossing-lane. Real data were collected, like flow density and percentages of vehicles changing direction at the crossing lane. Test site is shown on Fig. 5.

Traffic flows in simulation were of 1650 veh/h for vehicles going straightforward, and of 2390 veh/h for vehicles entering test site from the South. Travel time over the test site was evaluated in simulation, for vehicles going straightforward only, because vehicles turning right or left are leaving Stop&Go mode for this maneuver. Different percentages of equipped vehicles were also simulated, to assess impact of Stop&Go on different time horizons. These percentages were set to 20, 40 70 and 100%, using a whole manual simulation as reference.

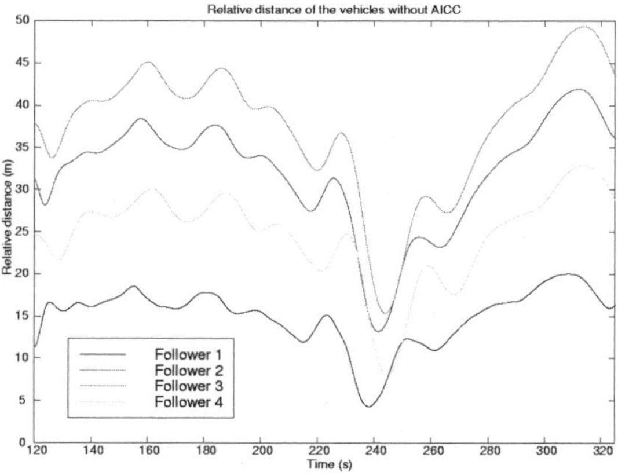

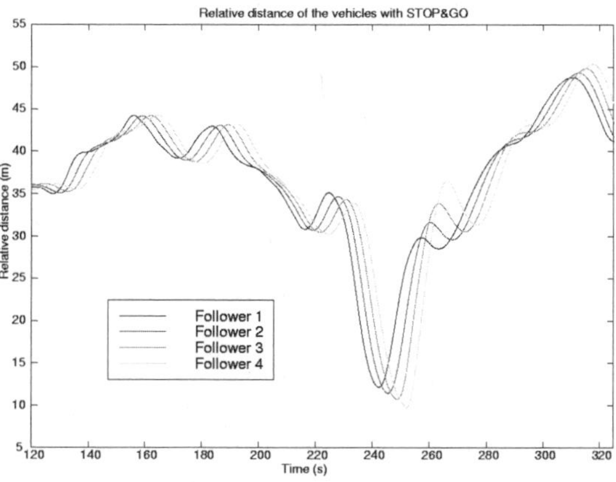

Figure 4. Single-lane platoon behavior in Stop&Go mode

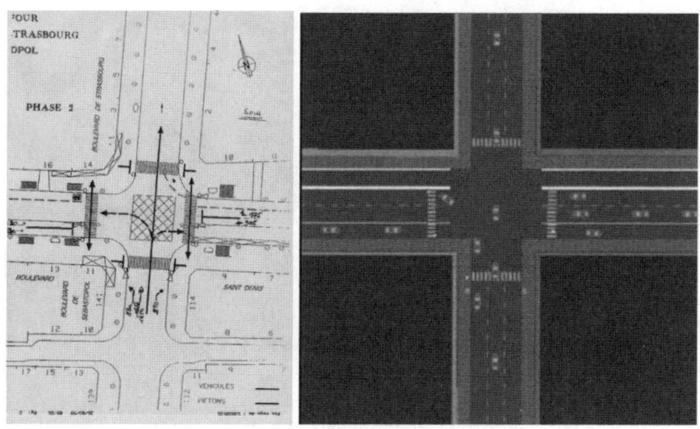

Figure 5. Test site map and simulation layout

We also assessed the influence of the headway time used in the control law, using three different distance setups, noted h, h_- and h_+ on the tables : h is the standard value of headway used during Stop&Go controller development. h_- and h_+ are respectively shorter and longer distance setup with one meter offset.

The following graphs present the travel time analysis, with mean and extremes values, for each percentage of equipped vehicles.

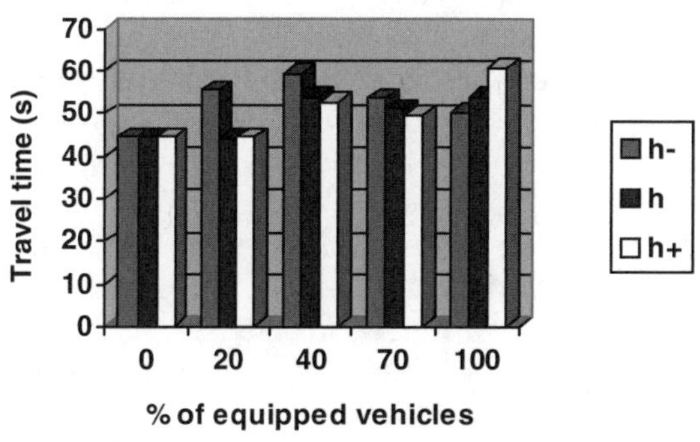

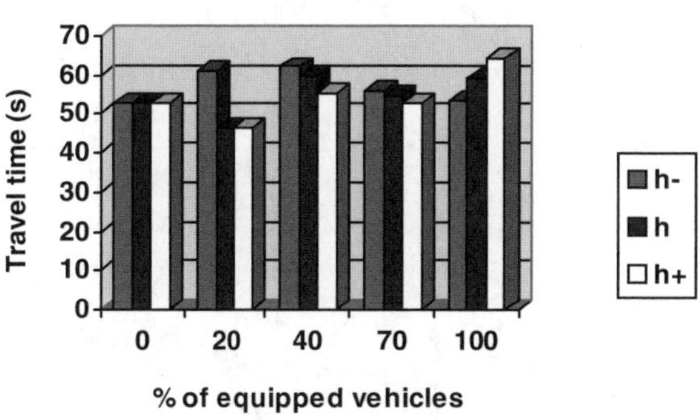

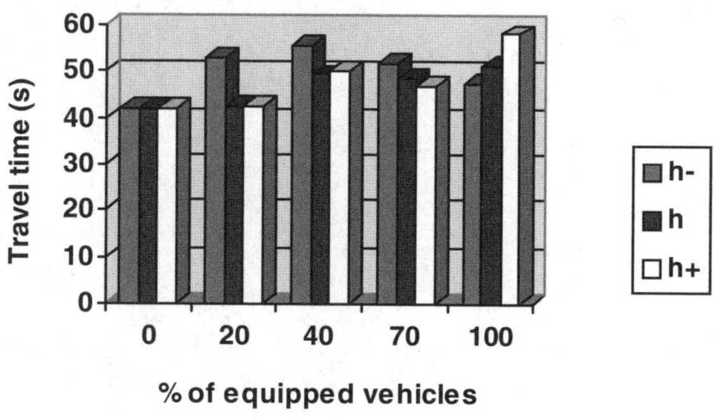

Figure 6. Fluid traffic simulations results

This first type of simulation, with Stop&Go vehicles among fluid traffic (average speed between 30 and 45 km/h), implies greater travel times for the considered avenue when equipped vehicle are inserted in the traffic. The main cause is the large headway time used in automatic control, for safety reasons. Simulations of mixed traffic with manual and automatic driving show no direct correlation between headway time and travel time, whereas in full automatic traffic, travel time increases with the following distance.

Simulations of 20 or 40% of equipped vehicles with a short headway control law (h_-) show a rise in the travel time of 25 to 35%. String instability with mixed vehicles can explain such a decrease in the traffic flow: an automated vehicle trying to follow a manual driven car at short distance will generate higher perturbations in the string, and then lower the speed of the whole traffic. If further simulations confirm this result, respect of the traffic flow would be another reason for the use of safe distance policy. However, distance setup should be limited, with regard to cut-in situations.

In a second time, simulations focused on traffic jam situations (average speed around 17 km/h), which is the scenario where Stop&Go driving greatly improves driving comfort. Results are illustrated on Fig. 7.

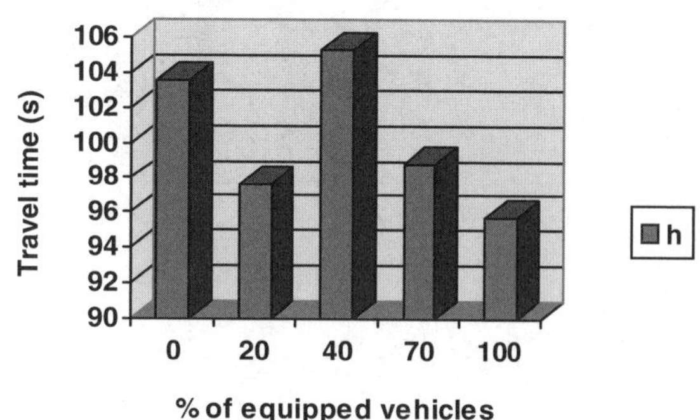

Figure 7. Traffic jam simulations results

Impact of ACC is not always positive in traffic jam situation, even if improvement of travel time appears in most cases. The first parameter is the reaction time of ACC system, which is shorter than in manual driving. It could then be awaited an increase of the traffic flow in traffic jam. On the other side, higher distance setup in automatic mode trends to reduce traffic flow. Influence of these two parameters can explain the limited efficiency of Stop&Go control on traffic jams reduction.

Further simulations will highlight other parameters of the control law which can increase traffic flow, at any percentage of equipped vehicles. Specific design of distance setup combined with the use of enhanced short distance sensors could also be more effective in traffic jam situation.

CONCLUSION

Although the evaluation of ACC algorithms developed for Urban Drive Control is not yet completed, we have already seen that the performances in terms of comfort and safety are largely dependant on the control algorithms and that fine tuning will be needed. We have also observed that traffic flow can be influenced by the percentage of vehicles equipped with ACC and that the benefits or disbenefits depend also on the control parameters.

REFERENCES

1. M. McDonald, G. Marsden, M. Cremer, L. Dens, T. Vaa· *Deployment of Inter-urban ATT Test Scenarios (DIATS). Review and Evaluation.* 4th ITS Congress, Seoul, Korea. Oct. 1998.
2. E.J. Hardman. *Motorway Speed Control Strategies Using SISTM.* Eighth International Conference On Road Traffic Monitoring And Control, 23-25 April 1996. Conference Publication No. 422. 1996. pp169-72. Institution Of Electrical Engineers, Savoy Place, London, United Kingdom.
3. B. van Arem, A.P. de Vos, M.J.W.A. Vanderschuren. *The microscopic traffic simulation model MIXIC 1.3.* TNO-report INRO-VVG 1997-02b, Delft, January 1997.
4. S. Donikian. *Driving Simulation in Virtual Urban Environments.* Driving Simulation Conference DSC'97, Lyon, France, September 1997.
5. A. Hochstädter and M. Cremer. *Investigating the potential of convoy driving for congestion dispersion.* In Proc. Of the 4th Ann. World Cong. On Intelligent Transport Systems, Berlin, October 1997.
6. S. Espié, F. Saad, B.Schnetzler & al (1994) - *Microscopic traffic simulation and driver behaviour modelling : the ARCHISIM project.* VTI Konferenz. In Proceedings of the Strategic Highway Research Program (SHRP) and Traffic Safety on Two continents.
7. C.E. Hewitt, P. Bishop, R. Steiger (1973) - *A universal modular ACTOR formalism for artificial intelligence* In Proceedings or the 3rd IJCAI. Stanford. California.

8. F. Saad (1993) - *Driver strategies in car-following situations*. Fifth International Conference on Vision In Vehicles. University of Glasgow. Scottland. Ed. Elsevier.
9. M. Cremer, C. Demir, S. Donikian, S. Espie, M. McDonald. *Investigating the impact of AICC Concepts on Traffic Flow Quality*. 5th World Congress on Intelligent Transport Systems, Séoul, Corée du Sud, October 1998.
10. G. Moreau, S. Donikian. *From psychological and real-time interaction requirements to behavioural simulation*. Eurographics Workshop on Computer Animation and Simulation, Lisbonne, Portugal, September 1998.
11. S.B. Choi, J.K. Hedrick. *Vehicle longitudinal control using an adaptive observer for automated highway systems*. Proc. of the American Control Conference, 1995.
12. D. Yanakiev, I. Kanellakopoulos. *Variable time headway for string stability of automated heavy-duty vehicles*. Proc. of the 34th conference on Decision & Control, 1995.

CONTACT

Michel Parent
INRIA/LARA
BP 105
78153 Le Chesnay Cedex
France
Tel. 33 1 39 63 55 93
Michel.Parent@inria.fr
http://www-lara.inria.fr

980606

An Adaptive Cruise Control Using Wheel Torque Management Technique

Satoru Kuragaki, Hiroshi Kuroda, Toshimichi Minowa, Mitsuo Kayano, Tokuji Yoshikawa, Hiroshi Takenaga, Kouzou Nakamura and Kazuaki Takano

Hitachi Ltd.

ABSTRACT

This paper describes a longitudinal control method with an Adaptive Cruise Control (ACC) system using a wheel torque management technique. The wheel torque management technique can control vehicular speed by the following procedure without tuning parameters. First, the ACC module calculates a command speed from a desired headway distance and from output data of the radar sensor. Secondly, it calculates a required wheel torque to take the command speed, current speed and running resistance into consideration. Thirdly, the management module controls actuators based on the command wheel torque and characteristics of each vehicle. If the required wheel torque is positive, the management module orders adjustment of the throttle opening position and a change of the gear ratio in the automatic transmission. If the command wheel torque is negative, the management module activates the electronic brake in accordance with the magnitude of the command wheel torque.

This ACC system was installed on a test vehicle. Experiments showed the vehicle follows a preceding vehicle at the speed of the command speed within ±0.3[m/s] deviation.

INTRODUCTION

Recently, ITS (Intelligent Transport Systems) technology is being developed for manufacturing plants and other users. ACC (Adaptive Cruise Control) system which provides safety and convenience is one of the most important examples of ITS technology. ACC keeps a safe headway distance and provides comfortable driving. [1],[2] A valuable component of ACC is longitudinal control.[3]-[6]

A control technique for the power train has also been developed, based on wheel torque.[7] This technique actuates an electronically controlled throttle valve and automatic transmission cooperatively in order to improve acceleration feeling and get better shifting performance and fuel economy.

This paper describes longitudinal control of a prototype ACC system which adds a speed controller and a headway controller to the system based on the wheel torque management technique. The new method controls has a special feature to control speed without using tuning parameters.

A PROTOTYPE ACC SYSTEM CONFIGURATION

The configuration of a vehicle with ACC is shown in figure 1. The ACC-installed system is designed to have the same configuration manual driving. For manual driving based on a wheel torque management technique, the required wheel torque is determined from the operating stroke of an accelerator pedal. The engine and the transmission are controlled cooperatively by the required wheel torque. For the ACC, the engine and the transmission are cooperatively controlled to correspond with a desired headway distance which is changed by the vehicle speed and the measured headway distance detected by a mm-wave radar sensor. The purpose of ACC is to keep a safe distance from a preceding vehicle by controlling the brake and the power train, which consists of the engine and the transmission. That is to say, expansion from manual driving to ACC using the same configuration can be realized, since the controlling logic of the power train is coordinated for manual driving and the ACC.

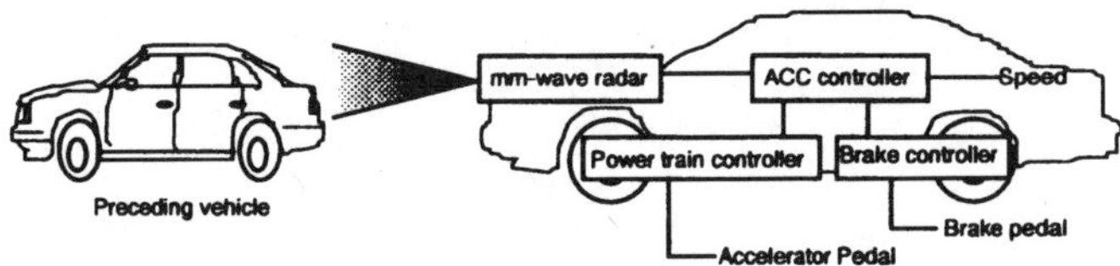

Figure 1. ACC system configuration

BUILDING UP ACC SYSTEM

A block diagram of the proposed ACC system is shown in figure 2. Its function is based on the wheel torque management technique and it has special features to control vehicular speed which are described in the following.

Firstly, the wheel torque management is shown in the lower part of the block diagram. The wheel torque manager selects from an electrically controlled throttle, an automatic transmission or an electrically controlled brake to send commands depending on the required wheel torque. In the following two cases, the required wheel torque is chosen alternatively by the driver or the speed controller. In the manually driven system, the throttle valve opening and transmission ratio are calculated from the required wheel torque T_{rd} which is determined from accelerator pedal angle, vehicular speed and vehicular acceleration (or deceleration). In the other drive system which is treated later, the required wheel torque T_{rc} is calculated from a speed controller. When the selected required wheel torque T_r is larger than a threshold, the throttle valve opening and transmission ratio are calculated and the valve is operated. When the required wheel torque T_r is less than the threshold, the electrically controlled brake is required. These two cases of driving operations are executed by the same software that selects actuators to work. That is to say, it is not necessary to change the software program in the wheel torque manager when the ACC or other systems are added to the manually driven system. By using the wheel torque management technique, the ACC and the manually driven system can be realized with the same architecture.

Secondly, a conventional cruise control function is achieved by adding a speed controller to the wheel torque manager. The speed controller calculates the required wheel torque T_{rc} from the command speed v_c and a speed of the installed vehicle v_o (own speed). If a driver uses the cruise control function in the midst of manual driving, the driver pushes a switch to start the cruise control function. At this time, the command speed v_c would be set to v_o and the speed controller would try to regulate speed of the vehicle toward v_c. The speed controller computes the required wheel torque T_{rc} and sends it to the wheel torque manager continuously.

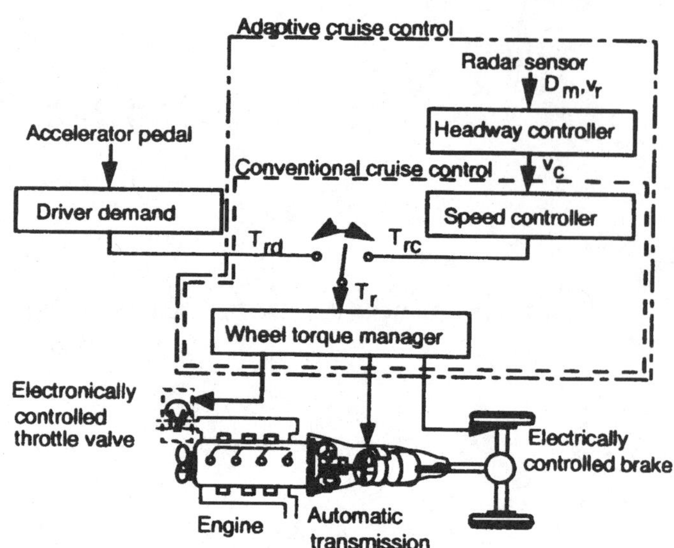

Figure 2. Building up an ACC

Finally, the ACC function, which consists of a radar sensor and a headway controller, is added to the conventional cruise control function. The headway controller sets itself a desired headway distance D_d which corresponds to the speed of the installed vehicle v_o. The mm-wave radar can measure headway distance D_m and relative speed vr of the installed and preceding vehicles. The headway controller computes a command speed v_c with a desired headway distance D_d, a measured headway distance D_m, the speed of the installed vehicle and a characteristic of the speed controller. If the ACC function is started, the headway controller calculates the command speed vc and sends the vc to the speed controller. Therefore, the vehicle tries to keep the desired headway distance D_d.

DESIGN OF SPEED CONTROLLER USING WHEEL TORQUE MANAGEMENT TECHNIQUE

SPEED CONTROLLER – As stated above, the speed controller calculates the required wheel torque T_{rc} from the command speed and the speed of the installed vehicle. The wheel torque manager actualizes wheel torque based on the required wheel torque. Then, the vehicle has the speed that the actualized wheel torque is balanced with the resistance of the driving vehicle. In order to design the speed controller, transfer function of the power train and resistance of the driving vehicle are necessary.

The transfer function of the power train is determined as follows. The required wheel torque which shapes the step function is set for the wheel torque manager, and the wheel torque sensor measures step response of the wheel torque. Then, the transfer function of the power train is described by equation (1) with first order delay and lag time.

$$G_{PW}(s)=\frac{e^{-Ls}}{1+sT_1} \qquad (1)$$

In the test vehicle, L=0.12 and T_1=0.08.

The running resistance is calculated from variance of speed which is measured in the following experiment. The test vehicle is driven at a speed which is the fastest speed possible to make the running model. Recording transition of speed begins at the time to change wheel torque to zero. The transition of acceleration (deceleration) is computed from the recording, and running resistance from to calculated vehicle weight and the transition of acceleration (equation (2)).

$$R(v)=a_1v^2+a_2v+a_3 \qquad (2)$$

In the test vehicle, a_1=-0.3327, a_2=-19.708, a_3=-222.07.

In order to facilitate use of equation (2), it can be approximated as equation (3) using a Taylor series .

$$R(v)\approx a_4v+a_5 \qquad (3)$$

An example of approximating speed is 22[m/s], a_4=-34.35 and a_5=-60.97.

A speed controller can be designed to make a feedback loop with equations (1) and (3). In this case, the speed controller has an I-PD structure as shown in figure 3.[8],[9] Its characteristics of open loop gain and phase are shown in figure 4. Gain margin is 27.2 dB and phase margin is 60 deg.

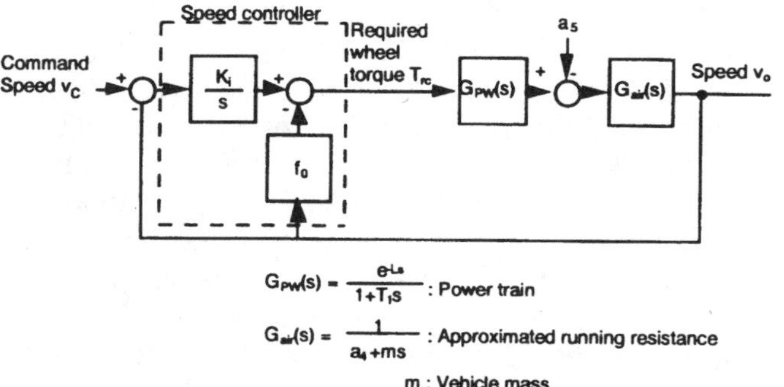

Figure 3. Block diagram of speed controller

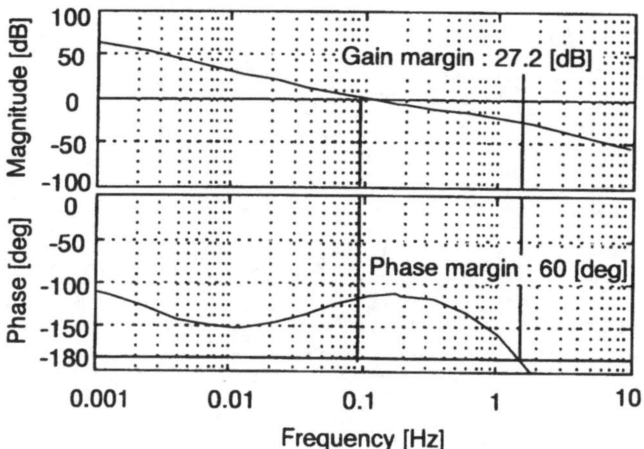

Figure 4. Open loop characteristics of the speed controller

HEADWAY CONTROLLER – The headway controller basically calculates command speed, using equation (4). It has an I-PD structure as shown in figure 5.

$$v_c=K_j\frac{1}{s}(D_d-D_m)-\left(F_1D_m+F_2sD_m+F_3s^2D_m\right) \quad (4)$$

Relative speed v_r is differentiation of measured headway distance D_m. The mm-wave radar can measure relative speed and headway distance simultaneously. Therefore, equation (4) can be changed to equation (5).

$$v_c=K_j\frac{1}{s}(D_d-D_m)-\left(F_1D_m+F_2V_r+F_3sV_r\right) \quad (5)$$

Each coefficient K_j,F_1,F_2 and F_3 is determined using computer simulation in consideration of power train, running resistance and the speed controller. Under the condition that the preceding vehicle decreases its speed from 20[m/s] to 11[m/s] with -2.5[m/s^2] deceleration, a set of coefficients that headway distance does not overshoot the desired headway distance is selected. The headway controller's characteristics of open loop gain and phase are shown in figure 6. Gain margin is 30 dB and phase margin is 63.4 deg.

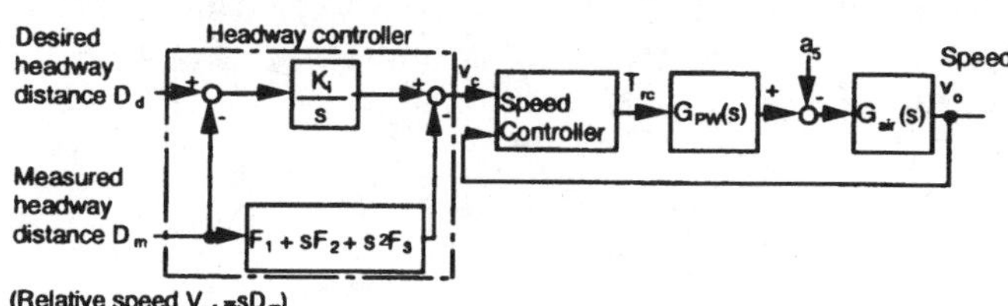

Figure 5. Block diagram of headway controller

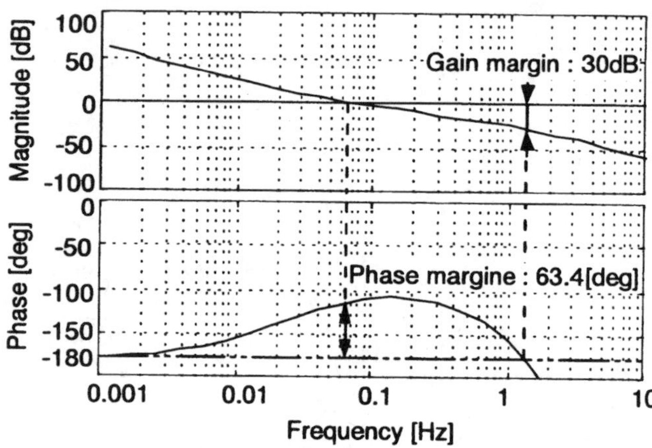

Figure 6. Open loop characteristics of the headway controller

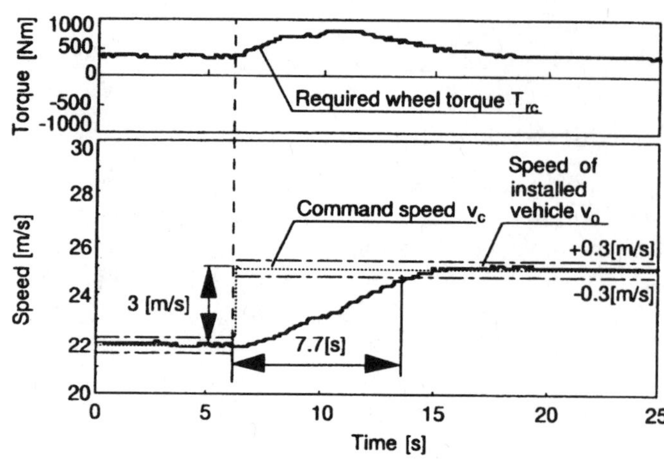

Figure 7. Experimental results of cruise control (Command speech is changed)

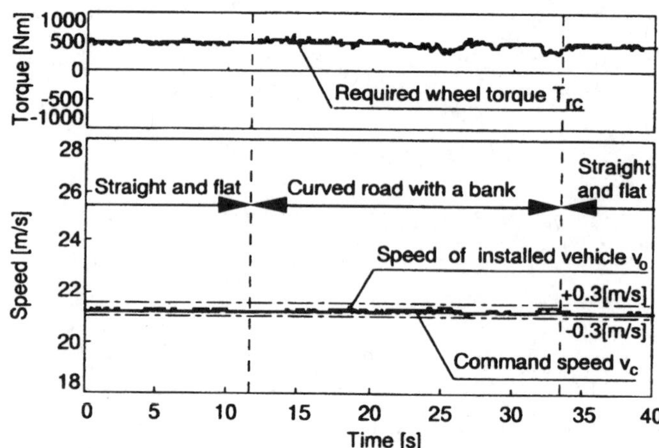

Figure 8. Experimental results of cruise control (Command speech is fixed)

TEST RESULTS

CONVENTIONAL CRUISE CONTROL RESULTS – This ACC system was implemented in a test vehicle. The test results of the conventional cruise control function are shown in figures 7 and 8. For the function, important requirements are stability and transition characteristics of speed. When the command speed jumps to 3[m/s] discontinuously, the target time of accelerating to the command speed is set between 7 to 10 seconds, so that a driver does not feel any time lag or roughness. Under the fixed command speed condition, the target value of speed deviation is set to ±0.3[m/s], so that a driver does not sense any variation of speed.

Target characteristics of the speed when the command speed v_c is changed from 22[m/s] to 25[m/s] are shown in figure 7. The vehicular speed vo follows v_c by increasing required wheel torque T_{rc} smoothly. In this case, it takes 7.7[s] to increase the vehicular speed v_o to the command speed v_c.

An example of stability characteristics of the speed when the running load changes quickly is shown in figure 8. In this case, the data are gotten on a curved road with a bank when the test vehicle climbs up a slope of 1.5%. The speed controller regulates the vehicular speed v_o within ±0.3[m/s] of the v_c while the vehicle runs on the curved road.

ACC RESULTS – Results of ACC characteristics of required wheel torque, speed and headway are shown in figure 9 for the ACC system. The ACC is designed to follow the speed of the preceding vehicle v_p and to keep a proper headway distance at the same time. At time t=0 the ACC is started, at time t_1 the preceding vehicle increases its speed v_p, at t_2 the preceding vehicle decreases speed v_p by braking and at t_4 v_p is kept at a constant speed. After starting the ACC, the preceding vehicle accelerates and v_p is increasing. The required wheel torque T_{rc} shows its peak value at the beginning of acceleration, and it keeps a constant value during the preceding vehicle's acceleration. During this acceleration, v_o and D_m follow v_p and D_d, respectively. On and after t_2, the preceding vehicle decelerates with about -2.5[m/s^2], the v_p is decreased and T_{rc} is less than zero. The electrically controlled brake operates to keep the measured headway distance the same as desired it. In this situation, the deviation from D_d is -3 meters which is the largest number in this test. On and after t_3, the preceding vehicle accelerates gradually, and deviation from D_d is 3 meters.

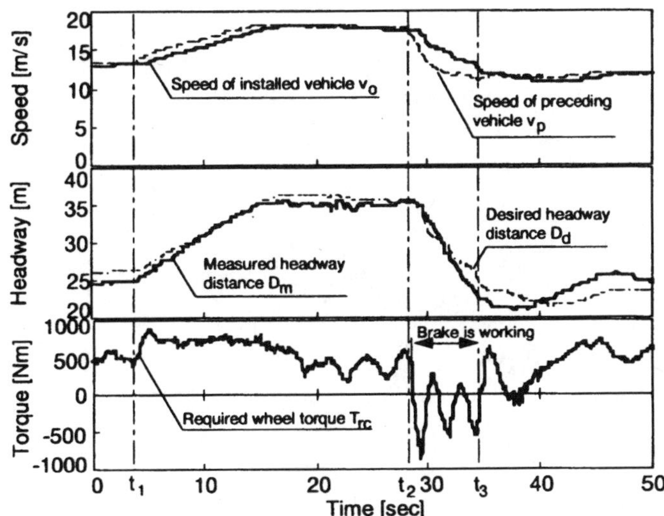

Figure 9. Experimental results of ACC

CONCLUSION

An ACC using a wheel torque management technique has been developed and its performance has been investigated by using a test vehicle. The results of the investigation are summarized as follows.

1. The ACC system can be built with three controllers. First, the headway controller calculates a command speed from a desired headway distance and output data of the radar sensor which are measured headway distance and relative speed. Secondly, the speed controller calculates a command wheel torque to take the command speed, current speed and running resistance into consideration. Thirdly, the wheel torque manager controls actuators based on the required wheel torque and characteristics of each vehicle.
2. When using the test vehicle, the conventional cruise control with the wheel torque management technique regulated the vehicular speed v_o within the command speed v_c ±0.3[m/s] deviation.

REFERENCE

1. Watanabe, T.; Kishimoto, N.; Hayafune, K.; Yamada, K.; Maede, N., "Development of an Intelligent Cruise Control System", Proc. of the 2nd World Congress on Intelligent Transportation Systems, 1995
2. Hayashi, Y.; Hayafune, K.; Yamada, K., "System Safety Study on Intelligent Cruise Control",Proc. of 4th World congress on Intelligent Transportation systems, 1997
3. Fancher, P.; Bareket, Z., "Evaluating Headway Control Using Range Versus Range-Rate Relationships", Vehicle System Dynamics, 1994, pp.575-596
4. Fujioka, T.; Baba, J., "Control System for platooning -Comparison between Sliding Control and PID Control -"(in Japanese), Proceedings of JSAE, 1995, pp.49-52
5. Hoess, A.; Hosp, W.; Doerfler, R.; Rauner, H., "Longitudinal Autonomous Vehicle Control Utilizing Access to Electronic Throttle Control, Automatic Transmission and Brakes", SAE961009, 1996
6. Winner, H.; Witte, S.; Uhler, W.; Lichtenberg, B., "Adaptive Cruise Control System Aspects and Developing Trends", SAE961010, 1996
7. Minowa, T.; Kimura, H.; Ozaki, N.; Ibamoto, M., "Improvement of Fuel Consumption for a Vehicle with an Automatic Transmission Using Driven Power Control with a Powertrain Model", JSAE Review 17, 1996, pp.375-380
8. Kitamori, T., "A Method of Control System Design Based upon Partial Knowledge about Controlled Processes" (in Japanese), Transactions of the Society of Instrument and Control Engineers vol.15 No.4 pp.549-555, 1979
9. Shigemasa, T.;Takagi, Y.;Ichikawa, Y.;Kitamori, T., "A Practical Reference Model for Control System Design" (in Japanese), Transactions of the Society of Instrument and Control Engineers vol.19 No.7 pp.592-594, 1983

973184

Radar Based Adaptive Cruise Control for Truck Applications

Jerry D. Woll
Eaton VORAD Technologies

ABSTRACT

Radar based collision warning systems (CWS) for heavy trucks have been in production and on the road in the United States for approximately two years. A short description of these systems is presented with actual driver performance data and accident reduction data as experienced by various U.S. national fleets using these systems. The next application of radar sensors is for Intelligent Cruise Control (ICC) or also known as Adaptive Cruise Control (ACC). This paper describes the operation of adaptive cruise control and presents the associated benefits to the driver

The radar technology has been enhanced and the application has been extended to include radar controlled adaptive cruise control for heavy trucks This has been made possible by 1) technology improvements in radar systems, plus 2) the addition of the standard SAE J1939 data bus for engine controllers on most U.S diesel engines. The SAE J1939 data bus allows electronic control of engine speed by the radar system plus in many cases, control of engine retarder braking to assist in vehicle slowing while in adaptive cruise control operation.

This paper described the radar operation, radar enhancements and the benefits of adaptive cruise control as experienced by drivers. The most significant radar enhancement, called monopulse radar. is presented Comparisons are made between standard cruise control operation on heavy trucks and adaptive cruise control

COLLISION WARNING SYSTEM: BACKGROUND

The Eaton VORAD model EVT-200 Collision Warning System (CWS) is a forward-looking, radar based detection system for heavy trucks and buses. It has been in production for two years with approximately 3000 systems installed on commercial heavy truck fleets. The radar system scans the area in front of the vehicle to detects objects and vehicles and generate alarm lights and tones to warn the driver of hazardous situations The system measures the range (distance) and the closing rate (relative speed) to vehicles and objects in its field of view. The system can determine if the truck is approaching slower moving traffic at a hazardous rate and warn the driver accordingly. Most forward moving collisions result from momentary driver inattention or distractions and the rapid detection of hazards by the radar warning system can give the driver the valuable time to take corrective action to avoid a collision.

It has been shown that if an extra 0.5 seconds of warning can be provided to a driver, 60% of forward collisions can be avoided and if 1.0 seconds of extra warning time can be provided, the driver can avoid 90% of forward collisions. Providing this extra warning time is precisely the primary purpose of the CWS.

The EVT 200 system includes smaller radar sensor(s) located on the side of the truck for vehicle detection in the blind spot areas of the truck Theses sensors supplements the side view mirrors to aid the driver in making safer lane change maneuvers The radar system is robust and fully complies with the SAE J1455 recommended environmental standards.

The components of the collision warning system are shown in Figure 1

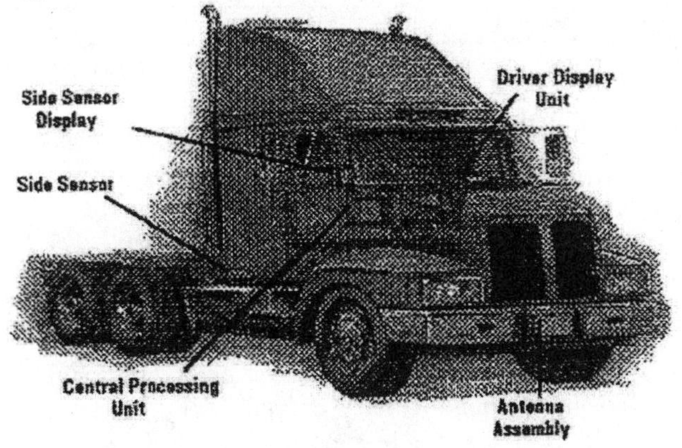

Figure 1 - EVT-200 CWS Components

The radar system uses information from other systems on the truck to supplement the radar tracking data to accurately determine hazardous situations The radar has input connections for the brake signal, speedometer input signal, and steering position. Heavy trucks do not typically have a sensor for steering position, so the CWS includes a steering position sensor that is mounted on the steering column shaft Truck input data can come from discrete connections to individual devices on the truck, i e. the brake light circuit, the speedometer and the steering position sensor or some of the data can come from a data bus such as the SAE J1857 or SAE J1939.

The specifications for the EVT-200 CWS forward looking radar are shown in Table 1.

Radar Characteristic	Specification
Radar Type	FMCW (FSK)
Operating Frequency	24.725 GHz
Frequency Bandwidth	15 MHz
Range	1 - 110+ meters, ±3%
Closing Rate	0.4 - 160 km/h, ±0.5%
Field of View	
Azimuth	4 degrees
Elevation	5 degrees
Transmitted Power	0.5 milliwatts
Power Requirements	+12 or +24 VDC, 15 watts
Antenna Size	15 cm H x 20 cm W x 5 cm D

Table 1 - EVT-200 CWS Specifications

The EVT-200 system includes a data recording capability for recording driver and vehicle operating parameters that are used for vehicle operations management. maintenance management and accident reconstruction. There are other on-board trip recording systems on the market for recording vehicle data, but only the EVT-200 system includes radar data on other vehicles in proximity to the truck This gives unique data on average following distances, near misses, vehicle cut-ins, heavy braking incidents, etc. A full description of the data recording capability and the accident reconstruction feature is provided in reference [1]

ACCIDENT REDUCTION

Actual experience with collision warning systems in real-world truck fleet operations have shown that significant reductions in accidents result from installation of the systems In addition to the direct accident reductions from the warnings provided to drivers, the CWS has been shown to actually modify driver behavior to produce 1) greater following times and distances and associated safer driving effects, 2) a reduction in hard braking incidents, and 3) a reduction in fuel consumption.

Truck and bus fleets have accumulated over 800,000,000 kilometers of highway experience with the collision warning systems. This large experience base has produced significant statistics and case studies on accident reduction Accident reduction is the result of two CWS factors which include 1) actual collision warnings given by the CWS to drivers. and 2) improved driver awareness and driver behavior modification by the CWS leading to safer following distances.

Fleet Type	Number of Trucks	Km Driven With CWS (Millions)	Accidents per Million Km without CWS	Accidents per Million Km with CWS	Accident Reduction Percentage
Private Carrier	20	17.0	1.3	0.0	100%
For Hire Carrier	170	37.8	3.7	2.4	34%
Truckload Carrier	350	55.8	0.5	0.0	100%
Leasing Company	9	0.5	19.7	0.0	100%
Beverage Distributor	58	2.2	29.6	0.0	100%
Totals	**607**	**109.3**	**2.2**	**0.3**	**86%**

Table 2 - Accident Reduction Results for Various Fleet Types

Regardless of factor relevance, fleet managers credit the accident reduction results to use of the CWS Table 2 shows actual documented case studies of accident reduction results from use of the collision warning systems by various selected fleet types The drivers of these fleet trucks are professional truck drivers performing their normal daily driving assignments. They are not test drivers so it not usually possible to hold all variables constant for experimental data purposes All fleet users of the CWS have experienced positive results None of the fleets have reported any negative effects from use of the CWS

COST REDUCTIONS

Use of collision warning systems on truck fleets has demonstrated several areas of cost savings for fleet owners. In addition to the obvious cost savings from the above demonstrated accident reduction statistics, collision warning systems reduce costs by increasing the average following times/distances and by reducing engine idle time. Following too closely generates more brake use. engine wear and wastes fuel. Data and case studies have shown that trucks with collision warning systems reduce hard braking occurrences (braking at level of 0.25 to 0.50 G's or greater) by up to 37%; reduce occurrences of closing on slower vehicles by 97%, and reduce the amount of road time spent following within 1 to 2 seconds by 80%. Fuel economy improvements of 2 to 10% are achieved by users. For one test fleet, it was shown that their average fuel consumption of 7.45 MPG could be improved by 24.8% to 9.3 MPG if, 1) all following times under 2 seconds could be avoided, and 2) all idle time was eliminated. Specific cost saving data resulting from reduced engine wear and reduced brake wear is not yet available.

ENHANCED ADAPTIVE CRUISE CONTROL

The next generation truck radar product will be released in 1998. This enhanced product is referred to as the model EVT-300 Collision Warning System and has added capabilities and features. The new radar system has all the collision warning features described above but adds monopulse operation and the powerful new feature of fully automatic adaptive cruise control.

The standard cruise control on trucks requires the driver to set the speed and engage the cruise control. When the truck overtakes a slower moving vehicle, the driver must disengage the cruise control by applying the brakes or shutting the cruise control off. The driver then must re-set and engage the cruise control when the traffic clears. In higher traffic situations, the repetitive engage/disengage activity by the driver often makes standard cruise control inconvenient and the driver simply stops using it.

The adaptive cruise control function places the radar system in the cruise control loop and allows the radar system to control the speed of the truck to maintain a pre-determined following distance from a lead vehicle. The system can thus adapt the truck speed to fit the traffic situation and reduce speed from the cruise control "set speed" to accommodate slower moving vehicles without the driver disengaging the cruise control. When the slower moving vehicle increases speed or leaves the lane , the truck will automatically increase speed back to the previously selected "set speed". It has been shown that the use of cruise control can be extended by up to 80% of time in interstate driving situations. At any time, the driver can over-ride the radar cruise control by manually applying the accelerator or by manually applying the brakes.

The two major developments that have led to the new cruise control capability for heavy trucks are 1) the maturing and real-world testing of the vehicle radar technology, and 2) the implementation of the SAE J1939 data bus standard in the trucking industry and major engine manufacturers. Vehicle data required by the radar system, such as speed, rpm, torque and brake signals, are readily available on the J1939 data bus and the engine, transmission and retarder brake controls can be exercised by the radar system via the J1939 data bus.

The adaptive cruise control software of the radar system can also control deceleration devices such as the Jacobson engine retarder ("Jake" brake) if it is accessible via the J1939 data bus. The use of speed retarder controls such as the Jake brake plus the standard throttle control, extends the speed difference range that can be handled by the automatic cruise control system when overtaking other vehicles.

The Eaton VORAD cruise control system, called SmartCruise®, is fully operational on several demonstration vehicles including three light vehicle platforms and two heavy truck platforms. Eaton VORAD has tested and evaluated radar based cruise controls systems that employ throttle control only, throttle control coupled with commanded down shifting, throttle control coupled with automatic braking, and throttle control coupled with commanded engine retarder braking on heavy trucks (Jacobson or "Jake" braking).

In late 1995 the U.S. Army Tank-Automotive Research, Development and Engineering Center tested the Eaton VORAD radar system in both collision warning applications and intelligent cruise control applications for military convoying, operational safety improvements and controlled vehicle spacing over a six month period. The installations included 10 vehicles at Fort Hood, Texas, 6 vehicles at Fort Stewart, Georgia and 6 vehicles at Hunter Army Airfield, Georgia. The types of vehicles tested with the system included the 1) M915/916 truck tractor, 2) the HEMTT truck and, 3) the M939 tractor. The CWS equipment was also endurance tested at the Aberdeen Proving Grounds. Conclusions from the Army evaluation report included the following:

- CWS and ACC use would reduce personnel injury and loss of life
- it was a cost effective means to increase safety on military tactical wheeled vehicle
- it enhanced driver performance in adverse weather conditions and night time operations
- it reduced vehicle accidents and downtime
- it leads to safer and more efficient convoy missions
- system is rugged enough for very harsh terrain

Eaton VORAD Technologies working the Hitachi Limited, Japan has developed a 60 GHz monopulse radar system for Japanese truck and light vehicle applications in collision warning and adaptive cruise control.

MONOPULSE RADAR SYSTEM

The new radar system includes an advanced technology feature called "monopulse" radar operation. The proven EVT-200 system uses a fixed beam system with a forward looking radar field-of-view beamwidth of 4 degrees in azimuth (horizontal beamwidth) by 5 degrees in elevation (vertical beamwidth). The fixed beam technology works well for the collision warning function; however, a radar system that can accurately measure the angles to forward vehicles offers advantages for adaptive cruise control and can handle a wider range of highway geometry.

The primary advantage of the monopulse feature is the simultaneous, continuous, and independent measurement of azimuth angle to all vehicles as well as the precise range and closing rate measurements of the fixed beam system. The added azimuth angle dimension provides improved vehicle detection and enhanced vehicle tracking, the capability to define and discriminate between lanes, and gives improved performance in turns when coupled with a turn/steering sensor.

The monopulse feature of the enhanced CWS employs two antennas separated by a small distance instead of the single antenna of the fixed beam system. This two-antenna system gives a stereo-graphic forward view similar to the way that the two eyes of a human are used to detect the angle off center of objects. The monopulse system allows the measurement of the azimuth angle to each forward vehicle over a 12 degree range to an accuracy of ± 0.1 degrees. The 12 degree angle range has been shown to be sufficient to permit accurate vehicle tracking around all standard curves of the interstate highway system while in typical cruise control following distances. Thus, the new radar system can accurately determine 1) the range/distance, 2) the closing rate, and 3) the azimuth angle to every vehicle within the forward looking field-of-view width of 12 degrees. References [2] and [3] provide more detailed technical information on the theory of operation for the monopulse radar system

Monopulse systems have advantages over switched beam antenna systems and mechanically scanned antenna systems. The monopulse system provides continuous tracking data on all targets within the monopulse detection azimuth range without having to interrupt the data flow while switching beams or mechanically rotating the antenna. The monopulse system can continuously over-sample target data to refine and filter position data as a steady stream of data. Switched beam and mechanically scanned systems must interrupt the data flow and clear the data channels each time the antenna beam is switched or rotated, and then restart the target data flow and processing from scratch. These systems must also wait until the antenna is again aimed at a specific target in order to get the next data update on that particular target, which can slow the update rate. These momentary gaps or blinks in data processing reduces system sensitivity and increases data latency for switched beam and scanned systems

The monopulse system requires that more radio frequency (RF) power be delivered the antenna than the fixed-beam system. Added power is required in order to fill the 12 degree wide radar beam of the monopulse antenna with the same energy density level as the 4 degree wide fixed-beam antenna beam pattern.

MONOPULSE SYSTEM BENEFITS

The benefits of the monopulse system can be shown in the following three traffic scenarios:

1. Better in-lane detection. The upper diagram of Figure 2 shows the typical lane detection coverage for a fixed beam radar system. Since the radar beam is conical in shape, it gets wider as the distance increases and has to approximate the narrow lane. The lower diagram shows the zone of detection for the monopulse system. Since the angle to all vehicles is known, a squared-up lane detection zone can be mathematically created to accept vehicles within the azimuth versus range lane limits and reject vehicles outside the lane zone.

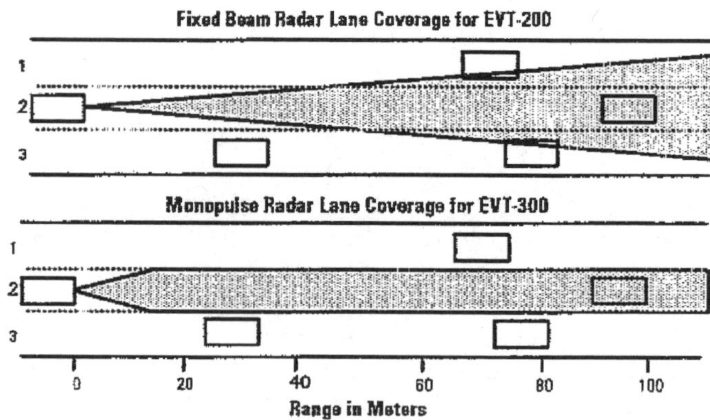

Figure 2 - Monopulse vs. Fixed Beam Lane Coverage

2. Better lane coverage in curves. The monopulse system includes an accurate steering sensor that can measure truck turning angles to ± 0.1 degrees. Combining this information with the monopulse radar angle measuring capability allows the radar system to calculate the detection zone for a specific lane in a curve. Figure 3 shows how the monopulse system can mathematically determine a curved lane detection zone for better tracking of vehicles around curves

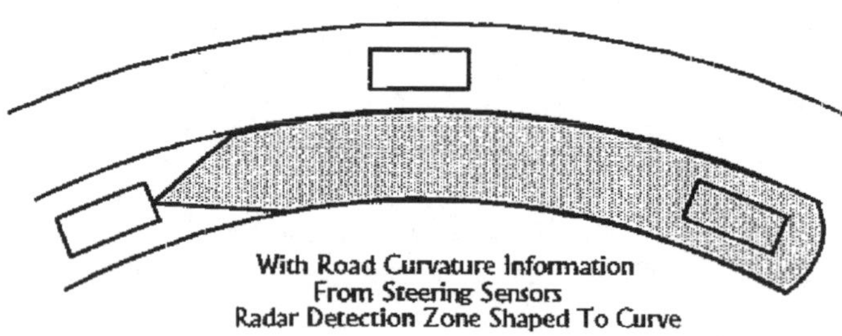

With Road Curvature Information
From Steering Sensors
Radar Detection Zone Shaped To Curve

Figure 3 - Monopulse Lane Coverage on Curve

3. Better vehicle cut-in coverage. In order to minimize out-of-lane detection for the fixed beam radar system, it is necessary to make the beamwidth as narrow as possible. As shown in Figure 4, the narrow beam of the fixed beam system is very narrow in close to the truck. This means that a close-in vehicle cutting in front of the truck must travel nearly to the center of the lane before it is detected by the radar system. The 12 degree wide beam of the monopulse system, as shown, can detects the close-in cut-in vehicle much earlier than the fixed beam system.

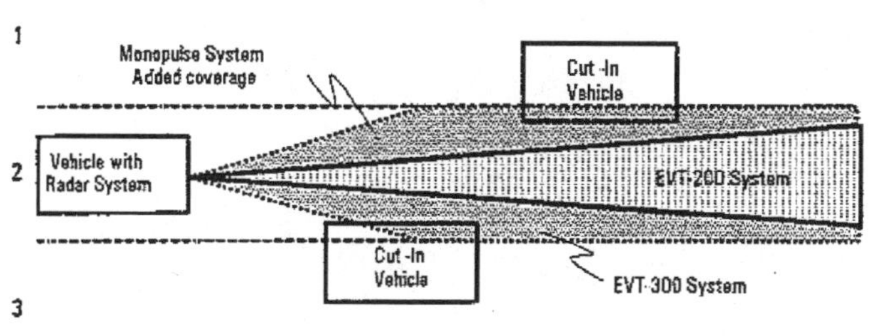

Figure 4 - Vehicle Cut-In Coverage of Monopulse System

DATA RECORDING

The EVT-300 radar system will also have extended data recording capability. Vehicle and radar data is stored on battery backed memory that can be removed from the truck and downloaded for use in operations reports or accident reconstruction reports. A PC based software program is provided for use by the customer to run the Vehicle Information Management System (VIMS™) for his fleet. The VIMS program provides a full set of vehicle performance reports to manage the day-to-day operations of the fleet for maximum efficiency. Data on fuel usage, rpm vs. engine loading, average speed, maximum speed, distance traveled, engine idle time, hard braking events, brake application profiles, average following distances, number of radar alarms given, etc. can be displayed in the reports. Standard reports include:

- Performance Summary Report
- RPM/Speed Summary report
- Trip Segment Report
- Vehicle Productivity Report
- Brake/Fuel Use Report
- CPU Operational Status Report

A secondary use for the stored data, if desired by the customer, is for accident reconstruction. A moving data window of about 20 minutes in duration is stored in non-volatile, removable memory and is available to describe truck and radar activity during the period leading up to and including the accident. This data can be used to generate detailed reports of the traffic scenario in front of the truck as well as the performance activity of the truck and driver just prior to an accident or other incident of interest.

SUMMARY

Technology exists and production systems are available for forward-looking, radar based sensors that are used to provide collision warnings to drivers of heavy trucks and can be used to automatically control truck speed while in cruise control mode thus maintaining adequate following distances and adapting to varying traffic situations. Truck accidents are significantly reduced by use of collision warning systems generating a very short Returns On Investment (ROI) through reduced safety related costs and fixed costs.

The EVT-200 Collision Warning System has been in production for over two years and has demonstrated that significant accident reductions are achieved by use of the system. In 1998, the Eaton VORAD model EVT-300 Collision Warning System will be introduced through truck manufacturers (OEMs) with the automatic adaptive cruise control, SmartCruise®, feature for speed and following distance control of the truck while in cruise control operation. This feature has been very popular with test drivers desiring to use cruise control. Drivers have found that driving is less fatiguing with adaptive cruise control and use of the system typically leads to greater/safer following distances than would normally be maintained manually by the driver.

Monopulse radar operation provides significant improvement in vehicle radar performance for adaptive cruise control by measuring the azimuth angle to forward vehicles and thus handles a greater range of highway geometry and traffic scenarios.

REFERENCES

[1] Woll, Jerry D., "Vehicle Collision Warning System with Data Recording Capability", SAE Technical Paper Number 952619, SAE International Truck and Bus Meeting and Exposition, Winston-Salem, North Carolina, November 13-15, 1995.

[2] Woll, Jerry D., "VORAD Collision Warning Radar" Proceedings of the IEEE 1995 International Radar Conference, Alexandria, Virginia, May 8-11, 1995. IEEE Catalog Number 95CH-3571-0.

[3] Woll, Jerry D., "Monopulse Doppler Radar for Intelligent Cruise Control", SAE Technical Paper Number 972669, 1997 SAE Future Transportation Technology Conference, San Diego, California, August 6-8, 1997

ABOUT THE AUTHOR

Jerry Woll was Vice President of Engineering for Eaton VORAD Technologies, San Diego, California, a vehicle radar development and manufacturing company. He was with VORAD Safety Systems and Eaton VORAD Technologies for six years. Prior experience includes 10 years as Vice President of Engineering for Teledyne Ryan Electronics, San Diego, California, where he directed the design and development of Doppler radar systems for military aircraft applications. He completed 20 years service as an officer in the Civil Engineer Corps of the U.S. Navy where he specialized in electronic and computer engineering projects. Mr. Woll received a BSEE degree from Purdue University, a MSEE degree from the University of Michigan, and a MS degree in Computer Science from the Naval Postgraduate School, Monterey, California. He is a registered professional engineer in the states of Indiana and California, and a member of Tau Beta Pi and Eta Kappa Nu engineering honorary societies. Mr. Woll is co-inventor on five patents involving radar technology and has published and presented several technical papers for SAE and IEEE.

972655

Macroscopic Analysis of Traffic Flow of Automated Vehicles

H. Raza and P. Ioannou
University of Southern California

ABSTRACT

In the first part of this study a macroscopic traffic flow model of automated vehicles is developed by using the microscopic control laws that govern the longitudinal motion of individual vehicles together with the dynamics of the interconnection with other vehicles. The developed model is used in this paper to analyze the steady state behavior of automated traffic flow for different operating conditions. The analysis indicates that some of the proposed modes of AHS which operate without a traffic flow controller may not be effective in avoiding traffic congestion problems resulting from traffic flow disturbances. The model also predicts the existence of shock waves in extreme cases for the same modes of AHS. The results of this analysis can be used as guidelines for designing macroscopic as well as microscopic control laws. Finally, some of these phenomena predicted by analysis of the model were validated with the help of simulations.

1 Introduction

With the development of near term automatic vehicle following concepts such as intelligent cruise control (ICC) and cooperative driving, vehicles will be able to follow each other automatically in the longitudinal direction. The modeling and analysis of traffic flow consisting of such vehicles is important in order to come up with traffic flow control strategies. In the previous chapter we have developed a model that describes the macroscopic behavior of automated traffic flow. The model is applicable to a wide variety of automatic vehicle following concepts including IMVF. Since the model is based on the deterministic microscopic dynamics, we can use the dynamics representing different vehicle following concepts to analyze their macroscopic properties.

In particular we have used the model to compare the stability properties of equilibrium states of the system operating under time and fixed distance headway policies. The analysis indicates that in both cases the equilibrium states are only locally attractive. In the presence of disturbances, the system operating under time headway policy will cause congestion problem, i.e., the operating density will be higher than the desired one. Furthermore, the recovey from this congestion requires some cooperative control laws. The fixed distance headway policy, on the other hand, can recover without any external assisstance.

Due to speed dependent density distribution, in the case of time headway policy, the system can end up in shock waves if a locally steady traffic approaches a region with lower steady speed. Finally, we have given an argument in the favor of infrastructure control that these potential problems can be avoided by introducing an active feedback through the roadway controller. The main result of this analysis is that some proposed modes of AHS which do not require roadway assisstance has only a limited region of operation where the desired performance can be guaranteed. The involvement of infrastructure can significantly enhance the region of useful operation. In addition to the results shown through the analysis of model, we have confirmed some of these phenomena through simulation of the model.

The paper is organized as follows: An analysis of the equilibrium states of the automated traffic flow, by using the model developed in [1], is given in section 2. The issues related to simulation of the model are discussed in section 3.

2 Analysis of Automated Traffic Flow

In this section we will analyze the model developed in [1], which is summarized in Appendix A, to study the properties of automated traffic flow especially their equilibrium states. Since the model developed in this study is independent of the implementation details of a particular system, it can be used to compare the properties of different automatic vehicle following concepts. In this way the macroscopic behavior of these systems can be studied by choosing the appropriate microscopic dynamics governing these concepts. As an example we will compare controller designs based on time headway and fixed distance headway policies, in terms of the convergence properties of their desired equilibrium sets. Similarly different control designs within the same category can be compared by selecting appropriate dynamics in terms of transfer functions $W_1(s)$ and $W_2(s)$ in Table 1.

For simplicity, we will consider only a single lane highway with no lateral traffic flow. In the absence of lane changes, the desired headway h_m will be assumed to be constant, hence the only input to the model in Table 1 is the desired speed $V_m(x,t)$ for section m. The main objective of this analysis is to show that there are operating conditions under which the system will end up in undesirable steady state leading to congestion or interrupted flow. In extreme cases these disturbances may lead to shock waves if vehicles are operating in automatic following mode without some kind of global control. We will formulate the main results of this analysis in the form of following propositions; the proof is given by the analysis to follow.

Proposition 2.1 *The automatic vehicle following controllers designed with the constraints* **C–II** *and* **C–III** *are not sufficient to make the desired equilibrium point globally attractive.*

Proposition 2.2 *Under the time headway policy, if the system is in undesirable equilibrium state, convergence to the desired set require cooperative control laws. However, for the fixed distance headway policy, the system will return to it's desired equilibrium state if the disturbance is removed and this convergence can occur without any external control laws.*

Proposition 2.3 *Under the time headway policy, there are operating conditions in which shock waves are produced if the vehicles are operating without infrastructure control.*

These propositions outline one of the major difference in macroscopic properties of control laws designed with the two different headway policies, time headway and fixed distance headway in this case. To prove these claims, we will derive the steady state solution of the system represented in Table 1 for different operating conditions. We will consider the stationary and non-stationary flows as two special cases of interest. We will show that the system formulation in Table 1 restricts the steady state speed distribution to be identically constant in both cases. However, it permits non-stationary density distribution in steady state, which captures a rich class of operating conditions. These cases are discussed below in detail.

2.1 Stationary Flow

Since we are considering a single lane highway, we will drop the subscript y from the notation in Table 1. For stationary flow conditions to exist it is required that at any fixed point there are no variations in traffic flow rate, i.e., traffic appears as stationary to any static observer. The stationary flow conditions are satisfied if:

$$\frac{\partial}{\partial x}q_m(x,t) = 0 \;\forall t \quad \Rightarrow \quad \frac{\partial}{\partial t}k_m(x,t) = 0 \;\forall x. \tag{1}$$

Now we can solve the system in Table 1 for steady state:

$$\dot{k}_m(x,t) = 0 \quad \Rightarrow \quad \frac{\partial}{\partial x}v_m(x,t) = 0 \tag{2}$$

Also combining (2) with the requirement that $\dot{v}_m(x,t) = 0$ and with the assumption that $v_m(x,t) \not\equiv 0$, we get:

$$\frac{\partial}{\partial t}v_m(x,t) = 0. \tag{3}$$

From (2) and (3), we have that at steady state:

$$v_m(x,t) = \bar{V}_m \tag{4}$$

where $\bar{V}_m > 0$ is any constant. Since at steady state:

$$\dot{k}_m(x,t) = \frac{\partial}{\partial t}k_m(x,t) + v_m(x,t)\frac{\partial}{\partial x}k_m(x,t) = 0 \tag{5}$$

and we are considering stationary flow, i.e., $\frac{\partial}{\partial t}k_m = 0$ $\Rightarrow \frac{\partial}{\partial x}k_m = 0$, hence:

$$k_m(x,t) = \bar{K}_m \tag{6}$$

where $\bar{K}_m > 0$ is any constant. First, we will consider time headway policy, in this case, under stationary flow conditions, $\bar{K}_m$ is not arbitrary but is related to $\bar{V}_m$ in (4) as:

$$\bar{K}_m = \frac{1}{h\bar{V}_m + l} \tag{7}$$

where h is the constant time headway. As expected for stationary flow conditions, the model produces static speed and density distributions as steady state solutions. Furthermore, the set of equilibrium points, $\mathcal{E} = \{\bar{V}_m, \bar{K}_m\}$, is not unique. Next we will isolate the set of equilibrium points into desirable and undesirable ones and will identify the region of attraction of the desirable set. This analysis will help us to identify the operating conditions under which the system may end up in the undesirable region as pointed out by proposition 2.1.

2.1.1 Structure of Equilibrium States

If we assume that under steady conditions the desired speed $V_m(x,t) = V_m$, where $V_m > 0$ is any constant, then for time headway policy, the desired equilibrium point is unique and is given as:

$$\mathcal{E}_d = \{V_m, K_m\},\ K_m = \frac{1}{hV_m + l} \tag{8}$$

We will show that the desired equilibrium point $\mathcal{E}_d \in \mathcal{E}$ and derive the relationship between $\mathcal{E}_d$ and $\mathcal{E}$ which is dictated by the properties of transfer functions $W_1(s)$ and $W_2(s)$. This relationship is given by the following lemma.

Lemma 2.1 *If the automatic vehicle following controllers satisfy the constraints* **C–II** *and* **C–III** *then:*

$$||v_m(x,.)||_\infty \leq ||V_m(x,.)||_\infty \ \ \forall\, x$$

and in steady state $v_m(x,t) \leq V_m(x,t)$.

Proof: If we assume normal operating conditions within a platoon, then we have, $\delta_m(x_{ij},t) = G_\delta(s)v_m(x_{i(j-1)},t)$, where $G_\delta(s)$ is a stable, proper, minimum phase transfer function. The transfer function relating $\delta_m(x_{ij},t)$ and $\delta_m(x_{i(j-1)},t)$ can be found as:

$$\begin{aligned}\frac{\delta_m(x_{ij},t)}{\delta_m(x_{i(j-1)},t)} &= \frac{\delta_m(x_{ij},t)}{v_m(x_{i(j-1)},t)}W_1(s)\frac{v_m(x_{i(j-2)},t)}{\delta_m(x_{i(j-1)},t)}, \\ &= W_1(s),\end{aligned} \tag{9}$$

where $v_m(x_{ij},t) = W_1(s)v_m(x_{i(j-1)},t)$. Similarly, we can show that $\frac{v_{r_m}(x_{ij},t)}{v_{r_m}(x_{i(j-1)},t)} = W_1(s)$. From constraint **C–III**, that guarantees platoon stability, it is required that:

$$||w_1(t)||_1 \leq 1, \tag{10}$$

where $w_1(t) = \mathcal{L}^{-1}\{W_1(s)\}$. Now from 1 by using the condition (10), we have:

$$\begin{aligned}&||v_m(x_{ij},.)||_\infty \leq ||V_m(x_{i1},.)||_\infty;\ j\in\mathcal{J},\ i\in\mathcal{I} \\ \Rightarrow\ &||v_m(x,.)||_\infty \leq ||V_m(x,.)||_\infty\ \forall x.\end{aligned} \tag{11}$$

Now to prove the second part of the lemma, we will differentiate between the desired speed V and the actual speed followed by the platoon leader V_{d_1} given in [1]. The constraint **C–II** on $W_1(s)$ and $W_2(s)$ guarantees that $\lim_{t\to\infty} v_m(x_{ij},t) = V_{d_m}(x_{i1},t)$, where $V_{d_m}(x_{i1},t)$ is the actual speed followed by the platoon leader of platoon i in section m. Now since:

$$V_{d_m}(x_{i1},t) = \min(V_m(x_{i1},t), V_l(t)) \tag{12}$$

where $V_l(t)$ is the speed of the vehicle in front of platoon leader. Hence, it follows that in steady state $v_m(x,t) \leq V_m(x,t)$.
□

Now for time headway policy, Lemma 2.1 implies that in steady state:

$$\bar{V}_m \leq V_m\ \Rightarrow \bar{K}_m \geq K_m. \tag{13}$$

Since we are assuming positive velocities only, the plot of the equilibrium states $\mathcal{E} \in \mathcal{R}^2$ is shown in Figure 1, here K_j is the density at traffic jam conditions, when $\bar{V}_m = 0$. To show that the desired equilibrium point $\mathcal{E}_d$ is contained in the set $\mathcal{E}$, we will write the expressions for $\frac{\partial}{\partial t}v_m(x,t)$ and $\frac{\partial}{\partial x}v_m(x,t)$, by using Table 1, as given below:

$$\begin{aligned}&\frac{\partial}{\partial t}v_m(x,t) = \dot{v}_m(x_{ij},t) + \Big\{\dot{k}_m(x_{ij},t) \\ &[v_m(x_{i(j-1)},t) - v_m(x_{ij},t)] + k_m(x_{ij},t) \\ &[\dot{v}_m(x_{i(j-1)},t) - \dot{v}_m(x_{ij},t)]\Big\}(x - x_{ij})\end{aligned} \tag{14}$$

$$\begin{aligned}&\frac{\partial}{\partial x}v_m(x,t) = k_m(x_{ij},t)\,[v_m(x_{i(j-1)},t) - \\ &v_m(x_{ij},t)]\end{aligned} \tag{15}$$

From (14) and (15) we see that the conditions given in (2) and (3) are satisfied if and only if:

$$\begin{aligned}&\dot{v}_m(x_{ij},t) = 0 \\ \text{and}\quad &v_m(x_{ij},t) = v_m(x_{i(j-1)},t)\ i\in\mathcal{I}, j\in\mathcal{J}\end{aligned} \tag{16}$$

Since we want to find the region of attraction of the desired equilibrium point, we will again differentiate between V, the desired speed, and V_{d_1}, the speed followed by the platoon leader, given in [1]. Now from 1 we have that the conditions given above are satisfied if and only if the desired speed, $V_{d_m}(x_{i1},t)$, is constant for all i. The desired speed $V_{d_m}(x_{i1},t) = V_m$ if $k_m(x,t) \leq K_m$ for all x. Hence the region of attraction of $\mathcal{E}_d$ is:

$$k_m(x,t) \leq K_m \tag{17}$$

This region is mapped in Figure 1 and proves proposition 2.1 for the time headway policy. Now we will show the same result for the fixed distance headway policy. In this case the desired equilibrium states are:

$$\mathcal{E}_d = \{V_m, K_m\},\ K_m = \frac{1}{X_{r_d} + l}, \tag{18}$$

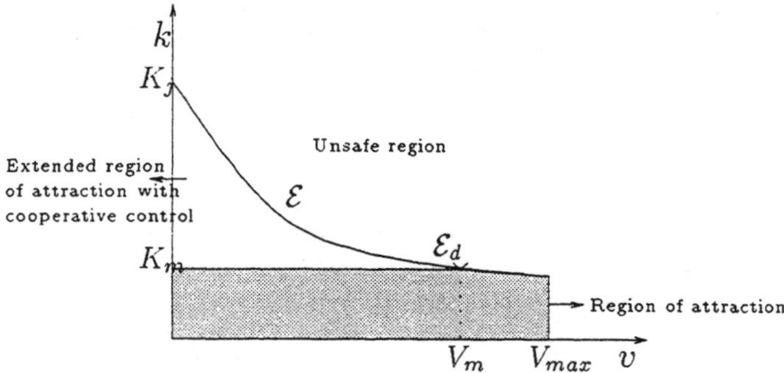

Figure 1: Region of attraction for stationary flow under time headway policy.

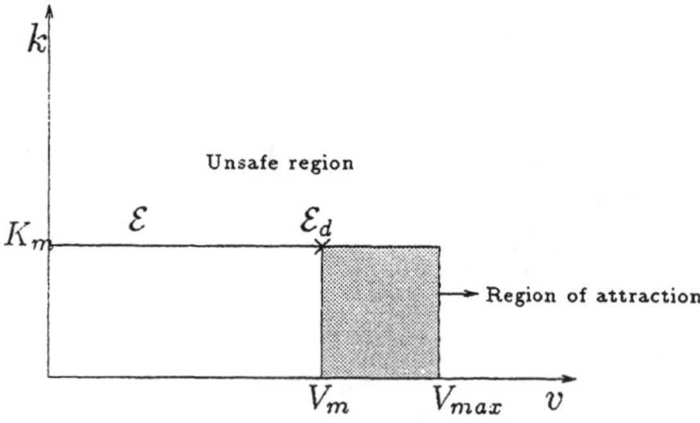

Figure 2: Region of attraction for stationary flow under fixed distance headway policy.

where X_{r_d} is the desired spacing, which is fixed and independent of the operating speed. Since Lemma 2.1 is independent of a particular control design, it also applies to the controllers designed with the fixed distance headway policy satisfying the constraints **C–II** and **C–III**. In this case we have that:

$$\bar{V}_m \leq V_m \text{ and } \bar{K}_m = K_m. \tag{19}$$

The plot of the equilibrium states in this case is shown in Figure 2. The equilibrium state density is fixed, which is a property of this control law, however, the equilibrium speed can be lower than the desired one, if $v_m(x,t) < V_m(x,t)$ for some x. Which proves proposition 2.1 for the fixed distance headway policy.

To prove proposition 2.2, we will start by identifying different regions shown in Figures 1 and 2. The constraint **C–II** imposed on the vehicle following controllers guarantees that, in Figure 1, the set $\mathcal{E}$ is asymptotically attractive for all trajectories within the domain, $V_m \leq V_{max}$. The region above the equilibrium set $\mathcal{E}$, given as:

$$k_m > \frac{1}{h\bar{V}_m + l} \tag{20}$$

is unsafe, as the minimum safety distance policy is violated. Since the vehicle following control laws are designed to guarantee local safety, these trajectories are rejected at the microscopic level. Any transient in this region will eventually be terminated on the set $\mathcal{E}$. From (17) it is obvious that the desired equilibrium point is only locally attractive. In case of a disturbance, the system will end up in undesirable state with $\bar{K}_m > K_m$. Now to recover from this state it is required that:

$$\dot{k}_m(x,t) < 0 \text{ when } \bar{K}_m > K_m. \tag{21}$$

Since $\dot{k}_m = -k_m \frac{\partial v_m}{\partial x}$, to satisfy (21) it is required that there is a strict positive spatial gradient in the speed distribution which cannot be guaranteed without some kind of cooperation between the vehicles.

On the other hand, for fixed distance headway policy, Figure 2, the equilibrium set $\mathcal{E}$ is asymptotically attractive for all of trajectories above or below this set. Furthermore, since the density remains equal to the desired one, the recovery to the desired set will occur if the disturbing condition is removed, without any need for external cooperation. Since

$$\begin{aligned} &\bar{K}_m = K_m \text{ (always)} \\ \text{and} \quad &\bar{V}_m < V_m \text{ when } v_m(x,t) < V_m \text{ for some } x, \end{aligned}$$

$\mathcal{E} \to \mathcal{E}_d$ when the disturbance is removed, which proves proposition 2.2.

In the next section we will extend some of these results to the case of non-stationary flow.

2.2 Non-Stationary Flow

In this section we assume non-stationary flow conditions, i.e., $\frac{\partial}{\partial x} q_m(x,t) \neq 0$ or $\frac{\partial}{\partial t} k_m(x,t) \neq 0$ for some $x \in [0, L_m]$. Again for steady state we require $\frac{\partial}{\partial x} v_m(x,t) = 0$ and $\frac{\partial}{\partial t} v_m(x,t) = 0 \Rightarrow v_m(x,t) = \bar{V}_m$. Since at steady state:

$$\dot{k}_m(x,t) = \frac{\partial}{\partial t} k_m(x,t) + v_m \frac{\partial}{\partial x} k_m(x,t) = 0.$$

By substituting $v_m = \bar{V}_m$ in the equation above we get:

$$\frac{\partial k_m}{\partial t} + \bar{V}_m \frac{\partial k_m}{\partial x} = 0. \tag{22}$$

Since in this case $\frac{\partial}{\partial t} k_m \neq 0$, the solutions of (22) have the form:

$$k_m(x,t) = f_m(x - \bar{V}_m t) \tag{23}$$

where $k_m(x,0) = f_m(x)$ is the initial condition and $x - \bar{V}_m t = \xi$ is the characteristic line, along which

$k_m(x,t)$ has a constant value $f_m(\xi)$. Hence we have a wave traveling to the right with a constant velocity $\bar{V}_m$ that carries the non-constant density distribution $f_m(x)$, since at time $t = 0$ if we have $k_m(x_0, 0) = f_m(x_0)$ then at time $t_1 > 0$ for $x_1 = x_0 + \bar{V}_m t_1$ we have $k_m(x_1, t_1) = f_m((x_0+\bar{V}_m t_1)-\bar{V}_m t_1) = f_m(x_0) = k_m(x_0, 0)$.

In the following we will do an analysis of the equilibrium states of the system for the non-stationary flow conditions.

2.2.1 Structure of Equilibrium States

Since in this case the steady state density distribution is non-uniform, $f_m(x - \bar{V}_m t)$, whereas the speed distribution, $\bar{V}_m$ is constant, the equilibrium states, for the time headway policy, consist of the following set:

$$\mathcal{E} = \{\bar{V}_m, (0, \bar{K}_m]\}, \; \bar{K}_m = \frac{1}{h\bar{V}_m + l}. \tag{24}$$

In this case the set of desired equilibrium states is:

$$\mathcal{E}_d = \mathcal{E}|_{\bar{V}_m = V_m}. \tag{25}$$

Hence the effect of non-stationary flow conditions at steady state is to enlarge the set of desired equilibrium states. As expected, the set $\mathcal{E}_d = \{V_m, (0, K_m]\}$ given in (25) reduces to a single point $\{V_m, K_m\}$ for homogeneous density. In this case the same kind of arguments can be used to show that the region of attraction is:

$$k_m(x,t) \le K_m. \tag{26}$$

Similarly, the results given for fixed distance headway policy, in the case of stationary flow conditions, hold for non-stationary flow, which proves proposition 2.1. It can be easily shown that the same kind of congestion recovery characteristics exist for the two flow conditions considered here, which extends the proof of proposition 2.2 for non-stationary flow. As discussed before, an extension of this region, in the case of time headway policy, can be achieved with the help of a macroscopic controller.

Till now we have assumed that it is always possible for the system to attain a uniform speed profile. It is not true in general, that the system can reach the steady state with a constant speed V_m. In the following we will discuss the situation in which a locally steady traffic approaches to a somewhat different operating conditions downstream. If we assume that there is no involvement of infrastructure to help avoid this potentially discontinuous situation then in some cases shock waves may be produced.

2.3 Shock Waves

In the previous section we have shown that for non-stationary flow conditions, the density distribution at steady state is a wave traveling to the right with a constant velocity. The implicit assumption of obtaining continuous solutions in (23) is that there is no obstruction for this wave, i.e., all the sections downstream section m are operating at the same (or higher) constant velocity. However, this may not be true in general. If the wave (23) happens to come across another wave generated by density fluctuations in some other section which is operating at a speed different than $\bar{V}_m$ then there will be some interaction between these two waves. This interaction may cause a shock wave in an attempt to match the conditions at the interface of two waves. Without loss of generality, we can assume the two sections to be $m = 1$ and 2, with the density waves as:

$$k_1(x,t) = f_1(x - \bar{V}_1 t), \tag{27}$$
$$k_2(x,t) = f_2(x - \bar{V}_2 t). \tag{28}$$

Since k is constant along the characteristic line which is a function of the initial condition ξ, two waves will meet at a point (x_s, t_s), where:

$$x_s = \bar{V}_1 t_s + \xi_1 = \bar{V}_2 t_s + \xi_2,$$
$$\Rightarrow \quad t_s = \frac{\xi_2 - \xi_1}{\bar{V}_1 - \bar{V}_2}, \tag{29}$$

where $\xi_2 > \xi_1$, $\Rightarrow t_s > 0$ if $\bar{V}_2 < \bar{V}_1$. Hence the waves (27) and (28) meet at a positive time given by (29). In this case the continuous solutions given in (27) and (28) fail to exist beyond the time t_s. Furthermore, the assumption of constant speeds $\bar{V}_1$ and $\bar{V}_2$ is no longer valid near the interface of two waves. Hence (22) no longer holds around the discontinuity. But, in general, the law of conservation of vehicles always holds, i.e.,

$$\frac{\partial k}{\partial t} + \frac{\partial q}{\partial x} = 0 \tag{30}$$

where k and q are the density and flow around the region of discontinuity. We will rewrite (30) in a form which is similar to (22) but permits the speed to be discontinuous. If we denote the curve of discontinuity to be $x = \phi(t)$ and since $q(k) = kv$, we can write:

$$\frac{\partial k}{\partial t} + \frac{\partial q(k)}{\partial x} = 0$$
$$\Rightarrow \quad \frac{\partial k}{\partial t} + \frac{dq}{dk}\frac{\partial k}{\partial x} = 0. \tag{31}$$

We propose that (31) can be written as:

$$\frac{\partial k}{\partial t} + v\frac{\partial k}{\partial x} = 0 \tag{32}$$

where $v(x,t)$ is the speed in the region of discontinuity and is given as:

$$v(x,t) = \begin{cases} \bar{V}_1 = \frac{dq}{dk} & \text{for } x < \phi(t) \\ \bar{V}_2 = \frac{dq}{dk} & \text{for } x > \phi(t). \end{cases} \tag{33}$$

However, $\frac{dq}{dk}$ fails to exist at the curve of discontinuity, $x = \phi(t)$, due to jump in the values of q and k caused by discontinuity in v. As given in (33), $v(x,t)$ has limits from below and above, i.e.,

$$\lim_{x\uparrow\phi} v = \bar{V}_1 \text{ and } \lim_{x\downarrow\phi} v = \bar{V}_2.$$

Now we can use the technique given in [2] to derive the relationship between the speed at the discontinuity and the jump in the values of k and q. Since k and q are also function of speed, in the case of time headway policy, we can rewrite (30) as:

$$\frac{\partial k(v(x,t))}{\partial t} + \frac{\partial q(v(x,t))}{\partial x} = 0. \tag{34}$$

If we assume the discontinuity to be contained in the region $[a,b]$, then integrating (34) over this region we get:

$$\int_a^b \frac{\partial k(v(x,t))}{\partial t} dx + \int_a^b \frac{\partial q(v(x,t))}{\partial x} dx = 0, \tag{35}$$

$$\Rightarrow \frac{d}{dt}\int_a^b k(v(x,t))dx + [q(v(b,t)) - q(v(a,t))] = 0.$$

Since by construction, $a < \phi(t) < b$, and v goes from $\bar{V}_1$ to $\bar{V}_2$ across the curve $\phi(t)$, we can rewrite (35) as:

$$\frac{d}{dt}\left[\int_a^\phi k(v(x,t))dx + \int_\phi^b k(v(x,t))dx\right] + [q(v(b,t)) - q(v(a,t))] = 0. \tag{36}$$

Using Liebnitz rule and replacing $\frac{\partial k(v)}{\partial t}$ with $-\frac{\partial q(v)}{\partial x}$, we get:

$$\left[k(\bar{V}_1)\dot{\phi} - \int_a^\phi \frac{\partial q(v)}{\partial x}dx\right] - \left[\int_\phi^b \frac{\partial q(v)}{\partial x}dx + k(\bar{V}_2)\dot{\phi}\right] + [q(v(b,t)) - q(v(a,t))] = 0,$$

$$-\dot{\phi}\left[k(\bar{V}_2) - k(\bar{V}_1)\right] + \left[q(\bar{V}_2) - q(\bar{V}_1)\right] = 0, \tag{37}$$

where $\dot{\phi} = \frac{d\phi}{dt}$ and is given as:

$$\frac{d\phi}{dt} = \frac{[q(\bar{V}_2) - q(\bar{V}_1)]}{[k(\bar{V}_2) - k(\bar{V}_1)]}. \tag{38}$$

Hence the speed of propagation of the discontinuity or shock, $\frac{d\phi}{dt}$, is equal to $\frac{\Delta q}{\Delta k}$, where Δq and Δk are jump in the values of q and k across the discontinuity. It should be noted that the shock wave $\phi(t)$ can travel upstream or downstream depending on the signs of Δq and Δk.

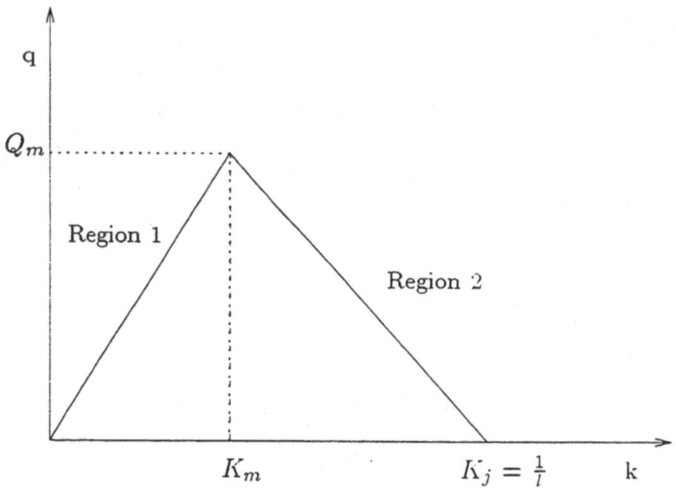

Figure 3: Fundamental diagram for automated traffic flow under time headway policy.

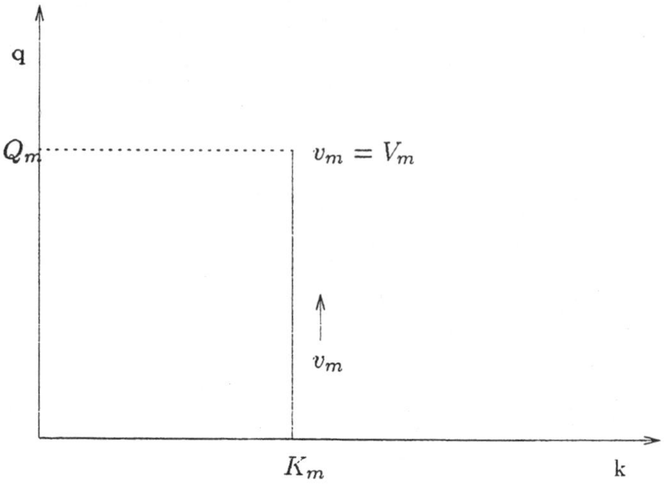

Figure 4: Fundamental diagram for automated traffic flow under fixed distance headway policy.

The analysis given above is valid only for time headway policy, as the assumption in (34) that k is a function of speed $v(x,t)$ is not true for fixed distance headway policy. This proves proposition 2.3. At this time it is not clear whether the speed dependence of the density distribution is the necessary condition for existence of shock waves. Hence the proposition 2.3 does not imply that the fixed distance headway policy is free from shock waves. However, the analysis of fundamental diagram for the two headway policies can be used to show that indeed fixed distance headway policy will not result in shock waves.

The fundamental diagrams showing the relationship between the steady state flow and density for the two headway policies are shown in Figures 3 and 4. The region 1 shown in Figure 3 corresponds to the region of attraction of the desired equilibrium point, when $k_m < K_m$. In this region the speed is constant at V_m and flow increases to Q_m as the density increases to it's maximum permissible value K_m. The region 2 in Figure 3 results from congested traffic when $k_m > K_m$. The time headway policy has $q - k$ characteristics which are very similar to those of human driving, where the variations of $\frac{\Delta q}{\Delta k}$ give rise to shock waves. However, as shown in Figure 4, this phenomenon cannot occur in fixed distance headway policy. This is due to preservation of density distribution under all operating speeds. Hence if the disturbance, causing a reduction in speed, is removed the system can recover to it's normal speed without an outbreak of shock waves. During recovery stage in the case of time headway policy, the increasing speeds of downstream vehicles will result in reduction in relative spacings of upstream vehicles, causing cyclic reductions in speed and hence shock waves.

At this point we will make the following remark.

Remark

- As we have seen above, without active involvement of infrastructure there are situations in which the undesirable phenomena observed on current highways such as congestion and shock waves will show up for some automatic vehicle following concepts. Hence the modes of operation of AHS which require less cooperation between vehicles and infrastructure, such as ICC (mixed traffic) and autonomous individual vehicles, have a restricted range of operation in which the required traffic throughput can be achieved. However, as shown above, some of these undesirable effects can be sufficiently attenuated with the help of macroscopic control laws.

In the next section we will present the results produced by simulation of the model for particular scenarios considered in the analysis.

2.4 Simulation Results

In this section we will validate the macroscopic properties of automated traffic flow predicted by the analysis of the model in section 2. Since no macroscopic data from automated traffic flow is available to do this job, we will use simulation results only. In particular we will simulate the situations in which the undesirable effects outlined in propositions 2.1-2.3 can be visualized.

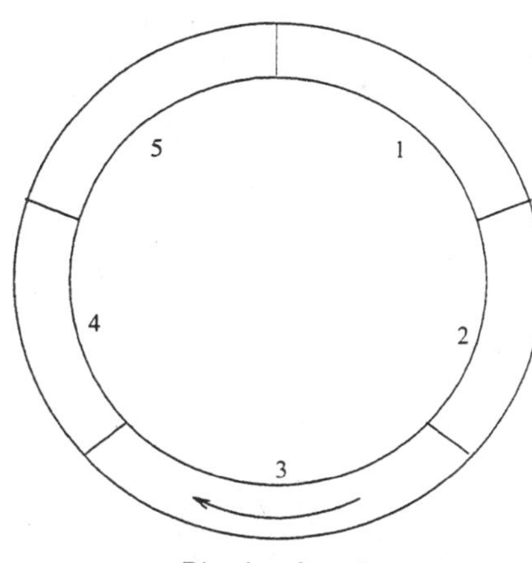

Figure 5: A single lane circular highway used for simulation.

For simplicity we have assumed a single lane circular highway shown in Figure 5. The highway is subdivided into five sections, $M = 5$, each with an initial length of 500 meters. The vehicles are assumed to be traveling in platoons of uniform size, $n_i = 5$. Different scenarios used for simulations are described below.

2.5 Scenario 1

In this scenario we will demonstrate the existence of shock waves for automated traffic flow, when vehicles are traveling under time headway policy. The transfer functions $W_1(s)$ and $W_2(s)$ are selected from the longitudinal vehicle following control design in [3]. The nominal highway speed is assumed to be 20 m/s with a constant time headway of 0.5 seconds.

For this scenario we assume that a disturbance exists in section 3, which causes the vehicles in that section to decelerate to a speed of 10 m/s. The rest of the sections are operating at their nominal speed. This disturbance is removed after 10 seconds so that the disturbed vehicles can resume their normal speed. The plots of the speed and density distribution functions are shown in Figures 6 and 7.

The speed distribution function in Figure 6 shows that, even though the disturbance is removed, the system cannot return back to its desired equilibrium point. The density distribution in Figure 7 indicates the presence of shock waves. These waves are generated as the system is trying to recover to its normal state. The vehicles at the point of disturbance with open space in front of them are returning to their normal speed, which causes a reduction in the relative spacings of the upstream vehicles. These vehicles then have to reduce their speed again, this cyclic variations is speed results in a shock wave. In this case this wave is traveling upstream with an approximate speed of 10 m/s which is exactly as predicted by the analysis of the model.

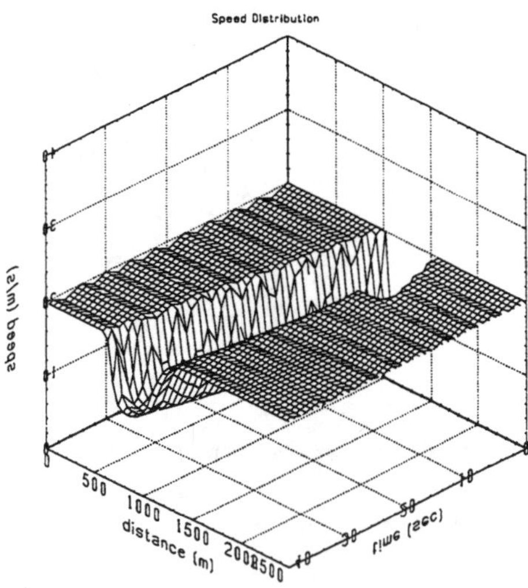

Figure 6: Speed distribution function for time headway policy. The system is distrubed from $t = 0$ to $t = 10$ seconds, after the disturbance is removed the system is not able to recover till $t = 40$ seconds.

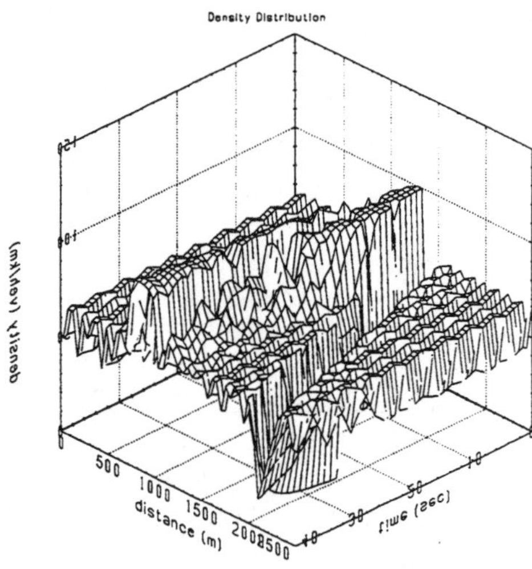

Figure 7: Density distribution function for time headway policy. The plot shows that shock waves are generated as the system is recovering to it's normal state.

2.6 Scenario 2

In this scenario, we have selected the same kind of operating conditions as were created for scenario 1. The only difference in this case is that the vehicles are traveling under fixed distance headway policy with a constant headway of 10 meters. The transfer functions $W_1(s)$ and $W_2(s)$ are selected from the longitudinal vehicle following control design in [4].

The plots of the speed and density distributions are shown in Figures 8 and 9. The speed distribution function in Figure 8 indicates that the system returns to its normal operating point within few seconds after the disturbance is removed. The density distribution functions in Figure 9 shows that no shock waves are created during this recovery process.

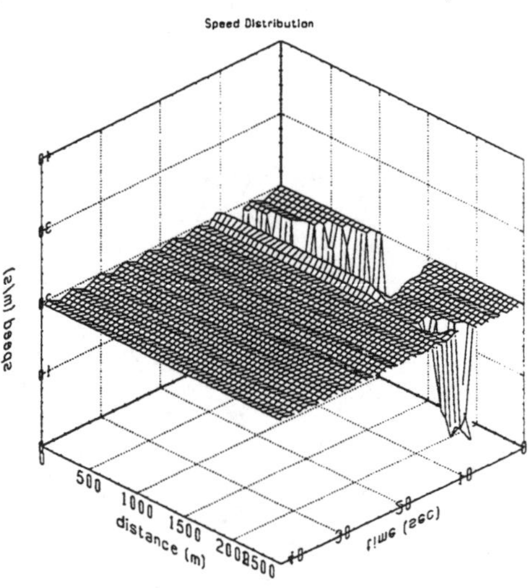

Figure 8: Speed distribution function for fixed distance headway policy. The system is distrubed from $t = 0$ to $t = 10$ seconds, after the disturbance is removed the system returns to it's desired equilibrium state.

3 Conclusion

In this paper we have used the model developed in the first part of this study [1], to analyze the macroscopic

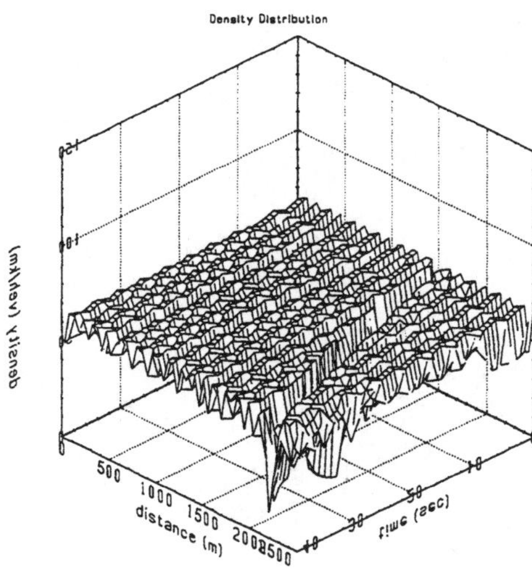

Figure 9: Density distribution function for fixed distance headway policy. The plot shows that no shock waves are generated as the system is recovering.

properties of automated traffic flow for different operating conditions. In particular we have compared the convergence characteristics of equilibrium states of time and fixed distance headway policies. The analysis indicates that under time headway policy the system has a limited range of operation within which the desired performance can be guaranteed. The system in this case is susceptible to congestion and shock waves in some situations. It is shown that these undesirable phenomena can be eliminated with the help of cooperative control laws. Hence the analysis proves that some proposed modes of AHS may not be effective in reducing the traffic congestion problem. Finally some of the undesirable phenomena predicted by the analysis of the model were also shown through the simulation of the model.

Acknowledgments

This work is supported by the California Department of Transportation through PATH of the University of California. The contents of this paper reflect the views of the authors who are responsible for the facts and accuracy of the data presented herein. The contents do not necessarily reflect the official views or policies of the State of California or the Federal Highway Administration. This paper does not constitute a standard, specification or regulation.

References

[1] H. Raza, P. Ioannou, "Macroscopic Traffic Flow Modeling of Automated Highway Systems" To appear in *Proc. of The 5th IEEE Mediterranean Conference on Control and Systems*, July 1997.

[2] F. John, *Partial Differential Equations*, 4th edition, Springer-Verlag, New York, 1982.

[3] P. Ioannou, Z. Xu, "Throttle and Brake Control System for Automatic Vehicle Following". *IVHS Journal*, vol. 1(4), pp. 345-377, 1994.

[4] J. K. Hedrick, et. al, "Control Issues in Automated Highway Systems", *IEEE Control Systems*, vol. 14, no. 6, pp. 21-32, Dec. 1994.

Appendix A

Table 1: Global Macroscopic Model

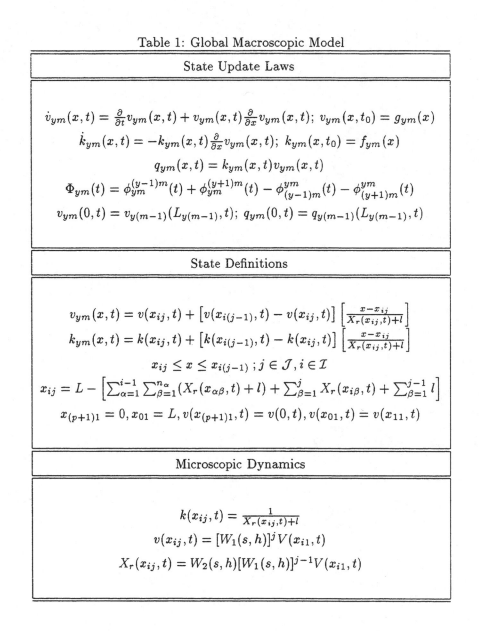

State Update Laws
$\dot{v}_{ym}(x,t) = \frac{\partial}{\partial t}v_{ym}(x,t) + v_{ym}(x,t)\frac{\partial}{\partial x}v_{ym}(x,t);\ v_{ym}(x,t_0) = g_{ym}(x)$ $\dot{k}_{ym}(x,t) = -k_{ym}(x,t)\frac{\partial}{\partial x}v_{ym}(x,t);\ k_{ym}(x,t_0) = f_{ym}(x)$ $q_{ym}(x,t) = k_{ym}(x,t)v_{ym}(x,t)$ $\Phi_{ym}(t) = \phi_{ym}^{(y-1)m}(t) + \phi_{ym}^{(y+1)m}(t) - \phi_{(y-1)m}^{ym}(t) - \phi_{(y+1)m}^{ym}(t)$ $v_{ym}(0,t) = v_{y(m-1)}(L_{y(m-1)},t);\ q_{ym}(0,t) = q_{y(m-1)}(L_{y(m-1)},t)$
State Definitions
$v_{ym}(x,t) = v(x_{ij},t) + \left[v(x_{i(j-1)},t) - v(x_{ij},t)\right]\left[\frac{x-x_{ij}}{X_r(x_{ij},t)+l}\right]$ $k_{ym}(x,t) = k(x_{ij},t) + \left[k(x_{i(j-1)},t) - k(x_{ij},t)\right]\left[\frac{x-x_{ij}}{X_r(x_{ij},t)+l}\right]$ $x_{ij} \leq x \leq x_{i(j-1)}\ ; j \in \mathcal{J}, i \in \mathcal{I}$ $x_{ij} = L - \left[\sum_{\alpha=1}^{i-1}\sum_{\beta=1}^{n_\alpha}(X_r(x_{\alpha\beta},t)+l) + \sum_{\beta=1}^{j}X_r(x_{i\beta},t) + \sum_{\beta=1}^{j-1}l\right]$ $x_{(p+1)1} = 0, x_{01} = L, v(x_{(p+1)1},t) = v(0,t), v(x_{01},t) = v(x_{11},t)$
Microscopic Dynamics
$k(x_{ij},t) = \frac{1}{X_r(x_{ij},t)+l}$ $v(x_{ij},t) = [W_1(s,h)]^j V(x_{i1},t)$ $X_r(x_{ij},t) = W_2(s,h)[W_1(s,h)]^{j-1}V(x_{i1},t)$

970458

Tests Characterizing Performance of an Adaptive Cruise Control System

P. Fancher, Z. Bareket, S. Bogard, C. MacAdam, and R. Ervin
University of Michigan Transportation Research Institute

ABSTRACT

The tests described here have been used to provide a preliminary checkout of the control functionality of a prototype adaptive cruise control (ACC) system being used in a field operational test of intelligent cruise control. The results presented provide an initial characterization of the headway control performance of the ACC system. The inputs to these tests are the speed of the preceding vehicle. The results of the tests are based upon measurements of range, range rate, velocity, transmission shift commands, and velocity commands resident within the ACC system. Numerical performance measures are derived from these data and used to characterize system performance quantitatively. Results from these types of tests could be used in assessing differences in headway control characteristics associated with various ACC systems.

INTRODUCTION

This paper addresses methods for characterizing the headway control performance of advanced vehicle control systems known as "adaptive cruise control (ACC)" systems. People involved with Intelligent Transportation Systems (ITS) may also refer to these systems as "intelligent cruise control (ICC)" and "autonomous intelligent cruise control (AICC)" systems. These systems all employ headway controllers and they are meant to provide safer following distances and the convenience of less stressful driving. (See references [1] through [6].)

The methods presented here do not address tests of sensors, per se, and the broad set of ambient conditions, target attributes, or roadway geometry under which sensing performance would be assessed. Nevertheless, without a sensor that functions acceptably in typical roadway environments, it is very difficult and practically useless to try to perform the functional tests described here. The methods described here rely on having a sensor that will perform satisfactorily on limited access highways.

The approach employed here for characterizing ACC systems is based upon identifying generic, fundamental tasks that these systems may be expected to perform. The set of tasks described in the paper are related to the following operational situations:

- closing-in on a preceding vehicle from a long range.
- changing to a new headway in response to changing the system's headway setting.
- responding to a preceding vehicle that decelerates to a lower speed.
- responding to a vehicle that suddenly appears in the path of the ACC vehicle.
- responding to a close approach to a preceding vehicle

This set of test situations do not cover all aspects of ACC driving. However, they are important situations and they provide a good basis for checking the performance of existing ACC systems. A more extensive set of procedures could be developed and documented for providing a more complete characterization of ACC systems.

In order to check and evaluate system performance in these types of situations it is necessary to define: (1) the input (essentially the behavior of the preceding vehicle), (2) the initial conditions for starting the test, (3) the conditions which apply during a test run, and (4) the performance signatures and measures used to characterize system performance. Examples of each of these items (inputs, initial conditions, run conditions, and measured results) are presented and discussed in this paper.

The example results illustrate the performance of a prototype system. They are not meant to be examples of excellent performance from a control system perspective. However, they do represent levels of performance that are sufficient for indicating that the ACC system functions properly. Experience has shown that drivers can readily understand and use ACC systems that have control capabilities similar to those illustrated here [7]. The intention of the paper is to provide descriptions and example results for tests that are useful for characterizing certain important functional aspects of the performance of ACC systems in general. These characterizations are needed for studying and understanding the influences of system properties with respect to driver observations and driver-vehicle-system performance in field operational tests representing typical driving environments.

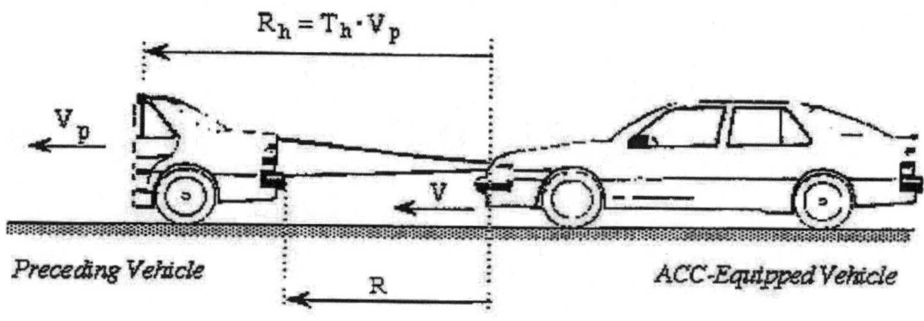

$dR/dt = R_{dot} = V_p - V$

Figure 1. Headway control variables for ACC systems.

The proposed tests are objective tests that do not depend upon driver opinion. Operational testing is needed to obtain subjective measures of the quality of ACC driving with a particular ACC system. In that regard not all drivers like ACC systems. Obviously people who are trying to pass most of the other vehicles on the road will find that ACC tends to hinder them regardless of the details of how the system operates. The driver gives up part of the control task to an ACC system. However, for drivers who are willing to travel at a speed close to the average speed of travel, experience has shown that they will enjoy having the functionality provided by an ACC system in uncongested (free flowing) freeway traffic [7].

The concluding section of the paper examines the purpose and meaning of this set of tests. Changes in testing philosophy that may be required to account for technological advances in sensing, control authority, and communicating with the driver are also addressed in the concluding section.

PRELIMINARY COMMENTS ON THE TESTS

Example results are presented in this paper based upon a prototype ACC system that is being employed in a U.S. Field Operational Test (FOT). Ten of these prototype ACC systems are implemented in ten 1996 Chrysler Concorde sedans employing ODIN-4 infrared ranging sensors. (Further information on the FOT is given in the Acknowledgments section and reference [1].) Characterization testing is an integral portion of the protocol for releasing vehicles into use by lay drivers in the FOT.

The proposed tests are controlled in reference to the speed of the preceding vehicle. It is desired that the speed of the preceding vehicle be approximately 66 mph or 60 mph in certain tests. If the tests are done without a cooperative preceding vehicle (a confederate vehicle), it will be necessary to accept the speeds of the preceding vehicles encountered on the highway. Nevertheless, the test procedures are intended to be robust enough to be useful even if the speed of the preceding vehicle is not well controlled. The procedures are also intended to be useful even if they are performed on normal grades and curves as encountered on limited access highways. However, curvature and grade will influence quantitative measures of performance to the extent that straight level sections of roadway are desired when consistent numerical results are needed. (For information on the influence of grades see reference [10].) If a confederate vehicle is available, its cruise control should be used for controlling and changing speed. For the ICC FOT [1], it has been convenient to use a '96 Chrysler Concorde as the confederate vehicle. In that way the results are fairly repeatable, both test-to-test and time-to-time.

The following primary data signals (and their measured equivalents) are used in performing and evaluating the test results (see Figures 1 and 2 below):

- Vp = velocity of the preceding vehicle
- Th = the ACC system's headway time setting
- R = range from the front of the following vehicle to the rear of the preceding vehicle
- Rdot = time rate of change of range; relative velocity between the two vehicles
- Vc = an output of the headway control unit; velocity command to the engine controller
- Shift = an output of the headway control unit; shift command to the transmission controller
- δ = percent of full throttle position
- V = velocity of the following vehicle
- Vdot = acceleration (including deceleration) of the following vehicle
- Vset = the driver's desired velocity when the road is clear; the speed set by the driver
- Rh = the desired headway distance determined by Th and Vp

The time histories of these variables provide performance signatures for the characterization tests. Also, R versus Rdot plots are useful for interpreting results [8].

In addition, the computed quantity "Headway Time Margin", symbolized as Thm, is useful for interpreting results The equation for Thm is:

$$Thm = R / V \qquad (1)$$

In steady following with V = Vp, Thm should be equal to the headway time (Th) used in the headway controller. Whether the following vehicle is closing-in (Rdot < 0) or following (Rdot = 0; that is, V = Vp), Thm represents the reaction time within which the following driver would need to match any deceleration profile of the preceding vehicle in order to avoid a crash. The derived quantity Thm is of fundamental importance in this characterization procedure. Specifically, the goal of the headway control system is viewed as trying to cause Thm to approach Th.

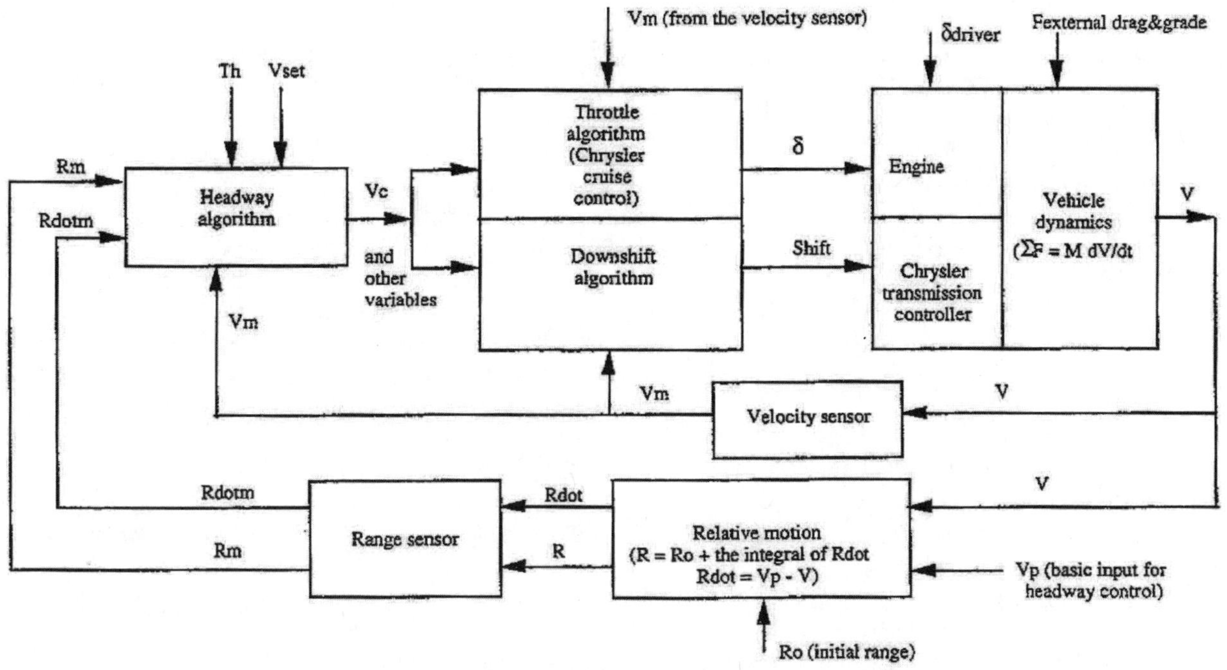

Note: Symbols ending in m refer to the measured version of the variable involved.

Figure 2. Diagram showing elements and interaction variables for an ACC system.

OVERVIEW OF THE ELEMENTS OF THE HEADWAY CONTROL SYSTEM TESTED

The headway control system is viewed as an overall closed-loop control-system composed of the following control units, dynamic elements, and sensors:

- headway controller
- engine controller (including a cruise control system that responds to Vc)
- transmission controller (that responds to shift commands)
- the vehicle as a dynamic body
- the kinematics of relative motion between a preceding and a following vehicle
- a sensor for detecting R and Rdot
- a sensor for detecting V

The interactions (communications) between these elements are illustrated in Figure 2. The quantities appearing on the lines of interaction in the figure are measured and used in the characterization test procedures. Because sensors are an inherent and crucial part of this system and its performance, Figure 2 includes sensor blocks and thereby emphasizes the difference between the inputs and the outputs of the sensors. (Symbols ending in "m" identify those variables associated with sensor outputs.)

The following types of tests have been used to characterize basic functional aspects of the system portrayed in Figure 2.

TEST 1: CLOSING-IN ON A PRECEDING VEHICLE

This test examines basic properties associated with the transition from (a) operating in a manner similar to that of a conventional cruise control to (b) operating in a headway control mode. At long range the ACC system does not adjust speed. However, when the ACC vehicle closes-in on the preceding vehicle, the headway control feature is automatically activated. The system slows the ACC vehicle to the speed of the preceding vehicle and maintains a distance determined by the preselected headway time. Further insight into this test may be obtained by examining the test procedures and example results that follow.

Input -

- Vp = 60 mph (88 ft/s, 26.8 m/s) The preceding vehicle is traveling at a steady speed that is less than that of the approaching ACC vehicle.

Initial conditions for the ACC vehicle -

- V = 70 mph (103 ft/s, 31.3 m/s)
- Vset =70 mph
- Th = 1.4 s (implies 123 ft at 60 mph, 37.5 m at 96.6 kph)
- R > about 350 ft (107 m)

Run conditions - Starting from appropriate initial conditions operate the ACC system until a following condition (V = Vp and R = 1.4 Vp) is established. Other vehicles should not intervene between the ACC vehicle and the preceding vehicle. Ideally the test should be performed on a straight road with no grade. (This test is not a large challenge for this ACC system but a relative velocity (V-Vp) equal to 18 mph (8.0 m/s) would be.)

Example results - Figure 3 has a horizontal axis representing time in minutes. The process of slowing from the ACC vehicle's initial velocity to Vp takes many seconds. This test may take 30 to 60 seconds to perform. In this case the preceding vehicle was sensed before 6.8 minutes and the data are presented for about 0.9 minutes (54 s) — until approximately 7.7 minutes into the trip involving these tests.

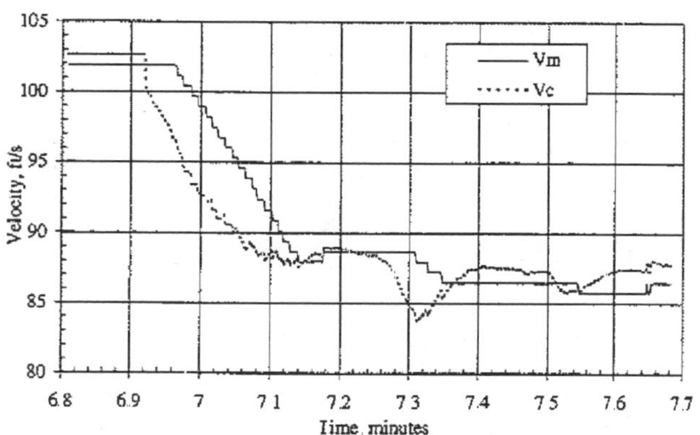

Figure 3. Vm and Vc versus time, closing from long range.

The vertical coordinate in the figure represents velocity in ft/s. Both the measured velocity, Vm, of the ACC vehicle and the velocity command, Vc, signal from the headway controller are plotted versus time in Figure 3. Vm appears as a series of "stair steps" because the least significant bit used in communicating velocity information represents 0.5 mph (0.7 ft/s, 0.22 m/s). When the preceding vehicle is first detected, the ACC vehicle is using Vset and not range and range-rate to determine its speed. Examination of Figure 3 shows that approximately steady following of the preceding vehicle is attained at 7.4 minutes. After 7.4 minutes, Vm and Vc are within about 2 ft/s (0.6 m/s) of each other.

The figure shows that in the start of the test (6.9 - 7.1 minutes) Vm lags Vc because the resolution of velocity (0.7 ft/s plus any dead zone in the cruise control) can mean a certain level of difference even when the ACC vehicle is using Vc to adjust its speed. In addition, there are lags and thresholds in the cruise and engine controllers (the implementation of the throttle algorithm in this ACC vehicle depends upon the hardware and software that comes with the vehicle in its O.E.M. state). Furthermore, the dynamics of the vehicle (essentially, mass times acceleration equals the sum of the forces acting on the vehicle) influences the difference between V and Vc. Due to all of these factors, one may observe time differences in Figure 3 of up to 6 s (0.1 minutes) between when Vc reaches a particular value and when Vm reaches that same value.

(These differences between Vc and Vm may be observed at times throughout all of these tests. Nevertheless, the process of controlling headway is slow enough that it appears that drivers accept these differences as being insignificant to the process of controlling headway. After all, the driver has no idea of the value of Vc. The driver only perceives range, range-rate, and velocity and hence the lag between Vc and Vm would only manifest itself to the driver to the extent that it causes the driver to think that the vehicle responds too late to a preceding vehicle. The results of the FOT will show if drivers think the response is too late but past experience indicates that it is reasonable to expect that many drivers will accept the performance given by this type of system [7].)

Figure 4 is a phase plane plot of range versus range rate for this test. Time is not directly shown in this plot, however the direction of increasing time is shown using arrowheads.

In closing from long range, R decreases as expected. Rdot is the derivative of R and hence is negative for decreasing range.

The range between the vehicles starts at 350 ft (107 m) in the example data. The value of range-rate stays at approximately 15 ft/s (10 mph, 4.5 m/s) until the range decreases to approximately 230 ft (70 m). At this point on the range versus range-rate trajectory, the headway control algorithm starts reducing the speed of the ACC vehicle and thereby causing the range-rate to decrease. In this case the value of range-rate actually fluctuates momentarily rather than changing uniformly towards the end of the test. These types of fluctuations in measured Rdot can be caused by small changes in the speed of the preceding vehicle and/or perturbations caused by grade or wind gusts, or sudden control adjustments occurring because Vm or measured Rdot cross a resolution or dead-zone boundary. The trajectory ends at approximately 125 ft (37.6 m) which is the headway range corresponding to 60 mph and the selected headway time of 1.4 s.

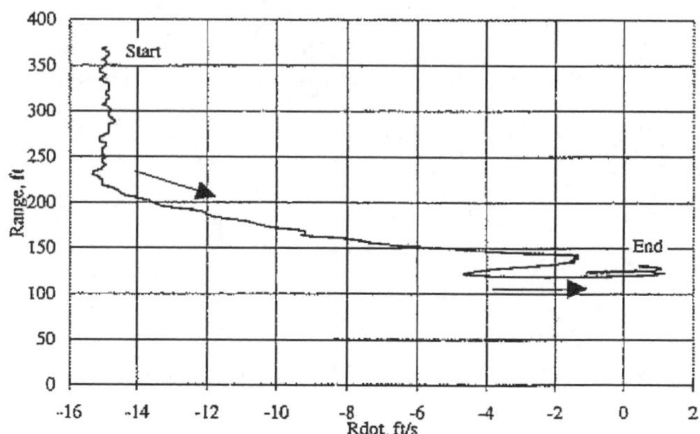

Figure 4. Range versus Range-Rate, closing from long range.

Figure 5 is a plot of headway time margin, Thm, versus time during this test. At the beginning of the sequence (before the data starts) the vehicles are separated by more than 3.5 seconds. At about Thm = 2.3 seconds, the time history of Thm goes from a linear relationship to a curved, somewhat-exponential approach to the selected headway time Th = 1.4 s. The overall resolution of the system is such that typical variations in speed and grade will cause headway time margin Thm to be within 10 percent of Th when nominally steady following conditions are reached. Usually, headway time margin Thm eventually reaches a value that is within ± 0.1 seconds of Th.

TEST 2: CHANGING TO A NEW HEADWAY (Th, HEADWAY TIME ADJUSTMENT)

The purpose of this test is to see how the ACC vehicle responds when headway is adjusted. The vehicle being tested has three settings for headway time. The driver interface contains three buttons for selecting different headway times with the right button labeled "Farther", the left button labeled "Closer", and the center button unlabeled. By pushing these buttons the driver can select nominal headway times of 2.0, 1.0, and 1.4 seconds, respectively. These settings cover the range of headway used by drivers that tend to travel at the speed of adjacent traffic [9]. The test cases (A through C below) pertain to changes between these levels of headway time.

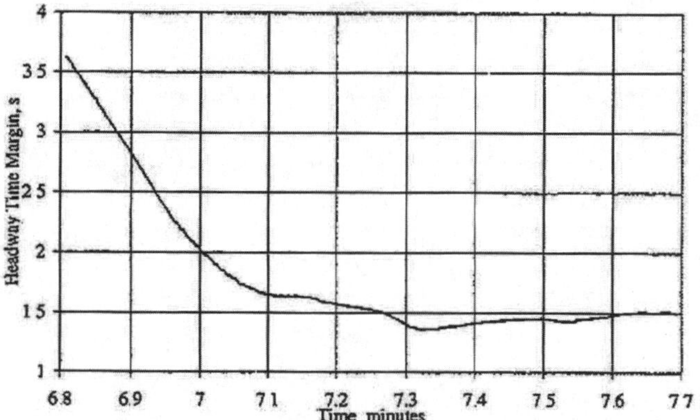

Figure 5. Headway Time Margin (Thm) versus time, closing from long range.

CASE A.

Input -

- Vp = 66 mph (97 ft/s, 29.5 m/s)
- Th = 2.0 s

Initial conditions -

- V = 66 mph
- Vset = 70 mph (103 ft/s, 31.3 m/s)
- R = Th Vp = 194 ft (59.2 m) for 66 mph

Run conditions - Follow the preceding vehicle for several seconds. (That is with V = Vp and R = 2.0 Vp. The range should look fairly constant to the driver.)

When traffic permits, change the Th button setting from farther to closer (2.0 to 1.0 s) and record the transient as well as the ensuing steady state condition. This test will cause the vehicle to change to a shorter range of approximately 97 ft.

Example results - Figure 6 shows time histories of the velocity command Vc and the measured velocity response Vm. Note that the vehicle speeds up and then slows down in order to adjust the headway range between the vehicles. The values of Vc and Vm are approximately equal at the beginning and the end of the test. The test lasts for approximately 0.7 minutes (42 s). The velocity command Vc jumps to the level of the set speed Vset when the shorter headway is requested by the driver because the headway algorithm determines that a large speed change is needed to meet the system's goals. After speeding up to shorten the headway, the ACC vehicle decelerates to re-assume its initial speed value. The maneuver comes to an end as the velocities V and Vc become nearly equal to Vp and a steady state following mode is re-established at the new headway time.

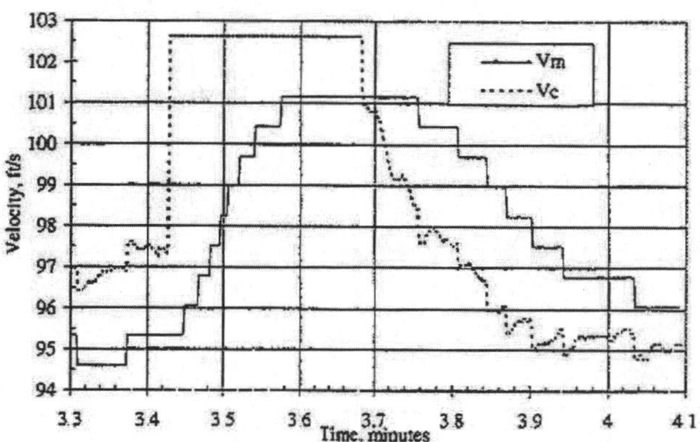

Figure 6. Vc and Vm versus time, changing from Th = 2.0 to 1.0 s.

Figure 7 is a plot of range versus range rate for this test. The range decreases to satisfy the reduced Th selection. Since the velocity of the preceding vehicle is nominally constant, the relative acceleration is approximately equal to the acceleration of the following ACC vehicle. For this test the most negative value of Rdot is approximately -6 ft/s (-1.8 m/s) and the change in range is approximately 120 ft (36m).

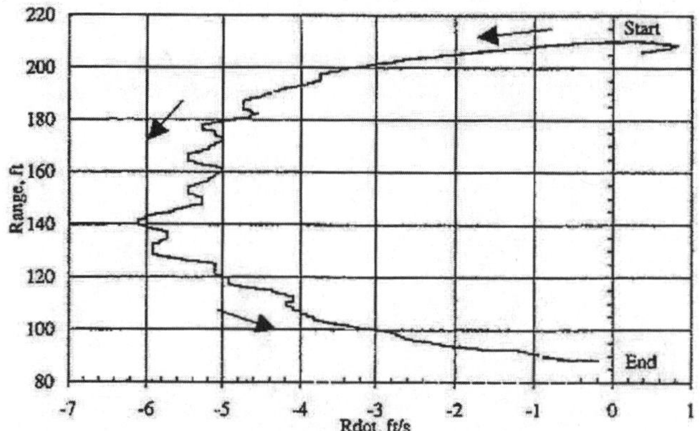

Figure 7. Range versus Range-Rate, changing from Th = 2.0 to 1.0 s.

Figure 8 shows the headway time margin Thm = R/V. Aside from some rounding of the wave form at the beginning and end of the transient response, the headway time margin changes fairly linearly during the transient with a slope of approximately 3.14 s/minute for this test.

CASE B. (Inverse of case A, initial Th = 1.0 s and final Th = 2.0 s)

Input -

- Vp = 66 mph (97 ft/s, 29.5 m/s)
- Th = 2.0 s, from Th = 1.0 s initially

Initial conditions -

- V = 66 mph
- Vset = 70 mph (103 ft/s, 31.3 m/s)
- R = Th Vp = 97 ft (29.6 m) for Th = 1.0 s initially

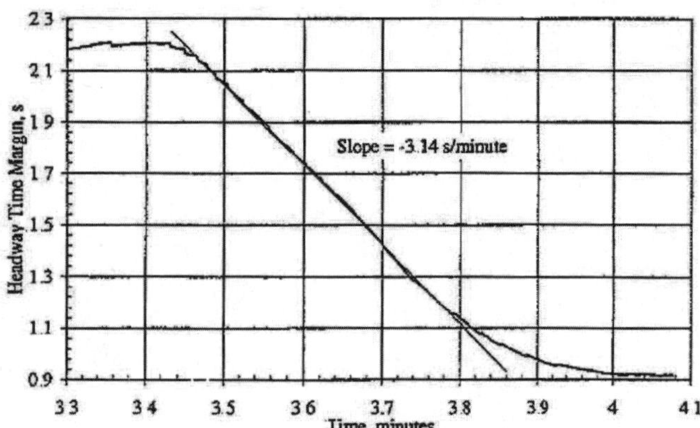

Figure 8. Headway Time Margin (Thm) versus time, changing from Th = 2.0 to 1.0 s.

Run conditions - same general idea as Case A except this case will cause the vehicle to change from a short to a longer range

Example results - Figure 9 shows Vm and Vc. At the start of the data presented, Vc is much less than Vm because the headway time has just been changed from 1.0 to 2.0 seconds. At about 5.8 seconds, Vc and Vm are about equal but Vc is on its way back up to 66 mph and Vm is still decreasing as needed to increase range. There is about a 1 or 2 ft/s difference between Vm and Vc at the end of the data portrayed in the figure. This is within the velocity correction capability (dead zone) of the system.

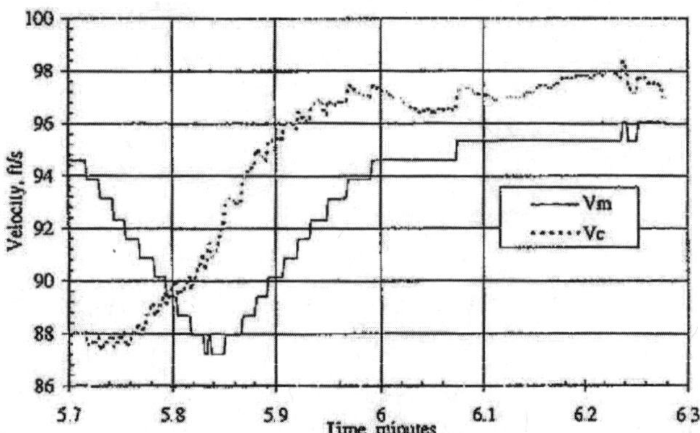

Figure 9. Vc and Vm versus time, changing from Th = 1.0 to 2.0 s.

Figure 10 presents the range versus range-rate diagram for this example. The maximum range-rate is 8 ft/s This means that the ACC vehicle slows down considerably as it widens the headway range by approximately 100 ft (30.5 m) in this case. Examination of the data for cases A and B indicates that this system increased headway (from Th = 1.0 to 2.0 s) in approximately 1/3 less time than it required to shorten headway by the same increment (compare Figures 8 and 11 as well as Figures 7 and 10).

Examination of Figure 11 indicates that the maximum slope of the headway time margin is approximately 6.3 seconds/minute, or in other words, the slew rate employed in increasing headway time is about twice as fast as that employed in decreasing headway time.

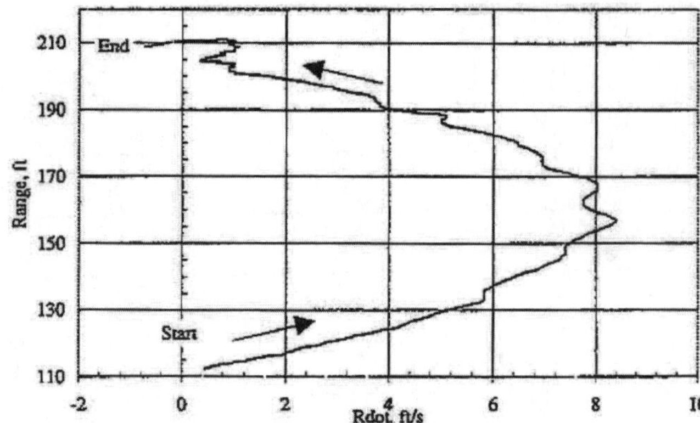

Figure 10. Range versus Range-Rate, changing from Th = 1.0 to 2.0 s.

CASE C. (Same as Case A except final Th = 1.4 s)

Example results - None shown because they are much like those for Case A except the change is smaller. (The test simply confirms that when the button for Th =1.4 s is pressed, the system performs as it should.)

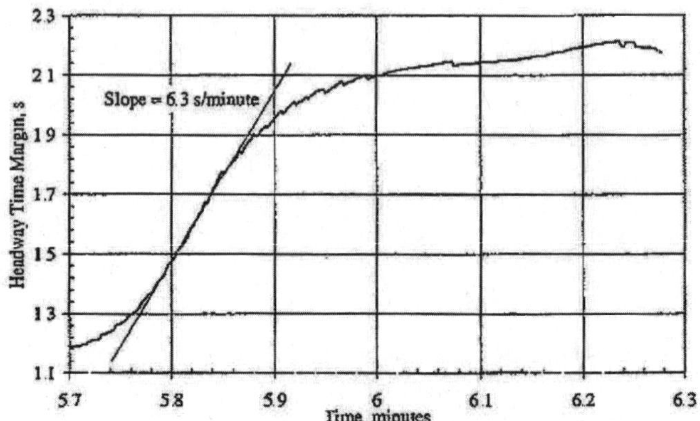

Figure 11. Headway Time Margin (Thm) versus time, changing from Th = 1.0 to 2.0 s.

TEST 2 SUMMARY - The series of test results presented in Figures 6 through 11 indicate the nature of the changes in range and range-rate that accompany changes in headway time. The range versus range-rate diagrams indicate that the vehicle slows down or speeds up as needed to achieve the new headway. A plot of R/V versus time is useful for examining the rate at which the headway change takes place. At steady state operation, R/V equals the headway time requested by the driver. At the end of the transient to steady headway, the R/V signature should not show much over- or undershoot of the steady state headway level. Preliminary results from the operational test program and other studies [7] indicate that these observed transition times from one headway time to another are generally acceptable to many drivers. However, it is not known what values of transition times are preferred by various types of drivers whose driving styles range from aggressive to passive behavior.

TEST 3: LEAD VEHICLE DECELERATING.

The purpose of this test is to see that the controller responds properly when the lead vehicle decelerates moderately.

Input - The velocity of the preceding vehicle is changed during this test. The preceding vehicle begins by driving in conventional cruise control at 66 mph in **3rd gear**. The driver presses the coast button until 60 mph is reached. The coast button is released. The lead vehicle maintains 60 mph until the test is finished.

Initial conditions for the ACC vehicle -

- V = 66 mph
- Vset = 70 mph
- Th = 1.4 s (implies Rh = Th Vp = 135.5 ft, 41.3 m)
- The ACC vehicle should be following the preceding vehicle (that is, V = Vp and R = 1.4 Vp)

Run conditions - The ACC vehicle is to slow down in response to the deceleration of the preceding vehicle. The run is to be continued until steady headway-keeping is re-established. (V = Vp and R = 1.4 Vp) A level section of roadway is desirable if repeatable, quantitative results are required

Example results - In Figure 12, the velocity command Vc starts out approximately equal to Vm. At about 9.64 minutes, Vc decreases because it is following the reduction in Vp from 66 to 60 mph (96.8 to 88 ft/s, 29.5 to 26.8 m/s). Vm drops below 88 ft/s before recovering to approximately 87 ft/s at the end of the test data. The vehicle speed needs to drop below 88 ft/s in order to re-establish the selected headway time. (See Figure 14 to see the excursion in headway time margin.) This maneuver causes a downshift from fourth to third gear in order to slow the ACC vehicle. The downshift command occurs at approximately 9.81 minutes. It lasts for 4.5 seconds.

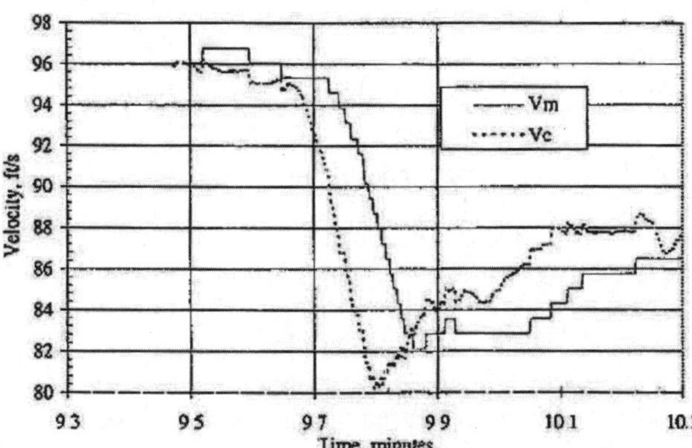

Figure 12. Vm and Vc versus time, lead vehicle decelerating.

The range versus range-rate diagram for this test is presented in Figure 13. These data show that range rate decreases to a minimum of approximately -7 ft/s while range is decreasing, and, increases to a maximum of about 3 ft/s while range is increasing. The minimum range is 91 feet on the way to a final range of about 137 ft.

The minimum range does not occur at Rdotm equal to zero because there is about a second lag in Rdotm compared to the derivative of Rm as measured by the sensor. Nevertheless, the ACC system performs its intended function. The system re-establishes an acceptable headway range and range-rate in response to a speed change from 66 to 60 mph by the preceding vehicle.

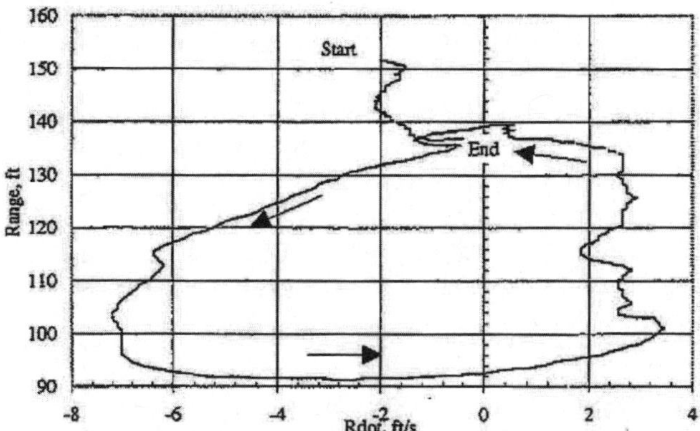

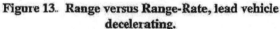

Figure 13. Range versus Range-Rate, lead vehicle decelerating.

Figure 14 presents the time history of the headway time margin Rm/Vm. In this case the headway time margin dips to 1.05 seconds before it increases to over 1.4 seconds. Changing from 1.6 seconds to around 1.4 seconds will take a long time because changes due to errors in range (with Vm = Vp) have a time constant of about 11 seconds in this system.

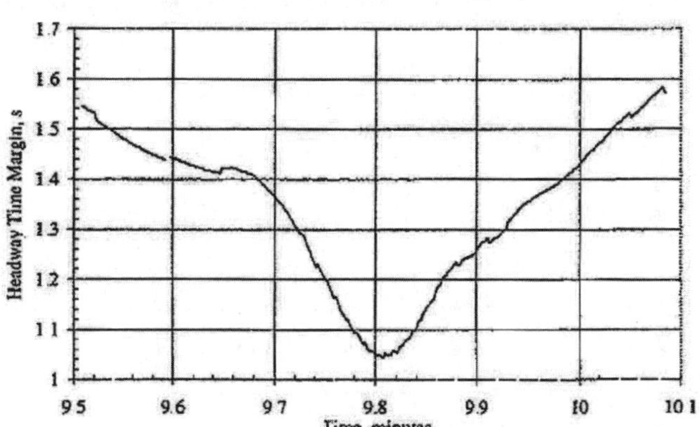

Figure 11. Headway Time Margin (Thm) versus time, lead vehicle decelerating.

TEST 4: CUTTING BEHIND THE LEAD VEHICLE.

The purpose of this test is to check the controller's response when a preceding vehicle suddenly appears in the path of the ACC vehicle. A downshift command is to be expected from this system configuration. (A similar test could be arranged with the "preceding" vehicle cutting in front of the ACC vehicle and then slowing down, but the logistics of this arrangement are difficult to control. Of course, the cut-in by the preceding vehicle cannot be done practically without a confederate preceding vehicle. Furthermore, since the characterization value of the test is equal in either scenario, it is preferable to do the easier test.)

Input -

- Vp = 60 mph

Initial conditions for the ACC vehicle -

- V = 60 mph
- Vset = 70 mph
- Th = 1.4 s
- The equipped vehicle should be following. (V = Vp and R = 1.4 Vp)

Run conditions - The driver of the ACC vehicle is to move to an open adjacent lane and start to overtake the preceding vehicle. When the range gets to approximately 2/3 to 1/2 of the original gap, the driver of the following vehicle is to pull back in behind the preceding vehicle. The test is continued until following is re-established or until the driver brakes.

Example results - The data shown in Figure 15 start at the time when the driver of the ACC vehicle has just pulled in behind the preceding vehicle at a close range. This maneuver simulates the sudden cut-in of a slower moving vehicle in front of the ACC vehicle. (Such a situation often occurs during merging at entrance ramps.)

The measured velocity decreases during the first part of the headway adjustment. Then the commanded speed rises to match the speed of the preceding vehicle and is trailed by the measured speed

There is a command to shift to third gear at about the 15.6 minute mark. The down shift lasts for 6.9 seconds until about the 15.7 minute mark.

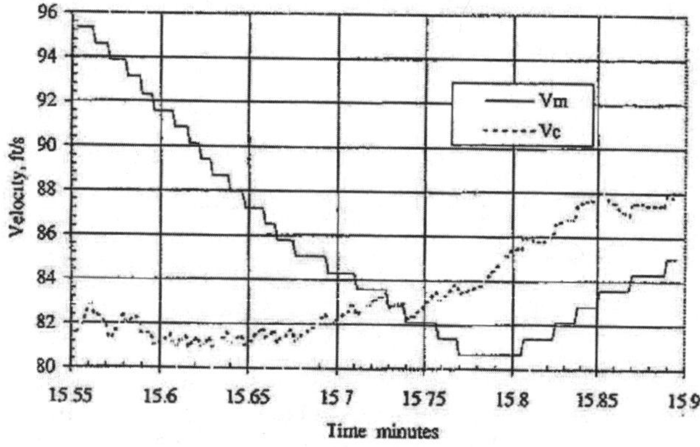

Figure 15. Vm and Vc versus time, cutting behind the preceding vehcile.

The range versus range-rate diagram (Figure 16) shows that the minimum Rdotm is about -12 ft/s in this test. The maximum is about 6 ft/s. In this case there was a relatively near encounter with the range minimizing at less than 70 ft. (Nevertheless, this rather short range for ACC driving is not extraordinary relative to the minimum headway values employed in normal driving. Just as in normal driving a sudden deceleration of the preceding vehicle could precipitate a crash if the driver of the ACC vehicle is not very alert.) Starting from where the preceding vehicle is first detected by the sensor, the test will produce about 3/4 of a complete loop in the range versus range-rate diagram. The final range is approximately what it was when the test started. (The data do not show the range when the test started because the preceding vehicle is not in view of the sensor when the ACC vehicle is in the adjacent lane.)

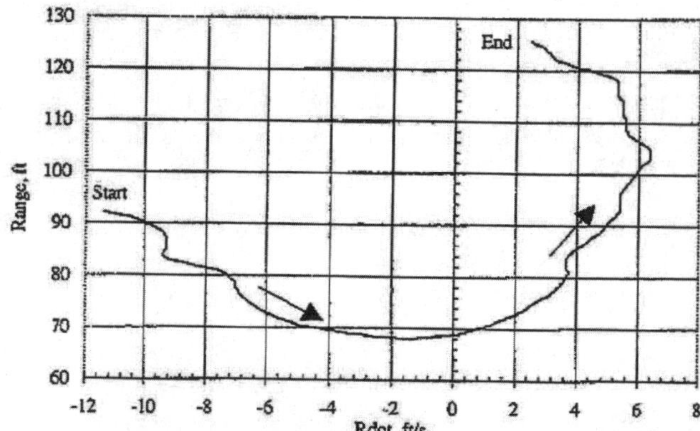

Figure 16. Range versus Range-Rate, cutting behind the preceding vehicle.

Figure 17 shows that the headway time margin dips to approximately 0.76 seconds then returns to the neighborhood of 1.5 seconds. The increasing portion of the Thm response is similar to that shown earlier for cases in which the headway time abruptly increased.

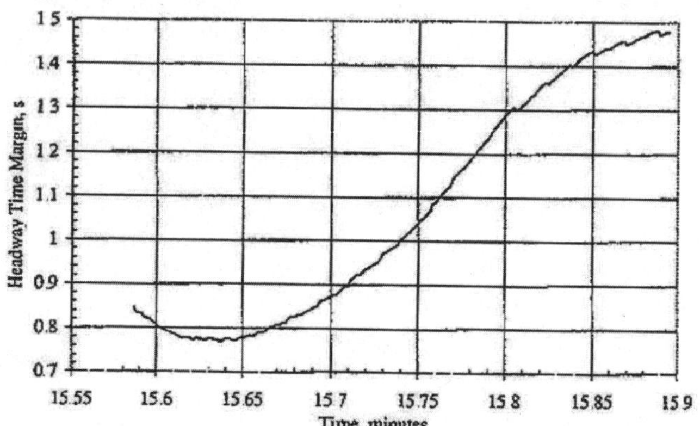

Figure 17. Headway Time Margin versus time, cutting behind the preceding vehicle.

MANUALLY ACCELERATING.

The purpose of this test is to exercise the accelerator pedal override capability as well as to check the ability of the system to correct for a moderately-near encounter. This test may cause the control system to downshift the transmission while the driver is accelerating the ACC vehicle. Nevertheless, once the accelerator peddle is released by the driver, the ACC vehicle should slow down towards a proper following condition in a manner that is characteristic of the operation of this headway control system.

Input -

- Vp = 60 mph

Initial conditions for the ACC vehicle -

- V = 60 mph
- Vset = 70 mph
- Th = 1.4 s (implies Th Vp = 123 ft)

- The ACC vehicle should be following. (V = Vp and R = 1.4 Vp)

Run Conditions - The driver of the ACC vehicle is to accelerate and partially overtake the preceding vehicle. When the range gets to approximately 2/3 of the original gap, the driver of the following vehicle is to release the accelerator pedal. The test is continued until steady- state following is re-established or until the driver brakes. (This test could be viewed as an aborted passing maneuver but it is probably better to view it as a means to simulate a near encounter. In practical operation, near encounters can happen for many reasons including merges or other events that cause the sensor to pick up a preceding vehicle for the first time at close range.)

Example results - The data in Figure 18 indicate that Vm increases rapidly at the start of the test. This is due to the driver pushing on the accelerator pedal. Vm starts to decrease rapidly when the driver releases the accelerator pedal. At this time Vc is much less than Vm and it also decreases rapidly until it reaches a commanded speed of about 78 to 79 ft/s. Vm eventually reaches about 79 ft/s and then increases towards Vc which has reached a fairly steady value near 88 ft/s.

There is a downshift command at about 12.92 minutes. It lasts for 9.2 seconds. The downshift accounts for the relatively rapid change from acceleration to deceleration of the ACC vehicle during the time from 12.9 to 13.1 minutes.

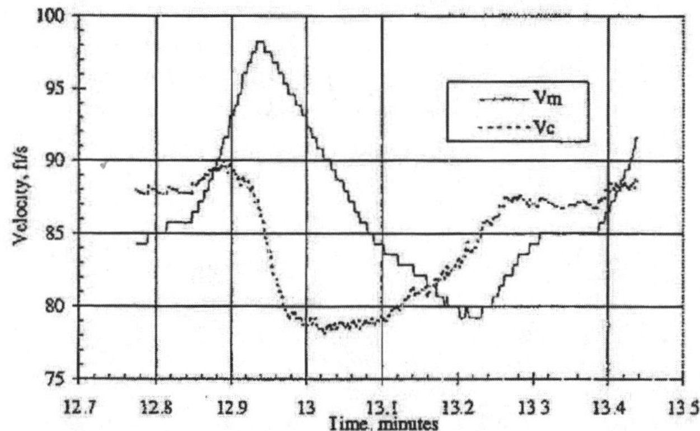

Figure 18. Vm and Vc versus time, manually accelerating.

Data for range versus range-rate are presented in Figure 19. These data show that the trajectory in the range versus range-rate space is nearly a closed-loop. (Ideally it would be a closed loop.) The minimum Rdotm is approximately -12 ft/s and the maximum is about 8 ft/s. The minimum range is close to 50 ft (—perhaps a little closer than the test driver intended but not something that would scare the driver.)

The last 3/4 of the trajectory in Figure 19 has a form similar to the trajectory shown in Figure 16. These maneuvers tend to be very similar after either their cut-in or accelerating phases. The cut-in or accelerating actions simply set up the conditions for the remainder of the test. (Perhaps the cut-in test could be omitted without losing any valuable information with regard to checking the operation of this ACC system. The manually accelerating test is much easier to perform than the cutting-in behind test, especially if other vehicles are using adjacent lanes.)

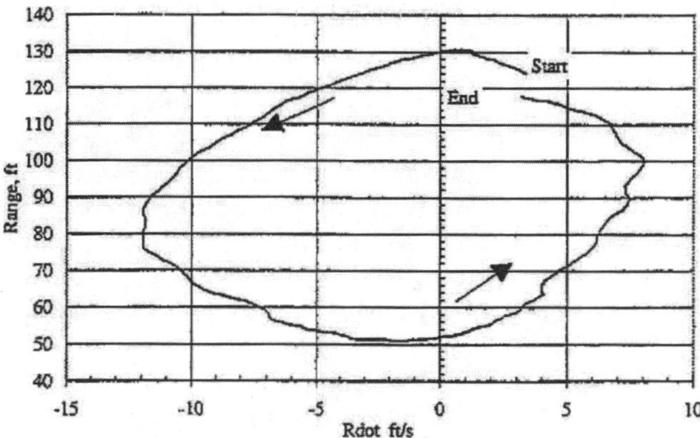

Figure 19. Range versus Range-Rate, manually accelerating.

Figure 20 shows that the headway time margin goes from about 1.5 seconds to a low of about 0.6 seconds and then back to about 1.4 seconds in this test. This is all done in approximately 0.45 minutes (27 seconds).

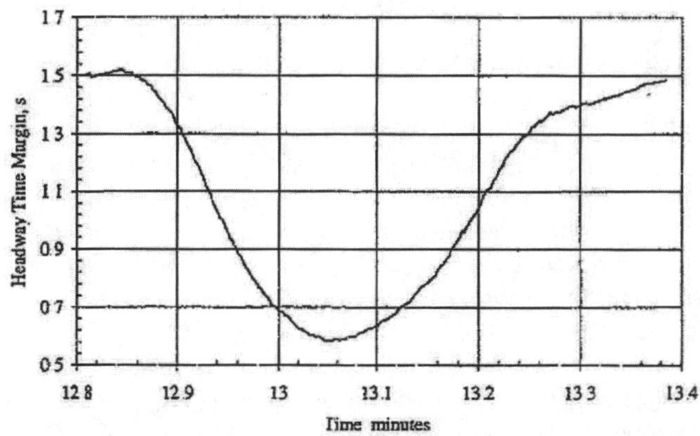

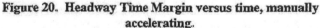

Figure 20. Headway Time Margin versus time, manually accelerating.

CLOSING REMARKS

The test scenarios presented in this paper serve as a practicable means for characterizing and periodically reconfirming the performance of the ACC vehicles used in the field operational test that is currently underway [1]. They provide performance signatures that can be examined to quantify features that serve as performance measures for ACC vehicles. Since the test conditions do not control for grade and traffic condition, the results will differ from time to time and place to place. Nevertheless, since the functionality of adaptive cruise control does not depend upon high levels of performance from a control system perspective, the results of these tests are sufficient to answer basic questions concerning the control algorithms such as: Does the vehicle slow down when it should? Does the vehicle speed up as it should? Does headway time adjust as it should?

These tests can be done on curves or with vehicles in adjacent lanes if the sensor operates properly. If the sensor is out of alignment (or not functioning properly on curves), it will be apparent to the driver as well as producing "glitches" in the test data. Furthermore, the driver readily senses if targets are missed. Fortunately, the sensor seldom misses targets and the driver appears to have sufficient time to observe such situations if they occur.

In summary, the types of tests described in this paper indicate that this ACC system reaches selected headway times with a resolution of approximately ten percent. In the tests proposed here, the system is able to correct for disturbances in speed or range-rate that cause range-rate to reach a closing rate of approximately 10 mph (-15 ft/s, - 4.5 m/s). The system is able to keep the headway time margin above 0.6 seconds in the sudden encounters involved in these tests. Changes in headway time are achieved smoothly with little overshoot or undershoot. When closing in from long range, the ACC system starts to adjust speed at 200 to 300 feet away (depending upon the level of headway time selected) when the preceding vehicle is traveling at highway speeds. And finally, the ACC system downshifts when it needs to achieve a higher deceleration than that available from the natural retardation of the vehicle.

Procedures to account for advances in sensing, control authority, and communicating with the driver.

Anticipated advances (including optimistic dreams) for ACC systems include sensors that can identify almost all objects in the projected lane of travel, controllers and actuators that allow the brakes to be used to achieve greater control authority, and driver interfaces that provide the driver with greater situation awareness and warnings of impending risks. As the capabilities of ACC systems advance, the ability of the driver to supervise and to compensate for situations that are beyond the system's state of intelligence will lessen. It may be that drivers simply will not have time to react if a high level of deceleration is vested in a system having imperfect sensing and decision making performance. A prime example of concern involves sudden severe braking as may result from a false alarm. Within the intelligence built into the ACC system, a situation that appears benign to a person could be treated as an immediate threat. A challenge for developing tests for more advanced systems may not lie in developing control system specifications in a conventional manner but rather in developing specifications regarding an intelligence test involving sensing skills, recognition abilities, decisions concerning control actions, and finally the ability to act as sensibly and effectively as good drivers do now.

ACKNOWLEDGMENTS

The Intelligent Cruise Control (ICC) FOT is sponsored by the National Highway Traffic Safety Administration (NHTSA) in a cooperative agreement partnership with the University of Michigan Transportation Research Institute (UMTRI), Leica AG, Michigan Department of Transportation, and Haugen Associates. The Volpe National Transportation Research Center is serving as the independent evaluator for NHTSA and the U.S DOT's Joint Program Office in this FOT.

The Chrysler Corporation provided communication access (inputs and outputs) to their cruise control (engine controller) and their transmission controller so that these control units could be used in assembling a prototype ACC system.

REFERENCES

1. "Intelligent Cruise Control (ICC) Field Operational Test." National Highway Traffic Safety Administration, Cooperative Agreement No.: DTNH22-95-H-07428, September 30, 1995.

2. Fancher, P., Ervin, R., Bareket, Z., Johnson, G.E., Trefalt, M., Tiedecke, J., Hagleitner, W., "Intelligent Cruise Control: Performance Studies Based Upon an Operating Prototype", *Proceedings of IVHS America 1994 Annual Meeting,* pp. 391-399, Atlanta GA.

3. Sayer, J.R. et al., "Automatic Target Acquisition Autonomous Intelligent Cruise Control (AICC): Driver Comfort, Acceptance, and Performance in Highway Traffic", *Proceedings of the Society of Automotive Engineers International Congress and Exposition,* SAE Technical Paper No. 950970, Special Publication SP-1088, Detroit Michigan.

4. Becker, S., et al., "Summary of Experience with Autonomous Intelligent Cruise Control (AICC)", Parts 1 and 2, First World Congress on Applications of Transport Telematics and Intelligent Vehicle-Highway Systems, pp 1828-1843, Paris France.

5. Watanabe, T., Kishimoto, N., Hayafune, K., Yamada, K., Maede, N., "Development of an Intelligent Cruise Control System. "Steps Forward", *Proceedings of the Second World Congress on Intelligent Transport Systems,* 1995, Yokohama Japan.

6. Winner, H., Witte, S., Uhler, W., Lichtenberg, B., "Adaptive Cruise Control System Aspects and Development Trends", International Congress & Exposition Detroit, Michigan, February 26-27, 1996. SAE Technical Paper Series #961010.

7. Fancher, P., Bareket, Z., Sayer, J., Johnson, G., Ervin, R., Mefford, M., "Fostering Development, Evaluation, and Deployment of Forward Crash Avoidance Systems (FOCAS)", Annual Research Report ARR-5-15-95, NHTSA Contract No DTNH22-94-Y-47016, May 1995.

8. Fancher, P., Bareket, Z., "Evaluating Headway Control Using Range Versus Range-Rate Relationships", *Vehicle System Dynamics,* 1994, pp. 575-596.

9. Fancher, P., Sayer, J., Bareket, Z., "A Comparison of Manual Versus Automatic Control of Headway as a Function of Driver Characteristics", 3rd Annual World Congress on Intelligent Transport System, Orlando, FL, October 14-18, 1996.

10. Ervin, R., Stein, J., Bogard, S., Zachariou, N., Kleinsorge, K., "Evaluating Adaptive Cruise Control Designs In Light of the Stochastic Nature of Encroachment Conflicts", 3rd Annual World Congress on Intelligent Transport System, Orlando, FL, October 14-18, 1996.

970170

Driver Car Following Behavior Under Test Track and Open Road Driving Condition

R. Wade Allen and Raymond E. Magdaleno
Systems Technology, Inc

Colleen Serafin, Steven Eckert, and Tom Sieja
Ford Motor Co.

ABSTRACT

This paper describes the results of an experiment concerning driver behavior in car following tasks. The motivation for this experiment was a desire to understand typical driver car following behavior as a guide for setting the automatic control characteristics of an ACC (Adaptive Cruise Control) system. Testing was conducted under both test track and open road driving conditions. The results indicate that car following is carried out under much lower bandwidth conditions than typical steering processes. Dynamic analysis shows driver time delay in response to lead vehicle velocity change on the order of several seconds. Typical longitudinal acceleration distributions show standard deviations of less than 0.05 g (acceleration due to gravity). Distributions of time headway (following distance divided by following vehicle speed) show conservative behavior by some subjects while others had median values on the order of 1.0 second, and significant occurrences of following between 0.5 and 1.0 seconds.

INTRODUCTION

The driving task can be broadly categorized according to control, guidance and navigation functions that determine vehicle path and speed profile. Control covers psychomotor functions that stabilize vehicle path and speed against various aerodynamic and road disturbances and assist in traffic interactions such as car following. Guidance involves perceptual and psychomotor functions coordinated to follow delineated pathways, adhere to implied speed profiles, interact with traffic and avoid hazards. Traffic control devices, including road markings and signs provide a significant input to the guidance level in path following and speed selection. Navigation involves higher level cognitive functions applied to path and route selection and decisions regarding higher level traffic interactions (e.g., avoiding congestion).

A considerable range of past research has focused on driver steering control and following delineated pathways with more limited attention to speed selection and control. The research discussed in this paper concerns driver headway and speed control during car following. The speed control aspects of car following can relate generally to driver closed loop response to aerodynamic disturbances and roadway geometry. The guidance aspects of car following include perception of lead vehicle headway and relative velocity and closed loop control of following distance. This research was motivated by a desire to understand the dynamics of driver headway control as a guide for setting the automatic control characteristics of Adaptive Cruise Control (ACC) Systems.

BACKGROUND

Past research on car following has dealt with driver headway control models and measurements of driver behavior. Pipes [1] carried out fundamental work in this area, and Bekey, et al. [2] provided a useful summary of past work and further analysis on the general problem of driver lead car following. These early control models assumed that during car following the driver attempts to minimize velocity differences with a lead vehicle (i.e., a well defined stimulus). Recent work on ACC (Adaptive Cruise Control) systems by Fancher, Bareket, et al., (3) and Sayer, Fancher, et al., [4] has produced some data on velocity, range and range rate distributions of drivers during car following.

Data collected by Chandler, et al. [5] has shown that the driver can be characterized according to a closed loop bandwidth (gain or crossover frequency) of 0.37 rad/sec and a time delay of 1.5 seconds in responding to changes in lead vehicle velocity. Note that this bandwidth is a factor of 10 slower than compensatory steering bandwidth, e.g. Allen [6]. Torf and Duckstein [7] also have collected data on driver detection times for several levels of lead car acceleration. They found detection times of 1.9 seconds for a lead car acceleration of 2.5 ft/sec^2, and 2.5 seconds at an acceleration of 1.6 ft/sec^2. By regression analysis they also determined that response time decreased by 0.8 seconds for each increase of 1 ft/sec^2 in lead car acceleration. This may relate to the amount of time required to sense a velocity change (i.e., higher accelerations give more rapid change in lead car range and range rate).

SIMPLE CROSSOVER MODEL — The early speed control models cited above [1,2,5] can be summarized with the classical Crossover Model of McRuer and Krendal [8] as illustrated in Figure 1. Here, the driver responds to velocity errors with throttle commands such that vehicle longitudinal acceleration is proportional to the error. In this model the driver/vehicle response is simplified to a gain (the proportionality constant between velocity errors and longitudinal acceleration), time delay between velocity error and acceleration, and a pure integration to derive vehicle speed from longitudinal acceleration.

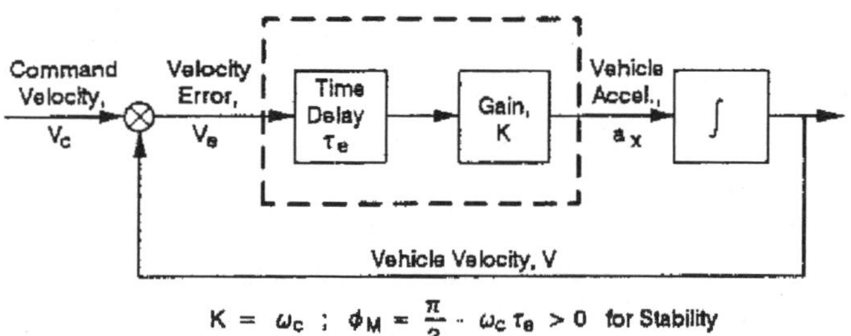

Figure 1. Simple "Crossover" Control Model for Speed Control

The Crossover Model for human control systems is efficient for experimental measurement as it can be compactly characterized by two parameters, the gain or crossover frequency (ω_c) and the time delay (τ_e)[8]. If we take the Fourier transform, e.g. Truxal [9], of the equations describing the Figure 1 system we have the following transfer function:

$$F\left(\frac{V}{V_e}\right)_{j\omega} = \omega_c e^{-j\omega\tau_e}$$

where (1)

$$\omega_c = K \text{ and } j = \sqrt{-1}$$

In the crossover model characterization of manual control system dynamic behavior, crossover frequency is a measure of the system (driver/vehicle) bandwidth, and the product of crossover frequency and time delay is a measure of system damping:

Crossover Frequency = $\omega_c \approx$ Bandwidth

Phase Margin (system damping) = $\phi_M = \pi/2 - \omega_C x \tau_e$ (2)

In the above equation ω_C is given in radians/second, τ_e is expressed in seconds and ϕ_M is given in radians. When Phase Margin goes much below unity (1.0 radian or about 60°), the system response is oscillatory. Phase Margin goes to zero, the system becomes unstable.

The Crossover Model is a convenient means for simply characterizing manual control system behavior that can easily be derived from FFT transfer function data. Even though we may postulate more complicated engineering control system models, the crossover model provides a simple basis for summarizing the dynamic behavior of a compensatory system. These two key parameters, crossover frequency (ω_C) and phase margin (ϕ_M), provide a means for characterizing the bandwidth and damping of the closed loop manual control system that can be conveniently statistically analyzed to provide a summary of typical behavior and variation across a group of subjects.

In this research it is of interest to simply characterize the dynamic coupling between the following and lead vehicles. The above crossover model parameters can also be interpreted in terms of a closed loop natural frequency by using the Pade approximation for a time delay, e.g. Truxel [9]:

$$e^{-j\omega\tau_e} = \left(j\omega\tau_e +\right)^{-1}$$

where (3)

$$j = \sqrt{-1}$$

Given the above approximation, we can then derive the closed loop transfer function which is given by:

$$\frac{\omega_c / \tau_e}{(j\omega)^2 + j\omega/\tau_e + \omega_c/\tau_e} \quad (4)$$

where the closed loop natural frequency (ω_n) and damping ration can be expressed as follows:

$$\omega_n = \sqrt{\omega_c / \tau_e}; \zeta_n = 1/2\sqrt{\omega_c \tau_e} \quad (5)$$

EXTENDED CROSSOVER MODEL — The above simple crossover model can be extended to include maintenance of a desired headway as illustrated in Figure 2. Here, a command feed-forward for headway has been added with the additional parameter a which is low frequency (i.e., long time constant) effect. The extended crossover model controls to minimize velocity errors (V_e) just as with the simple crossover model. In addition, the extended crossover model also develops an additional headway error term (R_e) which is also minimized, but at a much slower rate than the velocity errors.

The extended crossover model has a bandwidth that is approximately equal to the simple crossover model. Because of the higher frequency dynamics of the low frequency a term the phase margin now has an extra component:

Phase Margin = $\phi_M = \pi/2 - \omega_c x \tau_e - \alpha/\omega_c$ (6)

In the above formula, α is expressed in the units 1/second and can be interpreted as the low frequency bandwidth for headway distance control. This extra phase component allows a simple means for identifying the α parameter in transfer function phase data.

APPROACH

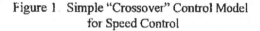

The data processing and analysis used in this paper involves frequency domain procedures designed to identify transfer functions and parameters for crossover models described above. These procedures start with time histories of key

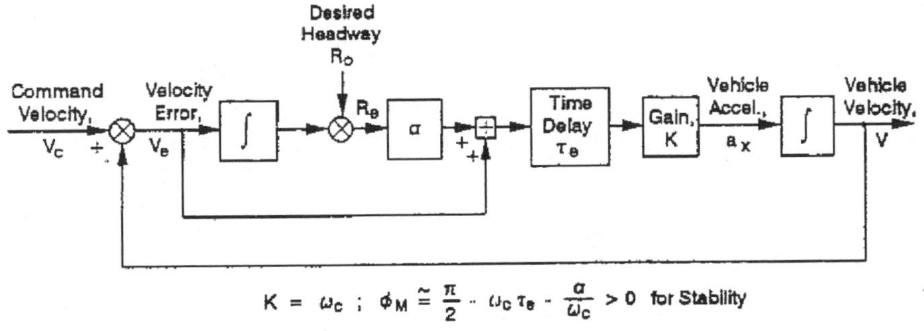

Figure 2. Extended Crossover Model for Speed and Headway Control

variables (e.g., throttle, speed, range) that define the basic human/machine system dynamic response. These time histories are then transformed using FFT (Fast Fourier Transform) procedures to give frequency domain transfer functions between key variables as discussed in Bendat and Piersol [10] and Randall [11]. The FFT procedures are analogous to linear regression analysis procedures that define the relationship between a dependent variable and an independent variable in terms of correlated and uncorrelated components.

With FFT analysis the correlated response between independent and dependent time histories then defines a transfer function that expresses an input/output relationship (e.g. driver throttle response to changes in lead vehicle headway) between key system variables. Given a transfer function, parameter identification procedures can then be used to identify key system characteristics such as driver/vehicle time delay and gain in response to lead vehicle velocity changes.

Measured time histories of key variables were recorded during experimental runs and converted to binary form including scaling constants to allow for maximum efficiency in processing and storage. The time histories were initially manually screened to locate regions of artifact free response, and to screen out segments containing drop outs in sensor response. This was particularly important regarding the range sensor data in both the test track and open highway experiments. The range signal would drop out if range became too large or a combination of lateral position and road curvature caused the lead target vehicle to exceed the limits of the sensor azimuth field of view.

Good sections of time history response were identified for further FFT processing. Additional preprocessing was carried out by applying taper windows to minimize transient artifacts associated with selecting data time windows where the time histories are abruptly started and stopped. The data were then processed by an advanced FFT routine that provided power spectra and transfer functions and coherence functions between selected variables. The coherence function is the equivalent of a linear correlation function, and defines what percentage of an output signal in a given frequency region is linearly correlated with an input signal. Typically the coherence values are used to select transfer function points that are reliable (high coherence) and reject unreliable measurements (low coherence) as indicated in the example transfer function plot in Figure 3.

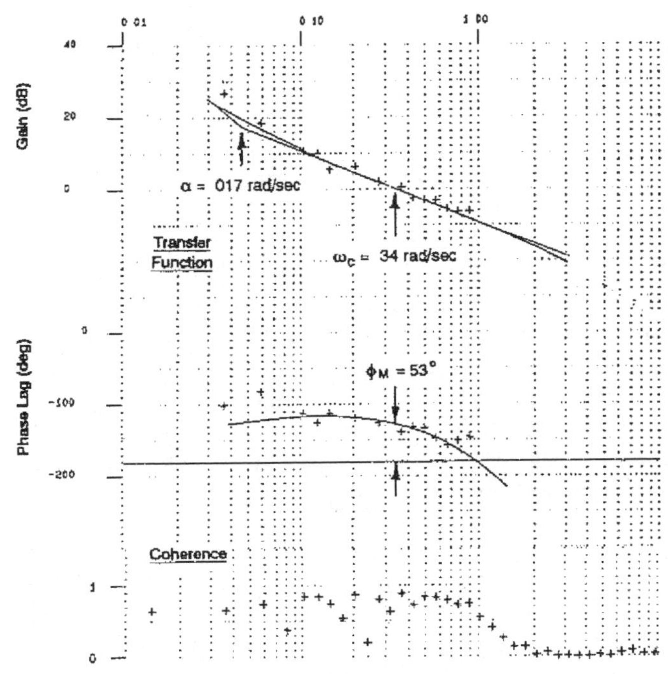

Figure 3. Example Plot of FFT Results and Crossover Model Parameter Identification

Transfer function and coherence data were plotted as indicated further on to highlight reliable transfer function data and to allow for simplified parameter identification. If it is assumed that the driver/vehicle system can be described by the simple gain and time delay model used by previous investigators, then these parameters can be easily identified from transfer function plots such as Figure 3. The gain is identified from the amplitude plot at the zero dB crossover point, and the time delay is obtained from the phase plot in the region of crossover. The α parameter in the extended crossover model is identified in the low frequency region well below crossover based on increased phase shift with decreasing frequency. The Figure 3 transfer function was derived by taking the ratio between the range signal FFT (driver input) and following vehicle velocity (driver/vehicle response) and analytically accounting for the kinematic integration between velocity and range.

An example of the vehicle dynamics for longitudinal speed control are illustrated by the transfer function plot in Figure 4. This vehicle transfer function was derived by taking

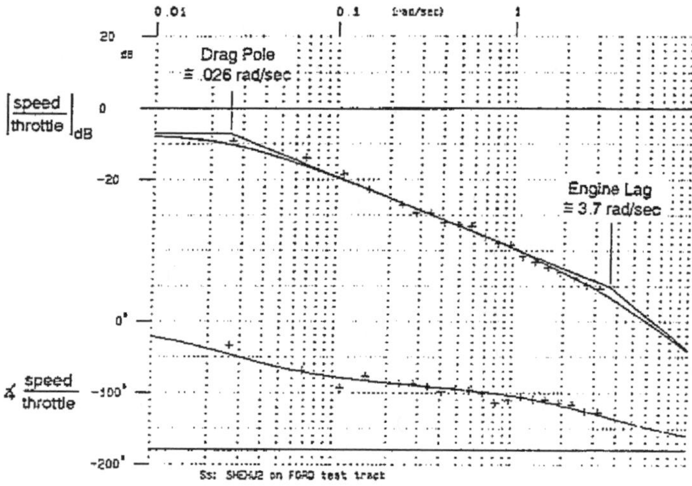

Figure 4. FFT Identification of Longitudinal Vehicle Dynamics Transfer Function

the ratio between the vehicle velocity FFT (output) and the throttle signal (input). The transfer function model fit to the FFT data involves a low frequency pole associated with vehicle aerodynamic drag and a high frequency pole associated with engine throttle response lag. The Figure 4 data show that longitudinal vehicle dynamics can be approximated over a wide frequency range by a pure integration as assumed in the crossover models of Figures 1 and 2.

Distributions of longitudinal acceleration and time headway (lead vehicle range divided by following vehicle headway) were derived directly from any artifact free time history data. In long test track or open road runs, the time series were screened for artifacts (mainly range dropouts), and the distributions were based on the remaining data.

METHODS AND PROCEDURES

TEST TRACK EXPERIMENT — Twelve Ford employees (seven men and five women) took part in the study. The human use research protocol for this study required the participants to be company employees. A reasonable distribution of age and gender was achieved as indicated in Table 1a.

Two test vehicles with automatic transmissions were utilized in the study; the lead vehicle was a midrange four door sedan and the follow vehicle was a midrange sport coupe. The follow vehicle was instrumented with a radar sensor mounted on the center of the front bumper to measure the distance of the lead vehicle with respect to the follow vehicle. Throttle angle (degrees), brake pressure (psi), and velocity (mph) of the follow vehicle were also recorded. Custom-written data acquisition software was used to collect and record data at a frequency of 20 Hz on an IBM PC-compatible computer located in the trunk of the follow vehicle. During testing, an IBM Thinkpad was used to view the data as it was collected. Interference from other vehicles on the test track as well as lap completion times and the time at which climate control tasks were performed (as explained below) were recorded and time-synched with the data file.

The low speed test track at the Ford Dearborn Proving Grounds, shown in Figure 5, was used in the study. The track is 4.3 kilometers long and has six curves varying in radii from 606 to 241 meters. Participants were greeted by the experimenter at their workplace and driven to the test track in the follow vehicle. They were first given a brief overview of the study and then filled out a consent form indicating their willingness to participate in the study and a biographical form which provided the experimenter with information regarding personal characteristics (e.g., date of birth, occupation, etc.) and driving habits (e.g., vehicle driven, annual mileage, etc.).

The test participants were instructed to follow the lead vehicle as they normally would as if they were driving in traffic. They were told that the objective of the study was to evaluate the usability of a climate control system in order to encourage natural car following behavior. The driver of the lead vehicle produced what appeared to be a random speed profile during the study. A majority of the time the lead vehicle driver used cruise control inputs to maintain uniform acceleration and deceleration rates; brake pedal and accelerator pedal inputs were used three times. The speed of the lead vehicle ranged from 30 to 60 mph for all of the laps. The number of speed changes per lap ranged from two to five. An example lead vehicle speed profile for a lap is indicated in Figure 5.

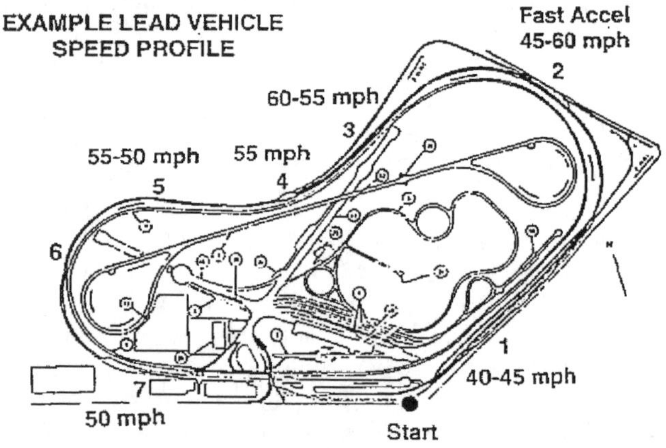

Figure 5. Ford Low Speed Test Track

Each participant drove six laps around the test track. On the final three laps, each participant performed a total of nine tasks using the climate control system as instructed by the experimenter. Examples of some of the tasks included increasing the temperature three degrees, checking the outside temperature, and decreasing the fan setting to the minimum output. At the end of the session, participants were driven back to their workplace. Each test session lasted approximately one hour.

OPEN ROAD EXPERIMENT — Researchers at the University of Michigan Transportation Research Institute (UMTRI) collected manual control data under open highway conditions. The manual control condition was one of three that was investigated; the other two conditions involved driving using conventional cruise control and driving using adaptive cruise control where vehicle speed and headway is controlled relative to a forward vehicle in the same lane.

Thirty-six drivers (18 men and 18 women equally divided into three age groups (20-30 years, 40-50 years, and 60-70 years), were recruited from a local driver and vehicle licensing office to serve as participants. The subjects drove a 1993 compact imported sedan, instrumented with an infrared headway sensor, around a 88.5 kilometer (55 mile) route in Southeast Michigan that took approximately 50-60 minutes to complete. The highway route and average traffic density conditions are summarized in Figure 6. The study was run

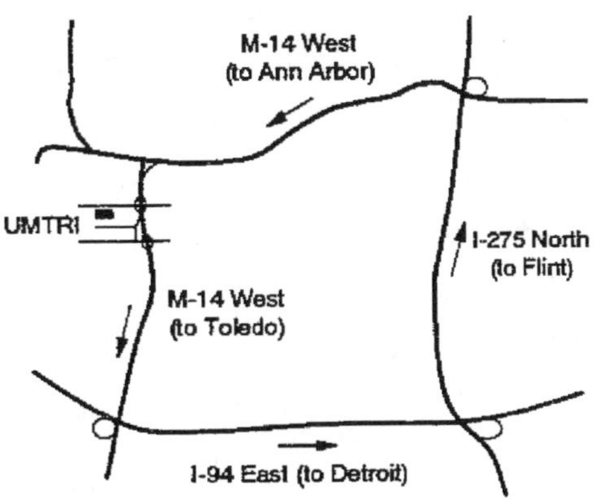

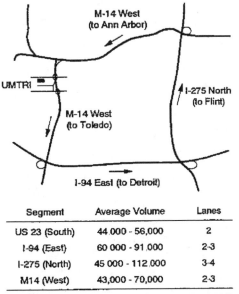

Segment	Average Volume	Lanes
US 23 (South)	44,000 - 56,000	2
I-94 (East)	60 000 - 91 000	2-3
I-275 (North)	45 000 - 112,000	3-4
M14 (West)	43,000 - 70,000	2-3

Source: Michigan Department of Transportation (1993)

Figure 6. Open Road Test Route

during non-peak travel times, and due to the open road conditions was less controlled than the Ford test track study. While a variety of data were recorded, the following six measures were supplied for analysis herein: acceleration, engine throttle position, brake pedal depression and velocity of the instrumented test vehicle, and range and range rate to lead vehicles

RESULTS

DATA ANALYSIS — Data on vehicle speed, longitudinal acceleration and lead vehicle range and range rate were collected on a lap top computer and stored in data files. This data was subsequently analyzed using several time series analysis programs. Figure 7 shows a time series for a good test track data set This time series was analyzed with FFT procedures which resulted in the transfer function data shown previously in Figure 3. The transfer function estimates represent frequency points that reached a coherence value of .65 or greater in the analysis procedure. The transfer function estimates span the crossover frequency region (.34 rad/sec). The model fit gives reasonable representation of the FFT data, and is consistent with both simple and extended crossover model interpretations.

Figure 8 a) shows a typical time trace of one subject's data during the open road experiment Range dropouts are apparent in the data which limit FFT analysis. However, time windows were identified as indicated where reasonable FFT analyses could be obtained. Figure 8 b) shows a time expansion of data selected for FFT analysis. Data quantization can be noted here, which illustrates digital resolution in range, range rate and speed. The range drop outs plus quantization place some limitation on the quality of subsequent FFT analysis of the open road data.

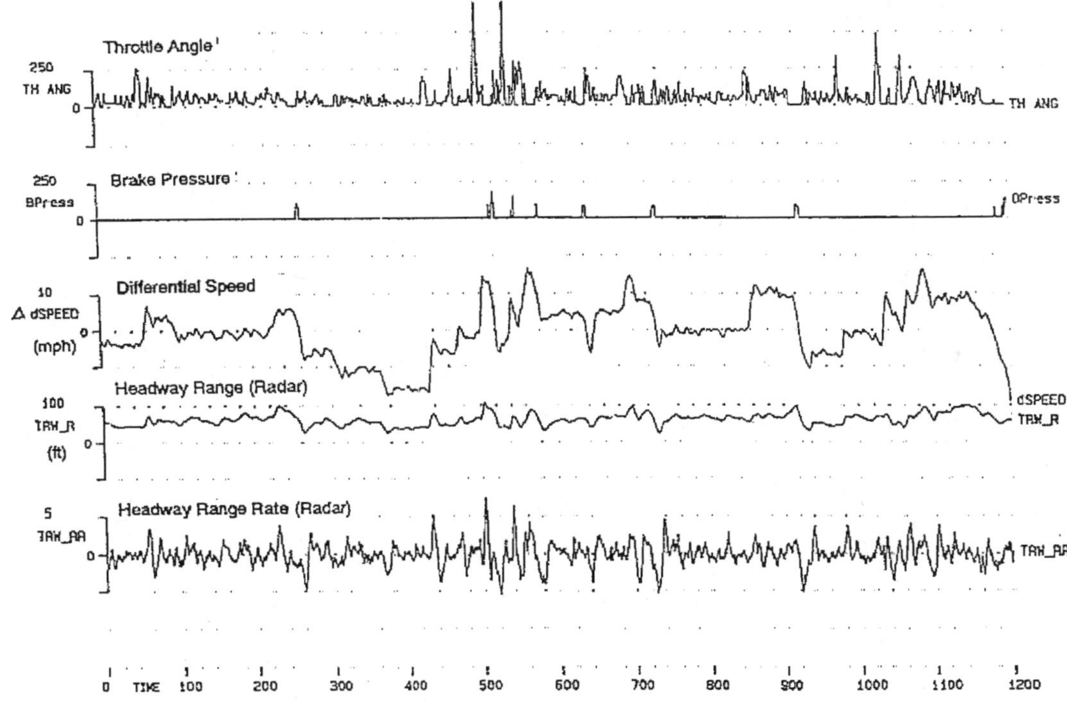

Figure 7. Example Test Track Time History Data

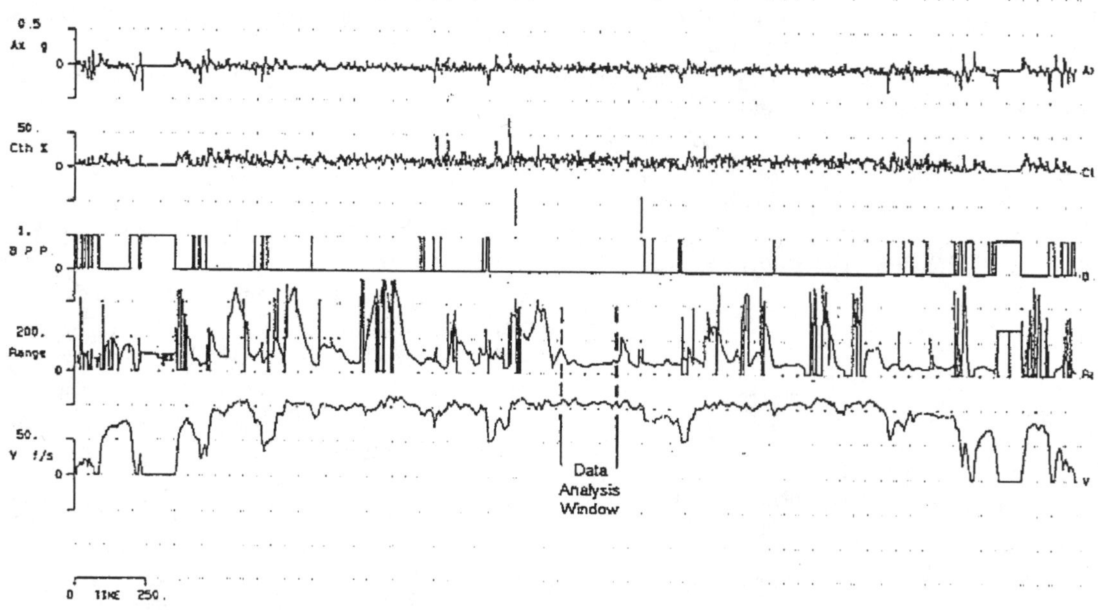

a) Complete Run

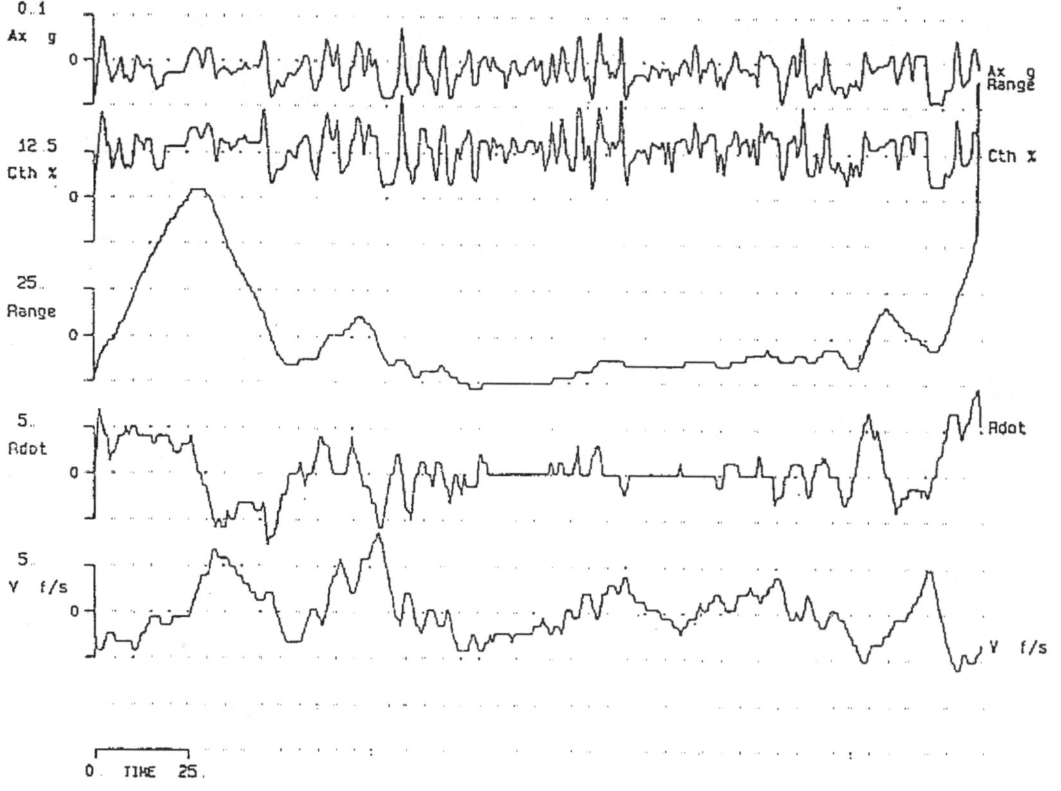

b) FFT Segment

Ffigure 8 Example Open Road Time History Data

DYNAMIC COUPLING — Simple crossover model (crossover frequency, phase margin and time delay) data is summarized for both the test track and open road experiments in Table 1. Note that the average crossover frequency is .21 rad/sec and phase margin is 0.7 radians for the test track data and 0.76 radians for the open road data. Equivalent time delays, as derived from the crossover frequency and phase margin, are 3.28 and 4.96 seconds respectively for the track and road data. If the open road time delay data outlier at 11.47 seconds is ignored, the track and road data sets are quite comparable. The phase margins indicate loop closures that range from critically damped to slightly under damped. The closed loop bandwidth and damping defined by Equation 5 were calculated for the track and road data and are also summarized in Table 1. Here we see that the closed loop damping is quite stable across subjects for both sets of data and indicates a slightly under damped condition

TABLE 1. SIMPLE CROSSOVER MODEL DATA

a) Test Track

Subject		Headway			Simple Crossover Model			Closed Loop Coupling	
Gender	Age (yrs)	R_o (ft)	U_o(mph)	T_h(sec)	ω_c	ϕ_m((rad)	τ_e	ω_n	ζ_m
M	34	76.80	36.80	1.42	0.25	0.87	2.79	0.30	0.60
F	34	71.50	41.60	1.17	0.16	1.05	3.27	0.22	0.69
F	26	100.20	40.70	1.67	0.20	0.87	3.49	0.24	0.60
F	32	70.50	36.00	1.33	0.21	0.65	4.41	0.22	0.52
F	37	72.20	39.90	1.23	0.36	0.73	2.33	0.39	0.55
M	31	91.70	39.60	1.58	0.20	1.05	2.62	0.28	0.69
M	37	105.00	39.00	1.83	0.20	0.44	5.67	0.19	0.47
M	38	100.00	36.00	1.89	0.12	1.05	4.36	0.17	0.70
M	45	80.00	40.30	1.35	0.18	0.87	3.88	0.22	0.60
M	32	61.60	45.20	0.93	0.34	0.92	1.90	0.42	0.62
F	45	68.00	40.60	1.14	0.29	0.61	3.31	0.30	0.51
F	50	117.50	40.60	1.97	0.18	0.73	4.65	0.20	0.55
$\bar{X}$	33.92	84.58	36.64	1.35	0.21	0.76	3.28	0.27	0.59
σ_X	6.89	17.68	2.58	0.33	0.07	0.19	1.09	0.076	0.075

b) Open Road

Subject		Headway			Simple Crossover Model			Closed Loop Coupling	
Age(yrs)	Gender	R_o (ft)	U_o(mph)	T_h(sec)	ω_c	ϕ_m((rad)	τ_e	ω_n	ζ_m
20-30	F	110.00	54.29	1.38	0.35	0.79	2.24	.395	.565
20-30	F	62.10	73.47	0.58	0.24	1.05	2.18	.332	.691
20-30	M	118.00	62.52	1.28	0.22	0.38	5.39	.202	.459
40-50	F	185.10	66.12	1.90	0.24	0.52	4.36	.235	.489
40-50	F	128.00	71.29	1.22	0.15	1.05	3.49	.207	.691
40-50	F	72.90	60.95	0.81	0.12	0.79	6.55	.135	.564
40-50	M	97.20	59.93	1.10	0.13	0.87	5.37	.153	.598
60-70	F	101.20	53.61	1.28	0.29	0.52	3.61	.283	.489
60-70	M	134.20	63.81	1.43	0.11	0.37	11.47	.098	.445
	$\bar{X}$	112.08	62.89	1.22	0.21	0.70	4.96	.227	.554
	σ_X	36.21	6.77	0.38	0.08	0.26	2.84	.096	.093

For the test track data there is some tradeoff between driver dynamic behavior and performance. Figure 9 illustrates that driver time delay decreases and crossover frequency increases with decreasing headway time. This result is consistent with more aggressive control for shorter headway times. Multiple regression analysis was performed with headway (T_H) as the dependent variable and crossover frequency (ω_c), phase margin (ϕ_M) and effective time delay (τ_e) as independent variables. The results are summarized in Table 2, which shows that the slopes of crossover frequency and time delay are a significant function of headway time, while phase margin (a measure of closed loop control damping) is not dependent on headway time. These results indicate that driver dynamic behavior is generally related to headway time, with shorter headways leading to more aggressive driver control.

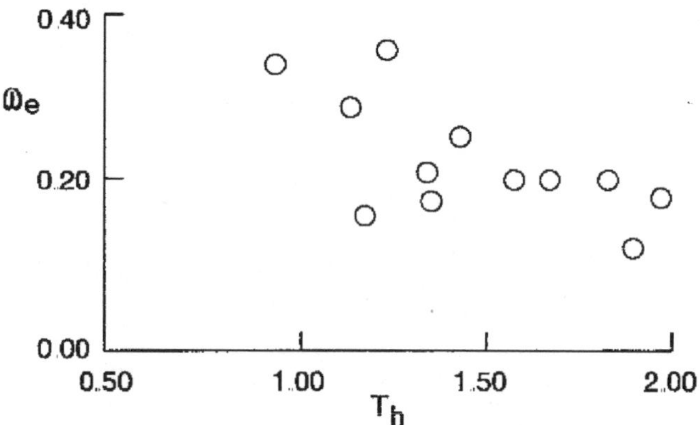

a) Crossover Frequency

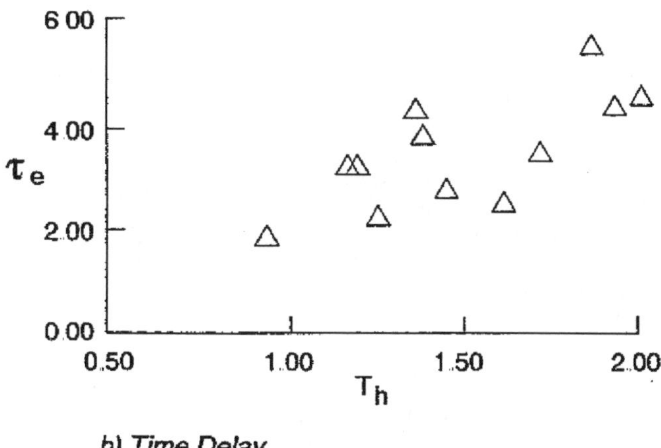

b) Time Delay

Figure 9. Test Track Crossover Frequency and Time Delay Data vs. Headway Time

The test track FFT data was also used to fit the low frequency parameter α (Figure 2) associated with outer loop hadway control (low frequency data quality was too variable in the road set to permit reliable α identification). Since a accounts for some of the open loop phase lag, the associated driver time delays are somewhat reduced as summarized in Table 3. Here we see that α, which is the equivalent of the bandwidth of the headway or range control loop, is an order of magnitude lower than the inner velocity control loop bandwidth given by the crossover frequency ω_c.

CONTROL AND HEADWAY DISTRIBUTIONS — Distributions of longitudinal acceleration for both the track and road experiments are summarized in Figure 10. Here we see that the acceleration distributions during car following are remarkably similar between subjects and between test track and open road. Maximum values are less than 0.3 g, and standard deviations are less than 0.05 g (1.0 g equals the acceleration due to gravity or 32.2 ft/sec^2). The variation is greater on the open road probably due to the more varied driving conditions. The closed throttle deceleration of modern aerodynamically designed passenger cars is on the order of 0.1 g which probable explains the lower distribution limit. The distributions appear to be reasonably symmetrical, and the upper distribution limit indicates conservative use of engine throttle to match lead vehicle velocity and maintain headway.

Given the longitudinal acceleration described above, the driver can still choose to follow a lead vehicle at any desired distance. Typical time headway distributions are shown in Figure 11. Here we see more variability between drivers in headway time than in their longitudinal acceleration distributions. We also note that the open road drivers exhibit more variability than the test track drivers. Some subjects spend a significant portion of their car following exposure at headway times of less than 1.0 seconds which might be considered fairly risky behavior. The oft stated rule of thumb of a minimum of one car length (approximately 15 feet) for each ten miles per hour of speed (approximately 15 feet/sec) gives an equivalent headway time of 1.0 seconds.

Range and velocity limits were applied to the open road headway data in Figure 11b in order to make the following conditions more consistent with the test track conditions. In Figure 12 we show open road distributions without any range or velocity limits. Here we see that occurrence of large time headways increases dramatically. In Figure 12 we also compare our instrumented vehicle headway distributions with data collected on the highway with loop detectors as presented by Farber [12]. Here we see that the open road instrumented vehicle data is generally consistent with the ensemble data collected at a single location. The instrumented data presented here does show significant variations between drivers, which may be an important consideration when analyzing the effectiveness of crash avoidance systems.

CONCLUSION

We have successfully analyzed open road car following data and validated the general findings of a test track experiment of driver car following behavior. The overall objective of the manual headway control experiment was to measure the dynamic coupling drivers achieve with respect to a lead vehicle. We have a consistent measurement of this coupling under both test track and open highway driving conditions. The open road data appears to be less constrained which may be due to the influence of more uncontrolled variables such as the occurrence of interacting traffic and the drivers' general task demands.

TABLE 2. TEST TRACK REGRESSION ANALYSIS DATA

a) Using 2 independent varialbes 1) τ_e 2) ϕ_m

Regression Statistics	
Multiple R	0.7679
R Square	0.5897
Adjusted R Square	0.4985
Standard Error	0.2333
Observations	12

Parameter Fit Statistics			
Parameter	Standard Error	t Stat	P-value
Intercept	0.5426	0.0127	0.9900
Variable 1	0.7545	3.5639	0.0060
Variable 2	0.4249	1.4217	0.1888

b) Using 2 independent variables 1) ϕ_m 2) ω_c

Regression Statistics	
Multiple R	0.7288
R Square	0.5312
Adjusted R Square	0.4270
Standard Error	0.2494
Observations	12

Parameter Fit Statistics			
Parameter	Standard Error	t Stat	P-value
Intercept	0.4702	5.6796	0.0003
Variable 1	0.4061	-1.3336	0.2150
Variable 2	1.0833	-3.1613	0.0115

TABLE 3. EXTENDED CROSSOVER MODEL DATA FROM TEST TRACK EXPERIMENT

Subject		Extended Crossover Model	
Gender	Age (yrs)	α	τ
M	34	0.00604	1.82491
F	34		
F	26	0.00594	1.76988
F	32	0.02459	2.67972
F	37	0.03268	1.55385
M	31		
M	37	0.12298	1.91245
M	38	0.02238	2.10306
M	45	0.00616	1.74523
M	32	0.00793	1.40859
F	45	0.00896	1.97839
F	50	0.00662	2.71962
$\bar{X}$	33.92	0.02	1.52
σ_x	6.89	0.04	0.43

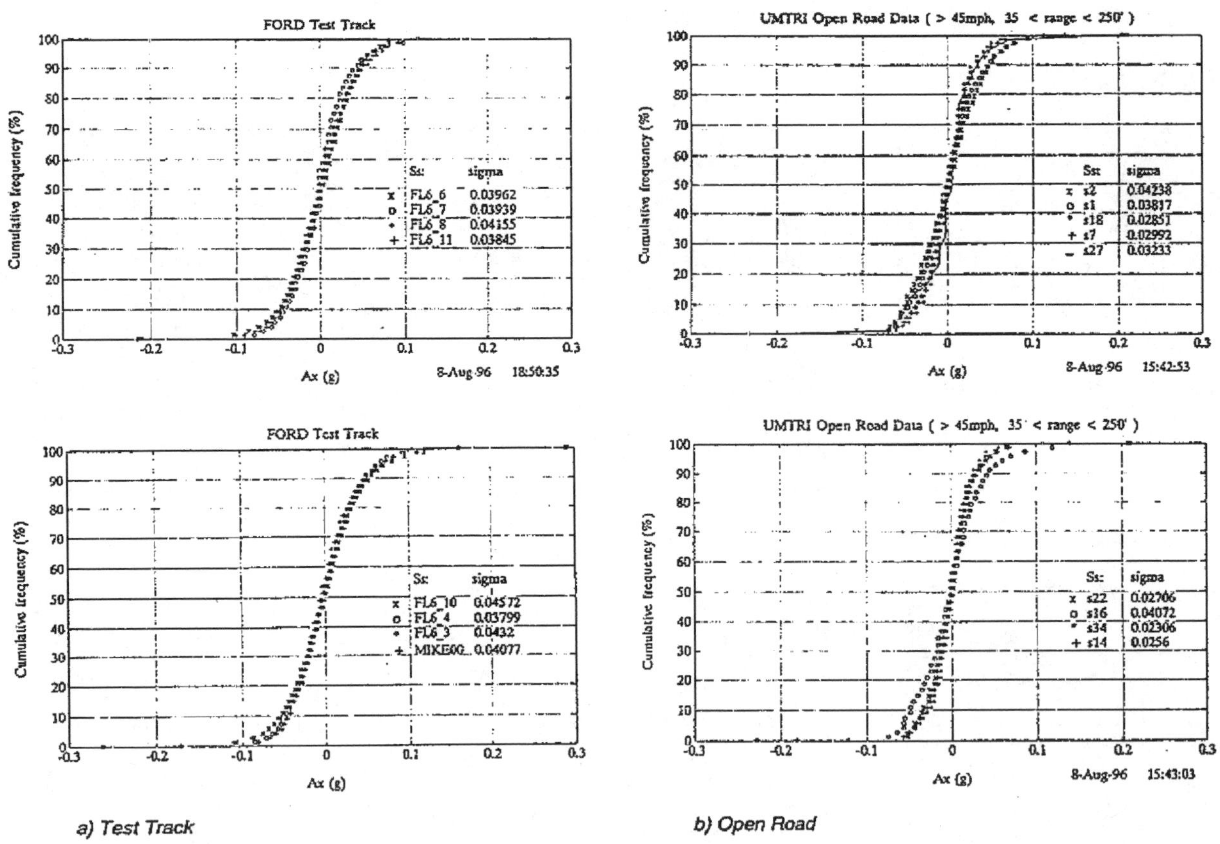

Figure 10. Longitudinal Acceleration Distributions Under Test Track and Open Road Conditions for a Number of Subjects

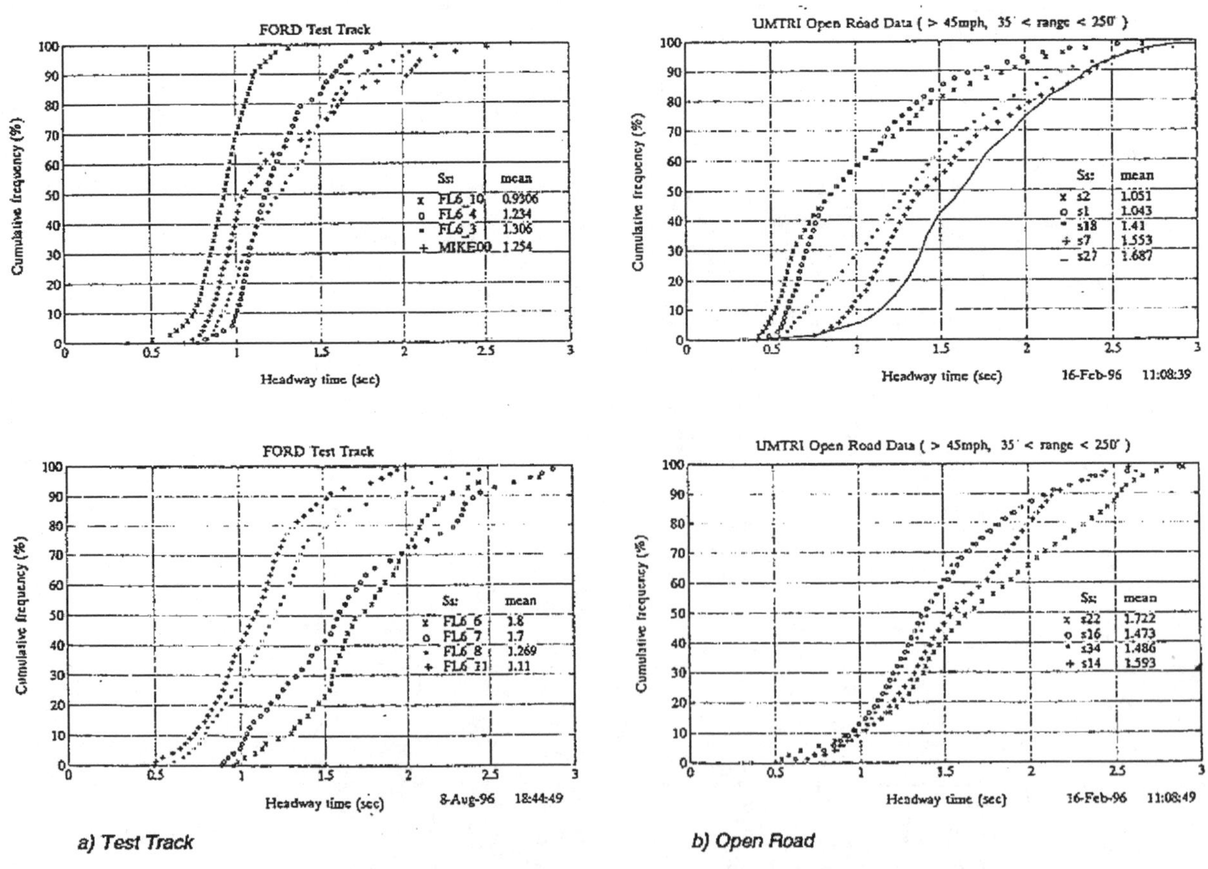

Figure 11. Headway Time Distributions Under Test Track and Road Conditions.
Open Road Data Limited to Greater than 72 kph (45mph) and Range Interval of 10-80 m (35-250 ft)

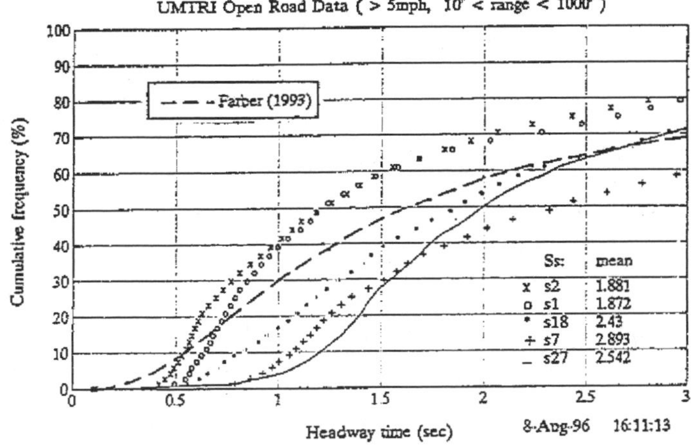

Figure 12. Open Road Headway Time Distributions Under Near Full Range Conditions: Speed Greater than 8 kph (5mph) and Range Interval 3-300 m (10-100 ft)

This study has identified driver headway control characteristics that are quite slow compared to other control processes such as steering for path following and maintaining lane position. The driver exhibits time constants and time delays on the order of several seconds to tens of seconds that limit the stable control bandwidth that can be achieved in maintaining headway. These continuous control time constants and time delays are probably due to processes associated with range and range rate perception, and should not be confused with discrete reaction times associated with braking which are considerably shorter.

ACKNOWLEDGMENTS

This work was sponsored by the National Highway Traffic Safety Administration. Mr. Michael Perel of the Office of Crash Avoidance Research served as the Contracting Officer's Technical Representative. We gratefully acknowledge the open road car following data provided by Dr. James Sayer of the Human Factors Division of the University of Michigan Transportation Research Institute

REFERENCES

1. Pipes, L.A. (1953), "An Operational Analysis of Traffic Dynamics," *Journal of Applied Physics*, vol. 24, pp. 271-281.

2. Bekey, G.A., Burnham, G.O. and Seo, J. (1977), "Control Theoretic Models of Human Drivers in Car Following," *Human Factors*, vol. 19, no. 4, pp. 399-413.

3. Fancher, P.S., Bareket, Z. (1995), "Evaluation of Human Factors and Safety Performance in the Longitudinal Control of Headway," Proceedings of the Second World Congress on Intelligent Transport Systems, Intelligent Transport Systems World Congress, Yokohama, Japan

4. Sayer, J.R., Fancher, P.S., et al. (1995), "Automatic Target Acquisition Autonomous Intelligent Cruise Control (AICC): Driver Comfort, Acceptance, and Performance in Highway Traffic, SAE Paper 950970, Society of Automotive Engineers, Warrendale, PA

5. Chandler, F.E., Herman, R., and Montroll, E.W. (1958), "Traffic Dynamics: Studies in Car Following," *Operations Research*, 6, pp. 165-184.

6. Allen, R.W. (1982), "Stability and Performance Analysis of Automobile Driver Steering Control," SAE Paper 820303, International Congress & Exposition, Detroit, MI.

7. Torf, A.S. and Duckstein, L. (1966), "A Methodology for the Determination of Driver Perceptual Latency in Car Following," *Human Factors*, vol. 8, no. 5, pp. 441-447.

8. McRuer, D.T. and Krendal, E.S. (1974), "Mathematical Models of Human Pilot Behavior," AGARD-AG-188.

9. Truxal, J.G. (1955), *Automatic Feedback Control System Synthesis*, McGraw-Hill, New York.

10. Bendat, J.S. and Piersol, A.G. (1971), *Random Data: Analysis and Measurement Procedures*, Wiley-Interscience, New York.

11. Randall, R.B. (1987), *Frequency Analysis*, Bruel & Kjaer, Denmark.

12. Farber, E. and Paley, M. (1993), "Using Freeway Traffic Data to Estimate the Effectiveness of Rear-End Collision Countermeasures," *The Proceedings of the 1993 Annual Meeting of IVHS America*, 14-17 April, Washington, DC.

961667

Intelligent Cruise Control - Issues for Consideration

James R. Sayer
University of Michigan Transportation Research Institute

ABSTRACT

With the development and introduction of advanced vehicle control systems such as intelligent cruise control (ICC) and forward collision avoidance systems (FCAS), many safety and human factors issues specific to these control systems are being raised. This paper addresses some issues that, to date, are still matters for discussion and consideration amongst system designers. Aimed principally at the implementation of ICC, some items naturally lend themselves to the design of forward collision avoidance systems as well. Specific issues discussed include: seat belt lock-out systems, foot placement sensing, and adjustable headway.

INTRODUCTION

Recently, both the ISO TC204/WG13/N4.1 and the SAE Safety and Human Factors Committee have been active in addressing issues associated with the standardization of intelligent cruise control (ICC) operating characteristics. The author has reviewed drafts of the considerations for standardization, and offers observations and insight based upon ICC research conducted at the University of Michigan Transportation Research Institute. While many of the issues being considered for standardization of ICC systems are not addressed in this article, several new items are raised.

ICC DEVELOPMENT ISSUES

Initiation of Following

The two potential modes of initiating following are automatic and manual control, and ICC systems can readily be designed to allow for either option. Automatic initiation of following requires that a system recognize when a proceeding vehicle comes into range, and assume full ICC system operation when the system is in an "engaged" mode (i.e., the ICC system is attempting to maintain the speed selected by the driver). Manual initiation of following, or driver initiation, would require the driver to acknowledge the presence of a proceeding vehicle and perform some positive action to commence ICC system operation. Should the mode of initiating following (manual or automatic) be standardized?

The likelihood that ICC systems will be linked with other advanced vehicular control systems, such as forward collision warning and forward collision avoidance, suggests that ICC should automatically initiate following. Collision avoidance systems, which by their nature will require automatic initiation to be truly effective, are conceptually very similar in the minds of drivers who have experienced ICC. In particular, ICC systems are often viewed by the layperson as a form of collision avoidance system.

Defining levels of control authority

Perhaps one of the most challenging tasks for ICC and CAS developers is defining the point where intelligent cruise control systems end and forward collision avoidance systems begin. It can be a fuzzy line between ICC and FCAS. At what level of deceleration authority does an ICC system become a FCAS?

A great deal of discussion has taken place regarding active braking and ICC systems. Specifically, some system developers believe that active braking will be required in order that ICC systems be marketable. Yet how will drivers be able to differentiate between ICC and FCAS. Specifically, what is the level of deceleration authority that should be assigned these similar, yet different, control systems. The level of deceleration authority associated with each of the two systems should be distinctly different such that drivers will not be confused as to which system is evoked. There is also an issue related to the transfer of training from one vehicle/system to another.

Differentiating between ACC and FCAS raises a larger, more fundamental, question related to the definition of ICC, FCAS, and even forward collision warning systems (FCWS). This will be particularly true if low decel cues are to used for FCWS. Defining the levels of control authority that each of these systems will evoke is a pressing safety and human factors issue. How drivers differentiate between an

ICC system with moderate braking authority and a FCAS with moderate braking, without having to rely solely on secondary displays, must be addressed.

Seat-Belt Lockout

What level of deceleration is necessary to dislodge a driver or passenger from their seat if they are not wearing a seat belt? The potential appears to exist for the development of ICC systems that have sufficiently high levels of deceleration authority to allow an un-belted driver or passenger to "submarine" under the dashboard, or into the rear of the front seat. There is the additional concern with an ICC system that the driver's legs may not be positioned to provide bracing against the floorboard. A casual observance of drivers in ICC equipped vehicles confirms that drivers are often without their feet positioned near the brake or accelerator pedals.

Because there is the potential for drivers to become dislodged from their seat under moderate levels of deceleration resulting from either an ICC system, FCWS, or FCAS, seat-belt lockouts should be considered for standardization. A system that mitigates a collision through the use of moderate deceleration could leave the driver in a vulnerable position to regain control of the vehicle. Systems providing longitudinal deceleration should consider requiring seat belt use during system activation.

Foot placement sensors

Drivers frequently position their feet away from the brake and accelerator pedals when driving in either the conventional cruise or ICC modes. As a result, their reaction time in responding to events will be lengthened if use of either pedal is required. Knowing the relative position of a drivers' right foot, or potentially both feet, could be beneficial in determining the response of either an ICC system or FCAS.

In the case of an ICC system implementation, knowing the position of the driver's feet could permit the modification of the system's control algorithm. Specifically, an ICC control algorithm could be designed to automatically increase headway time when drivers position their feet away from the pedals. The increase headway time would help counter the lengthening of driver reaction time associated with foot re-positioning to the pedals.

Similarly, in the case of FCAS, the levels of system deceleration could be modified on the basis of predicting the likelihood that a driver is prepared to guide the vehicle out of a potential collision. Information on the position of the driver's feet could be used, in part, in determining whether longitudinal deceleration or a lateral maneuver is a better approach towards mitigating a collision.

Fixed vs. Driver-Selectable Headway.

In a fixed headway system there is a single level of headway between the proceeding car and the ICC equipped vehicle. In a driver-selectable system the headway is determined by the driver. Should ICC systems use fixed or driver-selectable headways?

Early on-road evaluation of a fixed-headway ICC system resulted in comments from lay drivers regarding the need for driver-selectable headway. While individuals noted that the fixed headway they evaluated was a "safe" following distance (1.4 s), they also experienced frequent cut-ins by other vehicles as this headway was large in comparison to surrounding traffic.

A recent study that examined preferences for ICC driver-selectable headway times found a wide range of preferred settings that were based upon both individual preferences and traffic conditions. When given the opportunity to adjust the constant time headway of an ICC equipped vehicle between 0.7 and 2.5 s, a dramatic difference in preference was observed across age groups (see Figures 1 - 3). Specifically, four younger drivers (22 - 30) tended to select shorter headway times compared to four middle-aged (41 - 52) and four older participants (69 - 74) when driving on highways and expressways in moderate traffic (note: a floor effect due to the limit on the lower bound of 0.7 s was observed).

Given the range of preferred headway settings observed, and safety considerations, driver-selectable headway is recommended. Although a minimum headway time will likely be required. However, the use of continuous, or finely incremented, control of headway time is not recommended. Three or four headway-time settings, over the range of 1.0 to 2.0 s, are thought to be the limit on the number of headway values people can readily discriminate while driving. However, this issue requires additional investigation.

DISCUSSION AND CONCLUSION

While many issues remain to be addressed, some new, and perhaps controversial, items have been raised. Possibly the most challenging task ICC, FCAS, and FCWS developers face is the design of systems that are capable of working both independently and in cooperation with one another. The ability to successfully convey vehicle status to the driver, maintain the requisite level of vehicle control authority, and develop a system requiring a minimum amount of driver training remains a formidable objective.

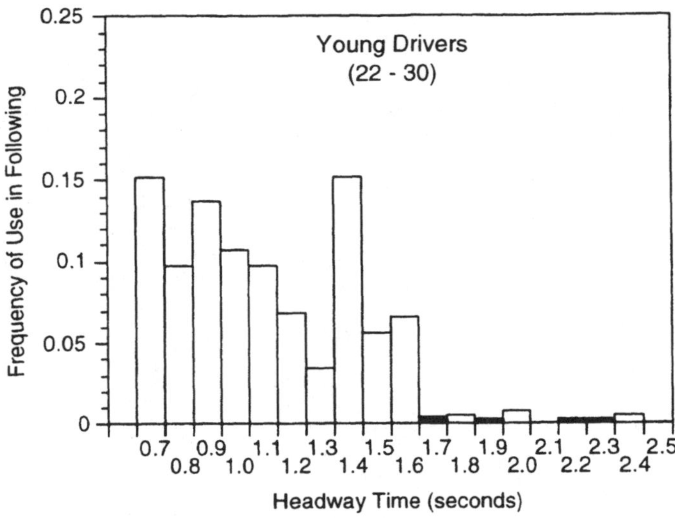

Figure 1. ICC headway time selection of young drivers.

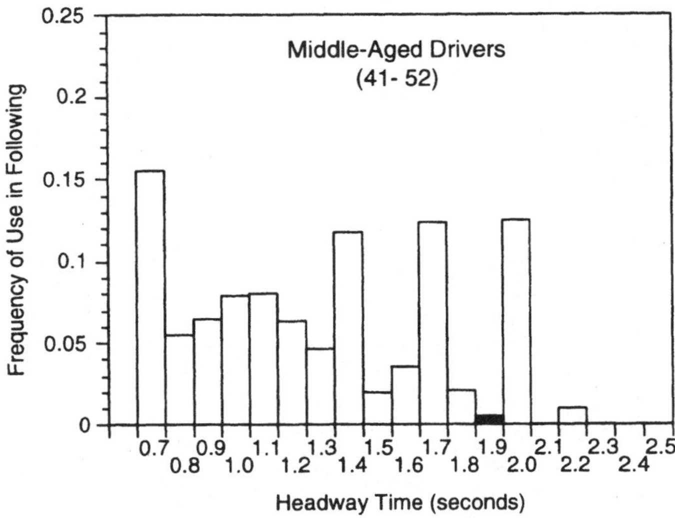

Figure 2. ICC headway time selection of middle-aged drivers.

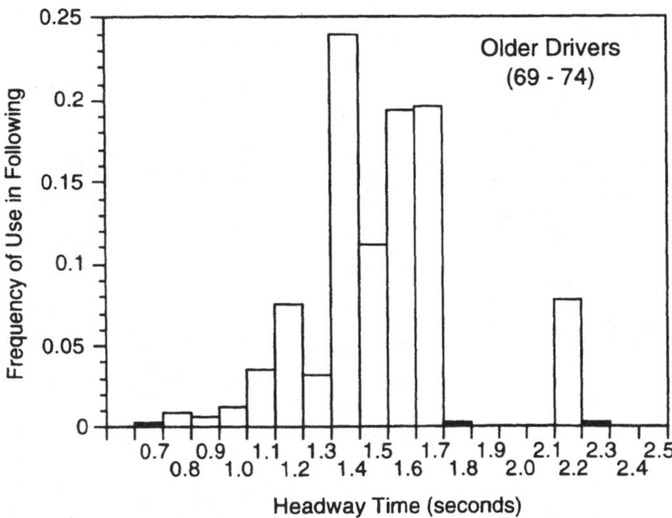

Figure 3. ICC headway time selection of older drivers.

961010

Adaptive Cruise Control System Aspects and Development Trends

Hermann Winner, Stefan Witte, Werner Uhler, Bernd Lichtenberg
Robert Bosch GmbH

ABSTRACT

This paper is based on the experiences with Adaptive Cruise Control (ACC) systems at BOSCH. Necessary components (especially range sensor, curve sensors, actuators and display) are described, roughly specified, and their respective strength and weaknesses are addressed. The system overview contains the basic structure, the main control strategy and the concept for driver-ACC interaction. Afterwards the principal as well as the current technical limits of ACC systems are discussed. The consequences on traffic flow, safety and driver behavior are emphasized. As an outlook, development trends for extended functionality are given for the next generation of driver assistance systems.

INTRODUCTION

Recently several companies independently demonstrated driver assistance systems for longitudinal control. These systems called (Autonomous) Intelligent Cruise Control (AICC / ICC) or Adaptive Cruise Control (ACC) extend the conventional cruise control by also enabling the driver to automatically follow a slower preceding vehicle. Thus, the vehicle can automatically flow with other cars in dense traffic while keeping a safe distance. In this paper the structure and the functionality of ACC systems are discussed in detail with emphasis on the BOSCH experiences.

Although development of ACC systems began in the late seventies [1,2], marketing is now possible after significant progresses in both sensor and signal processing technologies. Sensors, on the one hand, need to measure accurately the distance and relative speed to preceding vehicles, be easily and cheaply producable, and must meet the strict requirements of the automotive market. On the other hand, the signal processing must guarantee the desired resolution of the processed data while keeping rigorous timing constraints. Progress in these areas was partly triggered by the PROMETHEUS project, an European research project involving all European car manufacturers, initializing similar activities in the US and Japan.

In this paper, we describe the main components which typically make up such an ACC system. The control strategy and the system architecture of the ACC system used in the prototype vehicles at BOSCH are discussed. Then the technical and principal limits, as well as the simulated effects on the traffic flow are pointed out. Last, the system experience and the future development trends are presented.

ACC COMPONENTS

OVERVIEW - The ACC system is built as a distributed system using common Electronic Control Units (ECUs) plus one additional ECU which contains the Range Sensor and the ACC controller. The different ECUs are connected via a CAN data bus. The actual components are displayed in Fig. 1.

The combined Range Sensor and ACC controller is mounted in the front of the car. The Curve Sensor helps to predict the future course of the vehicle. A Man-Machine-Interface (MMI) includes all the interfaces of the ACC system to the driver: the operation switches, the display and the pedals (accelerator, brake). The actuators in the ACC system are controlled by the slightly modified standard ECUs for engine control (EGAS, EDC), transmission control and active brake control (small addition to ASR or Vehicle Dynamic Control (VDC)). An electronic brake control system is optional depending on the characteristic traffic conditions. In Europe, frequent acceleration and deceleration phases result in an unsteady traffic flow, while in the US the traffic situation is more homogeneous. In unsteady conditions a significant gain

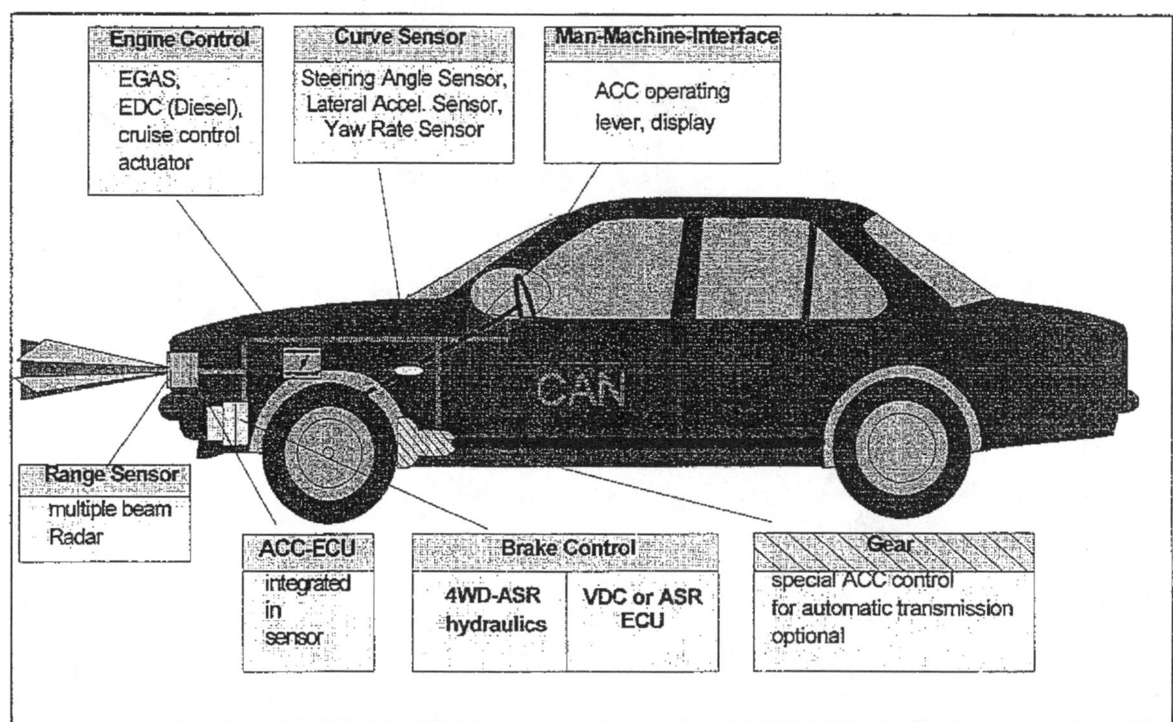

Fig. 1: Basic ACC components

of functionality is achieved by the active brake control.

RANGE SENSOR - The range sensor is the key component of ACC. It has to supply the ACC controller with data about the position and speed of preceding vehicles relative to the ACC equipped vehicle. The considered ACC system contains a mm-wave Radar sensor in the 76,5 GHz frequency range. With the FMCW modulation (frequency modulated continuous wave) resolutions of better than 1m distance and 0,5 m/s in relative speed are achieved. Not only the values for distance and relative speed directly used in the ACC controller (see Sec. on ACC Controller) are of interest; the lateral position or the angle relative to the vehicle's longitudinal axis is important to select the relevant preceding vehicle. An angular resolution of better than 1° within a range of ±5° can be achieved using multi-beam techniques. This results in sufficient detection quality for straight and curved roads. Multiple target values are passed to the ACC controller after signal processing, pre-selection, tracking and filtering for further selection and computation.

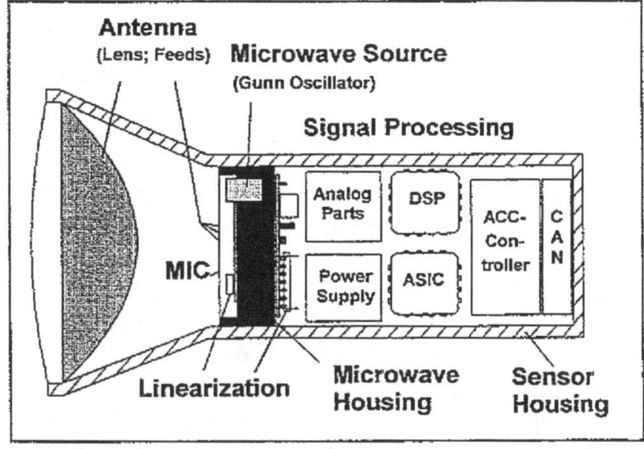

Fig. 2: Basic components of the ACC-RADAR-Sensor

A semi-planar technology is used for the transceiver to meet the requirements of high integration, high reliability and low cost. The average output microwave power is very low (< 1 mW) due to simultaneous multi-beam measurements. Although the unit contains the 76,5 GHz transceiver, the signal processing and the ACC controller, the entire unit is reasonably small for integration in the front part of the vehicle.

In comparison to other sensor concepts only mm-wave Radar sensors are sufficiently robust against bad weather influences. There is only a small degradation by fog and rain. Detection range will always remain higher than the human visibility for the specified detection range (150 m). It should be noted that for bad weather robustness it is necessary to mount the Radar antenna so that it cannot be covered by snow.

CURVE SENSORS - To detect and select the "relevant" preceding vehicle it is essential to estimate the future course of the ACC car. Fig. 3 shows two typical

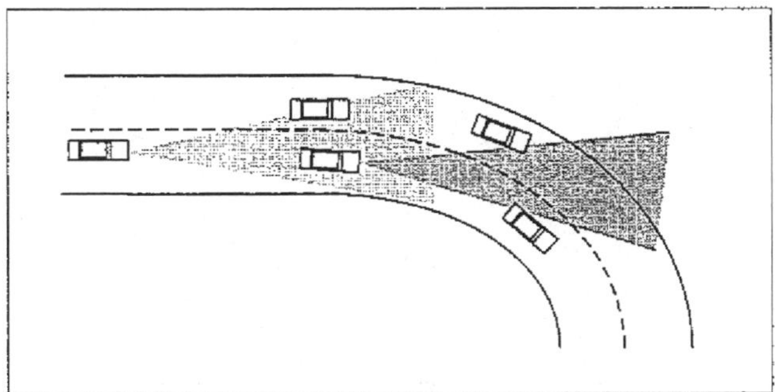

Fig. 3: Problems arising when selecting the relevant preceding car

examples where a wrong "target" will be selected without a proper course prediction.

In the simplest case, course prediction assumes movement in a straight line. Under this assumption, no dedicated curve sensor is needed. It is obvious that this way of predicting the course does not work in curves or during lane changes.

In a more complex case, a constant course is assumed, meaning constant speed and curvature. This works well most of the time, since estimation errors usually only occur at the beginning and end of curves. Several ways of sensing the actual curvature are commonly used today [3]: evaluation of the relative difference of the wheel revolutions, using a steering angle sensor or measuring the lateral acceleration. A yaw rate sensor which is needed for Vehicle Dynamic Control (VDC) systems can also be used. All methods possess characteristic errors Hence a combination is most robust.

A higher level of curve prediction can be provided by using navigation systems (digital maps and course calculations). The limits of this technique depend on the agreement of the maps with the actual road and on the system's capability in determining the car's actual position. The prediction is faulty in construction areas and for new roads. Moreover, today's systems do not have a position resolution which is sufficient for ACC course prediction. Furthermore, the price has to be significantly reduced to guarantee a broader distribution. Technically, the use of navigation systems has very interesting prospects.

Several high-tech Radar development laboratories promise a road and lane prediction purely based on the Radar information Stationary objects like reflector posts and crash-barriers detected by the signal processor are used to reconstruct the road boundaries. Little is known, however, about the quality and robustness of these new techniques so far.

Extracting road markers from video images is another way to predict the road course. Lane classification of the detected objects is possible by combining a video system with an angle resolving distance sensor. Lane prediction using video seems to be the most promising from a technical point of view in spite of current limitations. First, ambiguous lane markers as in construction areas can not be distinguished. Second, visibility in bad weather and darkness is limited. In general, the prediction range will be limited to about 80m.

ACTUATORS

Engine Control - There are several suitable means of controlling the engine: separate or integrated electronic throttle control (EGAS), combined throttle control with engine management, pneumatic or electric cruise control actuators and EDC systems for diesel engines. These possibilities combined with the different engine types result in a large variety of ACC systems. Application expenses are reduced, however, by using modular control concepts and general interfaces based on physical quantities e.g. engine torque.

Transmission Control - Electronic transmission control in vehicles with automatic transmission improves the overall ACC comfort significantly. Furthermore, in cars without electronic brake control, it is possible for the ACC to shift down to decelerate with the engine. Hence, the number of necessary driver interventions due to the "normal" engine deceleration capability is reduced. Acceleration and deceleration capabilities in vehicles with manual transmission are limited by the current gear. If the clutch is disengaged, the ACC system is either temporarily or permanently switched off.

Brake Control - Active brake control is based on the hydraulic systems used for standard traction control (4WD-ASR) or VDC and does not require a smart booster. This system allows a quiet and comfortable deceleration control, but still can automatically switch to ABS if necessary. Since the required safety levels are comparable to ASR and VDC-systems, the same safety mechanisms are utilized. Deceleration might be restricted to small values to limit the potential hazards due to unnecessary automatic braking. Alternatively only a slow increase of the deceleration is permitted (see Sec. Range of Operation)

OPERATION AND DISPLAY - Operation of the ACC system is similar to the conventional cruise control: Switches are used to turn the system on or off, to resume and to set the speed. Additionally the desired time gap representing a speed dependent following distance is a main operation variable. To establish the basic principle of total driver priority, the driver is also able to intervene in the system by applying the brakes, turning the ACC off, or by using the gas pedal to increase the delivered engine power. In vehicles with manual transmission, the driver can pause or shut off the ACC by pushing the clutch. After engaging the clutch ACC could be automatically resumed. This depends on the preferences of the car manufacturer.

The information which is displayed in the front panel includes (see the sample realization in Fig. 4)

- the set speed, since the driver might forget the set value after a longer period of following slower traffic,
- the set time gap, and
- the actual ACC mode, i.e. whether the car is in Following Control mode (symbolic vehicle is lit) or Speed Control mode (symbolic vehicle not lit).

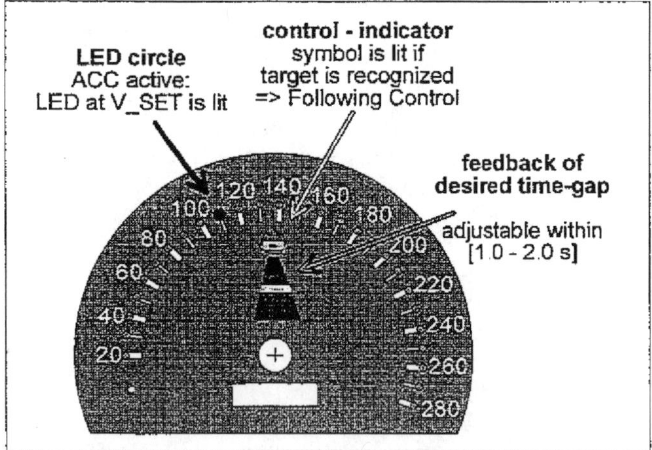

Fig. 5: Sample display of an ACC system

The last feature is intended especially to support learning and supervision of the ACC system.

Another interface element is a warning device. Normally a loudspeaker is used to request that the driver takes over control. This happens if the deceleration capability of the ACC is insufficient due to the imposed limitations discussed earlier (see Sec. on Brake Control).

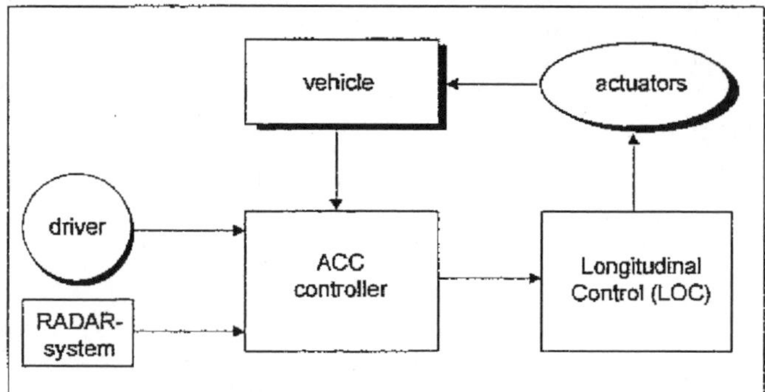

Fig. 6: Basic control loop of an ACC system

ACC CONTROLLER - The first control step is to select the relevant preceding vehicle (see Fig. 6). The expected course of the ACC equipped vehicle will be determined using the speed and the course curvature (see Sec. on Curve Sensors). The Radar sensor supplies the distance, relative speed and angle of multiple objects representing different preceding vehicles to the ACC controller. Comparison of the object data with the expected future course is used to select the relevant vehicle. Generally this is the closest vehicle driving in the same direction along that course. Then the values for distance and relative speed of this relevant vehicle are fed to a (non-linear) control part (Following Control), which has to reduce the relative speed as well as the difference between the actual and the set distance to zero. In the case of a car pulling in from the side, the distance control is very smooth to increase comfort and to react like a human driver whereas the speed will be adjusted significantly faster. The Speed Control is a parallel branch to the Following Control and dominates only if no relevant vehicle is detected. In this case it works like a conventional cruise control. In addition, the Speed Control limits the Following Control to avoid following a car which is faster than the set speed. The output of the entire ACC controller is a desired longitudinal

SYSTEM ARCHITECTURE

OVERVIEW - The ACC function can be split into three major parts (see Fig. 5): 1) the ACC controller computing how the vehicle should accelerate, 2) the Longitudinal Control (LOC) which manages the actuator systems to achieve the desired acceleration and 3) the Man-Machine-Interface enabling the driver to operate, supervise and intervene.

The functional structure has to be implemented in real vehicles bringing up questions concerning integration and interfaces.

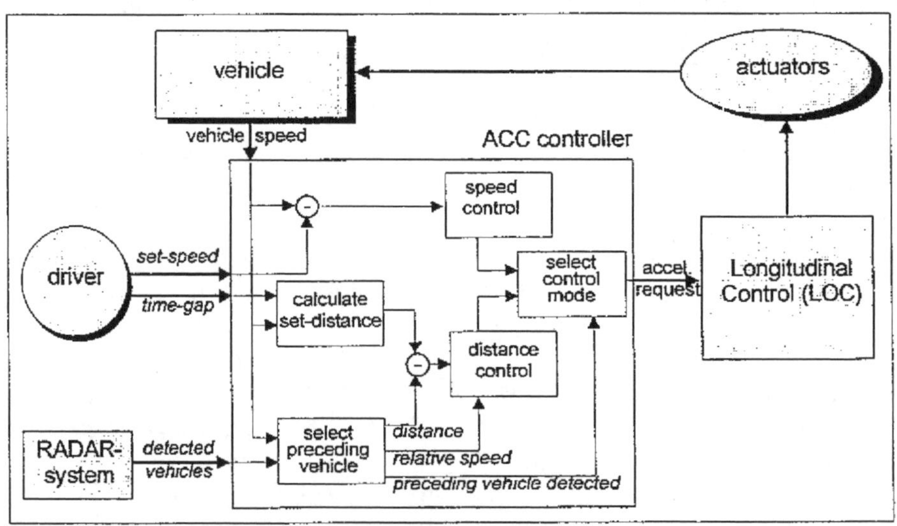

Fig. 4: Closer look at the ACC controller

acceleration-over-ground which has to be realized by the various vehicle subsystems.

LONGITUDINAL CONTROL (LOC) - The Longitudinal Control has to manage the actuator systems in order to achieve the desired acceleration calculated by the ACC controller. Depending on the set value of the acceleration either the drive train or the brakes have to be activated. An estimated road inclination is considered in this selection. In addition, limits of the actuation range of the drive train and the brake system must be known or calculated. After the active actuation branch is selected, the corresponding set values are computed.

The active brake system can either be:

- a deceleration control with an autonomous, closed control circuit using wheel speed sensors. The set value for deceleration is then directly derived from the set acceleration of the ACC controller, or
- or a brake force control mostly based on a pressure control loop with a pressure sensor. In this case the deceleration control happens on a higher level and will be a part of the Longitudinal Control.

Different functional structures of the drive train control are used if the car has manual or automatic transmission. For manual transmission the Longitudinal Control is demanding an engine torque. This can also be done with automatic transmission, but a coordination of the Longitudinal Control and the transmission control is more comfortable. In this case the Longitudinal Control sends a drive train torque command to the transmission control. This by itself computes a suitable gear and engine torque corresponding to the current gear shift strategy.

MAN-MACHINE-INTERFACE - In spite of all the technical aspects of ACC the driver will remain the master of the system retaining full responsibility for driving the car. The driver has to activate, operate, supervise and, if necessary, intervene or switch off the ACC. He also selects the major control parameters set speed and set time gap.

At least one switch is necessary to start the ACC function. This may be a separate switch or could have further functionality. As in conventional cruise control, the driver can adjust the desired maximum speed. Additionally, the driver must be able to control the set distance value. This set distance is proportional to the vehicle speed. It represents a constant time gap between the preceding vehicle and the ACC vehicle under stationary conditions. Consequently, this time gap is the set value. Again these two functions can be combined in one operation device.

Implementing ACC without a driver adjustable set time gap leads to a unsolvable dilemma: if the ACC time gap is very large, then ACC control will not be accepted by the customer because of the uncommon long distances. If on the other hand the ACC time gap is well tuned for the majority of ACC users under normal conditions, then this time gap will be too small in bad weather conditions for example. Thus, the set time gap must be adjustable so that the driver can take on full responsibility for driving the car when using ACC.

The driver is still part of the control circuit even after activating ACC. However, instead of operating the gas and brake pedal he has to supervise ACC. This requires some kind of information feed back. The most important feed back is the actual vehicle acceleration and acceleration rate of change to which the driver is highly sensitive. Via this "information channel" the driver is well informed about the state of the ACC controller. Other necessary information for the driver is the value of the set speed and set time gap. Very helpful for supervising especially during the learning phase is a "vehicle detected" signal. It indicates that a relevant vehicle for following has been recognized. An indication of insufficient deceleration capability during the actual traffic situation is helpful. The driver is warned if the preceding car decelerates too rapidly or the speed difference is too high while approaching. Such a signal, e.g. as an acoustical information, tells the driver to take over control. Another cause for the driver to take over control can be an automatic switch off of the ACC function, which must be clearly indicated. This can occur in case of system failure or in case of an intended switch off e.g. to avoid an engine stall in manually shifted vehicles.

IMPLEMENTATION - For the different functions within the entire ACC system a concept for integration in the vehicle was developed. Evaluation of potential concepts was done taken the following criteria into account:

- no impact on vehicle safety,
- no reduction of availability of the basic functions of the vehicle,
- low hardware effort,
- low application effort,
- only small component variations.

All these criteria can be fulfilled by slightly modifying the existing ECUs and adding one new ECU combining the Range Sensor and ACC controller. Splitting the Range Sensor and ACC controller would lead to a high external communication rate or to move ACC controller functions into the sensor. Then the sensor would have about the same workload as a combined sensor - controller unit.

The output of the ACC controller block, the desired acceleration, is an invariant command which can be used for every vehicle. The next functional block, the Longitudinal Control, is more dependent on the vehicle's actual equipment. However, at least for the introduction phase of ACC, while it will be sold as an option, the Longitudinal Control will be computed within the ACC/Sensor ECU (see also Sec. on Technical Trends).

The commands to drive train control or brake control, the output of the Longitudinal Control, can be different quantities. For example brake deceleration or brake torque, drive train torque or indicated engine torque could be used depending on the actual components These commands are sent via a data network like CAN to the actuator subsystems to achieve the active automatic intervention. These will be received by the standard ECUs, i.e. brake control by the ECU for traction control or Vehicle Dynamic Control. The engine power control has to carry out the torque demand of the ACC Longitudinal Control. In all cases the actuator control systems are fully functional even when ACC is not working properly. Therefore, their availability, reliability and safety are not affected by the ACC system. This assumes, that the driver must have the normal access to these subsystems not only via ACC.

A standard interface with a data set defined in physical units allows an independent development of different actuator systems, e.g. engine power control systems for different engines including gasoline and Diesel types. Ideally, the same ACC/Sensor ECU could be used for a gasoline or Diesel engine, with or without automatic transmission, with Vehicle Dynamic Control or mere traction control. On the other hand the same actuator system can be used for different ACC systems, e.g. of different car manufacturers.

LIMITS

RANGE OF OPERATION - A lower speed limit is introduced for safety reasons to prohibit an automatic (positive) acceleration at low speed. This should avoid a dangerous approach to an obstacle that is outside the lateral sensor range, but well inside the collision region of the vehicle. This constellation is typical for crossing pedestrians in urban areas or nonaligned cars in traffic jams. Usually, lower speed limits of about 40 km/h are used.

As mentioned above there are upper and lower limits for the set time constant. The upper limit of 2 s is of no importance for the safety of the system, but it makes no sense extending this limit to higher values because very few drivers will select a larger time constant. The lower limit is far more relevant for the system safety. A minimum value must allow the driver to safely take over control of the vehicle in emergency situations. It must also be acceptable for the majority of drivers. Experiences made during the testing phase of ACC systems have shown that values of about 1.0 s are reasonable.

Active braking must be restricted to moderate values to prevent the driver from getting into an unexpected situation caused by an ACC system reaction. Either the deceleration or the deceleration rate of the active brake have to be limited. Tests have shown that reasonable limits are 2.5 m/s^2 for the maximum deceleration and 1.0 m/s^3 for the deceleration rate of change. The latter meaning a change in deceleration of 1/10 g in 1 s. By this "smooth" braking the driver is never surprised by the car's reaction on changing traffic situations; he will not be overstrained in case he has to intervene during automatic braking. As a consequence ,however, the ACC system is not capable of making an emergency braking.

Mainly for the same reasons as with braking, but also in order to make the control of the car more comfortable, the maximum positive acceleration is limited to a value of 1.0 m/s^2.

TECHNICAL LIMITS - All ranging sensors - independent of their basic technical principle - have only limited range, as well in longitudinal as in lateral direction. Typical range values under ideal environmental conditions are 150 m for longitudinal and 10° for lateral range. However, these values will be further reduced in two ways: Either by weather conditions or by geometrical obstruction.

The longitudinal range of optical sensors is far more influenced by weather conditions than those of Radar sensors. They are physically limited in the same way as is the human eye, e.g. by rain, fog or snow. Under some special conditions (e.g. wet roads after heavy rainfall), optical sensors cannot detect vehicles that the human eye can see. This causes major problems because the driver does not expect the system to be "blind" in this situation. This almost never happens with Radar sensor. But even those are limited under certain conditions, especially if an absorbing or reflecting medium like snow covers the sensor. This also means detection drop outs with optical sensors.

Limitations due to geometrical obstructions are characteristic for all autonomous ranging sensors existing today. Tops of hills and bottoms of valleys naturally limit the longitudinal range. Crash barriers, walls and other side obstacles act in the same way in curves. Vehicles in the same or adjacent lanes can reduce both the longitudinal and the lateral range by hiding objects in front of them.

Other limitations of today's systems arise from difficulties in predicting the course far in front of the ACC equipped car. This is mainly due to two reasons: 1) errors in determining the actual value of the road curvature and 2) parts of roads with non-constant curvature. Whereas it is difficult to improve the determination of the actual road curvature (better filtering of the sensor signals usually implies increased filtering delays) the latter difficulty might at least partially be overcome by integrating video or navigation systems.

PRINCIPAL LIMITS - Although - as mentioned above - there are many ways to predict the course of the ACC car, one major problem can hardly be overcome: Lane changes intended by the driver are only predictable with a low probability. In the given sample situation the subsequent dilemma for the ACC arises: Approaching a vehicle in the same lane with high velocity on a multi-lane highway will, with high probability, lead to a passing maneuver. If this is desired, automatic braking to adjust to the preceding car would be undesirable. On the other hand, if the ACC waits until the decision is obvious, the distance to the car ahead may already be too small. Therefore it is too late to decelerate the own car in time to follow its predecessor. The situation gets far more complicated, if the car in front begins to pass or following traffic does not allow the intended passing.

The described situation is typical for principal limits of a technical system. It can not take on the responsibility of directing the vehicle in the general traffic. This results in restricting the functionality of the system. These limitations must be transparent to the driver. If the driver always understands the system behavior, he is able to decide on his interventions in time.

EFFECTS ON TRAFFIC FLOW

To estimate the effects of ACC equipped cars (ACC-cars) on traffic flow, simulations of traffic with ACC equipped and non-equipped cars can be used. The simplest ACC relevant traffic situation that can be investigated is driving on a single lane road in a line of traffic. In this chapter results of microscopic traffic simulations are shown presenting effects of ACC systems on single car behavior and the overall traffic flow.

In order to investigate mixed traffic (human drivers and ACC cars), it is necessary to have a validated driver model for longitudinal control. Empirical investigations led to an "action-point model". In this model changes in acceleration are not continuous. Acceleration jumps only occur at "action points" with a minimum absolute value of about $0.1\ m/s^2$ to $0.25\ m/s^2$. A driver changes the acceleration of the car, either if a "static condition" or a "dynamic condition" is satisfied. "Static condition" means that the difference between the actual distance and a desired following-distance exceeds a driver specific threshold value. A "dynamic condition" is fulfilled if the "time to collision" or "time to double"* becomes smaller than a threshold value depending on perception and attention of the driver. To get different driver behavior statistical distributions are used. Details of the driver model are given in [5].

In order to evaluate the degree of harmonization of the traffic flow, the acceleration noise *ACN* in time interval *T* is introduced as

$$ACN = \sqrt{\frac{1}{T} \cdot \int_0^T \left(a(t) - \bar{a}\right)^2 dt} \ ,$$

with acceleration *a(t)* and the corresponding mean value $\bar{a}$. *<ACN>* represents the ensemble mean value, approximated by using a set of simulations of the same experiment. To show the influence of an ACC car on a line of traffic, <ACN> was calculated for different car positions in the line. Fig. 7 shows the *<ACN>*-values for two setups of 20 cars. The first consists only of non ACC equipped cars, in the second, one ACC-car is located at position 10. In both cases the leader car drives with constant speed of 30 m/s.

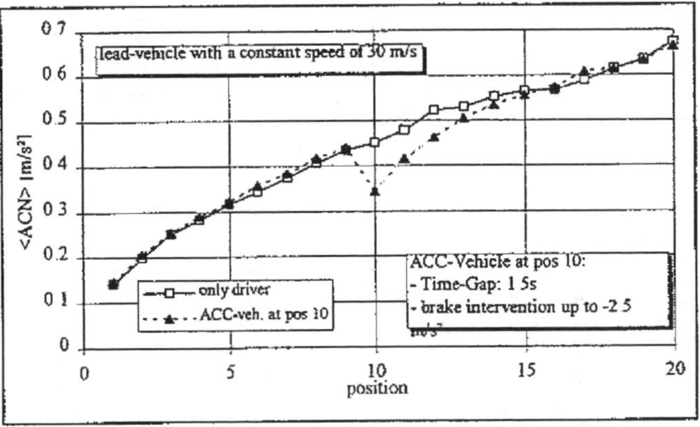

Fig. 7: Acceleration noise <ACN> dependent on the position of the car in a line of traffic. Comparison of a setup with "driver-cars" only and another setup with one ACC-car at position 10.

Acceleration noise is increasing with increasing car position in the line. A single ACC equipped car however (e.g. at position 10, see Fig. 7) decreases acceleration noise at this position, but even additionally for the four to five cars behind it. Hence, the effect of ACC equipped vehicles is the harmonization of vehicle acceleration, due to a continuous time and acceleration control and due to

* „time to collision" is defined as the time a following vehicle needs to reach the preceding vehicle, keeping the relative acceleration at the actual value. „time to double" is defined equivalently.

larger average time gaps between the ACC car and the car in front.

Another relevant point for ACC algorithms is platoon stability. It is well known, that driver behavior does not lead to platoon stability. Investigations of different ACC systems performed during the PROMETHEUS project showed ACC control algorithms to behave nearly the same like drivers and to exhibit increasing instability with decreasing value of the set time gap. To our knowledge this is still the case for almost all present ACC systems. This is uncritical as long as the amplification of acceleration fluctuations by ACC systems is smaller than those by drivers. All this was true for the ACC-algorithm we used for simulations.

Following distances of ACC cars are determined by the set time gap. These time gaps very often exceed drivers' values. Consequently you would assume ACC cars to reduce traffic flow. On the other hand ACC systems lower acceleration noise. The resulting harmonization is expected to lead to a macroscopic stabilization of traffic. Overall an increase or only a minor decrease of traffic flow should come out.

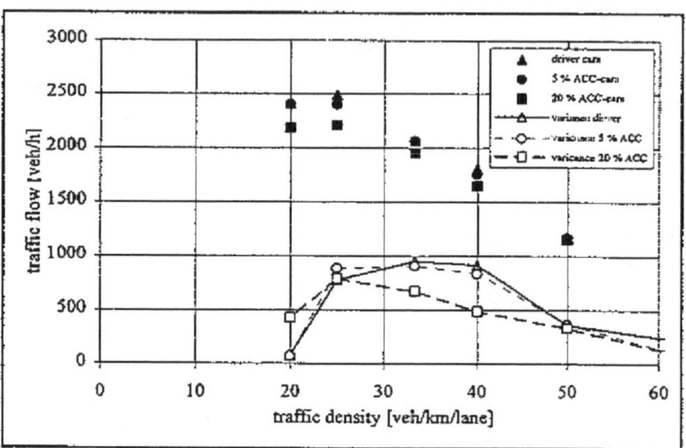

Fig. 8: Maximally achievable traffic flow for traffic systems with different amounts of ACC equipped cars (set time gap: 1.5 s). Simulations were done on a closed track (spatial periodic boundary conditions).

To estimate this effect, traffic simulations on a single lane closed track of variable length L and a fixed number of N = 100 vehicles were done. By variation of L different mean traffic densities were realized*. In the simulation only passenger cars (car length = 4.5 m) were used, and the maximum speed of the cars was distributed evenly in the interval 35 m/s .... 40 m/s. The distribution of inter-vehicle distances of "driver-cars" were fitted to measured data of short traffic lines. In longer lines of traffic occurring at high densities, some drivers switch over to larger distances to reduce their workload. Taking this into consideration the simulated traffic flow data for 100 % driver cars has to be interpreted as maximum possible values.

The simulation data in Fig. 8 shows a slight decrease of traffic flow with introduction of ACC cars, together with a macroscopic traffic harmonization. The later can be seen in a decrease of the variance of traffic flow, which is most significant at high densities. Increasing rates of ACC equipped cars decrease traffic flow due to larger time gaps. However, penetration rates of less then 5% to 10 % nearly do not have any macroscopic effect. Even the noticeable decrease of traffic flow for 20 % ACC cars may not represent reality because of two reasons: First, our driver model is based on short line driver behavior as mentioned above; second, future ACC algorithms may reach platoon stability even for smaller time gaps.

In summary, the main effect of ACC systems on traffic flow will be local harmonization which also influences non-equipped cars. The reduction of acceleration noise results in a more constant and therefore a more comfortable driving for all drivers. Additionally this may reduce the number of critical situations. Together with the larger time gaps of ACC cars this may lead to an enhanced driver safety.

EXPERIENCES

BOSCH has tested its own ACC system on over 40.000 test kilometers. The technical functionality as well as the safety of the system was demonstrated in real-world traffic situations. Test drivers felt significantly relieved on long distance travel - especially on highways, but also on major state and county roads - and praised the gain of comfort.

Test persons familiar with conventional cruise control adjusted very quickly to the operation of the extended functionality of our ACC system. Drivers without that experience required a short learning period to get used to the operation. After this adjustment phase, the users felt comfortable especially since the ACC system behavior was comprehensible due to the slow acceleration and deceleration changes. With active brake control, it was typically possible to drive long periods even in dense traffic without any driver interventions (up to 50 km on highways). Situations the system could not handle were only rarely encountered, because drivers generally intervene well before based on their respective driving experience. Therefore, it seems that the ACC system does

* A closed track is of course an „artificial" environment, but it has some advantages: it is possible to fix the mean traffic density to a predefined value without the need of many cars, therefore saving calculation time for investigations.

not affect the drivers' ability to judge dangerous situations

The test drivers felt relieved by the ACC assistance, because tasks rather difficult for humans like distance and speed measurements are taken care of by far superior ACC sensors. Hence, the attention of the driver shifted from observing mainly the preceding vehicle to a broader view of the general traffic situation enabling him to better predict traffic flow and dangerous situations.

The test persons not only reported feeling more comfortable, but also safer. This is probably based on the transparent ACC system behavior and the increased gaps between cars. It is interesting to note that even though the gaps get wider, fewer cars than expected pull in. We think this is due to the continuous control and consequently, the relative small variations of the gap. Does it happen anyway, the driver is still less distracted, because the ACC takes on the responsibility to adjust the gap.

Tests in the US showed the usefulness of the ACC even without active brake control. In Europe, on the other hand, the experiences revealed the necessity of active braking due to the dense traffic conditions. Without common driver interventions made it practically impossible to use the ACC continuously over a longer period of time. The driver could only feel the intended relief with active brakes.

Overall, the experiences with the ACC system can be summarized as:

easy to learn, easy to handle, easy to master.

TECHNICAL TRENDS AND DEVELOPMENT DIRECTIONS

INTEGRATION ASPECTS - In these days many developments in the automotive sector are characterized by achieving an ever increasing level of system integration. This is also the case for ACC. The Longitudinal Control function as described above is expected to be removed from the ACC ECU so that it is available to other systems. E.g. ACC and VDC systems can use a common LOC to realize their low level vehicle control functions. In a later stage the Longitudinal Control function will be integrated into an overall vehicle system architecture. Work on such a system architecture is in progress at present.

FUNCTIONAL IMPROVEMENTS - It can be expected that performance of Radar sensors will improve continuously. This implies increasing longitudinal and lateral range as well as higher separation capability of objects. A very interesting feature seems to be Radar imaging (see also Sec. on Curve Sensors) which is still in a very early stage. A lot of development work has still to be done.

A better target selection performance is to be expected with the integration of video systems by providing ACC with a more reliable course prediction and lane classification of objects. Although the basic algorithms for these tasks are known they have to be modified and further developed in order to be fast and robust enough. At the same time they should only require moderate hardware resources. Camera systems with sufficient dynamic range are under investigation, too. Much research effort is spent on these systems especially in Stop&Go-ACC activities but a definite solution to all problems mentioned is not to be seen today.

FUNCTIONAL EXTENSIONS

Stop&Go-ACC - As a next step following the series introduction of ACC systems, everybody expects the ACC functionality to be expanded towards Stop&Go. Then, the ACC application also assists the driver in traffic jams on highways and in urban areas which will particularly benefit people in congested regions. However, this requires the solution of a sensor as well as an actuator (or control) problem during the development stage.

The development of ACC sensors was mainly focused on detecting more distant vehicles (> 10 m). The Stop&Go extension necessitates the complete coverage of the near range meaning at least a few times the entire width of the car in a range of up to 30 m. Obviously, this is impossible to achieve with a single sensor in the front end of the vehicle (see Fig. 9). The arrangement and sensor types for this task are tested now, but it is too early to predict the final arrangement.

Furthermore, to extend the ACC functionality to

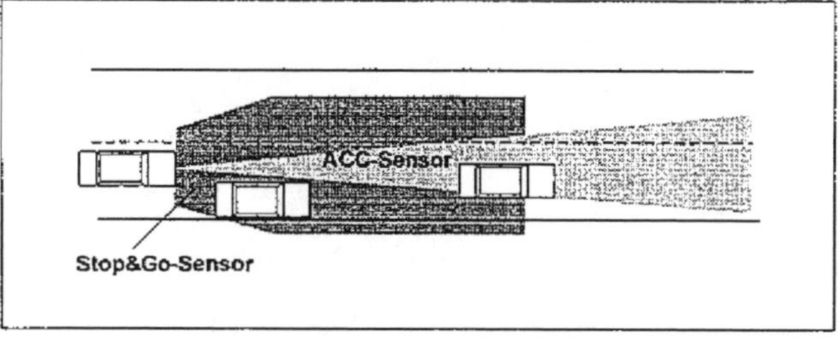

Fig. 9: Example for detection problems of nonaligned cars, typical in Stop&Go conditions

Stop&Go, an electronically controlled brake as well as an automatic transmission or coupling device are essential. No special requirements are necessary for the latter devices, but an automatic idle position during the stop phase would be advantageous.

The controlled brake has to obey stiffer requirements. On one side, higher deceleration values are needed at lower speeds. On the other side, the control strategy evidently has to consider the unsteady deceleration behavior during stopping maneuvers resulting in possible changes of the control variables and concepts.

Collision Warning - Using the ACC sensors for additional functions of course seems to be very attractive. But although technical progress in sensor technology is expected it is doubtful that Collision Warning with acceptably low false alarm rates and sufficient reliability can be achieved. The danger of the situation to be evaluated by the system primarily depends on the future course of the vehicle: In most cases a collision is avoided by a maneuver of the driver implying lateral motion of the car. However, anticipating this would require knowing the driver's actual and future intentions. Up to now no technical concept has been presented achieving this even only to a small extent. Thus these systems will not be able to distinguish a passing maneuver from a real collision situation (see also Sec. on Principal Limits) leading to either a high false alarm rate or low reliability.

CONCLUSIONS

The positive reaction of the test persons and the experience with a prototype ACC system at BOSCH gives us the confidence to expect ACC to be a useful driver assistance system. Thus, the ACC system will be developed further and a worldwide market introduction is planned within this decade. Furthermore, because of the strict exhaustion laws in many countries and the demand for more safety which require electronic throttle or diesel control and VDC systems it seems reasonable to expect the additional ACC system costs to be reduced significantly. Consequently, more people will be able to afford such an ACC system opening a high volume market and further opportunities for future extensions resulting in more safety and comfort.

REFERENCES

[1] Ackermann, F., "Abstandsregelung mit Radar," *Spektrum der Wissenschaft*, June 1980, p. 24-34, Weinheim, Germany, 1980

[2] Leutzbach, W.; Steierwald, G., Felderprobung autarker Abstandswarnsysteme, Final Report of the BMFT Project, BMFT, Bonn, Germany, 1981

[3] Ishikawa, T.; Sasaki, H.; Doi, A.; Adachi, T.; Teranaka, I.; Seni, H., "Development of an Auto-Brake System for the Collision Avoidance," *Mazda Technical Journal*, 12/1994, Japan,

[4] Winner, H.; Witte, S.; Uhler, W.; Lichtenberg, B., "System Aspects of Adaptive Cruise Control Systems," Proceedings of ATA-EL 95, Belgirate, Italy, May 9-10, 1995

[5] Witte, S., Einflüsse von Fahrerverhalten und technischen Abstandsregelsystemen auf den Kolonnenverkehr, Ph.D. Thesis, (to be published 1996)

961009

Longitudinal Autonomous Vehicle Control Utilizing Access to Electronic Throttle Control, Automatic Transmission and Brakes

Alfred Hoess, Werner Hosp, Reiner Doerfler, Hans Rauner
Siemens Automotive

Abstract

Different realizations of adaptive cruise control systems (ACC) have been tested. Firstly, only throttle access has been realized. In addition to this, the second realization utilizes access to the automatic transmission ECU. Finally, the third realization includes access to the brakes. Essentially, the first two versions are characterized by different states (e.g. acceleration, hold speed, deceleration), while the third version is based on continuous longitudinal vehicle control, e.g. using fuzzy methods [1].

Practical results showed high system stability for all three ACC versions. Advantages and disadvantages of each realization have been worked out based on simulated and measured results. Measurements showed that the first two solutions are sufficient to handle many traffic situations. However, in comparison with these versions, the third realization turned out to be the most powerful one.

1. Introduction

A test vehicle has been equipped with a three beam radar sensor [2]. Lateral beam characteristics are displayed in Fig. 1. Beam width (-3 dB) is about 3°, while the offset of adjacent beams is about 3.3° [3]. Utilizing this sensor, cars are detected at distances up to 170m, trucks at distances of about 200m. Pedestrians are detected up to about 75m.

Extensive test rides lead to the conclusion that a five beam radar sensor providing an individual beam width of 2° (-3dB) and an offset of adjacent beams of 2.5° is best suited for ACC. This kind of sensor that is currently under development covers an angular field of ±5°. Caused by higher antenna gain, pedestrians are detected at distances up to 110m.

2. Hardware Platform

The ACC hardware platform is shown in Fig 2. A twoprocessor system is used. While a digital signal processor is responsible for sensor signal processing, a micro-controller is used for acquisition of other vehicle sensor information, realization of actuator access, communication with other ECUs, driving a man machine interface as well as for the adaptive cruise control algorithms themselves [3].

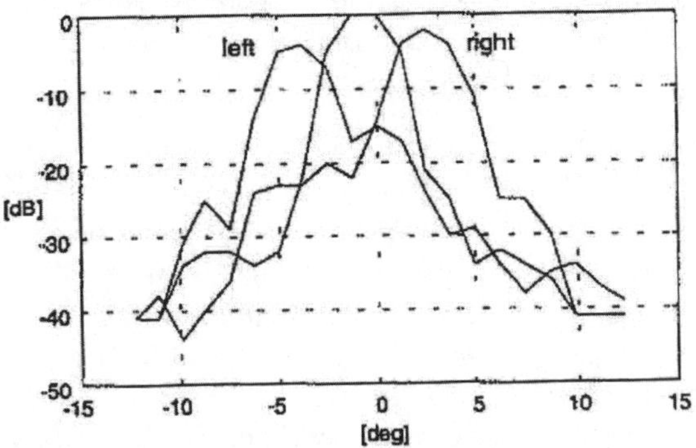

Fig. 1: Lateral radar beam sensitivity measured using a small corner cube reflector.

The headway sensor provides information about the distance and the relative speed of potential obstacles ahead. For classification of the danger potential of each object the road's actual radius of curvature needs to be known. This information can be estimated in several ways: Using wheel speed sensors, a steering wheel position sensor, a gyro sensor or a video camera. While the first three methods are only capable of detecting curves, when the car is already driving through the bend, the fourth method is able to forsee curves. However, due to the complex video signal processing and environmental problems, a video camera supported lane detection system is not suitable for the first generation low-cost ACC systems.

The following digital inputs are acquired: Cruise command switches, brake switch, driving style and road conditions. At present, driving style and switches adjust the safe distance within the legal range.

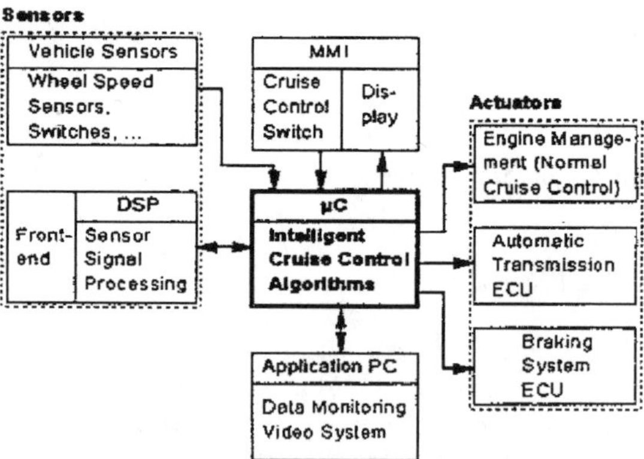

Fig. 2: Block diagram of ACC hardware.

Vehicle longitudinal control is realized indirectly by accessing the throttle via a conventional cruise control system (CC), by accessing the automatic transmission ECU as well as the braking system. Different versions of ACC systems have been realized and tested:

- Version 1:
  ACC functions are executed by only having access to the conventional cruise control system, e.g. via the engine management. Activated ICC can be in one of the following three states: decelerate (DC), hold speed (HS) and accelerate (AC). In AC mode the set speed value of the conventional cruise control system behind ACC is increased. Different acceleration states (marked AC1 AC2 and AC3) have been realized by switching the gear program characteristics between 'winter' (AC1), 'economy' and 'sport' (AC3). In HS mode set speed values are not modified. In DC mode, CC is switched off. It is automatically re-engaged when a state transition to HS or AC is initiated by ACC.

- Version 2:
  In addition to version 1, access to the automatic transmission ECU is enabled. This access is used for shifting down the automatic transmission while decelerating, thus increasing the engine's torque and leading to higher deceleration. Dependent on the number of downshifts, different deceleration states are realized that are marked DC (similar to version 1, i.e. all gears available), DC4 (gear program 4: only gears 1 to 4 enabled), DC3 (gear program 3) and DC2 (only the lowest two gears allowed)

- Version 3:
  In addition to version 1 limited brake access is allowed. Due to the fact, that a 100% error free distance sensing cannot be guaranteed by any available distance sensor, brake access has to be limited. Otherwise, a false alarm from a virtual obstacle in a very short distance could result in emergency braking, thus endangering the following vehicles. The continuous acceleration control is available using an electronic throttle control system (ETC).

The first two versions have been realized only by modifying the wiring of the input signals of available ECUs in the vehicle. No severe safety related problems occured. In contrast, for realization of the third version the booster of the braking system has been modified.

An application system has been developed for optimization of sensor signal processing and longitudinal control strategies. Most important data are faded into the video image from the road scene ahead of the vehicle. Additionally, all relevant data are recorded on hard disk, thus allowing an exact reconstruction of the the traffic situation later on in the lab.

Since the driver is fully responsible for his car, adaptive cruise control functions are automatically disengaged when the driver brakes. In order to improve safety this is done by both hardware and software. This also applies to the cruise control's OFF tip switch. In these cases ACC is not re-engaged automatically, which in contrast is the case when the driver accelerates. As soon as the driver doesn't accelerate any more, e.g. after overtaking another vehicle, ACC is automatically activated.

3. ACC Control Strategies and Results

Primary objective of ACC is distance control if a vehicle is detected ahead. Vehicle speed is adjusted according to automatically adapt and keep a recommended safety distance. If no vehicle is detected the ACC system acts like a conventional cruise control system (see Fig. 3)

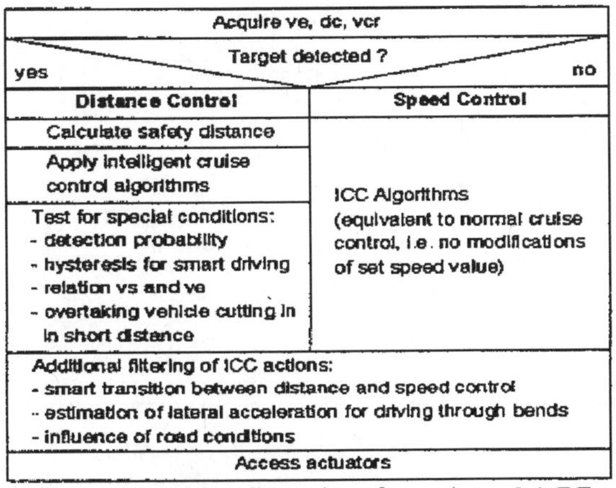

Acquire ve, dc, vcr

Target detected ?

yes / no

Distance Control	Speed Control
Calculate safety distance Apply intelligent cruise control algorithms Test for special conditions: - detection probability - hysteresis for smart driving - relation vs and ve - overtaking vehicle cutting in in short distance	ICC Algorithms (equivalent to normal cruise control, i.e. no modifications of set speed value)

Additional filtering of ICC actions:
- smart transition between distance and speed control
- estimation of lateral acceleration for driving through bends
- influence of road conditions

Access actuators

Fig. 3: Algorithm flow chart for activated ACC.

The recommended safety distance for distance control is computed as following: Frequently, the rule of thumb

$$\frac{d_s}{m} = \frac{1}{2}\frac{v_e}{km/h} \qquad (1)$$

is used, where d_s represents the recommended safety distance and v_e is vehicle speed. This rule is well suited for following another vehicle at almost the same speed. When there is a speed difference, however, additional parameters have to be taken into account:

$$d_s = d_0 + v_e T_s + \frac{v_e^2}{2a_{e\,max}} - \frac{v_c^2}{2a_{c\,max}} \qquad (2)$$

with

d_0 remaining distance for $v_e = v_c = 0$

T_s time constant (obviously, T_s=1.8s and $v_e = v_c = 0$ results in eq. (1))

v_c absolute speed of vehicle ahead

$a_{e\,max}$ maximum vehicle deceleration

$a_{c\,max}$ maximum deceleration of vehicle ahead.

T_s is one parameter that is used to adapt the ACC system to the driving style [3,4]. Presently, these parameters are set by the driver using switches. Depending on switch configuration, T_s values ranging from 1.2s (sports driver and dry road) to 2.7s (cautious driver) are chosen. Algorihms based on observation of driving history (driver behavior and interventions in typical traffic situations can be used for an automatic adaption of the driving style to the driver.

Common to all ACC versions is the flow chart described in Fig. 3. Basically, vehicle speed v_e, target distance d_c and relative speed v_{cr} are used as inputs for ACC algorithms At first, the recommended safety distance is computed (eq. (2)) Prior to accessing the actuators, the following special conditions are tested:

- During calculation of the most critical obstacle a detection probability is computed for every target depending on road radius of curvature and target distance as well as the tracking and prediction counters. This information is classified. Depending on the detection probability, ACC actions may be limited. While no limitations are necessary for very high detection probability, ACC actions are increasingly limited for decreasing detection probability. This principle has proven useful in order to avoid strange ACC actions for low probability targets where false alarms are more likely than for high detection probabilities. While the comfort is improved (unnecessary actions that may be well recognized by the driver are avoided), at the same time the ACC dynamic range is reduced (maximum deceleration only for confirmed objects).
- Additional hystereses have been implemented for smart driving. ACC actions that are well recognized by the driver are eliminated for low differences between desired and measured distance and speed values.
- In distance control mode the ACC system tends to adapt vehicle speed according to maintenance of the correct safety distance. Relation of vehicle speed v_e and set speed v_s is tested permanently in order to ensure limitation of v_e to v_s.
- A special situation occurs, when an overtaking vehicle is cutting in at too short distance Depending on speed difference, an additional distance credit is computed, thus avoiding unusual system reactions, e.g. unnecessary rapid deceleration.

Independent of ACC control mode, ACC actions to be applied are further filtered:

- Algorithms for a smart transition between distance and speed control mode have been implemented, ensuring smart driving, e.g. when a target is detected for the first time or when it is lost for a short period of time.

- Having information on the road's radius of curvature and on vehicle speed, lateral acceleration is estimated assuming quasi-stationary conditions. Depending on lateral acceleration permitted actions are limited in order to avoid rapid acceleration or deceleration while driving through bends.

- Finally, according to driving style and road condition information ACC actions are limited, thus avoiding rapid deceleration or acceleration on slippery roads.

3.1 ACC Realizations 1 and 2

Obviously, ACC realization 1 is a reduced version of realization 2. Therefore, description of the algorithms is combined. Longitudinal control is realized by switching between possible states. A three-dimensional characteristic state mapping is used for determination of the required ACC state. Necessary inputs are represented by classified values of vehicle speed v_e (6 classes), relative speed v_{cr} (11 classes) and difference d_r between desired distance d_s and obstacle distance d_c (11 classes). State mapping contents are state numbers: -3 (equivalent to AC3), -2 (AC2), -1 (AC1), 0 (HS), 1 (DC), 2 (DC4), 3 (DC3) and 4 (DC2). A detailed description of control algorithms is given in [5].

Fig. 4 illustrates ACC behavior in a situation where the test vehicle is following a vehicle ahead. Desired speed and acceleration are adapted within acceptable tolerances. Since relative speed is slightly higher than the desired speed, measured distance becomes increasingly less than the desired distance. As soon as a specific tolerance is exceeded the system is switched to moderate deceleration (state no. 1) for a short time ($t \approx 10$ ... 12s). A little bit later, the preceeding vehicle starts overtaking another vehicle in front of it ($t \approx$ 14s). Consequently, the slower vehicle is detected at a distance of about 100m. Relative speed is measured to be about -7m/s. Deceleration is initiated. Since relative speed is rather low, no downshifts are necessary. Adaption to desired speed and distance is very comfortable, because the situation can be handled simply by closing the throttle.

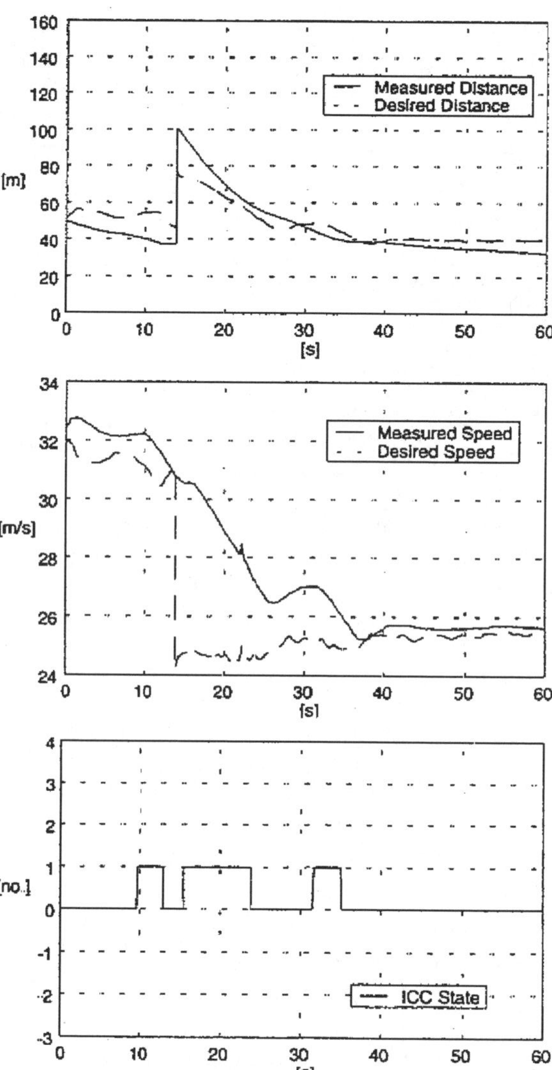

Fig. 4: Vehicle ahead starts overtaking a slower vehicle in front of it. ACC adapts test vehicle speed to the slower vehicle.
-3: AC, highest acceleration
0: HS, hold speed
+3: DC, gear program 3, high deceleration

Fig. 5 indicates an approaching manoeuvre to a rather slow vehicle ($v_{cr} \approx$ -14m/s) that is detected at a distance of about 130m ($t \approx 1.5$s). This situation can only be handled by applying maximum available deceleration (downshift to gear 3, state 3). Switching the automatic transmission system back to program 'D' (state no. 0) takes some time. As a consequence vehicle speed is reduced more than required resulting in necessity for moderate acceleration (state no. -1, $t \approx 22s$).

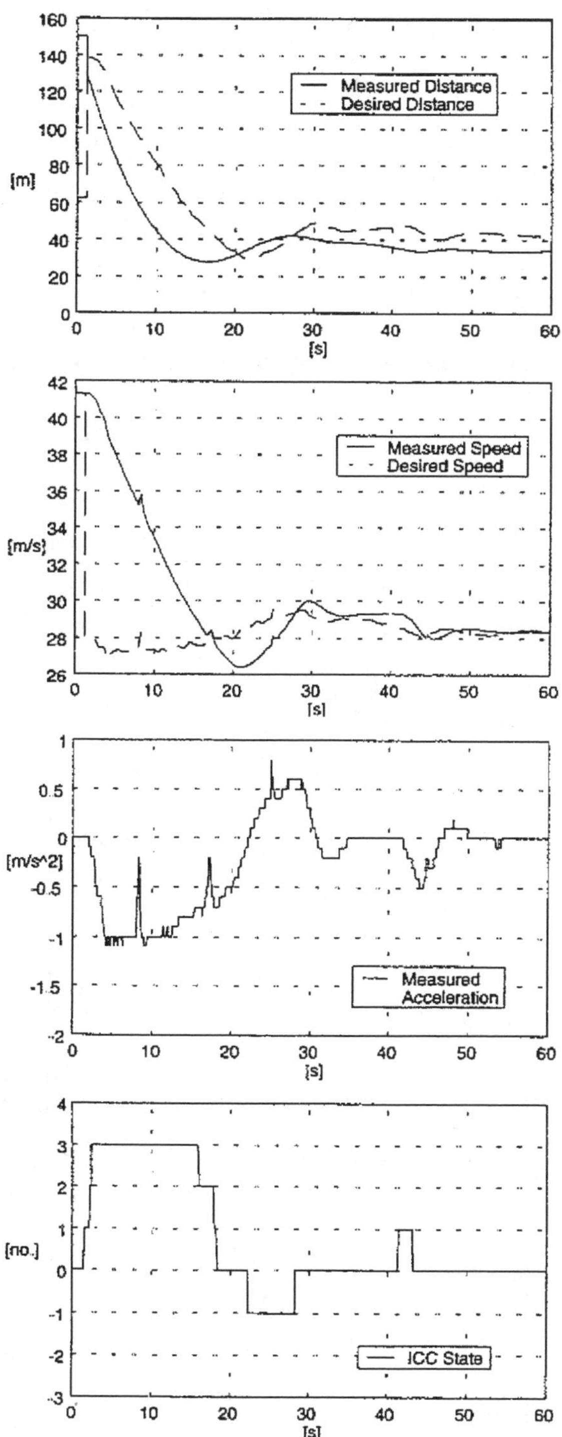

Fig. 5: Approaching a rather slow vehicle. Demand for downshift to gear 3.

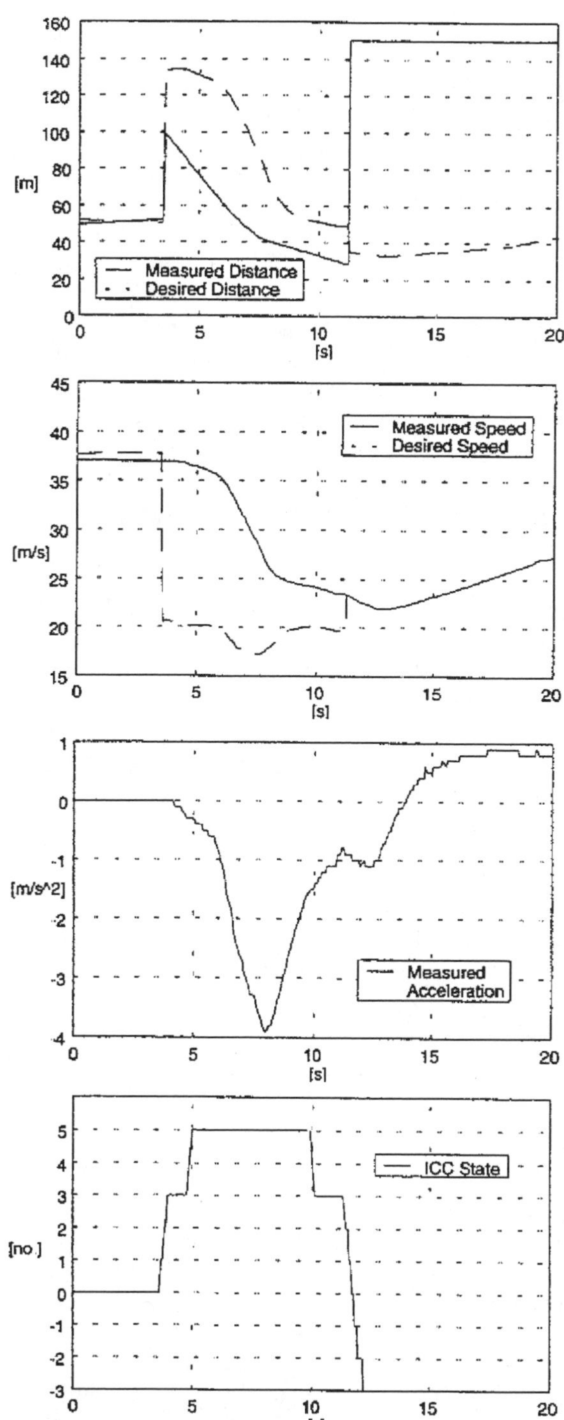

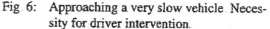

Fig. 6: Approaching a very slow vehicle. Necessity for driver intervention.

Fig. 5 also illustrates limited deceleration capability even for plain terrain. Closing the throttle (state 1) leads to $a_e \approx -0.5 m/s^2$, while shifting down by one gear (state 2) results in $a_e \approx -0.75 m/s^2$. Even a downshift by 2 gears (state 3) only yields a deceleration of about $a_e \approx$ -1m/s². Further downshifts are not possible due to the fact that they demand too high engine rpm. Obviously, deceleration values depend very much on the vehicle itself (e.g. weight) as well as on the engine's torque.

The example in Fig. 6 points out limited deceleration capability. The test vehicle is approaching a very slow vehicle ($v_{cr} \approx$ -18m/s). Due to driving through a bend, the vehicle is detected for the first time at a distance of about 100m ($t \approx$ 3s). Although ACC immediately shifts down the automatic transmission (state 3) the situation can't be handled automatically. The test vehicle driver has to brake ($t \approx$ 5s). Consequently, ACC is completely switched off (state 5). ACC continues operation after re-engaging the system ($t \approx$ 10s). Due to overtaking the vehicle in front, at $t \approx$ 12s the vehicle isn't detected any more (default distance 150m) resulting in acceleration (AC3, state no. -3).

3.2 ACC Realization 3

Having given an ACC specific maximum deceleration a_{eACC} and a slower vehicle ahead driving at constant speed v_c, the situation can be handled automatically only if the vehicle is detected at a distance

$$d_c > d_{s0} + \frac{(v_{e0} - v_c)^2}{2a_{eACC}} \tag{3}$$

where

$$d_{s0} = d_0 + T_s v_c \tag{4}$$

with d_{s0} being the safety distance for speed adaption ($v_e = v_c$) and v_{e0} being the initial vehicle speed.

For targets detected at shorter distance than the d_c value in eq. (3), the actual distance can become shorter than the required safety distance d_{s0} for speed adaption. For detection distances lower than

$$d_{\min} = \frac{(v_{e0} - v_c)^2}{2a_{eACC}}$$

automatic braking is not able to avoid a rear-end collision. As a consequence, the driver has to brake.

For handling the situation in Fig. 6 without violation of d_{s0} an ACC deceleration of 2.3m/s² is necessary, while for a 50% violation of d_{s0} an automatic deceleration capability of 1.9m/s² is sufficient.

ACC version 3 is essentially based on computation of the required deceleration for best adaption to the vehicle in front, i.e. driving with the same speed in recommended safety distance. Accees to the brakes is necessary only for higher decelerations than about 0.5m/s², which represents the deceleration with closed throttle (plain terrain). Automatic braking is limited to 2.5 m/s². For higher decelerations, the driver has to brake himself.

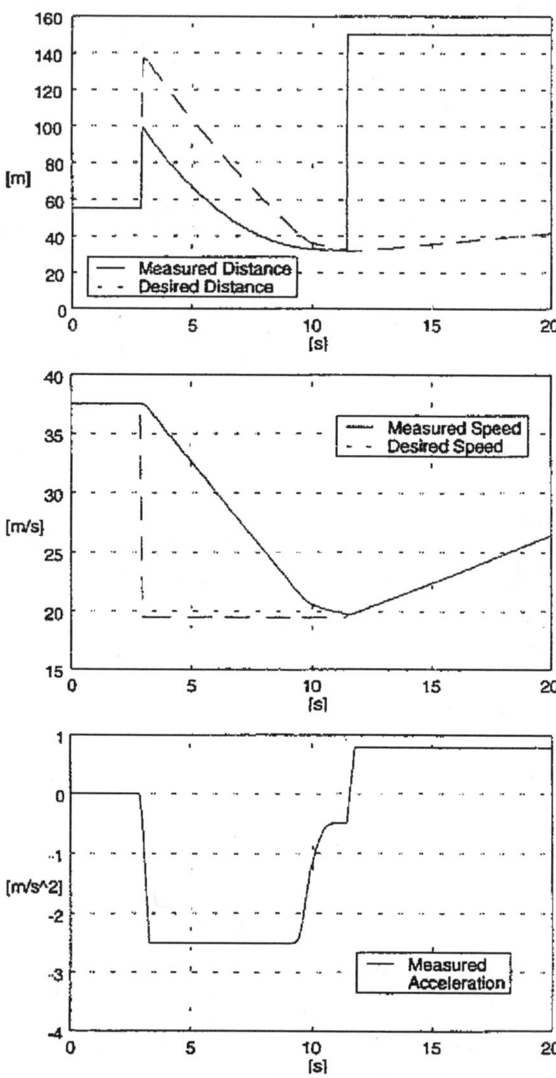

Fig. 7: Simulated result of the situation in Fig. 6 using ACC realization 3

Fig. 7 illustrates simulation results obtained outgoing from the traffic situation in Fig. 6. Even when an ACC reaction time of roughly 0.4s is assumed, the situation could be handled automatically. At first maximum deceleration is applied. Since a safety factor has been introduced, reduction of brake pressure is started ($t \approx 9s$). After additional two seconds, brake access is no more required (deceleration less than 0.5m/s²).

4. Comparison

ACC realization 1 is the most limited solution. Deceleration capability is very limited (0.5m/s² for plain terrain). When driving down a hill, in some cases no deceleration is obtained. ACC dynamic range is not sufficient. Relative speeds of about 8m/s can be handled automatically (plain terrain). Control comfort in these situations is very satisfactory, since only throttle access is used and no rapid reactions can occur.

ACC realization 2 includes the advantages of version 1 for low speed differences. ACC dynamic range is increased by downshifts of the automatic transmission. Deceleration values of about 1 to 1.5m/s² have been measured. Relative speeds of up to 15m/s² can be handled. While a downshift by one gear doesn't decrease comfort very much, downshifts by more than 1 gear are clearly recognized. Hence, comfort is not very satisfactory in the latter situations.

While vehicle modifications for these two solutions are not very much safety related, realization 3 is safety critical due to modifications of the braking system. While the upper systems are based on state control, version 3 enables analog control capability resulting in much smarter driving and increasing comfort. ACC dynamic range is limited according to the maximum allowed brake access (eq. (3)). If a vehicle ahead is reliably detected at a distance of 120m, relative speeds of more than 20m/s can be handled automatically.

5. Conclusion

The ACC systems described in this paper have proven to be very useful, particularly when the comfort aspect is considered.

Most traffic situations can be handled automatically. However, there are some situations that cause problems which have to be solved by the driver (e.g. if approximation to other vehicles is too fast or if vehicles ahead are detected at rather short distances, e.g. while driving through bends).

For this reason as well as due to the fact, that a 100% liability (100% detection probability, 0% false alarm rate) of the distance sensor can't be guaranteed, ACC can only be a driver assisting system without any claim for collision avoidance. Therefore, the driver remains fully responsible for his car in all situations. As a consequence, all automatic functions are overridden by driver actions.

References

[1] Driankov D., Hellendoorn H., Reinfrank M., "An Introduction to Fuzzy Control", Springer Verlag, 1993

[2] Hoess A., Hosp W., Rauner H., "Comparison of radar and infrared distance sensors for adaptive cruise control applications", ...

[3] P43 39 920.7

[4] P44 02 080.5

[5] Hoess A., "Realisation of an intelligent cruise control system utilizing classification of distance, relative speed and vehicle speed information", IEEE Symposium Proceedings of "Intelligent Vehicles 1994", Paris, to be published

ACC SENSORS

Overview

2006-01-0142

Test Methods and Results for Sensors in a Pre-Crash Detection System

Charles Birdsong, Peter Schuster, John Carlin, Daniel Kawano, William Thompson and Jason Kempenaar
California Polytechnic State University

ABSTRACT

Automobile safety can be improved by anticipating a crash before it occurs and thereby providing additional time to deploy safety technologies. This requires an accurate, fast and robust pre-crash sensor that measures telemetry, discriminates between classes of objects over a range of conditions, and has sufficient range and area of coverage surrounding the vehicle. The sensor must be combined with an algorithm that integrates data to identify threat levels. No one sensor provides adequate information to meet these diverse and demanding requirements. However the requirements can be met with an optimal combination of multiple types of sensors. Previous work considered criteria for evaluating various sensors to find an optimal combination. This work presents test methods and results for selected sensors proposed for use in a pre-crash detection system. The test methods include static and dynamic telemetry testing to identify the range, accuracy, reliability and operating conditions for each sensor. Each sensor is evaluated for its ability to discriminate between classes of objects. The tests are applied to ultrasonic, laser range finder and radar sensors. These sensors were selected because they provide the maximum information, cover a broad range and region and are commercially viable in passenger vehicles.

INTRODUCTION

Motor vehicle crashes are the leading cause of death for persons of every age from 2 through 33. Since the 1960s, introduction of passive safety equipment (e.g. seat belts, air bags, crush structures) has dramatically reduced accident rates, injury severity and the number of fatalities, however the absolute number of deaths and injuries remains high. Since 1993, every year nearly 6 million motor vehicle crashes have consistently resulted in over 40,000 deaths in the US alone (NHTSA 2005). Certain conditions (weather, lighting, impairment, distraction) limit drivers' effectiveness at recognizing and responding to dangerous situations. For example, 50% of fatal accidents occur outside of daylight hours, and 12% during inclement weather. Driver distraction is cited as a contributing cause in half of all accidents.

In order to significantly reduce accident severity and occurrence, future safety technologies must move beyond 'passive.' To support this, vehicles will require new exterior pre-crash sensors to create an electronic awareness of the traffic situation. Pre-crash sensing may well have the most impact in reducing injuries from nighttime accidents involving impaired drivers. However, the advanced safety features enabled by pre-crash sensing will provide a significant benefit in all cases of poor lighting, bad weather, or driver distraction.

Figure 1 illustrates some near-term safety benefits of pre-crash sensing. Current vehicles (top half of the figure) do not have any means of anticipating a crash. In the short time frame (approximately 10-20 ms) after a crash is detected by acceleration-based sensors the options for deploying safety technologies is limited. Currently airbags are deployed approximately 10-20 ms after impact and must be inflated rapidly so that they are in place to protect the passenger. If the crash could be anticipated then additional time would be available to deploy new safety technologies such as audible alarms, seatbelt pre-tensioners, automatic door locks, seat stiffeners, seat position control, window closing, slower airbag inflation rates, and pre-crash braking (Lyons & Taskin 2000, Spies 2002, Knoll et al. 2004). The result would be increased vehicle crash survival rates. In addition, pre-crash detection will reduce the incidence of unnecessary airbag deployment. Studies show that unnecessary airbag deployment can cause greater injuries than a minor crash would cause (Jones 2002).

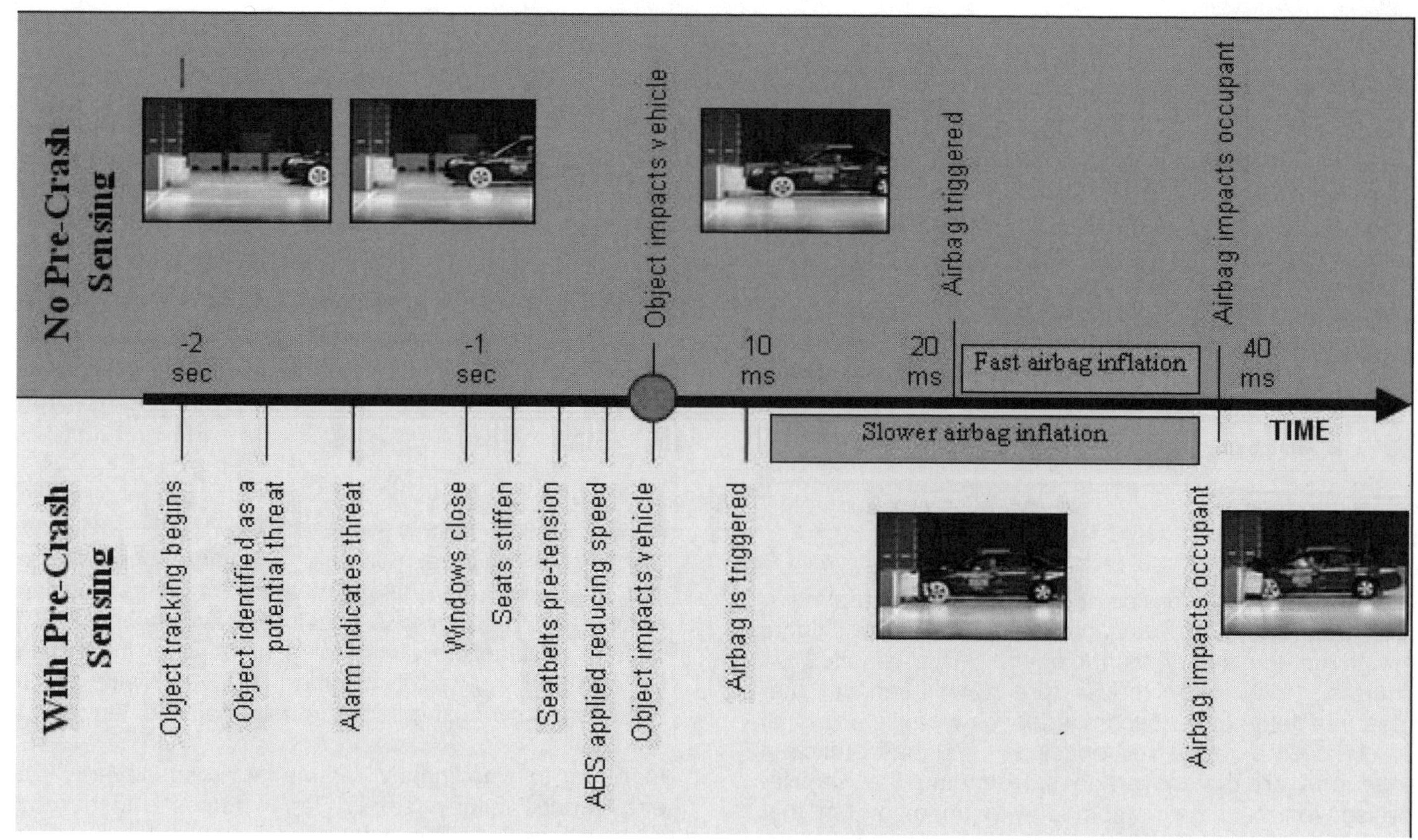

Figure 1: Timelines for collisions with and without pre-crash sensing

Beyond the passive safety technologies shown in Figure 1, an advanced pre-crash sensing system will also be capable of directing future accident-avoidance technologies. For example, an automated braking system could augment a driver's braking force if the sensor determines more deceleration is necessary to stop the vehicle before impact. With increased sensor robustness, this system could be used to automatically apply the brakes when an imminent crash is predicted; regardless of whether braking is already applied.

This type of technology is not new. Certain external sensors have already been adopted into passenger vehicles, reducing the costs and broadening consumer acceptance. For example, ultrasonic sensors are used as parking aids on many vehicles, passive infrared sensors have been used to aid vision at night, and radars are used in adaptive cruise control (ACC) systems to maintain safe following distance when cruise control is active. These sensors are used in a passive sense and not to actively avoid or aid in a crash event. However it has been proposed that they could be integrated with intelligent real-time algorithms to do so (Knoll *et al.* 2004). This requires an accurate, fast and robust pre-crash sensor that measures telemetry, discriminates between classes of objects over a range of conditions, and has sufficient range and area of coverage surrounding the vehicle. The sensor must be combined with an algorithm that integrates data to identify threat levels. No one sensor provides adequate information to meet these diverse and demanding requirements. However the requirements can be met with an optimal combination of multiple types of sensors. Previous work considered criteria for evaluating various sensors to find an optimal combination (Carlin, et. al. 2005).

To support the development of future integrated pre-crash sensing systems, this paper presents methods for testing individual sensors in a pre-crash detection system. In most cases, the proposed sensors were not developed for pre-crash detection, but may be adapted to this use. As a result, sensor performance for this application is not already known. Pre-crash detection is a new function that is distinct from other types of sensor applications so new test protocols are required.

The objective of a pre-crash sensor is to provide telemetry and object discrimination data at a suitable range and rate to predict a crash event. Accuracy, reliability and environmental factors must be considered as well. Test methods can be collected into general categories of static, dynamic, and object discrimination with specific procedures defined in each category. In addition to the test methods, preliminary test results are presented in this paper. These are intended as examples that can be used for a broad range of proposed pre-crash sensors.

STATIC TESTS

Static tests measure the performance of sensors while both targets and sensors are stationary. This is expected to provide a measure of the optimal sensor performance since there is no relative motion. Static tests include range, accuracy, and reliability. Each of these criteria is evaluated for sensitivity to multiple objects, vibrations, and environmental factors.

RANGE, ACCURACY, AND RELIABILITY

Distance Range measures the minimum and maximum distances at which the sensor can detect objects with reasonable accuracy. The sensor manufacturer usually provides this information for certain standard objects, with a factor of safety to account for environmental conditions and other factors. Under ideal cases a sensor's range may exceed the manufacturer's specification significantly. The test method involves placing a target a fixed distance from the sensor and comparing the sensor output with the distance measured using a tape measure. The range can depend on the shape, surface finish or material of the target. For example a LIDAR may have a longer range for reflective surfaces compared with a dispersive surface. An ultrasonic sensor may have longer range with large flat surfaces (walls) versus smaller curved surfaces (pole, ball, human). Minimum range information is also important because the most critical measurement for a pre-crash sensor triggering irreversible countermeasures is distinguishing a near miss from an actual crash event. Long-range data is less sensitive because far objects represent less of a threat (and proposed long-range countermeasures are currently reversible).

Field of View (FOV) Range measures the angular detection range of the sensor. LIDAR measures in a straight line (narrow beam), but RADAR and ultrasonic sensors have a cone of coverage. A signal is broadcast and reflected by the target and the reflection is used to obtain the telemetry data. The FOV is important in designing a pre-crash sensor to avoid blind spots near the sensor where critical measurement is needed. Also, if multiple sensors are used, the FOV can be used to develop an algorithm to more effectively integrate output signals. The FOV test method involves placing a target at specific positions at pre-identified distance and angle from the centerline of the sensor. The sensor output is compared to a target distance measured with a tape measure and protractor from the center of the sensor. The results can be reduced into a map that shows the area of coverage in detail. Typically the data from the periphery of the angular range is unreliable and the FOV is defined by the locations where the data is accurate and repeatable. Figure 2 provides an example of the output map obtained from testing an Ultrasonic sensor.

Accuracy indicates how well the sensor predicts the telemetry data compared to a known value. The data in Figure 3 shows range test results with an ultrasonic sensor for various objects. The graph records the absolute deviation of the measured distance of the target predicted by the sensor compared to the measured distance with a tape measure. The results indicate that the ultrasonic sensor has accurate range from about 0.1 meters up to 4 meters with little sensitivity to different target objects. Beyond 4 meters some objects can be measured while others cannot. The difference is likely due to the ability of the target surface and shape to reflect the ultrasonic waves back to the sensor.

Reliability is defined to be the probability that the sensor will not fail (i.e. return erroneous results) in any given measurement. A safety sensor is expected to have extremely high reliability. However, for the purposes of a new safety technology that is intended to enhance (significantly) the already-proven performance of passive safety systems, the important aspect of reliability is that the system should do no harm. In other words, while the long-term goal is a system that can detect virtually all objects in virtually all conditions, a short-term aim is to detect as many as possible, with NO false detections. False positive detections are undesired because they might be used to trigger irreversible deployments or potentially drastic avoidance maneuvers. So, in the initial system requirements, avoiding false positives is more important than detecting every real contact.

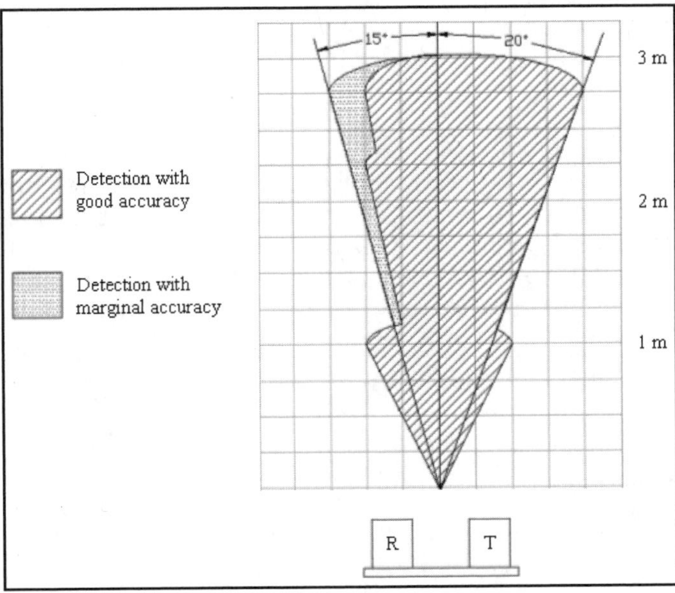

Figure 2: Ultrasonic rangefinder sonic cone map

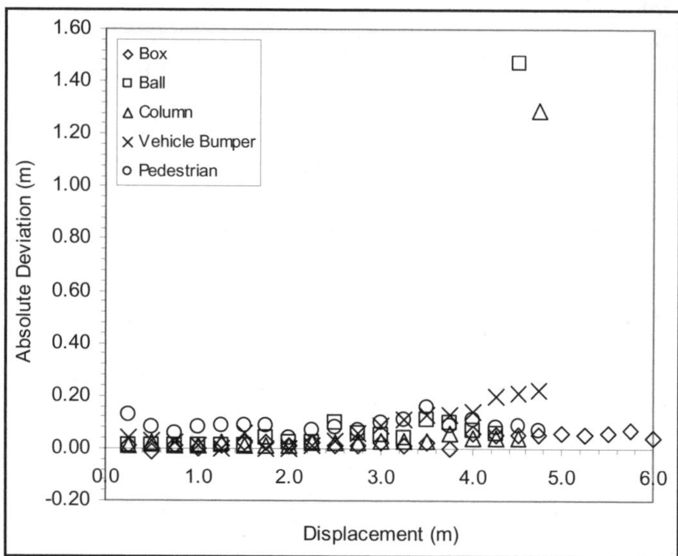

Figure 3: Ultrasonic rangefinder absolute deviation as a function of displacement for various target objects in static tests

The static test results for a LIDAR are presented in the figures below. Figure 4 shows that the accuracy of the LIDAR is well within in the ±0.30m claim of the manufacturer. In fact, on average all of the data falls within ±0.20m of the actual object distances. In general, it appears that the LIDAR tends to slightly overestimate the distance for most objects while underestimating for a pedestrian.

The absolute deviation remains within ±0.20 m as distance is increased, and as a result, the percent error in the distance measurement decreases as distance is increased (Figure 5). When ranges are less than 5 m, the ±0.20 m accuracy causes significant errors. Beyond 5 m, the effect of this accuracy is much less important.

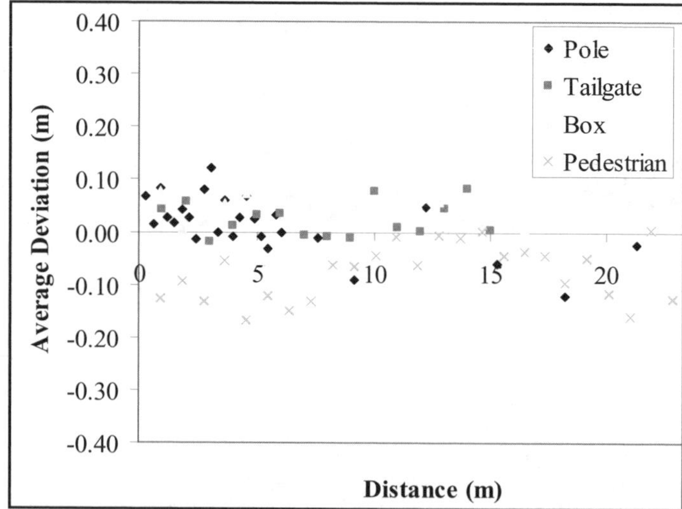

Figure 4: LIDAR absolute deviation as a function of distance for various objects in static testing

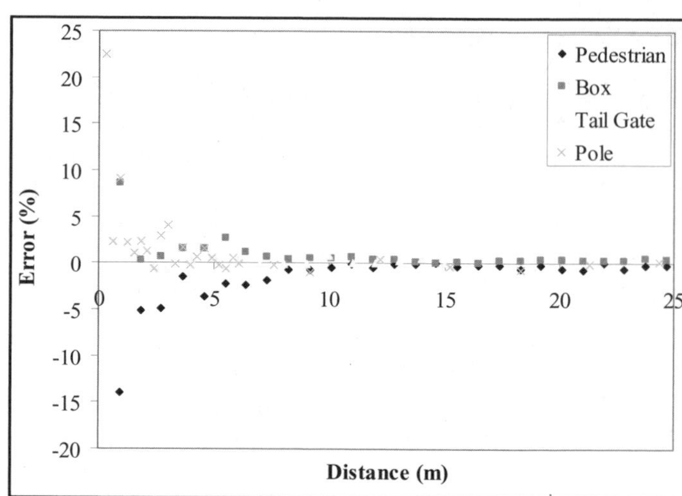

Figure 5: LIDAR percent error in distance measurement as a function of distance for various objects in static tests

SENSITIVITY OF RESULTS

<u>Multiple Objects</u> - These tests are intended to determine the sensor's ability to differentiate between the target (typically the object presenting the greatest threat to the vehicle) and other objects within range. In the real-world scenario, multiple objects will always be present, and a sensor must have some way of either (a) tracking multiple objects (e.g. most radar systems), or (b) selecting and reporting data on the most important objects (e.g. ultrasonic sensors give distance to only the closest object). Multiple object testing is currently underway

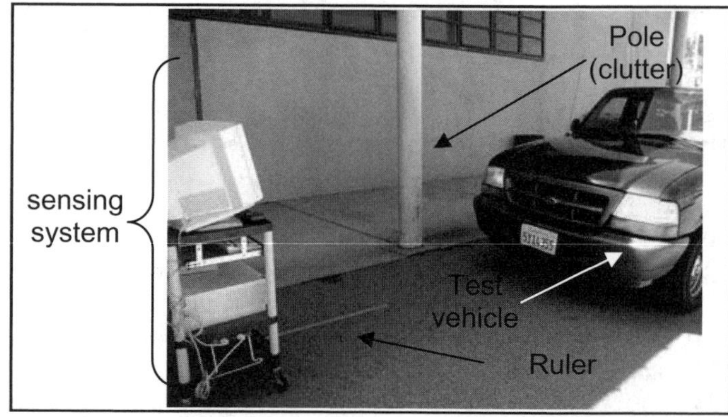

Figure 6: Experimental setup for multiple object static testing used in all sensor types

Environmental Factors - The environmental issues faced by an external automotive sensor are well understood. Many sensors proposed for a pre-crash system will have already been subjected to these conditions to evaluate their durability. However, evaluating the *performance* of the sensors under adverse conditions, and particularly under conditions known to cause issues for the tested sensor, are key to understanding the best way to integrate a number of sensors into a single system.

Vibration - Vibration inputs into the exterior sensors depend to a certain extent on the specific vehicle and locations chosen for a particular application. However, as with environmental factors, typical automotive vibration loads are well understood and many sensors will already have been evaluated for durability. But, the performance of the sensors under these predicted vibrations is critical for evaluating their input to the integrated system.

DYNAMIC TESTS

Dynamic tests measure the performance of the sensors as the target or sensor moves during the test. Under some conditions the sensor's performance is degraded when there is relative motion. Dynamic tests are performed with controlled, usually fixed, velocities of the target object. Actual distance is determined using a separate, direct measurement scheme. In addition to determining the accuracy of a sensor under these circumstances, the dynamic tests enable additional assessment of sensitivity to direction of motion, near misses, detection time, and multiple objects.

Figure 7 shows the test setup for a simple 1 m/s test of the Ultrasonic system using a string pot, while Figure 8 and Figure 9 give typical results. As the figures show, overall the sensor accurately measures the displacement of the test object (with occasional scatter), with the exception of the pole (95 mm diameter) as a target. Multiple trial runs with the pole indicated that the sensor consistently underestimates the displacement of the pole.

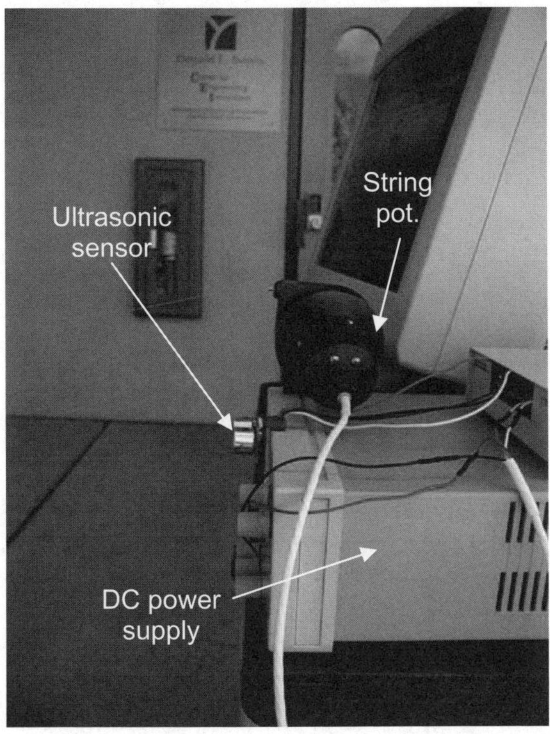

Figure 7: Ultrasonic sensor dynamic tests with string pot.

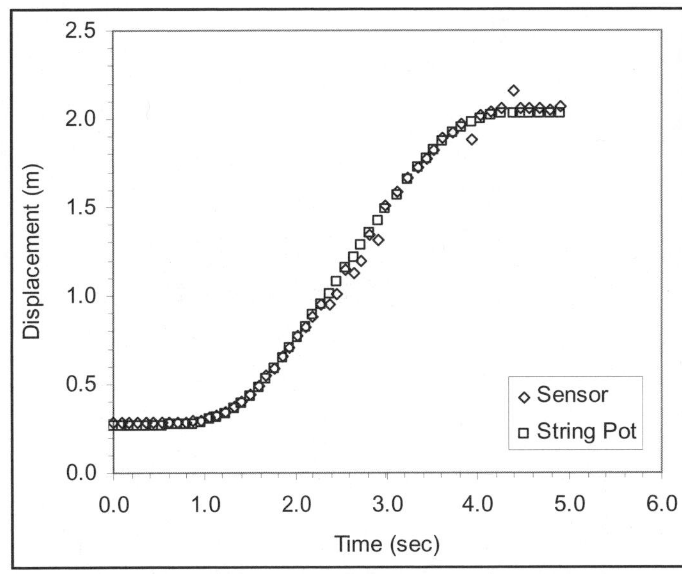

Figure 8: Typical results for dynamic test of ultrasonic sensor compared with string pot.

<u>Time to Detection</u> – A related performance criteria evaluated through dynamic testing is the time it takes a sensor to detect an object when it enters the FOV. Two conditions will be considered – motion laterally into the FOV from outside the angular range, and motion longitudinally into the FOV from outside the distance range.

<u>Near Miss</u> – For a system that triggers irreversible deployments or avoidance maneuvers, the sensors must be capable of predicting when a collision becomes unavoidable (i.e., no maneuvering can prevent it from occurring). The key criterion here is the difference between an impact and a near miss. For a head-on collision with significant offset, this may not be apparent until a few meters before contact. This criterion will be measured by assessing how the sensor output data changes for longitudinally moving objects located progressively further from the sensor centerline.

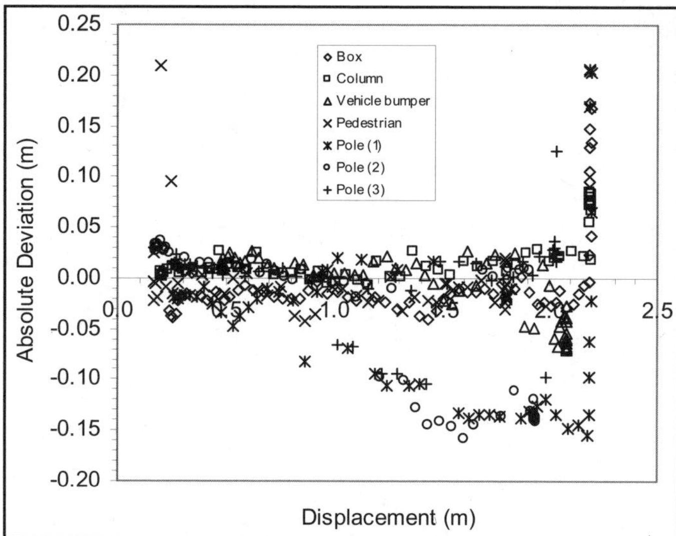

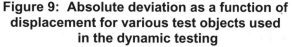

Figure 9: Absolute deviation as a function of displacement for various test objects used in the dynamic testing

Sensitivity to Direction – Many of the dynamic tests will be performed with object motion either directed longitudinal (parallel to the centerline of the sensor FOV), or transverse (perpendicular to the centerline of the sensor FOV). However, additional sensor tests are required to evaluate objects traveling within the FOV on trajectories between these extremes. Tests will be performed for motion vectors every 30° between 0° and 90°.

Multiple Objects – The goal of the dynamic multiple object tests is to determine how well a system responds when objects appear to join with and separate from each other in the FOV, or when the primary threat target changes from one object to another as relative positions change. The tests performed will include both lateral and longitudinal movement of two or more objects within the field of view.

OBJECT DISCRIMINATION

Object discrimination tests assess an additional aim of pre-crash sensing systems – the ability to distinguish between types of objects. The goal of these tests is to identify whether a particular sensor exhibits any differences in output signals with different objects (all other conditions held constant). The categories of objects for which different vehicle responses may be desired are summarized in Table 1. Sensor responses to each of these types of objects will be measured initially in static tests.

Table 1: Object types for discrimination tasks

Type of object	Size	Mass	Type	Example object
Wide high mass	Wide	High	Hard	Tree, vehicle, walls
Narrow high mass	Narrow	High	Hard	Tree, pole
Wide low mass	Wide	Med	Med	Brush, billboard, motorcycle
Medium high mass	Med	Med	Soft	cow, moose, pedestrian, cyclist
Medium low mass	Narrow	Med	Hard	Signpost
	Med	High	Hard	Boulder, Barrier
Small high mass	Narrow	Low	Soft	Small animals, cones

The first set of testing evaluated the LIDAR reported signal strength. Since signal strength is related to the surface color and texture of the target, it may be useful for object discrimination. However, initial test results shown in Figure 10 indicate a weak correlation between object type and signal strength (Figure 10).

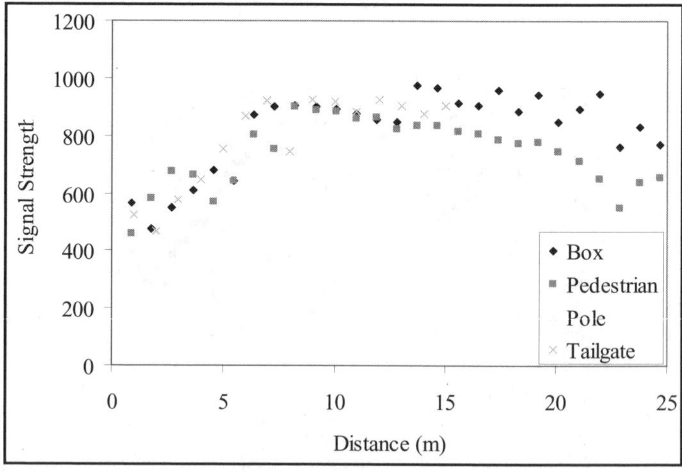

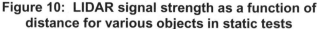

Figure 10: LIDAR signal strength as a function of distance for various objects in static tests

These results also indicate one major limitation of the LIDAR: it does not detect certain objects. For example, in the static test for the Ultrasonic sensor, the flat black bumper of a pickup truck was used rather than the tailgate. Upon targeting the bumper, the LIDAR returned a signal strength of zero. Further investigation has found that the range finder is not good at sensing black objects in general. The sensor could not detect a black trash bag or the black plastic back of a chair; however, it could detect the black nylon of a backpack. More testing in this area is probably needed; the black objects are probably simply absorbing most of the laser energy and reflecting very little. It was noticed that the laser would also return signal strength of zero when targeting some dark, flat panels held at certain angles to the beam.

CONCLUSION

A series of tests have been designed to assess the performance of individual sensors relative to the requirements of pre-crash sensing. A selection of test results for an Ultrasonic and LIDAR sensors have also been presented. The data to-date indicate that these sensors are complementary in performance (at significantly different ranges), but are insufficient to form a complete sensor system. Since the LIDAR sensor cannot detect all types of objects, it does not provide enough data at the long range. In addition, testing has not yet identified a viable method to discriminate between object types – a long-term goal of any pre-crash sensing system.

These test results will be used to direct the design of a pre-crash sensing system integrating the responses of multiple sensors. In particular, to address the issues identified with the two tested sensors, a Radar sensor is currently being tested. The resulting system should take advantage of the strengths of each and overlap the weaknesses of others. Combined with an intelligent algorithm the system should provide real-time information to an automobile computer to enable improvement in current safety technology and facilitate development and deployment of the next generation of safety technologies. The end results is that vehicle crash survivability will be increased, saving lives.

ACKNOWLEDGMENTS

This work was funded by a grant from the California Central Coast Research Partnership.

REFERENCES

1. Carlin, J., Birdsong, C., Schuster, P., Thompson, W. and Kawano, D., (2005), "Evaluation of Cost Effective Sensor Combinations for a Vehicle Pre-Crash Detection System," SAE Commercial Vehicle Engineering Congress & Exhibition, Chicago, November 1-3, 2005.
2. Jones RC (2002), "Technologies for Static Airbag Suppression Systems", 6th International Symposium on Sophisticated Car Occupant Safety Systems, Karlsruhe, Germany, December 2-4, 2002.
3. Knoll P, Schaefer BJ, Guettler H, Bunse M, Kallenbach R (2004), "Predictive Safety Systems – Steps Towards Collision Mitigation." SAE 2004 World Congress, Detroit, MI, USA.
4. Lyons CT & Taskin I (2000), "A low-cost MMIC based radar sensor for frontal, side or rear automotive anticipatory pre-crash sensing applications," IEEE Intelligent Vehicles Symposium, Dearborn, MI, USA.
5. NHTSA (2005), "Traffic Safety Facts 2003." DOT HS 809 775, www.nhtsa.dot.gov.
6. Spies HD (2002), "What is Achievable Today and in the Near Future? - Overview on Technologies: Radar, Video, IR." 6th International Symposium on Sophisticated Car Occupant Safety Systems, Karlsruhe, Germany, December 2-4, 2002.

2002-01-1883

Multi-Level Sensing and Situation Awareness Evaluation for Adaptive Collision Countermeasure Activation

Kwaku O. Prakah-Asante, Mike K. Rao and Gary S. Strumolo
Ford Research Laboratory, Ford Motor Co.

ABSTRACT

Integrated, microprocessor-based, predictive crash systems provide opportunities for significant improvements in automobile safety. Consequently, next generation safety systems will incorporate various kinds of engineering concepts such as radar and laser-based sensors as well as vision-based electronic imaging systems that track the distance and closing velocity of objects detected to be on a potential collision path with a vehicle. A discussion on the synergies obtained from the integration of sensor systems for enhanced performance of safety products is presented. A multi-level situation awareness approach to assess the potential for imminent collision, and activate safety actuator systems to meet the challenges of improved safety, is presented.

INTRODUCTION

Recent developments in the automotive industry have focused on applying multiple sensor information on the vehicle environment to assist in intelligent activation of safety systems [1,2,3]. These safety systems incorporate pre-crash sensing and intelligent algorithms to recognize the environment immediately around the vehicle, evaluate the hazard potential, and decide on what systems to deploy. It is therefore important to capitalize on the best mix of technologies to deliver an affordable and reliable system, that is able to meet performance specifications under various driving scenarios. Improved perception of the driving situation, other vehicles, obstacles, and enhanced judgment on appropriate countermeasures in collision imminent situations are required.

The focus on developing improved technologies to obtain information from the front, side and rear sides of the vehicle is depicted from statistics from a report by the National Highway Traffic Safety Administration [4] shown in Figure 1. 43.9 % of light trucks crashes were caused by frontal impacts, side impacts accounted for 30%, and 23.8% of all light truck crashes were caused by rear impacts. The requirements for improved occupant protection therefore includes methods to obtain information about the type of crash and the direction, to compensate for frontal, oblique, side and rear impacts.

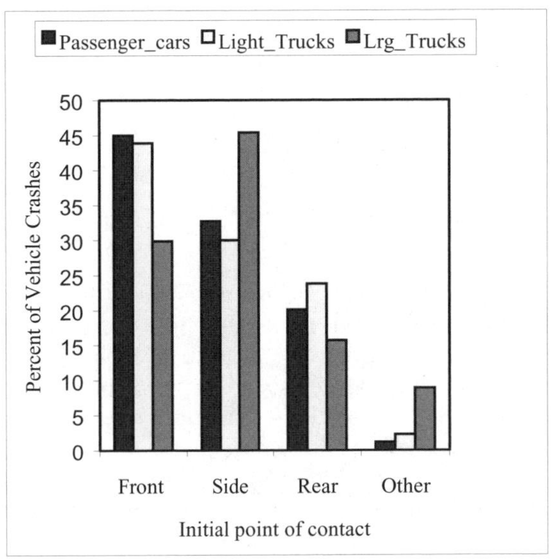

Figure 1. Vehicle crashes by type and point of impact

Robust algorithm development, vehicle integration, human factors, and system evaluation play important roles in the development process, as illustrated in Figure 2. Remote sensor information, model-based vehicle path estimation, and driver-in-the-loop models, are coupled to form an integrated multi-level network for evaluating potential collisions. Component safety countermeasures can then be activated based on a hierarchical evaluation of occupant protection requirements.

Presented in section two of the paper is a discussion of sensor systems for object detection and advantages obtained from the integration of multiple sensing systems. Section three presents situation awareness approaches to assess the potential for imminent collision and countermeasure activation. Conclusions are presented in section four.

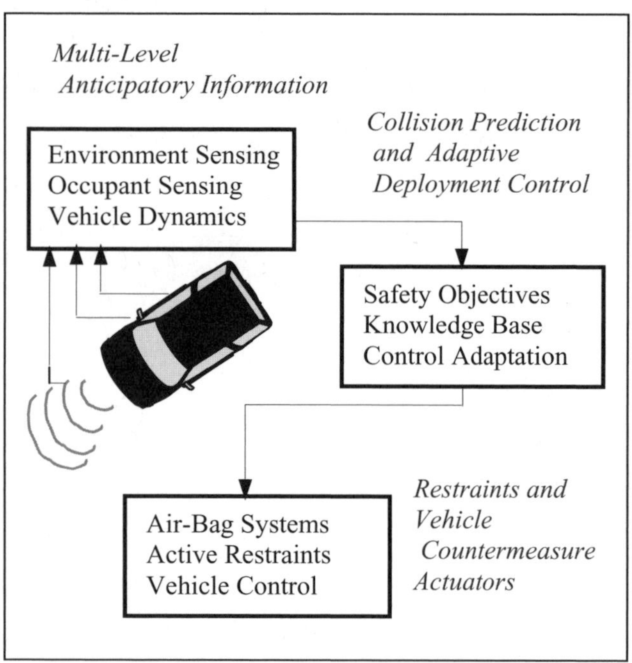

Figure 2. Advanced Safety Systems

MULTI-SENSOR SYSTEMS

This section presents an overview of the functional requirements of pre-crash sensor systems, and typical sensor systems incorporated on vehicles to meet required improved performance of safety systems. A discussion on the synergies obtained from the integration of multiple sensor systems for improved performance is presented.

The functional requirements for pre-crash sensing systems for targeted vehicle implementation include :

- determination of the relative closing speed of obstacles within close proximity of the vehicle to within 1%
- adequate spatial observation zones in azimuth and elevation to obtain adequate coverage around the vehicle
- strategic placement of sensors to obtain accurate distance measurement and direction of impact
- minimal detection time for signal processing, image processing, obstacle discrimination, and identification
- ability to detect the minimum size of an obstacle that can be considered as a threat to the vehicle in case of a crash
- ability to estimate the size, or key features indicative of the harzard type
- Fast update rates of less than 20 ms
- Sizing requirements, packaging and costs

The sensing systems are required to recognize a wide range of objects, operate in rainy weather, foggy conditions, and varying environment conditions. Example scenarios encountered in the driving environment are shown in Figure 3. Curved roads, multiple lanes, intersections, and a variety of roadside objects, constitute complex driving situations. Radar -based, lidar, vision, and vehicle dynamics sensing systems are used to meet the requirements of pre-crash sensing for adaptive collision countermeasure control. Figure 4 shows a schematic of a potential spatial coverage for vehicle environmental sensing. Sensors mounted on the front, side and rear of the host vehicle are used to determine potential target distance and speed, roadway obstacles, vehicles in adjacent lanes, and to track preceding vehicles on winding lanes.

For a typical radar sensor system, the amount of energy received from a target depends on the average transmitted power, the effective antenna gain, the range of the target, the dwell time on the target, and the Radar Cross Section (RCS). The RCS accounts for the reflectivity and directivity of the target. These related parameters have to be optimized to obtain reliable radar designs for near zone detection. Radar systems meet most of the requirements for the operating environment for pre-crash sensing, however radar systems are not as effective in determining object characteristics, including size. Camera systems with advanced image processors are advantageous in characterizing and identifying objects in complex driving environments. Processing logic is effectively used to estimate key object features. Inclement weather conditions, which might be detrimental to vision performance, leads to the rational behind the integration of radar and vision systems to capitalize on their synergy. The relationship between the driver and the vehicle is also important in the development of a multi-level sensing system. Information obtained from sensing of the driving operation, and driver behaviors are important in the development of driver-in-the-loop algorithms. Driver-in-the-loop methods can also improve the reliability and robustness of collision countermeasure decision-making.

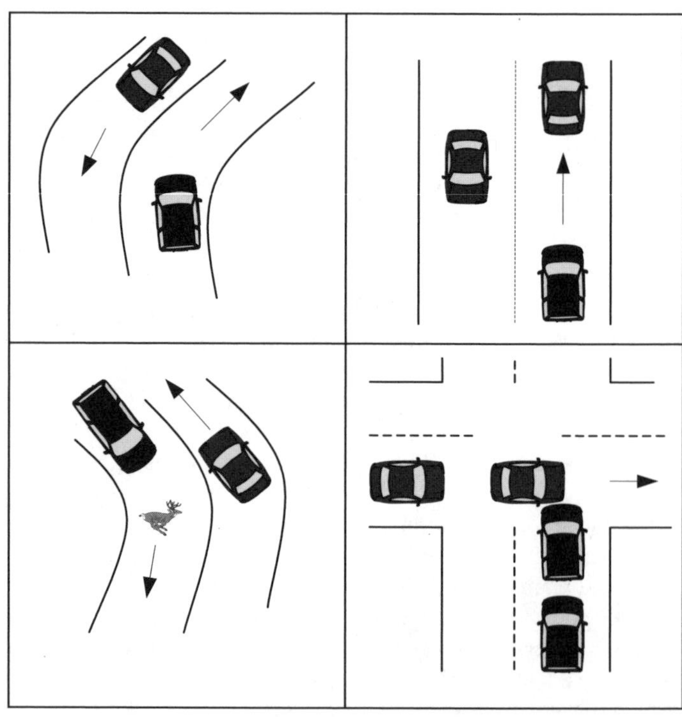

Figure 3. Scenarios encountered in driving environment

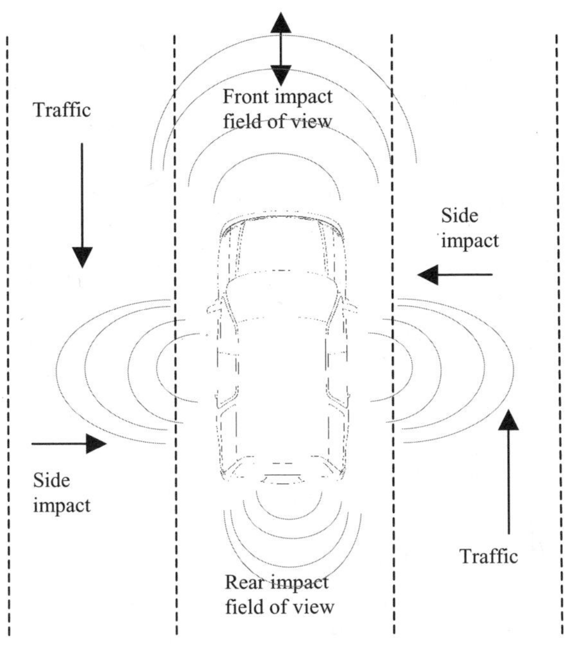

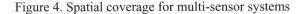

Figure 4. Spatial coverage for multi-sensor systems

In order to meet the objectives of vehicle exterior sensing, a fusion of sensors to detect obstacles and perform added discrimination and classification might be necessary, depending on the application. Multi-level sensing enhances the ability to determine the threat potential of an obstacle. Tailored activation of safety systems for improved occupant protection can then be effectively achieved.

Figure 5 illustrates a framework for a multi-level sensor system. Object kinematic information from radar, vision sensors, vehicle dynamics, and driver-in-the-loop models, are coupled to form an integrated system for evaluating potential collisions. The attributes for the particular automobile are used to determine the sensor suite. The sensing systems for a particular automobile should be chosen to meet the specification for actuation of the particular countermeasure device. The economic and societal implications involved particular to the sensor suite should be critically evaluated, and the integrated system designed within the limitations of the proven sensor performance.

As depicted in Figure 5, a combination of radar, vision, vehicle dynamics and driver characteristics may be required for a Level 1 sensing and actuation system where, for example, a non-reversible countermeasure is required to be deployed. The input requirements for the situation awareness and collision countermeasure decision-making are designed to accommodate a system with only radar, or vision object kinematic information, or both. The multi-sensor approach provides an aggregate method to effectively evaluate potential collision situations, to determine the potential for imminent collision. Safety systems may then be activated according to the potential for impact. To account for fail safe conditions particular safety devices are only activated if minimum sensing requirements are satisfied. The output manipulating signal for countermeasure activation based on Level 1 and Level 2 sensing are given by,

$$u_1 = f[L_1, \beta_1(\lambda_1, \tau_1)] \quad (1)$$

$$u_2 = f[L_2, \beta_2(\lambda_2, \tau_2)] \quad (2)$$

where u_1 , u_2 are functions of the sensing level L_1, L_2 and the countermeasure device dynamic characteristics β_1 and β_2. The countermeasure characteristics are functions of the time constants τ_1, τ_2 and the required deployment times λ_1 and λ_2. Subsequently, for the nth level sensing and actuation system the output manipulating signal for countermeasure activation is given by,

$$u_n = f[L_n, \beta_n(\lambda_n, \tau_n)] \quad (3)$$

Section three of the paper presents situation awareness approaches to assess the potential for imminent collision, and decision-making for collision countermeasure activation.

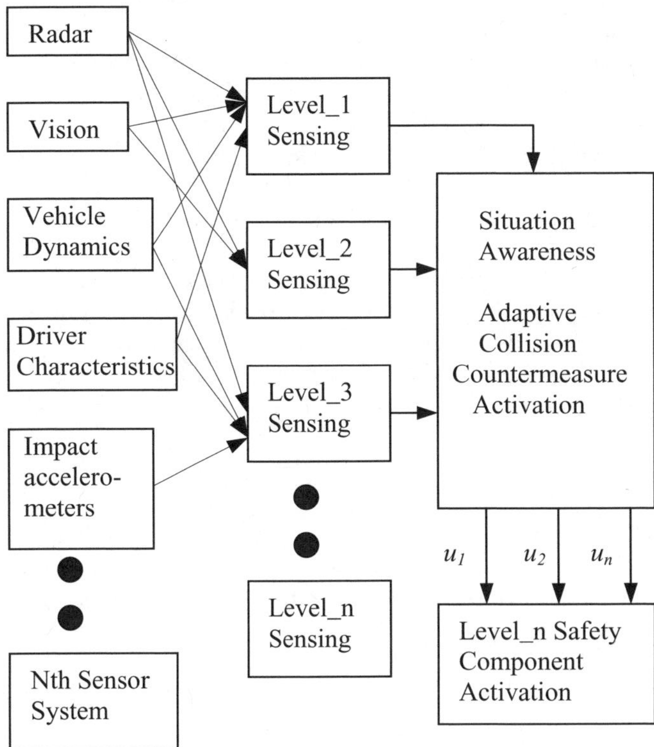

Figure 5. Multi-level sensor systems framework

SITUATION AWARENESS & ADAPTIVE COLLISION COUNTER MEASURES

The objective of intelligent control of vehicle safety systems is to avoid potential crash situations and, in case of a crash, optimize occupant injury mitigation. Collision countermeasures, under investigation in the industry, therefore, include systems that avoid collisions, and ones that respond when a collision is imminent. This section discusses situation awareness and adaptive collision countermeasures for imminent and early crash deployment control of safety restraint systems.

For restraint system activation or autonomous braking decision-making in near-zone applications, discrimination of a threat/no-threat assessment of obstacles in the vehicle environment has to be achieved with very high levels of confidence. The multi-level sensing requirements for the safety system as discussed in the previous section, coupled with the occupant injury mitigation requirements sets the foundation for algorithm development. Figure 6 shows the architecture for situation awareness and collision countermeasure activation based on the supervisory impact anticipation and control framework presented in [5]. The multi-level sensor information obtained is processed by microprocessor-based algorithms to determine the obstacle kinematic states, the host vehicle path, and occupant characteristics. The input information are used for impact determination. These algorithms determine the potential for impact and the signal is sent to the safety systems before an imminent collision. In addition, the adaptive countermeasure output from computation is sent to the local restraint control module with information about the potential for impact, and the potential severity, to assist in tailored restraint systems deployment should a collision occur.

Consider the case where situation awareness and safety systems decision making are to be made from short range pulsed radar sensors, yaw rate, steering wheel information, and occupant driving characteristic feedback information. The equations governing the relative velocity (range rate) determined from the obstacle range obtained from the radar is given by,

$$\dot{r} = v_r \quad (4)$$

$$\dot{v}_r = a_r \quad (5)$$

where r is the range from the host vehicle to a potential object, v_r the relative velocity, and a_r the acceleration. The vehicle dynamics equations based on a bicycle model [6] is given by,

$$\dot{\psi} = \frac{aFy_1 - bFy_2}{I} \quad (6)$$

$$\dot{v}_{h\_lat} = \frac{Fy_1 + Fy_2}{m_h} - U_h \psi \quad (7)$$

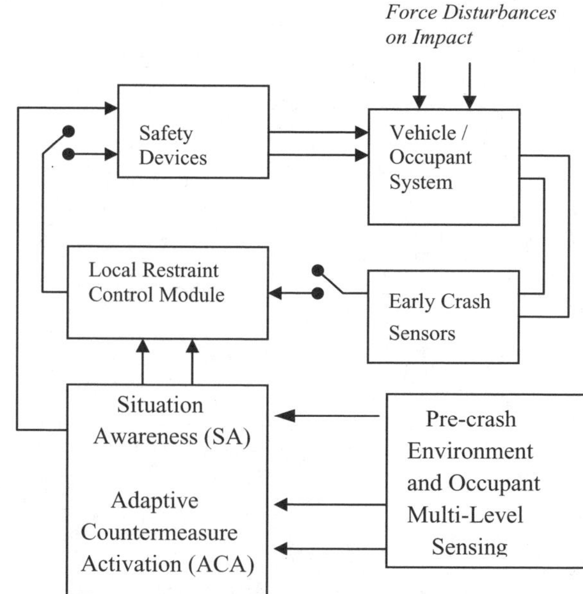

Figure 6. Situation Awareness and Collision Countermeasure Architecture

$$\dot{\delta} = \psi \quad (8)$$

where $\dot{\psi}$ is the yaw-rate, F_{y1} and F_{y2} are tire forces, a is the distance from the front axle to the vehicle center of gravity, b is the distance from the rear axle to the vehicle center of gravity. The yaw moment of inertia is given by I, and the host vehicle lateral velocity v_{h_lat}. U_h represents the host vehicle longitudinal speed, and m_h the mass, while δ represents the steering wheel angle. The host vehicle position (x_h, y_h) is readily deduced as a function of the vehicle longitudinal speed, lateral speed , and steering angle, or yaw rate.

$$\dot{x}_h = U_h \cos\delta - v_{h\_lat} \sin\delta \quad (9)$$

$$\dot{y}_h = U_h \sin\delta + v_{h\_lat} \cos\delta \quad (10)$$

Equations 4 and 5, together with the vehicle dynamics equations 6-8, are combined with the vehicle position in a state-space representation form

$$\begin{aligned} \dot{\underline{x}} &= A\underline{x} + B\underline{u} + F\underline{w} \\ \underline{y} &= C\underline{x} + \underline{v} \end{aligned} \quad (11)$$

where A is the state matrix, B the matrix for the input u, F the input noise matrix, and C the output matrix. The input random noise disturbance and measurement noise are represented by w and v, respectively. The state variables of the host vehicle system are given by,

$$\underline{x} = [r \;\; v_r \;\; \psi \;\; v_{h\_lat} \;\; \delta \;\; x_h \; y_h]^T$$

A Kalman filter in the form

$$\dot{\hat{\underline{x}}} = A\hat{\underline{x}} + B\underline{u} + K(\underline{y} - C\hat{\underline{x}}) \quad (12)$$

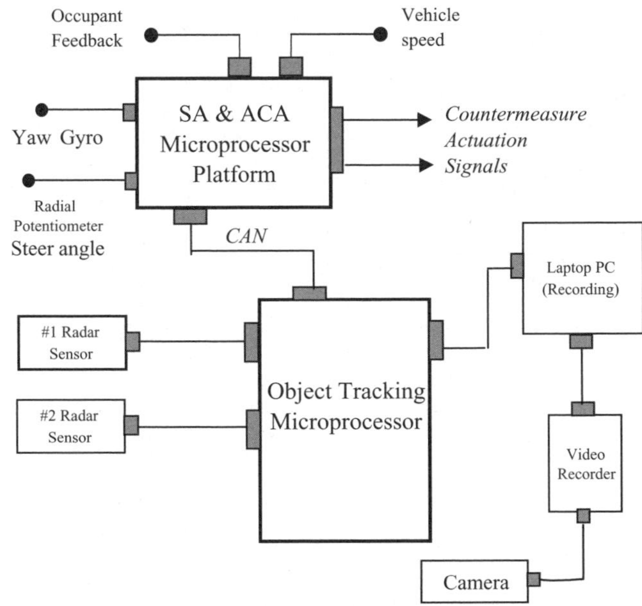

Figure 7. Schematic of hardware components

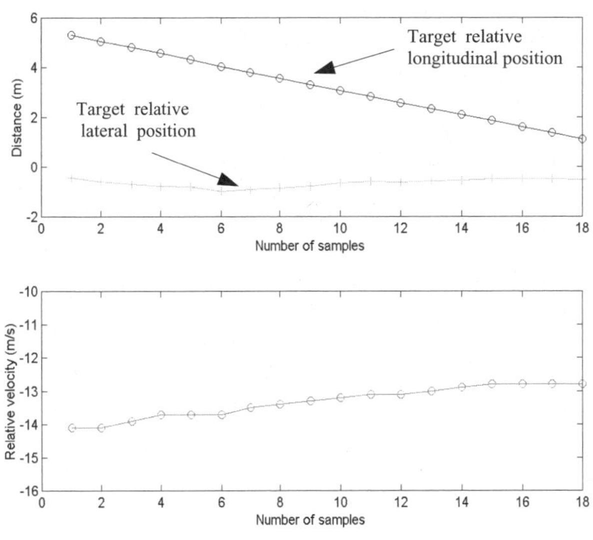

Figure 8. Obstacle relative position and velocity with respect to host vehicle

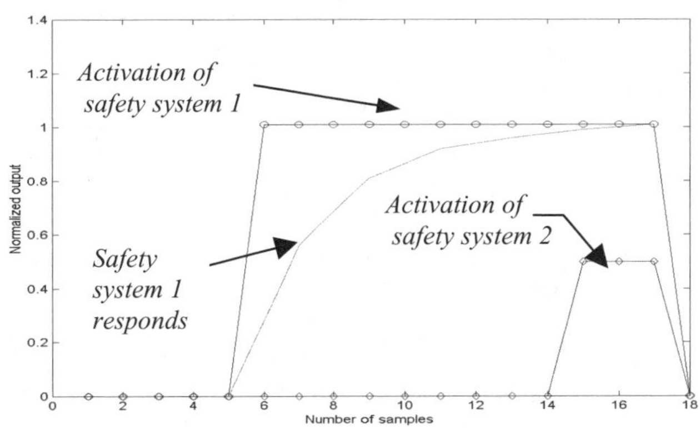

Figure 9. Activation of respective safety systems based on performance specifications

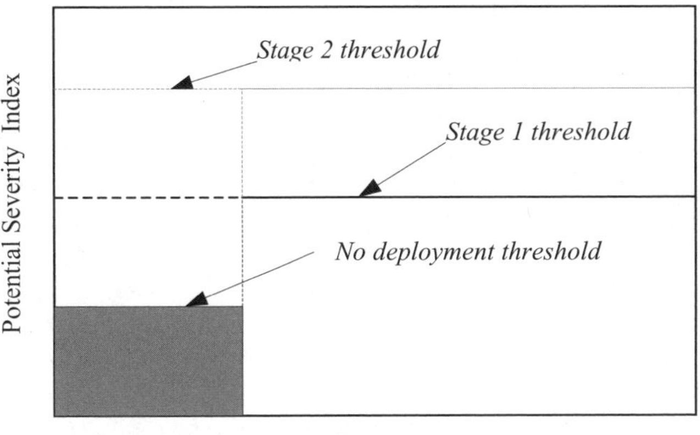

Figure 10. Pre-arming of multi-stage safety systems based on multi-level sensing

can subsequently be designed to filter the yaw rate and steering wheel measurements, predict the path of the vehicle, and estimate the velocity of the potential target. K is the gain matrix optimally chosen to minimize the error of the estimates due to process and measurement noise. The estimated parameters are then used to predict the potential for impact, and subsequent countermeasure activation.

Shown in Figure 7 is schematic of example hardware vehicle components used for evaluating the performance of algorithms developed for predicting the potential for collision and adaptive activation of countermeasures. Short range 24 GHz pulsed radar signal outputs, vehicle dynamics yaw rate, steering wheel information and driver feedback information are integrated to form a multi-input multi-output system configuration. Figure 8 shows the real-time results from an imminent crash situation with the obstacle relative position and velocity with respect to the host vehicle. The host vehicle approaches the target object with a velocity between 12.5 to 14 m/s.

Figure 9 is a plot indicating activation of two safety systems based on their respective performance requirements, and their multi-level sensing requirements. Once imminent crash was deduced, and the countermeasure specific deployment criteria met, an activation signal was sent to the corresponding safety device to assure complete deployment of the safety system before collision occured. Safety system 1 is deployed 14 sample times before impact, while safety system 2 is deployed 5 samples times before impact. To account for fail safe conditions particular safety devices are only activated if minimum sensing requirements are satisfied as presented in the section on multi-sensor systems. The activation signal sent to the safety device based on the potential for impact, therefore, accounts for the multi-level sensing requirements, and the safety device dynamics which is a function of the countermeasure time constant and the required deployment time (Equation 3). Figure 10 shows criteria for pre-arming safety systems with multiple stages of activation sensing based on multi-level and situation awareness prediction. For safety systems that are required to activate only after impact, pre-arming eliminates the time required to sense and discriminate the impact and therefore allows activation of the restraint system components on early impact. Arming of the safety system depends on minimum closing velocity, velocity dependent potential severity, and occupant characteristics. The pre-armed safety systems are activated once collision is confirmed by accelerometers. Multi-sensor systems and associated situation awareness and collision countermeasure integrated systems undergo extensive verification for various driving conditions, and scenarios, to meet the objectives of improved safety.

CONCLUSIONS

This paper presented multi-level sensing and situation awareness evaluation approaches to assess the potential for imminent collision, and to activate collision countermeasures. The complex nature of the vehicle environment requires the effective combination of sensor systems coupled with countermeasure characteristics to tailor activation to meet the requirements of occupant protection. Deployment decision-making for multiple pre-crash activated safety systems should be made within the limitations of sensor performance to minimize false alarms. Sensor performance monitoring is essential to determine confidence levels for activation of respective safety systems. Results from real-time data were used to demonstrate tailored activation of safety systems for frontal imminent collision. Safety systems of the future will incorporate several multiple sensing systems with a broad field of view around the vehicle targeted towards improved occupant and pedestrian protection, and enhanced vehicle-vehicle interactions.

REFERENCES

1. Groush, T., "Radar sensors for Automotive Collision Warning and Avoidance," SPIE Vol 2463, Pages 239-247 1995.
2. Hermans, F.J, "Road Prediction Using Video for Integrated Driver Support," Computing and Control Engineering Journal, pages 169-175, 1999.
3. Higashida, H et. al, "Fusion Sensor for an Assist System for Low Speed in Traffic Congestion Using Millimeter-Wave Radar and Image Recognition Sensor," SAE 2001-01-0800.
4. NHTSA, *Traffic Safety Facts*. U.S. Department of Transportation., 1998.
5. Prakah-Asante, K.O., Rao, M.K., Morman, K.N., Strumolo, G.S., "Supervisory Vehicle Impact Anticipation & Control of Safety Systems," IEEE CCA/ISIC Publication, pages 326-330, 2001.
6. Margolis, D.L., Asgari J.,"Multi-purpose Models of Vehicle Dynamics for Controller Design," SAE 911927.

1999-01-1234

Driving Course Prediction Using Distance Sensor Data

Werner Uhler, Michael Scherl and Bernd Lichtenberg
Robert Bosch GmbH

ABSTRACT

The assignment of vehicles detected by distance sensors to lanes relative to the own vehicle is an important and necessary task for future driver assistance systems like Adaptive Cruise Control (ACC). The collective motion of objects driving in front of the vehicle allows a prediction of the vehicle's own driving course. The method uses not only data of the host vehicle to determine its own trajectory but as well data from a distance sensor supplying distances and angles of objects ahead of the vehicle to determine the trajectories of these objects. Algorithms were developed using an off-line simulation, which was fed with recorded data obtained from a real ACC vehicle. The results show a significant improvement in the quality of the predicted driving course compared to other methods solely based on data of the host vehicle. Particularly in situations of changing curvature, e.g. the beginning of a bend, the algorithm helps to improve the overall system performance of ACC.

INTRODUCTION

Present and future driver assistance systems, e.g. ACC or Collision Warning/Avoidance, have a common challenge in evaluating the current traffic situation. They detect vehicles and other objects around the car using some kind of distance sensor. This sensor gives information about the location of detected objects relative to the vehicle. Knowledge of their position relative to the lanes however implies more information about the course of these lanes in front of the car. This problem is described in /1/.

There are several ways to obtain the lacking information. A large class of methods determines the actual curvature of the car's trajectory. Today's systems mostly use standard in-car sensors, like wheel speed sensors generating the curvature from the difference and the mean of the wheel speeds. Alternatively a yaw rate sensor together with the vehicle speed can give the same information. A steering angle sensor can be used to assist both methods. Fundamental are two assumptions. First the car's trajectory is assumed to be closely related to its lane. Second the lane's actual curvature is assumed to be constant. Violation of the first assumption has minor consequences because in many cases predicting the vehicle's trajectory is even more relevant than predicting its lane, e.g. during lane changes. However, this is not true for the second assumption. At the beginning or the end of a curve serious errors occur in predicting both the car's trajectory and it's lane. Obviously these systematic errors can not be overcome using a local determination of the curvature alone.

A second class of methods uses sensors to look ahead of the car. Commonly known is the detection of lane boundaries by a video sensor, see e.g. /2/. This way the curvature of the lane can be measured and does not have to be predicted. Additional information about the car's location in the lane, lane width, type of lane boundaries etc. is provided. However the measuring distance is restricted to about 50-80m due to camera optics and camera resolution forcing the system to predict values for larger distances. In addition the performance of video sensors is easily degraded by weather conditions and daytime, e.g. dusk or dawn. Also well known are radar sensors detecting the boundaries of the road, see e.g. /3/ and /4/. Using this method for lane prediction requires the sensor to have a good lateral resolution making them more expensive. Furthermore, knowing the location of standing objects near the road boundary does not mean knowing the course of the lanes because information about their number and the width is lacking. A common feature of these truly predictive systems seems to be the considerable additional cost.

Third, a navigation system can be used to predict the lanes. It is easy to estimate that the precision in determining the own cars position must be in the range of a typical lane width in order to assign other vehicles to the correct lanes. Today standard navigation systems have a worst case precision of around 50m even if they are GPS based. Use of differential GPS does mean a considerable improvement. Still, these systems have difficulties in urban areas and when using up-to-date maps. However it seems promising to use navigation data to enhance lane prediction and provide information about intersections etc.

A very promising way to support lane prediction is to integrate information about other vehicles' trajectories. An example is given in /5/. Of course, these trajectories usually differ from the course of the lane like the own car's trajectory does. But here we have the chance of using many trajectories allowing for a statistical evaluation. By this method cars making lane changes or leaving the road can be separated from other data. In this paper we describe a method of deriving predictive lane information from recorded position data of other vehicles.

DESCRIPTION OF THE ALGORITHM

FUNDAMENTALS – The basic idea of the method presented here is to measure the location of other vehicles in front of the own car driving in the same direction. The positions of each of these vehicles are recorded separately. In every time step these positions are transformed into the actual vehicle coordinate system. Thus for each object we have at any time a number of positions representing its trajectory relative to the host vehicle's present position and coordinate system.

Let us make some fundamental definitions of lateral offsets of other vehicles relative to the host vehicle. The definitions are illustrated in Fig. 1.

1. The *actual lateral offset* is the lateral distance between the other vehicle's present position and the host vehicle's position when reaching this position. This value can not be measured in the present because you would have to know the host vehicle's exact trajectory in the future.
2. The *historical lateral offset* is defined as the lateral distance between the host vehicle and the other vehicle's recorded position at the host vehicle's present position.
3. The *predicted lateral offset* is the lateral distance between the other vehicle's present position and the host vehicle's predicted position at the distance of the other vehicle.

As the actual lateral offset can not be measured it is approximated by the predicted lateral offset which is then used to determine the relevance of other vehicles for the host vehicle's motion. Vehicles with a predicted lateral offset bigger than half a lane width are considered not to be relevant for the host vehicle's motion[1]. However, this requires a precise prediction of the host vehicle's trajectory. As mentioned above local predictions suffer from systematic errors at the beginning and the end of curves.

On the other hand the historical lateral offset can be used as well. It can be easily determined using the recorded data of the other vehicles. The fundamental assumption is that significant changes in it's value, i.e. changes of about half a lanewidth or more, do occur only very rarely. It is obvious that lane changes of other vehicles result in systematic errors whereas the method is not affected by varying lane curvature.

A major drawback of using historical lateral offsets alone should be mentioned: New objects entering the detection area of the distance sensor in the far range require a long time until a historical lateral offset can be assigned to them, i.e. the host vehicle must first reach the original position. This has serious consequences when approaching significantly slower vehicles. As an illustration imagine a car traveling at half the speed as the own car being detected at a range of 100m. Reaching this position the other car's distance has reduced to 50m. ACC or e.g. Collision Warning/Avoidance has to decide on the other car's relevance for its own safe and comfortable motion much earlier. Consequently additional predictive information about the course of the lanes ahead

1. Very sophisticated algorithms are used to filter these values taking into account both measurement errors of inertial or video sensors as well as those of the distance sensors.

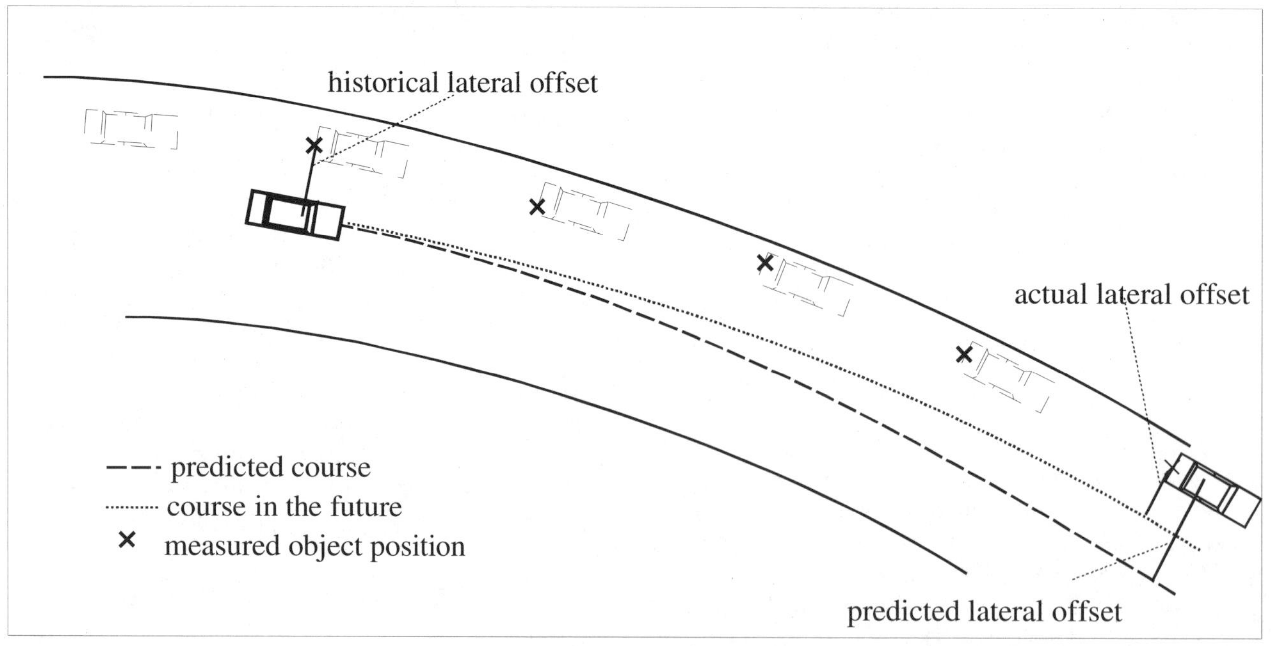

Figure 1. Definitions of lateral offsets

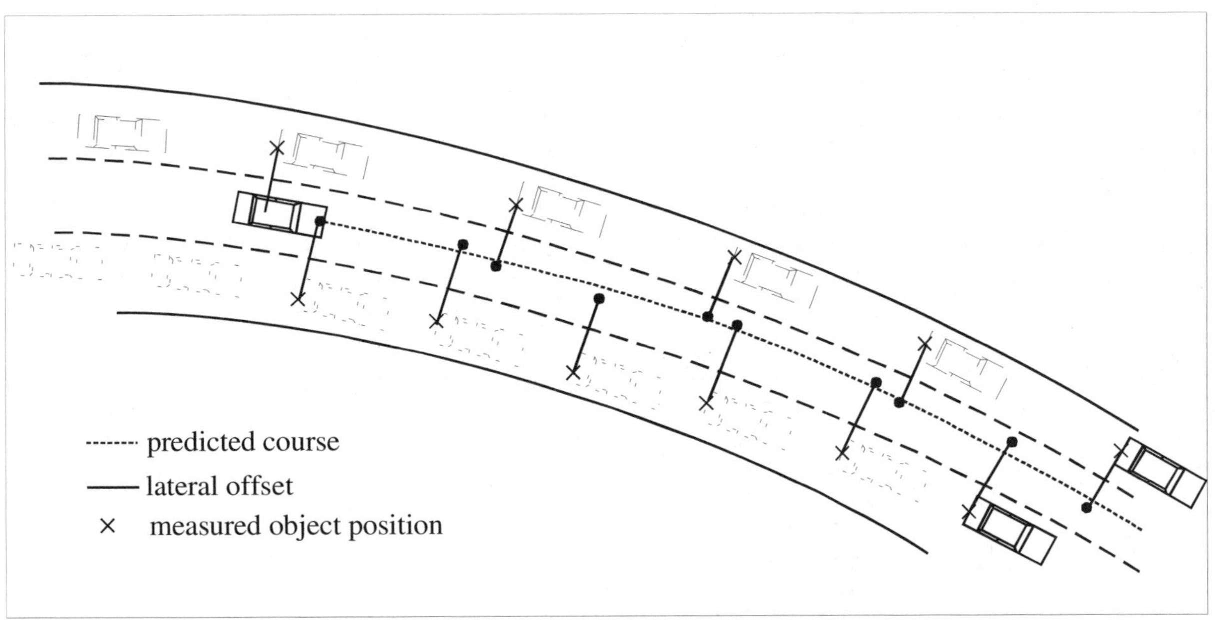

Figure 2. Bird's eye view of method 1

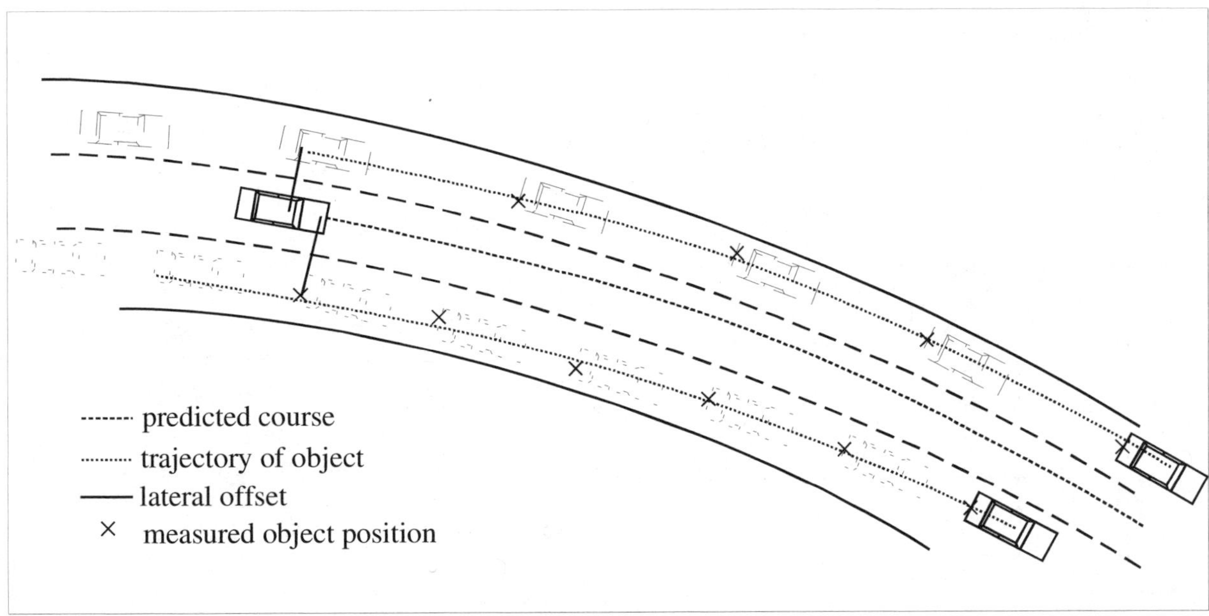

Figure 3. Bird's eye view of method 2

must be taken into account to achieve a reliable system performance.

Fortunately we can get the lacking information. Two different methods are illustrated in Fig. 2 and 3.

The basic idea of the first method is to construct a single predicted trajectory using all data about other vehicles. If no lane changes occur other vehicles' trajectories are identical to the prospective one of the host vehicle except for a lateral shift. Consequently the measured positions of each vehicle for which a historical lateral offset has been determined are shifted laterally by the negative value of their historical lateral offset. This gives a number of points ahead of the host vehicle representing a superposition of all measured trajectories shifted to the origin of the host vehicle's coordinate system. Now a model trajectory can be fit to these points resulting in a predicted trajectory for the host vehicle. Statistical fluctuations can be expected to be compensated provided a sufficient number of vehicles has been measured. In this case systematic errors due to lane changes will also be suppressed to a certain degree.

The second method which we believe to be more efficient considers each trajectory of the other vehicles separately. This method is illustrated in Fig. 3.

A model trajectory is fitted to the measured positions of each vehicle. The relevant parameters like lateral offset and curvature of this trajectory can be derived from this fit. These parameters can be treated statistically in order to eliminate extreme or unplausible values. This results in mean values for the parameters which in most cases allows a prediction of the host vehicle's trajectory with a real preview.

The most prominent differences between both methods are obvious. On the one hand the second method requires a minimum number of measured positions for each trajectory to allow a reliable fit. In the first method even single measurement points can be used, provided a historical lateral offset has been measured for this object. On the other hand this is the most serious restriction of this method: Use of measured data is limited to those objects where the historical lateral offset has been determined.

DATA ACQUISITION – In each time step position data for all vehicles detected by the distance sensor are collected. The tracking of the distance sensor assigns an identification number to each object. Data belonging to one identification number are grouped together forming a trajectory of the respective object. To illustrate this imagine that other vehicles are placing "markings" on the road at their position at distinct times. The trajectory is then defined by the positions of these markings belonging to one object. Data is added to the trajectory when a new marking is created. Data is removed from the trajectory when the host vehicle passes one of the markings.

An efficient way for storing this data is to use ring buffers, one for each object. These ring buffers can be viewed to form a "data matrix" each row possessing a start and an end pointer, see Fig. 4.

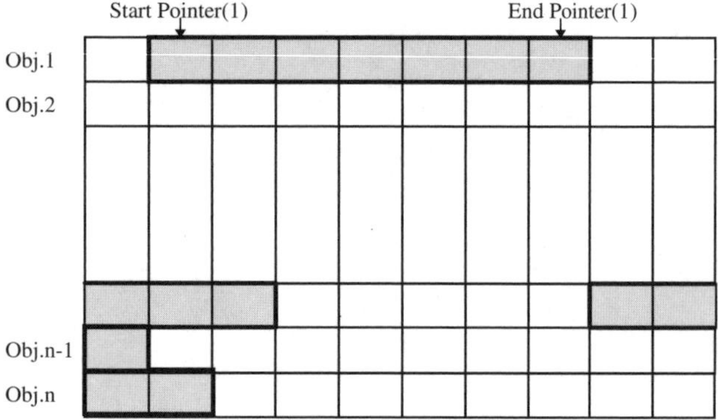

Figure 4. Object list

Entering new object data means shifting the end pointer of the corresponding row for one entry and storing the data at this place. Removing data of an object is reflected by shifting the start pointer for one entry.

For a new object an empty row in the data matrix is used. If no row is empty it has to be decided whether an occupied row shall be cleared or whether the new object has to be rejected (see below). If an object suddenly disappears (e.g. by leaving the detection area of the distance sensor) it's corresponding data can be used until the host vehicle has reached the last measured position.

Data are collected during the motion of the host vehicle. This means that measured relative positions of objects correspond to different vehicle coordinate systems. From time step to time step the host vehicle is translated and rotated. Data collected during earlier time steps have to be transformed to the actual vehicle coordinate system. This can be achieved by a transformation compensating both translation and rotation of the host vehicle, see Fig. 5.

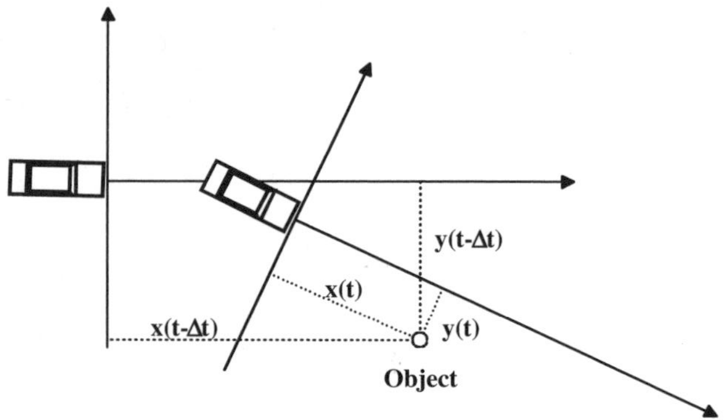

Figure 5. Transformation

For a small time step Δt it can be shown[2]

$$
\begin{aligned}
x(t) &= (x(t-\Delta t) - v(t)\cdot\cos(\omega(t)\Delta t)\cdot\Delta t)\cdot\cos(\omega(t)\Delta t) \\
&\quad + (y(t-\Delta t) - v(t)\cdot\sin(\omega(t)\Delta t)\cdot\Delta t)\cdot\sin(\omega(t)\Delta t) \\
y(t) &= -(x(t-\Delta t) - v(t)\cdot\cos(\omega(t)\Delta t)\cdot\Delta t)\cdot\sin(\omega(t)\Delta t) \\
&\quad + (y(t-\Delta t) - v(t)\cdot\sin(\omega(t)\Delta t)\cdot\Delta t)\cdot\cos(\omega(t)\Delta t)
\end{aligned}
$$

where $x(t)$, $y(t)$ denote the components of the fixed position (a "marking" on the road) with respect to the host vehicle's coordinate system at time t, $v(t)$ is the host vehicle's speed at time t and $\omega(t)$ it's yaw rate. So at any time step the values of $v(t)$ and $\omega(t)$ are measured and the values of $x(t-\Delta t)$, $y(t-\Delta t)$ are updated to $x(t)$, $y(t)$.

Very crucial is the quality of the used yaw rate signal. A constant offset leads to errors seriously effecting $y(t)$, whereas $x(t)$ is relatively robust. Additive white noise results in fewer difficulties because the contributions of this noise are partly compensated from time step to time steps. This can be nicely illustrated by calculating the trajectory of a closed path, see the "Measurements" section of this paper.

The maximum look ahead distance in time required by ACC is around 5 s. Using an optimized yaw rate signal we could estimate the maximum error in calculating the lateral position of the host vehicle over this time to be around 0.5 m. In most cases the actual error is significantly below.

Another crucial point is the quality of the objects' lateral offsets as provided by the distance sensor. Usually new objects are detected in the far range of the distance sensor where particularly the quality of the lateral offset measurement is relatively poor. Both methods described above have to use these first measurements for an early determination of the object's lateral offset. Thus it is obvi-

2. In this approximation sine and cosine can well be replaced by their quadratic approximations.

ous that the accuracy of the distance sensor determines the reaction time and quality for new objects for both methods.

STATISTICAL EVALUATION OF THE CURVATURE AND LATERAL OFFSET – In this chapter we will describe how lane prediction data is calculated from the measured and transformed position data.

Method 1 uses data from all vehicles with a calculated historical lateral offset. Each position is shifted in y-direction by the negative value of the corresponding historical lateral offset. In other words, all trajectories are shifted towards the host vehicle. Now a model trajectory is fit to all these data positions by a least mean squares fit[3], see Fig. 2. For simplicity, we neglect the side slip angle and use $y(x) = c_0 + c_2 x^2$ as a fit curve with fit parameter c_2 and $c_0 = 0$ which proved to be sufficient in all cases we have investigated. Treating c_0 as a fit parameter makes the determination of c_2 less robust against measuring errors e.g. due to sensor noise. Finally the curvature κ of the lane ahead is determined via $\kappa = 2\ c_2$.

Method 2 is more sophisticated. Position data of each vehicle is treated separately, i.e. a model curve is fit to each vehicle trajectory[3], see Fig. 3. This model curve is again $y_k(x) = c_{k,0} + c_{k,2}\ x^2$ but now both $c_{k,0}$ and $c_{k,2}$ are treated as fit parameters. The index k denotes the number of the trajectory representing the number of the corresponding vehicle.

The fit parameter $c_{k,0}$ can be viewed as the lateral offset of vehicle k. This is a major advantage of method 2 over method 1: A lateral offset of a vehicle can be predictively determined if the host vehicle has not yet reached the first position of the other vehicle. Moreover it should be noted that this lateral offset is the lateral distance between the car's present position and a fit curve to many measured values. As a consequence this value is relatively robust against single measuring errors.

It is easy to imagine that fit parameters for different trajectories have different qualities. Qualities are affected by e.g. distance and distribution of measured positions, number and variation of measured values belonging to the respective trajectory, plausibility of parameter values etc. This shall be illustrated for distance and distribution of measured values with the examples in Figure 6.

This kind of reasoning can be extended to all other cases.

Consequently to each of the values $c_{k,0}$ and $c_{k,2}$ a quality is assigned. This facilitates comparing $c_{k,0}$ with values derived from other methods e.g. as described in the introduction. In addition, these qualities allow merging these values to have a unified interface to the particular assistance system.

3. If qualities for the measured positions are available, e.g. if provided by the distance sensor, they can be taken into account during the fit procedure.

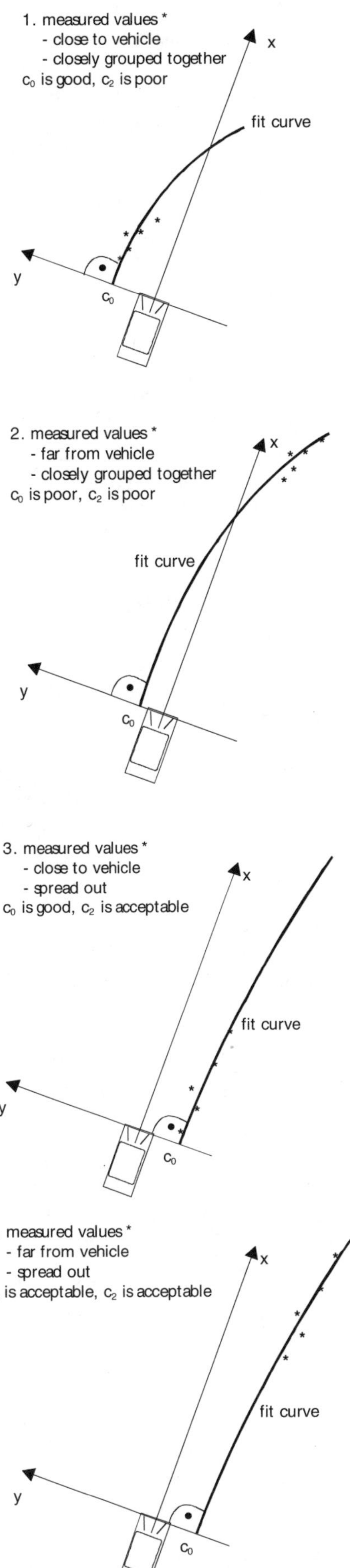

Figure 6. Examples for different distributions of measured values

Concerning the $c_{k,2}$ an optimum value for the curvature of the lane ahead can be derived using the corresponding qualities. The contribution of a particular $c_{k,2}$ should be according to its quality, i.e. values with low quality should contribute only little. Moreover the curvature must be robust against values from cars performing lane changes. All this can be achieved by filtering the $c_{k,2}$ with a weighted median filter, the qualities serving as weights. The median filter is known to be robust against extreme values. In our case this means a lane change of a vehicle is disregarded given the other measured vehicles keep to their lanes.

MEMORY MANAGEMENT – To implement the method in an ECU the use of computer memory should be limited. Therefore the data matrix should be kept small. This means that only a few vehicle trajectories can be managed at a time. In case more vehicles are measured than can be stored in the data matrix it has to be decided which trajectories shall be used.

In general new objects are written to empty lines of the data matrix. But if the data matrix is full and a new vehicle turns up we have to estimate the usefulness of all trajectories for lane prediction in the future. Imagine the new vehicle overtaking the host vehicle with a high relative speed. This vehicle can be expected to produce a long trajectory ahead in a relatively short time. Thus it will be very valuable for lane prediction. In contrast a much slower vehicle will not give a trajectory extending over the whole sensor range thereby reducing its value considerably.

Estimation of this usefulness has to be applied to all trajectories in the data matrix as well as to the predicted trajectory of the new vehicle. In other words we have to predict the corresponding qualities of the trajectories. However, for a new vehicle only those contributions to the quality related to its motion are directly predictable. Thus to compare a new vehicle with an existing vehicle only these contributions are taken into account.

In each time step the predicted qualities of all existing trajectories and the predicted quality of a possible new vehicle are calculated and compared. If the latter exceeds any of the first the entry in the data matrix with the least predicted quality is replaced by the new object.

On the other hand objects are deleted from the data matrix after reaching the last position or alternatively if only less than a minimum number of recorded positions are available.

MEASUREMENTS

EXPERIMENTAL ENVIRONMENT – To develop and optimize all algorithms synthetic data as well as real traffic data were used. The latter were recorded in a real ACC vehicle equipped with a radar sensor supplying object distances up to 150 meters and lateral position within an angle of about ± 5 degrees. Additional sensors provided host vehicle data like speed, yaw rate, etc. Vehicle and distance sensor data were recorded in real-time using the CAN (controller area network) interface and stored in a data file. Additionally all traffic scenarios were recorded by a video system.

In a second step, the data file was used as input for offline simulations of the driving course prediction algorithm implemented in Matlab™. The development of all algorithms, optimization and visualization of the results was done using Matlab™.

The optimized algorithms were coded using the C programming language and implemented on the vehicle computer to test the system under real-time conditions. Our experimental setup is shown in Fig. 7.

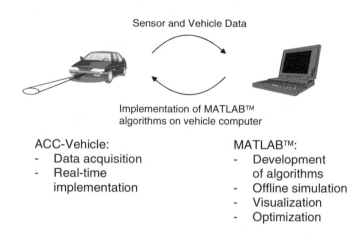

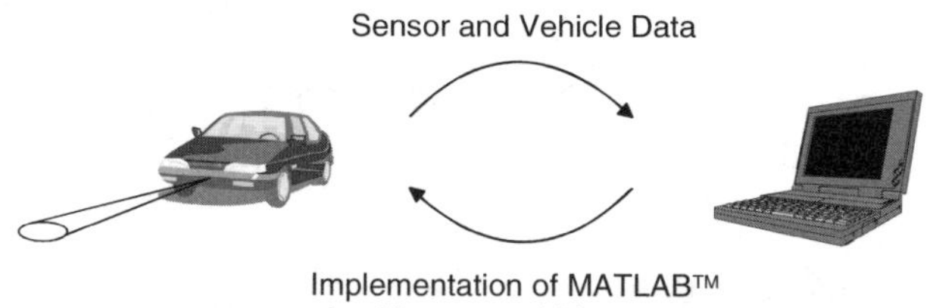

ACC-Vehicle:
- Data acquisition
- Real-time implementation

MATLAB™:
- Development of algorithms
- Offline simulation
- Visualization
- Optimization

Figure 7. Experimental environment

RESULTS OF MEASUREMENTS – The driving course prediction algorithm uses sensor data of the host vehicle to calculate its own trajectory. This is necessary to transform all recorded positions to the actual vehicle coordinate system. Since there are several different sensors, which allow a determination of the yaw rate, an assessment of 4 possibilities was made.

The yaw rate can be derived from

- a yaw rate sensor,
- a lateral acceleration sensor,
- a steering angle sensor,
- the wheel speed difference of the front (non powered) axle.

A test drive was performed along a motorway cloverleaf. The vehicle trajectory formed a closed track and took about 120 seconds. During the test drive all signals named above were recorded. Figure 8 shows the calculated trajectories based on the yaw rate signals derived from the four sources. In every case the car is starting at the origin heading to the positive x-direction. It is easily seen that the yaw rate sensor supplies the signal with the best long term stability. Both position and direction at the end of the measurement fit best to the starting point after an integration time of about 120 s. Taking into account that the usual integration time of the host trajectory is shorter than 5 seconds, the obtained accuracy of the lateral position proves to be smaller than 0.5 m. As the measuring error of the distance sensor for the lateral position is in the same order this is regarded to be sufficient. Therefore, both driving course prediction methods are based on the yaw rate sensor.

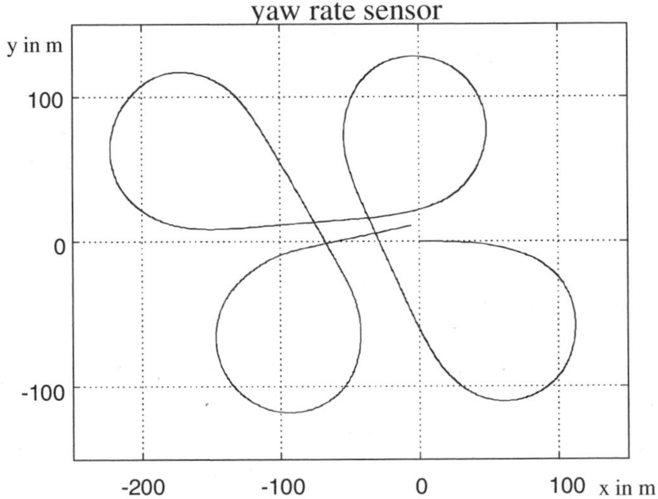

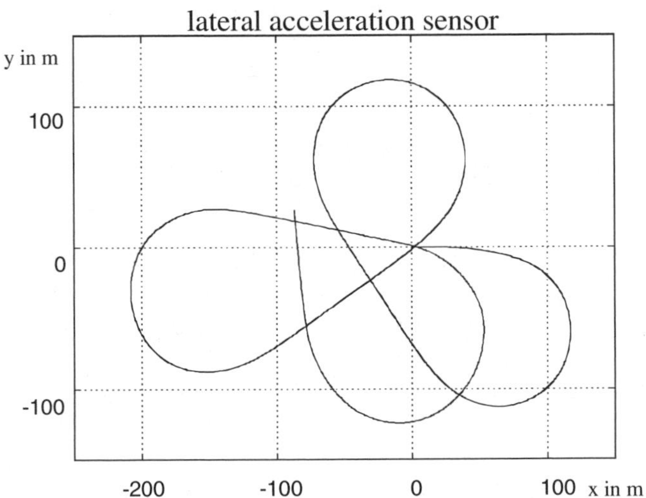

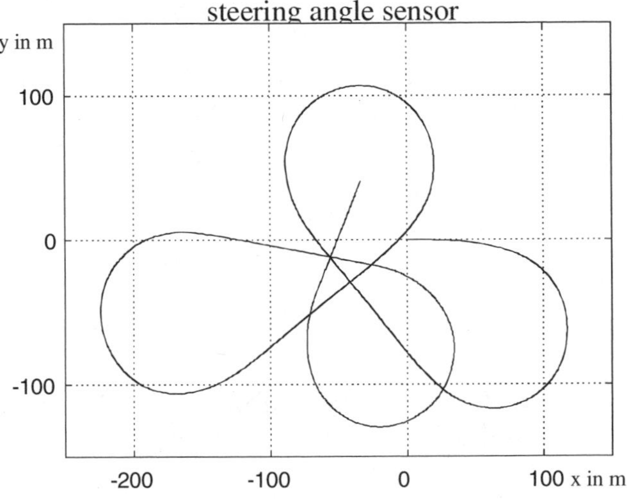

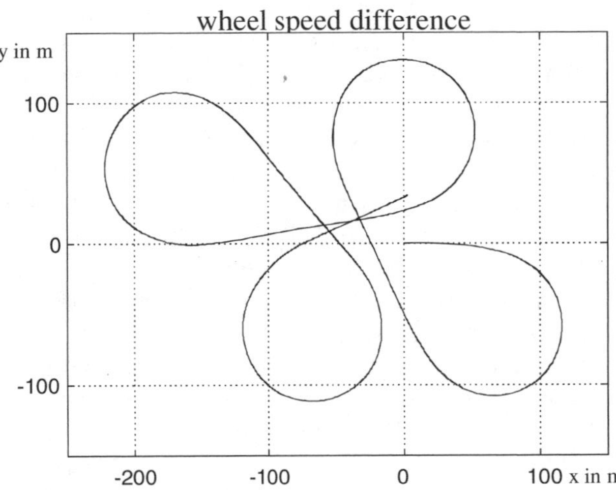

Figure 8. Host trajectories derived using different yaw rates

To illustrate the potential and robustness of the driving course prediction, Figure 9 shows results for both methods. The recorded traffic situation is the beginning of a right-hand curve on a 3 lane motorway in rather dense traffic. The host vehicle is driving in the middle lane. The predicted curvatures of methods 1 and 2 are plotted over time. Also, the curvature derived from the yaw rate signal as well as a reference curvature is shown. The reference curvature is obtained by an offline calculation using the integrated trajectory of the host vehicle. It is the mean of curvature values over a time interval of $\pm$ 1.0 s with respect to the current position. The time shift of about 0.2 s between reference and yaw rate curvature is due to a filtering delay of the latter. Looking at the results of the predicted curvatures compared to the reference curvature both methods can be seen to recognize the curve significantly earlier, i.e. about 1 s. (The reason for the failure of method 1 at times bigger than 48.5 s will be discussed below.) This fact shows clearly the potential of both methods to recognize changes in curvature ahead of time and thus help to avoid wrong lane assignments of other vehicles.

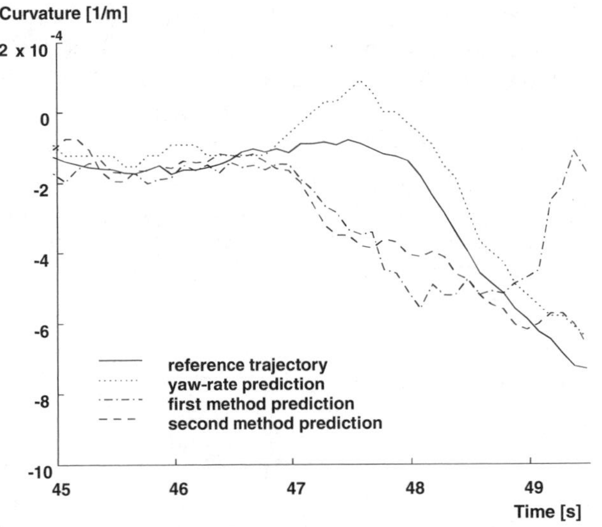

Figure 9. Results of driving course prediction

Figure 10 shows the situation from a bird's eye view in the vehicle coordinate system at times t = 48.2 s and t = 49.6 s. All recorded positions of objects in front of the own vehicle are marked with an "x". The shifted positions of all relevant objects for method 1 are indicated by appropriate arrows. The actual positions of the different objects are marked with an "o". The dotted lines represent the trajectories of every single object. At t = 48.2 s it can be seen that both methods supply a right bend curvature while the yaw rate still yields a straight course prediction as discussed above. At t = 49.6 s the own vehicle has entered the curve and the yaw rate based curvature fits the result of method2. Surprisingly method1 now deviates significantly from reality. This is due to a severe error of the radar sensor in measuring the lateral position of the vehicle on the right lane. It's measured distance is about 88 m and its measured lateral position is about 4 m putting it on the left(!) lane. Since method 1 includes this point in it's least squares fit the result is rather poor. Method 2 on the other hand uses a median filter. The trajectory with the erroneous position yields a quite different curvature and has a low quality compared to all other trajectories. Thus it is disregarded by the median filter. Consequently method 2 has a much better robustness against sensor errors than method 1.

The same arguments apply to robustness against lane changes of other vehicles. The trajectory of the lane changing vehicle yields a curvature much different from those of other objects. Again, the median filter of method 2 makes sure this trajectory has no or only little influence on the result, provided a sufficient number of other vehicles is measured.

An important feature to keep memory consumption low is the selection of relevant objects in case the object list is full up. This selection is based on a predicted quality the object is supposed to have a certain time ahead. Fig. 11 shows a comparison of actual and predicted qualities of single object trajectories. It has to be mentioned that the overall quality of a single trajectory consists of two factors: a predictable and a non predictable part. The selection of objects is of course solely based on the predictable part. From Fig. 11, showing the predictable parts only, the predicted qualities can be seen to be shifted to earlier times compared to the actual ones. This proves the prediction to work as expected. It should be noted that the rise and decrease times are much shorter, compared to the real qualities. This is due to the fact that the prediction cannot anticipate a vehicle's first detection. It then immediately jumps to the value the real trajectory will show in the future resulting in a steep rise.

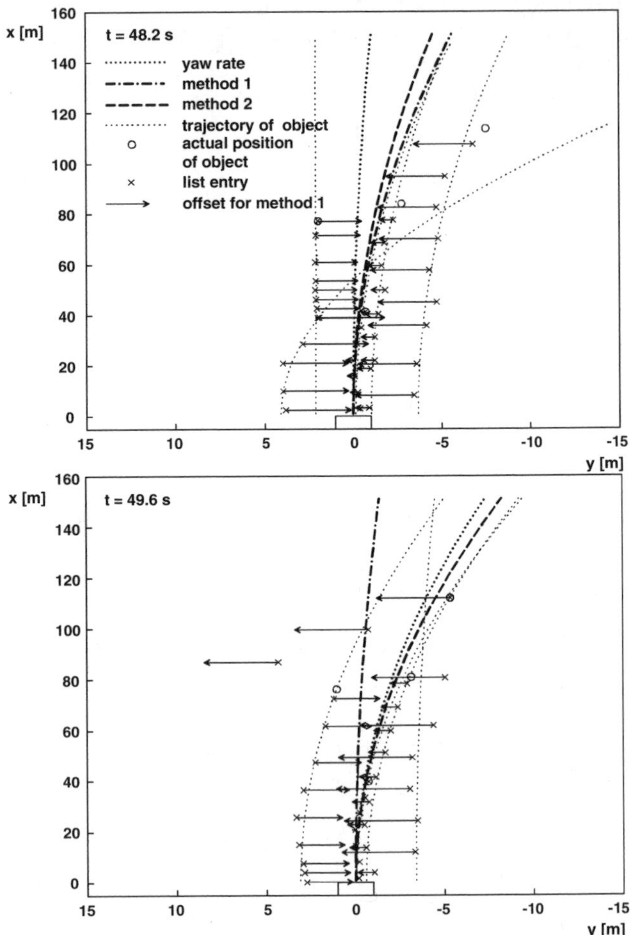

Figure 10. Situation from bird's eye view at fixed times

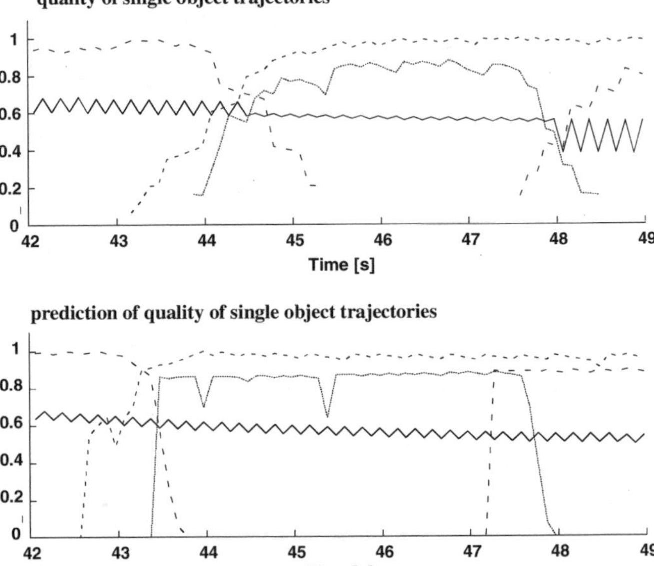

Figure 11. Actual and predicted qualities of single trajectories

CONCLUSION

In this paper we have presented two methods to predict a host vehicle's trajectory based on measured and recorded position data of other vehicles. The quality of the prediction is determined by the number of tracked vehicles, their number of lane changes and the quality of the signals from the distance sensor. The prediction is not affected by lane changes of the host vehicle and by varying lane curvature, e.g. when entering or leaving a curve. The preview time is typically more than 1 s depending on the constellation of the vehicles ahead.

The second method seems to be very promising. It analyzes each vehicle's trajectory separately, extracts the corresponding parameters and assigns a quality. A statistical analysis based on these values calculates representative trajectory parameters to predict the host vehicle's motion. This method has been shown to be robust against singular events like lane changes of other vehicles and against measuring errors of the distance sensor given a sufficient number of recorded vehicles.

The accuracy of the signals from the distance sensor is crucial for the quality of the results. If the quality of the lateral position is too poor even the fit procedure of the second method cannot compensate measuring errors. The sensor must have a reliable object tracking to allow the recording of long trajectories being the most valuable for prediction. In addition, an efficient object clustering should be implemented, i.e. the classification of many reflections from one vehicle - typically a truck - as one object. Otherwise, the allocated memory for the data matrix will be exhausted too early.

Of course, the way of prediction presented here can not replace other methods like, e.g., use of yaw rate sensors. However, it does effectively support systems using only a local determination of the host vehicle's trajectory by providing a real look-ahead in cases when other vehicles are present.

ACKNOWLEDGMENTS

The authors would like to thank Hermann Winner, Robert Bosch GmbH, for contributing part of the initial ideas, and Harald Michi, Robert Bosch GmbH, for his intensive cooperation during the whole project.

REFERENCES

1. Winner, H.; Witte, S.; Uhler, W.; Lichtenberg, B.; "System Aspects of Adaptive Cruise Control Systems", Proceedings of ATA-EL 95, Belgirate, Italy, May 9-10, 1995.
2. Goldbeck, J.; Draeger, G.; Hürtgen, B.; Ernst, S.; Wilms, F., "Lane Following Combining Vision and DGPS", Proceedings Intelligent Vehicles 1998, Stuttgart, Germany, 1998, to be published.
3. Lakshmanan, Kaliyaperumal: LEXLUTHER: An algorithm for detecting roads and obstacles in radar images, IEEE 1997
4. Rebora, C.; Saroldi, A.; Anerdi, G.; Re Fiorentin, S., "Road Recognition Method for Anticollision Radar System", Proceedings of the 2nd World Congress on Intelligent Transport Systems 95, Yokohama, Japan, Nov 9-11, 1995, p 1057-1062.
5. Schiffmann, Widmann: Model-based scene tracking using radar sensors for intelligent automotive vehicle systems, IEEE 1997

ACC RADAR SENSORS

2006-01-1463

Compact High-resolution Millimeter-wave Radar for Front-obstacle Detection

K. Natsume, Y. Miyake and K. Hoshino
DENSO CORPORATION

C. Yamano
DENSO IT LABORATRY, INC.

ABSTRACT

We propose a novel millimeter wave radar system and object detection algorithm for automobile use by using advanced null scanning method. Generally, null scanning method can achieve a higher resolution and a more compact sensor size compared to beam scanning method, but needs huge computing power. We introduced the theory of forgetting factor into it and developed a new null scan algorithm. It achieved a high lateral object separation ability of less than 3 degree, and a quick response under feasible computing power in simulation and test vehicle. These technologies enable compact and high performance radar for advanced safety system.

INTRODUCTION

We developed an automobile millimeter-wave radar for front-obstacle detection in 2003. [1][2] And we are working to further miniaturize, reduce costs for installation in popular and small cars, and improve object detection performance.

As for miniaturization, although large and luxury cars have space for a millimeter-wave radar and therefore have increasingly been equipped with one, further miniaturization is indispensable if the millimeter-wave radar is to disseminate among small and popular cars, which have limited space.

As for radar performance, high azimuth resolution performance is crucial for the radar to work satisfactorily in complex road environments, such as on urban roads. Generally, however, higher azimuth resolution performance involves larger antennas. Simultaneously realizing both miniaturization and high azimuth resolution performance is an extremely difficult technical challenge.

With the aim of providing a solution to this challenge, this paper reports on a developed millimeter-wave radar system that combines the frequency-modulated continuous wave (FMCW) technology and switched digital-beamforming (DBF) technology, with advanced signal-processing technology that uses a null-scan algorithm also developed for application to our radar system.

MAIN SECTION

1. Configuration of Millimeter-wave Radar

Figure 1 shows the configuration of our millimeter-wave radar.
The antenna, radio-frequency (RF) module and signal-processing circuit board, all planar in shape, are laid one over another. Since this radar system does not contain any components that would make the system large, such as mechanical components for the mechanical scanning system and lens antennas for the lens system, the entire construction is small in depth. The FMCW technology is used for detecting the distance and relative velocity.

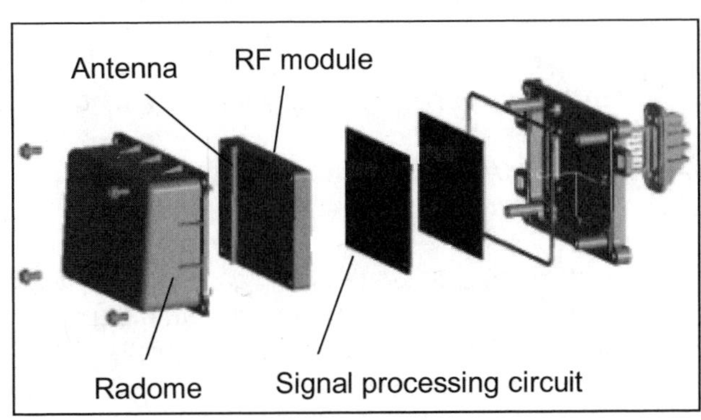

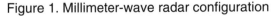

Figure 1. Millimeter-wave radar configuration

2. Switched Digital Beamforming

We regard digital beamforming (DBF) as the most promising method for detecting the horizontal azimuth of an object ahead, for two reasons: it allows compact construction suitable for installation on vehicles; and it enables higher detection performance with the advancement of digital signal processing technology. However, DBF generally requires a large number of expensive monolithic microwave ICs (MMICs) since it is necessary to install a receiver, such as a mixer, for each receiving antenna channel. Moreover, possible performance differences among the multiple receivers can deteriorate azimuth detection performance. To solve these problems, a 76 GHz radio-frequency (RF) switch has been installed to switch the receiving antenna channels in turn so that the radar operates as if it had only one receiver, as shown in Figure 2. This system is called "switched DBF." With this system, the receiving antenna channels received signals as they are switched at the timing synchronized with the sampling of the AD converter by a clock signal from the microprocessor. Signals received through the receiving antenna channels switched at MHz order speed are sent to the microprocessor to perform signal processing for azimuth detection.

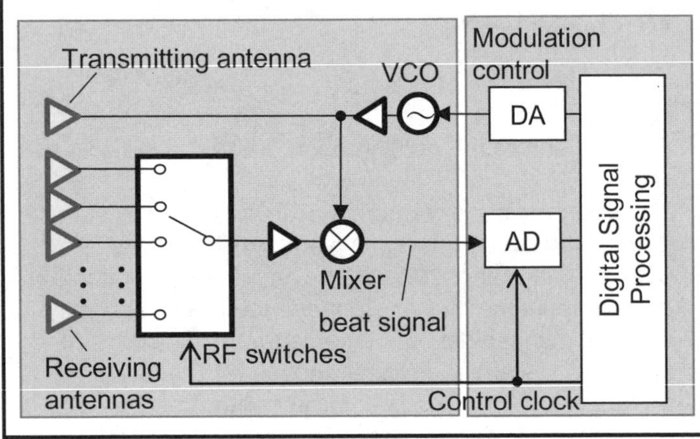

Figure 2. Radar Block Diagram

3. Azimuth Signal Processing using Null Scanning

This section describes the azimuth signal processing method for use with the switched DBF.

High azimuth resolution is an essential requirement of a front-object detection radar system. An automobile radar, which is used where there are many reflecting objects in the surrounding environment, such as guardrails and other vehicles, is required to detect a target (vehicle) ahead separated from the surrounding objects. On urban roads where the distance between the vehicle ahead and guardrails or other roadside objects can be small because of narrow lanes, the automobile radar is required to provide especially high azimuth resolution performance.

Two DBF signal processing methods exist that are applicable to the developed radar system: beam scanning and null scanning. Table 1 compares these two methods. Beam scanning has the advantage of requiring small computing power but has the disadvantage of using a beam width proportional to the overall antenna width. In other words, a large antenna width is necessary to achieve the high azimuth resolution performance required of a front-object detection radar. This prevents compact construction of the radar. In contrast, null scanning has the potential of high azimuth resolution with a narrow antenna width.

In view of the above, the following paragraphs describe the MUltiple SIgnal Classification (MUSIC), a typical null-scanning signal processing method.[3][4] Figure 3 shows the conventional MUSIC flowchart. The MUSIC method enables high resolution for azimuth detection but involves operations for integrating past receiving-signal data, called "spatial smoothing" or "time smoothing." The desired resolution cannot be obtained unless integration is carried out with a sufficient number of snapshots (data volume). In addition, the MUSIC method requires an extremely high computing power. These drawbacks of the MUSIC method provide the following challenges if applied to the automobile radar, and it has no prospects for practical automobile use.

· Sufficient number of snapshots

On an actual highway, an automobile radar would often experience a scene where the azimuth of a target changes suddenly due to vehicles suddenly cutting in. Time-smoothing with a sufficient number of snapshots would result in poor detection response and a delay in target detection. Spatial-smoothing permits reduction in the required number of snapshots without damaging the detection response. However, spatial-smoothing results in a decrease in the number of effective receiving-antenna channels, and therefore a decrease in the maximum number of detectable objects, which is smaller by one than the number of antenna channels. This would hamper simultaneous detection of multiple objects.

· Computing power

The processing element for automobile use is required to provide high operating reliability, such as high temperature resistance. However, its processing speed is not high. The amount of required operations must therefore be suppressed to a level suited to the automobile microprocessor.

In view of this, we propose a new MUSIC method suitable for application to our automobile millimeter-wave radar. To develop this new method, we clarified the number of snapshots required for the radar, and have applied forward-backward spatial smoothing and the concept of the forgetting factor. The following paragraphs describe the proposed MUSIC method.

Table 1. Comparison between Beam Scanning and Null Scanning

	Beam Scaning	Null Scaning
Required antenna width	Wide	Narrow
Resolutio	Low	High
Required CPU power	Low	High
Snapshot	Not needed	Needed
Spectrum pattern	Target1 Target2 Power -15 -10 -5 0 5 10 15 Direction	Target1 Target2 Power -15 -10 -5 0 5 10 15 Direction

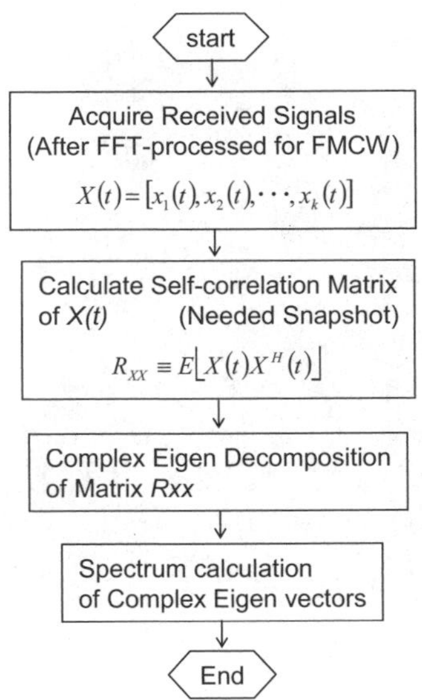

Figure 3. Conventional MUSIC Flowchart

4.1 Required Number of Snapshots

The number of snapshots required by an automobile millimeter-wave radar is calculated using simulation. Figure 4 shows the relationship between the number of snapshots and azimuth resolution using the MUSIC method. It can be understood that e.g. 12 or more snapshots are needed to separate two targets with azimuth difference of 3 degrees under the condition of SNR = 10 dB. Considering the response and computing power, however, it is practically difficult to obtain 12 snapshots with the automobile radar, as mentioned earlier. It is therefore necessary to decrease the required number of snapshots. To this end, we use forward-backward spatial smoothing and the concept of the forgetting factor.

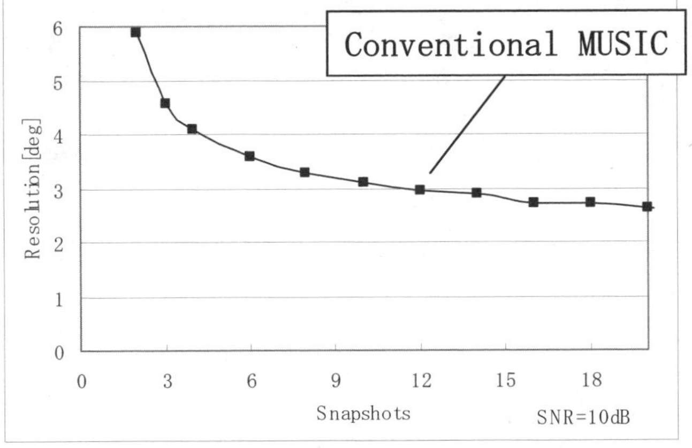

Figure 4. Resolution Characteristic of Conventional MUSIC

4.2 Forward-Backward Spatial Smoothing

The receiving-signal vector is set as:

$$X(t)=[x_1(t),x_2(t),\cdots,x_k(t)] \tag{1}$$

Forward correlation matrix of $X(t)$ is expressed as:

$$R^f{}_{XX} \equiv E\lfloor X(t)X^H(t)\rfloor \tag{2}$$

Backward correlation matrix $R^b{}_{xx}$ of receiving-signal vector $X(t)$ is calculated as follows:

$$X_b(t)=\lfloor x^*{}_k(t),x^*{}_{K-1}(t),\cdots,x^*{}_1(t)\rfloor \tag{3}$$

$$R^b{}_{xx} \equiv E\lfloor X_b(t)X_b^H(t)\rfloor \tag{4}$$

Forward-backward spatial smoothing is carried out as follows:

$$R^{fb}{}_{xx} = \frac{R^f{}_{xx} + R^b{}_{xx}}{2} \tag{5}$$

With this smoothing operation, the same resolution as with two snapshots can be achieved using receiving-signal vectors for one cycle shot without adversely affecting the detection response. Moreover, since the forward-backward spatial smoothing requires real-number operations only, the number of eigen decomposition operations, which accounts for the majority of the MUSIC algorithm, can be decreased by about 85%.

4.3 Concept of the Forgetting Factor

The required number of snapshots can be decreased by integrating the correlation matrices for the past multiple cycles, on a one-to-one basis. However, this method can result in deteriorated response due to influence from the past data. The concept of the forgetting factor is used to prevent this response deterioration. When the self-correlation matrix for the last cycle is expressed as $R^{fb}{}_{xx}(t-1)$, the self-correlation matrix for the present cycle as $R^{fb}{}_{xx}(t)$, and the forgetting factor as $\alpha(< 1)$, the self-correlation matrix used for MUSIC algorithm R_{xx} can be set as:

$$R_{xx} = \alpha R^{fb}{}_{xx}(t-1) + (1-\alpha)R^{fb}{}_{xx}(t) \qquad (6)$$

Multiplication of the last-cycle self-correlation matrix $R^{fb}{}_{xx}(t-1)$ by the forgetting factor α provides a satisfactory smoothing effect while minimizing the influence from past data. As a result, it is possible to decrease the required number of snapshots without deteriorating the detection response.

Figure 5 shows the proposed MUSIC Flowchart.

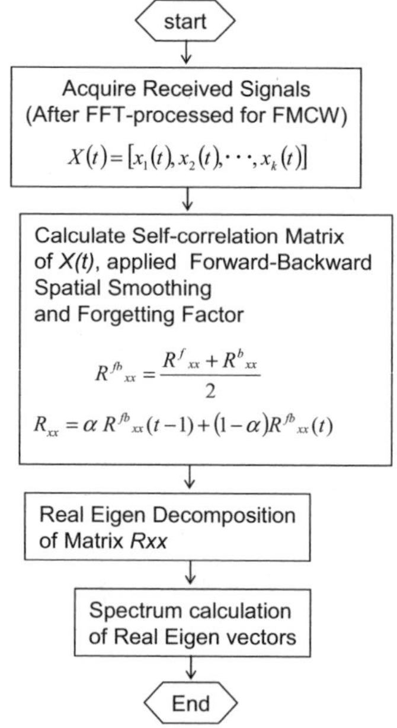

Figure 5. Proposed MUSIC Flowchart

5. Results

Figure 6 shows the simulated resolution with the proposed MUSIC that uses forward-backward spatial smoothing and forgetting factor α=0.5. It is clear that the proposed MUSIC can achieve an azimuth resolution of 3 degrees or less using three snapshots. This resolution is equivalent to using 18 snapshots with the conventional MUSIC algorithm. The resolution has improved twofold presumably due to the effect of forward-backward spatial smoothing, and threefold presumably due to the effect of the forgetting factor, with the same number of snapshots. Also clear from the response simulation result shown in Figure 7 is that the radar using the proposed MUSIC can accurately follow a target that is cutting in 20 m ahead of the host vehicle from an adjacent lane in 1 s, i.e., at a lateral speed of 3.5 m/s.

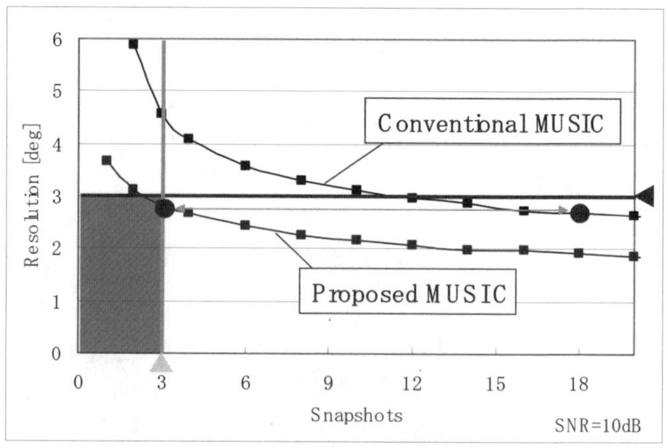

Figure 6. Resolution Characteristic of Proposed MUSIC

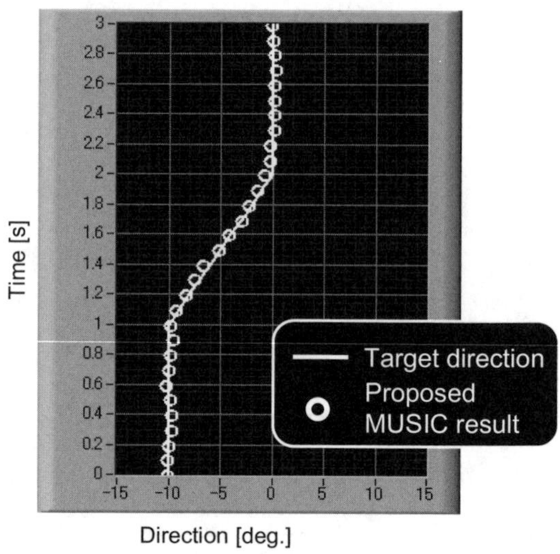

Figure 7. Results of Response Simulation

For on-vehicle verification, a test vehicle equipped with the developed millimeter-wave radar was driven on a Japanese highway while receiving-signal data were processed using the proposed algorithm. Figure 8 shows a scene viewed through the windshield of the test vehicle. Reflection beat signals, received by multiple receiving antennas of the switched DBF radar, were FFT-processed in the time direction in accordance with the principle of FMCW, and then processed by the proposed MUSIC method in the direction of the azimuth. Figure 9 shows the processing results, which verify the effectiveness of our proposed algorithm; the signals reflected by the small car ahead are separated at a high resolution from those reflected by the guardrail with an azimuth difference of about 3 degrees from the small car.

Figure 8. Test Scene

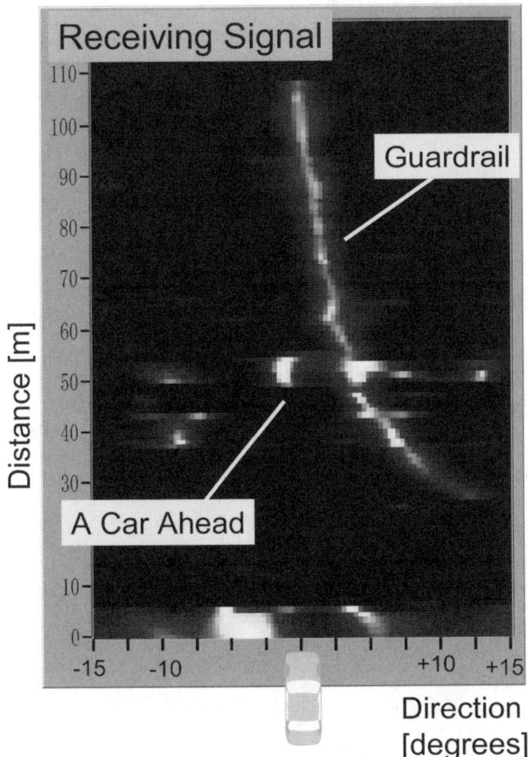

Figure 9. Processing Results

As for the computing power, the required operating time was measured with the proposed and conventional MUSIC algorithms installed separately in a 32-bit RISC microprocessor (200 MIPS) for automobile use. The operating time with the proposed algorithm was 33 μs per cycle of MUSIC, compared with 220 μs with the conventional algorithm. If the time required for FFT and other processing operations is added, the total operating time will be 100 ms, which indicates that the proposed null-scanning (MUSIC) algorithm is practically applicable to an automobile millimeter-wave radar.

The radar specifications are shown in Table 2, and the RF specifications in Table 3.

Table 2. Radar Specifications

Parameter	Value
Range	2 … 150 m (zero relative velocity)
Relative velocity	-200 …. 100 km/h
Azimuth angle range	-10 …. +10 degrees
Azimuth angle resolution	< 3 degrees
Processing cycle time	100 ms
Size	< 350cc

Table 3. RF Specifications

Parameter	Value
Operating frequency	76 … 77 GHz
Modulation principle	FMCW
Azimuth scan principle	Switched Digital Beam Forming (Advanced MUSIC)
Average output power	2 mW

CONCLUSION

We have developed an automobile millimeter-wave radar that uses switched digital beamforming and a high-resolution null-scanning algorithm for application to the radar. Due to the characteristics of these technologies, the developed radar provides a superior azimuth resolution of 3 degrees or less, which promises improvement of obstacle detection performance. Moreover, since the developed radar is implemented in compact body and requires low computing power feasible with an automobile microprocessor, it has high prospects for installation in popular and small cars.

Our future challenge is to further improve our radar system and algorithm by adding an object-detection tracking process. The results of the road test conducted for the present study not only verify the high resolution of the developed millimeter-wave radar in detecting vehicles ahead, but also implies its applicability for detecting roadside objects, such as guardrails. In the future, we intend to develop new applications that utilize road configuration information.

REFERENCES

[1] H.Mizuno, et al.: A Forward-looking Sensing millimeter-wave Radar, JSAE Society Automotive Engineers Japan Spring Conference No.33-04,167 (2004)

[2] S.Tokoro, et al. : Electronically Scanned Millimeter-wave Radar for Pre-Crash Safety and Adaptive Cruise Control System, IEEE International Conference on IV, p.304-309 (2003)

[3] Y.Kikuma: Adaptive Antenna technique, ohmsha (2003)

[4] R.O.Schmidt, "Multiple emitter location and signal parameter estimation", IEEE Trans. Antennas and Propagat., vol.AP 34(no.3)", pp.276-280 (1986)

CONTACT

Kazuma NATSUME

DENSO CORPORATION

Vehicle Integrated System R&D Dept.

Mail to: natsume@rd.denso.co.jp

2005-01-1478

Radar-based Target Tracking Method: Application to Real Road

Shunji Miyahara
Visteon Japan, Ltd.

Jerry Sielagoski and Faroog Ibrahim
Visteon Corporation

ABSTRACT

Principle of the target tracking method for the Adaptive Cruise Control (ACC) system, which is applicable to non-uniform or transient condition, had been proposed by one of the authors. This method does not need any other information rather than that from the radar and host vehicle. Here the method is modified to meet more complex traffic scenarios and then applied to data measured on real highway. The modified method is based on the phase chart between the lateral component of the relative velocity and azimuth of a preceding vehicle. From the trace on the chart, the behavior of a preceding vehicle is judged and the discrimination between the lane change and curve-entry/exit can be made. The method can deal with the lane-change of a preceding vehicle on the curve as well as on the straight lane. And it is applied to more than *20* data including several road/vehicle conditions: road is straight, or turns right or left; vehicles are motorbikes, sedans and trucks. The algorithm could identify a target vehicle during the lane change and curve-entry/exit successfully. The trace of the data on the chart was found to be similar to what is expected in the analysis.

INTRODUCTION

Adaptive Cruise Control (ACC) systems have been introduced into Japanese market since the middle of the 1990s, European market since the end of the 1990s [1] and US market since 2001, respectively. The ACC automatically keeps the distance between a host and preceding vehicles by throttle and brake control, and the distance is measured by a laser or millimeter wave radar.

Although the history of ACC products is relatively long, the number of vehicles with this system in a market is still very low. There are several reasons. The cost problem is a dominant reason, but will eventually be solved as that in other new products was. The frequency of usage is another reason and depends on traffic conditions and applicability. Regarding the applicability, the present ACC has a serious drawback. The ACC can judge whether a preceding vehicle is a target or not only when the vehicle and a vehicle with ACC are on the lane with the same curvature. Namely, the ACC works properly on only uniform road conditions. And the ACC cannot distinguish the lane-change and curve-entry. To solve this inherent drawback, it has been proposed to add lane marker detection by a vision system [2] and to use fusion systems [3-6]. Since these approaches increase the cost and difficult to be applied under adverse weather, they seem impractical. The path prediction by the radar was also proposed [7], but it is insufficient for non-uniform and the transient road conditions. Therefore the author proposed a principle of the new method based on the phase chart between the relative velocity and the azimuth angle [8], which can expand the applicability without additional devices.

Here the authors have modified the method to improve the applicability and applied to real data measured by a millimeter wave radar. The modification and application results are described.

DRAWBACK OF CONVENTIONAL ACC

When the host vehicle is following a target vehicle changing to the adjacent lane or a preceding vehicle changing to the lane of the host one as shown in Fig.1 (a) and (b), it is difficult for the ACC system to distinguish the lane-change from the curve-enter/exit shown in Fig.1 (c) and (d). Especially (a) and (c) in Fig.1 are difficult to distinguish. The wrong judgment accelerates the host vehicle and might cause a dangerous accident. Or, it keeps the host vehicle in the following mode even though there is no target vehicle.

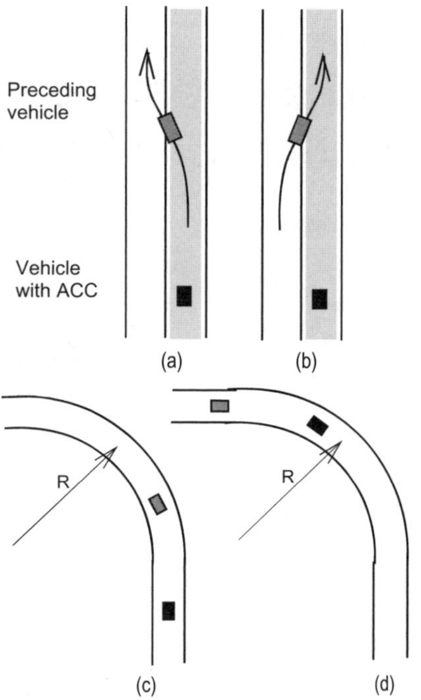

Figure 1: Lane-change and curve-entry/-exit. A host vehicle follows the preceding vehicle.

CONCEPT OF METHOD

The author proposed a new method utilizing the ACC information (range, relative velocity and azimuth angle), the velocity and steering angle/yaw-rate of the host vehicle [8]. The method is based on the quasi time-independent phase-chart between:

- *Azimuth angle* of the preceding vehicle against the bore-sight of the host one and
- *Relative velocity* of the preceding vehicle against the host one.

CONCEPT

The behavior of the azimuth angle is shown in Figs.2 (a) and (b). The angle can detect the change like the curve-entry and lane-change of a preceding vehicle. But it cannot distinguish one from the other since the amount of the angle change depends on the radius and/or the range. Therefore, as additional information, the relative velocity vector is proposed. They are perfectly different in the curve-entry and lane-change. But it seems difficult for only the vectors to distinguish the lane change from non-change. Namely, the combination of the azimuth angle and relative velocity seems promising for the identification of the curve-entry and the lane-change.

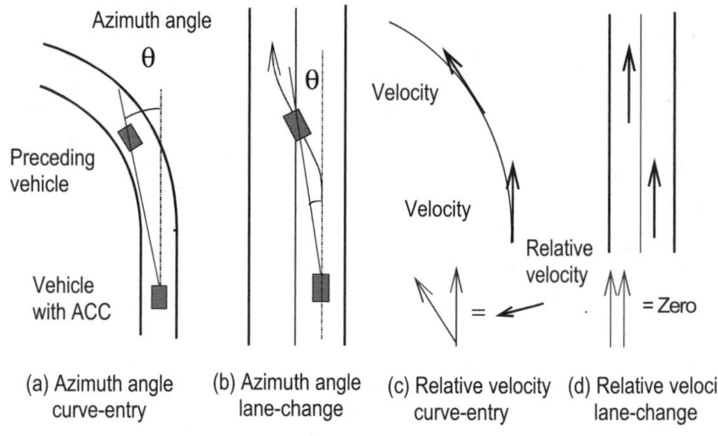

Figure 2: Azimuth angle and relative velocity.

METHOD FOR TARGET TRACKING

The original method [8] is focused on the basic situations shown in Fig.1. But on actual roads, drivers often encounter the lane change on the curve with large radius. So the method is modified to meet this change as well as the basic situations. The modified method is described here.

SELECTION OF RELATIVE VELOCITY

As the relative velocity, the lateral component of the velocity is used in the phase chart instead of the absolute value. The lateral component is shown in Fig.3. The lateral component is not influenced by longitudinal component of the velocity, which is not necessary for lane change and curve-entry/exit detection.

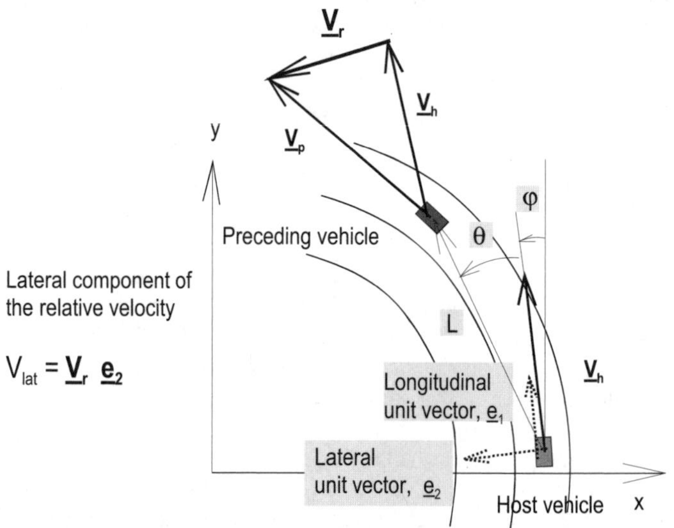

Figure 3: Lateral component of the relative velocity. L, $\underline{V}_h$, $\underline{V}_p$, $\underline{V}_r$, V_{lat}, $\underline{e}1$ and $\underline{e}2$ are the distance between the host and preceding vehicles, velocities of host, preceding vehicles, the relative velocity, the lateral component of the relative velocities and unit vectors, respectively.

THEORETICAL EXPRESSION

The mathematical relation between the azimuth angle and relative velocity is considered. The velocity of host and preceding vehicles are assumed to be the same. The positions of the vehicles are expressed by Eqs.(1) and (2) (refer to Fig.4 (a)).

$$(x_h, y_h) = (R \cos \phi_h, R \sin \phi_h) \tag{1}$$

$$(x_p, y_p) = (r \cos \phi, r \sin \phi) \tag{2}$$

where (x_h, y_h), (x_p, y_p), R, r, ϕ_h and ϕ is the positions of the host and preceding vehicles, the radius and angles of their traces, respectively. The angle ϕ_h is expressed by Eq.(3).

$$\phi_h = \phi - L/R \tag{3}$$

where L is the distance between the host and preceding vehicles.

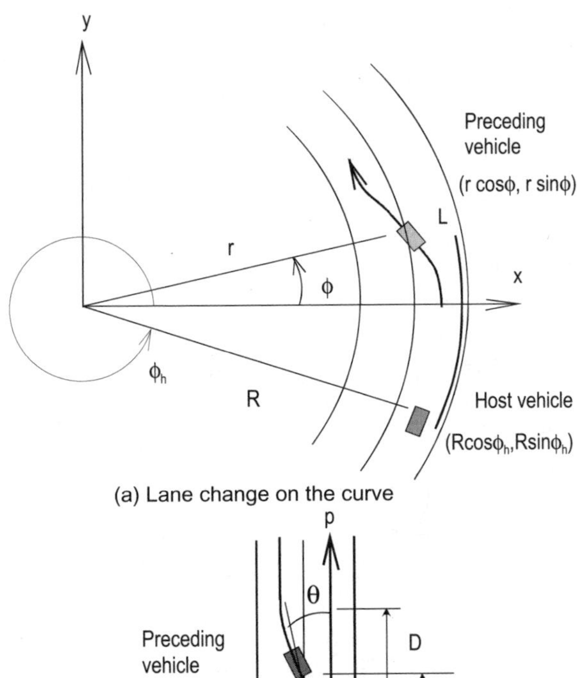

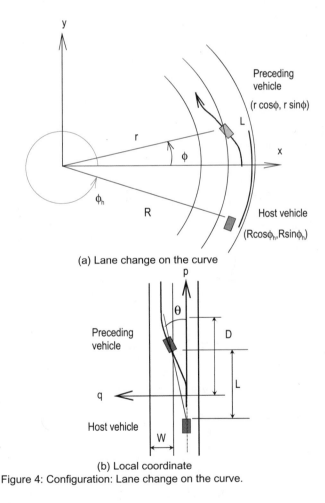

(a) Lane change on the curve

(b) Local coordinate

Figure 4: Configuration: Lane change on the curve.

Consider the lane change in the local coordinate shown in Fig.4 (b). The distance between the vehicles along p-direction is L [m]. The lane-change distance is

$$D \text{ (m) } (= Vp * 4\sim8 \text{ sec}). \tag{4}$$

The trace of the target during the lane-change is assumed as follows:

$$q = (W/2) \{ 1 - \cos (\pi p/D) \}, \quad 0 < p < D \tag{5}$$

where W and D are the width of a lane and the distance necessary for lane-change. The relation among Eqs.(2), (3) and (5) is expressed by Eq.(6) by assuming that $R >> D$ and W.

$$R \phi = p \tag{6}$$

$$r = R - q \tag{7}$$

where R and ϕ are positive for the left curve and negative for the right curve, respectively. Substitute Eqs.(6) and (7) into Eq.(5).

$$r = R - (W/2) \{ 1 - \cos (\pi p/D) \}, \quad 0 < p < D \tag{8}$$

Here the both vehicles are assumed to run at the same angular velocity ω. And the velocity vectors of the host and preceding vehicles, $\underline{V}_h$ and $\underline{V}_p$, are expressed as follows:

$$d\phi/dt = d\phi_h/dt = \omega \tag{9}$$

$$\underline{V}_h = V_0 (-\sin(\phi - L/R), \cos(\phi - L/R)) \tag{10}$$

$$V_0 = R \omega \tag{11}$$

$$\underline{V}_p = \frac{d}{dt} (r \cos \phi, r \sin \phi)$$

$$= (dr/dt \cos \phi - r \omega \sin \phi, dr/dt \sin \phi + r \omega \cos \phi) \tag{12}$$

Here dr/dt is calculated by using Eq.(8). Substitute Eqs.(8) and dr/dt into Eq.(12), $\underline{V}_p$ is calculated. $\underline{V}_h$ is given by Eq.(10). The relative velocity, Eq.(15), is expressed by applying Eqs.(13) and (14).

$$\phi << 1, \quad L/R << 1 \quad \text{and } W/R << 1 \tag{13}$$

$$\sin \phi \approx \phi \quad \text{and} \quad \cos \phi \approx 1 \tag{14}$$

$$\underline{V}_r = \underline{V}_p - \underline{V}_h \approx V_0 (-(\pi W/2D) \sin(\pi p/D) - L/R, \ 0) \tag{15}$$

The lateral component of the relative velocity, V_{lat}, is given by Eq.(16).

$$V_{lat} \approx V_0 \{(\pi W/2D) \sin(\pi p/D) + L/R\} \tag{16}$$

By using Eq.(17), the relation between the azimuth angle and the lateral component of the relative velocity is given by Eq.(18).

$$\theta \approx L/2R + (W/2L) \{ 1 - \cos(\pi p/D) \} \quad (17)$$

$$\{(\theta - L/2R - W/2L)/(W/2L)\}^2 + \{(V_{lat}/V_0 - L/R)/(\pi W/2D)\}^2 = 1 \quad (18)$$

The relation is expressed by an elliptic equation in the phase chart as shown in Fig.5. In the chart, the uniform road conditions, where both vehicles are on the straight lane or in the curve, are single points, and the non-uniform road conditions, where one of them is on the straight lane and the other in the curve, draw the elliptic curves. When turning to the right, the azimuth angle becomes negative. The way to detect the lane change on the basis of this trace is called "Method Lane" here.

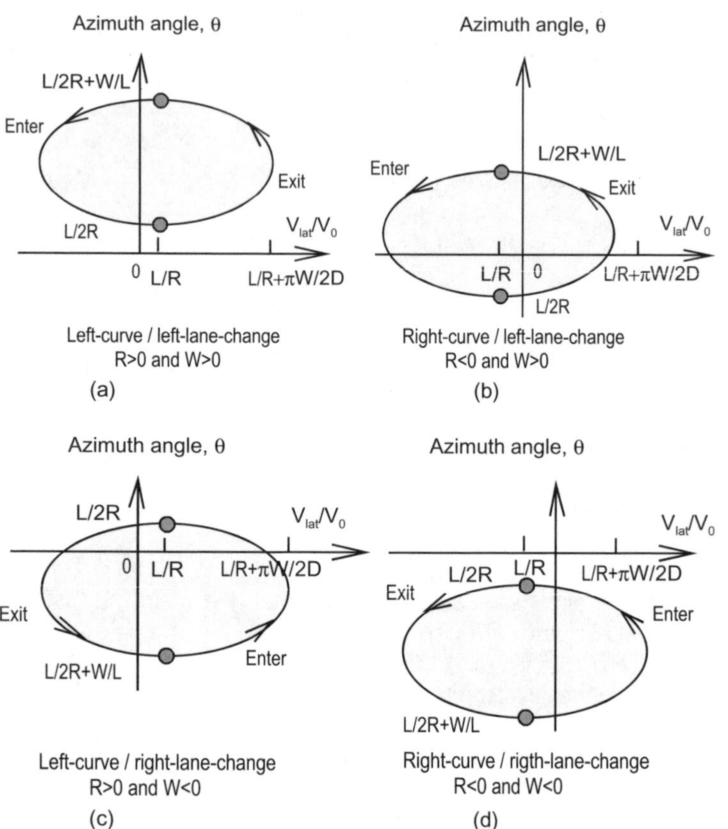

Figure 5: Phase chart for the lane change on the curve (Method Lane). Horizontal and vertical axes are the lateral component of the relative velocity and azimuth angle, respectively. *R*, *W* and *L* are the radius of a curve, the width of lane and the distance between host and preceding vehicles, respectively.

The relation in the curve-entry/exit is investigated in the same manner as the lane change. The relation is given by a parabolic equation, Eq.(19), and shown in Fig.6.

$$\theta = \{ (V_{lat}/V_0 - L/R_0)^2 - (L/R_0)(L/R_0 - L/R) \} / \{ 2L(1/R - 1/R_0) \} \quad (19)$$

where R and R_0 are the radius of the curves on which the preceding and host vehicles are running, respectively. The way to detect the lane change on the basis of this trace is called "Method Curve" here.

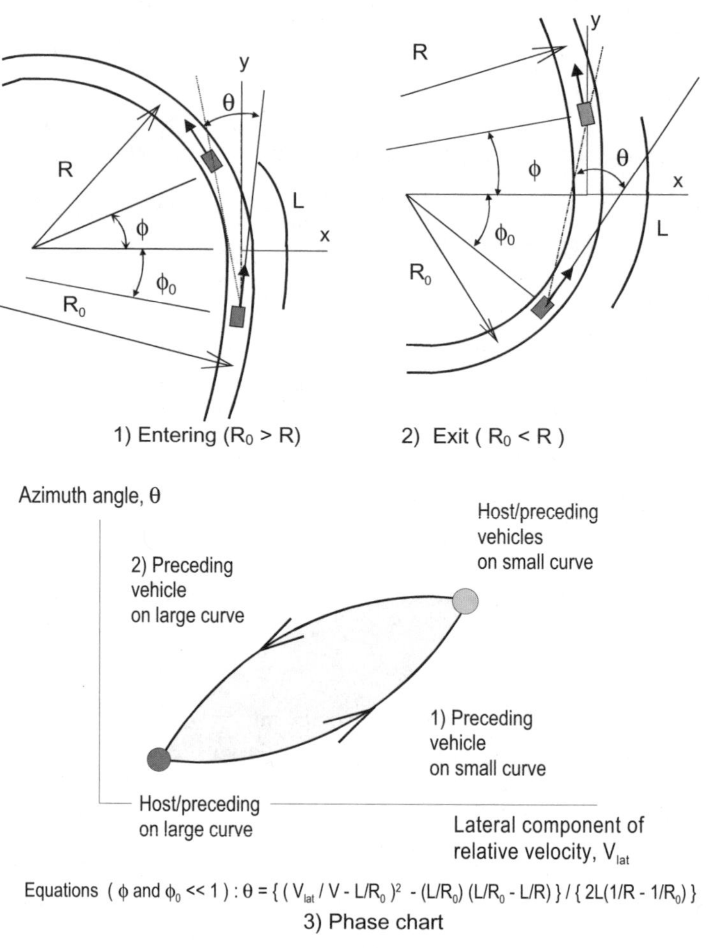

Figure 6: Phase chart for the curve-entry/exit (Method Curve). This curve to curve expression includes the curve-entry/exit. Left turn: R, R_0, ϕ and ϕ_0 positive, Right turn: R, R_0, ϕ and ϕ_0 negative.

ALGORITHM FOR THE METHODS

The proposed methods are expressed by theoretical relations, Eqs.(18) and (19). Here the algorithms on how to use the relationships are described.

Time series data ($V_{lat}(\tau)$, $\theta(\tau)$), $\tau = t-n, t-n+1, \ldots, t$ are used. Regression based on the quadratic or elliptic equations is applied to the data. By comparing the residual of the regression curve with a criteria, it is judged whether this is a lane change or not, or curve-entry or not. One advantage for using these methods is that they do not require a great deal of experimental data for determining the criteria since the algorithms are based on the theoretical relation, not empirical data.

The lateral component of a relative velocity used in the algorithms is calculated as shown in Appendix A.

REGRESSION

Method Lane

The regression for Method Lane, expressed by Eq.(18), is as follows: The regression curve is expressed by Eq.(20).

$$\left(\frac{X-a-c}{a}\right)^2+\left(\frac{Y}{b}\right)^2=1 \qquad (20)$$

$$X=\theta \qquad (21)$$

$$Y=V_{lat}/V_0-L/R: \qquad (22)$$

$$a=W/2L,\ b=\pi W/2D \text{ and } c=L/2R \qquad (23)$$

The velocity of the host vehicle V_0, the radius of curve R are obtained from the host vehicle. Range L and azimuth angle θ are measured by a radar. V_{lat} is calculated from L, θ and yaw rate. The elliptic equation is converted into simple quadratic equation, Eq.(24), for regression.

$$Z=Y^2=a_0+a_1X+a_2X^2 \qquad (24)$$

If Eqs.(25-27) is satisfied, this is judged as lane-change.

$$\sigma_Z/\mu_Z<c_Z \qquad (25)$$

$$\left|\frac{W^*-Width\_lane}{Width\_lane}\right|<c_{lane} \qquad (26)$$

$$W^*=2L*\sqrt{\frac{(a_1^*/a_2^*)^2}{4}-a_0^*/a_2^*} \qquad (27)$$

where σ_Z, μ_Z, W^*, $Width\_lane$, a_0^*, a_1^*, a_2^*, c_Z and c_{lane} are the standard deviation and average of Z, the estimated lane width, the preset lane width, the estimated regression coefficients and the criteria, respectively. The judgment on entering or exiting from the host lane is made on the basis of the time derivative of the compensated azimuth angle, where the angle on the future path estimated from yaw-rate is taken zero.

Method Curve

The regression for Method Lane is as follows: The regression curve is expressed by the parabolic equation as shown in Eq.(19). This equation is expressed by the equation by Eq.(28).

$$Y=a_0+a_1X+a_2X^2 \qquad (28)$$

where X, Y, a_0, a_1 and a_2 are the lateral component of the relative velocity, azimuth angle, the constant, linear and quadratic coefficients of the regression curve, respectively. By applying $(V_{lat}(\tau), \theta(\tau))$, $k=t-n, t-n+1,..,t$ to (X,Y), the estimated value a_2^* and standard deviation σ_{a2} of the coefficient a_2 are calculated. If Eqs.(29) and/or (30) are satisfied, this is judged as curve-entry.

$$\sigma_{a2}/a_2^*<c_{a2} \qquad (29)$$

$$\sigma/\text{Average of } Y_i<c_\sigma \qquad (30)$$

where c_{a2} and c_σ are the criteria. From the time dependence of the azimuth angle $\theta(\tau)$, the curve-entry or –exit can be distinguished. Additionally, from the estimated value a_2^*, the radius R can be estimated. The judgment on the curve-entry and –exit is made by time derivative of azimuth angle.

EVALUATION BY REAL DATA

The proposed methods based on the phase chart are evaluated through real data. A vehicle with 77 GHz radar is run on the highway in Detroit in US. The range and azimuth data are collected with the velocity and yaw rate data of the vehicle. Those data are applied to the developed methods.

MEASURING SYSTEM

The radar and CCD camera are installed on the grill and rear view mirror of a vehicle as shown in Fig.7. The radar information (range, relative velocity and azimuth angle), CCD image and vehicle information (velocity and yaw rate of the host vehicle) are sampled every 0.1 [sec]. The output of a radar, camera, velocity and yaw-rate are synchronously measured. The camera data is not used in these methods, but as a monitor.

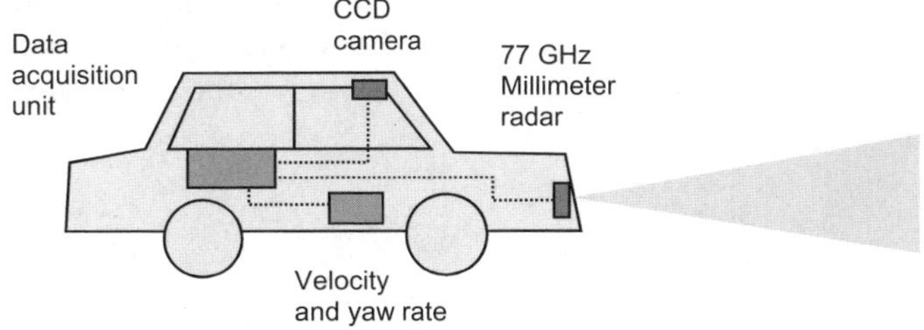

Figure 7: Measuring system. Range and azimuth angle obtained from the radar, velocity and yaw rate are used in the methods. Camera is used as a monitor.

CONDITIONS

The condition for the road, vehicles and radar is shown in Table 1. The condition for the operation is shown in Table 2. The criteria previously described are as follows: c_{a2}, c_z and c_{lane}, are *0.25*, *0.5* and *0.4*, respectively.

Table 1: Condition for road, vehicles and radar

Item	Specification
Road:	Highway near Detroit
Vehicle:	
Type of host vehicle	Sedan
Velocity	about 120 [km/h]
Radar:	
Frequency	77 GHz
Installation	Front grill
Azimuth angle	+/- 6.0 [degrees]
Azimuth angle resolution	< 0.3 [degrees]
Range	1 to 150 [m]
Range resolution	< 3 [m]
Resolution of relative velocity	< 0.15 [km/h]

Table2: Condition for the operation

Item	Specification
Calculation pitch [sec]	0.1
Measuring pitch for radar, yaw rate and velocity [sec]	0.1
Number of data for regression	10 to 40

EVALUATION BY OFF-LINE DATA

The methods are evaluated for the lane-change, the curve-entry, curve-exit and slow-down of a preceding vehicle. The data is at first colleted on the road and applied to the methods in laboratory.

Method Lane and Method Curve

Lane change

A motorcycle changed the lane as shown in Figs.8 (a) and (b). The trace of host and preceding vehicles are shown in Fig.8 (c). The result for this lane change detection is shown in Fig.8 (d). The change started at t = *3* [sec] and completed at t = *6* [sec]. Method Lane detected the change at t = *5.5* [sec] and Method Curve did not respond to this change. Namely both methods worked ideally.

(a) Motorcycle on the center of a lane at t = *0.19* [sec]

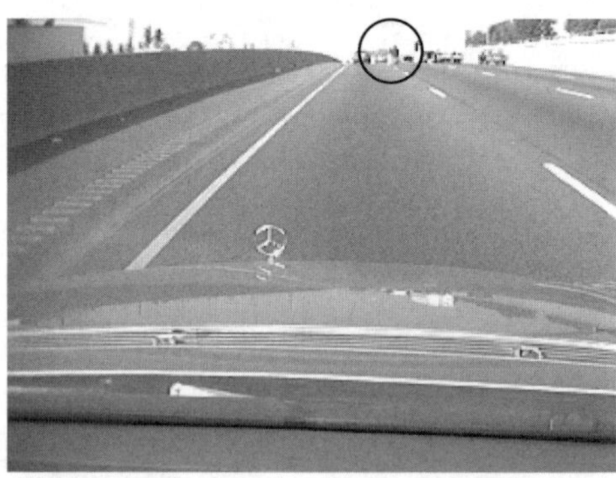

(b) Motorcycle changing the lane at t = *4.0* (sec)

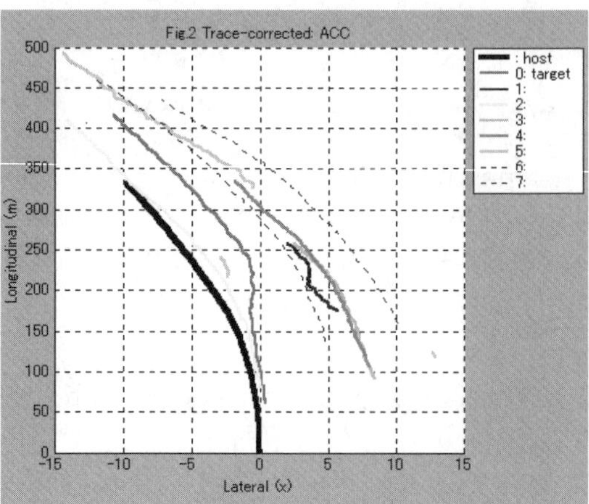

(c) Trace of vehicles: black-host vehicle, red-motorcycle

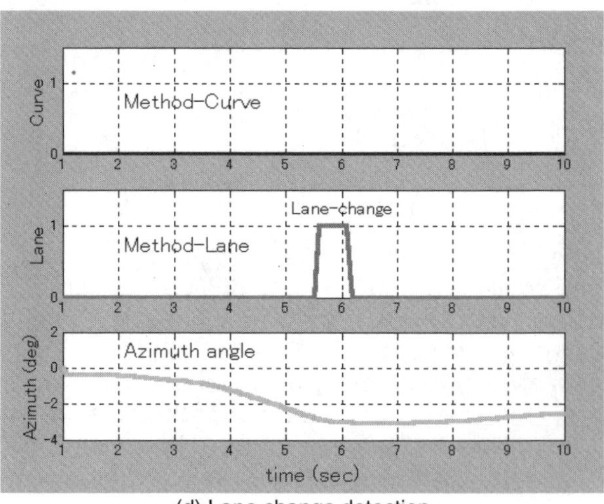

(d) Lane change detection

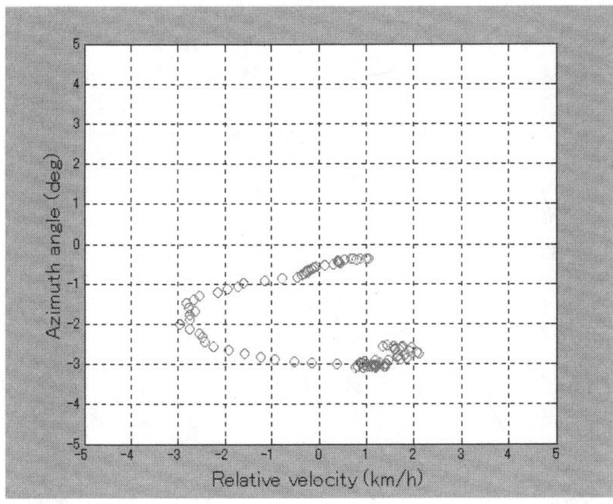

(e) Phase chart: azimuth angle and lateral component of relative velocity

Figure 8: Lane change detection: Target is a motorcycle. Range, velocity and relative velocity are *60* to *80* [m], *120* [km/h] and *0* to *3* [km/h], respectively. The lane change is detected at t = *4.5* [sec].

(b) t= *5* [sec]

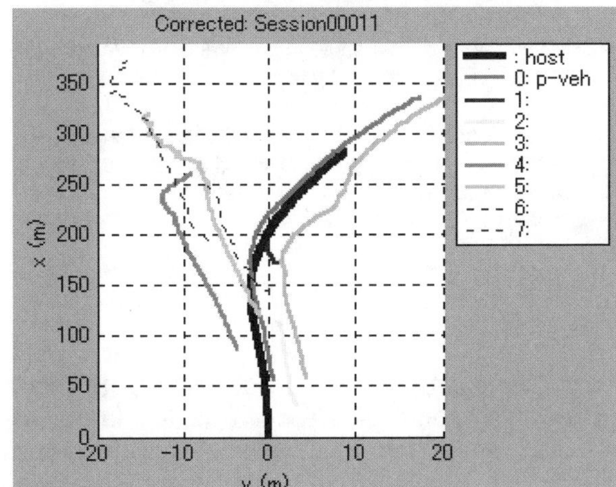

(c) Trace of vehicles: black-host vehicle, red-sedan

The phase chart is shown in Fig.8 (e) and looks similar to those in Fig.5. By comparing with Fig.5 (c), this chart shows the left-curve and right-lane-change. This result agreed with the trace in Fig.8 (c). The road looks straight, not left-turn from the picture of Fig.8 (b). This discrepancy seemed to come from the offset of yaw-rate.

Curve enter

A sedan entered the curve as shown in Figs.9 (a) and (b). The trace of host and preceding vehicles are shown in Fig.9 (c). The result for this lane change detection is shown in Fig.9 (d). The sedan entered the curve at t = *3.0* [sec] and the host entered at t = *4.5* [sec].

(a) t= *0* [sec]

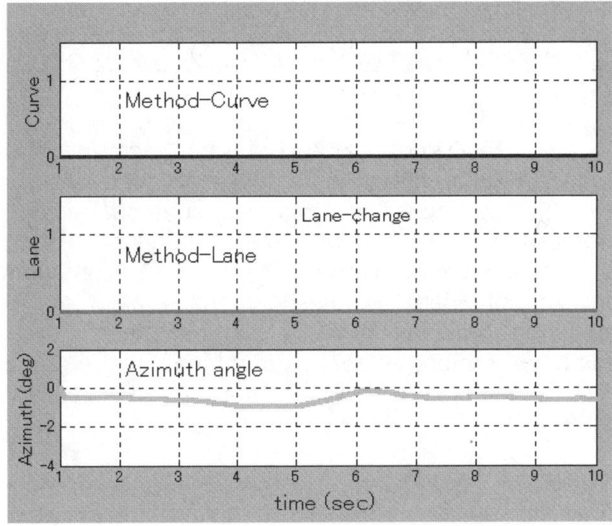

(d) Lane change detection

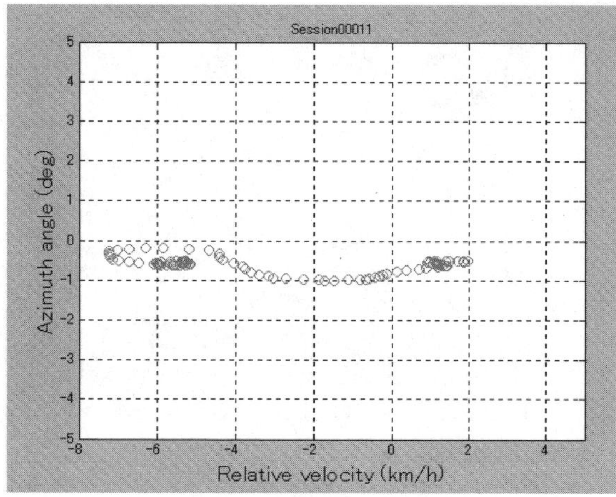

(e) Phase chart: azimuth angle and lateral component of relative velocity

Figure 9: Curve entry detection: Target is a sedan. Range, velocity and relative velocity are 50 to 55 [m], 103 [km/h] and 0 to 1 [km/h], respectively. The curve entry is not detected since the radius of the curve is too small.

Method Curve and Lane did not respond to this enter. Because this radius of the curve is too large, Method Curve did not respond. Fig.9 (e) shows the small azimuth angle change. Namely both methods worked properly. In near future the methods will apply to the curve with small radius.

Target identification by combination of Methods and yaw rate

The combination of the proposed methods and yaw-rate based target identification is necessary for a total system. As one example, a combined method, where the methods work in non-uniform and transients conditions, and the yaw-rate based target identification works in uniform conditions, is investigated. The algorithm for the switching between them is not described here. The combined method is applied to a lane change and curve entry in Fig.8 and Fig.9. And then is also applied to a curve exit.

The method is applied to a lane change. The results are shown in Fig.10 (a), the first *30* [m] cannot be calculated since there is no accumulation of data. At *y = 160* [m], the combined method judged that the preceding vehicle was no more a target. The judgment is correct. Green and red mean that the preceding vehicle is a target or not a target, respectively.

The method is applied to a curve entry. As shown in Fig.10 (b), the method judged that the preceding vehicle was a target for all the way. The judgment is correct.

The method is also applied to a curve exit. The pictures for curve exit are shown in Figs. 11 (a) and (b), respectively. The result is shown in Fig. 11 (c). This method correctly identified a target.

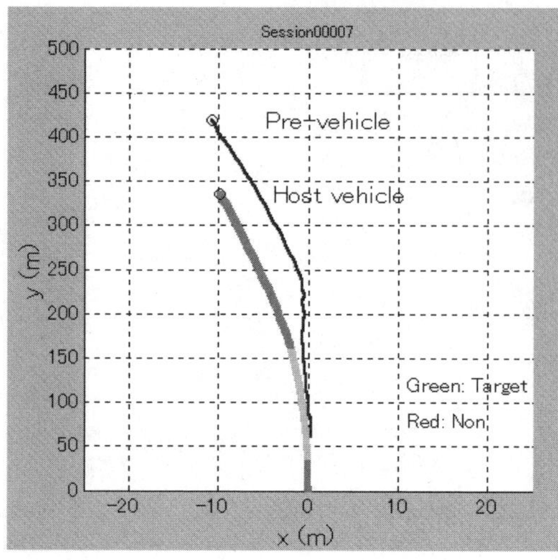

(a) Lane change for Fig.8. In the position between *30* and *160* [m], the preceding vehicle is a target and in that between *160* and *340* [m], the vehicle is no more a target. Time: *0* to *10* [sec].

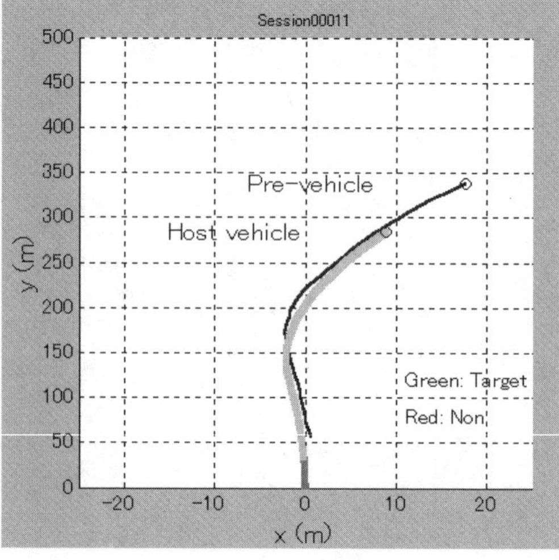

(b) Curve entry for Fig.9. Preceding vehicle has been a target. Time: *0* to *10* [sec].

Figure 10: Target identification by the combination of Method Curve, Method Lane and yaw-rate based target identification. It is applied to a lane change and curve entry.

(a) Curve exit: on the curve at t =*2* [sec]

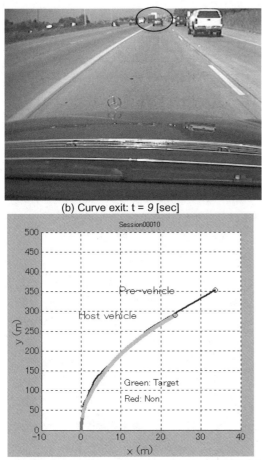

(b) Curve exit: t = *9* [sec]

(c) Curve exit: The preceding vehicle has been a target from the beginning through the end. Time: *0* to *10* [sec].

Figure 11: Target identification by the combination of Method Curve, Method Lane and yaw-rate based target identification. It is applied to a curve exit.

DISCUSSION

LONGITUDINAL COMPONENT OF REATIVE VELOCITY

In the modified methods, the lateral component of the relative velocity is used instead of the absolute velocity. The reason is that the methods should not respond to longitudinal relative velocity change. Methods were applied to other *20* scenarios. The results were satisfactory. Namely this component is suitable for the chart.

CONCLUSION

The principle of the target tracking methods for the Adaptive Cruise Control (ACC) system had been proposed. Only the radar and host vehicle information can discriminate the lane change and curve-entry/-exit. Here modifying the methods to meet the actual scenarios, they are applied to actual data. The modified methods could identify the lane change. And the combination of the methods and yaw-rate could exactly identify whether a preceding vehicle is a target or not in lane change and curve-entry/exit.

ACKNOWLEDGMENTS

The authors thank Sam Rahaim and Tim Tiernan, Visteon Corporation, for the technical discussion with them on this development.

REFERENCES

1. W. D. Jones, “Keeping Cars from Crashing”, IEEE Spectrum, pp.40/45, Sept., 2001.
2. K. Hanawa and Y. Sogawa, “Development of Stereo Image Recognition System for ADA”, Proceedings IEEE Intelligent Vehicles Symposium 2001, pp.177/182, 2001.
3. M. Beauvais and S. Lakshmanan, “CLARK: a heterogeneous sensor fusion method for finding lanes and obstacles”, Image and Vision Computing, 18, pp.397/413, 2000.
4. H. Higashida, R. Nakamura, M. Hitotsuya, K. F. Honda and N. Shima, “Fusion Sensor for an Assist System for Low Speed in Traffic Congestion Using Millimeter-Wave and an Image Recognition sensor”, 2001 SAE, 2001-01-0800, 2001.
5. T. Kato, Y. Ninomiya and I. Masaki, “An Obstacle Detection Method by Fusion of Radar and Motion Stereo”, IEEE Trans. Intelligent Transportation Systems, vol.3-3, pp.182/188, Sept. 2002.
6. N. Shimomura, K. Fujimoto, T. Oki and H. Muro, “An Algorithm for Distinguishing the Types of Objects on the Road Using Laser Radar and Vision”, IEEE Trans. Intelligent Transportation Systems, vol.3-3, pp.189/195, Sept. 2002.
7. W. Uhler, M. Scherl and B. Lichtenberg, "Driving Cource Prediction Using Distance Sensor Data", SAE 1999-01-1234, 1999.
8. S. Miyahara, “A Method for Radar-Based Target Tracking in Non-Uniform Road Condition”, 2003 SAE, 2003-01-0013, 2003.

APPENDIX A: RELATIVE VELOCITY

The calculation of the lateral component of a relative velocity is described. As show in Fig.3, the position of the preceding vehicles is expressed by Eq.(A1). The velocity is obtained by differentiating it as shown in Eq.(A2).

$$\underline{P}_p = \underline{P}_h + \begin{pmatrix} \cos\varphi & -\sin\varphi \\ \sin\varphi & \cos\varphi \end{pmatrix} \begin{pmatrix} \cos\theta \\ \sin\theta \end{pmatrix} L \qquad \text{(A1)}$$

$$\underline{V}_p = \underline{V}_h + \frac{d}{dt}\left\{ \begin{pmatrix} \cos(\varphi+\theta) \\ \sin(\varphi+\theta) \end{pmatrix} L \right\} \qquad \text{(A2)}$$

where $\underline{P}_p$, $\underline{P}_h$, $\underline{V}_p$ and $\underline{V}_h$ are the position and velocity vectors of the preceding and host vehicles, respectively. The relative velocity is expressed by Eq.(A3).

$$\underline{V}_r = \underline{V}_t - \underline{V}_A = \frac{d}{dt}\left\{\begin{pmatrix}\cos(\varphi+\theta)\\ \sin(\varphi+\theta)\end{pmatrix} R\right\} \qquad \text{(A3)}$$

The lateral components of the relative velocity is expressed by Eq.(A4) and can be simplified as shown in Eq.(A5).

$$V_{lat} = \underline{V}_r \bullet \begin{pmatrix}\cos(\varphi+\pi/2)\\ \sin(\varphi+\pi/2)\end{pmatrix} \qquad \text{(A4)}$$

$$= \frac{dL}{dt}\sin\theta + L\cos\theta\frac{d}{dt}(\varphi+\theta) \qquad \text{(A5)}$$

The azimuth angle θ and range L are measured by the radar. The direction of the host vehicle, φ, is obtained by integrating the yaw rate.

2004-01-1594

Highly Reliable High Power Diode Laser for Laser Radar Application

Kinya Atsumi, Katsunori Abe, Hisaya Kato and Katsunori Michiyama
DENSO CORPORATION

ABSTRACT

In 1997, we have applied laser technology to the world's first practical adaptive cruise control (ACC) system. The ACC system is based on 2-dimensional scanning laser-radar-sensor technology that is supported by highly reliable high power diode laser. Now, we have developed 34W output power multiple-quantum-well (MQW) diode laser. The power of 870nm near IR diode laser is twice as high as conventional one, thus it meets the strong needs for robust detection of the reflective laser beams from the moving vehicle ahead. Furthermore, Au-Sn-Ni a new alloy solder has been employed to sustain high degree of vibration and thermal shock to raise reliability. The acceleration life-tests at high temperature pulsed operation demonstrate the high reliability of developed 34W high power diode laser.

INTRODUCTION

The developments in the direction of vehicle safety have taken the form of making cars more intelligent in terms of performance. The innovations in the modern cars are based on new technological developments in electronics. Adaptive cruise control system utilizing scanning laser-radar-sensor is one of such innovation. The sensor must detect targets ahead and measure the distance precisely. The high power pulsed diode laser that becomes the most important part as an "eye" of the laser-radar-sensor. The longer life-time of diode laser is strongly desired as it is used as a vehicle safety equipment. Semiconductor diode laser is a device which has become successful as winning product with large-scale production. With the increasing emphasis on higher output power of diode lasers, various new application fields have been developed. For example, the diode lasers are used for industry as the welding light source. There has been even a long history of diode laser research that explains how to overcome the difficulties of reliability to avoid the crystal degradations induced by high optical density. Securing reliability with keeping initial characteristics is the most substantial. We have been engaged in the development of fabrication technology emphasizing the highly reliable diode lasers which includes epitaxial growth, electrodes, solders, wafer-processing, die- and wire-bonding and reliability test, etc. Developed laser-radar-sensors have shown good results in Japanese and North American ACC market.

A HIGH POWER DIODE LASER FOR SCANNING LASER-RADAR-SENSOR

15W-CLASS DIODE LASER

High performance pulsed AlGaAs/GaAs diode laser has been developed since 1985 as the light source of the scanning laser-radar-sensor for automobile application. It has been put on the market as ACC system in 1996. The schematic diagram of diode laser is shown in Figure 1. As for the diode laser structure, MQW was optimized in the active region to achieve highly efficient current-output power. The die is mounted on cupper heat-sink and wires are bonded.

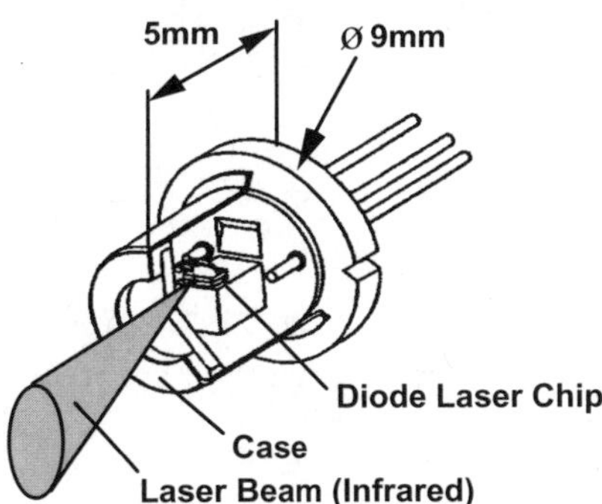

Figure 1. High power diode laser

The assembled structure of diode laser is extremely sensitive to damage that has been induced in the active region during the assemble processes. Therefore, we have established a low damage mounting process to assure high reliability. An acceleration life-tests at high temperature were carried out under the test conditions shown in Table 1. Figure 2 shows the results of the acceleration life-tests. There is little change in the diode laser output power after 10,000 hours in spite of acceleration condition is around 10 times toward the common use condition. Figure 3 shows a life-test under the identical conditions as in Figure 2, however a pressure has been applied in the range of 0.7N by the collet during die-bonding to the center part of the die.

The output power decreases with surprising speed in a short operation period around 200 hours though there aren't any differences between the samples in visual inspections.

Table 1. Summary of life-time test conditions

Light output power	15W
Temperature	90°C
Pulse width	50ns
Repetition frequency	8kHz

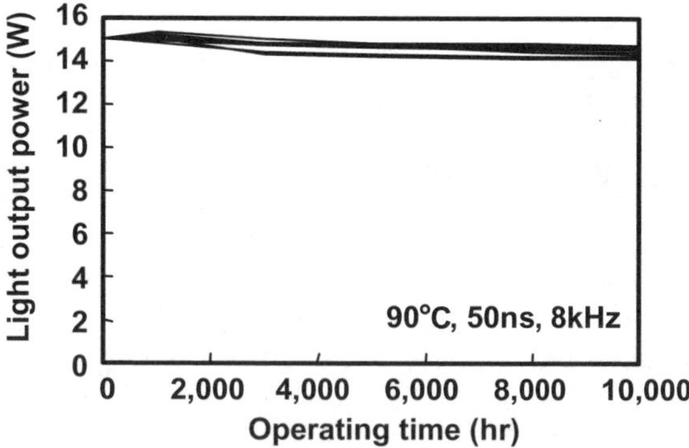

Figure 2. Life-time test of the diode lasers with low damage die-bonding conditions

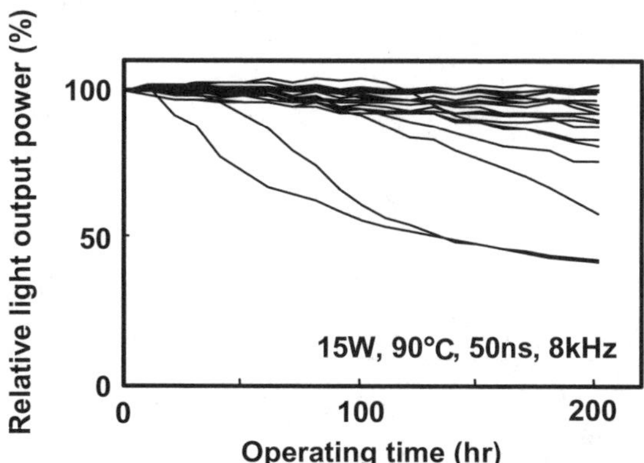

Figure 3. Life-time test of the diode lasers under the 0.7N pressure die-bonding conditions

The active region of the degraded diode laser was observed by the transmission electron microscopy (TEM) as shown in Figure 4. As evident form the TEM images that many dislocations are generated underneath the collet pressing point. It clearly states that the stress at the active region has a great influence on the life-time of the diode laser. For the improvement in reliability of diode laser, it is important to develop the mounting technology that does not give the damage to the diode laser die. We have developed the ternary Au-Sn-Ni solder to get rid of pressurization to a die during die-bonding period. The newly developed Au-Sn-Ni solder material enables die-bonding in a good wettability between the die and cupper heat-sink without any pressure by the collet. Figure 5 shows the Au-Sn-Ni phase diagram obtained from differential scanning calorimetery (DSC). As shown in this figure, when Ni content is 2.5 wt%, the temperature of melting point of this solder is at the minimum point.

The lower melting point of the solder reduces residual stress in the diode laser die. Thus, optimum additional quantity of Ni contribute to lower melting point and good wettability. Consequently no damage die-bonding is attained. Furthermore, all reliability tests, such as vibration, high temperature preservation and heat-shock which are demanded as an automobile application, has been satisfying.

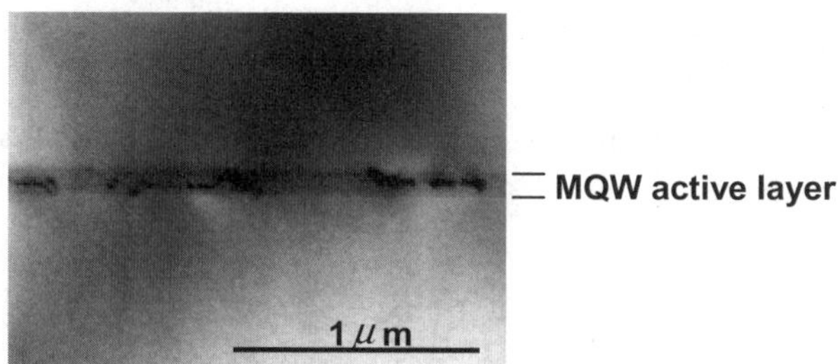

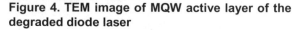

Figure 4. TEM image of MQW active layer of the degraded diode laser

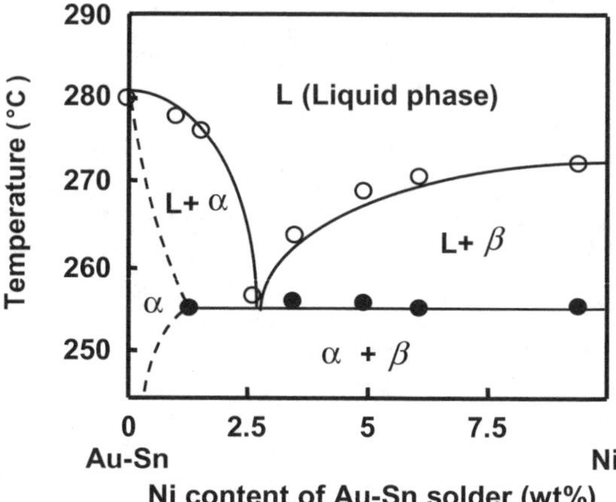

Figure 5. Phase diagram of Au-Sn-Ni alloy

34W-CLASS DIODE LASER

2-dimensional scanning is performed using a hexagonal mirror. The individual faces of hexagonal mirrors have its own angles, as shown in Figure 6. The ability of detection ahead is around 120m.

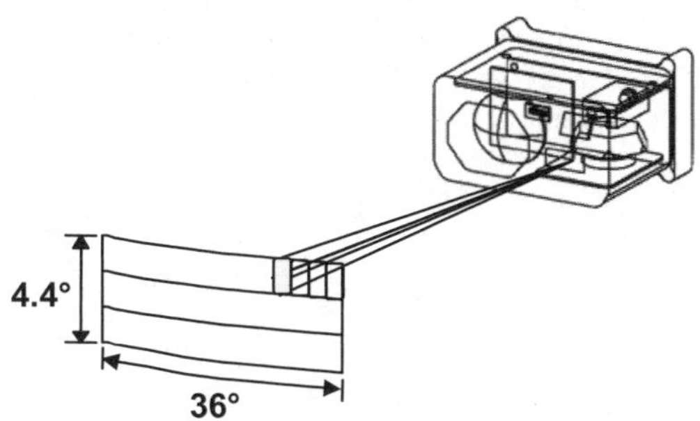

Figure 6. Schematic diagram of 2-dimensional scanning laser radar

To expand horizontal detection angle of the sensor from ±8° to ±18°, the duty became severe due to the increment value of frequency. And the beam size was redesigned to expand. The laser power has to be increased from 15W (conventional power) to 34W so that the density of power can be kept specific level. While the SN ratio of sensor and the robustness over environment can be improved. The relationship between driving load and the operating parameters can be expressed as

$$L \propto I^2 F W \exp(-E_a / K_B T) \quad (1)$$

Where as these parameters are defined as

L: Driving load, I: Current, F: Frequency, W: Pulse width, E_a: Activation energy, k_B: Boltzmann constant, and T: absolute temperature

Each driving load of the high power (34W-class) and conventional (15W-class) laser-radar-sensors are compared in Table 2. The driving load estimation is based on the equation (1). The total load rate became as severe as 17 times in comparison with conventional type.

Table 2. Comparison of drive load of conventional and high power type laser-radar-sensor

	Conventional type	34W-class	Load rate
Repetition frequency	1	2.06	2.06
Pulse width	1	1.17	1.17
Light output power	1	2.27	(2.27)
Drive current	1	1.81	3.27
Temperature	1	1.08	2.16
		Total	17.0

LIFE-TIME TEST OF 34W-CLASS DIODE LASER

In the early stage of the development of diode laser, the laser power was 15W. Now, it is nearly double in just 6 years. The appearance of new degradation modes will be predicted in high output power operation. To improve and ensure reliability, we systematically investigated the specific degradation modes to understand the degradation mechanism. High temperature acceleration life-test was carried out at 34W output power to realize the new degradation modes. The operating conditions and the test results are shown in Figure 7. The acceleration condition is about 21 times toward Table 1 conditions. The test results show that there are several diode lasers which didn't satisfy the requirement of life-time. We have investigated the changes of near field pattern (NFP) at the facet to clear the failure mode.

FAILURE ANALYSIS

(A) DEGRADATION OF DIODE LASER

It is well known in semiconductor diode lasers, that two types of typical failure modes exist. The first one is the catastrophic optical damage (COD) and the other one is the dark line defect (DLD). COD is related to the phenomenon in which the crystal melts down due to the optical absorption at the facet. Thus, COD strongly depends on optical output power. COD elongates rapidly along the travel direction of laser light in the crystal. COD occurs at the moment when output power exceeds the critical level. There are two kinds of COD degradation, which are called static and dynamic COD. The former one occurs suddenly when injection currents are increased and latter one happens suddenly during long-term operation under constant current. The static COD is two or three times larger than that of the dynamic COD in general. Dynamic COD tends to be easy to cause because the diode laser facets oxidized gradually in long-term operation.

On the other hand, DLD is a phenomenon in which the point defects inhering in the crystal grow along the crystal direction slowly with increasing electric current and temperature. Figure 8(a) indicates that the degradation results, which occurred during life-time test of 15W-class diode laser. It is evident from Fig. 8(a) that deterioration moves gradually from the center of the diode laser die. It also shows that the width of NFP becomes narrow suddenly after around 500 hours and diode laser hardly emit till 1,000 hours. It is difficult to conclude the mode of degradation form the data shown in Figure 8(b). It is quite likely that a new degradation mode appears in the life-test of 34W-class diode laser. A detailed analysis of the crystal is necessary to define the degradation mode because it is hard to estimate the difference form just appearance. Therefore, we attempted to visualize the crystal defects using the electron beam induced current (EBIC) images.

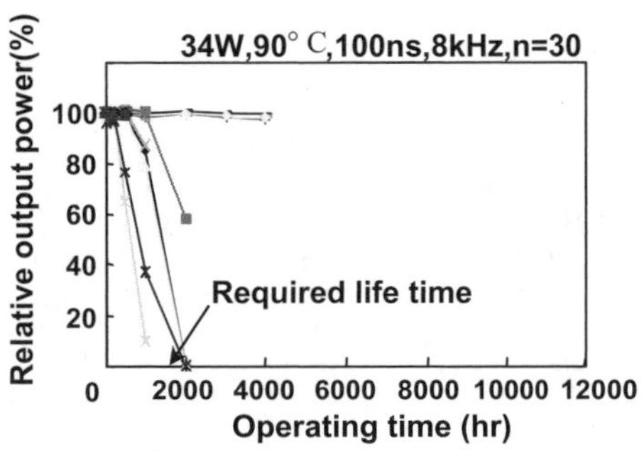

Figure 7. Results of the acceleration life-time test

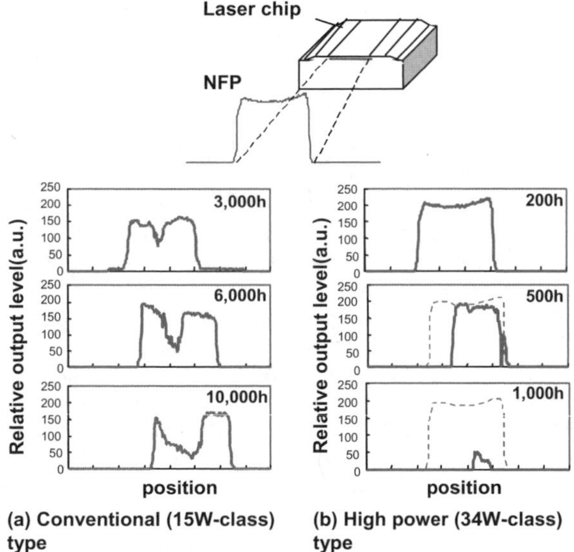

(a) Conventional (15W-class) type

(b) High power (34W-class) type

Figure 8. NFP under the life-time test

(B) VISUALIZATION OF DISLOCATIONS

The EBIC image gives better understanding at the high power diode laser. The results of the EBIC analysis are shown in Figure 9. Usually, the defects appear as dark spots or lines in the EBIC image. The EBIC results clearly indicate that the failure mode in 15W power diode laser is DLD due to correspondence of dislocation along the <001>direction as shown in Figure 9(a). With the extension of DLD, a part of NFP intensity decreases and the light output fades away. Further, it is clear from Figure 9(b) that the complex failure mode is responsible for the degradation under the 34W-operation. The complex phenomenon is related to the COD and DLD degradations. Based on the life-time test and EBIC analysis, we proposed the failure mechanism related to the complex phenomenon. Accordingly, at first the dynamic COD occurs at the facet during life-time test and develops as a molten part inside the crystal along the <01-1> travel direction of the diode laser light. The DLD is induced at the end point of COD. It is peculiar in the wide stripe laser like this case. COD itself doesn't influence optical output because of its propagation direction corresponds to lasing direction that is perpendicular to the facet. It is DLD, which reduce optical output power as dislocations have got across the active layer. However it takes several hundreds of hours to decrease the output power as shown in Figure 9(b) as the propagation speed of DLD is very slow. This is the main mechanism of the failure mode happened under 34W-operation. Such a failure mechanism was reported for the first time for high power semiconductor diode lasers. Therefore, it is very important to suppress COD generation and improve reliability of the conventional diode laser.

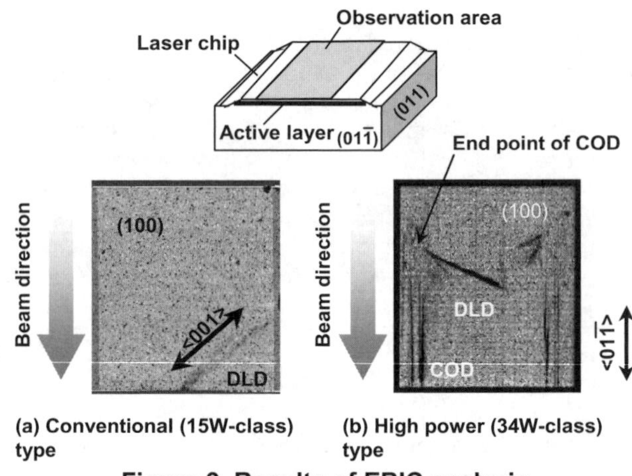

(a) Conventional (15W-class) type

(b) High power (34W-class) type

Figure 9. Results of EBIC analysis

SUPPRESSION OF COD

COD can be suppressed if the optical density and absorption at the vicinity of a facet is decreased and/or by improved the facet coating of the diode laser. The prevention of facet oxidation is effective way to suppress the COD generation. However, the existences of laser light enhance the facet oxidation and thus generate COD. Therefore, it is extremely important to reduce light density and prevent oxidation at a front facet to get a long life-time product.

REDUCTION OF OPTICAL DENSITY

In order to adjust the reflectance (front and back facets) of light, facets are coated and separated from the atmosphere. To reduce optical density, the reflectance coating design is very significant by the selection of specific thickness and the refractive index of front facet coating layer. Figure 10 represents the facet coatings and amplitude of internal light calculated by the following equations.

$$P_+(z) = \exp\left\{\frac{z}{2L}\ln\left(\frac{1}{R_f R_r}\right)\right\} \quad (2)$$

$$P_-(z) = \exp\left\{\frac{L-z}{2L}\ln\left(\frac{1}{R_f R_r}\right)\right\} \quad (3)$$

Where as these parameters are defined as

Rf: Reflectance at front facet, Rr: Reflectance at rear facet, $P_+(Z)$: Amplitude of laser light, $P_-(Z)$: Amplitude of laser light, L: Cavity length of diode laser, and Z: Position in the cavity of diode laser.

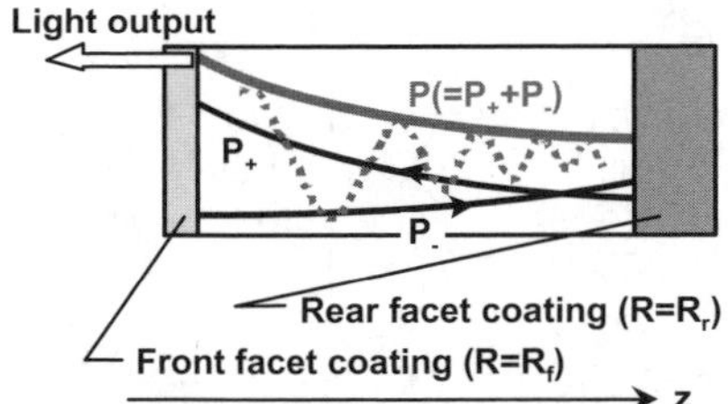

Figure 10. Principle of facet coating and amplitude of light

Static COD level related to optical density and reflectances at the front facet are shown at Figure 11. Optical density is calculated by equation (2) and (3) and normalized by that of uncoated facet. Static COD level has been proven on the condition of 0.15 % duty when the pulse width was 200ns and reflectance of back facet was constant as 90%. It can be seen from Fig. 11 that the COD level goes higher as the reflectance becomes smaller at the front facet. The dark points are experimental data of static COD level and the solid line is calculated data of optical density in arbitrary units (a.u.) related to reflectance at the front facet. Thus in comparison with the reflectance of 18% and 15%, the latter can reduce the optical density by more than 11%. As the result, the static COD level is improved about 10% level.

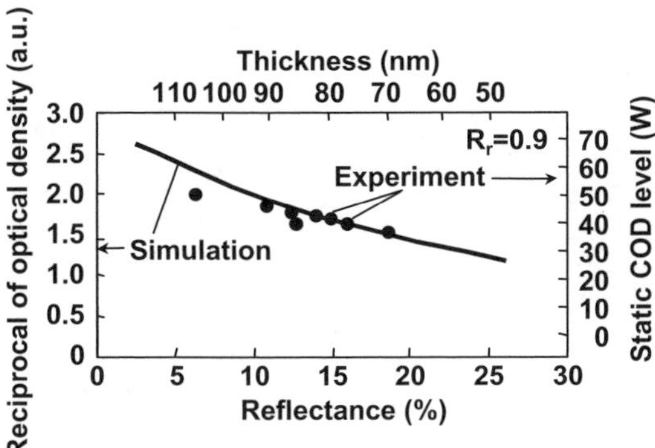

Figure 11. Static COD level and reflectance at front facet

REDUCTION OF OPTICAL ABSORPTION

The COD is induced easily with the facet oxidation as this causes light absorption. The cleaved facets are naturally oxidized. The most important thing is to reduce the time of the facets being exposed to the atmosphere. Figure 12 represents the relation between static COD level and atmosphere exposure time. The result suggested that COD strongly depended on exposure time. COD level could be improved around 30% level if the above two things are performed. 30% improvement of a critical static COD level implies that the dynamic COD level will be increased and eventually leads to improve its reliability.

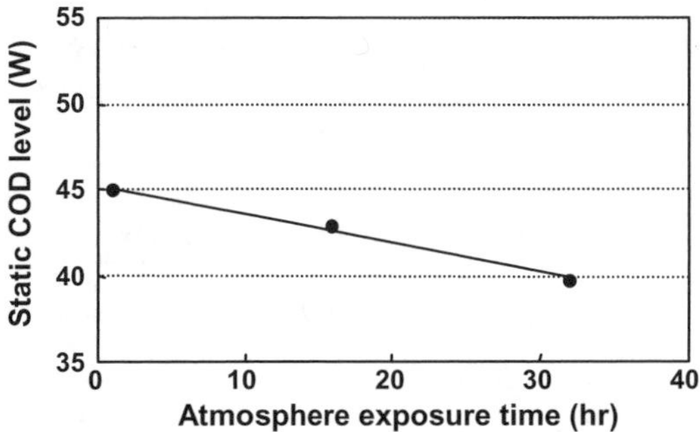

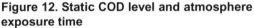

Figure 12. Static COD level and atmosphere exposure time

LIFE-TEST AT 34W-OPERATION OF IMPROVED DIODE LASER

We have redesigned the high power diode laser and tested its reliability as shown in Figure 13. The reflectance of the front facet has been determined as 15%. Test conditions are shown in Table 3. The acceleration condition is about 8 times toward 34W operating conditions of the actual laser-radar-sensor as seen in Table 2. The diode laser was operated at 34W under the repetition frequency of 27kHz. The pulsation width was 35 ns and ambient temperature was 90°C. Remarkable progress has been achieved in comparison with the result of Fig. 7. This is still a result until 1500 hours, but the prediction time in a market achieves above the 10,000 hours because it is an acceleration examination.

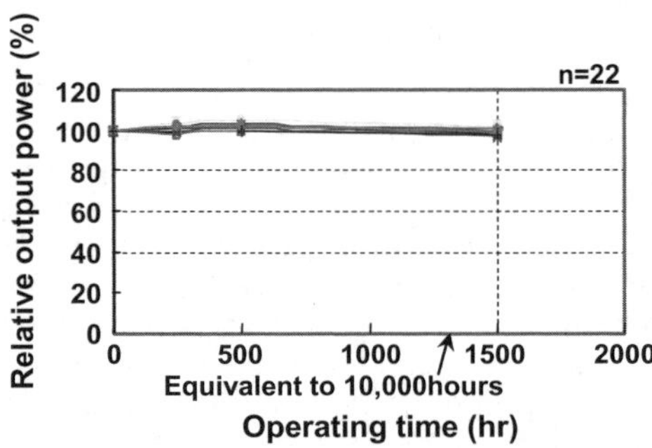

Figure 13. Result of the life-time test at 34W-operation

Table 3. Summary of life-time test conditions

Light output power	34W
Temperature	90°C
Pulse width	35ns
Repetition frequency	27kHz

CONCLUSION

A complex degradation mechanism of the high power 34W-class diode laser under the accelerated conditions has been proposed based on the life-test and EBIC image analysis. To prevent failure, two approaches were applied in this present work. One approach is to redesign the reflectance of front facet. The COD level was increased by reducing the value of reflectance to 15% in comparison with a conventional value. The other one is by solving the oxidation matter at the front facet in the fabrication processing of diode laser. Shortening exposure time of the front facet under the atmosphere was found to be very effective in increasing the COD level. These accomplished results meet the robust demanded level of the automobile application. The developed diode laser has been put on the market this year as the laser-radar-sensor for ACC system. Furthermore, we predict that this laser radar technology contributes greatly to the vehicle safety field in a future automobile society.

ACKNOWLEDGMENTS

The authors would like to acknowledge Prof. H. Yonezu, Y. Kimura, N. Matsushita and Y. Goto for their useful discussions.

REFERENCES

1. N.Furui, H.Miyakoshi, M.Noda, K.Miyauchi, "Development of Scanning Laser Radar for ACC", SAE SP-1332 No.980615 (1998) 71-76

2. K.Osugi, K.Miyauchi, N.Furui, H.Miyakoshi, "Development of Scanning Laser Radar for ACC system", JSAE Review 20 (1999) 549-554

3. H.Miyakoshi, N.Furui, T.Miyakoshi, M.Noda, K.Osugi, K.Miyauchi, "Development of Adaptive Cruise Control System" TOYATA Technical Review Vol.48 No.2 (1999) 88-93

4. Y.Kimura, N.Matsushita, H.Kato, K.Abe, K.Atsumi, "High Power Pulsed Diode Laser for Automotive Scanning Radar Sensor", Proceedings of SPIE Vol.3888 (2000) 759-766

5. F.P.Dabkowski, D.R.Pendse, R.J.Barret, A.K.Chin et al., "Reliability of High Power AlGaAs/GaAs QW Laser diodes", SPIE Vol.2886 (1996) 36-49

6. F.P.Dabkowski, D.R.Pendse, R.J.Barret, A.K.Chin, "Evaluations of As-Fabricated GaN Based Light Emitting Diodes", SPIE Vol.2886 (1996) 59-66

CONTACTS

Kinya Atsumi
DENSO CORPORATION
Research Laboratories. 500-1, Minamiyama, Komenoki, Nisshin, Aichi, 470-0111, JAPAN

Tel. +81-561-75-1099
Fax. +81-561-75-1193
E-mail:katumi@rlab.denso.co.jp

2004-01-1122

Electronically-Scanning Millimeter-Wave RADAR for Forward Objects Detection

A. Kawakubo, S. Tokoro, Y. Yamada, K. Kuroda and T. Kawasaki
Toyota Motor Corporation

ABSTRACT

Recently, the development of advanced automotive technology for excellent safety and convenience has become more active. Efforts have focused on the development of active safety technology. Pre-Crash Systems, such as passenger protection systems activated before a collision or collision speed reduction system, which are categorized between active safety systems and passive safety systems, have been a subject of focus. In such systems, surround sensing technology to predict a collision is the key issue.

We developed an electronically scanning millimeter-wave (MMW) RADAR, which uses Digital Beam Forming (DBF) technology, as one of the first in the world for automotive applications.

INTRODUCTION

To meet drivers' needs for "more convenient and safer driving," the automotive industry has been promoting the development of systems that leverage Intelligent Transportation Systems (ITS) technology.

As a typical driver convenience system, the Adaptive Cruise Control (ACC) system was commercialized in Japan in 1995, and is prevailing gradually throughout the world.

Meanwhile, active safety technologies designed to prevent collisions using ITS technology have been studied.

For example, Toyota Motor Corporation has been participating in the Advanced Safety Vehicle (ASV) Program started in 1991 under the initiative of the Ministry of Land, Infrastructure and Transport (the Ministry of Transportation at the time), and studying the possibility of commercializing active safety systems that use ITS technology. One of the most important core technologies for ITS is obstacle detection technology. For the Toyota ASV, we have developed an optimal obstacle detection system by combining MMW RADAR, which detects distance and speed accurately and operates well even in inclement weather or dusty conditions, with an image sensor, which identifies objects with higher accuracy. However, this experimental system faced challenges in terms of mass production. [1]-[5]

Various factors hamper mass production of the active safety system. For one, although the system requires a sensor that has as high recognition capability as that of human eyes, such a sensor has not yet been established at a reasonable size and feasibility suitable for mass production.

To cope with this challenge, we have limited the operational range of the active safety system to just before a collision, and have developed an obstacle detection system that can detect preceding vehicles more than 100 m ahead of the host vehicle (for ACC) and obstacles just in front of the host vehicle (for active safety system) simultaneously by using only one MMW RADAR. Through these measures, we have succeeded in commercializing an obstacle detection RADAR system that has solved the typical challenge regarding performance, feasibility and size.

By adopting phased array antenna technology for the first time in the world as an automotive RADAR, and by incorporating a new MMW circuit and new signal-processing, we have successfully achieved an electronically scanning MMW RADAR system that has compact size and yet provides high recognition performance. The developed RADAR system can be applied to a variety of vehicles.

This paper describes the MMW RADAR developed based on the above-mentioned new concept.

MAIN SECTION

We chose a MMW RADAR for the forward object detection which is needed for ACC as a driver convenience system and for the Pre-Crash Safety (PCS). Fig.1 shows the system configuration of ACC and PCS, and Fig.2 shows the system block diagram.

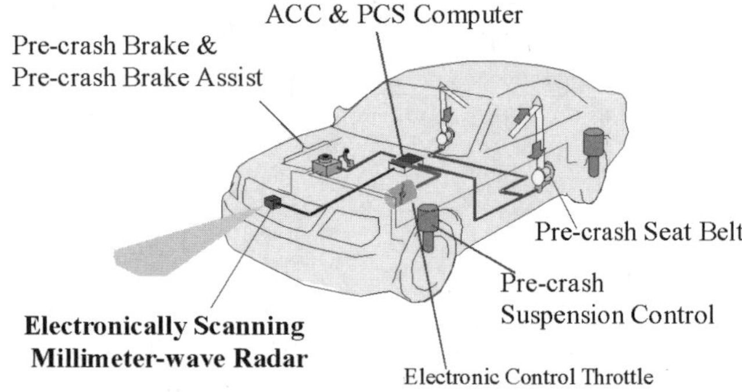

Fig.1: ACC and PCS system

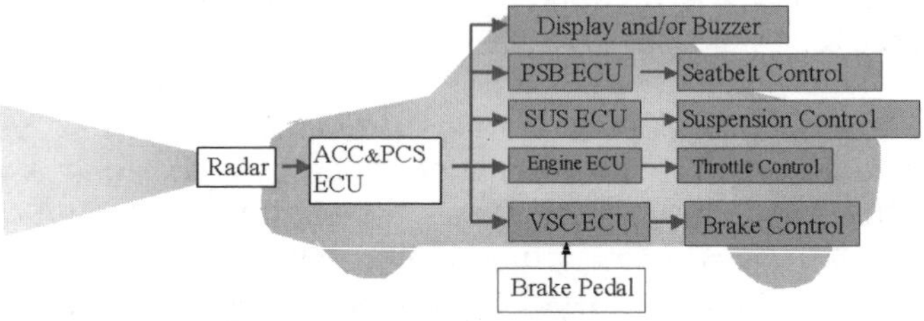

Fig.2: Block diagram of ACC and PCS systems (ECU: Electronic Control Unit)

To simplify the system, the ACC and PCS share the MMW RADAR and control computer. In addition, the brake control for ACC, and that for Pre-crash Brake (PB) and Pre-crash Brake Assist (PBA) share the vehicle stability control (VSC) brake actuator. This also helps streamline of the system configuration.

1. ACC System

ACC provides not only the conventional cruise control function of maintaining the vehicle speed set by the driver, but also a distance control function, that is, when detecting a preceding vehicle running at a lower speed than the host vehicle, the host vehicle is automatically decelerated to maintain the headway time set by the driver. (See Fig.3)

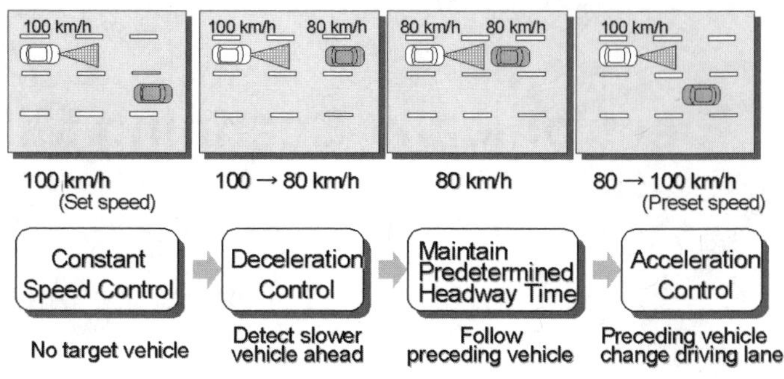

Fig.3: System functions of ACC

There are several types of forward object detection sensors such as LIDAR(Light Detection of Ranging), MMW RADAR, image sensors and ultrasonic sensors. In the beginning, LIDAR was used for ACC by considering required performance and feasibility. ACC employing a MMW RADAR has also become commercially available recently. MMW RADAR has wider working capabilities against adverse environmental conditions and longer detecting range than LIDER. Its use will gradually increase as feasibility improves.

Requirements for ACC are as follows.

- Stable detection of a vehicle at long range
- Distinguishing preceding vehicles from vehicles in adjacent lanes
- Compact size to fit in limited space

2. PCS System ([6] [7])

The developed MMW RADAR has been applied to the Pre-crash Seatbelt (PSB), PBA and PB features of PCS.

Requirements for PCS are as follows.

- Stable detection of a vehicle at short range
- Accurate azimuth angle to predict unavoidable collisions
- Small size to fit in limited space
- Wider working capabilities against adverse environmental conditions
- Accurate time for collision measurement

PSB has the following function. When the PCS computer judges a collision unavoidable on the basis of object information sent from MMW RADAR, seatbelt motor is activated, and retract seatbelts to restrain occupants just before the collision. This function enhances the ocupant protection performance in collisions. (See Fig.4)

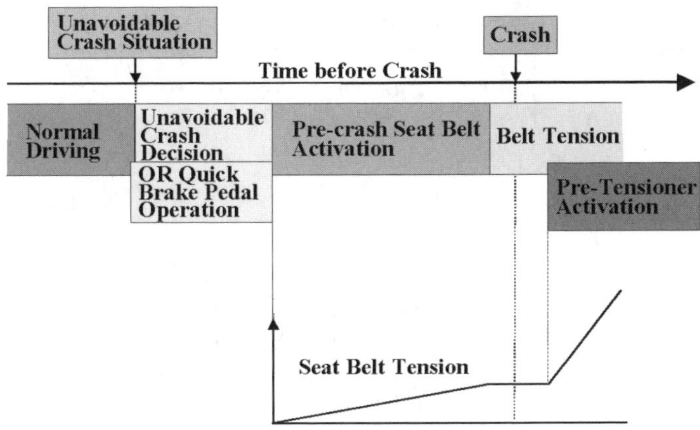

Fig.4: Activation of pre-crash seatbelt

The function of PBA is as follows. When an unavoidable collision is predicted, PBA increases the hydraulic pressure of the brake system in accordance with the driver's braking force, thereby enhancing the response of PCS and reducing the collision speed. (See Fig.5)

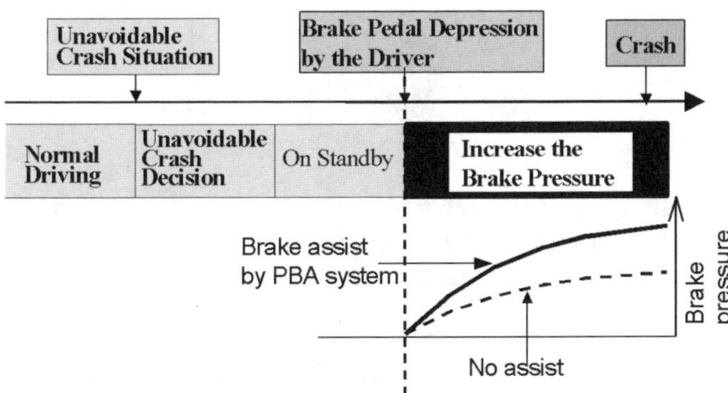

Fig.5: Activation of the pre-crash brake assist

PB backs up PBA. Even when the computer has determined that a collision is unavoidable, if the driver does not press the brake pedal, PBA will not be activated. In such a case, PB is activated to decelerate the vehicle. Also when required, PB is activated to work together with PBA. (See Fig.6)

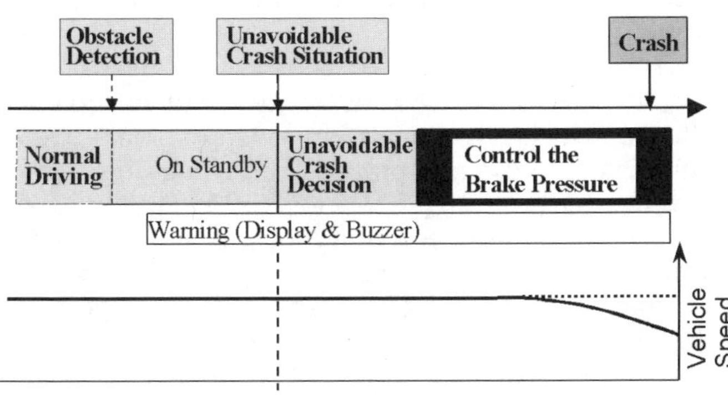

Fig.6: Activation of the pre-crash brake

3. Millimeter-wave RADAR

For ACC, we already developed LIDAR as forward object detection sensor.[8] LIDAR was developed first because the hardware feasibility was optimal at the time. In consideration of applying to PCS, MMW RADAR, which has wider working capabilities against adverse environmental conditions, was chosen.

As is mentioned in the preceding section, MMW RADAR has wider working capabilities even in inclement weather or dusty conditions. However, it has a potential drawback in that a larger and more complex structure is needed to get higher resolution. By employing the phased array antenna system, we have successfully developed a MMW RADAR that is physically compact and yet delivers higher object-recognition performance. Fig.7 shows the configuration of the developed RADAR.

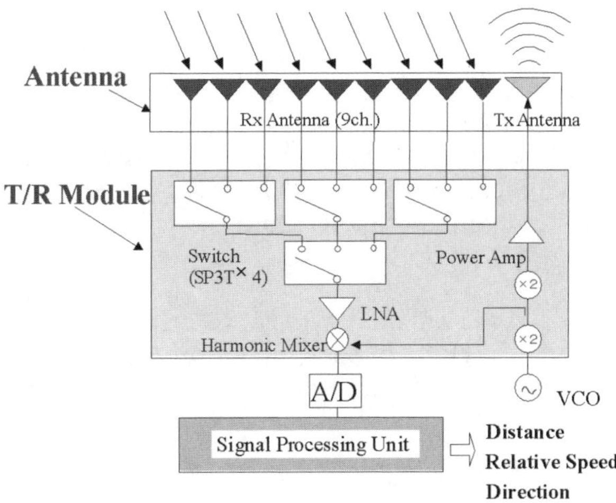

Fig.7: Configuration of developed Millimeter-wave RADAR

3.1 Switched Phased Array Antenna and Millimeter-wave Circuit

Phased array antenna carries out beam scanning by controlling the electrical phase difference between adjacent receiving (RX) or transmission (TX) antenna channels, and determines the direction of a detected obstacle by analyzing the phase difference. As such the obstacle can be detected precisely without any mechanical moving parts. However, this method requires complex antenna and MMW circuit configurations. In a conventional phased array antenna system for RX antenna, a receiving circuit is required for each channel, as shown in Fig.8, resulting in a large and complex MMW circuit. This type of phased array antenna system is used for military application. [9]-[12]

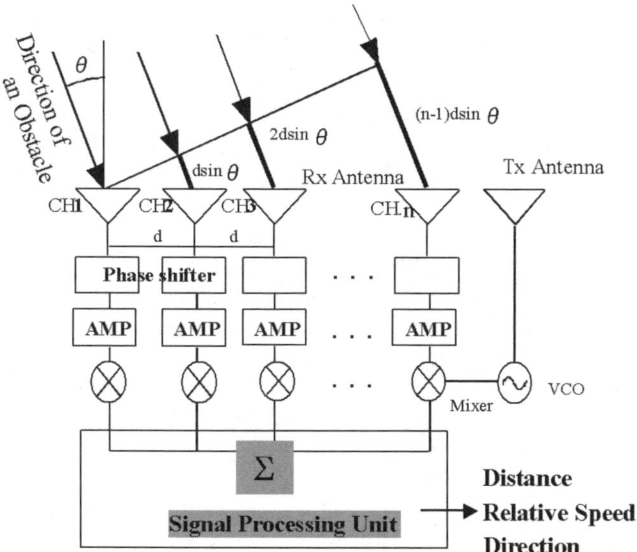

Fig.8: Typical circuit configuration of phased array antenna

As a measure to solve this difficulty, a switched phased array antenna system has been adopted(see Fig.7). A beam switching type system would also have similar circuit configuration to Fig.7. However, to apply it to a phased array antenna, higher operational performance is required for MMW circuit.

For a phased array antenna system, RX channels must be switched at high speed to minimize the time difference between RX antenna channels. (See Fig.9)

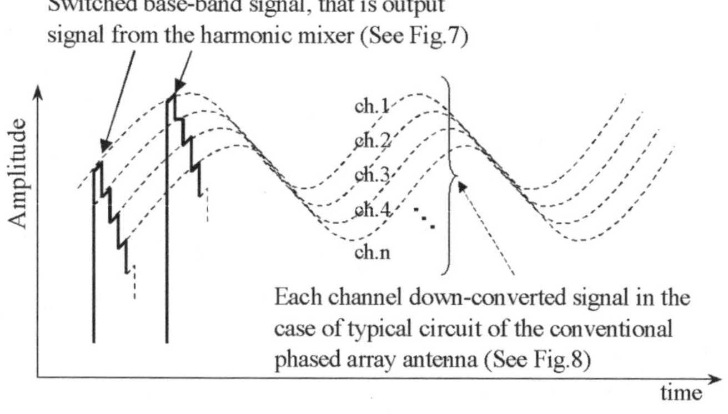

Fig.9: Switched base-band signal in the case of switched phased-array-antenna

To ensure good waveform response to the high-speed switching, the circuit needs to be responsive to signals of a wide frequency range from direct-current (DC) to some switching frequency (say, 5 MHz). This means that the phased array antenna system cannot use a high-pass filter (HPF) or bandpass filter (BPF) of baseband circuit which is generally used to remove leakage signal observed as DC or very low frequency for each channel in a MMW circuit. This could be solved by dividing a down-converted beat signal (mixture of receiving signals) into the receiving signals of the respective channels and then passing each of them through a HPF or BPF. (See Fig.10)

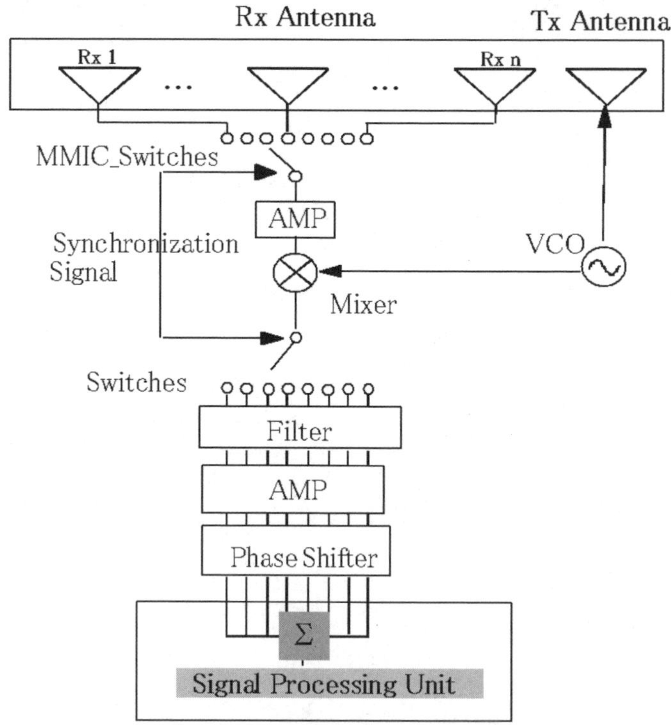

Fig.10: Another example circuit configuration of switched phased array antenna (case where beam signals are synthesized in the time domain)

This approach would however make the circuit configuration too complex. We therefore decided to provide secure isolation between RX antenna channels and TX antenna in the MMW circuit, thereby eliminating the need for passing signals through a HPF or BPF to suppress leakage. For this purpose, we have developed a MMW switch MMIC (monolithic microwave IC) that provides low loss and high isolation performance, as well as various switch MMICs with high signal-to-noise ratio (SNR).

3.2 Switched Phased Array Antenna and FM-CW Technology

In many cases, a phased array antenna system synthesizes receiving signals in the time domain before sending them to a signal processor. If receiving signals are mixed by switching RX antennas like our phased array antenna system, it will be necessary to divide the down-converted beat signal back into receiving signals for respective channels and then synthesize them, as shown in Fig.10. This would again make the circuit configuration too complex as in the case described in Section 3.1. We have coped with this difficulty by adopting frequency-modulated continuous wave (FM-

CW) technology to detect the distance and relative speed of obstacles.

The distance and relative speed detection using the FM-CW technology is based on the frequency-domain data, not on the time-domain data. Therefore, it is not necessary to take the step of synthesizing receiving signals in the time domain before conversion to frequency-domain signal. That means receiving signals can be synthesized directly in the frequency domain. Each receiving signal can be converted to frequency-domain signal simply by A/D converting the mixed signal as shown in Fig.7 and processing it using appropriate software. Such circuit configuration is easy to implement. Using this method, we could successfully eliminate the complex circuit for synthesis operation in the time domain.

3.3 Digital Beam Forming (DBF)

The method adopted for our system to detect the direction of an obstacle is to use scanning beams formed by digital beam forming (DBF) like mechanical scanning system. (See Fig.11)

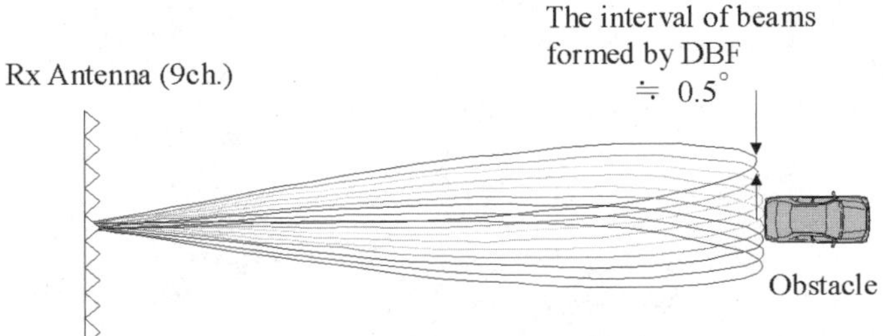

Fig.11: Electronic beam scanning using DBF technology

To detect the direction of receiving signal with higher accuracy for a phased array antenna, there are various higher resolution methods, such as Linear Prediction (LP) or MUltiple Signal Classification (MUSIC) technique. However, none of the existing techniques is practical for automotive application at the present time. For use in automobiles, the direction detection technique must meet various requirements regarding the microprocessor: the microcomputer must withstand the automotive environmental conditions; a new advanced algorithm is necessary to enable one or two microprocessors to perform all necessary operations within some 100 ms. No existing technique meets these requirements. We have adopted the DBF technology, leaving the above-mentioned microprocessor challenges to future development and improvements.

Even with the DBF-based direction detection, it would be difficult for a single automotive-specific microprocessor to complete necessary operations in 100 ms if the conventional algorithm were used. In this regard, we have developed an efficient algorithm as follows:

[Step 1] Based on the power spectrum obtained by fast Fourier transformation (FFT) of each receiving signal before DBF synthesis, the frequency range where an obstacle is likely to exist is extracted using steps i) and ii): (See Fig.12)

i) Mean receiving-signal power is computed for each RX channel, and frequencies at which receiving power exceeds a specified threshold value are extracted.

ii) Pre-DBF synthesis is performed for several directions of the host vehicle (for example, the directions are 0, -3 and +3 degrees in the case of driving on a straight road), and frequencies at which the power of synthesized receiving signals exceeds a specified threshold value are extracted.

[Step 2] Based on the obstacle data detected in the last operation, such as distance and relative speed, the frequency domain where an obstacle is likely to be detected in the next operation is estimated.

[Step 3] DBF is performed only for the frequency range extracted in steps 1 and 2, and its surroundings.

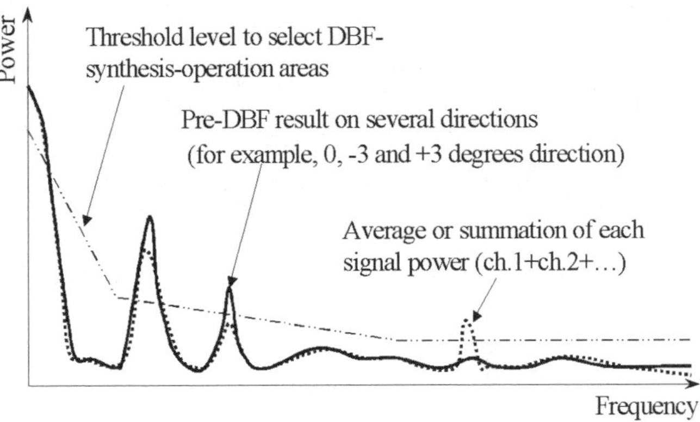

Fig.12 Selection of DBF-synthesis-operation areas in frequency domain

The conventional algorithm performs DBF synthesis for all frequency ranges of actual driving scenarios. Analytical study has proved that such algorithm often carries out the synthesis process unnecessarily for frequencies at which only noise and clutter exist that need not be detected. Our new algorithm has been developed with attention focused on this fact. Owing to this algorithm, operation from A/D sampling to DBF analysis has been reduced to less than one-third of conventional one.

We have combined this algorithm with various other efficient algorithms to complete operations of DBF synthesis and obstacle recognition (distance, relative speed and direction of obstacle) in 100 ms by a single automotive-specific RISC microprocessor.

Table 1 gives the specification of MMW RADAR having the features described above, and Table 2 gives the comparison with other RADARs. Fig.13 shows its construction. Fig.14 and Fig.15 show the photographs of the MMW RADAR sensor assembly. Table 2 shows the developed RADAR is the best from the view point of wide FOV(Field of View), long range, and small size.

Table 1: Specification of electronically scaning millimeter-wave RADAR

Item	Description
Type of Radar	FM-CW, Phased Array
Center Frequency	76.5GHz
Transmitter Power	10dBm
Range	2~150m
Relative Speed	-200~+100km/h
FOV (Field of View)	-10~+10deg
Calculation frequency	10Hz
Size	W107 x H77 x D53mm

Table 2: Comparison with competitor's millimeter-wave radar

Vehicle supplier	**TOYOTA**	A	B	C	D
Radar type	**FM-CW**	FM-CW	Pulse-doppler	FM-CW	FM-CW
Scanning type	**Electron-ical (DBF)**	Mono pulse	Mono pulse	Mechan -ical	Mechan -ical
Number of beams	**41**	3	3	17	21
FOV (deg)	**-10~ +10**	-4~ +4	-4.5~ +4.5	-8~ +8	-5~ +5
Range (m)	**2~150**	2~120	5~150	5~150	3~150
Size (cc)	**440**	800	700	840	2000

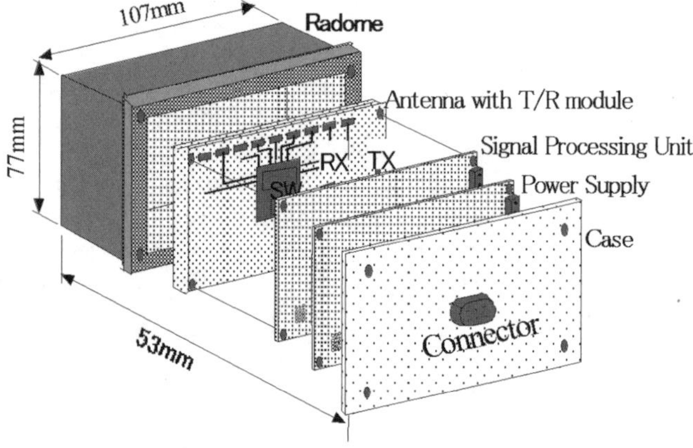

Fig.13: Structure of millimeter-wave RADAR

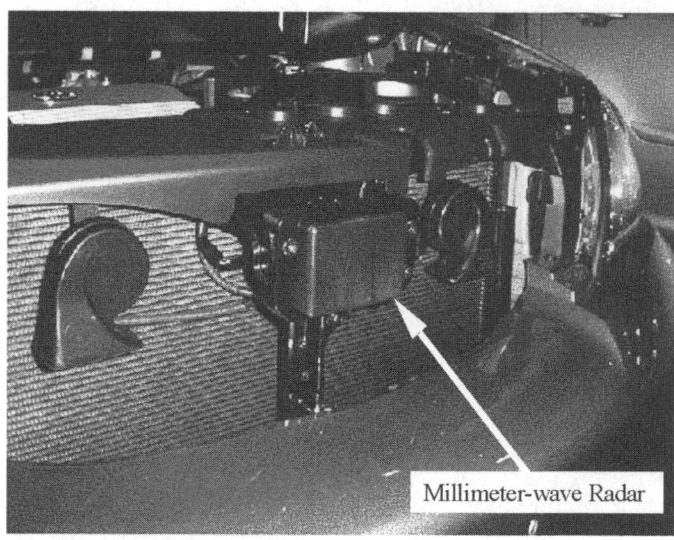

Fig.14: Millimeter-wave RADAR sensor assembly installed in a vehicle

Fig.15: Skeletal model of millimeter-wave RADAR sensor assembly

The automotive MMW RADAR that we have developed and successfully commercialized provides higher functionality and higher resolution, and yet is the smallest in size, due to use of the switched phased array antenna, as well as the various new ideas and elements described above.

3.4 Detection of Preceding Vehicles and Obstacles

For actual vehicle control with ACC, PCS, etc., it is not sufficient to obtain information from the above-mentioned MMW RADAR, such as the distance, relative speed and direction of each object. It is also necessary to obtain the longitudinal kinetic data of the host vehicle, such as the speed, and the lateral kinetic data of the host vehicle, such as the steering angle and yaw rate, and to complete the algorithms for recognition of obstacles or preceding vehicles.

For ACC, the most important information is whether the detected object is in host vehicle lane or not. The ACC system determines the target to follow by calculating the position relationship between the host vehicle driving path presumed by the yaw late information and the location of the object that MMW RADAR recognizes by comparing their distance, direction and relative speed. (See Fig.16)

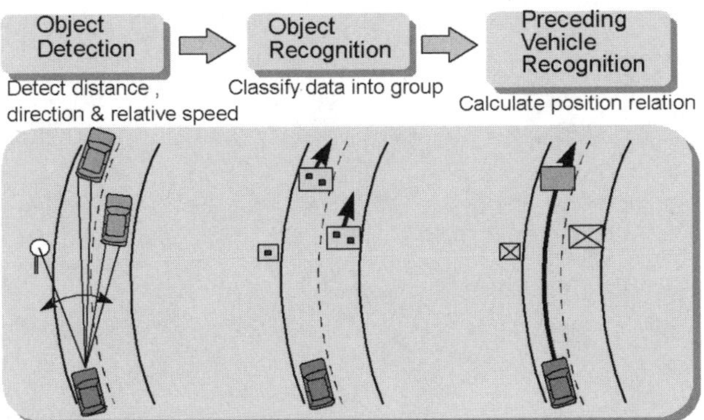

Fig.16: Recognition Method

Although MMW RADAR recognizes a preceding vehicle by the way mentioned above, it could potentially mis-detect targets in some limited situations. For example, MMW RADAR possibly detects a mirror object from a wall which dose not really exist. Because the wall acts as a mirror for radio waves when the distance and direction of the object are in a certain range. In such a case, if the host vehicle goes on curved roads or is changing lanes, ACC may follow the mirror object by mistake. (See Fig.17)

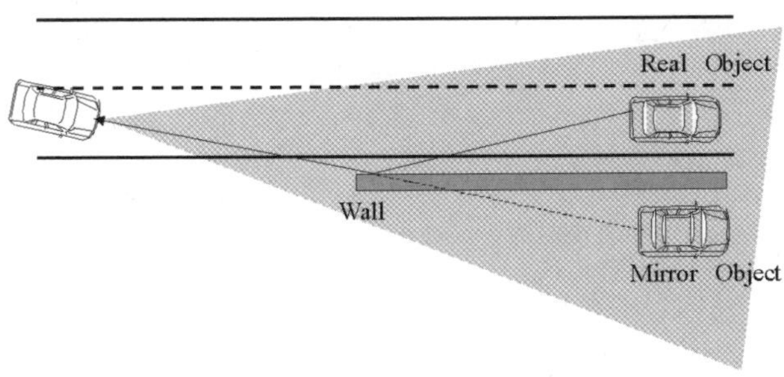

Fig.17: Mirror Object

This mirror object has the same distance and relative speed but different direction as the real object. When such objects exist, MMW RADAR distinguishes as mirror objects by the position relationship and recognition of the wall reflections to help prevent mis-detection.
Furthermore MMW RADAR has a tendency of detecting a vehicle's inner edge when the vehicle is seen obliquely. As a measure against this behavior, this RADAR revises the target vehicle position based on its rotational angle which is estimated by the curve radius and target direction. By applying additional techniques, the ACC can reliably distinguish preceding vehicles from mirror objects.

PCS identifies an obstacle using the following algorithm. When the host vehicle faces an oncoming vehicle as shown in Figure 18, the ECU determines whether the oncoming vehicle is an obstacle or not, on the basis of the time to collision (TTC) in which most drivers would not be able to avoid a collision even with rapid steering or braking. If the host vehicle driver begins steering to avoid the collision or if the oncoming vehicle driver begins to steer his/her vehicle laterally relative to the host vehicle earlier than the TTC, the ECU determines that the oncoming vehicle is not an obstacle. If not, it allows the PCS features to be activated later than the TTC.

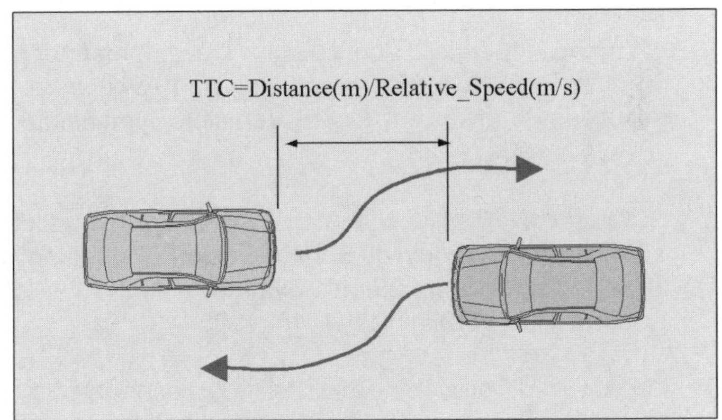

Figure 18: TTC (Time-to-Collision) in Which Most Drivers Would Not Be Able to Avoid a Crash Even with Rapid Evasive Action

In the developed safety system, the ACC & PCS ECU carries out the process of identifying preceding vehicles or obstacles as the post-process of the MMW RADAR, as shown in Figure 2.

CONCLUSION

By limiting the operational range of the active safety system to the range just before a collision, we have successfully developed and commercialized a compact, high recognition performance, and feasible MMW RADAR that can be shared with a convenience system such as ACC. Although the developed RADAR is still limited in its applications, it has certainly allowed us to make the first step toward the realization of active safety systems.

Our future tasks are to develop a more advanced MMW RADAR system by applying some methods with higher azimuth resolution and expanding the detecting area, and to add upgrade application systems for wider deployment of ITS and ASV.

ACKNOWLEDGMENTS

In closing, we would like to express our sincere gratitude to Denso Corporation and Mitsubishi Electric Corporation for their cooperation in developing the MMW RADAR

REFERENCES

1. S.Tokoro "Automotive Application Systems of a Millimeter-wave RADAR." TOYOTA Technical Review Vol.46 No.1 Sep., 51-56, 1996

2. T.Matsumoto, N.Yoshitsugu and Y.Hori "TOYOTA Advanced Safety Vehicle(TOYOTA ASV)." TOYOTA Technical Review Vol.46 No.1 May, 56-63, 1996

3. Y.Yamada, S.Tokoro and Y.Fujita "Development of a 60 GHz RADAR for Rear-end Collision Avoidance." Proceedings of the Intelligent Vehicles Symposium, 207-212, 1994

4. H.Satonaka, Y.Hashimoto, Y.Yamada and T.Kakinami "A Study of Sensor Fusion Technology for Collision Avoidance System." ITS World Congress '95 Vol.III, 1108-1115, 1995

5. M.Kawai "Collision Avoidance Technologies." Proceedings of the International Congress on Transportation Electronics, SAE P-283,94C038, 305-316, 1994

6. K.Fujita, T.Enomoto, R.Kachu, H.Kato, H.Fujinami, K.Moriizumi "Development of Pre-Crash Safety System" The 18th ESV Conference, Paper No.544-W, 2003

7. S.Tokoro, K.Kuroda, T.Nagao, T.Kawasaki, T.Yamamoto "Pre-Crash Sensor for Pre-Crash Safety" The 18th ESV Conference, Paper No.545-W, 2003

8. N.Furui, H.Miyakoshi, M.Noda, K.Miyauchi "Development of a Scanning Laser Radar for ACC" SAE No.980615, 1998

9. H.Steyskal "Digital Bemforming Antennas" Microwave Journal, Jan.1987, pp107-114

10. P.Barton "Digital Beamforming for Radar" IEEE Proceedings, Vol.127, Pt. F, August 4, 1980

11. W.Humbert and H.Steyskal "A Recent Evaluation of the Digital Beamforming Tested at Rome Laboratory" Rome Lab, TR-93-198, September 1993

12. B.Wardrop "Digital Beamforming in Radar Systems – A Review" Military Microwave Conf. Proc., UK, 1984

2004-01-0177

New Algorithm for Multiple Object Detection in FM-CW Radar

Shunji Miyahara
Visteon Japan, Ltd.

ABSTRACT

A new practical algorithm is proposed for multiple object detection in automotive FM-CW radars. They are radars for ACC (Adaptive Cruise Control) radar, collision avoidance, pre-crash safety, side-object detection, etc. This algorithm can provide the distance and relative velocity of objects without the ambiguity of distance and relative velocity, an inherent problem of FM-CW. Since it is simple, straight-forward and fast, it is suitable for automotive application, in which the update time is less than *100* [msec]. This algorithm is based on two down chirp frequency sweeps with small slope-difference. Since the difference is small, the correct pairs of beat frequencies are obtained automatically. Because of the down chirps, the polarity of beat frequencies owing to the distance and the doppler becomes the same for an approaching object and then the distance and the velocity are uniquely determined. Namely the distance and velocity information for multiple objects can be calculated without the ambiguity in a simple manner.

INTRODUCTION

Automotive applications of millimeter wave radar systems are gradually spreading into a market in Japan, US and Europe because of the high performance under adverse weather conditions. They are adaptive cruise control (ACC), pre-crash safety and collision warning systems. The expectation for the better performance and lower cost of the systems is getting larger and larger. In the applications, the azimuth angle is getting wider and several vehicles have to be detected even in instantaneous angle during the azimuth angle scanning. To manage multiple vehicles properly, FM-CW (Frequency Modulated Continuous Wave), multiple-frequency CW with monopulse and doppler principles and FM pulse doppler methods [1] are used in the systems [2-9]. The first one requires the high linearity of VCO (Voltage Controlled Oscillator). The second one seems to have the problem on the detection of multiple stationary objects because it depends on the doppler shift. The third one seems to have a problem on the range accuracy because it is based on the range window. The late improvement of the linearity and cost of the VCO encourages the use of FM-CW and makes it the most popular method in an automotive market.

FM-CW is an effective method for objects with low relative velocity, but has in principle the ambiguity on the separation of the range/distance and velocity for a single object with wide relative velocity range and the identification of the correct combination of beat frequencies for multiple objects. Especially in the automotive applications, the relative velocity ranges from *–150* [km/h] to *150* [km/h] and this results in the difficulty of the separation of the range and velocity and in the identification of the correct combination. So far the several methods to overcome these problems have been proposed, but seem so complicated and not practical. For instance, the insertion of flat frequency is added to two chirps, and exact combinations of beat frequencies and the resolution of the ambiguity are made. But it is so complicated and not practical. Therefore an algorithm based on two chirp frequency sweeps with small slope-difference is proposed. This algorithm can identify the correct pair from several combinations and provide the distance information automatically for multiple objects. Therefore the distance and velocity for multiple objects can be calculated without ambiguity. Here the principle and examples of the algorithm are described.

CONVENTIONAL FM-CW RADAR

The radar in automotive application is shown in Fig.1. The received radar signal is processed and the distance and relative velocity are obtained. The distance and velocity are used for the vehicle distance control and warning for safety.

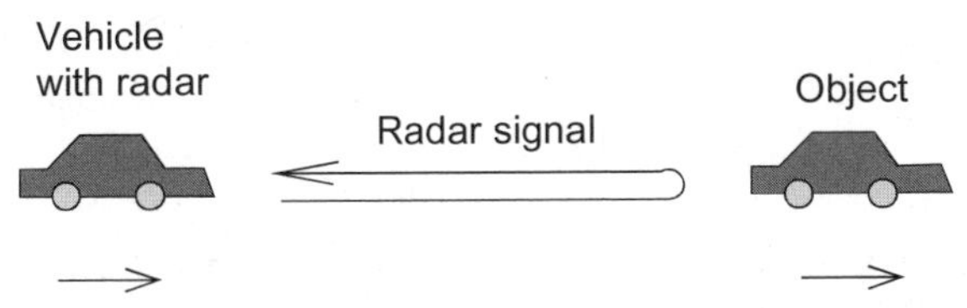

Figure 1: Radar application in automobile.

CONVENTIONAL TECHNOLOGY

Here it is assumed that the principle of the signal processing is the FM-CW [1]. The transmitted and received waves are expressed as shown in Fig.2. Linearly frequency modulated RF signal is transmitted and the signal reflected from objects is received. Both signals are mixed and the beat signal is obtained. The beat frequencies are given by Eq.(1) and (2).

$$f_{b\text{-}up} = | f_r - f_d | \quad \text{for up-chirp} \qquad (1)$$

$$f_{b\text{-}down} = | f_r + f_d | \quad \text{for down-chirp} \qquad (2)$$

f_r and f_d are given by Eq.(3) and (4).

$$f_r = | (2R/c)\ (df/dt) | \qquad (3)$$

$$f_d = 2\,V/\lambda \qquad (4)$$

where *R*, *c*, *df/dt*, *V* and λ are the distance between the object and vehicle with radar, the velocity of RF wave, the rate of change of the carrier frequency, the relative velocity (approaching is assumed positive) and wavelength, respectively.

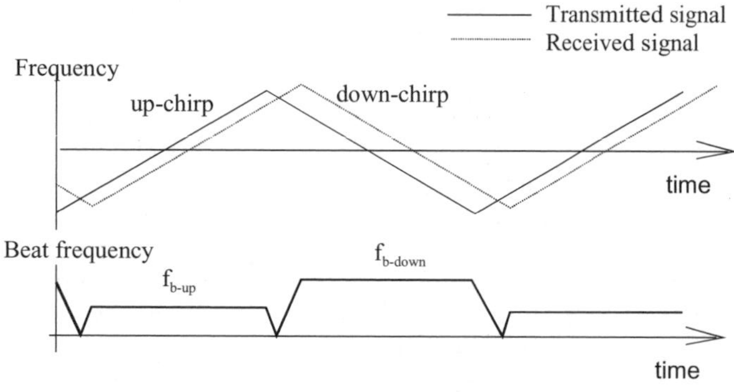

Figure 2: Principle of FW-CW radar.

In the automotive application, the amplitude of the range frequency f_r and Doppler frequency f_d is comparative and the both cannot be determined uniquely. Because only the absolute values of the summation and difference of the frequencies are measured as shown in Eqs.(1) and (2). In automotive applications, the f_r and f_d are ranging from *10* to *80* kHz and from *0* to *20* kHz, respectively. This can lead to the ambiguity.

Therefore the separation of the both frequencies needs some unmodulated continuous wave as shown in Fig.3 [6]. Since the f_d is measured in the period of the unmodulated wave, the ambiguity between f_r and f_d is resolved. But this procedure becomes so complex for multiple targets.

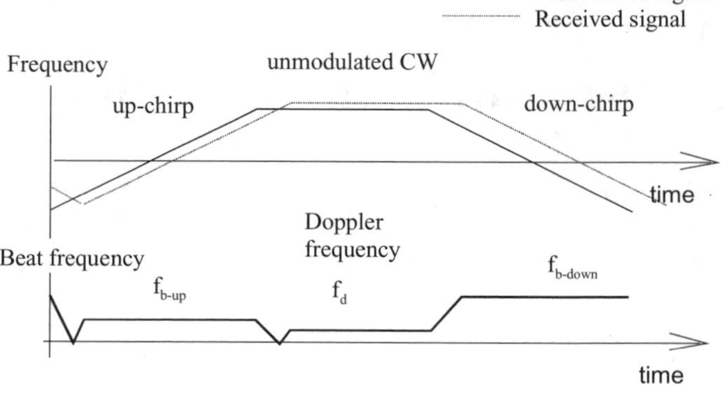

Figure 3: FW-CW radar including unmodulated CW. Single object.

NEW ALGORITHM

To overcome the ambiguity of the f_r and f_d in multiple objects, the author proposes a unique and practical algorithm based on dual down-chirps. The modulation of the algorithm is shown in Fig.4.

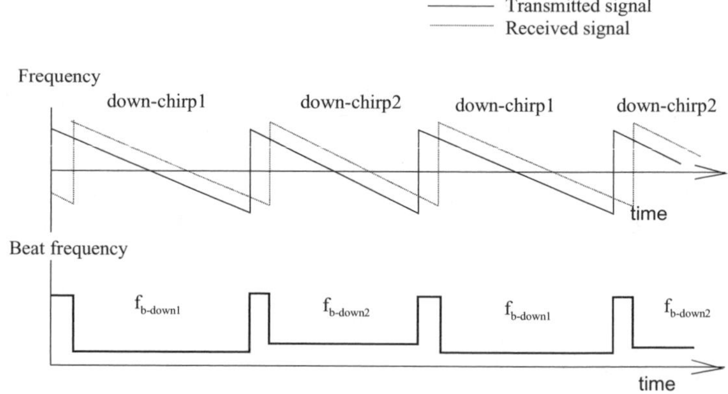

Figure 4: Dual down-chirps with small difference of slope. Single object.

The slope difference of the chirps are small so that the order of the beat frequencies, $f_{b\text{-}down1}(n)$ and $f_{b\text{-}down2}(n)$, *n*= *1*, …, *N*, where *N* is the number of targets, is not changed. The beat frequencies for both chirps are expressed by Eqs.(5) through (8) by using Eqs.(1) to (4).

$$f_{b\text{-}down1} = | f_{r1} + f_d | \quad \text{for down-chirp1} \qquad (5)$$

$$f_{b\text{-}down2} = | f_{r2} + f_d | \quad \text{for down-chirp2} \qquad (6)$$

$$f_{r1} = | (2R/c)\ (df/dt) | \qquad (7)$$

$$f_{r2} = | (2R/c)\ (df/dt)\ (1+\delta) | \qquad (8)$$

Since the δ is small, the polarity of "f_{r1} + f_d" and "f_{r2} + f_d" can be assumed not to be changed. By using Eqs.(5) and (6), the difference of $f_{b\text{-}down1}$ and $f_{b\text{-}down2}$ is given by Eq.(9). The distance R is calculated without the ambiguity.

$$df_b = | f_{b\text{-}down1} - f_{b\text{-}down2} | = (2R/c) \, | (df/dt) \, \delta | \qquad (9)$$

The f_d is calculated as shown as follows: The f_{r1} and f_{r2} are calculated by using Eqs.(7) and (8). The f_d is given by Eqs.(10) and (11).

$$f_d = f_{b\text{-}down1} - f_{r1} \quad \text{for } f_{b\text{-}down1} < f_{b\text{-}down2} \qquad (10)$$

$$f_d = - f_{b\text{-}down1} - f_{r1} \quad \text{for } f_{b\text{-}down1} > f_{b\text{-}down2} \qquad (11)$$

Here δ is positive.

In automobile application, the distance is positive and the relative velocity usually ranges from *–50* km/h (departing) to *+150* km/h (approaching stationary objects). The polarity of f_{r1} and f_{r2} is always positive (*10* to *80* kHz) and f_d ranges from *–7* to *20* kHz. Therefore if the down-chirp is chosen, the polarity of "f_{r1} + f_d" and "f_{r2} + f_d" is positive with high probability. And the most dangerous condition, in which the velocity is positive high value, definitely has the positive value of "f_{r1} + f_d" and "f_{r2} + f_d". Therefore the down-chirp is better.

<u>Examples</u>

The conventional and proposed FM-CWs are compared. The modulation is shown in Fig.5. An example is shown in Fig.6. The beat frequency is shown in Fig.7. The conditions of the calculation are shown in Appendix A. In the conventional FM-CW, the order of the beat frequencies for objects is different in the down- and up-chirps. This requires another analysis for identifying the correct pair of the beat frequencies corresponding to each object. This is a troublesome job.

In the proposed FM-CW, the order of beat frequencies is the same. And so the calculation in Eqs.(9) through (11) can be made for each object in a straight-forward way.

Another example is shown in Fig.8. The beat frequency is shown in Fig.9. In the conventional FM-CW, the beat frequencies corresponding to each object cannot be identified and additional measurements are required. But in the proposed FM-CW, the order of beat frequencies are the same. And so they are identified easily and the correct pairs are obtained.

Namely the proposed FM-CW algorithm is so simple and quick that this becomes practical for the automobile application.

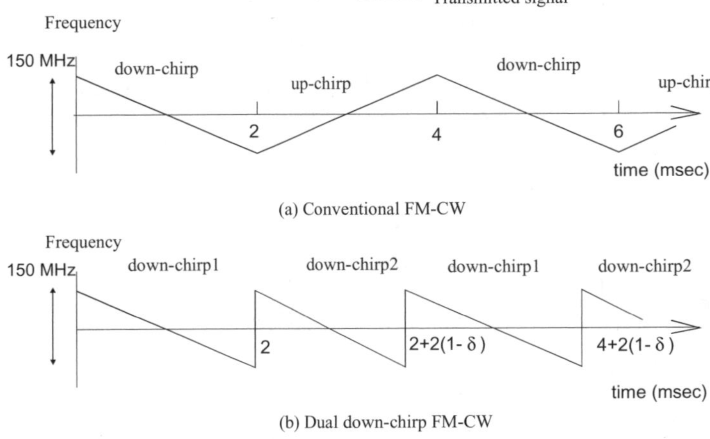

Figure 5: Modulation of conventional and dual down-chirp FM-CWs.

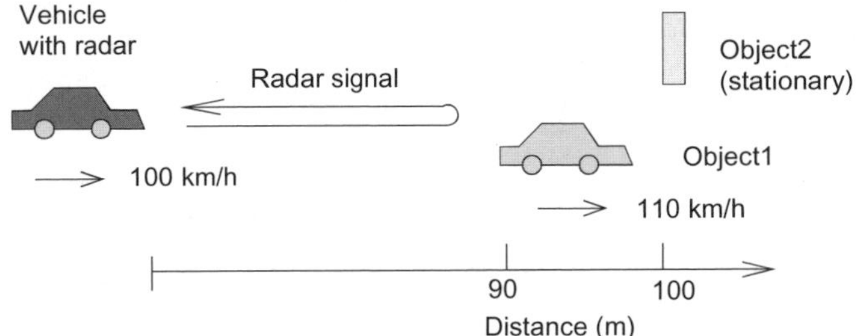

Figure 6: Example 1. Two objects.

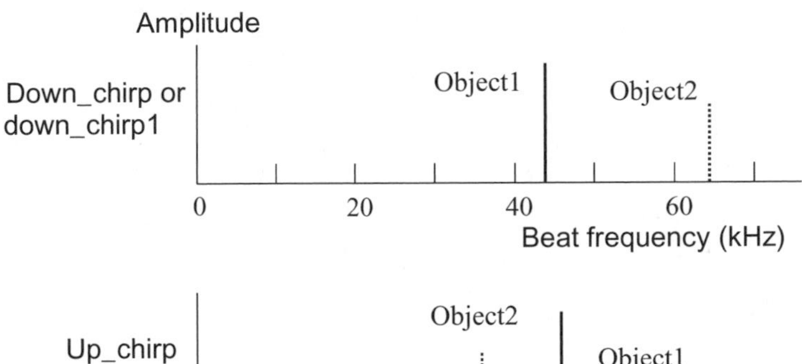

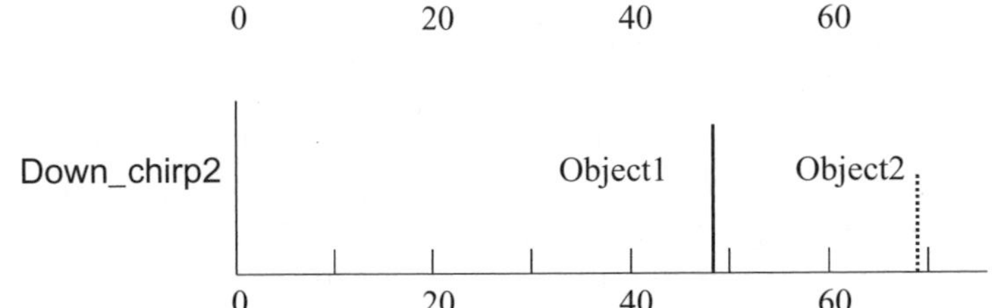

Figure 7: Beat frequency for Example 1. δ = 0.1. The top figure shows the beat frequency for the down-chirp in the conventional and the down-chirp1 in the dual down-chirps. The middle one shows the frequency for the up-chirp. And the bottom one shows the frequency for the down-chirp2 in the dual down-chirps.

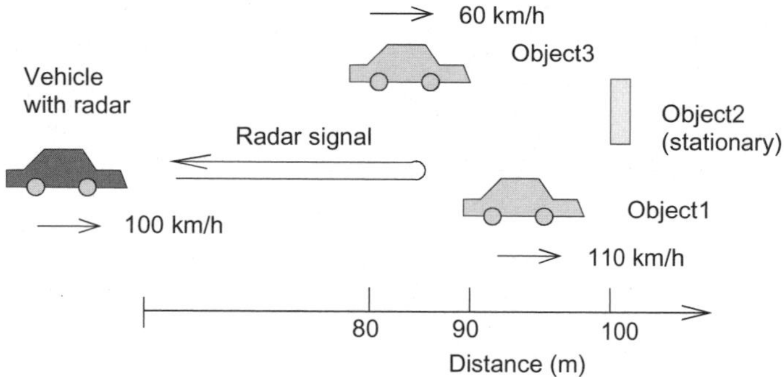

Figure 8: Example 2. Three objects.

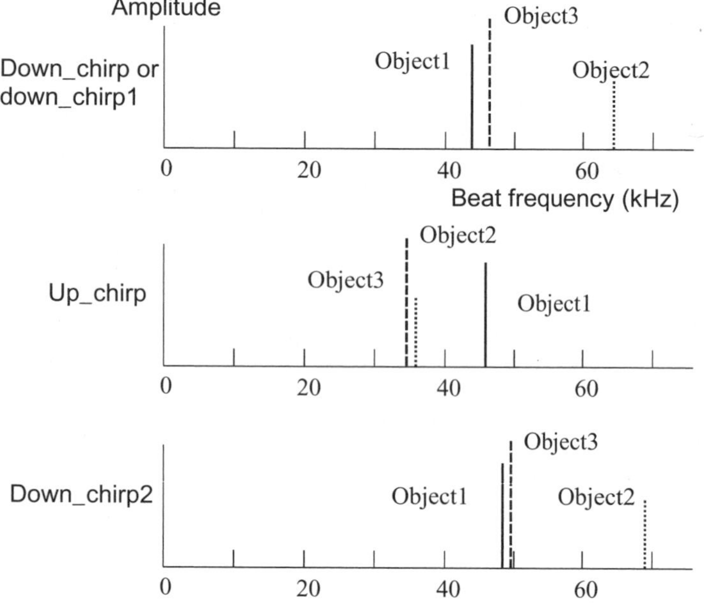

Figure 9: Beat frequency for Example 2. $\delta = 0.1$. The top figure shows the beat frequency for the down-chirp in the conventional and the down-chirp1 in the dual down-chirps. The middle one shows the frequency for the up-chirp. And the bottom one shows the frequency for the down-chirp2 in the dual down-chirps.

DISCUSSION

DOWN-CHIRPS FOR RESOLUTION OF UMBIGUITY

The proposed algorithm uses the dual down-chirps. The down-chirps always gives the positive value for "$f_{r1} + f_d$" in the right-hand of Eq.(5) or (6) for approaching objects. In an example shown in Fig.10, "$f_{r1} + f_d$" is positive for the relative velocity > *-70* [km/h]. This nature can provide a unique velocity and relative velocity for an approaching single object. In automotive applications, the detection of an approaching object is much more important than that of a departing object.

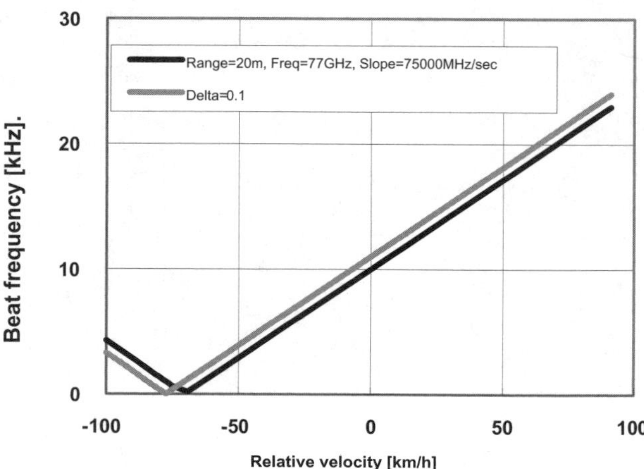

Figure 10: Beat frequency $|f_{r1} + f_d|$ and relative velocity. Range= *20* [m], frequency = 77 [GHz], bandwidth = *150* [MHz], modulation rate = *250* [Hz] and $\delta = 0.1$.

DOWN-CHIRPS FOR CORRECT PAIRS OF BEAT FREQUENCIES

For plural objects in an instantaneous radar beam angle, a conventional FM-CW has a difficulty to find out the correct pairs of beat frequencies from various combinations. The proposed algorithm, however, worked well for the correct pairs as shown in Fig.7 and 9. Here the validity for the correct combination is analyzed in more general way. It is assumed that there are three vehicles or objects at different distances in the beam angle of *3* [deg] as shown in Fig.11(a).

The beat frequency at the distance of *25*, *50* and *75* [m] is shown in Fig.11(b). The overlap of beat frequency is shown in Fig.11(c). The probability of the wrong combination between the objects (POW) is considered by assuming that the relative velocity distributes uniformly from *–100* to *100* [km/h]. The vehicles at *25* and *50* [m] have a possibility of overlap in frequencies from *10* to *28* [kHz]. The vehicles at *25* and *50* [m] have the frequency for the relative velocity > *-20* [km/h] and < *20* [km/h], respectively, as shown in Fig.12. The POW in Area *A* is *0.218* by referring to Appendix B. The overall POW is *0.078* (*7.8*%). It is small but not enough. The POB is improved if δ is reduced. But too small δ causes inaccuracy in Eq.(9) or requires severe linearity and accuracy of VCO. Namely δ should be determined through a field test.

The POB can be calculated for objects at *50* and *75* [m] in a similar manner. The order of POB is the same order of the above one.

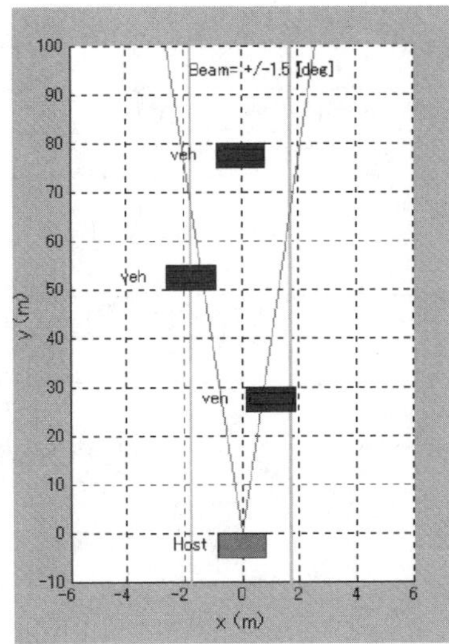

(a) Multiple vehicles: Instantaneous azimuth angle of radar beam= *3* [deg]. Length and width of vehicles = *5* and *1.7* [m], respectively. Width of lane = *3.5* [m].

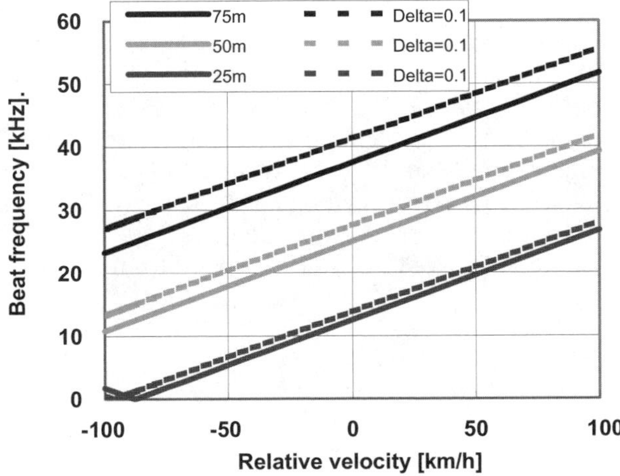

(b) Beat frequencies with distance and relative velocity

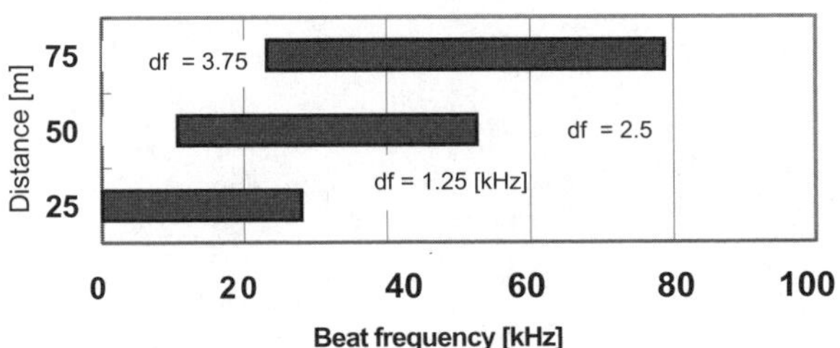

(c) Overlap of beat frequency. 'df' is the beat frequency difference between two chirps.

Figure 11: Beat frequency and relative velocity for multiple objects. Positive values of the relative velocity mean the approaching. Range= *25*, *50* and *75* [m], frequency = *77* [GHz], bandwidth = *150* [MHz], modulation rate = *250* [Hz] and $\delta = 0.1$.

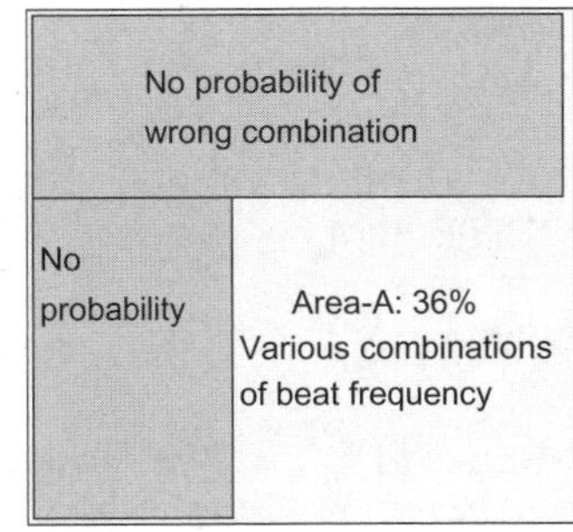

Figure 12: Probability that wrong combinations might exist. Objects are at *25* and *50* [m]. Relative velocity ranges from *–100* to *100* [km/h]. Positive value means the approaching. Frequency = *77* [GHz], bandwidth = *150* [MHz], modulation rate = *250* [Hz] and $\delta = 0.1$.

USE OF AMPLITUDE OF BEAT FREQUENCY

In the algorithm, the combination is determined by the order of the beat frequencies. To reduce the probability of the wrong combination, the amplitude of beat frequencies can be used. This amplitude information is effective when the ratio of the distances of objects is large. Namely if one object is very near, its correct pair of beat frequencies is easily identified.

DIFFERENT TYPE OF DUAL DOWN-CHIRPS

In Fig.5, the bandwidth is constant. But in actual application, the sweep time for each chirp can be constant. This might be easy since the processing interval is constant.

CONCLUSION

The most popular principle for the object detection is based on FM-CW in automotive millimeter wave applications. The FM-CW is suitable for the distance measurement for plural objects with small relative velocities, since the velocities do not introduce the ambiguity. But in the application like ACC, the relative velocity change from *–150* km/h to *+150* km/h. This results in the ambiguity between the distance and relative velocities of the objects. So far several methods to overcome this problem have been proposed, but so complicated and not practical. Therefore the author proposed a simple and quick algorithm, which is based on the dual down-chirp frequency sweep with small slope-difference. Since the difference is small, the correct pair of beat frequencies in the dual chirps for multiple objects can be identified automatically. And the down chirps remove the ambiguity between the distance and relative velocity for an approaching object. Therefore the distance and velocity information for multiple objects can be calculated without ambiguity in straight forward. The effectiveness of the proposed algorithm was explained through some scenarios. And the probability of the correct pair identification was calculated and it was shown that this algorithm is promising.

ACKNOWLEDGMENT

The author thanks P. Zoratti, Visteon Co., for the technical discussion on the algorithm.

REFERENCES

1. M. I. Skolnik, Introduction to Radar Systems, McGraw-Hill, 2nd edition, 1980.
2. W. Ulke, R. Adomat, K. Butscher and W. Lauer, "Radar Based Automotive Obstacle Detection System", SAE 1994 World Congress, 940904, 1994.
3. W. Prestl, T. Sauer, J. Steinle and O. Tsschernoster, "The BMW Active Cruise Control ACC", SAE 2000 World Congress, 2000-01-0344, 2000.
4. B. Riley, B. Schwartz, K. Shipp, J. T. Zumberge and G. Kuo, "Development of a Controlled Braking Strategy for Vehicle Adaptive Cruise Control", SAE 2000 World Congress, 2000-01-0109, 2000.
5. M. Mitsumoto, N. Uehara, S. Inatsune and T. Kirimoto, "Target Distance and Velocity Measurement Algorithm to Reduce False Targets in FMCW Automotive Radar", IEICE Trans. Communication, Vol.E83-B, No.9, pp.1983/1989, Sept. 2000.
6. M. Mitsumoto, T. Kirimoto, N. Uehara and S. Inatsune, "FMCW Automotive Radars using only In-phase Channel", SAE 1999 World Congress, 1999-01-0486, 1999.
7. I. J. Langheim, J-F. Henrio and B. Liabeuf, "ACC Radar System with 77 GHz MMIC Radar", Haus der Technik, Essen 1999
8. M. Nakamura, K. Takanoand and H. Kuroda, "76GHz FSK Monopulse Radar for ACC", 7th ITS World Congress, 2000.
9. K. Fujimura, M. Hitotsuya, S. Yamano and H. Higashida, "76GHz Millimeter-wave Radar for ACC", 32nd ISATA, 99AE019, pp.175/182, 1999.

APPENDIX A: CONDITIONS OF FM-CW CALCULATION

Conditions for FM-CW are shown in Table A1. The examples of the Doppler and range frequency are shown in Table A2 and A3.

Table A1: Frequency and band

Freqency (GHz):	77.0
Frequency band (MHz)	150.0
Sweep time (up&down) (ms)	4.0

Table A2: Doppler frequency

Velocity (km/h)	25.0	50.0	100.0	150.0
Doppler freq (kHz)	3.6	7.1	14.3	21.4

Table A3: Range frequency

Distance (m)	25.0	50.0	100.0	150.0
Beat freq (kHz)	12.5	25.0	50.0	75.0

APPENDIX B: WRONG COMBINATION OF BEAT FREQUENCY

Probability of the wrong combination of beat frequency between the ranges at *25* and *50* [m] shown in Fig.11. The frequency overlaps between *10* and *28* [kHz]. The frequency widths, which are the difference of beat frequencies in two chirps for each object, are *1.25* and *2.5* [kHz] for objects at *25* and *50* [m], respectively. The widths exists uniformly and random in *18* [kHz] (=28-10). The probability of wrong combination is that of the overlap of the widths and is obtained from Eq.(B1).

$$P = \frac{(a+b)L - \{(a+b)^2 - ab\}}{(L-a)(L-b)} \qquad \text{(B1)}$$

where L, a and b are the overlap frequency range, and frequency widths at *15* and *50* [m], respectively. Eq. (B1) holds for $L \geq a+b+\max(a,b)$. For $L=18$, $a=1.25$ and $b=2.5$, $P=0.218$.

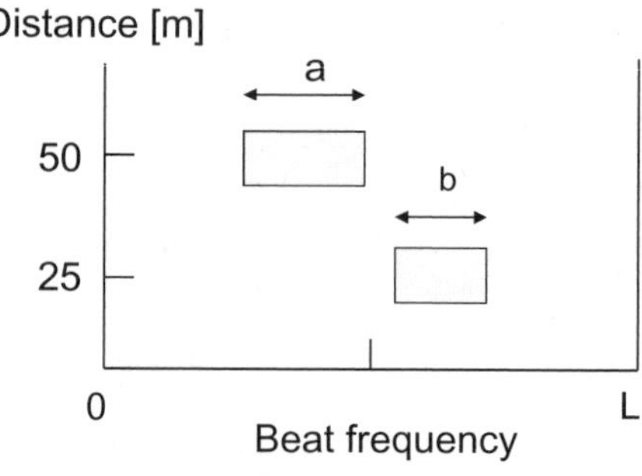

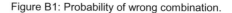

Figure B1: Probability of wrong combination.

2003-01-0195

Radar Based IVC System

Michael Wagner and Jürgen Dickmann
DaimlerChrysler Research & Technology

Josef Büchler
MicSenS

Volker Winkler, Uwe Siart and Jürgen Detlefsen
Technische Universität München

ABSTRACT

In the last years short distance radar (SDR) systems were developed for advanced safety applications. Near future production cars are expected to be equipped with multiple SDR sensors to allow an all around sensing of the vehicle's environment and therefore offer a versatile tool for occupant as well as pedestrian protection. On the other hand, another way to make traffic more safe is to establish inter-vehicle communication (IVC) systems that are able, for example, to inform the following traffic about possible hazards. This paper proposes an innovative device approach, the communication radar, for the first time. A basic concept for a SDR based communication system for IVC is decribed. The system is based on a 24 GHz pulse SDR sensor and is designed to allow simultaneous sensing over a range of 20 m and communication at 1 Mbit/s up to 200 m range. Appropriate signal processing schemes were developed in order to minimize the disturbances between communication and sensing as well as disturbances from other systems of the same type. From the communication point of view, separated channels for data exchange, protocol handling, and emergency notification allow as much flexibility as possible for IVC needs. Since SDR systems radiate in limited angular ranges, a selective communication direction is easily established. In this way it is possible to exchange different content to different partners.

INTRODUCTION

One of the most interesting challenges for automotive engineers is the vision of a collision free traffic. A first step into this direction was the market introduction of adaptive cruise control (ACC) systems. Such systems use radar sensors mounted at the front of the vehicle to detect objects in the vehicle's path. Throttle control and limited braking are used to control the distance to the vehicles ahead to an adequate extent. However, these devices are only capable in scenarios where possible hazards are in front of the vehicle and within its limited angle of aperture.

Short distance radar (SDR) systems mounted all around the vehicle are able to observe the full surrounding of a vehicle by a larger angular aperture. Such systems are commonly recognized to be powerfull devices for providing valuable information about the near ambient in order to increase the functionality of integrated safety systems. Possible applications include advanced pre-safe functionality, parking aid, blind spot detection, stop-and-go driving, among others. Therefore a wide spread market penetration of SDR can be expected. Of course, SDR systems are stand-alone devices, which are only aware of neighboring vehicles and their dynamics by detection and tracking.

Another promising approach to more safety on the road is to establish inter-vehicle communication (IVC) systems in order to communicate safety relevant data to neighboring vehicles such as acceleration, steering, identification, emergency notifiction, etc. The

IVC approach to enhanced safety systems is naturally only feasible if a sufficent penetration of compatible systems is on the road. This might be a serious problem for market introduction strategies.

In this paper, we propose a system that combines the advantages of both application areas, single sensor and cooperative systems. Our approach enhances the SDR sensor capability by its ability of simultaneous communication in one device, and thereby largely bypassing the problems of market introduction for IVC.

MOTIVATION

IVC systems show high potential for supporting integrated safety systems,, as they enable the systems to react to possible hazardous situations very early and thereby protecting the driver and other road-users. Moreover, with such systems it is possible to collect floating car data like position, speed, and acceleration of neighboring vehicles and building up an up to date picture of the on route traffic. With such systems, build up with commercial communication systems like WLAN or adapted systems, the overall data load on heavy crowded roads or in cities will be naturally very high. Safety relavant data, like advanced pre-safe warnings, might reach the affected communication partners delayed, i.e. a deteministic safety algorithm cannot rely only on this data. Directed communication would be very helpful in such a situation, because, for example, normally a driver is not interested in traffic jams he has just passed. On the other hand, for cooperative driving systems, a precise knowledge of the position of the own and neighboring vehicles is necessary but is not available from today's GPS or DGPS systems.

Radar based IVC, as proposed in this paper, combines the possibility of directed communication with simultaneous sensing capabilities. This enables cooperative driving systems to also take non-cooperative road users into account. Moreover, due to the fact that such systems can operate autonomously as sensors, there is a high potential for easily bringing such systems into the market, since the sensing functionality independently brings more safety and comfort to current vehicles. Additionally it should be stressed, that due to the fact that these two functionalities are combined in a single apperatus, fusion algorithms, combining the respective informations, can be established without significant time delay.

DESIGN GOALS

The major goal of the concept is to allow communication with cooperative systems within the communication range, while simultaneously detecting and tracking cooperative as well as non-cooperative objects within the sensing range. In order to establish these simultaneous functionalities, it has to be ensured that neither is the sensing significantly disturbed by communication nor is the communication significantly disturbed by sensing. Furthermore it has to be guaranteed that two devices in line of sight do not significantly interfere each others' functionality.

For typical SDR applications a sensing range of 20m is specified, whereas complete range scans are to be perfomed with an update rate of 10ms. For more precise information on the dynamics of each detected object, additionally the doppler frequency information is to be processed within a relative speed span of $\pm$50 m/s.

On the other hand, a maximum communication range of 200 m for safety relevant applications seems to be reasonable. The necessary maximum data rate highly depends on the application used. For emergency notification like airbag activation, only a few data bytes have to be send, but with a high demand on reliability and a defined maximum delay time. Other applications might need higher data rates, say up to 1 Mbit/s, with lower requirements on reliability. Even though such situations can be theoretically handled by means of protocol strategies, a system design that inherently treats these two application classes separately would be favourable, since it leads to lower system complexity and hence to higher reliability.

BASIC CONCEPTS

ALTERNATIVES FOR THE COMMUNICATION LINK

Principally, several possibilities for radar based IVC systems can be imagined. Among others one could think of the following:

Time-slotted communication / sensing

A controller enables either sensing or communication. This would be the easiest way to establish radar based communication. Clearly, the whole spectral band would be available for either functionality in the respective time slots. On the other hand, the synchronization of two or more communication partners would take too much time, so that this approach would be definitely not suitable for safety relevant applications.

Information hidden in sensing signals

This approach would use the sensing signals as the carrier for the communication signals. For example, in case of a continuous wave (CW) radar, the information could be embedded in the wave form. This possibility would only lead to poor data rates and the communication partners sensing strategy must be fully synchronized.

Spectral separation

Here, the two functionalities are seperated by their spectral content. A good compromise has to be found in order to fullfill the requirements of sensing resolution and data rate.

Quasi spectral separation

In the case of a pulsed radar system, the communication signal can be embedded in the power density spectrum of the pulse train, such that there is almost no interference between the signals. The spectral power content of a pulse within the respective frequency band is low at its edges. Therefore, the communction signal could be placed in this region (see figure 1) without significantly being disturbed by the pulse signals or disturbing the pulse signals. The communication partners are only needed to be synchronized with respect to the communication signals, i.e. they must not be aware of the sensing strategy of their partners.

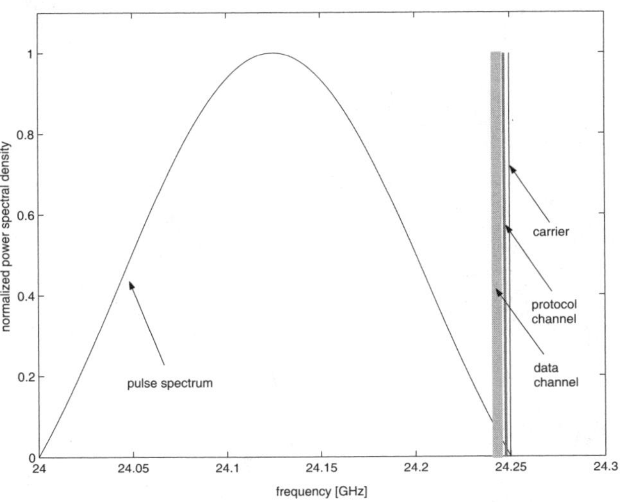

Figure 1: Diagram of spectral power layout

As indicated in figure 1, separated frequency bands are reserved for protocol and user data. This is favourable as it allows easy synchronization. A carrier signal is added to allow the adoption of carrier sense schemes from standard communication protocols. Additionally, the carrier might be modulated in amplitude in order to provide an extra channel for emergency notifications, which need to be transmitted without unnecessary protocol overhead.

PRI STAGGERING

Of course, a necessary demand for a communication radar system is that its functionality is not disturbed by the presence of other systems of the same type, i.e. the communication partner. This can be established by staggering the pulse repetition interval (PRI) in a quasi random manner. Due to this measure, pulse trains directly or indirectly received from other radar systems can be eliminated by integration while reflections of self generated pulses are preserved.

SENSING STRATEGY

The whole sensing range R is devided into

$$M = R/\Delta R \tag{1}$$

cells of length ΔR, corresponding to the demanded range accuracy for the radar system. Each time a pulse is transmitted, one range cell is observed for possible reflection signals. The whole observation range is thereby scanned within M consecutive observations. Let $F_U = 1/T_U$ denote the update frequency for the radar system to deliver range information to some electronic control unit (ECU) and T_P denote the (averaged) PRI. Then

$$N = \lfloor T_U/(MT_P) \rfloor \tag{2}$$

complete range scans can be performed within each update cycle.

DOPPLER ANALYSIS

With the above presented sensing strategy doppler analysis can be established with the following considerations. Due to staggering, there are no evenly sampled data points available, so that an ordinary fast fourier transform (FFT) would lead to distorted results. A method for estimating the spectral content of unevenly spaced data is as follows. Let

$$\bar{x} = \frac{1}{N}\sum_{i=1}^{N} x_i \quad \text{and} \quad \sigma^2 = \frac{1}{N-1}\sum_{i=1}^{N}(x_i - \bar{x})^2 \tag{3}$$

denote estimates for the expectation and variance of data samples x_i collected at corresponding unevenly spaced times t_i, $(i = 1, \ldots, N)$. Lomb's normalized periodogram is defined for any positive $\omega = 2\pi f$ as

$$P(\omega) = \frac{1}{2\sigma^2}\left\{\frac{\left[\sum_i (x_i - \bar{x})\cos\omega(t_i - \tau)\right]^2}{\sum_i \cos^2\omega(t_i - \tau)} + \frac{\left[\sum_i (x_i - \bar{x})\sin\omega(t_i - \tau)\right]^2}{\sum_i \sin^2\omega(t_i - \tau)}\right\} \tag{4}$$

where τ is selected to satisfy

$$\tan 2\omega\tau = \frac{\sum_i \sin 2\omega t_i}{\sum_i \cos 2\omega t_i}, \tag{5}$$

which makes $P(\omega)$ independent of jointly shifting the sample times t_i by any constant value. Clearly, this algorithm is not well suited for real time implementation of doppler analysis, since an operation count of order N_p^2, where N_P denotes the number of desired frequencies, is needed. Instead, real time algorithms, adopted from the Lomb normalized periodogram, should be used, that approximate $P(\omega)$ to any desired precision. Here, the operation count is comparable to that of FFT algortihms, i.e. only of order $N_p \log N_P$, see e.g. [1].

SIMULATION RESULTS

Let r denote the ratio of the communication signal transmission power to the peak radar pulse transmission power and a_C denote the decoupling of the receiver and transmitter. Furthermore JM_R and JM_C denote the necessary Signal-to-Noise-plus-Interference ratios at the receiver for the radar and communication system to work properly. The maximum ranges for communication and sensing depend on $J = JM_R + JM_C + 2a_C$ and are presented for various parameters in figure 2 for a specific radar cross section (RCS) of 0.3 m^2 (e.g. a pedestrian). Calculations have shown, that if transmitter and receiver are decoupled sufficiently, say a_C = 40 dB, the curve for J = 160 dB can be achieved. Figure 2 indicates, that in this case sufficient simultaneous radar and communication ranges are reached even for small RCS.

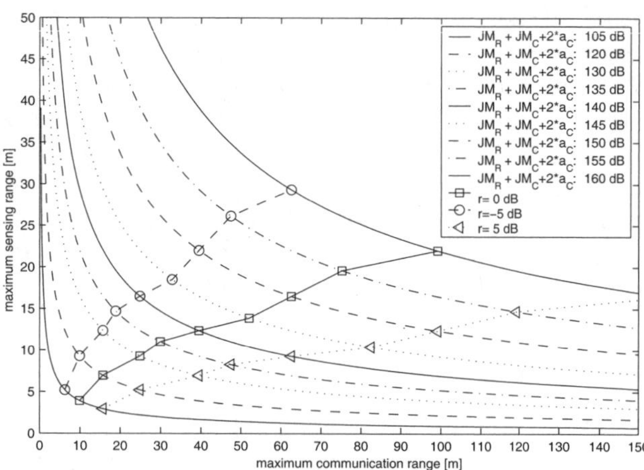

Figure 2: Range diagram for a RCS of 0.3 m^2

CONCLUSIONS

A new system concept for radar based IVC system, which provides simultaneous radar sensing and communication capability to vehicles in order to supply substantial information for future safety systems, was presented for the first time. In contrast to conventional communication systems, radar based IVC allows directed communication to cooperating partners. Since communication and sensing are implemented in a single apparatus, a fusion of the information obtained from either functionality can be easily provided without considerable time delays. In oder to establish both functions simultaneously, a strategy for protecting the radars from sensing pulses of cooperative partner was presented. Additionally a scheme for doppler analysis for staggered PRIs was indicated.

ACKNOWLEDGEMENT

This work is partly funded by the German Federal Ministry of Education and Research (BMBF) as a part of the FleetNet project. The authors would like to thank Dr. Walter Franz, project manager of FleetNet, for valuable comments and discussions on this topic.

CONTACT

Please do not hesitate to contact the first author
DaimlerChrysler AG
Reasearch & Technology REM/CC
Michael Wagner
Wilhelm-Runge-Strasse 11
89081 Ulm / Germany
michael.mi.wagner@daimlerchrysler.com
for any questions and/or comments regarding the contents of this publication.

REFERENCES

[1] William H. Press, Saul A. Teukolsky, William T. Vetterling, and Brian P. Flannery. *Numerical Recipies in C — The Art of Scientific Computing.* Cambridge University Press, Cambridge, 2nd edition, 2002.

2003-01-0015

Electrically Scanned Millimeter Wave Automotive Radar With Wide Detection Region

Masaru Ogawa, Kiyosumi Kidono and Yoshikazu Asano
TOYOTA Central R&D Labs., Inc.

ABSTRACT

This paper describes an electrically scanned millimeter wave automotive radar with a wide detection region in a field of view (FoV) and near range. The wide FoV is realized by introducing a beam forming technique to a target search under a low signal-to-noise ratio condition. The short minimum detection range is realized by eliminating a detection error peculiar to frequency-modulated continuous wave radar for a close target. An experimental radar has been developed to confirm the wide detection region. The radar accomplishes the FoV of 40 degrees in azimuth and the minimum detection range of 0.5m.

INTRODUCTION

Millimeter wave automotive radars with electrically switched beam antennas have been developed as forward-looking sensors for adaptive cruise control (ACC) and other systems [1]. Daimler Chrysler has already been launching 'Distronic' system, which is an ACC system with the millimeter wave automotive radar, since June 1999 [2]. Other passenger vehicle manufacturers put the same systems on the market in succession.

We also have developed an electrically scanned millimeter wave automotive radar for ACC [3], [4]. The radar possesses the field of view (FoV) of 20 degrees in azimuth and the detection range of 5 to 150m. However, they are not sufficient for driver assistance systems, such as stop & go system, collision warning system and collision mitigation system, which operate on an urban road as well as on a highway.

A wider FoV is required because vehicles on a sharp bend and cut-in vehicles have to be detected promptly in those systems. A shorter minimum detection range is also required because a distance between vehicles is short on an urban road.

This paper proposes solutions for widening the FoV and shortening the minimum detection range. Moreover, the effectiveness of the solutions is confirmed experimentally.

SOLUTIONS FOR WIDENING FIELD OF VIEW AND SHORTENING MINIMUM DETECTION RANGE

Solutions for realizing wider FoV and shorter minimum detection range are proposed on the basis of the electrically scanned automotive radar already developed [4]. The structure of the radar is equivalent to that of a fundamental holographic radar as shown in Figure 1. The wave form is a frequency-modulated continuous wave (FMCW) with both an ascending phase and a descending phase. Figure 2 shows the flowchart of the signal processing. In the result of Fourier transformation, the peaks corresponding to the targets are searched. And then the angle in azimuth as well as the range and the relative velocity is detected for each target on the basis of the peak values.

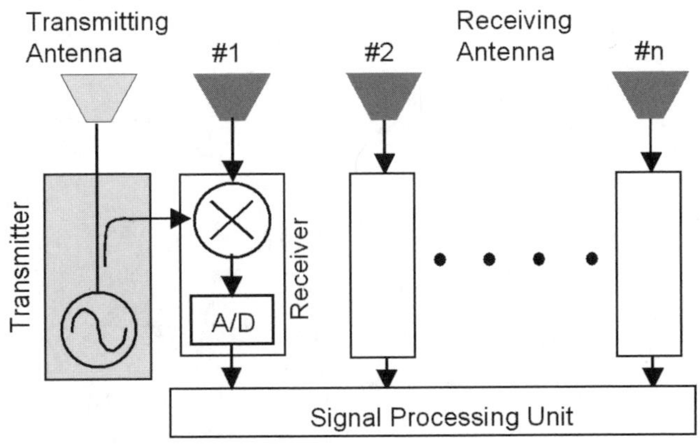

Figure 1. Configuration of fundamental holographic radar.

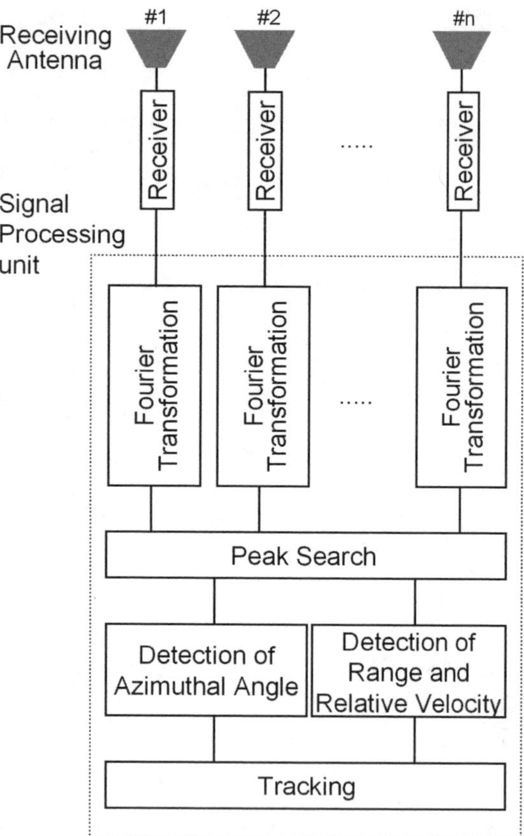

Figure 2. Flowchart of signal processing in fundamental holographic radar.

SOLUTION FOR WIDENING FIELD OF VIEW

A beam forming technique is introduced to the above signal processing for realizing the wider FoV. The technique is used not to the direction finding as usual but to the peak search under a low signal-to-noise ratio (SNR) condition.

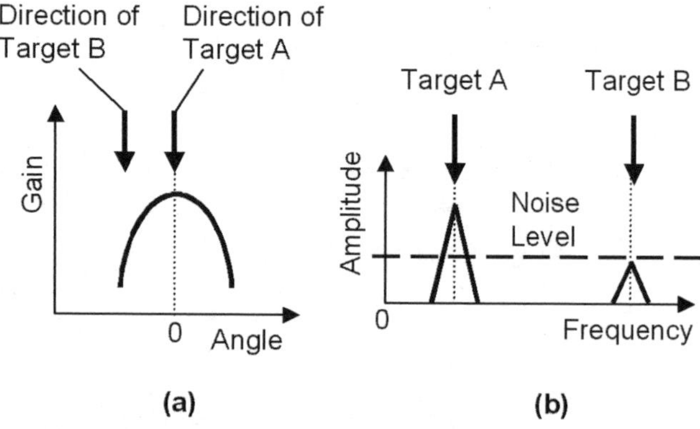

Figure 3. A beam pattern of receiving antenna (a) and result of Fourier transformation of signal received by the antenna (b).

Figure 3 shows a beam pattern of the receiving antenna in the fundamental radar in Figure 1 and the result of Fourier transformation of the signal received by the antenna in an ascending phase. The peak to the target A located in the same direction as the antenna beam is distinct, while the peak to the target B located in the low gain region is hard to be searched because of a low SNR condition. It follows that the FoV concentrates on the region where the gain is relatively high.

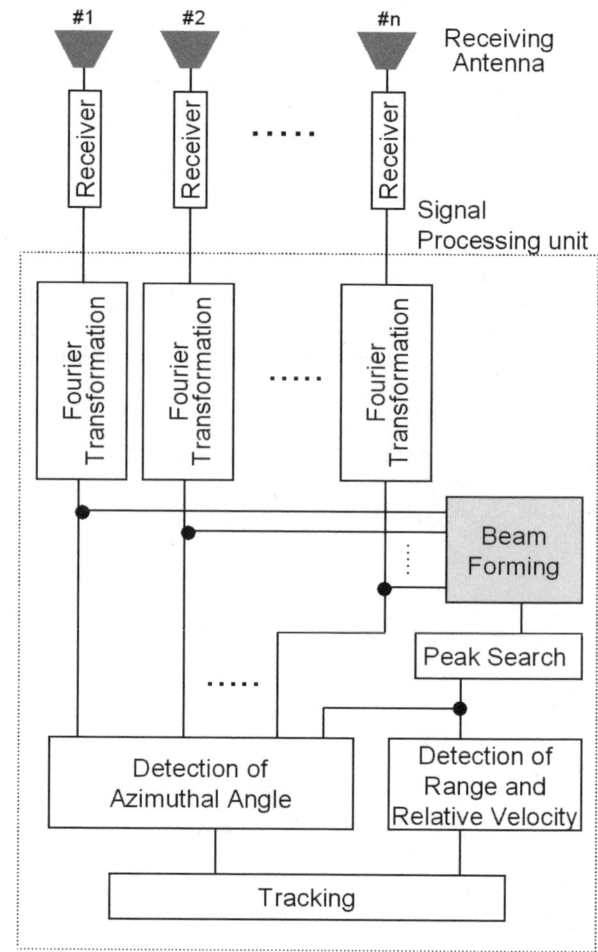

Figure 4. Flowchart of signal processing to which beam forming technique is introduced for widening FoV.

To improve the low SNR condition, the beam forming is added after the Fourier transformation process as shown in Figure 4. On the basis of the signal received by the plural antennas, such signal as is received by an antenna with a beam pattern towards the direction of the low gain region is synthesized in the beam forming process. The beam pattern and the result of the synthesized signal are shown in Figure 5. The peak to the target B becomes distinct, which represents that the target in the low gain region in Figure 3(a) comes to be detected by the introduction of the beam forming process. Consequently, the introduction of the beam forming process is said to be available to widening FoV.

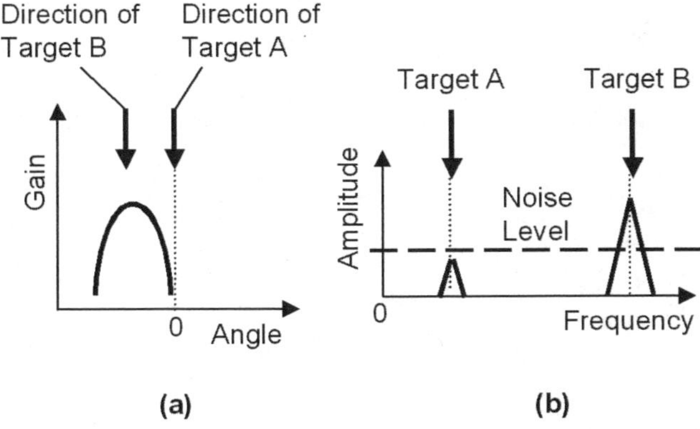

Figure 5. A beam pattern formed by signal processing (a) and result of Fourier transformation of signal received by the antenna with its pattern (b).

SOLUTION FOR SHORTENING MINIMUM DETECTION RANGE

A method for deciding a detection error peculiar to FMCW radar is introduced to the signal processing. The detection error occurs for a close target and impedes the detection of the target. Thus the occurrence of the error is the reason why the decrease of the minimum detection range is hard.

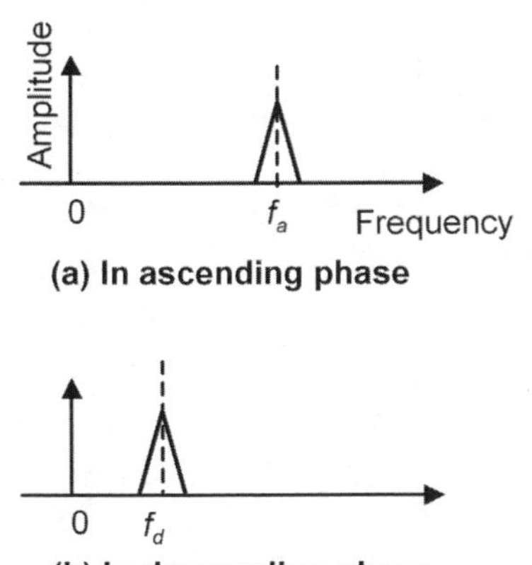

Figure 6. Result of Fourier transformation in single target case.

Figure 6 shows the result of Fourier transformation of the received signal in the case where single target exists. f_a and f_d are the peak frequencies in the ascending phase and the descending phase, respectively. The frequency becomes low as the target approaches; the difference between the frequencies depends on the relative velocity of the target. From the pair of the peak frequencies, the range and the relative velocity are obtained. Figure 7 shows the result for a close target. The peak frequency in the descending phase is wrongly detected as a positive value f_d, although the frequency should be negative theoretically. If f_d is substituted for $-f_d$, the incorrect range and relative velocity would be obtained. That is the detection error.

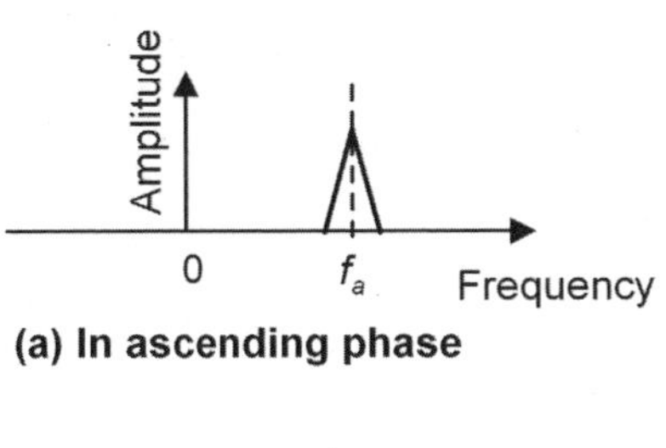

(a) In ascending phase

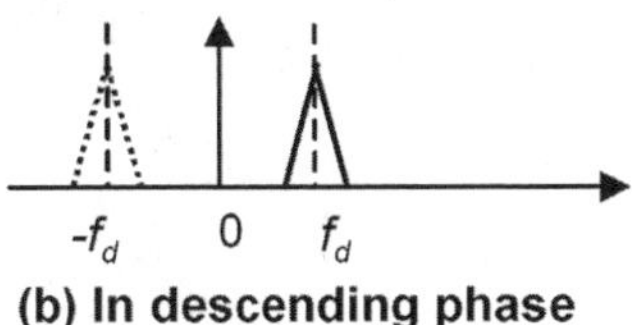

(b) In descending phase

Figure 7. Result of Fourier transformation in a close target case.

To acquire the correct range and relative velocity in the close target case, a decision process for deciding the detection error is added to the signal processing. The decision is based on both azimuthal angles of the target computed from the peak values in both the ascending phase and the descending phase. The signs of these angles are different each other under the occurrence of the detection error. Thus the detection error can be decided by the examination of the signs, and then the wrong peak frequency can be corrected. Therefore, the decision process makes it possible to detect the close target correctly. Consequently, the introduction of the decision process of the detection error is said to be available to shortening the minimum detection range.

CONFIGURATION AND SPECIFICATION OF EXPERIMENTAL RADAR

An experimental radar for confirming the effectiveness of the above solutions has been developed.

Figure 8 shows the configuration of the radar. It is equivalent to the fundamental holographic radar with a transmitter and nine receivers as shown in Figure 1. The experimental radar is simplified by the antenna switching [4]. In the radar, a frequency-modulated wave in a 76 GHz band is generated and transmitted through the selected antenna. For the period of the transmission from the antenna, three receiving antennas are switched in order. Through each receiving antenna according to the antenna switching sequence as shown in Figure 9, the reflected wave from a target is fed to the mixer. The base-band signal output from the mixer in the time division manner is digitized, and then fed into the signal processor unit. The range, the relative velocity and the azimuthal angle of each target are obtained with the signal processing including the fast Fourier transformation and a super resolution technique [5]. The principal specifications of the radar are listed in Table 1.

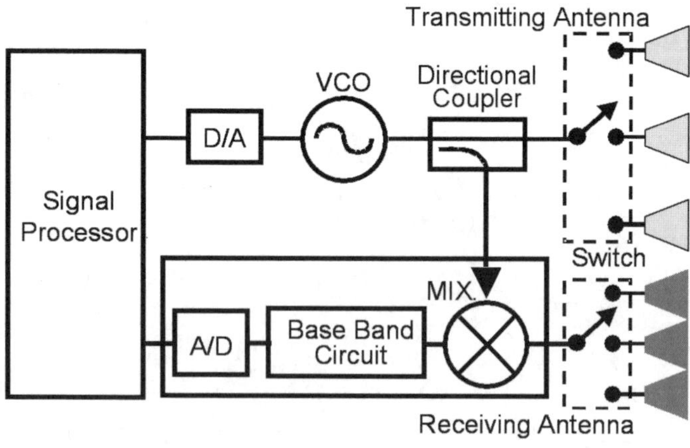

Figure 8. Configuration of experimental radar.

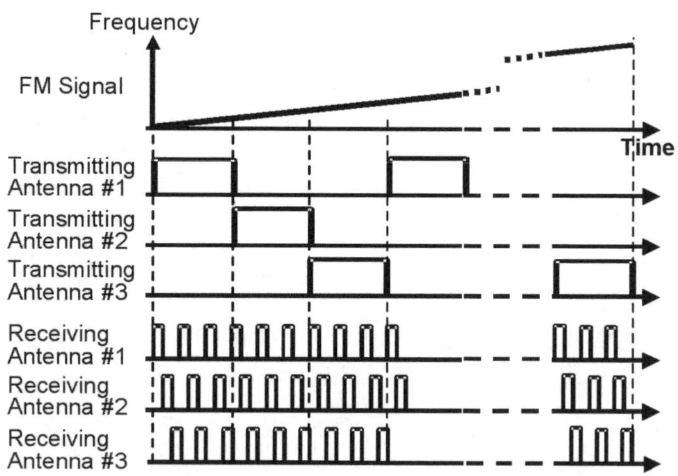

Figure 9. Sequences of antenna switching signals. The antenna whose switching signal is high is selected.

Table 1. Principal specifications of experimental radar

Wave Form	FMCW
Center Frequency	76.5 GHz
Frequency Modulation Bandwidth	200 MHz
Beam Width of Transmitting Antenna	40 degrees in azimuth 4 degrees in elevation
Beam Width of Receiving Antenna	47 degrees in azimuth 4degrees in elevation
Interval of Transmitting Antenna	4.2 wavelengths
Interval of Receiving Antenna	1.4 wavelengths
Period of Frequency Modulation	5.5 msec
Switching Period of Transmitting Antenna	1.8 μsec
Switching Period of Receiving Antenna	0.2 μsec
Polarization	45 degrees linear
Update Rate	10 Hz

PERFORMANCE OF EXPERIMENTAL RADAR

The experimental radar is evaluated in this section. In the evaluation, the standard reflector with the RCS value of 14.6 dBsm at 76.5 GHz is used as a target.

Figure 10 shows the experimental result of the azimuthal angle detection. The horizontal and vertical axes show the azimuthal angle where the target is set and the angle detected by the experimental radar, respectively. The detection error means the difference between the set angle and the detected angle. The target can be detected within the region of 40 degrees with the accuracy of less than 0.5 degrees.

Figure 11 shows the experimental result of the detection range in the region of less than 10m. The detection error means the difference between the set range and the detected range of the target. This figure represents that the minimum detection range is 0.5m and that the accuracy is less than 0.3m. The experiment also confirms that the maximum detection range is 120m with the same accuracy.

Consequently, the experimental radar accomplishes the FoV of 40 degrees and the minimum detection range of 0.5m.

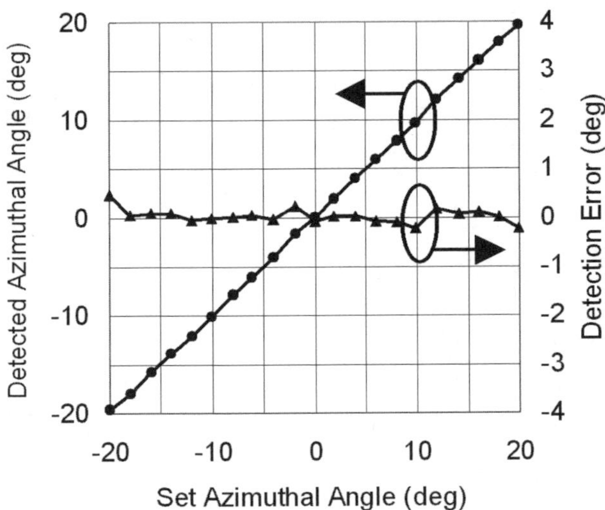

Figure 10. Experimental result of azimuthal angle detection.

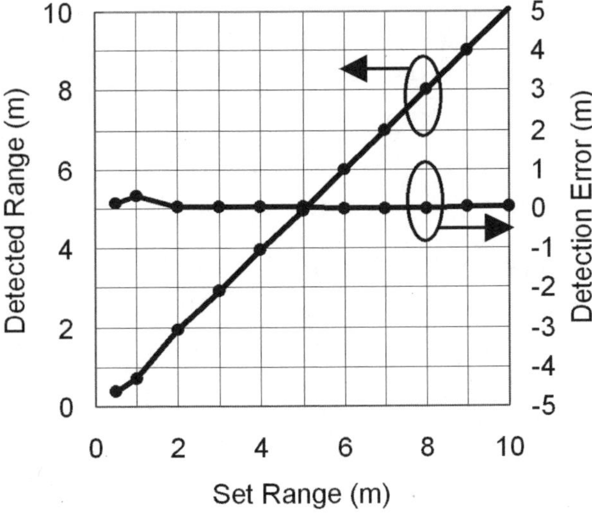

Figure 11. Experimental result of range detection.

CONCLUSION

The solutions for realizing the wider detection region in the FoV and the near range have been proposed on the basis of the electrically scanned automotive radar already developed. The FoV can be widened using the beam forming technique to the target search under the low SNR condition. In addition, the minimum detection range can be shortened using the method of eliminating the detection error peculiar to FMCW radar for the close target.

Moreover, the experimental radar has been developed to confirm the effectiveness of the proposed solutions. The experimental radar accomplishes the FoV of 40 degrees in azimuth and the minimum detection range of 0.5m. As compared with the electrically scanned automotive radar already developed, the FoV is widened by twice and the minimum detection range is shortened by one tenth.

The automotive radar with the wide detection region will open up new vistas on the realization of the driver assistance systems, such as stop & go system, collision warning system and collision mitigation system.

ACKNOWLEDGMENTS

The authors would like to thank Dr. K. Nishikawa and Mr. S. Ohshima, Research-Domain 21 (ITS), TOYOTA Central R&D Labs., Nagakute, Aichi, Japan, for valuable assistance and discussions.

REFERENCES

1. J. Wenger, “Automotive MM-Wave Radar: Status and Trends in System Design and Technology,” *IEE Colloquium on Automotive Radar and Navigation Techniques*, Feb. 1998.
2. Holger H. Meinel, “Automotive Millimeter wave Radar, status, trends and producibility,” *Technical Digest of 2000 Topical Symposium on Millimeter Waves*, pp. 5-9, March 2000.
3. S. Ohshima, Y. Asano, T. Harada, N. Yamada, M. Usui, H. Hayashi, T. Watanabe, and H. Iizuka, “Phase-Comparison Monopulse Radar with Switched Transmit Beams for Automotive Application,” *1999 IEEE MTT-S*, no. TH2A-3, June 1999.
4. Y. Asano, S. Ohshima, T. Harada, M. Ogawa, and K. Nishikawa, “PROPOSAL OF MILLIMETER-WAVE HOLOGRAPHIC RADAR WITH ANTENNA SWITCHING,” *2001 IEEE MTT-S International Microwave Symposium Digest*, vol. 2, pp. 1109-1112, May 2001.
5. R. L. Johnson and G. E. Miner, “Comparison of Superresolution Algorithms for Radio Direction Finding,” *IEEE Trans. on Aerospace and Electronic Systems*, vol. AES-22, no. 4, pp. 432-442, July 1986.

2003-01-0014

A Design of Millimeter-Wave Radar Dynamic Range With Statistical Analysis

Shinsaku Noda, Koichi Kai, Naohisa Uehara and Masahira Akasu
Automotive Electronics Development Center, Mitsubishi Electric Corporation

ABSTRACT

A way to design the STC performance for automotive millimeter-wave radar is proposed. With a statistical analysis on the data achieved in an experiment at a practical driving situation, the probability distribution of the received signal according to the distance is obtained. The experiment was carried out using FM-pulse Doppler radar we developed. Based on the obtained characteristics, a necessary compression of radar dynamic range is specified. With designed STC in the proposed way, the cost of the radar has been reduced while achieving a wide detection area up to 150m.

INTRODUCTION

Upon developing millimeter-wave radar for automotive applications, such as ACC (Adaptive Cruise Control) system, we encounter many problems in designing the dynamic range of the radar.

Automotive radar must have a large dynamic range. A detection range that extends from as short as a few meter distances to as long as over 100m distances is required. Usually, STC (Sensitivity Time Control) process is applied to the radar. It controls the receiver gain according to the distance between the radar and the target, and works to compress the dynamic range of the received power. We are developing a millimeter-wave radar using FM-pulse Doppler method.[1] One of advantages of FM-pulse Doppler method comparing to FM-CW (Frequency Modulation Continuous Wave) method, which is popular method for automotive radar because of its high distance resolution, is an applicability of STC operation. Designing of STC needs the information about the received power reflected from the target.

With respect to automotive application, we must take into consideration various targets such as small motorcycles, large-sized trucks, or pedestrians for some situations. In addition, the RCS (Radar Cross Section) of these targets fluctuates. Thus, it is difficult to estimate the exact RCS.

Considering all things mentioned above, the receiver has to achieve a very large dynamic range. The radar, therefore, costs much for high-resolution A/D converters or processing unit.

In this paper, we considered the received power or RCS as a random value that had some probability distribution. The kind of probability distribution was obtained by a statistical analysis on the achieved data in the experiment. And we designed STC parameters based on obtained statistical characteristics.

STATISTICAL ANALYSIS ON RECEIVED POWER

To obtain the statistical characteristics of received power in practical situations, we made experiments using FM-pulse Doppler radar we developed. Achieved data were statistically analyzed, and the probability distributions were estimated with distribution tests.

FM-PULSE DOPPLER RADAR

In the experiment, we used the FM-pulse Doppler radar we had developed as a sensor. Also, the radar was the object to be improved with respect to STC performance. Figure 1 shows the structure of FM-pulse Doppler radar.

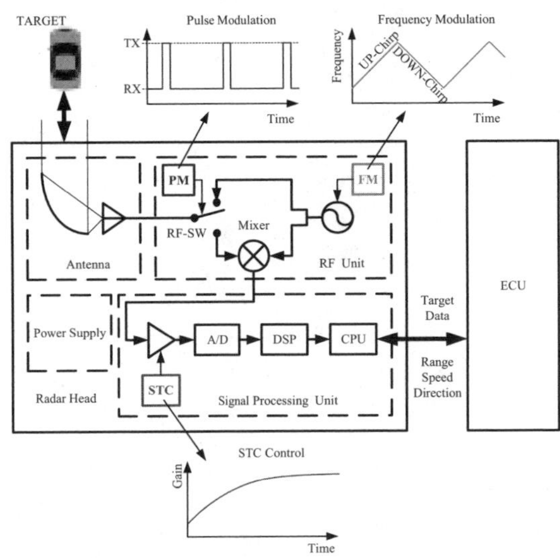

Figure 1 Structure of FM-pulse Doppler radar

FM-pulse Doppler radar has advantages of both FM-CW radar and pulse Doppler radar. The distance accuracy of FM-pulse Doppler method is based on that of FM-CW method. As well known, FM-CW method is generally adopted as automotive radar for its good performance with respect to the distance accuracy. However, FM-CW method has an ambiguity problem when receiving plural targets. Two or more beat frequencies have a possibility of causing wrong combination for calculation of the distance and the speed. Combining pulse Doppler radar operation with FM-CW radar gives a solution to the ambiguity problem. Measuring the delay time of the reflected pulse signal results in a rough distance to the target. Then, an ambiguity problem in FM-CW operation can be reduced. Moreover, pulse Doppler method has an advantage of an applicability of STC operation.

Our radar has a variable gain amplifier for STC operation as figure 1 shows. Especially in this experiment, to measure the received power which only the distance influences, the gain of the variable gain amplifier was set to constant value.

The detection area of the radar used in the experiment is shown in figure 2.

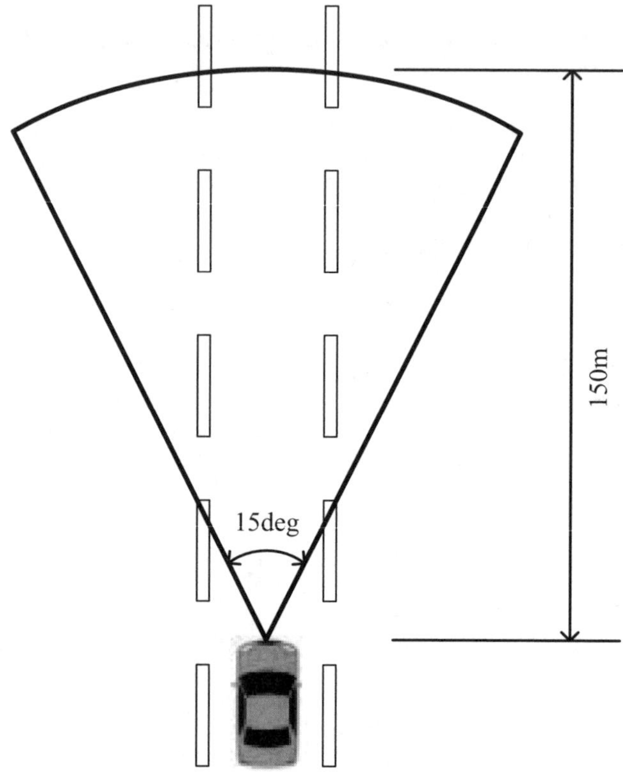

Figure 2 Radar's field of view

DATA AQCUISITION

The experiment was carried out on a highway with normal congestion condition of traffic. The radar was mounted on the test car. The test driver's driving manner was quite normal and typical. Most of the experiment time, the test car was following the other car at a constant speed, sometimes passed a slow car, and so on. The period of the experiment was about 40min, and the driven distance was about 60km. Table 1 shows the conditions of the experiment.

Table 1 Conditions of the experiment

Situation	Highway in normal congestion condition
Driving	Typical driving manner
Experiment time	About 40min
Driven distance	About 60km

During the experiment, the radar was reporting the target information including a distance to the target, a relative speed, signal amplitude, and an azimuth direction.

DATA ANALYSIS

The main purpose of the experiment was to obtain the relationship between the distance and received power, which denoted the signal amplitude. Therefore we extracted these data from achieved data. To obtain the characteristic of signal amplitude versus distance, the distance inside the detection area shown in figure 2 was divided into some ranges. Each range was specified to have a range of 10m. After that, the signal amplitudes were extracted at each distance range. Then extracted amplitude data were statistically analyzed using distribution test to obtain the probability distribution that the amplitude data had. Figure 3 shows the data analysis procedure.

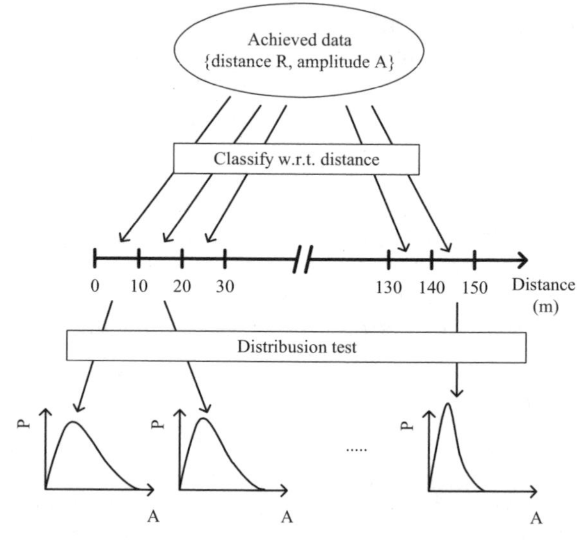

Figure 3 Data analysis procedure

We adopted the distribution test using AIC (Akaike Information Criterion) as statistical analysis. This distribution test maximizes the likelihood with respect to assumed probability distribution. We assumed two probability distributions. They were Gamma distribution and Ricean distribution. As generally known, a received power reflected by fluctuating target has special case of Gamma distribution. As for Ricean distribution, we considered that the received power had a typical value and a random factor was added to the typical value. Foregoing typical value was considered as a value calculated by radar equation given by

$$P_r = \frac{G_t G_r \lambda^2 S}{(4\pi)^3 R^4} P_t \qquad (1)$$

where P_r is the received power by receiving antenna, G_t and G_r are the antenna gains of transmitting and receiving antenna, λ is the wave length of the carrier frequency, S is RCS of the target, R is the distance between the radar and the target, and P_t is the transmitted power. The fluctuation of receiving power might be considered as the fluctuation of RCS S. Ricean distribution is known as the distribution of a mixed signal of a constant value and a random signal that has a normal distribution. Equation (2) gives a probability density function of Gamma distribution, and equation (3) gives the one of Ricean distribution.

$$p_G(x) = \frac{1}{\Gamma(\beta)} \alpha^\beta x^\beta e^{-\alpha x} \qquad (2)$$

$$p_R(x) = \frac{x}{\sigma^2} e^{-\frac{x^2 + A^2}{2\sigma^2}} I_0\left(\frac{xA}{\sigma^2}\right) \qquad (3)$$

where Γ is Gamma function, I_0 is 0th order modified Bessel function.

To give an example, the data analysis at distance range of 120m to 130m will be shown. First, amplitude data within a distance of 120m to 130m were extracted. Figure 4 shows the histogram of those data.

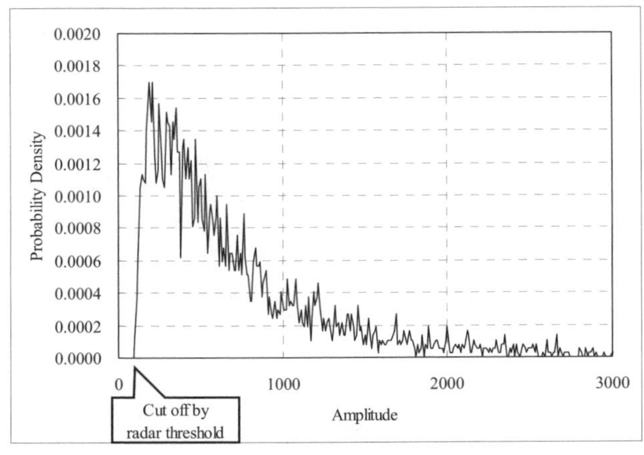

Figure 4 Histogram of extracted data (R=120 to 130m)

Next, two AICs with respect to Gamma distribution and Ricean distribution were calculated from extracted data. At each calculation, parameters of probability density functions, α, β, A, σ, were optimized to minimize each AIC. As a result, AIC of Gamma distribution was 34748, and AIC of Ricean distribution was 34880. Comparing these AICs, Gamma distribution was found to be more suitable for the distribution of extracted amplitude data. Figure 5 shows the result of the distribution test. Moreover, we found that the fitting of a probability distribution could describe the statistical characteristic of smaller region of amplitude that was cut off by the threshold for target detection.

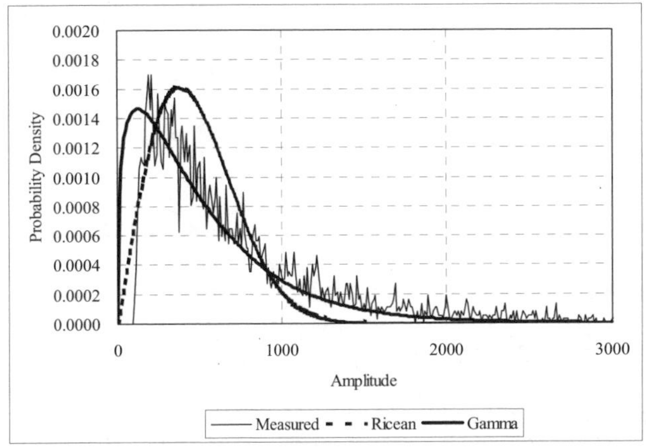

Figure 5 Result of distribution test

Obtained parameters of Gamma distribution are bellows.

$$\begin{cases} \alpha = 0.002602 \\ \beta = 1.322 \end{cases} \qquad (4)$$

Then, we considered about practical amplitude range at each distance. We defined the practical amplitude range as the range whose accumulative probability was from 5% up to 95%. Figure 6 shows the accumulative probability of the estimated probability distribution and its practical amplitude range we defined. Using numerical calculation, practical amplitude range was found to be 45 to 1398. And the mean value M was calculated to be 508 by

$$M = \int_0^\infty x p_G(x) dx = \frac{\beta}{\alpha} \qquad (5).$$

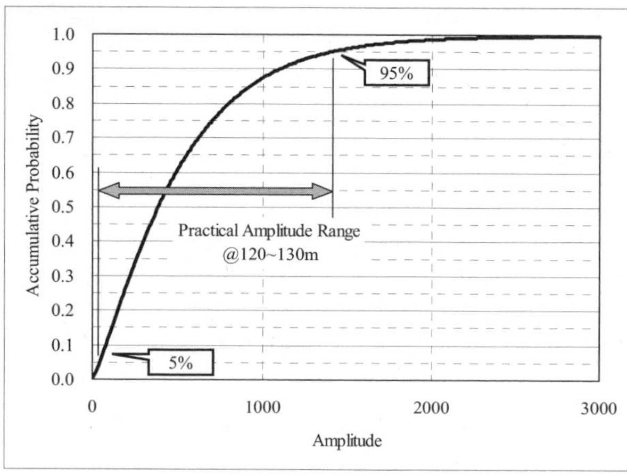

Figure 6 Accumulative probability of Gamma distribution

The above is the procedure to calculate the practical amplitude range for one distance range. The other practical amplitude ranges for its corresponding distance range were achieved similarly. The result of statistical analysis on all distance range is shown in figure 7, and table 2 shows the estimated probability distribution corresponding to the distance.

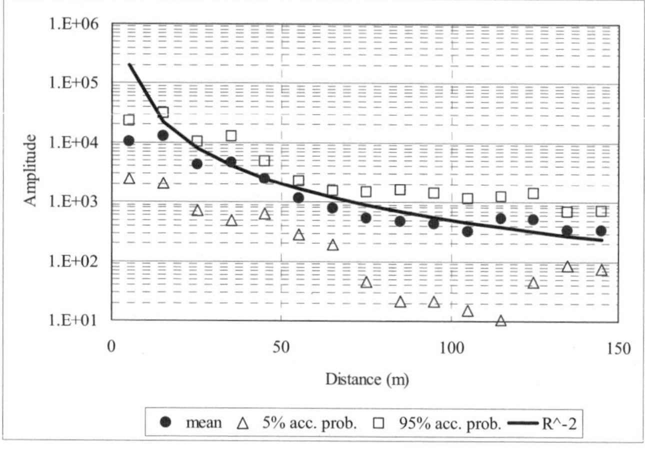

Figure 7 Result of statistical analysis

Table 2 Estimated probability distribution

Range	Distance	Probability Distribution
Near	~40m	Gamma
Middle	40m~70m	Ricean
Far	70m~	Gamma

In figure 7, a curve inversely proportional to square distance is also drawn as a reference. (Amplitude doesn't have a dimension of power, but of voltage). The result suggests bellows.

- The practical received signal has 70dB of dynamic range approximately.
- The received signal tends to be minimum at a distance of about 100m.
- At the near distance range, the amplitude of the signal is smaller than estimated value based on the radar equation (1).

As for the distance where the received signal takes the minimum value, we should take into consideration about an influence of multi-path cancellation. And as for reduction of the amplitude at near range, a reduction of RCS because of the decrease of reflecting area against the beam width should be considered.

DESIGN OF STC PARAMETERS

In this section, the design of STC parameters using the foregoing result of the experiment will be described.

COMPRESSION OF DYNAMIC RANGE

We found that the received signal in a practical situation with the detection area up to 150m had a dynamic range of about 70dB. To consider a margin, we think the radar should achieve a dynamic range of 80dB. On the other hand, to achieve a dynamic range of 80dB without STC operation, 14-bit or more resolution A/D converter is needed, and such an A/D converter costs much. Thus, we chose 10-bit A/D converter that has 60dB of dynamic range. Then we specified the dynamic range compression by STC to 20dB, that was a difference between 80dB of a practical received signal range with a margin and 60dB of the dynamic range of A/D converter.

IMPLEMENTATION OF STC OPERATION

To simplify the circuitry of the radar, 1 stage RC network filter was applied to control of the receiver gain as shown in figure 8.

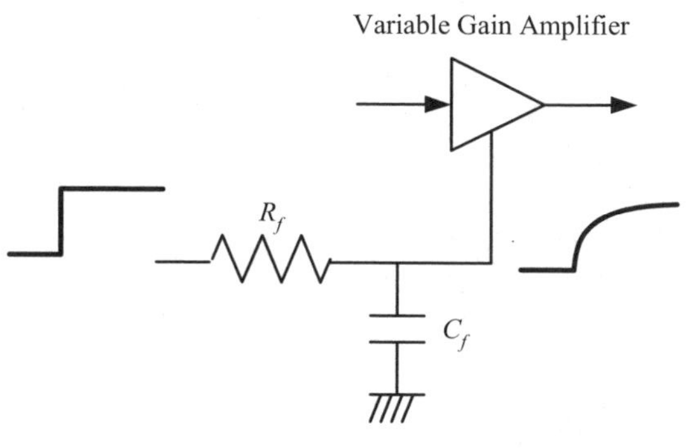

Figure 8 Gain control circuit for STC

A rectangular step function generated by a logic gate is shaped at RC filter, and output voltage is supplied into gain control terminal of the variable gain amplifier.

The variation of the gain can be tuned at the variable gain amplifier, and it was set to 20dB as mentioned above.

As for the time constant of the RC filter ($T=R_fC_f$), one policy is that the gain at the time corresponding to the distance of 70m (=467ns) should be almost maximum gain. Because the received signal at 70m tends to decrease as shown in figure 7. On the other hand, too small time constant makes no matter with respect to the purpose of STC operation. Finally, time constant was specified experimentally to 220ns.

Figure 9 shows the expected amplitude range with STC designed in this way.

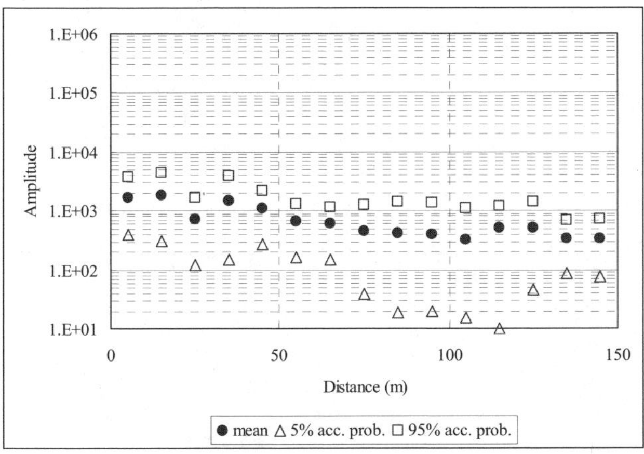

Figure 9 Estimated amplitude range with designed STC

As a result, we achieved 53dB of modified practical receiving amplitude range with the designed STC, and it satisfies the 60dB of a dynamic range of A/D converter.

CONCLUSION

We proposed an effective way of designing STC parameters using a statistical analysis on the practical received signal. We obtained the statistical characteristics of the received signal in practical situations. And we designed STC parameters based on the obtained characteristics. A reduction of a dynamic range succeeded to reduce the cost with lower resolution A/D converter. Moreover, we have found an advantage in a cost of FM-pulse Doppler radar over FM-CW radar for its applicability of STC operation.

REFERENCES

1. N.Uehara, K.Kai, S.Honma, T.Takahara and M.Akasu, "High Reliability Collision Avoidance Radar Using FM-Pulse Doppler Method," SAE 2001 World Congress, 2001-01-0803, 2001
2. S.Honma, T.Takahara, M.Akasu and S.Sato, "Offset Paraboloidal Reflector Antenna for Millimeter-Wave Radar," Seoul 2000 FISITA World Automotive Congress, F2000I408, 2000
3. M.Skolnik, "Introduction to Radar Systems 2nd Edition," McGraw-Hill, 1980
4. T.Hayter, "Probability and Statistics for Engineers and Scientists," Anthony J. Hayter PWS, 1996

2003-01-0013

A Method for Radar-Based Target Tracking in Non-Uniform Road Condition

Shunji Miyahara
Visteon Asia Pacific, Inc.

ABSTRACT

In the Adaptive Cruise Control (ACC) system, the conventional target tracking method depends on the yaw rate/steering angle information and is effective for the uniform road condition, where the host and target vehicles are on the roads with the same curvature. But it cannot work on non-uniform road conditions where the target vehicle and host vehicle are on the road with different curvature like curve-entry and lane change. Therefore a new method to track a target vehicle in non-uniform conditions has been developed. It is based on the locus on the phase chart between the azimuth angle and relative velocity, which are obtained from the radar and host vehicle information. It can express the path of the target vehicle in non-uniform conditions exactly since the locus can be expressed theoretically. The theory of the method and the simulation results are shown here. The performance for the curve-entry, curve-exit and lane-change is satisfactory.

INTRODUCTION

Since the middle of the 1990s, the vehicles with the Adaptive Cruise Control (ACC) system based on the laser radar have been introduced into the Japanese market. At the end of the 1990s, the vehicles with the system based on millimeter wave appeared in European and Japanese market [1]. Although the history is relatively long, the popularization of the system is still very low. There are several reasons. They are cost, performance, frequency of usage, etc. The cost problem is dominant, but will eventually be solved as that in other new products were. The frequency of usage depends on traffic conditions and applicability. Regarding the performance, the ACC has a serious drawback. The ACC can judge whether a preceding vehicle is a target or not only when the vehicle and vehicle with ACC are on the lane with same curvature. Namely, the ACC works properly on only uniform road conditions. And the ACC cannot distinguish the lane-change and curve-entry. This drawback limits the applicability of the ACC. The more the view angle is wider, the more serious the drawback becomes.

So far it is proposed to add a lane marker detection by vision system [2] and fusion systems [3-6] to solve this drawback. Unfortunately these approaches increase the cost and cannot be applied under adverse weather. The path prediction by the radar was also proposed [7], but it is insufficient for non-uniform and the transient road conditions. Therefore the authors propose a new method to solve this drawback by using the potential information of the ACC itself.

The proposed method is based on the phase chart between the relative velocity and the azimuth angle.

DRAWBACK OF CONVENTIONAL ACC

The situations of the preceding and host (ACC) vehicles are divided into the four cases. They are depicted in Fig.1. A), both of them are before the curve; B), preceding vehicle entering the curve and the host one on the straight line; C), both are in the curve; D), the preceding vehicle exits from the curve and the host is still in the curve; and E), both are out of the curve.

Case A and E do not have a problem identifying the target. Case C can estimate the curvature by the yaw-rate and/or steering information of the host vehicle itself and identify whether the previous vehicle is in the same lane as the host one.

But there are no effective methods to identify the target in Case B and D because the information of the host vehicle, yaw-rate and/or steering, cannot be used for the lane prediction.

When the host vehicle is following a target vehicle changing to the adjacent lane or a preceding vehicle changing to the lane of the host one as shown in Fig.2 (a) and (b), it is difficult for the ACC system to distinguish the lane-change from the curve-enter/exit shown in Fig.2 (c) and (d). Especially (a) and (c) in Fig.2 are difficult to distinguish. The wrong judgment accelerates the host vehicle and might cause a dangerous accident. Or, it keeps the host vehicle in the following mode even though there is no target vehicle.

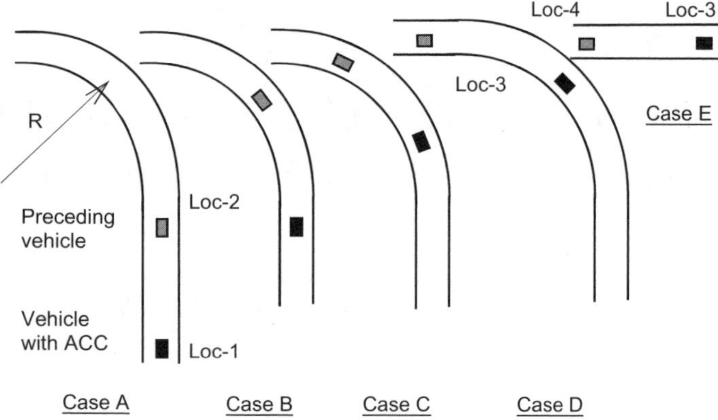

Figure 1: Relation of the preceding and host (ACC) vehicles regarding the curve.Loc-1: far-end of straight line, Loc-2: starting point of the curve, Loc-3: end point of the curve, Loc-4: far-end of the other straight line.

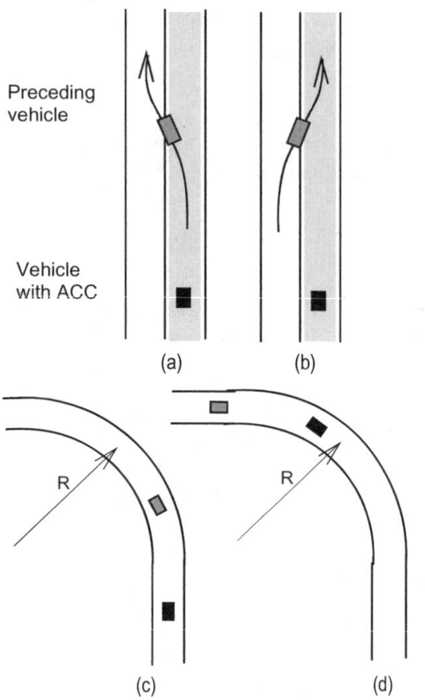

Figure 2: Lane-change and curve-entry/-exit. A host vehicle follows the preceding vehicle.

PROPOSED METHOD

The author proposes a new method for the host vehicle to follow the target before, in and after the curve by overcoming the drawbacks previously discussed. This new method utilizes the ACC information, the steering angle/yaw-rate of the host vehicle, relative velocity and the azimuth angle of the preceding vehicle against the bore-sight of the ACC. The method is based on the quasi time-independent phase-chart between:

- *Azimuth angle* of the preceding vehicle against the bore-sight of the host one and
- *Relative velocity* of the preceding vehicle against the host one.

CONCEPT

The behavior of the azimuth angle is shown in Fig.3 (a) and (b). The angle can detect the change like the curve-entry and lane-change of a preceding vehicle. But it cannot distinguish one from the other since the amount of the angle change depends on the radius and/or the range as shown in Fig.4. Therefore, as additional information, the relative velocity vector is proposed. The vectors are shown in Fig.4 (c) and (d). They are perfectly different in the curve-entry and lane-change. But it seems difficult for only the vectors to distinguish the lane change from non-change as seen from Fig.4 (d). Namely, the combination of the azimuth angle and relative velocity seems promising for the identification of the curve-entry and the lane-change.

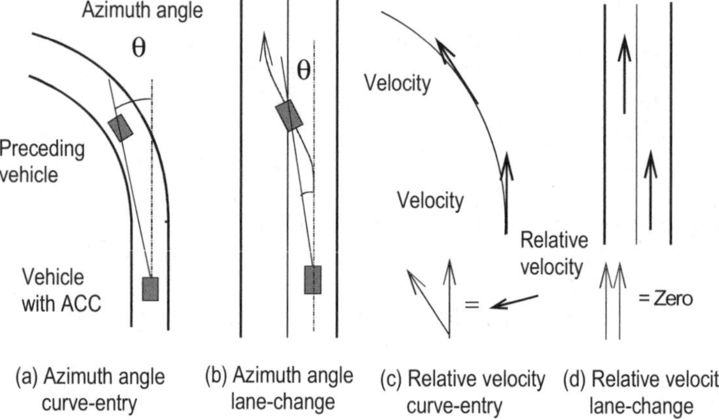

Figure 3: Azimuth angle and relative velocity.

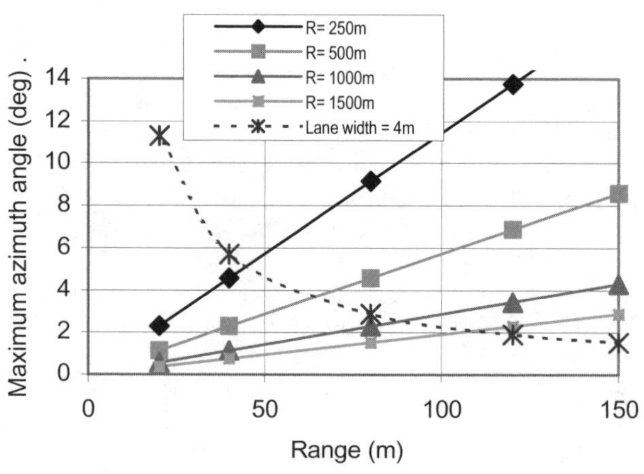

Figure 4: Maximum azimuth angle for curve-entry with radius R and lane-change.

THEORETICAL EXPRESSION

The mathematical relation between the azimuth angle and relative velocity is considered. The positions of the preceding and host vehicles are expressed by Eqs.(1) and (2) (refer to Fig.5 (a)).

$$(x_p, y_p) = (-R\,(1-\cos\phi\,),\ R\sin\phi\,) \qquad (1)$$

$$(x_A, y_A) = (\,0,\ R\,\phi - L) \qquad (2)$$

where (x_p, y_p), (x_A, y_A), R, L and ϕ are the positions of the preceding and host vehicles, the radius of the curve, the distance along the road and the angle shown in Fig.5, respectively. Assuming that the velocity of the both vehicles are the same, the azimuth angle (counter-clockwise), the relative velocity and the absolute value of the velocity are expressed by Eqs.(3-5), respectively.

$$\theta = \tan^{-1}\,(2\,R\sin^2\phi/2\ /\ (\,R\sin\phi\ - R\,\phi\ +\ L)) \qquad (3)$$

$$(v_x, v_y) = V\,(\,-\sin\phi\,,\ (\cos\phi\ - 1)) \qquad (4)$$

$$V_r\ = 2\,V\ \mid \sin\phi/2\mid \qquad (5)$$

where V is the absolute value of the velocity of the vehicles. Assume that ϕ is small enough. The azimuth angle and relative velocity are approximated by Eqs.(6) and (7).

$$\theta\ =\ (\,R\,\phi^{\,2}\,/\,2\,)\,/\,L \qquad (6)$$

$$V_r = \ V\mid\phi\mid \qquad (7)$$

From Eqs.(6) and (7), the relation is obtained as shown in Eq.(8).

$$\theta = \ (\,R\,/\,2\,L\,)\ (V_r\,/\,V)^{\,2} \qquad (8)$$

Regarding the curve-exit shown in Fig.5 (b), the similar relation is given by Eqs.(9) and (10).

$$\theta = \ -\,(R/2L)\ (\,V_r\,/\,V\ - L/R\,)^2 + L/2R,\ \phi>0 \qquad (9)$$

$$\theta = \ -\,(R/2L)\ (\,V_r\,/\,V\ + L/R\,)^2 + L/2R,\ \phi<0 \qquad (10)$$

The radius R and angle ϕ are positive for turning to the left and negative for turning to the right. The relation is expressed in the phase chart shown in Fig.6. In the chart, the uniform road conditions, where both vehicles are on the straight lane or in the curve, are single points, and the non-uniform road conditions, where one of them is on the straight lane and the other in the curve, draw the quadratic curves. When turning to the right, the azimuth angle becomes negative.

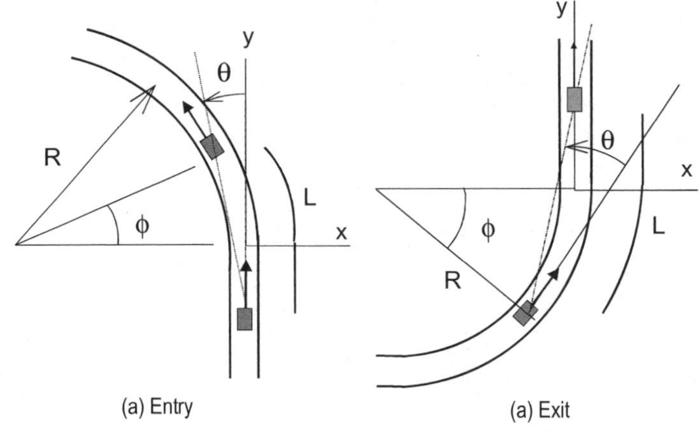

Figure 5: Azimuth angle and relative velocity.

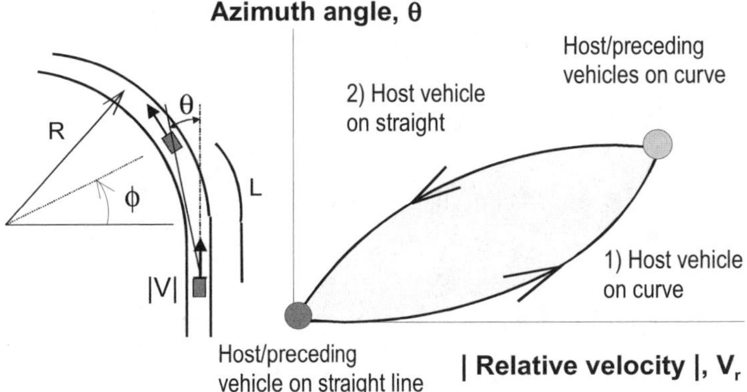

Equations ($\phi \ll 1$) :
1) θ = (R/2L) (V_r / |V|)², 2) θ = - (R/2L) (V_r / |V| - L/|R|)² - L/2R

Figure 6: Phase chart for the curve-entry and –exit (Method Curve).

The relation in the lane change is considered by referring to Fig.7. The locus of the preceding vehicle is assumed to be expressed by Eq.(11).

$$q = (W/2)\ \{\ 1 - \cos\,(\pi p/D)\ \} \qquad 0 < p < D \qquad (11)$$

By assuming that the velocity along the longitudinal direction is the same and that the azimuth angle θ is small enough, the relation is expressed by Eq.(12).

$$\{(\,\theta - (W/2L))/\,(W/2L)\}^2 + \{\,(V_r/Vp)\,/\,(\pi W/2D)\,\}^2 = 1 \qquad (12)$$

where W, L, D, V_r and Vp are the width of lane, the range, the length for the lane-change, the absolute value of the relative velocity and the velocity along the longitudinal direction, respectively. The phase chart for the lane-change is shown in Fig.8. In the chart, the stationary conditions, where both vehicles are running straight, are single points, and the transient conditions, where the preceding vehicle is changing the lane, draw the elliptic curves. If the vehicle turns right, the azimuth angle becomes negative.

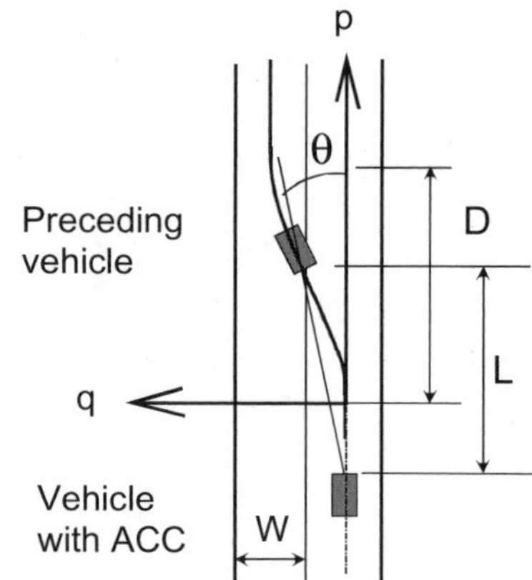

Figure 7: Lane change.

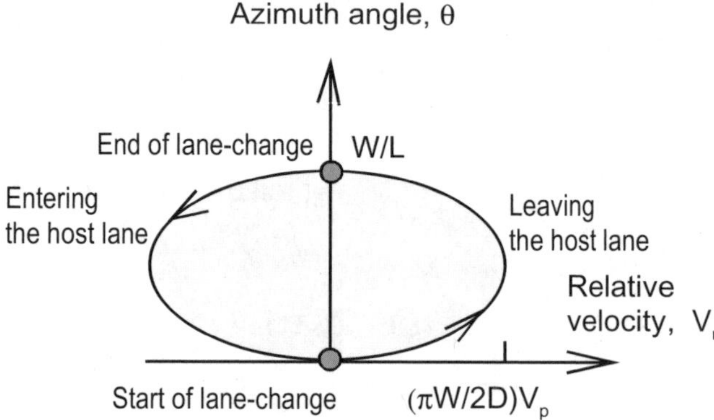

Figure 8: Phase chart for the lane-change (Method Lane). W, L, D and V_p are the width of a lane, the range, the distance for the lane change and the velocity of the host and preceding vehicles, respectively. Refer to Fig.7.

ALGORITHM FOR THE METHODS

The proposed methods can be expressed by theoretical relations like Eqs.(8-10) and (12). And it is possible to identify a target vehicle in "non-uniform" or "transient" road conditions by using the relationship. Here the algorithm on how to use the relationship is described.

Time series data $(V_r(\tau), \theta(\tau))$, $\tau = t\text{-}n, t\text{-}n+1, \ldots, t$ are used. Regression based on the quadratic or elliptic equations is applied to the data. By comparing the residual of the regression curve with an criteria, it is judged whether this is the curve-entry or not, or lane-change or not. One advantage for using these methods is that they do not require a great deal of experimental data for determining the criteria since the algorithm is using the theoretical relation, not empirical data.

The relative velocity used in the algorithm is calculated as shown in Appendix A.

REGRESSION

<u>Method Curve</u>

The regression for Method Curve is as follows: The regression curve is expressed by Eq.(13).

$$Y = a_1 X + a_2 X^2 \qquad (13)$$

where Y, X, a_1 and a_2 are the azimuth angle, relative velocity, the linear and quadratic terms of the regression curve, respectively. By applying $(V_r(\tau), \theta(\tau))$, $k=t\text{-}n, t\text{-}n+1,\ldots,t$ to (X, Y), the estimated value a_2^* and standard deviation σ_{a2} of the coefficient a_2 are calculated. If Eq.(14) is satisfied, this is judged as curve-entry.

$$\sigma_{a2} / a_2^* < c_{a2} \qquad (14)$$

where c_{a2} is the criteria. From the time dependence of the azimuth angle $\theta(\tau)$, the curve-entry or –exit can be distinguished. Additionally, the estimated value a_2^*, the radius R can be calculated.

<u>Method Lane</u>

The regression for Method Lane is as follows: The regression curve is expressed by the elliptic equation as shown in Eq.(12). This equation is transformed by the quadratic equation by Eq.(15).

$$Z = Y^2 = a_1 X + a_2 X^2 \qquad (15)$$

where Y, X, a_1 and a_2 are the relative velocity, azimuth angle, the linear and quadratic terms of the regression curve, respectively. By applying $(\theta(\tau), V_r(\tau)^2)$, $k=t\text{-}n, t\text{-}n+1,..,t$ to (X,Z), the estimated value a_2^* and standard deviation σ_{a2} of the coefficient a_2 are calculated. If Eqs.(16-17) is satisfied, this is judged as lane-change.

$$\sigma_Z / \mu_Z < c_Z \qquad (16)$$

$$\left| \frac{W^*}{W^* - Width\_lane} \right| < c_{lane} \qquad (17)$$

$$W^* = -4\,L\,a_2^* / a_1^* \qquad (18)$$

where σ_z, μ_z, W^*, *Width_lane*, L, a_1^*, a_2^*, c_z and c_{lane} are the standard deviation and average of Z, the estimated lane width, the measured range, preset lane width, the estimated regression coefficients and the criteria, respectively.

EVALUATION BY SIMULATION

The proposed methods based on the phase chart are evaluated through simulation.

CONDITION

The path is comprised of a straight, curve and straight road as shown in Fig.9. The radius of the curve is 500 [m]. The preceding vehicle leaves the host vehicle's lane and returns to it in the first straight road.

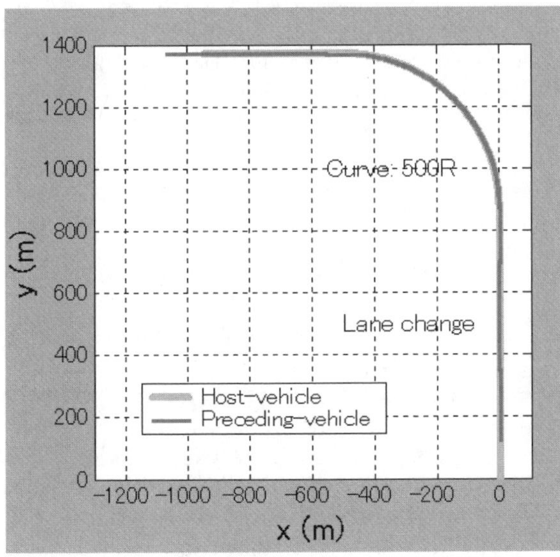

Figure 9: Path of the host and preceding vehicles in the simulation. The preceding vehicle leaves the host vehicle's lane and returns to it around $y = 500$ [m].

The condition for the vehicles, radar and road is shown in Table 1. It is assumed that the radar works ideally and the preceding vehicle is a point reflector.

Table 1: Condition for the vehicles, radar and road

Item	Specification
Velocity	
-Host nad preceding vehicles [km/h]	108
-Distance [m]	120 or 60
Radar	
-Range [m]	150
-Azimuth angle [deg]	-8 to +8
Dimension	
-Lane width [m]	4
-Preceding vehicles	point reflector

The condition for the operation is shown in Table 2. The criteria previously described are as follows: c_{a2}, c_z and c_{lane}, are 0.25, 0.1 and 0.25, respectively.

Table2: Condition for the operation

Item	Specification
Calculation pitch [sec]	0.1
Yaw rate [deg/sec]	calculated from the path shown in Fig.9
Number of data for regression	10 to 40

The inputs for this simulation are the range, azimuth angle of the preceding vehicle from the host vehicle, the yaw-rate of the host vehicles and the velocity of both vehicles.

SIMULATION

The simulation is made on Matlab/Simulink. A plot of the azimuth angle and the absolute value of the relative velocity as a function of time is shown in Fig.10. After filtering the velocity, they are expressed by the phase chart as shown in Fig.11. The locus is similar to that in Figs.6 and 8.

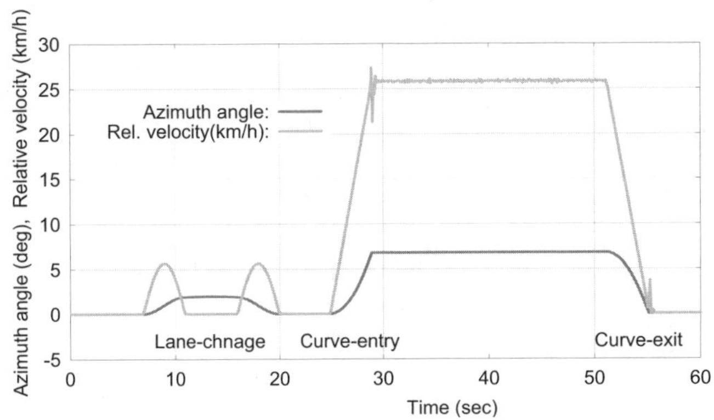

Figure10: Azimuth angle and absolute value of the relative velocity. Distance= 120 [m]. Velocity= 30 [m/sec].

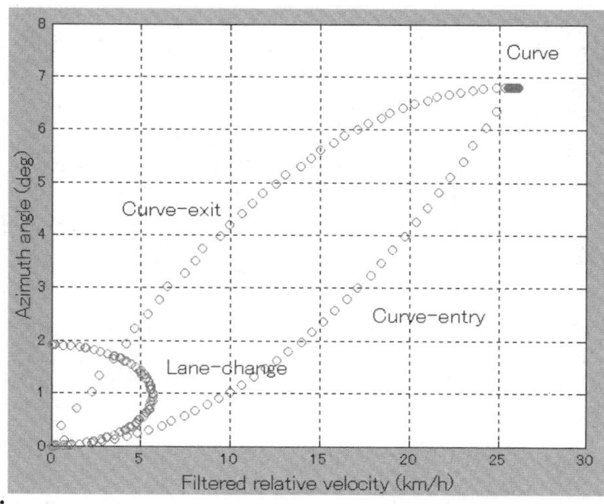

Figure 11: Phase chart between azimuth angle and filtered relative velocity. Distance= 120 [m]. Velocity= 30 [m/sec].

The simulation on Method Curve and Method Lane is made. When the lateral deviation from the host vehicle path is less than the half of the lane-width (4.0 [m]) and vehicle-width (1.7 [m]), the preceding vehicle is judged as not being in the host lane. The results with the conventional yaw-rate based target identification are shown in Fig.12. Both methods worked precisely. Method Curve detected the curve-entry and –exit, and showed no-response to the lane-change. Method Lane detected the lane change from the host lane and the entry to the lane, and showed no-response to the Curve-entry and –exit. The conventional yaw-rate based method responded to the lane change and curve-entry/-exit and could not distinguish one from another.

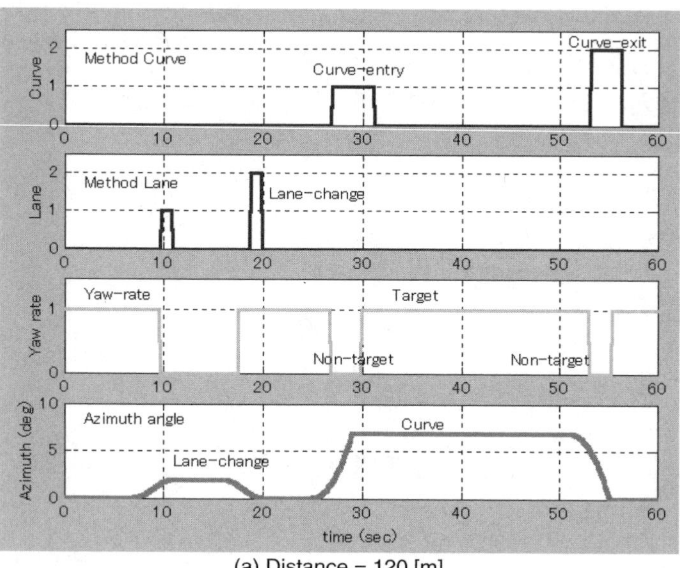

(a) Distance = 120 [m]

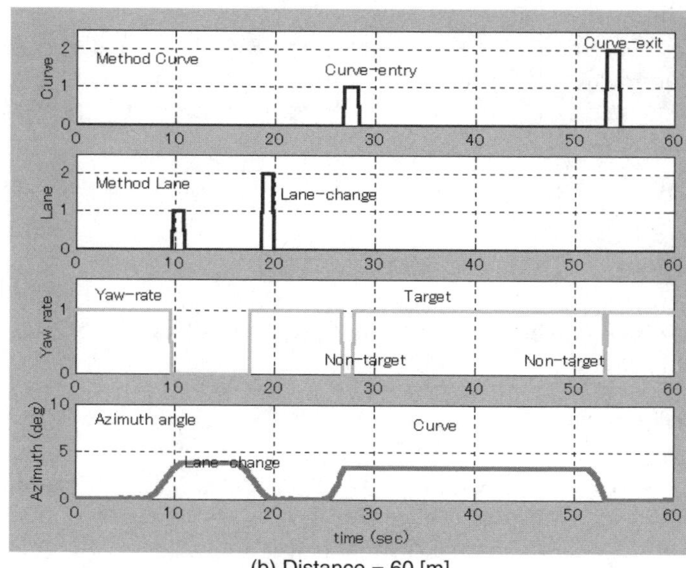

(b) Distance = 60 [m]

Figure 12: Curve and lane-change detection by Method Curve and Method Lane. Curve: Curve-entry and –exit correspond to "1" and "2", respectively. Lane: Exit and enter correspond to "1" and "2", respectively. Yaw-rate: Target and non-target correspond to "1" and "0", respectively. The preceding vehicle is judged based on the yaw-rate.

COMBINATION OF THE METHODS AND YAW-RATE

In actual application, the combination of the proposed methods and yaw-rate based target identification is necessary. As one example, a combined method, where the methods work in non-uniform and transients conditions, and the yaw-rate based target identification works in uniform conditions, is investigated. As shown in Fig.12, the methods works well in the transient and non-uniform conditions and the yaw-rate works well in uniform conditions. The algorithm for the switching between them is not described here, but only the results of the combined method are described as shown in Fig.13.

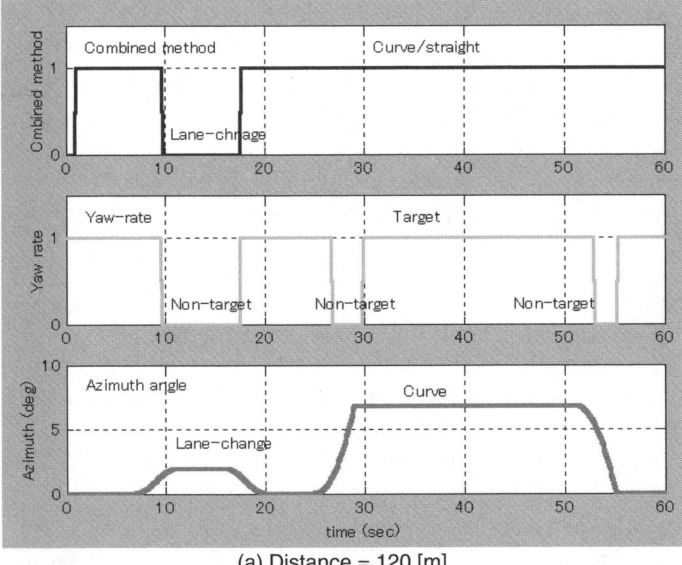

(a) Distance = 120 [m]

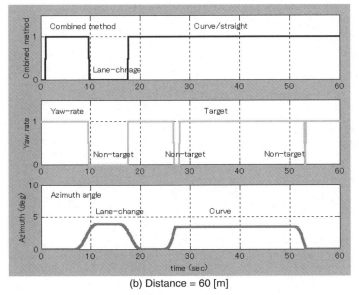

(b) Distance = 60 [m]

Figure 13: Target identification by the combined method. Combined: Target and non-target correspond to "1" and "0", respectively. Yaw-rate based identification: Target and non-target correspond to "1" and "0", respectively.

At the distance of *120* and *60* [m], the combined method identified the target exactly. Namely, it distinguished the curve-entry/-exit and the lane-change and worked well through all the path. The yaw-rate based identification could not work at the curve-entry and -exit. The combined method judged that there was no target around the time of zero. The judgment is delayed since the accumulation of data is necessary for the regression.

DISCUSSION

CRITERIA

For the actual application, the criteria for the judgment by Method Curve and Method Lane in Eqs.(14), (16) and (17) should be determined on the basis of road tests since the noise level for radar system and yaw-rate depends on hardware and road condition.

VALIDITY OF THE THEORETICAL EQUATIONS

The equations Eqs.(8-10) and (12) hold true if the velocities of the vehicles are almost the same and the angle ϕ is small enough. These assumptions seems to be applicable on the highway and do not limit the applications of the proposed methods. In the actual calculation of the equations, the distance along the road L is replaced the range measured by the radar. This does not introduce the error if the angle ϕ is small enough.

ALTERNATIVE METHOD FOR CURVE

Method Curve is designed for the transition between the curve and straight courses. In general, the Method Curve-2 is proposed for the transition from curve to curve as shown in Appendix B. This can be applied for the transition between curves with large and small radius. The drawback of this method is that it determines the present radius by the yaw-rate or steering angle. The evaluation of this method is in progress.

FILTERING OF RELATIVE VELOCITY

The filtering of the relative velocity is one of the important factor in the proposed methods. The noisy data will result in the curve and lane-change detection error. Since the relative velocity is calculated from the position of the host and preceding vehicles, the yaw-rate measurement influences the relative velocity calculation, (refer to Appendix A). To remove the un-stability shown in the time of *29* and *55* [sec] in Fig.10, adequate filtering is necessary.

CALCULATION OF RELATIVE VELOCITY

Here the relative velocity is calculated from the positions of vehicles to show the principle of the proposed method schematically. Practically, a following calculation shown in Eq.(18) is better.

$$\underline{V}_r = \frac{d}{dt}\left(\underline{P}_p - \underline{P}_A\right) = \frac{d}{dt}\left\{ L \begin{pmatrix} \cos(\theta + \varphi) \\ \sin(\theta + \varphi) \end{pmatrix} \right\} \quad (18)$$

where $\underline{V}_r$, $\underline{P}_p$, $\underline{P}_A$, L, θ and φ are the relative velocity vector, the position vectors of host and preceding vehicles, the range, the azimuth angle from the host vehicle to the preceding vehicle and the direction of the host vehicle, respectively.

CONCLUSION

In the Adaptive Cruise Control (ACC) system using the radar, the conventional yaw-rate based target tracking is confined to the uniform road conditions. In order to apply to non-uniform (curve-entry or –exit) and transient road conditions (lane-change), new methods called Method Curve and Method Lane are proposed. They are based on the phase chart between the azimuth angle and relative velocity. In the curve-entry, -exit and lane change, the relationship between them is expressed by theoretical equations: The curve-entry/–exit and the lane-change are expressed by the quadratic and elliptic equations, respectively. Namely, the deviation of the measured value from the equations tells whether the preceding vehicle is in the curve-entry or lane-change. In the simulation, the validity of the methods is demonstrated. The methods detect the non-uniform and the transient road condition exactly. And it is shown that the combination between the methods and yaw-rate can achieve the target identification through various road conditions. The proposed methods are undergoing road testing.

ACKNOWLEDGMENTS

The author thanks Sam Rahaim, Jerry Sielagoski and Faroog Ibrahim, Visteon Corporation, for their technical discussion on this development.

REFERENCES

1. W. D. Jones, “Keeping Cars from Crashing”, IEEE Spectrum, pp.40/45, Sept., 2001
2. K. Hanawa and Y. Sogawa, “Development of Stereo Image Recognition System for ADA”, Proceedings IEEE Intelligent Vehicles Symposium 2001, pp.177/182, 2001.
3. M. Beauvais and S. Lakshmanan, “CLARK: a heterogeneous sensor fusion method for finding lanes and obstacles”, Image and Vision Computing, 18, pp.397/413, 2000.
4. H. Higashida, R. Nakamura, M. Hitotsuya, K. F. Honda and N. Shima, “Fusion Sensor for an Assist System for Low Speed in Traffic Congestion Using Millimeter-Wave and an Image Recognition sensor”, SAE2001, 2001-01-0800, 2001.
5. T. Kato, Y. Ninomiya and I. Masaki, “An Obstacle Detection Method by Fusion of Radar and Motion Stereo”, IEEE Trans. Intelligent Transportation Systems, vol.3-3, pp.182/188, Sept. 2002.
6. N. Shimomura, K. Fujimoto, T. Oki anf H. Muro, “An Algorithm for Distinguishing the Types of Objects on the Road Using Laser Radar and Vision”, IEEE Trans. Intelligent Transportation Systems, vol.3-3, pp.189/195, Sept. 2002.
7. W. Uhler, M. Scherl and B. Lichtenberg, "Driving Cource Prediction Using Distance Sensor Data", SAE 1999-01-1234, 1999.

APPENDIX A

The relative velocity is calculated as shown in Fig.A1. The azimuth angles, $\theta(n-1)$ and $\theta(n)$, and ranges, $L(n-1)$ and $L(n)$, are measured by the radar. The velocity of the host vehicle is measured and the direction of the host vehicle, $\varphi(n-1)$ and $\varphi(n)$, are obtained by integrating the yaw-rate.

At first, the position of the host vehicle is calculated by using the velocity and direction. By using the position, the range and azimuth angle, the position of the preceding vehicle is calculated. Next, the time derivative of the positions is calculated and becomes the velocity of the vehicles. And the difference of the velocity becomes the relative velocity, $\underline{V}_r(n-1)$.

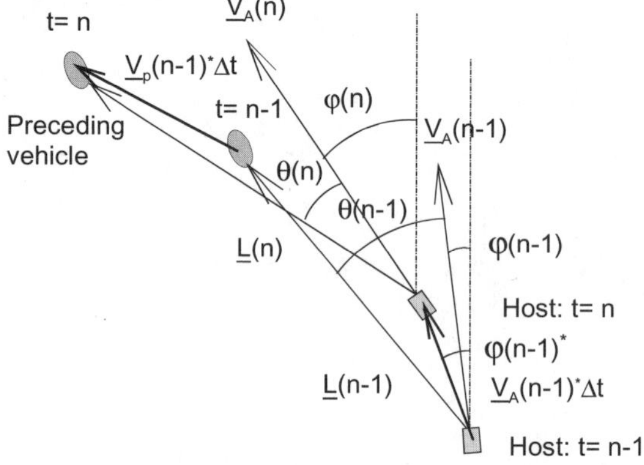

$\underline{V}_A(n-1)^* = (\underline{V}_A(n-1)+\underline{V}_A(n))/2$ Average velocity of host vehicle
$\underline{V}_p(n-1)^* = (\underline{L}(n)+\underline{V}_A(n-1)^*\Delta t-\underline{L}(n-1))/\Delta t$ Average velocity of preceding vehicle
$\underline{V}_r(n-1)=\underline{V}_p(n-1)^*-\underline{V}_A(n-1)^*$ Relative velocity

Fig.A1: Relative velocity. $\underline{V}_A$, $\underline{V}_p$, $\underline{L}$, θ and φ are velocity vectors of host and preceding vehicles, vector from host to preceding vectors, azimuth angle measured by radar and direction of host vehicle, respectively.

APPENDIX B

The method shown in Fig.6 is confined to straight-to-curve conditions. It is modified to fit to the transition from curve-to-curve (Method Curve-2). The curvature where the host vehicle runs is estimated from the yaw-rate or steering angle. The positions of the preceding and host vehicles are expressed by Eqs.(B1), (B2) and (B3), by referring to Fig.B1,

$$(x_p, y_p) = (-R\,(1-\cos\phi),\ R\sin\phi) \tag{B1}$$

$$(x_A, y_A) = (-R_0\,(1-\cos\phi_0),\ -R_0\sin\phi_0) \tag{B2}$$

$$L = R\phi + R_0\,\phi_0 \tag{B3}$$

where R, R_0, ϕ and ϕ_0 are the radius and angles, and positive for the left turn and they are negative for right turn. $R_0\phi_0$ and $R\phi$ are path-length and non-negative. The polarity of the azimuth angle is counter-clockwise. The azimuth angle and the relative velocity are approximated by Eqs.(B4) and (B5).

$$\theta = \{ z^2 + (-2L/R_0)\, z + L^2/R_0R \} / \{ 2L(1/R - 1/R_0) \} \quad \text{(B4)}$$

$$\phi + \phi_0 = V_r / V = z \quad \text{(B5)}$$

where V_r and V are the relative velocity and the velocity of vehicles, respectively. The phase chart is shown in Fig.B2.

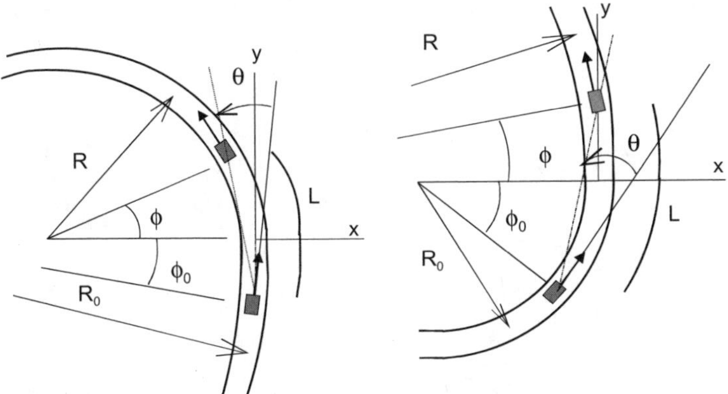

Fig.B1: Method Curve-2: This method can detect the transition between curves.

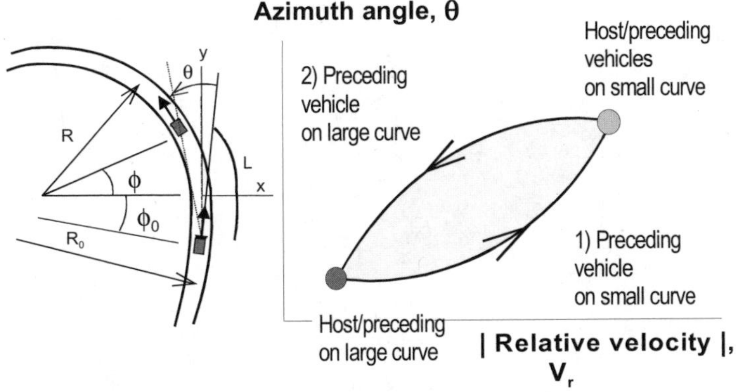

Equations (ϕ and $\phi_0 << 1$):

$$\theta = \{ (V_r/|V| - L/R_0)^2 - (L/R_0)(L/R_0 - L/R) \} / \{ 2L(1/R - 1/R_0) \}$$

Fig. B2: Phase chart: Curve to curve (Method Curve-2).

2002-01-1071

On Board Doppler Sensor for Absolute Speed Measurement in Automotive Applications

Thierry Ditchi and Stéphane Holé
Laboratoire des Instruments et Systèmes d'Île de France, Université Pierre et Marie Curie

Céline Corbrion and Jacques Lewiner
Laboratoire d'Électricité Générale, École Supérieure de Physique et de Chimie Industrielles

ABSTRACT

Many automotive applications, like anti-lock braking systems (ABS), anti collision radars, airbags, require an absolute speed accurate measurement, especially in high risk situations. On-board Doppler sensors may provide a better answer to such a problem than sensors which measure the speed of rotation of the wheels. Indeed the latter can for instance slide on wet or icy roads. However, conventional Doppler sensors cannot operate when the beam emitted by the radar does not encounter a scattering obstacle on the road surface.

In this paper, we present solutions, tested by simulations and by experiments, which drastically increase the probability of having reflecting obstacles in the antenna footprint of Doppler sensors, leading to accurate measurements.

INTRODUCTION

Many automotive applications, for instance anti-lock braking systems (ABS), anti collision radars and airbags, require a good knowledge of the absolute speed of the vehicle for any kind of ground surfaces. Measurements based on the rotation of the wheels may not reflect the reality, particularly in dangerous situations. This is the case, for instance, when the wheels are sliding on an icy or very wet road surface. Indeed in this case even though the wheels do not rotate, the vehicle may still have a significant speed. This can lead the safety systems of the vehicle to take erroneous decisions.

On-board Doppler sensors seem well suited to solve such problem since they give a measurement of the absolute speed of the vehicle, relative to ground. In such systems, and as is shown in Figure 1, an antenna emits towards the road surface a wave which is partially back scattered by the ground obstacles. The reflected wave frequency is shifted by an amount f_d proportional to the vehicle speed and to the cosine of the angle α under which the obstacle is seen by the antenna. For this reason and in order to make accurate measurements, conventional Doppler sensors use a narrow beam to well define the emission and reception angles. Unfortunately, the measurement can only be achieved if there is at least one scattering obstacle in the antenna footprint. However in the above-mentioned dangerous situations, the obstacle density may be so small that the measurement cannot be performed continuously.

In order to increase the probability that the wave emitted by the radar encounters a scattering obstacle, we have proposed to use a broad beam emission [1], but in this case, the angle α becomes an additional unknown variable. The use of a variable frequency allows the determination at the same time of the vehicle speed and of the angle α [2]. This makes accurate speed measurements possible in situations where narrow beam sensors would not operate, but it requires costly hardware and sophisticated data processing.

In the present paper, we propose a new approach using a broad beam antenna with a single frequency [3-5]. This leads to devices which can be easily mass-produced taking advantage of the development of Monolithic Microwave Integrated Circuit (MMIC) technology [6] and the acceptance of microwaves in automotive applications [7].

In the following section, the principle of this absolute speed sensor is introduced. In the next part, the tools developed in order to test this principle are presented. The signal analysis techniques are then explained and the validity and the accuracy of the solutions are discussed.

PRINCIPLE

The principle of the measurement is shown in Figure 1. A wave of frequency f_0 is emitted towards the ground during a time slot ΔT. This wave is reflected by the scattering obstacles on the road surface, present in the antenna footprint.

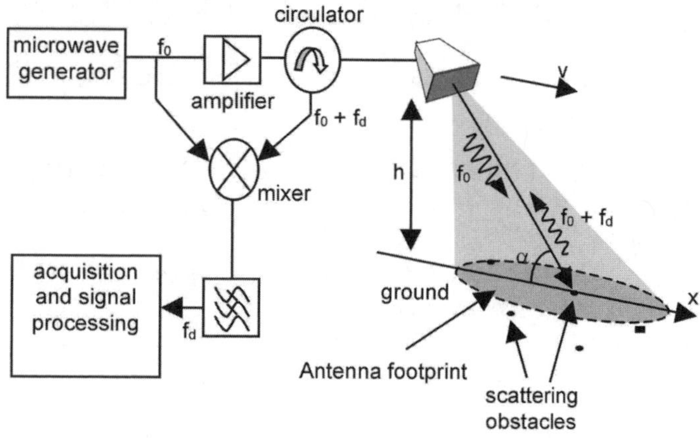

Figure 1: Principle of a Doppler effect speed sensor.

The Doppler frequency shift f_d of the reflected signal associated to a particular obstacle is given by:

$$f_d(t) = \frac{2\ f_0\ v\cos(\alpha)}{c}\ , \qquad (1)$$

where c is the propagation speed of the wave and v the absolute speed of the vehicle. Since the relative position between the scattering obstacle and the sensor changes during the time slot, due to the vehicle movement, the Doppler frequency associated with a ground obstacle also changes [8]. This variation depends on three parameters: i) the vehicle speed v , ii) the obstacle position x at the beginning of the time slot relative to the projection on the road surface of the sensor, and iii) the height h of the sensor above the road. If the time slot is chosen to be short enough so that the speed of the vehicle can be considered constant during this time and since the frequency f_0 of the emitted wave is constant, then the frequency variation of the Doppler signal is only due to the vehicle movement. Thus, the time dependent Doppler frequency $f_d(t)$ can be expressed as:

$$f_d(t) = 2\ f_0\ v \Big/ \left(c\sqrt{1 + h^2/(x - v\,t)^2} \right) \qquad (2)$$

In this expression, the vehicle speed has been chosen positive if the vehicle approaches the obstacle and negative otherwise.

Examples of Doppler frequency variations as derived from equation (2) are plotted on Figure 2 for different values of the parameters v and x.The vehicle speed v can be determined by fitting this analytical function with the experimental Doppler frequencies associated to an obstacle during its displacement relative to the vehicle. This fitting is carried out by adjusting the two parameters (v and x) of equation (2).

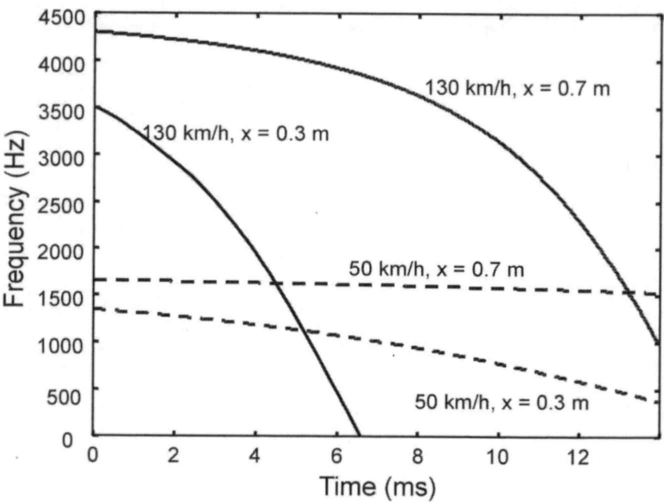

Figure 2: Time dependence of the Doppler frequency for different values of the parameters v and x.

An example is shown on Figure 3. The vehicle speed is equal to 70 km/h, and a unique obstacle is present in the antenna footprint. Its position at the beginning of the measurement is 35 cm. The dotted line represents the experimental frequency evolution and the solid line is obtained by the above described adjustment process. The best-fit parameters in this case are 35 cm for the position and 70.1 km/h for the velocity.

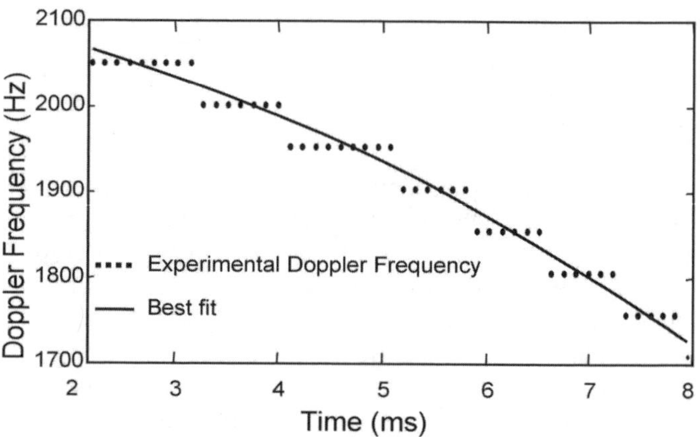

Figure 3: Comparison of the measured Doppler frequency with the analytical one with the parameters obtained by the best fit procedure.

IMPLEMENTATION

The frequency evolution of the Doppler signal during the time slot ΔT is determined using time-frequency methods [9]. For each slot, we use a Fast Fourier transform (FFT) algorithm on moving windows of duration δT here after defined as analysis windows. These windows overlap in order to enable a good frequency tracking.

The accuracy of the speed measurement is directly dependent on the accuracy of the determination of the Doppler frequency. In order to reach a good precision, we need a high spectral resolution technique and as constant as possible a Doppler frequency. These two conditions may not be easy to fulfill at the same time. Indeed since the spectral resolution is inversely proportional to the duration δT, this would favor large δT. Unfortunately, a large δT leads to a significant vehicle displacement during the measurement and thus to a large variation of the Doppler frequency. A satisfactory compromise has been found for the moving window duration δT. It corresponds to a displacement of the vehicle within 5 to 10 cm. For similar reasons, the main direction of the antenna beam results from an other compromise. In order to have a small variation of α during the time slot, one would favor small angles. However, if the angle α is small, the amplitude of the reflected wave is also small. A satisfactory compromise has been found. It corresponds to $\alpha = 35°$.

The possible speed variations during the time slot ΔT, due to acceleration or braking, lead to uncertainties on the speed determination. They must thus be limited by using sufficiently short windows. When the speed of the vehicle is less than 100 km/h and considering a maximal acceleration of 14 m/s^{-2}, which corresponds to an hard braking reducing the speed from 100 km/h to 0 km/h in 2 s, we choose $\Delta T = 10$ ms which leads to an absolute error smaller than 0.5 km/h. For speeds above 100 km/h, we choose $\Delta T(ms) = v(km/h) / 10$. This leads to a relative error equal to 0.5%.

EXPERIMENTAL SETUP AND SIMULATIONS

In order to test the accuracy and the validity of the principles presented in this paper, we carried out simulations and made real measurements.

An experimental evaluation system has been developed to allow measurements with one or multiple obstacle configurations, with an optimal reproducibility. It is illustrated in Figure 4. A belt, which represents the road surface, is driven by a motor-pulley system, and its linear speed can be adjusted in the range 0-90 km/h. Scattering obstacles are fixed on the belt. Their number, shape and distribution can be set. Furthermore, this distribution can be discrete or continuous in order to simulate any kind of road surfaces. A device based on optical barriers is used in order to have an accurate speed reference. An antenna with main axis oriented at a 35° angle from the belt surface was used to emit a wave at a frequency of 19 GHz.

In addition to the experimental system, we have developed a simulation program. It makes it possible to precisely analyze the influence on the measurement of numerous parameters such as vehicle speed and acceleration, noise, road profile, antenna diagram, height above the road, duration of the time slot etc... The number, repartition and shape of the obstacles can be

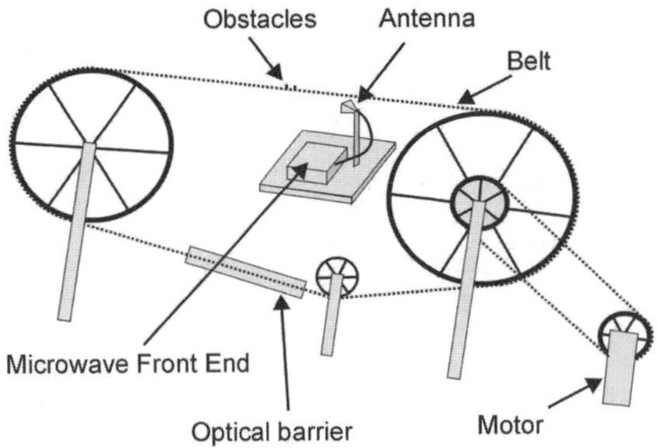

Figure 4: Laboratory set-up.

introduced in the program in order to allow the simulation for different road surfaces. These obstacles can be positioned anywhere on the road surface. The radiation pattern of the antenna and the influence of the antenna-obstacle distance on the signal amplitude can also be introduced. Colored noise of settable levels can be added to the signal in order to simulate noise from electronic components or mechanical vibrations.

SIGNAL ANALYSIS AND SPEED DETERMINATION

The Doppler signal depends on the scattering obstacles in the antenna footprint. If there is only one scattering obstacle in the antenna footprint, the Doppler frequency is non-ambiguous. If there are several widely distributed scattering obstacles, the associated frequencies are well separated. In both cases, a spectral analysis based on the Fourier transform with zero filling allows the determination of the frequencies associated to all the obstacles. An example is presented in Figure 5. One can see essentially two series of Doppler frequencies representing two obstacles.

If several obstacles are closely distributed in the antenna footprint, the associated frequencies are also close to each other and their contributions overlap in the global Doppler signal. Each obstacle produces an elementary spectrum which depends on the duration of the analysis windows δT and on the window function used to compute the FFT. For instance, using flat top windows leads to sinus-cardinal (sinc) functions as the elementary spectra. The decomposition of the calculated Doppler spectrum in elementary spectra allows the determination of the frequencies associated to each obstacle [2].

Once the frequencies associated to the different obstacles have been found for each moving window within the time slot, the procedure described above to fit equation (2) must be implemented. Two approaches have been investigated, either collecting in series the Doppler frequencies generated by each obstacle, or using a Radon-like Transform.

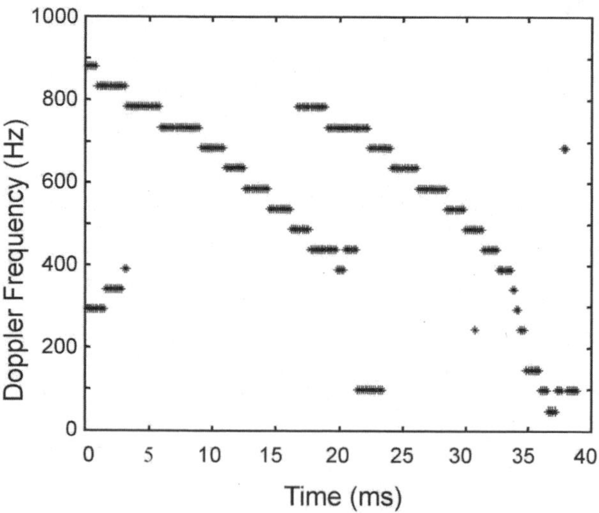

Figure 5: Example of Doppler frequency evolution with two scattering obstacles on the ground.

ASSOCIATION IN SERIES

The frequencies associated with the same scattering obstacle seen at several positions during the time slot are organized in order to form series. The determination of these series takes into account the speed measured at the previous time slot, the maximum possible values of the vehicle acceleration and also the fact that, during a measurement, the number of scattering obstacles in the antenna footprint may change. An example of such an association is shown on Figure 6 where two obstacles are identified.

Once the series have been determined, we fit the analytical function (2) to each of them. If the vehicle has a height sensor, the fit is done by only varying two parameters: the speed (v) and the obstacle position (x) in the analytical function. If no height sensor is available, there are three fit parameters: the speed, the position and the height above the road surface. The parameters for which there is the best fit between the frequency series and the analytical function are chosen as the solutions of the problem.

The optimization is achieved by minimizing an error function associated to the difference between the theoretical and the experimental frequencies. In order to avoid weak local minima of the function, we combine a Monte-carlo method with a gradient method.

This approach leads to a speed of 99.8 km/h for the first obstacle and of 99.4 km/h for the second one for a real speed equal to 100 km/h, which leads to a relative error equal to 0.4%.

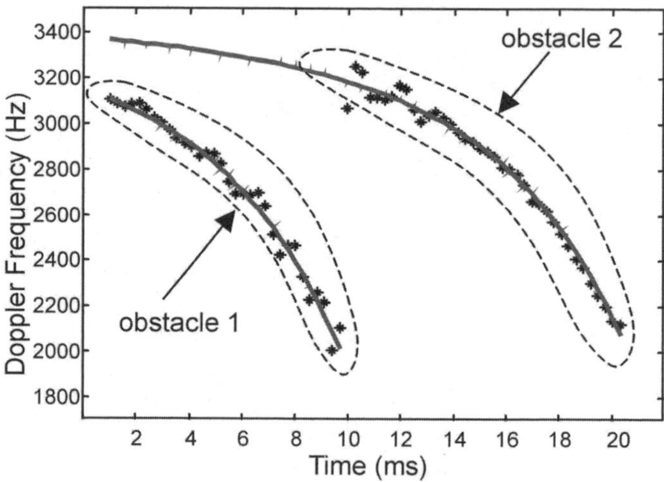

Figure 6: Frequency association by obstacle and fitting.

RADON-LIKE TRANSFORM.

The association in series and the fitting process can be performed by a modified Radon transform. The standard Radon transform [10] allows for the detection of linear feature in a noisy image. The modification we have developed allows for the detection of function (2) features in the image representing the Doppler frequencies versus time such as shown in Figure 6. The result of the transformation gives an other image. In this image the coordinate of one point is (x,v) and the color coded amplitude of each point is proportional to the probability that an obstacle at the initial position x has a relative speed v. Each point of the image of coordinate (x,v) is calculated by determining the number of Doppler frequencies versus time points laying on the $f_d(t,x,v)$ function. In this case, the Radon-like transform R(x,v) can be expressed as

$$R(x,v) = \iint I(t,f_d)\,\delta\left(f_d - \frac{2\,f_0\,v}{c\sqrt{1+(h/(x-vt))^2}}\right) dt\,df_d \quad (3)$$

where $I(t,f_d)$ is the image representing the variation of the experimental Doppler frequency with time and δ is the Dirac's function. As an example, applying this transform to the data of Figure 6 leads to Figure 7.

It can be seen that the speed of each obstacle can be derived directly. The darkest points give the higher probability to have an obstacle at position x with a velocity v. The Radon-like transform presented in Figure 6, leads to an estimated velocity of 101 km/h for the first obstacle and of 100.5 km/h for the second one for a real speed equal to 100 km/h, which corresponds to a relative error of 0.7%.

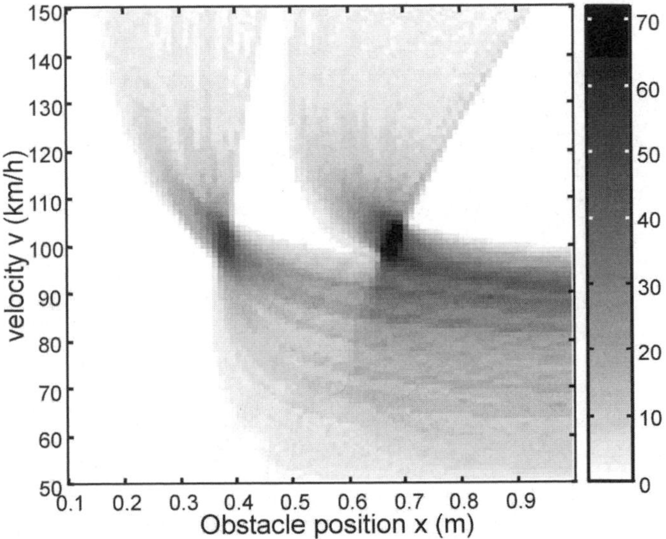

Figure 7: Radon-like Transform of the image shown in Figure 6.

If the third parameter h must be determined at the same time, the Radon-like transform can still be applied. A three dimensional image is then built where each point has three coordinates (x,v,h).

One major difficulty in the association in series is the choice of the convenient series. The Radon-like transform can help making this choice since the position of each obstacle is clearly identified. However as the resolution of Radon-like transform is increased to obtain the best accuracy in the estimation, the time it takes for the processes also increases. For real-time estimations, a coupling of the two methods is possible. First a low resolution Radon-like transform is performed to obtain a first estimation of each obstacle position x_i and velocity v_i. These informations are then used to associate the closest points to $f_d(t,x_i,v_i)$ in the ith series. Finally the parameters (x,v) of $f_d(t)$ are adjusted to obtain the best fit. The coordinates (x,v) give the accurate estimation of the velocity. In this case, the number of operation necessary to compute the velocity is mainly due to the time-domain frequency analysis. It requires roughly 10^6 operations to compute the 1024 point FFT of the 100 analysis windows. The low resolution Radon-like Transform and then the optimization need only less than 10^5 operations. Such an algorithm is directly implementable in real time (in less than 50 ms) with most of the actual DSP's.

RESULTS AND DISCUSSION

COMPARISON BETWEEN NARROW AND BROAD BEAM SENSORS

The broad beam sensor presented above is very accurate when one only or a limited number of obstacles are present in the antenna footprint, situations associated with a high risk (snow, water, etc…). It is now possible to compare the performances of standard narrow beam Doppler sensors with the present broad beam sensor. Figure 8 shows the speed uncertainty for both types, as a function of angle of view of a unique scattering obstacle in the antenna footprint. The apertures of the narrow beam and of the broad beam antennas are respectively 10° and 34°. It can be seen that the use of a broad beam makes it possible to determine the speed for a much larger interval of obstacle positions than in the case of narrow beam sensors. In the illustrated case, for h=30 cm, the broad beam sensor leads to an accuracy of ± 0.5 % over a 50 cm range of obstacle position (from 14 to 64 cm), whereas the same accuracy of ± 0.5 % is obtained over a 7 cm only range for the narrow beam sensor (from 36 to 46 cm).

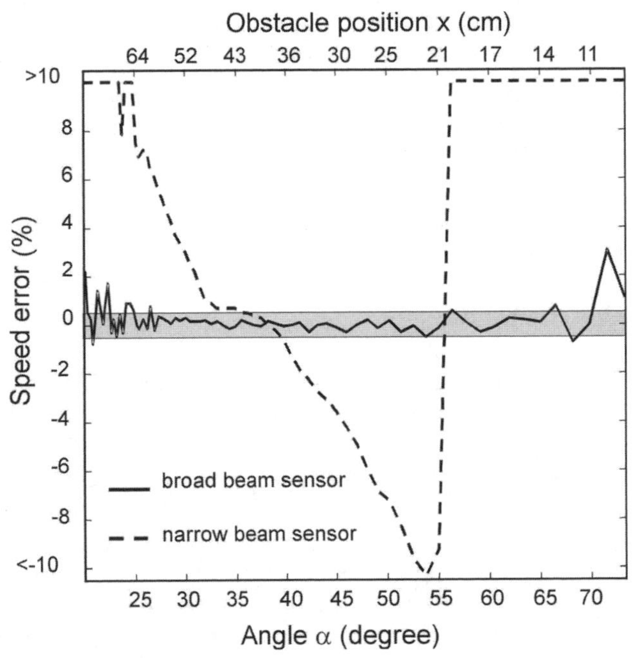

Figure 8: Comparison between broad and narrow beam sensors.

Thus when the obstacle density is larger than one obstacle every 10 cm, which does not correspond to a high-risk situation, then narrow beam Doppler sensors can be applicable with a good accuracy [5].

SENSITIVITY TO HEIGHT

The height h above the road surface is also a parameter of equation (2). Until now, it has been assumed to be known although its value can fluctuate due to the vertical movements or bad conditions of the road surface. Simulations have been performed to test the influence of such variations on the speed determination accuracy. The height variations around its average value can reach $\pm$ 5 cm in the case of an automobile with a 1 to 2 Hz frequency oscillation. An error of $\pm$ 5 % on height h, i.e. 1 cm for a height of 20 cm, leads to a maximum speed error of $\pm$ 0.5 %. This variation of 1 cm can only be reached in a time larger than 25 ms. Thus these height variations can be neglected since the time slots have been chosen less than 20 ms.

Another factor must be taken into account: the variation of the average height, due for instance to variations of the vehicle load, the suspension aging, the chafing of the tires, etc... Such variations can typically reach 10 cm for a normal height of 20 cm. Using only the theoretical height in the calculations leads to a maximal error of 6%. It is therefore necessary to determine this third parameter along with the speed and the position of the obstacle. These three parameters can be determined by a best fit procedure between equation (2) and the experimental time dependent Doppler frequency data. This usually leads to speed errors less than 4%. In order to improve this result, the two and three parameter optimization procedures can be combined. Indeed, it is possible to use some heights determined at some previous time slots by three parameter fittings, in order to calculate an average height value. This value is then used to perform a two parameters fitting. After the two parameters optimization has been carried out, the error becomes smaller than 2.5%.

CONCLUSION

A Doppler sensor using a single fixed frequency and a broad beam of emission is particularly well suited for high-risk situations in automotive applications. We have shown that it combines the advantages of broad beam of emission Doppler sensors, i.e. a high probability of having a reflecting obstacle in the antenna footprint, and of single frequency emission devices, which allows easy implementation. It has been shown that the accuracy of this sensor is very high for low density obstacle distributions. It gives accurate results in a large range of obstacle positions in comparison with narrow beam sensors. A modified Radon Transform allows a better automation of the process to separate frequency contributions due to several obstacles present in the antenna footprint. Finally, the same sensor can also give the value of the vehicle height above the road.

REFERENCES

1. J. LEWINER, E. CARREEL: "Method and apparatus for measuring the speed of a moving body ", US patent US 5 751 241, May 1998.
2. C. CORBRION, T. DITCHI, S. HOLÉ, E. CARREEL, J. LEWINER, "A broad beam Doppler effect sensor for the measurement of the absolute speed of a vehicle", 8th European Automotive Congress, Bratislava, Slovak republic, june 2001.
3. C. CORBRION, T. DITCHI, E. CARREEL and J. LEWINER, " Procédé et dispositif pour mesurer la vitesse d'un mobile ", French patent, FR 00 06494, 2000.
4. C. CORBRION, " Etude de nouveaux capteurs de vitesse absolue à effet Doppler et à grande ouverture angulaire ", PhD thesis, Université de Paris 6, December 2000.
5. C. CORBRION, T. DITCHI, S. HOLE, E. CARREEL and J. LEWINER, "A broad beam Doppler speed sensor for automotive applications", Sensor Review, Vol. 21, pp. 28-32, January 2001.
6. L.H. ERIKSSON, S. BRODEN: "High Performance Automotive Radar", Microwave Journal, pp.. 24-38, October 1996.
7. P. HEIDE: "Commercial Microwave Sensor Technology: An Emerging Business", Microwave Journal, pp 348-352, May 1999.
8. N. KEES, M. WEINBERGER, J. DETLEFSEN: "Doppler measurement of lateral and longitudinal velocity for automobiles at millimeterwaves", IEEE MTT-S digest, vol. 2, pp. 805-808, June 1993.
9. P. FLANDRIN, "Temps-Fréquence", Ed. Hermes, Paris, 1998.
10. A.C. COPELAND, G. RAVICHANDRAN, and M.M.TRIVEDI, ``Localized Radon Transform-Based Detection of Linear Features in Noisy Images,'' *Proc. IEEE Conf. on Computer Vision and Pattern Recognition*, Seattle, WA, pp. 664-667, June 1994.

CONTACT

Thierry Ditchi, Assistant Professor, Université Pierre et Marie Curie, Laboratoire des Instruments et Systèmes d'Ile de France (LISIF)
Tel: (33) 1 40 79 45 71, thierry.ditchi@espci.fr

Stéphane Holé, Assistant Professor, Université Pierre et Marie Curie, Laboratoire des Instruments et Systèmes d'Ile de France (LISIF)
Tel: (33) 1 40 79 45 71, stephane.hole@espci.fr

Céline Corbrion-Filloy, Assistant Professor, Ecole Supérieure de Physique et de Chimie Industrielles (ESPCI), Laboratoire d'Electricité Générale (LEG)
Tel: (33) 1 40 79 45 91, filloy@optique.espci.fr

Jacques Lewiner, Professor, Ecole Supérieure de Physique et de Chimie Industrielles (ESPCI), Laboratoire d'Electricité Générale (LEG)
Tel: (33) 1 40 79 45 31, jacques.lewiner@espci.fr

2002-01-0820

Millimetre-Wave Automotive Radar Advance Path Measurement

E. G. Hoare, P. S. Hall, R. Hill and S. H. Tsang
University of Birmingham

C. Thompson and S. Fu
Cranfield Univ.

N. Clarke
Jaguar Cars Ltd.

ABSTRACT

Millimetre wave radar sensors are being actively developed for automotive applications including Intelligent Cruise Control (ICC), Collision Warning (CW), and Collision Avoidance (CA). Knowledge of the road geometry is of fundamental importance to these future intelligent automotive systems. The interest in such systems is evidenced by manufacturers now starting to incorporate radars in production luxury vehicles. Determination of the road geometry, day and night, under all weather conditions, is a challenging problem requiring both fundamental research and systems studies.

Current automotive radar systems rely heavily on the use of extrapolating yaw rate data generated within the vehicle to produce a prediction of the path of the road ahead. This use of historical data is only satisfactory if the road trajectory is uniform. Sudden discontinuities in the path, such as bends, cause this method of path prediction to produce significant errors. The ROADAR project has developed algorithms to measure, rather than predict, path trajectory ahead of the host vehicle, based on image processing techniques of the radar return signals. This approach has the benefit of all weather performance and additional high resolution range and velocity data. ROADAR has also quantified the electromagnetic mechanisms responsible for radar reflection at 76 GHz by measuring the complex dielectric constant of samples a variety of different road surfaces and roadside furniture targets.

1 Background

Knowledge of the road geometry, and associated objects such bridges and signs, ahead of a vehicle has been found to be of fundamental importance to future intelligent automotive systems [1,2,3,4]. The intense worldwide drive to incorporate such systems is evidenced not only by manufacturers in the US, Europe and Japan incorporating radars in their vehicles, but also by the increased number of papers offered to journals and conferences concerned with future systems. Determination of the road geometry ahead of the radar equipped vehicle, under all conditions, is a fundamental requirement for effective system operation. This work is part of a Foresight Vehicle Link project collaboration between The University of Birmingham, Cranfield University and Jaguar Cars.

Automotive radars used for intelligent cruise control and collision avoidance are required to detect target vehicles ahead of the radar equipped host vehicle and accurately determine which lane these vehicles occupy. This is achieved by correlating measured target vehicle radar position data with predicted road path data. Vehicle position data measured by the radar can be accurate to ? 0.5 m in range and better than ? 0.3 deg in angle using the best available sensors. Any error in the path prediction immediately introduces errors in apparent lane position of target vehicles, thus determination of both the position of the target vehicle on the carriageway and future road trajectory have been significant parameters for this study.

2 Data collection

Data collection has been undertaken using vehicle mounted, mechanically scanned 76 GHz and 94 GHz radars. The radar characteristics of motorways, highways and urban streets have been recorded for analysis. 94GHz radar measurements have been taken to increase the database of radar signatures at different millimeter wavelengths and to understand if there is any advantage to using higher frequencies. The data collection exercise has also recorded data from the Motor Industry Research Association (MIRA) proving ground at Nuneaton to quantify the radar returns from specific road types, surfaces, road furniture types and objects such as potholes. The position and characteristics of the test track scenes have been measured and recorded to provide correlation with the radar image. This has enabled us to accurately identify and quantify the scatterers that produce road edge and other reflections.

The example shown in Fig.1 is the radar image of four 30 cm diameter in-path pot holes, approximately 75 mm deep, recorded on the MIRA test track. It can be seen that these show up as large targets. Such radar returns may have significant implications for collision warning systems.

3 Off-Line Analysis Of Data For Road Edge Detection Algorithm Development

A novel algorithm for road edge detection has been developed, [5]. The important features are summarised as

?? The algorithm uses thresholding and peak detection for data pre-processing followed by a linear Hough transform and curve fitting and outputs road radius of curvature and distance to either road edge.

?? The algorithm has been demonstrated on single radar frames, multiple frames taken along a 2km stretch of road, and split frames to improve performance in multiple radius scenarios.

Data was obtained from the test vehicle, together with synchronised video to enable correlation. Vehicle yaw rate sensor[6] and GPS data were also recorded.

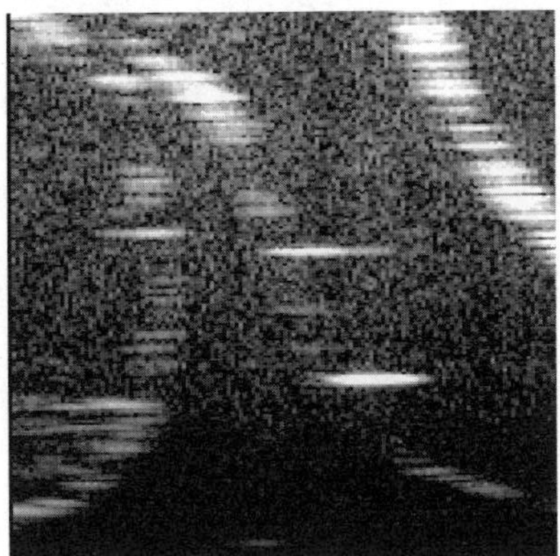

Fig 1. 30cm diameter in-path pot holes on MIRA test track.

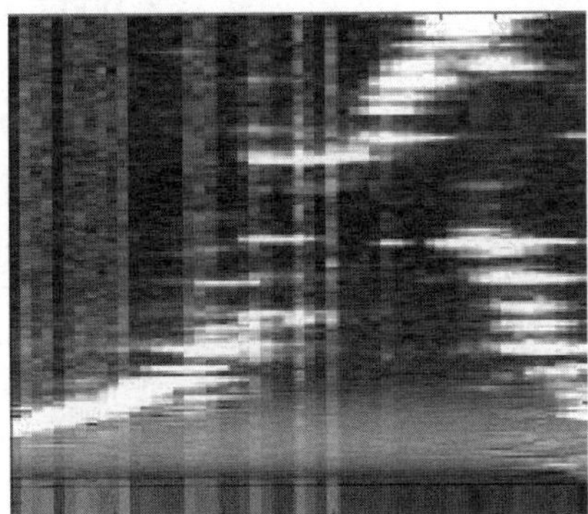

Fig 2. Raw radar image.

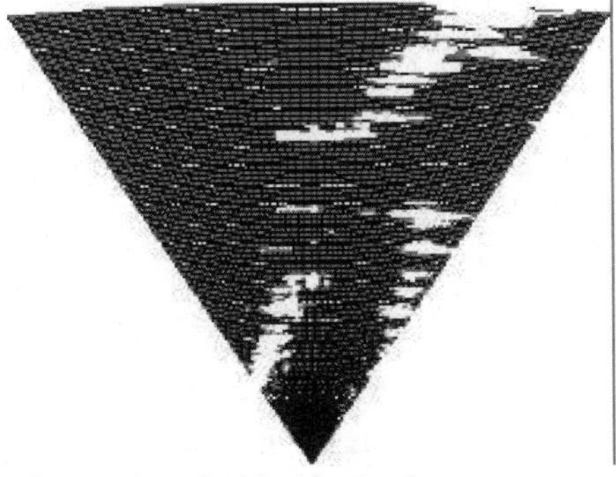

Fig 3. Thresholded radar image.

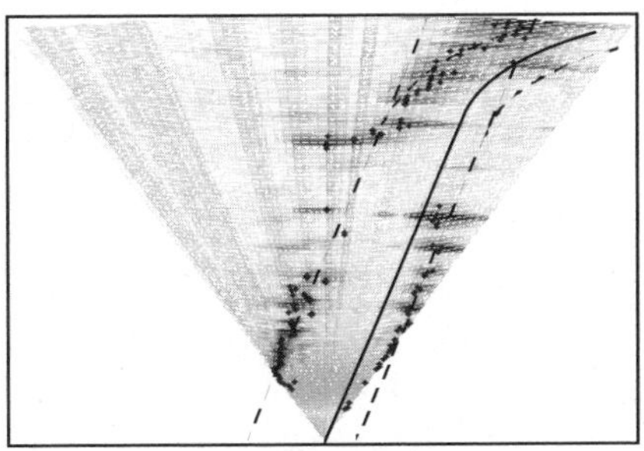

Fig 4. Predicted trajectory

Subsequent correlation with digital map database allowed road radius curvature to be computed from yaw rate, map and radar to compare relative accuracy.

Figs 2,3 and 4 show three stages in the algorithm applied to a single radar frame. The raw data is of a single carriageway road that is initially straight out to approximately 100m and the turns to the right. In this case a split frame process was used and the predicted trajectory indicated the road shape well. Table 1 shows the relative accuracy of the radius of curvature computation for a single frame with full frame processing.

	Radius of curvature
APM	1315.8m
GPS	1357.5m
Digital map	1031.9m
Yaw rate	1428.6m

Table 1. Radius of curvature

When applied to a set of frames taken over a 1.78km stretch of the A46 near the Jaguar Research Centre in Coventry, UK, the results of Fig 5 and 6 were obtained. Fig 5 shows the road boundary offsets compared to those obtained from the video images. Agreement is within 1m and it is clear that the vehicle is in the inner of this two lane carriageway. Fig 6 shows radius of curvature compared to that deduced from the map database. It was found that this measurement was extremely sensitive to the algorithm parameters, in particular, the widths of the peak detectors and the Hough transform windows. Fig 6 was obtained by tuning these for optimum performance frame by frame.

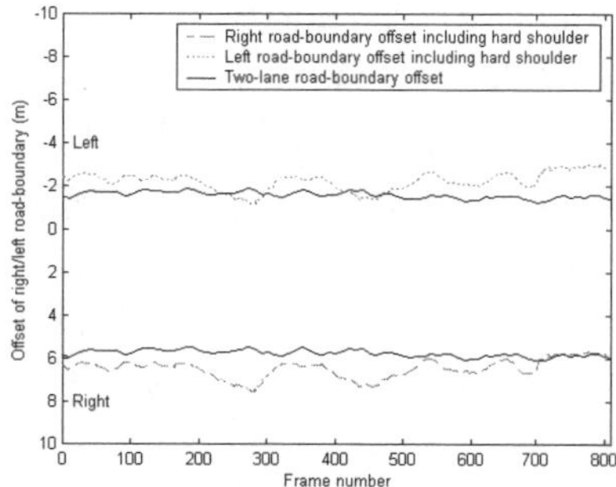

Fig 5. Road boundary offsets. Dotted – radar, solid – video.

However the parameter values show significant correlation with the radius of curvature and it is believed that automatic adaption of the parameters based on the output of the previous frame will provide good results in a real time system.

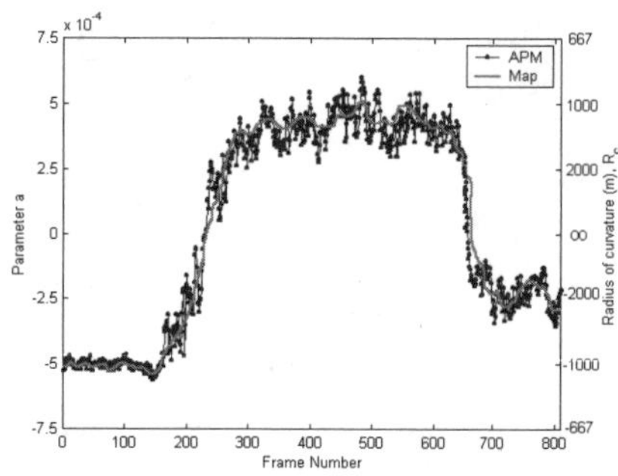

Fig 6 Road radius of curvature, Dotted-radar, solid – map.

4 Off-Line Analysis Of Images For Algorithm Development For Detection Of Other Features

The high level of reflection from the barrier in the central reservation means that significant ghosting from moving targets can take place. Algorithmic procedures were established to allow such ghosts to removed. Fig.7 shows the radar image of a railway bridge, footbridge and truck and car targets, with path data overlaid.

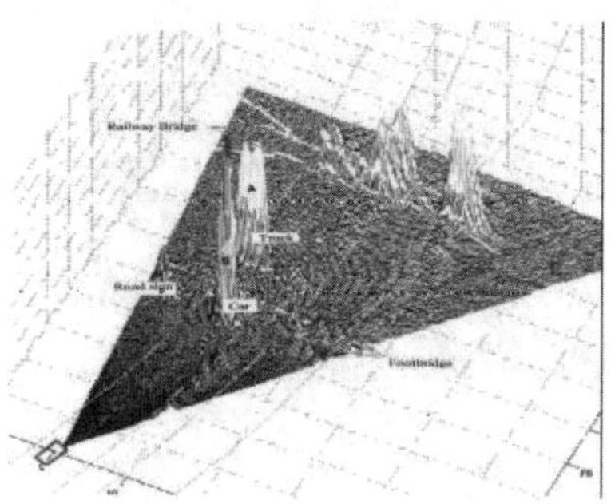

Fig 7 Radar image of railway bridge, footbridge and vehicle targets.

The bridge data shows that at long range a bridge appears as an extended target in azimuth and as the range reduces the passage under the bridge is detected. This occurs at approximately 60m with the antenna parameters used in the experimental radar. Algorithm development has the potential to use this information, in addition to the tracking of targets through the extended bridge reflection to identify the presence of bridges.

5 Algorithms in an Application Demonstrator

Fig.9. shows a video image taken from the test vehicle during a run on the A46. The accompanying image is the combination of the radar data overlaid on a digital map of the same. Host vehicle position is derived from differential GPS. The path prediction is shown in yellow and the two bridges and vehicle targets can be clearly identified.

6 Texture analysis

Under conditions when high reflectivity road infrastructure is absent an alternative processing technique was investigated. The radar data was analysed using texture analysis and region growing using self-organising maps. Data in a high-dimensional feature space were projected into a 2D array of nodes in a neural net in such a way as to maintain spatial relationships present in the data. The features used were small areas of radar image normalised to remove the effects of mean pixel intensity, leaving only textural information. An example of segmentation is shown in Fig 8. This demonstrates that the method can detect "missing" boundaries where the reflectons are weak.

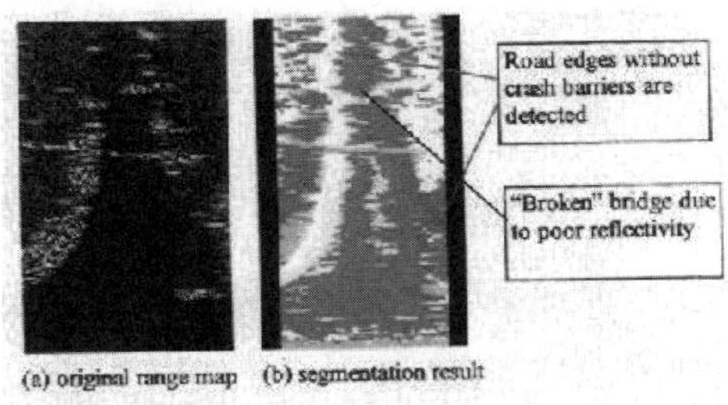

Fig 8. Texture analysis of radar data.

7 Conclusions

Encouraging performance has been obtained from a relatively simple road edge algorithm which is easy to implement and fast in operation. Further work to include adaptive parameter tuning is necessary. The work to characterise returns from other road objects will allow further enhancement of the algorithm. Other work on texture based methods is complimentary and could improve the performance of this type of edge finding algorithm particularly when there are no strong reflectors but merely road material changes at the boundary.

Fig 9 Video and corresponding radar /map image.

8 References

1. F. J. J. Hermans, "Road prediction using video for integrated driver support," *Computing and Control Engineering J.*, pp.169-175, 1999.
2. P. A. Barber and N. J. Clarke, "Advanced collision warning systems," in *IEEE Colloquium (Digest)*, Stevenage, UK, no.234, pp.2/1-2/9, 1998.
3.
4. C. F. Lin and A. G. Ulsoy, "Vehicle dynamics and external disturbance estimation for future vehicle path prediction," in *Proc. of the American Control Conference*, vol.1, pp.155-159, 1995.
5. M. J. Richardson, P. A. Barber, P. King, E. G. Hoare, and D. C. Cooper, "Longitudinal driver supports system," in *IMECHE Autotech-97*, pp.87-97, 1997.
6. S. H. Tsang, E. G. Hoare, P. S. Hall, and N. J. Clarke, "Automotive radar image processing to predict vehicle trajectory," *IEEE International Conf. on Image Processing*, vol.3, pp.867-870, 1999.
7. P. A. Barber, P. King, and M. Richardson, "Road lane trajectory estimation using yaw rate gyroscopes for intelligent vehicle control," *Trans. of the Institute of Meas. and Control*, vol.20, no.2, pp.59-66, 1998.

9 Acknowledgements

The authors wish to acknowledge the contribution made by the following individuals and organisations: Reflecting Roadstuds, Halifax (Cats eyes), Varley & Gulliver, Birmingham. (Crash barrier manufacturers.), Lila Tachtsi & Chris Holt, Civil Eng Dept, Univ of Bham (Ashphalt samples), RMC Aggregates, Bromsgrove. (Tarmac samples)

Figure 7 and Figure 9 courtesy of P. A. Barber and H. Bendafi, Jaguar Research.

10

Contact

Dr E G Hoare
The University of Birmingham,
Edgbaston,
Birmingham B15 2TT, Uk
e.g.hoare@bham.ac.uk

2002-01-0398

Development of Short Range Radar for Automotive Applications

Shigekazu Okamura, Katsuhisa Kodama, Katsuji Matsuoka and Masahira Akasu
Mitsubishi Electric Corporation

ABSTRACT

We have many traffic accidents and related fatalities every year and safety issue is focused very much as well as environmental issue. As for frontal collision, some products of Adaptive Cruise Control (ACC) System and headway distance warning system have been developed and introduced to the market in Japan, U.S, and Europe. In the other hand, the systems to reduce side and rear collision, for example, which assist driver's maneuvers in lane change situation at high speed, are under development. And efforts to make restraint systems such as airbag and seat belt more effective is also needed in order to increase passive safety and reduce related fatalities, for example, smart airbag using additional sensors.

Corresponding to these situations, we made a plan to develop short-range radars for these automotive applications, Blind Spot Detection System (BSD), Parking Aid System (PA), and Pre-crash Detection System (PC). And we developed a prototype pulse radar for a kind of BSD, Side Obstacle Warning System (SOWS), as the first generation of our short-range radar. In this paper, the configuration of this pulse radar is described and test results derived from evaluation tests are shown. Finally, the challenges related to improvement of this radar are discussed.

INTRODUCTION

SHORT-RANGE RADAR AND ITS APPLICATIONS

During the last decade, the many efforts to apply radar technologies to automotive area have been made. As for Long-range radar that has maximum range of above 100m, automobile manufacturers have already introduced Adaptive Cruise Control Systems with millimeter-wave radar to Japanese and European markets.

In the other hand, because there are some challenges for short-range measurement with radar, automobile manufacturers have not introduced applications using short-range radar to the market yet. But some system concepts such as Blind Spot Detection System (BSD), Parking Aid System (PA), Pre-crash Detection System (PC) for Smart Airbag and Stop & Go Application (ACCS) and sensor requirements for these systems are proposed (Table 1). [1]

Table 1. Performance requirements for different short-range radar applications [1]

Item	PA	BSD	ACCS	PC
Distance Range	0.2 ~ 5.0 m	0.2 ~ 5.0 m	0.2 ~ 20 m	0.2 ~ 20 m
Distance Accuracy	0.1 m	0.1 m	0.1 m	0.1 m
Distance Resolution	0.2 m	0.2 m	0.2 m	0.2 m
Relative Speed Range	-40 ~ +40 km/h	-40 ~ +40 km/h	-180 ~ +180 km/h	-180 ~ +180 km/h
Relative Speed Accuracy	4 km/h	4 km/h	2 km/h	2 km/h
Relative Speed Resolution	4 km/h	4 km/h	2 km/h	2 km/h
Measurement Cycle	100 ms	50 ms	30 ms	2 ms

Based on these requirements, we made an application map from the perspective of sensor performance and reliability shown in Figure 1. We added Side Obstacle Warning System (SOWS) in this map, which is our first target application of short-range radar. In the next section, we explain the detail of this system.

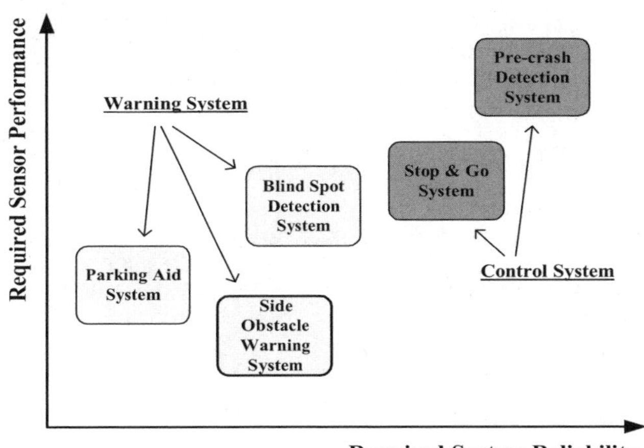

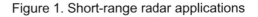

Figure 1. Short-range radar applications

SIDE OBSTACLE WARNING SYSTEM (SOWS)

A Side Obstacle Warning System is intended to supplement the interior and exterior rear-view mirrors, not eliminate the need for such mirrors. The system is intended to detect vehicles to the sides of the subject vehicle (Figure 2). When the subject vehicle driver indicates the desire to make a lane change, the system will evaluate the situation and warn the driver if a lane change is not recommended. The system will not take any automatic action to prevent possible collisions. Responsibility for the safe operation of the vehicle remains with the driver.

This system has three main functions; side obstacle detection and ranging, warning decision, and display and/or beeping.

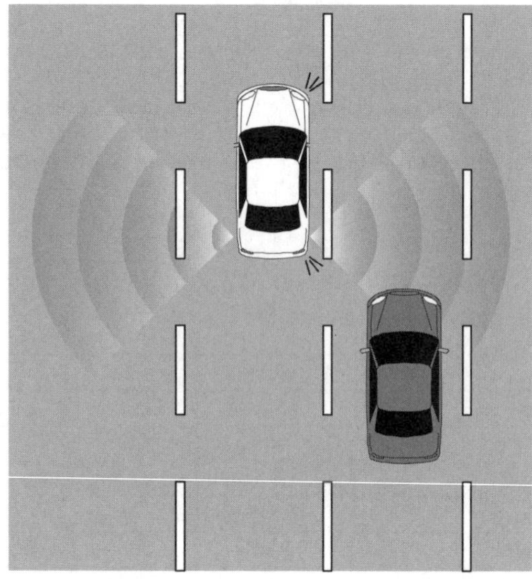

Figure 2. Side Obstacle Warning System

SOWS radars equipped on the both side of the subject vehicle detect a vehicle and measure distance between subject vehicle and obstacles. According to the information from the radars, the system evaluates a situation around the vehicle and decides if warning is necessary or not. Under the danger situation, the system warns the driver using display and /or beeping.

PROTOTYPE RADAR FOR SOWS

Prototype radar for SOWS is a pulse radar using ASK modulation. In this section, we introduce outline of this radar and its hardware structure and show its evaluation test results.

OUTLINE

Figure 3 is a photograph of the prototype radar. Specifications of this radar are summarized in Table 2.

Figure 3. Prototype radar

Table 2. Specification of prototype radar

Item		Specification
Operation Frequency		24.125 GHz
Modulation		Pulse (ASK)
Distance Range		Max. 6 m
Range Accuracy		0.5 m
Beam Angle	Horizontal	- 45 - +45 degrees
	Vertical	- 17 - +17 degrees
Measurement Cycle		50 ms

HARDWARE STRUCTURE

Functional block diagram of the radar is shown in Figure 4.The radar consists of five main parts; a redome, two horn antennas, a signal processing circuit board, and a RF module assembled on rear cover.

We chose horn antennas as transmission and receiving antennas because of their isolation performance. Its radiation pattern in E-plane and H-plane is shown in Figure 5.

The signal processing circuit board has five circuits; power supply circuits, signal amplifiers, a comparator, signal-processing unit with 16bits microprocessor, and single wired CAN communication interface circuit.

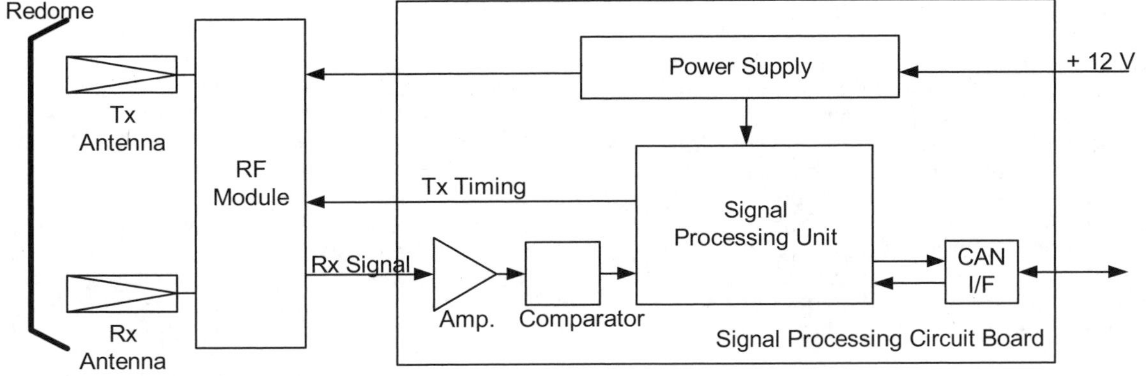

Figure 4. Block Diagram

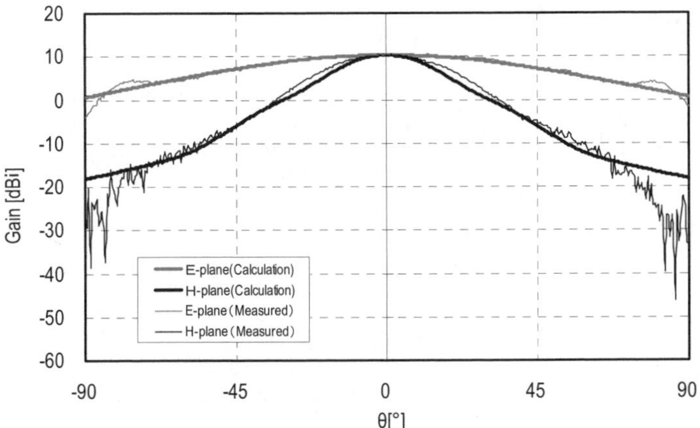

Figure 5. Radiation pattern

The signal-processing unit provides "Tx Timing Signal" to RF module. Using this signal, the RF module performs amplitude modification to the carrier wave of 24.125GHz generated by dielectric resonator and transmits it via horn antenna. Then the reflection wave from surrounding objects is detected and transformed to "Rx Signal" by the envelope detector in the RF module. "Rx Signal" is sent to signal amplifiers and digitized by a comparator. The signal-processing unit reads data from the comparator every pre-determined time and performs detection and ranging procedures.

EVALUATION TESTS AND RESULTS

In order to evaluate basic performance of the prototype radar, we have performed several tests on our probing ground.

Detection Area

At first, we measured maximum range for a corner reflector of 1m^2 RCS at several directions to verify its detection area. The result is shown in Figure 6. At each direction between –30 degrees and +30degrees (30degrees step), maximum range is about 9m or more.

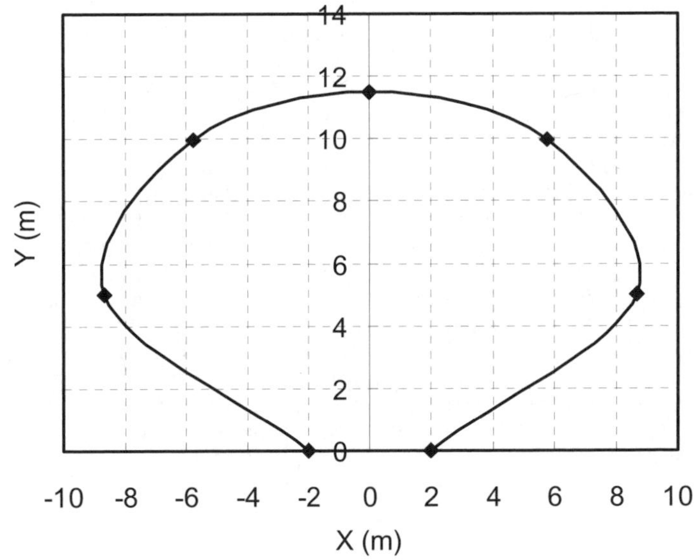

Figure 6. Detection area for corner reflector of 1m^2 RCS

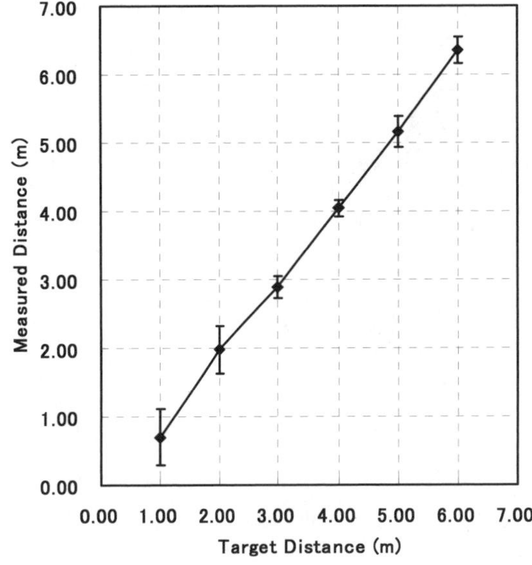

Figure 7. Range accuracy for corner reflector of 1m^2 RCS

Range Accuracy

Next, we carried out measurement of range accuracy for a corner reflector of $1m^2$ RCS in front of the radar. The result is shown in Figure 7. The deviation is below 0.5m at the all measurement point. But there is a trend that the detection range is shorter than the actual distance at the nearer distance. This is influence of the dependence of received signal amplitude on the distance. Because the received signal amplitude becomes small and the rise time of the signal gets long, if a constant threshold level to detect a signal is used, the time when the signal crosses the threshold level gets delayed. This is the first challenge of this radar.

Range-cut and Discrimination

In the usage for SOWS application, the radar is required to make distinction between obstacle on the adjacent lane and on the far side lane. So, we checked the detection range for the target vehicle that runs on the adjacent lane and on the far side lane to verify the performance of the discrimination. We set the radar 0.9 m away from the edge line of the adjacent lane and recorded the detection data from the radar while the target vehicle run on the adjacent and far side lane. The result is shown in Figure 8. Numbers with parenthesis on the right-hand graph of Figure 8 indicate the course on the left-hand figure on Figure 8. As the figure shows, when the target vehicle is around the nearest range, the radar can discriminate the vehicle on the far side lane from on the adjacent lane using range-cut method if appropriate threshold range, which is correspondent to lane width, is set. But when the vehicle is away from nearest range, the detection range is longer than actual range. This is the second challenge.

CHALLENGES

According to the results as described above, there are two challenges related to detection and ranging performance. They are reduction of influence by receiving signal amplitude and reduction of range accuracy dependence on the detection direction.

In addition, there is a challenge based on radar type, interference between radars. In the case of pulse radar like our prototype radar, it is impossible to distinguish the transmission signals from subject radar to ones from other radars theoretically and the radar makes fault detection under the circumstances that there are other radars around the subject radar.

CONCLUSION

We have developed the prototype of SOWS radar, which is a kind of pulse radar as the first generation of our short-range radar. We have also performed the evaluation tests and verified that it has good performance for the SOWS application and some challenges in detection and ranging performance.

In the next step, we will carry out experiments on the road in order to verify the performance of the radar equipped in the vehicle and examine the influences by road components such as guard rail, side wall, and so force. And then, we are going to improve anti-interference performance as well as detection and ranging performance.

REFERENCES

1. M. Klotz, H. Rohling, "A high resolution radar system for parking aid applications", 5th International Conference on Radar Systems, Brest, France, 1999

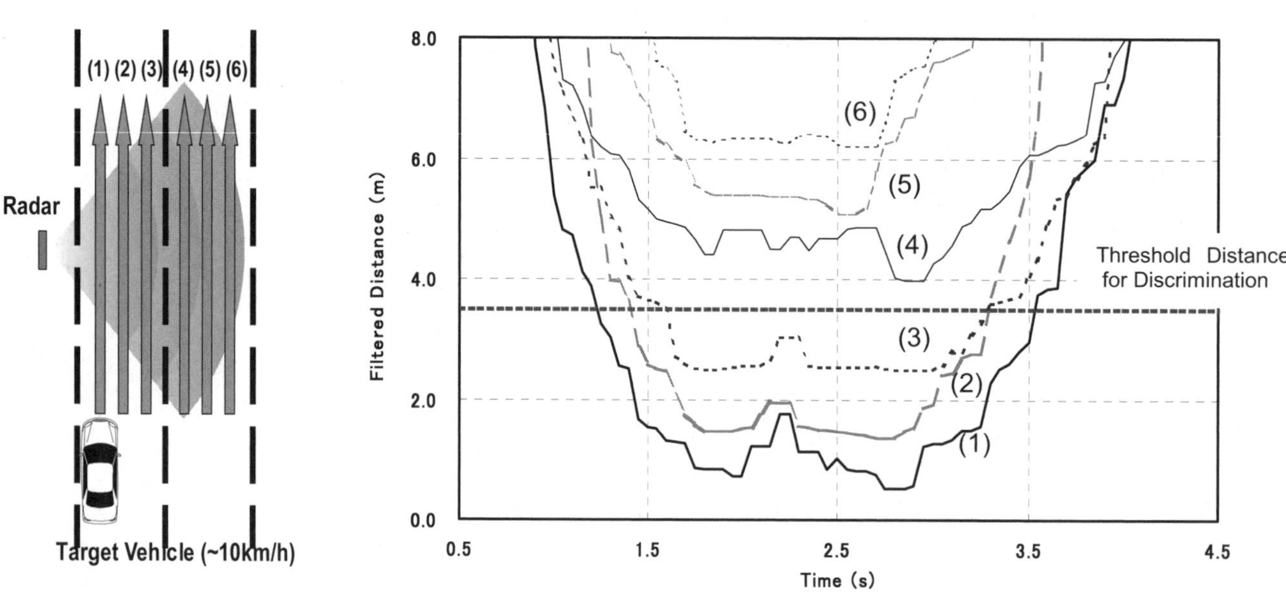

Figure 8. Range-cut and Discrimination

2001-01-0803

High Reliability Collision Avoidance Radar Using FM-Pulse Doppler Method

Naohisa UEHARA, Koichi KAI, Shinichi HONMA, Toshiyuki TAKAHARA and Masahira AKASU
Mitsubishi Electric Corporation, Automotive Electronics Development Center

ABSTRACT

The vehicular collision avoidance millimeter-wave radar that uses an FM-pulse Doppler method is proposed. This radar is constituted with the FM-CW radar method and the pulse Doppler radar method. This radar method has combined the advantages that the precision of the measurements of distance and speed of the target that the FM-CW radar method provides, and the low target mis-recognition probability that the pulse Doppler radar method provides. The millimeter-wave radar using this method was produced using comparatively simple circuits The experimental data that was obtained with this radar and with the FM-CW radar are compared with each other. The effectiveness of the FM-pulse Doppler method was investigated using data obtained from on the road environment using a target vehicle and some objects.

INTRODUCTION

The Millimeter-wave radar suitable for the vehicular collision avoidance system has been developed. This millimeter-wave radar is an indispensable sensor to compose the ACC (adaptive cruise control) system [(1)]. The 76.5GHz millimeter-wave radar for the collision avoidance system measures the distance, the speed, and the direction, to the target vehicles that run forward as well as road obstacles. The millimeter-wave radar has the characteristic by which the target can be detected stably in bad weather like rain and fog compared with the infrared laser sensor. Recently semiconductor technology and electronic circuit technology in a high-frequency band are remarkably advanced. Therefore, a high function and efficient radar sensor can be more easily produced. Thus, the condition to achieve the millimeter-wave radar for the vehicular application has been satisfied. The millimeter-wave radar has been marketed as a sensor of ACC.

It is demanded that the vehicular collision avoidance radar faultlessly detect the position and the speed of the target vehicles. When the millimeter-wave is used for the vehicular radar, it is not avoided that the target detection performance is deteriorated by the clutters, that is, the unnecessary reflection wave interfering from the other obstacles. It is required to decrease this interference to compose the practicable-collision avoidance radar system.

We have developed the vehicular radar system [(2)(3)]. To improve the target-detection reliability of the collision avoidance millimeter-wave radar, we adopted the FM-pulse Doppler method [(4)(5)]. In addition, we produced the millimeter-wave radar system.

In this paper, the FM-pulse Doppler radar method, the trial production of the radar system and some experimental results are mentioned.

RADAR PRINCIPLES

Figure 1 shows the block-diagram of the FM-pulse Doppler radar method. The FM-pulse Doppler radar is called the FMICW (frequency modulated interrupted continuous wave) radar [(4)]. This radar consists of a millimeter-wave-oscillator, a frequency modulator, a pulse modulator, an antenna, a receiving mixer and a signal-processing unit. The millimeter-wave that is oscillated by the millimeter-wave-oscillator is frequency-modulated by the frequency-modulator. This millimeter-wave is pulse-modulated using the pulse-modulator, and radiates through the antenna. The millimeter-wave that is reflected with the target is received to the radar. The received wave is down-converted at the mixer and becomes an IF (intermediate frequency) signal. The amplitudes of the IF signal are sampled at a specific interval time (the "range gate") that is set in the radar system. The sampled signals are arranged in a time series in each specific range gate. The time series of sampled amplitude signals are frequency analyzed, such as a FFT (fast Fourier transform). The distance and the speed of the target are obtained from the analyzed frequency spectrum.

The FM-pulse Doppler radar thus has the advantage over the FM-CW radar method and the pulse Doppler radar method. Moreover, the radar system can complement the mutual faults. The measurement principle of the FM-CW radar and the pulse Doppler radar is shown as follows.

FM-CW RADAR

The FM-CW (frequency modulation continuous wave) radar is a comparatively easy circuit composition. This radar can exactly measure a distance and a relative speed of the target at the same time. Therefore, the FM-CW radar is widely used in the collision avoidance-millimeter-wave radar.

The operation principle of the FM-CW radar is shown in figure 2. The millimeter-wave that has been frequency-modulated is radiated through the antenna. In the receive-mixer, the received signal is mixed with the radiate signal. As a result, the radar obtains the beat signal as an IF signal. This beat signal of frequency *fb* has the information of the time delay caused by the distance between the radar and the target, and the information of the Doppler shift caused by the relative speed of the target.

A distance and a relative speed of the target are obtained as follows.

1. Two FM waveforms (linearly frequency-modulated waves) with different time-frequency relationship are alternately radiated from the radar.
2. Two kinds of beat signals obtained from the received reflection wave from the same target and the radiation wave are frequency-analyzed.
3. A distance and a relative speed of the target are obtained from the combination operation of two beat frequencies, that is, *fb1* and *fb2*.

In the example of Figure 2, the radar radiates two FM waveforms alternately. The one is the "up-chirp" wave (positive time-frequency relationship) and the other is the "down-chirp" wave (negative time-frequency relationship).

The distance *R* and the relative speed *V* of the target are obtained by operating the combination of the beat signals obtained from the above.

$$R = \frac{(f_{b1} + f_{b2})c}{8 f_m \Delta f} \qquad (1)$$

$$V = \frac{(f_{b2} - f_{b1})c}{4 f_0} \qquad (2)$$

where, *c* is the speed of light, *1/fm* is the period of the frequency modulation, Δf is the frequency deviation and *f0* is the center frequency.

Figure 2(a) shows the case that the relative speed of the target is zero. The frequency *fb1* and *fb2* of the beat signals obtained from two kinds of chirp waves are equal. Figure 2(b) shows the case that the relative speed of the target is not zero. In this case, because of the Doppler effect, the frequency *fb1* and *fb2* of the beat signals are different. In either case, the operation procedure for the distance and the speed of the target is the same.

Then, using the FM-CW radar, the distance and the relative speed of the target are obtained at the same time by radiating two kinds of chirp waves and signal-processing two kinds of reflection waves from the same target. On the other hand, when two or more targets and objects exist, the beat signals obtained from them are observed over many frequencies, at the same time. Therefore, the wrong combination of the beat frequencies that obtained using both chirp-waves of the same target, causes mis-recognition of the targets. It is important to combine pairs of the beat signals faultlessly to decrease the mis-recognition of the targets.

PULSE DOPPLER RADAR

The operation principle of the pulse Doppler radar is explained. Figure 3 shows the procedure of the pulse Doppler radar. The millimeter-wave that has been pulse-modulated and its width is τ is radiated through the antenna. The reflected wave at the target is received at the radar, which is involved in the time delay corresponding to the distance from the target. After radiating the millimeter-wave, the radar receives the reflection wave in order time in each time-divided window that width is *tg*. The window of time width *tg* is called a "range gate". For a specific range gate, only the data of the target that exists in distance ΔR, which corresponds to the time Δt, will be received. The distance *R* of the target is given by

$$R = \frac{c\Delta t}{2} \qquad (3).$$

The relative speed of the target is obtained as follows.

1. For a specific range gate, the beat signal is obtained from the reflection wave received from the target and the radiation wave. The amplitude of the beat signal is sampled.
2. Many sampled data are arranged in the time order.
3. This time series sampling data is frequency-analyzed, such as a Fast Fourier Transformation.
4. The signal frequency *fb* obtained on the frequency domain is a Doppler frequency which originates at a relative speed of the target.

The relative speed *V* of the target is given by

$$V = \frac{2 f_0}{c f_b} \qquad (4).$$

Thus, using the pulse Doppler radar can obtain the data of a distance and a relative speed of the target, in each range gate. Therefore, the pulse Doppler radar has low probability of the mis-recognition of the target when plural targets and objects exist. The radar radiates the pulsed wave. Accordingly, when the signal is received, the radar stops the radiation of the millimeter-wave.

Therefore, it is suppressed that the radiated millimeter-wave is directly received to the receiver. As a result, this radar can share the radiation antenna and the reception antenna without saturating the receiver.

As for the pulse Doppler radar, the target range resolution, that is, the unit of the output of the range is the distance that corresponds to the range gate. To obtain a practicable target range resolution as the vehicular collision avoidance radar, the radiation pulse width and the width of the range gate should be narrowed. Using present millimeter-wave technology and signal-processing technology, it is difficult to fill this condition with a simple and low-priced circuit. Moreover, the pulse Doppler radar is inferior to the FM-CW radar concerning interference with other similar radar.

FM-PULSE DOPPLER RADAR

We adopted the FM-pulse Doppler radar as the vehicular collision avoidance radar. This aims to improve the detection reliability of the target.

As shown in figure 1, this radar radiates the millimeter-wave that is frequency-modulated and pulsed. The reflection wave from the target is influenced by the Doppler shift caused by a relative speed of the target, and the time delay corresponding to the distance of the target. In every range gate, the radar obtains the beat signals of these received waves and the radiated waves. The width at the range gate is chosen to be a length of the target vehicle. Only the reflection wave from the target that nearly corresponds to one vehicle will be included in the signal observed at a specific range gate. Therefore, the FM-pulse Doppler radar can decrease the mistaken combination of the beat frequency. As a result, even if plural targets and objects exist, the mis-recognition of the target can be decreased. When the reflection wave from the target is received, the radar stops radiating the millimeter-wave. Then, the FM-pulse Doppler radar can decrease interference in the receiver of the radiation wave. Therefore, this radar can improve deterioration in the radar detection performance. In addition, this radar can obtain a practicable range resolution as vehicular collision avoidance by processing the signal that is in the same range gate, same as the FM-CW radar. Thus, the FM-pulse Doppler radar has the advantage of the FM-CW radar and the pulse Doppler radar. It can complement the fault of each other. This is an appropriate radar for the vehicular collision avoidance system.

OUTLINE OF THE TRIAL PRODUCT

We produced the radar system using the FM-pulse Doppler method. Figure 4 shows the radar head. This radar is composed of an antenna, an RF (radio frequency) circuit, a signal processing unit and a power supply circuit. The RF circuit can compose comparatively easily by adding the pulse generator and the RF switch for the pulse modulation to the RF circuit of the FM-CW radar. The size of this radar head is 114mm width, 92mm height and 83mm depth, and the mass is 0.65kg. This radar head can output a position (distance and direction) and a relative speed of two or more target vehicles.

EXPERIMENTAL RESULT

We produced the vehicular collision avoidance millimeter-wave radar system that used the above-mentioned radar head and installed the system in a vehicle. We then measured the target detection performance and recorded the data as follows.

Using the FM-CW radar and the FM-pulse Doppler radar, the targets on the road were observed respectively. As targets, one vehicle and two or more metallic poles were placed in front of the radars at an arbitrary distance. The beat signals that had been obtained by the observation were frequency-analyzed. The frequency spectra obtained from both radars respectively were then compared.

Figure 5(a) and (b) show the obtained frequency spectra. Figure 5(a) shows the spectrum of the FM-CW radar. Two or more signals caused with a target vehicle and some metallic poles are observed at the same spectrum. It is difficult to select the target-vehicle signal from these signals. Figure 5(b) shows the spectrum of the FM-pulse Doppler radar. This spectrum shows the signal at the range gate that corresponds to the distance where the target vehicle exists. In this case, only the signal from the target vehicle is obtained. The metallic poles are at a distance that is different from the target vehicle. So, the signals from metallic poles are observed at a different range gate than the range gate where the target vehicle is observed. Therefore, only the signal of the vehicle is in the spectrum at the range gate with the target vehicle. A target distance and relative speed are obtained by combining and operating the beat frequencies obtained from two kinds of the chirp-waves and observed at the same range gate. The FM-pulse Doppler radar has distance measurement and speed measurement performances equal with the FM-CW radar and can decrease the mis-recognition of the target. Therefore, the FM-pulse Doppler radar is an appropriate method of the vehicular collision avoidance millimeter-wave radar

CONCLUSION

The millimeter-wave radar using an FM-pulse Doppler method is proposed. It is shown that this radar is useful as the vehicular collision avoidance millimeter-wave radar system according to the measurement data. The FM-pulse Doppler radar can measure precisely a target distance and a relative speed. This type of radar can diminish the target mis-recognition probability. Therefore, the FM-pulse Doppler radar can be used for not only the vehicular collision avoidance radar system to warn of vehicles forward but also the cruise control system of the vehicle.

REFERENCES

1. H. H. Meinel, "Millimeterwaves for automotive applications," Proc. of 26th European Microwave Conference, pp.830-835, 1996.
2. S. Honma, T. Takahara, M. Akasu and S. Sato, "Offset Paraboloidal reflector Antenna for Vehicular Collision Avoidance Radar," SAE International Congress and Exposition, 1999-01-1237, 1999.
3. S. Honma, T. Takahara, M. Akasu and S. Sato, "Offset Paraboloidal reflector Antenna for Millimeter-Wave Radar," Seoul 2000 FISITA World Automotive Congress, F2000I408, 2000.
4. R. H. Khan and D. K. Mitchell, "Waveform Analysis for High-Frequency FMICW Radar," IEE Proc.-F, Vol. 138, No.5, pp. 411-419, October 1991.
5. F. E. Nathanson, Radar Design Principles, McGRAW-HILL BOOK, New York, 1969.

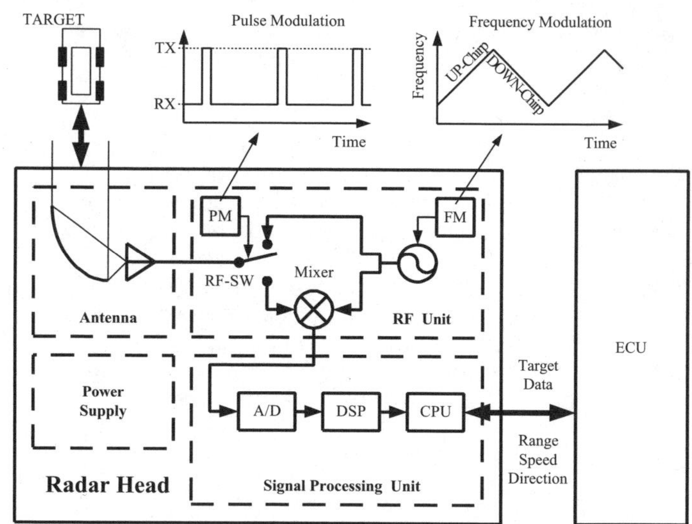

Figure 1 FM-pulse Doppler radar system

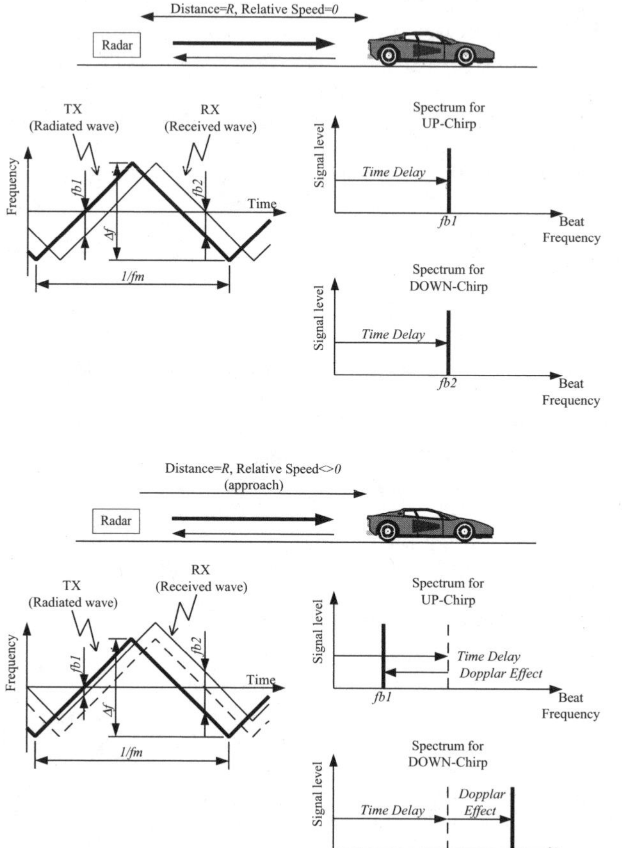

Figure 2 Signal processing of FM-CW radar system (a) Relative speed=0, (b) Relative speed<>0 (Approaching)

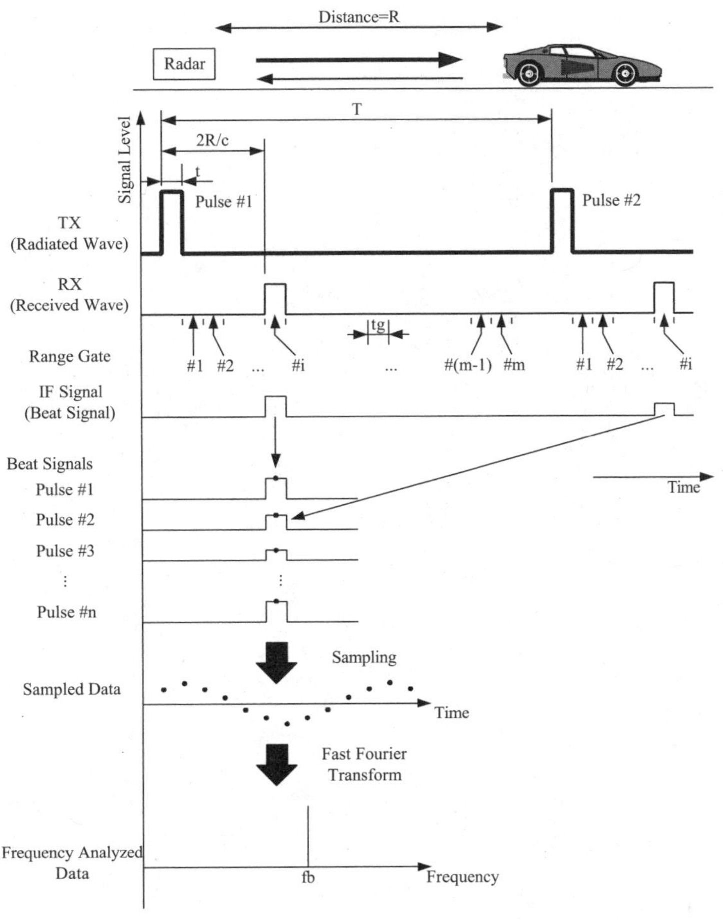

Figure 3 Signal processing of pulse Doppler radar system

Figure 4 FM-pulse Doppler radar head (Trial product)

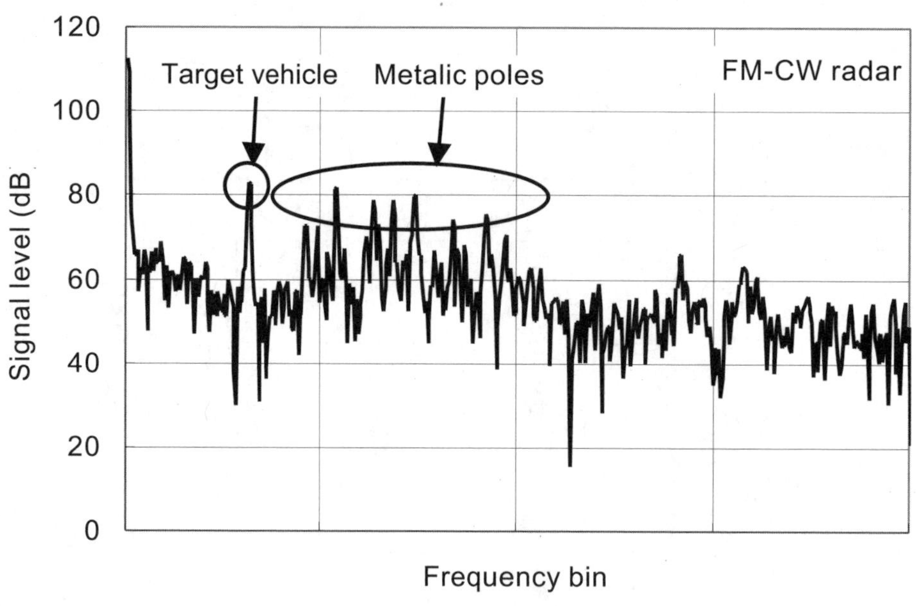

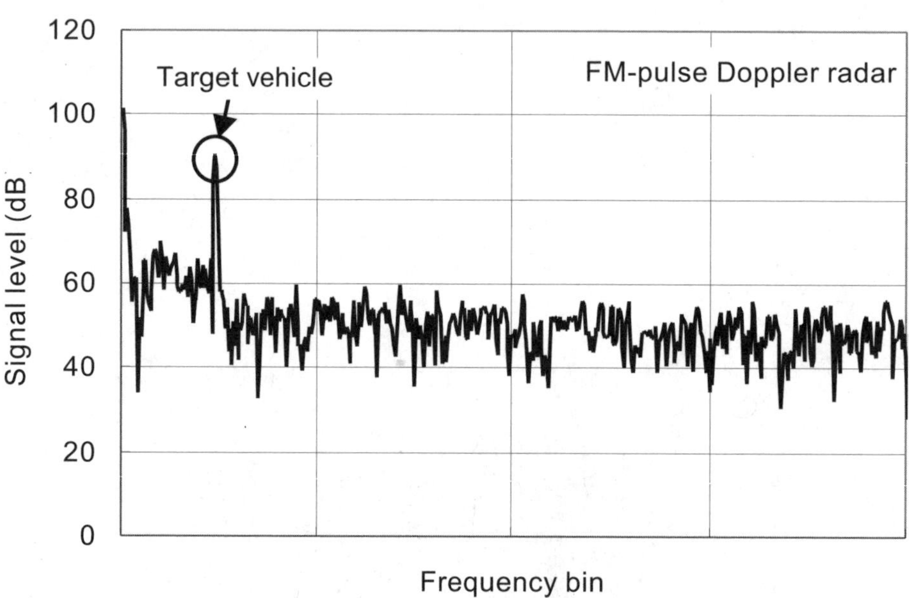

Figure 5 Spectra of the targets (Experimental results) (a) FM-CW radar, (b) FM-pulse Doppler radar

2001-01-0800

Fusion Sensor for an Assist System for Low Speed in Traffic Congestion Using Millimeter-Wave Radar and an Image Recognition Sensor

Hirofumi Higashida, Ryuichi Nakamura, Masaki Hitotsuya, Kanako F Honda and Nobukazu Shima
Fujitsu Ten Ltd.

ABSTRACT

A traffic congestion support system is one of the remarkable driving safety features in ITS (Intelligent Transport Systems) technology. We have developed a fusion sensor, combining a millimeter-wave radar and a stereo camera, for use as a forward recognition sensor that is an integral part of the system. The fusion sensor is introduced below.

INTRODUCTION

The recent increase in demand for greater driving safety has encouraged many ITS development efforts, some of which have already resulted in commercial products. One of the most remarkable and promising features of ITS technology is the traffic congestion support system that reduces the driver's burden and prevents rear-end collisions on congested roads. Such a system is not possible without a forward recognition sensor, which represents a critical sensing technology. We succeeded in developing a forward recognition sensor combining a millimeter-wave radar and stereo vision recognition technologies.

TRAFFIC CONGESTION SUPPORT SYSTEM

SYSTEM OPERATION - We will present the basic concept of the system before explaining the system's operation. An application called STOP&GO, an extension of the existing ACC, is commonly considered for supporting driving safety in ITS. However, automatically starting a vehicle from zero and stopping it when it runs at high speed involves some technical problems. It is also likely to require special awareness on the part of the average driver. In other words, such an application is likely to be misunderstood by drivers as automated driving, and this tendency increases as higher technologies are involved.

To preclude this type of misunderstanding, we believe the driver himself or herself should always be in control of the car, and that the driver must have the discrete option of engaging and disengaging a support system.

Figure 1 shows this concept in terms of the vehicle's function and the scope of control.

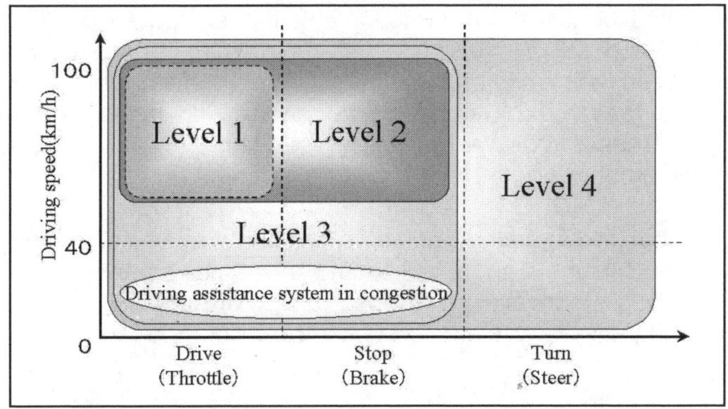

Figure 1. Positioning of driving safety support system

Level 1 or Level 2 applies to the existing ACC while STOP&GO is thought to correlate to Level 3. Level 4, if ever realized, would represent automated driving.

As mentioned above, however, many technical problems need to be resolved before Level 3 can be achieved. In addition, a product based on this level will not be accepted in the market if it is held responsible for accidents and other mishaps.

Under these circumstances, our development efforts were based on a system specialized to reduce the driver's burden in traffic congestion by limiting control to a range from a vehicle speed of 0 km/h to a given upper limit (for example 20 km/h).

Figure 2 shows the typical operation of our system.

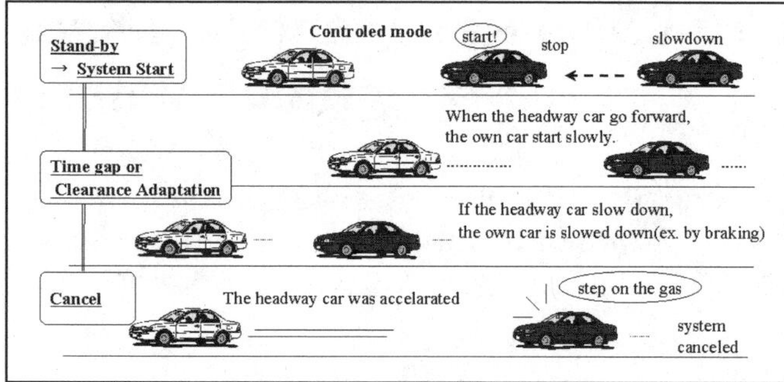

Figure 2. Typical system operation

Control is introduced by operation of the driver's switch when the vehicle speed is zero and a forward obstacle is detected.

Once control is introduced, and the distance from the forward car is clear, the vehicle runs up to the upper speed limit while maintaining a minimum distance. When the forward car stops, for example, and the distance decreases, the brakes are engaged and the vehicle stops automatically.

When the forward car starts and the distance is clear, the vehicle runs without exceeding the upper control speed limit. The driver may choose to operate the accelerator and the system shifts to the control quit mode.

SYSTEM CONFIGURATION - Figure 3 shows the system configuration.

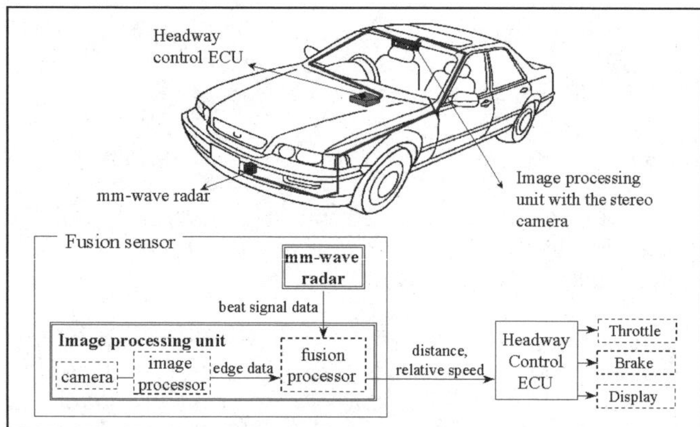

Figure 3. System configuration

This system is configured with a sensing block consisting of a millimeter-wave radar, CMOS sensor stereo camera, a signal and image processor, a control ECU and actuators that control the engine throttle and brakes. Only the sensing block is introduced in this report.

PURPOSE OF DEVELOPMENT OF THE FORWARD RECOGNITION SENSOR - The following functions are considered necessary for a sensor in the traffic congestion support system:

- Range of detection: A wide angle of detection within a near distance
- Distance accuracy: Accuracy equal to or better than that of the ACC
- Speed accuracy: Accuracy equal to that of the ACC
- Positional accuracy: High accuracy to detect edges of an obstacle
- Obstacle detection: Detection not only of vehicles and motorbikes, but also pedestrians and bicycles

We realized that two or more sensors had to be combined to meet the above requirements, and this concept led to the development of a fusion sensor combining a scan type millimeter-wave radar and a stereo camera.

We chose a millimeter-wave radar because it can detect obstacles of any kind having a minimum dielectric constant in any weather, and can be used directly as the conventional ACC sensor. We chose a stereo camera because it offers the highest cost performance as a sensor with a wide range of detection and high degree of accuracy in detecting the edges of obstacles.

FUSION SENSOR CONCEPT

CONCEPT OF DATA FUSION - One of the essential issues in the development of a fusion sensor is attaining the lowest possible cost. Using several sensors may ensure very high performance, but will not be acceptable commercially if the cost is high.

Figure 4 shows our concept of data fusion.

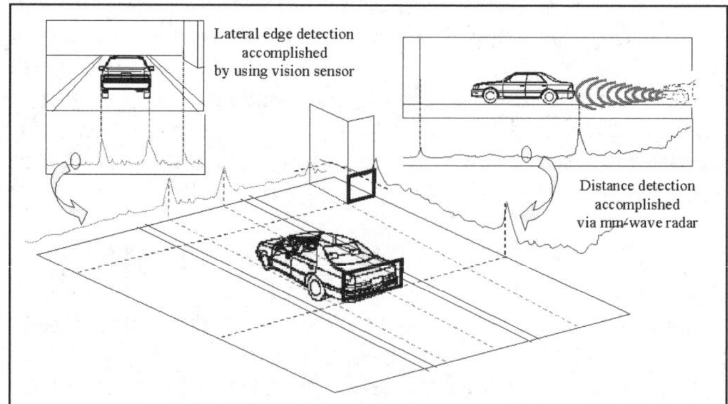

Figure 4. Concept of data fusion

Conventional vision sensors were designed for two-dimensional (and sometimes three-dimensional) detection of an obstacle from the forward view. The data were used to determine the distance, side positions, speed, and even the direction of travel. This required very accurate cameras and lenses as well as fast processing devices. Consequently, costs were high, and there have been few efforts which have led to control sensors for commercial use.

We attempted to use a vision sensor only for detecting the vertical edges, in order to determine the side position, and then to fuse the obtained data with distance information taken from a millimeter-wave radar in order to detect the position of an obstacle.

In this way, we managed to substantially reduce the required accuracy of detection of the vision sensor. The result is a low cost sensor for use in a traffic congestion support system.

MAIN FEATURES AND TARGET SPECIFICATIONS OF THE MILLIMETER-WAVE RADAR - For the millimeter-wave radar, we decided to rely on the specifications from the conventional product designed for the ACC system rather than developing new ones. This makes it possible to deploy a traffic congestion support system by simply adding a stereo camera and an image processing ECU to the existing ACC system. We believe this provides users more options.

An FM-CW type millimeter-wave radar was chosen for our purpose since the distance to the obstacle and the relative speed can be detected instantly, whether the obstacle is moving or still. The mechanical scan of the antenna also makes it possible to detect other vehicles in adjacent lanes at sharp curves.

Table 1 shows the main specifications of the millimeter-wave radar.

Table 1. Specifications of the millimeter-wave radar

Item		Condition	Specification
Longitudinal range		Target: 10dBsm, corner reflector on asphalt road at normal temperature	5m to 140m
Object recognition			2m to 5m, reported by flag
Azimuth angle			16 deg.
Relative speed			-100km/h to +200km/h
Accuracy	Distance		±1m or ±5%, whichever is larger
	Angle		±0.5 deg.
	Relative Speed		±5.5km/h or ±5%, whichever is larger

MAIN FEATURES AND SPECIFICATIONS OF THE VISION SENSOR - Table 2 shows the specifications of the vision sensor.

Table 2. Specifications of the vision sensor

	Item		Specification
Camera	No. of pixels		640x480 (black/white)
	Interface		Digital
	Angular field of view		40 deg.
ECU	Recognition cycle		100 msec
	Obstacle detection		Vertical edge of the closest end to the forward car
	Accuracy	Distance	±20% (2-12m)
		Angle	±1.0 deg.
	Shape and structure		Integrated camera and ECU (planned for future)

We combined the vision sensor with the high distance accuracy millimeter-wave radar to meet the necessity for ease of installation, low cost, and high ranging performance. The vision sensor contains a horizontal stereo camera using CMOS image sensors placed 200mm apart from each other for installation behind the rear view mirror. The stereo camera and the ECU are separated at the present, although they will be integrated in the future. Figure 5 shows the developed vision sensor.

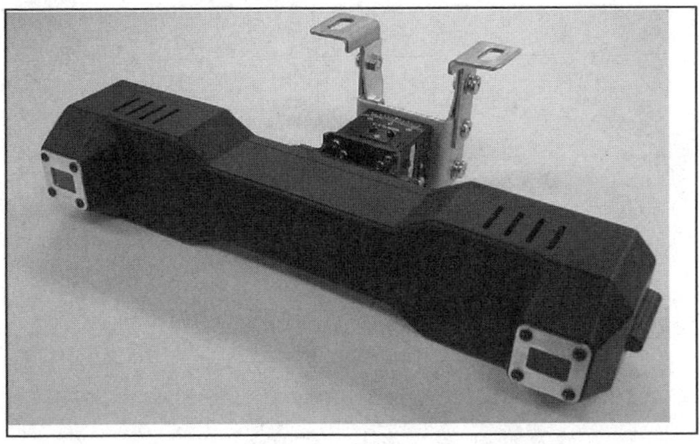

Figure 5. Developed vision sensor

We used a common correlation operation method for distance measurement, but we made special efforts to reduce the processing burden of the CPU as much as possible by pattern matching pictures from the two image sensors, showing the vicinity of large edges, extracted by filtering (see Figure 6). The sensor also features logics such as camera shutter speed control and gain control for optimum imaging, night and day judgment and discrimination between the road surface and three-dimensional obstacles for higher recognition performance, as well as a fail-safe feature for determining non-recognition conditions.

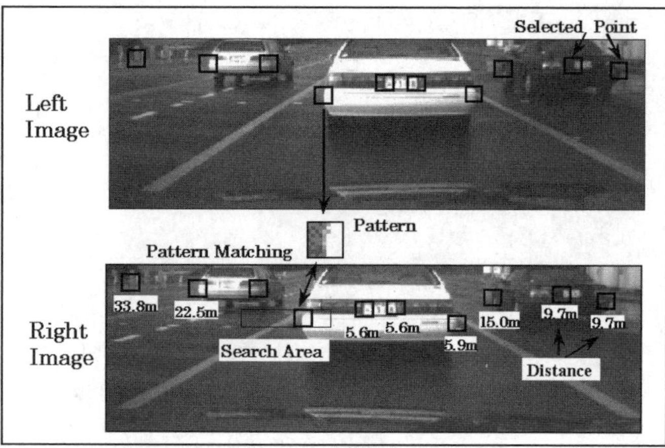

Figure 6. Matching method

SPECIFICATIONS OF THE FUSION SENSOR - Table 3 shows the specifications of the fusion sensor.

Table 3. Fusion sensor specifications

The following specifications must be met in the vehicle's own lane, as shown below:

Item	Distance accuracy	Relative speed accuracy	Cut-in response	Obstacle detection
Specification	±20% or±2m (whichever is larger)	±2km/h	Less than 500msec	Distance and speed of the obstacle edge to own car's center in the control area

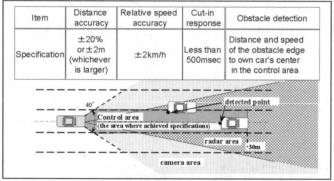

40°
Control area
(the area where achieved specifications)
detected point
radar area
30m
camera area

The distance, speed, angle, and response accuracy of the sensor was set such that the vehicle can slow down at the maximum decelerating speed. The accuracy was also chosen such that the G fluctuation of deceleration would not be uncomfortable to the driver.

The sensor output method varies by the specific area of an obstacle to be controlled. The output data of the fusion sensor is limited to the single target selected last. For the purpose of our system, we decided that the distance to and speed of a single point, closest to and in front of the moving vehicle, were all that were necessary.

CONTENT OF DEVELOPMENT - The data fusion technique is presented below.

As explained in the section on the data fusion concept, the distance and lateral position (angle) of the vertical edges of the obstacle are supplied from the stereo camera, while the distance and the angle of the estimated center of the obstacle are received from the millimeter-wave radar. In reality, the millimeter-wave radar supplies the reflected power information for every beam detected by scanning. Figure 7 shows the method of calculating the position and the size of an obstacle from the received data. As shown, the power of the millimeter-wave radar near each vertical edge is integrated to calculate the probabilities of obstacles existing on the right and left sides of the vertical edge. When there is a significant difference in the probabilities between the both sides of a given vertical edge, that edge is assumed to be an edge of an obstacle and its shape is determined accordingly. Then, the likelihood of the shape of the obstacle is studied in a time series analysis. Once the shape is established, complement is used as needed, even if the camera failed to capture a vertical edge, so that detection can be performed without interruption.

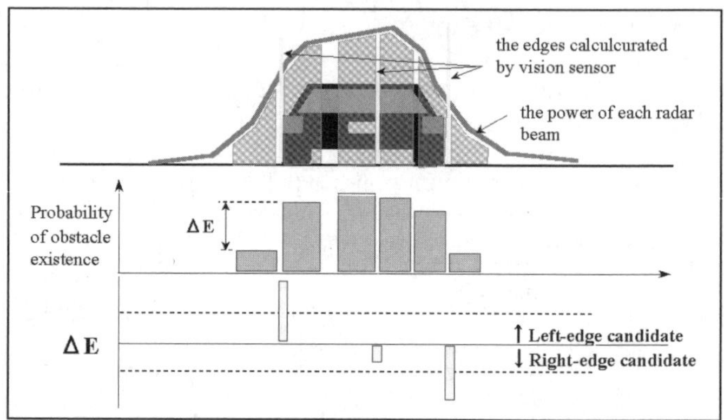

Figure 7. Data fusion technique

EVALUATION RESULTS

RESULT OF QUANTITATIVE EVALUATION OF THE FUSION SENSOR - Figure 8, 9 shows the result of quantitative evaluation of the fusion sensor.

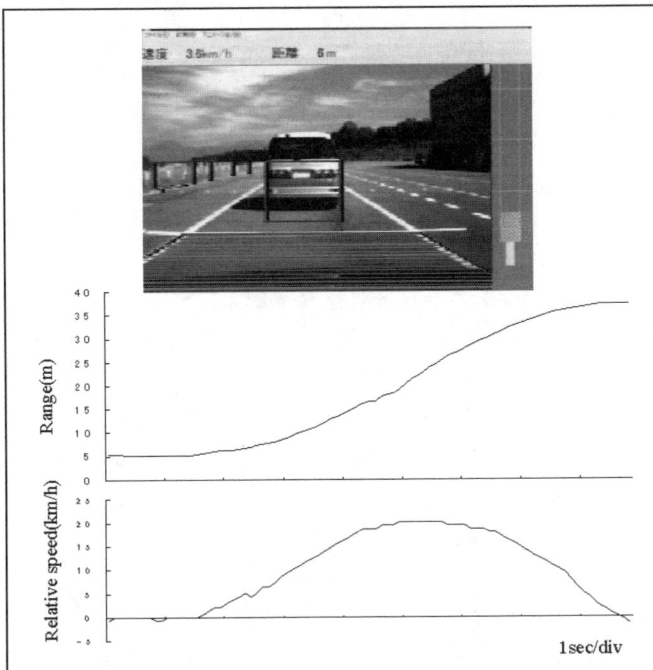

Figure 8. Example of the result of recognition for a departing vehicle

Figure 9. Picture showing vehicle detection by the fusion sensor

RESULT OF ON-BOARD EVALUATION AS A TRAFFIC CONGESTION SUPPORT SYSTEM - Figure 10 shows an example of the result of on-board evaluation of the system.

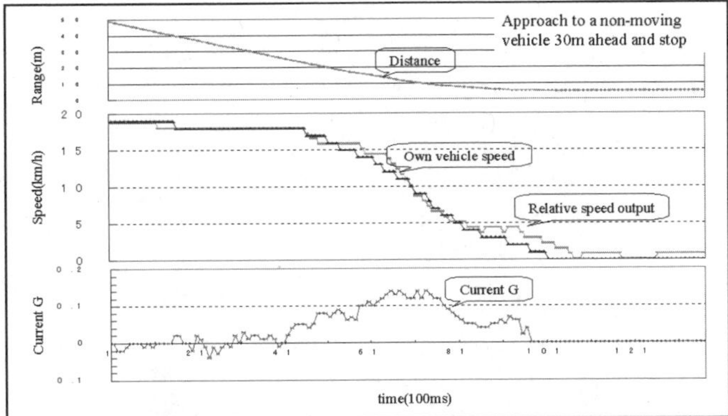

Figure 10. Example of the result of on-board evaluation of the system (deceleration relative to a non-moving vehicle)

CONCLUSION

A forward recognition sensor was developed for use in a traffic congestion support system that is drawing considerable attention as a post-ACC driving safety support application. The sensor uses the millimeter-wave radar from the ACC so that the existing application can be upgraded with the addition of a stereo vision camera, requiring only a minimum cost increase. The new system also reduces the post-processing burden, since only a single point is selected for control in the direction of travel.

The sensor was integrated in a traffic congestion support system for testing purposes and proved to be adequately effective. We believe higher performance can be achieved by further improving the response of the actuators and other components.

REFERENCES

1. K.Fujimura, M.Hitotsuya, S.Yamano, H.Higashida, “76GHz Automotive Radar for ACC”, 6th ITS World Congress, No.3118(1999)
2. M.Hitotsuya, K.Fujimura, S.Yamano, H.Higashida, “Practical Approaches to the Automotive Millimeter-Wave Radar”, Convergence ‘98, SAE Paper No. 98C042 (1998)

1999-01-2923

76 GHz Automotive Millimeter-wave Radar Using Spread Spectrum Technique

Hiroshi Endo, Yasushi Aoyagi, Toshihide Fukuchi, Hiroaki Takahashi, Yoichi Iso, Kiyoshi Inoue and Haruhiko Ishizu
The Furukawa Electric Co., Ltd.

Ryuji Kohno
Yokohama National University

ABSTRACT

Automotive radar is one of the most important key technologies in sensors for Intelligent Transport Systems (ITS). It is considered very important to conduct analysis of the results which the radar took under various road conditions. In this paper, we shall report the results of a 76GHz automotive millimeter-wave radar using SS modulation technique, which were evaluated on roads under various situations. For example, multi-path was observed from the results that were analyzed from inside a tunnel. We believe that the results are very useful for development of the object discrimination algorithm.

INTRODUCTION

Intelligent Transport Systems (ITS) are under development worldwide as a means of reducing loss of life and limiting economic and environmental costs. Of the technologies used in ITS, millimeter-wave radar is an important element, and the preparations for legalizing it, including frequency assignment ,have already begun in Japan, USA and Europe. It has attracted attention as a replacement for infrared laser radar currently in use, since its performance is unaffected by weather. Automotive millimeter-wave radars are utilized for Collision Warning Systems, Adaptive Cruise Control (ACC) Systems and Automated Driving Systems [1], and we are expecting them to be adapted for further performances. In the case of ACC, it has been required to correctly detect a target located in the same lane as the radar equipped vehicle. Particularly if we correctly detect objects in complicated road environments, the development of a superior algorithm has been necessitated. Thus, it is extremely important to study millimeter-wave propagation characteristics in complicated road situations.

In this paper, we shall report on the data analyzed from the received signals in complicated road situations for 76 GHz millimeter-wave radar using SS technique.

AUTOMOTIVE MILLIMETER-WAVE RADAR USING SPREAD SPECTRUM (SS) TECHNIQUE

THE PRINCIPLE AND FEATURES OF SS RADAR – Fig. 1 shows the principle of measurement of SS radar. In SS radar, transmission signals are modulated using PN codes, and then transmitted through the transmission antenna. The signal reflected from a target located ahead of the radar equipped vehicle has a time delay that corresponds with the two-way range delay, the doppler shift corresponds with the range rate between the radar equipped vehicle and a target ahead; and that signal that is received by the reception antenna. The PN sequences have an auto-correlation function as shown in Fig. 1 [2]. Utilizing these characteristics, SS radar can measure range from the phase difference of PN sequences. The range rate can be measured by frequency analysis when the correlation peak is detected. In this method, accurate ranging and multiple target separation are possible due to the detection method using the auto-correlation characteristics of PN sequences. Moreover, SS modulation has excellent interference capabilities since the demodulation process using PN sequence spreads undesired signals or interference in the channel and thus suppresses those signals.

If we considered the automotive radar based on the reasons mentioned above, the SS method has superior features compared with FMCW radar in the following;

- Accurate ranging is possible,
- Multiple target separation is possible;
- Interference suppression has good capabilities.

Additionally it has been reported that it is easier to develop a millimeter-wave oscillator for the SS method than that of the FMCW method since compensation is provided by the reception down-convert mixer in the SS method [3].

For the features mentioned above, we have developed automotive millimeter-wave radar using the SS method [4]-[8].

THE PROTOTYPE CONFIGURATIONS AND SPECIFICATIONS – Table 1 shows the specifications of the prototype radar and Fig. 2 shows the hardware configurations. Our prototype radar consists of antennas, millimeter-wave circuits, IF circuits and signal processing circuits.

Table 1. Radar Specifications

Modulation	Direct Sequence-SS
Frequency	76.5 GHz
Transmission Bandwidth	480 MHz
Transmission Power	4 dBm
PN-sequence	M-sequence, 255chip, 40 Mcps
Antenna Width Sidelobe Level	3.9°(Az,Total) -40dB

Antennas – A compact, high efficiency, high gain and low sidelobe antenna is required when we consider installing the radar into a passenger vehicle. From the viewpoint of low sidelobe, two micro-strip antennas were used as the transmitter and the receptor. Uniform sidelove level was obtained with the mechanical beam scanning method even when the beam was scanning. The prototype radar has a sidelobe level of less than –40 dB.

Millimeter-wave circuit – Waveguide discretionary components were used to improve the design flexibility in this prototype radar. The InP type Gunn diode was used as the millimeter-wave oscillator. The 3dB-directional coupler was used as the allotter of electric power for the transmission and the reception. The power amplifier was installed into the transmission circuit to cover the loss of the up-converter. For these reasons, the prototype radar has obtained a transmission power of 4dBm. At the reception circuit, the down-converter was used to convert the received signals to IF band signals.

IF circuit – In the IF circuit for SS modulation and demodulation, 1 GHz band signal is being used. The phase noise of 1GHz oscillator has achieved approximately -100 dBc/Hz at 25 kHz offset. Generally, the phase noise level of the millimeter-wave oscillator is greater than that of the IF oscillator. However, in the case of SS method, compensation for the phase noise of oscillator is provided. Therefore, the SS method's good performance for range rate measurement is dependent on the characteristics of the IF circuit.

Signal processing – FPGA (Field Programmable Gate Array) was used as the PN generator for spreading. The sequence is M-sequence. Its chip rate is 40 Mcps and length is 255 chips. The filter-bank was used to record every doppler frequency in the reception circuit for data analysis. The filter-bank consists of 8 filters of from FB#1 to FB#8. It has such characteristics that it can separate the signal reflected by the roadside from the whole reception signal since the minimum driving speed on expressways is 50 km/h in Japan.

EXPERIMENTAL

EVALUATION SYSTEM – Fig. 3 shows the evaluation system. The RF unit consists of antennas and a millimeter-wave circuit that were place near the front grille of a vehicle. The IF and signal processing circuit were set inside the cabin. Measured data was recorded on a personal computer and data recorder, and the situation evaluated was recorded on video tape.

RESULTS AND DISCUSSION

Single beam – To study the fundamental detection performance, a single beam was used in the first experiment. The experiment condition was that a target was located at range of approximately 70 m in front of the radar equipped vehicle on a expressway. On curved roads, data were obtained using the manual beam steering technique. Fig. 4 shows the evaluated results. Fig. 4-(A), -(B) and -(C) represent the detection results of every filter-bank,FB#3,FB#4 and FB#5, and show the range of from -100 km/h to -50 km/h, from -50 km/h to 0 km/h and from 0 km/h to 50 km/h, respectively. The X-axis shows the time and the range of the X-axis is approximately 8 minutes. The Y-axis shows the range from 47 m to 107 m. The change of the background color's brightness means that the beam was being steered. In Fig. 4-(B) and -(C), an object detected at approximately 70 m ahead. Moreover, it was also confirmed that objects were moving far ahead of the radar equipped vehicle. These are targets, which have higher range rates than that of the radar vehicle, moving in a different lane. These targets were detected by both filters since characteristics of the filters slightly overlapped. On the other hand, It can be seen that zonation objects were detected in Fig. 4-(A). These zonation objects had a range rate that corresponded with the self range rate of the radar equipped vehicle. These were noteworthy when detected inside tunnels and sound insulated walls. From the results shown in Fig. 4, it was found that it is possible to separate the mobile objects from those data of stationary objects existing on the road by utilizing the filter-bank.

Beam scanning – Next the experiment of the fixed 3 beam position was carried out to investigate multiple beam detection performance. Fig. 5 shows an example of data evaluated. Fig. 5-(a) shows the photograph of the conditions of a right directionally curved road having a radius of approximately 1000 m inside a tunnel. Fig. 5-(b) shows the analyzed results of the adjacent 3 beam called #2, #3, and #4 in that same situation. The X-axis is the range rate and the Y-axis is the range in all graphs. Beam #3 detects objects in the frontal direction. Beam #2 and #4 detect those to the left and right directions, respectively. The brightness of graphs represents the distribution of reception intensity. In this situation, it can be confirmed that the target is detected by beam #4 since the target is on the right. However, beam #2 could see the object which had the same range and range rate as those detected by beam #4. This phenomenon can be explained by a model like that shown in Fig. 6. It was such a model that produced the reflection signal from the target that was reflected at roadside again and detected as a multi-path reflection in beam #2. Based on the above assumption, we believe that the multi-path reflection wouldn't be separated in spatial domain if radar has a wide width beam. Optimum beam width of our radar will be investigated, but more importantly we need to develop the algorithm for reduction of multi-path reflection.

CONCLUSION

We fabricated a 76 GHz prototype automotive millimeter-wave radar using an SS modulation technique and evaluated it under various situations on the road. From the results of the fundamental detection experiment, it was found that it is possible to separate the mobile objects from those data of stationary objects existing on the road by utilizing the filter-bank. Moreover, from the results of the 3 beam scannig, multi-path reflection from the roadside and inside tunnels was obtained. We believe that the obtained results are valuable for the development of the necesarry algorithm in the near future.

REFERENCES

1. T. Tokoro "Automotive Radar and Its Applications" Journal of the 1997 IEICE Vol.80, No.9 (1997)
2. J. K. Holmes "Coherent Spread Spectrum Systems" Krieger Publishing Company, pp.379-381 (1990)
3. S. Noda, K. Inomata and T. Fukae "A Study on Automotive Millimeter-wave Radar using SS Technique" Proceeding of the 1997 IEICE General Conference, SA-4-4 (1997)
4. K. Hashimoto, H. Endo, Y. Aoyagi, H. Ishizu and R. Kohno "Evaluation of Fundamental Performance for 60 GHz Automotive Radar using SS Method" Proceeding of the 1996 IEICE General Conference, B-115 (1996)
5. H. Endo, Y. Aoyagi, T. Fukuchi, K. Inoue, H. Ishizu and R. Kohno "76 GHz Automotive Radar using SS Method" Proceeding of the 1997 IEICE General Conference, SA-4-5 (1997)
6. Y. Hanada and R. Kohno "Evaluation of DOA Estimation Using Multi-beam Antenna in using Spread Spectrum Radar" Proceeding of the 1997 IEICE General Conference, SA-4-1 (1997)
7. H. Ishizu "Millimeter-wave Automotive Radar using Spread Spectrum Technology" Microwave Workshops and Exhibition '97, pp.200-205 (1997)
8. Y. Aoyagi, T. Fukuchi, H. Endo, K. Inoue, H. Ishizu and R. Kohno "An Evaluation of Angle Measurement Method for 76 GHz-band Spread Spectrum Radar" Trans. IEICE A, Vol.J81-A,No.4(1998)

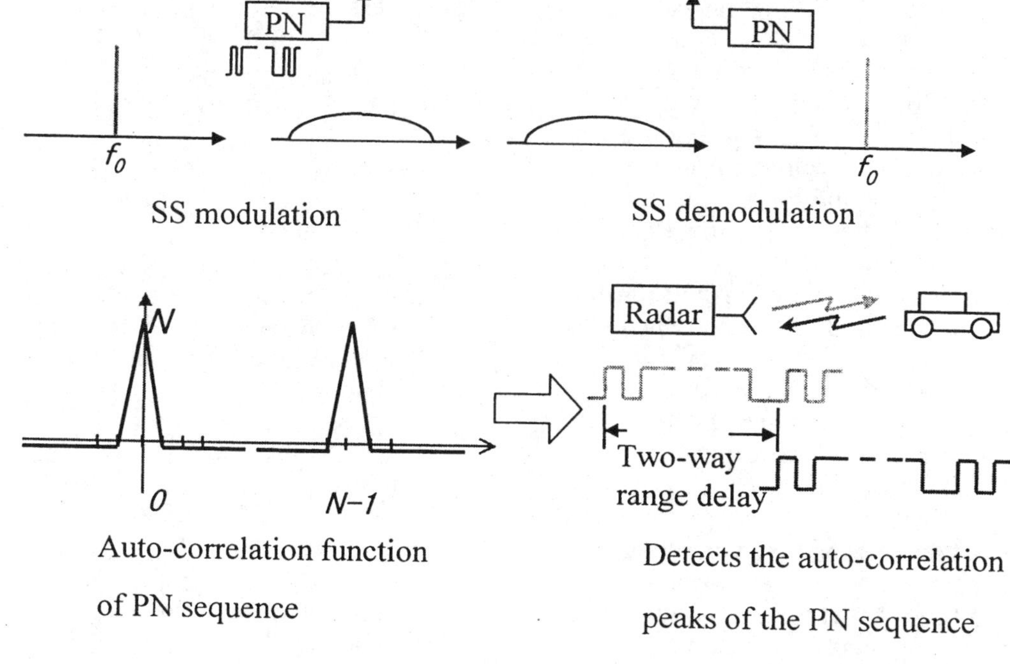

Figure 1 : Principle of Spread Spectrum radar.

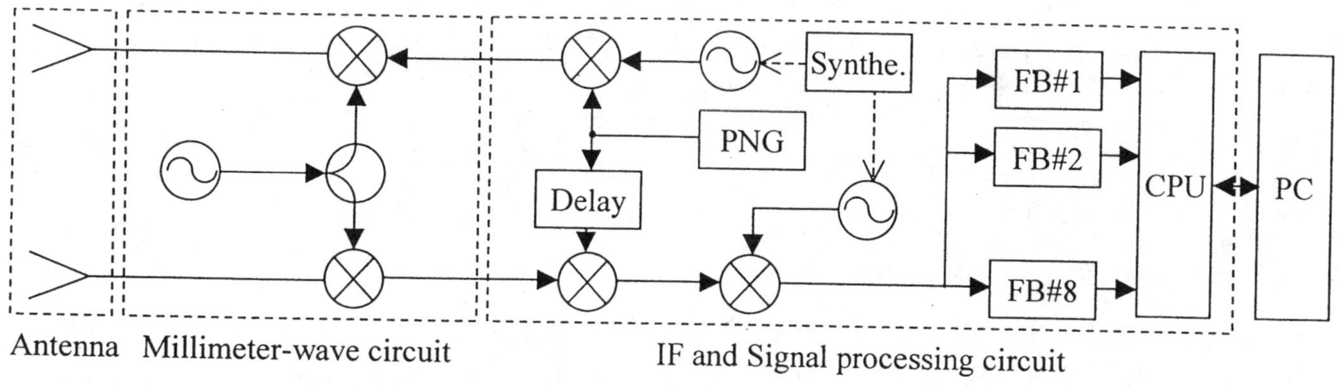

Figure 2 : A brief hardware configurations of our SS radar.

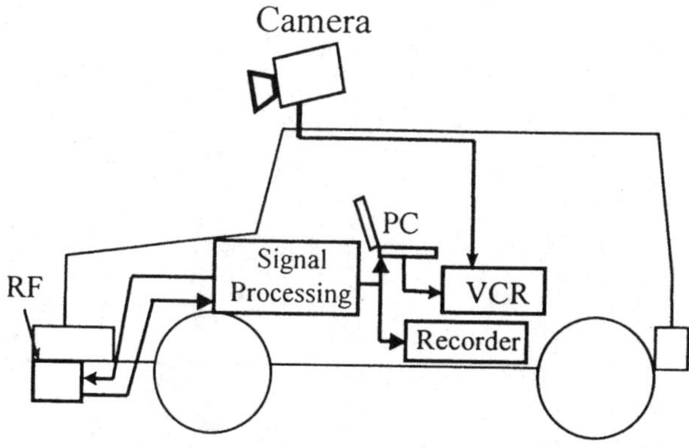

Figure 3 : Evaluation system for field tests.

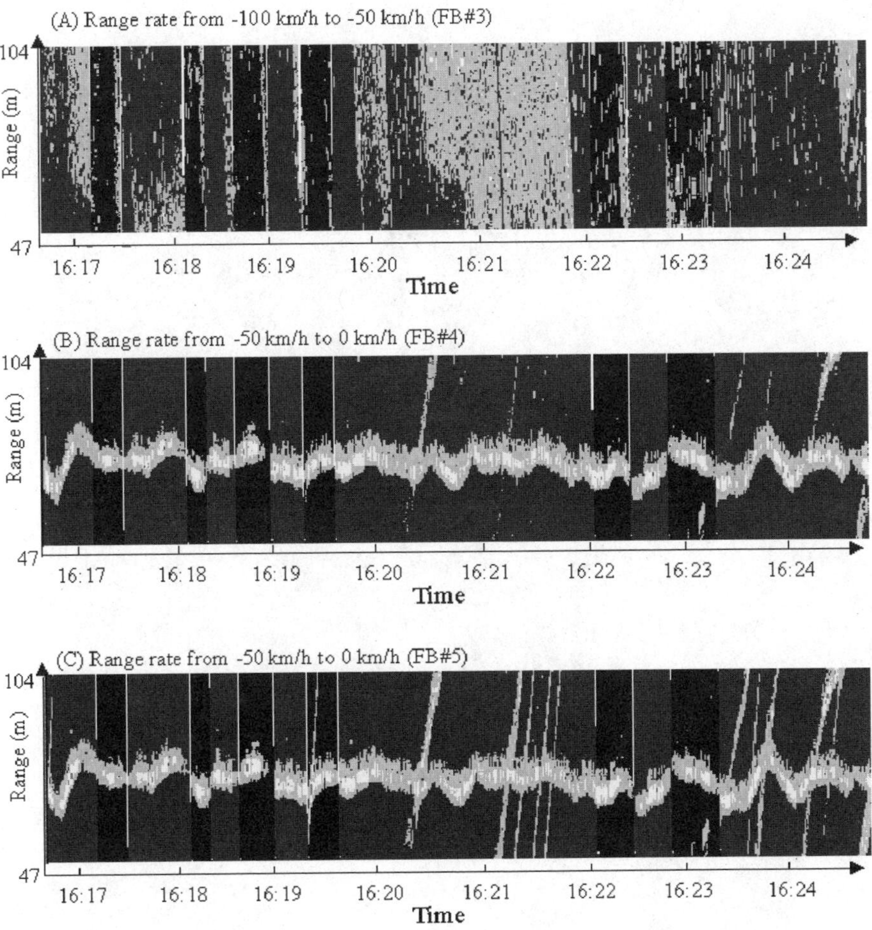

Figure 4 : Experimental results of steered single beam. (A), (B) and (C) represent the detection results of FB#3, FB#4 and FB#5, respectively.

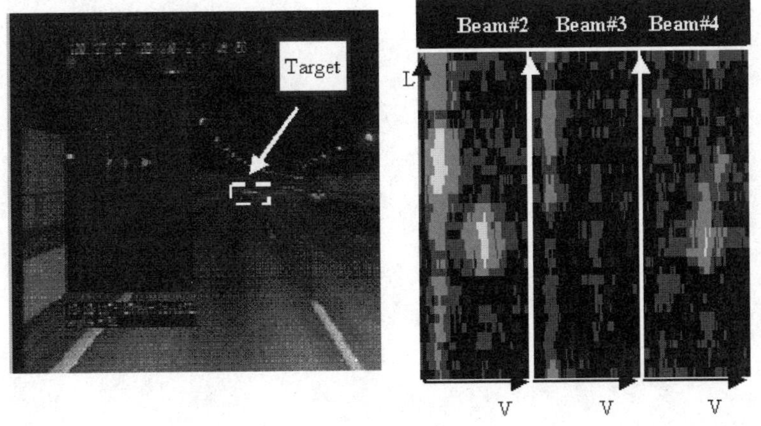

Figure 5 : An example of data obtained inside a tunnel. The left photograph shows a situation evaluated in this situation. The graphs on the right show analyzed results detected by the positions of 3 beams, #2,#3 and #4.

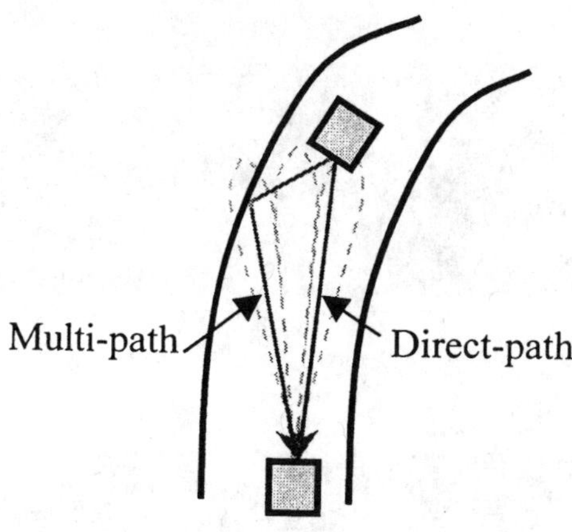

Figure 6 : A model of multi-path reflection.

1999-01-1239

Radar-Based Near Distance Sensing Device for Automotive Applications

Martin Kunert
SIEMENS AG

ABSTRACT

This paper highlights the generic idea of a synergetic system approach and first test results of a radar-based near distance sensing device actually developed at Siemens Automotive. Due to the limited space in the vehicle's front and rear region a multi-functional sensor system for different applications is envisaged.

Technical requirements for near-term driver assistant functions are described and the necessary system architecture to handle those applications is roughly specified. Practical strength, limits and shortcomings of the realized systems and first test results are addressed.

INTRODUCTION

GENERAL MOTIVATION – Since 1991 ultrasonic-based parking aid systems turned up on the automotive market with continuously increasing numbers. By transmission of acoustic wave packages vehicles became capable to get in contact with the near vicinity around the car for the first time.

Actually systems like ACC based on 77 GHz microwave technology appear on high-class vehicles, which scan an observation zone in front of the vehicle from 1m to 150m with an aperture angle of about 10°. For next generation ACC with Stop & Go the observation angle before the vehicle must be enlarged by an important amount, which demands a broad looking, near distance sensing device.

Furthermore smart restraint systems of future generations with reversible actuators (e.g. pneumatic airbag, motor-driven seat-belt pretensioner, etc.) require a so-called precrash sensor, which alerts the restraint ECU of an imminent object coming frontal or aside onto the car several milliseconds before crash occurrence.

The surveillance of the vehicle's blind spots and an indicator of the presence and speed of an object within this area not covered by the rear view mirrors will support the driver during lane-change operation or low speed maneuvering. Especially the fast growing number of elder drivers will benefit of such a driver assistant device.

All those applications described above have one system component in common, the near distance sensing device. The radar-based near distance sensing portfolio is shown graphically in Figure 1.

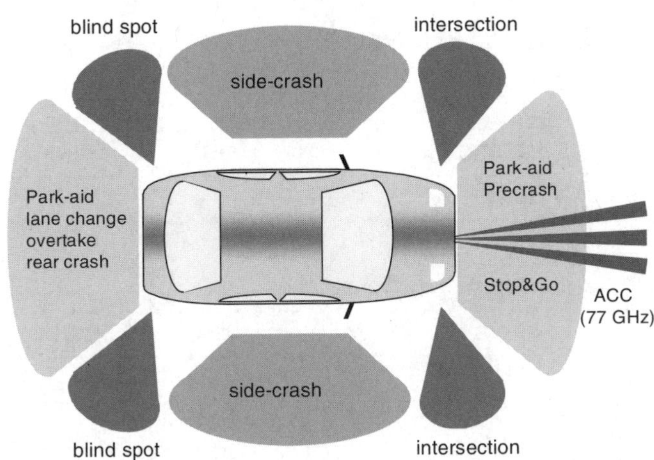

Figure 1. Radar-based Near Distance Sensing Portfolio

SYNERGETIC SYSTEM APPROACH – Due to limited mounting space, cost aspects and distributed, multi-functional architecture concepts a proximity sensing device must provide sufficient flexibility to fulfill the different demands for near field applications. This idea in mind Siemens Automotive started a development project to explore the benefits and limits of a multi-functional sensor approach for a cross-application system approach interacting with several vehicle subsystems on demand. To get an idea of the performance of such a multi-mode, multi-functional sensor it is necessary to specify the coarse requirements of each application envisaged.

COARSE SPECIFICATION OF DIFFERENT DRIVER ASSISTANT FUNCTIONS – According to the prevailing driving situation the requirements for a sensing devices will change for each different function. The basic parameters are detection range limits, range accuracy, relative speed limits, speed accuracy, object discrimination distance (i.e. the capability to detect and separate two distinct targets), observation zone angle, object detection capability and new object detection time.

A preliminary specification of these parameters is given for the following systems:

Parking Aid System

Table 1. Parking aid system basic parameter list

Parameter	Min	max
Detection range	0.2 m	1.5 m
Distance accuracy	0.02 m	
Object discrimination distance	0.15 m	
Relative speed	-5 m/s	+5 m/s
Speed accuracy	0.5 m/s	
Observation zone	Vehicle width ± 30 deg.	
Azimuth angle accuracy	5 deg.	
Object detection capability	Plastic tube	
Object detection time		100 ms

Precrash sensing System

Table 2. Precrash sensing system basic parameter list

Parameter	Min	max
Detection range	0 m	5 m
Distance accuracy	0.05 m	
Object discrimination distance	0.20 m	
Relative speed	- 5 m/s	- 55 m/s
Speed accuracy	1 m/s	
Observation zone	Vehicle width ± 50 deg.	
Azimuth angle accuracy	10 deg.	
Object detection capability	Motorbike	
Object detection time		10 ms

Stop & Go System (extension to ACC)

Table 3. Stop & Go system basic parameter list

Parameter	min	max
Detection range	0 m	20 m
Distance accuracy	0.5 m	
Object discrimination distance	0.75 m	
Relative speed	-27 m/s	+27 m/s
Speed accuracy	1 m/s	
Observation zone	vehicle width ± 50 deg.	
Azimuth angle accuracy	5 deg.	
Object detection capability	Motorbike	
Object detection time		150 ms

Blind Spot Surveillance System

Table 4. Blind spot surveillance system basic parameter list

Parameter	min	Max
Detection range	0 m	10 m
Distance accuracy	0.1 m	
Object discrimination distance	0.5 m	
Relative speed	-27 m/s	27 m/s
Speed accuracy	1 m/s	
Observation zone	± 30 deg.	
Azimuth angle accuracy	Presence detection	
Object detection capability	Living beings and medium sized objects	
Object detection time		150 ms

It must be annotated that the above given basic parameter lists are only a preliminary, coarse specification derived from different articles and discussions with several car manufacturers and suppliers working on the respective subjects.

RADAR BASED NEAR DISTANCE SENSING SYSTEM

Among the different physical realization principles for near distance measurements radar based devices outline several advantages compared to acoustic, optical or thermal methods:

- Invisible mounting behind non-conductive materials
- All weather operation capability
- Conform with harsh environment constraints
- Very fast, parallel operation possibility
- Low interference with same or similar systems
- Small or no performance deterioration during important environment variations
- Precise and redundant information achievable

Microwave radar systems are therefore very suitable for outside vehicle sensing tasks and seem to have the potential to fulfill the necessary requirements of the different applications already mentioned in Table 1 to Table 4.

SYSTEM ARCHITECTURE AND PHILOSOPHY – The varying demands of the different system functions require a flexible sensor concept, which can adapt its performance limits accordingly. To cover the complete vehicle's front or rear surface a distributed sensor system consisting of at least two radar devices placed at the carbody's outer dimensions (e.g. the bumpers right and left corner) is obligatory. The usage of a smart control and processing unit, either implemented with a microcontroller or an

ASIC, in the radar front-end guarantees the desired flexibility for a multi-functional operation. A common ECU communicates both with each radar front-end module via a local communication protocol and with the vehicles infrastructure by the appropriate gateway link.

SYSTEM BLOCK DIAGRAM – The near distance sensing system consists of two functional module types (see Figure 2), the ECU and a given number of smart radar modules, and can be easily extended by adding further radar modules.

The microwave front-end module consists of a high frequency circuit, two patch antenna, a microcontroller with some glue electronics and some signal conditioning stages. The microcontroller provides all necessary control commands, samples the received radar signals and conducts basic signal processing algorithms.

The ECU gathers the preprocessed, condensed information from the front-end modules via a dedicated, local bus. The data exchange to all relevant subsystems on the vehicle's infrastructure is managed exclusively by the ECU with the respective, subsystem specific protocol. This communication link is also used to provide the near field sensing ECU with vehicle specific information, e.g. steering angle, reverse gear or driving speed.

The bi-directional high-speed CAN-Bus between front-end modules and ECU manages both control and information exchange and avoids data package collisions on the communication link by ECU bus mastering. Special command sequences of the ECU cause the radar modules to conduct a special function task and send back the information in a specific order and time frame.

Alternatively, event-triggered data transmission of the radar front-end devices, previously set in a scanning operation mode by the ECU module, can be established for time-critical applications like precrash sensing.

TECHNICAL SPECIFICATION – From the many possible radar operation principles a combination of pulse, Doppler and FMCW radar is selected to best match the varying performance requirements of the envisaged functions.

Among the possible operating frequency bands, stipulated by national and international regulations, the ISM frequency band from 24.00 GHz to 24.25 GHz is selected for the near field sensor.

Table 5 shows an preliminary overview of important sensor parameters.

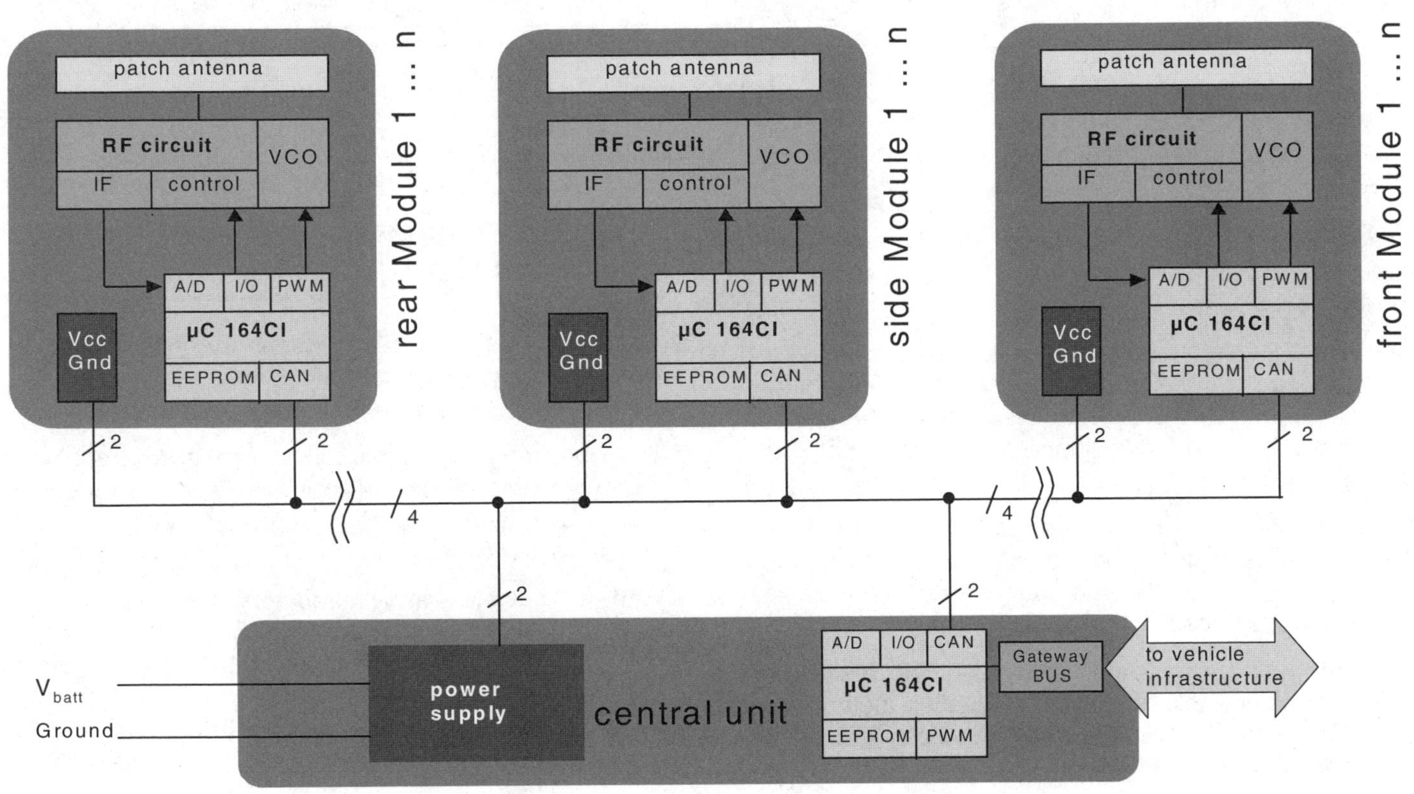

Figure 2. System Block Diagram

Table 5. Microwave front-end system parameters

Parameter	Value
Center Frequency	24 GHz
Modulation	Pulse, Doppler, FMCW
Output power (e.i.r.p.)	1 μW
Number of beams	1
Azimuth beam width (3dB)	ca. ±70°
Elevation beam width (3dB)	ca. ±10°
Range (Mode 1)	0 .... 2 m
Range resolution (Mode 1)	0.05 m
Range (Mode 2)	0 ... 20 m
Range resolution (mode 2)	0.5 m
Velocity limits	- 27 m/s ... 55 m/s
Velocity resolution	0.5m/s
Update rate	ca. 50 Hz

PHYSICAL RADAR CHARACTERISTICS – With a homodyne RF-mixer the received signal is directly transferred into the baseband and by using the simplified equations for distance (eqn. 1) and speed (eqn. 2)

$$f_{range} = \frac{4 \cdot \text{ÄF}}{c_0 \cdot T_m} \cdot range \qquad (1)$$

$$f_{doppler} = \frac{2 \cdot \text{cosè}}{\text{ë}} \cdot speed \qquad (2)$$

the following frequency vs. range and frequency vs. speed relations are valid for a given $T_m = 5$ ms and different ΔF values:

It is obvious that for the different application requirements the Doppler and range frequency contributions vary by an important amount. To cope with this immense frequency range variations a flexible, function-specific signal processing is necessary.

The main implementation interest lies in the task to realize as much as possible only by software or command level means and keep the necessary hardware modifications as small as possible.

Furthermore, industrialization constraints like maximum sample frequency, tolerances, compensation methods or calculation power limits influence the reachable hardware concept for a series production.

NECESSARY DISCRIMINATION CAPABILITY – The discrimination capability to separate two adjacent objects doesn't depend on the used radar principle, but only on the applied transmitted signal bandwidth.

The dualism between pulse-Doppler and FMCW radar systems yields the simple relation that their respective discrimination performance is theoretically identical if the same bandwidth is used. As a rule of thumb a pulse radar with a 1 ns transmit signal is equivalent in target separation with a FMCW radar runs with a 1 GHz frequency span.

Practically there are several advantages when the FMCW principle is selected, especially for bandwidth, data processing and observation (or better integration) time reasons.

Table 6. Homodyne mixer frequency for different ranges and speeds

range	f_{range} @	f_{range} @	f_{range} @	speed F_{center}	$f_{Doppler}$ @
ΔF	220 MHz	1 GHz	2 GHz	F_{center}	24 GHz
0.1 m	59 Hz	268 Hz	536 Hz	0.1 m/s	16.1 Hz
0.2 m	118 Hz	536 Hz	1074 Hz	0.2 m/s	32.2 Hz
0.3 m	177 Hz	805 Hz	1611 Hz	0.5 m/s	48.3 Hz
0.4 m	236 Hz	1074 Hz	2148 Hz	1 m/s	161 Hz
0.5 m	295 Hz	1342 Hz	2685 Hz	2 m/s	322 Hz
0.6 m	354 Hz	1611 Hz	3222 Hz	5 m/s	805 Hz
0.7 m	413 Hz	1879 Hz	3758 Hz	10 m/s	1611 Hz
0.8 m	472 Hz	2148 Hz	4295 Hz	15 m/s	2416 Hz
0.9 m	532 Hz	2416 Hz	4832 Hz	20 m/s	3222 Hz
1 m	591 Hz	2685 Hz	5369 Hz	28 m/s	4510 Hz
2 m	1181 Hz	5369 Hz	10.7 kHz	30 m/s	4832 Hz
5 m	2953 Hz	13.4 kHz	26.8 kHz	40 m/s	6443 Hz
10 m	5906 Hz	26.8 kHz	53.7 kHz	56 m/s	9020 Hz
20 m	11.8 kHz	53.7 kHz	107 kHz	81 m/s	13 kHz

As frequency bandwidth allocation by government institutes is always a matter of concern, large frequency bands over 1GHz are unfortunately not available.

The only remaining possibility to achieve larger bandwidth is to use the so-called spread spectrum methods, which cover large frequency ranges with very poor mean transmission power.

With this guideline as a mandatory rule a radar sensor can be designed which profits from all the benefits of both pulse- or frequency-modulated principles by using a special kind of low power, high discriminating technique for the near vicinity and a classical high power, medium resolution principle for far field operation up to ca. 20 m.

RADAR SIGNAL PROCESSING TECHNIQUES – Both a flexible radar operation concept and sophisticated signal processing algorithms are necessary to cover the main performance requirements described in Table 1 to Table 4. The frequency values shown in Table 6 vary over several decades, thus making a common, unique signal processing method for all function modes rather difficult.

The main idea to solve this problem is to tune the appropriate radar parameters according to the desired speed or distance range.

The RF-mixers beat frequency contribution for small distances below 2m with low maneuvering speeds (i.e. parking aid function) needs a high frequency span ΔF of more than 1GHz with moderate transmission power to get sufficient object discrimination and range accuracy.

For medium distances from 2m up to 20m with higher relative speeds (i.e. ACC with Stop & Go) a frequency span ΔF of several hundred MHz is enough to achieve range resolution and target separation around 0.5 m. For this function the very large beamwidth of each sensor and the relative short distance between them is a handicap which will probably need some hardware modifications to overcome these problems.

The described smart sensor concept with a microcontroller to handle the parameter tuning and data processing activities is capable to manage all necessary tasks.

MULTI-MODULE TRIANGULATION – The angular resolution of the near field radar system is attained by applying the triangulation method between the radar modules. At least two modules with a sufficient space between them are necessary to conduct the triangulation principle. Because of the limited beamwidth of the first prototypes and in order to avoid ambiguity situations a configuration with three radar modules is taken for the first test runs.

The basic idea of the rudimentary triangulation algorithm is shown in Figure 3.

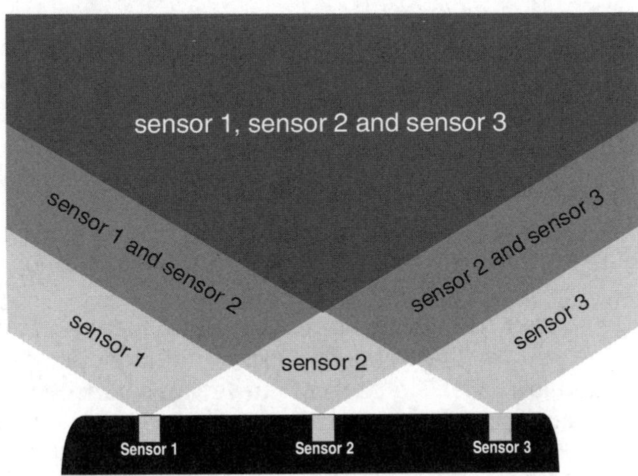

Figure 3. Triangulation chart with 3 radar modules

It is obvious that the aperture of the sensor beam mainly influences the angular resolution.

Dependent on the actual position only one, two or three sensors can detect an object within their observation zone. When two radar modules see a target at least angular information can be calculated by adequate algorithms.

With the help of a priori information and time history analysis high redundancy and position accuracy can be achieved in dynamic scenarios. This holds true for both point-scatterers and in a wider sense also for distributed, larger objects.

FIRST TEST RESULTS – With the above-described radar signal processing and triangulation procedures first test runs with three radar modules were conducted.

The beam width of each sensor is ca. ± 50 degrees, the maximum detectable distance is 5m and the frequency span ΔF is 1.5 GHz, yielding a target discrimination capability of ca. 0.25m. The sweep time of the linear up- and down-ramp is set to 2 ms and the signal is sampled at a 30 kHz rate.

With the help of a zero-padded, 256 point Zoom-FFT a range resolution below 0.025 m can be reached. Due to the still reduced observation zone of the radar modules triangulation is only possible behind a distance of ca. 0.35 m from the sensor line. Within this zone there is actually only range information by one sensor available, as it is sketched in Figure 3.

The following radar signals are recorded from a scenario shown in Figur 4. Two corner reflectors with 1 m^2 RCS are positioned in a distance of 1m and 1.3m from the sensors.

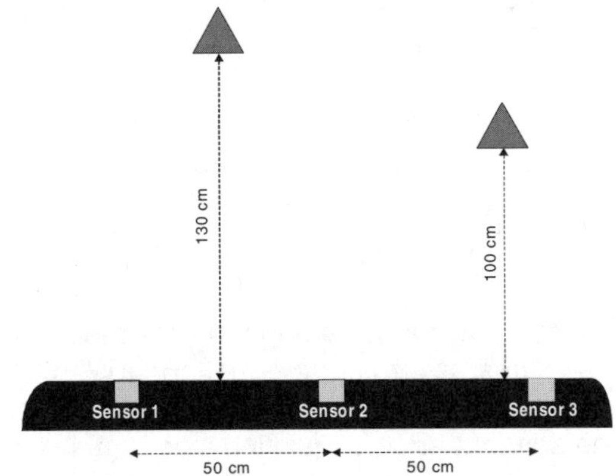

Figure 4. Test configuration with 3 modules and two reflectors

The signals of the up- and down-sweeps of sensor 1 to 3 are plotted in Figure 5 to Figure 7.

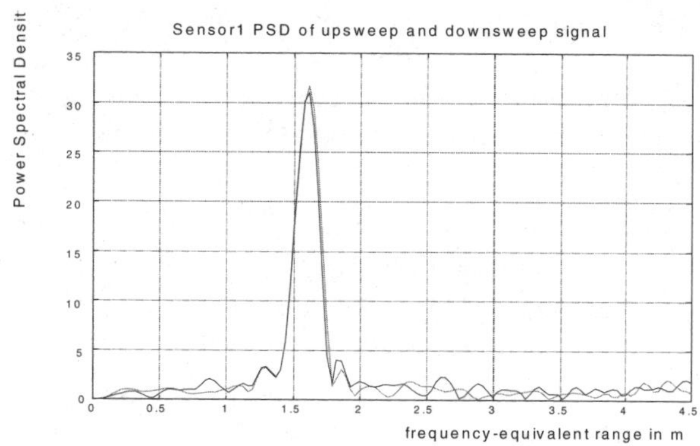

Figure 5. Frequency plot of scenario in Figure 4

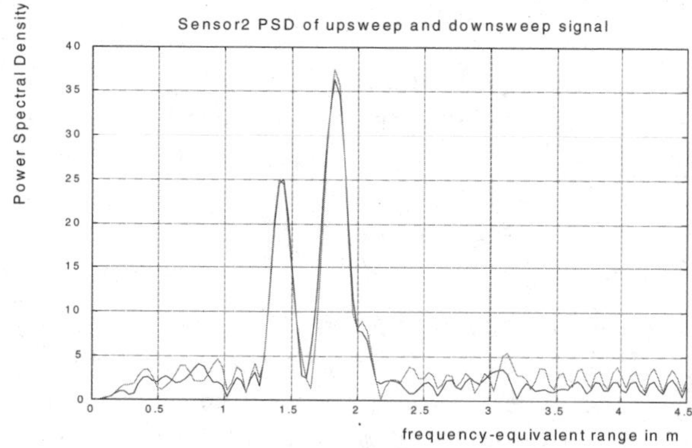

Figure 6. Frequency plot of scenario in Figure 4

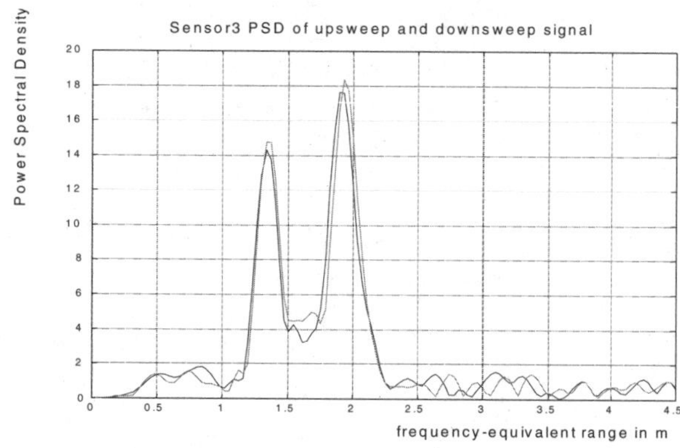

Figure 7. Frequency plot of scenario in Figure 4

The frequency axes in Figure 5 to Figure 7 are calibrated in distance values according to equation 1. With the distance information extracted from the frequency spectrum of the three sensors the triangulation algorithm is capable to determine the position of the two corner reflectors within a few centimeters or degrees, respectively.

A second test trial with a distributed target type, a passenger car, is shown in Figure 8 to Figure 10.

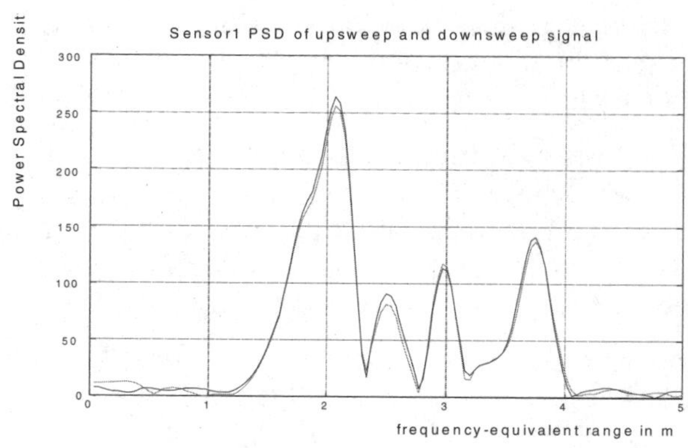

Figure 8. Sensor 1 frequency plot of vehicle scenario

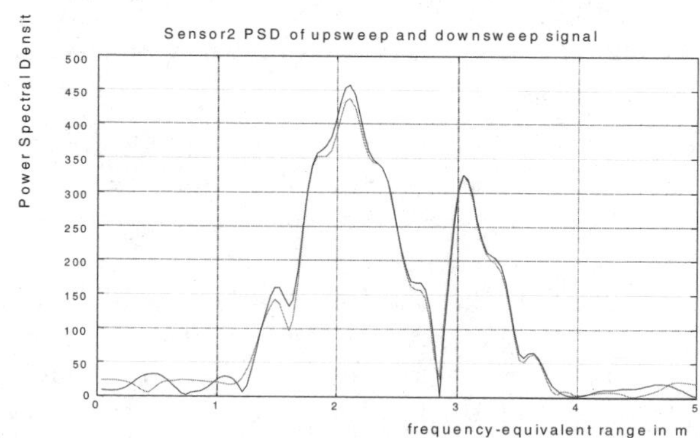

Figure 9. Sensor 2 frequency plot of vehicle scenario

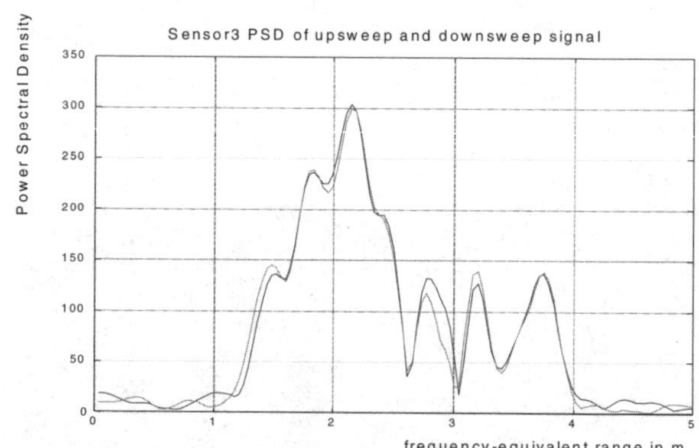

Figure 10. Sensor 3 frequency plot of vehicle scenario

A distributed object results in several frequency peaks distributed over the frequency axis. The interference of high and low reflecting parts of the vehicle's surface produces a characteristical spectrum, which depends on the viewing angle and distance to the reflection point.

The actual design of the developed radar front end is shown in Figure 11.

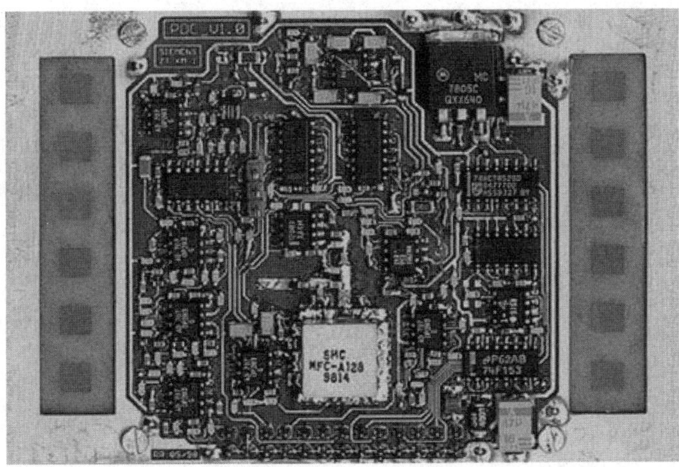

Figure 11. Radar module prototype (original size)

CONCLUSION

The presented near distance radar concept has the potential to handle the various demands of future driver assistant and safety functions.

The multi-functional system approach holds true for both limited mounting place to position the otherwise necessary different sensor devices for each application and also for overall system cost.

The first test results with the existing radar prototype show the feasibility of the taken development path. With the steadily increasing calculation power also "deeper buried" radar information will get accessible in the future.

The rapidly advancing progress in RF components pushed by other commercial market segments will provide competitive, cost-effective solutions right now.

REFERENCES

1. M. Skolnik, "Radar Handbook" 2nd edition, Mac Graw Hill, 1990
2. M. Kunert, "Automotive FMCW Radar – A global system approach with modern methods" INPT Toulouse, 1996
3. J. Detlefsen: "Radartechnik", Springer-Verlag Berlin, 1989.
4. P. Lowbridge et.al.: "A Low Cost mm-Wave Cruise Control System for Automotive Applications", Microwave Journal, October 1993.
5. B. Zimmermann et.al.: "24 GHz Microwave Close-Range Sensors For Industrial Measurement Applications", Microwave Journal, May 1996.
6. C.G. Bachman: "Radar Sensor Engineering" Lexington-Books, Toronto 1982
7. S.A. Hovanessian: "Introduction to sensor systems" ARTECH House, INC., Norwood 1988

DEFINITIONS, ACRONYMS, ABBREVIATIONS

ΔF :	frequency span
C_0 :	speed of light
T_m :	FMCW radar sweep time
$\cos\theta$:	inclination angle of radar beam
λ :	wavelength of radar sensor
ACC :	**A**daptive **C**ruise **C**ontrol
ASIC:	**A**pplication **S**pecific **I**ntegrated **C**ircuit
CAN:	**C**ontroller **A**rea **N**etwork
ECU:	**E**lectronic **C**ontrol **U**nit
e.i.r.p.:	**e**quivalent **i**sotropically **r**adiated **p**ower
FFT:	**F**ast **F**ourier **T**ransform
FMCW:	**F**requency **M**odulated **C**ontinuous **W**ave
ISM:	**I**ndustrial, **S**cientific, **M**edical
RCS:	**R**adar **C**ross **S**ection
RF :	**R**adio **F**requency

1999-01-1237

Offset Paraboloidal Reflector Antenna for Vehicular Collision Avoidance Radar

Shinichi Honma, Toshiyuki Takahara, Masahira Akasu and Shinichi Sato
Mitsubishi Electric Corp.

ABSTRACT

An offset paraboloidal reflector antenna for vehicular collision avoidance radar is designed and evaluated. The antenna is designed to use at 77GHz band, and to have suitable gain and beamwidth for the vehicular collision avoidance radar. The properties measured and calculated are compared and confirmed to agree well.

The offset paraboloidal reflector antenna is low-loss and has large degree of freedom of antenna design, compared with such as a microstrip antenna. So, using this type of the antenna for the radar system contributes to miniaturize, to make light weight, and to be easily mass-produced of the radar system.

INTRODUCTION

One of the ITS (Intelligent Transport Systems) key systems, vehicular collision avoidance radar systems using millimeter-wave have been developed in recent years. In these radar systems, microstrip antenna or lens antenna are usually used. The microstrip antenna and the lens antenna are useful for mass-production because of their simple structure. But it is difficult to minimize an antenna aperture area because of low antenna efficiency.

For high antenna efficiency, light weight and low cost, we have developed the radar head using an offset paraboloidal reflector antenna. In this paper, the design and the performance evaluation of the paraboloidal reflector antenna are shown.

RADAR EQUATION AND ANTENNA EFFICIENCY

In a radar system, a received power P_r of the radar antenna from the target is derived by the radar equation;

$$P_r = P_t \frac{G^2 \lambda^2 \sigma}{(4\pi)^3 R^4} \tag{1}$$

where, P_t is a transmitted power from the radar, G is the antenna gain, λ is a wavelength, σ is a radar cross section of the target, R is a range between the antenna and the target. If a minimum input power S_{min} of the receiver is given, the maximum radar range R_{max} is obtained by

$$R_{\max} = \left(\frac{P_t G^2 \lambda^2 \sigma}{(4\pi)^3 S_{\min}} \right)^{\frac{1}{4}} . \tag{2}$$

The antenna gain G is obtained by

$$G = \frac{4\pi A}{\lambda^2} \eta \tag{3}$$

where, A is an antenna aperture area, η is an antenna efficiency. In the case that the same antenna gain G is required, we can miniaturize the antenna aperture area A (that is the antenna size), if higher antenna efficiency η is obtained. Generally, the antenna efficiency of the microstrip antenna is less than the efficiency of the reflector antenna.

ANTENNA STRUCTURE

The vehicular collision avoidance radar will be operated in W-band (75-110GHz). The antenna in this paper is designed to operate at 76.5GHz. Figure 1 shows the configuration and the coordinate system of the offset paraboloidal reflector antenna. This antenna has an offset paraboloidal reflector and a pyramidal horn. Figure 2 and Figure 3 show these antenna components, that is, the reflector and the pyramidal horn, respectively.

A radar head for a vehicle should be designed as small as possible since it is to be mounted on the vehicle. In order that the antenna be miniaturized, it is selected that an aperture diameter D of the paraboloidal reflector is 40mm.

The offset angle β of the reflector and the subtended angle φ of the reflector are 64and 31, respectively. So that the pyramidal horn does not cause the blockage of the wave reflected by the reflector. The pyramidal horn, which is the primary radiator of the antenna, is placed on the reflector focus. The antenna radiates a linearly polarized wave. In order that the polarization plane is tilted at an angle of 45toward the ground, the pyramidal horn is rotated on its beam axis.

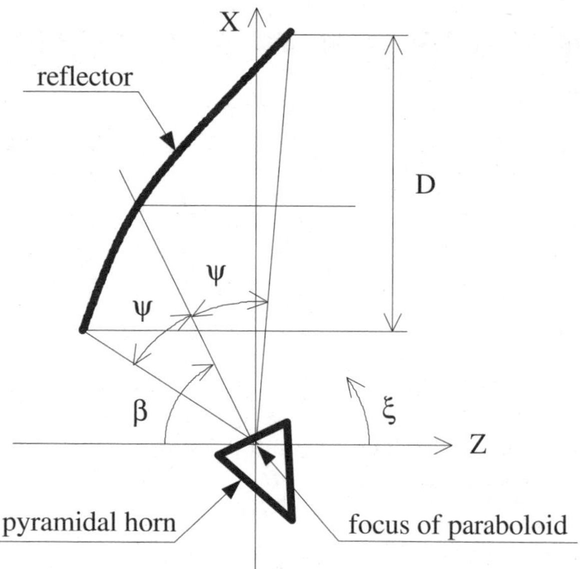

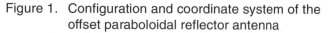

Figure 1. Configuration and coordinate system of the offset paraboloidal reflector antenna

The material of the reflector is resin and the reflector surface is plated with metals. The pyramidal horn is made of a block of metal. The weight of the reflector is 6.0 grams and the pyramidal horn's weight is 2.5 grams. The light weight of the reflector and the horn contribute to the light weight of the radar head. Figure 4 shows the offset paraboloidal reflector antenna.

We designed this antenna, electrically and mechanically. A simulation software was developed and has been used for the electrical design.

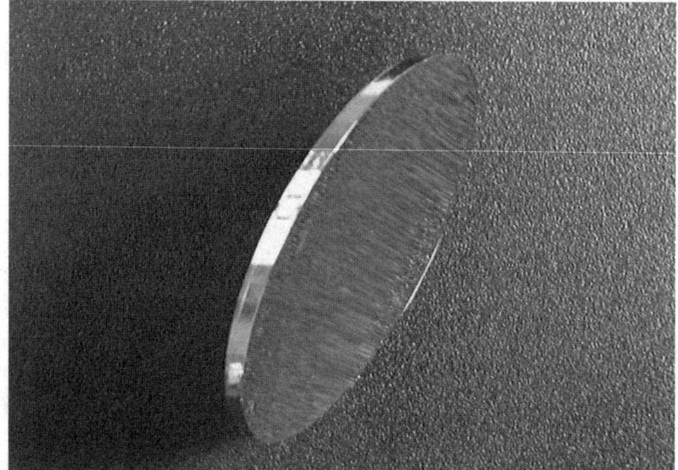

Figure 2. Picture of the offset paraboloidal reflector

Figure 3. Picture of the pyramidal horn

Figure 4. Picture of the offset paraboloidal reflector antenna (only antenna components are shown)

RADIATION CHARACTERISTICS

The offset paraboloidal reflector antenna can be reciprocally used as a transmitting antenna and a receiving antenna. So, we use only one antenna for the radar system. This helps to miniaturize the radar head.

The characteristics, such as radiation pattern and gain, were measured in our anechoic chamber. Figure 5 shows the calculated and measured radiation patterns (beam direction is 0) of the antenna. The calculated and measured antenna gains G are 28.5dBi and 28.8dBi, respectively. The calculated and measured beamwidths of the antenna are 6.5and 6.6, respectively. A good agreement between calculated and measured results is obtained.

The efficiency η of this antenna is 70.5%. This is very high in comparison with the efficiencies of the microstrip and the lens antennas, because there are no dielectric materials between the reflector and the horn. By using the reflector antenna instead of the microstrip antenna or the lens antenna in the radar system, the increase in the maximum detectable range for a given transmission power is obtained. Conversely a highly efficient antenna requires less input power at the antenna feed point for the same maximum radar range. Less costly RF circuits may result.

The beam direction of this antenna can be controlled by inclining the horn axis. Figures 6 and 7 show the radiation patterns in the case of the beam directions shifted to +3.8and-3.8, respectively. The measured gains for the +3.8beam and the -3.8beam are 28.6dBi and 28.4dBi, and the measured beamwidths for each beam are 6.5and 6.6, respectively. In this range of beam scanning angle, the beam directions can be controlled without changing the gain and beamwidth significantly.

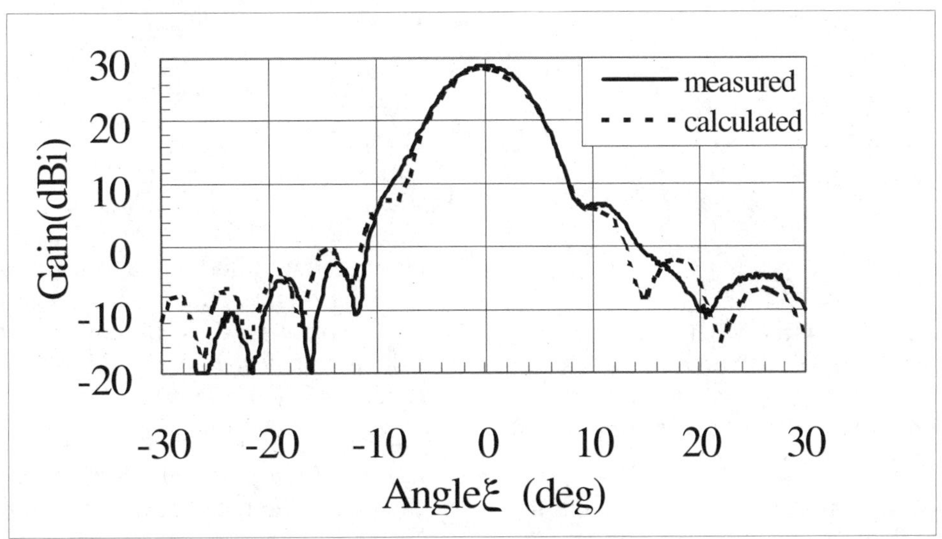

Figure 5. Radiation pattern of the paraboloidal reflector antenna (beam direction = 0deg.)

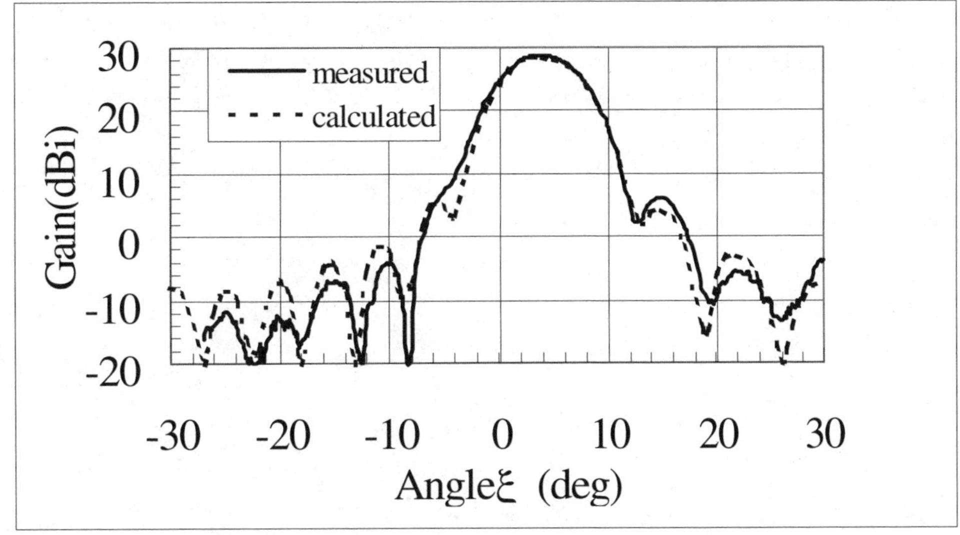

Figure 6. Radiatioin pattern of the antenna (beam direction = +3.8deg.)

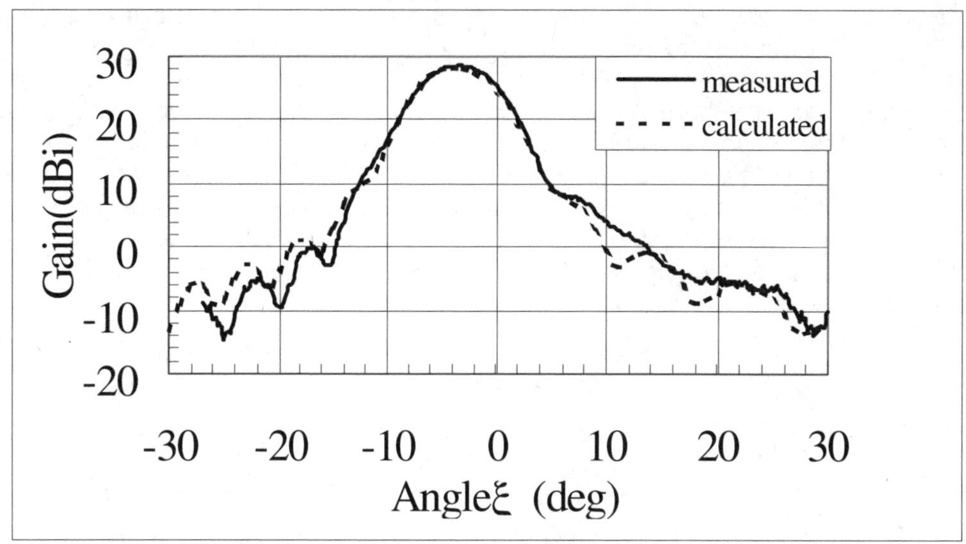

Figure 7. Radiation pattern of the antenna (beam direction = -3.8deg.)

CONCLUSION

An offset paraboloidal reflector antenna for vehicular collision avoidance radar has been designed and evaluated at 76.5GHz. This antenna has been designed to have suitable gain and beamwidth for the vehicular collision avoidance radar.

This antenna has been evaluated by measurement of the radiation patterns and gains. The measured and calculated characteristics have been compared. It has been confirmed that this type of antenna is useful to the vehicular collision avoidance radar system.

The offset paraboloidal reflector antenna, compared with an antenna such as a microstrip antenna, has low-loss characteristics and has a large degree of freedom of the antenna design. The reflector and the horn of the offset paraboloidal reflector antenna are easy to manufacture. Consequently, this type of antenna is facilitates the mass-production of the radar system.

We will be constructing a vehicular collision avoidance radar system using this type of antenna and we will be evaluating the radar system on the vehicle.

CONTACT

E-mail:honma@hime.melco.co.jp

FAX:+81-792-96-1992

1999-01-1044

Development of a Compact Scan Laser Radar

Shoichi Tanaka, Tetsuya Nakagawa, Masahira Akasu and Yukio Fukushima
Mitsubishi Electric Corporation

William Bracken
Mitsubishi Electronics America Inc.

ABSTRACT

This paper relates to a distance detecting sensor, specifically a scan radar laser used for a vehicle distance warning system or an intelligent cruise control system. In developing the scan laser radar, we used a light-based scan-action system working via an electromagnetic actuator and ICs in place of the internal circuitry for substantial parts count reduction. The compact scan laser radar is smaller in size and lower in price with higher performance than its predecessors(1). This has made it possible to offer a lower-priced, compact, lightweight, and easy-to-install scan laser radar.

INTRODUCTION

Deliberate effort is being made to develop various intelligent transport system (ITS) programs envisaged for the 21st century, and one of its objects is supporting traffic safety. Today, with particular emphasis being given to vehicular safety – installation rate increasing for ABS, air bag, and other safety systems – expectation is growing for preventive safety systems for reducing driving errors and preventing accidents.

A major component of preventive safety system is a sensor that detects the distance between vehicles. A distance detecting sensor (radar) which applies millimeter wave or light is well known. However, the millimeter-wave radar has such hurdles to overcome as price and size and thus has yet to be established as a general-purpose radar. The laser radar is already in commercial use as the warning device(2) and controlling device for distance between vehicles in trucks, busses, upscale cars, etc. To use the laser radar as the controlling device for distance between vehicles, the radar must have accurate information of the preceding vehicle, its movement, existence of any obstacles, and road contours. As can be noted from Figure 1, the radar scans horizontally toward the moving direction with narrow light to measures distance. Scanning horizontally up to an object for distance measurement while measuring its horizontal position is the main stream of this technology today. (1) (3)

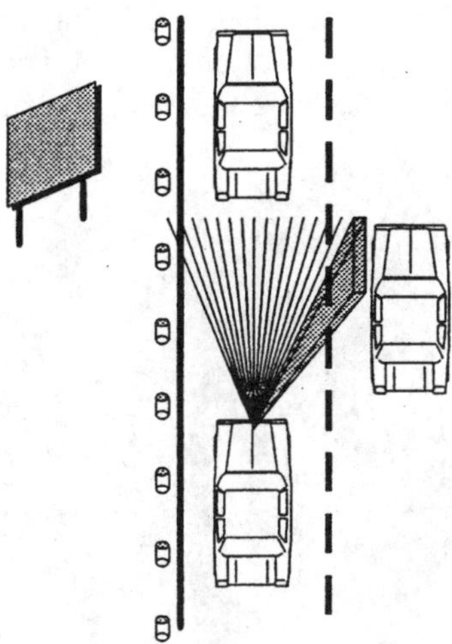

Figure 1. Scanning

However, the conventional scan laser radar cannot be said satisfactory yet in price and size for installation in small vehicles, mass market cars, or low-price models. If it is to be in wider use, it is necessary to realize a low-priced scan laser radar that is compact, lightweight, and easy to install.

Recognizing that need, we employed a light scan system with the electromagnetic actuator and ICs in place of the internal circuitry to achieve substantial reduction of parts count, thereby developing the compact scan laser radar that is smaller, lower-priced, and higher in performance.

PRINCIPLE OF DISTANCE MEASUREMENT

As shown in Figure 2, to measure distance by laser beam, the time is taken from the moment of transmitting laser pulses to the moment of receiving the returning beam reflected from the object.

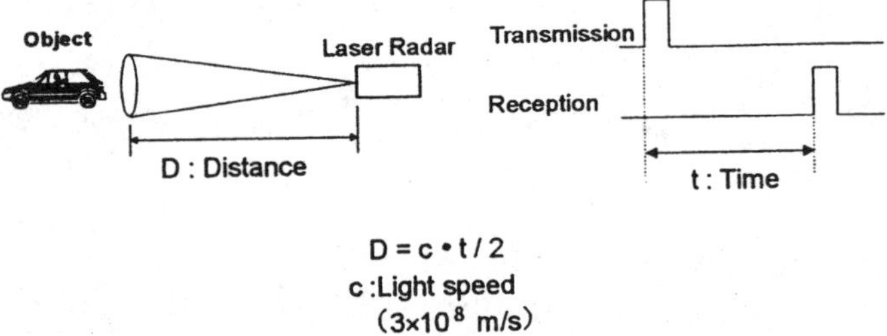

Figure 2. Basic Principle of Laser Radar

To meet the need of measuring distance in several directions at high speed, the scan laser radar uses a single distance measurement process which calculates the distance by the time period of single transmission and reception.

STRUCTURE

The external appearance of the Compact Scan Laser Radar which was developed is shown in Photo 1. Figure 3. is the composition of the Compact Scan Laser Radar. The Compact Scan Laser Radar consists of a laser transmission section, light reception section, scanning mechanism section, stain detection section and case.

Photo 1. Compact Scan Laser Radar

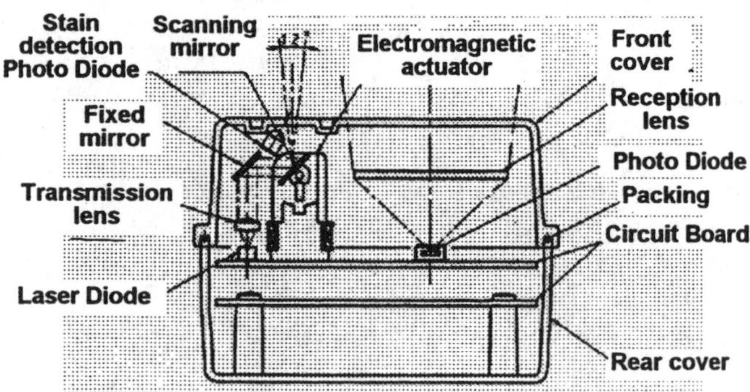

Figure 3. Composition of Compact Scan Laser Radar

LIGHT TRANSMISSION SECTION – The laser diode in light transmission section emits the infrared light of 850 nm wave length, in 100µs cycle. The transmission light specifications are shown in Table 1. Besides, in order to improve the angle resolving power and detection performance, the transmission lens forms a very narrow light beam on a horizontal line.

Table 1. Transmission Specifications

Light Output	11W
Light Wave Length	850nm
Transmission Period	100µs
Transmission Angle (Horizontal)	4°
Transmission Angle (Vertical)	0.05°
Pulse Width	25ns

LIGHT RECEPTION SECTION – Using the reception lens, the light reception section condenses the aforesaid laser pulse light, and receives light with the PIN diode. The reception lens employs a short focal length (f = 18 mm) Fresnel lens to achieve downsizing. In addition, reception sensitivity has been increased to reduce the reception area. The reception specifications are shown in Table 2.

Table 2. Reception Specifications

Reception Area	1000mm^2
Reception Angle (Horizontal)	14°
(Vertical)	7°
Detectable Peak Light Wave Length	900nm
Reception Sensibility	0.6A/W

SCANNING MECHANISM SECTION – The scanning section consists of a scanning mirror and an electromagnetic actuator. Laser pulse light emitted from the transmitter is irradiated to the transmitting scanning mirror through the fixed mirror. The scanning mirror attached on the electromagnetic actuator is rotated to direct laser pulse light horizontally in the forward direction. The laser pulse light is reflected on the object forward, returned to the laser radar and received at the light reception section.

Regarding the electromagnetic actuator, as shown in Figure 4, the scanning mirror and the permanent magnet are attached on the rotation shaft around which they move. The permanent magnet is mounted so that its magnetizing direction agrees with the rotating direction. This changes the direction and strength of current flowing in the electromagnetic coil provided nearby, magnetizes the core tip according to the amperage, and permits the scanning mirror to operate in the rotating angle proportional to the amperage. The rotation shaft is fixed using ball bearings, resulting in good response with low hysteresis. Figure 5 shows the relation between driving current and rotation angle.

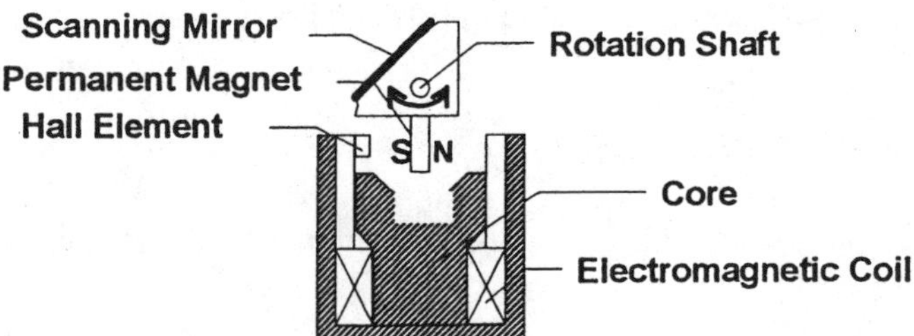

Figure 4. Electromagnetic Actuator

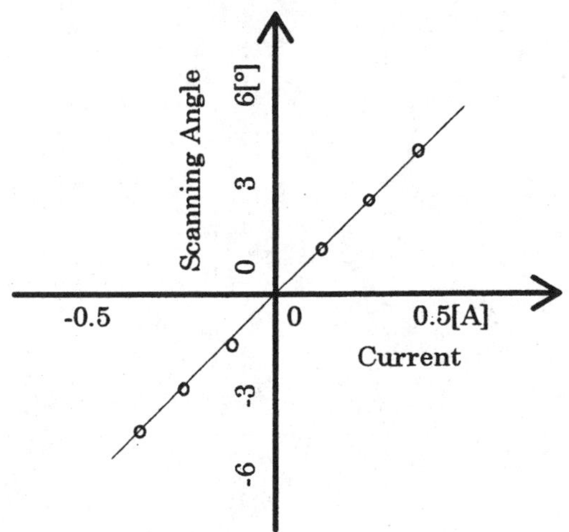

Figure 5. Scanning Angle-Current

In the vicinity of the permanent magnet, is provided the Hall element that detects the magnetic flux density of the magnet, permitting detection of rotation angle.

Thus, the scanning mirror and peripheral components can be realized by simplified construction, and the rotation unit which is non-contact and compact can be detected with ease, resulting in an extra-compact, highly accurate, and highly durable scan system.

STAIN DETECTION SECTION – When the front cover of laser radar surface becomes stained , the laser pulse beam is scattered which deteriorates distance detection performance. In the transmission light section, there is a photo-diode equipped to detect stain or haze on the transmission window, by monitoring a portion of the scattered light.

CASE – The laser radar case employed is a plastic one that is lightweight, low-cost, and has sufficient strength and durability for practical service. The case consists of the front cover and rear cover. The front cover, which is required to transmit light, is made of a non-crystalline plastic. In addition, the front cover has a pigment added which cuts off visible light, forming an infrared light absorbing filter.

OPERATION

Figure 6 shows the operation block diagram of the compact scan laser radar. Receiving control data from the external laser radar control unit, the scan laser radar becomes ready to detect distance per control signal, drives the laser diode, and emits the beam. Then the scan laser radar drives the electromagnetic actuator to rotate the scanning mirror, and emits laser beam for horizontal scan. After laser beam reflected from the object ahead is received and undergoes photoelectric conversion by the photo diode, it is amplified and input to the time measuring circuit. The time measuring circuit detects distance by measuring the time from light transmission to reception and speed of light, and corrects distance according to reception level at that time. The laser beam scanning directions and the measured distance are averaged and sent to the laser radar control unit as distance data, together with respective scanning directions.

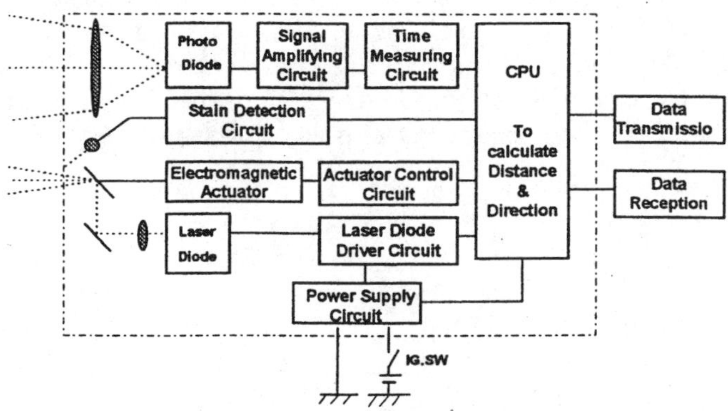

Figure 6. Operation Block Diagram

ELECTROMAGNETIC ACTUATOR CONTROL – Referring to Figure 7, in the electromagnetic actuator control circuit, the delta wave driving signals that determine transmission beam scan timing are amplified by the actuator driver circuit in accordance with gain control signals. The Hall element provided near the moving magnet (permanent magnet) of the electromagnetic actuator is used to detect the rotation angle. Gain of the actuator driver circuit is changed to suit that rotation angle, thus to determine a certain rotation angle. This is how the feedback control works.

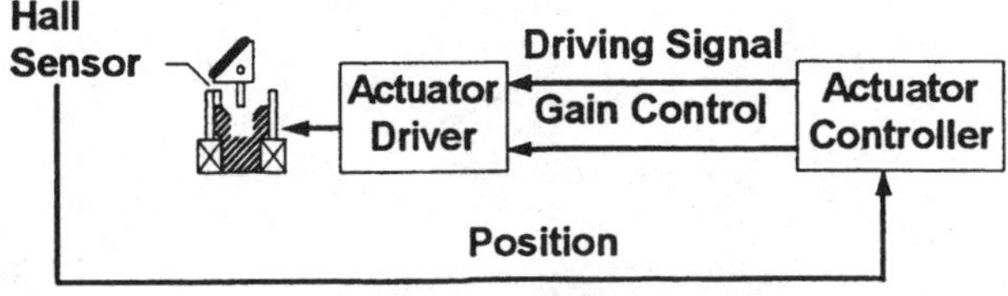

Figure 7. Electromagnetic Actuator Control

Figure 9 shows delta wave driving signals. As can be noted, the electromagnetic actuator is driven to rotate the scanning mirror. In accordance with this rotating light, transmission laser pulse light scans forward horizontally through the scanning mirror. During this one scanning, the present method detects distance in the same scanning direction every time by scanning only one direction. Regarding the driving signals, the distance measuring section is twice the returning section and the electromagnetic actuator makes fast return. The measuring period for the driving signals keeps linear, providing the scanning mirror a constant scanning angle speed. To drive the electromagnetic actuator, gain is set so that one rotation of the scanning mirror cycles the scanning transversely to make the laser pulse beam travel through a 12° range. The above control assures a transmission beam scanning angle of little fluctuation.

CORRECTION BY RECEPTION LEVEL – The laser radar calculates time from transmission to reception and measures distance. Judgment of reception is made by detecting signal wave startup on the basis of a predetermined threshold level. Therefore, as shown in Figure 8, distance measurement error occurs depending on reception signal level. Measured distance becomes greater as reception level decreases. A correction on measured distance based on the reception signal level improves measurement accuracy. Assuming measured distance as D, distance accuracy as L, and necessary correction as T (L), then corrected distance D' can be expressed:

$$D' = D - T(L)$$

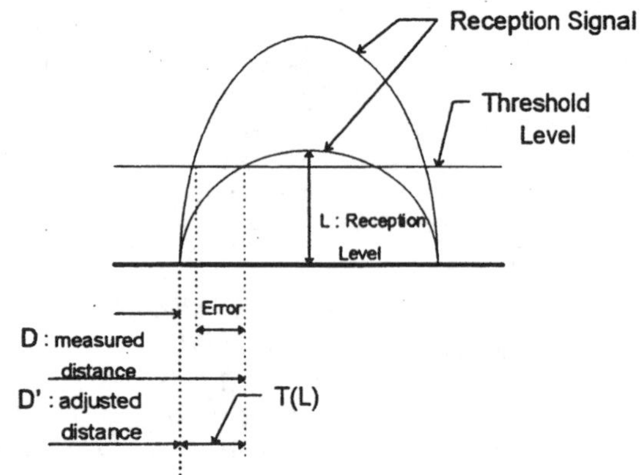

Figure 8. Correction by light reception level

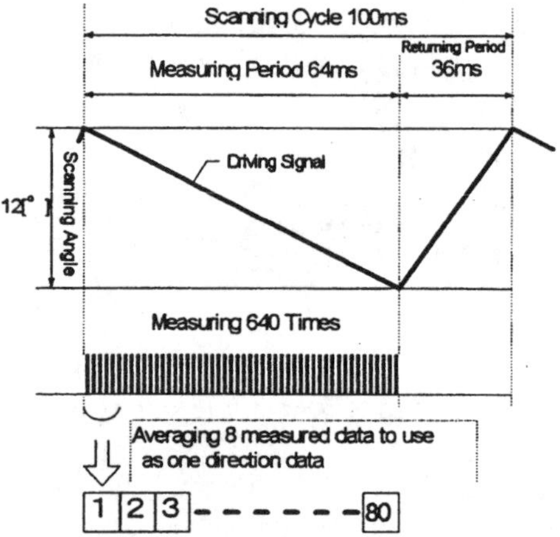

Figure 9. Scanning Process

DETECTION OF EACH DIRECTION – Figure 9. shows the timing of computing distance for a cycle of one scan. One scanning cycle of Scan Laser Radar is 100 ms. Within this cycle, the distance detection section is 64ms, in which 640 instances of distance detection are conducted. 8 instances each are averaged resulting, in distance data for 80 directions. The scanning angle is 12°,thus the angle resolving power of one direction is 12/80 = 0.15 [°]

SPECIFICATIONS

Specifications of the Compact Scan Laser Radar are shown in Table 3.

Table 3. Specifications of Compact Scan Laser Radar

Power Supply	10V
Maximum Current	0.7A
Temperature Range	-30~85°C
External Dimensions	100×52×70mm
Weight	0.3kg
Maximum Detection Distance	more than 100m*
Horizontal Detection Angle	12°
Vertical Detection Angle	4°
Distance Resolution	0.15m
Angular Resolution	0.15°
Distance Measuring Period	0.1s

*target:Φ51mm Reflex Reflector

FEATURES OF COMPACT SCAN LASER RADAR

COMPACT, LIGHTWEIGHT, AND LOW-PRICED

Use of Electromagnetic Actuator – To scan transmission laser pulse light, the system uses a simplified, moving-magnet electromagnetic actuator. This has allowed providing direct rotation without using any link mechanism with the motor, leading to the scan system with substantial reduction in size, weight, and sound, resulting in increased durability.

Use of Specialized ICs for Internal Circuitry – Specialized ICs are used in place of the analog circuitry such as the reception signal amplifier circuit and the time measuring circuit for distance detection. This has led to considerable cut in electronic components count, and has made it possible to downsize the surface-mount area as well as electronic components, and realize a more compact, lower-priced, and higher-reliability laser radar system.

Upgraded Reception Sensitivity – As the laser radar reception area is increased, the stronger reflected beam is receivable from the object with higher detection capacity. However, too large a reception area is a factor that affects downsizing. With the present system, specialized ICs are used in place of the signal amplifier circuitry in the light reception section, S/N ratio is raised to improve reception sensitivity, achieving reduction of the reception area with no deterioration of detection performance. This also saved the size of the laser radar.

Use of Plastic Case – Changing the laser radar case to the plastic one also has reduced its weight and cost. Because of the necessity to allow infrared laser pulse alone to pass through, the non-crystalline plastic having the effect of filtering infrared light is used for the front portion of the case.

UPGRADING OF PERFORMANCE

Faster Distance Measuring Cycle – The laser radar distance calculation circuit operates at higher speed and the electromagnetic actuator is more responsive, thus realizing faster distance measuring cycle.

Higher Distance-Measuring Accuracy – The strength of signals the laser radar receives decreases as detection distance increases and increases, to an excessive degree, as detection distance decreases, indicating that the signal strength range is extensive. Consequently, when the laser radar receives the beam reflected from a highly reflective object at a close distance, reception signals become saturated. In this case, distance cannot be corrected by light reception level, resulting in deteriorated distance accuracy. To counter this, we arranged to monitor signal strength at the prior-to-saturation stage in order to extend the dynamic range for detecting reception signal strength(Figure 10), thus enabling correction by light reception level even when excessive signal strength at a close distance is input. This has improved distance measuring accuracy.

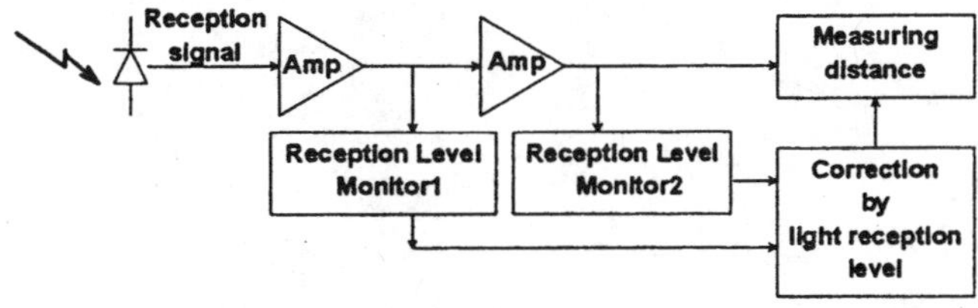

Figure 10. Monitoring light reception level

PERFORMANCE

ACCURACY OF DISTANCE – Accuracy of distance by the developed Compact Scan Laser Radar was measured. The 51mm reflex reflector, as the object, was placed at varied distance points on the forward direction of laser radar, and the distance to the object was measured. The results are shown in Figure 11. The accuracy of distance is within ±1 m, as shown in the figure.

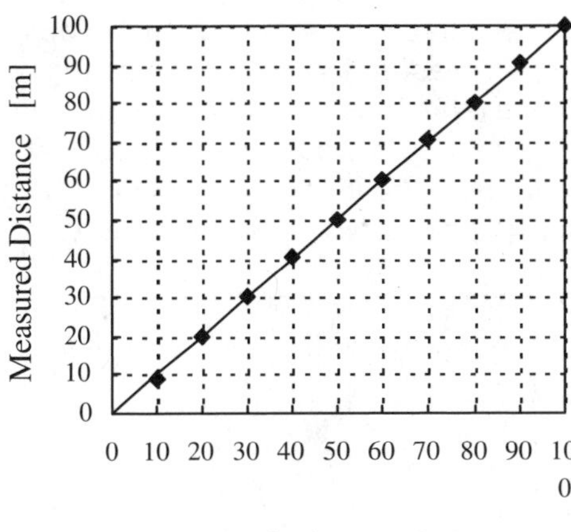

Figure 11. Accuracy of distance

DETECTION RANGE – Detection range of the compact laser scan laser radar was measured. Figure 12 shows the detectable range with the 51mm reflex reflector used as the test object. The detectable angle is 12 horizontally and 4 vertically, as shown.

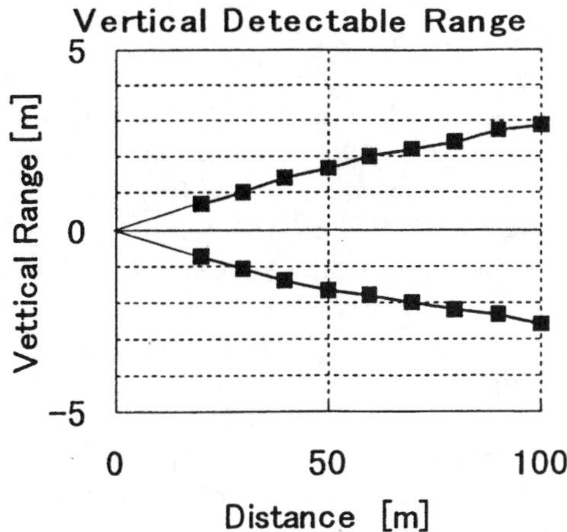

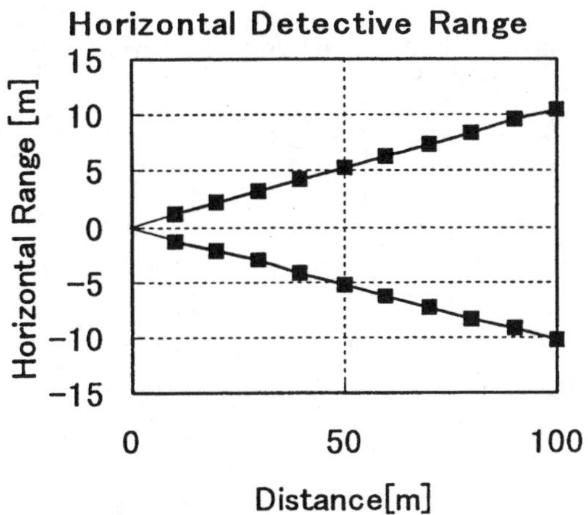

Figure 12. Detectable Range

SCAN PATTERN – The scan pattern of the scan laser radar was measured. Detection angle in each detecting direction was measured with a 51mm reflex reflector placed 100 m ahead of the laser radar. The result is shown in Figure 13. Note that the angle of each detection direction changes linearly, indicating that the transmission beam is capable of linear scanning.

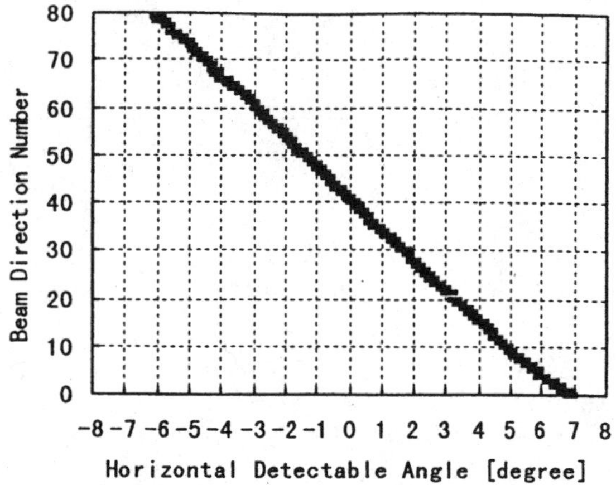

Figure 13. Scan Pattern

CONCLUSION

We have developed a low-price scan laser radar for warning of and controlling distance between vehicles. Downsizing and weight reduction of the laser radar made it easier to install in vehicles. The features of this laser radar are expected to lead to its wider use and play a further important role for preventive safety in the future.

REFERENCES

1. Shoichi Tanaka, Masahira Akasu, William Bracken, "Development of a Scan Laser Radar", SAE, Paper 970172
2. Yanagisawa, "Development of a Laser Radar System for Automobiles", SAE, Paper 920745
3. Kazuma Kaneko, Koichi Kai, Masahira Akasu, "Trial of Target Vehicle Detection by Using Scanning Laser Radar", SAE, Paper 970177

972669

Monopulse Radar for Intelligent Cruise Control

Jerry D. Woll
Eaton VORAD Technologies

ABSTRACT

This paper describes the Eaton VORAD Technologies monopulse radar system and its application to intelligent cruise control (ICC) systems using the SmartCruise® ICC for light and heavy vehicles. The advantages of monopulse radar for continuous, independent measurement of the azimuth angles to multiple highway obstacles and vehicles are discussed. A comparison of the monopulse radar system to switched beam systems and mechanically scanned systems is presented. In addition, this paper describes the narrow band Doppler radar principles employed in Eaton VORAD radar technology and discusses its advantages over wide-band modulation techniques. The unique interference avoidance scheme of the radar system is presented. Radar sensor technology is compared with other sensor technologies and the advantages of radar are also discussed.

BACKGROUND

Eaton VORAD Technologies has been manufacturing and marketing radar based collision warning systems for the heavy truck and bus markets for over three years. Over 4500 systems have been sold and installed. Over 5500 professional drivers have experienced over 900,000,000 kilometers with the radar systems giving Eaton VORAD the largest vehicle system mileage data base, the largest driver human factor feedback data base, and the most extensive collision warning data in the world. This wealth of information has led to many product improvements and is the basis for the next generation radar system which includes monopulse operation and the SmartCruise® intelligent cruise control capability. Eaton VORAD has 18 issued patents and over 15 patents in process relating to their radar system technology. Additional information on the Eaton VORAD system and its predecessor VORAD system can be found in references [1], [2], [3] and [4].

RADAR TECHNOLOGY

There are several technologies under investigation for possible use in vehicle sensors detecting obstacles and vehicles in front of a host vehicle at long distances (up to 150 meters), as well as for detecting obstacles at shorter ranges (up to 10 meters) near the host vehicle for blind spot and lane change warning and back-up collision warning. The long range sensor on the front of the vehicle is typically referred to as a Forward Looking Sensor (FLS) and the short range sensors on the sides and the back of vehicles are referred to as Near Obstacle Detection Systems (NODS).

Potential technologies for the sensors include radar, laser, video, infrared, and ultrasonic. Light based systems such as laser, video and infrared have the demanding and often difficult requirement of maintaining a clean unobstructed lens, and typically have the same limitations as the human eye with regard to penetrating adverse weather such as fog, dust and rain, and therefore offer little help to the driver under such conditions.

Laser based systems are able to focus the transmitted energy into very narrow beams due to its high frequency and very short wavelengths. It is often necessary to scan the laser beam or diffuse the beam with a lens to fully cover a traffic lane. The strongest laser reflections from target vehicles usually come from the taillight lenses or the license plates. If these surfaces are dirty or covered with snow or mud, the effective range of the laser system can be significantly reduced. Of course, if the lens of the laser system itself is dirty or coated with mud or snow, system performance is also significantly degraded or non-operational. Some laser systems have problems at sunrise or sunset when the sun is shining directly into the detector lens. Sunlight has frequency components in the same range as the laser frequency which can cause false alarms or sensor blindness under certain conditions. Laser systems must also be designed to consider human eye-health safety issues, as do all laser products. The health issue is sometimes handled by powering the laser down while the vehicle is stopped and only allowing the laser to activate after the vehicle reaches a forward speed of 8 to 15 km/h.

Video systems hold some promise as vehicle sensors in the distant future; however, at this time the complex signal processing associated with automatic video target recognition and tracking for multiple targets is prohibitive in cost. As mentioned earlier, video systems also have performance limitations with regard to lens contamination and adverse weather. In addition, since video systems are passive, they require an external source of light to illuminate the targets. This can be a problem at night when only the headlights are available for target illumination. Further, long range target distance measurement accuracy is limited for video systems. To get range in a video system, two lenses/cameras separated by a fixed distance in a stereo operational mode are required. Range is then determined by triangulating the target distance with reference to the separation distance of the two camera lenses. With the distance between the camera lenses typically small (several centimeters) for mounting behind the center rear view mirror, it is difficult to accurately measure target range beyond 30 to 50 meters.

It is very difficult to project an infrared or ultrasonic energy beam out to 150 meters while traveling at highway speeds, and therefore, infrared and ultrasonic systems have potential for only NODS applications. Infrared, however, still has the requirement for a clean lens, and some precaution must be taken if the sensor is exposed to direct sunlight since sunlight includes infrared frequency components. Ultrasonic sensors also have potential for NODS applications, but their poor directionality and high false alarm rates have thus far limited them to bumper-mounted parking aids with a maximum range of 2 to 3 meters. Ultrasonic sensors typically operate at a frequency between 40 KHz and 50 KHz and are therefore susceptible to false alarms from common noise sources that produce frequencies or harmonics in the ultrasonic frequency band - hissing from air brake operation, jingling keys, tire noise on wet roads, etc. Ultrasonic sensors do offer better operation in adverse weather than light-based systems since they do not require a clear sensor surface. Nevertheless, a layer of ice or mud over the sensor surface may render ultrasonic sensors non-operational.

For these reasons, radar offers the best solution of all technologies, and the general industry trend is towards radar technology for vehicle sensors. With recent FCC approval of 46.8 GHz and 76.5 GHz for vehicle applications, radar sensor antennas can be reduced in size to accommodate all vehicles including small automobiles. Radar offers the best all-weather operation with good ability to penetrate fog, dust, rain and snow. Radar sensor surfaces can tolerate typical highway buildup such as dirt, bugs, salt spray, snow and ice better than any other technology. In fact, radar is the only technology that allows the sensor to be physically located behind plastic surfaces such as bumper facias. This has great appeal to vehicle stylists who want to totally conceal such sensors. Radar systems also offer excellent target discrimination with the ability to measure range, range rate, and azimuth angle to multiple targets. Table 1 presents a comparison of vehicle sensor technologies.

Technology→ Performance Feature↓	Ultrasonic	Infrared	Laser	Video	Radar
Long Range Capability	Poor	Poor	Good	Poor	Good
Target Discrimination	Poor	Poor	Fair	Fair	Good
Minimizing False Alarms	Poor	Poor	Fair	Fair	Good
Temperature Stability	Poor	Good	Good	Good	Good
Darkness Penetration	Good	Good	Good	Poor	Good
Adverse Weather Penetration	Poor	Poor	Poor	Poor	Good
Low Cost Hardware	Good	Good	Fair	Poor	Good
Low Cost Signal Processing	Good	Good	Fair	Poor	Good
Sensor Surface Dirt and Moisture Performance	Fair	Poor	Poor	Poor	Good
Vehicle Application	NODS	NODS	FLS/NODS	NODS	FLS/NODS

Table 1 - Technology vs. Performance

PRODUCTION RADAR

The model EVT-200 is the current production radar system from Eaton VORAD. This unit is a multiple-frequency modulated system that uses a very narrow bandwidth and thus is extremely spectrum efficient. The narrow-band system was developed by Eaton VORAD to operate in the existing FCC Part 15 unlicensed band with an authorized bandwidth of only 100 MHz. The new FCC vehicle radar frequencies of 46.8 GHz and 76.5 GHz will permit bandwidths of 200 MHz and 1000 MHz respectively. While the new frequencies allow more bandwidth for radar systems, Eaton VORAD has found that there are significant advantages to staying with a narrow-band system. The current Eaton VORAD production radar system is a fixed-beam system operating at a frequency of 24.725 GHz. The 3 dB half-power beamwidth is 4 degrees in azimuth and 5 degrees in elevation with an antenna aperture size of 15 cm high by 20 cm wide. At 76.5 GHz the antenna aperture size is about 7 cm in height by 12 cm in width. The smaller antenna aperture size can reduce the sensor package size to approximately 8 cm high by 13 cm wide by 6 cm deep.

The current production unit is a Doppler based radar system using continuous wave (CW) transmission with frequency modulation (FM) operation from a frequency modulation switching technique (frequency shift keying, FSK) to independently and simultaneously measure range and closing rate for an unlimited number of detected targets. Target closing rate (range rate) is measured directly from the Doppler frequency shift in the reflected signal, and target range is measured by comparing the frequency phase of the Doppler frequencies on the reflected signal on each of at least two different transmitted frequencies. The EVT-200 system employs a powerful digital signal processor (DSP) chip to calculate a 4096 point Fast Fourier Transform (FFT) to identify, discriminate, and track multiple targets.

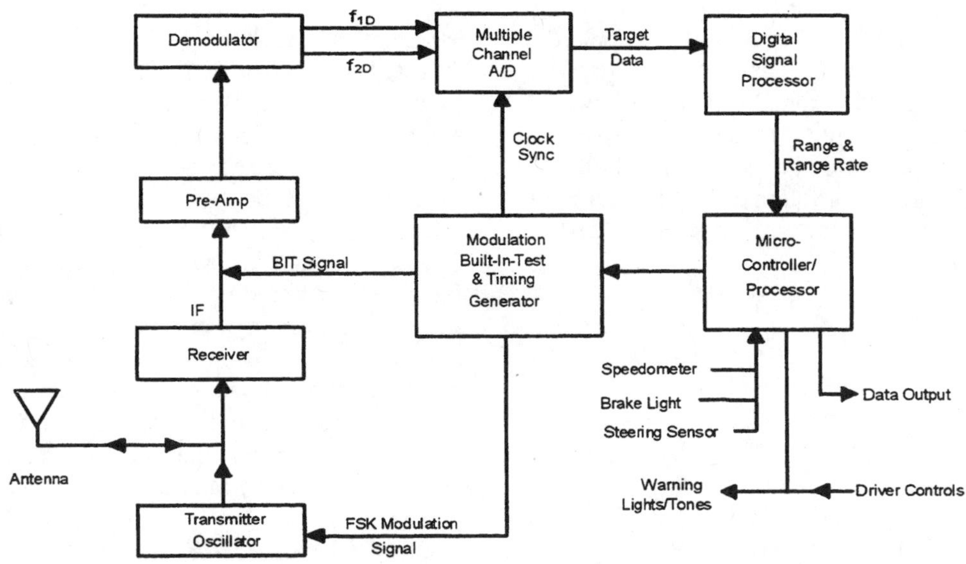

Figure 1 - Eaton VORAD Radar System Block Diagram

The EVT-200 uses a etched-patch, flat antenna for both transmit and receive, and a gallium arsenide (GaAs) GUNN diode oscillator with a balanced Schottky diode mixer receiver and associated circuitry on a microwave integrated circuit (MIC) soft-board substrate. The transmitter power delivered to the antenna is typically only 0.5 milliwatts, making the system highly efficient in power as well as bandwidth. Figure 1 presents a block diagram of the EVT-200 production system.

The Eaton VORAD FM-CW (FSK) modulated radar transmission is similar to that shown in Figure 2. At least two different frequencies, f_1 and f_2, are transmitted at a time-shared switched rate of about 100 KHz. The two frequencies are only about 500 KHz apart which results in the very narrow bandwidth of operation for the system. Traditional FMCW radar systems require 300 MHz to 500 MHz of modulation bandwidth to achieve range resolution/accuracies of 0.5 to 1 meter. This is 600 to 1000 times more bandwidth than the Eaton VORAD system requires.

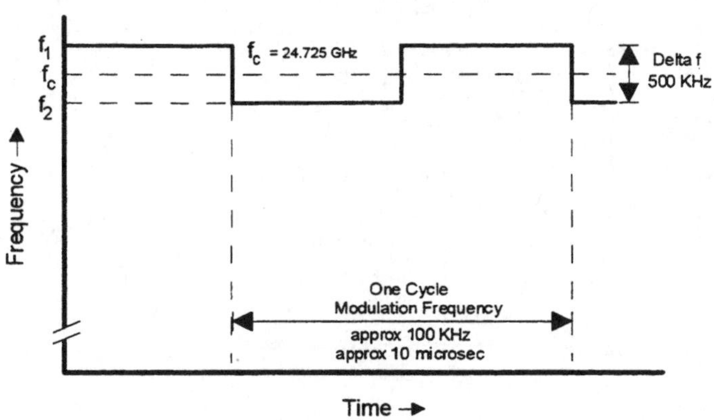

Figure 2 - Eaton VORAD FM-CW (FSK) Modulation

The two transmitted frequencies, f_1 and f_2 , when reflected from a target, will generate two Doppler signals, f_{1D} and f_{2D} as shown in Figure 1 at the output of the demodulator. Closing rate is determined directly by the frequency of the Doppler signal on either f_{1D} or f_{2D} at 45 Hz per km/h. Range is calculated by comparing the phase of f_{1D} to the phase of f_{2D} with a range of 1.5 meters per degree of phase difference. The frequency spectrum for received radar signals for either transmitted frequency is shown in Figure 3. Each target is represented by a Doppler frequency component as shown. The height of the frequency component relates to the strength of the return signal, and the frequency is directly convertible to the closing rate by dividing by 45 Hz/km/h. The system can differentiate between targets down to a speed difference of only 0.4 km/h. In highway scenarios, vehicle targets cannot maintain speed matches of less than 0.4 km/h for more than a few milliseconds. System software trackers maintain accurate vehicle target tracking through momentary speed matches of multiple targets.

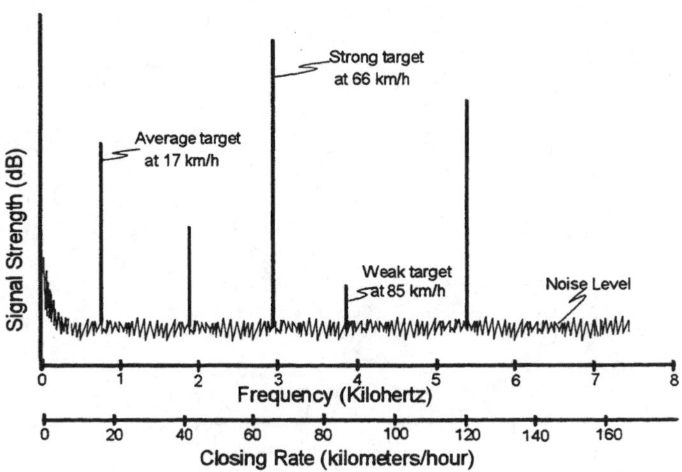

Figure 3 - Doppler Frequency/Target Spectrum

Target range is measured by comparing the Doppler frequency phase of f_{1D} to the phase of f_{2D} as shown in Figure 4. The phase difference is related to round trip signal travel time and travel time is related to target distance by the speed of light. The maximum range that can be measured with this technique is the round-trip range equivalent of 180 degrees of phase shift, or approximately 1.5 meters/degree times 180 degrees or approximately 270 meters.

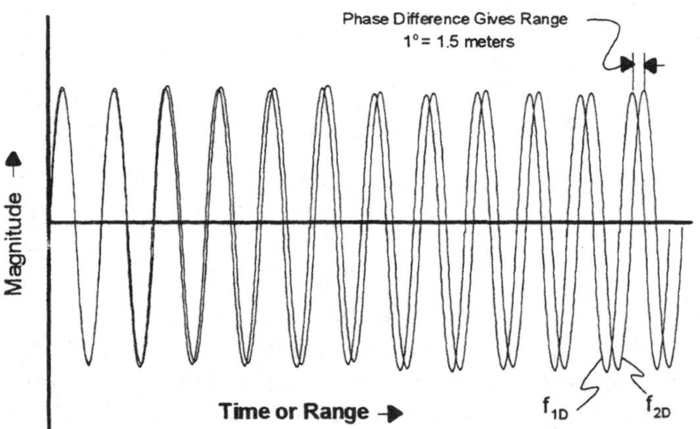

Figure 4 - Range from Doppler Frequency Phase Difference

INTERFERENCE AVOIDANCE

The narrow frequency bandwidth of Eaton VORAD system technology enables it to be one of the best technologies for avoiding interference from other vehicle radar systems or other RF in-band sources in general. Radar systems that require 300 MHz to 500 MHz of modulation bandwidth will find it more difficult to operate within the 1000 MHz bandwidth allowed by the FCC for 76.5 GHz. The Eaton VORAD system, with a modulation bandwidth of less than 1 MHz, has no problem finding a quiet zone within the 1000 MHz band to continue safe operation. Wide bandwidth radar systems may claim to be interference free because of the improbability of any two radar systems having synchronized modulation signals, or they may claim to have a coded or correlated signal recognition. These techniques do reduce interference possibilities; however, they do not account for the increase in noise floor created by the other radar systems and that reduces the overall system signal-to-noise ratio, thus reducing its detection capability for weaker targets. Eaton VORAD has a patented scheme for frequency hopping to avoid interference and thus assure continuous operation in the presence of potential interfering RF sources.

MONOPULSE RADAR SYSTEM

A monopulse feature has been added to next generation Eaton VORAD radar systems now nearing market introduction. The primary advantage of a monopulse feature is the simultaneous, continuous, and independent measurement of azimuth angle to all targets as well as the range and closing rate measurements described in the previous section. This added dimension provides for improved target recognition and tracking, plus it allows lane definition/discrimination and improved performance in turns when coupled with a turn/steering sensor. Moreover, monopulse operation gives excellent performance for intelligent cruise control applications. Eaton VORAD is developing monopulse systems at several operating frequencies including 24 GHz, 47 GHz, 60 GHz and 77 GHz. The block diagram for the monopulse system is shown in Figure 5.

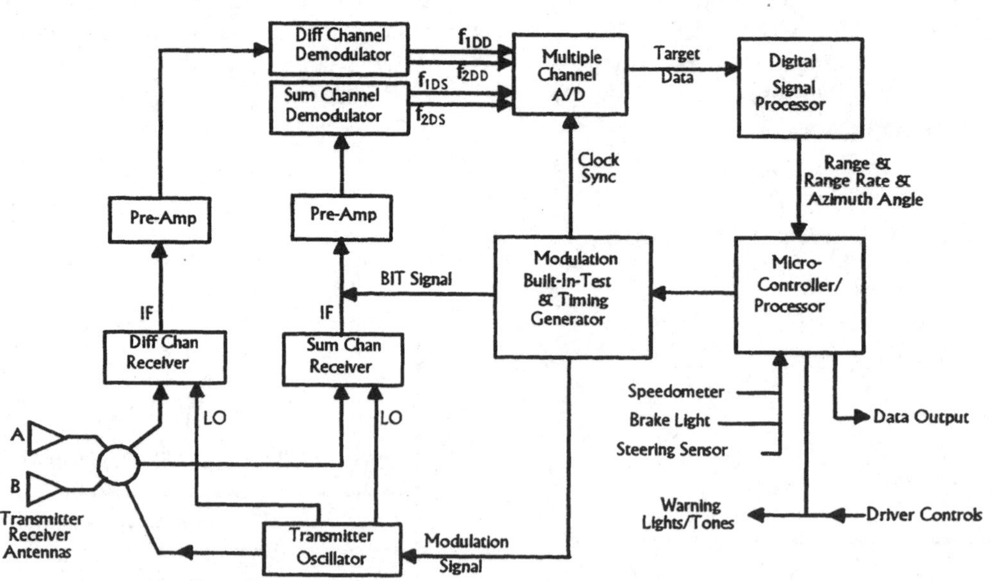

Figure 5 - Monopulse Radar System Block Diagram

As can in Figures 1 and 5, the major difference between the monopulse system and the fixed beam system is that the monopulse system splits the single antenna into two antennas, A and B, and adds a second receiver channel. The transmitted signal is fed out both antennas as if they were one single combined antenna. However, on the receive side, the received signal is split between antenna A and antenna B, which are physically separated by a few centimeters. This separation of the two receive antennas gives a stereo-vision perspective to the radar. By comparing selected properties of the signals from the two receive antennas, azimuth angles to vehicle targets can be calculated.

The theory of operation for the monopulse feature consists of combining the return signals from antenna A with antenna B in a particular way. Within the microwave circuitry, the return from antenna A is added to the return from antenna B giving the sum signal which is processed in the sum channel of the system. The return signal from antenna A is also subtracted from the return signal from antenna B giving the difference signal which is processed in the difference channel of the system. As seen in Figure 5, there are now four (4) Doppler channel frequencies available (f_{1DS} and f_{2DS} from the Sum channel and f_{1DD} and f_{2DD} from the Difference channel). Target azimuth angle information is determined by comparing the signal strength (gain) on one of the Sum channel Doppler signals with the strength of the corresponding Doppler frequency on the Difference channel. This is shown graphically in Figure 6.

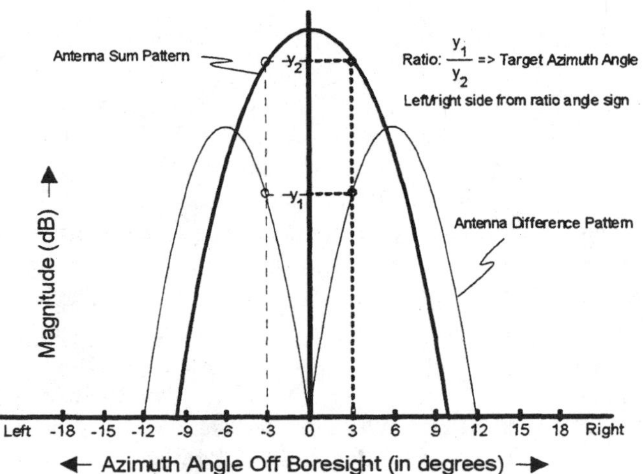

Figure 6 - Monopulse Sum and Difference Patterns

From Figure 6, it is seen that the Difference pattern/channel has a deep notch in signal strength at boresight (straight ahead or 0 degrees) while the Sum pattern/channel has it maximum strength at boresight. By comparing the ratio of the signal strengths of the Sum and Difference channels, the angle off boresight can be determined. There are actually two angles off boresight with the same signal strength ratio, one on the left side and one on the right side. However, the system is mathematically able to determine if the target is on the left or right side and resolve the angle redundancy. The monopulse system can measure azimuth angle over a range from approximately 6 degrees on the left to 6 degrees on the right (total of 12 degrees) with an angle accuracy and resolution of 0.1 degrees. Thus the three key target data parameters are measured as follows:

Closing Rate: The closing rate is calculated directly from any one of the four Doppler channel frequencies (f_{1DS}, f_{2DS}, f_{1DD} or f_{2DD}) by dividing the frequency by 45 Hz/km/h. This provides a four way redundancy to verify closing rate calculations.

Range: Range is calculated by measuring the phase difference between either f_{1DS} and f_{2DS} or between f_{1DD} and f_{2DD}. This provides a two way redundancy to verify range calculations.

Azimuth Angle: Azimuth angle to the target is calculated by comparing the signal strength values between f_{1DS} and f_{1DD} or between f_{2DS} and f_{2DD}. This provides a two way redundancy to verify azimuth calculations.

The azimuth angle capability of the monopulse feature permits the radar system to track targets around typical interstate radius curves, to minimize false alarms by skewing the detection zone in turns and to shape the detection zone to accurately fit a traffic lane. This makes the monopulse system the ideal sensor technology for both intelligent cruise control and collision warning applications.

Monopulse systems have other advantages over switched beam antenna systems and mechanically scanned antenna systems. The monopulse system provides continuous tracking data on all targets in the monopulse detection range of about 12 degrees without having to interrupt the data flow to switch beams or mechanically rotate the antenna. This allows the monopulse system to over-sample continuous target data to refine and filter position data as a steady stream. Switched beam and mechanically scanned systems must interrupt the data flow and clear the data channels each time the antenna beam is switched or rotated, and then restart the target data flow and processing from scratch. These systems must also wait until the antenna is again aimed at a specific target in order to get the next data update on that particular target, which can slow the update rate. These momentary gaps or blinks in the processing reduces system processing sensitivity and increases target data latency for switched beam and scanned systems.

The monopulse systems requires that more radio frequency (RF) power be delivered the antenna than the fixed-beam system. Added power is required in order to fill the 12 degree wide radar beam of the monopulse antenna with the same energy density as the 4 degree wide fixed-beam antenna beam pattern. Additional information on the theory of operation of Eaton VORAD monopulse radar system can be found in references [5] and [6].

INTELLIGENT CRUISE CONTROL

Eaton VORAD is an established leader in the field of intelligent cruise control systems and has a patent on an autonomous cruise control system. The Eaton VORAD cruise control system is registered under the name of SmartCruise® and is fully operational on several demonstration platforms including three light vehicle platforms and one heavy truck platform. The next generation Collision Warning System (CWS) product for heavy trucks will feature monopulse radar technology and SmartCruise®. Eaton VORAD has extensive experience with radar based cruise controls systems that employ throttle control only, throttle control coupled with commanded down-shifting, throttle control coupled with automatic braking, and throttle control coupled with commanded engine retarder braking on heavy trucks (Jacobson or "Jake" braking). Monopulse radar sensors for intelligent cruise control are available at 24 GHz for heavy trucks and at 77 GHz for automobiles and other light vehicles.

Eaton VORAD has been selected by the National Highway and Traffic Safety Administration (NHTSA) to conduct an operational test for intelligent cruise control systems on heavy trucks. Under this project, a number of operational heavy trucks at three nationally known commercial fleets will be equipped with Eaton VORAD collision warning and intelligent cruise control systems for studying driver benefits and changes in driver behavior over a two year test period.

The U.S. military has extensively tested the Eaton VORAD systems in both collision warning applications and intelligent cruise control using SmartCruise® for military convoying, safety and automatic vehicle spacing. The systems were endurance tested at the Aberdeen Proving Grounds with excellent results, showing that Eaton VORAD commercial products meet full military requirements for rough terrain and adverse environment operation.

As further verification of this technology, Eaton VORAD Technologies has formed a joint development effort with the Hitachi Corporation in Japan for the development of 60 GHz monopulse radar systems for Japanese vehicle applications in collision warning and intelligent cruise control.

REFERENCES

[1] Murphy, Donald O., Woll, Jerry D., "A Review of the VORAD Vehicle Detection and Driver Alert System" SAE Technical Paper Number 922495, SAE International Truck and Bus Meeting and Exposition, Toledo, Ohio, November 16-19, 1992.

2] Woll, Jerry D., "A Review of the Eaton VORAD Vehicle Collision Warning System", SAE Technical Paper Number 933063, SAE International Truck and Bus Meeting and Exposition, Detroit, Michigan, November 1-4, 1993.

[3] Woll, Jerry D., "Radar Based Vehicle Collision Warning System", SAE/IEEE Technical Paper Number 94C036, SAE/IEEE Convergence International Congress on Transportation Electronics, Dearborn, Michigan, October 17-19, 1994.

[4] Woll, Jerry D., "Vehicle Collision Warning System with Data Recording Capability", SAE Technical Paper Number 952619, SAE International Truck and Bus Meeting and Exposition, Winston-Salem, North Carolina, November 13-15, 1995.

[5] Woll, Jerry D., "VORAD Collision Warning Radar" Proceedings of the IEEE 1995 International Radar Conference, Alexandria, Virginia, May 8-11, 1995. IEEE Catalog Number 95CH-3571-0.

[6] Woll, Jerry D., "Monopulse Doppler Radar for Vehicle Applications", Proceedings of the Intelligent Vehicles '95 Symposium, Sponsored by the IEEE Industrial Electronics Society, Detroit, Michigan, September 24-25, 1995.

ABOUT THE AUTHOR

Jerry Woll is Vice President of Engineering for Eaton VORAD Technologies, San Diego, California, a vehicle radar development and manufacturing company. He has been with VORAD Safety Systems and Eaton VORAD Technologies for six years. Prior experience includes 10 years as Vice President of Engineering for Teledyne Ryan Electronics, San Diego, California, where he directed the design and development of Doppler radar systems for military applications. He completed 20 years service as an officer in the Civil Engineer Corps of the U.S. Navy where he specialized in electronic and computer engineering projects. Mr. Woll received a BSEE degree from Purdue University, a MSEE degree from the University of Michigan, and a MS degree in Computer Science from the Naval Postgraduate School, Monterey, California. He is a registered professional engineer in the states of Indiana and California, and a member of Tau Beta Pi and Eta Kappa Nu engineering honorary societies. Mr. Woll is co-inventor on five patents involving radar technology and has published and presented several technical papers for SAE and IEEE. His office is at Eaton VORAD Technologies, 10802 Willow Court, San Diego, CA 92127.

970177

Trial of Target Vehicle Detection by Using Scanning Laser Radar

Kazuma Kaneko, Koichi Kai, and Masahira Akasu
Mitsubishi Electric Corp.

ABSTRACT

In vehicle distance warning systems using fixed beam laser radar false alarms often occur on curved roads. To solve these problems, we attempted to detect the target vehicle correctly by using a scanning laser radar on curved roads. This scanning laser radar has the advantage that it is able to measure the distance and direction of obstacles on roads.

In this paper, we explain the following three items. The first is the configuration of the experimental system which we developed. The second is the method of target vehicle detection by using reflectors located along roads. The third is the performance of this experimental system.

INTRODUCTION

To prevent rear-end collisions, the development of vehicle distance warning systems and of auto-brake systems using fixed beam laser radar have been reported [1, 2]. Since false alarms often occur on curved roads with these systems, they cease alert and braking functions there. Accordingly they do not have sufficient performance for practical use.

A weak point of conventional systems is that fixed beam laser radar is unable to measure the direction of obstacles on roads. Because of this, conventional systems often lose the target vehicle and often mistake the guardrail for the target vehicle on curved roads. To solve these problems scanning laser radar has recently been developed in Japan [3, 4, 5]. Scanning laser radar has the advantage that it is able to measure not only the distance but also the direction of obstacles on roads.

We attempted to detect the target vehicle in the lane of travel on curved roads by using this scanning laser radar. To construct the vehicle distance warning system and the auto-brake system with sufficient performance, it is important to be able to detect the target vehicle correctly even on a curved road.

APPROACH FOR A TARGET VEHICLE DETECTION

To detect the target vehicle in the lane of travel, it is necessary to decide the range of the lane of travel. The shape of a lane usually agrees with the shape of the road. Accordingly, if a system could recognize the shape of a road, it could decide the range of the lane of travel based on the shape. On Japanese expressways, there are many reflectors located along curved roads (delineators). Because these delineators have superior reflection characteristics, the scanning laser radar is able to detect them at a long distance. We considered that it would be possible to recognize the shape of a road based on the locations of the delineators.

The experimental system that we developed has the following functions.

1. It detects delineators located along roads.
2. It estimates the shape of a road based on the locations of delineators.
3. It calculates the range of the lane of travel based on the road shape and detects the target vehicle in the lane of travel.

SYSTEM CONFIGURATION

The configuration of the experimental system is shown in Figure 1. The experimental system consists of the scanning laser radar, a speed sensor, a Personal Computer (PC), a data recorder, a video camera, a Video Tape Recorder (VTR), and a synchronizer. The scanning laser radar measures the distance and direction of obstacles on

the road, and outputs them to the data recorder. The speed sensor senses the speed of the vehicle and outputs it to the data recorder. The data recorder records data from the scanning laser radar and the speed sensor and plays back the recorded data. The video camera films the road situations and outputs a video signal to the VTR. The VTR records the video signal from the video camera and plays back the recorded video signal. The synchronizer synchronizes the data recorder and the VTR operations. The PC detects the target vehicle based on the outputs of the scanning laser radar and of the speed sensor and superimposes images of the recorded road situation on a display at the same time.
The images of the road situations and the vehicle ahead are used to judge whether the target vehicle is detected correctly, and nor to detect the target vehicle.

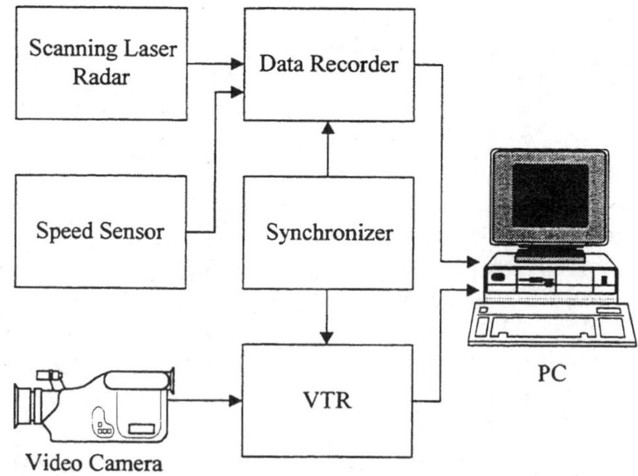

Figure 1. Block Diagram of The Experiment System

PERFORMANCE OF SCANNING LASER RADAR - The scanning laser radar which is the main sensor of the system has the following specifications.

- Vertical beam angle of 4 degrees.
- Scanning angle of 12 degrees.
- Horizontal angle resolution of 12/80 degrees.
- Scanning interval of 150 ms.
- Laser wave length of 850 nm (Infrared).

The vertical beam angle was decided in consideration of the vehicle pitching due to acceleration or braking and of bumpy roads [6]. The scanning laser radar conforms to the IEC regulation of Class 1.

Figure 2 is a photograph of the scanning laser radar. The scanning laser radar is 154 mm wide, 54 mm high, and 90 mm deep. In Figure 2, the large window is for reception, and the small window is for transmission.

Figure 2. Appearance of Scanning Laser Radar

PROCESS OF TARGET VEHICLE DETECTION

In this section, we explain the method of target vehicle detection. The data that we use for detecting the target vehicle are the distance and the direction measured by the scanning laser radar and the speed of the vehicle. A data flow diagram from the start of process to the end is shown in Figure 3.

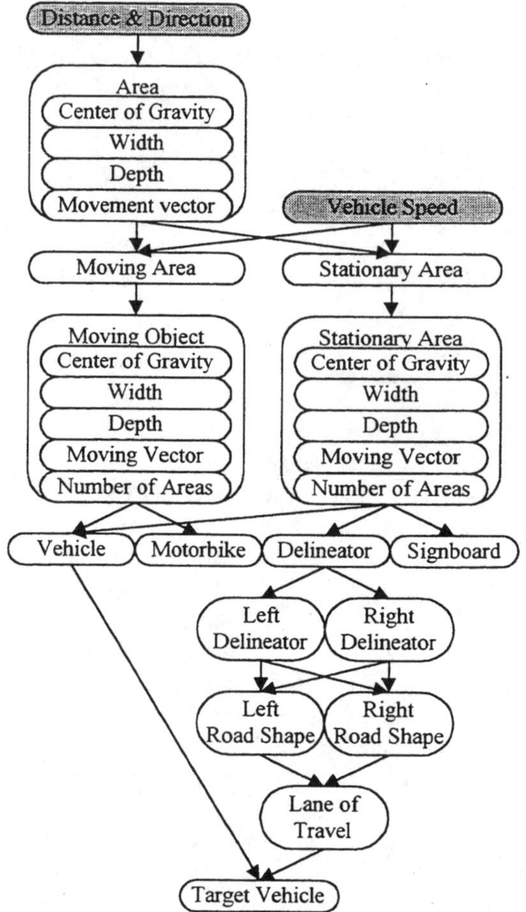

Figure 3. Data Flow Diagram of Target Vehicle Detection

AREA EXTRACTION - Figure 4 is a conception diagram of measurement by the scanning laser radar. When the scanning laser radar measures an obstacle having a certain width such as a vehicle, it detects the distance by plural beams. If the distances measured by adjacent beams are almost equal there is a high possibility that this is one object. We call this part an area, and do it with base unit of process. The PC extracts areas and calculates center of gravity, width, and depth for each area.

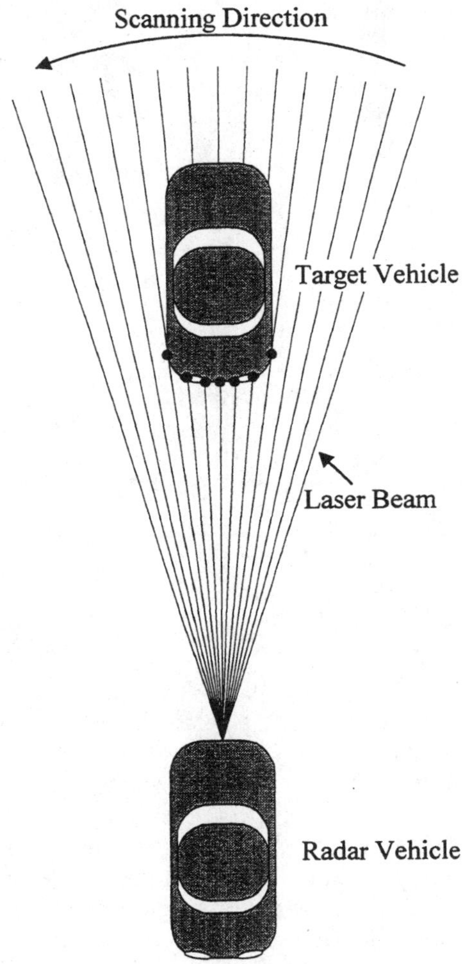

Figure 4. Measurement by Scanning Laser Radar

MOVEMENT OF AREA - When the scanning laser radar measures a passing vehicle, the distances measured by the scanning laser radar get longer by degrees. On the other hand, in the case of an approaching vehicle, the distances measured by the scanning laser radar shortens by degrees. Therefore the relative location changes of obstacles on roads are equivalent to movements of extracted areas. The PC examines which area extracted in the previous scan corresponds with the area extracted in the present scan.

STATIONARY/MOVING AREA DECISION - The movement distance of the radar vehicle during a scanning period is calculated based on the scanning period and the speed of the radar vehicle. The movement of the radar vehicle and the length of the movement vector of the area are compared. If both values are about the same, this area is judged to be a stationary area. If the values are different, this area is judged to be a the moving area.

AREA COMBINATION - In the case of a vehicle a long distance away, the scanning laser radar is able to detect only reflex reflectors with their superior reflection properties [7]. Therefore, only two reflex reflectors having the same movement vector are detected by the scanning laser radar. In consideration of this, plural areas which have about the same movement vector are combined as one object. After combination, the center of gravity, the width, the depth, movement vector, and the number of combined areas are calculated again for every combined area. But, combination is not done when the width or the depth of the area after combination becomes very big. After this processing, we call both combined areas and non-combined areas objects.

RECOGNITION OF VEHICLES - The stationary objects and the moving objects which satisfy all the following conditions are judged to be vehicles.

1. An object composed of two or more areas.
2. An object width of the Wo of more than 1 meter and less than 2 meters.
3. An object depth Do of less than 3 meters.

RECOGNITION OF MOTORBIKES - Moving objects which satisfy all the following conditions are judged to be motorbikes.

1. An object composed of one area.
2. An object width Wo of more than 50 centimeters and less than 1 meter.
3. An object depth Do of less than 2 meters.

We do not include stationary objects as motorbike decision objects here, because it is difficult to distinguish stationary motorbikes and delineators on roads by using only the outputs of the scanning laser radar and of the vehicle speed calculation unit.

DELINEATOR EXTRACTION - There are two type of object found along roads. One is delineators, and the other is sign boards. We are able to use only delineators to estimate the road shape. Accordingly, it is necessary to distinguish between delineators and sign boards.

The ability to distinguish between delineators and sign boards is based on the difference between the width of a delineator and that of a sign board. If the width of a stationary object is less than threshold alpha, the PC judges that the stationary object is a delineator candidate. If the width of stationary object is not less than threshold alpha, the PC judges that the stationary object is a sign board. Next, the PC sets up the window of width 2Ww and of depth 2Dw around the circumference of the delineator candidate. If there is just one delineator candidate inside the window, the delineator candidate in the center of the window is judged to be a delineator.

LEFT-RIGHT SEPARATION OF DELINEATORS - The delineators extracted by the above process include delineators established along the right and left of roads. To estimate the road shape, it is necessary to separate the delineators installed along the left from delineators along the right. We developed a method of separating delineators into right and left based on the loci of the delineator. An explanation of this method follows.

The PC computes the loci of a delineator based on the present position and the last three positions of the delineator. Figure 5 shows the conceptual figure of the loci of a delineator. We will explain this method by using the example of Figure 5.

The PC seeks for locus a_0-a_{-3} which has the shortest distance, and computes a straight line L of a delineator of which the present position a_0 and the position a_{-3} of three scans previous are connected. The intersection point P between the straight line L and the X axis is computed. If the x coordinate value of the intersection point P is a minus, locus a_0-a_{-3} is judged to be a delineator installed along the left of the road. If the x coordinate value of the intersection point P is a plus, locus a_0-a_{-3} is judged to be a delineator installed along the right of the road. As for the example in Figure 5, locus a_0-a_{-3} is judged to be a delineator installed along the left of the road.

The PC next seeks for a locus b_0-b_{-3} whose distance is shortest after locus a_0-a_{-3}. The straight line L is defined in equation (1). The distance S_b in the X axis direction between the position b_0 and the straight line L is calculated by equation (2). Here (x_b, y_b) are the coordinate values of the delineator b_0. If distance S_b is more than threshold beta, locus b_0-b_{-3} is judged to be opposite to locus a_0-a_{-3}. If distance S_b is smaller than threshold beta, locus b_0-b_{-3} is judged to be on the same side as locus a_0-a_{-3}.

$$y = ax + b \tag{1}$$

$$S_b = |\frac{y_b - b}{a} - x_b \tag{2}$$

The same processing is done for locus c_0-c_{-3}. As for the example in Figure 5, locus a_0-a_3 and locus c_0-c_{-3} are judged to be delineators installed along the left of the road, and locus b_0-b_{-3} is judged to be a delineator installed on the right of the road.

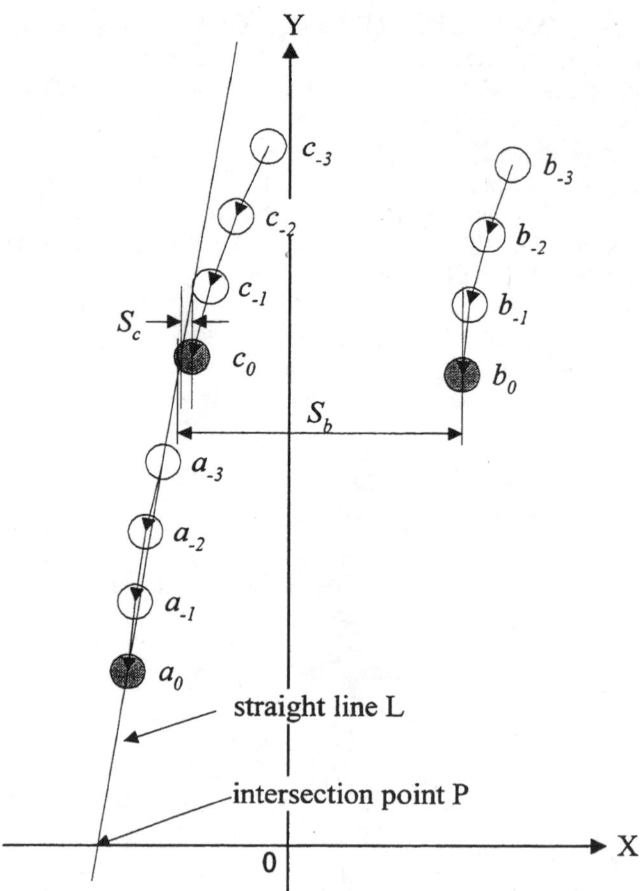

Figure 5. Example of Left-Right Separation of Delineators

ESTIMATION OF ROAD SHAPES - We consider a road shape to be a combination of straight and curved lines. We devised a method of estimating the road shape by using a quadratic curve which is the simplest curved line. Vehicles usually travel along a road in the same lane except for lane changing. Therefore, we supposed that a road shape is parallel to the track of the vehicles traveling along it. In accordance with this supposition, the quadratic curve shown in equation (3) is computed by the method of least squares. Then, the road shape is approximated by computing the quadratic curve. Figure 6 is a outline of the quadratic curve shown in equation (3).

$$x = a \cdot y^2 + c \tag{3}$$

The process which computes the road shape is as follows.

Step 1 - As the number of loci which are available for computing the quadratic curve increases, the estimation precision of the road shape becomes higher. Therefore, a comparison is made between the number of loci which are installed along the right side of a road and the number of loci along the left side. The side which has more loci is the standard side for estimating the road shape.

Step 2 - The quadratic curve shown in equation (3) is computed based on the loci of the standard side.

Equations (4) and (5) are coefficient a and coefficient c of the quadratic curve computed by using the method of least squares.

$$a = \frac{N \cdot \sum_{i=1}^{N} x_i \cdot y_i^2 - \sum_{i=1}^{N} y_i^2 \cdot \sum_{i=1}^{N} x_i}{N \cdot \sum_{i=1}^{N} y_i^4 - \sum_{i=1}^{N} y_i^2 \cdot \sum_{i=1}^{N} y_i^2} \tag{4}$$

$$c = \frac{\sum_{i=1}^{N} x_i \cdot \sum_{i=1}^{N} y_i^4 - \sum_{i=1}^{N} y_i^2 \cdot \sum_{i=1}^{N} x_i \cdot y_i^2}{N \cdot \sum_{i=1}^{N} y_i^4 - \sum_{i=1}^{N} y_i^2 \cdot \sum_{i=1}^{N} y_i^2} \tag{5}$$

where N is the number of the loci of the standard side, and (x_i, y_i) are the coordinate values of the delineator Di contained in the locus.

Step 3 - The road shape on the opposite side is computed based on the quadratic curve of the standard side. It is computed by moving the quadratic curve of the standard side along the X axis. The distance to be moved along the X axis is calculated based on the loci on the opposite side by using the method of least squares. The road shape on the opposite side is not computed when there is no locus on the opposite side of the road.

Step 4 - The road shape of an expressway does not change rapidly, it changes gradually. Therefore, the difference between the current shape of the quadratic curve and the last one is small. When there is a large difference between the shapes of these two curves, the number of the current loci is compared with the number of the loci the last time. If the number of the loci the last time is greater than that at present, it is judged that the reliability of the road shape the last time is higher than the current one. In this case, the last quadratic curve is adopted for the road shape at present. However, if the number of loci at present is more than that at the last time, it is judged that the reliability of the current road shape is higher than the last time. In this case, the current quadratic curve is adopted as the road shape.

Steps 1, 2, and 4 are done for both sides of the road when the number of the loci which are installed along the right side of the road is the same as the number along the left side.

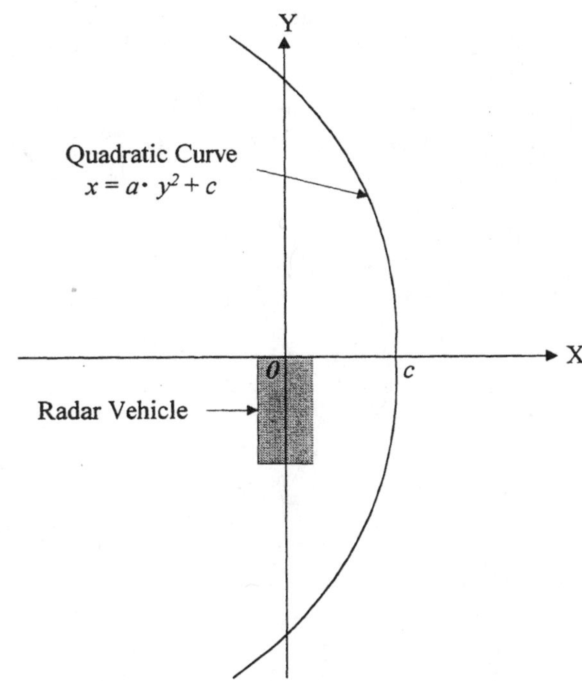

Figure 6. Outline of the Quadratic Curve

RECOGNITION OF A TARGET VEHICLE - In accordance with the supposition that the road shape and the shape of the lanes are similar, the range of the lane of travel is calculated by the following method.

The estimated road shape is moved to the origin of the coordinates along the X axis. Then the road shape, which is moved to the origin of the coordinates, is considered to be the center of the lane of travel. The range of width W_l is set on both sides from the center as shown in Figure 7, and it is regarded as the range of the lane of travel.

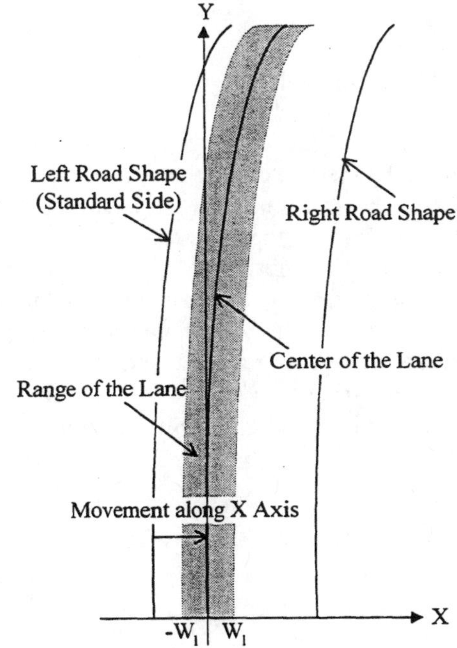

Figure 7. Range of the Lane of Travel

A reliability distribution is set within the range of the lane of travel. Figure 8 shows the reliability distribution. The reliability distribution has a maximum value in the center of the lane of travel, and has a minimum value at both ends of the range of the lane of travel. The reliability decreases further as the distance from the center of the lane of travel becomes bigger.

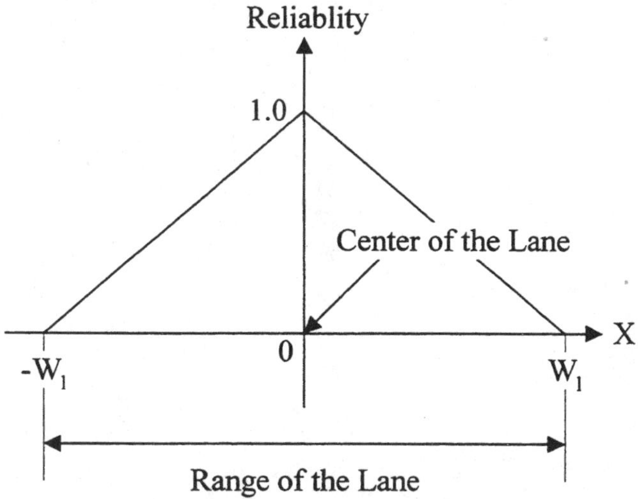

Figure 8. Outline of Reliability Distribution

The reliability of vehicles in the lane of travel are calculated and they accumulate at every scan. However accumulated reliability has an upper limit. When the accumulated reliability exceeds the upper limit, the accumulated reliability is held at the same value as the upper limit. The fixed value is subtracted from the accumulated reliability of vehicles out of the lane of travel at every scan. Finally, the vehicle which has the maximum value of accumulated reliability is recognized as the target vehicle.

DRIVING TEST DATA RECORDING

We installed the developed experimental system onto a vehicle. Figure 9 show a photograph of the vehicle with the experimental system. The scanning laser radar is installed on the front bumper, and the video camera is installed inside near the front window. We drove the vehicle on an expressway with the experimental system running. We recorded the output of the scanning laser radar and of the speed sensor in the data recorder, and recorded the road situation during driving with the VTR. The various conditions of the driving test are shown in Table 1.

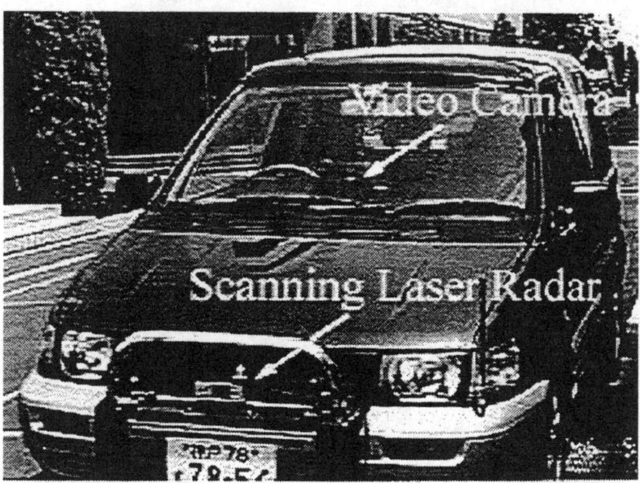

Figure 9. Photograph of Vehicle with Experimental System

Table 1. Conditions of Driving Test

Date	May 17, 1996
Time	11:30 - 15:00
Weather	Clear
Location	Maizuru Expressway Yokawa I.C. to Kasuga I.C.
Speed	around 100 km/h

EXPERIMENTAL RESULTS

We played back the data from the scanning laser radar and the vehicle speed calculation unit which were recorded as above and performed the following experiments. The correct target vehicle selection was determined based on the image data corresponding to the recorded data.

RELATIONS BETWEEN LANE WIDTH AND RECOGNITION RATE - We examined the change in the target vehicle recognition rate when the lane width W_1 was changed. The data used for the experiment was selected from the total. Data 1 is data during the driving on straight roads. In data 1, the distances to the target vehicle range from around 40 m to 60 m. Data 2 is data during driving on curved roads. In data 2, the distances to the target vehicle range from around 45 m to 70 m.

Figure 10 shows relations between the lane width W_1 and the recognition rate. The horizontal axis is the lane width, and the vertical axis is the recognition rate. The solid line is the recognition rate of data 1, and the dotted line is the recognition rate of data 2.

The following is obvious from Figure 10; the improvement in the recognition rate is small even if lane width W_1 is expanded to more than 3.6 m. The lane width of a Japanese expressway is 3.6 m. This value corresponds to the lane width 3.6 m of the above experimental results. If lane width W_1 is made wider than 3.6 m, the possibility that the PC will mistake vehicles in the adjacent lanes for vehicles in the lane ahead arises. Therefore, the appropriate lane width for recognizing target vehicles is 3.6 m.

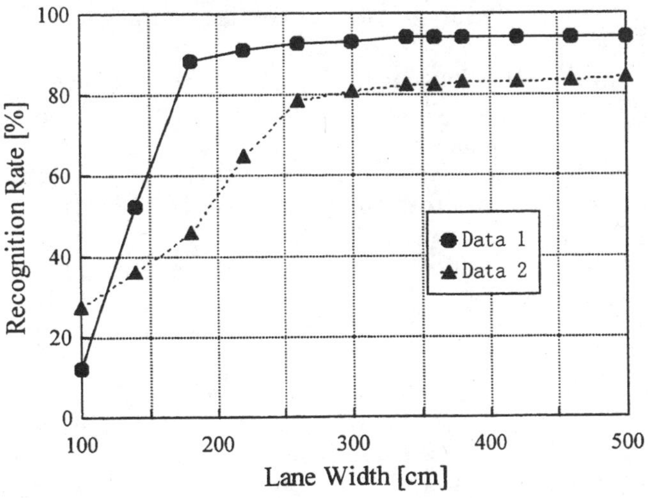

Figure 10. Relations between Lane Width W_l and Recognition Rate

PERFORMANCE ON STRAIGHT ROADS - We selected a section of data from driving on straight roads from the total recorded data. The time of the chosen data is 151.8 seconds which is calculated from 1012 scans and a scanning period of 150 ms. We calculated the recognition rate of the target vehicle using this data. The lane width W_l is 3.6 m. The target vehicle recognition rate on straight roads was calculated as 94.1 %.

Figure 11 shows example of the recognition results on straight roads. The two fan-shaped areas in Figure 11 are the detection areas of the scanning laser radar, and the pivot of the fan-shaped area is the location of the radar vehicle. The outer arc of the fan-shaped area is equivalent to a distance of 150 m. The circles in the left fan-shaped area are the positions of obstacles which are measured by the scanning laser radar.

The central photograph in Figure 11 is the image of the road conditions made at the same time as the measurement results by the scanning laser radar. There is a vehicle in the lane ahead on an almost straight road. In this case, this vehicle is the target vehicle.

On the other hand, figures in right fan-shaped area in Figure 11 are the recognition results corresponding to the measured results by the scanning laser radar. The two gently curved lines are the estimated road shape and the gray rectangle means the target vehicle. Therefore, the recognition results in this example are correct.

Figure 11. Example of Recognition on Straight Road

We investigated the situations where the PC could not recognize the correct target vehicle and classified the situations into the following three kinds. The first situation (Error 1) is when the PC could not estimate road shapes. The second situation (Error 2) is when the PC could not recognize the target vehicle as a vehicle. The third situation (Error 3) is when the PC could recognize the target vehicle as a vehicle but could not recognize it as the target vehicle. Table 2 shows the relations between the above three situations and the number of occurrences.

Table 2. Type of Error and the Number of Occurrences (on Straight Roads)

Type of Error	Number of Occurrences
Error 1	6 times
Error 2	23 times
Error 3	28 times

PERFORMANCE ON CURVED ROADS - We selected a section of data from driving on curved roads from the total recorded data. The time of the chosen data is 151.8 seconds which is calculated from 1012 scans and a scanning period 150 ms. The recognition rate of the target vehicle was calculated from this data. The lane width W_l is the 3.6 m which is the same as the experiment on straight roads. The target vehicle recognition rate on curved roads was 86.7%. The recognition rate was lower than that on straight roads.

Figure 12 shows an example of the recognition result on curved roads. There are three vehicles in the lane ahead on the left curving road. The curved line which curved to the left is displayed as the correct road shape. The three vehicles are recognized correctly as vehicles, and the vehicle whose distance to the radar vehicle is the shortest is recognized properly as the target vehicle.

Figure 12. Example of Recognition on Curves

We investigated the situations that when PC could not recognize a target vehicle, and sorted these situations into three kinds in the same way as the experiment on straight roads. Table 3 is the number of occurrence of the above three situations. The number of occurrence of Error 1, Error 2, and Error 3 on curved roads was more than that on straight roads.

Table 3. Type of Error and the Number of Occurrence (on Curved Roads)

Type of Error	Number of Occurrence
Error 1	38 times
Error 2	37 times
Error 3	60 times

CONCLUSIONS

We attempted to recognize the correct target vehicle on a curved road, and developed an experimental system using scanning laser radar. The experimental system has the following functions.

- It detects delineators installed along roads. It estimates the road shape based on the arrangement of delineators.
- It calculates the range of the lane of travel by using road shapes.
- It recognizes the target vehicle from other vehicles in the range of the lane of travel.

We did a driving test on an expressway and recorded the output of the scanning laser radar, the speed data of the radar vehicle, and the image data of road conditions. Then, we played these data back and carried out target vehicle recognition experiments.

As a result of the experiments, the recognition rate on straight roads was 94.1 %, and the recognition rate on curved roads was 86.7 %.

Problems of the experimental system are as follows.

- It can not estimate road shapes in the section of complex road shapes such as junctions. So, it can not recognize the target vehicle.
- When there are few detectable delineators, the estimation accuracy of road shapes is low. Therefore, the recognition accuracy of the target vehicle is low, too.
- The recognition accuracy decreases during lane changing.

REFERENCES

[1] Hiroyuki Hayakawa, Mitsunori Maruyama, and Sinobu Yabuta, "Vehicle Distance Warning System for Passenger Cars", 1993 JSAE Spring Convention Proceedings, No. 931, pp. 57-60, May 1993, (in Japanese).

[2] Tetsuhiro Umeda, Katsuki Yamamoto, and Kazuo Matusima, "An Emergency Braking System for Rear-End Collision Avoidance - Driving Test Results on the Proving Ground -", 1993 JSAE Spring Convention Proceedings, No. 932, pp. 37-40, May 1993, (in Japanese).

[3] Yasuhisa Hiroshima, Hideo Araki, Toshio Ito, and Kunio Nishioka, "Development of Preceding Vehicles Recognition Algolism Using Laser Radar - Part 2: The Basic Technology for ASV (Advanced Safety Vehicle) -", 1993 JSAE Spring Convention Proceedings, No. 931, pp. 53-56, May 1993, (in Japanese).

[4] Ayumu Doi, Toyokatsu Teranaka, Tadayuki Niibe, Takeshi Takagi, Yasunori Yamamoto, and Hirofumi Seni, "Development of an Auto-Brake System for the Collision Avoidance", 1993 JSAE Autumn Convention Proceedings, No. 936, pp. 125-128, October 1993, (in Japanese).

[5] Takahiro Maemura, Tetsushi Mimuro, Yoshiki Miichi, and Toshiharu Hirai, "Recognition of Surroundings by the Mitsubishi ASV", 1996 JSAE Spring Convention Proceedings, No. 961, pp. 359-362, October 1993, (in Japanese).

[6] William J. David, "FMCW Sensors for Longitudinal Control of Vehicles", Systems and Issues in ITS, SP-1106 SAE, pp. 87-96, 1995.

[7] Tetsuo Teramoto, Kenji Fujimura, and Yasuhiro Fujita, "Study of Laser Radar", The Twelfth International Technical Conference on Experimental Safety Vehicles, 89-4B-0-020, May 1989.

970175

Automotive Radar Signal Source Using InP Based MMICs

Kazuoki Matsugatani, Kouichi Hoshino, Kunihiko Sasaki, Hiroshi Mizuno, Takashi Taguchi, and Yoshiki Ueno
DENSO Corp.

ABSTRACT

A 60GHz millimeter-wave signal source for automotive radar was developed with MMICs. This signal source consists of two MMICs; a 30GHz VCO and a 30GHz-to-60GHz frequency doubler. For the transistor of these MMICs, we used the InAlAs/InGaAs on InP pseudomorphic HEMT with a 0.5μm gate length. Because of the high electron mobility and the high sheet charge density, the HEMT performed with sufficient output power gain in the millimeter-wave frequency range. The oscillation frequency of the signal source was controlled from 58.403GHz to 59.373GHz linearly. These frequency characteristics will satisfy the specifications of the FMCW radar system.

INTRODUCTION

Recently there has been considerable interest in developing millimeter-wave radar for the intelligent cruise control and the collision avoidance systems. Various research on the automotive millimeter-wave radar has been carried out [1][2], but the automotive radar systems have not yet gone into production. Low productivity and the high costs of the millimeter-wave devices have prevented the practical use of the automotive radar.

The monolithic microwave/millimeter-wave integrated circuit (MMIC) is one potential solution. In the MMIC, all the devices such as transistors, transmission lines, stubs and condensers are integrated into the chip during the IC process. The MMIC technology enables the minimization of the millimeter-wave circuit, thus resulting in a reduction in cost and improvement in production yield.

In this study, we have developed a millimeter-wave signal source with MMICs. This signal source, being composed of a voltage controlled oscillator (VCO) and a frequency doubler, is for the automotive radar system in the 60GHz band. As the transistors in the MMICs, we used the high electron mobility transistors (HEMTs) with the InAlAs/InGaAs pseudomorphic heterostructure on the InP substrate. In order to achieve higher productivity, the gate length of the HEMT was set to 0.5μm, and was formed using conventional photo-lithography. Because of the high mobility and the high sheet charge density of the InAlAs/InGaAs pseudomorphic structure, the HEMT showed sufficient performance for the 60GHz millimeter wave system. In the following section, we describe the principle of the frequency modulated continuous wave (FMCW) radar, the structure and performance of the HEMT, the design of the MMICs and the performance of the signal source.

PRINCIPLE OF FMCW RADAR

We used the FMCW radar for the automotive application. The FMCW system has a simple configuration and requires less output power than other radar systems, such as pulsed radar [3]. In addition, the distance and the velocity of the target can be detected simultaneously. Figure 1 shows the principle of the FMCW system and Fig. 2 shows its configuration. In the FMCW system, the transmitted signal generated by the signal source is modulated in an alternating up and down frequency. The received signal is delayed in proportion to the distance, and its frequency is shifted in proportion to the relative velocity between the target and the radar sensor.

The received signal is mixed with the transmitted signal, and the beat signals f_{b1} and f_{b2} are generated. The frequency of the beat signal f_{b1} corresponds to the difference between the received and local frequencies in the up interval, and f_{b2} corresponds to the difference in the down interval. From these beat signals, the distance R and the relative velocity V are calculated by

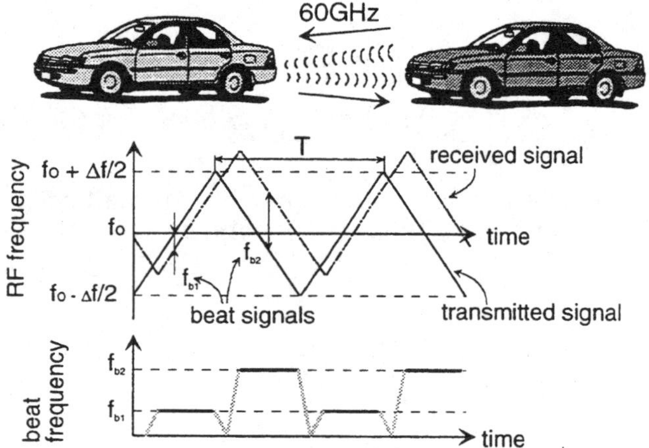

Figure 1: Principle of the FMCW radar

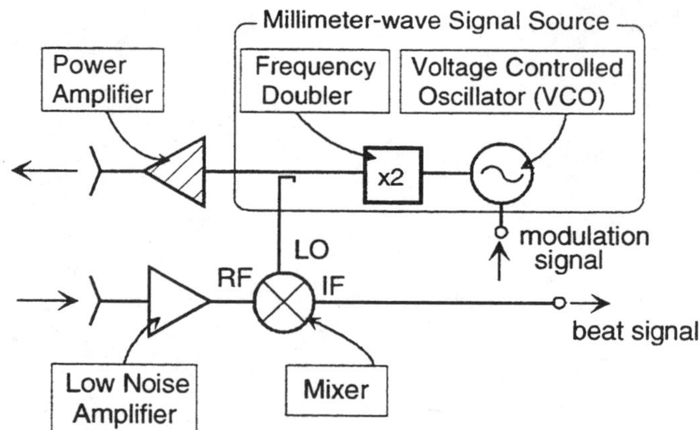

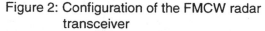

Figure 2: Configuration of the FMCW radar transceiver

$$R = \frac{cT}{8\Delta f}(f_{b1} + f_{b2}) \ldots(1)$$

$$V = \frac{c}{4f_0}(f_{b1} - f_{b2}) \ldots(2),$$

here c is the light velocity, Δf is the modulation bandwidth, f_0 is the central frequency of the transmitted signal and T is the interval of modulation.

From equations (1) and (2), we knew that the resolutions of the distance and the velocity depend on the precision of measuring the beat signal frequency. To improve the precision, maintaining linearity in the frequency sweep of the transmitted signal is critical. When nonlinearity exists in the up and down intervals of the frequency sweep, the spectra of the beat signals are spread, thus causing an error in the measured frequencies.

In developing our FMCW radar system, the modulation bandwidth Δf was required to be 100MHz within the 59GHz to 60GHz frequency range. Therefore, the central frequency f_0 was from 59.05GHz to 59.95GHz. In the VCO design, as described in the following section, we have tuned and optimized the feedback circuit in order to maintain the linearity within the 100MHz-wide frequency sweep.

HEMT STRUCTURE AND PERFORMANCE

For the active device of the MMICs we used a HEMT. Figure 3 shows the cross-sectional view of the HEMT. This HEMT is characterized by the 0.5μm-long rectangular gate electrode. In general, a 0.1 to 0.2μm T-shaped gate is used for the microwave or millimeter-wave transistors in order to achieve the high-speed switching. However, the formation of such a short and complex-shaped gate requires using the electron beam (EB) lithography technique. A gate longer than 0.5μm, that could be formed using the conventional photolithography technique, would be more easily produced than a T-shaped gate.

To attain sufficient output power gain in the HEMT for the millimeter-wave FMCW system with a 0.5μm-long rectangular gate, we used the InAlAs/InGaAs pseudomorphic heterostructure for the active layer. The heterostructure for the HEMT was grown using molecular beam epitaxy on the semi-insulating InP substrate. This structure consisted of a 100nm nondoped $In_{0.52}Al_{0.48}As$ buffer, 16nm nondoped $In_{0.80}Ga_{0.20}As$ pseudomorphic channel, 4nm nondoped $In_{0.53}Ga_{0.47}As$ subchannel, 5nm nondoped $In_{0.52}Al_{0.48}As$ spacer, 10nm Si-doped $In_{0.52}Al_{0.48}As$ donor, 10nm nondoped $In_{0.52}Al_{0.48}As$ Schottky barrier and 20nm Si-doped $In_{0.53}Ga_{0.47}As$ cap layer. Compared with the lattice-matched $In_{0.53}Ga_{0.47}As$ channel, the pseudomorphic channel had a higher electron mobility and a higher electron sheet charge density because of the high In content in InGaAs [4]. In addition, the $In_{0.53}Ga_{0.47}As$ subchannel, inserted at the InGaAs/InAlAs heterointerface, enhanced the electron mobility by reducing the electron diffraction. As a result, the excellent performance of the mobility, i.e., μ=13,000cm^2/Vs, and the sheet charge density of n_s=3×10^{12}cm^{-2} at room temperature were obtained. These values of μ and n_s were twice as high as those of the conventional AlGaAs/GaAs HEMT.

Figure 4 shows the measured output power gain of the InAlAs/InGaAs pseudomorphic HEMT. The gate length is 0.5μm and the total gate width is 50μm with two fingers. In spite of the longer gate, this HEMT showed good performance in the millimeter-wave frequency range. The maximum stable power gain G_{ms} was 15dB at 30GHz and 11dB at 60GHz, respectively. This performance was due to the excellent mobility and sheet charge density of the InAlAs/InGaAs pseudomorphic heterostructure.

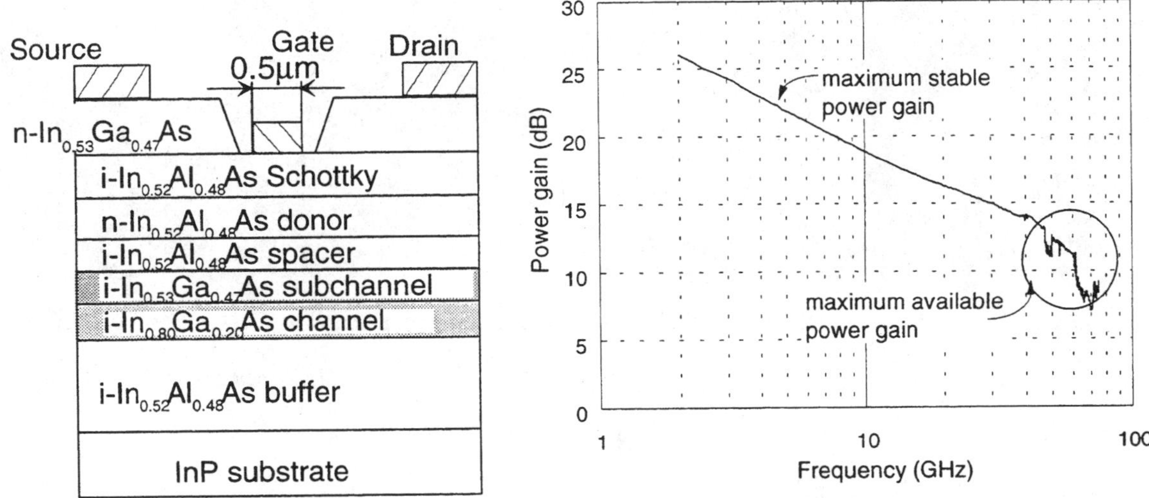

Figure 3: Cross-sectional view of the InAlAs/InGaAs pseudomorphic HEMT

Figure 4: Measured power gain of the InAlAs/InGaAs pseudomorphic HEMT

MMIC DESIGN

The 60GHz signal source consisted of two MMICs: a 30GHz VCO and a 30GHz-to-60GHz doubler. The schematics of these MMICs are shown in Fig. 5 and the micrographs of these MMICs are shown in Fig. 6. The InAlAs/InGaAs pseudomorphic HEMTs, described in the previous section, and the passive circuit elements formed by the coplanar waveguide (CPW) were used in the MMICs, and all the elements were integrated on the InP substrate. The circuits were designed based on the small signal scattering parameters of HEMTs and passive circuit elements. The following describes each MMIC design.

30GHz VCO - The VCO is composed of an oscillator and a buffer amplifier, and is integrated into the 3mm×1.7mm MMIC chip. The oscillator has a common-source series feedback configuration The gate length of the HEMT in the oscillator is 0.5μm; and the gate width is 13×4 μm. The transmission line L_r, being connected to the gate, works as a resonator. The capacitive stub L_s is connected to the source as the feedback element. The matching circuit, being composed of the line L_{d1} and the stub L_{d2}, is connected to the drain terminal. The gate bias V_{go}, being applied from the end of L_r, works as a frequency control voltage. The drain bias is applied from the end of L_{d2}.

The central oscillation frequency mainly depends on the length of L_r, and the feedback strength and the output power depend on both the output resistance of the HEMT $Re(Z_{ad})$ and the load impedance Γ_{load}. Tuning the output power to be maximum stabilizes the oscillation frequency, but the controllability of the frequency impaired. Because the linearity in the frequency sweep are important for the

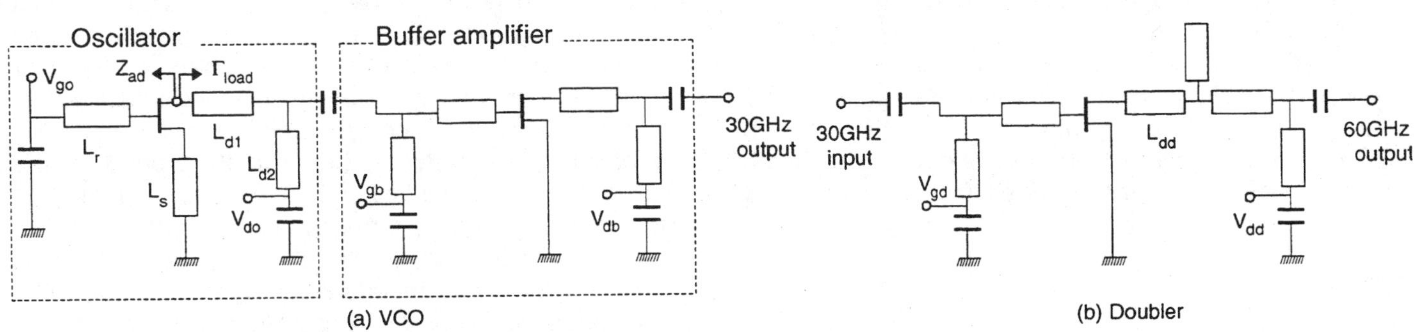

Figure 5: Schematics of the 30GHz VCO and the 30GHz-to-60GHz doubler

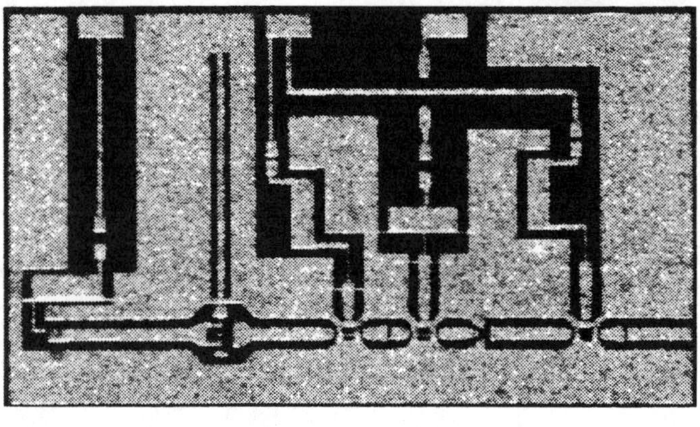

(a) VCO

(b) doubler

Figure 6: Micrographs of MMIC chips

FMCW signal source, we arranged the feedback and matching circuit to lower the output power in order to maintain the linearity.

The buffer amplifier is connected to the output terminal of the oscillator. This amplifier has a simple common source single-stage configuration. The gate length of the HEMT used in the amplifier is also 0.5μm, and the gate width is 25×2μm. The input and the output matching circuits are connected to the gate and the drain terminals, respectively. The gate bias voltage is applied individually, while the drain bias voltage, whose terminal is connected to the drain terminal of the oscillator HEMT, is applied from the same power supply as the oscillator.

30GHz-to-60GHz DOUBLER - The doubler has a common source configuration, and is integrated into the 2.7mm×1.7mm MMIC chip. The HEMT used in the doubler has the same structure as in the buffer amplifier of the VCO. A 30GHz input matching circuit is connected to the gate terminal. And a 30GHz shorted circuit and a 60GHz output matching circuit are connected to the drain terminal. The 30GHz shorted circuit is made using a quarter-wavelength open stub.

To improve the conversion gain of the doubler, we have inserted the phase delay line L_{dd} between the drain terminal and the 30GHz shorted circuit. The reflected 30GHz signal from the shorted circuit creates a standing wave in the inserted delay line, and is reinjected into the drain terminal of the HEMT. This reinjected signal, being converted into 60GHz by the HEMT, enhances the 60GHz output power. The length of the delay line L_{dd} was designed to create an efficient standing wave.

RESULTS

First, we investigated the output power of the VCO. To examine the relation between the oscillator circuit design and the output power, we made the experimental VCO-MMIC *without* the buffer amplifier. Table 1 summarizes the output resistance of the feedback circuit $Re(Z_{ad})$, the load impedance seen from the drain terminal of the HEMT Γ_{load} and the typical measured output power *without* the buffer amplifier in various designs. $Re(Z_{ad})$ and Γ_{load} are calculated from the individual scattering parameters of the HEMT, stubs, lines and condensers. The gate bias V_{go} was set so that the oscillation frequency was 29.75GHz. The drain bias V_{do} was 2.5V.

The feedback strength was set to the maximum in design A. This design generated the largest output power. Designs B or C, with the depressed feedback strength, generated a lower output power than design A.

Next, the linearity in the frequency sweep was examined. Figure 7 shows the measured oscillation frequency and output power as functions of the gate bias voltage V_{go}. The drain bias voltage V_{do} was maintained at 2.5V. Figure 7 (a) shows the data for the design-A VCO without the buffer amplifier. The output power was maintained at around 1dBm in the measured bias range, while the frequency was changed along the steplike curve. This nonlinearity is unsuitable for the FMCW signal source. Figure 7 (b) shows the data for the design-B VCO with or without the buffer amplifier. Depressing the feedback strength of the oscillator lowered the output power to -5dBm (plotted by the closed symbols). However, the linearity in the frequency sweep was drastically improved. By connecting the buffer amplifier to the oscillator, the power was increased to 2dBm and the linearity was maintaind (plotted by the open symbols). The central oscillation frequency was shifted about 600MHz, because the input impedance of the buffer amplifier affects the oscillator load impedance. Considering the importance of the linearity for the FMCW system, we adopted the design-B VCO with the buffer amplifier for

Table 1: Output resistance, source impedance and typical output power of the various VCOs, without buffer amplifiers.

Design	Re(Z_{ad}) (Ω)	Γ_{load} mag	Γ_{load} ang (deg)	Output Power (dBm)
A	-104	0.80	79.7	1
B	-96	0.87	84.2	-5
C	-68	0.91	93.3	-14.5

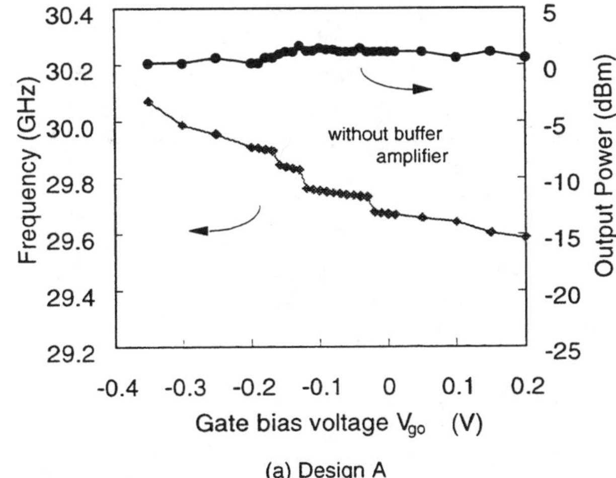

(a) Design A

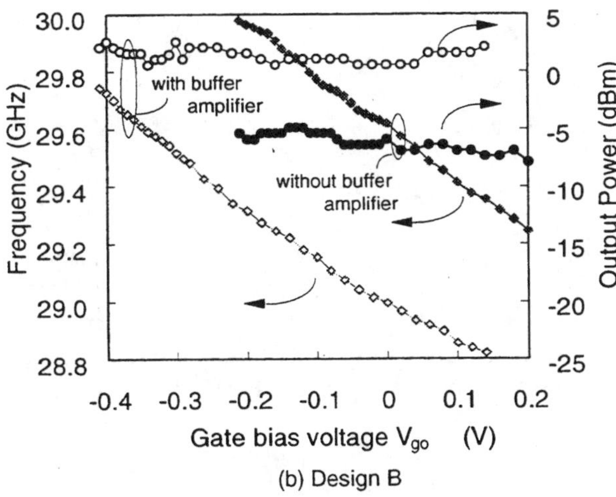

(b) Design B

Figure 7: Measured oscillation frequency and output power as functions of the gate bias voltage for the various VCOs.

the signal source. This VCO oscillated at 29.726GHz at V_{go}=-0.4V and 28.857GHz at V_{go}=+0.1V, with an output power changing from 1 to 2dBm.

Next, the performance of the doubler MMIC was measured. Figure 8 shows the output power and conversion gain of the doubler as a function of the input power. The input frequency was 29.75GHz and the output frequency was 59.5GHz in this experiment. The gate bias voltage V_{gd} was 0.2V and the drain bias voltage was V_{dd} 2.5V. Applying the signal with -14dBm to the doubler, the maximum conversion gain of 3.7dB was achieved. The doubler exhibited the positive gain up to 0dBm input power, and the maximum output power was 1dBm.

Finally, the total performance of the 60GHz signal source was investigated. The VCO-MMIC, which includes the design-B VCO with the buffer amplifier, and the doubler MMIC were mounted on the metal carrier and were connected by bonding wires. Figure 9 shows the output frequency and output power of the signal source as a function of the gate bias V_{go} applied to the HEMT of the oscillator. The maximum output frequency was 59.973GHz at V_{go}=-0.26V, and the minimum frequency was 57.897GHz at V_{go}=+0.12V. Within the bias voltage range from V_{go}=-0.2V to V_{go}=0V, the output frequency was controlled quite linearly from 59.373GHz to 58.403GHz. As described above, the FMCW radar under development requires a 100MHz modulation bandwidth within the 59GHz to 60GHz frequency range. This MMIC signal source, which generates 59.200±0.050GHz signals on changing V_{go} from -0.18V to -0.16V, will satisfy the specifications of the 60GHz FMCW radar.

The output power was varied from -5dBm to -3dBm by increasing V_{go}. This measured output power is about 4dB lower than the expected output power performance that we estimated from the VCO MMIC and the doubler MMIC. The reason we believe is that the bonding wire loses the signal power, and the maximum gain frequency of the doubler was lower when connected to the VCO.

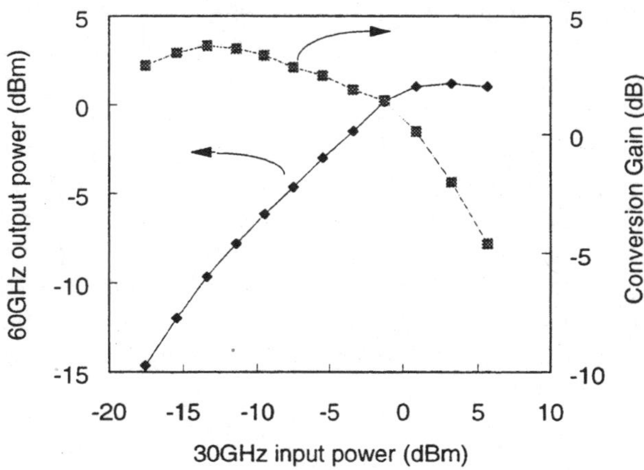

Figure 8: The second-harmonic output power and the conversion gain as a function of the input power for the 30GHz-to-60GHz doubler. (Input frequency f_{in}=29.75GHz)

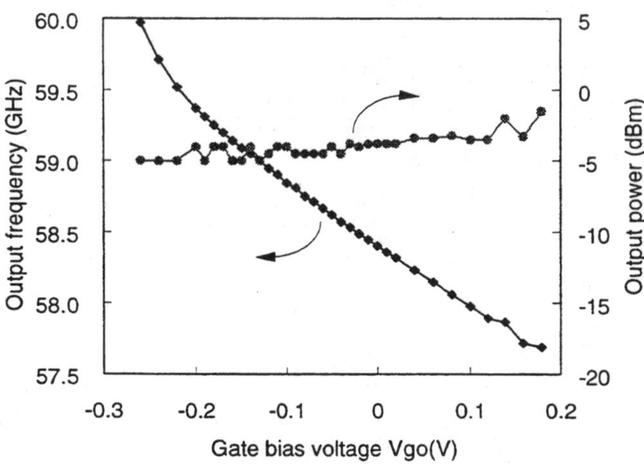

Figure 9: The output frequency and the output power of the 60GHz signal source

CONCLUSIONS

We have developed a 60GHz signal source for the automotive FMCW radar with a 30GHz VCO and a 30GHz-to-60GHz frequency-doubler MMIC. We used the InAlAs/InGaAs pseudomorphic HEMT on the InP substrate as the transistors in the MMICs. The gate electrode of the HEMT was a 0.5μm-long rectangular gate which could be formed using the conventional photolithography technique. Because of the high electron mobility and the high sheet charge density of the InAlAs/InGaAs pseudomorphic heterostructure, the HEMT showed excellent performance of the maximum stable power gain, i.e. G_{ms}=15dB at 30GHz and G_{ms}=11dB at 60GHz, in spite of the long gate length

The VCO-MMIC, with the maximum feedback strength, generated the largest output power but demonstrated the nonlinearity in the frequency sweep. To improve the linearity and to maintain the output power, we depressed the feedback strength and connected the buffer amplifier to the oscillator. The oscillation frequency of the VCO-MMIC was controlled from 29.726GHz to 28.857GHz by changing the gate bias voltage V_{go} from -0.4V to +0.1V, with an output power changing from 1 to 2dBm. The doubler MMIC demonstrated the largest conversion gain of 3.7dB at the -14dBm input signal level, and the maximum output power was 1dBm.

The 60GHz signal source was formed by connecting the VCO to the doubler with bonding wires. The output frequency of this signal source was varied from 59.973GHz to 57.897GHz by changing the gate bias of VCO V_{go} from -0.26V to +0.12V, with an output power changing from -5dBm to -3dBm. Within the bias voltage range from V_{go}=-0.2V to V_{go}=0V, the output frequency was controlled quite linearly from 59.373GHz to 58.403GHz.

REFERENCES

(1) E. H. Düll and H. J. Peters, "Collision Avoidance System for Automobiles". SAE Congress 780263, 1978.

(2) P. Martin, "Autonomous Intelligent Cruise Control Incorporating Automatic Braking". SAE Congress 930510, 1993.

(3) M. Kamimura, N. Shima, K. Fujiwara and Y. Fujita, "Millimeter-Wave Automotive Radar Using Digital Signal Processing". SAE Congress 930552, 1993.

(4) Y. Sugiyama, Y. Takeuchi and M. Tacano, "High Electron Mobility Pseudomorphic $In_{0.52}Al_{0.48}As/In_{0.8}Ga_{0.2}As$ Heterostructure on InP Grown by Flux-stabilized MBE". J. Crystal Growth, Vol. 115, 1991, P.509-514

970172

Development of a Scan Laser Radar

Shoichi Tanaka and Masahira Akasu
Mitsubishi Electric Corp.

William Bracken
Mitsubishi Electronics America, Inc.

ABSTRACT

This paper is concerned with a scan laser radar sensor used to measure distance. It s a basic component of a vehicle distance warning system or an intelligent cruise control system. An intelligent cruise control system requires not only the distance to the object, but also the ability to detect movement of the preceding vehicle and the existence of any other nearby obstacle. However conventional radar sensor mainly fixed beam technology and measure only distance. Therefore, it s insufficient for the application to an intelligent cruise control system. Our newly developed scan laser radar transmits an extreme narrow beam and scans both transmission direction and reception direction simultaneously at a high measurement time rate. This scan laser radar can measure the lateral position of objects with high accuracy and good reconstruction level.

INTRODUCTION

In recent years, the safety features of cars have received more serious attention. Examples of this increased attention are the installation of ABS and Air Bags. It is expected that the next level is the development of preventive safety systems to assist in the prevention of accidents.

One of the major components of this preventive safety system is a sensor for detecting distance between cars. As a distance detection sensor, those using applications of microwaves or light are well known, and the distance detection sensor using laser has already been put to practical use as a warning device of distance between cars. This warning device is used for large-sized trucks, buses and high class passenger cars [1]. But these distance detection sensors of traditional type are dominated by fixed beam types. The fixed beam can obtain distance to the object, but it rarely makes detection errors due to the forms of roads or the traffic conditions. Therefore, eventually the usage is limited within the warning device level capability. Expanding the usage to a control system for the distance between cars, requires not only the distance to the object, but also the information about the movement of the preceding vehicle or the existence of any obstacle or forms of roads. Additionally, it is necessary to measure the object position on a horizontal line with good reconstruction performance. The concept is shown in Figure 1. If the image of distance as shown in the figure is available, by processing the data of distance and direction, reflectors on a road and cars can be identified and the data about road shape is also available by the direction from roadside reflectors.

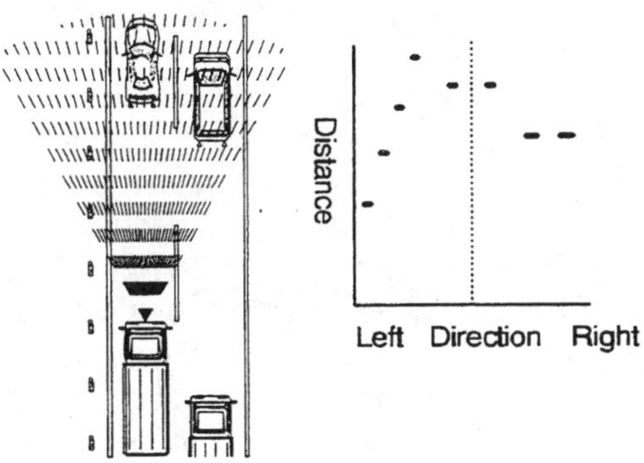

Figure 1.Concept of Scanning

We developed the Scan Laser Radar, which transmits a very narrow light beam on the horizontal line, and measures the distance at a very high speed. This is achieved by scanning the directions of both transmission light and reception light simultaneously in the forward directions.

PRINCIPLE OF DISTANCE MEASUREMENT

The principle of measuring distance by laser beam, as shown in Figure 2, is to measure the time period from the moment of laser pulse transmission to the moment of receiving reflected beam from the object.

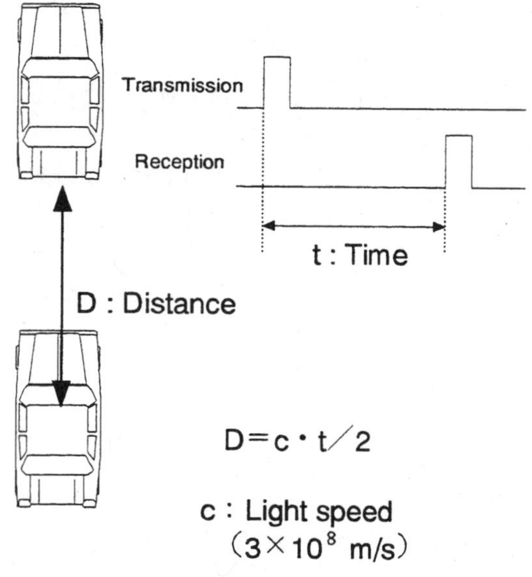

Figure 2.Basic Principle of Laser Radar

In the case of the Scan Laser Radar, due to necessity for measuring distance of various directions in high speed, a single distance measurement process system is employed, in which distance is computed by measuring the time of each process of transmission and reception of light. In this method, a counter is used, however, due to very high speed of light, 3×10^8 m/s, only 7.5 m resolving power is available even by a counter of 20 MHz. Therefore, by using the electric linear discharge circuit as shown in Figure 3., we could obtain the resolving power to below 7.5 m. In other words, before distance measurement, the capacitor for electric discharge is charged. Discharging during the time period from the moment the receiving pulse is detected to the moment of the next count-up, then this discharged volume is converted to distance, and by this method the resolving power of below 7.5 m is obtained. Being represented by N as the detected counter value, H as measured discharged volume and Hmax as discharged volume of one count (equivalent to the measured distance of 7.5 m), measured distance, D is;

$$D = 7.5 \times N + 7.5 \times (H/H_{max}) \text{ [m]} \quad (1)$$

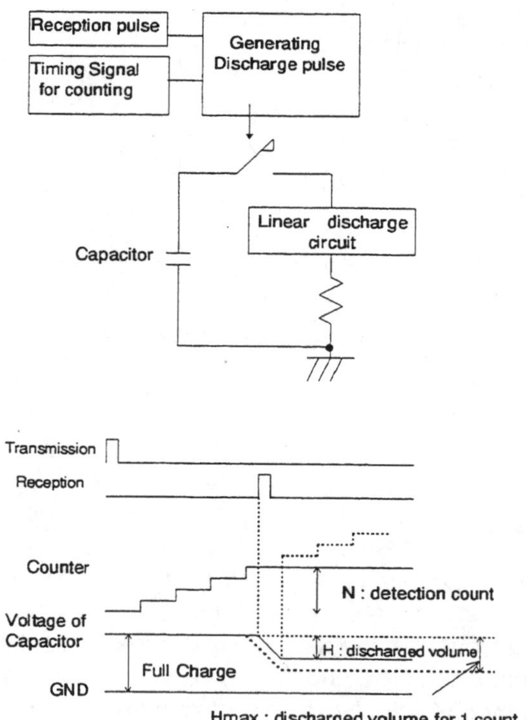

Figure 3.Discharge Process

STRUCTURE

The external appearance of the Scan Laser Radar which was developed is shown in Photo 1. Figure 4. is the composition of the Scan Laser Radar. The Scan Laser Radar consists of a laser transmission section, light reception section, scanning mechanism section and stain detection section.

Photo 1.Scan Laser Radar

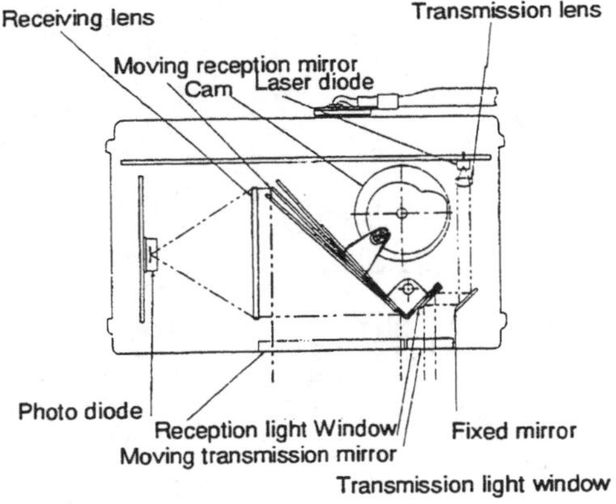

Figure 4.Composition of Scan Laser Radar

LASER TRANSMISSION SECTION - The laser diode in laser transmission section emits the infrared ray of 850 nm wave length, in 160 μ s cycle. The transmission light specifications are shown in Table 1. Besides, in order to improve the angle resolving power and detection performance, the transmission lens forms a very narrow light beam on a horizontal line. Transmission beam patterns are shown in Figure 5.

Table 1.Transmission Specifications

Light Output	9W (18W at high mode)
Light Wave Length	850nm
Transmission Period	160 μ s
Pulse Width	18ns

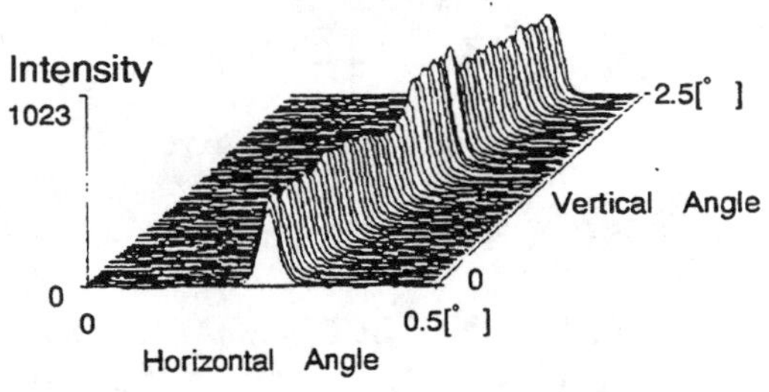

Figure 5. Transmission beam patterns

LIGHT RECEPTION SECTION - The light reception section cuts visible light by infrared filter, and collects the above mentioned laser pulse by receptive lens to receive at the PIN diode. Fresnel lens of f = 40mm is used as the receptive lens, and the reception light specifications are shown in Table 2.

Table 2.Reception Specifications

Reception Area	$2000mm^2$
Reception Angle (Horizontal)	6°
(Vertical)	6°
Detectable Peak Light Wave Length	900nm
Reception Sensibility	0.6A/W

SCANNING MECHANISM SECTION - The scanning mechanism section consists of scanning mirror, stepping motor and cam-link mechanism. Laser pulse light emitted from the laser transmission section is irradiated on the scanning mirror for radiation via the fixed mirror. By driving the stepping motor, this scanning mirror makes transverse vibrating motion via the cam-link mechanism, to scan laser pulse on the horizontal line forward. The scanning laser pulse light is reflected on the objects forward and returned to the laser radar sensor, where it is reflected by the scanning mirror and received in the light reception section. As shown in Figure 4, scanning mirrors of both transmission and reception are supported by one solid material to make both transmission light axis and reception light axis scanning on the same direction simultaneously. This permits the scanning angle to be widened. By detecting the shade installed on the scanning mirror through a photo-interrupter, the position of the origin point of scanning is detected.

Scanning action is shown in Figure 6. As shown in the figure, one rotation of stepping motor makes one cycle of scanning mirror transverse vibrating motion to make laser pulse beam travel in the range of 12 ° . Laser radar measures distance only in forward direction of transverse vibrating motion. This is for reconstruction of distance detection of same scanning direction every time, by scanning only one direction. The cam is designed to form the longer section of the forward direction, which is five times longer than the returning section.

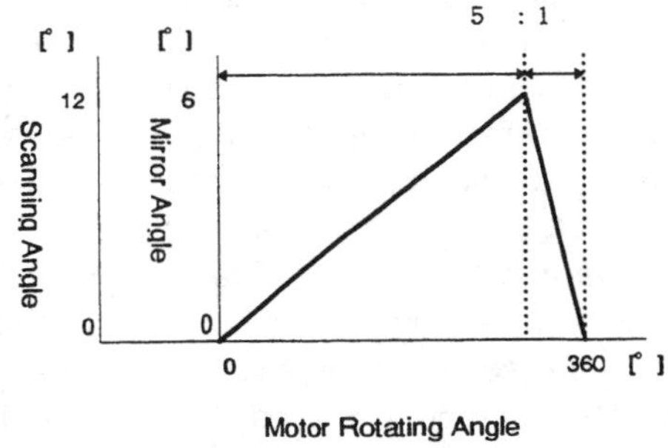

Figure 6.Scanning Process

STAIN DETECTION SECTION - When the front glass of laser radar surface becomes stained , the laser pulse beam is scattered which deteriorates distance detection performance. In the transmission light section, there is a photo-diode equipped to detect stain or haze on the transmission window, by monitoring a portion of the scattered light.

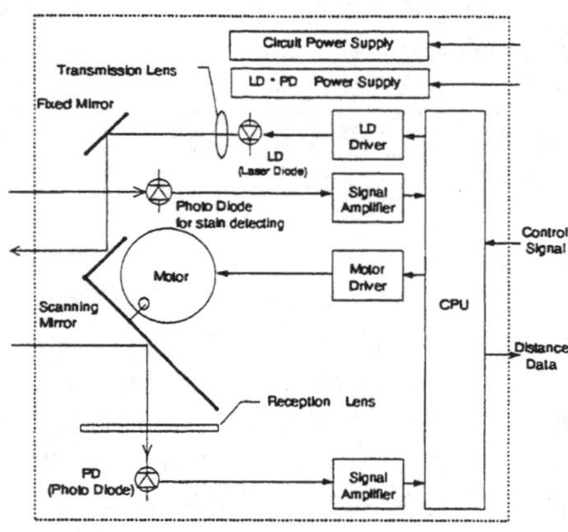

Figure 7. Operation Block Diagram

Figure 7. is an illustration of the circuit block of the Scan Laser Radar. This sensor needs 2 power supply, i.e., power supply for circuit and power supply for transmission and reception light systems. The external laser radar control unit can operate this sensor to detect distance by the signal. In distance detection mode, the CPU in the sensor activates the laser diode for transmission light, drives the motor, makes scanning mirror in transverse vibrating motion and scans forward. When reflected laser light from the objects forward is received, it is changed to the electric signal by the photo diode. It is amplified and input to the measurement process circuit. In the measurement process circuit, distance is computed from the velocity of light and the duration of time between transmission and reception of light, and at the same time, correction of distance is made by light reception level. After the averaging process of detected distances, it is transmitted to the laser radar control unit as the distance data, together with each scanning direction.

CORRECTION BY LIGHT RECEPTION LEVEL - The laser radar detects distance by measuring the duration of time from transmission light to reception light, but the existence of light reception is judged by detecting a signal wave lifted up above the designated threshold. As shown in Figure 8., an error is made by the level of reception signal. When light reception level is low, the detected distance indicates greater distance. Then, an adjustment by the level of reception signal is made on the detected distance to improve the precision level. Being represented by D as the detected distance, L as the light reception level and T(L) as the adjustment for error, then, distance after correction D' is;

$$D' = D - T(L) \quad (2)$$

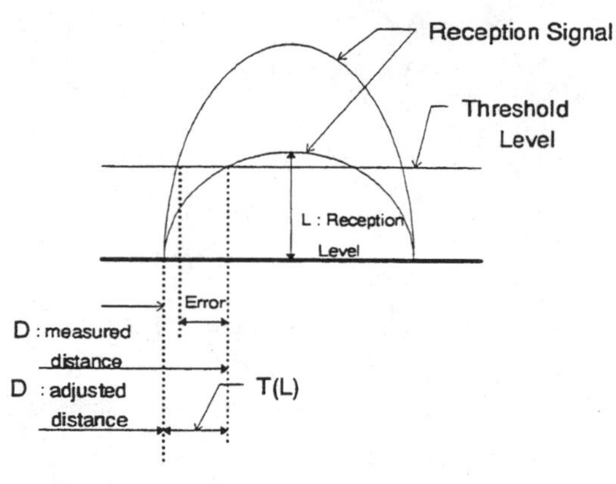

Figure 8.Correction by light reception level

DETECTION OF EACH DIRECTION - Figure 9. shows the timing of computing distance for a cycle of one scan. One scanning cycle of Scan Laser Radar is 150 ms. Within this cycle, the distance detection section is 125ms, in which 800 instances of distance detection are conducted. 10 instances each are averaged resulting, in distance data for 80 directions. The scanning angle is 12 ° ,thus the angle resolving power of one direction is 12/80 = 0.15 [°]

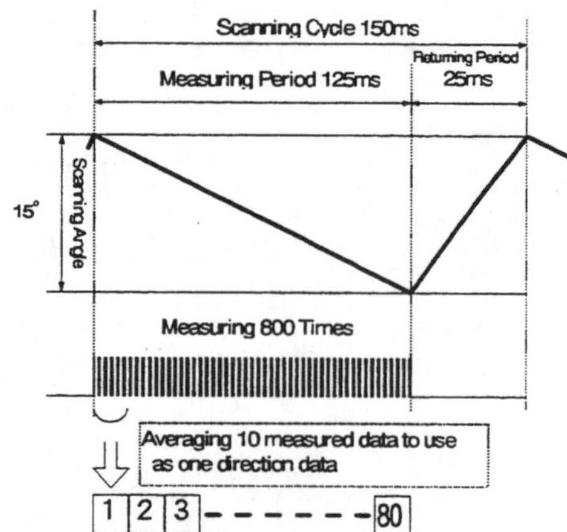

Figure 9.Timing Chart

FAIL-SAFE COUNTERMEASURE

COUNTERMEASURE AGAINST STAINING - As mentioned previously, staining on the front glass of the laser radar sensor is detected by monitoring a part of scattered light on the transmission window. A stain detection signal is transmitted to the laser radar control unit.

COUNTERMEASURE AGAINST INTERFERENCE - There is a possibility of other infrared rays causing interference resulting in a distance detection error. Therefore, It is designed to detect interference. The interference detection signal is sent to the laser radar control unit. In case of detection interference, the CPU in the sensor shifts the timing of transmission light for preventing the interference.

COUNTERMEASURE AGAINST RAINY WEATHER - Since the laser radar uses infrared laser light, its performance is deteriorated in bad weather. In order to secure distance detection performance even in a poor environment such as rainy weather, the output power of the laser pulse transmission power is doubled.

COUNTERMEASURE AGAINST COUNTER LIGHT - When very strong ray like sun counter light irradiates directly onto the laser radar. Then distance detection becomes difficult. In this case, monitoring the volume of irradiated light, and if the volume is extraordinarily big, a counter light detection signal is transmitted to the laser radar control unit.

SPECIFICATIONS

Specifications of the Scan Laser Radar are shown in Table 3.

Table 3. Specifications of Scan Laser Radar

Power Supply	10V
Maximum Current	0.7A
Temperature Range	-30~60℃
External Dimensions	154×54×90mm
Weight	0.76kg
Maximum Detection Distance	more than 100m∗
Horizontal Detection Angle	12°
Vertical Detection Angle	4°
Distance Resolution	0.15m
Angular Resolution	0.15°
Distance Measuring Period	0.15s

∗target: Φ51mm Reflex Reflector

PERFORMANCE

ACCURACY OF DISTANCE - Accuracy of distance by the developed Scan Laser Radar was measured. The φ 51mm reflex reflector, as the object, was placed at varied distance points on the forward direction of laser radar, and the distance to the object was measured. The results are shown in Figure 10. The accuracy of distance is within ±1 m,as shown in the figure.

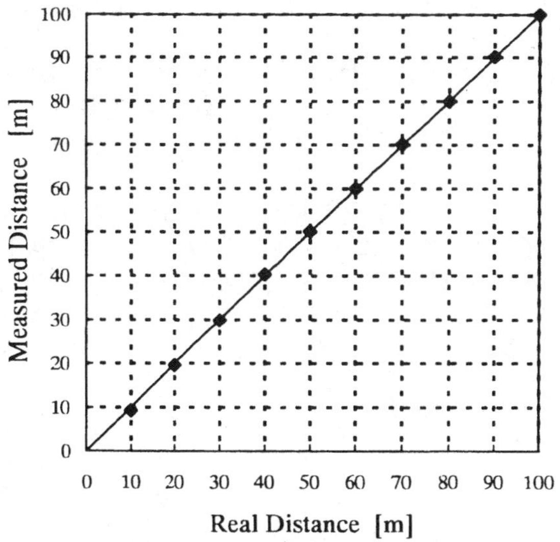

Figure10.Accuracy of distance

STABILITY OF DISTANCE - The above mentioned reflector is placed the same at 30 m on the forward direction of the laser radar and the stability of detected distance was measured by measuring the change of time. The result is shown in Figure 11. And as shown in the figure, the dispersion range of distance was within ±0.3 m, i.e. , distance detection was done with a good reconstruction level.

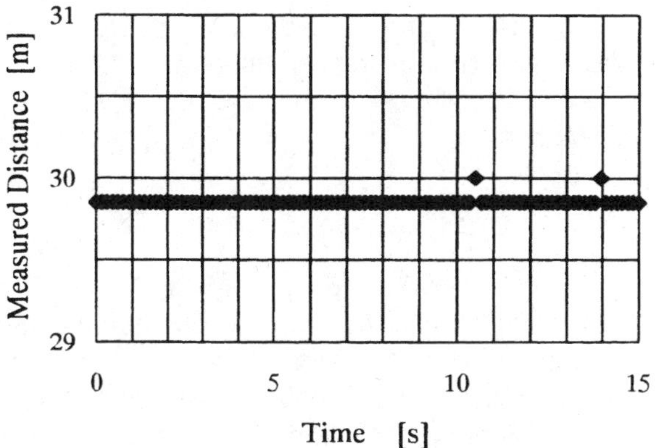

Figure11.Stability of distance

INFLUENCE OF WEATHER - Since an infrared ray is used for the laser radar, its performance is deteriorated in poor weather conditions. The splash made by a car running ahead in rainy weather or fog results in fine particles of small diameter floating in the air. This situation results in a scattering of the laser beam and a reduction in detection performance, specifically. The detection performance of the Scan Laser Radar in fog is shown in Figure 12. This figure shows the maximum detectable distance of the object, φ 51 reflector, compared to the transmissivity of fog.

The broken line in the figure indicates sight distance and was constructed from the equation below.

$$\text{Visibility} = (-1 \times \ln T) \times (1/\ln(1/\varepsilon)) \quad (3)$$

T : Transmissivity of fog

ε : 0.05

As shown in the figure, the detection performance of the Scan Laser Radar is slightly better than sight distance, and it is understood that it detects fog itself when the transmissivity becomes 35%, or lower.

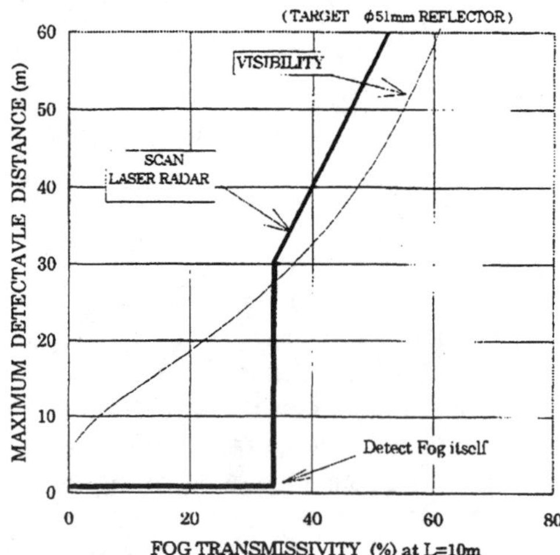

Figure 12. Maximum Detectable Distance in fog

SAFETY - The safety standard of laser beam was determined using regulation, IEC825. The Scan Laser Radar satisfies the Class 1 level standards of the regulation.

CONCLUSION

We have developed a Scan Laser Radar with high angle resolving power. By this method, the object is recognized, and motion of the car ahead and shape of the road are known. We are confident that the Scan Laser Radar can be used for the control system of distance between cars, and such control will play an important role in preventive safety.

REFERENCES

1. Yanagisawa, "Development of a Laser Radar System for Automobiles", SAE, Paper 920745

MISCELLANEOUS ACC SENSORS

2006-01-0347

Multi-beam Lidar Sensor for Active Safety Applications

Norbert Höver and Bernd Lichte
Hella KG Hueck & Co.

Steven Lietaert
Hella Electronics Corporation

ABSTRACT

This paper describes a multi-beam infrared sensor technology (*IDIS®*) with unprecedented robustness to environmental influences, which was originally designed for the comfort application Adaptive Cruise Control (ACC).
The paper shows that beside ACC an optimal functionality for safety applications such as Precrash and Collision Mitigation can be provided by the *IDIS®* sensor, which has a good lateral resolution by principle and can clearly identify width and outlines of vehicles and road obstacles, a feature which is extremely important for these applications.
An outlook is also given on data fusion aspects between this Lidar sensor and camera systems, which further improve functionality and availability of the safety functions.

INTRODUCTION

At present, Advanced Driving Assistance Systems (ADAS) represent one of the most innovative branches of modern vehicle development. The United States and the European Union have joined forces with the automotive industry to strive towards a drastic reduction in the number of traffic accident casualties. At the same time, vehicle manufacturers are conscious of the fact that vehicle safety functions are an excellent differentiating feature and sales argument.

The long-term objective is the development of a vehicle that avoids accidents autonomously. On the way to achieving this objective, attempts have been made to detail driver assistance systems in elementary individual applications, making them technically feasible while also making them easier to bring home to consumers. These applications have all been designed to take the pressure off drivers and make driving easier for them and aim to increase safety for both vehicle passengers and other road users. Initially, driver assistance functions were actually introduced to the market as pure convenience functions (e.g. ACC).

However, when ACC systems are active, the safety of vehicle passengers and other road users automatically increases as equipped vehicles are kept a safe distance apart and are slowed down earlier than the drivers would often actively do themselves.

In addition, the sensors used for the ACC systems are also able to detect critical driving situations such as imminent rear-end collisions, either working alone or in interaction with other sensors, and to autonomously intervene in longitudinal vehicle control. They will in future be able to intervene in lateral vehicle control as well. For this reason it is only natural and sensible to use the information provided by these sensors as a functional extension for the realization of safety-related functions, a task which presents a special challenge to development particularly under the aspects of technical performance, reliability and costs.

In comparison to widespread radar technology, Lidar (Light Detection and Ranging) sensors with a high lateral resolution offer high potential since they are in a position to detect not only the distance to an object but at the same time uniquely the lateral position and dimensions of this object. This paper initially describes the working principle and structure of a low-cost multi-beam ACC Lidar sensor which has uniquely high performance due to high availability even under the most adverse of weather conditions. It then goes on to present the advantageous implementation of active safety functions such as Precrash and Collision Mitigation as a functional extension of this sensor and demonstrate the positive effects it has on accident situations. The final section deals with the potentials resulting from fusion with other sensors.

ACC MULTI-BEAM LIDAR (*IDIS®*)

TECHNOLOGY AND OPERATING PRINCIPLE

The primary aim in the development of the *IDIS® (Infrared Distance System)* multi-beam sensor was to meet the requirements and specifications of an ACC system, which are mainly characterized by a long range, relatively small opening angle, good object separation and resolution as well as a sturdy design.

At present, the systems most widespread on the market for this application are radar systems which work in the 76 GHz frequency range and are based on a relatively complex GaAs technology. Much less expensive are optical Lidar systems which work according to the principle of time-of-flight measurement and use near-infrared laser diodes as transmitters and photo diodes as receivers. Lidar systems have a range of up to 200 m - comparable with radar systems - and as multi-beam sensors provide better lateral resolution on account of their working principle, but being optical systems they do react more sensitively to environmental influences and soiling. This has led to introduction of Lidar ACC systems into the market which do not fully exploit the possibilities offered by the technology and for example are switched off in the rain via the windscreen wiper.

For this reason, a technological approach was chosen for the development of the *IDIS®* which results in achieving the maximum possible tolerance against rain, spray and soiling.

The basis for this approach is the use of a multi-beam system where the transmitter consists of 12 or 16 high-power lasers which are typically built up monolithically next to one another and are mapped optically via a common lens (see figure 1).

Fig. 1 Optical transmitter system. Only three of 16 beam bundles are depicted

Each of the projected beams maps a rectangle of 1° azimuth and 3° elevation. The laser pulse power required is 50 W at a pulse width of approx. 10 ns.

On the receiver side there is another monolithic array, this time of photo diodes, with the same number of beams as the transmitter, which exactly maps the rectangle illuminated by the respective corresponding laser via a common receiver lens, making optimum energetic exploitation of the measuring signal possible. Avalanche Photo Diodes (APD) are used as receiver diodes providing significantly better signal-to-noise ratio and sensitivity than pin diodes. Figure 2 shows the resulting beam projection for the transmitting and receiving directions.

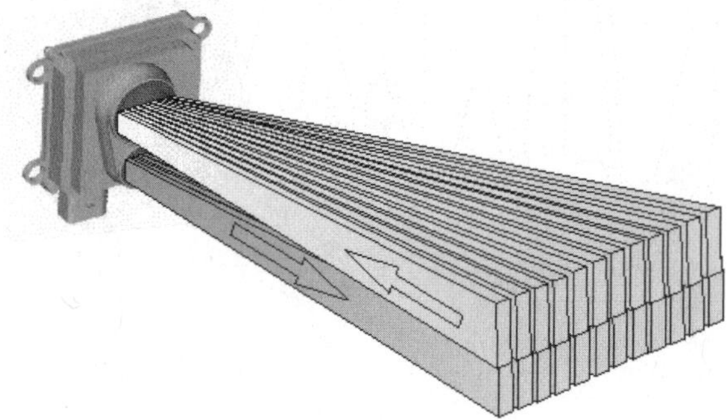

Fig. 2 Multi-beam ACC concept of corresponding transmitter and receiver

The advantages of the concept chosen are:

- no moving parts,
- extremely sensitive,
- excellent signal-to-noise ratio.

SIGNAL PROCESSING

In addition to optimum sensitivity, however, the type of downstream signal processing also plays a major role in sensor performance. Figure 3 illustrates typical backscatter curves as can be measured on the receiver side of an individual APD.

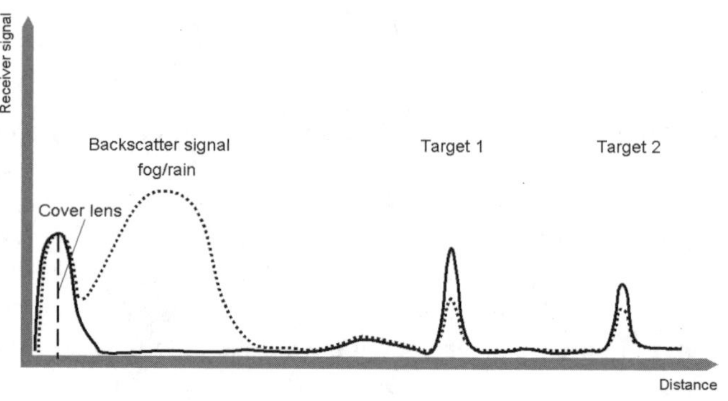

Fig 3. *IDIS®* Receiver Signal

The solid curve shows a typical signal image as produced by two vehicles driving behind one another in good weather conditions met by the same measuring beam (e.g. a motorbike at 100 m behind a truck at a distance of 150 m). The first pulse, which can be seen at very close range, represents reflection from the sensor's cover lens, and the intensity of this reflection serves as an indicator for the degree of soiling of the sensor.

The dotted line illustrates the same scenario with heavy spray in front of the vehicle. The water droplets in the air dampen the signals, which remain clearly detectable, however, and also produce a smeared reflection at close range. Classical Lidar measuring methods which only measure the time-of-flight to the first signal pulse are bound to fail in this situation and would react incorrectly to the spray signal and would no longer perceive the targets behind this spray.

For this reason, the *IDIS®* uses a measuring method which scans the whole length of the backscatter signal regardless of its shape. This both ensures the multiple target ability of the sensor and makes it possible to distinguish between so-called "hard" wanted signals and "soft" environment signals and their effect on sensor performance by a sophisticated analysis of the raw signal curves.

Once the raw targets have been determined in the individual beams, a subsequent tracking process across all the beams filters out the relevant stationary and moving objects from the input data, whereby information about distance, relative velocity, angular position and physical expanse of the objects is provided. Figure 4 demonstrates, with the example of a classical following scenario on highways, the allocation and the lateral resolution of the measuring channels to a target vehicle in different distances.

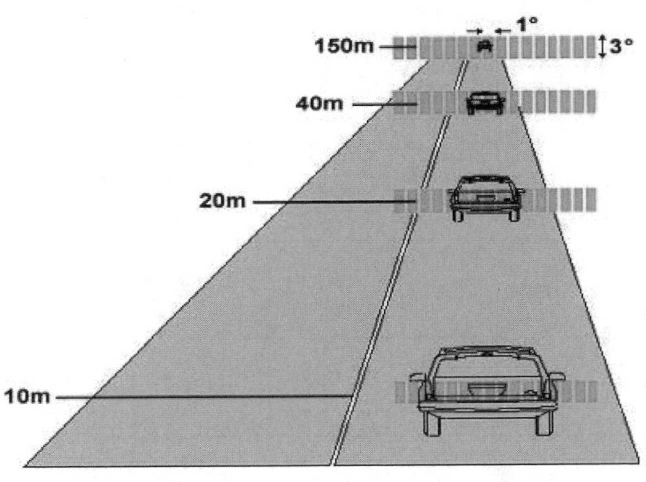

Fig. 4 *IDIS®* Multi-beam Projection

PERFORMANCE UNDER ADVERSE WEATHER CONDITIONS

As already emphasized above, a special focus of the sensor design work was dedicated to high availability and good performance even under the most adverse of weather conditions. If the damping curves of electromagnetic waves in the Radar and Lidar ranges (figure 5) are considered and compared, it can be seen that from a purely physical point of view comparable performance can be expected from both technologies under all weather conditions, which is clearly proven by the results achieved with the *IDIS®* in reality.

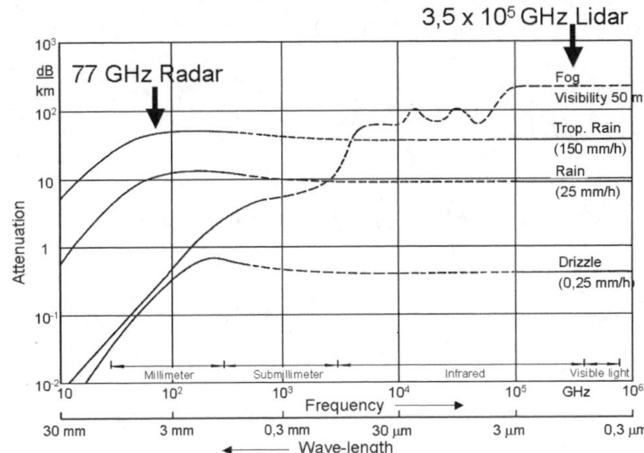

Fig. 5 Damping behavior of electromagnetic waves [1]

Clear differences in damping can only be seen in foggy conditions, Radar waves are capable of measuring through fog more or less without damping. In this situation, the range of Lidar sensors is roughly comparable to that of the human eye. At the same time however, the above described evaluation of the backscatter signal generated by the fog enables the *IDIS®* to detect the restricted visible range of the sensor and provide this information for use in pre-defined system-usage strategies, for example to switch off an ACC in such situations. In contrast, Radar systems allow drivers to "drive blind" since they cannot perceive the driver's visibility limitation. It is still disputed among experts, which behaviour is preferable regarding system and safety aspects.

In addition to the optical damping of the measuring path, soiling both of the targets and the host vehicle play an important role in sensor performance. Whereas target soiling and the lack of reflectors are not critical for the defined ACC ranges thanks to the measuring principle chosen and the high sensitivity involved, more major soiling of the sensor cover lens caused by snow, grit or dirt cannot be ignored, since the measuring beam has to penetrate this layer twice, once during transmission and once during reception. Photometric calculations [2] show, however, that at the critical large ranges this effect only contributes in reducing measuring sensitivity to the extent of the square root of the transmittance of the cover lens. The photos in figure 6 show the high ranges that can still be achieved even with the sensor cover lens extremely soiled.

Fig. 6 Ranges depending on soiling of the cover lens (left: d> 150 m, middle: d = 128 m, right: d = 102 m)

In practice, such extreme soiling hardly ever occurs since self-cleaning effects caused by rain and spray occur repeatedly on the vehicle front-end. If availability is to be increased for these rare cases, however, the sensor can also be coupled quite easily to the headlamp power wash system by an additional cleaning nozzle. As the sensor can measure the degree of soiling of its own cover lens, as detailed above, it is able to trigger the necessary cleaning process itself if and when required.

Table 1 shows a summary of the performance data of the *IDIS®* sensor.

Measurement range	Tracks:1-150m Raw-Data:1-200m
Field of view	16 °
Angular (lateral) resolution	1°
Distance resolution	0.1 m
Distance accuracy	1%
Velocity resolution	0.1 km/h
Velocity accuracy	1 km/h
Dimensions [mm]	W 105 x H 105 x D 76.5

Table 1. *IDIS®* specification

How this sensor with its specific properties can contribute to the implementation and realization of safety functions will be illustrated in the following section.

COMPARISON OF ADAS TECHNOLOGIES

A variety of sensors employing different technologies is used to detect objects in the area surrounding the vehicle. The properties of these different technologies are compared below with regard to their suitability for safety applications. The main focus of the safety functions under consideration is on Precrash and Collision Mitigation.

These sensors detect objects in the area around the vehicle and calculate their position as well as their relative velocity in comparison with the host vehicle. These data are then used to analyze the driving situation for current hazards. The following data are of particular interest for this analysis:

- Distance to the host vehicle,
- Relative velocity,
- Object width,
- Lateral position,
- Time to collision (TTC).

Optional information about the direction and the point of collision as well as about object classification are desirable.

Optical sensors and Radar sensors are the types mainly worth considering for perceiving the environment. At the moment, 76 GHz Long-Range Radar sensors (LRR), 24 GHz Short-Range Radar sensors (SRR), 24 GHz Universal-Medium-Range Radar sensors (UMRR), multi-beam lasers, laser scanners and mono cameras based on CCD or CMOS image sensors are the main types used. Table 2 below provides a brief summary of the main sensor technologies currently available for driver assistance systems. These systems mainly differ on the basis of range, field of view as well as number and type of directly measurable object attributes. Specifications can vary depending on the manufacturer and application.

	Range	Field of view	Measuring data
Multi-beam Lidar	120m -200m	16°	Distance Angle
IR scanner	30m	>120°	Distance Angle
76 GHz LRR	120m -200m	8°-16°	Distance Angle Speed
24 GHz SRR	30m	40°-80°	Distance Angle
24 GHz UMRR	50m	70°-120°	Distance Angle Speed
Camera (mono)	50m - 70m	20°-50°	Gray scale values

Table 2. Sensor technologies

Without going into details of the respective sensor principles, the various different sensor technologies will be evaluated and compared below in terms of their advantages for the safety applications dealt with in this paper. The calculation of the relevant object data presented above will be utilized for this purpose. All these sensor principles are currently undergoing ongoing development, which means future improvements in performance are to be expected.

MONO CAMERA

Video systems estimate object attributes in a model-based format using gray scale values. With this method, features are extracted from the gray scale values to form model hypotheses. These are then fed into a tracking process which calculates the object attributes. In comparison to Radar or Lidar sensors the object attributes are usually calculated significantly less accurately using this method and object detection is not as robust. On the other hand, cameras can classify objects well. If the image sensor system is provided with the object distance through fusion with a Radar or Lidar sensor, for example, the lateral position and width of an object are usually extremely well defined (see "Sensor fusion"). In addition, cameras are subject to limitations caused by the influence of the weather. Radar and Lidar sensors are less sensitive in this respect.

RADAR

Radar sensors can be divided into CW Radars (continuous wave) and pulse Radars. Pulse Radars measure the distance to the object directly using the time-of-flight of a brief pulse. Pure pulse radars determine the relative velocity through differentiation of this distance, whereas pulse Doppler Radars use the Doppler effect for this purpose. In any case, however, the object has to be tracked over several cycles this—alignment of receiver signals can be particularly problematic with short-range Radars with a large opening angle (range alignment). In contrast, CW Radars transmit continuously over a comparatively long period and receive simultaneously. Object distance measurement is not carried out directly, rather it is transferred into measurable frequency information through the modulation of the transmission frequency over time. This causes ambiguity in the evaluation since combinations of distance and relative velocity values have to be taken into consideration regarding the measured difference frequencies. This can result in ghost targets, particularly in scenarios where lots of objects are involved. Ghost targets originating from multiple reflections can also be observed with Radar sensors. Various measures such as plausibility considerations can be used to significantly reduce such ghost targets, but in certain situations in practice this phenomenon can still occasionally be observed.

Scanning methods using a mechanically swiveling antenna which scans the field of view step by step using a more or less thin beam have direct angle assignment and, with a respective resolution, provide good results for both the lateral position and width of the object. These sensors do not have a significant share in the market for cost reasons, however. Instead, a so-called multi-lobe method which works with stationary antennas is used. The individual antennas are inclined at several degrees against one another in the horizontal. This method results in relatively inaccurate lateral position determination and cannot be used to determine object width at all.

LIDAR

Optical sensors based on laser time-of-flight measurement can be divided into multi-beam sensors and scanners. Whereas multi-beam sensors use arrays of transmitting and receiving elements to cover different angle segments, scanners use a mechanically rotating system which directly represents the angle. Lidar sensors measure the distance directly and deliver good results for the lateral position and width of the object provided that the angle resolution is high enough. The relative velocity of the object is calculated indirectly through differentiation of the distance. Technology, weather conditions and soiling have already been dealt with before in detail. As far as weather conditions are concerned, the only significant differences to Radar sensor technology are to be found in fog conditions, whereby the *IDIS®* is in a position to detect this limitation of visible range.

EVALUATION

In summary it can be stated that mono cameras alone are not suitable for the safety functions considered here, since their capability to estimate distance and relative velocity is relatively poor. However, together with Radar or Lidar sensors which provide the object distance, they can significantly improve the determination of lateral position and width of an object as well as providing accurate object classification. Radar sensors (exception: scanning Radar sensors) are suitable for safety functions in as far as the lateral position and width of the object are not expressly required, otherwise fusion with camera or Lidar sensors is a better solution. In addition, ghost targets and losses of target which inherently occur due to the technology format represent a disadvantage in comparison to optical sensors. Lidar sensors are also suitable on their own for these safety applications, since they are the only ones which can determine all object attributes with very-good to good quality, and certain formats, as shown above using *IDIS®* as an example, are relatively insensitive to the influences of the weather and soiling. In addition, they are even in a position to recognize their own performance limitation. The only disadvantage in comparison to Radar sensors is the indirect calculation of relative velocity. For this reason, the next section will deal with the determination of relative velocity in more detail using the *IDIS®* as an example. The results presented above are summarized in Table 3.

	Lidar	Radar	Camera
Distance	++	++	-
Rel. velocity	+	++	-
Width	+	--	++ (fusion)
Lateral position	+	-	++ (fusion)
TTC	+	+	-

Table 3. Comparison of technologies

RELATIVE VELOCITY

In contrast to pure comfort systems such as ACC, safety systems make great demands on the dynamics of the object attributes in order to be able to directly detect emergency braking of a vehicle in front, for example. Since Lidar systems calculated relative velocity through differentiation, the filtering process has to consider these high dynamic requirements in order to compensate the disadvantage in comparison with Radar sensors which measure velocity directly using the Doppler effect.

In order to optimize the relative velocity calculation with the *IDIS®*, a 76 GHz Long-Range Radar sensor was used as a reference. The filter design was carried out using Matlab/Simulink combined with an automatic code generation and ported onto a micro controller using integer arithmetic with the aid of the wave digital filter concept [3]. Wave digital filters are robust against the quantization of filter coefficients and ensure that the required transmission behavior is only slightly modified by the porting process. In addition, parasite effects caused by the limitation of word length are systematically avoided.

Figure 7 shows the result of the filter design in a real driving scenario where the vehicle driving in front carries out a full braking maneuver following moderate deceleration. The dotted line shows the previous, conventional relative velocity calculation of the *IDIS®* which is completely aligned to comfort, and the solid line shows the new, considerably improved relative velocity calculation. The dashed line shows the Radar sensor measurement. A significant improvement was achieved with the aid of the above method. At low remaining ripple in the signal, which also meets the demands of pure comfort systems such as ACC, nearly the same dynamics are achieved as with Radar sensors, so that the disadvantage is practically eliminated. In the case of pure safety applications, slightly larger signal ripple is acceptable so that in these cases the filtering can be designed even more dynamically. If several applications are to be represented with one sensor, the use of application-specific filtering is recommended.

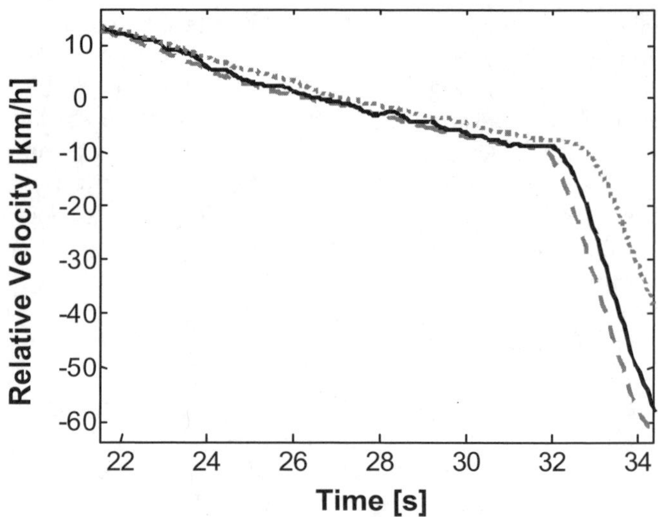

Fig. 7 Comparison of relative velocity

ACTIVE SAFETY CONCEPT

In modern vehicles, so-called *passive safety systems* such as belt tensioners or airbags contribute to increasing passenger safety by intervening during the accident to alleviate the consequences of the accident. In contrast, *active safety systems* intervene before the accident happens and can be further classified as follows: *Precrash systems* prepare the vehicle for collision directly before the accident with the intention of lessening the consequences of the accident. *Driving assistance systems* such as ASR, ABS or ESP support drivers in critical driving situations, helping them to master the situation and return to a normal, non-critical driving situation. Seen from the point of view of the time line, *driver assistance systems* such as ACC or LDW provide support even earlier and reduce the probability of an accident by avoiding critical driving situations in the first place. We will now take a closer look at the Precrash and Collision Mitigation systems.

PRECRASH SYSTEM

Precrash systems provide information such as relative velocity or TTC to a downstream actuator system directly before an imminent accident. In this way the information can be used to achieve optimum timing of the triggering of various actuators (e.g. belt tensioners). This is of major importance with a view to the greatest possible protective effect. These data can also be used to reduce the airbag trigger threshold and optimize ignition timing. In addition, the position of the passengers can be improved (e.g. active headrest) and even the vehicle structure can be adapted (e.g. by a crash box or the extension of additional bumpers). Reversible safety systems can be activated before 100 % collision probability is established. Further non-reversible functions are triggered by contact and acceleration sensors working with redundancy.

On the basis of the object data from around the vehicle and the data of the host vehicle, the decision is made as to whether objects will lead to an accident or not. For this, the time to collision (TTC) and the point of collision are calculated for the objects. In addition, the vector of relative velocity, the distance, the lateral position and the width of the objects are required. Together with the stopping distance and the critical escape routes of the host vehicle, a "probability" for an imminent collision is estimated.

COLLISION MITIGATION

Beyond this passive support of passenger protection, informations about the surrounding of the vehicle can be used for preliminary warning systems and active reduction of the kinetic collision energy. A first step towards this is the pre-conditioning of the braking system, for example by pre-filling of the braking system and application of the brake pads on the brake discs when a critical driving situation is detected on the basis of the sensor and vehicle data. In addition, the triggering threshold and maximum deceleration threshold of the braking assistant can be adapted to the driving situation. If the driver applies the brakes in such a situation, the quickest possible braking reaction is provided with optimum deceleration values.

The consistent further development of the measures described above leads to the so-called automatic emergency brake (AEB). The automatic emergency brake is defined as an automatic braking intervention with maximum deceleration in the event of an accident that is no longer physically avoidable. Consequences of the accident are mitigated by reducing driving speed and thus the kinetic energy at the time of the collision as much as possible - the AEB has a similar effect to an extended crash crumple zone. In other words, the application only intervenes when the driver can no longer avoid collision by braking nor by steering maneuvers. The connection between these two criteria is illustrated in the following figure for a normal car as the host vehicle and a truck as the target object with assumption of an ideal brake deceleration and an ideal lateral acceleration. The distance at which the respective criterion would trigger the AEB has been mapped against relative velocity. It can be seen clearly that at higher relative velocities the triggering point is determined by the steering criterion.

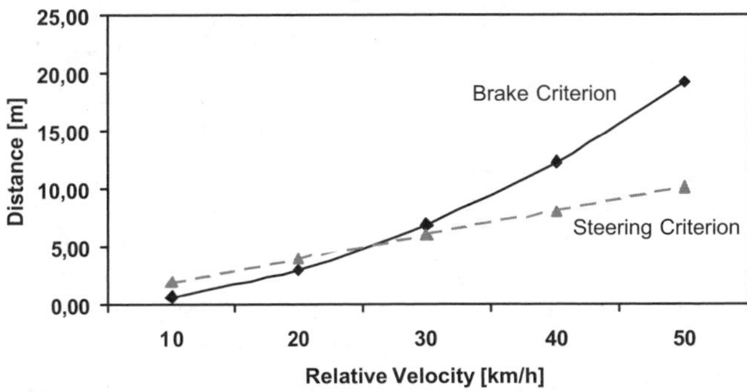

Fig. 8 Comparison of brake and steering criterion

To realize this application, the vehicle data and course prediction are initially used to calculate the braking distance and the smallest possible escape routes. If the braking distance is no longer sufficient and the escape routes overlap with the object, the driver can no longer avoid collision and the AEB is activated. Along with the relative velocity vector and the distance, the lateral position and width of the object are absolutely crucial for this calculation. If there is no object width data available, the critical moment for the steering criterion is delayed – there is no change to the braking criterion – and the benefit is extremely reduced since the reduction of relative velocity depends quadratically on time (see figure 9).

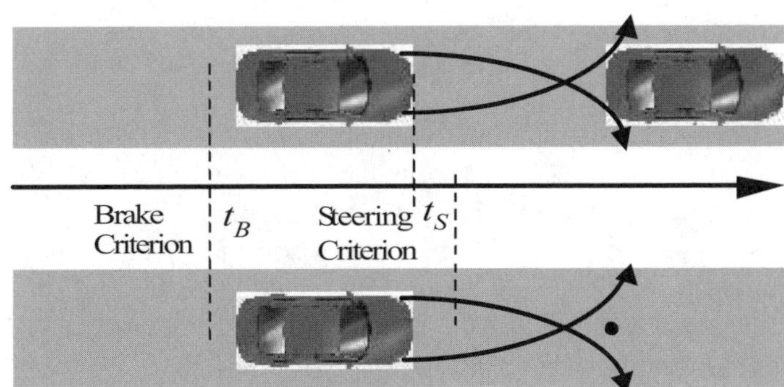

Fig. 9 Influence of object width

BENEFIT OF ACTIVE SAFETY SYSTEMS

This section will discuss the benefit of these active safety systems on the basis of statistical data.

Once every minute, someone dies somewhere in the world as the result of a traffic accident. Thus, for example, more than 93,000 people were killed in the USA, Europe and Japan in 1998. According to [4] human error plays a role in approx. 95 % of all traffic accidents. Driver assistance systems which support drivers and take the pressure off during driving have a high potential for avoiding such accidents, particularly in view of the fact that increasing traffic density is leading to more complex traffic situations and even greater pressure on the driver. Therefore, a purely comfort system such as ACC which automatically controls the distance to the vehicle in front has a safety effect, because more than 25 % of all accidents are rear-end collisions [5].

A survey by the German Federal Statistics Office [5] shows further that the number of accidents involving vehicles with ESP is significantly lower. Just as today ESP intervenes in vehicle dynamics only once the situation becomes critical and the vehicle threatens to get out of control, airbags are also only triggered once a collision has already been taken place. Typical reaction times are 5 ms in these cases. Despite of this extremely short time required for the triggering of measures which reduce the effects of accidents, it is indisputable that airbags have made a major contribution in mitigating the results of accidents. Due to this extremely short time between the detection of the accident and a possible reaction by the system, the potential of current systems is limited, however. Driver assistance systems provide a much greater potential for avoiding accidents because they can expand this very short time interval by using sensors to map the area around the vehicle. This puts them in a position to analyze the surrounding of the vehicle and detect hazardous driving situations in order to provide the best possible support for drivers in their driving maneuver in the respective situation. In this way, both the current traffic situation and the objects in the area around the vehicle can be taken into account when calculating measures to avoid or to mitigate the seriousness of collisions.

Next, the theoretical potential of an automatic emergency brake will be examined as a further example. The data used in the following were taken from [6]. Frontal collisions with stationary obstacles were exclusively used for the investigation. The fall in the numbers of injured persons and the reduction of the severity of injury were estimated on the basis of the reduction of collision speed through AEB. In addition, the initial velocity and the braking deceleration were considered in the investigation along with collision velocity so that cases could also be considered where drivers had already started to apply the brakes themselves before the accident. An ideal sensor system and a system delay of 300 ms were assumed for the AEB. The injury severity is divided into MAIS classes (Maximum Abbreviated Injury Scale) (see table below).

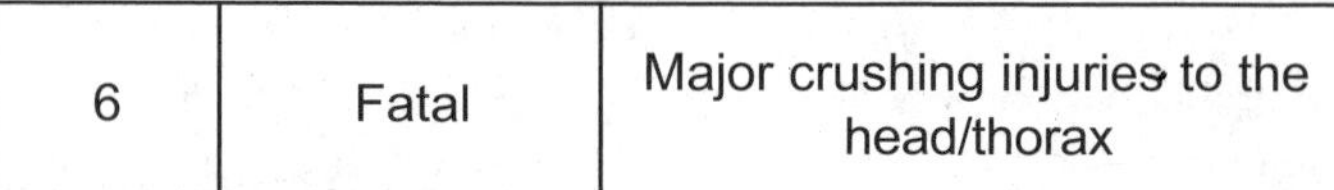

MAIS	Injury Severity	Example
1	Minor	Bruising
2	Moderate	Slight concussion
3	Serious	Heavy concussion
4	Severe	Dangerous bleeding
5	Critical	Serious head injuries
6	Fatal	Major crushing injuries to the head/thorax

Table 4. Injury Scale

Figure 10 shows how an AEB would reduce injury severity under the above-mentioned pre-conditions. According to this, the number of extremely critically injured persons whose injuries usually prove fatal is reduced by approx. 32 %. The group with critical injuries would be reduced by approx. 21 % and the group with severe injuries still by another approx. 10 %.

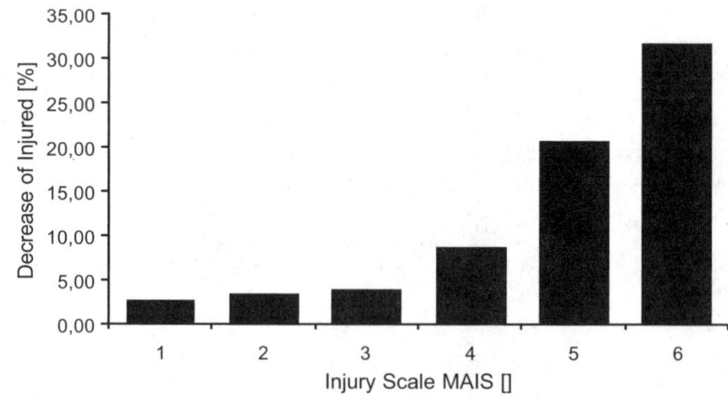

Fig. 10 Reduction of injury severity by AEB

If the fact that in critical scenarios quite often only fractions of a second are decisive as to whether or not a collision occurs is also taken into consideration, it becomes quite clear that there can be no doubt that active safety systems have an enormous potential for avoiding accidents.

SENSOR REQUIREMENTS

Assuming that the safety functions Precrash and Collision Mitigation presented above should cover the complete area in front of the vehicle taking all scenarios into account, this leads to a sensor with the following properties being required: The sensor should ideally have a field of view of 180° and be able to measure all the object attributes mentioned above as perfectly as possible. In addition it should be insensitive to the influence of weather conditions and have a sturdy object tracking. Such a sensor, however, cannot be realized at realistic cost at the moment.

To totally abandon the introduction of such safety systems for this reason is surely the wrong approach, however, since even a restricted sensor system can represent the above safety functions in its field of view and thus still make a contribution to improved traffic safety. For this reason, this paper will go on to describe an integrated approach which uses the ACC sensor (*IDIS®*) with a relative narrow opening angle to represent the above safety functions. It is interesting that even this narrow opening angle covers a large proportion of the statistically relevant accident scenarios.

INTEGRATED APPROACH

As outlined above, active safety systems have a great potential for increasing traffic safety. Lidar sensors in particular, which are good at calculating the lateral position and width of the object as well as the distance and relative velocity, are especially suitable.

The *IDIS®* multi-beam sensor was primarily developed for the ACC application. With its opening angle of 16°, however, it is also very suitable for active safety systems. Figure 11 illustrates the measures described above as a complete application. Limited to the field of view these safety functions can be represented as add-ons to the ACC, which means that no significant new hardware costs are incurred and subsequently customer benefits are considerably increased. A negative aspect is the small opening angle.

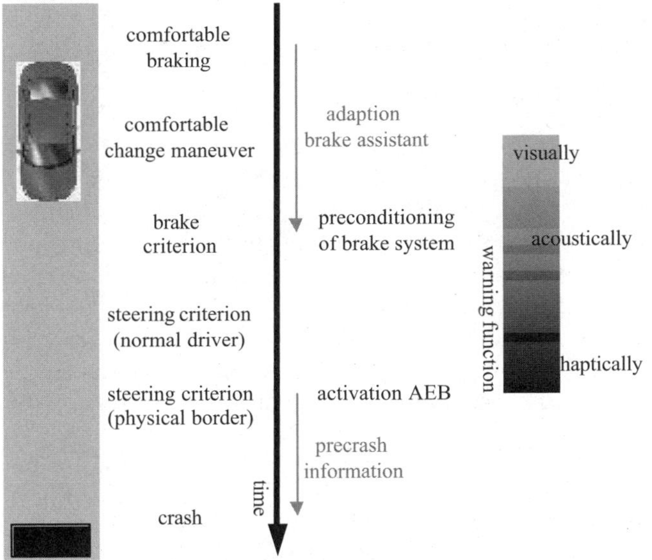

Fig. 11 Integrated approach

Taking into account, however, that more than half of all rear-end collisions are caused by drivers not paying enough attention when driving straight ahead, it is possible to cover a large share of the statistically relevant accident scenarios using the *IDIS®* only. In such scenarios it is indeed possible to use sensors developed for ACC such as *IDIS®* and, to a limited extent, 76 GHz Long-Range Radar sensors with a relatively narrow opening angle for active safety systems. In order to be able to cover further accident-prone scenarios, it is advisable to use a sensor system with sensors of different technologies in order to achieve a good synergy. From the *IDIS®* point of view, the camera and/or 24 GHz Short-Range Radars are ideal for this purpose. The following section will deal with the fusion of camera and *IDIS®* in more detail.

SENSOR FUSION CAMERA - *IDIS®*

Whereas in the short-term, particularly from a cost point of view, the functional extension of one single ACC *IDIS®* sensor can already achieve a considerable increase in safety, the information from several different sensors will be connected through data fusion in the mid to long-term future to improve the field of view and provide redundancy. Over time and with appropriate market penetration of driver assistance sensors, central data fusion units will become established in vehicles for this task, whereby a first step will be the decentralized fusion between two individual sensors.

The following section illustrates which additional potential will result in particular for the realization of the described safety functions by the fusion of *IDIS®* data with an image processing system for LDW (Lane Departure Warning).

VISION SENSOR FOR LANE DEPARTURE WARNING

The original LDW-system is based on a forward looking CMOS-Imager with a wide-angle lens and a separate image processing unit. The sensor works mainly in the visual spectrum and needs no additional, special light source at night.

In contrast to distance sensors it delivers a matrix of grey-values (Table 5) representing the brightness distribution of the scenery, leading to a 2D pattern- or template-based signal processing for object detection without the information of depth (geometric model).

Sensor resolution (pixels)	640H, 480V
Opening angle	45 °H, 22 °V
Grey value	12 bit
Range	50..70 m
lateral res. (d:50 m, f:5,7 mm)	0.07 m
Cycle time	40 ms

Table 5. LDW Camera Specification

The lane-detection task is based on a mixed feature-model-based image processing approach. By sensing the position of lane boundaries like white lane markings in front of the car, it estimates lane assignment, curvature ahead and ego-position of the vehicle in its own lane track. For reproducible system operation this assumes driving environments with "model"-like characteristics. Much investigation has been devoted to the image processing task, yielding a combination of an edge- and area-based lane marking detection algorithm adaptable to most road and illumination conditions.

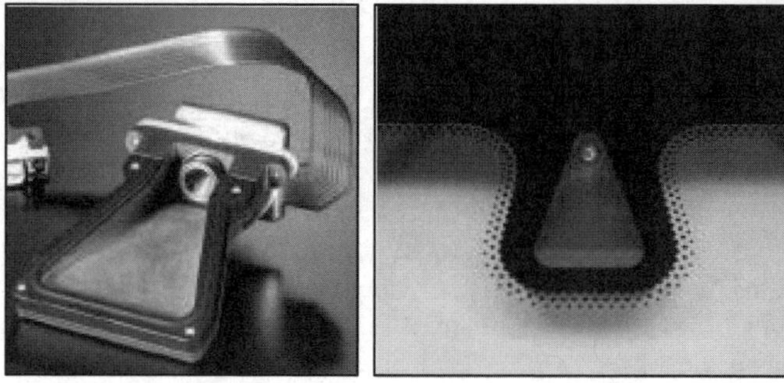

Fig. 12 Vision sensor for LDW. Best mounting position is behind the upper windscreen due to perspective view of the road ahead

FUSION CONCEPT

The method presented shows, how fusion of the LDW sensor with the *IDIS®* provides a more exact and robust calculation of static and lateral object parameters such as width, relative position in the lane and lateral velocity with comparatively low computing power.

If the topology of the two sensors is considered (see figure 13) it can be seen that both complementary and redundant covering areas exist.

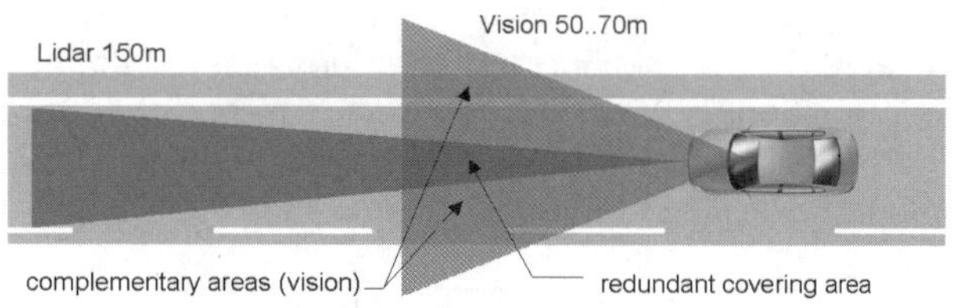

Fig. 13 Sensor covering areas and ranges.

The lane assignment of detected objects is regarded as the first step towards fusion of LDW and ACC systems in particular. In this case, the lane parameters sensed by the LDW image sensor are interpolated onto the distance of the objects observed and the lane assignment is checked on the basis of overlap of object position and lane position. In this way a distinction can be made between objects relevant for ACC longitudinal control and objects in the adjacent lane.

Much more complex than this complementary addition of LDW and ACC is redundant object detection using both sensor technologies and the fusion of the sensor data. In this case, the objects initially detected by the distance sensor are transmitted with their describing parameters as object lists to the image sensor system via a fusion CAN (see figure 14) which then opens up a search window in the camera image using the distance and angle information.

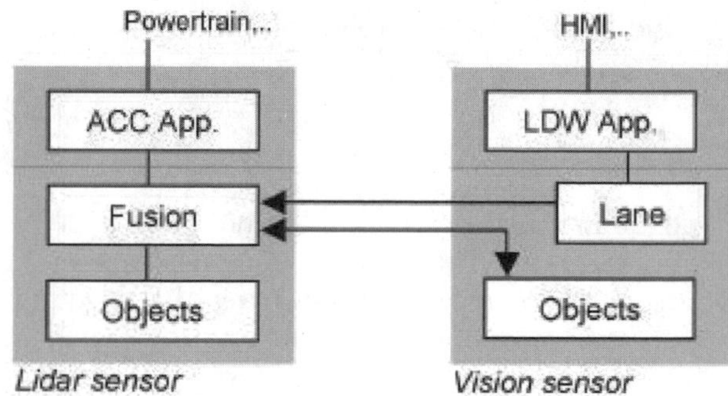

Fig. 14 Lidar/vision sensor cluster and the partitioning of the function blocks.

The vision sensors' task is now to detect and track all objects, which are initiated by the *IDIS®*, and to return the determined vision-based track lists, plus additional lane information to the *IDIS®* for the fusion task. Objects which drift in the vision sensor's right and left complementary areas will be tracked for a certain life time only by image processing to bypass short time object loss of the *IDIS®*, e.g. in narrow curves. In addition, objects that enter the vision area from left or right (near cut-in) can also be recognized initially by the LDW sensor.

The image processing methods used are based on horizontal and vertical edge detection, while the resulting edge candidates are analyzed concerning their attributes and must be arranged in certain geometrical orientation, e.g. the U-pattern [7]. This works during day-time and under good conditions. Because at night or in low-light situation additional features(like the tail-light of the vehicles) have to be detected, a multiple geometrical model approach for object segmentation has been chosen.

Finally, Kalman filtering is used to track the objects by the LDW system in parallel to the *IDIS®* tracking.

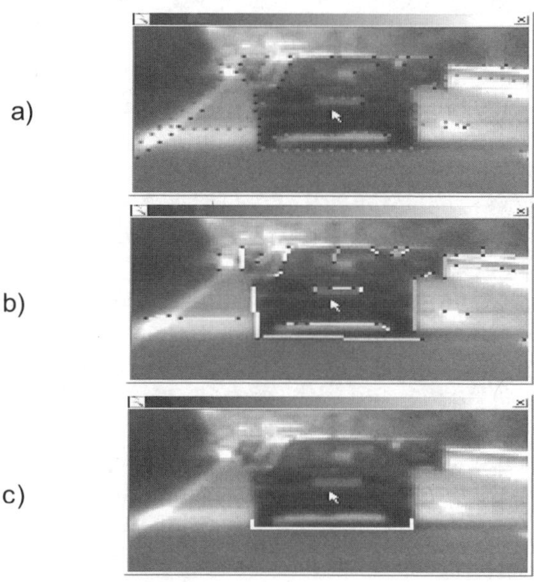

Fig. 10 Object detection a) horizontal and vertical edges. b) segments based on grouped edges. c) tracked object.

The target attributes, which are finally linked together in the central fusion process, differ in quality and accuracy depending on the sensor's physical principle. For example, the distance measurements are better performed by the lidar sensor than by the vision system. At this point, fusion is cooperative and feature-complementary by simple assembling of predefined sensor measurements, assuming that these measurements are constantly available.

On the other side, object features are often competitive due to the different situation- and weather-depending availability of the sensor systems (quality factor $Q_{m,Sensor}$). In this case the merging of features, which is described elaborately in [8], leads to better results.

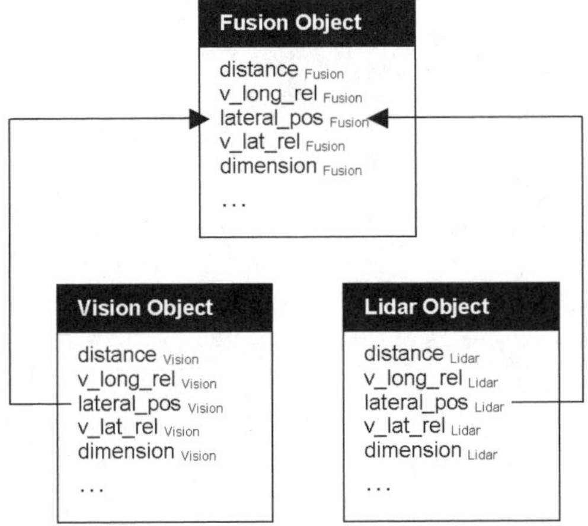

Fig. 15 Merging of competitive fusion features

RESULTS

The vision-based object detection capabilities are illustrated in figure 16, which shows a lane-change maneuvre of a relevant track ahead. The small bottom line represents the object width measured by the Lidar, the top thick one is the fusion object attribute target width, drastically improved by the vision system. The actual range in the given frame is about 60 m, so the accuracy improvement of the fusion step depends primarily on the resolution of the vision sensor.

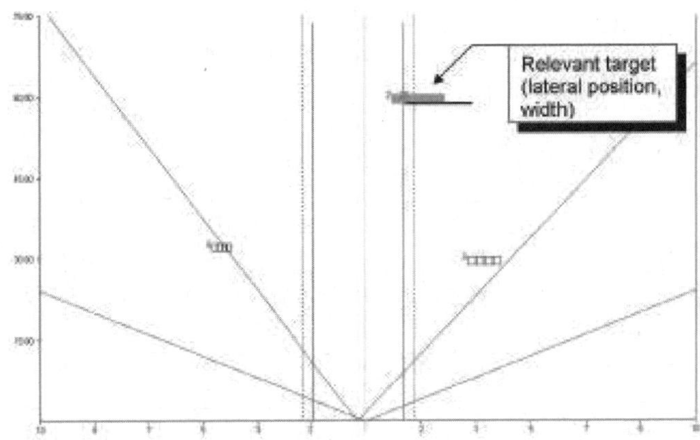

Fig.16 Fusion example with improved lateral target position and width

This example gives an idea of the functional improvements which can be achieved both for comfort and safety applications by this fusion approach.

Due to the given proceeding, the functional structure of both sensors can be preserved in most aspects, which means low modification and variation of the single sensor system. Especially sensor-specific signal processing and object tracking tasks remain in each device. A close system-internal data connection between this two tasks ensures an optimum system performance without facing the problems of a centralized fusion architecture.

CONCLUSION

As driver error plays a role in the vast majority of traffic accidents, active safety systems which can reduce reaction times prior to accidents offer significant potential to help reduce collision injuries, particularly of the extremely critical nature. Of the available object-detection technologies required for these systems, Lidar has been shown to provide an excellent balance of cost (allowing for potentially higher market penetration) and performance, especially regarding lateral position and object width which are ultimately necessary for effective collision mitigation systems. The IDIS® multi-beam infrared sensor offers the additional advantage of good performance under all weather conditions and detection of restricted visibility for use in driver alert strategies. As system cost can greatly affect the implementation of such beneficial active safety systems, a single IDIS® ACC sensor with relatively narrow opening angle can deliver a significant increase in safety when Pre-Crash and Collision Mitigation are implemented as an add-on to ACC. When fused with a forward-facing camera, not only are the base convenience functionalities of both units (e.g., ACC and Lane Departure Warning) enhanced, but the functionality of the active safety systems can also be greatly increased.

REFERENCES

1. Neunzig, D.: „Abstandsregelsysteme – Auf dem Weg von Komfort zur Sicherheit", IIR Fachkonferenz Fahrerassistenzsysteme, Stuttgart, Oct. 2003.
2. Boehlau, C.: „Multi-beam Lidar ACC – Approaching the Start of Production", ISAL 2005, Darmstadt.
3. Fettweis, A.: "Wave Digital Filters: Theory and Practice, Proceedings of the IEEE", Vol. 74 (2), 1986
4. N.N.: Fatality Analysis Reporting System (FARS), NHTSA, Web based Encyclopedia, 2001
5. Unfalldaten des Statistischen Bundesamtes (1998-2001).
6. Kopischke, S.: Entwicklung einer Notbremsfunktion mit Rapid Prototyping Methoden, Dissertation, TU Braunschweig 2000.
7. Gern. A., Franke U., Levi P.: "Advanced Lane Recognition – Fusing Vision and Radar", Proceedings of the IEEE Intelligent Vehicles Symposium 2000, Dearborn (MI).
8. Thiem, J., Mühlenberg, M.: „Datafusion of two Driver Assistance System Sensors", AMAA 2005, Berlin.

CONTACT

Norbert Höver

Address: Hella KGaA Hueck & Co., GE-ADS, Beckumer Str. 130, 59552 Lippstadt/Germany, Phone: +49(0)2941/38-8446, E-mail: Norbert.Hoever@hella.com

Steven Lietaert

Address: Hella Electronics Corp., 43811 Plymouth Oaks Blvd., Plymouth Twp., MI 48170, Phone: 734-414-5018, email: Steve.Lietaert@hna.hella.com

Dr. Bernd Lichte

Address: Hella KGaA Hueck & Co., GE-ADS, Beckumer Str. 130, 59552 Lippstadt/Germany, Phone: +49(0)2941/38-8393, E-mail: Bernd.Lichte@hella.com

2001-01-2517

The Role of Vision Sensors in Future Intelligent Vehicles

Lisa Hamilton, Lawrence Humm, Michele Daniels and Huan Yen
Delphi Delco Electronics Systems

ABSTRACT

The advancement in CMOS imaging sensors has enabled low-cost and high quality cameras that are making their way into future automobiles. Vision sensors can be deployed in a car to perform a variety of functions, including driver monitoring for workload management; passenger monitoring for intelligent airbag deployment; pedestrian and object recognition for precrash sensing; lane marker and roadway tracking for lane/roadway departure warnings; and general scene and object recognition to improve ACC/FCW/CA (adaptive cruise control / forward collision warning / collision avoidance) system robustness through sensor fusion. Possible system implementation and key performance requirements for vision sensors in these applications are discussed.

INTRODUCTION

During the past three decades, the automotive industry has undergone a great deal of changes. Besides the usual evolvement of exterior styling and interior features, the single most significant change is the ever-increasing use of electronics in cars. Traditionally, automotive technology is the domain of mechanical engineering and only accessories such as radio receiver and playback devices have any significant electronics content. However, due to a combination of technology advancement, vehicle manufacturers' market share competition, government legislation, and consumer pull, electronics is beginning to have a strong presence in cars. At the same time period, low cost microprocessors are becoming abundant and the idea of electronic control has migrated beyond engine control into other vehicle systems as well. To accomplish these control functions requires a wide range of sensors, signal processing electronics, algorithms, and actuators. Again, automotive engineers turned to electronics for answers. This evolution has since snowballed into the optimistic projection that the electronics content of cars will soon reach 10 to 15 percent of a car's value.

As we march into the new millennium, several major automotive systems are under development and will be rolled out within the next decade or two. Of particular interest is the integrated safety system (ISS). The vision is to equip the vehicle with adaptive cruise control, collision warnings, collision avoidance, pre-crash sensing, advanced safety interiors, pedestrian protection, rollover sensing, driver monitoring, etc. as a complete system. In so doing, the sensor information is shared among the various subsystems and the overall system will have performance superior to the sum of individual systems. This system approach is realizable only through advanced electronics that greatly increases the capability for sensing, computing, control, and communications. In this article, we will examine a small segment of this enabling technology, namely the vision sensor (camera), to see how the advancement in image sensing and processing may impact future intelligent vehicles.

THE INTEGRATED SAFETY SYSTEMS (ISS)

Delphi launched its ISS concept during the 2000 SAE Congress [1]. Briefly, the driving situations can be described in terms of a state diagram as shown in Figure 1. We used five states to describe what could happen if we deviate from safe driving.

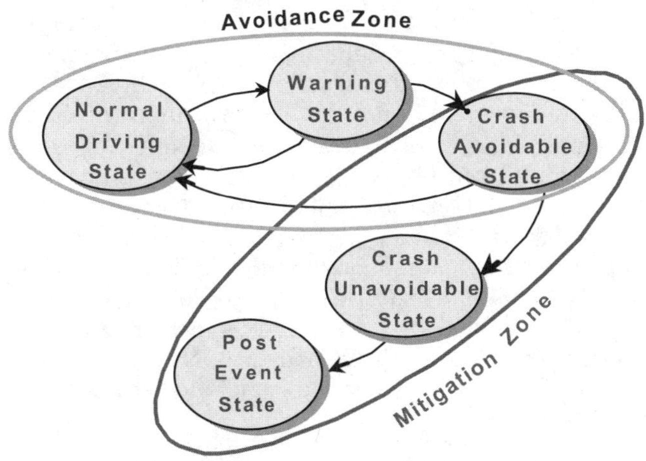

Figure 1. Integrated Safety System State Diagram

The five states and their brief definitions are listed below:

- Normal Driving State -- Enable the driver to stay comfortable, alert, and be aware of the driving environment (Subsystems that are active during this state include: ACC, driver monitoring system, night vision, etc.)

- Warning State -- Threat detection and warning to enable appropriate action (Subsystems that might be activated during this state include: collision warning, lane/roadway departure warning, etc.)
- Collision Avoidable State -- Vehicle control enhancements to supplement the driver's actions as the probability of a collision increases (Subsystems that are actively engaged during this state include: collision avoidance, suspension control, rollover prevention, etc.)
- Collision Unavoidable state -- Optimize protection to occupants, pedestrians, and property immediately before, during, and after a collision event (Subsystems that are most active during this state include: anticipatory crash sensing, advanced safety interiors, etc.)
- Post Event State: Neutralize risks to occupants and rescuers following a collision and provide assistance to rescue efforts (Subsystems that might be in action include: mayday system, fuel/power shutoff, etc.)

Typically, we should be spending well over 99% of the time in the normal driving state and well under 1% in the warning and the crash avoidable states. These three states constitute the so-called Avoidance Zone, meaning the vehicle with its electronic gadgets will do all it can to assist the drivers to stay away from a crash. In the Mitigation Zone, the vehicle once realizes that a crash is imminent will deploy appropriate interior or exterior mechanisms to minimize bodily harms to both the occupants and the pedestrians. Furthermore, in the Post Event State, the telematics equipment in the car will activate calls to summon emergency services, shut off engine, shut off gasoline, and also disconnect power if a fire threat exist. Thus, the future vehicle will be equipped with an array of sensors that in essence form an electronic cocoon around the car that will sense any dangerous situations dynamically and issue warnings or take actions to avoid the situation. A sketch of the ISS vehicle is shown in Figure 2. The sensors involved are microwave and millimeter wave radars, cameras, ultrasonic transducers, and laser- or LED-based devices. Behind the sensors are signal processing electronics and algorithms. In most cases, multi-mode sensors will be used and the information from these different sensors will need to be fused to extract the most reliable information for actions. In a vehicle equipped with all these sensors there will be a data network in place to facilitate information sharing and transmission of command signals.

Besides sensing the exterior traffic conditions and obstacle detection, sensors are also needed for interior driver monitoring and passenger recognition/position sensing. These informations will be used for driver alertness indication and workload management or fed to the smart airbag deployment mechanism to adjust its firing schemes. For better accuracy, again, multi-modal sensor arrangement is typically required to account for most real world scenarios. Again, microprocessors are used for signal processing as well as to execute the decision algorithms.

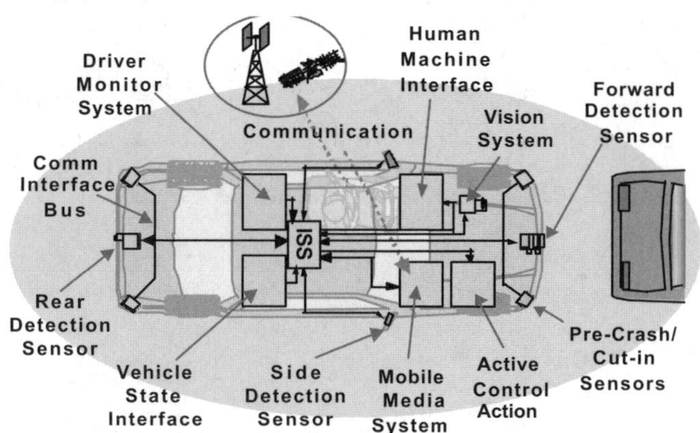

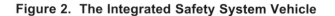

Figure 2. The Integrated Safety System Vehicle

THE NEED FOR EXTERIOR VISION SENSORS

Figure 3 shows an example of a complex roadway scenario often encountered during driving. It is not hard to envision that without the complement sensor suite of radars and the vision system, it would be difficult for a vehicle system to discern whether the trees, the road sign and the lamp posts are stationary vehicles directly in the path of the host vehicle.

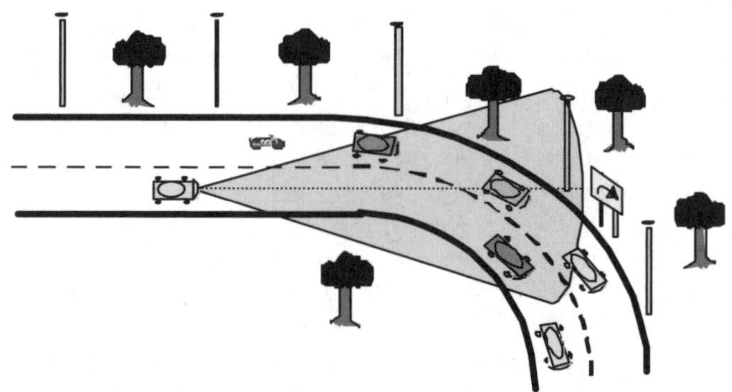

Figure 3. Example of a complex roadway scenario

For Collision Warning (CW), Collision Avoidance (CA), and Adaptive Cruise Control (ACC) functions to perform properly requires a suite of path algorithms (i.e.: host path estimation, target in-path prediction/estimation, and target selection) using radar and conventional on-board sensor information (i.e.: yaw rate and speed). These algorithms use radar data to provide accurate estimates of the range, range rate, and angular position of roadway and roadside objects within the sensor's field-of-view, and on-board host vehicle sensors to estimate the roadway radius-of-curvature. This approach has proved to be adequate for ACC applications that are limited to moving vehicular objects. However, this approach is not adequate for FCW (Forward Collision Warning) applications that are heavily dependent on the detection and in-path discrimination of long range stationary objects. The current sensor suite does not provide enough information to readily discern lane boundaries or to reliably reconstruct the road geometry ahead of the host vehicle. In the absence of lane boundary information, host lane position, and long-range forward curvature, it is difficult to reliably anticipate changes in road curvature ahead of the host (i.e.: curve entry/exit transitions), and to differentiate between lane change maneuvers and curve entry/curve exit maneuvers. Consequently, without the incorporation of a long-range vision-based lane tracking system to augment present collective sensors, it will be difficult to develop robust and accurate FCW systems.

On the other hand, vision system alone, though provides the information of host lane position, the target lane positions, and road information (number of lanes, roadside structures, traffic lights and signs, etc.), is not ideal as a primary sensor for ACC, FCW and CA applications because of its vulnerability to inclement weathers, as well as the nature of the information extraction process. To accurately estimate the closing speed of the object ahead, a priori knowledge of the geometrical dimensions of the object is required or a stereo vision (two cameras located slightly apart) system is necessary. In addition, vision systems rely on the analysis of successive images to determine the relative range and range rate of the objects ahead and hence has a longer response time.

HIGH DYNAMIC RANGE CAMERA DEVELOPMENT

For automotive applications, it is critical that a relatively high dynamic range (HDR) camera be used to handle the real world scenes encountered in normal driving. For example, a transition from bright daylight to an underpass/tunnel and vice versa present a severe challenge for any vision system since it is vital to discern whether there is a potential hazard just inside or just outside of the tunnel before entering or exiting it. Also, during early morning and late afternoon hours when traveling in a direction that looks right into the sun, the driver especially needs help and the camera must be able to deliver clear images.

CCD cameras have been around for quite some time now. They are known to have very high sensitivity, and high resolution. However, CCD cameras are also known to be susceptible to blooming because of over exposure and pixel saturation. Recent progresses in CMOS technology has made smart cameras possible. These cameras have local processing capability at the pixel level such that each pixel is capable of adjusting its exposure level in real time and the entire image information can be preserved with very high dynamic range. Of course, real life displays will have problem handling such a scene. Fortunately, further signal processing can render the scene to an image with compressed intensity distribution so that all key features are still preserved. There are several competing implementations being pursued today like the TFA Local Adaptive Sensor [2,3], the logarithmic compression, and others. Besides a good camera, the key to a successful vision system is actually the algorithm for object detection and recognition. This is an area generally falls under computer vision. The issues here are many and complex. The difficulty is in picking out objects from a two-dimensional image that is subject to interference from shadows, occlusions, distortions, etc. Figures 4(a) and 3(b) show the scenes recorded by a HDR CMOS camera and a CCD camera, respectively. These pictures clearly show the power of the high dynamic range camera even though the print media does not do justice to its full capability.

Figure 4(a) Image from a HDR CMOS camera

Figure 4(b) Image from a CCD camera

For lane/roadway departure warning systems, the camera typically does not look beyond 20-30 meters ahead of the vehicle. Furthermore, the camera is typically looking down at an angle of about 5-10 degrees as the goal here is to detect the lane markers/roadway-to-shoulder transition and decide if the vehicle is in lane. In this configuration, the dynamic range is still important as the lighting condition for the road varies widely particularly from an overcast day to a wet night with plenty of light reflections off the road.

LANE SENSING SYSTEM

Lane sensing systems typically perform two levels of operations, *lane detection* and *lane tracking*. At the lowest level, lane detection is a feature extraction process that detects the location of lane markers, road edges, or other significant road features. During the lane detection process, search windows are placed about the predicted road position, based on the detected road structure in the previous image frame. Edge detection or matched filter techniques are typically employed to extract low-level lane marker features. Hough transform or linear approximation techniques are often employed to group these features and to pre-select trackable lane marker features. This process typically provides an estimate of the host lateral lane position as illustrated in Figure 5.

Figure 5 shows a sequence of three pictures taken with the host vehicle at slightly different lateral positions within a lane. The lane sensing algorithm estimated lane boundaries are overlaid on the road scene in each case. Figure 5(a) shows the case where the host vehicle is traveling right down the middle of the lane. The intersection of the two estimated lane boundaries appears to lie roughly in the middle of the lane also. Figure 5(b) shows the case where the host vehicle was traveling down the lane at about 0.5 meter to the right of the center line. The intersect of the estimated lane boundaries clearly moves to the right. Figure 5(c) shows the case where the host vehicle at 1 meter off center to the right, and the intersect point appears to shift proportionally. This information can be exploited to indicate host lateral lane position to increase the robustness of the ACC/FCW systems.

Figure 5(a) Vehicle at the center of the lane.

Figure 5(b) Vehicle is 0.5 meter off to the right

Figure 5(c) Vehicle is 1 meter off to the right

Lane tracking is a statistical model-based process that tracks and extrapolates the host vehicle's state and forward road curvature. It involves the tracking of lane and road features from frame to frame, given an existing road model. During the lane tracking process, the dynamic state of the road in both the horizontal and vertical dimensions is estimated, tracked, and extrapolated for the road ahead. A dynamic model of the road (e.g. clothoidal curves with constant/piece-wise curvature, quadratic curves, concentric circular arcs) is fit to the lane marker features to reject those which violate width and curvature constraints. The remaining lane marker features are fed to an extended Kalman filter, which continuously updates the road model parameters such as road width, horizontal curvature, vertical curvature, and slew angle.

Most lane sensing systems are sensitive to camera mounting, vehicle pitch and vibration, and vertical road curvature. Vehicle/camera motion during frame integration can adversely affect the lane detection process by smearing image features across multiple pixels and causing image distortions. In addition, vehicle/camera motion and vertical road curvature can cause distortions during the dynamic update of the predicted host vehicle and road models.

In general, Lane Departure Warning and ACC/FCW/CA applications have very different requirements. Lane Departure Warning applications require a lane detection range of 8 to 15 meters. At these ranges, the lane sensing algorithms are more tolerant to vehicle vibration, pitch, and jitter, and less sensitive to image blur. On the other hand, ACC/FCW/CA applications require accurate estimates of road curvature and a lane detection range out to 75-100 meters ahead of the host vehicle. At these ranges, lane sensing systems are very sensitive to camera mounting, vehicle pitch and vibration, and changes in the overall vehicle state (e.g. tire pressure, vehicle load, etc.).

Both Lane Departure Warning and ACC/FCW applications require robust lane sensing systems that are self acquiring, tolerant to vehicle pitch and vibration, and able to dynamically calibrate their camera position/world model. Such systems must also be robust enough to handle the following: (a) image clutter (e.g.: shadows from roadside clutter and other vehicles, extra painted lane markings, roadway curves, and off ramps), (b) variations in the color and shape of the vehicular and lane marker objects (e.g. white and yellow dashed lines and continuous lines of varying contrast, reflective bumps, etc.). In addition, these vision systems must have enough contrast resolution to operate under a variety of illumination and environmental conditions (e.g. cloudy days, sunny days, headlight illumination at night, light-pole illumination at night, tunnel entry/exit, rain, fog, mist, and snow).

INTERIOR USE OF VISION SENSORS

As part of the ISS system, advanced safety interior features are making their way into modern vehicles. One key component is a smart airbag system that deploys only if the passenger seat is occupied and only if it is safe to do so. For example, depending on the size of the occupants (adult/children, male/female, etc.), the type of infant seat and its orientation, the position of the occupants (too close to the dashboard/feet or hand on the dash, etc.), the airbags will be either deployed with full force, partial force, or not at all. For best results, the occupant position should be monitored dynamically. Given the infinite possible scenarios in real life, the challenge for realizing a robust occupant recognition and position monitoring system is enormous. Many different approaches are under development including the use ultrasonic sensors, infrared sensors, LED arrays, and weight-based sensors among others. In general, to increase the probability of making correct decisions, a multi-sensor approach is required. An example is the use of an infrared LED array together with a weight-based sensor.

Because of its ability to capture a large amount of information in parallel, vision systems appear to be an ideal candidate to address this application. By choosing a wide field-of-view optics, the vision system can cover a large space within the vehicle thus avoiding any dead space compared to existing techniques. Furthermore, if a stereo imager pair is used, we can also obtain a 2-D range map that will greatly increase the robustness of the recognition algorithm. The competitiveness of the vision system for this application was hampered by the perceived high cost of cameras and the need for high performance computing equipment to carry out the necessary signal processing. Both of these factors are changing rapidly because of the advancement in CMOS and microprocessor technologies. We fully expect the vision system will be deployed in vehicles in the very near future.

Vision systems can also be used for other vehicle interior monitoring tasks such as driver alertness monitoring and safety/security monitoring. Drowsy driver has long been recognized as one of the significant risk factors for traffic accidents. Some characteristics of drowsiness are nodding of head, decrease of the eye-lid opening, and the blank stare look. These characteristics can be detected by the use of a camera and associated processing electronics. A number of studies have been carried out over the past twenty years on this subject [4]. To date these systems remain largely as clinical and laboratory tools. However, technological advancements in electronics have enabled some of these systems to be packaged in a way that is compatible with vehicular deployment.

FUTURE OUTLOOK

The advancements in affordable high dynamic range vision sensors and in powerful image processing software/hardware have opened the door for a wide array of applications in future intelligent vehicles. Although this paper deals mostly with applications of self-contained systems in the vehicle, It is recognized that vision systems have already been widely deployed in the highway infrastructure for traffic monitoring purposes. In the future, on-board vision systems in vehicles will not only be able to recognize cars, pedestrians, roadway objects, lanes, and roadway boundaries, but also be able to comprehend the information presented by the infrastructures. For example, vision systems will be used to recognize the traffic signal state, read the traffic signs (stop, yield, lane narrowing, detours, etc.), read the speed limit marked either on the road surface or posted by the road, and eventually also understand the overhead signs for traffic routing. For this vision to become reality, further progress in pattern recognition and image processing are necessary.

REFERENCES

1. Stephen N. Rohr, Richard C. Lind, Robert J. Myers, William A. Bauson, Walter K. Kosiak, and Huan Yen, "An Integrated Approach to Automotive Safety Systems," SAE 2000-01-0346, 2000.
2. M. Bohm, F. Blecher, A. Eckhardt, B. Schneider, S. Benthien, H. Keller, T. Lule, P. Rieve, M. Sommer, R.C. Lind, L. Humm, M. Daniels, N. Wu, and H. Yen, "High Dynamic Range Image Sensors in Thin Film on ASIC Technology for Automotive Applications," D.E. Ricken and W. Gessner (eds), Advanced Microsystems for Automotive Applications, Springer-Verlag, Berlin, pp. 157-172 (1998)
3. T. Lule, H. Keller, M. Wagner, M. Bohm, C.D. Hamann, L. Humm, and U. Efron, "100,000 Pixel 120 dB Imager for Automotive Vision," Proceedings of the Conference on Advanced Microsystems for Automotive Applications (AMAA), Berlin, 18-19 March, 1999.
4. Wierwille, W.W. "Overview of Research on Driver Drowsiness Definition and Driver Drowsiness Detection," 14th International Technical Conference on Enhanced Safety of Vehicles (ESV), Munich, Germany, 1994.

971128

Infrared Technology for "ACC" and Future Advanced Applications

Georg Otto Geduld and Wilfried Mehr
Automotive Distance Control Systems GmbH

To be an assistance for the driver and make his journeys more comfortable are the aims of the first "ACC" (Adaptive Cruise Control). It is the first step of a new area for the automotive future. ODIN is the name of the ACC-sensor made by ADC GmbH Switzerland, which based on infrared light (IR). There are full of parameters to describe the situation in front of a vehicle. Developing an ACC-sensor, needs to define this parameters exactly. What are the requirements? This will be discussed in the first section of the lecture.
The near IR is out from research and already a cheap and reliable technology. Due to the close relation between the visible light the IR technology is predestinated for an forward looking sensor. The differences between other technologies will be illustrated. ODIN has been quite a success for many ACC application at the automotive industry. ADC still improve their knowledge and wants to present how we come up to the requirements of ACC.
In the second section of the lecture, the vision of advanced driver assistance systems, equipped with infrared and supplementary technology will be described. If the ACC is a very simple comfort system, the next generation of systems will be more and more safety systems. On the path to collision avoidance, the goal at the horizon, a lot of sub-functions have to be developed, tested, compared and adapted to the behaviour of the human driver. Stop&Go, emergency braking, city ACC, lane keeping support, fall a sleep warning, blind spot supervision, pass over support are all sub functions to the final goal. Single beam-sensor solution, which are comparable with a blind stick in front of a vehicle, are no longer sufficient for the high demands to failure redundancy and reliability of such systems. Simple driving path estimation solutions with on-board systems has to be replaced with detection systems for the driving trajectory. Future driver assistance and safety systems have to deal not only with licensed vehicles. They also have handle situations with (dangerous) obstacles, children and animals "Simple" measurements of range and range rate to the relevant object have to be supplemented with traffic scenario interpretation modules. ADC GmbH Switzerland is prepared to join your future in safe and reliable advanced driver assistance systems.

INTRODUCTION

To be an assistance for the driver and make his journeys more comfortable are the aims of the first "ACC" (Adaptive Cruise Control). The requirements for this application are formed all over the world at this time. Almost every automotive company discuss ACC solutions and there are certain about the introduction of this technology.
Leica, well known for his infrared technologies (IR), develop one of the first sensors for ACC named „ODIN". Out of this business, the company "Automotive Distance Control Systems GmbH Switzerland" (ADC GmbH) was founded. Up to now we have more than 1Mio km experience with our sensor and their implementation.

THE REQUIREMENTS OF ACC AND HOW DOES THE ADC INFRARED SENSOR AND OTHER TECHNOLOGIES COME UP TO THEM.

REQUIREMENTS OF THE DRIVING SYSTEM

In general ACC are suitable in every kind of vehicles if it is a van, a car or anything else. The only thing you need is a cruise control system. Cruise control systems controls the speed by the throttle and by the gear unit. First ACC also use this way. Nowadays also active brakes supports modern ACC systems.

Throttle Break Gear Unit	ACC Control-Unit	Forward Looking Sensor

Figure 1: Functional path of a ACC driving system

REQUIREMENTS OF THE FORWARD LOOKING SENSOR

Range of view

Automotive companies demand that an driving assistance system should react and drive like the human being would do it. Therefore a sensor has to identify vehicles in front of it in the same way as the human eye. The human being has two typically areas for observing the situation in front of the car (see Figure 2). The first overview are made till 300m. The area where the human being reacts is shorter. It various on many reasons as like traffic situation or actual relative speed to the vehicle in front. At high relative speed, studies show, that most of the people react between 100 and 150m. Out of this point the detection zone of a forward looking sensor has to reach at least 100m.

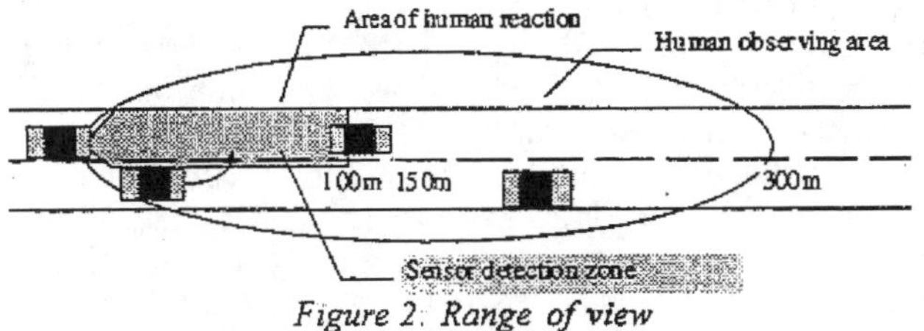

Figure 2: Range of view

As shown in Figure 2 the detection zone needs to cover the near and far field in the same way. This enable the system to react on all cut in and cut out situations. In addition the zone must clearly be related to the lane in order to decide which obstacle right in the own lane or not.
Curves reduce the maximum range of view, but the driver should be able to use the ACC-system in curves above 500m as well as on straight highways.

The sensor of ADC was adapted step by step to the needs of ACC-technology. To reach that high demand on the range of view ADC decide to use five independent beams (see Figure 3) which are sufficient to detect all object in the predicted path. The gaps between the beams are small enough to ensure that, in the detection range, no vehicle can be partially in a gap without being in a beam also. To enhanced the range of view at curves the sensor measure the actual angular velocity and move the whole set of beams in the direction of the curve.

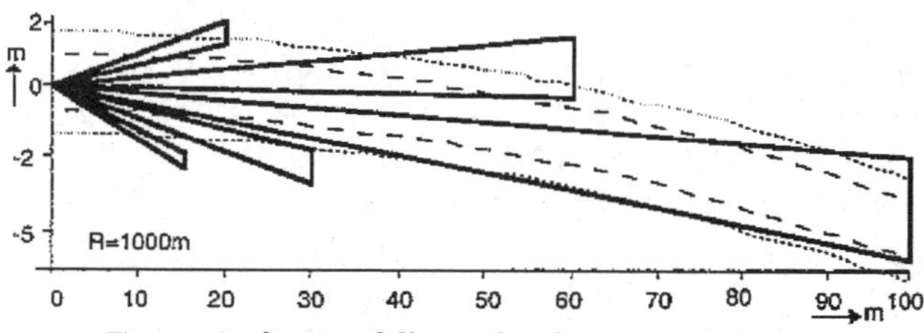

Figure 3: Sensor follows the direction of curves

The minimum measurable distance is 0m and under optimal conditions maximum detection is more than 150m. The decision if an obstacle is in or out of the own lane based on the distance of the obstacle, actual curve radius the adjusted lane width and the signal intensity of each beam. This combination of information are able to avoid wrong target detection.

Reliability of detection

To reach a very comfortable system you have to avoid wrong reactions. That needs a high reliability of detection. But the reflection properties of vehicles are quite different. Additionally to bad reflecting cars the weather conditions also take influence on the amount of the detectable signal. Extremely bad weather condition, which reduce the view of the human being, should be indicated by ACC-Sensors. They can call on the driver to take over the control or adapt the velocity of the vehicle. As like as the signal for bad weather it is usefully to indicate a dirty sensor, which also affects the reliability of detection.

There are values, assumed by the automotive companies, which describe the detection requirements of an forward looking sensor. They demand that less than 1% of the vehicles are detected below 80m.

The performance of ODIN is conceived to detect a worst case obstacle up to 100m at good weather condition. The reflectivity of the worst case target is equal to a small vehicle without a number plate and retroreflectors. Detection performance is also a function of the transmission factor of the media through which the infrared signal is transmitted (frontglass, cover, air etc.). Given a transmission factor of 100% with a clean frontglass and clear weather conditions the minimum allowed transmission factor is 25% to satisfy the requirements of ACC. A lots of test drives on the road under normal conditions confirm this data.

Great water drops as like rain and snow affects microwave technology. Weather conditions as like fog, which really reduce the visibility of the human being are detected by ODIN. So it can be reported a kind of visibility index to the ACC system, which adapt the velocity of the vehicle.

Reaction time of ACC-Sensors

For all requirements the human being still sets the level. Also for the reaction time of forward looking sensors. But in this point electronic is faster than the driver. ODIN reach at the moment reaction times around 0.3 seconds.

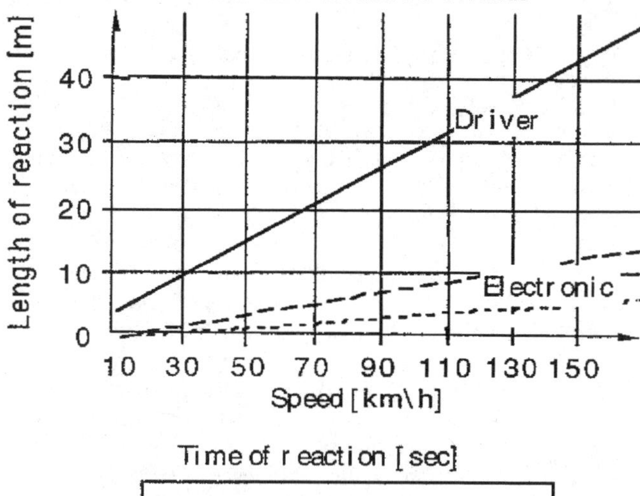

Figure 4: Reaction time of driver and sensor

Mutual interference

The desired requirements in this point are defined. No mutual interference should be appear between ACC controlled vehicles.

Both technologies radar and infrared right in this point in state of engineering. ODIN use a random coded signal to avoid this interference. This technology already reach a high performance.

Align -and adjustment

Not only the functionality of ACC sensors are important for the automotive industry. The same position obtain the align -and adjustment. The production costs are not allowed to increase by an complicated adjustment-process. The companies would like to adjust the sensors with already used proceedings. The same requirements are valid for the service stations.

In this point infrared technologies has an advantage against radar. With cheap technologies like CCD cameras the infrared beams of ODIN becomes visible for the human being. The projection image of the sharp beams can be adjust to the vehicle or for the headlamp implementation to the bright-dark border of the dimmed headlamp. This doesn't exceed the serial costs for the industries and make the adjustment for the service station cheap and comfortable.

Add on functions of ACC sensors

Automotive companies are interested in additional information which could be obtained by forward looking sensors. One is the information about headlamps and their covering with dirt.

Only a sensor implementation based on infrared technology could return a signal about the degree of dirt which after can start a cleaning process. ADC already made experiences with an full integrated sensor in a headlamp

The other add on function which is in conjunction with ACC sensors are the load levelling measurement. The ACC system should not have any influence to the detection reliability due to the variance of elevation. ACC should be independent from load levelling.
The elevation detection zone is defined by the beam heights of 2 degree and the maximum pitch angle of the vehicle. Elevation up to +/- 1 degree can be tolerated without noticeable performance degradation. This elevation range can only be established at vehicles equipped with a load levelling system. In this case, the sensor can use an additional road sensing beam measuring the angle between sensor and ground (see Figure 5). The distance measured by this beam may be used to compensate slow changing pitch levels of the vehicle. Additionally, this feature reduces accuracy requirements for the sensor mounting adjustment during production.

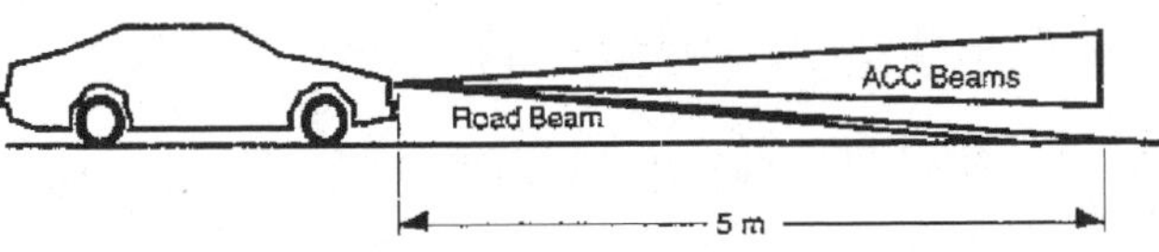

Figure 5: Load levelling sensor

Influence of sensor to the environment

Today every development should be considered by the influence for the human being. ACC sensors transmit electron magnetic waves and it is absolutely necessary to know how they take effect to the environment. Infrared sensors transmit light, which medically influence are well known and strictly specified. ODIN is designed to the laser class 1. That means that everybody can be in front of the sensor without damaging his healthy. Microwave technology like radar are not in this good position, as the long term influence isn't known.

ADVANCED DRIVER ASSISTANCE SYSTEMS

SYSTEM DESCRIPTIONS

Stop & Go

As a next step after ACC the functionality will increase to lower speed and the automation of the Stop&Go traffic. Stop&Go in the sense of this discussion is driving in a range between approximately 0 m and 20 m within a speed between 0 kph and 40 kph. The stop as well as the automatic "Go" is part of this function. This however is a minor expense of the longitudinal control as an additional requirement for a safe and a reliable functionality of the obstacle detection in the whole zone ahead the subject vehicle. Not only vehicles have to be detected, also pedestrian, children, toys and small pets and animals have to be considered.

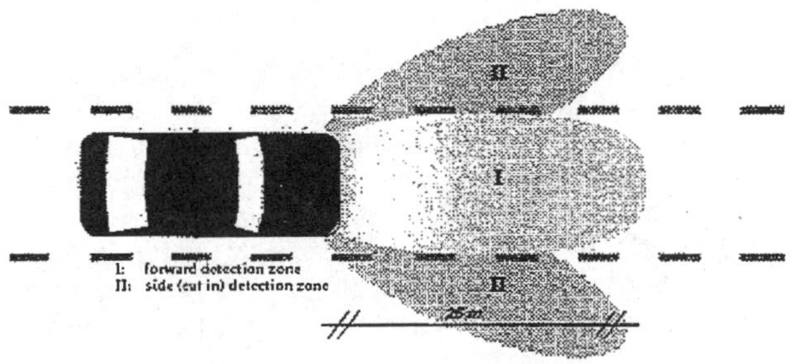

Figure 6 Stop&Go detection area

Lane keeping

Lane keeping support stands as a synonym for a couple of different system solutions and feasible products. Warning devises witch acoustically simulates the pass over of a rumple stripes are also included, as fall a sleep warning devices which detect for example the curvy driving behaviour. Systems which actuate the steering and give the feeling of driving on a railway-line or systems which take over the whole lateral control is also under development. Requirements for this function are also different as the mentioned products. Simple systems which detects the white lane's bedside the subject vehicle are the first step to detect the actual position and may be direction related to the road geometry. Advanced systems have to handle information between objects just in front up to the fare range on not only straight roads. Not only well designed and white painted road marks have to be considered. Also dirt or missing lines under different daylight situations and atmosphere conditions has to be managed.

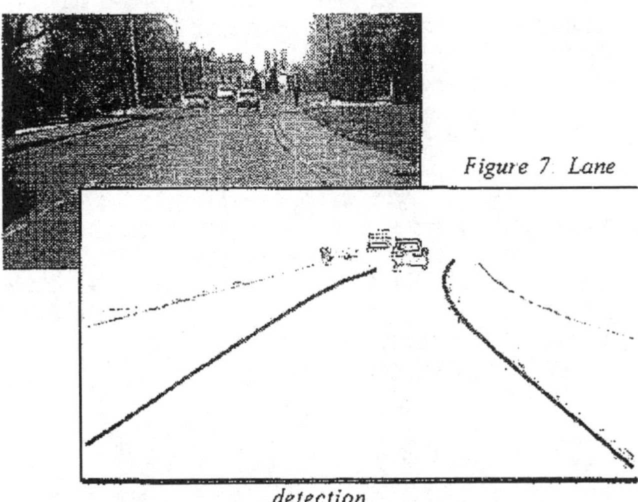

Figure 7 Lane detection

Emergency braking

The requirement's of the detection of an emergency braking situation are very pretentious if the driver should get the possibility to act in without a braking manoeuvre as long as possible. Emergency braking in this case means to prevent an accident or to reduce the damaging of the object inside the braking path, without restraining the driver using a different possibility to prevent damage or danger. The determination of the environment conditons includes the road status (highway, urban road with on-coming traffic, etc.), road geometry, road surface condition or friction, possible driving dynamics (load of vehicle, lateral dynamic capability, etc.), reaction time of the driver (differences between drivers, condition of the driver, etc.) and minimal/optimal time to collision for initiating the manoeuvre. Also the traffic scenario has to be interpreted, so that no other participant (other vehicles, pedestrian, cycles, etc.) are in danger.

<u>City ACC</u>

City ACC is a combination of ACC, Stop&GO and infrastructure communication. ACC on urban area has additional requirements to the detection capability and reliability. Not only co-operative vehicles in the same driving direction have to be considered. Objects like pedestrians, bicycles as well as oncoming traffic is part of the urban scenario. Urban area deals as well with different road geometry, more complex traffic scenarios and traffic management devices. Near field target detection in front of the whole vehicle is required. Detection or communication with the infrastructure to collect information like traffic signs and lights, dynamic and static speed limits, zebra crossings, etc. has to be established. In this case there will be a difference between autonomous and infrastructure based systems. The system initiated "Go" has to be discussed under this conditions. Up to now, it is an open question how to handle the automatic "Go" after a stop in front of a traffic light or a zebra crossing.

<u>Blind spot observation, rear view and lane merging</u>

Blind spot observation as well as rear view observation uses the technology of forward looking systems to create information about vehicles in the blind spot zone or behind the subject vehicle. The goal of blind spot observation system is the support or automation of lane merging and/or changing. Rear view observation supplements the blind spot zone to the rear of the vehicle. Fast approaching vehicles which obvious will overtake the subject vehicle has to be detected. Lane merging support gives the driver the opportunity to change the lanes in a very comfortable and save manner. The system has to consider the traffic in front, rear and side. In this case the sensibility of the systems is sufficient if vehicles, motor bikes and cycles are detect able. The geometry of the detection zone has to be adapted to the requirements of the systems.

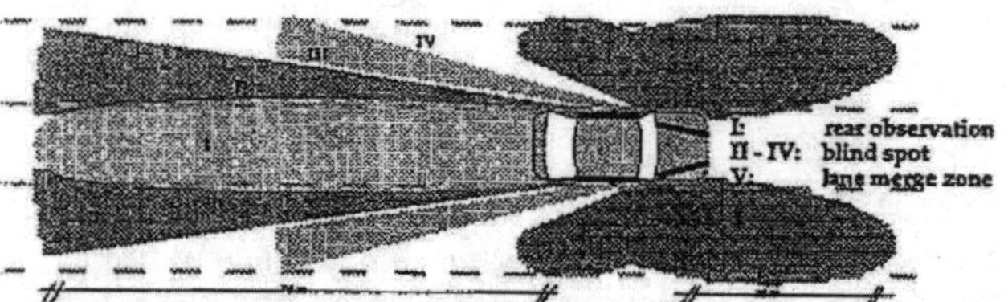

Figure 8: Blind Spot, Rear View and merging zone

<u>Driving support</u>

A combination of the above mentioned systems could support the driver by all of the ordinary driving tasks. Maybe the whole bunch of situations will not be handled 100 %, but driver information should help to introduce the necessary required action done by the driver. First tests with such systems show the need to design a feasible HMI (Human Machine Interface) to prevent misunderstanding and create trust to the systems. As more safety impact as well as the degree of atomisation grows up, as more is the responsibility at the system side.

<u>Collision avoidance</u>

Collision avoidance is the final goal of all of the developoment of driver assistance systems. The knowledge of today however leads to the opinion, that these goal slides away like the horizon. To avoid a collision, emergency braking is one possible reaction to minimise damage on persons and material. In most of the situations it is easier and better to pass the obstacle. This however assumes the knowledge about on-coming traffic or traffic beside the subject vehicle. To leave the road and use for example a meadow could be also the right decision to minimise damage, but only in the case, that there are no children playing...

REQUIREMENTS TO FUTURE ASSISTANCE SYSTEMS

<u>Difference of ACC in case of the environment data measurement</u>

ACC, one of the first introduced driver assistance system takes nearly no responsibility away from the driver. Like as the standard CC, ACC is a support device to increase the comfort to the driver. Only a part of the extensive driving tasks will be take over by the system.

Each of the additional functionality's has an increased impact to the safety and takes more responsibility away from the driver. Even Stop&Go, an apparently simple system extension, causes major responsibilities at the system side. Extensive evaluation of the HMI has to established, so that the responsibilities for acquired actions are relay obvious for the driver.

To achieve the requirements to this increased responsibility, not only simple telemetric sensors like blind sticks are sufficient. To guarantee a liable system solution, multi sensor systems (sensor fusion), communication (infrastructure-vehicle; vehicle-vehicle), advanced detection area combined with an advanced detection capability as well as traffic scenario interpretation and traffic management tasks will be necessary to reach the common high sophisticated goal inside the European research activities.

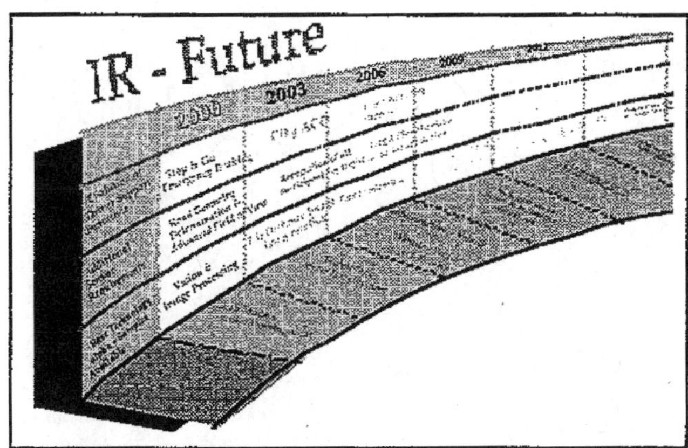

Figure 9: Advanced Driver Assistance Systems and their Technology

Near view observation zone

Zone among 0 and 25 m in front of the whole front-end of the vehicle.

Depending of the defined application different requirements could be solve the detection request. For simple acquisition of obstacles a primitive light barrier or ultra sonic solution could be sufficient. This solution could manage the inner circle, just one ore two meters in front of the vehicle. For control functions of the vehicle (like Stop&Go) a measurement of distance, relative velocity and lateral position is required. Together with an image processing device, a simple laser pointer and a scene interpretation and detection device this highly reliable task could be solved in an adequate manner. Depending on the application definition, not only vehicles, but also pedestrians, children, pets and toys have to be detected, if an automatic "GO" is part of an Stop&GO function.

For a future step into "City ACC" or "Urban Drive Control" not only the vehicle just in front has to be observed. Also the over next vehicle or vehicles on the neighbour lines are relevant for a driver accepted control strategy. In this case, telemetric sensor solutions are not more sufficient. Only communication systems (vehicle-vehicle; vehicle -infrastructure) will help to solve to acquire the needed information about position and vehicle dynamic data. This data has to include not only longitudinal information, but also lateral movement of the relevant vehicles. Discrete optics, image interpretation are means to achieve the requirements.

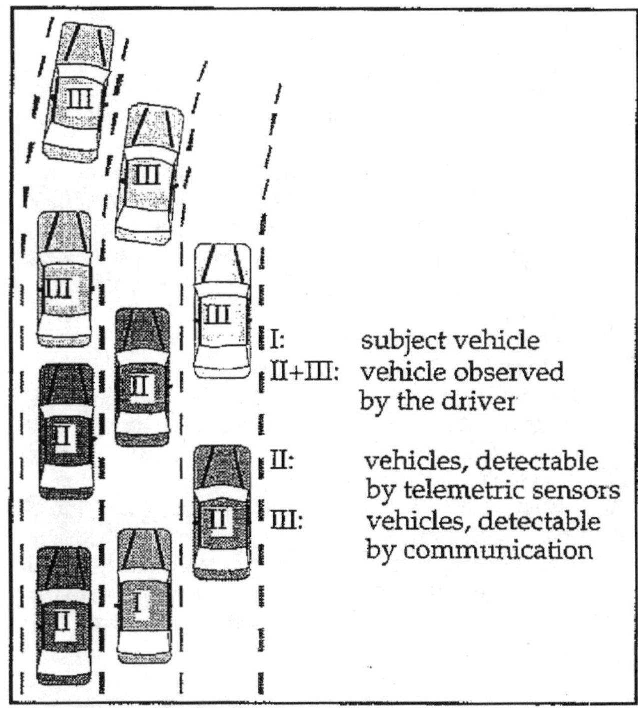

Figure 10: Traffic observation zone (urban area)

The far field of observation:

Today sensors deal with a range approximately of 150 m. These are the requirements of ACC to get a sufficient following capability as well as enough detection distance for approaching capability. However the observation zone of an ordinary driver is spread up to 300 m. He also observes the neighbour lanes, infrastructure, situations and movements beside the road. If necessary the possible driving trajectory independent whether it is on the road or not is also part of the consideration.

This leads to the requirement to interpret the available area. It has to be distinguished between objects with influence the own driving path and areas, which are considered to move on without disturbing or danger the other traffic participants. To solve the whole breadth of requirements, sensor fusion could be one of the solutions. More output power in a different wave length (between 1.5 µm and 15 µm) help to detect week obstacles under poor weather conditions. Lane detection, vehicle dynamic's calculation, scene interpretation combined with trajectory prediction has to handle situations in the same manner as a strong driver will do. Also navigation and communication have a lot of sub information to deliver to get the whole picture of the actual traffic scenario.

Detection capability

The detection capability is the second part which has to be improved.

Not only poor targets have to be illuminated. Also objects which are relevant to reduce the risk of driving or vehicles not in the direct field of view of any scene analysing sensor system have be considered. In some not very seldom cases, communication and navigation (even with infrastructure) have to help to look around corners, to calculate with vehicles not in the direct detection zone of a sensor or to detect non co-operative targets. More output

power, different wave length, combination of technology (infrared, radar, computer vision) are the key to get more and more rid to the requirements.
For reaching a well driver acceptance, not only the vehicles direct in front of the subject vehicle has to considered Like an experienced driver, a future driver assistance system has to observe the whole relevant driving environment. This is the only way to reach the final goal of collision avoidance.

Advanced scenario interpretation

The third part will be the advanced scenario interpretation. The human driver is able to weight the same vehicle configuration total different in different environments and traffic flow conditions. The concluded reaction is than different at the vehicle reaction and dynamic. Also the near and relevant environment (urban area, highway condition, etc.) have to be considered to design acceptable system solutions. This is a research area for the next decades. A lot of real traffic analysis has to be done. However to reach a sufficient solution, most of the on board sensors has to be developed.

Driver model and interpretation

Last but not least, the driver acceptance of new and advanced assistance system solutions have to be based on human driver modules which represents the behaviour, the weakness and the strength of different drivers. Not only perfect technical solutions will be bring enough benefit to the driver. Also the perfect completion of different strengthens (technical and human) will bring a sufficient solution. HMI of driver assistance systems is one of the deciding component for success or failure of the system solution.

A.D.C. - Automotive and Distance Control Systems GmbH is prepared to join your future in safe and reliable advanced driver assistance systems

ACC NOW AND IN THE FUTURE

Adaptive Cruise Control—Current State and Future Aspects

Peter M. Knoll
Robert Bosch GmbH

SUMMARY

Today's common adaptive cruise control (ACC) is a driver-supporting convenience function that can be viewed as a preliminary stage for vehicle guidance and collision avoidance. Long-range radar (LRR) and light detection and ranging (Lidar) are used for the ACC function. With a range up to 200 m and superior signal quality, LRR is the key technology and main enabler for future predictive safety systems (PSS).

The second generation of ACC enhances convenience and has opened a path to safety functions. For such functions, additional sensors are needed if strong vehicle interaction is made. Their signals are fused with the long-range signals of the ACC sensor.

Video technology has been introduced for systems such as night vision improvement and lane detection warning. Passive infrared sensing based on thermal radiation sensors is used in some cars. Information derived from these cameras may help to verify an obstacle detected by the ACC long-range sensor. Mid- and short-range sensors currently are based on various radar and optical sensing technologies, as well as on emerging new technologies.

Active safety systems demand high performance and reliability. With further improvement in sensor performance and sensor data fusion, collision-avoidance and collision-mitigation functions will become realistic.

INTRODUCTION

Sensors to detect the vehicle environment are already in use today (e.g., ultrasonic parking aids and ACC sensors). New sensors, mainly video cameras, are being developed at a rapid pace and have been introduced for early applications. New functions are being implemented rapidly because of their importance in safety and convenience applications. In 2005, the first application of short-range radar (SRR) sensors occurred with the introduction of the Brake Assist Plus system in the new Mercedes S-Class vehicles.

Airbags and modern restraint systems play a dominant role in achieving a high standard of passive safety in modern vehicles. Active safety systems such as antilock braking systems (ABS), electronic stability program (ESP), and hydraulic brake assist (HBA) help the driver avoid accidents in critical situations. An important aspect in developing active and passive safety systems is the capability of the vehicle to perceive and interpret its environment, recognize dangerous situations, and support the driver and his or her driving maneuvers in the best possible way.

There will be an ongoing stepwise approach from today's convenience and first safety systems to tomorrow's safety systems with ACC as the basis. ACC and the next ACC generation, ACCplus, controls the speed of a vehicle and the safe distance to a vehicle in front.

The second step has been started with predictive safety systems (PSS). These systems interact with the vehicle to prepare it for critical situations and to warn the driver of a dangerous traffic situation as soon as possible. The goal, in the best case, is to avoid a potential accident or to mitigate the consequences of an unavoidable accident.

Microsystems technology plays an important role during the introduction of active safety systems. Various sensors (ultrasonic, radar, Lidar, and video) all contribute to gaining relevant and reliable data about surrounding vehicles. Sensor technology, sensor data processing, sensor data fusion, and appropriate algorithms for function development allow the realization of accident avoidance and mitigation.

EU GOAL OF FATALITY REDUCTION

In 2004, more than 85,000 persons were killed in road traffic accidents in Europe, the United States, and Japan, leading to a socioeconomic damage of more than 500 billion.

With more than 40,000 fatalities per year in the European Union (EU), the European Commission in 2001 defined the Road Safety Action Plan, with the challenging goal of reducing fatalities in Europe by half until 2010. However, today more than 1.4 million accidents still occur each year on EU roads. Current research indicates that human error is involved in almost 93% of accidents, with a cost of around 200 billion, or 2% of the EU gross domestic product (GDP). Traffic congestion now affects 10% of the European road network and costs 50 billion per year, or 0.5% of the EU GDP. Investigations show that up to 50% of fuel consumption is due to traffic congestion or poor driving habits. These problems will be solved through information and communication technologies. "Intelligent" systems can help drivers avoid accidents and can even call emergency services automatically in the event of a crash. The systems also can be used in electronic traffic management systems or to optimize engine performance, thus improving energy efficiency and reducing pollution.[1]

SENSORS FOR SURROUND SENSING, ACC, AND PREDICTIVE SAFETY

By making use of electronic surround vision technologies, many driver assistance systems can be realized. Today, components needed for these systems—highly sensitive sensors and powerful microprocessors—are available or are under development. As a result, the realization of the "sensitive" automobile is approaching rapidly. Sensors scan the environment around the vehicle, derive warnings from the detected objects, and perform driving maneuvers, all in a split second faster than the most skilled driver. With a timely warning, an earlier reaction by the driver can be achieved. Going one step further, active driver assistance systems enable a vehicle reaction that is much faster than the normal reaction time of the driver.

Sensor technologies and the sensors based on them vary considerably. One prominent distinctive feature is the detection area. Figure 1 shows detection zones for a typical "sensitive" vehicle.

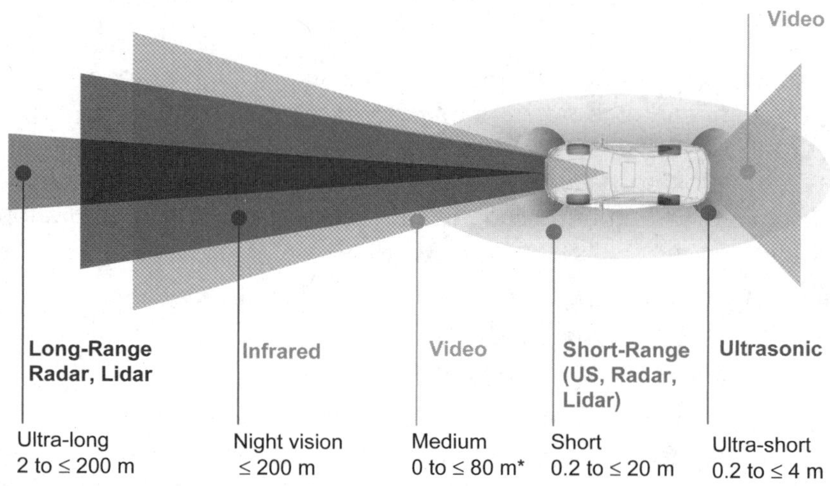

* Object detection up to 80 m

Fig. 1: Detection zones of surround sensors.

The following sensors are available or are under development:

- Ultrasonic sensors are common as reversing and parking aids. In the future, they also will support many new functions in the field of parking assistance.
- LRR sensors are used for the ACC.[1] Such sensors, with a narrow lobe and an opening angle of ±8°, detect obstacles in front of the "own" vehicle and measure the distance and relative speed to vehicles in front.
- Lidar sensors are in common use In Japan. They have poorer performance than radar sensors, especially in adverse weather conditions and with water spray in particular. However, Lidar sensors do have some cost advantages. As a consequence, radar sensors are more common in upper-class vehicles (also in Japan), whereas Lidar sensors are more common in medium- and lower-class vehicles.
- Video technology was introduced in the Mercedes S-Class in 2005 with a system for night vision improvement. The camera meets all the requirements for automotive components regarding temperature range and robustness and can be used for daytime applications as well. A powerful CPU significantly improves the picture quality of the night vision system. Other systems for night vision enhancement, based on either near-infrared or far-infrared technology, have already been introduced in Japan and the United States.
- Short-range sensors build a virtual "safety belt" around the car. Short-range radar (SRR) was also introduced in the Mercedes S-Class 2005. It is used in the front of the vehicle to detect short cut-ins, thereby improving the overall performance of the ACC system in the low speed range. Alternatively, Lidar and ultrasonic technology may be used. However, ultrasonic technology, with a detection distance far below 10 m, limits its application to very low speed ranges. In the rear of the vehicle, SRR sensors also are a substitute for ultrasonic sensors for parking aid.
- Range imagers are at the stage of entering the market today. In principal, they have a high potential for supporting active and passive safety functions in the future. However, many technological problems must be solved before these technologies can become part of an automotive safety system.

LONG-RANGE RADAR (LRR) SENSORS

LRR sensors based on 77 GHz were introduced into the market in 1999 with the Mercedes S-Class, and BMW followed one year later. Today, second-generation LRR sensors are found in vehicles.

Radar ("radio detection and ranging") uses electromagnetic waves to measure the distance between a radar antenna and an obstacle. The simple form of the radar equation expresses the maximum radar range R_{max} in terms of key radar parameters and the target's radar cross section

$$R_{max} = \sqrt[4]{\frac{P_t G A_e}{(4\ )2 S_{\min}}}$$

where

P_t = transmitted power [W]

G = antenna gain

A_e = antenna effective aperture [m^2]

σ = radar cross section of the target [m^2]

S_{min} = minimum detectable signal [W]

To measure a distance with radar, a flight-time measurement of the electromagnetic waves is made. The flight time t_{flight} is the duration between the emission of a transmitter signal and the reception of its echo from the target, with

$$t_{flight} = 2\frac{d}{c}$$

where

d = distance between the sensor and obstacle

c = velocity of light (300,000 km/sec)

The relative speed between the target and the "own" vehicle is of basic importance for ACC. It can be measured with the Doppler effect. A signal transmitted by the "own" radar is subject to a frequency shift $f_{Doppler}$ when it is reflected by an object moving toward or away from the "own" system

$$f_{Doppler} = 2\frac{f_c v_{rel}}{c}$$

where f_c = carrier frequency (76.5 GHz).

For a relative speed of 1 m/s, the frequency shift is roughly 510 Hz.[2]

The principal hardware architecture can be demonstrated using the Bosch second-generation LLR shown in Fig. 2. The lower substrate carries the RF components; the upper one carries the low-frequency electronics. Four patches with "polyrods" emit four radar lobes, which are focused with a dielectric lens covering the sensor.

Fig. 2: 77-GHz radar sensor control unit (SCU) for ACC.

This sensor control unit (SCU) combines the sensor and the ECU for the ACC system. The first-generation series was introduced in 2000; the second generation was introduced in 2005.

Frequency modulation continuous wave (FMCW) is the most common modulation form used. It varies the radar frequency linearly over time. Distance and relative velocity of objects can be calculated using the difference frequencies of outgoing and incoming signals of various frequency "ramps." Another modulation form is pulse modulation, which is combined with a time-of-flight measurement.

FMCW offers some cost advantages. All radar SCUs are able to measure the data of a plurality of objects in parallel.

Angular resolution is derived using the signals from all four lobes by comparing the peak heights of one object in two or more lobes. Thus, within an opening angle of ±8°, objects can be detected in front of the "own" vehicle, and their distance, relative velocity, and lateral position can be estimated.

Scanning Radars allow the measurement of the obstacle with good accuracy.

LIDAR SENSORS

In principle, Lidar sensors work similar to radar but emit near-infrared light instead of microwaves. The light is modulated only in intensity, not in frequency. Figure 3 shows a block diagram of a Lidar sensor system.

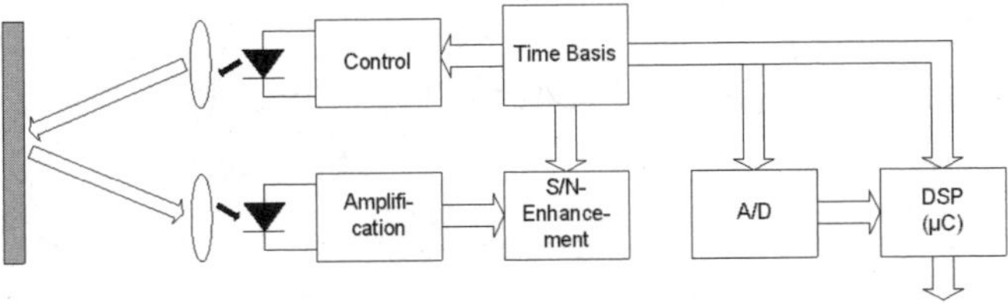

Fig. 3: Lidar block diagram.

The modulated infrared light emitted by the Lidar sensor is reflected by an object and is received by one or more photodiodes. Modulation forms can be rectangular, sinusoidal, or pulses. The modulator sends the modulation information to the receiver. The received light can be compared with the emitted light to either measure phase differences or flight times in order to calculate the distance of the object. The S/N ratio depends strongly on the modulation. The best values are obtained with pulse modulation. For long-range Lidars, pulse modulation is a must. Typical values for pulse widths are in the nanosecond range, resulting in pulse lengths in the meter range. By using signal evaluation algorithms, distance accuracies of centimeters can be achieved.

Lateral and vertical resolutions can be realized either by multibeam geometries or by mechanical scanning. Mechanical scanning has the advantage of a very fine resolution obtained by using only one emitting and one receiving element. Beam deflection is achieved either by rotating mirrors or by moving the focusing optics of the emitter and/or the receiver.

In contrast to most radar sensors, Lidars do not measure the object velocity directly. Instead, this signal is calculated by differentiating (or filtering) the distance signal to result in a certain delay time and a reduced signal quality. On the other hand, the good lateral resolution of scanning Lidars shows superior quality compared to typical radars today.

A big issue is weather performance. Lidars as optical sensors, of course, have drawbacks in spray and mist situations.[3]

SHORT-RANGE RADAR SENSORS

Short-range radar (SRR) sensors can be used in the future to build a "virtual safety belt" around the car. They have a detection range between 2 and 20–50 m, depending on the specific demand for the function performance. Objects are detected within this belt, their relative speeds to the "own" vehicle are calculated, and warnings to the driver or vehicle interactions can be derived. Functions may be realized based on the SRR alone or by sensor data fusion with ACC or other sensors.

Today, 24 GHz is the frequency used to operate SRR sensors. Two different technologies are involved. Ultra-wide-band (UWB) sensors emit very short pulses and therefore require a large bandwidth. Narrow-band sensors require a bandwidth of only 0.125 GHz (ISM-band). UWB sensors offer superior distance accuracy and object separation capability compared to narrow-band sensors. Especially for low-speed applications such as ACC Stop&Go, these sensors fulfill all requirements.

When development of UWB-SSR sensors began, they were not allowed to be used in any country. But in 2002, the 24-GHz UWB (ultra-wide band with 5-GHz bandwidth) was released for use in the United States. The European release was made in 2004, however, it is permitted only until mid-2013, but a worldwide harmonization is evolving. After 2013, the 79-GHz frequency band with 4-GHz bandwidths may be used in Europe. The release came in 2004, too.

Figure 4 shows a graphical sketch of an SRR sensor.

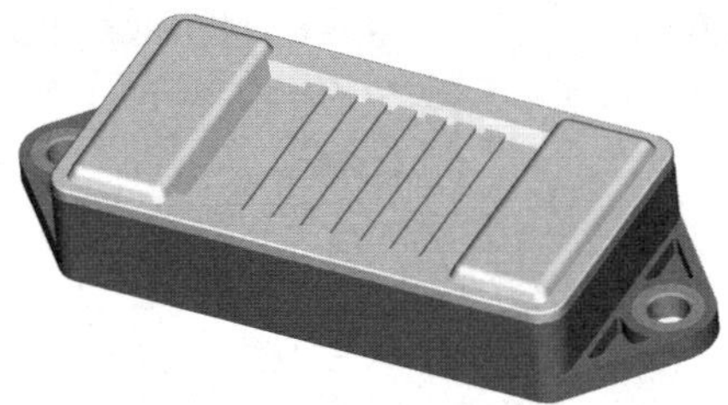

Fig. 4: Short-range radar (SRR) sensor.

Although the introduction of the SSR sensor probably will be driven by one or two single functions, investigations have shown that eight sensors (depending on the size of the car) allow coverage of an almost complete surround view with all its functionality. This multiple use of sensors also is necessary to reduce the cost of the system.

VIDEO SENSORS

Two main application classes can be identified for video sensors. One is where a picture taken by a camera is enhanced by the system and is presented to the driver (object detection is performed by the driver). The other is where object detection and object classification also are done by the system.

An example of an automotive camera (Fig. 5) is the current setup of the Robert Bosch camera module. It is fixed on a small printed circuit board with camera-relevant electronics. On the rear side of the camera board, the plug for the video cable is mounted. The whole unit is placed onto the windshield-mounted adapter.

Fig. 5: Video camera module.

This is the first CMOS video camera with full automotive qualification. The ECU either shows the driver a familiar and high-quality picture or automatically extracts features and objects from the images. For both applications, intelligent picture processing is necessary.

The current concept is a power PC with a clock frequency of 400 MHz and 700 MIPS. Other than consumer electronics, the night vision ECU currently represents the most powerful ECU in automotive applications.

RANGE IMAGERS

Range imagers are a newly evolving technology with characteristic features of both Lidar and video sensors.[4] A range imager can be thought of as a video sensor with the added ability to measure the distance to the next object in each picture element (pixel), which gives a three-dimensional representation of the surrounding world. Figure 6 shows a block diagram of a range imager system.

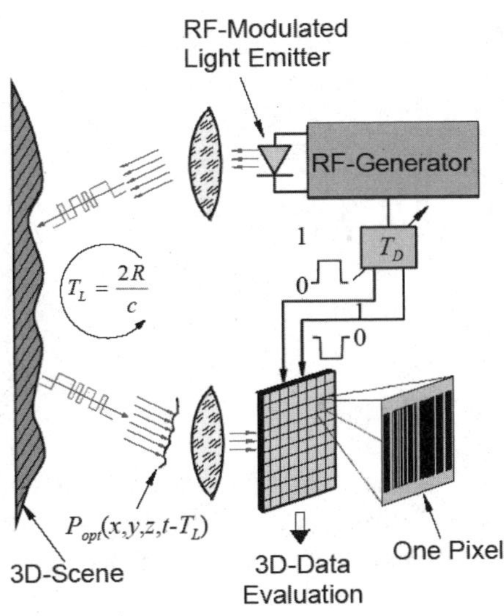

Fig. 6: Range imager block diagram [4]

There are several range imager technologies that differ in some details. At present, the most prominent technology in the automotive field is the "photonic mixing device" (PMD) developed cooperatively by the University of Siegen (Germany) and Audi. Figure 6 illustrates its technological principle: modulated light is emitted by near infrared lamps.

A special imager chip measures both, the brightness of a pixel and the time of flight of the infrared light pulse emitted by the light emitter. In this way, a stereoscopic picture with distance information can be generated.

The entire scene in front of the sensor must be illuminated with modulated light. For longer ranges (>5–10 m), powerful infrared lamps are needed, able to be modulated in the megahertz range. This results in high power dissipation. Eye safety is a limiting factor for the measurement range. Because modulation precision is critical to the quality of the distance measurement, lighting is a technological challenge.

SENSOR DATA FUSION

The radar setup used for ACC has excellent longitudinal accuracy, but the horizontal resolution is rather poor due to the limited number of radar lobes (e.g., four in the Bosch system). The radar system receives reflections only from a target in front and cannot distinguish among relevant objects (e.g., a bicycle) and non-relevant objects (e.g., an aluminum can on the road).

Video has a good lateral resolution due to the high number of pixel cells per line. For cost considerations, a mono-camera approach has been used in the introduction phase of the video technology. It enables a good mono-object detection (MOD) to be made, but its longitudinal measurement accuracy is poor. Due to the high resolution of the imager chip, a video picture processing unit can give reliable information about the size of an object and therefore a good prediction of its relevance.

Radar and video combine optimally (Fig. 7), resulting in a reliable mono-object verification (MOV) with high accuracy for both the distance and the width of the object.

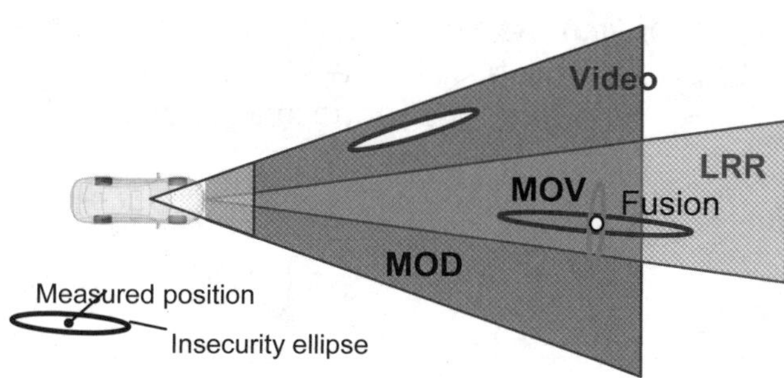

Fig. 7: Data fusion of radar and video.

Radar: High distance accuracy, low lateral resolution.
Video: Low distance accuracy, high lateral resolution.

SURROUND SENSING SYSTEMS AND DRIVER ASSISTANCE SYSTEMS

Figure 8 shows the enormous range of driver assistance systems on the way for use in the "safety vehicle." These systems can be subdivided into two categories: (1) safety systems with the goal of collision mitigation and collision avoidance, and (2) convenience systems with the goal of semi-autonomous driving.

Driver support systems without active vehicle interaction can be viewed as a preliminary stage to vehicle guidance. They warn the driver or suggest a driving maneuver. One example is the Bosch parking assistant. It gives the driver steering recommendations for parking optimally into a parking space. Another example is a night vision improvement system. Because more than 40% of all fatalities occur at night, this function has high potential for saving lives. Lane departure warning systems also can contribute significantly to the reduction of accidents. Almost 40% of all accidents are due to unintended lane departures.

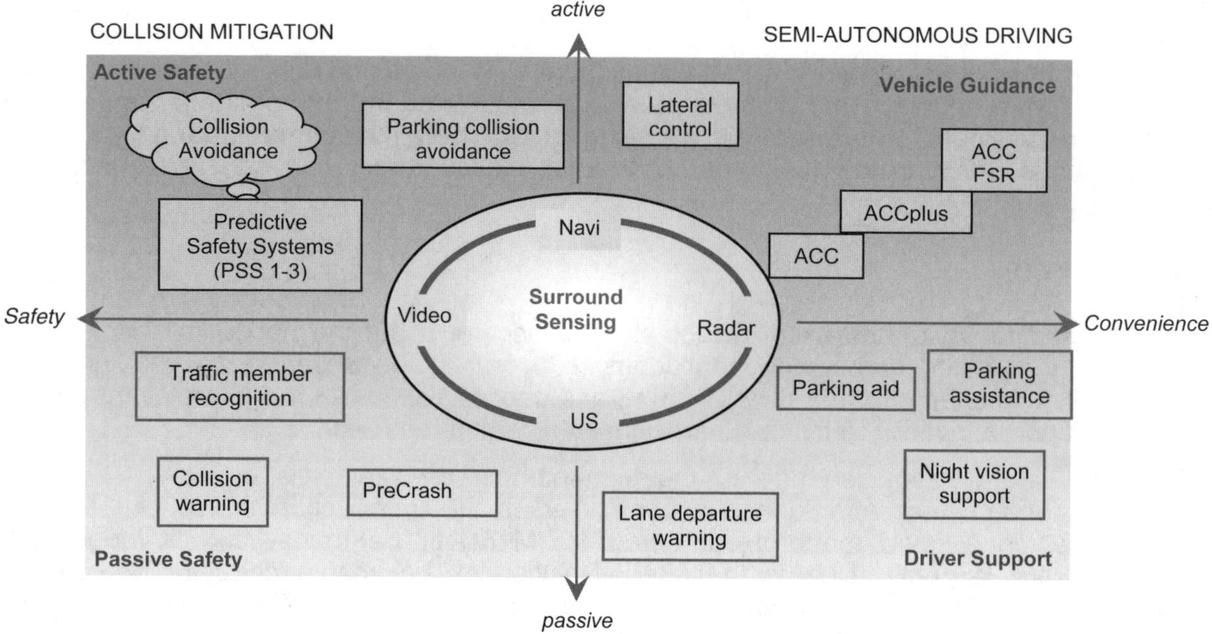

Fig. 8: Driver assistance systems on the way to the "safety vehicle."

ACC belongs to the group of active convenience systems and is being developed further to better functionality. If longitudinal guidance is augmented by lane keeping assistance (also a video-based system for lateral guidance) and use is made of complex sensor data fusion algorithms, automatic driving is possible in principle.

Passive safety systems contain the predictive recognition of potential accidents and the functions of pedestrian protection.

The highest demand regarding performance and reliability is put on active safety systems. They range from a simple parking stop, which automatically brakes a vehicle before reaching an obstacle, to predictive safety systems (PSS) in three stages, ranging up to an automatic emergency braking in the case of an unavoidable collision.

SENSOR TECHNOLOGY USABILITY

How well suited are these sensor technologies for the different applications shown in Fig. 8? Of course, there can be no general answer. Generally, even similar applications differ fundamentally in certain requirements, depending on the car manufacturer or the dedicated vehicle. Thus, only some general guidelines can be given.

LONG-RANGE APPLICATIONS

The only technologies with a range of 150 m or more today are 77-GHz radar and Lidar. Radar presently is the only technology found in ACC and predictive safety systems in Europe and the United States. Lidar and radar both are common in Japan.[1,4,5]

Radar and Lidar technologies have some fundamental differences, such as cost, signal quality, and weather performance. These characteristics should be taken carefully into account when designing convenience or safety systems that rely on the signals of these sensors. Predictive safety systems must work in high dynamic situations and must show high availability in all situations. This leads to a clear preference for radar technology. Due to its outstanding performance, radar is the key component for existing and future predictive safety systems.

At present, Lidar sensors offer cost advantages over radar, so they seem better suited for applications in mid- and low-class vehicles. But it is expected that this cost gap will decrease significantly (or even be closed) for future generations of these sensors. Until then, when using Lidar not only for convenience-oriented systems but also for safety-related systems, the performance of the particular sensor should be checked carefully against the requirements for the system.

MID-RANGE APPLICATIONS

For maximum ranges between 50 and 80 m, almost all technologies discussed here are suitable. 77-GHz and 24-GHz radar, Lidar, video, and range imagers can be adapted using suitable antennas or optics to measure in this range. Which technology fits best depends on features such as detection area, signal quality, availability, cost, and so forth.

The following are typical mid-range applications:

- Stop&Go-ACC and enhanced congestion support
- Support of predictive safety systems
- Pedestrian protection
- Lane departure warning/lane keeping support
- Lane change assistance
- Traffic sign recognition[3]

SHORT-RANGE APPLICATIONS

The maximum range of ultrasonic sensors is limited to about 5 m. Therefore, no ACC-related applications are reasonable.

VIDEO SYSTEM

Video technology is being introduced first for convenience functions that provide transparent behavior to and intervention by the driver. Figure 9 shows the basic principle of operation for a video system.

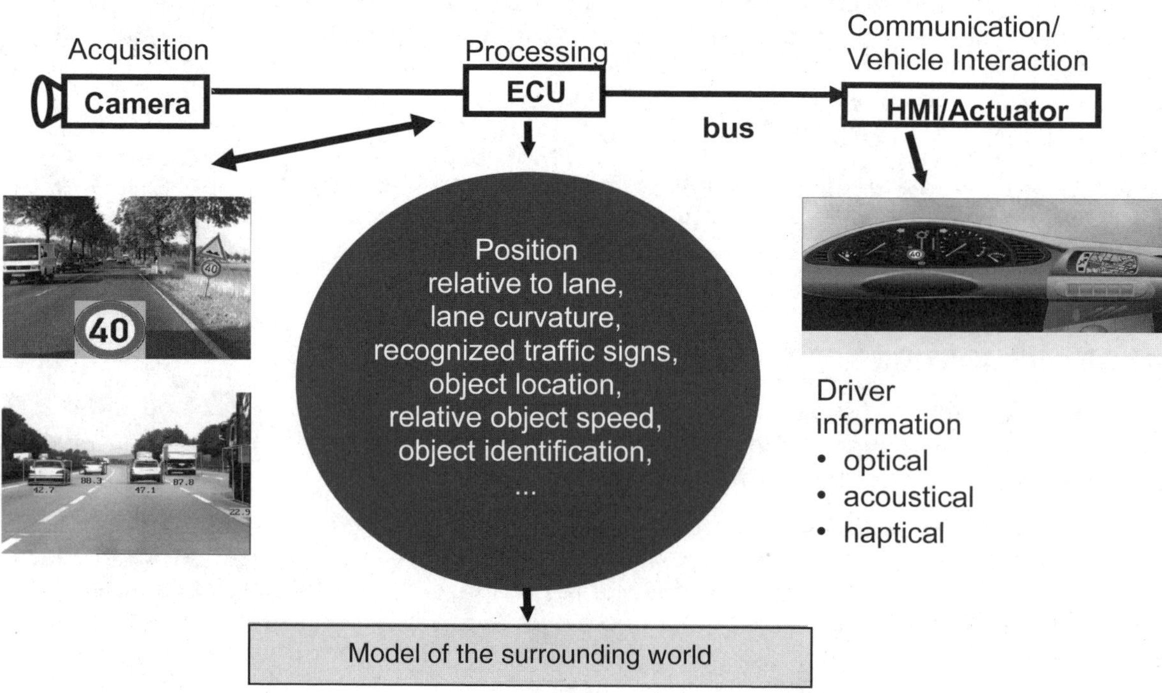

Fig. 9: Basic principle of a video sensor and functions being considered.

The enormous potential of video sensing is intuitively obvious from the performance of human visual sensing. Already, a respectable number of information and related functions can readily be achieved by computerized video sensing. The following are some of them:

- Lane recognition and lane departure warning, position of "own" car within the lane
- Traffic sign recognition (e.g., speed, no passing), with an appropriate warning to the driver
- Obstacles in front of the car, collision warning
- Vehicle inclination for headlight adjustments.

Future video sensors will be used for better object detection and, in the long term, for object classification as well. New methods of picture processing in conjunction with high dynamic imagers will further improve the performance of these systems.[6] In addition to measurement of the distance to the obstacle, the camera can assist the ACC system by performing object detection or object classification. Special emphasis is being put on night vision improvement during the introductory phase of video technology.

A high benefit can be achieved with a tail camera to detect objects approaching quickly from behind if this information is accompanied by a warning signal to the driver when he or she intends to pass.

ACC, FUTURE ACC GENERATIONS, AND PREDICTIVE SAFETY FUNCTIONS

ACC was the first function with limited vehicle interaction on the market. The radar sensor measures the distance to the vehicle ahead and maintains the safety distance by interaction with the brakes and the accelerator. With today's systems, the braking deceleration is limited to 2.5 m/sec². Figure 10 shows the main components of the system.

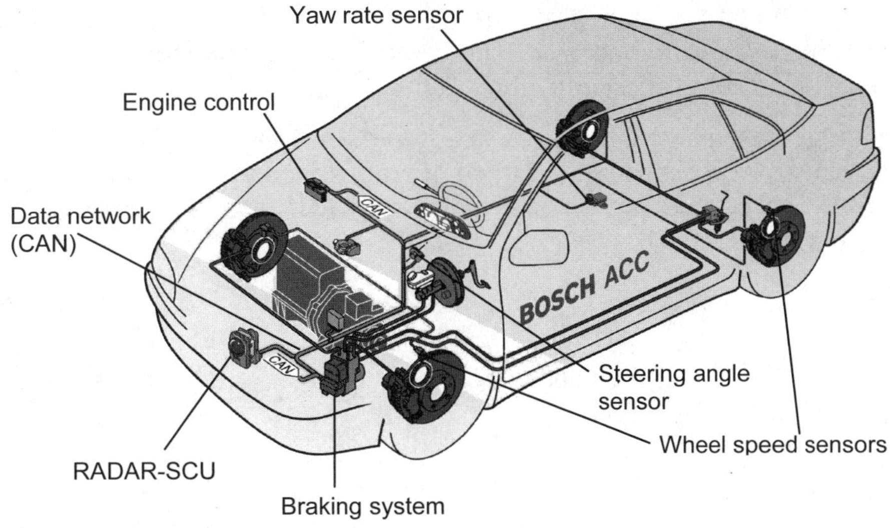

Fig. 10: ACC system structure.[7]

The radar SCU is integrated into the bumper. It interacts directly with the braking system and with the engine management system via a CAN bus. Speed, steering angle, and yaw rate are the input data. Yaw is needed to predict the course of the "own" vehicle and, thus, to avoid both false alarms from vehicles in adjacent lanes and unwanted acceleration in sharp curves.

The system must be activated by the driver. Today's vehicles are using a switch at the steering wheel. A display in the instrument cluster shows the status of the system. The driver also can choose the safe headway within legal limits. The system is deactivated automatically if the driver pushes the brake pedal. The system also can be switched off by the driver.

Figure 11 shows the basic function of the ACC system.

Fig. 11: Basic function of the ACC system.

With no vehicle in front or a vehicle in a safe distance ahead, the "own" vehicle cruises at the speed that has been set by the driver (Fig. 11, top). If a vehicle is detected, ACC adapts the speed automatically in such a way that the safety distance is maintained (Fig. 11, middle) by interaction with the brakes and the accelerator. In the case of a rapidly approaching speed to the vehicle in front, the system also warns the driver. If the car in front leaves the lane, the "own" vehicle accelerates to the previously set speed (Fig. 11, bottom).

To avoid excessive curve speeds, the signals of the ESP system are considered simultaneously. The ACC system will reduce the speed automatically. The driver can override the ACC system at any time by activating the accelerator or with a short activation of the brake.

Most systems in use today are active at speeds greater than 30 km/h. To avoid too many false alarms, stationary objects are suppressed. With improved second-generation ACC systems, this convenience function also can be used on smaller highways. ACCplus is a further consecutive step, braking the car down to a speed of zero.[7]

BENEFITS OF ACC

Today's ACC systems are convenience functions enabling the driver to drive more relaxed and safely. The following are the main benefits of ACC:

- ACC keeps a safe distance from the vehicle in front by interaction with the engine management and brake systems. Almost 20% of all accidents are rear-end collisions.
- ACC avoids dangerous driving errors of the type "following too closely." A study of the EU (INVENT)[17] has shown that 70% fewer situations of extreme and significant following too closely occur (see Fig. 12).

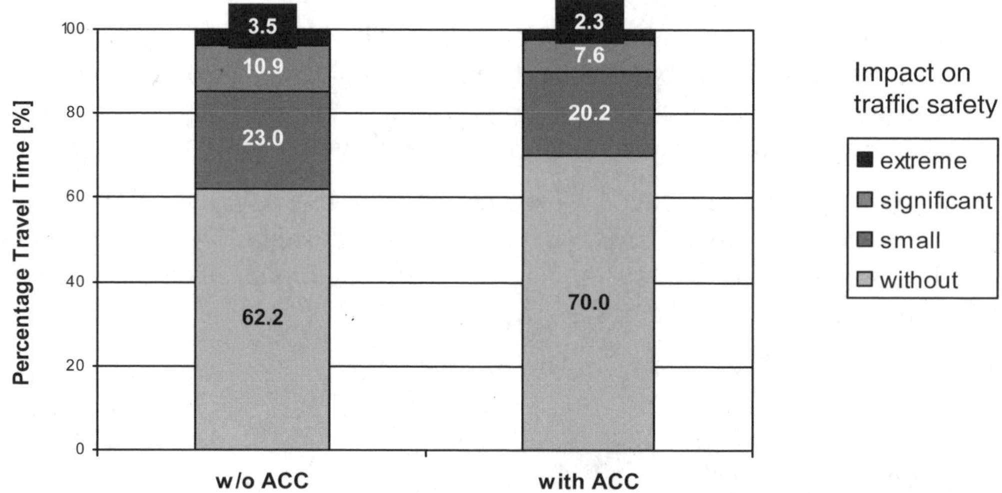

Fig. 12: Driving error of "following too closely" without and with ACC.[17]

- ACC warns the following traffic in time. Before the driver can react and step on the brake, ACC starts braking. The braking lights are activated and warn the following traffic.
- ACC helps the driver in the routine of longitudinal control. Drivers drive more attentively and are more relaxed. This has been shown with a study performed during the EU-funded project SANTOS. An internal study by DaimlerChrysler (2002) has shown a 40% improvement in reaction time.
- ACC has accident avoidance potential. According to the SeiSS (SocioEconomic Impact of Safety Systems) EU study, 4,000 accidents could be avoided in Europe if only 3% of the vehicles were equipped with ACC.[8]

- ACC helps to harmonize traffic flow. A simulation study of the University of Dresden, Germany, shows that at a penetration rate of only 10%, the probability of traffic jams is significantly reduced. With 20% penetration, most traffic jams can be avoided.[9]
- ACC can improve traffic flow. Depending on the headway gap, a 30% increase in traffic flow can be achieved.[10]
- ACC helps save gasoline. According to a vehicle test (Audi A8, 4.2 l), gasoline consumption can be reduced by more than 10% with frequent use of ACC.[11]
- ACC has a high development potential. ACC is the basis for new predictive safety systems that help to avoid and mitigate accidents, especially rear-end collisions.

ACCplus

ACC with extended functionality, ACCplus, may use additional medium-range sensors to extend the lateral vision of the system, particularly for short cut-ins. The first system of this kind was launched in late 2005 in the Mercedes S-Class and is called Distronic Plus. The system is based on sensor data fusion of the LRR sensor with SRR sensors. The system also is used for the safety function "Brake Assist Plus," a collision-mitigating system, warning the driver of hazardous situations by tightening the safety belt and by performing braking with a medium brake deceleration.

In early 2006, Bosch marketed the ACCplus function based on an LRR sensor alone. Both systems control the speed of the vehicle between 0 and 200 km/h. The Bosch system offers a strong braking jerk instead of automatic braking. Investigations have shown that drivers react quickly to this kind of warning, saving a few hundred milliseconds of reaction time. To avoid uncomfortable braking maneuvers, the vehicle must be equipped with a comfort-optimized system.

For re-acceleration, the driver simply pushes the accelerator pedal. An automatic restart also may be made within a certain time limit.

Figure 13 shows the ACCplus system architecture as chosen by DaimlerChrysler for the Mercedes S-Class model year 2005.

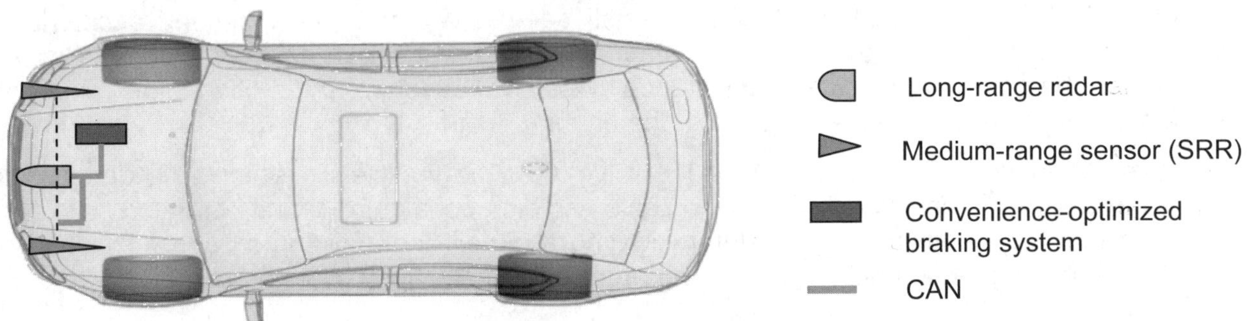

Fig. 13: System architecture of the Distronic Plus system.

The overlap of the detection areas of the two different sensor types allows an improvement in detection performance.

ACC LOW-SPEED FOLLOWING

The next step in ACC function development will be made with a low-speed following (LSF) function that makes use of the fusion of the LRR with a medium-range sensor. A good combination might be an SRR sensor with improved performance and/or a video camera (see the paragraph on Sensor Data

Fusion). A combination of three sensor types (LRR, Lidar, and SSR) and a video camera is possible in principle but is unlikely due to high costs.

The ACC LSF function will allow complete longitudinal control covering all speed ranges and urban traffic situations as well. Figure 14 shows the system architecture.

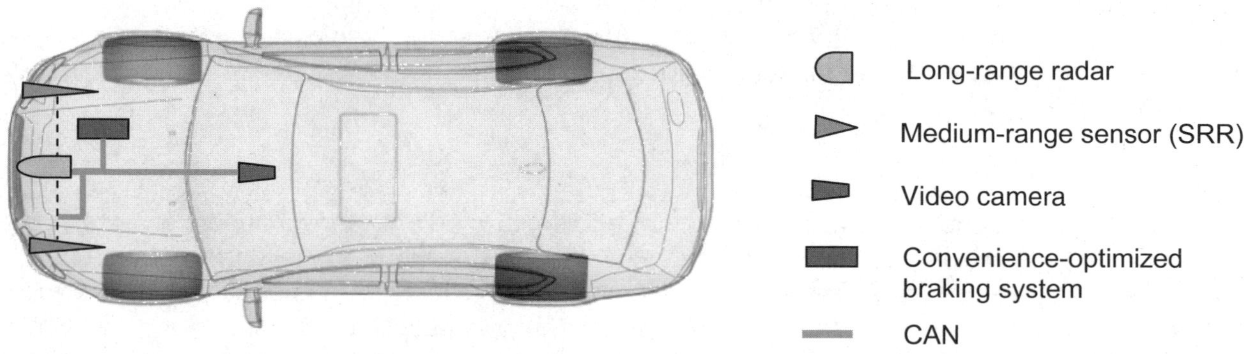

Fig. 14: System architecture of the ACC FSR.

COMBINATION OF ACC WITH NAVIGATION

The predictive location of curve radii within defined distances in front of the vehicle is possible using digital maps. Through interpolation, the curvature of the road can be calculated up to about 50 m ahead. A necessary precondition is high-quality and accurate digital maps. With additional information (e.g., the number of lanes and road types), additional applications will be possible. Development of this system is ongoing.

ACC-BASED SAFETY SYSTEMS

In critical driving situations, only a fraction of a second may determine whether an accident occurs or not. Studies[12] indicate that about 60% of front-end crashes and almost one-third of head-on collisions would not occur if the driver could react only one-half second earlier. Every second accident at intersections could be prevented by faster reactions. An early warning to the driver results in an earlier reaction by the driver. Active driver assistance systems with vehicle interaction allow a vehicle reaction that is quicker than the normal reaction of the driver.

Predictive driver assistance systems speed up the driver's or the vehicle's reaction to a dangerous situation. With the signals of surround sensors, objects and situations in the vicinity of the vehicle can be incorporated into the calculation of collision-mitigating and collision-avoiding means. The earlier the systems can recognize a potential accident, the more effectively those systems can carry out their functions.

Predictive safety systems (PSS) support the driver in situations where there is a risk of rear-end collisions. In PSS systems, the active brake functions—ABS, ESP, and HBA—are combined with adaptive cruise control (ACC).

MIGRATION SCENARIO

Predictive driver assistance systems have been introduced with convenience systems. Safety systems have not been addressed because of lack of experience in the field. Another factor is that vehicle buyers do not want to spend a lot of money for safety features. They expect a high standard of safety in a vehicle without having to buy safety options. Convenience systems of the type described earlier make use of new, high-performance sensors, allowing the realization of safety functions, too. ACC, with its outstanding performance in measurement of distance and relative speed, therefore is the most important basis for entering the field of safety functions. In a further step, video technology helps to enhance the performance of the systems.

PREDICTIVE SAFETY SYSTEMS

Inattention is the cause of 68% of all rear-end collisions. In 11%, inattention plus following too closely are the cause, and 9% of rear-end collisions are caused by following too closely alone. These statistics[13] show that 88% of rear-end collisions can be influenced by longitudinal control systems. To counteract these collisions, more detailed information is needed about the circumstances of the different kinds of accidents. The new German GIDAS database (GIDAS = German In-Depth Accident Statistics) gives detailed information about the braking behavior in accidents (Fig. 15[14]).

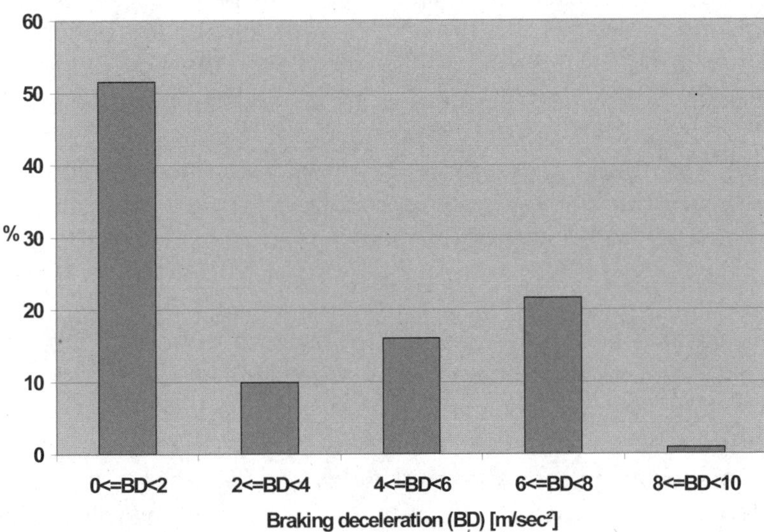

Fig. 15: Braking behavior during collision accidents.[14]

In more than 50% of collisions, drivers do not brake at all (braking deceleration [BD] between 0 and 2 m/sec^2). Real emergency braking (BD above 8 m/sec^2) happens in only 1% of accidents. In all other cases, only partial braking occurs. This analysis confirms that inattention is the most frequent cause for collisions and shows the high collision-avoidance and collision-mitigation potential of predictive driver assistance systems if the braking process of the driver can be anticipated or if a vehicle interaction can be made by the vehicle computer.

Predictive safety systems will pave the way to collision avoidance with full interference in the dynamics of the vehicle. These systems are being introduced in three stages.

PREDICTIVE BRAKE ASSIST

In the first stage, the system prepares the braking system for possible emergency braking. In situations where there is the threat of an accident, predictive brake assist prepares for it by building up the brake pressure, bringing the brake pads into very light contact with the brake discs, and modifying the hydraulic brake assist. The result is that the driver gains important fractions of a second until the full braking effect is achieved. If the driver then undertakes emergency braking, he or she gets the fastest possible braking action with the maximum deceleration and thus the shortest stopping distance.

If the driver does not need to brake, these preparatory measures are withdrawn. If an accident occurs nonetheless, the system can reduce the side effects and save lives. A typical situation that can lead to an accident is when a much slower vehicle moves out into the lane in which you are driving. If you are driving at 140 km/h and the vehicle in front is traveling at only 80 km/h and suddenly moves into your lane 40 meters ahead of you, the predictive safety system prepares for emergency braking in only one-fifth of a second—before you have even noticed the slow-moving obstacle. In the event of emergency braking, the driver benefits from the more rapid operation of the braking system, enabling him or her to avoid an accident. Without the predictive safety system, a serious accident would have occurred under these circumstances.

Bosch introduced this first generation of the predictive safety system in 2005. The system architecture for this system is the same as that shown in Fig. 13.

PREDICTIVE COLLISION WARNING

In more than half of all collisions, drivers crash into an obstacle without braking. The second generation of predictive safety systems not only prepares the braking system as already described, but also gives a timely warning to the driver about dangerous traffic situations, thereby helping to prevent accidents in many cases. To do this, the system triggers a short, sharp operation of the brakes. Studies of drivers have shown that a sudden braking impulse is the best way to get the driver's attention to what is happening on the road. Drivers react directly to the warning and immediately step on the brake. Alternatively or additionally, the system also can warn the driver by means of optical or acoustic signals, or by a brief tightening of the normally loosely fastened safety belt.

In the preceding case where a slow-moving vehicle suddenly moves into the lane in front of you, the extended predictive safety system prepares for emergency braking in only one-fifth of a second. The difference from the first generation of the safety system, however, is that the driver also is given a warning if he or she does not change course or brake within the next one-third of a second. In this case, the driver can still avoid a crash by moving out of the lane. If the driver only brakes, the driver can at least considerably reduce the speed of the vehicle. Vehicles without driver warning—and therefore without braking—will crash into each other. Therefore, the predictive safety system significantly reduces the speed of collision and thus the severity of the accident. Depending on the information coming from the sensors, the system in many situations will even warn the driver early enough so that the accident can be prevented simply by braking. Series launch of the second generation of the predictive safety system with the warning function occurred in mid-2006.

PREDICTIVE EMERGENCY BRAKING

The third developmental stage of the predictive safety system will not only recognize an unavoidable collision with a vehicle in front but also will trigger automatic emergency braking with maximum vehicle deceleration. This will reduce the severity of an accident when the driver has failed to react to the previous warnings or has reacted inadequately. Automatic control of vehicle function demands a very high level of certainty in the recognition of objects and the assessment of accident risk. To be able to recognize reliably that a collision is inevitable, further metering systems (e.g., video sensors) will have to support the radar sensors. It also will be necessary to create the legal basis for the use of such systems for traffic on public roads.

In their highest levels of refinement, active systems intervene in steering, braking, and engine management to avoid collisions with an obstacle. Here, the vision goes to the collision-avoiding vehicle, which then makes computer-assisted driving maneuvers for crash avoidance.[15]

The system architecture for both systems—predictive collision warning and predictive emergency braking—corresponds to that shown in Fig. 14.

ACCIDENT AVOIDANCE POTENTIAL OF DRIVER ASSISTANCE SYSTEMS

Calculations and estimations show that with the first two steps of PSS, almost 20% of fatalities could be avoided in Germany.

Stimulated by the EU Commission, the SeiSS study was performed under the guidance of the VDI/VDE IT GmbH organization, and the University of Cologne, Germany.[8] The study estimates the socioeconomic benefit of some driver assistance systems by calculating a cost/benefit factor. Included in the study is not only an estimate of the socioeconomic benefit of accident prevention and mitigation but also by avoidance of traffic jams and gas consumption during waiting caused by accidents. Currently, the study is being extended to other driver assistance systems.

Meanwhile, the Road Map Working Group of the EU Safety Forum has published the "Final Report and Recommendations of the Implementation of the Road Map Working Group." It is based on the SeiSS study and contains details about accident avoidance potential. The report also gives a recommendation for the introduction of driver assistance systems with the highest potential for accident avoidance and accident mitigation.

HUMAN MACHINE INTERFACE ASPECTS

The human machine interface (HMI) of ACC and PSS systems must be designed in such a way that the driver always feels that the system is providing support in the best way and that he or she has full control of the vehicle and is always in the loop. The driver must never have the impression of being taken over by a system that he or she does not understand. A skillful HMI design therefore is essential for the acceptance of these systems by the driver.

The EU Commission currently has a communication under preparation: a renewal of the 1999 "European statement of principles on human machine interface." It aims at a common approach of the European industry to the problem of the driver's interaction with the new safety devices in the car in order to guarantee that the growing complexity of the safety systems does not pose a safety risk in itself. This statement of principles was made for driver information systems and shall be applied to driver assistance systems in the future as well.[16]

CONCLUSION

ACC is established in the market and still has enormous potential for a stepwise functional improvement versus convenience and safety. ACC is the most important driver assistance function and the basis for predictive safety systems.

The political institutions have defined worldwide their goals to reduce fatalities significantly in the next years.[7]

Estimates show that many collisions can be avoided or mitigated if only the driver reacts faster. To achieve this, sensors are needed to scan the environment of the vehicle and to measure the distance to and the relative speed of detected obstacles. Early warnings then can be given to the driver, and interactions with the vehicle can be made to avoid or mitigate the accident. Explorations of these potential developments of predictive safety systems have been made and are ongoing.

Safety systems, in particular, have high demands in performance and reliability of obstacle detection.

High-performance sensors, such as radar and video, allow reliable detection of relevant objects. With a parallel use of the sensors for active and passive safety functions, additional synergies can be explored.

Accident-free traffic will remain a vision, but many developments are aimed at introducing stepwise driver assistance functions that allow the driver to drive in a more relaxed manner and more safely in future vehicles.

REFERENCES

1. Winner, H.; Witte, S.; Uhler, W.; Lichtenberg, B.: "Adaptive Cruise Control—System Aspects and Development Trends," SAE Paper No. 961010 (1996).
2. Knoll, P.M.: "Radar Sensors" in "Sensors for Automotive Technology," Chapter 7.7, Wiley-VCH Editor (2003).
3. Uhler, W.; Knoll, P.M.: "Surround Sensors—Enablers for Predictive Safety Systems," Convergence 2006, Paper No. 06SS – 43.
4. Schwarte, R.; *et al.*: "A New Electro-Optical Mixing and Correlating Sensor: Facilities and Applications of This Photonic Mixer Device (PMD)," SPIE-EOS: Sensors, Sensor Systems, and Sensor Data Processing, Vol. 3100, Munich, Germany (1997).
5. Knoll, P.M.; Schaefer, B.-J.: "Predictive Safety Systems—Steps from Convenience Towards Collision Avoidance and Collision Mitigation," ITS Congress, Hannover, Germany (2005).
6. Seger, U.; Knoll, P.M.; Stiller, C.: "Sensor Vision and Collision Warning Systems," Convergence, Detroit, MI (2000).
7. Knoll, P.M.; Sailer, U.: "How Driver Assistance Systems Pave the Way to the Safety Vehicle," ATA EL 2004 Conference, Parma (2004).
8. Baum, H.; Geißler, T.; Grawenhoff, S.; Schneider, J.; Schulz, W.H.: "Exploratory Study on the Potential Socio-Economic Impact of the Introduction of Intelligent Safety Systems in Road Vehicles" (2005), http://www.escope.info.
9. Treiber, M.; Helbing, D.: "Micro Simulations of Freeway Traffic Including Control Measures," at Automati-Sierungstechnik 48 (2000), Oldenbourg Verlag.
10. Shladover, S.: PATH programme, University of California (2005).
11. "Vehicle Test of Audi A8 with 4.2 Liter Engine," Auto Motor and Sport 5/2006.
12. Enke, K.: "Possibilities for Improving Safety Within the Driver Vehicle Environment Loop," 7th International Technical Conference on Experimental Safety Vehicle, Paris (1979).
13. NHTSA Report (2001).
14. GIDAS database: Braking Behavior at Accidents, http://www.gidas.org.
15. Knoll, P.; Schaefer, B.-J.; Guettler, H.; Bunse, M.; Kallenbach, R.: "Predictive Safety Systems—Steps Towards Collision Mitigation," SAE Paper No. 04AE-30 (2004).
16. Knoll, P.M.: "Predictive Safety Systems: Convenience—Collision Mitigation—Collision Avoidance," Convergence 2006, Paper No. 06SS-35.
17. INVENT Report AP3100—Appendix.